The New Illustrated
EVERYMAN'S
ENCYCLOPAEDIA

Consultant Editor: John Paxton

Editor of *Everyman's Dictionary of Abbreviations* and *The Statesman's Year-Book*

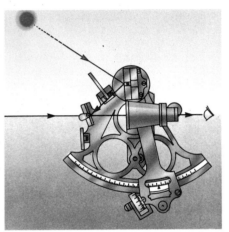

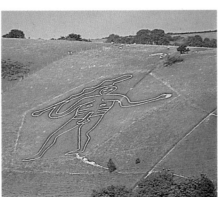

VOLUME SIX

Acknowledgements

The publishers would like to thank the following individuals
and organisations for their kind permission to reproduce the
photographs in this book.

Bryan & Cherry Alexander 1621 below; **The J. Allan Cash Photolibrary** 1707; **BBC Hulton Picture Library** 1445, 1504, 1517, 1580, 1635, 1673, 1679, 1691; **The Bridgeman Art Library** (Bodleian Library, Oxford) 1533, (Galleria Borghese, Rome) 1579, (Musée Cluny, Paris) 1546, (Detroit Institute of Arts) 1528, (Glasgow Art Gallery and Museum) 1712, (Kenwood House, London) 1646, (Victoria & Albert Museum) 1536, 1587, 1700; **British Tourist Authority** 1509, (Adam Woolfitt) 1637; **Bruce Coleman Ltd.** (B & C Calhoun) 1607, (E. Crichton) 1624, 1686 above, (G. Cubitt) 1483, (A. Deere-Jones) 1521, (N. Devore) 1626, 1681, (M.P. Kahl) 1501, (S. Navarrini) 1538, (S. Prato) 1605, (W. Schmidt) 1513; **Essex Institute, Salem, Massachusetts** 1697; **E.T. Archive** 1699, (Villa Valmarana, Virenza) 1575, (Wellington Museum) 1677 above; **Greg Evans** 1515; **Mary Evans Picture Library** 1557, 1569; **Joel Finler** 1677 below; **Paul Forrester** (National Trust) 1675; **Glasgow Art Gallery & Museum** 1685; **Ronald Grant Archive** 1656; **Sonia Halliday Photographs** 1503 below, 1663 right, 1690; **Robert Harding Picture Library** 1444, 1455, 1587, 1612 above, 1617, 1644, 1650, 1663 left, 1664, 1669, 1672, (Art Institute of Chicago) 1511, (British Museum) 1547, (Collection Duke of Wellington) 1472, (Museum & Art Gallery, Leicester) 1661, (National Portrait Gallery, London) 1702, (W. Rawlings) 1689, (Russian Museum, Leningrad)

1551, (Sassoon) 1457, 1545, 1621 above, 1668 above, (A.C. Walthem) 1503 above; **Michael Holford** 1602, 1647, 1706, (G. Clyde) 1593, 1640, (Guildhall Museum, London) 1653 right, (E. Hurwicz) 1686 below, (National Gallery, London) 1578, 1616, (Pollocks Toy Museum) 1590, (Statens Historiska Museum, Stockholm) 1653 left, (Victoria & Albert Museum) 1642, (Walker Art Gallery) 1454; **Anwar Hussein** 1559; **Hutchison Picture Library** 1479 above, (F. Green) 1574 (M. Macintyre) 1477, 1479 above; **Jelu de Paume, Paris** 1439; **Mansell Collection** 1583; **The Mayor Gallery, London** 1668 below; **Jon Moss** 1570; **National Gallery, London** 1611, 1638; **National Portrait Gallery, London** 1447, 1510, 1519, 1666, 1698; **Picturepoint** 1449, 1459, 1463, 1496, 1549, 1585, 1592, 1715; **Ian Robson** 1466; **Ronald Sheridan's Photo Library** 1492, 1534, 1556, (Alan Eaton) 1541; **Tate Gallery** 1495; **Topham Picture Library** 1442, 1479 below, 1563, 1597, 1649, 1682, (Geographical Magazine) 1719; **ZEFA** 1531, 1694, (B. Croxford) 1461, (Damm) 1717, (R. Everts) 1491, 1610, (R. Halin) 1601, 1643, (G. Heilmann) 1625, (K. Kerth) 1612 below, (Knight & Hunt) 1608, (Orion Press) 1450, 1582, (Photri) 1489, (J. Rushmere) 1723, (K. Scholl) 1522, (G. Sirena) 1581, (R. Smith) 1535, (S. Warner) 1623. © DACS 1984 1528, 1668 below

ILLUSTRATIONS BY
Clyde Surveys
Hayward & Martin
Ian Stephen
Linden Artists
Oxford Illustrators Ltd
Wayne Ford

This edition published 1984 by
Octopus Books Limited
59 Grosvenor Street, London W.1.

under licence from
J.M. Dent & Sons Limited
Aldine House, 33 Welbeck Street, London W.1.

ISBN 0 86273 157 7

Printed and bound by
Graficromo S.A.,
Cordoba, Spain.

The New Illustrated
EVERYMAN'S
ENCYCLOPAEDIA

VOLUME SIX

Sesostris (incorrectly Usertsen), Greek corruption of Egyptian Senusret or Senusert. There were three kings of this name in ancient Egypt, all of the 12th Dynasty: *Sesostris I* (c.1971 BC); *Sesostris II* (c.1897 BC); and *Sesostris III* (c.1878 BC); second, fourth, and fifth kings respectively of the dynasty.

Sesshū (1420–1506), important Japanese painter, a pupil of the Zen-Buddhist monk, Strubun. Much influenced by the Chinese landscape painters of the Sung period and by travel in China, 1467–69, he developed a powerful naturalism and freedom of brushwork employing vigorous marks and splashes. His work strongly affected succeeding generations of Japanese painters.

Sessions, Roger (1896–), US composer. His music displays a highly wrought contrapuntal fabric and throughout his career became increasingly chromatic; in 1953 he adopted 12-note serialism. Among his works are the operas *The Trial of Lucullus* and *Montezuma*, eight symphonies, violin and piano concertos, two string quartets, and three piano sonatas.

Sesson (1485–1570), self-taught Japanese painter, greatly influenced by Sesshū, and chiefly known for his mist-shrouded lyrical landscapes in broad monochrome.

Set, Seth or Setekh, Egyptian god of the desert, whose symbol was an unidentified animal with long ears and a tail. Set was often execrated because he was hostile to his brother Osiris and Horus.

Set Off is a defence, in English law, to an action, by means of which a defendant is allowed to meet the plaintiff's claim (wholly or partly) by 'setting off' a claim against the plaintiff. It exists only in respect of mutual debts, and a debt accruing due after the issue of the plaintiff's writ cannot be pleaded as set off, though it can be pleaded as a counterclaim. A set off differs from a counterclaim in that it is a defence and not a cross-action.

Set Theory, created by Georg Cantor, is the branch of mathematics which provides formal rules for dealing with sets, relations between sets, and relations between sets and members (or elements) of sets. A = all positive integers less than 100; B = all poems written by Wordsworth, are examples of sets. The fact that an object *s* is a member of a set *S* is denoted by the symbol $s \in S$; $s \notin S$ means *s* is not a member of *S*. If all the members of a set, *E*, are also members of another set, *F*, then *E* is a *subset* of *F*, denoted by $E \subset F$. For example A★ = all positive integers less than 100 which are divisible by 7; B★ = all poems more than 500 lines long written by Wordsworth, are subsets of the sets defined earlier. Any set *S* is also a subset of itself, $S \subset S$. The 'empty' or 'null' set, denoted by   has no elements and is a subset of every set (saying that   is not a subset of a set *S* would imply that   had an element that was not in *S*, but   has no elements).

Given two sets, *E* and *F*, it is possible to form the set that consists of all the elements of both sets together (the *union* of *E* and *F*, denoted by $E \cup F$) and the set that contains only elements that are common to both sets (the *intersection* of *E* and *F*, denoted by $E \cap F$).

When a set is denoted by a list of its elements, curly brackets are used. For example, the set of all positive integers less than 5 is denoted by $\{1, 2, 3, 4\}$. When writing out a definition of a set it is usual to employ the following notation:
$H = \{x \in G | x$ has a specified property$\}$
which means '*H* is the set consisting of all elements *x* from the set *G* for which it is true that *x* has a specified property'. For example, *A* above can be defined by
$A = \{x \in N | x < 100\}$
where *N* is the set of all the positive integers.

Sète, French port in the *département* of Hérault, on the Mediterranean, separated from the mainland by a shallow lagoon. It is connected by canal with the interior, and is the most important French Mediterranean port after Marseilles. It has fishing, metallurgical, oil-refining, and shipbuilding industries. Population (1975) 40,179.

Seton, Ernest Thompson (1860–1946), Canadian naturalist, writer, and artist. He is best known for his books about wild life, and for his foundation of the Woodcraft League in the USA. Among his chief works are *Animal Heroes*, 1906; *Wild Animal Ways*, 1916; and *Lives of Game Animals*, 1925. *The Trail of an Artist-naturalist*, 1940, is an autobiography.

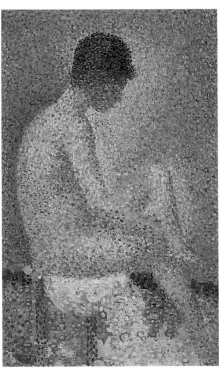

Georges Seurat. Model in Profile, *1887.*

Setter, dog which has been trained to assist in taking game, sitting or crouching instead of pointing, like the less active but more keenly scented pointer. The breed was long known as the spaniel, from which it is descended. There are three varieties, the English, the Scottish, Gordon or black-and-tan and the Irish. The height in all three breeds varies from 61 to 68 cm and the weight from 27 to 32 kg.

Settlement. In English law settlements may be classified into: marriage settlements; family settlements; separation deeds; and voluntary settlements. The most usual classification under English law, however, is that between the strict settlement and the trust for sale. The former provides for the 'tying-up' of land in one family, the latter for the management and enjoyment of the money which is invested in the property.

Setúbal, town situated 29 km south-east of Lisbon, Portugal. It is a fishing port, and has fish-curing, cement, distilling, and shipbuilding industries. There is a trade in oranges, muscatel grapes, and salt. Population (1970) 50,730.

Seurat, Georges Pierre (1859–91), French painter. In 1884 his painting *La Baignade* (now in the Tate Gallery, London) refused by the official Salon, was exhibited at the Salon des Indépendants, organised that year. Their president, Signac, initiated Seurat in the methods of the Impressionists. *Un Dimanche d'été à la Grande-Jatte*, 1886, is declared 'the first picture executed entirely in the divisionist technique' (Art Institute of Chicago). Inspired by the colour researches of Chevreul, Seurat gained effect by using a stipple of the three primary colours, an extension of the Impressionist theory. *Cirque*, 1891, the last of his works, shows the geometric scheme of composition he had developed. He produced remarkable drawings, rich in effects of light and shade.

See also IMPRESSIONISM.

Sevastopol, or Sebastopol, city in south-west Crimean *oblast* of the Ukrainian SSR, USSR, an important Soviet naval base on the Black Sea, and a seaside resort. It was founded in 1783, and was almost completely ruined during the sieges of 1854–55 and 1941–42, falling on both occasions. Population (1980) 308,000.

Seven Days' Battle. This was a famous series of engagements during the American Civil War, when Federal troops under Gen. G. B. McClellan were in sight of Richmond, the Confederate capital, in the summer of 1862, and it looked as if they might, by a bold stroke, capture it. McClellan, however, was always cautious, and was suddenly ordered to abandon his position and bring his army back near Washington.

Seven Sages, famous Greek law-givers, tyrants, and others who lived between 620 and 550 BC. Each was noted for a wise maxim: Cleobulus of Rhodes—'Moderation is the chief good'; Periander of Corinth—'Forethought in all things'; Pittacus of Mitylene—'Know thine opportunity'; Bias of Priene—'Too many workers spoil the work'; Thales of Miletus—'Suretyship brings ruin'; Chilon of Sparta—'Know thyself'; and Solon of Athens—'Nothing to excess'.

Seven Sleepers of Ephesus, heroes of a celebrated legend told by Gregory of Tours in *Miraculorum Liber*. To avoid the persecution of Decius (AD 250), seven Christian soldiers took refuge in a cave, which was blocked up by their pursuers. They fell asleep and awoke nearly 200 years later, in the reign of Theodosius II (447). Having explained the significance of their experience, they returned to the cave to sleep until Judgment Day, and Theodosius absolved all bishops who had been persecuted for believing in the Resurrection.

Seven Week's War. The partition of Schleswig-Holstein, which had been won by Austria and Prussia from Denmark in 1864, led to various disputes between Austria and

Prussia for the hegemony of the German Confederation. The two sides armed for the struggle, the smaller German states siding with Austria, while Prussia was in alliance with Italy, who in return was promised the province of Venetia. In 1866 Bismarck mobilised the Prussian army and occupied Holstein, Hesse, Saxony, and Hanover. The subsequent battle fought at Sadowa between the Prussians and the Austrians was a decisive defeat for Austria. Against the Italians the Austrians were initially more successful but Garibaldi's Volunteers were victorious at Ampola and Bezzana. To secure the mediation of France, the Austrian Emperor, Francis Joseph, ceded Venice to Napoleon III, who then offered it as a gift to Italy. Both Italy and then Prussia refused Napoleon's mediation except on the basis of a new Germany under Prussian leadership, from which Austria would be excluded. The Prussians took Frankfurt and advanced on Austria. The peace of Prague with Austria (23 September) excluded Austria from Germany and imposed a war indemnity. A plebiscite in Venice (19 October) declared for union with Italy and, on 7 November, Victor Emmanuel entered the city in triumph.

Seven Wonders of the World, were held to be the pyramids of Egypt; the hanging gardens of Semiramis at Babylon; the temple of Artemis at Ephesus; the colossus at Rhodes; Phidias's chryselephantine statue of Zeus at Olympia; the Mausoleum at Halicarnassus; and the lighthouse on the island of Pharos at Alexandria.

Seven Years' War, or Third Silesian War, name given to a period of war (1756–63), fought in Europe by Frederick II the Great of Prussia, aided by subsidies and troops from Great Britain against a coalition of Austria, Russia, France, Sweden, and Saxony, and by Great Britain against France, later aided by Spain on sea and on land, mainly in North America and India. While the continental war is of great importance in military history on account of Frederick's masterly campaigns, the British war laid the foundation of British naval supremacy, of the Indian Empire, and of the final withdrawal of French rivalry in North America. At the close of the war the Peace of Paris (1763) left Great Britain practically the sole colonising power and in control of the seas.

Seventh-Day Adventists, see ADVENTISTS.
Severalty. In the English law of real property, a freehold estate in severalty is that which the owner holds in his own right, without being joined in interest with any other person.

Severini, Gino (1883–1966), Italian painter. In 1910 he was one of the leading Futurist painters but by 1917 was working in a Cubist manner. Later he turned to decorative work in fresco and mosaic.

Severn (Welsh *Hafren*), river of England and Wales, which rises on the slopes of Plynlimmon in Wales. It intersects Powys and enters Shropshire near the Brythen Hills. It then flows through the counties of Hereford and Worcester and Gloucestershire, widening considerably at Newnham, its waters thenceforth forming a long estuary to the Bristol Channel. It is 336km long. The River Severn from Gloucester to Sharpness is tortuous and has many shifting shoals and sand banks. Consequently, the Sharpness and Gloucester ship canal was opened for traffic in 1827. Above Gloucester the river is navigable by barges of up to 350t capacity to Worcester, and 150t capacity to Stourport. The drainage area is 11,420km². The river flows rapidly in the reaches below Newnham, and is subject to a tidal wave about 2m in height known as the Severn bore.

Severus, Lucius Septimius (AD 146–211), Roman emperor, 193–211. After holding various commands under Marcus Aurelius and Commodus he was appointed commander-in-chief of the army in Pannonia and Illyria. These troops proclaimed him emperor on the death of Pertinax. Having secured the throne Severus turned against Pescennius Niger, who had been saluted emperor by the legions of the east. Niger was defeated near Issus and put to death soon afterwards (194). Severus next laid siege to Byzantium, which was not taken until 196. He was now undisputed master of the Roman world. Severus proved himself a patron of letters, and did much to restore and improve the capital. In 208 he went to Britain; after nearly three years of successful campaigning and reform he died at Eboracum (York).

Sévigné, Marie de Rabutin-Chantal, Marquise de (1626–96), French letter-writer. In 1644 she married the Marquis de Sévigné, her unhappy married life being terminated in 1651 by the death of her husband in a duel. As a widow she was able to move freely in Parisian society, enjoying a wide circle of literary and influential friends. She was devoted to her children and the letters to her daughter (first published in 1725) 'written from Paris or Brittany' are outstanding for their style and the picture they give of life and thought in contemporary French society.

Seville (Spanish *Sevilla*), capital of the province of Sevilla, Spain, and the principal city of Andalusia, on the River Guadalquivir. It was an important town in Roman times. Later, it was for a time the capital of the Visigoths, and in 712 it was taken by the Moors. Ferdinand III of León and Castile captured it in 1248. In the 16th century it had the monopoly of trade with the West Indies, and it became a centre of art and letters.
Seville is one of the most beautiful cities of Spain, an important port and also the most important industrial city in Andalusía, with aircraft, shipbuilding, textile, and food industries. Population (1981) 653,833.

Sèvres, a porcelain from the national porcelain factory of France (c.1738–present day). Originally established at Vincennes in 1738, it moved to Sèvres in 1756. From the beginning it enjoyed royal patronage and in 1753 was granted the monopoly of porcelain manufacture in France.

Sewage, liquid waste discharged into a sewerage system (a network of pipes or sewers) to be carried away for disposal. Sewer-pipes are usually made of vitrified clay or precast concrete; surface water sewers have much larger capacities than foul sewers to cope with the run-off from heavy storms.
Sewage flows by gravity wherever possible, aided by pumps. In coastal areas it is discharged directly into the sea through long outfall pipes. In inland areas it is screened to remove large solids, then passed slowly through sedimentation tanks to remove most of the organic solids as sludge. It is then oxidised by bacterial action. The clear liquid produced can then be discharged safely into rivers. The residual sludge can be broken down further by bacteria in a digestion tank to produce methane gas to provide heat. The remaining inoffensive material can be returned to the land as a fertilizer and soil conditioner.
In areas not connected to a sewage system, sewage flows to a septic tank—an underground container, connected to an individual building. Here the solids settle out and the liquid leaches into the soil to be purified by soil bacteria. The remaining sludge in the tank is converted to humus by anaerobic bacteria.

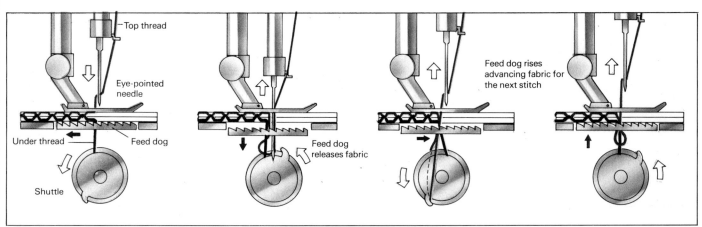

Sewing-machine, the lock-stitch process was patented by Singer in 1851. The basic procedure remains the same for today's high-speed machines.

Sewell, Anna (1820–78), English writer. Her mother, Mary (Wright) Sewell, was herself an author, but the family's life was clouded by poverty. An accident in Anna's childhood left her crippled. Her only book, *Black Beauty: the Autobiography of a Horse*, a perennial children's classic, was published in 1877.

Sewing-machine, a device for sewing mechanically. It uses a different principle of stitch formation from hand sewing. Although in the past attempts were made to devise such a machine, success was not achieved until the mid-19th century, when the American inventors Elias Howe and Isaac M. Singer devised their lock-stitch machines.

The basis of the lock-stitch sewing-machine is the eye-pointed needle, which conveys a bight of thread through the cloth without itself having to pass right through. An under-thread, carried on a spool underneath the machine, is passed through the loop, and tightened. Single-thread chain-stitch machines also exist. These pass a bight of thread through the cloth as before; the bight is held so that at its next stroke the next bight passes through the previous one. Such a stitch is easily undone. The double thread chain stitch machine uses an underthread and is more secure.

Modern sewing-machines produce many types of stitch, and their speeds have been increased up to 10,000 stitches a minute. The invention of the sewing-machine revolutionised the garment industry and brought home-dressmaking within the reach of millions.

Sex, in plants and animals, including man, is the basis of a type of reproduction that results in every individual being slightly different from every other. In contrast, asexual reproduction produces populations of identical or clonal individuals. Sexual reproduction involves the fertilisation of a female gamete (egg or ovum) by a male gamete (sperm in animals, pollen nucleus in flowering plants). The fertilised egg forms the zygote which develops into a new individual. The details of the process vary enormously in different organisms but the result is always the same: offspring which resemble their parents in all their main features but differ in minor points. Thus a cat can only produce kittens, but there is often considerable variation between kittens in the same litter. This variation is important because it gives the species an evolutionary potential; it provides a range of types on which natural selection can act. This is believed to be the reason why sexual reproduction is almost universal throughout the plant and animal kingdoms. See also ASEXUAL REPRODUCTION; BIOLOGY; FLOWER; REPRODUCTION; SEXUALITY, HUMAN.

Sex Determination. In a few animals, such as the garden snail, the earthworm, and the fresh-water hydra, the male and female sexes are combined in one individual, which is said to be a hermaphrodite. Most animals, however, have separate male and female sexes, though hermaphrodite individuals may occur as exceptions.

The normal method of sex determination is by the distribution of the sex chromosomes, which are of two kinds, X and Y. Typically, the female has two X chromosomes, i.e. XX, in the nuclei of the body cells, as well as a certain number of pairs of ordinary chromosomes; the male has one X and one Y, i.e. XY, together with the same number of ordinary chromosomes as the female. During the maturation of the gametes (sperms or eggs) the pairs of chromosomes separate, so that the total number is halved; each egg receives one X chromosome, while approximately half the sperms receive an X and half receive a Y. Approximately half the eggs will be fertilised by X sperms; each resulting zygote (fertilised egg) will have XX and will develop into a female. The remaining eggs (approximately 50 per cent) will be fertilised by Y sperms, so that each zygote will have XY, and will become a male. In this way the numbers of males and females in the offspring are maintained approximately equal.

In birds, butterflies and moths, caddis flies and certain fishes, the above arrangement of sex chromosomes is reversed: the male is XX and the female XY.

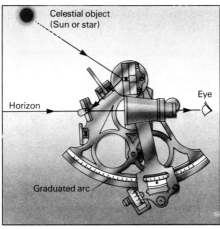

Sextant, used in navigation for finding latitude.

Sextant, an instrument for measuring the angle between two directions. The name implies the presence of a graduated arc extending over one-sixth (Latin *sextus*) of a circle (60°). The sextant as we know it appears to have been devised by several people at once, particularly Thomas Godfrey of Philadelphia (November 1730) and John Hadley in England (May 1731).

The modern marine sextant contains a graduated arc, a movable arm, two mirrors, and a small telescope. One mirror, the index glass, is fixed. The other, the horizon glass, has one half clear glass and is movable. To find the altitude of a celestial object the observer points the telescope so that he can see the horizon through the clear part of the horizon glass. He then adjusts the instrument so that he sees the celestial object, reflected via the index glass to the mirror part of the horizon glass, which is apparently in contact with the horizon. He can then read the altitude on the graduated arc.

Sexton, a contraction of sacristan. After the Reformation the sacristan's duties in the Church of England largely disappeared, and the sexton has declined into a person who prepares the graves, cares for the churchyard, sweeps the church, and performs similar offices.

Sexual Deviation, see SEXUALITY, HUMAN.
Sexual Intercourse, see SEXUALITY, HUMAN.
Sexuality, Human. The part sex plays in human relations, in love, and in our image of ourselves as effective men or women, gives it an importance in human terms far beyond its essential purpose of ensuring the continuation of the species.

The biological basis of sexuality in humans is the same as in animals. However, unlike animals, humans have no special season for birth, hence no mating season. Thus in humans, the pleasures of sexuality have taken on a significance largely disconnected from the essential reproductive purpose.

Masculinity and Femininity. Every society has an image of the ideal behaviour for men and women, and tries to make individuals fit into certain patterns, according to their sex. This stereotyping ignores the overlap of characteristics between the sexes. The male and female sexual organs develop from the same rudimentary organs in the embryo. Every person has the same sex hormones, only the proportions differ in men and women.

Psychosexual Development. Sexuality in humans brings us great bodily pleasure. From earliest infancy, the infant experiences pleasure and pain as he feels and explores his body, and is caressed and handled. Infants seem to develop through phases of awareness and concern with certain aspects of the body, classified by psychologists as oral, anal and genital. The oral phase centres on the pleasures of sucking, and the relationship to the mother's breast. The anal phase involves the pleasures and discomfort of defecating, and eventually the ability to produce or withhold, perhaps the infant's first experience of power. The greatest pleasure is discovered in normal exploration and play with the genitals. Genital preoccupation becomes latent during the years from about age 6–11, then reawakens around puberty to continue during adult life.

Homosexuality may result from distortion of normal psychosexual development. Although the person may feel secure in his own sex, he or she is attracted to members of his own sex more than the other.

A different problem is *transsexuality*, in which the person is convinced, even though his body and chromosomes indicate that he is male or female, that he or she is really a member of the other sex. Many transsexuals undergo 'sex-change operations' to alter their external genital organs. Transsexuality should not be confused with *transvestism*, which is the dressing in clothes of the opposite sex, usually for erotic pleasure.

Paedophilia is sexual play or intercourse with a child. It is proscribed by law.

The Sexual Act. Sexual arousal in the male causes the penis to become engorged with blood, making it hard and erect. The friction of intercourse increases this pleasurable tension until, at the climax (orgasm), the seminal fluid is ejaculated, followed by a softening of the penis and general relaxation. Sexual arousal in the female causes secretions to flow in the vagina, lubricating the tissues to facilitate entry of the penis. The clitoris, a similar structure to the penis, becomes hard and erect, and as excitement increases, tension and intensely pleasurable feelings build up until, at orgasm, the uterus and vagina contract rhythmically, then all the organs relax. The female's secretion corresponds to the male's erection in that both make penetration possible.

In children, and often between adults, sex acts are aimed only at erotic pleasure. Children start with masturbation, which is caressing the external genital organs to produce sexual excitement and usually orgasm. Masturbation is also resorted to by adults for various reasons. Sex play between children, and petting or mutual caressing by adolescents, whether engaged in out of curiosity or for pleasure, is part of learning about sex and the human relations connected with it.

See also HOMOSEXUALITY.

Seychelles
Area: 404 km²
Population: 64,035
Capital: Victoria

Seychelles, archipelago of 92 islands in the Indian Ocean, with a land area of 404 km², forming an independent republic situated 1000 km north-east of the Malagasy Republic, between 3°38′ and 5°45′S and 52°55′ and 53°50′E. Mahé, with an area of 144 km², is the largest island of the Granitic group, followed by Praslin, Silhouette, and La Digue. There is also an Outer or Coralline group.

Almost all the granite islands are dominated by mountains which rise sharply from the sea to heights of 610 and 910 m. Mahé, 8 km across at its widest, has a chain of peaks, the highest, Morne Seychellois, reaching 905 m. The population was estimated at 64,035 in 1981; 86 per cent is concentrated on Mahé. Victoria is the capital and chief town. Aldabra, Farquhar, and Desroches in the western Indian Ocean are islands attached to the Seychelles.

About half the total land area of the Seychelles is under tree or shrub crops, the remaining land being unsuitable for agriculture, or under forestry. Coconut palms and cinnamon trees have been the two mainstay crops.

Since the *coup d'état* of 5 June 1977 Seychelles has been ruled by a president and seven ministers appointed by him; there is no prime minister.

The new flag is divided horizontally red over green by a wavy white stripe, with red of double width.

History. The islands were occupied by the French in 1756, and later the group was named Seychelles in honour of the Viscomte Morau de Seychelles, controller-general of finance under Louis XV. In 1794 Mahé was captured by the British and in 1810, after the capture of Mauritius, Seychelles was formally incorporated as a dependency of that colony. In 1897 the Seychelles was separated from Mauritius and given its own governor. An elected governor was introduced in the late 1960s and in 1976 Seychelles became independent and joined the Commonwealth. After a coup in 1977 the office of prime minister was replaced by that of president, and government by decree was introduced.

Seymour, Lady Jane (c.1509–37), Queen of England, third wife of Henry VIII, and mother of Edward VI. She was a lady-in-waiting first to Catherine of Aragon and then to Anne Boleyn. She married Henry a few days after Anne's execution in 1536. She died in 1537, a few days after giving birth to her son.

Seymour, Lynn (1939–), Canadian-born ballerina of the Royal Ballet. Seymour, who excels not only in classical works but also in intensely dramatic rôles and in the broadest of broad comedy, has been fortunate in having throughout her career a choreographer to exploit her great gifts—Kenneth MacMillan has done for her what Ashton did for Fonteyn.

Sfax, seaport city on the Gulf of Gabès, Tunisia, 130 km south of Sousse. Its chief articles of trade are cotton and woollen goods, olive oil, fruit, phosphates, and sponges. Population (1974) 100,000.

Sforza, famous Italian ducal family.

Francesco Sforza (1401–66) succeeded his father in command of the *condottiere.* Francesco defeated the Venetians, hereditary enemies of Milan, and was acknowledged duke of Milan in 1450. His rule was most beneficent.

Galeazzo Maria Sforza (1444–76), succeeded Francesco Sforza as duke of Milan on the latter's death in 1466. He was a cruel and dissolute despot, and was assassinated.

Gian Galeazzo Sforza (1468–94), son of Galeazzo Maria, succeeded to the Duchy under his mother's regency.

Ludovico Sforza, surnamed il Moro (the Moor) (1451–1508), husband of Beatrice d'Este, supplanted, and probably poisoned, his nephew, Gian Galeazzo. He was betrayed in 1500 to Louis XII of France.

Sgraffito (Italian, scratched work), form of pottery and house decoration which was very general in prehistoric times throughout the Mediterranean area, and which has been revived in central Italy and Switzerland since the 15th century. The wall is coloured black or dark brown, and then receives a coat of light plaster on which a design is traced so that the dark paint shows through. The modern practice in commercial art of executing black-and-white drawings by 'scraper-board' is based on the same principle, except that the scratching is performed on black over a base of white, producing an effect similar to reproductions from wood engravings.

's Gravenhage, see HAGUE, THE.

Shaanxi (Shensi), an inland province of northern China to the west of Shanxi. It is bounded on the north by the Ordos Desert of Inner Mongolia and on the south by the Daba Shan (mountains). Most of the province lies north of the Qinling Shan and, like neighbouring Shanxi province, consists of a dissected upland covered by deposits of wind-blown loess. It is a rather remote area with a hard climate and relatively short growing periods for crops. The most populated part of Shaanxi is the Weihe valley, a tributary of the Huanghe, flowing eastwards at the foot of the Qinling Shan. The valley is well watered and extensively irrigated, with winter wheat, tobacco, and cotton being the major crops. In the extreme south of the province the Han valley has an almost subtropical climate and besides wheat, corn, and rice, fruit crops such as apples, pears, apricots, and grapes are produced. The capital is Xi'an in the Wei valley. Xi'an is an ancient capital of China but more recently it has been developed into a major industrial city. Area 195,800 km²; population (1972) about 22,000,000.

Shaba, formerly Katanga, province of south-eastern Zaire bordering on Zambia. It is one of the most important mining districts in the world for copper, zinc concentrates, and cobalt. Lubumbashi is the provincial capital, and Likasi and Kolwezi are important mining centres. Area 497,000 km²; population (1974) 3,072,600.

Shabbi, Abu'l-Qasim al- (1909–34), Tunisian poet, a contributor to *Apollo*. He is recognised as one of the finest Arabic poets writing between the world wars, in spite of his tragically short life, for his single volume of verse, *Songs of Life*, published

Seychelles. The islands are of continental origin. Mahé is the largest in the group.

in 1955. Usually described as a Romantic poet, the intensity of his vision transcends his own experience and problems to those of his society and humanity at large.

Shache (Chinese *Suoche*; Turkish *Yarkand*), walled town and oasis in Sinkiang Uighur (*Xinjiang Uygur*) autonomous region of China, on the River Yarkand about 160 km south-east of Kashi. A very old trade centre with bazaars, caravanserais, and many mosques, it is also the centre of an irrigated agricultural region producing grain, fruit, and oil palm. Population (1970) around 90,000.

Shackleton, Sir Ernest Henry (1874–1922), British explorer. He commanded the British Antarctic expedition, 1908–09. On 1 January 1908 his expedition left New Zealand in the *Nimrod*. He established a base near Mount Erebus, whence, on 20 October 1908, he started over the ice with sledges and three men, with provisions for 91 days. On 9 January 1909 they reached 88° 23′S, 156 km from the South Pole, a record far surpassing that established on Scott's first expedition. Mount Erebus was climbed and the magnetic pole reached. In 1914–16 he intended to cross Antarctica from Coats Land to McMurdo Sound; but the ship *Endurance* was crushed in ice and abandoned; and the party were rescued only after Shackleton and five others had voyaged to South Georgia in a 7-metre boat. In September 1921 Shackleton left London in the ship *Quest*, for a three-year tour in Antarctica. He died on board, and was buried in South Georgia.

Shad, alose, or allice, *Alosa*, a genus of fishes of the herring family Clupeidae, order Clupeiformes, found on both sides of the North Atlantic. They enter rivers to spawn.

Shadow Clock. The earliest surviving time-measuring devices provided with actual time scales were shadow clocks, the oldest known example being an Egyptian one of about the 10th to 8th centuries BC. In appearance something like a T-square, this instrument comprised a longish base with a shorter cross-piece standing up on a short arm at right angles to it. It was placed in the morning so that the cross-piece lay north and south, with the base pointing towards the west. The shadow from the cross-piece would thus fall on the base—in the early hours near the end, and gradually creeping nearer to the cross-piece itself, until the sun was at its zenith. As soon as noon had been registered the instrument was reversed in order to measure the afternoon hours in similar manner, morning and afternoon being divided into six hours each on a scale along the base.

See also SUNDIAL.

Shadow Puppets, flat figures held between a light and a translucent screen. Puppets of this kind have been developed mainly in oriental countries, where various traditions have been established.

A shadow show is featured in Ben Jonson's comedy, *A Tale of a Tub*, 1633, but it was not until towards the end of the 18th century that this form of puppet theatre played any large part in Europe.

The shadow theatre is an art form capable of great fantasy, and has attracted a number of contemporary puppeteers, notably Lotte Reiniger who exploited this medium in films.

Shadows. The shadow of an object formed by an extended light source is divided into two regions. No light rays reach the umbra, or shadow proper, so that this is in principle completely dark, but light from some parts of the source reaches the penumbra.

Shadwell, Thomas (c.1642–92), English poet laureate and dramatist. His first play, *The Sullen Lovers*, based on Molière's *Les Fâcheux*, was produced at the theatre in Lincoln's Inn Fields in 1668. After other adaptations he wrote *Epsom Wells*, a coarse but well constructed comedy, which was successful at Dorset Garden in 1672. *The Squire of Alsatia* was presented in 1688 and *Bury Fair* in 1689. Among his other comedies, which show comic power based on Jonson's theory of 'humours', are *Royal Shepherdess*, 1669, *The Humorists*, 1671, and *The Miser*, 1672.

Shadwell supported the cause of the middle-class Whigs, and when Dryden attacked them in *Absalom and Achitophel* and *The Medal*, Shadwell scurrilously assailed him in *The Medal of John Bayes*, 1682. The punishment which this evoked in Dryden's *MacFlecknoe* and the second part of *Absalom and Achitophel*, in which Shadwell figures as 'Og', gave him an unenviable immortality. However, at the Revolution, he replaced Dryden as poet laureate.

Shaffer, Peter Levin (1926–), English dramatist and novelist. Shaffer came to prominence with *Five Finger Exercise*, 1958, a domestic drama set in a rich middle-class home. This was followed by *The Private Ear and the Public Eye*, 1962, and *The Royal Hunt of the Sun*, 1964, an epic play about the Spanish conquest of Peru. The highly successful farce, *Black Comedy*, 1965, was followed by a philosophical play, *The Battle of Shrivings*, 1970, *Equus*, 1973, a psychological study of a boy who deliberately blinds horses, and *Amadeus*, 1979 an examination of the gulf between morality and the creative drive, focused on Mozart and Salieri. He has written television and screen plays (including *Lord of the Flies*, with Peter Brook), and novels with his twin brother Anthony Shaffer, who is chiefly known for his highly successful stage thriller, *Sleuth*, 1970, which was later filmed.

Shaftesbury, Anthony Ashley Cooper, 1st Earl of (1621–83), English politician. Shaftesbury sat in the Barebones Parliament, and was appointed one of the Protector's council of state. From 1655 he was in constant opposition to Cromwell. At the restoration of Charles II, he was made chancellor of the Exchequer, and a privy councillor. After the fall of Clarendon, Lord Ashley formed one of the Cabal ministry. In April 1672 he was created earl of Shaftesbury, and in November following was raised to the office of lord chancellor. In 1673, however, he supported the Test Bill and was dismissed from office. Shaftesbury now openly joined the ranks of opposition as a champion of toleration for dissenters and national liberties. The Habeas Corpus Act was for long known as Shaftesbury's Act.

After the fall of Danby, Shaftesbury was made president of Temple's new Privy Council (1679), and he now tried to exclude James, Duke of York, from the succession in favour of Monmouth. When Monmouth and Lord William Russell refrained from the open rebellion advocated by Shaftesbury, the latter fled to Holland on 18 November 1682, and died there a few months later.

Shaftesbury, Anthony Ashley Cooper, 3rd Earl of (1671–1713), English politician and philosopher, grandson of the first Earl of Shaftesbury. In 1693 he entered Parliament, but he resigned his seat in 1698. He distinguished himself in the House of Lords; but after the accession of Anne he never took any part in public life.

Shaftesbury's *Characteristicks of Men, Manners, Opinions, Times*, published in 1711, reveal his religious scepticism, and he was attacked as a Deist by Berkeley and others. His genuinely lofty sentiment gives value to his ethical speculation, the best account of which is in his *Inquiry concerning Virtue in two Discourses*, 1699. His aesthetic speculations are to be found in *Notion of the Historical Draught or Tablature of the Judgment of Hercules*.

Shaftesbury, Anthony Ashley Cooper, 7th Earl of (1801–85), British politician. He entered Parliament as member for Woodstock in 1826. Reform in poor law, the treatment of lunatics, and the condition of factory operatives were subjects with which he was connected. Largely through his efforts a Ten Hours Bill was passed in 1847. He was the champion in Parliament of the movement for ragged schools and for nearly 40 years was chairman of the Ragged School Union. His was the influence behind Lord Palmerston's bill for the care and reformation of juvenile offenders. The Lodging House Act, which he piloted through the Upper House (he had succeeded to the earldom in 1851), was designed to improve the dwellings of the people.

Shag, *Phalacrocorax aristoclis*, a bird, related to the cormorant, in the order Pelecaniformes. It is smaller than the cormorant, with a green tinge to its plumage and in the breeding season has a crest.

Shah, word meaning ruler or prince, that was applied particularly to the ruler of Iran. In his own land he was also called shahinshah (king of kings).

Shah Jahan (1592–1666), fifth of the Mogul emperors of India, in whose reign Mogul power reached its height. Although able and artistic, Shah Jahan was ruthless; he executed all his male collaterals during the wars of succession and, a zealous Muslim, he persecuted Hindus in the early part of his reign. Prodigal court expenditure created terrible famines for his people. His age was the golden period for Muslim architecture in India; he built the Taj Mahal at Agra as a mausoleum for his favourite wife; the palace and Great Mosque at Delhi; and the celebrated Peacock Throne. He founded the modern city of Delhi between 1639 and 1648. In 1657, while Shah Jahan lay dangerously ill, civil war broke out between his four sons. Aurangzeb, the victor, confined his father in the citadel of Agra, where he died in December 1666.

See also INDIA, *Architecture*.

Shah of Iran, see MOHAMMED RIZA SHAH PAHLAVI.

Shahn, Ben (1898–1969), US painter. Shahn

was apprenticed to a lithographer but also attended New York University, the City College of New York, and the National Academy of Design. Many of his paintings and graphic works reflect Shahn's involvement in social issues.

Shakers, popular name of the United Society of Believers in Christ's Second Appearing, founded about 1747 in England by James and Jane Wardley. They were joined by Ann Lee (1736–84) of Manchester, who claimed to be Jesus Christ in his second appearance. In 1774 the sect moved to America, and three years after the death of Ann Lee the society was established on a communistic basis.

Shakespeare, William (1564–1616), English dramatist and poet, born at Stratford-upon-Avon. His father, John Shakespeare, a leading citizen of the town, was a glover and general businessman. The young Shakespeare almost certainly attended Stratford Grammar School. He married, at the age of 18, Anne Hathaway, who was then aged 26. It is not known what Shakespeare did between this period and 1592, by which time he was established in the London theatrical world. From 1594 onward he was an important member of the Lord Chamberlain's Company of actors. In 1603 the Company became the King's Men. By 1597 Shakespeare was prosperous enough to purchase New Place, the second largest house in Stratford and by 1613 had apparently retired permanently to Stratford. He died on 23 April 1616, and was buried in the chancel of Holy Trinity, Stratford.

The dates of composition of the plays are partly conjectural, but the general chronology has been widely agreed by scholars. The early years in London till about 1594–95 witnessed Shakespeare's first attempts at the chronicle-history (*Henry VI*, 1, 2 and 3, and *Richard III*); at farce based on a classical model (*The Comedy of Errors*); at romantic comedy of character (*The Two Gentlemen of Verona, The Taming of the Shrew*); at sensational Senecan revenge tragedy (*Titus Andronicus*); at sophisticated wit-comedy (*Love's Labour's Lost*); and at romantic tragedy (*Romeo and Juliet*). Although they can all be faulted, the striking feature of the early plays is the imaginative power Shakespeare brings to his experiments with established forms and conventions.

The plays written between 1595 and 1600 reveal Shakespeare's development towards full maturity as an imaginative artist and dramatic craftsman. These include the histories of *Richard II, King John, Henry IV* 1 and 2 and *Henry V*. In this same period Shakespeare wrote a number of comedies centring on love and sexual relations, and often featuring the resourceful good-sense of the heroines. These include *A Midsummer Night's Dream, The Merchant of Venice, Much Ado About Nothing* and *The Merry Wives of Windsor. As You Like It* and *Twelfth Night* are his masterpieces in the genre of romantic comedy. The sadness and bitterness which run as undercurrents through them come to the surface in the so-called 'dark comedies' or 'problem plays' which Shakespeare wrote between c.1601 and c.1605. These are *Troilus and Cressida All's Well That Ends Well* and *Measure for Measure.*

Between c.1601 and c.1605 Shakespeare produced the four great tragedies. *Hamlet*, the first of them, is perhaps the single best-known play ever written. At the centre of the play is Hamlet's alienation from the life going on, apparently normally, around him, for only he knows the truth about his father's murder. *Othello* continues Shakespeare's preoccupation with truth and its deceptive simulacrum. *King Lear* is perhaps the most emotionally powerful of all his plays, while *Macbeth* is a story of crime and punishment.

Shakespeare. The frontispiece to the First Folio.

Antony and Cleopatra and *Coriolanus*, which immediately followed the great tragedies, may be considered with *Julius Caesar* (which was written just before them) as comprising a distinct group of 'Roman' plays. *Timon of Athens*, written at roughly the same time as *Coriolanus*, is very uneven in quality. Experimental features are especially evident in *Pericles*, which initiates the final period of Shakespeare's work, and which includes *Cymbeline, The Winter's Tale, The Tempest,* and *Henry VIII*. Certain similarities in theme and technique link these plays closely together. They characteristically present some tragic or poignant complication which is ultimately resolved—in the form of the reconciliation and reunion of antagonists.

As a poet, Shakespeare is chiefly remembered for his sonnets, which he wrote mainly in the earlier part of his life. They were published in 1609. He also wrote two narrative poems, *Venus and Adonis* (1593) and *The Rape of Lucrece* (1594).

Shakhty (formerly *Aleksandrovsk Grushevski*), city in Rostov *oblast* of the RSFSR, USSR, in the Donets Basin 60 km north-east of Rostov-on-Don. It is a centre of coal-mining (anthracite) and electricity production of the East Donbas, and was founded as a coal-mining settlement in 1839. Population (1980) 212,000.

Shale, a rock showing a fissility along bedding planes formed by the compaction and consolidation of clay or fine sediments from which the water has been expelled by the weight of overlying sediments.

Shale Oil is the oil obtained by the destructive distillation of oil shale. It is sometimes called synthetic crude oil or syncrude, once it is extracted. Oil shale is a stratified sedimentary rock in which are found numerous fragments of fossil plants and animals. The shale, although containing as much as 35 per cent organic matter, does not contain any oil. The organic material, kerogen, is similar to a precursor of oil, and may be removed from the rock by heating, which decomposes it and forms a complex oily liquid (shale oil) which differs from both crude oil and asphalt. Shale oil is distilled from the shale, and is processed in a similar way to petroleum.

Shaliapin, Feodor Ivanovich (1873–1938), Russian bass singer. He made his operatic début at Tiflis in Glinka's *Life for the Tsar*. Later he sang at St Petersburg as Ivan the Terrible in Rimsky-Korsakov's *Maid of Pskov*. His favourite roles included Don Basilio in Rossini's *Barber of Seville* and Leporello in Mozart's *Don Giovanni*; his performances were as remarkable for his acting as for the magnificence of his voice. He made his New York début in 1907 and he first appeared in London in 1913.

Shallot, a plant allied to the onion. It was long considered to be a different species from the onion, *Allium cepa*, but is now considered to be a variety of it (var. *aggregatum*).

Shamanism, name which loosely embraces the main religious beliefs and practices of the indigenous peoples of North Asia, the Eskimoes and the Lapps. The shaman, mistakenly called medicine-man, is believed to make contact with Divinity during trances in ecstatic rituals, to converse with spiritual beings, and thus ward off evil influences, cure sickness, bring rain, foretell the future, etc. His position in society and his powers to heal have sometimes been seen to parallel those of psychotherapists in Western Society. See also ECSTASY; TABOO; WITCHCRAFT; YAKUTS.

Shamrock, several trifoliate plants, notably *Trifolium dubium*, the white *T. repens* and *Medicago lupulina*, one of which Saint Patrick is said to have used to illustrate the doctrine of the Trinity. The shamrock is the national badge of Ireland. Wood-sorrel, *Oxalis acetosella*, is sometimes also known as shamrock.

Shandong (Shantung), maritime province of north-east China whose eastern half forms a peninsula separating the Gulf of Bohai from the Yellow Sea. Its relief consists of two upland areas separated by a central depression about 80 km wide. Fishing has always been a major industry, and a wide variety of crops are grown including wheat, maize, cotton, tobacco, peanuts, and fruit. The province is famous for its silks and its wines. The Huanghe crosses the province and enters the sea in the north. In recent years the province's mineral resources, chiefly coal and iron-ore, have been intensively developed, and an oilfield has been discovered at Shengli in the

Huanghe delta. The capital of the province, Jinan, is the major manufacturing centre. Qingdao and Yantai are the largest ports. Qufu, the birthplace of Confucius, lies in the south-west. Area 153,300 km²; population (1972) about 60,000,000.

Shanghai, the largest city in China, situated at the mouth of the Changjiang delta. Formerly a place of only minor significance, in 1842, in accordance with the Treaty of Nanjing, Shanghai was chosen as a treaty port to be opened to international trade.

As a treaty port, Shanghai developed rapidly during the second half of the 19th century as the commercial outlet for the whole of the Yangtze basin. It grew into a large international port and also a considerable light-manufacturing centre, particularly in textiles and other consumer goods. An important shipbuilding and ship-repairing trade developed. The so-called 'international settlement' was a foreign enclave within Shanghai established by the Western powers. It was here that China's first urbanised labouring class grew up after the First World War, and it was the scene of much political unrest. Shanghai has now become China's second-largest iron and steel producer after Anshan in Manchuria. Most of this new industry is situated at Wusong. Shanghai has also become a major refining centre for copper, lead, and zinc. Chemicals, plastics, synthetic fibres, and fertilisers are other industries now represented there. There is also an oil refinery which processes crude oil from the Daqing field in Manchuria. The population of the city is estimated (1970) to be about 11,000,000.

Shankar, Ravi (1920–), Indian sitar player who studied under Ustad Allauddin Khan of Maihar; outstanding as an exponent and teacher; founder of music schools in Bombay and Los Angeles. He has composed music for many films, including Satyajit Ray's *Apu* trilogy. His experimental work includes the *Sitar Concerto*. Shankar is the author of *My Music, My Life*, published in 1968.

Shankly, Bill (1915–81), Scottish footballer and outstanding football manager. As a wing half he gained five full caps for Scotland. He turned professional with Preston North End in 1932 and after the Cup Final of 1938 he became a manager, first with Carlisle, then Grimsby, Workington and Huddersfield. He joined Liverpool in 1959 and led them to the First Division title. During his 15 years with Liverpool the Club won three League Championships, two FA cups and one UEFA cup.

Shannon, longest river of Ireland; it rises in the Cuilcagh Mountains, County Cavan, 105 m above sea-level. It flows through Loughs Allen, Boderg, Forbes, Ree, and Derg, past Limerick into the Atlantic. It is 350 km long, and its estuary is 110 km long and 3–16 km wide, navigable by large vessels as far as Limerick.

Shansi, see SHANXI.

Shantung, see SHANDONG.

Shanxi (Shansi), an inland province of northern China, bounded on the west and south by the Huanghe, on the north by the Great Wall of China and on the east by the Taihang Shan (mountains). Together with neighbouring Shaanxi province to the west, Shanxi consists of a dissected plateau between

500 and 2000 m in height covered by wind-blown superficial deposits known as loess. The Fenhe valley is the major area of settlement and within it is the city of Taiyuan, the capital of the province. Agriculture in the valley is largely dependent upon irrigation, the principal crops being winter wheat, kao-liang, and millet. Cotton and hemp are also grown. Large coal-mines have been developed at Datong in the north of the province, at Xishan west of Taiyuan, at Fenxi, and at Yitang. Taiyuan is now one of China's most important iron- and steel-producing centres and its population exceeds one million. Datong is a major railway junction and coal-mining centre. It also has cement industries and engineering works. Area 157,000 km²; population (1972) about 20,000,000.

Shap Fells, granitic upland in Cumbria, England, crossed by the main railway line and motorway (M6) to Scotland. Height 422 m.

Shapley, Harlow (1885–1972), US astronomer. At Mount Wilson observatory Shapley worked on globular clusters and from their distribution showed that the Sun was some 50,000 light years from the centre of the Milky Way, not near it as had hitherto been supposed.

Shares, see STOCK; STOCK EXCHANGE.

***George Bernard Shaw,** photographed in 1925.*

Shariah (Arabic, road leading to a water-hole), Islamic religious law, incorporating all the practical aspects of Mohammed's religious and social teachings. The Shariah is drawn from four sources: the Koran, the Sunna or traditional life of Mohammed, *ijma* or the consensus of opinion of the Ulema on any question, and *qiyas* or analogy, the last being sought only when none of the first three criteria was applicable. The various schools of interpretation predominate in different parts of the Muslim world.

Shariah courts today are mostly restricted to cases concerning marriage, the family, inheritance, and the like.

Sharjah, see UNITED ARAB EMIRATES.

Shark, fish in the order Selachii, of subclass Elasmobranchii in class Chondrichthyes, the fish that have a cartilaginous instead of a bony skeleton. Subclass Elasmobranchii includes the sharks and rays (Batoidei). Both

have five to seven pairs of gill slits, but in the sharks these open on the side, while in the rays they open underneath the flattened body. The pectoral fins of rays join the body in front of the gills, forming a wide flap, but in the sharks the forward edge is free and attached behind the gills. Sharks and rays are living fossils, as many genera today closely resemble fossil sharks of the Jurassic period. There are over 200 living species of shark and more than 300 species of ray.

All sharks are carnivorous, but two species, the basking shark, *Cetorhinus maximus*, and the whale shark, *Rhincodon typus*, filter plankton from the seawater, living entirely on these microscopic organisms and, perhaps, small fish. Others eat crustacea, fish, squid, sea birds, rubbish from ships and carrion.

Male sharks have specially adapted fins, called claspers, with which they insert sperm into the females. Pregnant females ready to give birth congregate in preferred nursery areas. These vary from shallow bays to the deep ocean, according to species. Some species are oviparous, others are ovoviviparous, and a few are viviparous.

The white shark, *Carcharodon carcharias*, is probably the most dangerous shark known to man. It grows to 12 m.

See also DOGFISH.

Sharon, plain on the coast of Israel, which stretches from Jaffa to Caesarea Philippi, about 65 km long. The 'roses' for which it was famous in ancient times are supposed to have been narcissi. The present-day Rose of Sharon is a *Hypericum*.

Sharp, Cecil (1859–1924), musical researcher, famous for his collections and arrangements of folk-songs, country dances, morris dances, etc. He founded a school of music at Adelaide, Australia and the English Folk Dance Society (renamed English Folk Dance and Song Society).

Sharp, character in musical notation which indicates that a note is to be sung or played a semitone higher than its natural pitch. The sign occurs before the note to be sharpened in the case of accidentals. The sharps occurring regularly in the key chosen by the composer apply throughout unless contradicted by another accidental. A double sharp (X) indicates that the pitch is to be raised by a whole tone.

See also NOTATION.

Shastri, Lal Bahadur (1904–66), Prime Minister of India (1964–66). He was active for the Indian National Congress from 1921 and served a time in prison in 1930. He was general secretary, UPCC, 1935–38; minister of police and transport UP, 1947; general secretary of the Indian National Congress, 1951; minister for transport and communications in the Indian government, 1957–1958; commerce and industry, 1958–61; home affairs, 1961–63; minister without portfolio, 1964; and became prime minister on 12 June 1964, on the death of Nehru. He died in Tashkent in the USSR.

Shatt-al-Arab, see EUPHRATES.

Shaw, George Bernard (1856–1950), English playwright, born in Dublin, of a genteel but poor Protestant family. He had little formal education but when he went to London in 1876 he studied voraciously. He became a socialist and in 1884 joined the newly created Fabian Society. He wrote reviews, pamphlets and music, drama and art criticism for a number of papers during the 1880s and 1890s. He began to champion Henrik Ibsen and took Ibsen and Shakespeare as models for a new drama which would be in vital contact with contemporary life and problems.

During the 1890s Shaw began to supply the public with the didactic 'problem' plays he believed were needed. *Arms and the Man*, 1894, was a satire on romantic attitudes towards war. *Mrs Warren's Profession* examined the social nature and implications of prostitution, without any of the romantic melodrama of previous 'women-with-a-past' plays. Other works of this early period are *Candida*, 1895, *The Devil's Disciple*, 1897, *Caesar and Cleopatra*, 1898, *John Bull's Other Island*, 1904, *Man and Superman*, 1905, *Major Barbara*, 1905 and *The Doctor's Dilemma*, 1906. As a counter-balance to his treatment of serious issues, Shaw developed a comic technique which relied on brilliantly witty serio-comic dialogue and playfully ironic inversion of audience expectations about character and situation. As a result, he contrived to be at once a leader of the intellectually serious and progressive English theatre and a successful popular playwright.

The years before the First World War produced a number of lightweight but popular comedies, including *Misalliance*, 1910, *Androcles and the Lion*, 1912, and *Pygmalion*, 1913. *Heartbreak House*, written during the war, is regarded by some critics as his finest play. In *St Joan*, 1923, the chronicle-history which is—with *Pygmalion*—his best-known and most revived play, Shaw examined the implications of religious belief. With *The Apple Cart*, 1929, he began to write a number of 'political extravaganzas', including *Too True to be Good*, 1932, *On the Rocks*, 1933, and *The Millionairess*, 1936. He refused all honours except the Nobel Prize for literature, which he was awarded in 1925.

Shaw, Richard Norman (1831–1912), British architect. He created an immense practice, which included many country mansions; town-houses; churches; Albert Hall Mansions, the first large block of flats in London (1879); the Gaiety Theatre; New Scotland Yard (1888); and the Piccadilly Hotel (1905). He had great influence on late 19th-century English architecture.

Shaw, Robert Archibald (1927–78), British actor, novelist and dramatist. Shaw was best known as an actor who appeared in classical roles with the Royal Shakespeare Company and in major parts in modern plays in both London and New York. Examples of the latter are Blackmouth in *Live Like Pigs* by John Arden and Aston in *The Caretaker* by Harold Pinter. He also achieved fame as a film actor, appearing as Henry VIII in *A Man for All Seasons*, 1966; *The Birthday Party*, 1968; *Battle of Britain*, 1969; and *Figures in a Landscape*, 1969, for which he also wrote the screenplay. His novels include *The Hiding Place*, 1959, for which he won the Hawthornden prize; *The Sun Doctor*, 1961; and *The Man in the Glass Booth*, 1967. He was married to the actress Mary Ure, who died in 1975.

Shawl, article of dress worn over the shoulders, or head and shoulders, as a wrapping. For many centuries this simple garment remained in constant use among women of almost all nationalities and classes, both for themselves and for their babies. The decline in its use for adult wear coincided with the advent of cheap, machine-made clothing and the invention of weather- and water-proof coats.

Shawm, woodwind instrument, the forerunner of the oboe, with a double-reed mouthpiece and a wide bell. The largest sizes had a curved crook similar to that of the bassoon.

Shawnee, North American Indians of the Algonkian linguistic group, noted for their extensive migrations through the east and south of the USA. Most of the 5000 survivors live in Oklahoma.

Shawqi, Ahmad (1868–1932), Egyptian poet, one of the greatest of the modern period, usually known as *Amir al-Shu'ara'*, Prince of Poets. His early career was spent at the court of the Khedive 'Abbas II, much as a court poet in the old Arabic tradition. He was exiled from Egypt during the First World War, and returned an enthusiastic supporter of Egyptian nationalism. Although bitterly attacked by some for his associations with the Khedive, his literary reputation is safeguarded by the quality of his poetry, collected into four volumes and known as the *Shawqiyyat*. He also wrote some of the earliest drama in literary Arabic.

Shcherbakov, see RYBINSK.

She-oak, see CASARINACEAE.

Shearwater, about 15 species of bird in the family Procellariidae, in order Procellariiformes. All the species are oceanic, and either dark above and white below or all dark. They are related to the albatrosses and petrels and get their name from their habit of skimming low over the sea on still wings. Shearwaters breed colonially in burrows, often in huge numbers. The Manx shearwater, *Puffinus puffinus*, is a common breeding bird in parts of the British Isles, Italy and Greece.

Sheba, the name given in the Bible to a state (modern Yemen) in southern Arabia which was rich because it controlled the trade route, especially for incense. The story of Solomon and the Queen of Sheba occurs in 1 Kings x and in the Koran, and is well known to Arab writers, who call her Bilqis. The royal house of Ethiopia claimed descent from this union.

Shechem, see NABLUS.

Sheene, Barry (1950–), British motorcyclist. He won his first 500cc world championship in 1976, following a remarkable recovery from injuries received in a spectacular 175 mph crash at Daytona the previous year. He retained the title in 1977, but in July 1982 badly smashed both legs during a test session at Silverstone. He has since signed a contract with Suzuki to return to competitive racing.

Sheep, a ruminant animal of the genus *Ovis*, family Bovidae (the cud-chewing animals) of order Artiodactyla (the cloven-hoofed mammals), which has been domesticated from the earliest times. Wild sheep occur in various parts of the world, the mouffion is still in a semi-wild state in the islands of Sardinia and Corsica.

Britain has long been one of the chief sheep countries of the world, and its breeds have been valued highly. The two most notable breeds of sheep which owe nothing to British blood are the Merino and the Astrakan. Mention should also be made of the milk-yielding sheep of France, the most notable breed of which is the Larzac; its milk is used chiefly in the production of Roquefort.

Existing British breeds are usually classified as (1) mountain and moorland and (2) lowland. The chief mountain and moorland breeds are Blackface, Welsh Mountain, Rough Fell, Lonk, Derbyshire Gritstone, Swaledale, Exmoor Horn, Dartmoor, Cheviot and Herdwick. Most of the lowland longwool breeds are hybrids, improved in the past by crossing with the Leicester, originally a large, heavy-fleeced slow-maturing animal.

Sheep Ked, *Melophagus ovinus*, insect belonging to the family Hippoboscidae (suborder Cyclorrhapha) in order Diptera. They are ectoparasites of sheep, and feed on their blood.

Sheepdog Trials and demonstrations are very popular events at agricultural shows. The International Sheepdog Society holds annual trials in England, Scotland, Wales, Ireland and the Isle of Man to select a team from each country to compete at the International Trials held in England, Scotland and Wales in turn. Twelve dogs with the highest points are selected in England, Scotland and Wales and four in Ireland and the Isle of Man. These dogs are run on the national course which is the same as the qualifying course at the International Trials. Shepherd classes are also competed for, and there are contests for 'brace' or double dogs and a driving championship at the International Trials.

Sheerness, former naval base, seaside resort, and industrial port on the Isle of Sheppey, Kent. Container and roll-on/roll-off systems operate.

Sheffield, city of South Yorkshire, England. Its importance is due to the production of special steels and steel products. It is noted for its cutlery and hand tools.

Situated on the coal measures, with workable seams within the city boundary, Sheffield is bisected by the Don and its tributaries.

Iron was worked in the vicinity in the 12th century, and Sheffield was famed for its knives by 1400. The invention by Boulsover in 1742 of the method of coating copper with silver to form 'Sheffield plate', established an industry which flourished until it was superseded by electroplating in the 1850s. In 1740 Huntsman invented the process for making crucible steel and later established his works at Attercliffe. Sheffield now makes alloy and special steels to withstand high pressures or temperatures, to be acid-resistant, or possess other unusual qualities. Most were invented in Sheffield laboratories and works (including stainless steel). Population (1981) 477,142.

Sheffield Plate, see SILVERSMITHING.

Sheikh (Arabic *shaikh*), Arabian and Muslim title, used to designate chieftains, lesser magistrates, and scholars. The word literally means an elder, and denotes a dignity that has no very precise significance. Basically it is little more than *primus inter pares*; thus chiefs of tribes and heads of villages are both called sheikhs. *Shaikh al-Islam* was originally a title of honour granted to theologians which came to be the prerogative of the mufti of Istanbul.

Shekel, a Babylonian unit of weight, and the name used in the Bible for silver coins of approximately the same weight circulating in ancient Israel. The shekel was only struck by the Jews themselves during their first and second revolts against Rome (AD 66–70 and 132–35). The shekel became the currency of Israel in 1980.

Shekinah, or Shechinah (Hebrew, dwelling or presence), expression frequently occurring in the Targums and Talmud to denote the divine presence, the idea being developed in Jewish Rabbinical thought after Old Testament times. The original conception grew from the description of the presence of the Lord in the holy of holies in the tabernacle, indicated by the cloud enveloping it as the manifestation of God, which was thought of as the light behind the cloud.

Shelduck, *Tadorna tadorna,* handsome, brilliantly plumaged member of the duck family, Anatidae, in the order Anseriformes. It is found naturally on European coasts and in central and eastern Asia, but is often kept on ornamental waters. The name refers to a shield-like patch on the breast. The drake is about 60 cm long, the head and neck are glossy green and the rest of the plumage is chiefly black and white, with rich chestnut breast and a bronze patch on the wing.

Shell, the hard covering of an animal, including the carapace of a tortoise, crab or lobster; more correctly confined to the calcareous structures characteristic of phylum Mollusca. A typical mollusc shell is composed of carbonate of lime mixed with conchiolin, an animal substance similar to chitin. The shell is secreted by the mantle, a fold of skin which envelops the mollusc's body. Additions to the shell are formed only by the edge of the mantle and, since growth is discontinuous, lines of growth are shown on the exterior surface.

Shells are divided into two main groups, univalves, which are all in one piece, as in the whelk and snail, and bivalves, which consist of two distinct portions, as in oysters and mussels. Both types show wide diversity in shape, colour and surface conformation.

In bivalves the shell valves may be similar, as in the cockle, or dissimilar, as in the scallop, in which one is strongly convex, while the other is flat. The valves are hinged at the top by an elastic ligament or membrane, which exerts a pull on the areas to which it is attached. This pull is countered by the contraction of muscle bands that stretch between the valves. An empty shell shows distinctive scars at the points of attachment of these muscles. Accurate closing of the valves is often ensured by the development of interlocking teeth or ridges at the top margins.

Univalves, like limpets, winkles, top shells, necklace shells, whelks, screw shells, spindles and conelets, are among the most common of seashore objects. The largest univalve shells are the spindle-shaped tulip shells of the shores of South Carolina, which may be 60 cm long, and the West Indian pink conch, or fountain shell, weighing up to 1.8 kg.

Univalves include many tropical and sub-tropical forms of great beauty. Special mention may be made of the volutes, olives, harp-snails, cones and wing-snails.

The most generally distributed bivalves include oysters, mussels, scallops, cockles, trough shells, gapers and the long narrow razor-shells. Among the many large and interesting bivalves of tropical and sub-tropical waters are the pearl mussels, the brightly coloured thorny oysters and the clams, in some species of which a single valve may weigh over 90 kg.

Shell-shock, a term for traumatic neurosis that was widely used during the First World War to describe various neurotic syndromes which are now recognised as anxiety states and anxiety hysterias. While it is true that the onset of symptoms was, in some cases, associated with some specific incident, such as proximity to a shell-burst, many more occurred in areas remote from shell-fire. In the majority of cases the appearance of symptoms merely marked the point where the breaking stress had been reached after a prolonged period of tension, even if the latter had been unsuspected.

See PSYCHOPATHOLOGY.

Percy Bysshe Shelley by Amelia Curran, 1819.

Shellac, a substance secreted by the lac insect, and more especially a resin prepared from the secretions. Shellac was used in the production of gramophone records before the advent of vinyl plastics. Dissolved in alcohol or acetone, shellac is used as a lacquer.

Shelley, Mary Wollstonecraft (1797–1851), English novelist, the daughter of the philosopher William Godwin and Mary Wollstonecraft, and second wife of the poet Percy Bysshe Shelley.

Mary Shelley is best known as the author of the weird and brilliant tale of horror *Frankenstein: or, The Modern Prometheus,* 1818, which of all novels written in the 'gothic' style has had the most striking influence.

Shelley, Percy Bysshe (1792–1822), English poet. In 1810 he entered University College, Oxford, but soon after matriculating he joined Thomas Jefferson Hogg, the future biographer, in the production of a pamphlet, *The Necessity of Atheism,* 1811, which gave so much offence that he was sent down.

In 1813 he published *Queen Mab,* and came under the influence of the radical William Godwin. At this time Shelley and his wife, Harriet, with whom he had eloped in 1811, drifted apart, and in 1814 Shelley eloped to Switzerland with Godwin's daughter Mary. In 1816, he married Mary Godwin, issued the memorable *Alastor,* and travelled in Switzerland and France. After living for some time at Marlow, and then near Windsor, Shelley and his wife proceeded to Italy.

His contact with Italy was a landmark in Shelley's intellectual development. Here he composed *The Cenci,* 1819, 'Ode to the West Wind', 1819, *Rosalind and Helen,* 1819, and *Prometheus Unbound,* 1820; while at Pisa he wrote many of his finest short lyrics, and also *Epipsychidion,* 1821, *Adonais,* 1821, his elegy on the death of Keats, and *Hellas,* 1822. He continued to champion the cause of freedom in England and Italy, while he read Greek literature incessantly, mastered Spanish, Italian, and German, and translated Calderón, Dante, and Goethe. In July 1822, while sailing to Spezia, his boat foundered in a storm and he was drowned.

Shelley is often pictured as an ethereal visionary. This view fails to take account of his development from the over-simplified theories of his youth, his great learning, or his readiness to risk involvement with the pain and injustice of the world. In *A Defence of Poetry,* written in 1821, but unpublished until 1840, Shelley declared his belief in poetry as a moral force. Many of his poems were radical and reforming in aim; but, though these excited much contemporary interest and contain stirring passages (such as his eulogies on freedom in *Hellas*), Shelley is chiefly remembered as one of the greatest lyric poets.

Shellfish, popular unscientific name which includes edible molluscs (phylum Mollusca) such as the whelk, periwinkle, oyster and mussel, as well as such crustaceans (phylum Arthropoda, class Crustacea) as the crab, lobster, prawn and shrimp.

Shelta, or Shelter, Shelterox, Sheldru, Sheltru, is apparently a corruption of Irish *bēlra* or *bērla* (or *bēarla*), meaning speech, language, jargon. It is a mysterious form of speech, of uncertain origin, used by Irish gypsies, although it seems not to be connected with Romany. It draws on English as well as Irish for its vocabulary.

See also IRELAND, *Language.*

Shema, central prayer of Judaism (Deut. vi. 4–9). It is the affirmation of the One God, to be loved and taught to all, prominent in all public and private prayer of Jews, and recited at the death bed.

Shenandoah, river of Virginia and West Virginia, USA, a tributary of the Potomac, which joins it at its passage through the Blue Ridge, after a course north-east for 325 km.

Shenandoah Valley Campaign. The valley of the River Shenandoah in north-west Virginia. It was the scene of many conflicts during the Civil War and became especially famous in 1864. Gen. U. S. Grant, with 150,000 Federal troops, was confronting Gen. Robert E. Lee, with 75,000 Confederates. Grant sent his best cavalry general, Philip Sheridan, to lay the whole valley waste, so that it could not afford a field for Confederate operations. On 5 October Sheridan began his famous raid down the Shenandoah Valley. Pursuant to orders, he destroyed everything the enemy might use. The devastation of the valley prevented further movements there by either side.

Shensi, see SHANXI.

Shenstone, William (1714–63), English poet. *Poems upon Various Occasions* was published in 1737, and this was followed by *The Judgement of Horatio*, 1741, and *The School-mistress*, 1742, a humorous imitation of Spenser. After 1745 Shenstone took up landscape gardening which earned him a wider reputation than his poetry.

Shenyang (Mukden), largest city of Manchuria, capital of Liaoning province, China, and the main railway junction for south Manchuria. North of the city is the burial ground for Qing emperors. It is the most important machine-building centre of the heavily industrialised north-east, besides being the main trading city for the whole of that area. It also has important copper, zinc, and lead refineries. Population (1970) 3,500,000.

Shepard, Alan (1923–), US astronaut. On 5 May 1961 he became the second man to enter space. His space capsule was fired from Cape Kennedy 180 km into space, and Shepard maintained communication with the ground throughout his 15-minute flight. In 1971 he made a lunar landing in *Apollo 14*, and during a 33½-hour exploration gathered samples from the Moon's surface and set up scientific equipment.

Shepard, Ernest Howard (1879–1976), British artist and cartoonist. Shepard produced illustrations for A. A. Milne's *Winnie-the-Pooh*, 1926, Kenneth Grahame's *The Golden Age*, 1928, and *The Wind in the Willows*, 1931, which continue to be the standard versions even in modern editions. He published an autobiography, *Drawn from Memory*, 1957.

Shepherd's Dog, see OLD ENGLISH SHEEP-DOG.

Shepherd's Purse, *Capsella bursa-pastoris*, a cosmopolitan plant belonging to the Cruciferae and characterised by its two-valved fruits. The plant is extraordinarily adaptable, and, being self-fertilised, is able to flower and seed the whole year round.

Sheppard, David Stuart (1929–), English cricketer and churchman. He played in 22 Test matches before his retirement in 1963, and captained England in 1954. He played for Sussex, 1947–62. He was ordained into the Church of England in 1955 and was warden of the Mayflower Family Centre in Canning Town, 1957–69. He succeeded Dr John Robinson as suffragan bishop of Woolwich in 1969, and in 1975 was appointed bishop of Liverpool. His publications include *Parson's Pitch*, 1964, and *Built as a City*, 1974.

Sheppard, Jack (1702–24), English criminal. In July 1724 he was caught, and in the following month was tried and condemned to death. He escaped twice, but was caught drunk, and watched day and night until his execution at Tyburn on 16 November. He was a popular hero, and Ainsworth made him the subject of a novel, *Jack Sheppard*.

Shepparton, town of Victoria, Australia, centre of the fruit-growing area in Goulburn valley, 182 km north of Melbourne, in one of the main irrigation districts. Industries include engineering, sawmilling, metal casting, ham and bacon curing, and fruit canning for export. Population 19,110.

Sheppey, Isle of, an island off the North Kent coast, England, at the mouth of the Thames, joined to the mainland by a bridge over the River Swale since 1959. Both arable farming in the north and grassland farming in the south on reclaimed marshes are important; the latter still grazes many sheep. Sheppey, Anglo-Saxon in origin, means Sheep Island. Sheerness is the main town.

Sheraton, Thomas (1751–1806), English furniture maker and designer. His fame rests on his published works, the *Cabinet-Maker and Upholsterer's Drawing Book*, 1791–94, and *The Cabinet Dictionary*, 1803. His name has been associated with the style of furniture fashionable during the 1790s and at the beginning of the 19th century.

Sherbrooke, town of Quebec, Canada, at the junction of the Magog and St Francis rivers, 160 km east of Montreal. Sherbrooke is in the heart of a farming, mining and lumbering area. It has cellulose, asbestos, paper, machinery, and cloth-making industries. Population (1980) 73,900.

Shergar, racehorse, foaled in 1978. He is a bay stallion with a white blaze. In 1981 he won the Epsom Derby from Glint of Gold by 10 lengths, the easiest victory in over 200 years of the race. He followed this up with victories in the Irish Sweeps Derby and the King George VI and Queen Elizabeth Diamond Stakes, but finished only fourth in the St. Leger. He was retired to the Aga Khan's Ballymany Stud in Ireland, being owned by a £10 million syndicate. He was kidnapped for ransom, and effectively disappeared in 1983.

Sheridan, Richard Brinsley (1751–1816), English dramatist and politician, born in Dublin. In 1770 his family moved to Bath, and he later settled in London. In 1775 *The Rivals* was produced at Covent Garden, establishing his reputation. The following year he acquired a share in Drury Lane Theatre, and in 1777 produced there *The Duenna*, an opera with music by his father-in-law, Thomas Linley, and *The School for Scandal*. The latter play is regarded by many as the most brilliant comedy of manners in the language. It was followed by *The Critic*, 1779. Sheridan entered Parliament in 1780, supporting the Whigs, and was under-secretary for foreign affairs in 1782 and secretary to the Treasury in the coalition ministry of 1783. He was treasurer of the Navy in the 'All the Talents' administration, 1806–07, and in his last years was receiver of the Duchy of Cornwall. In 1799 his last play, *Pizarro*, appeared. In politics Sheridan distinguished himself as an orator during the impeachment of Warren Hastings (1787). As a dramatist his fame rests chiefly upon *The Rivals* and *The School for Scandal*.

Sherif, or Shereef (Arabic *sharif*, noble), in Islam, a title given sometimes to descendants of the family to which Mohammed belonged, but usually confined to his direct descendants, of whom there are two branches: the off-

spring of Hasan and Husain. Though the majority are unimportant, sherifs have ruled in many places. But only Jordan and Morocco now have sherifian kings. The sherifs (or properly, *ashraf*) are to be found in all groups of Islamic society, and until recent times had considerable personal prestige.

Sheriff and Sheriff Courts. In the Norman judicial and financial administrative system in England the sheriff of each county (from the old English for shire-reeve) was the accredited representative of the central authority and the special nominee of the king. Henry I limited these powers, which were much abused.

The duties of the sheriff today are purely civil and include acting as returning officer for county elections; summoning juries for the High Court and attending judges on circuits. In Scotland, although the office of sheriff had the same origin as in England, its judicial functions developed separately. The sheriff principal is now the chief local judicial officer; his jurisdiction extends in most cases to an area comprising two or more counties. In the USA the sheriff is a county official, generally popularly elected, and a resident of the county. His duties can be compared with those of the police in England.

Sherman, Roger (1721–93), American patriot, one of the signatories of the Declaration of Independence, and one of the committee of five who drafted it. He was also a member of the Constitutional Convention of 1787, where he introduced the famous 'Connecticut Compromise'.

Sherman, William Tecumseh (1820–91), US general. He resigned from the army in 1853 to conduct a banking business at San Francisco but, on the outbreak of the Civil War, joined the North, and after taking part in the battles of Bull Run (1861) and Shiloh (1862), was, in 1863, made head of the army of the Tennessee, and in 1864 commander in the West. He took Atlanta on 1 September 1864, and later in the same year abandoned his base and marched 483 km across Georgia to the sea. In 1865 he again abandoned his base and marched to Richmond, defeating Johnston and co-operating with Grant. Johnston surrendered to Sherman in April 1865, thus bringing the war to an end.

Sherman Anti-Trust Act (1890), passed by the Congress of the USA with the intention of breaking up the monopolies of the day. The act was named after John Sherman, American financier and Republican statesman. The act forbade 'every contract, combination in the form of trust or otherwise, or conspiracy, in restraint of trade', and declared it to be an offence to 'establish or attempt to establish a monopoly'. At the outset the courts had a difficulty in interpretation, and they therefore tended to liberality of interpretation. Successive presidents, too, failed to enforce the act. Anti-trust action is now a prime feature of US economic policy. See also COMPETITION; MONOPOLY.

Sherpa (feminine *Sherpari*), Mongolian people who originally migrated from Tibet to Solo Khombu, in north-east Nepal. The word 'Sherpa' means 'man from the east'. The Sherpas have earned fame as mountain porters on Himalayan expeditions. Tenzing Norgay, who climbed Everest in 1953, is a Sherpa. Wheat is grown in Solo; barley and potatoes in Khombu. The potato is the staple food. Sheep, goats, and yaks are bred. The Sherpas are estimated to number 85,000. They are Buddhists of the Red Hat sect.

Sherrington, Sir Charles Scott (1857 –1952), British physiologist of the nervous system. In 1932 he was awarded the Nobel Prize for medicine jointly with E. D. Adrian. His greatest contribution to physiology lay in his study of the physical basis of mind; he anticipated Pavlov in the discovery of the nervous phenomenon labelled by the latter 'conditioned reflex'.

See also BEHAVIOURISM.

Sherry, wine from the region which centres round Jerez de la Frontera in Andalusia. Sherry is remarkable for the variety of types into which wines, apparently identical, develop of their own accord. It owes its character to a secondary fermentation or *flowering* which would be disastrous in the case of other wines. When the flowering of the wine is over, it is introduced into the solera, a complicated system of blending and maturing. There are two main categories of sherry. First the clean, dry wines which are apéritifs; manzanillas, very dry indeed; finos, very nearly as dry, and usually fuller-flavoured; and amontillados. The second category, the olorosos, are fuller and rounder wines, very rich in flavour and scent. Sherry is not fortified until its fermentation is complete, and it is naturally one of the driest of wines.

See also SPANISH WINES.

's Hertogenbosch (French *Bois le-Duc*), capital of the province of North Brabant, Netherlands, situated at the confluence of the Aa and Dommel, 45 km south-east of Utrecht. It has an important cattle market. 's Hertogenbosch had its origins as a hunting-lodge of the dukes of Brabant. Population (1981) 88,585.

Sherwood Forest, ancient royal forest, extending from Nottingham to Worksop, England, and long associated with stories of the outlaw Robin Hood.

Shetland, archipelago off the north coast of Scotland. The archipelago, which was formerly a county and is now administered by the Shetland Isles Islands Council, contains over 100 islands, of which 17 are inhabited. It lies some 80 km north-east of the Orkney Islands. The largest island is Mainland, and others include Yell, Unst, Fetlar, Bressay, Papa Stour, and Whalsay. The islands form a group 110 km long, and have a total area of over 1400 km². They are for the most part bleak, hilly, and clad in moorland. The climate is moist, cool and windy. In summer there is almost perpetual daylight, but the winter days are very short.

The archipelago was under Norse domination from the 9th to the 15th centuries, and a strong Scandinavian flavour is retained. Crofting and fishing are the traditional occupations, the former concentrating on sheep, and locally, on ponies, while the latter supports a fish-processing industry. Shetland woollens are well known, and the hosiery industry is an important source of income. Oil discoveries off the north-east of Shetland have resulted in the growth of an oil extraction support industry, and oil is piped ashore to Sullom Voe, 35 km north of Lerwick. Population (1981) 26,716.

Shevchenko, Taras Hryhorovych (1814– 61), Russian writer, the most celebrated Ukrainian poet. For participation in the Brotherhood of Saints Cyril and Methodius, a secret Pan-Slav society, he was banished in 1847 for ten years and forbidden to write or paint. His most famous work is *Kobzar*, 1840, a collection of poems in popular romantic style.

Shield, an article of defensive armour. It was usually carried on the left arm, leaving the right arm free for striking. Although shields disappeared from the battlefield long ago, they have been revived to protect riot police. In heraldry, the shield bears the distinctive charges and forms the most important part of a coat-of-arms.

See also ARMOUR.

Shigatse, second largest city of Tibet, on the south bank of the Brahmaputra, 225 km west of Lhasa. It stands 3596 m above sea-level. The nearby Tashilumpo monastery with its 3500 priests was the palace of the Pachen Lama, who was second to the Dalai Lama in temporal power but superior in spiritual power before China took control over Tibet in 1951.

Shihkiachwang, see SHIJIAZHUANG.

Shih Tzu (Chinese, lion dog), an ancient Tibetan dog similar to the pekingese. The head is broad and round, the legs are short and muscular, the tail is heavily plumed and carried over the back, the coat is long and dense.

Shiite, or Shiah, a member of that division of Islam which follows Ali, the son of Abu Talib as the first legitimate successor of Mohammed; they called themselves the party (Arabic *shia*) of Ali. The orthodox Shiites recognise a series of 12 imams, the last of whom disappeared, 'went into occultation', from which he will return to fill the earth with righteous-

ness as it is now filled with injustice. The Shiites observe the five daily prayers but add to the call, 'Come to the best of work'; they have developed their own system of law, which differs only in small points. One peculiarity is that they allow temporary marriage; a man gives a woman money and they separate on the agreed date. They have their own collections of 'traditions', reports of what Mohammed said and did. Shiah became the state religion of Persia about 1500, under the Safawid Dynasty; it is common in Iraq, North India, and East Africa.

Shijiazhuang (Shihkiachwang), city in Hebei province of China, situated to the east of Taiyuan at the foot of the Taihang Shan; it has become a commercial centre and a collecting point for the region's agricultural produce. Its first industries were textiles and food processing, followed in the 1960s by chemicals and light engineering. Population (1970) 950,000.

Shikoku, island of Japan. With an area of 18,787 km², it is the smallest of the four main islands, and is separated from Honshū by the narrow Inland Sea. Population is largely concentrated in the small coastal plains which front the Inland Sea, and its largest cities are Matsuyama and Takamatsu.

Shilling, English silver or cupro-nickel coin, equal in value to one-twentieth of a pound or to 12d. The first shilling issued by Henry VII in 1504 was the first English coin to bear a realistic portrait of the sovereign. The shilling is still in use today as the decimal 5p piece.

Shillong, capital of Meghalaya state, India, situated on the Brahmaputra river at 1593 m above sea-level. Rebuilt since the 1897 earthquake destroyed most of the town, Shillong is a local trade centre and an important military base. Population (1971) 73,529.

Shetland. *Lerwick is the port and principal town of the islands.*

Shiloh, Ephramite city, Joshua's head-quarters and place of the first sanctuary of Israel in which the ark was kept. Samuel was brought up there by Eli under whom the ark was captured by the Philistines at Ebenezer, about the middle of the 11th century BC, and Shiloh destroyed by fire (1 Sam. iv). This has been confirmed by excavation. Previously unwalled, the city was walled and became populous during the early Iron Age, which suggests the date of the conquest under Joshua as c.1200 BC.

Shiloh, Battle of, two days' conflict in the American Civil War, 6–7 April 1862, between the Confederates under Johnston and the Federals under Grant. The latter won a great victory on the second day. The battle-field was near the Tennessee River.

Shimonoseki, seaport city of Yamaguchi-ken, Japan, on the Inland Sea. It was opened to foreign commerce in 1890, and is an important commercial centre with a good harbour. It is one of the largest fishing ports in Japan, and is noted for its tinned marine products. Industries include ship-building, chemicals, and metals manufac-turing. Population (1979) 262,000.

Shin, a school of Buddhism in Japan, foun-ded by Shinran Shonin (1173–1262). It is the culmination of the Pure Land teaching and is one of the two largest Buddhist schools in Japan today, the other being Zen.

Shingles, *Herpes zoster,* an inflammatory skin affection, characterised by the formation of vesicles along the course of a cutaneous nerve. The skin eruption usually disappears in a few weeks, but the accompanying neuralgic pain may persist for months, especially in older people. Shingles is caused by a virus infection, the virus being identical to that which causes chicken-pox.

Shinto (the way of the gods) is the in-digenous religion of Japan. Unlike major world religions, basic Shinto does not affirm a timeless absolute or universal law as the basis of existence but rather stresses all con-crete forms of existence. A Shintoist reveres reality as it reveals itself in form, rather than in any ultimate principle or cause. Nature in particular creates for a Shintoist a spiritual sense of communion and he imbues trees, mountains, lakes and rivers and all other forms of nature with spiritual essences called *kami* (a term both singular and plural). *Kami* are at the heart of Shinto and are not so much 'beings' as the 'beingness' of an outstanding and awe-inspiring place, person, animal or object. The word itself means 'great' and it applies to harmful as well as benign in-fluences. In simple Folk Shinto the *Kami* are regarded as deities, with Amaterasu, the sun-goddess, heading the hierarchy, and shrines abound everywhere for their worship and appeasement. Intellectual Shintoists regard the *Kami* as a form of life-giving myth which enriches and harmonises the Japanese people. The elaborate rituals practised at the shrines emphasise the oneness of matter and spirit, for Shintoists believe that all material objects are expressions of spiritual powers.

The origins of Shinto lie in Japanese pre-history. In course of time it was influenced by Buddhism, Confucianism (particularly with regard to ritual and decorum) and Christian-ity, but it continued to retain its most vital

Ships and Shipbuilding. *Modern ship construction in Nagasaki, Japan. Pre-fabricated sections of steel hull are built on site and welded together to form the complete ship.*

beliefs. At present it is expressed in four main ways: Imperial Shinto, Sect Shinto, Shrine Shinto and Folk Shinto. Imperial Shinto is forbidden to the general public and is centred round the rites performed by the Emperor of Japan, who is believed to be a direct descen-dant of Amaterasu, the sun-goddess. Sect Shinto is a term used for 13 groups formed during the 19th and 20th centuries which eventually received government recognition as branches of Shinto. Shrine Shinto is per-haps the most representative and the most religious of all the Shinto groups. Its priests lay great emphasis on rituals and mystical rites which they perform in the thousands of shrines dedicated to the different Kami. Folk Shinto is a general term which covers the many superstitious and semi-shamanistic cus-toms of the remote country people of Japan.

Shinty (Gaelic *sintiag*, leap), a 12-a-side stick-and-ball game played almost exclusively in the Scottish Highlands and closely related to the Irish game of hurling from which it derives. It is also related to bandy and hockey. It was taken to Scotland by Irish Gaels some time in the Middle Ages. Shinty is played 45 minutes each way on a field 132 to 183 m long by 64 to 91 m wide, with sidelines and hail (goal) lines marked. In front of each hail a line 3·65 m long, parallel to the hail line and joined to it by quarter-circles, forms the 9-m area. The caman (stick) is shorter than a hockey stick, with a heavier blade, and is made of one piece of wood. The ball is leather-covered cork and worsted, 6·4 cm in diameter. Shinty is a game with more violence than hockey and played often at greater speed.

Shinwell, Emanuel Shinwell, Baron (1884–), British politician. He was respon-sible for the national organisation of the Marine Workers' Union. He was a Labour MP 1922–24, 1928–31, 1935–50, and 1950–70. As minister of fuel and power from 1945 to 1947 he carried through the nationalis-ation of the coal-mines. He was war minister in 1947 and minister for defence, 1950–51.

Ship-money, tax imposed by the British Crown upon seaports and trading towns which compelled them to provide and furnish warships to combat piracy or to pay money

for that purpose. It was first levied about 1007 to form a navy to oppose the Danes. It was levied by Charles I between 1634 and 1638 without the consent of Parliament and was extended to inland shires and towns.

In 1637 John Hampden refused to pay ship-money and, in a test case before the Ex-chequer of Pleas, 7 out of 12 judges decided that Charles was entitled to levy the tax. It was abolished in 1641.

Shipbuilding, see SHIPS AND SHIPBUILDING.

Shipping Routes. The shipping routes of the Roman Empire lay principally in the Mediterranean, linking Rome with Gades, Tarraco, Massilia, Carthage, Alexandria, etc. In the Middle Ages the centre of the Mediter-ranean shipping routes shifted from Rome to Venice, while in the northern seas the shipping routes radiated from the Hanse towns. Columbus opened the route to America in 1492, while the shipping routes to the Far East were for a long time in the hands of the Portuguese, following Vasco da Gama's voyage in 1498. The shortest trans-ocean routes are the east-west great circle tracks, which give the greatest saving of dis-tance in the higher latitudes.

From a shipping point of view, the most dangerous ice area is in the North-West Atlantic, where an International Ice Patrol Service is maintained. The most direct routes between European ports and Australia or New Zealand are through either the Suez Canal (opened in 1869) or the Panama Canal (opened in 1915).

Ships and Shipbuilding. Shipbuilding is one of the oldest crafts, and was apparently practised in prehistoric times. From the time of the Phoenicians the dominant ships were the oared galleys, designed for inland seas and coastal voyaging. From the 14th century the use of the mariner's compass meant that ships could venture further out to sea, and the development of large sailing ships was rapid. Wood was the main material used until the 19th century, when iron began to enter into the construction of ships; by 1840 wood had been practically superseded in shipbuilding except in North America.

The galley was an attempt to design a ship

that was independent of the vagaries of the wind. With the development of steam engines in the 18th century, their application to ships was a logical step. The first successful steamship was built by James Ramsey in America in 1786. Steamship development progressed rapidly through the early years of the 19th century, and in 1827 the Dutch vessel *Curaçao* made the first transatlantic voyage under steam. The first great iron steamship built was the *Rainbow*, launched in 1838, which traded from London to Ramsgate and Antwerp. Early steamships still used sails as auxiliary power, but this changed when screw propulsion, instead of paddlewheels, came in in 1839.

Screw propulsion has remained supreme ever since, though there have been many improvements in engines, including the introduction of internal combustion engines. For large ships steam turbines were the preferred motive power, but oil fired rather than coal fired as early steamships were.

In the 20th century, up to the 1950s, large passenger ships were the 'monarchs' of the seas, especially on the North Atlantic route. Since the development of air travel passenger liners have become largely uneconomic. The modern giants are the supertankers, designed to carry bulk petroleum. The largest tankers are more than 400,000 tonnes deadweight.

The years since the Second World War have seen the emergence of new types of propelling machinery, in the form of the gas-turbine and diesel engines. The future possibilities of nuclear power for marine propulsion are of the greatest interest. The first nuclear-powered vessel was the US submarine *Nautilus*, in 1955.

There have also been important developments in the use of stabilisers, to prevent ships from rolling. The activated fin type stabiliser decreases the overall hull resistance. In 1960 a new anti-rolling device, the flume stabilisation system, made its appearance. It employs a controlled flow of liquid in a specially designed tank system; by means of nozzles known as flumes, liquid ballast is made to lag the roll of the ship by 90°, thus damping the roll to a claimed reduction of 75 per cent.

Ship's Company. The designation of a ship's crew as her 'company' is of ancient origin, but today the term is more used in the navy than in the merchant service, where 'crew' is preferred. The ship's company of a warship, known as her complement, includes both officers and men and varies according to the size of her ship, her armament and equipment.

Shipton, Mother (c.1488–c.1558), reputed prophetess of Knaresborough in Yorkshire. Said to have been the child of a witch who consorted with the devil, she married, in 1512, Tobias Shipton, a builder, and lived for over 70 years. She is first mentioned in 1641 as having foretold the death of Wolsey; she is also said to have predicted the Civil War, the Fire of London in 1666, and the end of the world in 1881. Mother Shipton's cave can be seen at Knaresborough and the Dropping Well is still associated with her powers.

Shipwrecks, see WRECKS.

Shiraz, capital city of Fars province, Iran, on the highway from Tehran to Bushire. Grain, rice, pulses, tobacco, gum tragacanth, clarified butter, wool, skins, and carpets are the main products. There are manufactures of cotton goods, glass, attar of roses, and inlaid fancy articles. The tombs of the poets Sa'di and Hafiz are on the outskirts of the city. Population (1971) 410,000.

Shire, see COUNTY.

Shitta Wood, or shittim wood, derived from some species of acacia, from which the Tabernacle was largely constructed.

Shiva, see ŚIVA.

Shizuoka, or Shidzuoka, city and capital of Shizuokaken, Japan, 150 km south-west of Tokyo. The centre of a tea and mandarin orange trade, it is also noted for the production of tinned food, textiles, and furniture. Population (1979) 455,000.

Shkodër (Italian *Scutari*), town of Albania near the south-east end of Lake Scutari, and connected with the Adriatic Sea via the Buenë (Boyana) river. It has a large trade in wool, tobacco, maize, and skins, and its manufactures include cement, alcohol, and cigarettes. Population (1978) 62,500.

Shlonsky, Abraham (1900–73), Israeli poet, born in the Ukraine. He settled in Palestine in 1921. One of the first Symbolists in Israel, his poetry concerns the development of his new land and its people's attitudes.

Shock, a state of collapse following injury. It is the result of a diminution of the effective circulating volume of the blood, due to loss of blood from external haemorrhage, to loss of plasma (as in extensive burns), or to loss of blood through leakage into damaged tissues.

Treatment of shock consists in measures to restore the circulating volume of blood, and, medically, the principal treatment is blood transfusion. First-aid treatment consists in arresting haemorrhage when present and covering wounds.

Shock is sometimes used to describe a condition of acute mental distress, such as occurs upon the sudden death of a close relative or the witnessing of an accident.

Shock, Electric, injury caused by an electric current, see RESUSCITATION.

Shockley, William Bradford (1910–), Anglo-US physicist, taught at MIT 1932–36 before joining Bell Telephone Laboratories. Working with J. Bardeen and W. H. Brattain, he discovered the junction transistor in 1948. The three men shared the Nobel Prize for physics in 1956.

Shoddy, kind of soft woollen goods made from old woollen rags. Dewsbury is the English centre of the industry. The term is also applied to the waste thrown off during the process of wool manufacture. In common parlance the word has come to refer to any poor material; also used figuratively.

Shoemaker, Willie (1931–), American jockey, three times champion of the USA. In terms of money won in a single season, he has been the top jockey ten times. The great years of his career were 1953 and 1970; in the former he rode a record of 485 winners and in the latter he rode his 6,033rd winner to take the record held until then by Longden.

Shoes, see BOOTS AND SHOES.

Shofar, ancient Jewish wind instrument, made of a flattened ram's horn, still used in the synagogue today.

Shogun, abbreviation of Seiitaishogun, which was the highest rank of the Japanese samuari or warrior class. From 1192, when Minamoto no Yoritomo was made the first shogun of the Kamakura Shogunate government, until 1867, when Tokugawa Yoshinobu, the 15th shogun of the Tokugawa Shogunate government, restored to the emperor the reins of national government, the shogun was in reality the ruler of Japan, although the emperor retained nominal supremacy.

Shola, or sola, *Aeschynomene aspera*, a pithy-stemmed, Indian, leguminous swamp plant, used for making light helmets once worn by Europeans in the tropics.

Sholapur, town in Maharashtra state, India, 340 km south-east of Bombay, and an important cotton textile centre. Population (1981) 514,461.

Sholokhov, Mikhail Aleksandrovich (1905–84), Soviet novelist. He published several stories about the Don Cossacks in 1925, but became famous in 1928 with the publication of the first volume of his four-volume masterpiece *The Silent Don*, a realistic historical epic showing the life of the Don Cossacks on the eve of, and during, the First World War, and in the first five years after the October Revolution. It is regarded as one of the masterpieces of Socialist Realism. Sholokhov was awarded the Nobel Prize for literature in 1965.

Shooting. Despite the invention of gunpowder and the resultant use of primitive 'hand-gonnes' in the 14th century, it was not until the latter part of the 17th century that shooting for sport, as we understand the term today, began to emerge.

Lowland game shooting. In Britain this comprises pheasant (1 October to 1 February inclusive) and partridge (1 September to 1 February). The methods used are 'driving' in which teams of beaters send pheasants from woodlands or partridges across open ground over guns sited much as for grouse, or 'walking-up' with or without dogs in which birds of either species are flushed from fields of winter fodder or root-crops or from young forestry plantations and are shot going away. *Rough shooting.* The shooters have no human assistance and the quarry may be game, woodcock, snipe, wildfowl, hares, rabbits or woodpigeons. Rough-shooters customarily operate in pairs, shooting over dogs, of which spaniels are the most effective.

See also CLAY-PIGEON SHOOTING; GUN; PISTOL SHOOTING; RIFLE SHOOTING.

Shooting Star, see METEOR.

Shooting, Target, see CLAY PIGEON SHOOTING; PISTOL SHOOTING; RIFLE SHOOTING.

Shop Steward, also known as shop secretary, or works representative, local representative in the UK of the members of a trade union employed in a single place of work, e.g. a factory or 'shop'. They are an important link in the local organisation of a trade union. The increasing tendency for wage-bargaining at factory level to supplement national bargaining has strengthened their position in certain industries.

Shore, Peter David (1924–), British politician. He was elected Labour MP for Stepney in 1964. Since 1974 he has represented Stepney and Poplar. He first entered the Cabinet in 1967 as secretary of state for Economic Affairs. In March 1974 he became secretary of state for Trade, but, following his prominent rôle as an anti-Marketeer in the referendum of 1975, he was appointed secretary of state for Industry. He was Secretary of State for the Environment from 1976 to 1979 and Opposition spokesman on Foreign Affairs from 1979 to 1980 and on Treasury and Economic Affairs from 1980.

Shore, see SEASHORE.

Shoring (from *shore*, a prop, term used for temporary support of a structure). The three main types of shoring are raking, flying or horizontal shoring, and dead shoring (or vertical or needle shoring). Shoring is used mainly to support the loads of a wall or structure during alterations.

See also UNDERPINNING.

Short-circuit, a condition when two or more terminals of a source of electrical energy, or two or more conductors between which a potential difference exists, are connected together through a path of negligibly small resistance. Short-circuit of overhead transmission lines may occur as a result of flash-over between lines; short-circuit of cables may occur by failure of insulation.

See also ELECTRICAL MACHINES; TRANSFORMER.

Short-sightedness, is a defect in vision due to a faulty structure of the eye. Parallel rays of light are brought to a focus in front of the retina owing to excessive distance between the surface of the cornea and the retina, or a too great convexity of the crystalline lens. Thus an indistinct image is thrown on the retina. This defect is corrected by the use of spectacles with concave lenses adjusted so that parallel rays are focused on the retina as in ordinary vision. Short-sightedness often has hereditary connections.

See also REFRACTION, ERRORS OF.

Short Ton, see METROLOGY.

Shorthand, the art of writing, with the aid of certain signs, more quickly and in less space than by means of longhand. The expressions 'shorthand', 'stenography', and 'longhand' became generally used in England during the 17th century.

Some systems are light-line; that is to say, the strokes are of even thickness. Others employ some thickening to express certain sounds. Nearly all shorthand systems are phonetic, i.e. a word is spelt as sounded and not as normally written. For instance, F is used for Ph (foto for photo), K for hard C (kat for cat). Consequently many systems have no complete alphabet; but those that do have one allow exact spelling when advisable.

Stenotypy (machine shorthand) is a system of recording speech on a special typewriter first developed in the late 19th century and now much used in North America for court reporting. Letters (or groups of letters) represent phonetic syllables and words.

In the 20th century systems have been developed for rapid note-taking in which ordinary roman characters are used but words are drastically abbreviated. For example, 'Speedwriting', devised by Emma Dearborn (USA) about 1924, 'Dutton Speedwords' and 'Pitman Script'. These systems can be learned more easily than Pitman or Gregg shorthand but are not so rapid in use.

Shoshone, North American Indian peoples living in the Basin-Plateau area of Idaho, Utah, and Wyoming. There are many Shoshone peoples, commonly known by the whites as 'Diggers'. They now number about 7600.

Shostakovich, Dimitri (1906–75), Soviet composer. He had his first symphony performed before he was 20. One of the most original Soviet composers, he came into conflict with the authorities, especially over his realistic opera, *Lady Macbeth of the Mtsensk District*, 1934. A revised version, *Katerina Izmaylova*, was staged in 1962. By compromising judiciously he was able to go on expressing his individuality. His works include another opera, *The Nose* (based on Gogol), three ballets, much incidental and film music, 15 symphonies, 15 string quartets and other chamber music, piano works, and songs.

Shotgun, see FIREARMS.

Shoulder, region where the arm joins the trunk. The articulation of the humerus (armbone) with the scapula or shoulder-blade is an example of a ball-and-socket joint. The scapula is a flat, triangular bone with a depression called the glenoid cavity into which the head of the humerus fits. The shallowness of the cavity allows great mobility of the shoulder-joint, but renders it liable to dislocation. A certain amount of protection is afforded by the glenoid ligament, which forms a sort of lip about the cavity, increasing its depth, and the acromion, a process of the scapula which forms a protective arch overhanging the shoulder socket.

Shove-halfpenny, a form of the old game of shovel-board. Shovel-board or shoveboard is played, especially on ship's deck, by pushing or shoving discs (once pieces of money) with hand or cue along a board marked with transverse lines, the object being to play the disc so that it rests between each set of lines or in one of a number of squares chalked on the deck. In the contemporary game each player in turn strikes five metal discs on a board divided into nine 'beds'. Three discs in a bed fill it, and any disc placed in that bed by the same side afterwards counts for the opponents, except in the case of last point for game.

Shovell, Sir Cloudesley, or Clowdisley (c. 1650–1707), English admiral of the fleet. In 1692 he played an important part in the defeat of the French at Barfleur, and in 1704 he assisted Sir George Rooke in the storming of Gibraltar. His ship was lost with all hands off the Scilly Isles.

Shoveller, *Anas clypeata*, species of Anatidae (web-footed birds), order Anseriformes, which has a very wide distribution in all the continents, and is noted for the brilliant coloration of the male. The female is tawny, but the male is dark brown, with bright brown lower surfaces, green head, white neck, black and white wings, greyish bill, and orange feet. The bird is so named because of its bill which is long and spatulate. It is used for filtering out small organisms from sand and mud.

Show Jumping, an equestrian sport dating from the second half of the 19th century when riders, particularly cavalry officers, began to jump their horses competitively over artificial obstacles. It quickly became popular and in recent years it has become, largely through television, a major spectator sport.

There are many different types of competition, but basically there are only two kinds of obstacles: uprights, such as walls and gates, and spreads, such as parallel and triple bars. Faults are awarded as follows: a knock down, 4; fall of horse or rider, 8; first refusal, 3; second refusal, 6; third refusal, elimination. Time faults are incurred if the stipulated 'time allowed' is exceeded. When there is equality of faults at the end of a round, competitors are usually required to 'jump off'. Time is often used as a final deciding factor. The Olympic Games include both individual and team events. The courses for such competitions contain at least two 'combinations' —groups of 2 (a double) or 3 (a treble) obstacles in close succession which test a horse's ability to adjust his stride. The average height of Olympic fences is about 1·50 m, with spreads of up to 2·00 m and a 5·00 m water jump. International competitions at big shows such as Aachen, London, Rome, New York and Dublin are run under the rules of the Fédération Equestre Internationale. National competitions in Britain are run under the rules of the British Show Jumping Association. The most coveted individual trophy outside the Olympics is the King George V Gold Cup which is competed for annually at London's Royal International Horse Show.

Showboat, floating theatre found on major American rivers, especially the Mississippi and the Ohio, which travelled downstream, and moored for one or more nights near a town or settlement. The first showboat was built by the English-born actor, William Chapman (1764–1839), and he and his family put on popular dramas and music and dance shows. During the 19th century showboats became extremely elaborate, but because of the Civil War they almost disappeared. They were revived in the 1870s, showing melodramas and vaudeville acts. During the early decades of the 20th century the number of showboats declined, and only a few survive as museum pieces.

Shrapnel, type of ammunition, consisting, as originally constructed, of a spherical iron shell containing a large number of bullets, sufficient powder being mixed with the bullets to burst the shell when the fuse ignited the charge. It was invented in 1784 by Henry Shrapnel (1761–1852), an officer of the Royal Artillery, adopted by the British army in 1803, but not used in action until 1808.

Shreveport, city on Red river, in the northwestern corner of Louisiana, USA. The city lies close to a rich oil-field also yielding sulphur, and has become the centre of a large refining and chemical industry complex. The agricultural area nearby produces cotton, and there are processing and textile industries. Population (1980) 205,815.

Shrew, a small, mouse-like mammal of family Soricidae in order Insectivora. The common shrew, *Sorex araneus*, is about 8 cm long, with a long, supple, pointed snout bearing numerous stiff hairs projecting beyond the lower jaw; its fur is reddish-grey above and greyish beneath. It has glands which secrete a strong, unpleasant odour as a means of defence. It feeds on insects, worms, and often on members of its own kind killed after a fight. The pigmy shrew, *S. minutus*, is a rare and beautiful little animal with iridescent fur. The water shrew, *Neomys fodiens,* lives mainly on molluscs, and is essentially aquatic in habit, though only slightly modified for such a life; the feet are fringed with stiff hairs that aid in swimming. Shrews have worldwide distribution excepting Australasia and polar regions.

Shrewsbury, Charles Talbot, 12th Earl and only Duke of (1660–1718), English politician. After the accession of William and Mary, he was appointed secretary of state, and in 1694 was made a duke and head of the government. He was charged with negotiating with the Jacobites, and retired from office and went abroad in 1700. Ten years later, however, he returned to public life, and helped to secure the Hanoverian succession.

Shrewsbury, Earldom of. This earldom is one of the oldest in the English peerage. It was first granted to Roger de Montgomery in 1071. His son, Robert Bellême or Belesme, forfeited his estates and titles for rebellion in 1102. The title was revived in 1442 for John, 5th Baron Talbot, whose descendants still hold the title, which ranks as the premier earldom in the English peerage.

Shrewsbury, John Talbot, 1st Earl of (c. 1388–1453), English soldier. One of the most daring and distinguished warriors of his age, from 1420 onward he fought intermittently in the French wars, defeating the Burgundians at Crotoy (1437), recovering Harfleur (1440), and Bordeaux (1452). He was killed in an attempt to raise the siege of Castillon.

Shrewsbury, county town of Shropshire, England, on the River Severn, 244 km northwest of London. Offa made Shrewsbury part of his kingdom of Mercia at the end of the 8th century; in the Saxon and Norman periods it was frequently raided by the Welsh. The town retains much of its medieval character. Industries include precision engineering, malting, the manufacture of diesel engines, locomotives, machine tools, electrical equipment, and agricultural implements. Population (1981) 59,826.

Shrikes, or butcher-birds, as they are sometimes called from the way some of them impale small animals, lizards, frogs and insects on thorns, constitute the passeriform family Laniidae. They have long, sharply clawed feet and hooked beaks. Common species include the great grey shrike, *Lanius excubitor*, about 25 cm long, the lesser grey shrike, *L. minor*, a little smaller and the red-backed shrike, *L. collurio.*

Shrimp, *Crangon*, a genus of crustaceans. The common shrimp (*C. vulgaris*) is one of the most abundant crustaceans on European coasts, frequenting shallows in immense shoals, but also visiting deep water. It is greyish-brown dotted with dark brown, which gives it a very close resemblance to sand. It is about 5 cm long, and has a round, articulated carapace with two pairs of antennae; the 'tail' or telson is flat, laminated and hirsute; the eyes are prominent and close together. After boiling the cuticle becomes brown. Similar North American species are, in the Atlantic, *Crago septemspinosus*, and in

the Pacific, *C. franciscorum*. Large quantities of small prawns, which turn pink on boiling, are sold as shrimps.

Shriver, Robert Sargent, Jr. (1915–), US politician. He played an important rôle in the successful presidential campaign of his brother-in-law John F. Kennedy (1960). He was director of the Peace Corps (1961–66) and director of the Office of Economic Opportunity (1964–68); he also served as special assistant to President Johnson (1964–68). He became US ambassador to France (1968–70), and was the unsuccessful Democratic vice-presidential candidate in 1972.

Shropshire, English county on the Welsh border, bounded on the north by Cheshire, on the south by Hereford and Worcester, on the east by Staffordshire, and on the west by Powys. From 1974 until 1980 it was called Salop.

In the south and west the county is hilly. The principal river is the Severn. Near the northwest border are several lakes or meres. Geologically the county displays a greater variety of rocks than any other county in England; limestone and roadstone are quarried in large quantities. The chief industries are iron-founding, brick-making, agriculture, and general engineering. The Coalbrookdale area occupies an important place in the history of the iron industry. In the area of Dawley, Madeley, and Coalbrookdale a government sponsored new town is being planned to grow to a population of 250,000 by the year 2001 as Telford New Town. The greater part of the county, about four-fifths of its area, is devoted to agriculture. Forestry is also important. Area 3490 km². Population 354,400.

Shrove Tuesday, day before Ash Wednesday, and a day of preparation for Lent. The name denotes it as the time for shrift or shriving, i.e. confession before the Easter Communion. The pancakes appropriate to the day are almost the sole widespread survival in England of the merrymakings with which it was once celebrated.

Shrubs, woody perennials, in which the primary stem usually grows slowly compared with that of a tree, while the lateral branches develop more rapidly and at all levels above the ground without an obvious main trunk. The term is, however, often somewhat loosely applied. Shrubs are grown in gardens for the ornamental value of their foliage or bloom.

Shugborough, Staffordshire, England, the home of the Anson family, later to become Earls of Lichfield, from 1624 until the present day. The present late 17th-century house, with 18th-century alterations, contains plasterwork by Vassali and Joseph Rose. A group of neo-Grecian monuments in the park was built by James 'Athenian' Stuart.

Shumen, see KOLAROVGRAD.

Shunt, an electric conductor connected in parallel with a circuit for diverting part of the current. In shunt motors and generators, the field winding is connected in parallel with the armature. Galvanometers and most other meters depending on the movement of a fine coil of wire can be 'shunted' with a coil which takes the larger part of the current. Multi-range instruments are provided with

sets of shunts diverting known fractions of current.

See also ELECTRICAL MACHINES; ELECTRIC METERS.

Shute, Nevil, pseudonym of Nevil Shute Norway (1899–1960), Australian novelist. His best-known novels are *A Town Like Alice*, 1950, and *On the Beach*, 1957. Others are *Marazan*, 1926; *What Happened to the Corbetts*, 1939; *Pastoral*, 1944; *No Highway*, 1948; *The Far Country*, 1952; *In the Wet*, 1953; *Slide Rule* (autobiography), 1954; and *Beyond the Black Stump*, 1956.

SI Units, see METROLOGY.

Sialkot, town of Pakistan, some 120 km north of Lahore. It has been identified with the Indo-Greek city of Sagala and is the site of the mausoleum of the Sikh apostle, Nanak (d.1538). It is well known for its manufacture of sporting goods and surgical instruments. Population (1972) 212,000.

Siam, see THAILAND.

Siamese Cat, see CAT.

Siamese Fighting Fish, *Betta splendens*, a beautiful fish noted for its colour and elaborate behavioural displays. One variety, bred in Bangkok, is used for sport; two fish are allowed to fight and wagers are made on the outcome. The male builds a nest of bubbles and looks after the eggs. Domesticated fish are available for tropical fish enthusiasts.

Siamese Twins. The term is usually applied to twins who are united bodily but possess separate personalities. It includes partners who share various combinations of trunk and limbs. The internal organs may partly or wholly each be a mirror image of the other rather than a replica. It is usually assumed, but not proved, that conjoined twins are monovular (develop from the same ovum) and are due to fission of an embryo. Siamese twins may be joined at the navel, at the sternum (breastbone), at the head or at the pelvis. The place of fusion may include an important internal organ such as the stomach, intestine or liver, or the brains may be joined. The name is derived from Chang and Eng (1811–74), twins fused at the hip, born in Siam. The incidence of conjoined twins is not known exactly, and owing to the difficulties of their birth many are stillborn. Others are so handicapped by their abnormality that they survive only a short time. The treatment is that of surgical division at the place of junction, which is possible only if vital organs are not involved.

Sian, see XI'AN.

Sibelius, Jean (1865–1957), Finnish composer. His music evidences exceptional sensitivity to the harmonies and rhythms of nature. His reputation rests mainly on his seven symphonies, which are triumphs of organic musical thought whose progressive concentration resulted in the single-movement seventh symphony. No less mastery is shown in the symphonic poems *Pohjola's Daughter, The Oceanides* and *Tapiola.* Sibelius wrote much light music and theatre scores, a violin concerto, choral music, chamber music, piano works and songs.

Siberia, area comprising the Asiatic part of the USSR, excluding Central Asia. The main natural regions of Siberia are the West Siberian lowland between the Ural Mountains and the Yenisei river, the Central Siberian plateau between the Yenisei and Lena, and the mountainous regions of southern Siberia. The climate is almost wholly continental, the degree of continentality increasing from west to east, with very cold winters particularly in the north-east where the 'Cold Pole' lies. The Pacific coast differs in having a monsoonal climate. Large parts of Siberia are affected by permafrost, especially east of the Yenisei. All but one of the main rivers cross Siberia meridionally, originating in the mountains of the south and flowing into the Arctic Ocean; the exception, the Amur, flows west to east into the Sea of Okhotsk. Lakes are numerous in the west, but the largest is Baikal in the south-east. Vegetation follows latitudinal zones, with tundra along the Arctic coast, coniferous forest (the most typical Siberian landscape), wooded steppe, and steppe in the extreme south. Vegetation changes with altitude in the mountains.

Over half the population is urban; the chief cities are Novosibirsk, Omsk, Novokuznetsk, Krasnoyarsk, Irkutsk, Prokopyevsk, Barnaul, Kemerovo, and Tomsk.

Siberia has great natural resources—coal, iron ore, non-ferrous metals, gold, and diamonds; recently, numerous deposits of oil and natural gas have been discovered in the West Siberian plain. There are also vast forests (pulp-quality conifers in the north, lumber-quality in the south and the Far East) and fertile black earth soil in the south-west. The water-power potential of its great rivers, where some of the USSR's largest hydro-electric power stations have been built, is enormous. After the Russian conquest of Siberia which began in the 1580s, fur was the main attraction; metallurgy started in the 18th century, and gold-mining in the 19th. Modern industrial development began during the First World War, and has been particularly intensive since the 1930s. Siberia was a place of banishment for criminals and political prisoners from the 18th century and from the 1830s was the main region of corrective labour camps.

Sibiu (formerly German *Hermannstadt*), town of central Romania, on the River Cibin, capital of the province of the same name about 217 km north-west of Bucharest. In the 15th century Sibiu grew to be a major centre for Transylvania, and much later (1703–91 and 1849–65) was capital of the state. Parts of the medieval town are still preserved. The town is now a major industrial centre, producing machine tools, textile machinery, leather, textiles, paper, and foodstuffs. Population (1979) 156,854.

Sibyl, name of certain priestesses of Apollo, who prophesied under his direct inspiration. The most famous sold the Sibylline books to Rome, offering first nine, then six, then three for the same price.

Sichuan (Szechwan), one of the most important provinces of China, both in size and in population. It is located in western China, being essentially an elevated basin between high ranges of mountains. The name Sichuan means 'four rivers'. These are generally considered to be the Changjiang, which runs through the province from west to east, and three of its principal tributaries, the Minjiang, the Fujiang, and the Jialing.

In 1955 the former Sikang province was added to Sichuan. This territory in the west of Sichuan province is, however, very rugged and thinly populated.

Because it is protected from climatic extremes by the encircling mountains, the Sichuan basin has a generally mild climate which is very favourable for agriculture. Rice, wheat, and maize are the principal grain crops but other crops of importance include sugar, tea, oranges, and tobacco. The rivers are used for irrigation, the principal irrigated area being the large alluvial fan formed by the Minjiang near Chengdu which has been irrigated since the 3rd century BC. Sichuan is richly endowed with mineral resources. Coal underlies much of the province and is mined to the north and west of Chongqing. There is some production of petroleum and also natural gas at Lungnüsi. Iron-ore, copper, asbestos, mica, and salt are also mined. Sichuan is China's main producer of asbestos. Area 56,000 km². Population (1972) 75,000,000.

Sickert, The Old Bedford Theatre in the 1890s.

Sicily (Italian *Sicilia*), the largest and most populous island in the Mediterranean Sea, situated between latitude 36°38′ and 38°18′N, and between longitude 12°25′ and 15°40′E. It forms an administrative region of Italy (from which it is divided by the narrow Strait of Messina). Area 25,735 km². Population (1980) 4,999,032. The chief city is Palermo. Eighty per cent of Sicily is hilly or mountainous terrain averaging 150 m above sea-level over much of the interior, even higher along the north coast. The great volcano of Etna is the highest point. Most of the interior is devoted to poor crops of wheat with sheep and goats on the meagre pasture. The coastal plains are fertile and intensively cultivated producing vegetables (artichokes, tomatoes, cabbages), citrus fruits, and vines. The lack of industry has exacerbated problems of poverty and emigration.

Minerals found include sulphur, rock-salt, and petroleum. The fisheries (tunny, sardines, coral, and sponges) are important.

In AD 440 the island was conquered by the Goths, who had overrun Italy. A Saracen invasion occurred in 827 and by 878 they had become possessors of the entire island. The Saracens in turn were driven out by the

Normans under Robert and Roger Guiscard, who ruled in the island from 1072 to 1194. After 1194 the island passed under the domination of the German emperors. In 1265 Pope Clement IV invested Charles of Anjou with the Sicilian kingdom. Angevin rule ended in 1282 in Sicily with a popular revolution, known, because it broke out at the hour of vespers, as the Sicilian Vespers. Peter III of Aragon was invited to become king of Sicily, and Naples and Sicily were reunited in 1442 when Alfonso V, King of Sicily, won control of Naples. Throughout the second half of the 15th century, the 16th, 17th, and 18th centuries Sicily was ruled by Spain, the House of Savoy (1713–18), the Austrian Hapsburgs (1718–34), and then the Spanish Bourbons. In 1860 Garibaldi invaded and the island was annexed to the Italian state of Piedmont.

Sicily was granted a degree of regional autonomy in 1946. In 1953 oil was discovered offshore near Ragusa and Gela, and the establishment of a refining industry gave the economy of eastern Sicily a firmer base. Crime and emigration continue to provide sad indices of the island's social conditions.

See also MAFIA.

Sickert, Walter Richard (1860–1942), British painter and etcher. It was not until he was over 60 that his merit as an artist was recognised in England, although he was well-known in the rest of Europe. Sickert was one of the first British painters to appreciate the significance of Impressionism. In all his paintings he sought light, colour, and tone. He is noted for his pictures of Dieppe, Venice, and London streets, for scenes of the theatre and music-hall, and the more intimate aspects of domestic life; all treated with great verve and wit. Among his earlier works are a number of portraits, including the *George Moore* (Tate Gallery), *Charles Bradlaugh at the Bar of the House of Commons* (Manchester), and *Miss Hilda Spring as Imogen Parrot in 'Trelawny of the Wells'*. Other of Sickert's works include *The Camden Town Murder*, 1906, *Sinn Fein*, 1915, *Pulteney Bridge*, 1918.

Sickle-cell Anaemia, see ANAEMIA.

Sicyon, ancient Greek city-state in northern Peloponnesus between Corinth and Achaea. From the end of the 6th century BC until shortly before the mid-4th century, Sicyon was largely dominated by Sparta or Corinth. A succession of tyrants followed one another from 369 until 251, when Sicyon was freed by Aratus and made a member of the Achaean League. The glory of Sicyon, however, lay in the field of art. The school of painting established by Eupompus included Pamphilus and Apelles; and a long line of sculptors, beginning with Canachus, reached its climax in Lysippus.

Siddons, Mrs Sarah (1755–1831), British actress, the daughter of the provincial actor Roger Kemble and sister of John Philip and Charles Kemble. She married the actor, William Siddons, when 18 years of age. Garrick engaged her in 1775 to play at Drury Lane as Portia, but she was not successful in this and other parts. She went into the provinces and did not return to London until 1782, after which she was a favourite with the public until her retirement in 1812. In tragic roles she was at her best, her dignified presence and splendid voice being especially suited to those parts. Among her famous roles were Lady Macbeth, Constance in *King John*, Jane Shore in Rowe's tragedy, and Zara in Congreve's *The Mourning Bride*.

Side Drum, see DRUM.

Sidgwick, Henry (1838–1900), British philosopher. His theory of ethics is presented in his most important book, *Methods of Ethics*, 1874, where he adopted a hedonistic utilitarian position.

Sidi-bel-Abbes, a walled town 75 km by rail south of the city of Oran, Algeria; it occupies a most important strategical position, and trades in wheat, tobacco, and alfalfa. It was the headquarters of the French Foreign Legion until the French withdrawal in 1962 after independence. Population (1974) 151,000.

Sidmouth, Henry Addington, Viscount (1757–1844), British politician. He entered Parliament in 1784. He was appointed Speaker (1789–1801), and, on the retirement of Pitt in 1801, became prime minister. Addington was a weak prime minister and his ministry came to an end in 1804, when he was created Viscount Sidmouth, although he subsequently held lesser posts.

Sidney, Algernon (1622–83), English politician, entered the Parliamentary army, and fought against Charles I at Marston Moor. He later held several parliamentary posts, but retired from public life, 1653–59. After the Restoration he went abroad, returning to England in 1677. He was tried for treason for his alleged involvement in the Rye House Plot in November 1683, was found guilty and executed.

Sidney, Sir Philip (1554–86), English soldier, statesman, and poet. He was entrusted with missions to the Emperor and William the Silent, and in 1578 became known as a poet; Spenser dedicated the *Shepheardes Calender* to him. In 1583 he was knighted and in the same year married Frances Walsingham. He was made governor of Flushing in 1585, became involved in war, and while leading a charge received a fatal wound.

His literary work, all written between 1581 and 1584 but not published until after his death, is of the first importance. The *Apologie for Poetrie*, later renamed *Defence of poesy*, is the first example of literary criticism in English. His *Astrophel and Stella* started the vogue in England of the sonnet sequence; and his pastoral medley, *Arcadia*, written for his sister Mary, Countess of Pembroke, is the greatest of all the Elizabethan prose romances.

Sidon (modern Arabic *Saidā*), chief city of ancient Phoenicia, on the coast of Lebanon, 40 km south of Beirut. In the earliest times Sidon was the leading city of the Phoenicians. It suffered heavily during the Crusades, but once more experienced prosperity under the Druze prince, Fakr ed-Din (1595–1634), and again under Mohammed 'Ali (1832–40). Oranges and lemons are an important export. Fishing provides some employment, but the largest employer is the oil refinery, linked by pipeline to Saudi Arabia. The population are mostly Sunni Muslims. Population (1978) 24,740.

Siege, the 'sitting down' of an army or military force before a fortified place, for the purpose of taking it either by direct military operations or by starving it into submission.

Siegen, city in North Rhine-Westphalia, Federal Republic of Germany, on the Sieg, 93 km south-east of Düsseldorf. It was once a seat of the princes of Nassau-Oranien. There is a 13th-century hexagonal church, and a castle (now a museum). It was the centre of an iron-mining district, but now has office equipment and computer manufacturers. Population (1980) 112,500.

Siegfried, see NIBELUNGS.

Siegfried Line, name given by the Germans to the line of defence taken up by their armies in France in September 1918. The name was also given by the British to the West Wall in the Second World War.

Siemens, Ernst Werner von (1816–92), German electrical engineer. He became superintendent of the artillery workshops in Berlin (1844), and laid the first telegraph line in Germany between Berlin and Frankfurt am Main (1848). He founded the firm of Siemens & Halske.

Siena (ancient *Saena Julia*), Italian city and capital of Siena province, some 50 km south of Florence. It is built on three hills, 305 m above sea-level. In the 12th century it became a free city adhering to the Ghibelline faction. In 1559 it was annexed to the Duchy of Tuscany. The 'Palio' is held every August; the 17 divisions of the city (*contrade*) parade in medieval costume and compete in a horse race round the city's streets. The magnificent 12th–14th-century archiepiscopal cathedral contains a pulpit by Niccolò Pisano, and sculptures by Michelangelo, Donatello, and Bernini. Population (1974) 56,500.

Siena. *The Palio horserace and festival is held annually in the city streets.*

Sienkiewicz, Henryk (1846–1916), Polish novelist, author of *Quo vadis?*, 1896, a novel about Nero's Rome, popularised by several film versions. He received the Nobel Prize for literature in 1905. Probably the best-known Polish writer abroad, and the most translated, he began his career as a journalist, literary critic, and short-story writer. He was constantly on the move and most of his writing was done outside Poland.

Sierra Leone
Area: 71,488 km²
Population: 3,470,000
Capital: Freetown

Sierra Leone, Republic of, independent republic on the coast of West Africa, lying between 6°55′ and 10°N latitude. The sea coast, 336 km in length, extends from the border of the Republic of Guinea to the Mano river, on the border with Liberia. It is bounded on the west by the Atlantic, north and east by the Republic of Guinea, and south by Liberia. Area 71,488 km²

In the north-east lie two granite massifs, the Loma Mountains and the Tìngi Hills rising above 1800 m; Loma Mansa, the highest peak in West Africa, rises to 1948 m. Southwards and westwards from these mountains extends the main plateau of Sierra Leone. Along its western edge the Sula Mountains form a range of hills rising to 700 m. Below the plateau is a lowland zone, much of which is inundated during the wet season and is known as the 'bolilands'. Beyond these lowlands, the rivers have formed extensive deltas that have been partly drowned to form ria-like estuaries fringed by islands and lagoons. The Freetown peninsula, in marked contrast with the rest of the coastal zone of Sierra Leone and most of West Africa, forms an area of highland, rising to nearly 1000 m.

The total population in 1978 was 3,470,000. Except for Freetown, the capital, the development of large towns has only occurred since the Second World War. Agriculture is the main economic activity with most of the population producing their own food on small farms. Rice is the major staple crop. Cassava, sweet potatoes, maize, and sorghum are also widely grown, primarily for subsistence. Oil-palms are also important in most areas, and once provided the main exports, while cocoa and coffee provide sources of cash in the south-east. Cattle are largely confined to the north while some fishing is undertaken along the coast.

Mining now provides the chief exports, with diamonds of paramount importance. Bauxite mining in the Mokanji Hills began in 1963. Manufacturing is largely confined to food and timber products.

The currency unit is the *leone*.

In August 1975, parliament approved in principle a one-party constitution, which received popular approval in a referendum. The Executive President is elected for five years by the House of Representatives, and serves a maximum of two terms, sharing executive power with a Cabinet. The legislature is represented by a House of Representatives, dominated by the one official party, the All People's Congress (APC).

The official languages is English, but the indigenous tribal languages of Mende and Temne are widespread.

History. Discovered in 1462 by the Portuguese, the colony of Sierra Leone originated in the sale and cession in 1788 of a piece of land

1455

by 'King' Nembana to the 'free community of settlers, lately arrived from England'. The main purpose of the colony was to secure a home in Africa for freed slaves and homeless Africans from England. Although this first settlement proved a failure a new settlement became a Crown Colony in 1808. The Protectorate, forming the hinterland of the colony, was formed in 1896. Sierra Leone became an independent member of the Commonwealth in 1961. In 1967 an army coup overthrew the government of Dr Siaka Stevens but in 1968 a second army revolt opened the way for a return to civilian rule. A republican constitution was introduced in 1971, under which Dr Stevens became executive president. In 1975 the House of Representatives unanimously approved a motion calling for a one-party system of government and the introduction of a new constitution; both were effected in 1978.

Sierra Madre, name of the three principal mountain ranges of Mexico. The Sierra Madre Occidental runs along the west coast to join the Sierra Madre Oriental, which runs along the east coast, at about the 19th parallel in the centre of Mexico. From about this junction the mountain range continues southwards under the name of Sierra Madre del Sur, to the Isthmus of Tehuantepec. The Sierra Madre Occidental is the most formidable range of the three, being about 1280 km long, 320 km wide, with elevations mostly over 1800 m rising to over 3000 m.

Sierra Maestra, mountain range running along the extreme south-east coast of Cuba, extending from Cape Cruz to Guantánamo; the Pico Turquino (1974 m) is the highest point in Cuba.

Sierra Morena, mountain range in southern Spain, extending east to west between the Guadiana and Guadalquivir rivers.

Sierra Nevada, mountain range in southern Spain, mainly in the province of Grenada, but also extending into Almeria. Mulhacén (3477 m), its highest peak, is also the highest mountain in Europe outside the Alps and the Caucasus. The snowline is at 3000 m.

Sierra Nevada, mountain range in the USA, lying mainly in California, and forming the southern part of the chain of the mountains of the Pacific. The Sierra Nevada has a general ridge line at over 2500 m, above which protrude individual peaks, the highest of them being Mount Whitney (4418 m). The eastern side is faulted and very steep, and provides one of the swiftest natural transitions in North America, from snow-covered peak, through dense forest, to scrub and down to desert.

Sierra Nevada de Santa Marta, mountain group in the north-east of the department of Magdalena, Colombia, near the Caribbean Sea, rising to over 5400 m.

Sieyès, Emmanuel Joseph, Comte (1748–1836), French cleric and politician. He was one of the chief theorists of the revolutionary and Napoleonic eras. He became vicar-general and chancellor of the diocese of Chartres. His famous pamphlet, *What is the Third Estate?*, 1788, secured for him a place as one of the deputies of Paris to the States-General. Later he voted for the death of Louis XVI. He was, with Napoleon, one of the three consuls, but exercised little influence on practical politics.

Sight, Short, see REFRACTION, ERRORS OF; SHORT-SIGHTEDNESS.

Sigismund (1368–1437), Holy Roman Emperor from 1410, a son of Emperor Charles IV. He succeeded his father as margrave of Brandenburg (1378), and King of Hungary (1387). Sigismund was a prominent member of the Council of Constance (1414), which brought the Great Schism to an end, and was involved in the death of John Huss, an event which roused the Bohemians against him so that it was only after 17 years of war that Sigismund was able to enter their capital as king. Sigismund's character is still disputed by historians.

Sigismund, name of three kings of Poland. *Sigismund I* (1467–1548), became king in 1506. He waged war against the Teutonic knights (1519–21) and against Muscovy in support of Lithuania.

Sigismund II Augustus (1520–72), the son of Sigismund I, whom he succeeded. He was a tactful diplomatist, and through him the Union of Lublin with Lithuania was achieved. He was the last of the Jagellons.

Sigismund III (1566–1632), the nephew of Sigismund II and son of John III, King of Sweden. He was elected to the Polish throne in 1587, and succeeded his father in Sweden in 1592, although he was dethroned there in 1604.

Signac, Paul (1863–1935), French painter, associated with Seurat in the development of 'Neo-Impressionist' painting—the scientific use of spectrum colour. He painted with mosaic-like blocks of pure colour in many landscapes and seascapes of the Normandy, Brittany, and Mediterranean coasts.

Signals and Signalling are particularly important in military operations. Up to the early part of the 19th century armies used trumpets and bugles for short-range signalling, and runners and mounted dispatch riders for shorter distances. Since then the greater range of fire and therefore of distances led to the adoption of signalling by lamp, flag, semaphore and heliograph, but of recent years all communication is by field telephone or radio. Naval signalling is at least as old as the Battle of Salamis (480 BC), when a red cloak raised aloft was the signal for the Greek attack on the Persians. Modern flag signalling was pioneered by the British in the early 1800s, and adopted for commercial use in 1887 as the International Code. Individual navies retain their own private codes. Ships also use light signals and radio. Air operations are largely dependent on radio.

Coastguards have their own signals to warn of gales. By day a cone is hoisted: with the apex up it indicates a northerly gale, and with the apex down a southerly one. A triangle of lights is used at night.

See also SEMAPHORE; TELEGRAPHY.

Signal-to-noise Ratio, in radio and radar receivers, the ratio of the output to the noise arising in the receiver itself through thermal agitation in the transistors and other causes.

Signature, in music, (1) the time signature, indicating the rhythmic structure, is written on the stave at the beginning of the work, e.g. $\frac{3}{4}$, three crotchets to a bar; $\frac{3}{8}$, three quavers to a bar.

(2) Key signature, the tonic of the scale in which a composition is written, see KEY.

Signature Tune, a term originally used by dance bands for a popular tune of their own choice to identify them at the beginning and end of their acts; now extended to cover the tunes which identify particular series of programmes on radio and television.

Signet, or Privy Signet, one of the three legally recognised British royal seals for authenticating documents, the other two being the Great Seal and the Privy Seal.

Signet, Writer to the, member of a society of legal practitioners in Edinburgh who formerly had important privileges, now nearly all abolished. They are so named because they were originally clerks to the office of the king's secretary, their duties being to prepare all warrants or charters for sealing with the king's signet.

Signorelli, Luca (c.1441–1524), Italian painter. He was the pupil of Piero della Francesca, but less serene in style and one of the first to paint figures in violent action. His finest work is found in the chapel of S. Brizio, a part of the cathedral of Orvieto.

Sigurdsson, Jón (1811–79), Icelandic statesman and scholar; spent his life in fighting for the commercial and political freedom of Iceland and the cultural and economic advancement of his people. The abolition of the Danish trade monopoly was achieved in 1854 and a certain measure of home rule in 1874.

Sihanouk, King Norodom (1922–), former King and Prime Minister of Cambodia (now Kampuchea). As King of Cambodia he proclaimed his country independent in 1945. While on a visit to the USA in 1953 he made a forthright public speech demanding independence for Cambodia. He abdicated in favour of his father, Norodom Sumarit, who became king in March 1955, whilst he himself became Prime Minister. In 1960 his father died, so he became head-of-state as well. During the 1960s he managed to maintain a neutral stance between China and the US and kept the country uninvolved in the Vietnam conflict. Whilst on a diplomatic visit abroad in 1970, General Lon Nol staged a military coup to depose Sihanouk, thus allowing US forces to attack Viet Cong strongholds in Cambodia. Sihanouk went to Peking and formed a royal government in exile. There he became the figurehead of the Khmer Rouge guerrillas against Lon Nol, and resumed his position of head-of-state after the victory of the guerrillas in 1975. After one year as a Communist figurehead he resigned all his posts.

Sika (*Cervus nippon*), small deer of eastern Asia, often called the Japanese deer. It grows to between 70 cm and 100 cm at the shoulder and is distinguished by a very white patch on the rump. It has been successfully bred in Europe, while in Japan the species has been virtually wiped out by hunting. There are about a dozen sub-species, found in China and Taiwan.

Sikhs (Sanskrit *S'ishya*, disciple), community in the Punjab (India) State, which was divided between India and Pakistan in 1947, and again in 1966, numbering 10 million today. They are the probable descendants of the original inhabitants of the Indus valley. Originally a small religious community, gathering round their founder, Nanak (1469–1539), they

Sikkim. *Terraced cultivation is important to the economy because so much of the terrain is mountainous. The country is highly fertile and is known in Sikkimese as* Denjong, *The Valley of Rice.*

gradually grew into a nation because of their proselytising powers. Nanak, a humanitarian, aimed at combining Hindus and Muslims into one brotherhood by a unique blend of Hindu and Sufi beliefs. The climax of his thought was to be found in the concept of ineffable union with God, the Formless One, and his teaching about the path to this union is still the mystical heart of Sikhism, followed to this day by orthodox Sikhs. He appointed a disciple to follow him and the line of prophetic succession continued until the Tenth Guru, Govind Singh. The Sikh community thus gained their character from ten leaders, each of whom emphasised a particular aspect of the teaching, exemplified in his own life. Govind Singh, combated the Muslim power and religion, while he also repudiated the caste system of Hinduism. As a result of his teaching the Sikhs ultimately obtained political independence in 1764, but were defeated by the British in 1849.

Sikhs are divided into non-Jat Sikhs and Jats. The non-Jat Sikhs are strict followers of their religion and wear the five Sikh symbols: a steel dagger, a bangle, a comb, uncut hair, and short breeches. The Jats are less strict.

Sikkim, state of India, strategically located south of China, east of Nepal, and west of Bhutan. It lies on the southern slopes of the Himalayas and its Singalila range contains the third highest mountain in the world, Kanchenjunga (8578 m). Its forests are extensive. The population (1981) totals 315,682. The chief crops are maize, rice, millet, cardomom, and tea. Area 7107 km². The capital is Gangtok.

Sikkim was absorbed into British India in 1935, and after independence it became an Indian protectorate. In 1975, after a long period of strain between the two countries, India admitted Sikkim as the 22nd state of the republic. Its hereditary *chogyal* (ruler) was deposed.

Sikorski, Władysław (1881–1943), Polish statesman and soldier. In 1921 he was chief of the general staff and in 1922 prime minister, restoring order and obtaining general recognition of the Russo-Polish line of demarcation. But after Piłsudski's coup in 1926 he retired. In 1939, he left Poland to build up a Polish army abroad and on 30 September was nominated premier of the exiled Polish government and commander-in-chief of all the Polish forces abroad. In 1940 he established his quarters in London as chief of the Polish general staff. Sikorski was killed in an aeroplane crash at Gibraltar.

Sikorsky, Igor Ivan (1889–1972), Russian aeronautical engineer. He emigrated to the USA in 1919 and was naturalised there in 1928. He constructed and flew the first successful four-engined aeroplane in 1913. Sikorsky produced several four-engined bombers for the Russian Government (1914–1917). He made the first successful and practical helicopter in the Western Hemisphere (1939), and became one of the leading designers of helicopters.

Silage, see HAY AND SILAGE.

Silbury Hill, the largest ancient man-made mound in Europe, situated 1·5 km south of Avebury, Wiltshire, England, and probably contemporary with the Late Neolithic sanctuary there. It is about 40 m high and has a ditch surrounding it about 6 m deep which was used as the quarry for the building of the mound. Its purpose is still unclear, but it may have been a cenotaph; no burial or other significant finds have been traced.

See also BARROW.

Silchester, village in Hampshire, England, 11 km north of Basingstoke, the site of *Calleva Atrebatum,* cantonal capital of the Atrebates, a Belgic tribe which inhabited a large district south of the middle Thames from Surrey to north-east Wiltshire. The stone walls, enclosing some 40 ha, were added around AD 200

as a facing to a previously existing earthwork, which was itself a contraction of a larger enclosure, possibly 150 years older. Outside the walls are the remains of an amphitheatre. The town plan was recovered by extensive excavation in 1890–1909, when the sites of the forum, basilica, inns, a bath-house, a building (probably a Christian church), etc., were found.

Silenus, in Greek mythology, son of Hermes or Pan, an aged woodland deity or satyr, with a reputation for song, prophecy, drunkenness, and lechery. With other aged satyrs (collectively called *Sileni*), he was the companion of Dionysus, and always carried a wine-skin. He is represented commonly as a jovial old man, bald and puck-nosed, fat and intoxicated. Unable to trust his own legs, he is generally shown riding on an ass or supported by other satyrs.

Silesia (German *Schlesien*; Polish *Śląsk*; Czech *Slezsko*), region of Eastern Europe, lying in the middle and the upper Oder basin and bordered in the south by the Sudeten mountains. Since 1945 most of Silesia has been within the frontiers of Poland. It has a total area of about 50,165 km². Silesia is mainly lowland, but Schneekoppe (Polish *Śnieżka*) in the Riesengebirge (Polish *Karkonosze*) rises to 1603 m. It is extremely fertile, especially in the south and south-west, but its mineral deposits are of prime importance: its coalfields are among the most important in Europe, and there are rich deposits of iron, lead, and zinc. The metallurgical industries of the area are highly developed, and there are also manufactures of machinery, textiles, chemicals, glass, and paper. The principal towns are (in Poland) Wrocław (German *Breslau*), Opole (*Oppeln*), Katowice (*Kattowitz*), Bytom (*Beuthen*), Chorzów (*Königshütte*), and (in Czechoslovakia) Opava (German *Troppau*).

Silesia belonged to the Czechs in the 10th century, and to Poland from 990. It has since been contested between Poland, Austria, Czechoslovakia, and Germany.

Silica, silicon dioxide (SiO_2), occurs in nature as five distinct minerals: quartz, tridymite, cristobalite, opal, and lechatelierite.

Quartz, one of the most abundant minerals in the crust of the Earth. Quartz may occur in massive cryptocrystalline form. It is stable over a wide range of geological conditions, and is an essential constituent of silica-rich igneous rocks and many metamorphic rocks. As it is hard and very resistant to chemical weathering it is the most abundant mineral in sedimentary rocks, and forms the bulk of most sandstones. It also makes up a large part of hydrothermal vein deposits and granite pegmatites.

Quartz occurs in two distinct varieties, macrocrystalline and cryptocrystalline (the latter often classed as chalcedony). Macrocrystalline varieties include milky quartz, amethyst, rose quartz, citrine, smoky quartz, cat's eye, aventurine quartz, and ferruginous quartz, most of which are used as ornamental stones in jewellery.

Cryptocrystalline varieties (chalcedony): chalcedony is a group name for the compact varieties of silica composed of minute crystals of quartz with submicroscopic pores. They occur in massive form, often filling cavities in rocks or as nodules in sedimentary rocks. Varieties include agate, onyx, carnelian and sard, heliotrope and bloodstone, moss agate (mocha stone), jaspar, chert, flint, plasma, prase, chrysoprase, tiger eyes.

Tridymite, a high-temperature polymorph of silica, SiO_2, being stable at temperatures between 870° and 1470°C.

Cristobalite, the polymorph of silica stable at temperatures above 1470°C.

Opal, composed of a solidified colloidal gel of silica, usually containing a small percentage of water in submicroscopic pores. It may be colourless, white, yellow, red, green, blue, or black. Precious opal exhibits a delicate play of colours. Diatomite, a form of opal, is a deposit formed from the remains of siliceous organisms. It occurs in extensive beds and is mined for use as a filtering agent, an insulating medium, and a mild abrasive.

Lechatelierite, silica glass, unstable at temperatures below 1713°C. It is formed when lightning strikes in sand, fusing small amounts to glass; tubes of glass (fulgurites) several metres long may be formed in this way.

Silica Glass, or quartz glass, is fused vitreous quartz. It can be made either translucent or transparent to visible light. Unlike ordinary glasses it will also transmit much ultraviolet and infrared radiation. It has a small thermal expansion coefficient and may therefore be cooled and heated rapidly without breaking. It also has a much higher melting-point than either soda or borosilicate glasses. For these reasons it is used in scientific apparatus and in special lamp bulbs (e.g. quartz-iodine lamps).

Silicates, alkali metal salts formed when alkali metal carbonates are fused with silica at high temperatures. Carbon dioxide is driven off, and a complex mixture of silicates is left. A few silicates contain simple orthosilicate (SiO_4^{4-}) ions, but most are complex polymeric structures.

See also ZEOLITES.

Silicon, non-metallic chemical element, symbol Si, atomic number 14, atomic weight 28·086. It does not occur in the uncombined state, but in combination with other elements it is, with the exception of oxygen, the most abundantly distributed of all the elements, present to the extent of 28 per cent by weight in the Earth's crust. As the dioxide, silica, it occurs both free, and combined with various bases, as flint, felspar, sand, quartz, opal, chalcedony, etc. In combination with oxygen, and metals such as aluminium and magnesium, it occurs in clays and marls, and constitutes a large number of rocks. Silica, or silicon dioxide, occurs in nature in the amorphous form as opal, and in the diatomaceous deposits or 'kieselguhr' of Germany. It is formed when silicic acid is heated or by the action of an acid on sodium silicate. In the crystalline condition as quartz, silica forms prismatic crystals of the hexagonal system. As rock crystal, silica is occasionally cut and polished, and substituted as a gem for diamond. Silicon forms a series of spontaneously inflammable hydrides, analogous to the alkane hydrocarbons. These run from silane (SiH_4) to silico-hexane (Si_6H_{14}). It seems, however, that though silicon chemistry is in many ways similar to carbon chemistry, the ability to form long chains, characteristic of carbon compounds, is shown by silicon only to a limited extent. Investigations into the preparation of high polymers combining carbon and silicon units in the molecule have resulted in a new class of compounds, the siloxanes or silicones. They are non-conductors of electricity, and thus find use as insulators, and as they are insoluble in water, chemically very inert and able to withstand extremes of temperature, they find many very important practical uses as greases, oils, elastomers (silicon rubber), and water-repellent films. The silicates form fibrous structures, as in asbestos, and thin leaves or sheets, as in mica and talc. Silicon is also an important ingredient of steel, and silicon carbide is widely used as an abrasive and refractory material under the name of carborundum. Pure crystals of silicon have immensely valuable applications as semiconductor materials in the manufacture of transistors, solar cells, and other solid-state devices.

See also GLASS; IRON AND STEEL; SILICA GLASS.

Silicon chip, see COMPUTER.

Silicones, see SILICON.

Silicosis, see PNEUMOCONIOSIS.

Silk and Silkworms. Silk is a textile fibre obtained from the cocoon of the silkworm, of which *Bombyx mori* is the most important, but also from the silkmoths *Antheraea mylitta* of India and *A. pernyi* of China.

The larvae eat mulberry leaves and in about 5 weeks grow to about 8 cm in length and start to spin their cocoons. Most of the larvae are killed in their cocoons, only a few being required for egg production. The cocoon consists of about 900 m of continuous fibre, two parallel filaments being stuck together by a gum called seracin. To obtain the fibre the cocoons are softened in hot water, the ends found, and the cocoons unwound. The original yarns are then twisted together.

Silk is made of protein; it is very strong, stretches and recovers easily, and absorbs water readily. In processing, the gum (seracin) is removed but the silk is treated with tin salts or with other gums to increase its weight and reduce its price. It is used for very fine (thin) cloths and as a luxury fibre where its strength, lustre, softness, and water absorption are called for. Production has dropped greatly since the Second World War and many of its uses have been almost completely taken over by other fibres, particularly nylon.

Silk Screen, see SCREEN PROCESS PRINTING; SERIGRAPHY.

Sill, an igneous intrusion of sheet-like form, showing a conformable relationship with the bedding of the country rocks.

Sillitoe, Alan (1928–), English novelist. At first he thought of himself primarily as a poet, and published several collections of verse. However, he is most widely acclaimed for his novels and stories about working-class life, notably *Saturday Night and Sunday Morning*, 1958, and *The Loneliness of the Long Distance Runner*, 1959, both of which have been filmed from his own screenplays. Among his other works are the novels *A Start in Life*, 1970, and *Raw Material*, 1972.

Silone, Ignazio, pseudonym of Secondo Tranquilli (1900–), Italian novelist. He joined the newly founded Italian Communist party in 1921, but left it in 1930. Because of his anti-fascist activities he had to leave for Switzerland, where he lived from 1930 to 1944. He then returned to Italy and, as a socialist, edited the paper *Avanti*.

Silone's knowledge and understanding of peasant life are shown in his novel *Fontamara*, 1930. This is bitterly anti-clerical; but the conflict between Christian and revolutionary ideals is portrayed with greater sympathy in *Pane e vino*, 1937. Silone's writing is distinguished by human understanding and sympathetic irony in the handling of his subjects. Later works include *Il segreto di Luca*, 1956, and *Uscita di Sicurezza*, 1965.

Silphium, compass plant or pilot weed, a hardy perennial, belonging to the Compositae. *S. laciniatum* has the peculiarity while young of turning its leaf-edges north and south to avoid mid-day heat, and hence is called the compass plant. Other species are *S. perfoliatum* (*connatum*) and *S. terebinthinaceum*, prairie dock.

Silt, the mineral fraction of soils which is between 20 and 2 μm (0·02 to 0·002 mm) in size. The particles are irregular fragments, essentially micro-sands, with quartz as the dominant mineral. They add little to the nutrient content of soils and because of their small size may give rise to cultivation problems unless supplemented by clay, sand, and organic material.

Siltstone, an argillaceous rock composed of grains ranging in diameter from 0·004 to 0·06 mm.

Silures, ancient British people who inhabited what are now the counties of Gwent, the three Glamorgans, and the southern part of Powys. They opposed the Roman conquest, but were subdued by Scapula and his successors (48–78).

Silurian System, geological name of the third of the Paleozoic systems of strata occurring above the Ordovician and below the Devonian Systems. The Silurian began between 435 and 460 million years ago and ended about 405 million years ago. The Silurian is divided into the Llandovery series, at the base, followed by the Wenlock and Ludlow series. The Downtonian series, which occurs above the Ludlow, is classified by some authors as Silurian and by others as Devonian. The first jawed-fishes appeared in the Silurian, but the bulk of the fauna is made up of brachiopods, trilobites, crinoids, cephalopods, bivalves, and gasteropods. The graptolites died out in the British area before the end of the Silurian, but are found at higher horizons in continental Europe.

Silvanus, ancient Italian deity, originally of uncultivated fields and of forests, especially as protector of their boundaries. Later his patronage was extended to cattle, and he was identified with Pan and Faunus.

Silver, metallic chemical element, symbol Ag, atomic number 47, atomic weight 107·868; occurs in nature in the free state and in combination. Natural silver generally contains gold, copper, and other metals. Important ores are argentite, Ag_2S; pyrargyrite (ruby silver ore, Ag_3SbS_3); stephanite, Ag_5SbS_4; and horn silver, AgCl. Lead ores (galena) constitute one of the main supplies of silver. Mexico and the USA are the two great silver-producing countries, and yield about one-third of the world's output. There are several metallurgical processes for the extraction of the metal from its ores.

A relatively large proportion of the new silver produced is obtained during the refining of other metals, such as copper and lead.

Silver is a lustrous white metal (relative density 10·5, melting point 961·5°C), and is extremely malleable and ductile, being second only to gold. It has the highest conductivity for heat and electricity of all the metals. Two oxides of silver are known, the monoxide, argentic oxide, AgO, and a sub-oxide, argentous oxide, Ag_2O. The monoxide is the more important. The most important salt of silver is the nitrate, which is formed by dissolving the metal in nitric acid. Silver is a semi-noble metal because of its considerable resistance to corrosion, and is also of especially pleasing appearance and high reflectivity. It is unattacked by food-stuffs and fruit juices. For these reasons it has been used from ancient times for coinage and for domestic and ornamental articles. Pure silver alone being somewhat too soft for these purposes, an alloy containing 92·5 per cent silver and 7·5 per cent copper is used, and is known as 'sterling' from Old English *steorra*, star, with which some early Norman coins were marked. It is illegal to offer for sale articles which have not been assayed and 'hallmarked' to confirm that the silver content is at least of this quality.

Silver is also used as an electroplated coating on decorative and domestic articles, which are often made from 'nickel silver', also called 'German silver', an alloy of copper, nickel and zinc which does not in fact contain silver, hence EPNS (electroplated nickel silver). Silver is widely employed in the electrical and chemical engineering industries and is a constituent of silver solders.

Silver Thaw, American popular term for hoar frost, rime, and glazed frost.

Silverfish, (*Lepisma saccharina*) a member of the bristle-tail order of insects, Thysanura. Silverfish are found throughout the world in buildings, especially in kitchens, bathrooms, and other places where there are damp conditions. They are primitive insects, wingless at all stages of their lives, with three long segmented 'tails' and long antennae. They feed on such materials as spilled flour and scraps of paper.

Silverpoint, technique of drawing with an instrument pointed with silver on paper prepared with a gesso ground. It was used for the most exquisite work by Leonardo da Vinci, Dürer and early Flemish masters. It is little used today because modern paintings rarely demand intricate preparatory studies or favour the delicacy of touch achieved with this medium.

Silversmithing. Among ancient races the art of working gold or silver either by hammering or by casting, reached a remarkably high degree of skill, which was carried on through classical times to the Middle Ages. In England, as in the rest of Europe, the Church was the chief patron in the early Middle Ages, but from the 14th century onwards the extent of domestic patronage increased dramatically, as the inventories of kings and noblemen show. The Civil War saw the melting down of much plate, and most English plate now surviving dates from the Restoration on-

Silversmithing. A candelabrum made by Claude Duvivier from a design by Meisonnier.

wards. The dominant stylistic influence in this period is Dutch, but with the arrival of Huguenot refugees from 1685 onwards French influence also made itself felt. The British silversmith, for the last six hundred years, has been rigidly controlled in the quality of his metal. Sterling silver has throughout been the standard, except when an alloy of higher silver content (Britannia silver) was enforced. The first systematic use of a substitute for silver was the invention of Sheffield plate, by Thomas Boulsover in 1742; upon a sheet of copper he fused a thin sheet of silver, at first on one side only, then on both. This sheet was then worked into the forms current in silverware. The subsequent invention of electroplating (1840), enables many more people to purchase 'silver' domestic ware.

See also HALLMARKS.

Silves, town of Portugal, in Faro district 50 km northwest of Faro. It was the capital of Algarve under the Moors, from whom it was taken in 1242. The region produces figs, olives, vines, and almonds. Population (1970) 27,000.

Silviculture, or sylviculture (Latin *sylva*, *silva*, a wood; *cultura*, cultivation), the theory and practice of cultivating (growing and tending) forest crops. The silviculture of naturally-occurring forests of mixed species is much more complex than that of even-aged plantations of a single species, and has perhaps reached its highest form in the management of the 'selection' forests in Switzerland.

Sim, Alastair (1900–76), British actor. His first stage appearance was in 1930; subsequently he was associated as actor or producer with several of James Bridie's plays, including *Mr Bolfry, Dr Angelus* and *Mr*

Gillie. He made his screen debut in 1934, and among his films were *Happiest Days of your Life, Scrooge, The Belles of St Trinian's* and *Geordie*.

Simaroubaceae, family of 20 genera and 120 species of dicotyledonous shrubs and trees, mainly tropical and subtropical. The bark usually contains bitter compounds which have been used medicinally. The main genera are *Ailanthus* (tree of heaven), *Picrasma, Quassia* and *Simarouba*.

Simenon, Georges (1903–), Belgian novelist. A prolific writer of fiction, including ambitious psychological novels like *La Neige était sale*, 1948, he is internationally famous for his detective stories. His name is inseparably linked with that of Maigret, the *commissaire de police*, who figures in more than 70 of his tales.

Simeon, one of the tribes of Israel, descended from Simeon, the second son of Jacob and Leah. It played an important part in the conquest of Canaan, and it received the territory to the south of Judah, but was almost extinguished in wars against the Philistines, and absorbed into Judah, perhaps in the days of Samuel.

Simeon, a devout Jew in Jerusalem awaiting the Messiah. On seeing the infant Jesus brought into the Temple he uttered the hymn of praise, now known as *Nunc Dimittis*.

Simeon Stylites, Saint (from the Greek *stulos*, pillar) (390–459), Christian monk of Syria in the 5th century. He is reputed to have spent the last 37 years of his life on a pillar, 20 m high and 1 m wide at the top, erected near Antioch. He preached by day, and crowds of pilgrims flocked to receive his exhortations.

Simferopol, capital city and cultural centre of the Crimean *oblast* of the Ukrainian SSR, USSR, and the centre of a fruit-growing district. It has varied engineering and food industries. Founded in 1784 on the site of the Tatar settlement of Ak Mechet, it was the capital of the Crimean Autonomous Republic 1921–46. Population (1980) 307,000.

Simile (Latine *similis*, like), a comparison, definitely expressed, between two things of different kinds. Usually a simile is introduced by the words 'like' or 'as' (Kipling's 'He trod the ling like a buck in spring and he looked like a lance in rest', for example).

The simile is closely related to metaphor, but is explicit, whereas the metaphor's comparison is implicit.

See also FIGURE OF SPEECH.

Simla, capital of Himachal Pradesh state, India, situated on a ridge in the foothills of the Himalayas 2200 m above sea-level. A hill resort with sanatoria, it was a favourite summer retreat. Population (1971) 47,000.

Simms, William Gilmore (1806–70), US man of letters. He was the author of a poem, *Atalantis*, and several historical romances. Of these *The Yemassee*, 1835, is the most important, giving an account of a campaign which is otherwise virtually unknown, and dealing largely with Indian character and nature. The action of his revolutionary romances extends over the whole revolutionary period.

Simnel, Lambert (fl.1477–1534), English impostor. As a tool in the hands of an Oxford priest, Richard Symonds, he was put forward to impersonate Edward, the young Earl of Warwick, son of George, Duke of Clarence, who was a prisoner in the Tower. Symonds secured the support of Margaret, Duchess of Burgundy and other Yorkist leaders for his protegé and Simnel was taken to Ireland where Yorkist sympathies were strong. In 1487 Simnel was crowned Edward VI in Dublin Cathedral.

An armed force from Ireland, under the command of Sir Thomas Fitzgerald, landed in Lancashire, and marching upon the royal army, attacked it near Stoke-on-Trent (16 June 1487), where a battle took place in which Henry VII's forces were victorious, and Simnel and the priest made prisoners. It is traditionally said that Simnel was then made a scullion in the king's kitchens.

Simon, Claude (1913–), French novelist. His early novels were conventional. It was with *Le Vent*, 1957, *L'Herbe*, 1958, *La Route des Flandres*, 1960, and *Le Palace*, 1962, that he came to the notice of the public and was, misleadingly, classified as a 'new novelist'. The later novels (*Histoire*, 1967, *La Bataille de Pharsale*, 1969, *Les Corps conducteurs*, 1971, and *Triptyque*, 1973) have confirmed his reputation as among the most gifted novelists of his age.

Simon Magus (fl.c.AD 37), a magician (Magus) who became a Christian and offered St Peter money in exchange for the power of bestowing the Holy Spirit by laying on of hands; hence 'simony'.
See also SIMONY.

Simon of Stackpole Elidor, John Allsebrook Simon, 1st Viscount (1873–1954), British statesman. He entered Parliament as a Liberal in 1906 and was appointed solicitor-general in 1910. In 1913 he became attorney-general with a seat in the Cabinet. When the Coalition Government was formed in May 1915 he was appointed home secretary, but resigned in 1916 as he was opposed to conscription. A period of 15 years out of office followed during which Simon was a back-bench MP and devoted himself to his career at the Bar.

In 1930 he formed and led the National Liberal party with the object of supporting the newly formed government of Ramsay MacDonald and in 1931 took office as foreign secretary. In 1935 he was transferred to the Home Office and in 1937 to the chancellorship of the Exchequer. He became lord chancellor in the National Government of 1940. He played little part in politics after Churchill's defeat in 1945.

Simonides of Ceos (c.556–468 BC), Greek lyric poet. Having visited Hipparchus at Athens, he stayed for a time with Scopas in Thessaly, and returned to Athens at the beginning of the Persian wars. He moved to the court of Hieron at Syracuse about 476. The most famous of Simonides's surviving fragments is the epitaph on the Spartan dead at Thermopylae.

Simonstown, naval base in Cape Province, South Africa, on False Bay, 37 km south of Cape Town; it derives its name from Simon Van der Stel, an early governor of the Cape of Good Hope. In 1814 the British Admiralty made Simonstown the main base for the South Atlantic Naval Squadron. Under an agreement signed in 1955 Simonstown was transferred to South Africa, but Britain was guaranteed the fullest facilities in both peace and war, and in turn guaranteed the continued support of certain armaments to South Africa. In 1975 a British Labour government ended the agreement.

Simony (derived from Simon Magus), the purchase or sale of spiritual things. Early conciliar decrees prove that simony became common in the Church after the ages of persecution. The Council of Chalcedon (451) forbade ordination for money, and St Gregory the Great later denounced the same evil. Simony became widespread in the Middle Ages, especially by way of traffic in ecclesiastical preferment, which was repeatedly forbidden by such popes as Gregory VII as well as by the third Lateran Council (1179). Simony was treated in great detail by St Thomas Aquinas, and was vigorously condemned three centuries later by the Council of Trent. The Anglican canons of 1604 included provision against simony in the reception of benefices. The system of ecclesiastical patronage gave rise to simony in many cases, an abuse remedied by the English Benefices Act of 1898.

Simple Harmonic Motion (SHM), general name given to natural vibration and oscillation. It is the motion of a body under the influence of an opposing force directly proportional to the displacement of the body from a point in its line of motion. Thus it includes the oscillation of a weight supported by a spring, a pendulum, the string of a musical instrument, and wave motion in general. If a series of waves move regularly over a surface, any point on the surface will move up and down with SHM. If a pencil is moved up and down with SHM in contact with a piece of paper which is moved sideways at a uniform rate, a characteristic tracing is obtained. The curve can be obtained by plotting the graph of sin x.

Simplon Pass, Swiss Alpine pass between Brig in canton Valais and Iselle in Italy. The road over the pass was built between 1800–07 on Napoleon's orders. Altitude 2008 m.

Simpson, Sir James Young (1811–70), British physician who introduced chloroform anaesthesia. In 1847 he discovered the anaesthetic value of chloroform and its advantages over ether. He introduced it into his obstetric practice immediately finding himself in conflict with the Calvinists, who opposed the use of anaesthesia in childbirth. It was not until 1853 when Queen Victoria accepted the use of chloroform for the birth of Prince Leopold that criticism of Simpson died down. He published books and papers on gynaecology, obstetrics, anaesthesia, and homeopathy, and was also distinguished for writings on literature and archaeology.

Simpson, N(orman) F(rederick) (1919–), English dramatist. He first achieved success with *A Resounding Tinkle*, 1957, performed at the Royal Court Theatre, London. His next full-length play was *One Way Pendulum*, 1959, 'a farce in a new dimension', which continued the vein of satirical comic fantasy of his first play. A later full-length play was *The Cresta Run*, a farcical study of espionage. Simpson has also written short plays and revue sketches, and television and radio plays. He has clear affinities with some of the dramatists of the Theatre of the Absurd, especially Eugène Ionesco.

Sin, in Christian theology, is any word, deed, or thought contrary to the will of God. It may be variously analysed. There is Original Sin and Actual Sin, the sins we actually commit as distinct from an inherited infirmity and liability to do so.

Sinai, province of Egypt, a triangular peninsula at the head of the Red Sea. Area 62,000 km². The capital is El Arish. The peninsula is largely desert, occupied by a sparse nomadic population.

The modern significance of Sinai rests on its strategic importance as a buffer zone between Israel and Egypt, and the production of oil, begun in 1946, at Abu Rudeís. The peninsula was occupied by Israeli forces in the June War of 1967, but Egyptian forces re-established themselves east of the Suez Canal in the war of 1973. Israeli withdrawal from the peninsula was completed in 1982.

Sinai, mountain also known as *Horeb*, upon which the law was delivered to Moses. Its identity is not absolutely certain, but the weight of opinion favours Jebel Mūsā ('Mountain of Moses'), 2500 m. In the 6th century AD many Anchorites inhabited the region; but today there is only one monastery, the Orthodox Convent of St Catherine, which is believed to possess her relics. Here were discovered the great Codex Sinaiticus and the Syriac Codex of the Gospels.

Sinatra, Frank, (Francis Albert) (1917–), US singer and actor. He began in radio in 1936 and became a band singer. He made his first appearance in films in 1943 and won an Oscar for the best supporting actor in *From Here to Eternity* (1953). Other films include *High Society, Guys and Dolls, None But the Brave* and *Von Ryan's Express*.

Sinclair, Upton Beall (1878–1968), US novelist. A socialist, he turned his attention to capitalistic abuses, and in 1906 gained worldwide fame by his powerful novel, *The Jungle*. This was a bitter exposure of the methods existing in the stockyards and meat-packing plants of Chicago, and led to Congress passing the first national pure food law. In 1913 Sinclair investigated the abuses in the coalfields of Colorado, exposed them, and once more caused Congress to act. Out of his studies grew his novel *King Coal*, 1917.

Sinclair won the Pulitzer Prize in 1943 for *Dragon's Teeth*, 1942, which formed one of the Lanny Budd series (so named from its hero), a fictional account of world history from 1913 onwards in some ten books.

Sind, or Sindhu (indigenous name for the River Indus), province of Pakistan consisting mainly of the Indus Valley for the last 480 km of the river's course. The eastern part of the region is mostly the Thar Desert as far as the Indian frontier. The whole region is one of scanty rainfall, beyond the range of the monsoon, and dependent for water on canal irrigation. Rice, cotton, wheat, barley, oil-seeds, and vegetables are grown in the district. Salt is the main mineral product. Modern industries are making their appearance with the development of hydro-electric and natural gas power sources. Karachi has a ship-yard and varied industries. Sind was an administrative province of the Ommiad and Abbasid empires from 711 to 900. As the central authority weakened in Baghdad, the Arab governors established their own dynastic rule in Sind during the 10th century. The area passed into the control of the Moguls from 1591 to 1700, who were followed by two independent Sind dynasties from whom Sind was taken by the British, under Sir Charles Napier, in 1843.

Sind was part of the Bombay Presidency until 1937 when it was established as a separate province. After partition, in 1947, it became part of West Pakistan.

Sindbad the Sailor, one of the characters in the Arabian Nights. He is described as a wealthy citizen of Baghdad, who makes seven voyages, discovering, among other wonders, a roc's egg and the valley of diamonds.

Sindhi, Indo-Aryan language, spoken in the province of Sind, Pakistan, and in north-west India by some 7,000,000 people. The alphabet used by the Muslim majority is a Persian form of the Arabic, while the Hindu minority use a *devanāgarī* script.

Sine, see TRIGONOMETRY.

Sinecure, properly a benefice without cure of souls, an appointment within the church which has no duties. Certain cathedral offices, viz. canonries and prebends, are also called sinecures. By extension 'sinecure' is used in everyday speech to describe a post of profit which involves no work.

Singapore
Area: 616 km²
Population: 2,400,000

Singapore, island republic of 616 km², situated about 1°30′N of the equator, linked by a causeway to the southern tip of Malaya to which it previously belonged.

A granitic core rises to 177 m at one point and is surrounded by low-lying, often marshy land, much of which has been reclaimed. Land is Singapore's only appreciable resource: 16 per cent of the total area of 616 km² is cultivated, and 35 per cent in urban use. In 1980 the population totalled 2·4 million: 76 per cent Chinese, 15 per cent Malays, 7 per cent Indians and Pakistanis.

Agriculture is highly intensive and supplies all local needs of pork, poultry, and eggs.

Electronics, oil refining, and transport equipment (including shipbuilding and repair) are the main industries. The main industrial site is the 2835-ha Jurong Industrial Estate, with its own deep-water harbour and rail link, factories, and a new town. It is the regional headquarters, and a complete support base, for companies involved in mineral exploration and extraction in South-East Asia.

The unit of currency is the Singapore dollar, of 100 cents. Singapore is a major financial centre and has a recently developed tourist industry.

In December 1965 Singapore became an independent republic, with a president, a 12-member cabinet led by the prime minister, and a 51-seat (now 75 seats) parliament whose members are elected by universal suffrage.

An advisory presidential council exists to determine if legislation is discriminatory on racial or religious grounds or inconsistent with basic individual liberties, but has no

authority to examine any bill certified by the prime minister as affecting 'the defence or security of Singapore or relating to public safety, peace, or good order'.

The official languages are English, Chinese, Malay, and Tamil—of which English is the main language of education, administration, and commerce

History. In the 14th century Singapura (the Lion City) is mentioned as being a Malay capital, destroyed about 1391. In 1819, Stamford Raffles of the East India Company concluded a treaty with the nominal rulers of Singapore, Sultan Hussein and the Temenggong Abdul Rahman, allowing the company to establish a trading base near the Rochor river. In 1824 a treaty was signed ceding the entire island and most offshore islands to the company, and in 1832 Singapore was incorporated in the Straits Settlements. Between the two world wars the building of a great naval base at Singapore stressed the colony's strategic importance, and, in consideration of this, Singapore was made into a separate Crown Colony when the Straits Settlements were disbanded in 1946. Singapore was granted self-government in 1959. In 1963 Singapore joined the new Federation of Malaysia but racial and political tensions led to its secession in 1965. Singapore became a republic in 1965 and from 1966 the People's Action Party (PAP) government under the Prime Minister, Lee Kuan Yew, embarked on making Singapore a tightly-disciplined 'garrison state'. The British Far East Command ceased in 1971 and the British naval base was formally closed. The Singapore government now provides servicing facilities for foreign naval vessels but official policy is against the establishment of a naval base on the island by any power.

Singer Company, The, manufacturers of the sewing-machine invented by Isaac Merritt Singer (1811–75) in 1851. The business began in Boston, Massachusetts in that year by the formation of a partnership between Isaac Singer and Edward Clark. The Singer Company is now a multi-national diversified corporation. Isaac Singer was the first to initiate a system of credit terms, later familiarly known as hire-purchase.

Singer, Isaac Bashevis (1904–), Polish-born writer of novels, short stories and essays, now an American citizen. A member of a rabbinical family, he received a traditional Jewish education. He emigrated to the US in 1935. His novels, which are written in Yiddish and then translated into English, are penetrating studies of Jewish life in Poland and the USA. The include *The Slave,* 1962; *The Estate,* 1969; and *Shosha,* 1978. In 1978 he was awarded the Nobel Prize for literature.

Sinhalese, an Indo-Aryan language, the official language and script of Sri Lanka (Ceylon). It is the mother tongue of over 9,000,000 people (1972), three-quarters of the population of the island.

Sink-hole, a depression characteristic of karst areas which enables water to percolate into an underground drainage system. Various local terms used to describe this feature include swallow-hole, where the stream actually disappears into the depression, and pothole, where it leads into a cave system.

Sinkiang Uighur Autonomous Region (Chinese *Xinjiang Uygur Zizhiqu*) is situated in Western China and is the country's largest administrative unit. Sinkiang became an autonomous region in 1955 and consists of two basins separated from each other and encircled by high mountains. From north to south these are: the Altai Mountains (separating Sinkiang from the Mongolian People's Republic), Dzungaria, the Tianshan (with peaks to over 6100 m), the Talimupendi (Tarim Basin) (containing the Takla Makan Desert, Luobubo, and the Turfan Depression —c.275 m below sea-level), and the Kunlun Mountains separating Sinkiang from Tibet. Sinkiang has a frontier (some 2900 km) with the Soviet Union, and a 65-km frontier with Afghanistan (the Pamirs). The latter, with the western Kunlun (Karakoram), also separates Sinkiang from the Indian sub-continent. The main approach to the region from the rest of China is from Gansu across the Gobi Desert. Its external boundaries have all been fixed by international treaties, agreements, and protocols except for a length of about 240 km in the Pamirs facing the Soviet Union. The climate (especially of that portion north of the Tianshan) is extreme. The main

Singapore. *Modern skyscrapers contrast with the junks of the city's old waterfront.*

occupations are animal husbandry (by Kazakhs, Kirghiz, and Mongols) and farming (wheat, rice, maize, cotton, and fruit) on rich oases where streams from the mountains reach the plains. The mineral resources include petroleum, gold, coal, and iron-ore. The provincial capital is Urumchi (Wulumuqi). Area 1,642,000 km². Population (1980 est.) 12,560,000.

Sinking Fund, fund formed to pay off public debt, or company debt, or to replace capital equipment. The first public sinking fund was established in 1716 by Sir Robert Walpole.

See also BUDGET; PUBLIC DEBT.

Sinn Féin (We Ourselves), an Irish Republican movement. The party came to prominence in Ireland at the end of the First World War. The result of the 1918 general election showed how bitter feeling against England had become, for Sinn Féin (half of whose candidates were in prison) overwhelmed the old Irish Nationalist party. The elected members of Sinn Féin set up an independent Parliament (Dáil Éireann) in Dublin; the whole machinery of British administration had in fact broken down. Sinn Féin, in its original incarnation, declined rapidly in importance after de Valera resigned its presidency in 1926 to form Fianna Fáil. It continues, however, as the political wing of the Irish Republican Army and in the 1983 general election gained one Belfast seat in the House of Commons.

Sino–Japanese War (1894–95). Keen competition between Japan and China for markets in Korea was the real cause of this war. The resulting and thorough defeat of the Chinese was a startling revelation of the rise of Japanese power in the Far East. War was declared by Japan on 1 August 1894, actual hostilities having begun a week previously with the sinking of the transport *Kowshing*, a British vessel carrying Chinese troops.

In the battle of Pyong-yang (15 September), a Chinese army was routed with heavy loss. On 17 September, however, the Chinese navy fought stoutly, and the most important naval action of the war took place off the island of Hai-yang, when the Chinese fleet was defeated.

In February 1895, at the decisive battle of Wei-hai, the Chinese land and sea forces were utterly defeated. A treaty was signed at Shimonoseki in April and ratified in May at Chifu, under which Korean independence was recognised, and Liaotung, Formosa (Taiwan), and the Pescadores were ceded to Japan.

See also CHINA, *History*; JAPAN, *History*.

Sinop (ancient Greek *Sinope*), town and minor port on the Black Sea coast and capital of Sinop province, Turkey. It was founded in 630 BC by settlers from Miletus and became the greatest Greek commercial city on the Black Sea, as it was the terminus of a caravan route from the Euphrates. Julius Caesar established a Roman colony there in about 45 BC, but the port was already losing its trade to Ephesus, which was more favourably situated for Roman shipping. It was taken by the Turks in the 15th century. Population (1970) (town) 15,100; (province) 265,700.

Sintra, town of Portugal, 24 km north-west of Lisbon. It is known for its palaces, gardens, and Moorish remains. It is now a holiday resort. Population (1970) 20,320.

Sinus, a cavity or hollow space in the body, especially the nasal sinuses. There are four major pairs of nasal sinuses, found around the nasal cavity in the skull. Their function is uncertain, but it is thought they help to warm the air before it passes into the lungs, and help to make the voice resonant. They are lined with mucus membrane, and their secretions discharge into the nose. *Sinusitis* is inflammation of the mucus membrane, caused by bacteria or viruses. The symptoms are nasal discharge, and headache located near the involved sinuses.

Sioux, see DAKOTA.

Sioux City, city and county seat of Woodbury county, Iowa, USA, on the Missouri river where the Big Sioux and the Floyd enter it, 250 km north-west of Des Moines. It is a rail and highway centre with large stockyards, and a livestock and grain market; it does much meat packing and manufactures dairy products, flour, feed, and animal serums. Population (1980) 82,003.

Sioux Falls, city and county seat of Minnehaha county, South Dakota, USA, on the Big Sioux river. The river here falls 30 m and supplied water power for early industries. The city is a great wheat and livestock centre; it has important stockyards and fairgrounds. Population (1980) 81,343.

Siphon, bent tube with arms of unequal length used for drawing off liquid from one vessel into another. In use, the tube is first filled with liquid and placed so that the shorter arm dips into the vessel to be emptied. A soda siphon does not work by siphon action, but relies on the pressure of undissolved gas (carbon dioxide) to force the liquid out.

Siphonaptera, an order of the class Insecta, subclass Pterygota. These are the fleas. They are small, wingless, laterally compressed insects that usually have a hard cuticle. The antennae are in grooves, and the mouthparts piercing and sucking. The adults are ectoparasites of birds and mammals living mainly in their nests, burrows, or body covering. Most species are confined to a particular host species. The hindlegs are often especially large and long as an adaptation for jumping.

There are over 1800 species, only a few of which are important to man as vectors of disease, although many are indirectly important as they maintain the reservoir of disease among wild animals. Fleas are vectors of bubonic plague, murine typhus, and tularaemia, and they are also known to transmit myxomatosis virus to rabbits, and *Salmonella* food poisoning in mammals. The most important vectors belong to the genera *Leptopsylla*, *Nosopsyllus*, and *Xenopsylla*. All three genera are intermediate hosts of *Dipylidium caninum*, the dog and cat tapeworm.

The bites of several species cause allergic reactions with intense itching. *Ctenocephalides canis*, the dog flea, and *C. felis*, the cat flea, which both readily bite man, are very annoying in this respect. The bite of the human flea, *Pulex irritans*, also causes a severe reaction.

Sipunculida, a phylum of approximately 250 species of marine worms, also known as peanut worms. They have a cylindrical body divided into two parts and range in size from 2 mm to 70 cm long. There is a crown of short, hollow ciliated tentacles or lobes around the mouth. They live in sand, mud, rock crevices, or empty shells. Common species are *Golfingia* and *Sipunculus*.

Siqueiros, David Alfaro (1896–), Mexican painter and graphic artist, inspired in aim by the Mexican revolution. Principal works are mural paintings in Mexico City, dynamic and strongly proletarian in sentiment, of which *March of Humanity* (4600 m²) expresses most clearly his message. He has also painted many portraits.

Sir (French *sire*, a variant of *seigneur*, from Latin *senior*), official title of baronets and knights, which is prefixed to the Christian name of the bearer.

Siren, sound signalling apparatus. As used for fire warnings, air-raids, etc., the siren consists of three parts, viz., motor, rotor, and stator. Another type is especially used in lighthouses and lightships, and also in factories. This is the 'diaphone', of which several sizes are produced. It operates by compressed air fed to the instrument from an air storage tank.

Siren, the typical genus of tailed eel-like amphibians in the family Sirenidae. The species are characterised by having four-fingered forelimbs, three external gills on each side, no hind limbs and no eyelids. *S. lacertina* is the mud-eel, over 60 cm long, and occurs in North America. It resembles *Proteus*, except that teeth and hind limbs are absent in *Siren*.

Sirenia, the order of mammals which contains the sea-cows; many fossil forms have been found as well as the living species of the genera *Dugong* (or dugongs) and Steller's sea-cow, which attained a length of 10 m, but became extinct due to depredations of man within 50 years of its discovery in 1741. Sirenia inhabit various seashores and are purely vegetarian in diet. The mammary glands are pectoral in position, so that Sirenia may have been thought to be mermaids.

Sirens, nymphs whose songs irresistibly lured sailors to destruction, Odysseus plugged his men's ears with wax and tied himself to the mast, and so passed them in safety. When the Argonauts sailed by, Orpheus outsang the sirens, after which they threw themselves into the sea and became rocks.

Sirius, Alpha Canis Majoris or 'the Dog Star', a first magnitude star in Canis Major. The name Sirius is derived from the Greek word for 'sparkling', a description it fully warrants since, after the Sun, it is the brightest star in the sky. In ancient Egypt, where its hieroglyph was a dog, its reappearance in the early morning sky heralded the annual rising of the Nile. Sirius is double with an orbital period of 50 years. The eighth magnitude companion is sometimes known as 'the Dark Companion' since it was first detected by Bessel in 1850 from its gravitational effect on the observed proper motion of Sirius. It was seen for the first time in 1862 by Alvan Clark but it was not till the 1920s that it was recognised as a white dwarf, the first known example of such stars which have mean densities of the order of 100,000 times that of water.

See also ASTRONOMY; STAR.

Sirocco, see WIND.

Sisal, a textile fibre obtained from the leaf of *Agave sisalana*, which is indigenous to Mexico but is now also grown in Tanzania and Brazil. It is used for twine, especially for baler and binder machines, for floor coverings, and in millinery.

Siskin, *Carduelis spinus*, a bird species of the family Fringillidae, order Passeriformes, related to the goldfinch. Its colour is a greenish-yellow, and it is frequently seen in western and central Europe where it breeds, mainly in coniferous woods. In winter it is often to be seen in company with the redpoll, *Acanthis flammea*, in deciduous woods especially alder. It has recently taken to visiting bird tables.

Sisley, Alfred (1839–99), landscape painter of English parentage. He became acquainted with Monet and Renoir in the studio of the classical painter Gleyre. Sisley was a member of the Impressionist group, and his work shows the influence of the light-effects of Monet. He settled in Moret-sur-Loing but visited England in 1871 and 1874. He is known as one of the purest Impressionists. Well-known works include *The Square at Argenteuil* 1872 and *The Canal*, 1872.

Sistine Chapel, principal chapel of the Vatican at Rome. It was begun by Pope Sixtus IV in 1473, and is famous for the paintings which cover its walls and vault, notably those by Michelangelo including *The Creation, The Deluge* and *The Last Judgment*, and also masterpieces by Botticelli, Perugino and Pinturicchio. The voting of the cardinals at the election of a new pope takes place in the Sistine Chapel.

Sisyphus, legendary son of Aeolus and Enarete, and king of Corinth. He promoted navigation and commerce, but lived an evil life, for which he was punished in Tartarus, forever rolling a huge stone up a hill, which, at the top, always rolled back.

Sitar, fretted Indian lute. It has 6 or 7 main strings, and from 11 to 19 sympathetic strings. The main strings are plucked with a plectrum.

Sithole, Ndabaningi (1920–), Zimbabwe leader who founded the Zimbabwe African National Union (ZANU), the members of which originally formed the core of the guerrilla movement. He is a pastor of the Methodist Church. In 1959 he published *African Nationalism* and in 1964 was arrested for alleged incitement to violence. On 12 December 1974 he was conditionally released in order to participate in talks about Rhodesia's (Zimbabwe's) future. He helped to bring about the Rhodesian Zimbabwe settlement.

Sitka, town and former capital of Alaska, USA, situated on the west coast of Baranov Island, facing Sitka Sound, 160 km south-west of Juneau. Between 1804–67 it was the Russian capital. Since 1940 Sitka has been an important naval base; it is also a trading centre with fishing, lumbering, canning, and cold-storage operations. Population (1980) 7,803.

Sitting Bull (1835–90), famous chief of the Dakota Sioux Indians. During the American Civil War he led bands which attacked white settlers in Iowa and Minnesota. In a campaign against him Gen. G. A. Custer and his entire command were massacred. Sitting Bull fled to Canada, but returned in 1881 and lived at Standing Rock. During an attempt to arrest Sitting Bull in 1890, he was shot.

Sitwell, Dame Edith Louise (1887–1964), English poet and critic, sister of Osbert and Sacheverell Sitwell. In 1916 the first volume of *Wheels* appeared, an annual anthology of verse, which she edited until it was discontinued in 1921; it served as a showcase for her work and that of other young poets who were fighting an artistic revolt against the Georgians. An early series of poems called *Façade* was first recited by her at a public performance, accompanied by music composed by William Walton, in 1923. Later work, especially *Street Songs*, 1942, and *Song of the Cold*, 1945, is more preoccupied with religious themes and symbolism.

Sitwell, Sir Osbert (1892–1969), English poet and novelist, the brother of Edith and Sacheverell Sitwell. The First World War and subsequent peace excited Sitwell to bitter satire, both in prose and verse. In his two novels, *Before the Bombardment*, 1926, and *The Man Who Lost Himself*, 1929, he claimed to have originated the 'novel of reasoned action'. His verse is often caustic and mocking; however, his reputation chiefly rests on a series of autobiographical memoirs, *Left Hand, Right Hand!*, 1944; *The Scarlet Tree*, 1945; *Great Morning*, 1947; *Laughter in the Next Room*, 1948; and *Noble Essences*, 1950.

Sitwell, Sir Sacheverell (1897–), English poet and essayist, younger brother of Edith and Osbert Sitwell. His poetry is traditional in form and style, and reveals his preoccupations with art and music. His prose works include the seminal study *Southern Baroque Art*, 1924, *All Summer in a Day*, 1926, and *Far from My Home*, 1931.

Śiva (the Lord of Sleep), one of the creator deities belonging to the trinity of Brahma, Vishnu and Śiva. Profound Hindu understanding had embodied in Śiva the power of universal disintegration and dispersion. All that is born must die, is a law of the universe. Śiva, as the power of disintegration and death, is also the merciful redeemer who enables the weary soul to rest in its Source.

In images he is represented in either of two ways. In one he is a fearful destroyer, the embodiment of death: in the other he is the beginning of all creation, mysteriously dancing through the forests and scattering his seed to create unknown new worlds and beings. As new life, his symbol is the Lingam and his vehicle the bull.

Sivaji (1627–80), founder of Mahratta power, and a great Hindu hero and rebel. He revolted against the Bijapur rulers in 1646, and spent the rest of his life more or less continuously in a state of war. As a military leader he showed daring and resource; as a religious leader, he pointed the way to a Hindu revival while showing toleration towards Christians and Muslims.

Sivas, town and capital of Sivas province, Asiatic Turkey, situated on the Kızıl Irmak river and the railway and road from Ankara to Erzurum. The town is a major agricultural market centre and has food-processing industries. Population (1980) 172,864.

Six Acts, series of statutes passed in 1819 after the 'massacre of Peterloo' to prevent further popular disturbances—which ministers at the time considered presaged revolution. They prohibited meetings for military training, authorised the issue of warrants for the seizure of arms, limited meetings to draw up public petitions to not more than 50 people living in the parish where the meeting was to be held, allowed magistrates to seize seditious and blasphemous literature, dealt with procedure for bringing cases to trial, and imposed stamp duty on certain periodical pamphlets.

Sistine Chapel. *The vaulted ceiling was painted by Michelangelo between 1508 and 1512. The detail shows 'the creation of Adam by God and the separation of light from dark'.*

Sixth Form College, school or college in Britain for sixth-form pupils. The nature of the college may be defined by age, e.g. pupils aged 16–19, or by qualification—passes at 'O' level, and therefore by nature of work—post 'O' level standard. If only defined by age then both academic and non-academic courses are offered: if minimum entry qualifications are demanded then the college is essentially selective and academic. Although the sixth form college is a common pattern of organisation in Europe, there has been much opposition to it, particularly from teachers' organisations, in England.

Sixtus IV, Francesco della Rovere (b.1414), Pope, 1471–84, a Franciscan; he succeeded Paul II. He encouraged the spread of learning, began the Sistine Chapel and the Sistine Bridge, and was a patron of all the arts. He was involved in a conspiracy against the Medici which resulted in a war with Florence (1478) and urged the Venetians to attack Ferrara and then abandoned them.

Sixtus V, Felice Peretti, Pope, 1585–90, Franciscan preacher, and professor of theology at Rimini and Siena. His rule was characterised by a number of reforms. He brought order to the Papal States. He also built the Vatican library, and published a new edition of the Septuagint and of the Vulgate. He fixed the number of cardinals at 70.

Sjaelland (English, Zealand; German *Seeland*), largest island of Denmark, bounded by the Kattegat, the Great Belt, the Sound (Øresund), and the Baltic. The surface of the island is undulating and the soil fertile. Agriculture, dairy farming, cattle breeding, and fishing are carried on. The chief town is Copenhagen. Area 7225 km².

Skagerrak, arm of the sea situated between Norway and Jutland, connecting the Baltic and North Seas by means of the Kattegat. It varies between 112 and 145km in width, and is about 250km long.

Skaldic Poetry. *Skald* or *skáld* is the Old Icelandic word for poet and, used in a technical sense, it refers to the court poets of medieval Scandinavia. The earliest of these were Norwegian, but after the late 10th century, they were, without exception, Icelandic. The central theme of the skalds' poetry was praise of the kings or princes to whom they were attached. Later, their style was adopted by poets other than court poets and the term skaldic poetry is used of works composed in this style. Much of the corpus of skaldic poetry was composed in the pre-literary period and is preserved in Icelandic prose works of the 13th and 14th centuries, particularly in the *Snorra Edda* and *Heimskringla* of Snorri Sturluson and in sagas about poets such as Egils saga *Skalla-Grímssonar*.

Skalkottas, Nikos (1904–49), Greek composer. Only after his death was his music performed. His works include 36 *Greek Dances*, 19 concertos for various instruments, and the symphony *The Return of Ulysses*. Skalkottas was Greece's first composer of international stature.

Skanderberg (1404–68), Albanian hero who led a nationalist rebellion against the Turks (1444–68). The unity of purpose he was able to engender among the quarrelsome Albanian chieftains dissolved on his death and the country yielded again to Turkish domination.

Skåne, or Scania, old province in the south of Sweden, now included in the counties of Malmöhus and Kristianstad.

Skate, fish of the elasmobranch family Rajidae, suborder Rajoidei, which occurs in all temperate seas. The body of the fish is in the shape of a flattened disc, formed by its union with the greatly developed, fleshy pectoral fins; the tail is slender and usually bears two dorsal fins. The egg cases are oblong, and are commonly known as mermaid's purses. Several well-known species are *Raja radiata*, the starry skate; *R. oxyrhynchus*, the long-nosed skate; and *R. laevis*, the barn-door skate.

Skean-dhu, or sgean-dhu (Gaelic, black knife), short knife, usually worn with Highland dress and carried in the right stocking.

Skeet Shooting, see CLAY-PIGEON SHOOTING.

Skegness, largest seaside resort of Lincolnshire, England. It has 9km of sandy beaches. Butlin established his first holiday camp at Skegness. Population (1981) 14,452.

Skeleton, a rigid structure for the support or protection of the softer tissues of a plant or animal. When the skeleton is external, as in the shells of insects or other anthropods, it is called an exoskeleton; when it forms an interior framework for the support of surrounding tissues, it is known as an endoskeleton. In Man, the medial supporting structure is the vertebral column (spine); it consists of 33 *vertebrae* of which, in the adult, the lower 9 are fused to form the *sacrum* and the *coccyx*. The spine supports the skull, which consists of 22 bones, of which only the jawbone is movable. The organs of the chest are protected by the ribs, which articulate with the vertebrae behind.

The upper limbs hang from the shoulder-girdle, which consists of the *clavicle*, or collarbone, in front, and a flat, triangular bone called the *scapula*, or shoulder-blade, behind. They include the *humerus*, or bone of the upper arm; and the *ulna* and *radius*, the bones of the forearm.

The lower limbs articulate with the pelvic girdle. The arrangement of bones in the legs is somewhat similar to that of the arm bones. The *femur*, or thigh bone, is the longest bone in the body. The bones of the lower leg are the *tibia*, or shin bone, and the slenderer *fibula*. See BONE; JOINTS.

Skelmersdale, town in Lancashire, England, lying to the west of Wigan. It was designated a New Town in 1961, mainly for overspill from Liverpool; by 1981, its population had increased to 39,144.

Skelton, John (1460–1529), English poet. He was appointed tutor to the Duke of York (afterwards Henry VIII), and, taking holy orders in 1498, was given the living of Diss, Norfolk.

Most of his poetry is satirical, on political and religious matters, and in an idiosyncratic style of short rhyming lines. *Phyllyp Sparrowe* is a parody of the liturgical office for the dead, delivered upon a young lady's pet; *Speke Parrot*, 1521, *Collyn Clout*, 1522, and *Why Come Ye Not to Court?*, 1522, all combine attacks on the growing influence of Cardinal Wolsey with criticism of humanist learning. Skelton also wrote *Magnyfycence*, 1516, the first secular morality play in English, and

The Tunnyng of Elynour Rummynge, an energetic and realistic depiction of the drunken Elynour in an ale-house.

Skerries, several groups of rocky islets around the coast of Great Britain and Ireland. The name is specially applied to a group of islets off the north-west coast of Anglesey, in the Irish Sea.

Ski-bobbing, sport best described as cycling on snow, the rider sitting on a kind of bicycle frame fitted with short skis instead of wheels. The rider wears miniature foot-skis, not much longer than his boots. The foot-skis are fitted with metal claws at the heels to assist braking. One attraction is that it is easier to learn than ordinary skiing. Recreational ski-bobbers can easily attain speeds around 100 kmph. Leading racers have exceeded 160 kmph.

Ski Jumping, see SKIING.

Skiing, moving across snow with feet attached to shaped runners; skis originated in Scandinavia about 5000 years ago. Recreational skiing developed after 1896, when Mathias Zdarsky produced specially designed skis and bindings.

Alpine ski racing, so called because it originated on the ideal terrain of the European Alps, is now practised in more than 40 countries. The competitive sport comprises downhill, slalom and giant slalom events, with contestants individually timed and usually starting at one-minute intervals, the winner being the fastest to complete a course correctly. Combined titles are won by the best all-round performers in the three events. Downhill courses, designed to test courage and fitness, are set with length, steepness and degree of difficulty appropriate to the standard of competitors. The length of a senior course varies from 2·4 to 4·8km, with a vertical descent between 750 and 900m. A winner's average speed is usually between 65 and 80kmph.

Slalom courses, shorter than downhill, comprise a series of pairs of poles with flags, called 'gates', positioned at angles designed to test skill in turning and pace-checking, as distinct from the sheer speed in downhill events. A racer who misses a gate is disqualified unless he climbs back to pass through it. Senior courses can have 50 to 75 gates and a vertical drop between 200 and 300m. The distance between the two poles of each gate should be at least 3m and the distance between gates must be not less than 75cm. The flags are 1·8m above the snow and each pair is distinguished by red, yellow and blue colours.

Giant slalom courses blend characteristics of the downhill and slalom in one event. The trail is longer than the slalom, with wider gates set farther apart.

Nordic ski racing comprises long-distance cross-country running on undulating terrain of a kind which abounds in Scandinavia. Senior men's races are contested over 15, 30 and 50km, and women's over 5 and 10km. There are also team relay races. The course is roughly circular, starting and ending at the same point. A good racer can achieve an average speed around 16kmph.

Ski jumping, a highly specialised branch of nordic skiing, originated at Iverslokka, Norway, in 1866. Major events start from heights of 90 m and 70 m, competitors skiing in turn down a ramp, reaching up to 120 kmph before take-off. The winner is not necessarily the one who jumps farthest. A panel of five judges award marks for style and technique, which are assessed in conjunction with the distance cleared. Separate world ski-flying championships began in 1972, with emphasis on distance cleared and using higher take-offs.

The nordic combination is an event to test the overall ability of skiers in jumping and in 15 km nordic cross-country ski racing, winners being determined on a points basis.

Both alpine and nordic disciplines of skiing are governed by the International Ski Federation (FIS), founded in 1924.

Skiddaw, mountain in the Cumbrian Lake District National Park, England, and the highest point (930 m) of the area north of Keswick.

Skidmore, Owings and Merrill, US architectural partnership, founded in 1935, which has pioneered modern office design. The Lever Building, New York (1952), was an International Style building designed by one of the partners, Gordon Bunshaft and widely imitated.

Skikda, formerly Philippeville, Mediterranean port of Algeria. The port exports the agricultural and mineral products (iron ore, marble) of its hinterland and is an important sardine fishing port. A natural gas pipeline from the Sahara has its terminus here. Population (1974) 127,968.

Skimmer, or scissor-bill, *Rhynchops*, genus of birds with bills in which the lower mandible is longer and flatter than the upper, and fits into it like a penknife blade into its handle. There are three species found on inland and coastal waters in the tropics. They are related to the gulls and terns. They feed on small fish and other aquatic life taken from just below the surface of the water by skimming it with the beak, hence their name.

Skin, the outer, protective covering of the animal body. In human beings, it consists of two layers, the epidermis (cuticle or scarf-skin) above, and the true skin, the dermis (or corium), beneath. Both arise from the epithelium of the embryo. The *epidermis* consists of layers of epithelial cells, the outermost of which are dead horny scales or keratin, which are continually shed, while the lower layers actively multiply to replace them. The skin, in Man, is renewed continually and imperceptibly, but in some animals, such as the snake, it is cast in large portions or all at once. It is thickest on the palms of the hands and soles of the feet. Horns, hoofs, nails, hairs and feathers are all epidermal outgrowths.

The colour of the skin, and its darkening upon exposure to sunlight, is due to the pigment melanin, contained in special cells, the melanocytes, in the epidermis. The number of melanocytes is the same in all races of Man, but in the darker races they produce melanin more actively. The purpose of melanin is to protect the cells of the skin from the ultraviolet rays of the Sun.

The *dermis* is a layer of fibrous tissue merging gradually into the looser subcutaneous connective tissue underneath.

The skin is an excretory organ: its sweat glands pick up waste products from the blood and excrete them to the outside. It helps regulate the body temperature, through the evaporation of sweat which cools the body. In many fish, amphibia, and some other animals, the skin is the major excretory and respiratory organ. Skin is almost impermeable to water from the outside, but oils can enter, and some drugs or poisons can be administered by rubbing them on the skin. The skin is a major organ of sensation, with special receptors for pressure and pain. It protects the body from infection, both by providing an intact covering and by its active role in fighting invading organisms.

Skink, a lizard of the family Scincidae, the members of which live in Europe, Africa, Asia, and Australia. The common skink (*Scincus scincus*), which grows to a length of 23 cm, is found in the Sahara and along the shores of the Red Sea.

Skinner, Burrhus Frederic (1904–), US psychologist. Skinner has become famous as the most assertive of behaviourist psychologists, holding that his experiments with pigeons and other animals prove the existence of a reward principle governing all behaviour, including that of human beings. In *Walden Two*, 1948, reissued 1962, *Beyond Freedom and Dignity*, 1973, and other books, he has described a Utopia of beneficent control and manipulation which, however, many commentators find unconvincing and unpleasant.

See also SKINNER BOX.

Skinner Box, a device used to investigate 'conditioned' animal behaviour. It consists of a living-box with an object that an animal in the box can manipulate. The form of the object varies for different animals; for rats it is a lever which can be pressed, for pigeons a disc which can be pecked. When the animal moves the object sufficiently, a pellet of food may be delivered to it, thus reinforcing the action undertaken. This makes the animal more likely to repeat it. The lever/disc can initiate other stimuli such as opening a door, delivering water, giving electric shocks.

Skins, see FUR.

Skipjack, (*Euthynnus pelamis*), a species of small tunnyfish. It is a member of the mackerel family, Scombridae. It ranges the open ocean waters, usually in small groups.

Skipton, market town in North Yorkshire, England, 32 km north-west of Bradford. Manufactured products include cotton and rayon goods. The castle, dating partly from the 11th century, was a Civil War stronghold. Population (1981) 13,246.

Skirret, *Sium sisarum*, a species of the Umbelliferae. Its roots are tuberous, and are edible when boiled.

Skirt, popular garment falling from the waist to varying lengths; during the 1960s it reached its shortest ever with the mini-skirt.

See also DRESS.

Skittles, a target game dating from the Middle Ages which was originally introduced into Great Britain from Germany and became popular in public-houses. The rules varied considerably between areas, the game also commonly being known as 'kails' or 'nine-pins'. The basic principle is to bowl a ball or flat wooden 'cheese', weighing from 4·5 kg to 6·35 kg, down a lane or alley at the nine skittles evenly spaced in a diamond-shaped frame. The skittles are roughly cigar-shaped, about 30 cm high and weigh from 3 kg to 4 kg. There are two opponents or two opposing sides. Points are scored according to the number of skittles knocked down.

See also TENPIN BOWLING.

Skopje (Turkish *Üsküb*), capital of the republic of Macedonia, Yugoslavia, on the Vardar river, in the north-west of the great plain of Skopje. In pre-Roman times it was the capital of Illyria, and in the 10th and 11th centuries it was the capital of an independent Macedonian kingdom. Skopje has metallurgical and foodstuff industries. Population (1971) 389,000.

Skuas, birds of family Stercorariidae, in the order Charadriiformes, suborder Lari, the latter including the gulls and terns. Skuas are entirely marine, and very widely distributed, although their chief breeding grounds are on the islands of the north Atlantic, from the coast of Labrador to the Shetlands, and on the islands of the Antarctic. They average about 50 cm long, with long, well-developed wings and short, stout legs, and in colour are greyish above, white below; in character they are fierce, and will attack smaller birds to make them disgorge the fish they have captured. There are seven species. *Catharacta skua*, the great skua, and *Stercorarius parasiticus*, the Arctic skua or parasitic jaeger, are well-known species.

Skull, the skeleton of the head and face. It consists of the cranial cavity, or brain case, plus the bones of the face, which include the walls of the orbits (eye-sockets) and nasal cavity and form the roof of the mouth (hard palate), and a separate lower jaw or mandible. There are 21 bones forming the bulk of the skull, and in adult life they are united by immobile fibrous joints called sutures. In addition there are the ossicles of the middle ear within the temporal bone. The bones of the skull base develop in cartilage whereas the skull vault develops in membrane. At birth this ossification of the skull vault is not complete, leaving small membranous areas, notably the anterior and posterior fontanelles, which only close during the second year of life. This incomplete ossification and imperfect interlocking of the bones means that the skull is less rigid at birth and the slight mobility facilitates delivery of the baby.

The shape and size of the skull are used as means of classification by anthropologists and biologists. Thus the pre-human *Homo habilis* who lived about two million years ago had a skull (and therefore brain) volume of about 510 ml whilst that of modern *Homo sapiens* has an average volume of 1400 ml, reflecting a great increase in intellectual capacity. The notable features of the human skull are the large size of the brain case, the small size of the face, and the way the skull is poised on the vertebral column.

Skunk, an American carnivorous mammal in family Mustelidae of order Carnivora, with remarkably developed anal glands from which, when provoked, it ejects a foetid secretion. The common skunk (*Mephitis mephitis*) is about 70 cm long, including the tail, and black or dark brown in colour with white markings on the head and back. Its head is small, long and conical, and the ears short and rounded; the legs are short, and the animal burrows in the earth. Its food consists largely of small rodents and insects, but fruit and poultry eggs are often stolen. It is daring and fierce, and can inflict a nasty wound with its teeth, but its intolerable secretion is more feared. Its furry skin is purified and largely used by furriers.

Sky-diving, see PARACHUTING.

Skye, large and beautiful island in Highland Region, Scotland; the central part is very mountainous, rising to over 1000 m. The coastline is deeply indented by numerous sea-lochs, and most of the settlements are coastal. Crofting and tourism are the main sources of income, and large areas have been afforested. Area, 171,520 ha. Population (1971) 7183.

Skylab, launched on 14 May, 1973, was the first American space station. It was 26 m long and weighed about 70 tonnes. Three separate three-man crews spent a total of 171 days aboard carrying out scientific experiments; the third crew spent 84 days in orbit. The space station was abandoned after February, 1974, falling back to Earth on 11 July, 1979. See also SPACE TRAVEL.

Skylark, see LARK.

Skyros (Greek *Skíros*), island of Greece in the Aegean Sea, the largest of the Northern Sporades group, 40 km north-east of Euboea. The land is mountainous; sheep and goats are reared, but its mineral ores (chrome, iron, manganese, copper, gypsum, and lignite) are more important economically. Area 207 km²; population (1971) 2800.

Slade, Felix (1790–1868), British art collector. He bequeathed his collections of engravings, glass and pottery to the British Museum. Slade was also a noted book-collector, and left £35,000 for the endowment of art (Slade) professorships at Oxford, Cambridge and University College, London, the Slade School of art being called after him.

Slag, mixture of silicate, chiefly of lime and alumina, produced in many metallurgical operations. Blast furnace slag is chiefly calcium and aluminium silicate, and varies in character from a glass to a stony type. Some 20 million t of blast furnace slag are produced annually.

Slalom, see SKIING; WATER SKIING.

Slander, see DEFAMATION.

Slang, often used to describe colloquial language in general, more specifically describes the colloquial speech peculiar to certain groups. Slang is usually esoteric, understood within the group, but less intelligible to those outside. Slang may be humorous, obscene, witty, and both imaginative and repetitive.

Slates are fine-grained, low-grade metamorphic rocks with a highly developed cleavage due to parallel alignment of their constituent minerals, as a result of directed stress during metamorphism. The almost perfect cleavage enables slates to be split into thin laminae with great ease, thus enabling them to be used for roofing, for which purpose their durability and light weight make them eminently suitable.

Slave Coast, name formerly applied to that part of the coast of West Africa which lies between Ghana and the River Benin, now comprising the People's Republic of Benin and part of Nigeria.

Slavery, the condition of a human being who is the property of another. It may vary from the extreme 'rightlessness' of the Roman *servus*, whose labour could be exploited and his life taken by his master with impunity (although later, in the Christian era, this constituted murder), to the mitigated rigour of the *ascripti glebae*, or serfs of the soil of the later empire and the Middle Ages, who, though they passed with the soil and were bound to remain on it, had some of the position of freemen. Slavery may be a status to which a man was born, or be thrust upon him by debt, capture in war, or his own crimes; or, as in America, it may be rather the condition of having to perform compulsory labour at the will of a conquering people.

Slavkov, Czechoslovak town in southern Moravia. Under its German name, Austerlitz, it is famous as the scene of Napoleon's great victory over the Austrians and the Russians on 2 December 1805.

Slavonic Languages, or Slavic, branch of the Indo-European languages. There are three main groups of Slavonic languages: (1) the Eastern group, consisting of Russian (Great Russian), Belorussian (White Russian), and Ukrainian (Ruthenian, Little Russian); (2) the Western group, including Polish, Czech (and its close relative, Slovak), and Lusatian (or Wendish); (3) the Southern group, including Serbo-Croat, Slovene, Bulgarian, and Macedonian (this group is now separated geographically from the other Slavonic languages by a Hungarian- and Romanian-speaking area).

Slavophiles, members of a philosophic and political movement in 19th-century Russia which stressed its national peculiarities, tended to idealise the Russian past, and opposed Westernisation; politically the Slavophiles were liberal but not democratic, putting their faith in the virtues of the peasant communes.

Slavs, or Slavonians (native name *Slowene*, or *Slowane*, derived by some from *Slawa*, fame, but better from *Slowo*, a word, thus meaning 'speaking' or 'articulate', as distinguished from other nations, whom they called *Niemetz*, or 'Mutes'), general name of an ethnic and linguistic group of Indo-Europeans, whose settlements extend from the Elbe to the Kamchatka, and from the Arctic Sea to Dubrovnik on the Adriatic, the whole of east and south-east Europe being occupied by them. They were known to the ancient writers under the designations of Sarmatians and Scythians.

The Slavs may be divided into three groups: the eastern, western, and southern Slavs. The first comprehends Russians, Ukrainians, Belorussians; the second Poles, Czechs, Moravians, Slovaks, and Wends; the third Serbs, Croats, Slovenes, and Macedonians. They speak Slavonic languages, some written in the Cyrillic, and some in the Roman alphabet.

The Slavs are represented by ancient writers as an industrious race, living by agriculture and the rearing of flocks and herds, as hospitable and peaceful. The religion of the early Slavs seems to have been a kind of nature-worship. Christianity was introduced among the eastern Slavs in the 9th century by SS Cyril and Methodius. Today the eastern Slavs are members of the Eastern Orthodox Church, while the western and southern Slavs belong to the Roman Catholic Church. There was a short-lived and politically unsuccessful Pan-Slavic movement initiated by intellectuals in the 19th century. Today national politics and identities prevail.

Sleep, a recurrent state of inertia and unresponsiveness; the eyelids close, the pupils become very small, secretion of saliva, digestive juices and urine falls, and respiratory exchange and heat rate diminish. Consciousness is lost, but only temporarily, for any sufficient new stimulus will cause the return of wakefulness. Sleep is usually, in man, the concomitant of fatigue, whether physical or mental; less commonly it results from a monotonous repetition of a stimulus. Sleep may be induced by a variety of chemical agents such as barbiturates or anaesthetics.

Study of the EEG (electroencephalogram) tracings, which record the electrical activity of the brain, and physiological changes in sleepers has shown five different phases or stages of sleep, falling into two main categories: orthodox or non-rapid eye movement (NREM) sleep and paradoxical or rapid eye movement (REM) sleep. NREM sleep is characterised by large-amplitude, slow-frequency EEG tracings, a tense musculature, a regular heart beat, very few eye movements and a relative lack of reported dreams. REM sleep is characterised by small-amplitude, faster-frequency tracings, a relaxed musculature, an irregular heart beat and is rich in

Skylab in orbit. The large fin structures are photoelectric cells which generated power from the Sun's rays.

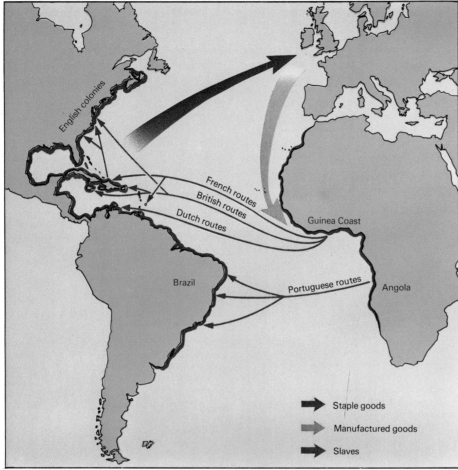

Slavery. The African slave 'triangle' of the 18th century. Plantations in the New World supplied staple goods which bought manufactured goods that were traded for slaves to work the plantations.

Staple goods

Manufactured goods

Slaves

reported dreams. During these periods eye movements occur (hence the name) and apparently correspond to the movements that the eyes of the dreamer make as he follows the scenario of his dream. Both types of sleep are essential. Selective deprivation of either state results in depression of measured performance and personality changes.

Function of Sleep. This is in part physiologically restorative, allowing spent energies to be recovered, but far more complex roles have been suggested for REM sleep. In psychoanalytic theory, sleeping and dreaming are essential for processing repressed material so that it can be integrated into the person's thoughts, feelings and memories, thus maintaining a healthy personality.

Others postulate REM sleep as analogous to the periodic clearing out of computer data storage banks, when material is scanned and either returned for storage or eliminated.

Sleep-walking, see SOMNAMBULISM.

Sleeping Sickness, see TRYPANOSOMIASIS.

Slessor, Kenneth (1901–71), Australian poet. Almost all Slessor's surviving poetry was written before the Second World War, when he was official war correspondent in the Middle East and New Guinea. As literary editor of the *Sun*, editor of the Sydney *Telegraph*, and finally as editor of *Southerly* (1956–1961), he became a benevolent elder statesman of poetry and journalism in Sydney.

Slickensides, grooved or ridged structures, or scratches, formed on rock surfaces by friction during earth movements. The surfaces of fault planes are often slickensided,

and the orientation of the slickenside is parallel to the direction of movement on the fault plane.

Slide Rule. An instrument invented about 1621 and widely used for making rapid approximate calculations until the appearance of cheap pocket-sized electronic calculators in the early 1970s. A slide rule has two pieces of equal length. One piece (the stock) forms a channel in which the other piece (the slide) can be moved. The working of the common slide rule is based on logarithms.

Sligo, maritime county in the Republic of Ireland, bounded on the north by the Atlantic, south-west and west by Mayo, east by Leitrim, and south-east by Roscommon. The Ox Mountains and Benbulben Range rise behind the coastal plain. The highest point is Truskmore (641 m) on the eastern boundary. Dairying and cattle grazing are the chief agricultural activities. There is some mineral wealth, including barytes, coal, lead, and copper. Area 1839 km²; population (1979) 54,610.

Sligo, market town, seaport and county town of County Sligo, Republic of Ireland, situated on the Garavogue river, between Lough Gill and the sea. It is one of the chief western ports of Ireland, the exports being barytes, lead and zinc concentrates, eggs, potatoes, and cattle; the imports include coal, timber, tar, motor spirit and oils, salt, manures, and provisions. The main industries are nylon and hospital products. Population (1981) 17,225.

Slim of Yarralumba and Bishopston,

William Joseph Slim, 1st Viscount (1891–1970), British soldier. After the First World War, he transferred to the Indian army. In 1942 he commanded the 1st Burma Corps, directing its fighting withdrawal to India and, later, as commander of the Fourteenth Army, his operations during 1944 marked the turning point of the Burma campaign and inflicted a crushing defeat on the Japanese. In September 1945 Slim was appointed commander of the Allied land forces, South-East Asia. In 1946 he became commandant of the Imperial Defence College and in 1948 chief of the Imperial General Staff. He became field marshal in 1949. He was governor-general and commander-in-chief of Australia from 1953 to 1960.

Slip, in induction machines, is the synchronous speed minus the rotor speed, divided by synchronous speed.

Slipware, name applied to objects of earthenware decorated with a semi-liquid clay mixture, known as 'slip'. Slip-covered earthenware is older than Chinese porcelain. Medieval Byzantine earthenware and similar wares from Cyprus led on to the superb creations of Bologna and Venice in the 15th century. In Egypt during the Mameluke period (13th and 14th centuries) the use of slip decoration was richly developed, and became popular in the 17th and 18th centuries in Europe.

Slipway, or slip, sloping rails running into the water of a river, dock, etc., carrying a cradle, used to draw vessels out of the water for inspection or repair. To minimise land use, the lower end may be enclosed by walls and a gate which can be shut to exclude the tide. This modification makes it a slip-dock. Slipways are used mostly for vessels of not more than 10,000 t instead of dry docks.

Sliven, town of eastern Bulgaria, capital of Sliven province, situated on the south-east slopes of the Balkan Mountains 64 km north-east of Stara Zagora. It is an agricultural centre, and manufactures textiles and carpets. Population (1979) 96,090.

Sloane, Sir Hans (1660–1753), Irish physician and naturalist. It could be said that he introduced the scientific method into medicine. He was a great believer in the importance of diet; and also helped establish the practice of inoculation for smallpox. He was a great collector of natural history specimens and books and manuscripts, and he left his collections to the nation. They formed the nucleus of the British Museum. He also has the distinction of inventing a recipe for chocolate mixed with milk ('Sir Hans Sloane's Milk Chocolate') which was used by Cadbury's until 1885.

Slocum, Joshua (1844–?1909), Canadian sailor. On 4 April 1895 he sailed from Boston on his voyage round the world alone. He anchored at Newport three years later, having completed his voyage. In 1909 he set off from Bristol, Rhode Island, in the *Spray*, for the Orinoco River and was never seen again. Slocum wrote *Sailing Alone Round the World*, 1900.

Sloe, see BLACKTHORN.

Sloop, small one-masted fore-and-aft rigged vessel, differing from a cutter in having a jib-stay and standing bowsprit. The name was also applied from 1676 to relatively small warships carrying guns on the upper deck only; then to a small corvette and, since the days of steam, to minor warships on trade-defence duties. In June 1947 the term sloop was abolished in the Royal Navy.

Sloth, any of several tree-dwelling mammals that hang upside down from branches and move extremely slowly. They belong to the family Bradypodidae in the order Edentata. There are six living species in two genera. *Bradypus* has four species of three-toed sloths, called ais. They have nine vertebrae in their necks instead of the usual mammalian seven, and can turn their heads almost completely around to see behind them. *Choloepus*, the unaus, includes two species of two-toed sloths. They all live in tropical America. Sloths have rounded faces, small ears and rudimentary tails. The body is about 70 cm long. The forelegs are longer than the hind-legs, and on the ground the animals cannot walk, but drag themselves along. The hair is brown, long, coarse and shaggy. An alga lives in the hair, and in damp weather turns it green so that it looks like grass, which helps the animal to blend in with its leafy background. Sloths are nocturnal animals.

Sloth Bear, *Melursus*, a large animal with a shaggy coat and a large white V on its chest. It feeds on termites, which it obtains by tearing their nest to pieces with its long claws. It devours the insects by scooping them up with a long tongue and protruding lower lip. It also eats fruits and honey. The young are carried on the mother's back when she is moving. The sloth bear inhabits the wooded parts of India and Ceylon. This animal is a bear, a member of family Ursidae, order Carnivora, not an ant-eater.

Slough, town in Berkshire, England, 32km west of London. Formerly a small market town, it has grown since the beginning of the 20th century into a large residential and industrial area. There are numerous light and precision engineering works, and motor-car, pharmaceutical, confectionery, and paint plants. Population (1981) 87,005.

Slovak Socialist Republic, constituent division of the federal republic of Czecho-slovakia since 1969. The capital is Bratis-lava. Area 49,014km²; population (1979) 4,914,554.

The greater part lies in the western Carpathians, but in the south-west is the fertile land of the Danube valley, and in the east is a plain of the River Tisza. It is mainly agricultural; the plains produce cereals, wine, fruit, and tobacco.

The Slovaks were conquered by the Magyars in the 10th century, and remained subject to the Hungarian sovereign until the collapse of Austria-Hungary in 1918. Slovakia then became part of the new republic of Czecho-slovakia. In 1938, after the Munich Pact, Slovakia secured a measure of autonomy, though losing territory to Hungary and Poland. The new Slovak government, led by Josef Tiso, abolished all political parties except the nationalist party. In March 1939 the Prague government, fearing that a declaration of Slovak independence was imminent, attempted to replace Tiso and his ministers by others friendly to Prague. This event provided Germany with a pretext for annexing Bohemia and Moravia, and Slovakia was declared an independent state under German protection.

After the outbreak of the Second World War, Slovaks abroad took part in the formation of a provisional Czechoslovak government under Beneš in London. At the end of the war Slovakia was incorporated in Czecho-slovakia.

See also CZECHOSLOVAKIA, *History*.

Slovakia, see CZECHOSLOVAKIA.

Sloth. *The two-toed sloth,* Choloepus didactylus, *lives in north-western S. America.*

Slovaks, Slavic people inhabiting the eastern region of Czechoslovakia, where they number about 4·5 million. From the 10th century until 1918 they were under the dominance of the Magyars. Until the 18th century the written language was a form of Czech, but it was then supplanted by the Slovak dialect. The Slovaks are independent peasants with a long-standing and rich tradition of which they are proud. The majority are Roman Catholics.

See also CZECHOSLOVAKIA, *History*.

Slovenia (Serbo-Croatian *Slovenija*), constituent republic of Yugoslavia, bounded by Italy, Hungary, Austria, and Croatia. The greater part of it was under Hapsburg rule from the 14th century until 1918. At the end of the First World War it was incorporated in the new kingdom of the Serbs, Croats and Slovenes, later renamed Yugoslavia.

Slovenia is mountainous, containing parts of the Julian, Savinje, and Karawanken Alps. The Julian Alps form the watershed for its rivers. Slovenia is rich in coal, mercury, and zinc. There is much stock raising. Vines and cereals are grown, but potatoes are the chief crop. The principal towns are Ljubljana (the capital), Maribor, and Celje. Area 20,250 km²; population (1981) 1,891,864.

Slow-worm, *Anguis fragilis*, a wormlike reptile usually about 30 cm long, of which half is tail. Internal traces of limbs indicate that it is a lizard. The colour varies a great deal, but usually the adult is brown above and black underneath, while its young are white with a black stripe running along the centre of the back. They inhabit bushes and feed upon earthworms and slugs. Their bite is harmless. They are timid creatures, and when frightened their muscles contract so rigidly that endeavours to bend the creature often cause breakage.

Slug, air-breathing molluscs (class Gastropoda, sub-class Pulmonata in which an external shell is either lacking or greatly reduced). Those belonging to the family Limacidae are without external shells, though most of them possess a small internal shelly plate or a few calcareous granules under the skin of the back. Like snails, they have a mouth composed of external fleshy lips and, within, a ribbon-like mass of teeth. They are mostly plant-feeders. They move by means of a flattened muscular part of the body called the foot. Slugs are hermaphrodites but cross-fertilising. Numerous eggs are laid in decaying vegetation. A common and destructive species is the grey field slug *Limax agrestis*. Other species include the bulb- or root-eating slug, the black slug, and the yellow or household slug. Another group of slugs, characterised by the small shell being external, hunt and destroy earthworms and insects, and are almost as beneficial as the others are injurious to cultivated crops.

Slumping, term used in geology to describe the collapse or flowage of soft or un-consolidated rock material under the influence of gravity. Slumping on land is associated with landslides and solifluction. Beneath the surface of the sea, sediment may accumulate in such great thicknesses that it becomes unstable, and the stimulus of earthquake shocks may make the surface layer slump, or slide down into deeper water.

Sluter, Claus (d. 1406), Flemish sculptor. He sculpted the Moses Well and the figures on the Chapel Portal at the Carthusian monastery at Champmol, outside Dijon, and the tomb of Duke Philip the Bold of Burgundy. Sluter was a master of portraiture, capable of bestowing extreme actuality also on imaginary figures, such as the prophets around the Moses Well, yet retaining a grandeur of conception, even in figures of the smallest proportions, as in the 'weepers' on the Duke's tomb.

Smack, a sailing vessel, having auxiliary steam or motor power, sometimes used for fishing, with a hold amidships. The term smack is also used for a small-decked or half-decked vessel.

Smallpox, or variola, a contagious infectious disease due to a virus and characterised by a skin eruption. Smallpox starts with headache, backache and febrile symptoms, followed in two or three days by a papular eruption mainly on the trunk, face and head. The eruption quickly becomes vesicular and then pustular, and after about a fortnight the pustules dry into crusts. When these separate the skin is usually left pitted, and the scars, or 'pockmarks', remain permanently. In mild cases the eruptions are scanty and discrete, but in more severe cases the eruptions are so numerous that they join together in a confluent mass. In an even more severe type of the disease, known as haemorrhagic smallpox, the vesicles become filled with blood. Fever and toxaemia are most severe in the immediate pre-eruption and in the pustular stages of the illness. The incubation period is from 12 to 14 days. In its most virulent form smallpox is a lethal disease. Even the less virulent forms have claimed victims among the unvaccinated, and on all occasions smallpox must be regarded as potentially dangerous.

Vaccination confers immediate and complete immunity for about two or three years, and a lesser degree of immunity for many years, if not for life. Isolation of victims, tracing, segregating and vaccinating immediate contacts, vaccination of the population exposed to risk, and disinfection of infected houses and contagious material, are the epidemiological measures used for stopping an outbreak.

Since the Second World War a huge World Health Organisation programme has been in operation to eradicate smallpox altogether. The programme has been extremely successful, total eradication being apparently achieved by 1980.

Smart, Christopher (1722–71), English poet. On leaving the University he went to London and lived by writing for periodicals. His *Poems on Several Occasions*, which contains 'The Hop Garden', was issued in 1752, and in the following year *The Hilliad* appeared, satirising John Hill, a personal enemy.

Smart eventually developed a form of religious mania and it was in confinement that he produced some of his best work, including *Rejoice in the Lamb* and his most famous poem, *A Song to David*, 1763. Unfortunate to the last, he died in the King's Bench prison, to which he had been committed for debt.

Smell, see NOSE.

Smelling Salts, a mixture of compounds usually containing ammonia which, when inhaled, acts as a stimulant and is used as a restorative.

Smelt, fishes of genus *Osmerus*, order Salmoniformes, found in Europe and North America. They bear close resemblance to the salmon in habit and appearance, but they are of smaller size, and their natural habitat is the sea, although they frequently enter rivers for spawning and thrive in fresh water. *O. eperlanus*, the common smelt, is considered a delicacy when fresh, and *O. mordax*, an American species, is also eaten.

Smelting, see METALLURGY.

Smetana, Bedřich (1824–84), Czech composer. He became conductor of the Hlahol choral society in Prague, and in 1866 of the provisional national theatre, where his first two operas, *The Brandenburgers in Bohemia* and *The Bartered Bride*, were produced that year. All the later ones were also produced there: *Dalibor*, 1868; *Two Widows*, 1874; *The Kiss*, 1876; *The Secret*, 1878; *Libuše*, 1881; *The Devil's Wall*, 1882; and the unfinished *Viola* (based on Shakespeare's *Twelfth Night*). None had the success of *The Bartered Bride*, which has remained the outstanding Czech national opera. Smetana created the Czech national symphonic poem with his cycle of six, *My Country*, and wrote choral and other orchestral works, two string quartets, a piano trio, piano pieces and songs.

Smethwick, town in West Midlands Metropolitan County, England, 5 km north-west of Birmingham, of which it is now effectively a suburb. Boulton, Watt and Murdock worked in Smethwick. Its principal industries are engineering, brewing, and the manufacture of weighing machines, metals, screws, nuts and bolts, and optical, technical, and domestic glass. There are also foundries.

Smew, *Mergellus albellus*, species of duck, family Anatidae, order Anseriformes. The male bird is chiefly white with black markings, the female is white with reddish markings, and both have a handsome appearance. They inhabit northern Asia and Europe from Kamchatka to Lapland, but do not touch North America.

Smiles, Samuel (1812–1904), British biographer and social reformer. Abandoning medicine he became editor of the *Leeds Times* and an active social reformer. His writings include *Life of George Stephenson*, 1857; the phenomenally popular *Self-Help*, 1859; and *Lives of the Engineers*, 1861.

Smirke, Sir Robert (1781–1867), the leading Greek Revival architect in England. He was trained by Sir J. Soane, then travelled in Italy and Greece. Starting practice about 1807, he designed Covent Garden Theatre, London's first Greek Doric building (1808–1809; destroyed 1856); the British Museum (1823–47); the General Post Office (1824–29; demolished 1913); and the east wing of Somerset House (1830–31).

Smith, Adam (1723–90), Scottish political economist. He published in 1759 his *Theory of the Moral Sentiments*, and in 1776 issued his *Wealth of Nations*, the foundation of all works on political economy. This is the first work in which the principles of political economy are set forth scientifically, and has had incalculable influence.

See also CLASSICAL ECONOMISTS.

Smith, Bessie (c.1895–1937), one of the greatest US blues singers. From 1923, the start of the classic blues period, she made many recordings, often with jazz instrumentalists such as Louis Armstrong. She starred in a film, *St Louis Blues*, 1929, her recording of that song being among her best known.

Smith, Harvey (1938–), British international show jumper. He represented Great Britain in the team event at the 1968 and 1972 Olympics. He has won numerous international show-jumping titles throughout the world, notably, in Britain, the John Player Trophy (seven times) and the British Jumping Derby (four times).

Smith, Ian Douglas (1919–), Zimbabwean politician. From 1948–53 Smith was a member of the Southern Rhodesia Legislative Assembly, and a member of the Federal Parliament, 1953–61. A former chief whip of the United Federal party, Smith resigned from it in 1961, and was a founder of the Rhodesian Front in 1962. He became premier and minister of external affairs and defence in April 1964. Smith represented the wing of his party which demanded immediate independence for Southern Rhodesia: when negotiations with Britain broke down, Smith made a unilateral declaration of independence in November 1965, which Britain considered illegal. In 1976, after ten years of 'illegal independence' Smith found himself under heavy pressure to reach an accommodation with the moderate wing of the African National Council on procedures to achieve black majority rule in Rhodesia. He continued as prime minister until 1979 when Rhodesia became independent Zimbabwe.

See also ZIMBABWE, *History*.

Smith, John (1580–1631), English adventurer and effective founder of Virginia, USA. In 1606 he joined an emigrant party destined for what is now the state of Virginia. The whole colony would have perished but for the energy and resourcefulness of Smith. While exploring the Chickahominy River he was taken captive by the Indians, his life being spared, according to his account, only when the Indian princess Pocahontas interceded on his behalf. Smith became governor of the colony. Later he explored and mapped the coast of the territory, which he named New England. He returned to England in 1609, continued to encourage colonisation, wrote books, and made maps.

Smith, Joseph, see MORMON CHURCH.

Smith, Sir Keith Macpherson (1890–1955), Australian airman. He served in the Royal Flying Corps in the First World War, and in 1919, with his brother Ross was the first to fly from England to Australia.

Smith, Maggie (1931–), British actress who first appeared at Oxford in 1952 as Viola in *Twelfth Night*. She has since made numerous appearances in plays by Shakespeare, Ibsen, Strindberg and others, taking both comic and tragic roles. Of her films *The Prime of Miss Jean Brodie*, 1968, is her best known, for which she was awarded an Oscar. She has also made numerous television appearances. More recently she has appeared in *Murder by Death*, 1976, and *California Suite*, 1979.

Smith, Richard (1931–), British artist. He has spent long periods in the USA and exercised considerable influence on the development of Pop Art, though it can be argued that he himself has never been a Pop Artist. His painting alludes to the scale and colour of commercial imagery but does not quote from or parody it.

Smith, Stevie, pseudonym of Florence Margaret Smith (1902–71), English poet. Her poetry—*A Good Time Was Had By All*, 1937; *Not Waving But Drowning*, 1957; *The Best Beast*, 1969; and many other collections—tackles serious themes through a calculated scattiness and seemingly casual manner.

Smith, Sydney (1771–1845), British cleric, author, and wit. He took holy orders in 1794, and later, while residing at Edinburgh, founded, with Jeffrey and Brougham, the *Edinburgh Review* in 1802. He came to London in 1803, and in the following year attracted attention by his lectures. He became a popular figure in society, and was a member of the Holland House set. In 1807 he wrote the *Plymley Letters* in favour of Catholic emancipation. He was rector of Foxton from 1806, and appointed a canon of St Paul's in 1831. He was one of the wittiest men of his day, and a sparkling conversationalist.

Smith, William Henry (1825–91), British politician and newsagent. He developed his father's newspaper agency into the prosperous business it is today, opening the firm's first railway bookstall at Euston in 1848. He entered Parliament in 1868, and nine years later became first lord of the Admiralty under Disraeli. When Salisbury became prime minister Smith was appointed first lord of the Treasury and leader of the House of Commons. *Punch* bestowed upon him the nickname 'Old Morality'.

Smithfield, situated a short distance north-west of St Paul's Cathedral, London, was originally a tournament ground and cattle market outside the city wall, and from 1868 has been the site of the principal London meat market. It has also been a fairground, a place of trial, and a place of martyrdom, mostly of Protestants under Mary I.

Smithson, British architects, Alison (1928–) and Peter (1923–), wife and husband. The term 'new brutalism' stems from them and epitomises their intention to present the structure and materials of their buildings without concealment by decoration. Hunstanton School, Norfolk, 1954, is the first example. Less 'brutal' buildings are the Economist Building in London, 1964, Robin Hood Gardens, Tower Hamlets, 1970, and the Garden Building at St Hilda's College, Oxford, 1970.

Smithson, James Macie (1765–1829), British founder of the Smithsonian Institution in Washington DC, USA. He devoted his life to scientific work, mainly chemistry and mineralogy. As a mineralogist he identified a new ore known as smithsonite. Smithson's will written in 1826 left the bulk of his estate to his nephew and any heirs he might have, but provided that if his nephew died childless, the money should go to the United States to found an institution bearing the Smithson name. His nephew died in 1835 without children and Smithson's money— 105 bags containing some 100,000 gold sovereigns, a great fortune in those days— was brought to America in 1838. The Smithsonian Institution on the Mall in Washington DC was established in 1846.

Smithsonian Institution, Washington DC, USA, owes its origin to the generosity of an Englishman, James M. Smithson, who in 1826 bequeathed over £100,000 to the US government to found an institution for 'the increase and diffusion of knowledge among men'. The Institution was formally organised in 1846 and the first building completed in 1855. From time to time various funds have been added to the original bequest. The US Congress has vested responsibility for administering the Institution in the Smithsonian Board of Regents, composed of the Chief Justice, the Vice President, three members of the Senate, three members of the House of Representatives, and nine citizen members.

Throughout its history, the Institution has carried on important scientific investigations and has conducted explorations in all parts of the world. It has administered the national collections and performed other educational public service functions. Some 4000 employees, including a staff of more than 500 professional scholars and scientists, work for the Institution. The Smithsonian operates three major history and science museums, six art museums, and various research establishments.

Smog, see AIR POLLUTION.

Smoke, see AIR POLLUTION.

Smoke Detectors. These devices are in general confined to places where the presence of smoke and visible vapours is unusual, e.g. ships' holds or aircraft. Three systems are in general use: (1) a system where a suction fan is used to draw air from the protected spaces to a centrally placed observation cabinet where a hidden light beam reveals the presence of smoke; (2) a system in which a beam of light (or infrared ray) is directed across the protected space to fall on a detector unit which utilises the photo-

electric cell as a means of completing an electrical circuit to sound an alarm; and (3) a system which is governed by the effect of smoke upon the electrical conductivity of the atmosphere.

Smoke detectors are increasingly being installed in homes to give early warning of fire, particularly since so many modern furnishing materials burn readily, giving off much noxious smoke.

Smoking. For some time it has been known that the inhalation of cigarette smoke causes cessation of ciliary action in the respiratory tract. This results in an increased number of dust particles, together with tar from the cigarette, entering the bronchioles. These particles are not swept upwards towards the trachea to be got rid of by swallowing but accumulate, eventually causing irritation leading to smokers' cough.

Tobacco smoke also causes acute constriction of the large airways, but it seems to have very little effect on the size or function of the small airways.

Carbon monoxide in cigarette smoke attacks the haemoglobin of the red blood cell, forming carboxyhaemoglobin which prevents oxygen uptake. Even when inhalation of neat smoke is stopped, it is about 112 days before the damaged red cells are replaced by fresh red cells from the bone marrow.

Carcinoma of the lung arises in the bronchus, and heavy smokers have been shown to have a death rate from carcinoma of the lung 30 times that of non-smokers. Causes of carcinoma of other tissues or parts of the body are not so clear cut.

It is not the nicotine content of the cigarette that is carcinogenic, this merely causes the craving for another cigarette, but the tar content which is inhaled that causes the problem; thus cigar and pipe smokers do not suffer to the same extent, although they are more liable to carcinoma of the mouth.

It is now believed that some people are more susceptible to cancer of the lung because they do not synthesise a sufficient quantity of an enzyme that renders this inhaled tar harmless before it has a chance to stimulate the cells to divide abnormally.

Smoky Mountains, see APPALACHIAN MOUNTAINS.

Smolensk, capital city, economic and cultural centre of Smolensk *oblast*, USSR, on the Dnieper. It has textile, food, instrument-making, and metal-working industries, and is an important transport centre. Known since the 9th century, it was Lithuanian, 1404–1514, then Muscovy's key western fortress, and an important commercial and administrative centre. Population (1980) 305,000.

Smollett, Tobias George (1721–71), Scottish novelist. He was for a short time a ship's doctor, but after 1743 he settled as a surgeon in London. In 1748 he published his first novel, *Roderick Random*, partly autobiographical, which stirred public concern about medical conditions in the navy, and then in quick succession came *The History of an Atom*, 1749, a skit on British politics, *Peregrine Pickle*, 1751, with vivid pictures of low life abroad, and *Ferdinand, Count Fathom*, 1753. *Sir Launcelot Greaves* appeared in 1762 and *Humphry Clinker*, the most genial of his

novels, about a Welsh family's tour of Scotland, in 1771.

Smollett is one of the leading figures among the novelists of the 18th century. Frequently involved in bitter controversy, extremely egoistical, and often recklessly malicious, he was, on one occasion, imprisoned for libel, an event which embittered him for the rest of his life.

Smooth Snake, *Coronella austriaca*, a common snake in southern and central Europe. It grows to a length of 60 cm, and it is brownish-red or grey in colour, with dark-brown spots along its back. It is ovoviviparous, producing live young. It is not venomous.

Smuggling includes offences of importing or exporting either goods on which duty and tax have not been paid or goods liable to prohibition.

See also BOOTLEGGING; PROHIBITION.

Smut, a plant disease caused by a fungus of the order Ustilaginales. When the spores remain for a time within the sorus, the disease is known as covered smut; that of barley being caused by *Ustilago hordei*; of oats by *U. kolleri*. Stinking smut or bunt of wheat is caused by *Tilletia foetida* and *T. caries*. Loose smut describes an infection when the spores are in an uncovered powder mass, freed by wind and rain.

See also PLANT DISEASES; RUST FUNGI.

Smuts, Jan Christian (1870–1950), South African soldier and statesman. In 1898 he became state attorney under President Kruger. In 1901 he was given supreme command of the Boer forces of Cape Colony, and proved a daring and able commando leader. In 1907, under British rule, he became colonial secretary of the Transvaal. Throughout the First World War Smuts was instrumental in quelling the pro-German separatist groups within the Union of South Africa and continued to work for Anglo–Boer co-operation. He became prime minister and minister for native affairs in 1919 and his government lasted until 1924. In 1933 Herzog founded a coalition government, with Smuts as deputy leader. On the outbreak of the Second World War Smuts advocated the co-operation of South Africa with the Allies, while Herzog and Malan urged neutrality. Smuts prevailed and formed a War Cabinet. Smuts became supreme commander of the Union defence forces in 1940, and was made a field-marshal in 1941. He helped to draft the UN charter in 1945. In the general election of 1948 Smuts was defeated and became leader of an Anglo-Afrikaner opposition, protesting vehemently against the government's policy of racial segregation.

Smyth, Dame Ethel (1858–1944), British composer. She lived much of her life abroad, and was active in the movement for women's suffrage. Her works include the operas *Fantasio*, 1898; *The Forest*, 1901; *The Wreckers*, 1906; *The Boatswain's Mate*, 1916; *Fête galante*, 1923; and *Entente cordiale*, 1925; and also choral, orchestral and chamber works.

Snail, air-breathing shelled molluscs of class Gastropoda forming a great number of species, some of which themselves include many varieties. With the slugs they are divided into two groups. One of these is characterised by a single pair of non-retractile tentacles, with the eyes at the base; a familiar example is the pond snail (*Limnaea stagnalis*). The members of the other group have two pairs of retractile tentacles, with the eyes at the summit of the upper pair. Snails are almost exclusively vegetable feeders, and are provided with cutting upper jaws and a rasping ribbon or radula in the mouth. Sea, land and water snails are found in all parts of the world, some land snails living at great altitudes. The sexes may be distinct, but snails are often hermaphrodite, cross fertilisation still being necessary. Many possess a structure not found in other molluscs: it is a beautiful crystalline body (Cupid's dart), which is ejected during copulation from a sac specially constructed for the purpose. Each snail shoots its dart at the other and each receives sperm from the other. *Achatina eulica* is the largest snail, being 15–22 cm from head to tail. The Roman snail (*Helix pomatia*) is a favourite table delicacy in France. Many snails hibernate in the ground or beneath leaves, and secrete a mucous plug to seal the aperture.

Snake, formerly Lewis, river of the USA, and biggest tributary (1670 km long) of the Columbia river. It rises as the South Fork in a lake 2375 m high in the Yellowstone National Park, Wyoming, and flows south-west through Idaho and then north to form the boundary between Idaho and Oregon and between Idaho and Washington. Navigation is hindered by rapids and falls, of which the chief are the Shoshone Falls (60 m).

Snake, the suborder Serpentes or Ophidia of order Squamata of class Reptilia. All have a long and vermiform body, and most are covered with scales. Traces of limbs are present in the boas and pythons. A marked characteristic of snakes is the distensible jaw, which enables the prey to be swallowed whole. Many snakes possess fangs (modified teeth) in the upper jaw, having grooves for the venom which runs from modified salivary glands where it is produced; the forked tongue is harmless. A popular classification is that of poisonous or non-poisonous. No external characteristics are known by which it is possible to distinguish at a glance those that are, and those that are not, venomous. With few exceptions all snakes are covered with scales, which are skin folds, and the whole skin is frequently shed; on the heads of some are plates similar to those of lizards. A snake's skeleton is composed of a great number of vertebrae and ribs; locomotion is effected partly by the passage of a lateral wave away from the head, and partly by the action of large scales on the under-surface of the body, each being attached to a pair of movable ribs. The gripping action and slight movement of the scales help locomotion. Most snakes are oviparous (lay eggs), but some, including the viper (adder), bring forth their young alive (viviparous). Snakes are of comparatively recent geological age, and are most numerous in the tropical countries. Some are only a few centimetres in length, while the anaconda is reputed to exceed 9 m. The majority of snakes are terrestrial, but there are also many species of amphibious water snakes (e.g. genus *Natrix* of family

Colubridae, non-venomous, all continents except South America) and of sea snakes.

Snake-bird, or darter, water birds of genus *Anhinga*, related to the cormorant and pelican, forming the family Anhingidae, in the order Pelecaniformes. They swim in lakes, rivers or seas with only the head on the long neck showing above water, moving sinuously, then darting forward to seize a fish, the neck vertebrae being specially adapted for flexibility. The snake-birds are widely distributed throughout Central and South America, southern Asia and Australia, and vary little in colour. *A. anhinga*, the American snake-bird, inhabits tropical regions; its general colour is greenish-black, the tail is tipped with brown, the wings marked with silvery-grey, and the feathers are small and soft. It is about 90 cm high.

Snake-bite. Snake venom is very toxic saliva containing a mixture of poisonous proteins. In general, viper venoms cause local swelling and pain and possibly haemorrhagic shock, whereas the venoms of elapids (cobras, mambas, kraits and the Australian taipan snake) cause paralysis of the muscles concerned with seeing, breathing and swallowing. Venomous snakes have two types of bite: one to paralyse the prey, in which case a large amount is injected and the prey rapidly dies; and the other to act as a defence in order for the snake to escape, only a small amount of venom being then injected.

Snake-charming. This has been practised in Egypt and throughout the East from the earliest times. It is still common in Egypt and in India, where the cobra is generally used. Snake-charming is usually an hereditary calling, and the success of the handler in making the snake perform rhythmic movements seems to depend upon a knowledge of the nature and peculiarities of the reptile. The fangs are usually first removed.

Snakes and Ladders, popular board game where players throw dice to enable their men to travel a journey of 100 squares to finish. At various points men alighting on a square containing the foot of a ladder can climb to the top. At other points the mouth of a snake requires the man to descend to the square occupied by the snake's tail.

Snakesbeard, *Ophiopogon*, a genus of perennials in family Liliaceae, with long narrow leaves and racemes of white or lilac flowers. *O. jaburan*, Japan, is sometimes cultivated. *O. japonicus* has edible starchy rhizomes (underground stems).

Snapdragon, see ANTIRRHINUM.

Snapper, several fishes in the family Lutjanidae of order Perciformes in the bony, ray-finned fish class Actinopterygii. They are tropical, carnivorous fishes, about 60 cm or more long. Many are red, but the species come in many colours. They are valuable edible fishes, especially one of the red species, *Lutjanus blackfordi*, the red snapper.

Sneezewort, *Achillea ptarmica*, a perennial herb of the Compositae, found in Europe, in Asia Minor and Siberia. The plant has a strong pungent odour. Its root-stock is long and creeping, and when reduced to a dry powder may be used as a substitute for snuff.
See also ACHILLEA.

Sneezing, violent expiration of air from the nose and mouth. It is caused by irritation of the nerve endings of the mucous membrane, either by nasal catarrh or by foreign substances, as in taking snuff. It is an involuntary reflex respiratory act, the stimulus being carried by the trigeminal nerve to the medulla, where it induces a reflex action. A quick inspiration occurs, followed by a violent expiration in which most of the air is driven through the nose. Sneezing may be induced by bright light. Paroxysmal sneezing occurs in hay fever.

Snipe, common name given to certain species of the family Scolopacidae, order Charadriiformes. They are closely related to the woodcocks. The birds inhabit marshes, which they probe with their long, straight bills for the worms, insects and molluscs on which they live. European species include the common snipe, *Gallinago gallinago*, about 25 cm long and mottled black and brown; *Lymnocryptes minima*, the slightly smaller jack snipe, and *G. media*, the great or solitary snipe, which reaches 30 cm in length. *G. delicata*, Wilson's snipe, is the commonest American species.

Snipers, formerly called sharpshooters. Their regular use only became possible with the general adoption of the rifle. Sniping is an economical method in static warfare of maintaining an aggressive attitude without great expenditure of ammunition, and was so used by the Boers in South Africa and by both sides during the trench warfare of 1914–18.

Snooker is played by two players, or four players in two partnerships, with 15 red and six coloured balls, and a white cue ball on a billiard table. One of the reds must be potted first, and this entitles the player to pot any coloured ball, which is returned to its specific spot on the table. Potted reds stay down, in the pocket(s). This procedure is followed, red and coloured alternately, until all reds are potted, leaving

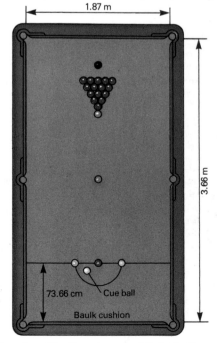

Snooker. *The dimensions of a full-sized table and the positions of the balls prior to play.*

on the table only the coloured balls which are then potted in order of their value. Snooker balls have the following values: red (1), yellow (2), green (3), brown (4), blue (5), pink (6), black (7). The word 'snooker' applies to the act of 'laying a snooker', an integral feature of the game. A player is said to be snookered with regard to any ball when a direct stroke to the ball he wants to play at is obstructed by one he may not lawfully strike. Since 1970 the professional side of the game has been governed by the World Professional Billiards and Snooker Association. The sport's popularity has grown enormously since the end of the 1970s, due largely to its exposure on television.

Snoring, an abnormal form of respiration that occurs during sleep. It is characterised by deep inspirations and a noise of low pitch caused by the vibration of the soft palate and uvula as the current of air passes. It is usually caused by the mouth falling open and may in that case be prevented by lying on the side. It may indicate a partial blockage of the nasal passage, e.g. by adenoids or catarrh, in which case medical treatment may prevent it.

Snow, C(harles) P(ercy), Baron of Leicester (1905–80), English novelist and scientist. During the Second World War he was a government science expert, and in 1945 was appointed a civil service commissioner. During the 1960s, he was a junior cabinet minister. In 1950 he married the novelist Pamela Hansford Johnson.
From 1935 to 1971 Snow was occupied in writing the 11-volume novel sequence, 'Strangers and Brothers', about the academic, public, and personal lives of Lewis Eliot, through which Snow analyses the effects and uses of power and bureaucracy in modern English society. His study, *The Two Cultures*, 1959, was a controversial attempt to argue that scientific and humanistic cultures have become separate and distinct.

Snow, John (1813–58), British anaesthetist and epidemiologist. He was the first specialist anaesthetist; before the introduction of chloroform he administered ether 152 times, but in the 11 years after 1847 he administered chloroform 4000 times. Snow wrote his distinguished book *On Ether*, in 1847, and his division of the stages of anaesthesia into five degrees was not improved upon for seventy years. He invented a chloroform inhaler in 1848. Snow was also interested in public health; by statistical and other investigations he proved in 1849 that cholera was transmitted by water infected with faecal matter.

Snow, see PRECIPITATION.

Snow-blindness. The glare from snow may cause acute conjunctivitis (inflammation of the lining of the eyelids) after long exposure. This condition is accompanied by acute pain and photophobia, and sometimes conjunctival haemorrhages. Those subject to it should wear dark glasses.

Snow-bunting, *Plectrophenax nivalis*, a bird species in the family Emberizidae, order Passeriformes, a winter visitor to central and western Europe from northern Europe and Siberia. Its plumage in winter is white with the upperparts rusty-brown, in summer

it is white and black. Breeding takes place in rocky and mountainous situations.

Snow-finch, or snow-bird, species of *Montifringilla*, birds in the family Fringillidae, order Passeriformes, distributed widely over the Ethiopian, Palaearctic and Oriental regions. The birds are about 15 cm in length and mainly white with grey and black markings. Only one species, *M. nivalis*, occurs in Europe.

Snow Leopard or ounce, *Leo uncia*, a species of the cat family Felidae in order Carnivora, from the mountains of central and southern Asia where it ranges to an altitude of 4000 m in summer. It is similar in shape and size to the leopard but with longer fur, up to 8 cm long. The snow leopard hunts a variety of small and medium-sized mammals which it traps after stalking them usually at night.

Snow-mobiling, sport on a motorised snow sled, developed since 1960 and most popular in North America, both for racing and as a holiday recreation at winter resorts.
See also WINTER SPORTS.

Snow-plough, machine for clearing snow from roads, railways, etc. Where a heavy snowfall has to be cleared a rotary plough is used, consisting of a number of cutting vanes arranged in a rapidly rotating wheel.

Snow-shoe, broad flat shoe used to prevent the feet from sinking beneath the snow; hide-webbing is mounted on a strong wooden framework.

Snowberry, *Symphoricarpos rivularis*, in the Caprifoliaceae, an American shrub bearing soft spongy white berries in autumn, planted and often naturalised in temperate countries. The name is also used for *Chiococca racemosa*, in the Rubiaceae, a West Indian evergreen shrub with fragrant white flowers, and for *Chiogenes hispidula* in the Ericaceae, a creeping evergreen shrub with bell-shaped flowers followed by white mealy fruits.

Snowden of Ickornshaw, Philip Snowden, Viscount (1864–1937), British politician. Snowden joined the Independent Labour party and was chairman from 1903 to 1906 and again from 1917 to 1920. He was made a privy councillor in 1924 and was chancellor of the Exchequer during the short Labour administration. In 1929 Snowden was again chancellor. After the 1931 general election he became lord privy seal—a post he resigned in 1932.

Snowdon, Antony Charles Robert Armstrong-Jones, Earl of (1930–), British photographer. On 6 May 1960 he married Princess Margaret and on 3 October 1961 was created Earl of Snowdon. They were divorced in 1978. He has continued his career as a photographer and designer.

Snowdon (Welsh *Eryri*), highest mountain mass in England and Wales, 16 km southeast of the Menai Straits, consisting of five main peaks, Y Wyddfa (1085 m), Carnedd Ungain (1065 m), Crib Goch (921 m), Y Lliwedd (898 m), and Llechog (884 m).

Snowdonia, mountainous region of North Wales, comprising three massifs above 1000 m divided by the passes of Llanberis and Nant Ffrancon: Snowdon, the Glyders, and the Carnedds (Carnedd Dafydd, Carnedd Llewelyn, etc.). Snowdonia was designated a National Park in 1951. It covers a total area of 2189 km²

Snowdrop, *Galanthus nivalis*, a perennial garden plant of the Amaryllidaceae from Europe and Asia, flowering in winter and early spring. The plant is bulbous and has two tapering leaves and one pendulous white flower at the top of the stem.

Snowflake, see LEUCOJUM.

Snowshill Manor, Gloucestershire, England, 5 km south of Broadway, a Tudor Cotswold manor house with an early 18th-century façade. Snowshill is primarily of interest because it belonged to Charles Paget Wade, an inveterate collector of clocks, toys, bicycles, orientalia, musical instruments, craft tools and bygones.

Snowy River, river of Australia, whose headwaters rise in New South Wales in the Great Dividing Range, the southern portion of which is known as the Snowy Mountains. The Snowy river begins near the north-east slope of Mount Kosciusko and reaches the sea in Bass Strait. The total catchment area is 13,493 km² and the maximum length of the river, 483 km.

Snuff, inhalant powder manufactured from ground tobacco leaves and stems (i.e. the mid-rib of the tobacco leaf). Cortes discovered that snuff was used by the Mexicans early in the 16th century, and the general habit of taking snuff in Europe started in Spain about 1620. In Britain, regular manufacture began in the middle of the 18th century and developed rapidly. In fashionable circles smoking gave way to the new craze, which persisted until largely ousted by the cigar early in the 19th century.

Snuff. A diamond-studded Regency snuff box.

Snyders, Frans (1579–1657), Flemish painter. He studied under the younger Pieter Brueghel and Henrick van Balen, then travelled in Italy for a time, and finally settled at Antwerp. He was one of Rubens's assistants. He excelled as a painter of still-life and animals and executed fine battle-pieces.

Soames, (Arthur) Christopher (John) Baron (1920–), British politician. He married a daughter of Sir Winston Churchill. Soames entered Parliament as a Conservative in 1950, and after holding junior office was minister of War, 1958–60, and minister of Agriculture, 1960–64. Between 1968 and 1972 he was British ambassador to France. From 1973 to 1977 he was a commissioner of the European Economic Community and Governor of Zimbabwe-Rhodesia from 1979 to 1980.

Soane, Sir John (1753–1837), British architect. He began private practice in London, and in 1788 was appointed architect to the Bank of England which he rebuilt from 1788 to 1833, his most important work. Other buildings include: Pitshanger Manor, Ealing (1800–03; now the public library); Dulwich College Art Gallery (1811–14; restored 1953 after war damage); and his own eccentric home, No. 13 Lincoln's Inn Fields (1812–13), which he bequeathed to the nation in 1835, together with his collection of antiques and a number of notable paintings.

Soap, substance which possesses detergent and cleansing properties. Chemically it is the salt of an alkali and fatty acid, and is commercially produced by boiling a blend of fats with an alkali. This is called saponification. Most commonly the alkali is sodium hydroxide, NaOH, but potassium hydroxide (for soft soaps), calcium hydroxide (for lubricant soaps), and other alkalis may be used as may organic bases, e.g. triethanolamine. The fatty acids are derived from natural animal and vegetable oils and fats. Chemically these are triglycerides, e.g. tallow and coconut oil, while lesser amounts of lard, groundnut oil, palm kernel oil, and palm oil are used. For soaps made from a given alkali, e.g. sodium hydroxide, the properties of the soap vary according to the oils and fats used, e.g. coconut soap, which has relatively short fatty acid chains, gives a quick, abundant lather, but dissolves rapidly, while tallow soap, which has longer fatty acid chains, wears away more slowly but gives less lather. Commercial soaps are usually made from blends of fats to give the desired properties, a typical blend for personal use being 80 parts tallow to 20 parts coconut oil.

Soap-berries, fruits of the American tree *Sapindus saponaria* in family Sapindaceae. They make a good lather in water due to the chemical saponin they contain, and are therefore used at times instead of soap.

Soapstone, see TALC.

Soares, Mario (1925–), Portuguese lawyer and leader of the Portuguese Socialist party. Having engaged in, and suffered imprisonment for, anti-régime activities during the premierships of Salazar and Marcelo Caetano, Soares came to prominence as leader of the Socialist party after the 1974 revolution. In 1976, President Eanes appointed Soares prime minister, an office that he held until 1979.

Sobers, Sir Gary (1936–), West Indian cricketer; a left-handed batsman and bowler, he first played for Barbados aged 16 and in his first Test match at 17. The most gifted all-rounder of modern times, he appeared in 93 Tests and scored more Test runs (8032) than any man in history, and also took 235 Test wickets. He captained West Indies a record 39 times between 1964–1965 and 1971–72, and when 21 years old made the world record Test score of 365 not out for West Indies v. Pakistan at Kingston in 1957–58. In his career he scored a record of 26 Test centuries. He was knighted in 1975.

Sochi, town in the Krasnodar *krai* of the RSFSR, USSR, on the Black Sea coast at the foot of the main Caucasus range. It has become the main Soviet health resort (sea bathing, sulphur springs), and extends along the Black Sea coast for a distance of nearly 40 km. Population (1980) 291,000.

Social and Cultural Ecology, the study of the social and cultural consequences of man's relationship with his physical environment. While not totally determinant, environment can impose constraints on the development of societies, e.g. climate can affect modes of production with consequences for political and ritual activities, and this relationship between ecology and society has recently received renewed interest from anthropologists.

Social Anthropology, see ANTHROPOLOGY.

Social Contact, general term for a group of theories which attempt to explain the nature of political authority in terms of a contract amongst the citizens, or between the citizens and their governors; this forms the basis for the justification, and terms of exercise of, political power. The contract derives its moral force from being one to which a free individual would reasonably consent.

Social Credit, economic doctrine proposed in the 1930s in the USA by Maj C. H. Douglas. He argued that 'poverty amidst plenty'—the great depression of the 1930s—was due to a flaw in the price system whereby all costs of production were not reflected in equivalent purchasing power. The state should therefore make periodic monetary gifts to its citizens to make good the alleged deficiency.

Social Democrats, name adopted by a number of west European left-wing political parties, standing generally for a mixed economy and pluralism of a liberal democracy. The earliest party, now the Social Democratic Party of West Germany was founded in 1863 and was originally a Marxist revolutionary organisation, but changed in the 20th century to a reformist people's party. Similar movements developed in Austria, Denmark, Finland and Sweden. In Italy the Social Democrats are an anti-Communist centre party, advocating economic control and some nationalisation. The British Social Democrat Party is a much more recent development. It was formally established as a centre party on 26 March 1981, by a group of former Labour politicians disenchanted with the militant radicalism of some of their colleagues.

Social Evolution. Influenced by Darwin, 19th-century anthropologists tried to develop evolutionary schemes to account for variations in the forms of society, assuming western society to be the 'highest' level of development. The ethnocentric assumptions on which this approach was based led to its rejection in the 1920s in favour of a structuralist approach but regained some favour in the 1940s and 1950s with the work of J. Steward in the USA and with French structural-Marxists.

Social Philosophy, that aspect of philosophy which brings philosophic methods to bear on the larger problems of social life and social history. It is closely related to political philosophy, from which it was scarcely distinguished until the 19th century. Its recognition as a separate aspect of philosophy was due to the growing consciousness of society as being more comprehensive than the state, which also led to the appearance of sociology as a separate study. All social philosophers envisage the

individual as placed in society and, at least in some degree, conditioned by it, and have considered the implications of the existence and activity of this more complex unit in the universe. As a result, the place and value of the individual in the universe have been radically reconsidered.

Social Security. In Britain the first step towards the creation of a system of state social security was taken by the passing of the National Assistance Act 1948, the fundamental purpose of which was to achieve the final replacement of the Poor Law by entirely new services founded on new conceptions of social welfare. Under the act a National Assistance Board administered a state scheme of financial aid for all people who fell outside the national insurance scheme, or whose requirements were not wholly met from that or any other source. The cost of this service falls on the Exchequer.

Social Stratification, a sociological concept which refers to societies as composed of distinct social strata or relatively permanent levels arranged in some kind of hierarchy. Different societies are stratified in different ways. Pre-industrial societies are not stratified in terms of social classes but of castes and of estates.

Social Worker, a very wide term with no settled meaning. In Britain it refers to those professionally trained or untrained who work in statutory or voluntary, permanent or temporary, agencies which operate public programmes of social welfare. Most social workers are now employed in local authority social service departments, and in the probation and after-care service.

Socialism, political doctrine and movement which advocates the partial or complete abolition of private property, and the establishment of society upon a basis of the common ownership of some or all of the means of production, distribution, and exchange. Sharing some of the sources of communism, socialism has evolved along different lines, to the point where it is claimed that it offers an alternative to the faults of unrestricted capitalism on the one hand and of communism on the other. Many parties and states now calling themselves socialist, are committed only to government intervention in the free market, and to egalitarian social welfare and taxation policies. As social democrats, rather than communists, they are also committed to the pursuit of such policies through political means, eschewing insurrection and non-constitutional activity, at least within states allowing freedom of political action and expression.

Socialist Realism, the 'basic method' of literature and art in Soviet Russia, defined as 'truthful, historically concrete representation of reality in its revolutionary development', which 'must be combined with the task of the ideological transformation and education of the working man in the spirit of socialism'. The concept of Socialist Realism was conceived by its creators, Stalin, Zhdanov, and Gorki, as a further development of Lenin's demand for the harnessing of literature to Party aims. Socialist Realism was first made obligatory for writers in 1932, when all existing writers' associations were dissolved by the Communist party and replaced by The Soviet Writers' Union.

Socialist Revolutionaries, Russian political party, formed in 1902 by adherents of revolutionary populism. Its programme, besides making common radical demands, aimed at a federal structure for the Russian state, self-determination for non-Russian peoples, and socialisation of the land. Assassination of leading government officials was a part of the Socialist Revolutionaries' tactics, and was carried out by an autonomous 'fighting organisation', for many years headed by the *provocateur* Azef. In 1917 a section of the party, Left Socialist Revolutionaries, split off, supported the Bolshevik seizure of power, and participated in the Bolshevik government until the Brest-Litovsk Treaty in 1918. The Socialist Revolutionaries had the majority in the Constituent Assembly which was dispersed by the Bolsheviks. The party was suppressed in Russia in 1922.

Society Islands, main group in French Polynesia, comprise Windward Islands (Tahiti, Mooréa, Mehetia, etc.) and Leeward Islands (Huahune, Raiatea, etc.) They were named by Captain James Cook when leading a Royal Society Expedition to Tahiti in 1769. Area 1673 km²; population (1977) 117,700.

Society of Friends, see FRIENDS, SOCIETY OF.

Society of Jesus, see JESUITS.

Socinus, Latinised surname of two celebrated Italian heresiarchs, the founders of Socinianism, which is akin to modern Unitarianism. Lelio Francisco Maria Sozini, or Loelius Socinus (1525–62), was keenly interested in theology, and in 1546 joined a secret society for the free discussion of theological matters. After having travelled through Europe, he finally settled at Zürich. Fausto Paolo Sozini, or Faustus Socinus (1539–1604), nephew of the preceding, had from his youth sympathised with his uncle's views. From 1579 until his death he lived in Poland, where the Minor (Reformed) Church adopted his theological scheme. Here he acquired a very considerable following. After his death his writings exercised considerable influence throughout Western Europe. Socinianism differs from Arianism in its denial of the existence of Jesus before his birth as a man. It differs from Unitarianism in holding that his birth was miraculous, and that Christ was then endowed with divine qualities.

Sociobiology, the study of social behaviour from the point of view that behavioural patterns in any animal have evolved by the same mechanism as physical features.

Sociology. The term 'sociology' was first used by Auguste Comte (1798–1857) who referred to it in the fourth volume of *Cours de philosophie positive*, 1839. His studies of change between types of society mark a significant and continuing interest in what has been termed 'evolutionary sociology'. The two most important sociologists working in this tradition in England were Herbert Spencer (1820–1903) and L. T. Hobhouse (1864–1929). The work of Hobhouse (*Morals in Evolution*, 1915; and *Social Development*, 1924) is probably the high-water-mark of this tradition. For much of the period between 1930 and 1950 sociology in Britain

was dominated by another tradition, namely that of the straightforward empirical description of social problems and conditions associated with the work of such earlier investigators as Charles Booth. There was little interest in the development of specifically sociological theory and the rich European theorising associated with Weber, Marx, Durkheim, Simmel, and Pareto (who together can be called the founding fathers of sociology) seemed to have little impact.

Since then, however, the situation has changed dramatically. Sociology has become a very well established feature of education in universities, polytechnics, and other institutions of higher education. Most universities have chairs in sociology and the subject is extremely popular with applicants for undergraduate and postgraduate places. As a response to this there has developed a keen interest in theory (some critics suggest that sociology only consists of detailed and repetitive discussion of the work of the founding fathers), in criticism of the existing social order, and in the development of specialised applications of sociology to particular problems and institutions.

The present state of sociological theory seems rich or chaotic, according to one's point of view. Marx, particularly early Marx, seems to some to be a source of considerable inspiration. Others, such as the so-called Frankfurt School (Habermas, Adorno, and others) build on and adopt a Marxian analysis. Functionalism, which will be discussed below, still enjoys prestige, whilst for sociologists who adopt a phenomenological perspective (attempting to suspend assumptions and examine social interaction as it takes place) the social structure seems to dissolve before a never-ending analysis of common-sense and taken-for-granted meanings. Yet other sociologists leave theoretical discussion and elaboration aside and concentrate on empirical work, on establishing the facts. This viewpoint was uppermost in the USA in the 1950s and early 1960s and was responsible for the quip that a sociologist was a man who spent a great deal of research money finding the way to a brothel. It is still, however, a significant viewpoint and some sociologists equate their discipline not just with empirical research, but with one particular method of conducting such research, i.e. the social survey.

This growth in theoretical positions has had at least two important effects on the developments of sociology. First, it has led to attempts to order the multitude of approaches and to suggestions that there are only two sociologies, one of consensus and the other of conflict; thus one has to choose where allegiance lies. Second, it has led to a steady, if not always steadying, criticism both of the existing social order (as repressive simply through the operations of its day-to-day business) and of sociological theories which are taken to support the repression. Of these the best known is structural functionalism.

Functionalism probably owes its origins to Emile Durkheim, who argued that social institutions exist for the purposes of fulfilling social needs.

Socotra, island in the Indian Ocean, 250 km north-east of Cape Guardafui, East Africa,

and near the entrance to the Gulf of Aden. Length east to west, 115 km; greatest breadth, 35 km; it now forms part of the People's Democratic Republic of Yemen. The island is mainly a lofty tableland, rising to above 1200 m, with a narrow coastal plain. Myrrh, frankincense, incense, aloes, and butter (ghee) are produced; cattle and goats are reared. The main settlement is Tamridah. It possesses a highly strategic submarine base. Area 3580 km²; population c.1200.

Socrates (469–399 BC), Greek philosopher, born at Athens. He left no writings so that our information about him depends on the records of others, chiefly his pupil Plato and Xenophon. Socrates grew to manhood while Athens was at the height of its glory.

The value of Socrates' contribution to philosophy is disputed. Some attribute directly to him much of the doctrine of his disciple Plato, but this view is rejected by many scholars, and indeed Socrates himself denied that he had any set of positive doctrines to teach. Nevertheless, it may safely be maintained that Socrates was the founder of the spiritual view of knowledge and conduct. He defined the soul as that in man which has knowledge, and also ignorance, good and bad. It was but a step from this conviction to the doctrine that goodness is knowledge (*epistēmē*). Socrates believed that he had a divine mission to convict men of sin (i.e. ignorance) by question and answer, examining systematically the fundamental assumptions from which discussion of conduct and morality arose, and insisting upon a strict definition of terms.

Following the expulsion of the Thirty Tyrants, Socrates was charged with impiety (*asebeia*) and corruption of Athenian youth. The second of these offences meant in effect Socrates' encouragement of the young to criticise the existing order. He was found guilty by a narrow majority, but by his attitude after the verdict he so enraged his judges that he was sentenced to death. The execution was delayed for 30 days, during the Delian festival, and during that time Socrates refused to avail himself of plans for his escape. He drank the hemlock in the spring of 399. The description of his last hours is found in the *Phaedo* of Plato, and is among the masterpieces of European literature.

Soddy, Frederick (1877–1956), British chemist. He was professor of inorganic and physical chemistry at Oxford (1919–36). His chief field of work was that of radio-activity. In 1913 he elaborated the theory of isotopes and, with Rutherford, stated the displacement law of radioactivity. In 1921 he won the Nobel Prize for chemistry. In later life he wrote on economics.

Söderblom, Nathan (1866–1931), Swedish Protestant theologian. In 1914 he was made archbishop of Uppsala. He wrote on historical and theological subjects, particularly *The Nature of Revelation*, 1903, *Origin of Belief*, 1914, and his remarkable Luther studies *Humour and Melancholy*, 1919. In 1931 Söderblom gave the Gifford lectures in Edinburgh, published in 1933 as *The Living God*. He was a leading advocate of the unity of the Christian churches. He also did much to promote international understanding and peace, and for this was awarded the Nobel Peace Prize in 1930.

Sodium, metallic chemical element, symbol Na, atomic number 11, atomic weight 22·9898, one of the alkali metals; occurs abundantly in nature as the chloride. Sodium chloride, or common salt, is found in sea-water and some lakes and springs. As the nitrate, sodium is found in Chile and Peru (Chile saltpetre), and as the fluoride (cryolite), $3NaF \cdot AlF_3$, in Greenland. It is also the constituent of many silicates, and is present in animal organisms and in plants. Sodium was first isolated by Sir Humphry Davy by the electrolysis of sodium hydroxide. It is manufactured by electrolysis of fused sodium chloride, the sodium collecting round the cathode while chlorine is evolved at the anode, or by electrolysis of fused silver hydroxide, which is Davy's original process adapted to modern electrical resources.

Sodium is a soft, silvery-white metal (relative density 0·97) which tarnishes instantly on exposure to air, forming a film of sodium oxide. (Because of this, it must be stored immersed in a liquid containing no oxygen, such as liquid paraffin.) Sodium is used either alone or in the form of the mercury amalgam, as a reducing agent for organic compounds, and is employed in the preparation of the peroxide and cyanide. Its potassium alloy, which is liquid at ordinary temperatures, has been used as a heat-transfer medium in nuclear reactors.

Sodium forms two oxides, the monoxide and the peroxide. The monoxide is a white amorphous compound produced by the partial oxidation of the metal in a limited supply of air. Sodium monoxide reacts with water to form the hydroxide: $Na_2O + H_2O = 2NaOH$. Sodium peroxide is a yellowish-white solid obtained by heating the metal in air in aluminium vessels. It decomposes water and forms sodium hydroxide. Oxygen is also evolved, and on account of this property the peroxide is used as an oxidising agent. With cold dilute hydrochloric acid, the peroxide forms hydrogen peroxide, which is used for bleaching. Sodium hydroxide (caustic soda) is manufactured by the electrolysis of brine, collecting round the cathode while chlorine is evolved at the anode. Sodium nitrate is an important fertiliser and sodium nitrite is used for preparing organic dyes. Sodium thiosulphate, $(Na_2S_2O_3$, 'hypo') is employed in photography. The most important of the artificially prepared compounds of sodium is the carbonate, commonly known as 'soda' (Na_2CO_3).

Sodium Chloride, common salt, NaCl, occurs in large quantities in sea-water and in extensive deposits of rock salt. It is either extracted by evaporation of brine, or mined, according to circumstances. Sodium chloride crystallises in cubes, is quite soluble in water, but almost insoluble in alcohol. It is used for seasoning and preserving food, for melting snow and ice on roads, and as a starting material in the manufacture of caustic soda and metallic sodium.

Sodium Sulphate, or Glauber's salt, $Na_2SO_4 \cdot 10H_2O$, compound prepared by heating salt with sulphuric acid, and crystallising the residue from water, from which it separates as colourless prisms. The 10 molecules of water of crystallisation are lost on prolonged exposure to the air. Sodium sulphate has a cooling, bitter and saltish taste, is a mild laxative and diuretic, and is present in the waters of Karlovy Vary, Cheltenham, etc. It is used in large amounts in paper-making processes, and as a constituent of some synthetic detergents.

Sodom and Gomorrah, two of the five 'cities of the plain', which now lie beneath the shallow waters of the southern end of the Dead Sea. Near Sodom Lot took up his residence, but fled before the destruction of the cities recounted in Gen. xix. 24 ff. The region is sulphurous and bituminous, and such places are liable to earthquakes and sudden eruptions of gas and oil, which may ignite spontaneously, giving off clouds of smoke.

Sodor and Man, title of the Anglican bishop responsible for the Isle of Man. It is a relic of the former Norse kingdom disbanded in 1266 when the Hebrides became part of Scotland.

Sofia, capital of Bulgaria, situated in the west of the country, some 480 km north-west of Istanbul and 320 km south-east of Belgrade. Its situation has made it an important crossroads for trade and communications throughout its history. The town was developed under the Byzantine empire, when the church of St Sofia was built. In 809 it was captured by Bulgaria and was given the name *Sredets*. It was named the capital of independent Bulgaria in 1879. Its main industries are engineering, textiles, chemicals, and electrical goods. Population (1978) 1,031,597.

Soft Drinks, originally an American term for non-alcoholic beverages to distinguish them from hard (i.e. alcoholic) drinks. The term is still used to denote non-alcoholic drinks, carbonated or still, containing natural or artificial flavouring and usually sweetened. Fruit drinks, soda water, tonic water, ginger beer, etc. are all considered soft drinks.

Carbonated or aerated waters and beverages, into which carbon dioxide is introduced under pressure, originated from the desire to imitate the naturally sparkling waters of certain springs. They were first attempted by Thurneysser in 1560, later by Hoffman, 1708, and Geoffroy, 1724. Joseph Priestley experimented, 1767–72, and proposed several improved methods, including the use of the pressure pump, successfully developed commercially by Paul, Schweppe, and Gosse.

Softball, a condensed version of baseball, is a very popular sport in many countries.

The ball is 30·16 cm to 30·79 cm in circumference and weighs 170 g to 184 g; far from being soft, it is as hard as a baseball. The bat must be under 86·36 cm long and 5·39 cm in diameter. The pitching distance is 14 m for men, 11·61 m for women and 18·3 m between the bases for both.

The rules of softball are similar to baseball, the principal differences being that the ball is pitched underhand and must be released below hip level with the wrist not further from the body than the width of a wrist. Seven innings are played. Base runners must remain in contact with a base until the ball leaves the pitcher's hand.

A further version of softball called 'Slow-pitch' has been developed in recent years and has grown in popularity.

Softwood, see TIMBER.

Sogne Fjord, inlet running eastward from the sea on the west coast of Norway. It is the longest (about 160 km), and also the deepest, in the country. The fjord is popular with tourists because of its magnificent panoramas of mountain scenery.

Soil may be defined as a naturally occurring body made up of mineral and organic constituents and differentiated into layers or horizons, each horizon having different chemical, physical, and biological properties. The initial stage of soil is the parent material. This consists of either solid rock and mineral materials or drift deposits (loosely consolidated material). Weathering processes act upon the parent materials to produce a mineral mixture of sands, silts, and clay. The vegetation growing on soils adds organic matter to the mineral parent material, and supports a diverse animal population, which adds further material as organic waste and other residues.

The unit of soil study is the *soil profile*, a two-dimensional section of soil. The profile is composed of several layers or *horizons*. For example, at the surface in a podsol soil the organic debris of dead leaves, twigs, etc. is termed the litter horizon; this litter undergoes chemical and biological breakdown in the fermentation horizon until it becomes humus.

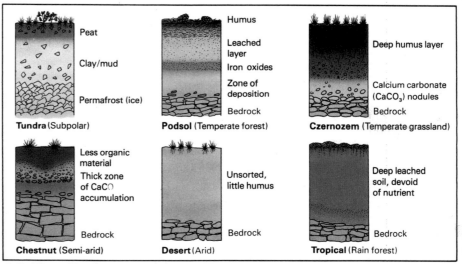

***Soil.** The profiles of six major soil classes. Although the nature of the parent rock is important, climate is the predominant factor in determining soil type.*

The terms topsoil and subsoil are popular expressions of the horizon concept. Most soils undergo successive waves of development, e.g. with the change from natural woodland to cropland which is later abandoned, and are thus not the result of a single set of interacting processes.

In their natural state soils are classified for moisture status on a five-point scale from excessively to very poorly drained. The pH value of soils ranges from three (acid) through seven (neutral) to nine (alkaline). Most agricultural and horticultural plants prefer a slightly acid soil for maximum yields.

See also CHERNOZEMS AND CHESTNUT EARTH SOILS; PODSOL SOILS.

Soil Erosion and Conservation. Soil erosion is the removal of soil particles from the Earth's surface by wind or water. It frequently results from the mismanagement of soil by people, and so should be distinguished from normal geological erosion—the breakdown of rocks by weathering and their removal by gravity, wind, water, or ice. Soil erosion can take weeks, or even hours. It may begin when forest or other vegetation cover is removed; or when crops are planted in rows running down hill, the spaces between the rows forming water channels.

Conservation depends on the type of erosion. Contour ploughing and terracing can reduce downhill erosion; wind breaks to protect soil from blowing away can be planted, or crops can be planted at right angles to the prevailing wind. Dunes can be stabilised by planting with vegetation, such as marram grass, which binds the sand into place. Mixed farming, which allows permanent pasture to be sown, is an excellent anti-erosion measure.

Soil-creep, imperceptible downward migration of soils under the influence of gravity. Its effects may be shown by the tilting of fences on hill slopes, and by the curving of tree-trunks, which change their direction of growth in an effort to remain vertical. Common manifestations of soil creep are terracettes about 25 cm wide.

See also SOLIFLUCTION.

Soiling, the accidental passage of small amounts of stool into the clothing. Although this often occurs in the aged and in persons with neurological disorders, it is most common in young children between five and ten years of age. The most common cause is a severe degree of chronic constipation.

Soilless Culture, the growing of plants in a compost which does not include soil. The first development of the soilless compost occurred at the University of California where a range of mixtures was recommended, of different ratios of sand and peat, all of which included fertilisers. The choice of mixture depends on the purpose for which it will be used, and varies for seeds and seedlings of different ages. Other soilless composts may include grit, perlite or vermiculite.

See also HYDROPONICS.

Soissons, French town in the *département* of Aisne, on the River Aisne. It saw the rise to power of Clovis I. It commands the north-east approaches to Paris, and has been sacked at least 15 times. Soissons has a large agricultural trade and metallurgical industries. Population (1975) 32,112.

Soke, word signifying jurisdiction, and especially the privilege of holding a court. It is thus used in Domesday Book. By extension it came to be used to describe the area under a particular jurisdiction; the word survives in the 'soke of Peterborough'.

Sokoto, capital of North-Western State, Nigeria. It grew from a small village into a military and administrative centre after the Fulani conquests over the Hausa states in the early 19th century and has remained an important regional centre for north-western Nigeria. Population (1971) 108,500.

Solanaceae, the tomato family, includes about 90 genera and 2000 species of dicotyledons, mainly herbaceous but including some shrubs. The flowers usually have five sepals, joined at their bases to form a tube, and five petals, also forming a tube, to which the usually five stamens are attached. The ovary is attached above the base of the petal tube and consists of two fused carpels; it ripens to give either a dry capsule fruit or a berry. Many Solanaceae are poisonous plants sometimes used medicinally; the most important are perhaps atropine, mainly from *Atropa* (deadly nightshade), hyoscyamine from *Hyoscyamus* (henbane) and nicotine from *Nicotiana* (tobacco). Other poisonous genera include *Datura* (thorn apple) and *Mandragora* (mandrake). The largest genus is *Solanum*, which includes the potato, *S. tuberosum*, the green parts of which are toxic. The tomato (*Lycopersicum esculentum*) and *Capsicum* (pepper) belong to related genera. A few Solanaceae are grown for their decorative flowers (*Petunia*), or fruits (*Physalis* and some species of *Capsicum*).

Solano, see WIND.

Solanum, chief genus of Solanaceae, native of tropical and temperate lands. It contains such important plants as the potato, *S. tuberosum* and the aubergine, *S. melongena*. The tomato, *S. lycopersicum*, is generally put in a separate genus *Lycopersicon*. Other cultivated members of the genus are the winter cherry (*S. capsicastrum*), Jerusalem cherry (*S. pseudocapsicum*) and the potato vine (*S. jasminoides*).

Solar, in a large medieval house, a sitting-room or parlour giving the owner's family some privacy from the communal life of the great hall.

See also HALL.

Solar Constant, the total radiant energy received from the Sun by unit area of a surface normal to the Sun and just outside the Earth's atmosphere when the Sun-Earth distance has its mean value. The presently accepted value based on observations made from very high flying aircraft is 1·950 calories per square centimetre per minute, i.e. 136·0 mW/cm².

Solar System, the region of space dominated by the Sun, a very ordinary star whose nearest stellar neighbours are over four light years away. Around the Sun revolves what is probably the debris of its formation and which includes nine planets, themselves attended by satellites, a host of minor planets, innumerable comets, meteors, and an extensive but extremely tenuous cloud of gas and dust, some of which we see as the zodiacal light. Of the total mass of the system, 99·86 per cent is concentrated in the Sun itself and 0·135 per cent in the planets, over two-thirds of it in Jupiter.

The solar system gives every indication of being a strongly unified system having a common origin and development. It is isolated in space; all the planets go round the Sun in orbits that are nearly circular and coplanar, and in the same direction as the Sun itself rotates. What the common origin may have been and how the solar system actually developed is, in spite of the many theories that have been advanced, still a mystery. The problem of the formation of the solar system seems to be a particular case of the more general problem of the formation of stars out of pre-existing nebulosity. In the case of the solar system the time at which the condensation took place seems to be fairly definite since the age of the system is the same as that of the Earth, the Moon, and the meteorites, viz., about 5×10^9 years.

Solarium (from Latin *sol*, sun), a glazed veranda or sun-parlour, acting as a sun-trap, especially in a sanatorium.

Solder and Soldering. Soldering and its counterpart, brazing, are joining processes applied mainly to metals but used also for joining metals to non-metals such as ceramics. The essential features of the processes are that a molten filler wets the surfaces to be joined, bridges gaps between them, and solidifies to form a joint. The filler may be either pure metal or an alloy but its melting point must be significantly below that of the parts being joined, so that (unlike welding) they are not fused during brazing. The distinction between soldering and brazing is one of temperature, soldering being carried out below an arbitrary temperature level and brazing above. This arbitrary temperature is normally taken as being about 500°C, which is slightly below the minimum melting point for fillers based on silver-copper alloys. The term 'soft soldering' is normally applied to soldering with a filler based on the lead-tin alloy system, while silver soldering and hard soldering are colloquial names given to brazing when a silver based filler is used. A solder is the filler used for soldering.

Soldier-bird, or blood-bird, *Myzomela sanguineolenta*, a species of the honey-eater family, Meliphagidae, order Passeriformes. It occurs in Australia, and its plumage is of brilliant scarlet and black.

Sole, a flat-fish, belonging to the family Soleidae, order Pleuronectiformes. A related family Cynoglossidae is known as tongue-soles. The best-known species is *Solea solea*, the common sole, which occurs in many parts of Europe. It attains a length of from 25 to 50 cm, and is the most highly valued of all food fishes. Other species are *S. lascaris*, the lemon sole, *S. minuta*, the little sole, and *S. variegata*, the banded sole. The American sole or hog-choker belongs to an allied genus, and is known as *Achirus fasciatus*.

Solenodon, either of two species of small West Indian mammals in family Solenodontidae of order Insectivora. They are about 28 cm long, with an almost equally long naked tail. They have shaggy hair, long, pointed snouts, and strong claws. They come out mostly at night, and eat insects, worms and other invertebrate animals. Their saliva is poisonous. The Cuban solenodon is in danger of extinction.

Solenoid, a coil of wire through which electricity is passed to create a magnetic field. See also ELECTRICITY, CURRENT.

Solent, The, western part of the strait between the Isle of Wight and the coast of Hampshire, England. It is 27km long by 1·6–8km wide, and famous for its yacht racing.

Sol-fa, Tonic, see GUIDO d'AREZZO.

Solferino, Italian village in Lombardy, 30 km north-west of Mantua. The French and Piedmontese defeated the Austrians here on 24 June 1859.

Solicitor, member of that branch of the English legal profession consulted directly by the public. Barristers can be consulted only through solicitors. To be admitted to the roll of solicitors it is necessary to pass law examinations and serve a period of articles (i.e. apprenticeship) with a practising solicitor.

Solicitor-General, in England and Wales, is the law officer of the Crown next below the attorney-general and acts as his deputy. The Crown is represented in Scotland by the solicitor-general for Scotland.

Solid. A solid possesses a definite shape and volume. In terms of the theory of phases of matter, the molecules of a solid are closely packed and the attractive forces exerted on an individual molecule by its immediate neighbours are so great that it has very little freedom of movement and remains 'attached' to its neighbours. The elasticity of solids is due to this characteristic; it is difficult to deform, and has the property of recovering its original shape after the stress is removed. The ultra-microscopic character of solids was revealed by X-ray analysis initiated by W. H. Bragg and his son, W. L. Bragg. They showed that crystalline materials consist of atoms (or ions) in regular arrays, and many solids, e.g. metals, that appear to be amorphous are polycrystalline, i.e. made up of many randomly orientated minute crystals.

Solidago, see GOLDENROD.

Solifluction, flow, under the influence of gravity, of soil and loose debris on the surface of the Earth. It is a phenomenon which generally occurs when the material is saturated with water, and particularly after the thawing of deeply frozen ground. The principal cause of movement is the alternate freezing and thawing of wet unconsolidated materials resulting in soil flow on slopes as low as 3°.

See also SOIL-CREEP; SOIL EROSION AND CONSERVATION.

Solihull, town in West Midlands county, England, 11km south-east of Birmingham. The borough is mainly residential but it includes Birmingham Airport, and the National Exhibition Centre, opened in 1975. Population (1981) 198,287.

Solingen, city in North Rhine-Westphalia, Federal Republic of Germany, 10km south-east of Düsseldorf. In the Middle Ages it was well known for its sword blades; nowadays it has an important cutlery industry. Population (1980) 166,600.

Sollya, the Australian bluebell creeper, a genus of family Pittosporaceae. They are evergreen twining shrubs with deep blue flowers in cymes. There are only two species: *S. fusiformis* and *S. parviflora*. Both are cultivated.

Solmisation, see GUIDO d'AREZZO.

Solo, see SURAKARTA.

Soloist, in music, instrumental or vocal performer of a work with piano, chamber or orchestral accompaniment. The solo part in a concerto is often particularly virtuosic, especially in 19th-century works such as the Liszt piano concertos. A soloist in vocal works takes the part of a particular character, for example in the Bach Passions, or is employed to sing arias and recitatives in contrast to the chorus, as in Handel's *Messiah*.

Solomon, third King of Israel, son and successor of David, reigning c.970–931 BC. Solomon has become a symbol of wisdom, pomp and magnificence. Although an autocrat, with vast numbers of oppressed slaves and a large harem of foreign women who introduced pagan cults into Israel, he did much to increase the prosperity of his kingdom by ruthlessly destroying his enemies and by greatly increasing international trade especially with Hiram of Tyre. He was a great builder particularly in Jerusalem and constructed the First Temple. He is reputed to have written the biblical books of Proverbs and Song of Solomon and to have been visited by the Queen of Sheba. His wisdom is illustrated by the story of two women who each claimed to be the mother of a living baby. Solomon swiftly discovered who was the true mother by suggesting they divided the baby in half. The real mother immediately gave up her claim to the child thus exposing the false mother.

Solomon (Solomon Cutner, 1902–), British pianist. He first appeared in public at the age of eight, playing a Mozart concerto, and made his first British tour at the age of nine, playing with leading orchestras. At 14 he retired for five years' study. He later played throughout Britain as well as on the continent. During the Second World War he undertook extensive recital tours abroad for the armed forces.

Solomon Islands, archipelago of Melanesia, in the west Pacific, stretching from north-west to south-east between 5° and 12°30′S and 155°30′ and 169°45′E. The Solomon Islands consists of six large islands, Choiseul, Ysabel, and Malaita (the northern chain) and Guadal-

Solomon Islands
Area: 29,785 km²
Population: 215,000
Capital: Honiara

canal, New Georgia, and San Cristobal (the southern chain), and countless smaller ones. The capital is Honiara on Guadalcanal.

The islands are of volcanic formation, and the coral reefs are only an adjunct to mountain massifs which rise to a height of 26,246 m. They are picturesque, with primeval forests of slender palms, coral gardens lining the translucent sea bottom and lovely lagoons. The total area of the Solomon Islands (formerly the protectorate) is 29,785 km² (land area). Population (1978) 215,000.

The chief crops are copra, timber, and tuna. Cocoa and chillies are also exported and an oil palm industry is being set up. Cattle raising is a new development and rice is grown for home consumption.

The 1974 constitution established the office of Governor, with a legislative assembly, whose elected members have chosen a chief minister and a council of ministers which is responsible to the legislative assembly. Internal self-government was instituted in January 1976 and full independence followed in 1978, when the Governor became Governor-General.

History. The first European known to have visited the Solomon Islands was a Spaniard, Alvaro de Mendana, who set out on a voyage of discovery in 1568.

The British sphere of influence in the Solomon Islands was recognised in 1886. A British protectorate over the Solomon group was set up by treaty with Germany in 1893. Many other islands were added to the Protectorate in 1898–99, including the Santa Cruz group, Rennell and Bellona; and in 1900 Choiseul, Ysabel, and some islands in the Bougainville Straits were transferred by convention from Germany to Great Britain. The northern Solomons (Bougainville, Buka, and some other islands) were captured from Germany by Australia in 1914 and mandated to

Solomon Islands. *The archipelago consists of hundreds of forested volcanic islets.*

Australia after the First World War.

Solomon, Wisdom of, Book of Wisdom. It is in the Apocrypha of the English Bible, but also included in the Roman Catholic canon. Solomon is not actually named in the book, but he is manifestly the speaker in chapters vi–ix, for he is the builder of the Temple in Jerusalem in ix. 7, 8. The Wisdom of Solomon is an exhortation to seek wisdom, first, because it brings salvation to the pious Jews: secondly, because of its divine essence; and thirdly, because the history of Israel shows how wisdom brought blessings to Israel and calamities to the heathen. Its most probable date is 100–50 BC.

Solomon's Seal, *Polygonatum,* a genus of herbaceous perennials in family Liliaceae, with handsome leafy stems and axillary bell-shaped flowers, followed by red or blue-black berries.

Solomos, Dionysios (1798–1857), Greek poet. He studied Greek poetry and in his long *Ode to Liberty,* 1823, the source of the Greek national anthem, vindicated the possibilities of the common language. There and in Corfu he wrote *Lambros, The Cretan,* and successive drafts of *Missolonghi, or The Free Besieged* but he completed none of them. The maturity of his thought and language was unparalleled in the Greek literary world of his day, and despite its sadly fragmentary nature his poetry still retains its appeal.

Solon (c.640–c.559 BC), Athenian legislator. On becoming chief archon (594), he cancelled debts, reformed the coinage and reorganised the constitution. He repealed the harsh laws of Draco and classified the citizens according to landed property. He was also a distinguished poet.

Solothurn, capital of the canton of the same name, Switzerland, on the River Aar, 30 km north of Bern. It is an important railway junction; industries include electrical engineering and watchmaking. Population (1974) 16,700.

Soloviëv, Vladimir Sergeevich (1853–1900), Russian philosopher and poet. He created the first comprehensive philosophical system in the history of Russian thought: the philosophy of all-unity. Partly by the study of philosophy and partly by personal religious intuition, Soloviëv abandoned his early atheistic materialism and accepted Christianity. He tried to revive the Christian humanism of such thinkers as Erasmus, St Thomas More, and St Francis de Sales, supplied a theological and philosophic justification for it, and urged that the principle of holiness should be introduced into every sphere of man's social life. His philosophy influenced Berdyaev and other Russian thinkers, and also Blok and the symbolist poets.

Solstice, strictly a moment when the Sun is farthest from the equator. The Sun is farthest north on 21 or 22 June as it enters the zodiacal sign of Cancer and is vertically overhead at midday at places on the Tropic of Cancer (latitude 23½° north). This is the time of midsummer and the longest day in the Northern Hemisphere and of midwinter and the shortest day in the Southern Hemisphere. Similarly midwinter/midsummer and the shortest/longest day occur on 21 or 22 December as the Sun enters the sign of Capri-

corn and is at its farthest south.
See also SEASONS.

Solti, Sir George (1912–), British conductor born in Budapest, where he studied with Kodály and Bartók; he later studied in Switzerland under Toscanini. He has been musical director of several great opera companies, including Covent Garden, 1961–71. A guest conductor in many European and American cities, he raised the Chicago Symphony to a position among the most acclaimed of world orchestras, especially through his recordings of romantic composers.

Soluble Glass, or water glass, is prepared by fusing silica (sand or flint) with sodium carbonate, or with carbon and sodium sulphate, when the sodium silicates may be dissolved out. It may also be prepared by digestion of silica and caustic soda under pressure. Soluble glass has been used for preparing artificial stone on buildings as a protection against weathering, for the manufacture of cheap varieties of soap, for preserving eggs and for fireproof cements.
See also SILICON.

Solutions, in physical chemistry, homogeneous mixtures of two or more substances constituting one phase, the composition of which can be continuously varied between certain limits. The most familiar solution is that of a solid (the solute) dissolved in a liquid (the solvent), but since matter exists in three distinct phases—solid, liquid and gas—and since matter in any state can be mixed with matter in every other state, at least theoretically, the following different classes of solutions are possible: (1) gas in gas; (2) liquid in gas; (3) solid in gas; (4) gas in liquid; (5) liquid in liquid; (6) solid in liquid; (7) gas in solid; (8) liquid in solid; (9) solid in solid; (10) more complicated solutions with the three stages of aggregation represented. When different substances are brought together they either act chemically on one another or they simply mix. It is this latter class only, where no chemical action takes place, that constitutes true solutions.
See also COLLOID; ELECTROLYSIS.

Solway Firth, in part the estuary of the River Esk, and in part an inlet of the Irish Sea. It separates England from Scotland. At its mouth the firth is over 40 km wide, but at its narrowest point only 3 km wide. The tides ebb and flow with great rapidity, creating a 'bore' of some 16 km/h.

Solzhenitsyn, Aleksandr Isaevich (1918–), Soviet writer. His story of life in a labour camp, *One Day in the Life of Ivan Denisovich* appeared in 1962. Subsequently his major work had to be published abroad, including his two best novels, *Cancer Ward,* 1962–66, which, based on personal experience, describes the inmates of a hospital ward for cancer sufferers and is also an allegorical statement about Stalin's Russia, and *The First Circle,* 1955–64 about a research institute staffed by political prisoners. Solzhenitsyn was awarded the Nobel Prize for literature in 1970.

In 1973 he wrote an open letter to the Soviet authorities, which perhaps contributed to his expulsion from the USSR in 1974. He has since published a history of Soviet labour camps, *Gulag Archipelago,* 1974–78. He now lives in Switzerland.

Soma, one of the plants from which the ambrosia of the Indian gods is said to be derived; hence it is sacred. Various plants with milky latex are said to have been the true *soma,* notably *Asclepias acida* and *Periploca aphylla.* In later Vedic literature *soma* is identified as the Moon God.

Somali, Cushitic people of the Horn of Africa, concentrated in the Somali Republic. They are nomadic pastoralists, traders and town dwellers and live in families, grouped in clans, under elective or hereditary chiefs. They are mainly Sunni Muslims of the Shafi'i sect. They number about 4 million.

Somalia
Area: 637,657 km²
Population: 3,640,000
Capital: Mogadishu

Somalia, or officially the Somali Democratic Republic, situated in the Horn of Africa (East Africa), bounded by Djibouti in the north, Ethiopia in the west, and Kenya in the south-west. The state is composed of the two former territories of British Somaliland and Italian Somaliland (Somalia). Area 637,657 km².

The north is occupied by an extension of the Ethiopian highlands, with peaks rising to 2400 m overlooking the Gulf of Aden; but in the south are lowlands crossed by rivers such as the Webi Shebeli which fall gently to the Indian Ocean.

The population totalled 3,640,000 in 1980. The capital and main town is Mogadishu.

Most of the population are pastoralists, depending mainly on their cattle, sheep, goats, and camels for their livelihood. Efforts are being made to expand rice growing in the river valleys, but at present irrigated agriculture consists mainly of plantation production of bananas for export and sugar for local use. Following the decimation of herds and flocks in the drought of the early 1970s, more people have had to turn to cultivation, often in new settlements, and also offshore fishing.

Few minerals have been found, though much oil prospecting has been undertaken, and the manufacturing sector is extremely small, mainly food processing.

The currency unit is the shilling, of 100 cents. The constitution provides for a President, elected by the National Assembly, with extensive executive powers; and a single National Assembly elected by universal suffrage. The sole legal party is the Somali Revolutionary Socialist Party.

The national and sole official language is now Somali.

History. The Democratic Republic of Somalia became an independent republic in 1960 when the former colonial territories of British Somaliland and Italian Somaliland united to form the Republic of Somalia.

On 21 October 1969, the army, led by Maj.-Gen. Muhamed Siad Barre, took control in a bloodless coup. Barre, acting as president, claims to have set the nation on the proper road to national unity through 'Scientific

Somalia. Mogadishu, the capital and chief port, was founded by Arab traders in the 10th century.

Socialism', a philosophy which aims at eradicating the divisive forces of tribalism and promoting economic development.

In 1979 a new constitution was approved by referendum, confirming the power of the sole legal party.

Somaliland, see DJIBOUTI; SOMALIA.

Sombrero, small island of Anguilla in the West Indies. It contains a lighthouse and lighthouse keeper and a handful of other residents. Area 5 km².

Somers, John, 1st Baron Somers of Evesham (1651–1716), English politician. He took part in the framing of the Declaration of Right in 1689, and became William III's most trusted minister, being in turn solicitor-general, attorney-general, lord keeper of the Great Seal, and in 1697 lord chancellor.

Somerset, Earls and Dukes of, titles held in the late Middle Ages by the Beaufort family and, since 1660, by the descendants of Edward Seymour, Duke of Somerset. The 1st Earl was John Beaufort (c.1371–1410), the eldest of the three sons of John of Gaunt. The Seymours descend from a Norman family. The 1st Duke of this line was Edward Seymour (c.1506–52), brother-in-law of Henry VIII and protector of England in the reign of his nephew, Edward VI.

Somerset, Edward Seymour, Duke of (c.1506–52), English statesman, Lord Protector of England. Henry VIII married his sister, Jane Seymour. On the death of the King in 1547, Somerset became protector during the minority of Edward VI, his nephew. He defeated the Scots at the battle of Pinkie in 1547. Somerset was a convinced Protestant and by the Act of Uniformity (1549) he tried to enforce the use of the first (and most extreme) Book of Common Prayer. Disagreements in the Privy Council threatened his position, first in 1549 when he was imprisoned in the Tower for a short time and again in 1551 when he was charged with high treason and executed.

Somerset, Robert Carr, Earl of, and Viscount Rochester (c.1589–1645), English courtier, favourite of James I. He married the divorced Countess of Essex in 1613. He lost his position when the circumstances surrounding the death of Sir Thomas Overbury were revealed. He and his wife were found guilty of murder and condemned to death, but reprieved and imprisoned until 1622.

Somerset, a maritime county in the south-west of England, bounded on the south-west by Devon, on the south-east by Dorset, on the east by Wiltshire, and on the north-east by Avon, while the Bristol Channel washes the northern and north-western shores. A large area north of the Mendip Hills was once Somerset but, since 1974, forms part of Avon. Somerset was originally part of the kingdom of Wessex, and figured largely in King Alfred's struggle with the Danes. Somerset contains many notable remains of Roman villas, abbeys, and castles, notably at Glastonbury and Dunster, while there is a celebrated cathedral at Wells. The Mendip caves have yielded many relics of prehistoric man.

Along the northern coast are low cliffs, with long sandy beaches and mud tracts at low tide, more especially in the north-west. The chief inlet is Bridgwater Bay; the only important harbour is at the mouth of the Parret, Somerset's principal river. Other rivers flowing through the county are the Axe, Exe, Brue, and Yeo. The most prominent surface features of Somerset are the Mendip Hills and the Quantock Hills. Due south are the low-lying moors, the second largest area of fen county in England, which includes Sedgemoor. The wild forest of Exmoor lies partly in the extreme west of the county and partly in Devon. Dunkery Beacon (518 m), the highest point in the county, is in this area.

The main occupations are agriculture and dairy-farming, including the manufacture of the famous Cheddar cheese. The numerous orchards of the county supply the cider- and perry-making industry. The holiday and tourist trade forms another important occupation, and many visitors are attracted both to the seaside resorts and to rural Somerset and its historic monuments. Burnham-on-Sea and Minehead are the principal coastal holiday resorts. Peat is cut in the Vale of Avalon. The principal towns are Wells, Taunton (the county town superseding the old capital, Somerton), Bridgwater, Yeovil, Frome, and Glastonbury.

Industries of the county include aircraft construction, the making of gloves, leather goods and shoes. The county is 345,799 ha in area; population (1981) 424,988.

Somerset House, a government building in the Strand, London, which formerly housed the General Register Office (of births, marriages, deaths), Inland Revenue, Valuation Office, Probate and Divorce Registery, and other public offices. The present building was erected by Sir William Chambers between 1776 and 1786. The General Register Office has now removed to St Catherine's House, Kingsway.

Somervell, Sir Arthur (1863–1937), British composer and educationist. He became professor at the Royal College of Music, and was later official inspector of music to the Board of Education. His songs, especially the cycles *Maud* (Tennyson), *A Shropshire Lad* (Housman), and *James Lee's Wife* (Browning), became his best-known works. He composed two masses, and choral and orchestral works and edited folk songs.

Somerset House occupies a site on which stood the palace of the Duke of Somerset.

Somme, river of northern France, rising near St Quentin, and flowing by Amiens and Abbeville to the English Channel. It is connected by canal with the Oise and the Scheldt. Length 245 km.

Sommerfeld, Arnold Johannes Wilhelm (1868–1951), German physicist, famous for work on atomic structure and the conduction of electricity in metals.

Somnambulism, sleep-walking, being up and about while asleep. It occurs in children and adults and is a totally unconscious activity in that the sleepwalker has no awareness of his behaviour.

Son et lumière (French: sound and light), open-air night-time entertainment set in a historic building or monument, using theatrical lighting effects and a simultaneous sound track, carrying music and an account of the history of the site. It was first used at the château of Chambord, France, in 1952.

Sonar, see ECHO SOUNDING.

Sonata, term designating both a type of composition and a musical form. In the 17th century the term implied an instrumental work in several movements for two or more players. A distinction grew up between the *sonata da chiesa*, suitable for performance in church, and the *sonata da camera*, a secular work, including dance movements. From about the mid-18th century the term was generally restricted to a work for one or two instruments. Sonata form derives from the older dance forms of the suite, where the first half ends in a key other than the tonic. In the 18th and early 19th centuries it is used regularly in a quick first movement, and often in other movements as well. Sonatas usually have three or four movements. The first movement tends to be quick. In the 18th-century sonata a minuet may occur as a middle movement or as a final movement. The rondo was a favourite choice for the last movement. The Romantic tendency to link movements was vividly illustrated by Liszt, whose Piano Sonata is in a single movement. The typical sonata form shows the following main outlines: a movement in two principal sections, the first called the exposition, and the second called the development. Two main thematic groups (the first and second subjects) make up the material of the exposition, with room for subsidiary themes and bridge passages. The first subject is in the tonic key. The second is usually in the dominant, in a movement in a major key, and in the relative major in a movement in a minor key. The exposition normally ends in a key other than the tonic. The development begins with a working-out of the foregoing material, leading to a 'recapitulation', where the first subject returns, possibly with new embellishments; the second subject now also appears in the tonic key. This necessitates a new transition between first and second subjects, and it is often here that the greatest point of interest or surprise of a sonata movement lies. The movement may end as the exposition ended, but in the tonic key; or a coda may be added. In modern times the key-relationships have ceased to have primacy, but composers often use the general configuration of the form. Sonata form is naturally not restricted to works called sonatas but occurs equally in trios, quartets, symphonies, etc.

Sondheim, Stephen (Joshua) (1930–), US lyricist and composer of popular music. He wrote the lyrics for the musicals *West Side Story*, 1957, and *Gypsy*, 1959, and the music and lyrics for *A Funny thing Happened on the Way to the Forum*, 1962; *A Little Night Music*, 1973; and *Sweeney Todd*, 1979. A revue featuring many of his songs, *Side by Side by Sondheim*, 1976, had successful runs in both New York and London.

Song, an art-form combining poetry and music, usually for vocal solo and accompaniment. The first phase of the modern art of song was the troubadour period (11th–14th centuries). In the 14th century French and Italian composers developed solo song with instrumental accompaniment, and the popularity of the lute and similar instruments in the 16th century led to the composition of songs in which the singer could accompany himself. This art reached its peak in England in the work of such composers as Dowland and Campion.

Opera in the 17th century led to the development of new forms such as recitative and aria, and to the perfecting of methods of using the voice. In the 18th century the ground was prepared for the art-song (*Lied*) of the 19th, when Schubert, Schumann and Brahms tended to cultivate strophic forms, whereas Wolf freed the vocal line from adherence to the musical structure. His example was followed by later composers.

In France outstanding contributions to song were made by Duparc, Fauré, Debussy, and Ravel. While the *Lied* tradition was carried into the 20th century by R. Strauss and Pfitzner, among others, Mahler aspired towards symphonic form. Other notable songwriters include Sibelius, Warlock, Finzi, Butterworth, Frank Bridge, and F. G. Scott. See also CANTATA; FOLK-MUSIC AND FOLK-SONG; MADRIGAL.

Song, Chinese dynasty (AD 960–1297). Its power extended over an area extending from the Great Wall in the north to the Island of Hainan in the south. Government was autocratic and the country was administered by an elite civil service.

Song of Songs (Canticles or Song of Solomon), the 22nd book of the Old Testament, a love poem attributed to Solomon but probably redacted if not compiled by a later hand. Some have made it a poetic drama, others reject its unity and make it a collection of love poems. Both Rabbis and the Church fathers overcame the problem of accepting love lyrics into the canon by using the allegorical method of interpretation, whereby the love-story is taken as an expression of God's love for his people.

Song Thrush, or mavis, *Turdus ericetorum*, a bird familiar throughout Europe, with a loud, sustained, richly varied song. It is about 20 cm long; the upper parts are light brown, the wing coverts tipped with reddish-yellow, and the yellowish neck and breast spotted with dark brown. It belongs to the family Muscicapidae of the order Passeriformes.

Songhay, descendants of the Songhai Empire which lasted from the Middle Ages until the 17th century; the 300,000 Songhay of Mali live on the River Niger below Tombouctou and are craftsmen, fishermen and farmers.

Sonic Boom, noise produced by shock waves from aircraft travelling at supersonic speeds. The disturbances in the atmosphere generated by a body in motion slower than the speed of sound (subsonic) are propagated away from the body at the speed of sound, and hence travel faster than the body itself. At supersonic speeds, however, the body moves faster than the waves it creates, and the waves are then attached to it. The waves are mostly concentrated at the nose and tail at a reasonable distance below the aircraft, and form an N-wave. These concentrated waves are shock waves and are of finite amplitude, and normally of infinitesimal thickness. As a supersonic aeroplane passes overhead at high altitude the shock wave pattern sweeps over the ground and is heard as one or two distinct bangs or booms. In many cases the sonic boom sounds similar to close thunder. The intensity of the boom at ground level depends on the aircraft size, speed, and altitude. Its character is greatly affected by atmospheric conditions.

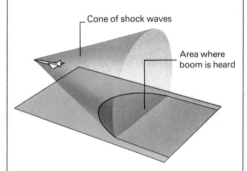

Sonic Boom. *The shock waves generated by supersonic flight form a cone with the aircraft at the apex.*

Sonnet (Italian, small sound), a poem of 14 lines, with a definite rhyme-scheme. The lines are in the prevailing metre of the language, in Italian, the hendecasyllable, in French, the alexandrine, in English, the decasyllable.

The original Italian or Petrarchan sonnet consisted of two parts—the first eight lines called the octave or octet, and the last six lines termed the sestet.

The early English employers of sonnet form were Surrey and Wyatt, followed by Spenser, Drayton, and Sir Philip Sidney. Spenser tampered with the rhymes in the octave, introducing a third rhyme, which was carried into the sestet. From these altered forms sprang the English sonnet, which was to win fame on its own account. The Shakespearean sonnet broke away entirely from Italian traditions.

With Milton the sonnet was once more written on its original model. From then onwards the sonnet received little attention from English poets until Wordsworth and Keats. Again it was the Italian sonnet form which was produced.

Soochow, see SUZHOU.

Soot, finely divided carbon resulting from incomplete combustion of organic matter, such as bituminous coal, wood, and oil. It contains some quantity of hydrocarbons and ammonium sulphate (when obtained from wood or coal), and has been used as a fertiliser.

Soper, Donald Oliver, Baron (1903–),

British Methodist minister. From 1926 to 1929 he was minister of the South London Mission, 1929–36 minister of the Central London Mission, and since 1936 he has been superintendent of the West London Mission, Kingsway Hall. A prominent pacifist and socialist, he is a prolific writer and a frequent speaker at meetings and on radio and television. He was made a life peer in 1965. He is also president of the League against Cruel Sports. His books include *Christianity and its Critics*; *It is Hard to Work for God*; *The Advocacy of the Gospel*; and *Aflame with Faith*.

Sophia (1630–1714), Electress of Hanover, daughter of the Princess Elizabeth of England and Frederick V, Elector Palatine of the Rhine, and granddaughter of James I (VI of Scotland). She married in 1658 Ernest Augustus, who became elector of Hanover in 1692. An Act of Settlement in 1701, settled the crown at the death of Anne upon the Princess Sophia and her heirs, 'being Protestant'. In June 1714 the Electress Sophia died suddenly, and on the death of Queen Anne, Sophia's eldest son succeeded to the throne of England as George I.

Sophia, Saint (Greek *Hagia Sophia*, Holy Wisdom), name of many churches, the most famous being Saint Sophia in Constantinople, built for the Emperor Justinian by Anthemius of Tralles and Isidore of Miletus, and consecrated in 538. The Holy Wisdom or Logos was a term used of Christ, to whom the churches of this name are dedicated.

Sophists, in ancient Greece, originally teachers of rhetoric and the art of disputation. They were not a school or sect, but a class of popular lecturers who aimed at imparting universal culture. After 450 BC the term covered anyone who taught for pay, and because of the repugnance felt for this practice by men such as Plato it began to acquire a derogatory meaning. It came to mean one who merely pretends to knowledge, or who attempts to make the worse appear the better cause.

Sophocles (496–406 BC), Athenian tragic poet. He won the tragic prize for the first time, with *Triptolemus*, in 468. In 440 he was one of the ten *strategoi* appointed to conduct the Samian war. Sophocles made three notable innovations in the drama. (1) He raised the number of the chorus from 12 to 15 but gave it a less direct share in the action than hitherto. (2) He introduced a third actor. (3) He produced trilogies the members of which were unconnected in subject. Only seven of his 123 plays are extant: *Ajax* (before 440); *Antigone* (440); *Electra* (between 440 and 412); *Oedipus Tyrannus* (c.431); *Trachiniae* (between 420 and 415); *Philoctetes* (409); *Oedipus Colonnus* (posthumous, 401). Besides these we possess more than 1100 fragments, including 400 lines of the satyric drama *Ichneutae* found in a papyrus at Oxyrhynchus in 1907.

Soprano, term in music denoting (1) the highest pitched voice, the usual compass being from C below treble clef to B above; (2) a singer with this voice.

Sopwith, Sir Thomas Octave Murdoch (1888–), British airman, yachtsman, and inventor. In 1910 he won the Baron de Forest £4000 prize for a flight from England to the Continent. His aircraft company (founded 1911) built several planes used in the First World War, and he assisted in the development of the Hawker Company's machines, the Hurricane, Typhoon and Tempest, in the Second World War.

Soranus of Ephesus (AD 98–138), Greek obstetrician and gynaecologist, the greatest of antiquity; his work was adopted by later writers and was unsurpassed for 1500 years. His obstetrical and gynaecological writings were published (Greek text) in 1838. He also wrote on fractures and on acute and chronic diseases.

Sorbonne, most famous of the colleges in the medieval university of Paris. It was founded in the mid-13th century by Robert de Sorbon (1207–74), chaplain to Louis IX, with the king's consent. The college was devoted entirely to theology and was regulated by the strictest discipline.

On the reorganisation of the University of Paris in 1808, the Sorbonne became the seat of the three faculties of literature, science, and theology. In 1823 the university library was moved to the Sorbonne. In 1868 the École des Hautes Etudes, and in 1897 the École des Chartes were established there. Reconstruction of the buildings was completed in 1889. Since 1969 the Sorbonne has lost its academic unity and is just a building shared by various colleges of the Paris University.

Sorbus, a genus of deciduous trees and shrubs found in Europe, North America and Asia, in family Rosaceae. *S. aria*, whitebeam, *S. aucuparia*, mountain ash or rowan, from Europe are widely cultivated. The genus is allied to, and used to be included under, *Pyrus*.

Sorcery, see MAGIC; WITCHCRAFT.

Sore Throat, a term used for many varied conditions characterised by pain in the region of the uvula, tonsils, pharynx, and larynx. Inflammation of the fauces, the region bounded by the soft palate, uvula, and tonsils, is due to micro-organisms. It may be caused by acute infection, either bacterial or viral, when it is often accompanied by other symptoms such as fever, chills, and headache. In young and middle-aged adults a sore throat sometimes persists for months, often with no other symptoms.

Sorel, Georges (1847–1922), French social philosopher. He became an engineer for the department of bridges and highways, but gave up his post in 1892 and began an intensive self-education. His outlook reflects the Anarchist philosophy of Proudhon and Bakunin, but denies any belief in progress and advocates instead a 'heroic conception of life'. Italian, Spanish, and German Fascism borrowed from Sorel's theories the concept of a corporate state and of a heroic myth to sustain popular enthusiasm.

Sorghum, a genus of annual or perennial grasses, in family Gramineae, native to warm countries. *S. vulgare*, probably African in origin, has several varieties, such as *saccharatus*, sweet sorghum, grown for its sugary sap and also for fodder. Sorghums grown for their long, stiff, branched panicles (*technicus*) are known as broomcorn; those grown for grain include *drummondii* (chicken-corn), and *caffrorum* (Kaffir corn). *S. halepense*, Johnson grass, is a perennial, grown for hay or pasture in mild countries, but is often a troublesome weed. *S. sudanensis*, Sudan-grass, and *S.*

virgatus, Tunis-grass, are annuals grown for forage.

Millet is generally similar to *Sorghum*, but is not very closely related botanically.

Sorocaba, town of Brazil, in the state of São Paulo, 90 km west of São Paulo city, on Sorocaba river. One of the leading industrial towns of the country, it has cotton and silk spinning mills, and manufactures cement, hats, footwear, alcohol, and fertilisers. There are also railway workshops and printing works. Population (1975) 208,287.

Sororate, institution in which a wife is replaced by her sister if she dies or is barren, because the husband's family feels that her family has failed to carry out the marriage contract of supplying a woman who will bear children for her husband.

The sororate was practised by Indians of the North American Great Basin. They also practised the levirate, by which a widow married her dead husband's brother.

Sorrel, various plants with a tangy, acid taste. *Rumex acetosa*, British sorrel, and *R. scutatus*, French sorrel, of the Polygonaceae, are sometimes grown as salad vegetables or substitutes for spinach. *Oxyria digyna* (Polygonaceae) is mountain sorrel; *Oxalis acetosella* (Oxalidaceae) is wood sorrel.

Sorrel-tree, *Oxydendrum arboreum*, a species of the Ericaceae from North America.

Sorrento, Italian town in Campania, on the Sorrentine Peninsula of the Bay of Naples, 30 km south-east of Naples. It is a popular tourist resort. Wine is produced and citrus fruit, fish and red vases; for all of which the town has been known since Roman times. Population (1974) 13,100.

Sortes Virgilianae, method of divination in which some sacred book was opened at random, deductions being drawn from the first passage which met the eye. Early Christian literature shows that many Christians used the Bible in this way, but the practice was condemned in several councils. Muslims frequently make use of the Koran for *sortes virgilianae*.

Sortilège, or casting of lots, a system of divination. A common method is to use pieces of wood or straw, which are marked and covered up, one or more being then drawn out at random.

Sosigenes (fl.1st century BC), Alexandrian astronomer and mathematician. He was employed by Caesar to reform the calendar and it appears from Pliny that he taught that the motion of Mercury is round the Sun. All that remains of his work consists of extracts from his *Revolving Spheres*, preserved in the 6th-century commentary by Simplicius on Aristotle's *De caelo*.

Sosnowiec, town of Poland, in Katowice province, on the River Czarna Przemsza, 10 km east of Katowice. It is a metallurgical centre, and has engineering, chemical, and other industries. Population (1979) 241,000.

Soteriology (Greek *sōtēriā*, salvation), branch of theology which deals with the salvation of mankind by Jesus Christ.

Soto, Fernando de (1496–1542), Spanish explorer, voyaged to Darien in 1519 and joined the expedition to Nicaragua in 1527. From the conquest of Peru, in which he seconded Pizarro, he returned home with 180,000 ducats, and as a result the Emperor

Charles V permitted de Soto to embark at his own expense on the subjugation of Florida. He set out in 1539 in search of El Dorado. In 1541 he discovered the River Mississippi, but his companions were decimated by disease and continual skirmishes with the Indians, and all the clues to the source of the treasure proved elusive. In 1542 de Soto died of fever and disappointment, and the remnants of his expedition eventually reached Mexico.

Sōtō, one of the two chief schools of Zen Buddhism in Japan, the other being Rinzai.

Soufflot, Jacques Germain (1713–80), French neo-classical architect. He studied for several years in Rome. In Lyons he made his reputation with the Hôtel Dieu, 1740. After further study in Rome, he returned to Paris, and in 1755 won the important competition for the church of St Geneviève.
See also PANTHÉON.

Soufrière (sulphur), name of several active and inactive volcanoes in the West Indies, among them Grande Soufrière on southern Basse-Terre Island, Guadeloupe, at 1484 m; La Soufrière at the north end of St Vincent in the Windward Islands, at 1234 m, and another on southern Montserrat in the Leeward Islands, at 914 m.

Soul (Greek *psyche*, Latin *anima*) religious concept of an immaterial element in man, capable of existence apart from the body, and immortal seat of the personality and of life, physical as well as intellectual, moral, aesthetic, and spiritual, in respect of which last it is sometimes called the Spirit.

Soult, Nicolas Jean de Dieu (1769–1851), Duke of Dalmatia, French soldier. He joined the French army as a private (1785). His promotion was rapid: after Fleurus he was made general of a brigade (1794). He commanded in Spain and Portugal, and after his defeats at La Coruña (1809), Albuera (1811), and Salamanca (1812), he displayed brilliant generalship in pitting his raw recruits against Wellington's veterans. After Waterloo he was banished till 1819. He was twice minister for war under Louis-Philippe, and was premier in 1832, and from 1840 to 1847.

Sound, term used to mean both the sensation received via the ears and the vibrations that cause the sensation. Everything that makes sound does so by vibrating. The surrounding medium (air, for example) vibrates and waves spread out in every direction. If they hit the tympanum (eardrum), it too vibrates and the vibrations are transmitted by small bones to detector cells inside the ear. Here, nerve impulses are set up and register in the brain as a sensation of sound. Human ears cannot detect vibrations slower than about 30 Hz. Middle C corresponds to 261 Hz. Human ears can also not detect frequencies above about 22,000 Hz. If (as for example, in outer space) there is no material to vibrate, sound cannot be conducted. Sound waves are *longitudinal*, i.e. the vibrations through which the waves are propagated take place in the direction in which the waves are travelling. The velocity with which sound travels in air at ordinary temperatures is about 340 m/s or 1200 km/h while its velocity in water is about 1400 m/s; in solids the velocity with which sound travels is considerably greater. Laplace showed that the velocity of sound in a gas is given by

the equation $V = \sqrt{(\gamma p/d)}$ where p is the pressure of the gas, d its density, and γ the ratio of the specific heat of the gas at constant pressure to its specific heat at constant volume. For air and other diatomic gases γ has the value of 1·41; for monatomic gases $\gamma = 1·67$. The velocity of sound in a solid vibrating longitudinally is given by the equation $V = \sqrt{(Y/d)}$ where Y is Young's modulus of elasticity for the solid. For a perfect gas, the velocity varies as the square root of its absolute temperature. Thus sound travels faster in warm air than in cold air.
Loudness. Common observation shows that loudness depends only on the amplitude or extent of the vibration of the sounding body.
Pitch. The pitch of a note is governed solely by the frequency with which the sounding body vibrates. The eight notes that comprise the *diatonic scale* of modern music are given below with their frequency ratios reduced to their simplest terms.

C D E F G A B c
24 : 27 : 30 : 32 : 36 : 40 : 45 : 48

The actual frequency of any note in the scale may be calculated from this table, since the frequency of C is 261 Hz.
Harmonics. If a string is plucked in the middle, the note emitted is called the *fundamental* note of the string. If it is damped at the middle and bowed elsewhere, it emits the octave of the fundamental note. When damped at a point one-third of its length from a fixed end, the note emitted has a frequency three times that of the fundamental. In general, if a string is damped at a point $1/n$ of its length from a fixed end, the note emitted has a frequency n times that of the fundamental, where n is any integer. This note is known as the $(n-1)$th overtone or *harmonic* of the fundamental note.
Ultrasonics. Vibrations of frequency beyond the audible range are called ultrasonic. Many animals and birds can emit and detect vibra-

tions inaudible to the human ear. For example, a bat avoids obstacles by emitting pulses of ultrasonic waves of frequency about 50,000 Hz. It emits about 60 pulses per second in flight, and these are reflected even by small objects. The bat is able to assess the direction from which the reflected waves come, and the interval between their emission and return; it can thus estimate both the direction and distance of obstacles, by means essentially similar to those used in radar. Ultrasonic waves in water are used for echo sounding.
See also ACOUSTICS; DECIBEL; DOPPLER, JOHANN CHRISTIAN; ECHO SOUNDING; NOISE.

Sound Ranging first assumed importance during the First World War, when it was employed to detect the positions of enemy gun batteries. The intervals that elapsed between the instants at which the sound of a gun reached three receiving stations were recorded, and from a knowledge of the velocity of sound in air and the exact positions of the three stations, the enemy battery could be located. The principle of sound ranging is today important in SONAR.
See also ECHO; ECHO SOUNDING.

Sound Recording and Reproduction. In the main systems of recording sound, sound waves are converted by a microphone into variable electrical signals (audio signals) which are then 'stored' either on a plastic disc or on magnetic tape. There is also a third method, used for the sound track on ciné film, which records the sound photographically.
The familiar record disc is produced from a pressing made from a master disc. This is cut by a stylus vibrated by the audio signals. The stylus cuts a spiral groove across the face of the recording disc, which captures the audio signals as a series of characteristic ridges. The disc is played back by means of another stylus in a record player. When this stylus is placed in the groove of the rotating disc, it vibrates. The vibrations are converted into electrical signals that are approximations of the original

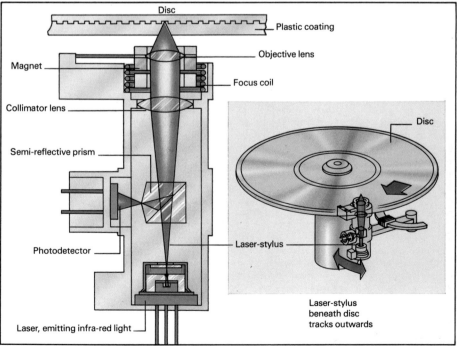

Sound Recording and Reproduction. *The microscopic pits on the underside of a compact disc are read by laser. The reflected light is converted by a photoelectric cell into an electrical signal and fed to an amplifier.*

audio signals. This system is known as analogue recording, since the ridges in the record groove are physical models or analogues of the audio signals.

A great improvement in the fidelity of reproduction has been brought about by digital recording methods. In this system the audio signals are converted into digital pulses, in which the signals are accurately represented by precise numbers. The playback signals can therefore be made virtually identical to the original audio signals, and the result is near-perfect reproduction.

Further refinement has been brought about by a totally new disc playback method. It uses a much more compact disc, typically 11·4 cm across, in which the digital pulses are stored in the form of microscopic pits beneath a plastic coating. The compact disc is played by a very low-powered laser beam instead of by a stylus. The beam picks up information as it is reflected from the pits. A photocell then converts the reflected beam into electrical signals which are fed to the speaker.

In ordinary tape recording the audio signals from a microphone are converted by a recording head (a form of electro-magnet) into variable magnetic signals. These in turn induce a pattern of magnetism in magnetic tape, which consists of a plastic ribbon coated with iron oxide or chromium oxide particles. On playback the magnetic pattern induces a corresponding electrical signal, which is a replica of the original audio signal.

As with disc-recording, digital techniques are becoming widespread in professional tape recording, resulting in an increase in fidelity. See also RECORD PLAYER; STEREOPHONY; TAPE RECORDER.

Soup, a liquid food made by boiling vegetables, bones and meat. Its main function in the diet is to stimulate the digestive juices. It is most usually served as a first course.

Sousa, John Philip (1854–1932), US bandmaster, author and composer. His compositions include numerous marches: *Stars and Stripes for Ever*, *Imperial Edward*, etc., operettas, waltzes and songs.

Sousse, seaport and commercial centre of central Tunisia. Fishing, especially sardines, is important, and other industries include textile milling, olive oil manufacture, and food canning. Population (1974) 90,000.

Soustelle, Jacques (1912–), French scholar and politician. He is an expert on Aztec civilisations. He joined Gen. de Gaulle in London during the Second World War, and became minister for information in 1945. He was the leading Gaullist deputy, and was governor-general in Algeria. He played a leading part in the events of 1958 that led to the establishment of the Fifth Republic. He quarrelled with de Gaulle over Algerian policy, and was exiled from 1962 to 1968.

Souterrains, or underground dwellings, have a very wide geographical distribution. They are found in China, Korea and Japan, in Iceland, Greenland and North America, and in one form or another in most countries of Europe. They vary as much in form as in distribution, and in date range from prehistoric to modern times.

In modern archaeology, souterrains are small underground caverns lined and roofed with boulders or stone slabs.

Other kinds of ancient monument to which the name souterrain has been wrongly applied in the past include pit-dwellings and storage-pits of the early Iron Age, common in the south of England. See also ARCHAEOLOGY.

South Africa
Area: 1,140,519 km²
Population: 24,000,000
Capital: Pretoria

South Africa, formerly Union of South Africa, now Republic of South Africa (RSA), independent state in the southernmost portion of Africa, comprising the four provinces of Cape Province, Natal, Orange Free State, and Transvaal. South Africa is bounded on the north-east by Mozambique, on the north by Zimbabwe, on the north-west by Botswana, and on the west by South-West Africa. South Africa administers South-West Africa (SWA, also known as Namibia) as an integral part of the republic. Area 1,140,519 km².

Most of South Africa is part of the vast interior plateau of southern Africa, with an average altitude of 1250 m. The lowland belt along the 3000-km long coast varies in width from 5 to 50 km, mainly about 150 m above sea-level. There are several great mountain ranges including the Drakensberg, Stormberg, Roggeveld, Bokveld, Nieuveld, and Kamiesberg. South Africa's two most important rivers are the Orange and the Limpopo. The Africans originating in the central and eastern parts of South Africa belong to four main groups, all Bantu-speaking: Nguni, Sotho, Shangaan-Tsonga and Venda.

Fundamental to the South African political system is the policy of apartheid, or separate development. As a result certain areas of the country are designated 'white', and others Bantu 'homelands'. Within the urban structure districts are similarly designated 'white', 'coloured' or African.

In 1979 there were an estimated 4,446,000 whites, 2,533,000 coloureds, 792,000 Asians, and 16,320,000 blacks in South Africa; the total population was 24,000,000. The main towns are Johannesburg, Cape Town (legislative capital), Pretoria (administrative capital), Durban and Port Elizabeth.

The biggest agricultural export is wool, followed by maize and maize products, sugar, preserved fruit and jam, citrus fruit, deciduous fruit, and hides and skins.

Normally South Africa produces enough wheat and other grains to be self-supporting. Cattle thrive, allowing meat and dairy produce to be exported in good years. In the western Cape there is an important wine industry, started over 250 years ago. In the last two decades South Africa has built up a big fishing industry.

The country is endowed with great mineral resources, and virtually every known mineral is found except oil. South Africa is the world's biggest producer of gold, gem diamonds, and antimony, and is important as a producer of other minerals: asbestos; beryl; chromite; industrial diamonds; manganese; platinum; uranium; and vanadium. Uranium is produced as a by-product of gold.

Local raw materials encourage the manufacture of cotton and wool textiles of every type, and there is an important clothing industry. All classes of light engineering are represented, and industries based on wood (furniture, paper, pulp, synthetic fabrics) are well developed. Vehicle assembly plants have been established and South Africa's aircraft and armaments industries have grown quickly.

Forty per cent of South Africa's manufacturing industries are located in the southern Transvaal, in the so-called Vaal Triangle, and other important areas are at Port Elizabeth-Uitenhage and Durban-Pinetown.

South Africa. The Holland Mountains near Somerset West in the south-west tip of the country.

The unit of currency is the *Rand* of 100 cents, introduced in 1961.

The head of state is the State President. He is elected by an electoral college consisting of the members of the House of Assembly and holds office for seven years. The executive government of the Republic is vested in the State President acting on the advice of the Executive Council which consists of ministers who must not number more than 18. The legislative power is vested in Parliament. There is an advisory Presidents' Council of white, Indian, coloured and Chinese representatives.

The official languages are English and Afrikaans.

History. The original inhabitants of the Cape when Bartholomeu Dian, the Portuguese navigator, first rounded the Cape of Good Hope in 1488, were the Bushmen, a nomad people, and Khoi-Khoi (Hottentots). In 1652 Jan van Riebeeck established the first staging post for east-bound ships of the Dutch East India Company. Around 1770 stock farmers, or Boers, moving east, encountered the Xhosa of the Nguni tribes, at the Great Fish River. This was the beginning of a black/white struggle in South Africa which is not yet resolved.

In 1795 when the British first occupied the Cape the total white population was only about 15,000. Dutch possessions in South Africa were later ceded to Britain by the Treaty of Amiens, 1814. British insistence on 'anglicising' the Colony was deeply resented. The Great Trek of 1834–38, when about 10,000 men, women, and children left the Colony in their covered ox-wagons, was an attempt to establish independent republics of which only the Orange Free State and the South African Republic (Transvaal) survived. Britain subsequently withdrew all claim to exercise authority north of the Vaal and Orange rivers.

After the discovery of diamonds in Kimberley in 1870 and of gold on the Witwatersrand in 1886 foreigners or 'uitlanders' flooded into the small republics to develop the mines. An attempt by the British to annex the South African Republic was defeated in the first Anglo-Boer War at Majuba Hill in 1881. The uitlander problem was behind the second Anglo-Boer war which started on 11 October 1899. When the war ended in the Peace of Vereeniging on 31 May 1902 most Boer homesteads and farms had been destroyed. To protect the women and children the British concentrated them in camps (hence concentration camps) where 26,000 died from disease. The tragedy created immense bitterness among Afrikaners and contributed to the later Anglo-Afrikaner political struggle which continues to this day.

Britain annexed the South African Republic and the Orange Free State but both were given responsible government in 1906 and 1907. A National Convention (1908–10) dominated by Lord Milner, Smuts, and Botha, and composed of white representatives of the four colonies, drafted a constitution for the Union of South Africa. In 1910 the Union of South Africa achieved independence within the British Empire, under the premiership of Gen. Louis Botha.

In 1934 the House of Assembly passed two Status Bills, which confirmed that the Union parliament was independent of legislative control by the British parliament. In 1936 the South African parliament adopted the Bantu Representation Act, removing Africans in Cape Province from the Voters' Roll. It also passed the Native Land & Trust Act 1936, allocating less than 14 per cent of South Africa's land as African 'reserves'.

At the outset of the Second World War Hertzog, leader of the fore-runner of the Nationalist Party, declared that South Africa would remain neutral. He was challenged by Smuts and on 4 September 1939 was defeated in parliament. Hertzog resigned and Smuts became premier.

Since Union in 1910 legislation under successive governments had increasingly restricted the civil rights and movement of Indians and blacks but it was the Malan government that elevated practice into a theory of apartheid or 'separate development'. The Defiance Campaign of 1952 was a non-violent mass movement aimed by blacks at drawing attention to the worst of their grievances. The campaign collapsed and most of its leaders and supporters were exiled or imprisoned.

In 1954 J. G. Strijdom succeeded Malan as prime minister and Dr H. F. Verwoerd succeeded Strijdom in 1958. On 31 May 1961, after tragic incidents at Sharpeville and Lange which had been followed by penal legislation, including the banning of the African National Congress and the Pan Africanist Congress, South Africa became a republic outside the Commonwealth.

At every election the Nationalists maintained their majority. In 1966 Verwoerd was assassinated and Balthazar Johannes Vorster became prime minister. South Africa intervened militarily in the Angolan guerilla war in 1976, action that destroyed South Africa's improving relations with black Africa. Pieter Botha, the former defence minister succeeded Vorster as premier in 1978.

In the 1970s several Homeland leaders such as Chief Buthelezi of KwaZulu and Chief Phatudi of Lebowa emerged as national African leaders urging a common programme of reform. Chief Mantanzima of the Transkei was the first to seek independence for his Homeland in 1976. New African-orientated organisations have sprung up, but have had their activities circumscribed by the banning of able leaders or limitation of funds.

Despite the establishment, in 1969 and 1968 respectively, of the Coloured Persons Representative Council and the South African Indian Council, the political equivalent of the Homeland Administrations, coloureds and Indians have no effective territorial base.

South African War, see BOER WARS.

South America, the southern portion of a continental mass lying between the Pacific and the Atlantic Oceans, joined to the northern portion by the isthmus of Panama. It comprises the ten republics of Brazil, Argentina, Venezuela, Colombia, Ecuador, Peru, Chile, Bolivia, Paraguay, and Uruguay, besides Guyana, Suriname and French Guiana. Its area is about 18,200,000 km². The extreme longitudes are Cape Branco, 35°W, and Punta Parina, 81°W, and the extreme latitudes Punta Gallinas, 12°30′N, and Cape Horn, 56°S.

South American Native Languages fall into four vast linguistic regions. The Chibcha or Muysca (*muhizca cehà*, body of five extremities, man) linguistic family comprises languages spoken in the southern part of Central America and in the north-west of South America, that is, from south Nicaragua through Costa Rica, Panama, Colombia, to north Ecuador. Cuna or Túle, a branch of the Chibcha, has its own ancient picture-writing, and is spoken by some 25,000 people on the Gulf of Darien (Panama). Another branch, Guaymi, is spoken north of the isthmus.

In the Caribbean area various languages and dialects are spoken by peoples inhabiting the tropical forests and grasslands extending from the Cordilleras to the Atlantic and from the River Plate to the Antilles. These languages belong to four main linguistic families: Arawak; Carib; Tapuya or Tabuya; and Tupi or Tupi-Guarani. The latter is the only native language of South America officially used in newspapers and public speeches.

The central Andean plateau, the region of the Inca Empire, extending from Ecuador to Chile, was inhabited by Quéchua-speaking peoples. In the northern part of the empire lived the Chimu, speaking a Mochica language not belonging to the Quéchua family. Their descendants, the Yunca, live along the coast, but Quéchua, subdivided into various dialects, is still the main native language.

The native population of the southern grasslands and forests, including the greater part of Uruguay, Argentina, and Chile, belongs to three or four linguistic families, comprising many languages. Of these the principal are Pampean, Tehuel-che or Patagonian, Araucan, Guaycurú, and Fuegian.

See also MEXICAN AND CENTRAL AMERICAN NATIVE LANGUAGES; NORTH AMERICAN NATIVE LANGUAGES.

South Australia, state of the Commonwealth of Australia bounded on the south by the Southern Ocean, with Queensland, New South Wales, and Victoria to the east, and West Australia on its western border. The total area of South Australia is 984,000 km². Most of South Australia is under 600 m in height, and the eastern half of the state is under 150 m. The area around Lake Eyre lies below sea-level and is the lowest elevation of the Australian continent. Much of the state is desert, chiefly the Great Victoria and Simpson deserts, which are covered by sand ridges. There are three ranges of mountains; the Mount Lofty Ranges (maximum height 727 m), the Flinders Ranges (maximum height 1165 m), and the Musgrave Ranges (1440 m). There are also wide expanses of flat or undulating land, particularly the Nullabor Plain in the south. Apart from the Murray river system, most of South Australia's drainage network operates intermittently, feeding into salt lakes such as lakes Eyre, Torrens, Frome, and Gardner.

The population in 1976 was 1,244,700. Adelaide, the capital and main commercial centre, had a population of 899,300. Other important towns of the state are Port Pirie, Whyalla, and Port Augusta. The number of aboriginals was 10,174.

Agriculture, severely restricted throughout most of the state by unreliable rainfall, is concentrated in the south-east, on the Yorke

Caribbean Sea
ARUBA (NETH.)
CURAÇAO (NETH.)
BARBADOS
GRENADA
TRINIDAD and TOBAGO
Barranquilla
Panama-Canal
Panamá
PANAMA
Caracas
Cuidad Bolívar
VENEZUELA
Orinoco
Georgetown
GUYANA
Paramaribo
SURINAM
FR. GUIANA
Cayenne
Medellín
Magdalena
Cauca
Bogota
Cali
COLOMBIA
Guiana Highlands
ATLANTIC
OCEAN
Quito
ECUADOR
Negro
Belem
Equator
Japura
Iquitos
Putumayo
Marañon
Amazon
Manaus
AMAZONAS
Fortaleza
Jurua
Purus
Madeira
Selvas
Tapajos
Xingu
Tocantins
São Francisco
Recife
PERU
BRAZIL
Lima
Cuzco
Mato Grosso Plateau
Salvador
Titicaca
Arequipa
La Paz
BOLIVIA
Goias Massif
Brasília
Brazilian
PACIFIC
Arica
Sucre
Highlands
Iquique
Belo Horizonte
OCEAN
PARAGUAY
Antofagasta
Pilcomayo
Paraguay
Paraná
São Paulo
Rio de Janeiro
Tropic of Capricorn
San Felix I. (Chile)
San Ambrosio I. (Chile)
Salta
Salado
Gran Chaco
Asunción
Curitiba
CHILE
ARGENTINA
Corrientes
Juan Fernandez Is. (Chile)
Mendoza
URUGUAY
Santiago
Montevideo
Buenos Aires
Rio de la Plata
Pampas
Colorado
Bahia Blanca
Temuco
ATLANTIC
Chiloé
OCEAN
Patagonia
Stanley
FALKLAND IS. (BR.)
Magellan's Strait
Punta Arenas
Tierra del fuego
SOUTH GEORGIA (BR.)
Cape Horn

SOUTH AMERICA

0 Km   500   1000   1500

peninsula and north of Adelaide as far as Peterborough. Main crops are wheat, barley, and hay. Viticulture is extensive: vines, which also yield raisins and currants for export, are grown under irrigation. Oranges and peaches are other important crops. Stock-raising is the traditional type of farming. Outside Adelaide the two most important industrial undertakings are steel and shipbuilding at Whyalla and the lead smelters at Port Pirie. Metal processing employs the largest percentage of the state's 118,000 employees in manufacturing.

The iron-ore deposits of the Middleback range are used to supply the steel industry at Port Kembla and Newcastle. South Australia also has the bulk of Australia's gypsum. Because of the arid climate large salt deposits are found around Port Augusta and Whyalla and from here two-thirds of Australia's salt requirements are met. The state has large deposits of oil and natural gas in the Gidgealpa and Moomba fields. There is a petrochemical complex at Redcliffe. South Australia also possesses large opal and pyrites deposits.

The parliament of South Australia consists of a Legislative Council and a House of Assembly. Responsible government is carried out by a governor and 12 ministers, members of the legislature, who form the Cabinet and are ex-officio members of the Executive Council.

In 1831 Major Baron suggested the desirability of forming a British settlement in the neighbourhood of the Murray river. The province was founded on Gibbon Wakefield's system of colonisation under an Act of 1834. The first colonists landed at Kangaroo Island but the settlement was almost immediately transferred to the mainland, where the province was proclaimed at Glenelg on 28 December 1836. The discovery of copper at Kapunda in 1842 and at the Burra in 1845 paved the way to prosperity. South Australia became a state of the Australian Commonwealth in 1901.

South Bend, city and county seat of St Joseph county, Indiana, USA, on the St Joseph river, 120 km east of Chicago. It manufactures automobiles, aeroplanes, machinery, foundry products, and has food-processing industries. Population (1980) 109,727.

South Carolina (Palmetto State), one of the 13 original states of the USA, with an area of 80,432 km². It is bounded on the north by North Carolina, on the east by the Atlantic Ocean, and on the south-west by Georgia. Along the coast is a belt of low swampy marine terraces, inland lies a series of parallel ridges and vales, while in the far west the surface rises to the rolling upland of the Piedmont plateau. All three divisions of the state carry considerable areas of forest, chiefly pine, poplar, oak, and hickory.

Traditionally agricultural, South Carolina has experienced a rapid industrialisation. There are about 1 million ha under crops, of which about 150,000 are under corn, 120,000 under cotton, and 25,000 under tobacco, the leading single source of farm income. South Carolina is the second biggest US producer of peaches after California. The state has a large share in the Southern textile industry, and other principal groups of manufactures are forest-based. In 1980 the population was 3,068,000.

The first permanent settlement in South Carolina was made by the English in 1670, and Charleston soon became the chief town, as well as serving as principal seaport. The colony remained under a proprietary government with North Carolina until 1729, when it became a separate Crown colony. The capital is Columbia.

South Dakota (Coyote State), state of the north-central USA, bordered on the north by North Dakota, on the east by Minnesota and Iowa, on the south by Nebraska, and on the west mainly by Wyoming. It has an area of 199,550 km². It was admitted to the Union in 1889 and its capital is Pierre. Most of the state's surface is made up of the Great Plains, rising gently from east to west and deeply dissected along the lines of the Missouri river and its tributaries to form the so-called 'badlands' topography which, on the White river, becomes so spectacular and castellated that the area has been designated a national monument. In the south-western corner of the state there is a dramatic interruption of this level surface, where the granitic Black Hills form a forested dome rising to over 2200 m in Harney Peak. The Black Hills were regarded as sacred ground by Indians, but as a source of gold by white men (South Dakota is today the US's largest producer of gold), and inevitably conflict ensued. Today the area is chiefly notable as a tourist attraction; it includes the Mount Rushmore Memorial.

South Dakota is bisected by the Missouri river. The eastern half of the state has an economy resembling that of the Corn Belt further east, with intensive livestock raising on fodder crops. West of the river, ranching on the natural range grasses is the dominant activity. The state developed no large urban centre; the towns are agricultural markets pure and simple. Population (1980) 690,178.

South Downs, see DOWNS, NORTH AND SOUTH.

South-East Asia, a subdivision of the continent of Asia that is broadly divided into two parts: mainland and insular. Mainland South-East Asia is usually defined as including Vietnam, Burma, Laos, Cambodia, Thailand, Malaysia, and Singapore; it consists in the main of north-south trending mountain ranges and valleys associated with some of the world's largest rivers, e.g. the Mekong and Irrawaddy. The insular sector includes Philippines, Brunei, and Indonesia, and either forms an island arc off the coast of Asia or part of the Asian continental shelf. The climate is predominantly tropical and the natural vegetation is forest. The area is very diverse culturally but similar in the type of agriculture that prevails, i.e. rice growing, and thus the economic development of most of the countries has been broadly along the same lines. The political fragmentation of the area and the internal and external struggles of the various states has been a notable feature of the region in the 20th century. See individual country entries.

South-East Asia Collective Defence Treaty, South-East Asian counterpart to the North Atlantic Treaty, signed in Manila on 8 September 1954 between Britain, the USA, Australia, New Zealand, Pakistan, France, Thailand, and the Philippines for their 'continuous and effective self-help and mutual aid'. The organisation was weakened by the refusal of India, Indonesia, and Sri Lanka to join it, changing attitudes in Australia and New Zealand, the collapse of US policy in Indo-China, the resignation of Pakistan from the organisation in 1973, and the refusal of France to participate after 1974. SEATO came to an end on 30 June 1977.

South Georgia, island in the South Atlantic Ocean lying between 54°00′ S and 54°55′ S and 35°45′ W and 38°05′ W. It is about 169 km long and 32 km wide with steep glaciated mountains and an indented coastline. It is part of the Falkland Islands Dependencies. James Cook landed here in 1775 and took possession for King George III, after whom the island is named. The island was occupied briefly by the Argentinians in 1982 during the Falkland crisis.

South Glamorgan, see GLAMORGAN, SOUTH.

South Island, see NEW ZEALAND.

South Korea
Area: 98,000 km²
Population: 37,019,000
Capital: Seoul

South Korea, or officially the Republic of Korea, came into being in 1948 when an independent republic was established south of the 38th parallel as a result of the UN-supervised elections. It is bounded on the north by North Korea, on the west by the Yellow Sea, on the south by the Korea Strait, and on the east by the Sea of Japan. It occupies the major part of the Korean peninsula. Capital, Seoul. Area 98,000 km². Population (1978) 37,019,000.

In recent years economic progress has been substantial, in large part because, as in the case of Taiwan, the US has been determined to turn South Korea into a showcase for capitalism in an Asian setting.

Agriculture remains the basis of the economy. The production of rice rose from 3 million t in 1955 to over 5·8 million t by 1978. In the production of other food crops, such as barley and sweet potatoes, there have been increases of the same order. Nevertheless, because of its dramatic increase in population, South Korea remains a food deficit area. Deep-sea fishing is important. Minerals include tungsten and anthracite. A wide variety of light consumer goods is now being produced. Additionally, the production of steel, fertilisers, and cement have increased markedly. The principal industrial cities are Seoul (the capital city) and Pusan. The official language is Korean. The national anthem is *The East Sea and Mount Paektu*.

The national flag has a disc divided horizontally by an S-shaped line, red above and blue below, on a white background with parallel black bars in each corner.

History. The Republic of Korea was established in the southern half of Korea on 15 August 1948. The Korean War, which broke out in June 1950 and ended in a truce signed in July 1953, ruined South Korea. The country lost 226,000 troops. South Korea's economic recovery was hindered under Syngman Rhee and Chang Myon by poor planning and inefficient execution, involving wide corruption. Since 1961 successive economic plans have been more capably worked out and implemented with increasing confidence. Capital has been provided almost entirely by foreign loans, mainly from the USA and Japan. Syngman Rhee's government was overthrown by popular demonstrations in April 1960, and a Democratic party prime minister, Chang Myon, presided over a year of political confusion, which was ended by a military coup in May 1961. The leader of the military junta, Park Chung Hee, was elected president, as candidate of a new party, in October 1963, and re-elected in May 1967, and, after amendment of the constitution, again in April 1971. In October 1972 President Park suspended the South Korean constitution and in November a national referendum approved what was called the Yushin, or 'Revitalisation', constitution. Normalisation talks have been held with North Korea since the early 1970s.

After a military take-over and period of martial law in 1980, a new constitution was approved.

See also NORTH KOREA, *History*.

South Orkney Islands, group of mountainous, ice- and snow-covered islands lying in the South Atlantic Ocean between 60°20′ and 60°50′S and 44°20′ and 46°45′W. They were discovered in 1821 by a joint British-American expedition. The islands lie within the British Antarctic Territory.

South Ossetian Autonomous Oblast lies in the Georgian SSR, USSR, on the southern slopes of the main Caucasus range. The economy is based on sheep and goat breeding, and some handicraft industries. The *oblast* was formed in 1922; capital, Tskhinvali. Area 3900 km². Population (1980) 98,000.

South Pole, see ANTARCTICA.

South Sea Bubble, name popularly given to a British financial scheme under which the directors of the South Sea Company made an offer to the government in 1720 to pay off the whole National Debt and to buy up the redeemable annuities, amounting to £800,000 a year, provided that the different public securities were consolidated into one fund in their hands and the government gave the company certain exclusive commercial privileges. The public, inflamed by the brilliant prospects of the gold and silver lands the directors said were awaiting exploitation in South America, rushed for the shares. The price of the shares eventually crashed and the failure assumed the proportions of a gigantic financial disaster. Sir Robert Walpole did much to restore national credit by arranging to assign £9 million of South Sea stock to the Bank of England, a like amount to the East India Company, and to repay the bonus of £7.5 million which the government received.

South Shetland Islands, archipelago of 12 islands lying 1000 km south-east of Cape Horn, between 61°S and 63°S and extending 450 km between 54°W and 63°W. The chief islands are Livingstone, Smith, Clarence, King George I, Elephant, and Deception. They were discovered and named by Capt. William Smith in 1819, and are now part of the British Antarctic Territory.

South-West Africa, or Namibia, territory of South Africa on the south-western coast of Africa, bounded on the north by Angola and Zambia, on the east by Botswana, and on the west by the Atlantic Ocean.

The country consists of a coastal desert region, the Namib desert, ranging from 100 to 160 km in width, mountainous central highlands, and the eastern Kalahari region. The Namib lies parallel with the Atlantic Ocean. It is mainly uninhabited, except for a few places such as the diamond workings at the mouth of the Orange river, and the ports of Lüderitz, Walvis Bay, and Swakopmund. The central plateau (average altitude 1100 m) is a watershed between the Namib and the Kalahari. The boundary rivers, such as the Orange, Cunene, Okavango, and Chobi, are the only permanent ones, but these do not rise in South-West Africa.

The country is very sparsely populated. The total population was about 908,800 in 1977, and 105,600 were whites. Bantu-speaking groups of the indigenous population include the Herero, Kakovelders, Ovambo, East Caprivians, Okavango, and a small group of Tswana; other distinctive groups are the Bushmen, Nama, Rehoboth Basters, and coloureds. The main towns are Walvis Bay, Windhoek (the capital), Lüderitz, and Swakopmund.

Cattle contribute 60 per cent of commercial agricultural output. There are 5 million karakul sheep, and South-West Africa is the leading exporter of pelts. By 1964 fishing was second to mining as an export earner.

Diamonds, mainly from alluvial deposits in the coastal belt, account for just over half the total mineral production. Base minerals include copper (especially from Tsumeb, lead, zinc, manganese, tin, vanadium and uranium. The Republic of South Africa has been responsible for the administration of South-West Africa (Namibia) since 1920, when the then Union accepted a mandate from the League of Nations to administer the territory as an integral part of the Union. There are four self-governing regional administrations: for Whites, the Ovambo, Kavango, and Lozi (Eastern Caprivi), covering 68 per cent of the population.

There is an elected Legislative Assembly of 18 members.

The official languages are English, German, and Afrikaans.

History. In the early 1880s F. A. W. Lüderitz, a German merchant, purchased part of the south-west African coast from local Nama chiefs and Germany gradually extended its authority over the whole territory. Following the First World War, South-West Africa came under League of Nations mandate, with South Africa as the administering authority. After the Second World War, the UN General Assembly proposed that the territory should be placed under the UN Trusteeship System. South Africa refused and since 1946 the United Nations has been trying by persuasion or demand to wrest South-West Africa from South African control.

The South West Africa People's Organisation (SWAPO), the Namibian organisation recognised by the African Liberation Committee of the Organisation of African Unity (OAU),

refuses to accept an apartheid policy in Namibia and since 1966 has engaged in intermittent guerrilla activity in the territory.

South Yorkshire, see YORKSHIRE, SOUTH.

Southampton, Henry Wriothesley, 3rd Earl of (1573–1624), English courtier, Shakespeare's patron. From 1590 he was prominent at court, and Shakespeare dedicated *Venus and Adonis* and *The Rape of Lucrece* to him. Southampton was involved in Essex's Irish conspiracy, and was sentenced to death. But the sentence was commuted to life imprisonment, and he was later freed and restored to royal favour by James I.

Southampton, seaport in Hampshire, England, on a peninsula between the Test and Itchen rivers, at the head of Southampton Water, 20 km south-west of Winchester. After the Saxon invasions Southampton developed into a port of some standing, but the old walled town was not established until the Conquest in 1066.

The modern importance of Southampton is due to its magnificent natural harbour, which enjoys a double tide, and to its docks. King George V graving dock was built primarily for the *Queen Mary* and can take vessels up to 100,000 t gross. The Ocean passenger terminal building was constructed especially for the transatlantic service which was at its height in the 1930s. Southampton is still the chief passenger port and, after London and Liverpool, the busiest cargo port in the UK. Population (1981) 204,406.

Southampton Water, inlet of the English Channel, stretching from the Solent and Spithead into Hampshire, England, for about 18 km. Its greatest breadth is 3·2 km.

Southcott, Joanna (1750–1814), English religious visionary. About 1792 she declared herself to be the woman of Revelation xii, and gave forth prophecies in rhyme, several collections of which were published. Her prescriptions for universal happiness are said to have been sealed in a box which her followers will only allow Anglican bishops to open. When one did so in 1927, it was found to contain nothing of interest or value.

Southend-on-Sea, seaside resort in Essex, England, at the mouth of the Thames, 60 km east of London, the second largest seaside town in the British Isles.

Southend has a pier 2 km in length, claimed to be the longest in the world. Industries include light engineering, boat-building, brick-making, sea-moss dyeing and processing; plastics, radio components, textiles, furniture, jewellery, paint and varnish are also manufactured. Population (1981) 156,683.

Southern Alps, mountain range of South Island, New Zealand, running 325 km southwards from Arthur's Pass down the west side of the island. The rock is largely a sandstone felspar combination called greywacke. Sixteen mountains rise above 3000 m, all situated near the centre of the range. The highest peaks are Mount Cook (3764 m) and Mount Tasman (3498 m).

Southern Bug, see BUG, SOUTHERN.

Southern Cross, see CRUX.

Southern Lights (or aurora australis), see AURORA.

Southern Rhodesia, see ZIMBABWE.

Southern Yemen, see YEMEN, PEOPLE'S DEMOCRATIC REPUBLIC OF.

Southey, Robert (1774–1843), English poet, editor, and biographer. He is sometimes regarded as one of the 'Lake Poets', more because of his friendship with Coleridge and Wordsworth and residence in Keswick than for any Romantic influence felt in his work. He was an early admirer of the French Revolution, whose aims he supported in the poem *Joan of Arc*, 1796. Southey's youthful radicalism later gave way to conservatism; in 1807 he obtained a small government pension, and in 1813 he became poet laureate, after Scott had refused the honour. Southey's *A Vision of Judgement*, 1821, an adulatory estimate of George IV, provoked Byron into his satirical answer, *The Vision of Judgement*, 1822.

Southey is best remembered for short poems such as 'The Battle of Blenheim' and 'The Inchcape Rock'.

Southport, town and seaside resort in Merseyside Metropolitan County, England, 24 km south-west of Preston. Southport has length rather than breadth; 10 km long and less than 2 km inland, it is built mainly on old sand dunes. The peat mosslands away from the coastal belt provide unsuitable foundations for houses and are best used as market gardening land. Southport is a popular residential town; several thousand use the fast electrified rail services to Liverpool daily and over a thousand commute to Manchester. Population (1981) 89,745.

Southsea, seaside resort and yachting centre in Hampshire, England, on the southern side of Portsmouth, of which it is part.

Southwark, a London borough created on 1 April 1965 and including the former metropolitan boroughs of Bermondsey and Camberwell. Population (1981) 211,708.

Soutine, Chaim (1894–1943), painter, born at Smilovitchi, Lithuania, associated with the School of Paris. He made his way to Paris after working in an art school at Vilna, and like his friend Modigliani led a Bohemian life. His paintings, which include portraits, landscapes, and still-life, are distinguished by expressive distortions of form and colour.

Sovereign, large gold coin valued at 20s., introduced by Henry VII in 1489 and issued by the Tudors and Stuarts. Also a modern British gold coin of the same nominal value first struck in 1817. The reverse design by Pistrucci shows St George and the dragon. The sovereign with the same reverse design is still being struck, although it is no longer in circulation.

Sovereignty, that relationship of authority which exists between the supreme (sovereign) legitimate power in a state and its inhabitants. The existence of such a relationship as a fact can be explained by invoking the political tradition of a country, into which all inhabitants, wittingly, or unwittingly, are to some extent introduced, and through which their attitudes to political authority are formed. Since the Second World War increasing international interdependence and the growth of the influence of multinational corporations on domestic economies has led to a drastic reduction in the sphere of autonomous sovereignty.

Sovetsk (formerly German *Tilsit*), city in Kaliningrad *oblast* of the RSFSR, USSR, on the Neman 100 km north-east of Kaliningrad. It has a timber and paper industry. It was founded in 1288 by Teutonic Knights as a castle, and has been a town since 1552. Population (1970) 38,000; mostly settlers from central European RSFSR.

Soviet Central Asia, see CENTRAL ASIA (SOVIET).

Soviet Far East, territory comprising the Primorski and Khabarovsk *krai*, the Yakutsk ASSR, and the Amur, Magadan, Kamchatka, and Sakhalin *oblasti* of the RSFSR, USSR. It is a region of rich mineral deposits, and was formerly an area of banishment and labour camps. Before 1938–45 there was also a large Japanese, Korean, and Chinese population, now expelled or departed. The territory was gradually annexed by Russia between 1649 and 1875. Area 6,215,900 km². Population (1975) 6,435,000; mostly Russians, Ukrainians, and Yakuts.

Soviet Russia, see RUSSIAN SOVIET FEDERATED SOCIALIST REPUBLIC; UNION OF SOVIET SOCIALIST REPUBLICS.

Soviet System, see SOVIETS.

Soviets (Russian *sovet*, council), organs of state power in the USSR. According to the Stalin constitution of 1936, 'soviets of toilers' deputies' are the 'political basis' of the state. Local, provincial, and republican soviets, and the Supreme Soviet of the USSR, are formally elected by universal, equal, direct, and secret vote. The elections are in fact fictitious because there is always only one candidate.

From 1917 to 1936 soviets were considered organs of the Dictatorship of the Proletariat. Stalin aptly described soviets as 'transmission belts from the party to the masses'. There has always been some uncertainty as to exactly how important the soviets are in the political system of the USSR, in spite of their theoretical importance. At the local level their activity includes mobilisation of voluntary labour, maintenance and expansion of communal services, housing, sanitation and transport. This corresponds fairly closely to local government services in other countries.

The Supreme Soviet of the USSR, although in theory the supreme legislature, or parliament, meets only twice a year for a few days at a time. It then rubber-stamps a backlog of legislation, much of it already in effect, initiated by the Politburo of the party or the Council of Ministers. Its votes have, to date, without exception, been unanimous. It has two chambers, with some 1500 deputies in all.

Soweto, the largest wholly Black urban complex of townships in Southern Africa, a suburb of Johannesburg where most of the inhabitants work. It is divided into tribal areas to prevent inter-tribal strife but has been held up as a prime example of African urbanisation and the acceptance of apartheid. However, African riots in 1976 that left over 100 dead and 1200 injured, and further subsequent unrest, have damaged this image.

Soya Bean, or soybean, *Glycine (Soja) max*, *G. hispida*, and *G. soja*, in the family Leguminosae; thought to have been derived from *G. ussuriensis*, which grows wild throughout much of East Asia. It is an annual plant with branching stems and trifoliate leaves, varying widely in shape, size and colour; and bears clusters of two to five pods. These vary in length from 3 to 7 cm and contain two or three seeds. The ripe seeds may be pale yellow, green, brown or black, or a combination of these colours. The seeds are very rich in protein, about 35 per cent by weight; those of medium size usually contain the most oil, about 18 per cent by weight. The stems, leaves and pods are normally covered with brown or grey hairs.

Many varieties have been developed and are cultivated in China for special purposes, which include production of flour, soy sauce, curd, milk and sprouts. In the western hemisphere mainly pale yellow beans of medium size are cultivated, and almost the entire crop is processed for oil and flour. The oil is used in edible products and, to a lesser extent, as a technical oil and the meal for animal feed. Relatively small quantities of the meal are used in the production of plywood glues, emulsion paints and washable wallpapers. It is also used as a fertiliser, particularly in Asia.

Soybean, see SOYA BEAN.

Soyinka, Wole (1934–), Nigerian author. He was resident playwright at the Royal Court Theatre in 1958, and in 1960 returned to Nigeria to study African dramatic arts. He was twice imprisoned for political acts, in 1965 and again in 1967. When released he resumed his post as director of the school of drama at Ibadan, resigning in 1972.

Soyinka has written a number of plays, all of which draw on Yoruba theatrical traditions as well as European (especially Brechtian) ones. He has also published volumes of poetry and novels. His novel *The Interpreters*, won the Jock Campbell Prize for Commonwealth literature, 1968.

Spa, town in Belgium, 27 km south-east of Liège in the Ardennes, with mineral springs. It was in the 18th century the most fashionable resort of this kind in Europe. It has a famous casino. A large factory produces every year about 50 million bottles of Spa water. Population 9500.

Spaak, Paul-Henri (1899–1972), Belgian statesman and lawyer. From 1935 to 1945 he was minister of foreign affairs in Pierlot's government, which he accompanied to London in 1940. He was foreign minister, 1946–50, and prime minister, 1950–54. During his term of office Spaak played a part in the promotion of the Benelux customs agreement (1944); the Treaty of Rome, under which the European Economic Community was established; and the negotiations for the North Atlantic Treaty.

He was equally conspicuous in the activities of the United Nations and was elected, in January 1946, as first president of the UN Assembly. Spaak led his party's opposition to the return of Leopold III, which took place in 1950. From 1954 he was foreign minister in van Acker's government. From 1957 to 1961 he was secretary-general of NATO, and he was deputy premier and foreign minister.

Space Travel dates from the launch of the first artificial space satellite, the Soviet *Sputnik I*, on 4 October 1957. The second *Sputnik* contained a live dog, Laika, and was the first stage towards manned space travel. This came on 12 April 1961 when Yuri Gagarin made one complete orbit of the Earth and landed back in the USSR. The US space programme began with the Explorer missions in 1958, leading to the flights of John

Space Travel. The Space Shuttle was designed as a reusable spacecraft. It was first launched in 1981.

Glenn and the Apollo programme. The longest manned flight to date is 140 days, achieved by two Russians on a *Salyut* orbiting station in 1978. Other notable feats have been 'walking in space', first performed by Leonov in 1965, showing the possibility of in-flight vehicle maintenance, and rendezvous between space-craft in orbit. A joint Soviet-American project culminated in a *Soyuz-Apollo* link-up in 1975. In 1968, as part of the Apollo programme men first orbited the Moon, and in July 1969, US astronauts Armstrong and Aldrin made the first Moon landing. Since 1972 the US space programme has centred on long-duration flights in the *Skylab* space-station, and the development of the *Space Shuttle*, a re-usable vehicle which can be flown back to Earth like an aeroplane. Unmanned shots have been used to explore conditions before subjecting humans to the unknown. For example, the US *Surveyor* and *Lunar Orbiter* craft respectively soft-landed and photographed the Moon from close range to aid selection of a suitable landing site, and the Soviet automatic car, *Lunokhod*, sampled the Moon's surface. Unmanned flights to Venus indicate that it is too hot for manned landings. The US *Mariner 4* in 1965 sent the first television pictures of Mars, later refined by other *Mariner* and *Viking* probes, to see if the Martian soil contains primitive organisms. Manned spacecraft design incorporates advanced environmental control and precautions against hazards. Collision with meteorites and space debris remains a peril. Another hazard is the heat generated on re-entering the Earth's atmosphere.

Spaghetti, see PASTA.

Spain
Area: 489,506 km²
Population: 37,700,000
Capital: Madrid

Spain (Spanish *España*, Latin *Hispania*, Greek *Iberia*), country of south-western Europe, forming with Portugal the Iberian Peninsula. It is bounded on the north by the Pyrenees, on the east and south by the Mediterranean Sea, in the north-west it has a coast on the Bay of Biscay, and on the west is bounded by the Atlantic Ocean and Portugal. Gibraltar lies at its extreme southerly point. Area 489,506 km².

Geologically the peninsula is an ancient raised landmass, the *meseta*, situated between high mountains of more recent development, the Pyrenees and the ranges of Andalusia. The *meseta* is drained by a series of parallel rivers, which flow from east to west. The most important of these is the Guadalquivir, which flows through Andalusia to the Atlantic and in navigable as far as Seville. The Ebro, the longest river in Spain, runs south-eastwards in a tectonic basin to the Mediterranean, providing irrigation for the plains of Aragon and Catalonia. The line of the Pyrenees continues parallel to the south coast of the Bay of Biscay in the Cantabrian Mountains. To the south-east the Cordillera Ibérica forms the watershed between the Duero and the Tajo on the

one side and the Ebro on the other. Further south are the Betic cordilleras which end in the rocky promontory of Gibraltar. The country is divided by three parallel ranges: the Sierra Morena separates the valleys of the Guadalquivir and the Guadiana; the mountains of Toledo separate the Guadiana and the Tajo; and the Sierra de Guadarrama separates the Tajo and the Duero.

The total population (including the Balearic and Canary Islands) is 37,700,000. Madrid is the capital, and other major cities are Barcelona, Valencia, Seville and Saragossa. Urban population has grown greatly since the 1930s. Except in the humid northern coastal region, natural conditions for agriculture are poor over much of Spain because of aridity, thin soils, and abrupt relief. Only 21 million ha can be considered arable out of a total area of over 50 million ha. Wheat production, often on unsuitable land, has been diminished in exchange for fodder crops, meat, and dairy products. Fresh fruit production has also been expanded. Oranges are an important export, as also are olive products (of which Spain is the world's largest producer) and wines such as Rioja, Valdepeñas, and Jerez.

Spain is rich in minerals. Coal, iron, lead, copper, tin, zinc and tungsten are important. Apart from tourism the most dynamic branches of industry have been vehicles, ships, machinery, metal products, and chemicals.

The unit of currency is the *peseta*, which has 100 *céntimos*.

The Spanish monarch enjoys wide constitutional powers in political and administrative matters. He appoints the President of the Government (prime minister) and, on the latter's recommendation, other members of the Council of the Realm. *Las Cortes*, the Spanish parliament, is bi-cameral.

Spain's only overseas territories are the Canary Islands and two small towns in North Africa: Ceuta and Melilla.

The official language is Spanish, although Catalan is widely spoken in the north-east, and Basque in the north.

History. The history of Spain begins with the Carthaginian invasion (238 BC). The Romans drove the Carthaginians from the peninsula, but nearly two centuries elapsed before they had mastered the whole country.

With the decline of the Roman Empire, the 'barbarians of the north' entered the peninsula (AD 409), and the Visigoths remained rulers of Spain until the beginning of the 8th century. However, the administration remained modelled directly on the Roman system.

The Muslim invasion began in July 711. Tarik, the Muslim general, crossed the straits, landed in the south of Spain, and immediately defeated Roderic, the last Visigothian King. By 718 the Muslims had reached the Pyrenees. But lack of unity among the Muslims enabled the Christian states in the north to keep their identity. Gradually Castile became the leading Christian power, and played the greatest part in the reconquest of the country. Sancho the Great of Navarra and his son Ferdinand I did much to unite the kingdoms of the north. Under Ferdinand the reconquest of Spain began. He died in 1065, and his possessions were divided amongst his three sons; but the greatest share of power passed to his second son, Alfonso VI. Against the Moors Alfonso's success was immediate, and he overran the whole of Muslim Spain, although with the invasion of the Almoravides from Africa, Alfonso had to give up some of his conquests. During the next hundred years the Christian conquest of Spain continued. In 1230 the crowns of León and Castile were finally united. The union of Spain was at last accomplished in 1479.

In 1519 Charles I was elected to the throne of his grandfather Maximilian the German Emperor, and ruled as Charles V. The royal power was definitely established, the monarchy became wholly despotic, and the constitutions of the various provinces were practically abolished. Philip II, his son, succeeded him and regarded himself as the Catholic champion of Europe. His power extended over Spain, the Netherlands, the greater part of Italy, the whole of South America, a large part of North America, possessions in the East Indies and in Africa. He possessed the finest fighting machine in Europe, both military and naval. He was broken by his fatal policy in the Netherlands, which aroused the hatred of France, by the cruelties of Alva in Flanders, which led to the revolt of the Netherlands, and by his quarrel with England, which led to the destruction of the powerful Armada.

The greatest days of Spain passed with Philip's death in 1598. The century which followed saw a rapid decline; the reign of Philip III witnessed the final declaration of the independence of the United Provinces.

During the reign of the childless Charles II (1665–1700) Europe waited for the division of the spoils at his death. France, Austria, and Bavaria had claims to the Spanish throne. By the will of Charles II the whole of the Spanish dominions were left to Philip of Anjou, grandson of Louis XIV, and he was proclaimed King of Spain in May 1700. This led, however, to the War of the Spanish Succession. By the Treaty of Utrecht, 1713, Spain lost its Italian possessions, the Netherlands, Minorca, and Gibraltar.

Ferdinand VI (1746–59) and Charles III (1759–88) initiated wide reforms and reformed the revenues; but in 1788 Charles IV became king, and Spain quickly declined. In 1807 a quarrel between Charles IV and his son Ferdinand culminated in an appeal to Napoleon. The crown of Spain was ceded to him; but the Spanish people recognised only their own chosen king, Ferdinand VII and the War of Liberation (Peninsular War) began. Joseph Bonaparte was finally driven out in 1813, together with all the French troops.

A constitution for Spain was drawn up in 1812 at Cádiz, but in 1814, when Ferdinand returned to Spain he restored absolute monarchy.

In 1833 his daughter Isabella succeeded him, but her reign was chaotic. From 1833 to 1839 the country was in a state of civil war (the first Carlist war), when supporters of Don Carlos, Isabella's uncle, sought unsuccessfully to establish their leader's claim to the throne. In 1868, Isabella abdicated in favour of Alfonso XII.

From 1868 to 1870, attempts to restore peace merely supplied France and Germany with a *casus belli* for the war of 1870. Amadeus I of Savoy was finally elected to the throne but resigned after three years. For a year Spain

became a republic, and then Alfonso XII was reinstated as king. In 1885 he died, and in the following May his son, Alfonso XIII, was born and was recognised as king. In 1898 the Cuban question gave rise to the war with the USA, leading to the loss of all Spanish territory in the West Indies and Philippines.

During the First World War Spain was neutral.

On 10 August 1917 a general strike, aiming at a Socialist Democratic republic, was declared. A military revolt broke out on 13 September 1923, under Primo de Rivera. The government resigned. The king was forced to recognise a military directorate, with Primo de Rivera as president, although the king later dismissed Primo.

Spain. Part of the old walled town of Granada.

Municipal elections in April 1931 resulted in a sweeping Republican victory, the king left the country, and a provisional Republican government was set up under Alcalá-Zamora, head of a conservative group within the Republican party. The provisional Republican government was confirmed by the general elections, held on 28 June 1931. On 14 July the *Cortes* began the task of drawing up the constitution. In November ex-King Alfonso was formally outlawed, and in December Alcalá-Zamora was elected president of the Republic.

In the general elections of February 1936, the newly formed Popular Front were swept into power. But Spain was moving towards complete chaos. Right (mainly Falangists) and Left extremists were fighting in the streets. Two opposite para-military formations were being trained: the Falangist clandestinely,

Socialists, Communists, and others openly.

The Civil War began in July 1936. So carefully prepared was the plan of the insurgents under Gen. Franco that revolt was almost simultaneous in the garrisons of Spanish Morocco, Madrid, Seville, Málaga, Burgos, and Saragossa.

After a fortnight of war the republicans held south-east Spain, much of north-east Spain and Madrid, Barcelona, Valencia, and Córdoba; Franco's forces held the rest of the country, including Seville, the area around Gibraltar, and Spanish Morocco. German and Italian planes and troops were sent to aid Franco.

Insurgent forces now advanced towards Madrid in the north. Irun fell on 4 September and San Sebastian on 12 September. Meanwhile in the south and west rebel forces were advancing towards the capital and to the relief of the besieged rebel garrison in Toledo. The historic siege of the Alcázar lasted from 1 August till 27 September, when the rebel troops succeeded in recapturing Toledo. The Republican government, under Largo Caballero, moved to Valencia, leaving Gen. Miaja in command in Madrid. Meantime the Republican forces were reinforced with the International Brigades. Early in February 1937 the city of Málaga was bombarded by rebel cruisers and it fell on 8 February.

The loss of Málaga and the pressure on Bilbao led to the fall of Caballero's government. A new Socialist government was formed under Negrin, but the effective head was Prieto, the defence minister.

On 25 August Santander was taken by the insurgents. The insurgent advance through the northern Spanish provinces continued, until on 21 October Gijon fell, and resistance in the north was virtually at an end.

Elsewhere fortunes fluctuated. After losing and recapturing Teruel, and advancing towards the coast, the insurgents decided to strike from Aragon to overrun the southern part of Catalonia. After a month the rebel forces drove a wedge between Barcelona province and the rest of Republican Spain. Offensives and counter-attacks in the spring and autumn of 1938 resulted in a general stalemate. On 23 December the rebel army advanced along a 161-kilometre front. By 21 January 1939 it had reached Tarragona and was well on the way to encircling the Republican eastern army. Gradually Republican resistance crumpled. Franco confined his activities to the investment of Catalonia, confident of victory. In March Col. Casado, commander of the Republican central army, seized power in Madrid and sent emissaries to Burgos to seek terms. Franco demanded unconditional surrender and negotiations were suspended.

Franco's Spain was modelled on Fascist Italy, as a national syndicalist state under himself as El Caudillo (Spanish equivalent of 'Führer'), with power to rule by presidential decree if necessary, but with a Cabinet buttressed by the political junta of the National Council. In the Second World War, though Franco's sympathies were with the Axis powers, he kept Spain neutral.

By 1948 the Western powers were reexamining their attitude towards Spain in the light of the far greater communist threat to their stability. In 1953, under a ten-year defence agreement signed with the USA, Spain was to receive arms and economic aid and to allow the Americans the use of naval and air bases in its territory. This agreement has been periodically renewed.

The militant Basque separatist movement, ETA (*Euzkadi Ta Azkatasuna*, Basque Homeland and Liberty) waged unremitting war in the north, and Catalan nationalism, though less active, was no less well established: thus the two economically most advanced areas of Spain presented the most critical political problems for Madrid.

In 1975 the death of Gen. Franco brought a restoration of the monarchy in the person of King Juan Carlos I, and the renewal of open political debate and party activity for the first time since the 1930s.

In 1977 the first general elections since 1936 were held. A new constitution came into force in 1978. In 1980 an attempt at solving the problem of separation was made, and autonomous zones were set up for Basques and Catalans.

Language. Spanish is a Romance language, closely related to Portuguese, Italian, and French. It is today spoken not only in Spain, alongside Catalan, the Basque Language and Galician—a Portuguese dialect—but also in all the countries once contained in the Spanish Empire, that is, all Central and South America, excepting Brazil and the Guyanas, the Philippines (where it has now largely been ousted by English and Tagalog), and in areas settled by Spaniards in Morocco. It is also widely spoken in the USA, notably by immigrant Puerto Ricans, and throughout Europe by migrant workers. The total number of Spanish speakers probably exceeds 140,000,000, and its geographical extension is second only to English.

Literature. The first great work of Spanish literature, a poem concerning the exploits of the Cid, is the *Cantar de mio Cid*, written about 1140. The 16th and 17th centuries, however, saw the finest literary flowering. Following Italian models, Garcilaso de la Vega, writing in metres new to Spain, established serious love poetry. The Salamancan theologian Luis de León wrote lyric poetry on moral themes, and St John of the Cross, friend and adviser of the mystic St Teresa, reached unprecedented heights of lyricism in his mystical poetry. In prose, the literary giant is Cervantes, author of *Don Quixote*. On the stage, 'cloak and dagger' drama predominated with plays by the fecund Lope de Vega, and Tirso de Molina, creator of the legendary figure of Don Juan. Calderon added to this tradition a cultured language, and in the field of one-act allegorical religious plays, *autos sacramentales*, far outstripped his rivals.

The 18th and 19th centuries produced no comparable development. The Romantic Movement was briefly influential, and Spanish novel-writing matured into a perceptive realism with Juan Valera (1824–1905), Pedro Alarcón, Maria de Pereda, who defended fresh, provincial life against 19th-century disbelief and materialism, and Benito Pérez Galdos, master of the modern novel. With the greater stylistic liberty of the early 20th century, however, a period of refined, musical poetry named *modernismo* emerged.

Two of the movement's most important poets were Juan Ramón Jiménez (who won the Nobel Prize in 1956) and Antonio Machado, while the period's greatest prose writer was Miguel de Unamuno.

The post-First World War period is remarkable for its poetry, above all that of García Lorca who, with Jacinto Benavente, was also a noted dramatist.

After the Civil War writers found themselves, following the death or exile of most of those authors already mentioned, in a cultural vacuum. Recurrent themes have been a sense of isolation and anguish, revolt against Americanised culture (post-1956), and attempts to discover new means of negotiating the horror of civil war and the emptiness of the resultant society and régime.

See also SPANISH-AMERICAN LITERATURE.

Spalding, market town in Lincolnshire, England, on the Welland, 23 km south-west of Boston. Spalding is a horticultural and agricultural centre; tulips and daffodils are grown in great quantity, and there are manufactures of agricultural implements and tractors. Population (1981) 18,223.

Spandau, German town at the confluence of the rivers Havel and Spree; since 1920 a suburb of West Berlin. It was one of the oldest towns of Brandenburg and a residence of the electors. It was famous for its state arsenal. Today its fame derives from the prison for Nazi war criminals.

Spandrel, in architecture, a near-triangular space between the curve of the arch and an enclosing rectangle.

Spaniel, important group of dogs characterised by large, pendulous ears and long, silky hair. The Cocker spaniel weighs up to 14 kg and is a good gun dog. The American cocker spaniel is, since 1940, a separate breed, but it was originally bred from English cockers in America. The weight is 10–12 kg. The English springer is, next to the cocker, the most popular of sporting spaniels. It weighs about 22·5 kg. Toy spaniels have long been kept as pets. A popular toy breed is the Japanese chin (also called Japanese spaniel), white in colour, marked with black or red. The Tibetan spaniel has several features in common with the Pekingese, but belongs to the group.

Spanish-American Literature. In South and Central America the dominant new language after the European conquests of the 16th and 17th centuries was Spanish and, with the exception of Brazil, where Portuguese was adopted, the literature produced in these countries was written in Spanish. Early Spanish-American literature consists largely of chronicles of the conquest, which also inspired poets such as the Spaniard Alonso de Ercilla, whose *La Araucana*, 1569–89, is based on his adventures in Chile. This the first work of real literary merit in Spanish produced in America.

The end of the 18th and the beginning of the 19th century saw the dawn of the movement for independence, and romanticism flourished at this time. Domingo Faustino Sarmiento, the vehement Argentinian publicist, advised his compatriots to turn their backs once and for all on Spain and seek inspiration in their native land. The masterpiece of this period, however, is *María* by

Jorge Isaacs. Juan Zorrilla San Martín (1855–1931), a native of Uruguay and author of a novel in verse, *Tabaré*, 1888, is considered the greatest Romantic poet of Spanish America. Towards the end of the 19th century a new modernistic tendency is found in Spanish America and for the first time Spanish-American writers make their contribution to world literature. The book that heralded the transition was *Azul*, a volume of verse by the Nicaraguan Rubén Darío, 1888. Realistic novelists of this period include the Chilean, Alberto Blest Gana (1830–1920), author of *Martín Rivas*, 1862, and *Durante la Reconquista*, 1897; the Colombian, Tomás Carrasquilla (1851–1941), with *Frutos de mi tierra* and *La marquesa de Yolombó*, 1928; and the Mexican, Frederico Gamboa, whose *Santa* was published in 1903. One aspect of writing in Spanish America has been the growth of *gauchesca* literature based on native folklore. One example is the Argentinian classic *Martín Fierro*, by José Hernández.

Poetry in the 20th century followed from the work of the *modernistas* and their leader, Rubén Darío who had claimed an independence for Latin American culture. This experimentalism culminated in the 1920s and 1930s with the work of, for example Pablo Neruda and César Vallejo. Political commitment and poetic experimentation were legacies which determined the work of the succeeding generation notably that of the Mexican Octavio Paz (1914–). The 20th-century novel continued at first to be realistic-descriptive, prolonging the characterisations and plot structures of the 19th century. Themes of social injustice continued to occupy succeeding novelists, but by the 1940s the influence of experimental European and United States fiction led to greater sophistication and technical skill. For example, Miguel Angel Asturias deals with the Guatemalan Indian, but from his myths and legends, not from the descriptions of an outsider. To themes of social oppression and man's insignificance in the face of nature were later added those of urban problems.

The mentor of most writers after 1945 is the Argentinian Jorge Luis Borges. Perhaps most representative of 20th-century writers, however, are the exuberantly imaginative Alejo Carpentier and the Colombian, Gabriel García Márquez, who won the Nobel Prize for Literature in 1982.

Spanish-American War, The, was the outcome of the conditions set up in Cuba by the political discontent in the island throughout the 19th century. On 15 February 1898, the US battleship *Maine* was destroyed by an explosion in Havana harbour with the loss of 266 lives. US public opinion at once accused the Spanish officials, and a resolution was passed by Congress declaring Cuba independent and empowering the president to make Spain relinquish its claims over the island. An ultimatum to this effect was sent to Spain, fixing 23 April as the last date for submission. Spain declared war formally on 24 April.

On 17 July Spain sued for peace. In 1899 a treaty was signed, and Spain evacuated Cuba, the Philippines, and other islands.

Spanish Architecture. Spain possesses many well-preserved remains of Roman buildings, the finest surviving monuments being the great bridge over the Tagus at Alcántara, built in AD 105. The Visigoths, who invaded Spain in AD 415, were converted to Christianity, and erected a number of small churches; but only a few remaining are original, among them S. Juan de Baños near Palencia (AD 661). When the Arabs invaded Spain in 711 influences from the Middle East and North Africa were introduced. In 786 the construction of the famous mosque at Córdoba was begun, through this became a Christian cathedral in 1236.

Meanwhile the Christian Visigoths had taken refuge in the mountains of Asturias in the north of Spain, where they built a number of churches, characterized by apses, round arches and stone barrel-vaulting. In the province of León, several 'Mozarabic' churches were built in the 10th century. A great boom in church-building began in north Spain in the 11th century; the finest Romanesque example is the cathedral of Santiago de Compostela (1075 onwards). Abreast of these, but over a long period, the Moors in the south built the Alhambra at Granada (c.1377).

Gothic churches in Spain are derived from French and German sources. They include the cathedral of Toledo, 1227.

The arrival of the Renaissance in Spain during the 16th century coincided with the 'Plateresque' style of which there are many examples in Salamanca and Zaragoza. The larger houses of this period focused on an internal courtyard (patio). The fully developed Italian Renaissance influence appears in Philip II's immense ecclesiastical palace, 'the Escorial', begun in 1559.

The Baroque style was welcomed enthusiastically and can be seen most picturesquely in the façade of the cathedral of Santiago (1738), and the royal palace at Madrid (1738).

After c.1750, Spanish architecture experienced a succession of architectural revivals and during the past hundred years, its most striking buildings have been those of Antoni Gaudi, including the huge and bizarre church of the Holy Family at Barcelona, begun 1883. Modern buildings have tended to follow the 'functional' fashions of other parts of Europe, but with respect for vernacular traditions.

Spanish Armada, see ARMADA, SPANISH.

Spanish Art. A genuine Spanish national art first began to develop with the Mozarabic style, a blend of Christian and Moorish elements, which began in the 9th century. With the advent of the Romanesque style Spain drew on a series of European influences which lasted throughout the Middle Ages and Renaissance.

Painting. The origins of painting in Spain are to be traced in illuminated manuscripts of the 9th and 10th centuries and in the remains of mural decoration. In the Romanesque period Spain was one of the great centres of painting and has more surviving examples of frescos from that time than any other country. By the 15th century a national type of painting had emerged, with the rise of the Seville school and such masters as Bartolomé Bermejo. Pedro and Alonso Berruguete are associated respectively with the introduction of the Renaissance and Mannerist styles into Spain. In the late 16th century Spain could boast her first genius in the art of painting, El Greco. Other important painters of the 16th century

Spanish Art. The altarpiece at Toledo Cathedral is in the Plateresque style, a form reminiscent of silverwork.

are Juan de Las Roelas, Luis de Vargas and Luis de Morales. The transition from Mannerist to Baroque heralded the great age of Spanish painting and in the 17th century Spain produced a host of important painters: Ribera, Zurbarán, Cano, Murillo, Velázquez and the religious sculptors Montañes and Cano. With the advent of the Bourbons in the 18th century, foreign influence again made itself particularly felt and regional influence waned. Spanish individualism asserts itself once more with Goya, after whom there comes a long decline. The work of modern Spanish painters, particularly Pablo Picasso, Juan Gris (Jose Gonzales) and the Catalonian Surrealists, Salvador Dalí and Joan Miró has been of significance in the development of 20th century art, although the most important painters have been largely expatriates. A new school of abstract painting developed in Spain itself in the 1940s, a leading figure being Antonio Tapies (1923–).

Spanish Broom, *Spartium junceum,* resembles the common broom but has smoother stems; it is the single species of its genus, which belongs to the Leguminosae. It flourishes in gardens and is native around the Mediterranean. Its flowers give a yellow dye.

Spanish Civil War, see SPAIN, *History.*

Spanish Main, name formerly applied to the Caribbean Sea, and to the north coast of South America from the Orinoco to Darien, also to the shores of the Spanish possessions in Central America.

Spanish Music. Spain possesses an unusually rich, varied and individual folk-music tradition. The dominance of the Moors in the southern part of the country from the 8th to 15th centuries caused Oriental elements to take deep root in popular song and dance; and the entry of the gypsies into the country during the latter century infused other distinctive elements—the *flamenco* style of singing, dancing and instrumental playing especially shows strong gypsy influence. Moreover the various Spanish regions, with their fierce

desire for separate identities, each developed their own unique musical characters. Spain is the home of very many kinds of dance-music, and two dance-types—the pavane and saraband—became an integral part of European music. The passacaglia also probably has its origins in a Spanish street-dance.

The first important Spanish composers, however, were the 16th-century composers of Church music, who followed the lead of the great Flemish composers. Cristobal Morales was one of the first to compose in this style, and the slightly later Tomas Luis de Victoria was one of the great European masters of his time, ranking with Byrd and Palestrina.

The *Zarzuela,* the distinctive national form of comic opera, came into being in the early 17th century and flourished until the 20th.

Towards the end of the 19th century a 'nationalist' style, drawing on the great store of folk-music, began to take shape, partly under the impetus of the researches of Pedrell (1841–1922). The pianist-composers Isaac Albeniz and Enrique Granados—the latter a pupil of Pedrell—were the harbingers of this school of composition. Manuel de Falla, another Pedrell pupil, wrote truly contemporary Spanish music. Falla's works—especially the ballets *El Amor brujo* and *El sombrero de tres picos (The Three-cornered Hat)*—had great international success and established a colourful and exotic style. Only in the last decade or so has there been some move to come abreast of 20th-century trends elsewhere, partly initiated by Christobal Halffter (1930–), who teaches at the Madrid Conservatoire. In Xavier Benguerel Spain has at least one respected figure among the European avant-garde.

Spanish Sahara, see WESTERN SAHARA.

Spanish Succession, War of the, 1702–14, fought by France, Bavaria, and Spain against Britain, Austria, Prussia, Denmark, Holland, and Portugal. Savoy fought for France first, but changed sides after 1703.

The war was caused by Charles II of Spain dying in 1700 without direct heirs, leaving his throne to a grandson of Louis XIV of France. Louis claimed his rights. The dangers of an ultimate union of France and Spain under one ruler were fully realised by the other major powers, but especially by William III of Britain, who formed the Grand Alliance, which declared war on France in May 1702. John Churchill, Duke of Marlborough, won the battles of Blenheim (1704), Ramillies (1706), Oudenarde (1708), and Malplaquet (1709).

A Franco-British armistice was signed (1712). The Peace of Utrecht (1713) finally ended the war proper, although Charles VI fought on until 1714. The war left the Bourbon Philip of Anjou as king of Spain, but it was agreed that no single person should ever rule both Spain and France.

Spanish Town, town of Jamaica, on the Rio Cobre, 18 km north-west of Kingston. Founded as Santiago de la Vega in 1525, it was the capital of Jamaica until 1871. Population (1970) 41,600.

Spanish Wines. Best known for fortified wines, such as Sherry and Málaga Wine, and cheap blended wines usually sold under a brand name, Spain does produce, in Rioja, a wine capable of excellence. Around the towns

of Haro and Logroño, along the valley of the river Ebro, both red and white Rioja wine is produced. The best wines are the red ones, and the best of these are the *reservas*. Aged for up to ten years in oak barrels, they have a unique velvety, refined quality.
See also WINE.

Spark, Muriel Sarah (1918–), Scottish writer. From 1947 to 1949 she was editor of *The Poetry Review*. She began by publishing critical biographies. Her poetry includes *The Fanfarlo and Other Verse*, 1952. However, she is best known as a novelist, her earlier books, *The Ballad of Peckham Rye*, 1960, and *Girls of Slender Means*, 1963, being humorous fantasies. Later novels dealt with deeper themes. Among her books are *The Prime of Miss Jean Brodie*, 1961, perhaps her best-known work; *The Mandelbaum Gate*, 1965 and *The Abbess of Crewe*, 1973. She is a prolific, far-ranging writer, witty, terse, and incisive.

Sparrow, a name given loosely to many small birds of various families, but applied particularly to the different members of the genus *Passer* in the family Ploceidae of order Passeriformes. They are natives of almost all parts of the Old World, but not of Australasia, and were introduced into America. The common sparrow, known usually as the house sparrow, is *P. domesticus*. The hedge sparrow or dunnock, *Prunella modularis*, is a species of Prunellidae, and is related to the nightingales and thrushes.

Sparrow-hawk, term often applied to *Accipiter nisus*, and in America to several other species of the family Falconidae, order Falconiformes, but especially to *Falco sparverius*, the American kestrel. The former occurs in Europe, Asia and North Africa, and is bluish-grey, with brown and white markings; the latter is reddish, with black and slate-grey markings.

Sparta, city and state of ancient Greece, situated in a plain on the right bank of the Eurotas, 32 km from the sea. The legendary founder was Lacedaemon, who called the city Sparta after his wife, daughter of Eurotas. Archaeological excavations have shown that Sparta was an important centre of Aegean civilisation during the 2nd millennium BC. By the 8th century, one section of the population was reduced to serfdom and the state was dominated by a ruling class of less than 10,000 persons (excluding women and children), forming an exclusively warrior caste called 'Spartiates'. Although there were two kings and a council of elders, in practice, affairs were largely in the hands of five ephors, who were elected annually.

By the time of the Persian invasion in 490 BC, the Spartan hegemony extended over Elis, Arcadia, Argolis, Sicyon, and Corinth; and Sparta was unanimously assigned the chief command. But after the final defeat of the Persians at Plataea (479), the haughtiness of Pausanias disgusted many of the Greek states, who transferred their loyalty to Athens. Sparta, however, recovered her supremacy (404) by the overthrow of Athens in the Peloponnesian War. She was herself defeated by the Thebans under Epaminondas at Leuctra (371), and the restoration of Messenia two years later completed the humiliation of Sparta. Following the Macedonian conquest of Greece, Sparta retained sufficient independence to refuse participation in the Asiatic campaigns of Alexander; but her power continued to decline. Sparta fell, with the rest of Greece, under Roman power in 146 BC.
The modern town of Sparta (modern Greek *Sparti*) is capital of the department of Laconia; population (1981) 15,915.

Spartacus (d.71 BC), in Roman history, leader of the third slave revolt. Originally a Thracian shepherd, he later served in the Roman army, but deserted and placed himself at the head of a brigand gang. Taken prisoner, he was sold to a trainer of gladiators. In 73 BC he persuaded his fellow gladiators to make a bid for freedom; about 70 of them broke out of their barracks and took refuge in the crater of Vesuvius. Chosen as their leader, Spartacus was soon joined by runaway slaves. Having defeated two Roman forces, they rose in number by the end of that year to 90,000, and were in possession of most of southern Italy. In 72 they defeated both consuls and made their way to the foot of the Alps. The slaves, however, would go no farther. Spartacus, obliged to retreat, was defeated and killed on the River Silarus by M. Licinius Crassus (71 BC).

Spasm, sudden involuntary contraction of a muscle. There are two varieties of spasm: tonic and clonic. In *tonic* spasm the contraction persists for some time, then relaxation may take place suddenly or gradually. In *clonic* spasm the contraction and relaxation succeed each other regularly. Contraction of muscle is brought about by efferent, or motor, nerve impulses. Spasm, being involuntary, occurs as a result of unpremeditated, uncontrolled nervous impulses which originate either in the motor nervous system itself or in reflex stimuli from the afferent, or sensory, nervous system. Thus muscle spasm occurs automatically in injury or inflammation due to the pain stimuli that travel up the sensory nerves from the affected part, transfer to the motor nerves, and return to the muscles in the affected part. This chain of impulses is known as a reflex action, and is nature's way of guarding the affected part against harmful movement.
A painful tonic spasm of a muscle or a group of muscles is called *cramp*. It is probably due to a local circulatory failure to remove the metabolic products of the active muscle fibres, and these products act as an irritant to the tissues.

Spassky, Boris (1937–), Soviet world chess champion; he joined the Young Pioneers Chess Club and in 1965 won the Candidates' Matches, making him challenger for the world title. He lost to the champion Petrosian but, after a second challenge, became world champion in 1969. Spassky was the first Russian world champion to lose the title to an American when in 1972 Bobby Fischer took the crown from him by 12½ points to 8½. In Belgrade, 1977–78, Spassky was defeated by Viktor Korchnoi in a match for the right to challenge the reigning world champion, Karpov.

Spastic, see CEREBRAL PALSY.

Spawn, the extruded egg mass of such oviparous animals as fish, amphibians, and molluscs. It is produced in very variable quantities (e.g. the ling lays about 150,000,000 eggs, and the American oyster 60,000,000 eggs), and is much preyed upon, even, as in the case of the stickleback, by the female herself; a variety of means have been devised for its protection. The name is also given to the mycelium of mushrooms and other fungi, seen as white threads in decaying matter.
In fish *spawning* is the reproductive phase, variously involving aggregation of the fish, courtship, extrusion of eggs and sperm into the water, and fertilisation of the eggs. Large migrations may precede spawning, as in salmon and herring. In some groups the spawn is not released, fertilisation being internal.

Spear, a weapon used by hunters and warriors of most races and ages. Its origin was a sharpened stick, later tipped with a head of worked flint and then bronze and finally iron. The metal heads of spears vary very greatly in size and shape at different periods.
See also ARMOUR.

Special Air Service, The, in the British army, consists of one regular and two Territorial Army regiments of highly-skilled troops whose main operational rôle is the harassment of the enemy behind his own lines. The regular element of the SAS is selected from all branches of the army, thus ensuring the presence of the widest range of military skills in the regiment.

Special Drawing Rights, a scheme which came into effect in 1970 under the auspices of the International Monetary Fund, to supplement international currency reserves and increase world liquidity. Participants, who must be members of the IMF, must, if asked by the Fund, provide convertible currency for another participant in exchange for SDRs, which are allocated in proportion to IMF quotas.

Special Education, term used for the provisions made to instruct groups of pupils who are regarded as handicapped (UK) or exceptional (USA). In Britain, the 1944 Education Act laid down that local education authorities should provide special education treatment either within ordinary schools or in special schools or classes. A number of categories were defined in regulations in 1953. They are: blind, partially sighted, deaf, partially deaf, educationally sub-normal, epileptic pupils, physically handicapped, pupils suffering from speech defects, and delicate children.
Similar categories exist in the USA; in addition the mentally gifted are frequently grouped with exceptional children.

Speciality Debt, one that is evidenced by deed or instrument under seal. Speciality debts enjoy priority in the order of payment of debts out of the assets of a solvent or insolvent estate over all simple contract debts.

Species. The plant and animal kingdoms are both divided into phyla, each consisting of several classes which are further subdivided into orders, families, genera, species and varieties. For most practical purposes, an organism is referred to by its generic and specific names: thus man is *Homo sapiens* (genus *Homo*; species *sapiens*), the daisy is *Bellis perennis* (genus *Bellis*; species *perennis*). This binomial system of nomenclature was devised by Linnaeus in the 18th century and has stood the test of time.

Traditionally, species are defined by the possession by their members of certain morphological characters not possessed by members of other species. Many modern biologists prefer a so-called 'biological' definition of the species, as a group of interbreeding populations which is reproductively isolated from other such groups. 'Populations', in this sense, are groups of individuals of the same kind living in the same area.

See also EVOLUTION; HYBRID; TAXONOMY.

Specific Gravity, see RELATIVE DENSITY.

Specific Heat of any substance, is the quantity of heat, today measured in joules, which will raise the temperature of unit mass of the substance through $1\,^{\circ}$C. Gases possess two specific heats, one at constant pressure and the other at constant volume. The specific heat of a body varies with the state of the substance, the presence of impurities, and the temperature. Thus the specific heat of ice at $0\,^{\circ}$C is 0.504 whereas that of water at $0\,^{\circ}$C is 1.000. Again, the specific heat of water varies from 1.000 at $0\,^{\circ}$C to 1.03 at $100\,^{\circ}$C. Dulong and Petit discovered that the product of the specific heat and the atomic weight is roughly the same for all elements at ordinary temperatures in the solid state. This product is termed the atomic heat and its average value is about 6.2.

Spectacles, glass or plastic lenses mounted in frames or half-frames (or rimless mountings) so as to be held before the eyes in cases of defective vision or eye-strain.

Aids to vision are now extensively used; convex lenses are used to correct hypermetropia (long sight), concave lenses for myopia (short sight), and cylindrical lenses for astigmatism. In cases of presbyopia (old sight) convex lenses are added to the distance correction, if any, to compensate for the loss of accommodation (ability to focus near objects), and prismatic lenses to correct muscle imbalance. The bulk of spectacle lenses are made of glass, a special hard crown of mean refractive index of 1.523 and specific gravity of about 2.6. Tinted lenses may be used to protect oversensitive eyes from glare or normal eyes from excessive glare. Bifocal or trifocal (multifocal) lenses are specially ground lenses that give presbyopic people the combined effect of lenses for distance and nearer range in one pair of spectacles.

Contact lenses made from glass or plastic, and worn in direct contact with the eye under the eyelids, can be used to correct visual defects for which no spectacles can be designed, and they also have cosmetic advantages. Although in theory a replacement for glasses in general, a satisfactory substitute for a presbyotic correction has not so far been evolved.

Spectrographic Analysis, determination of the composition of materials by studying their spectra. Large concave grating spectrographs known as polychromators are set up with as many as 30 exit slits, corresponding to the spectrum lines of many different elements. A reasonably accurate determination can be made in a few seconds if a computer is coupled to the instrument, so that continuous process control is possible in steel-making. The term can include other techniques, e.g. fluorescence and absorption

spectroscopy, which are directed more towards the study of molecular structure.

See also SPECTRUM AND SPECTROSCOPE.

Spectrohelioscope, an instrument invented by Hale which permits the visual observation of the Sun in monochromatic light. It is a modification of the spectroheliograph which was developed in the 1890s more or less independently by Deslandres in France, Hale in the USA, and Lockyer in Britain. Its purpose was to photograph the Sun in the light of a single spectral line, usually the red Balmer line of hydrogen or a violet line of ionised calcium.

Spectrophotometer, an instrument which measures a material's transmission of light of different wavelengths. Reflection spectrophotometers measure varying reflectivity through the spectrum of, e.g., pigments or coloured ceramics. A spectrophometer comprises essentially a light source with a continuous spectrum, a monochromator, a device for holding the sample to be measured, and a photoelectric detector, usually coupled to a recording system.

See also SPECTRUM AND SPECTROSCOPE.

Spectrum and Spectroscope. When a beam of light is passed through a prism, diffraction grating, or other dispersing agent, it is generally spread out in a fan-shaped beam which if made to fall on a white screen produces a coloured band of light known as a spectrum. Newton observed that the Sun's spectrum consisted of overlapping patches of violet, indigo, blue, green, yellow, orange and red, arranged in that order.

In a simple prism spectroscope the light falls on an entrance slit at the focus of the collimator lens, so that each point on the slit produces a beam of parallel light. The prism deviates different wavelengths through different angles and a telescope is used to view the spectrum. For quantitative scientific work it is usually necessary to record the spectrum photographically or photoelectrically. Spectroscopes using diffraction gratings give better results than prisms in respect of dispersion of wavelengths and resolving the smallest wavelength difference possible.

A solid hot body, e.g. a filament lamp, produces a *continuous spectrum*, containing all wavelengths in proportions depending on the temperature of the body. A single chemical element in gaseous form, e.g. sodium vapour, heated sufficiently, will produce light with a *line spectrum*; this consists of a number of sharply defined bright lines, indicating that only certain discrete wavelengths are being emitted, unique to the element in question and which form an identifying 'signature'. If light with a continuous spectrum is passed through a relatively cool gas or vapour, an *absorption spectrum* is obtained with dark lines at the wavelengths corresponding to the emission lines of the gas or vapour. Photons of visible and ultraviolet light, corresponding to transitions in the energy states of the outer electrons, produce *atomic spectra*.

Microwave spectroscopy uses the absorption of radio waves at wavelengths between about 1 and 300 mm. It has enabled bond lengths, dipole moments, and atomic masses to be calculated. Atomic clocks are made using these carefully regulated frequencies.

Speech, see VOICE AND SPEECH.

Speed Skating, see ICE SKATING; ROLLER SKATING.

Speedway, a form of motor-cycle racing held on dirt tracks. It originated c. 1902 in the USA and was first seen in Britain in 1927. It caught on quickly in Australia, and became widely popular in Britain, USA and Australasia in the 1930s. The first world championships were held in 1936. Each race is run by four riders (6 in Australia) over four laps, distances ranging from 275 m to 430 m. The machines are lightly built, have no brakes, one gear, and are limited to 500 cc.

Speedwell, see VERONICA.

Speenhamland System, method of outdoor poor relief adopted by the Berkshire justices in 1795 in response to widespread unemployment, high prices, and low wages particularly among agricultural workers. The parish was to supplement wages below an absolute minimum set by the justices, in accordance with the price of bread and the size of the man's family. The system spread to much of the south and east of England but its general effect was further to depress wages and greatly to increase the rate burden. The Poor Law Amendment Act of 1834 aimed to end such outdoor relief to the able-bodied poor; relief was only to be provided in workhouses and outdoor relief to be reserved for the very old or sick.

Speke, John Hanning (1827–64), British explorer. In 1844 he joined the Indian Army and served in the Punjab campaigns. In 1857–1858 he took part in an expedition led by Richard Burton to discover the source of the Nile, by journeying westward from Zanzibar. After Burton fell ill, Speke continued without him, to discover and name Lake Victoria, which he claimed to be the source of the great river. Burton challenged him bitterly and publicly over this, but Speke received the approval of the establishment and in 1860 was sent on a second expedition in the region. Speke was shot in a hunting accident in England, alleged by Burton to have been suicide.

Speke Hall, Merseyside, England. The present 16th-century house is a fine example of Tudor half-timbering.

Speleology, the study of caves, covering such topics as cave exploration and survey, the biology of cave life, the palaeontology of prehistoric finds in caves, and cave geology and geomorphology. Much of the work in this area is done by amateurs.

Spence, Sir Basil (1907–76), British architect. For nearly 20 years his work comprised houses, factories, theatres and the Scottish Pavilion at the Empire Exhibition, 1938. In 1951 he won the competition for Coventry Cathedral. Other work has included university buildings, the church of St Francis, Wythenshawe, Manchester, 1958; Hampstead Town Hall, 1958; replanning of the slum area of Gorbals at Glasgow with modern multi-storey residential flats; rebuilding of Knightsbridge Barracks, London; and the British Embassy at Rome.

Spencer, Herbert (1820–1903), British social philosopher, born at Derby, one of the major pioneers of sociology. Spencer published his first important work, *Social Statistics*, in 1851. Thereafter he was absorbed in applying the doctrine of evolution to man in society. His other main works are: *Principles of Psychology*; *First Principles*; *Principles of Ethics*.

Spencer, Sir Stanley (1891–1959), British painter. He studied at the Slade School from 1910 to 1914, and served in the First World War. His military service produced its effect on his painting, particularly evident in his greatest work, the mural paintings of the Memorial Chapel at Burghclere. For most of the remainder of Spencer's work two sources are responsible: Cookham, his birthplace, and the Bible. Among his other major works are *The Resurrection*, 1929 (Tate Gallery) and the series *Christ in the Wilderness*.

Spender, Stephen (Harold) (1909–), English poet and critic. He fought in the Spanish Civil War, and served in the London fire service during the Second World War. Spender was closely associated with W. H. Auden, Christopher Isherwood, Louis Macneice, and C. Day Lewis in the late 1920s and 1930s. His verse of that time shares their concern with socialism.

Later his work became more personal and introspective, and after his *Collected Poems*, 1955, he published only one further collection, *The Generous Days*, 1971. Increasingly his public literary activities have been as an editor and critic: he edited *Horizon*, 1939–41, and *Encounter*, 1953–67. Among his critical studies are *The Struggle of the Modern*, 1963, W. H. Auden: *A Tribute*, 1975, and *T. S. Eliot*, 1975.

Spengler, Oswald (1880–1936), German historical philosopher. In Munich, working as a schoolteacher, he finished his main work, *Der Untergang des Abendlandes*, 1918–23 (*The Decline of the West*, 1926–29), which, appearing immediately after Germany's defeat in the First World War, matched the mood of the hour. This, and the wide-ranging erudition of the author, gave the book an unexpected popularity, and it soon became world-famous. Spengler held that the different cultures of the world came to life, independent of one another, reached maturity, declined, fell, and died in identical cycles. This is essentially the view more recently put forward by Arnold Toynbee in his *Study of History*, though there it is expressed in less mystical and grandiose terms than Spengler's. According to Spengler, the civilisation of the West has entered its final phase, characterised by great-power conflicts, artistic sterility, the spread of pacifist and socialist ideas among the masses, etc. Later works, such as *Preussentum und Sozialismus*, 1920, and *Der Mensch und die Technik*, 1931, were less successful.

Spenser, Edmund (c.1552–99), English poet. The first great modern English poet, Spenser was admitted as sizar at Pembroke Hall, Cambridge. Little is known of his career at Cambridge.

It is known, however, that he formed a lasting friendship with two other Cambridge students, Gabriel Harvey and Edward Kirke. Harvey was a distinguished classical and Italian scholar, who influenced Spenser's ideas, but he was essentially a modernist who had no time for Spenser's interest in medieval chivalry and the romance tradition.

By 1579 Spenser had become acquainted with Sir Philip Sidney and his circle, and obtained a post in the household of Sidney's uncle, the Earl of Leicester. With Sir Philip Sidney, Dyer, and others, he formed a literary club, the Areopagus.

Shortly after moving to Leicester House he published (1579) the *Shepheardes Calender*, which was well received. This consists of twelve eclogues, one for each month of the year. In choosing such a work for his first major publication, Spenser was aligning himself with the major classical tradition, as represented by Virgil. In 1580 he went to Ireland where he lived until within a month of his death.

In 1595 Spenser published *Amoretti* and *Epithalamion*, celebrating his courtship and marriage to his second wife, Elizabeth Boyle. *Amoretti* is one of the most distinguished of the Elizabethan sonnet sequences. The *Epithalamion* is a richly ornate marriage ode in the classical manner.

Spenser's lasting claim to fame rests on the unfinished *Faerie Queene*. In the *Letter to Sir Walter Ralegh*, published in the 1590 edition of the poem, he explains that the work is 'a continued Allegory, or darke conceit'. In the person of Prince Arthur he intends to portray 'the image of a brave knight, perfected in the twelve moral vertues'. Arthur has a vision of the Faerie Queene, Gloriana, in whom, says Spenser, 'I conceive the most excellent and glorious person of our soveraigne the Queene, and her kingdome in Faery land'. So the allegory comprehends a celebration of Elizabeth and her court, England (and more particularly Protestant England, embattled against Catholic Spain), and at the same time an examination of chivalric virtue and romantic passion.

Stanley Spencer. St Francis and the Birds, *1935, is one of many biblical paintings.*

Speranski, Mikhail Mikhailovich, Count (1772–1839), Russian statesman. At the request of Alexander I he worked out a plan for the reform of the legislative and administrative system of the state. This plan was being carried out when Speranski was disgraced as a result of an intrigue and banished in 1812. In 1819 he was appointed governor-general of Siberia. In the reign of Nicholas I Speranski codified (1826–33) the existing Russian laws for the first time since the Code of Alexis Mikhailovich, prepared in 1649.

Sperm, short form of spermatozoa, the male reproductive cell. A spermatozoon or sperm cell seen under the microscope resembles a miniature, translucent tadpole. Spermatozoa are produced in the testes, and are carried in the secretion produced by the prostate gland, the substance being known as semen.

Sperm Oil, or spermaceti oil (iodine value 130 ± 20), is obtained from the sperm whale or cachalot. The crude oil is yellow to dark brown in colour, and has a fishy odour. Spermaceti separates on cooling, and the clear yellow oil which is left is purified by treatment with potassium hydroxide. Sperm oil forms a valuable lubricant for delicate machinery, since it does not readily become rancid or gummy. Spermaceti is used in cosmetics, ointments, candles, and textile dressing.

Sperm Whale, or cachalot, *Physeter catodon*, the only representative of its genus, is the largest toothed whale, males measuring up to 18 m long. It is common in both tropical and temperate waters. Each group of females is led by a dominant male. Sperm whales have massive blunt heads containing a cavity filled with oil which solidifies in air to form spermaceti, a white wax. Their teeth, about 40 in number, are all in the lower jaw and each is about 20 cm long and may weigh 2·7 kg. With this armoury the whales catch giant squids on which they feed, sometimes following prolonged titanic battles leaving the whales with permanent scars on their skin. Ambergris, found as a stinking grey mass in the gut of sperm whales, is a valuable base for many perfumes. Persistent exploitation has now reduced the numbers of sperm whales; the annual catch is limited by international agreement. There is a pygmy sperm whale (*Kogia breviceps*), rarely more than 3·7 m long, which resembles its larger cousin in both form and habit.

Spermatophya, or Phanerogamia, one of the main divisions of the vegetable kingdom, the seed-bearing plants, which include the Angiosperms and Gymnosperms.

Spermatozoa, see SPERM.

Sperry, Elmer Ambrose (1860–1930), US inventor. He developed the high-intensity arc searchlight. This searchlight became the standard for the principal armies and navies of the world, and has been used for many commercial purposes. The Sperry high-intensity arc was also applied to cinematography, both in the making of films and in their projection. Sperry was the leader in the application of the gyroscope to practical uses. His gyro compass was quickly adopted by leading navies of the world; following the First World War it became standard in the world's merchant fleets. His gyroscope ship stabiliser reduced the roll of vessels at sea. With his son Lawrence he developed a gyroscope aircraft automatic control for safety in flight. This auto-pilot led to the development of such instruments as the artificial horizon, directional gyro, and gyro-magnetic compass.

Spey, river of Scotland, one of the swiftest in Britain, and noted for its salmon. It flows from Badenoch, and enters the sea 6 km north of Fochabers. Length 176 km.

Speyer, or Spires (formerly *Spira*), city in the Rhineland-Palatinate, Federal Republic of Germany, at the confluence of the Rhine and the Speyer river, 17 km south of Ludwigshafen. Its site has been occupied for some 3000 years; there were Celtic and, later, Roman settlements (*Civitas Nemetum*) here. At the end of the 13th century it was made a free city of the empire. Fifty diets have been held in the city, and from 1513 until 1689 it was the seat of the supreme court of the empire. The term 'Protestant' comes from the protest of the reformers against the majority decision of the diet here in 1529. Electrical engineering, metallurgy, oil refining, and aircraft engineering are the main industries. Population (1971) 43,000.

Spezia, La, Italian seaport and capital of La Spezia province, situated some 80 km southeast of Genoa. It stands on a gulf, called the Gulf of La Spezia (Latin *Portus Lunae*), on the Riviera di Levante. Since 1861 La Spezia has been the main naval port of Italy, and it has shipyards, munitions and iron works, and oil refining and electrical industries. Shelley was drowned in the gulf here in 1822. Population (1979) 117,760.

Sphagnales, a family of Mosses, which contains one genus, *Sphagnum*. They are found in cold temperate zones, and are popularly known as bog mosses. The plants have erect stems with numerous leaves, and are moisture-absorbent. As they grow upwards the lower parts die without decaying, accumulate, and in time form moss beds of increasing thickness which eventually form peat. When dry, sphagnum moss is light, firm and elastic, and is used for packing plants, growing orchids, potting composts, and in emergencies for surgical dressings.

Sphalerite, the principal ore of zinc, usually found associated with galena. Sphalerite is zinc sulphide (ZnS), but substitution of iron for zinc occurs. When pure it is colourless, but increased iron content deepens the colour from yellow through yellow-brown to black. The resinous lustre is an aid to identification which may otherwise be difficult with twinned or distorted aggregates. Sphalerite occurs in hydrothermal veins and replacement bodies associated with galena and silver minerals.

Sphene, silicate of titanium and lime, occurring as a common accessory mineral in igneous rocks in which it occurs as tiny disseminated crystals, and also in metamorphic rocks. In colour it is dark brown, crystallises in the monoclinic system, and displays strong double refraction (hardness 5·5; specific gravity 3·5).

Sphenoid Bone, wedge-shaped bone lying across the base of the skull near its middle and taking part in the formation of the cavity of the cranium, the orbits and the posterior nares.

Sphere, a surface on which all points are the same distance (called the radius) from a fixed point called the centre; or the solid body consisting of such a surface and its interior. If the radius of a sphere is *r* then its volume is $4\pi r^3/3$ and its surface area is $4\pi r^2$. Any line segment from the centre to a spherical surface is called a radius. Any chord that passes through the centre is called a diameter. All diameters of a sphere have the same length (twice the radius of the sphere). If a plane passes through the centre of a sphere its intersection with the surface is called a

great circle. The radius of a great circle is the same as the radius of the sphere. Two great circles always intersect; the line of intersection is called an axis and it intersects the surface at two points called poles. The plane through the centre perpendicular to an axis is called an equatorial plane and it intersects the surface in a great circle called an equator. In Cartesian co-ordinates the equation of a sphere, centre (*a, b, c*), radius *r* is:

$$(x - a)^2 + (y - b)^2 + (z - c)^2 = r^2.$$

Sphere, the Celestial, see CELESTIAL SPHERE.

Spherical Aberration, see ABERRATIONS OF LENSES.

Sphincter Muscles, ring-like muscles whose action opens or closes certain orifices. The external *sphincter ani* closes the anus; the internal *sphincter ani* constricts the rectum; the *sphincter pyloricus* closes the pyloric orifice of the stomach; the *sphincter vesicae* constricts the urethral orifice of the bladder. The *sphincter pupillae* contracts the pupil in response to bright light.

Sphinx, fabulous monster, of Egyptian origin, figuring also in Greek mythology. In Egypt it was usually represented as a lion with a king's head, but later, as in Greece, it was a winged monster with a human female bust. One of the oldest and most famous examples is the Great Sphinx of Giza, near the group of pyramids. Subsequently it was often imitated on a smaller scale, and avenues of sphinxes frequently flanked the approaches to temples. In Greece, the most famous sphinx was that of Thebes in Boeotia, with a woman's head, lion's feet and tail, and bird's wings. She set the inhabitants a riddle and devoured all those who could not solve it. When it was at length solved by Oedipus, the sphinx destroyed herself.

Sphinx Moth, see HAWK-MOTH.

Spica, in astronomy, Alpha Virginis, a first magnitude star in Virgo. It is a spectroscopic binary with a period of 4·01 days.

Spice Islands, see MALUKU.

Spices, certain vegetable products which are used for flavouring foods. They all contain an essential oil which gives an aromatic odour. Their odour and flavour stimulate the flow of gastric enzymes which initiate the digestive process, but their nutritional value is negligible. They are derived from various parts of plants: the fruit, the seed, the stem, the flower-bud, the bark and the root. See also CONDIMENT.

Spider, Araneae, a large and very varied order in class Arachnida. Their most striking characteristic is the possession of a set of glands secreting a viscid fluid which hardens on exposure to the air to form a silky thread. These glands are numerous, and their secretion is made through many minute tubes on the under-surface of the spinnerets at the end of the abdomen. By means of their silky threads spiders construct their dwellings, some of them highly specialised and many of great beauty. The threads make webs and traps for the capture of prey, they serve for aerial transport, and are used as a safeguard against falling. Not all spiders use webs, however. Spiders are oviparous, and the female encloses her eggs in a silken bag which is sometimes carried about with her, sometimes concealed in the nest, and sometimes attached to solid objects. The young do not undergo metamorphosis. Spiders are predaceous, and bite the prey, then suck out the juices and soft parts.

Over 30,000 species, mostly small, are known, but a few tropical forms attain great size, for example, a body length of 9 cm. Probably the most feared are tarantulas, some of which are poisonous; their bite can cause local inflammation but rarely death. The water spider (*Argyroneta aquatica*) is remarkable for constructing a web below water; a bubble of air entangled in the web serves as a 'diving bell'. Wolf-spiders (Lycosidae) are a widely distributed group of very predaceous spiders. Many species are found in woods and commons; others are aquatic.

Sphinx. *The Great Sphinx at Giza was built around 2550 BC during the Fourth Dynasty.*

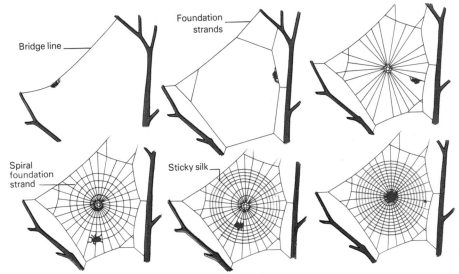

Spider. In constructing an orb web, strong foundation strands are laid down first, with the boundary threads attached to secure supports. The sticky, insect-trapping silk is then secreted from the outside inwards, while at the same time the spider ingests the spiral foundation strand.

Spider-crab, any crab of the family Majidae in class Crustacea. The carapace is much longer than it is wide. The legs are long, and often thick, in proportion to the body. *Macrocheira kaempferi*, the giant crab, is the largest arthropod known. It measures 4 m from one claw tip to the other.

Spiderwort, see TRADESCANTIA.

'Spiegel, Der', German political weekly magazine, founded in 1947. It achieved a large circulation and probed a number of controversial topics. As a result of one of these, the magazine's offices were raided by the police, and its editor, Rudolf Augstein, was imprisoned, 1962. A major government upheaval resulted.

Spike Island, island off Cobh in County Cork, Republic of Ireland. Formerly a prison, it is now a coastal-defence station.

Spina Bifida, failure in embryonic life of the closure of the *neural tube*, which forms the brain and spinal cord and their coverings. There is a striking regional variation in its incidence throughout the world and major efforts are being made to discover its cause.

The most severe form of neural tube malformation is *anencephaly*, where the brain and skull are rudimentary. Occasionally the back of the skull fails to close, resulting in a protrusion of the brain, or *encephalocoele*. *Meningocoele* and *meningomyelocoele* result from the failure of closure of the bony arch of the vertebral column, with a varying degree of overlying skin defect. This usually occurs in the lower part of the back, and the terms mean the protrusion, respectively, of meninges and of meninges and spinal cord through the defect. Depending on its severity there may be paralysis of the legs, and disturbance of bladder and bowel function ranging from minor to severe. Hydrocephalus is common. Occasionally the defect is so minor that it only affects the bony arch of the vertebrae (*spina bifida occulta*).

It is now possible to diagnose the condition in early pregnancy by examining a sample of amniotic fluid from around the foetus for the presence of a substance known as alpha-fetoprotein.

Spinach, *Spinacia oleracea*, a species in the family Chenopodiaceae, which grows wild in Asia. The plant is herbaceous, and the leaves are eaten as a vegetable; they are rich in vitamin C and iron.

Spinal cord, spinal medulla, the main nerve trunk of vertebrate animals. It is part of the central nervous system. It develops, like the brain, from the embryonic neural tube. In the adult the spinal cord is approximately 45 cm long; it runs in the vertebral canal, formed by the posterior arches of successive vertebrae, from the bottom of the skull where it is continuous with the medulla oblongata of the brain, to about waist-level in adults.

The spinal cord, like the brain, consists of nerve cells (grey matter) and their myelinated processes or nerve fibres (white matter). The grey matter is arranged in an H-shape around the central canal of the spinal cord, and it is surrounded in turn by the white matter which contains the ascending and descending tracts. There are long ascending and descending pathways in the spinal cord. They convey messages to the brain about the sensations of touch, pressure, vibration, proprioception (sense of position of one's limbs in space), pain, and temperature. They also convey instructions from the brain to the muscles. If by accident the pathways are severed there is paralysis and loss of sensation below the point of severance.

Spinal Nerves, the nerves arising from the spinal cord of a vertebrate animal, which leave it between the vertebrae. They are formed by the union of anterior (motor) and posterior (sensory) spinal nerve roots in the foramina (passages) between adjacent vertebrae. Man has 31 pairs of spinal nerves.

Each spinal nerve is attached to the spinal cord by a posterior (dorsal or sensory) root and an anterior (ventral or motor) root. Every root consists of a number of rootlets, each of which contains many nerve fibres.

Spine, see VERTEBRAL COLUMN.

Spinel, name given to a group of minerals which are double oxides of one or more divalent metals and one or more trivalent metals. They all crystallise in the cubic system. There are three series of spinel minerals, grouped according to their main trivalent metal; they are the spinel series, the magnetite series, and the chromite series. Spinel, $MgAl_2O_4$, is the commonest mineral in the spinel series. The crystals are octahedral and vary in colour from red to blue, green, brown, and black. Hardness is $7\frac{1}{2}$–8, specific gravity 3·58. Spinels are high temperature minerals, and are found as accessory minerals in basic igneous rocks and in highly aluminous metamorphic rocks. Magnetite $Fe^{2+}Fe_2^{3+}O_4$, the most important member of the magnetite series, is magnetic iron ore. It is famous as lodestone (Anglo-Saxon *Lōd*, way,). Chromite $Fe^{2+}Cr_2O_4$, is the chief member of the chromite series and is the chief source of chromium and its compounds. It normally occurs in massive form, black to brown in colour, with a metallic lustre. It occurs as an accessory mineral in ultrabasic igneous rocks, often as segregated masses and lenses.

Spinet, small keyboard instrument of the harpsichord family; it is distinguished in shape from other members of the family by its leg-of-mutton outline, and was probably named from a fancied resemblance of its quill plectra to spines (Italian *spinetta*, diminutive of *spina*, thorn). The spinet was a favourite instrument in Europe during the 16th to 18th centuries, and was also manufactured in America during the 18th century.

See also PIANOFORTE.

Spinks, Leon (1953–). American heavyweight boxer who won the world heavyweight title in his eighth professional fight, beating Muhammad Ali on a split points decision in Las Vegas in February 1978. He was stripped of the World Boxing Council (WBC) version of the title in March 1978 for refusing to defend against Ken Norton. In September 1978 he lost the World Boxing Association (WBA) version of the title to Ali. In June 1981 he challenged unsuccessfully for the WBC heavyweight title, losing in the third round to Larry Holmes.

Spinning, the textile processes leading to the production of yarn. There are two types of yarn, staple and filament; the first are made from relatively short (1–100 cm) fibres, the second from virtually continuous fibres. For man-made fibres, the term 'spinning' is also used to describe the production of textile fibre from the bulk raw material as well as the production and processing of short fibre to yarn. Each spinning method is designed to deal with fibres of certain properties, the average length and diameter of the fibres being the most important criteria.

Cotton fibres are passed through a carding machine to form a loose rope known as a sliver. These slivers are stretched or drawn by passing through a series of drawing machines. The final operation is the production of yarn from the final sliver by the insertion of twist. This is the spinning process proper.

In woollen spinning, carding produces a continuous thin web of fibres which is split into longitudinal strips, each 10–20 mm wide. These strips are spun into yarn without further processing.

Spinning of Synthetic Fibres. The production of synthetic fibre always leads to a liquid, usually slightly viscous. This liquid is carefully filtered, air bubbles are removed, and it is pumped through a spinneret, which consists of a plate perforated with one or more holes

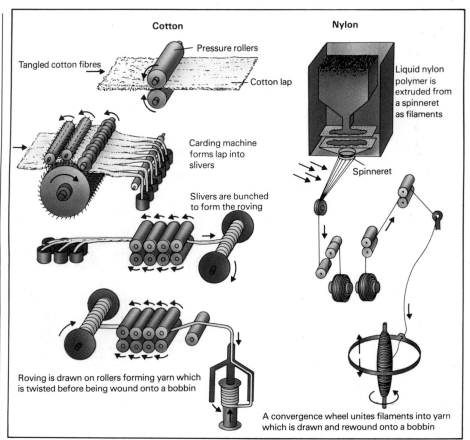

Cotton

Tangled cotton fibres

Pressure rollers

Cotton lap

Carding machine forms lap into slivers

Slivers are bunched to form the roving

Roving is drawn on rollers forming yarn which is twisted before being wound onto a bobbin

Nylon

Liquid nylon polymer is extruded from a spinneret as filaments

Spinneret

A convergence wheel unites filaments into yarn which is drawn and rewound onto a bobbin

Spinning. *The production processes involved in the manufacture of cotton and nylon show clearly the differences between the production of natural and synthetic fibres.*

usually of a circular shape. As the liquid or spinning dope leaves the holes in the spinneret it is hardened and becomes the fibre, which is pulled away by driven rollers.

Spinoza, Baruch, from 1656 known as Benedictus (1632–77), Jewish-Dutch philosopher. When he was 20 his unorthodox religious views led to his expulsion from the Jewish community in Holland. Spinoza made his living by teaching and grinding optical lenses. He refused a chair of philosophy at Heidelberg, the better to preserve his leisure and freedom. He lived a solitary abstemious life and was an assiduous correspondent.

Spinoza's Hebrew learning enabled him to become the founder of the historical explanation, or 'higher criticism', of the Bible. Spinoza regarded it as literature and not dogma. His philosophy is contained in his *Ethics*, not published during his lifetime, because of his reputation as an atheist. Set out in axioms and propositions in the pure rationalistic style, it is founded on a rationalised Judaism, the dualism of Descartes reconciled into monism, and the ideas of Hobbes. Spinoza defined the final cause or purposes at work in nature, and denied, in their ordinary sense, immortality of the soul, free will, and moral responsibility. Nature and God are identified, and all things, good or bad in human eyes, are integral parts of the divine being. Natural science could alone reveal what was fundamental and divine.

Spiracles, orifices at the ends of the tracheae (air-tubes) in insects. Respiration is carried on by means of the tracheae, which penetrate into all parts of the body, subdividing into smaller tracheoles. The arrangement of the spiracles on the body varies among groups

and life-stages. The spiracles are closed by valves actuated by special muscles. When the valves are closed, the air is driven by body contractions into the finer branches of the tracheal system.

Spiraea, in the family Rosaceae, a genus of deciduous shrubs, bearing white or pink to crimson flowers. It is distributed widely in the northern hemisphere and many species and hybrids are cultivated. Herbaceous spiraea are classed under *Aruncus* and *Filipendula*.

Spire, though commonly regarded as an ornamental feature, it was originally a normal pyramidal roof (as at Southwell Cathedral); but in Gothic times it was elongated to a much greater height. Sometimes an octagonal stone spire rises direct from a square tower without a parapet, the transition being made by means of 'broaches'.

Spires, see SPEYER.

Spirit (Latin *spiritus*, breath). Breath, apparently identical with life, provided a natural term for an invisible living power. This religious concept covers a variety of usages. Christian theologians from Irenaeus have taught the 'tripartite' nature of man, that he is an amalgam of body, soul, and spirit, the spirit being regarded as that part which is most open to divine influence, and which may survive death. Modern religious thinkers since Kierkegaard have identified man's spirit with his inner psyche or true self.

Spirit is also used to denote a superhuman order of being unlimited by space and time. According to the Bible, God himself is spirit. In Christian theology, the third person of the Trinity is the Holy Spirit, who first came to the disciples at Pentecost.

In contemporary Christian circles there has been a revival of the charismatic movement in which the Holy Spirit is invoked and people sometimes speak in tongues.

Spirit of Salt, name given to a solution of hydrochloric acid as prepared from sodium sulphate and common salt by Glauber in 1646.

Spiritualism, or Spiritism, a philosophy or religion, based on a belief in life after death and the possibility of communication between the dead and the living. It originated in America in 1848, and rapidly spread to other parts of the world. The movement was widely popularised by Conan Doyle, who in his writings and lectures claimed spiritualism to be 'a religion for those who find themselves outside all religions'.

There are two main groups of spiritualistic phenomena, mental and physical, and there are both mental and physical mediums (persons endowed with psychic awareness). In the presence of such persons, alleged supernormal phenomena take place, often when the medium is in a trance. Movement of objects without contact (telekinesis) is one type of physical phenomenon. Mental phenomena include information given by mediums which they could not have acquired through any normal means (clairvoyance and clairaudience).

Spit, a depositional feature formed along a coastline with marked longshore drift, often displaying one or more recurved ends. These are produced either by the interaction of different sets of wave trains from varying directions, or by wave refraction. Often the remnants of previous recurved ends can be identified in the form of beach ridges. In many cases lagoons and salt marshes form on the landward side of spits. When a spit links an island to the mainland, the feature is called a tombolo.

See also COAST.

Spithead, roadstead in the English Channel, between Portsmouth and the Isle of Wight. Here was fought in 1545 a battle between the English and French fleets, in which the latter was dispersed. More recently Spithead has been the scene of Royal Navy reviews.

Spitsbergen, Norwegian archipelago in the Arctic Ocean, lying between Zemlya Frantsa Iosifa and Greenland. The main islands are Spitsbergen, Edgeøya, Nordaustlandet, Barentsøya, and Prins Karls Forland. The land area of the group is about 62,050 km². The archipelago is grouped with a number of nearby islands, including Kvitøya, Kong Karls Land, Hopen, and Bjørnøya, under the name Svalbard. All the islands are mountainous; the highest peak is Newtontoppen, 1690 m, in the north-eastern part of Spitsbergen. There is much ice, generally in the form of long valley glaciers. Spitsbergen lies between 76°30′ and 80° N, latitude. At this latitude there is total daylight for 122 days; for 128 days there is either full sunlight or twilight only; and for a period of 115 days the sun does not rise above the horizon. The chief mineral is coal, some 850,000 t annually being mined, of which half is extracted by the USSR. Asbestos and copper are also found. The population of the islands in 1979 was 3,650, of whom 2,460 were Russian. The main centres of population are on the west coast of Spitsbergen at the capital of Long-yearbyen and the Russian mining settlements. The Norwegians maintain weather and radio stations on several of the islands.

Spitz, Mark Andrew (1950–), US swimmer who can claim to be his sport's most successful competitor ever on the basis of his feat at the Munich (1972) Olympic Games. He won seven gold medals (100 and 200 m freestyle and butterfly, 4 × 100 m and 4 × 200 m freestyle relay; and 4 × 100 m medley relay) all in world record times—a run unlikely to be equalled. He also won two freestyle team golds at the 1968 Games, and between 1967 and 1972 set 27 world records for freestyle and butterfly events.

Spleen, a lymphoid organ serving a number of functions including the formation of leucocytes and antibodies, removal of dead and dying cells, and storage of iron in the form of ferritin and haemosiderin. In some mammals, but not man, it plays a significant role as a reservoir of blood. Should the spleen have to be removed because of injury any of these functions can be taken up by other lymphoid and reticuloendothelial organs. See also LYMPHOID TISSUE.

Splints, structures made of wood, leather, zinc, aluminium, perspex or other materials so as to fit about a fractured or diseased limb in order to render it immovable. Modern treatment of the fractured limb is initially to immobilise it in an inflatable plastic splint as a first-aid measure, and then later to apply a more permanent and less bulky splint moulded to the shape of the limb. For this purpose plaster of Paris bandages, applied wet and then allowed to harden, are used as a rule, but more recently glass fibre bandages have offered a more waterproof and lighter alternative.

Split (Latin *Spalatum*), seaport in Croatia, Yugoslavia, the chief town of Dalmatia. The Roman emperor Diocletian built an immense palace here, to which he retired after his abdication in 305. In the 7th century the nearby town of Salona was destroyed, and the inhabitants began to develop a new settlement around the palace; more than 400 houses are crowded together inside the palace walls. Split has extensive shipyards and docks, textile and engineering industries, and a trade in wines and agricultural produce. It is a tourist resort. Population (1971) 114,000.

Spock, Benjamin McLane (1903–), US paediatrician. Spock is best known as a popular writer and television broadcaster on child psychology and development. His first book, *The Common Sense Book of Baby and Child Care*, reprinted in 1946 as *The Pocket Book of Baby and Child Care*, sold millions of copies in America alone and has been translated into 12 languages. Among his later books were *Dr Spock Talks with Mothers*, 1961, and *Problems of Parents*, 1963. He was amongst those who led opposition to the Vietnam war, the so-called Spock trial (in which Spock was acquitted) being one of the major focusing events of the anti-war movement.

Spode, Josiah (1733–97), British potter, apprenticed to Thomas Whieldon, established a pottery factory at Stoke-on-Trent in 1770. His son added porcelain in 1800 and stone-china in 1805 to its productions. In 1833 it became the still existing firm of 'Copelands'.

Spohr, Louis (1784–1859), German composer, conductor and violinist. His works include ten operas, ten symphonies, oratorios and violin concertos. His style mixes Classical idioms with chromatic harmonies, producing a lush effect which once made his music popular. His treatise on violin-playing appeared in 1832.

Spokane, city in the state of Washington, USA, 370 km east of Seattle. A fur traders' post was the first settlement on the site (1810). It was not until the 1880s, however, after the arrival of the Northern Pacific Railroad, that Spokane could exploit its position between the wheatlands of the Colombia plain and the minerals and forests of the mountains. It remains a route centre. Population (1980) 171,300.

Spoleto (ancient *Spoletium*), Italian town in Umbria, built on a hill 50 km south-east of Perugia. From 1247 to 1860 it belonged to the Papal States. It has a fine archiepiscopal cathedral (partly 11th century) containing frescoes by Pintoricchio and the tomb of Filippo Lippi. Population (1974) 18,000; municipality (1971) 37,400.

Spondias, a tropical genus of trees of the Anacardiaceae, which contains *S. dulcis*, sweet otaheite apple, and *S. lutea*, golden apple or Jamaica plum; the fruits are edible and fleshy.

Sponge, any of the invertebrate animals that make up phylum Porifera, the 'pore-bearers'. They are the most primitive of the multicellular animals, as they do not have distinct tissues or organs, and the individual cells that make up the organism retain some independence. There are about 5000 species, of which perhaps 150 live in fresh water; the others are all marine, living mostly in shallow water, but a few live at depths of about 5 km. A living sponge looks like a slimy mass from 1 mm to 2 m in diameter, often coloured bright red, orange, yellow, blue, or black. Sponges are always attached to a firm object, and the organism as a whole does not move.

There are three classes. Calcispongiae includes sponges with a calcium skeleton. They are mostly small, less than 10 cm high, and mostly live in shallow water. *Leucosolenia* and *Scypha*, simple, vase-shaped sponges that may grow in groups, are genera of this class.

Hyalospongiae, the glass sponges, have a siliceous skeleton of six-pointed spicules. They are usually symmetrical, 10 to 30 cm high and shaped like cups or urns. *Euplectella*, the Venus's flowerbasket, is an example. Most live at depths between 450 and 900 m.

Demospongiae contains most of the common sponges. They have a siliceous skeleton and are often brilliantly coloured. The boring sponges belong to this class, and also the freshwater sponges, which are mostly encrusting types, and may contain green algae. *Spongia* and *Hippospongia* are the commercial bath sponges. They are gathered by divers in the Gulf of Mexico, the Caribbean, and the Mediterranean; the living animals are allowed to die, and the cleaned spongy skeleton is sold.

Sponsors, godparents who present a child for baptism and make the baptismal confession and promises to keep the faith, in its name. According to the rule of the Church of England, every male child must have two godfathers and one godmother, while a female child has two godmothers and one godfather. In the Roman Catholic Church one sponsor, or at most two of different sexes, is required, both at baptism and at confirmation.

Spontaneous Combustion, burning which takes place without the application of any igniting agent. The conditions necessary for spontaneous combustion are the presence of a substance with a low temperature limit for flame, and a source of heat, such as slow oxidation, which eventually reaches that limit. Thus damp hay may burst into flame through the gradual rise in temperature caused by fermentation.

Spoonbills, together with the ibises form the family Threskiornithidae, order Ciconiiformes. They are characterised by their curious bills, which are long and flat, and are dilated at the end into the shape of a spoon. Their feet are adapted for wading, and the birds obtain their food, consisting chiefly of fish, frogs, molluscs and crustaceans, from shallow water. Spoonbills are found in all five continents.

Spoonerism, figure of speech comprising an accidental transposition of initial letters or syllables of two or more adjacent words. It owes its name to the Rev. W. A. Spooner (1844–1930), warden of New College, Oxford. Instances are 'Kinkering kongs their tatles tike' for 'Conquering kings their titles take'; 'Will nobody pat my hiccup' for 'Will nobody pick my hat up'; and 'You are occupewing my pie' for 'You are occupying my pew'. While some of the most diverting, including the first cited, may be attributed to Dr Spooner, most are apocryphal.

Spoons, made of pottery, were used in the Windmill Hill culture of the Neolithic period, and bronze spoons occur in the Early Iron Age, but in all probability these were for ritual and not utilitarian use. The name spoon, from the Old English *spon*, a chip, is a reminder that early spoons were made of wood. The form of spoon now in use came into fashion about 1750–60.

Sporades, group of islands in the Aegean Sea belonging to Greece. The Northern Sporades (Greek *Voríai Sporádhes*) are part of the department of Euboea. The main islands are Skyros, Skiathos, and Skopelos, where cattle rearing, fruit growing, and shipbuilding are the chief occupations. The Southern Sporades (Greek *Nótai Sporádhes*) was the name formerly given to the Dodecanese Islands.

Spore, a minute, generally single-celled structure by which the lower plants (algae, fungi, ferns, liverworts, mosses) and certain Protozoa characteristically reproduce. The essential feature of a spore is that it can germinate and produce a vegetative body without the need for fusion with another spore or other structure beforehand. In algae, ferns, liverworts and mosses, for sexual reproduction two kinds of spore are produced which differ in size and in behaviour. In the Fungi a great range of spore types exists; the classification of the group is largely based on spore form. The well-known fruiting-bodies of higher fungi form spores in colossal numbers, well seen when a dry puff-ball is compressed. In Bacteria resting spores, extremely resistant to temperature and chemicals, may be produced in adverse conditions; such spores can retain viability for years.

Sporophyte, see ALTERNATION OF GENERATIONS.

Sporozoa, a large and important class of microscopic unicellular parasitic animals, Protozoa, so called on account of the readiness with which they break themselves up into reproductive spores. The majority of them are minute, but their poisonous products give rise to deadly diseases in man and animals. The principal groups of Sporozoa are the gregarines, the coccidians and the haemosporidians. Gregarines occur only in invertebrates. Coccidians are found in mice, rabbits, frogs, insects, molluscs and lower animals. They reproduce by splitting and by the formation of spores after fertilisation by true spermatozoa. These two distinct processes of multiplication occur also in the haemospordia, a group of blood parasites, one of which, *Plasmodium*, causes malaria.

Sports, Book of, name given to a proclamation of James I in 1618, declaring, much to the fury of the Puritans, that certain games could be played after church on Sundays. In 1644 this book was ordered to be publicly burned by decree of the Long Parliament.

Sports Council, The, an independent body in England, established by royal charter in 1972. There are separate Councils in Scotland, Wales, and Northern Ireland. The main object of the Sports Council is to develop the knowledge and practice of sport in the interests of social welfare and the enjoyment of leisure among the public at large, and the encouragement of the attainment of high standards.

Through its grant-aid policy, the Sports Council encourages local authorities to provide projects of a regional and subregional nature, and finances experimental and prototype schemes to demonstrate the different ways in which facilities can be provided.

Spot-welding, see WELDING.

Sprain, wrenching of a joint, causing stretching or laceration of the ligaments. The most commonly sprained joint is the ankle, since it is, of all joints, the one which bears the most weight. The immediate effects of sprains are pain and loss of power in the joint. Swelling soon takes place. Where fracture is suspected the joint should be appropriately treated. In ordinary sprains swelling may be lessened by the application of cold water immediately after the injury. After the joint has swollen, however, hot water should be employed to ease the pain. The part should be well bandaged and rested.

Sprat, *Clupea sprattus*, a small member of the herring genus, order Clupeiformes. It is from 7 to 15 cm long, with smooth scales and a prominent lower jaw. It has a sharp, toothed edge to its belly. The sprat is a food-fish. Larger sprats are tinned and sold as 'brisling'.

Spring, the first of the four seasons, defined astronomically as the interval between the vernal equinox and the summer solstice but in popular usage taken to mean the period from mid-February till the end of April in Great Britain and from the beginning of March till the end of May in North America.

Spring, a flow of water rising from the point where the underground water-table reaches the surface. Seasonal movement of the water-table often causes this flow to be intermittent. Under certain geological conditions a line of springs may occur at approximately the same level affording a fairly reliable water supply to a group of settlements, hence the term 'spring-line villages'.

Spring Balance, see BALANCE.

Spring-tails, see COLLEMBOLA.

Spring Tide, see TIDES.

Springbok, *Antidorcas marsupialis*, a beautiful antelope found in central and southern Africa. It is of a tawny-red general colour with a white under-surface and head, and obtains its name from the long distances it can leap. This animal is the national emblem of the Republic of South Africa.

Springer, Axel (1912–), German publisher, whose publishing group publishes books, magazines and a number of Federal German newspapers such as *Die Welt, Bild Zeitung, Berliner Morgenpost*, and *Welt am Sonntag*; it also produces programmes for radio and television.

Springer, in architecture, the lowest voussoir of an arch.

See also ARCH.

Springfield, city and capital of Illinois, USA, 300 km south-west of Chicago, situated in a farming and coal-mining region. The tomb and monument of Abraham Lincoln are here in the city where he lived and worked before becoming president. Population (1980) 99,637.

Springfield, city in Massachusetts, USA, on the Connecticut river. The town was founded in 1635, but its growth dates from the establishment of an arsenal in 1777, since when its connection with small arms has been its best-known feature. Population (1980) 152,319.

Springfield, city in the state of Missouri, USA. It is a manufacturing centre in a region which contains few cities, and is the seat of Missouri State College. Population (1980) 133,116.

Springs, town in the Transvaal, South Africa, 47 km east of Johannesburg, centre of a number of gold-mines, two of which also produce uranium. Industries include the manufacture of alloy steels and non-ferrous products, paper making, cycles, sheet glass, electrical goods, and mining machinery. There is also a uranium plant. Population (1980) 153,974, including 49,752 whites.

Spruce, trees of the Coniferous genus *Picea*, of which there are numerous species in Europe, Asia and North America. The most important European species, *P. abies*, the common or Norway spruce, is sold commercially as European whitewood or deal, and is used for building, construction work, box making and the production of pulp for paper. Various North American species are also widely used for these purposes notably *P. sitchensis* the Sitka spruce.

Spur, a device fastened to the heel of a horseman's boot for goading the horse, the modern variety usually consisting of small blunt-pointed wheels called rowels. In the days of chivalry the use of the spur was limited to knights. It is among the emblems of knighthood.

Spurn Head, promontory at the south-east extremity of north Humberside, England, on the estuary of the Humber. Since the erection of groynes in 1864 the inroads of the sea have been checked to some extent. There are two lighthouses.

Sputnik, see SATELLITE, ARTIFICIAL.

Sputum, secretions from the lining or mucous membrane of the respiratory canal, usually consisting of saliva mixed with mucus from the nasal passage. If it is clear white in colour, this usually indicates a minor irritation of the respiratory tract. Purulent, yellowish sputum indicates more severe infection. In some diseases of the lung such as bronchiectasis, lung abcess, tuberculosis and carcinoma of the lung the sputum is purulent, blood-stained and offensive.

See also CANCER.

Spy, in war, is a person who, in order to obtain information for his own side, operates in enemy-held territory surreptitiously and under various forms of disguise. A spy, if captured, is put to death, but an officer or soldier in uniform must be treated as a prisoner of war. Military law, although distinct in ordering the death of a spy, is not clear in defining what constitutes one. The employment of spies in war is held to be legitimate by all states, but the spy himself is regarded as an outlaw, although spies are of two types, the renegade who sells his own country to the enemy for some reward or to further an ideology, and the spy who operates in the enemy territory to obtain information for his own side. Spies are employed by civil governments in peace-time, for the discovery of armament developments, etc., and are not unknown in the industrial world, in the discovery of trade secrets.

See also ESPIONAGE.

Spy, see WARD, SIR LESLIE.

Spyri, Johanna (1829–1901), Swiss author. She wrote many children's stories set in the Swiss mountains, among them *Heidi*, which has become most famous.

Squadron. The word is of Italian origin, and means a 'square' battle formation of companies of infantry or troops of cavalry in close order. In the Royal Navy the term is applied to administrative groups of warships, either working separately or attached to fleets. In the British army the term is used for a body of horsed cavalry, armoured troops, or engineers forming the sub-division of a regiment. In the RAF, a squadron is the smallest operational unit, consisting of both flying and ground personnel in numbers varying with particular functions.

Squall, Line. In an isolated thunderstorm the increase in wind and fall in pressure may be short-lived, but often the accompanying drop in temperature lasts longer, setting up a local cold front. This atmospheric activity can develop into a line squall caused by the sudden aggravation of unstable conditions by warm air being hindered in its path by friction on the ground surface, and being overrun by colder air. The line squall carries with it a characteristic roll cloud. The convection may be so fierce that a vortex develops and forms a funnel cloud as in the tornado. This funnel cloud or waterspout (over the sea) advances across the area affected with the squall.

See also WIND.

Square Dancing, term used for the American style of country dancing when a 'caller' tells the dancers which figure to perform. Originally the name referred to a dance performed by four couples standing in a square formation and was based on the cotillion and quadrille.

Square Measure, see METROLOGY.

Square-rig, rig of a ship whose principal sails are extended on yards, suspended horizontally at the middle, and can be set on either side at a greater or lesser angle with the keel, but not on one side as a fore-and-aft sail.
See also SAILS AND RIGGING.

Square Root, see ROOT.

Squash, see CUCURBITACEAE.

Squash Rackets, a racket-and-ball game for two or four players which evolved from rackets, almost certainly at Harrow School in the mid-19th century. There nearly every boarding house had a blank wall running at right angles to another which became used for a popular 'squashed' version of rackets using a soft, india-rubber ball. Players gaining in proficiency then proceeded to the hard-ball larger court game of rackets.

The court is 9·75 m long and 6·40 m wide; the front wall height (to the boundary line) is 4·75 m. Running along the bottom of the front wall is a board—known as the 'tin'—which serves the same purpose as the net at tennis. The object of the game is to hit a small rubber ball over the tin but under the front boundary line so that it evades an opponent until after it has bounced twice or forced the opponent to make a mistake. After service, the ball can be played off any of the four walls before and/or after hitting the front wall.

The player winning the toss serves on to the front wall from either of the two service boxes so that it rebounds into the opposite half of the court. Only the server can score, the receiver needing first to win a rally in order to become 'in hand' and then to win the next rally to score.

A game is won by the first player to reach a score of nine.

In the USA squash is played on a narrower court and some other dimensions vary; either player can score no matter who is serving.

Squid, a relative of the cuttlefish and, more distantly, of the octopus. It belongs to the mollusc class Cephalopoda (subclass Dibranchia, order Decapoda). Eight of its ten tentacles are short, and two are long, with suckers on the end for grasping prey. The squid swims by taking in water, then squirting it out forcefully, and also by means of its two lateral fins. The fins in the flying squid are strong enough to give it a gliding jump that occasionally lands it on the decks of ships. *Loligo vulgaris*, a common species, is eaten by man.

Squill, the dried, sliced bulb of white, or Mediterranean squill *Urginea maritima*, which contains glycosides with pharmacological activities similar to those of digitalis. It was used by Egyptian physicians in 1500 BC. However, it is less potent and is very poorly absorbed from the intestine. Squill has an irritant effect on the mucosal lining of the stomach when taken orally, and this causes a reflex expectorant action, hence its use in chronic bronchitis, but in larger doses causes vomiting. Red squill is used as a rat poison

in the form of a paste; the glycosides responsible are different from those with medicinal action.

Squill, see SCILLA.

Squinch, in architecture, a small arch built diagonally across the internal angles of a square structure, to carry a circular or octagonal dome or spire.

Squint, or hagioscope, slanting aperture cut through the walls of the chancel in certain medieval churches, so as to make the elevation of the Host visible from a side chapel.

Squinting, or strabismus. In correct vision the axes of both eyes correspond in direction and turn towards the object looked at. The motor muscles so act that any movement of one eye causes a harmonious movement of the other. Sometimes the axes of the eyes are not parallel and the eyes do not move harmoniously together, and this is known as squinting, or strabismus. It may take place upwards, downwards, inwards or outwards; both eyes may be affected, or it may be confined to one. It usually occurs in childhood, due to a defect in the muscles or nerves of the eye or to a unilateral refractive error leading to cortical malfunction. Excessive fatigue, fever or shock can be precipitating conditions, especially if a latent squint already exists.

Sri Lanka. Kandy lies in the interior.

Squire, Sir John Collings (1884–1958), English poet and critic. Squire was one of the leading Georgian poets. In 1913 he was literary editor of the *New Statesman*; from 1919 to 1934 he edited the *London Mercury*, a monthly magazine of literature and the arts to which he contributed under the name of Solomon Eagle. His verse includes *Collected Parodies*, 1921, *Poems in One Volume*, 1926, and *Selected Poems*, 1948.

Squire, abbreviated form of esquire. Originally a squire was the armour-bearer of a knight. In England the word later became popularly applied to the chief land-owner in a country district.

Squirrel, *Sciurus*, a genus of arboreal rodents in the family Sciuridae. *S. vulgaris*, the European or red squirrel, is widely distributed over Europe and parts of Asia. The body is reddish-

brown above and white below; the ears are large and tufted. The body is about 20 cm long, and the bushy tail only a little shorter. It feeds on fruits and shoots, and sometimes eggs and small birds. The grey squirrel, *S. carolinensis*, a native of eastern North America but introduced to Europe, is far more aggressive than the red one. The African ground or spiny squirrels belong to the genus *Xerus*. The flying-squirrels (*Pteromys*) of Asia have a membrane stretching from the forelimb to the hindlimb, which enables them to glide for distances up to 80 m.

Squirrel Monkey, monkey of the genus *Saimiri*, in the family Cebidae. There are two species, both of which are arboreal, insectivorous and gregarious; the long tail is non-prehensile and the face is small.

Sri Lanka
Area: 65,610 km²
Population: 14,470,000
Capital: Colombo

Sri Lanka (formerly Ceylon; Sanskrit *Sinhala*), island republic in the Indian Ocean. It is separated from India by the Gulf of Manaar and Palk Strait, but is virtually joined to the mainland by the submerged coral reefs and sandbanks known as Adam's Rama's Bridge, and by Rameswaram Island. It lies between 5°55′ and 9°50′N latitude and 79°40′ and 80°53′E longitude. Its length from Dondra Head to Palmyra Point (north to south) is about 428 km, and its width varies from 50 to 225 km. Area 65,610 km².

The island is dominated by its mountainous southern half. Its highest peak is Pidurutalagala (2524 m), although Adam's Peak (2243 m) is probably better known. The land slopes gradually down to the coast, except in the north where it forms an undulating plain. The coast is fringed by lagoons and sand bars. Ninety per cent of the country lies below 300 m. The country's rivers radiate from the central highlands like the spokes of a wheel. The main river is the Mahaweli (325 km long) but the majority are less than 150 km long.

The present population of Sri Lanka is around 14,470,000, composed of different races represented by the Sinhalese, Tamils, Moors and Burghers. Twenty-five per cent of the population is urban and concentrated in the region of Colombo (the capital). Other major towns are Jaffna, Kandy, and Galle.

The economy of Sri Lanka is dominated by agriculture. More specifically three crops: tea, rubber, and rice. Of the total cultivated area of 1·9 million ha, over 25 per cent is under rice cultivation and a further 25 per cent under tea and rubber. Of the other food crops cassava is the most important for domestic consumption. Industries include textiles, clothing, pharmaceuticals and food-processing. The most important minerals are gemstones and graphite.

Under the 1972 constitution Sri Lanka was declared to be a 'Free, Sovereign and Independent Republic'. It is a unitary state, whose sovereignty is exercised through the national State Assembly. The constitution was amended in 1977 to introduce an executive President, and a new Presidential republican constitution was formed in 1978.

The official language is Sinhalese, spoken by about 70 per cent of the population. Tamil and English are also widely used.

History. The legendary founder of the early kingdom is believed to be Prince Vijaya from Bengal. Between the 5th century BC and 10th century AD Anuradhapura was the capital and centre of civilisation. The turning point was the introduction of Buddhism in the 3rd century BC. Buddhism became not only the main religion but the main inspiration to cultural and spiritual life of the early civilisation, expressed in the numerous temples, stupas, and religious monuments which were built by successive kings.

With the growth of expansionist kingdoms in South India the Anuradhapura civilisation became involved in South Indian political conflicts. This led to the Cholyan invasion of the 11th century under Emperor Rajaraja the Great, who subjugated the northern part of the country.

The Cholyan invaders were expelled in 1070 by a resistance struggle led by Prince Vijayabahu who became king in 1070 and established himself in the new capital, south-east of Anuradhapura, Polonnaruwa. The Polonnaruwa phase of Ceylon history is notable for two kings, Vijayabahu and Parakramabahu the First, 1151 to 1186. Recurrent turmoil and erosion of the northern irrigation system led to the withdrawal of Sinhalese kings from Polonnaruwa to other sites; in the 15th century they established themselves at Kotte on the south-west coast near Colombo and in the 16th century in the hill capital of Kandy. The break-up of the centralised monarchy led to the establishment of a number of conflicting independent kingdoms. This opened the way for foreign invaders.

The period of European occupation began in 1505 with the landing of the Portuguese in Colombo after their arrival on the Malabar coast. In the middle of the 17th century the Dutch replaced the Portuguese in the maritime provinces of Ceylon. In the 18th century the kingdom of Kandy turned to the British East India Company for aid in dislodging the Dutch. On the outbreak of the revolutionary war in Europe the British occupied the maritime provinces and at the Peace of Amiens (1802) these territories were ceded to them. In 1815 they subjugated the Kingdom of Kandy, thus completing the British conquest of Ceylon.

The British period lasted from 1815 till 1948. Cash crops such as coffee and subsequently tea and rubber were introduced and vast plantations were opened up.

On 4 February 1948 the transfer of power was effected and Sri Lanka became independent. The independence constitution saw the appointment of a governor-general and the establishment of a Senate. The first Prime Minister was Mr D. S. Senanayake.

In 1956 the government of Mr S. W. R. D. Bandaranaike, leader of the Sri Lanka Freedom Party, pledged itself to a philosophy of democratic socialism. Following his assassination in September 1959, his widow Mrs Sirima R. D. Bandaranaike was elected Prime Minister in July 1960. She held office until 1977, except for the period 1965–70 when the United National Party was in power under the premiership of Mr Dudley Senanayake. In July 1977, after a general election marked by much violence and with an aftermath of civil unrest, the United National Party again came into power headed by J. R. Jayawardene. His policy has been to encourage foreign investment in industry and to find a constitutional solution to the problem of Tamil separatism.

Srinagar, summer capital of Jammu and Kashmir state, India, beautifully sited on the Jhelum river in the Vale of Kashmir, 1600 m above sea-level. To the north-east, the Dal Lake with its floating gardens and houseboats is an important tourist centre. Government factories and cottage industries produce carpets, silk, silver, leather, and copperware. Population 1981 est. 520,000.

SS Troops, see SA AND SS.

Stabat Mater, medieval Latin hymn on the seven sorrows of the Virgin Mary, so called from its opening words. There have been musical settings by Dvořák and Verdi.

Stabilisation (exchange rates), financial policy of counteracting wide fluctuations in the relative value of monetary units. The worldwide economic depression of 1930–32 brought the subject under discussion at the World Economic Conference in London in 1933, but with no practical results. Stabilisation of exchange rates after the Second World War was the aim of the Bretton Woods Agreements (1946), by which the International Monetary Fund was set up, which began work in 1947. By the agreement, fixed exchange rates of the other currencies (par values) were to be established with the dollar (and thus indirectly with gold, since the dollar had still a fixed value in gold); changes in par values (with certain exceptions) required the approval of the Fund. The stabilisation of exchange rates, to be effective without exchange restrictions, is dependent on internal financial stability, i.e. avoidance of inflation. See also EXCHANGE, FOREIGN.

Stability, property by which a structure tends to maintain its original position, and by which a moving system tends to recover its typical configuration when slightly disturbed.

See also EQUILIBRIUM.

Stachys, a genus of the Labiatae. It is worldwide in distribution, except for Australasia. Some species are known as woundwort. *S. sylvatica* is the hedge woundwort (with foetid leaves), and *S. palustris* the marsh woundwort. *S. affinis* is the Chinese artichoke which forms edible small white tubers on underground shoots. *S. byzantina (olympica)* is often grown in gardens for its decorative leaves, which are densely covered with white woolly hairs.

Stack, an isolated pinnacle of rock standing in the sea close to the coastline, produced where cliffs have retreated under marine abrasion, leaving scattered offshore remnants.

Stadholder, or Stadtholder, corrupt form of the Dutch *stad-houder* (stead-holder), a title formerly applied to a royal lieutenant or viceroy of a province, who was also a chief magistrate. It became a hereditary title in the House of Orange.

Stadium, Latin form of Greek word *stadion,* a *stade* being a standard measurement in ancient Greece. This was 600 Greek feet (about 185 m or 200 yds), the length of the first race in the original Olympic Games. The name was applied to the race itself and then to the place where the race was held, the sense in use today.

Staël, Madame de (1766–1817), or Anne-Louise-Germaine Necker, Baronne de Staël-Holstein, French novelist and essayist. Having published her *Lettres sur Rousseau,* in 1788, in 1792 the Revolution forced her to leave France, and for some years she travelled. A quarrel with Napoleon, against whom she intrigued constantly, led to her exile in 1803. She moved to Weimar, where she met and studied literature with Schiller and Goethe, and later to Berlin. She was again exiled in 1810, and had to seek refuge in Russia, Sweden, and London, where her masterpiece, *De l'Allemagne,* 1810, gained her access to intellectual circles. In 1814 she was welcomed to Paris by Louis XVIII.

Before her influence, German literature was unknown to France.

Staffa, small uninhabited island of the Inner Hebrides, Scotland, lying 11 km west of Mull. Its circumference is about 2·5 km. Geologically it is composed of volcanic basalt, and is remarkable for its numerous caves, with prismatic and columnar forms. The most famous are Fingal's Cave (70 m long), Clamshell Cave, McKinnon's or Cormorant's Cave, and Boat Cave.

Stafford, market town, and county town of Staffordshire, England, on the River Sow, in the green belt between Wolverhampton and Stoke-on-Trent. Stafford is an important rail centre. Its chief industries include electrical engineering, shoemaking, salt, adhesives, grinding wheels, concrete reinforcement, and other engineering products. Total population (1981) 55,497.

Staffordshire, a midland county of England, bounded on the north-east by Derbyshire, the east by Leicestershire, the south-east by Warwickshire, the south by the West Midlands county and Hereford and Worcester, the south-west by Shropshire, and the north-west by Cheshire. The surface generally is level, rising to hilly regions in the north and south-west. The hills in the north form part of the Peak district, and in the south include Kinver Edge; Cannock Chase includes a large open area in the middle of the county. The chief river is the Trent with its tributaries, the Churnet, Dove, Penk, Sow, and Tame. The county includes the great manufacturing district known as the Potteries. The Black Country, long famous for its metal industries, is no longer in Staffordshire but forms part of the separate West Midlands metropolitan county. Despite the great importance of its industries, much of the county depends on farming, particularly dairying.

Stafford is the county town. The University of Keele was established near the heavily populated area around Stoke-on-Trent. Besides the cathedral at Lichfield, there are many beautiful parish churches. Area 2716 km²; population (1981) 1,012,320.

Staffordshire Bull Terrier, a dog which differs from the modern bull terrier in several ways, and is a representative of the original fighting breed. Dogs weigh from 12·5 to 17·5 kg; their height is from 35 to 40 cm. The breed is unexcelled as a guard and an increasingly popular companion.

Stag-beetle, insect belonging to the family Lucanidae of the order Coleoptera (super-order Scarabaeoidea). They are so-called because most of the males possess enormous mandibles shaped rather like the antlers of a stag. The mandibles appear to be largely ornamental and cannot be moved by the jaw muscles. There are over 900 species within this family, including *Lucanus cervus*, the stag-beetle common to Europe and Asia. The males are much bigger than the females. The adult male *L. cervus* measures up to 80 mm in length. It is dark brown, with chestnut-coloured wing cases which completely cover its abdomen.

Stage, see ACTING; COSTUME, THEATRICAL; DRAMA; THEATRE.

Stagecoach, four-wheeled, four-horsed carriage with seats both inside and outside. It was used in England from the 16th century as a means of public transport, but did not become common-place until the 18th century. Journeys were divided into stages between which horses were changed. Stagecoaches were superseded by the railway; they remained important in the USA throughout the 19th century.

Staghound, foxhound used only for the purpose of hunting either the wild or 'carted' deer. The deerhound is a quite distinct breed.

Stahl, Georg Ernst (1660–1734), German chemist. In 1693 he was appointed professor of medicine at the University of Halle, where he also taught chemistry. Influenced by the ideas of Becher and Kunckel on combustion, he developed the theory of phlogiston, a substance which supposedly separated from objects when they burnt. The theory was finally discredited by Lavoisier.

Stained Glass. The art of stained glass reached its peak early, perhaps the finest of all windows being that presented to Poitiers Cathedral by Henry II of England in 1162. Superb displays of 12th- and 13th-century stained glass can be seen at Chartres, Bourges, Le Mans, Paris (Notre Dame and Sainte

Stalactites and Stalagmites in the Cueva del Agua, near Matienzo in northern Spain.

Chapelle), Laon and Canterbury. In the 14th century, stained glass began to yield its primacy as a decorative medium to painting, which increasingly was to affect stained glass design. Fine examples of this middle period are at York, Gloucester, Erfurt, Assisi, Florence (in the Cathedral some 15th-century glass was designed by Donatello, Ghiberti and Uccello), Milan, Seville and Cambridge (King's College Chapel). Renaissance glass in the 16th to 18th centuries used larger panes, often of white glass decorated with filigrees of black and gold ('silver stain') and impermanent enamels. Masterpieces are in Florence (Laurentian Library by Vasari), Auch, Westminster Abbey, and some Parisian churches and Oxford colleges. In the 19th century Munich glass was fashionable. Perhaps the best Gothic Revival stained glass

was English, especially that of the Burne Jones–Morris circle. In the 20th century, French painters including Matisse (at Vence) and Léger (at Audincourt) introduced 'abstract design', much used in postwar church-building in Germany (especially the Cologne Archdiocese) and England (Coventry Cathedral). A technical incentive has been the development of a fused glass technique and the use of cement and epoxy resin compounds for binding spalled slab glass.

See also GLASS-ENGRAVING.

Stainer, Sir John (1840–1901), British organist, composer and theorist. In 1872 he became organist at St Paul's Cathedral. Besides compositions for organ, church services and textbooks, he wrote several cantatas, and oratorios including *The Crucifixion*, 1877.

Stakhanov Movement, ideological movement among the workers and *kolkhoz* peasants in the USSR, aimed at raising the productivity of labour. It was originated in 1935 by the coal-miner A. Stakhanov on instruction of the Party authorities. Specially favourable conditions were given to selected workers, who, together with several assistants, achieved spectacular production results, which were used as justification for raising production targets for all workers.

Stalactites and Stalagmites are the colloquial names for columnar forms of chemical concretions known as speleotherms which occur in natural caves in limestone areas. Stalactites hang vertically from a cave roof and are initiated by the development of a single sheath of crystals surrounding a central passage of groundwater. As the water, saturated in carbon dioxide, drops from the roof it partly evaporates and results in a small precipitation of calcium carbonate forming around the edges. Each successive drop causes the deposit to grow, with later flow down the outer surface precipitating further layers of crystals thereby creating the extended conical form. Stalagmites grow upwards from the

Stained Glass. *The Rozenkranz window in Aachen Cathedral by Wilhelm Geyer.*

cave floor to the source on the roof in forms ranging from simple bosses to slender pillars. Curtain-like structures which form under suitable conditions are often banded with impurities to give white, blue, and red coloration. Marked variation in the rate of growth has been recorded, the average being around 0·25 mm a year.

Stalin, Joseph, real name Iosif Vissarionovic Dzhugashvili (1879–1953), dictator of Russia and of the world Communist movement, the most accomplished totalitarian ruler in modern history. He joined the Russian Social Democratic Workers' party in 1898 and the Bolshevik faction in 1903, and worked underground in Transcaucasia as an active but minor follower of Lenin until 1913, when Lenin and Zinoviev co-opted him into the Bolshevik central committee. This ensured his formal seniority when he returned to St Petersburg from banishment after the February Revolution in 1917. He was then second in the Bolshevik hierarchy in the capital, after Kamenev, and became editor of the party's newspaper 'Pravda'. Stalin followed Kamenev's conciliatory policy towards the provisional government, but when Lenin arrived from abroad accepted his plans for the seizure of power by the Bolsheviks. After the crisis over the Brest-Litovsk Treaty, in which the Left Communists and Trotsky opposed Lenin, Stalin became, apart from Sverdlov, Lenin's closest collaborator. During the Civil War he was a senior political commissar in the Red Army. He was a member of the Politburo from its foundation and in 1922 became general secretary of the Party's Central Committee.

By the time Lenin died Stalin had consolidated his hold on the party apparatus. In the inner-party struggle that ensued he joined forces with Zinoviev and Kamenev and defeated Trotsky, using the slogan of 'building socialism in one country first' as against Trotsky's 'permanent revolution'. He then, together with Bukharin and Rykov, defeated the 'new opposition' of Zinoviev and Kamenev and the 'combined opposition' of these two with Trotsky (Left Opposition), and finally defeated the Right Opposition of Bukharin and Rykov with the help of his own followers Molotov, Voroshilov, Kaganovich, Ordzhonikidze, and Kirov, whom he gradually promoted to the Politburo. He ruled together with them as undisputed leader of the victorious clique from 1929 until 1934, launching the Five-Year Plans, the collectivisation of agriculture, and the so-called 'cultural revolution', i.e. large-scale replacement of old intellectuals, whether liberal, technocratic, Populist or ex-Menshevik, by new ones hastily trained from among uneducated party members. From 1934, when an opposition emerged among his own followers led by Kirov, Stalin abandoned 'collective leadership' and established his personal rule. Constant purging of the party and state apparatus culminated in the Great Purge, aimed at the extermination of all potential and imaginary opponents.

Henceforth Stalin's rule was a reign of terror. In 1940 Stalin became officially the head of the government, in 1941 chairman of the State Defence Committee, commissar (later

minister) of defence and supreme commander-in-chief of the Soviet armed forces. He interfered personally with the work of the military commanders, and assumed the ranks of marshal and, later, generalissimo. The comparative relaxation of the political atmosphere in the war years was followed, from 1946, by the complete restoration of Stalinism as it had developed before the war and its imposition on the satellite countries of Eastern Europe. The last years of Stalin's rule were characterised by extreme obscurantism, xenophobia, chauvinism, and anti-Semitism.

Stalin Peak, see COMMUNISM PEAK.

Stalinabad, see DUSHANBE.

Stalingrad, see VOLGOGRAD.

Stalino, see DONETSK.

Stalinsk, see NOVOKUZNETSK.

Stall, in church architecture, an elevated seat in the choir enclosed by a high back and sides.

Stamford, handsome, stone-built market town on the River Welland in Lincolnshire, England. Burghley House, south of the town, was begun in 1575 by Lord Burghley. Agriculture, engineering, plastics, and timber and stone trades are important. Population (1981) 16,153.

Stamford Bridge, village in Humberside, England, on the River Derwent, 13 km north-east of York. It was the scene of the defeat of invading Norwegians under Harold III (Hardrada) by the English under Harold, on 25 September 1066.

Stamitz, Johann (1717–57), Bohemian composer. He was the founder of the Mannheim school of early symphonists. He wrote some 70 symphonies, which helped to establish the form used by Haydn and Mozart; he also wrote many concertos and much chamber music.

Stammering and Stuttering, fairly common forms of speech disorder, which are due to the uncoordinated action of the muscles around the larynx. In stammering there is a hesitation or delay in the pronunciation of a syllable, while in a stutter there is a machine-gun like repetition of the initial letters of a syllable. Stammering that originates in childhood is believed to be the result of physiological instability in the organisation of the neuromuscular apparatus concerned in speech. It may, however, be provoked or aggravated by emotional factors. The relatively frequent association of stammering with a family history of left-handedness has given rise to the theory that the condition is basically due to the incomplete dominance of the leading hemisphere of the brain.

Stamp Act, act passed in Britain in 1765, in spite of the protests of the New England colonies of America, by which the British government gave itself the right to levy a tax on all manner of documents, such as legacies, cheques, and receipts, as a means of raising revenue for colonial defence. The colonists, on the principle of no taxation without representation, denied the right of the home government to tax them. The Whigs repealed the act in 1766, but with a saving measure in the shape of an act declaring that England had full legislative and fiscal authority over the colonies.

Stamp Collecting, see PHILATELY.

Stamp Duty is a duty charged in Britain on certain documents. The principal statute is the Stamp Act 1891. It is not charged on transactions but only on instruments effecting transactions. Thus if a transaction can be effected orally, no duty is payable. The most common instruments attracting stamp duty are: (1) conveyances or transfers on the sale of land or other property, such as shares; (2) leases; (3) voluntary dispositions, e.g. conveyances of property into settlements; (4) policies of life assurance.

Standard, the uppermost and largest of the five petals composing the irregular corolla of papilionaceous flowers, such as the sweet pea. It overhangs the lateral wings and the 'keel'. In horticulture a standard tree or shrub is one grown on a single upright stem.

Standard, Royal, popular name of the British sovereign's armorial banner. See also FLAG.

Standard Deviation, see STATISTICS.

Standard of Living, a term used to indicate the amount of goods and services (utilities) enjoyed by a community or individually by its members. It can be assessed by investigating or measuring the kinds of, and expenditure on, food, housing, clothing, and other necessities or amenities in any section of the community.
See also COST OF LIVING; PRICE.

Standard Temperature and Pressure are 273·15 K (0°C) and 101,325 Pa (760 mm Hg).

Standing Orders, are, in Britain, the printed rules for regulating the proceedings of both Houses of Parliament, which, unless repealed, remain in force from parliament to parliament. They may be supplemented from time to time by sessional or temporary orders and resolutions. The standing orders which relate to the public business of the House of Commons are by no means a complete code of procedure but require to be more informally supplemented by unwritten precedents, general practice, and specific rulings from the Speaker. No special procedure is

Sir Henry Stanley as he was dressed when he met Livingstone at Ujiji.

involved in the making, suspending, or repeal of a standing order except that adequate notice must normally be given.

Standish, Myles (c.1584–1656), American colonist. He embarked in 1620 for New Plymouth in the *Mayflower*. He was chosen military captain of the colony in 1621, and defended it against the attacks of the Indians, notably at Weymouth, 1623.

Stanford, Sir Charles Villiers (1852–1924), Irish composer and teacher. He was the first professor of composition at the Royal College of Music and professor of music at Cambridge University.

Stanford was perhaps more influential as a teacher than as a composer. His compositions include eight operas; incidental and church music; many choral works; seven symphonies; five *Irish Rhapsodies* for orchestra; concertos; chamber music; piano works; and about 150 songs.

Stanhope, James Stanhope, 1st Earl (1673–1721), English soldier. In 1708 he was appointed commander-in-chief of the British forces in Spain. He captured Port Mahon, but was defeated and captured by the French in 1710 at Brihuega. In 1714 he was appointed one of the two principal secretaries of state.

Stanislavsky, Konstantin Sergeevich (1863–1938), Russian actor, producer and teacher. He began his career as an amateur, and by constant study, partly under the elder Kommissarzhevsky, became one of the most versatile actors his country has ever produced. He played in every form of drama, and even prepared for Opera. With Nemirovich-Danchenko he founded the Moscow Arts Theatre and opened a new era in dramatic production and acting. His method was seemingly natural acting as opposed to declamation. He produced many plays by Chekhov and Gorky, and was himself a splendid character actor. He published *An Actor Prepares*, 1948.

Stanley, Sir Henry Morton (1841–1904), assumed name of John Rowlands, British explorer and author. At the age of 15 he went to New Orleans, USA, where he met the benefactor whose name he took in preference to that of his natural father, and in 1861 entered the Confederate army. In 1867 he was appointed correspondent for the *New York Herald*, and accompanied Lord Napier's Abyssinian expedition. He next visited Spain, the Suez Canal, Palestine, Turkey, Persia, and India, and was sent to find David Livingstone, reaching Zanzibar in 1871. He came upon him at Ujiji, and together they explored the north end of Lake Tanganyika. In 1874 he circumnavigated Lake Victoria, passed down the Lualaba to its confluence with the Congo (Zaire) and then traced the course of that river to the sea. In 1879 he founded the Congo Free State. Stanley was a Liberal Unionist MP between 1895 and 1900 after reassuming his British citizenship. His works include *Through the Dark Continent*, 1878.

Stanley, capital of the Falkland Islands. Stanley is the only important settlement of the colony, and is situated on the coast of East Falkland. There is a good harbour and a wireless station. Population (1979) 1,000. A large garrison has existed since 1982.

Stanleyville, see KISANGANI.

Stannaries (Latin *stannum*, tin), the Court of the Stannaries of Cornwall and Devon was

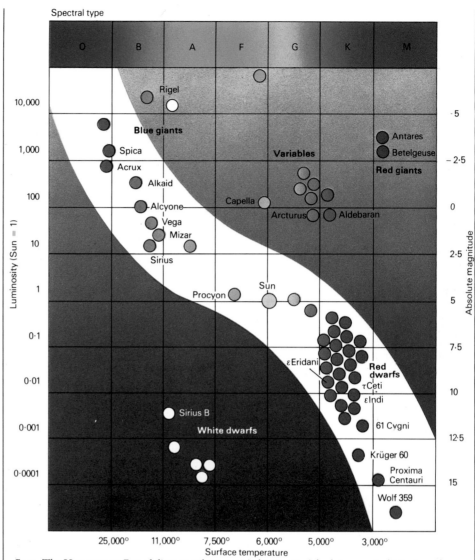

Star. *The Hertzsprung-Russel diagram relates a star's luminosity (absolute magnitude) to its surface temperature (spectral type). If stars found in open clusters are plotted on the diagram it is found that those in the 'adult' phase of their evolution lie in a broad band known as the main sequence.*

a court of record, with a special jurisdiction for the administration of justice among the tinners of those counties. The jurisdiction rested on an ancient privilege confirmed by royal charter in 1305, granted to the tin miners to sue and be sued in their own court so as to avoid being drawn from their business to the public detriment. The jurisdiction of the court was abolished in 1897.

Stansfield, Grace, see FIELDS, GRACIE.

Stanza, in prosody, Italian term meaning a collection of lines arranged in an ordered pattern connected by metre and rhyme to form a regular division of 'verse' of a poem.

Star, luminous body found, mainly in galaxies, throughout the observable Universe. Our local star is the Sun.

Stars are believed to originate in cool interstellar clouds. These consist mainly of hydrogen and helium but with traces of other elements and a sprinkling of dust grains. A star begins its existence as a volume of this interstellar matter gradually separating from the parent cloud. As it contracts gravitational energy is released as heat, slowly at first but at an increasing rate. As the star grows denser a smaller proportion of the heat generated can escape into space and its material warms up. The grains are first

vaporised and then their atoms, along with those of the former interstellar gas, are completely ionised. The star has become a sphere of 'perfect' gas consisting of a neutral mixture of free electrons and atomic nuclei. For a sphere with the mass and radius of the Sun, this theory implies a central temperature of about 24,000,000 K; but such a sphere could maintain the Sun's power output without appreciable change for a few tens of millions of years only. The crucial fact is that, as soon as the central temperature and density reach the point at which nuclear transformations can take place, energy is produced by the transformation of hydrogen into helium to replace that lost at the surface. The star has no need to contract further until its hydrogen is exhausted.

The nuclear transformations take place near the centre so the star gradually acquires an inert helium core (itself subject to gravitational contraction) surrounded by a thin shell of transforming hydrogen. As the core grows, the outer layers have to adjust themselves to maintain the mechanical and thermal equilibrium. The star expands, becomes a yellow giant, and consumes its hydrogen ever more quickly. What happens further depends on the mass of the star. If this is less than 1·2 times that of the Sun, the core becomes degenerate and the star, having shed its outer layers, becomes a white dwarf. If the mass exceeds this Chandrasekhar's limit, the core cannot become degenerate and development is catastrophic. As the core grows increasingly hot other nuclear transformations take place resulting in the helium being converted first into carbon and oxygen and then into heavier elements until iron, the most stable of all, is reached. Finally there is a supernova outburst that may leave behind it a pulsar which appears to be a rapidly rotating *neutron star*. But there is also a mass limit for neutron stars; if the central remnant has a mass more than twice that of the Sun it cannot collapse into the neutron star state but would have to form a black hole.

It is not possible to give an exact answer to the question 'How many stars are in the Galaxy?'. The estimated mass of the Galaxy is 200,000 million times that of the Sun. If most of this is condensed into stars, and if the greater number of these are like the stars near the Sun with an average mass 0·2 that of the Sun, the number of stars in the Galaxy may well be of the order of a million million. The number of observable galaxies in the Universe is almost certainly greater.

See also NOVAE; PULSARS; VARIABLE STARS.

Star Carr, one of the most important Mesolithic sites in Europe, situated 8 km south-east of Scarborough, Yorkshire. An occupation site of a hunting family, it has provided much evidence of the economy, lifestyles and natural habitat of its inhabitants. Red deer accounted for most of the meat diet, followed by roe deer, elk, wild ox and wild pig. The site may have been occupied on a seasonal basis, and its lakeside location used for fishing, the number of bone harpoons providing ample evidence for this.

Star Chamber, English high court of justice going back at least as far as Edward III's reign, the name being derived, perhaps, from a starry decoration on the ceiling. Under the Stuarts it became merely an instrument for enforcing the claims of the prerogative. Its abolition in 1641 deprived the Crown of a formidable weapon for the suppression of free speech and writing and for the enforcement of proclamations which the king had no right to make.

Star Clusters are groups of stars which are close together in space, share a common motion, and have a common origin. They may contain very many stars or only a few; their star densities may be as high as 1000 per cubic parsec or less than 1 per 100 cubic parsecs. In the former case their mutual gravitation may be expected to hold the cluster stars together almost indefinitely while in the latter what few stars there are will quickly dissipate into the general star field.

The Globular Clusters are very nearly spherically symmetrical, and contain an immense number of stars which are concentrated towards the centre where they are so close together that it is impossible to resolve them completely into individual stars even in the biggest telescopes.

The Open Clusters, of which the Pleiades, Hyades, and Praesepe may be taken as typical, are very much smaller than the globulars;

they contain very many fewer stars which are more widely scattered. They are relatively young objects and are found in the disc of the Galaxy, i.e., along the Milky Way.

Associations can be regarded as very extended open clusters with few members and as such must have formed recently. Two kinds are recognised though they may co-exist as in Orion. These are the O-associations containing O and B type stars and the T-associations whose members are T Tauri stars which are red eruptive variable stars newly formed from the surrounding interstellar matter.

Stara Planina (Balkan Mountains; ancient *Haemus*), sub-range of the central European mountain system, extending from the Iron Gate of the River Danube to the Black Sea. Most of the range, which is about 25–40 km broad and 603 km long, lies within Bulgaria. The highest mountain is Yumrukchal (2376 m). The chief pass is the Shipka.

Stara Zagora, town of central Bulgaria, capital of Stara Zagora province, lying south of the Shipka pass through the Balkan Mountains. Textiles, chemicals, tobacco, and foodstuffs are manufactured. The province is noted for its roses. Population (1978) 130,768.

Starboard (old English *steor*, rudder; *bord*, side) means the right-hand side of a ship as one faces forward; it is so named because it was the side on which the steering oar or steerboard was fixed in primitive vessels. At night a green light is carried on the starboard and a red light on the port side of a vessel.

Starbrook, David (1945–), British judo fighter. He won bronze medals at the 1971 and 1973 World Championships. He beat Rougé the following year at the Montreal Olympics on his way to winning a bronze medal. He has also won silver medals at the 1972 Munich Games and the 1973 European Championships. He has been winner of the British Open Championship nine times, and was British Olympic team manager at Moscow in 1980.

Starch, or amylum ($C_6H_{10}O_5$)n, carbohydrate, widely disseminated throughout the vegetable world. It occurs in rice and all kinds of grain in quantities up to 70 per cent, and also occurs in tubers, such as potatoes and arrowroot. It is insoluble in cold water, but swells and gelatinises in hot water, and is coloured blue with iodine. Boiled with dilute acids it is converted to dextrin and glucose and heated with diastase it forms dextrin and maltose, which are also formed by the action of saliva and pancreatic juice on starch. In green plants starch is formed from water and atmospheric carbon dioxide by the photosynthetic pigment chlorophyll; the necessary energy is derived from sunlight.

Starch occurs in two forms, α-amylose and amylopectin. α-Amylose consists of long unbranched chains of glucose molecules; the chains vary considerably in size and molecular weight which may be as high as 1 million.

Starch, Animal, see GLYCOGEN.

Starfish, animals of class Asteroidea in the phylum Echinodermata. They have a star-like shape, the rays of which usually number five; these are movable arms with skeletal structures, consisting of calcareous plates

transversely arranged and articulated with one another like vertebrae. The mouth is in the middle of the underside of the central disc. A wide furrow, the ambulacral groove, extends from the mouth to the tip of each arm. These grooves contain the tube feet, which are extensions of the water vascular system involved in locomotion. Movable spines protect these delicate structures. The upper surface bears the anus and the madreporite, a porous structure which allows communication between the water vascular system and the exterior. The precise role of the madreporite, and associated structures such as the stone canal, is poorly understood, but the water vascular system as a whole acts as a hydraulic system during locomotion. Elongation of the tube feet is brought about by forcing water into them. Upon contact with the substratum the centre of the terminal sucker of the foot is drawn in, causing adhesion by vacuum.

In some starfish, specialised jawed appendages (pedicellariae) are present. These are of several types but all basically function to capture small prey and in defence. Starfish are carnivorous, different species showing marked dietary preferences. Starfish show marked regenerative abilities and in some species asexual reproduction by splitting occurs. Most starfish species are dioecious (the animal is either male or female) with the eggs being fertilised outside the female, in the sea. A free-swimming, bipinnaria larva develops which settles and metamorphoses into the adult form.

Stark, Dame Freya Madeline (1893–), British explorer and writer. She worked on the *Baghdad Times* and published *Baghdad Sketches* in 1933. *The Valleys of the Assassins*, 1934, describes journeys in Persia and Luristan. She wrote *The Southern Gates of Arabia*, 1936, after explorations in the Hadhramaut. During the Second World War she worked for the Ministry of Information in the Middle East and North Africa. Her many other works include *Alexander's Path*, 1958, and *Minaret of Djam: An Excursion In Afghanistan*, 1970.

Starling, *Sturnus vulgaris*, a bird of the family Sturnidae, order Passeriformes, common in Europe. It is about 20 cm long, and the head, neck, back and underparts are a metallic glossy black. The feathers on the upper parts are tipped with buff, and the wings are greyish-black, with a reddish-brown fringe. The female is less glossy and lustrous than the male. A number of closely related foreign birds are known as starlings.

Starr, Ringo, see BEATLES.

Stars and Stripes, see UNITED STATES OF AMERICA.

Starvation, see FAMINE; FASTING; HUNGER.

Starwort, name used sometimes for stitchwort but more commonly for *Callitriche* (family Callitrichaceae), a genus of small aquatic plants whose oval leaves, sometimes floating, form a star-like pattern round the stem. They are found throughout the world.

State, autonomous system of political control exercised over citizens inhabiting a determinate geographical area. The system of control is derived from a formal structure of law which is backed up by coercive force of which the state has a legal monopoly. Administrative control is embodied in an organised system of

rôles and offices. The relationship between the individual citizen and the system of control can take various forms, from one in which the flow of influence is almost totally from authority to citizen (autocracy), to one of almost equal influence (democracy).
See also GOVERNMENT; SOVEREIGNTY.

State, Acts of, term used in English law to signify any prerogative act of policy in the field of external affairs. No action in tort lies in respect of an act injurious to the person or to the property of aliens outside Her Majesty's dominions done by any representative of the Crown and which is either previously sanctioned or subsequently ratified by the Crown. Such an act is an act of state.

State Trading, buying and selling at home or abroad by the state. It plays a great part in the economy of the USSR.
In Britain state trading received a great impetus during the First World War, and a still greater one during the Second World War, when the buying and selling of most industrial raw materials and foodstuffs were undertaken by the government in the interest of the national war effort.
See also NATIONALISATION.

States-General, name given to the various legislative assemblies of France prior to the Revolution. Six such bodies were established in the 14th and 15th centuries. The *États de Paris* (1614) did not meet again until 1785. These were strictly the last states-general held in France, for in 1789 they were transformed into the National Assembly.

States-General, legislative body of the Netherlands which, in 1814, superseded the National Assembly, which had itself been established in 1795 in place of the old States-General of the United Provinces.

Static, see ATMOSPHERICS.

Static Electricity, see ELECTROSTATICS.

Statics, branch of mechanics which deals with the action of forces in compelling a body to remain at rest or not alter its motion. See EQUILIBRIUM.

Statics, Graphic deals with the determination of stresses, tensions, etc., of frameworks and systems in equilibrium, by geometrical methods of construction. A force may be represented by a straight line of definite length, drawn in a given direction through a point and the resultant of any number of forces can be found by graphic construction. The method can be used to solve shear-force, bending-moment and other problems.

Stations of the Cross, or Way of the Cross, late medieval devotion originating in the pilgrimages to the Holy Land. In the 15th and 16th centuries in certain cities of Europe an exact topographical reproduction of the points of devotional interest seen by pilgrims in Jerusalem was attempted by means of shrines in various parts of the city. Reproductions subsequently lost all attempt at topographical meaning and, shrinking in size, came to consist of images or pictures showing various scenes from Christ's journey to Calvary. As such they eventually took permanent form, and are found as pictures, each surmounted by a cross, on the walls inside Roman Catholic churches. They are 14 in number, and the devotion consists in going from one to another and saying appropriate prayers at each. Sometimes 14 crosses are erected without pictures, but the devotion is made in the same way.

Statistics, branch of mathematics dealing with methods of collecting, recording and analysing numerical data; it also describes numerical data acquired by observation, measurement or experiment. A statistic is a number derived from summarising data collected. Economic and demographic statistics establish total values for simple counts of a defined kind such as population or export figures. They are usually presented as 'time series' – sequences of measurements made at regular intervals. Time series at intervals of three months or less are commonly subjected to 'seasonal adjustment' from a knowledge of previous years. Often 'index numbers' are used instead of actual figures; the value for a chosen 'base period' is designated 100 and figures for other times are expressed as percentages of it. Index numbers are particularly useful for comparing trends in different time series. Statistics about Individuals must be taken from a truly representative sample, and statisticians usually publish details of sampling methods and questionnaires used.
Unsorted 'raw' data is distributed into classes to determine the number of individuals in each class, the 'class frequency'. This can be presented as a series of rectangles; the graph obtained by joining the midpoints of the top of the rectangles is called a frequency polygon. Mean, median and mode are different 'typical' or 'central' values. The mean is the arithmetic average of the observed values and is the most useful for statistical theory; the median is the middle value exceeded by half the items in the sample; the mode is the most common value. Dispersion is measured by the 'variance', the arithmetic mean of the squares of the deviations from the mean. The positive square root of this is the 'standard deviation' and it is usual to work in units of standard deviation measured from the mean. A standard distribution has a mean of zero and a standard deviation of unity.
A most important use of statistical theory is in testing whether experimental data support hypotheses by comparing the standard deviations from sets of results for significant differences.

Stator, the stationary part of a rotating machine, alternator, motor, or turbine.

Statue of Liberty, see LIBERTY ISLAND.

Stauffenberg, Claus, Count Schenk von (1907–44), German soldier. He was severely wounded in the Second World War, and in 1944 was a colonel on the General Staff. Stauffenberg was one of the leaders of the unsuccessful attempt on Hitler's life on 20 July 1944, and it was he who placed the bomb in Hitler's bunker. He was shot the next day.

Staunton, Howard (1810–74), British chess champion between 1841–51; also an actor and Shakespearean scholar of some note. He defeated the strongest French and German chess players of the day. The pieces used in club and tournament play today were named after him by their designer, Nathaniel Cook.

Stavanger, city in the county of Rogaland, Norway, of which it is the county town. It lies 160 km south of Bergen, and was founded in the 8th or 9th century. It has a large fish-canning industry. There is an important shipyard, and much shipping is registered in Stavanger. The city is the centre of Norway's North Sea oil exploration and oil rig construction. Population (1980) 89,913.

Stave, or staff (music), see NOTATION.

Stavisky, Alexandre (1886–1934), naturalised Frenchman, of Russian birth, responsible for a financial scandal in France in 1934. He floated a very large sum in bogus bonds, in the name of the municipal credit establishment of Bayonne. Stavisky committed suicide after a warrant for his arrest had been issued. The scandal caused the fall of two governments, a general strike, and riots in Paris.

Stavropol (1935–44, *Voroshilovsk*), capital city, economic and cultural centre of Stavropol *krai*, 304 km south east of Rostov USSR, with food, and leather industries; it is the starting-point of the natural gas pipeline to Moscow. Population (1980) 265,000.

Steam, a dry, colourless and transparent gas formed by the evaporation of water at any temperature. The term is often used erroneously for the damp clouds of water droplets produced by the condensation of steam in a cooler atmosphere. Steam, or water vapour, is released by water or ice at all temperatures provided the atmosphere is not already saturated. The amount of vapour the atmosphere can hold increases with temperature.

Steam Distillation, process for purifying solids and liquids which are generally water-insoluble. It can be applied to systems in which the substance to be purified is volatile and the impurities non-volatile. Steam is passed into the mixture and volatilises the required product. The resulting mixture of steam and the product is condensed and the required material is recovered.

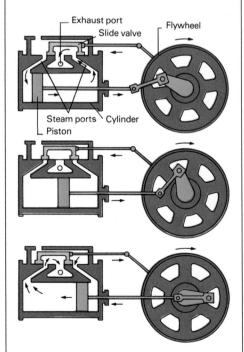

Steam Engine. *Three separate stages make up a complete cycle in the operation of the reciprocating steam engine.*

Steam Engine, mechanism powered by the expansion that takes place when water vaporises to form steam. In the traditional reciprocating steam engine, steam pressure acts on each side of a piston alternately. Steam is admitted slightly before both ends of each stroke, allowing the steam to exert its full pressure before the engine reaches dead centre. When the valve closes, the steam begins to expand and when the pressure has fallen sufficiently due to expansion, the exhaust valve opens. Some engines are still controlled by a slide valve which, when moved to one side, has one port open to compressed steam and one to exhaust. More modern is the piston valve in which steam and exhaust ports are cut. Independent poppet-valves, lift-valves or drop-valves, are common on high-efficiency stationary engines. Speed control, necessary because of varying steam pressure throughout the stroke, is achieved by using a flywheel and a governor, the latter maintaining an equilibrium at any engine speed.

Forms of Steam Engine. The *simple steam engine* is a single horizontal cylinder, using saturated steam and exhausting into the atmosphere. *Condensing engines* exhaust into a closed air-tight vessel in which steam is condensed to water almost instantaneously. Very low back-pressures can be attained, with corresponding increased efficiency. Condensers are of two types, surface and jet, the latter being more efficient and smaller. In *compound engines*, steam is partially expanded in a small high-pressure cylinder, passed to a receiver, then admitted to a larger low-pressure cylinder, where the rest of the expansion takes place. Advantages are a simpler valve gear and less condensation. A comparatively recent development is the *uniflow engine*. Steam flows one way only—in at the ends, usually via cam-operated drop valves, and out at the middle via exhaust ports cut in the cylinder wall.

Development. The first practical pumping engine was built by Savery in 1698, using the water as the piston. Newcomen's pumping engine, 1711, actuated a separate pump and was more effective. But the first efficient engine was Watt's single-acting engine (1769) which used a separate condenser, thus keeping the cylinder hot continuously. This success delayed the coming of the high-pressure non-condensing engine and Hornblower's compound engine (invented in 1781) and, as Watt's machines were beam engines, the direct-acting engine was a rarity until after 1825. With Watt's invention of the crank (1781), the steam engine came into extensive use. See also THERMODYNAMICS.

Steam Turbine, see STEAMSHIP; TURBINE, STEAM.

Steamship. The first practical steamboat was the *Charlotte Dundas* (1801), fitted with Watt's double-acting condensing engine, driving a stern paddle-wheel. The side-lever engine was the first true marine engine (as distinct from a land engine). The screw propeller was introduced on Brunel's passenger steamer *Great Eastern* (1840), and, being less vulnerable than the paddle-wheel, found great favour. Marine-engine design was thereby completely changed; the main shaft was now fore-and-aft, low down in the ship, and rotated at high speed. In 1872 the vertical marine-engine was adopted. This survived until the introduction of the steam turbine, and the diesel engine and gas turbine.

The first turbine-driven ship was the *Turbinia*

(1897). Today the main use for the steam turbine is on large tankers, aircraft carriers and container ships, where very high powers are required. Nuclear-powered ships use the reactor for raising steam and the steam turbine for propulsion.

See also PADDLE-STEAMER; SHIPS and SHIPBUILDING.

Stearic Acid, or octadecanoic acid, $CH_3 \cdot (CH_2)_{16} \cdot COOH$, a saturated fatty acid, occurs widely distributed as the glyceride in animal and vegetable fats and oils—usually associated with the glycerides of palmitic and oleic acids. It is most abundant in the more solid fats, particularly animal fats. Pure stearic acid is white, crystalline, insoluble in water but soluble in alcohol and ether, and has a relative density of $0 \cdot 85$ at its melting point $69°C$, whereas commercial stearic acid may be white or slightly yellowish in colour and have a melting point as low as $53°C$. Among the more important manufactured products in which stearic acid and its derivatives are used are foods, soaps, detergents, lubricants, protective coatings, gramophone records, polishes, cosmetics, toilet preparations, candles, matches, crayons, rubber compounds, and paper coatings.

See also FATTY ACIDS.

Steel, David Martin Scott (1938–), British politician and leader of the Liberal party since 1976. In 1965 he was elected Liberal MP for Roxburgh, Selkirk, and Peebles and was sponsor of the private member's bill to reform the law on abortion, 1966–67. From 1970 to 1975 he was Liberal chief whip. In 1976 he succeeded Jeremy Thorpe as leader of the Liberal party and was the first party leader in Britain to be elected by party supporters outside Parliament rather than by MPs.

Steel, see IRON AND STEEL; METALLURGY; ROLLING MILLS; STRUCTURAL STEELWORK.

Steel Drum, percussion musical instrument invented in the 1940s in Trinidad. Various materials were used initially but nowadays the bottoms of very large oil drums are always used. Small areas on the face of the drum are isolated by hammer and punch and are then tuned by hammering. Steel drums are used in sets, the highest or ping-pong with some 25 small areas, each producing a different pitch, the second pan with about 14, a pair of third pans each with 9 or 10 notes, and usually 4 bass pans with 4 or 5 notes each.

Steele, Sir Richard (1672–1729), English essayist and dramatist. His first, and most amusing, comedy, *The Funeral*, was produced at Drury Lane in 1701. In 1709 he founded *The Tatler* and, as Isaac Bickerstaff, a pseudonym borrowed from Jonathan Swift, contributed two-thirds of its essays. Several of the remainder were written by Addison, but Steele's are characterised by his easy, light style. In *The Tatler*, Steele produced the same mixture of entertainment and moral instruction (avoiding politics) which was later the great feature of *The Spectator*. For this journal, started by both writers in 1711, Steele invented many of the famous characters, such as Sir Roger de Coverley.

His last comedy, *The Conscious Lovers*, produced at Drury Lane in 1722, is one of the best English 'sentimental' comedies.

Although a successful dramatist, it is as an essayist that Steele is famous. In *The Tatler*,

Steele's individual work, he followed a favourite task, the reform of manners and the victory of culture over excess individualism.

Steen, Jan (1625/6–79), Dutch painter, who worked mainly in Leiden. He is associated primarily with merry or riotous drinking scenes. Steen was, however, more versatile than is generally realised, painting portraits, historical and religious works as well as genre scenes. He was one of the most prolific painters of the period.

Steeple, term applied to a tall tower, usually including its spire; especially applied to the spired towers of Sir Christopher Wren's City churches in London.

Steeplechasing (athletics). This event is now standardised at 3000 m (1 mile 1520 yards). It comprises 28 hurdles (0·91 m high) and a shallow water-jump (3·66 m square) in each of the seven laps. For horse racing, see POINT-TO-POINT STEEPLECHASES.

Stefan's Law, named after Joseph Stefan, Austrian physicist (1835–93), states that electromagnetic energy radiated from a heated body is proportional to the fourth power of its absolute temperature. Thus, if R is the amount of energy radiated per second from unit surface area of a body at an absolute temperature T, then $R = \sigma T^4$, where σ is Stefan's constant. Strictly the law applies only to 'black bodies', but it is frequently a good approximation to the radiation of other objects.

Stegosaurus, a genus of late Jurassic North American dinosaurs of the order Ornithischia. They were ungainly quadrupedal herbivores, with very small heads, a double row of triangular plates along the back, and spikes on the tail.

Stein, Gertrude (1874–1946), US poet and critic. In her works, influenced by the artists Picasso and Matisse, whose paintings she collected, she developed an abstract, experimental type of prose which in turn had some influence on later writers. In Paris she befriended and encouraged several expatriate American writers, including Ernest Hemingway. Her writings include *Three Lives*, 1908; *Making of Americans*, 1925; *Autobiography of Alice B. Toklas*, 1933, continued in *Everybody's Autobiography*, 1937; a study on Picasso, 1938; *Paris France*, 1940; and *Brewsie and Willie*, 1946.

Stein, Heinrich Friedrich Karl, Freiherr vom und zum (1757–1831), German statesman. He entered the service of Frederick the Great in 1780. He was later given a free hand as minister of the interior. His reforms included the abolition of serfdom, and the establishment of local self-government in towns. At the Congress of Vienna Stein pressed for a united Germany with a constitution excluding the princes, but was successfully opposed by Metternich.

Steinbeck, John Ernst (1902–68), US novelist and short-story writer. He first won attention with the appearance in 1935 of the ironically humorous *Tortilla Flat*. His reputation grew steadily with the publication of the novels *Of Mice and Men*, 1937, dramatised, 1939, and filmed, 1940, and, especially, *The Grapes of Wrath*, 1939, filmed in 1940. This novel, which won the Pulitzer Prize, tells of a refugee family from the dust-bowl of America, and is among the foremost of modern realistic fiction.

Among Steinbeck's other books are *Cannery Row*, 1945, and *East of Eden*, 1952. In 1962 he was awarded the Nobel Prize for literature.

Steinbok, or steenbok, *Raphicerus campestris*, a southern African antelope, reddish-brown in colour and about 60 cm high at the shoulder. It differs from the grysbok (*R. melanotis*) in having no lateral (false) hoofs.

Steiner, Rudolf (1861–1925), Austrian founder of anthroposophy. From 1902 he evolved a new study of the 'higher worlds', opposed to traditional occultism. His theories of education, using the arts therapeutically in the treatment of mental deficiency, had much influence, his pioneer school at Stuttgart (established in 1919) inspiring similar experiments in many countries, including Britain. His works include *Welt- und Lebensanschauungen des neunzehnten Jahrhunderts*, 1900–01; *Theosophie*, 1904; *Wie eflangt man Erkenntnisse der höheren Welten*, 1909; and an autobiography, *Mein Lebensgang*, 1925.

Stellenbosch, town of Cape Province, South Africa 48 km east of Cape Town, situated in a vine-growing valley, west of the Drakenstein Mountains. The site of Stellenbosch was selected by Simon Van der Stel, one of the earliest governors of the Cape. Stellenbosch is the wine centre of South Africa. Population (1970) 29,728 of whom 13,646 are whites.

Stem, the aerial portion of a plant supporting the leaves and flowers and conveying the food materials. In the first year of growth the stem is usually green, soft and herbaceous, but in the second year and later in a perennial plant or a tree it may become dark, hard and woody. Underground storage stems include tubers, corms and rhizomes which also serve to extend the plant. Above ground, stems may be erect, ascending, prostrate, creeping, climbing or twining.

Sten Gun, see SUBMACHINE-GUN.

Stencilling, art of forming letters or ornamental designs by means of a stencil. The required words or pattern are first cut out on a stencil or thin plate, which is then laid flat upon a surface and coloured over with a brush so that the surface below is marked as required. The advantage of stencilling is that any number of copies can thus be made from one plate. This method is used for colouring prints and decorating furniture, woodwork, cloth, etc.
See also PRINTMAKING.

Stendhal, pseudonym of Marie Henri Beyle (1783–1842), French author. His works are remarkable for their fineness of observation and for the extraordinary abundance of ideas. His critical works include *Histoire de la peinture en Italie*, 1817; *Rome, Naples et Florence*, 1817; *Racine et Shakespeare*, 1823–25; and *Promenades dans Rome*, 1829. His chief novels are *Le Rouge et le noir*, 1831; *La Chartreuse de Parme*, 1839; and the unfinished *Lucien Leuwen*, published 1894. Amongst a variety of miscellaneous works are his *Mémoires d'un touriste*, 1838. The *Journal de Stendhal*, 1888; *Vie de Henri Brulard*, 1890; *Souvenirs d'égotisme*, 1892; and his correspondence, all published posthumously, are valuable as autobiography.
Stendhal had the gift of psychological analysis, and it is for this, rather than for continuity and arrangement of plot, that his novels are so outstanding. Stendhal's reputation has risen considerably in modern times, and it has been appreciated that his work was a century in advance of its true era.

Stenmark, Ingemar (1956–), Swedish skier who has been World Cup champion on three occasions 1976, 1977 and 1978 and runner-up in 1980, 1981 and 1982. At the 1976 Winter Olympics in Innsbruck he turned in an erratic performance to take the bronze medal. But, at the Lake Placid Games in 1980 he took both the slalom and giant slalom titles. He turned professional shortly afterwards. By 1983 he held the record for the most number of World Cup wins (71).

Steno, Nicolaus, or Niels Stensen (1638–1686), Danish anatomist, geologist, and priest. He discovered the excretory duct of the paratid, and the ceruminous glands (*Observationes Anatomicae*, 1622). He was professor of anatomy at Copenhagen, 1672–74. Adopting Roman Catholicism he entered the priesthood, becoming a bishop in Germany in 1677.

Stenography, see SHORTHAND.

George Stephenson. The opening of the Stockton to Darlington Railway in 1825.

Stephen, Saint, first Christian martyr, a Jew of Greek culture, one of seven deacons set apart to minister to the Christian community in Jerusalem. He was charged with preaching 'against the Temple and the Law', and made a defence of his belief and conduct before the Sanhedrin, but was stoned by the angry crowd. His dying prayer led to the conversion of Saint Paul, who had taken part in his martyrdom.

Stephen (István), name of kings of Hungary in the Middle Ages.
Stephen I (c.970–1038), King of Hungary, instituted Christian monarchy in Hungary. Born a pagan, he was baptised and became Stephen. Stephen was recognised as king by the Pope Sylvester II and Emperor Otto III and was inaugurated at Christmas in 1000 AD. Hungarian tradition has it that the Pope sent a crown to Stephen for the inauguration. Stephen created a new social and political order, based on settled village life, agriculture, and land ownership, which the two sets of laws he issued helped to consolidate. His wars on Bavaria and on Poland were successful. Stephen was canonised in 1083; he was venerated for centuries as the law giver.
Stephen II (ruled 1116–31) waged many unsuccessful wars on his neighbours.

Stephen III (ruled 1162–72) had to fight off claimants who enjoyed the support of the Emperor Manuel of Byzantium and one of them was Stephen IV (ruled 1163–65).
Stephen V (ruled 1270–72) waged war on Ottokar II, King of Bohemia.

Stephen (c.1097–1154), King of England, son of Stephen, Count of Blois, and Adela, daughter of William I. He promised to recognise the claims of Matilda, daughter of Henry I, to the English throne, but on Henry's death usurped the crown (1135). Though a good soldier, Stephen lacked diplomatic tact: his reign was marked by civil war of an intermittent character. In spite of early concessions he made to the Church Stephen lost ecclesiastical support by his ill-judged attack on the Salisbury family. When his son, Eustace, predeceased him Stephen abandoned his attempt to found a new dynasty in England: at the Treaty of Wallingford (1153) he agreed that Henry, Matilda's son, should succeed him. His reign illustrates the immense power exercised by the Church, which, between 1135 and 1153, virtually played the rôle of kingmaker.

Stephen, Sir Leslie (1832–1904), English biographer and critic. A devoted Alpinist, he wrote on mountaineering, and collected his papers as *The Playground of Europe*, 1871.
In London he worked for the *Saturday Review* and the *Pall Mall Gazette*, and in 1866 began to contribute to the *Cornhill Magazine* (which he edited from 1871 to 1882) the essays known as *Hours in a Library*, 1874–79. His best book on religion is *An Agnostic's Apology*, 1893. Other works include biographies of Johnson, Pope, Swift, George Eliot and Hobbes, and he was editor of the *Dictionary of National Biography* from 1886 to 1891. Virginia Woolf was his daughter.

Stephenson, George (1781–1848), British inventor. In 1815 he invented, simultaneously with Sir Humphry Davy, a safety lamp. He designed a locomotive (which he called *My Lord*) which was successfully tried on the tramroads of the Killingworth Colliery in 1814. The projectors of the Stockton and Darlington Railway appointed him their engineer (1822), when their line, the first railway on which passengers and goods were carried by a locomotive, was opened on 27 September 1825. The success of this venture led to the employment of Stephenson in the construction of the Liverpool and Manchester Railway, which he carried successfully through Chat Moss. It was on this line that his improved invention, the *Rocket*, made its trial trip at 47 km/h. Until his death he was employed as a designer of railways, and during these years greatly improved upon his early locomotive.

Stephenson, Robert (1803–59), British engineer, son of George Stephenson. He travelled in South America, and returning to England in 1827 took part in the construction of his father's *Rocket*, and in the laying of the first railways in the country. In 1833 he became chief engineer on the London and Birmingham Railway. He was one of the greatest railway engineering experts of his time, specialising in the building of bridges, including the high-level bridge at Newcastle. He used a novel box girder type of construction in his bridge across the Menai Straits

(1850), and that still in original form at Conway (1848), in which the railway tracks were completely enclosed in parallel iron tubes.

Steppe, term applied particularly to the grasslands of the southern USSR, and generally to any similar areas in temperate zones where light rainfall, confined to spring and early summer, produces natural grassland with few trees, usually in continental interiors. The soil is deep and often rich in humus content, as in the 'black earth' areas of the Ukraine, though southern Siberia is less fertile. Grain is a major crop.
See also CHERNOZEMS AND CHESTNUT EARTH SOILS.

Stereochemistry, a branch of chemistry concerned with the spatial relations of the atoms in the molecule.
See also ISOMERS.

Stereophony, sound reproduction by two loudspeakers. All sounds come from only two speakers, but the ear is fooled, and receives an impression of a spread between the speakers. A note with equal intensity from each speaker will appear to come from halfway between them, while a note with all its intensity from one speaker and none from the other will be heard at the extreme edge of the sound image. One can listen to a recording of an orchestra and hear each instrument in its correct place.
Both records and tapes are now usually issued in stereo. On a stereophonic tape, each channel is in a separate part, and separate playback heads are used for each 'track'. A stereophonic record has one grove per side, with 'hill and dale' recordings on each wall. Thus the stylus vibrates up-and-down and side-to-side. These vibrations are decoded in the pick-up head, and two signals are passed to the stereophonic amplifier.

Stereotyping (Greek *stereos*, solid), processes used in the production of duplicate plates of type and photoengravings for use in letterpress printing. Originally implying the production of metal plates, the term now includes the making of rubber and plastic duplicates.

Sterilisation, the complete destruction of all forms of life. Certain substances, for example those to be injected into the blood-stream, or surgical instruments, must be sterile. This means that no forms of life—no bacteria, viruses or fungi, nor the cysts or spores by which they hibernate or reproduce—are present in them. Sterilisation may be done by several processes. *Autoclaving*, cooking the material to be sterilised in steam at a high pressure, is effective for surgical instruments, but would ruin more delicate things. *Filtration* is useful for delicate solutions, such as antibiotics. Other methods are *dry heat*, which must be greater and applied longer than the moist heat of the autoclave; *burning* of material to be discarded; *gamma radiation*; and *chemicals*, especially ethylene oxide gas.
Other methods are used where complete sterilisation is not necessary. Antiseptics are chemicals that either prevent micro-organisms from multiplying or kill most of them. Disinfectants are similar to antiseptics, but the term usually refers to chemicals used on table tops and floors. Preservatives in food slow down the growth of harmful micro-organ-

isms. Pasteurisation of milk kills the disease-producing organisms but not the others. Cooking also kills most micro-organisms.

Sterilisation (surgical) includes several procedures for making a person incapable of reproduction. These include vasectomy, cutting and tying of the vasa deferentia (the ducts leading from the testes to the urethra), in the male, and cutting and tying the Fallopian tubes in the female. Sterilisation in the male is a simple and quick operation and is reversible. In the female, cauterisation of the Fallopian tubes can be performed through the laparoscope, which is also a quick method. Clips are also put on the Fallopian tubes as a method of sterilisation.
See also BIRTH CONTROL.

Sterling (from the old English *steorra*, star, since some of the early Norman coins were marked with a small star), term applied in Britain to all lawful coins of the realm.

Robert Louis Stevenson, an 1887 portrait.

Sterne, Laurence (1713–68), English novelist. In 1760 he was appointed perpetual curate of Coxwold, where he lived happily in the house he called Shandy Hall. *The Life and Opinions of Tristram Shandy*, his masterpiece, was published between 1760 and 1767.
A decline in health (Sterne was a lifelong sufferer from tuberculosis) led to a tour of France and Italy, 1762–64, which provided much of the material for *A Sentimental Journey Through France and Italy*, which was published in 1768, shortly before his death.
Tristram Shandy was a revolutionary novel, precursor of the works of James Joyce and Proust in its handling of time and consciousness, though it has also been seen as a comic satire on the well-made novel of the earlier 18th century, and as a satirical reduction of claims made for rationality as the main principle of human order.

Sternum, or breastbone, a nearly flat bone, 15–20 cm long in the adult, which lies in the midline of the anterior wall of the thorax (chest). It can be felt beneath the skin throughout its whole length, from the root of the neck into the abdominal wall.

Steroids, a large group of naturally occurring cyclic, organic compounds, several of which have a profound effect on the body. Many of them can now be made synthetically, and are used in medical treatment. The most important examples of steroid compounds are the precursors of certain vitamins, cholesterol, and hormones.

Stethoscope, an instrument used in medical practice as a medium for auscultation (listening to noises made by the body). Respiratory, cardiac, arterial, venous, intestinal, foetal, and other sounds are conveyed to the ear of the examiner.

Stettin, see SZCZECIN.

Stevenage, new town in Hertfordshire, England, 48 km from London. Stevenage was the first new town to be designated under the New Towns Act 1964. It manufactures aircraft and electrical and plastic goods; together with engineering these form its chief industries. Population (1981) 74,365.

Stevens, Alfred (1818–75), British sculptor and decorative artist. His greatest work was the bronze monument to Wellington in St Paul's Cathedral. Other notable works were designs for mosaics of the Prophets under the dome of St Paul's and the vases and lions of the British Museum railings. He left a vast number of fine drawings (Tate Gallery) and some portraits of distinction; that of Mrs Collmann (National Portrait Gallery, London) being his masterpiece.

Stevens, Wallace (1897–1955), US poet. Stevens was one of the leading poets of American modernism. His poetry, collected in two volumes, *Collected Poems*, 1954, and *Opus Posthumous*, 1957, first appeared in *Poetry* (Chicago) in 1912, but he did not publish a volume until *Harmonium* in 1923.
His work, concerned with the status of the imagination and the power of a poetic fiction, evolved from a dandyish flamboyance to a spare, philosophical form; most of it is an examination of the poetic act itself.

Stevenson, Adlai Ewing (1900–65), US politician. He was one of the US delegates to the UN General Assembly, 1946–47. He was elected governor of Illinois in 1948. Stevenson was Democratic candidate for president in 1952. Though defeated by Eisenhower he retained his position as leader of his party. He again ran for the presidency in 1956, again being defeated by Eisenhower. Stevenson represented a more reflective trend in the Democratic party, as opposed to the New Deal radicalism of others. From 1961 he was US ambassador to the UN.

Stevenson, Robert Louis (1850–94), Scottish poet, novelist, and essayist. Educated at Edinburgh Academy and University, he studied law, was called to the Bar in 1875, but never practised. His early essays were published collectively as *Virginibus Puerisque* in 1881. On account of his delicate health (he suffered from tuberculosis), Stevenson travelled abroad, recounting his experiences in *An Inland Voyage*, 1878, his first book, and *Travels with a Donkey in the Cevennes*, 1879. He went to California in 1879 and married an American, Mrs Fanny Osbourne, 1880. To amuse his stepson Lloyd Osbourne, he began an adventure story about pirates and buried treasure; the tale was published in 1882 as *Treasure Island*. Its great success finally decided Stevenson's profession and his work afterwards showed growing confidence and skill. Other stories include *Kidnapped*, 1886, *The Black Arrow*, 1888, *The Master of Ballantrae*, 1889, and *Catriona*, 1893. Stevenson's poetry in *A Child's Garden of Verses*, 1885, reveals a rare feeling for the remembered emotions and thoughts of childhood, and also notable is *Underwoods*, 1887, a book of English and Scots verse. *The Strange Case of Dr Jekyll and Mr Hyde*, 1886, is both a thrilling tale of horror and a study in the duality of human nature.

In 1888 Stevenson sailed for the South Seas and settled in Vailima, Samoa, during the following year. Here his health improved and he worked steadily, interesting himself in the lives of the local people and the atmosphere of the islands. To the Samoans he was Tusitala, 'teller of tales'. He died in 1894 and was buried on Mount Vaea.

Stewart, Steuart, or Stuart, Scottish family tracing its descent from a Breton immigrant, Alan Fitzlaald, in the 11th century. His son, Walter (d. 1177), was made steward of Scotland by David I, and founded Paisley Abbey in 1163. The stewardship remained in the family, the various branches of which are descended from the seven sons of John (killed at Falkirk, 1298). The first royal Stewart was the son of Walter, sixth steward, and Marjory, daughter of Robert Bruce, and came to the Scottish throne as Robert II in 1371. The direct royal male line ended at the death of James V in 1542. His daughter, Mary, who adopted the spelling 'Stuart', claimed the throne of England by descent from Margaret Tudor, queen of James IV, and her son, James VI, became James I of England and progenitor of the royal line of Great Britain.

Stewart, Jackie (1939–), British racing driver. He began motor racing in Scotland as a hobby (1961) but his immediate success led to Grand Prix racing in 1965, and in that year he won his first Grand Prix in Italy, driving a BRM. Stewart's Matra won seven Grand Prix races in 1969, and in so doing he won the World Championship for the first time. Driving for the Tyrrell team, Stewart repeated this success in 1971 and 1973. In nine seasons of Grand Prix competition, Stewart won 27 Grands Prix, more than any other driver in history. He retired from the sport at the end of the 1973 season.

Stewart, James (1908–), US film actor. He has appeared in *Mr Smith Goes to Washington*; *The Philadelphia Story*; *Destry Rides Again*; *Winchester 73*; *Harvey*; *Rear Window*; *The Glenn Miller Story*; *The Man from Laramie*; *Anatomy of a Murder*; and many others.

Stewart Island, island off the south coast of South Island, New Zealand. The principal settlement is at Oban. It is mountainous and thickly forested, and is a holiday resort. Area 1735 km²; population (1971) 400.

Stewartia, camellia-like deciduous shrubs in the family Theaceae from Asia and USA, having creamy or white flowers. Species grown are *S. malacodendron*, *S. ovata*, *S. pseudo-camellia* and *S. sinensis*. Propagation is by seeds and cuttings.

Steyr, or Steier, Austrian town in the province of Upper Austria, at the confluence of the Enns and the Steyr. It manufactures motor cars, bicycles, cutlery, paper, and textiles. Population (1981) 38,898.

Stibnite, chief ore of antimony; antimony trisulphide, Sb_2S_3. Stibnite is orthorhombic and is often found in prismatic crystals showing vertical striations and spear-shaped terminations. It occurs in low-temperature hydrothermal veins and is mined in China, Mexico, Bolivia, and Algeria.

Stick Insect, insect placed with leaf insects, in the order Phasmatodea. Most stick insects belong to the family Phasmatidae. In common with the leaf insects, they mimic parts of plants, usually resembling the twigs of the vegetation on which they are found. The common stick insect, *Carausius morosus*, is a native of India. The adult, which measures about 8·5 cm in length, lacks wings and feeds on rose and privet leaves. The females are parthenogenetic.

Stickleback, the popular name given to small fishes of the order Gasterosteiformes. They have elongated, compressed slender bodies, always without true scales, but often protected by means of bony scutes (plates). The anterior dorsal fin is represented by isolated spines, and the ventral fin is formed of a strong spine and one or two soft rays. The sticklebacks are noted for their red breast when in season and their nest-building habit, the males constructing nests of leaves, twigs and grass, and binding them together by a mucus which they secrete. Nearly all the species are found in fresh water in Europe, Asia and America, are very pugnacious, and feed on spawn of other fishes.

Still-life. Vase of Tulips *by Cézanne, c.1890.*

Stiernhielm, Georg (1598–1672), Swedish poet. From about 1640 he was court poet to Queen Christina. He wrote sonnets, lyrics, and idylls, but his greatest achievement was a didactic allegorical poem, *Hercules*, 1647. A man of great learning, he has justly been called 'the father of the Swedish art of poetry', for he did much to harmonise traditional Swedish culture with literary styles adopted from the rest of Europe.

Stigmatisation (Medieval Latin, from Greek *stigma*, a mark), impression on certain individuals of the 'stigmata' or five wounds (in the hands, feet, and side) which Jesus received on the cross, generally held to be given miraculously as a favour to some of those specially devoted to the Passion. St Paul's words in Gal vi. 17 do not necessarily state that he bore the stigmata. The first certain instance and the only one generally recognised, is that of St Francis of Assisi. Since

that time over 300 instances are claimed, 29 during the 19th century, and Therese Neumann and Padre Pio in the 20th. Explanations of the phenomenon vary. The Roman Catholic Church does not treat stigmatisation as an incontestable miracle.

Stilicho, Flavius (c.365–408), Roman general and effective ruler of the Western Empire from 395 until 408. Theodosius I made him commander-in-chief of the army and before his death appointed Stilicho guardian of his young son, Honorius, who was to reign in the West. In 397 Stilicho took an army to Greece in order to defeat the invading Visigoths under Alaric, but failed to bring them to battle. In 401 Alaric invaded Italy and threatened Milan. Stilicho defeated the Visigoths at Pollentia (Pollenzo) and again in 403 at Verona.

In 405 Stilicho annihilated a vast horde of invading Germans, mostly Ostrogoths, led by Radagasius. By 408 his influence had declined. There was strong, though secret, opposition to him. Stilicho was imprisoned on Honorius's orders and beheaded later.

Still, see DISTILLATION.

Still-life, an art-form, consisting of inanimate objects grouped decoratively and generally represented illusionistically. It has sometimes been used as an adjunct, for example in the floral borders of medieval manuscripts or the candelabra of Van Eyck's *Arnolfini Wedding* portrait (National Gallery, London). A famous piece of trick *trompe l'oeil* painting is the still-life group in the centre of Holbein's *The Ambassadors* (National Gallery).

A prototype of 'successful' still-life is provided by Xeuxis' legendary bunch of grapes, so realistic that it deceived birds. An early example of 'pure' still-life is Jacopo de' Barbari's *Partridge with Gauntlets and an Archer's Bolt* (Munich). The genre reached a new expertise in the 17th century with painters such as de Heem and Snyders in the Low Countries, Zurbaran and the *bodegon* (tavern) painters in Spain, and Ruoppolo, the fruit-painter of Naples. Again in the 18th century still-life served painting as a whole by enabling Chardin to attain new heights in the study of the pictorial factor of 'tonality', e.g. in *The Attributes of the Arts* (Louvre). In this respect, Chardin was followed in the 19th century by a master of tonal still-life, Fantin-Latour. Yet again still-life served a pioneering role when Cézanne used it to attempt modelling with gradations of colour. In the 20th century, Picasso and Braque used it for their Cubist experiment with 'synthetic' drawing, which conflated many aspects of the same object so as to produce new flat-pattern effects.

See also FLOWER-PAINTING.

Stillbirth, see ABORTION.

Stilt, *Himantopus himantopus*, a long-legged wader bird of order Charadriiformes. It has a very wide distribution. The name is given to these birds by reason of their very thin, long pink legs which extend far behind the body. It lives in flooded areas and swamps, particularly where there is soft mud. The species is cosmopolitan, with separate subspecies in the USA, South America, Australasia and a wholly black subspecies found only on South Island, New Zealand.

Stilton, village in Cambridgeshire, England, 11 km north-west of Peterborough on the Great North Road. It gives its name to a slow-maturing, semi-hard, blue cheese. Population (1971) 910.

Stilwell, Joseph Warren (1883–1946), US soldier. Service in China and study of the language made him one of the foremost authorities in the USA on Chinese life. When Japan attacked the USA in 1941, Stilwell was chosen as US military representative in China. Chiang Kai-shek appointed him chief of staff, co-operating with the British forces in the defence of Burma. From October 1943 Stilwell conducted an advance of over 322 km, pushing the Japanese 18th Division back to their main base, Myitkyina. After an open breach with Chiang Kai-shek, Stilwell was given a home command in the USA. Later he commanded the American Tenth Army at Okinawa.

Stimulants, agents that increase activity. They may be general, exciting the body as a whole to a greater activity, or may affect particular organs, such as the heart, kidneys, liver, stomach, or brain. They are distinguished from tonics by their more immediate and transient action. The most common stimulants are alcohol, nicotine, ammonia, tea, coffee, various essential oils, strychnine, amphetamine, electricity, and heat and cold under certain conditions.

Stingray, any individual of the family Urolophidae, suborder Myliobatoidei, for example *Trygon pastinaca*, a ray of the Mediterranean and east Atlantic, in which a serrated poisonous spine is present on the whip-like tail. This spine projects upwards and backwards and may inflict a severe wound. Species of *Pteroplatea*, in the same family, are also able to cause deep and poisoned wounds.

Stinkweed, *Diplotaxis*, a small yellow-flowered plant in family Cruciferae, whose leaves have a foetid smell when crushed. It occurs as a weed in Europe.

Stinkwood, term applied to the wood of numerous plants, used especially in reference to *Gustavia augusta*, a species of Lecythidaceae. The wood has a foetid smell, and the tree occurs in tropical America.

Stipa, a genus of perennial grasses of family Gramineae. *S. gigantea* and *S. pennata*, feather grass, are ornamental plants of gardens. *S. tenacissima* is the esparto grass of Spain and North Africa, used in paper-making.

Stipend, originally the pay of soldiers, but now the annual allowance or income of an ecclesiastical benefice, and, in a wider sense, any settled pay for services daily, monthly, or annually. In the Roman Catholic Church stipend also denotes the fee a priest is entitled to for saying mass. 'Stipendiary' in a wide sense means one who performs services for a settled income, but specifically a paid magistrate.

Stippling, in interior decorating, the production of a finely granulated surface on paintwork, achieved by beating the wet surface with a flat-faced bristle brush. Use is made of stipplers with rubber plates or cylinders on surfaces of coarse texture. Stippling is used on oil-bound, quick-setting, non-glossy paint. An even change from one colour to another can be obtained by this method. In picture painting, drawing or engraving stippling is a method of obtaining effect by means of dots instead of solid areas of colour or tone, or continuous lines.

Stipule, a leaf-like projection at the base of a leaf and on either side of the stem. It may be a scale serving to protect a bud, a spinous protection against animals (e.g. acacia), or it may be large and green, and augment the photosynthetic capacity of the leaf (e.g. pea). Some stipules, for example on the smilax, are sensitive climbing tendrils.

Stirling, royal burgh (since 1226) and capital of the Central Region of Scotland, situated on the River Forth, 43 km north-east of Glasgow. Its strong strategical position made it the key to the Highlands. The castle was the birthplace and residence of several Scottish kings. The main industries are agricultural implements, fertilisers, carpets, textiles, and cigarettes. Population (1981) 38,638.

Stitch, a sharp pain in the side. It may be caused by pleurisy, by spasm of the respiratory muscles during violent exercise, or by intercostal neuralgia.

Stitchery, see EMBROIDERY.

Stitchwort, a cosmopolitan genus in the Caryophyllaceae. Their narrow radiating petals, white in colour, give the flower a star-like or stellate appearance. *S. media*, the common stitchwort, also called common chickweed is a common weed throughout the world.

Stoa, in Greek architecture, a detached colonnade.

Stoat, or ermine, *Mustela erminea*, a small carnivorous mammal, native of Europe, with a much elongated body covered with short fur. The stoat generally retains its reddish-brown colour in warm climates, but in winter in colder latitudes its fur becomes partially or wholly white and much denser, and is then highly valued by furriers. It is about 25 cm long, with a black-tipped tail about 12 cm long. It is closely related to the weasel, both being in family Mustelidae of order Carnivora.

Stock, abbreviation of stock gillyflower, *Matthiola incana*. All the garden varieties of the simple-stemmed stock, 10-week stock, Brompton stock, and queen's stock have been derived from *M. incana*. The wall-flower-leaved stock, *M. bicornis*, is a small plant, with narrow hoary leaves and dull brown flowers; it grows in Greece, and is the night-scented stock, which is grown for its fragrance by night.

Stock, term usually associated in the public mind with shares and dealings on a stock exchange, though negotiability on a stock exchange is not an essential incident of stock. *British Government Stock* (gilt-edged). The government invites the public to share in a loan. Each subscriber is allotted stock for his accepted contribution, e.g. Treasury Stocks, Exchequer Stock, Funding Loan, Consolidated Stock (Consols). Stock was also issued in exchange for proprietary interests in nationalised industries, e.g. British Transport Stock. Thereafter the stock may be bought or sold through a stock exchange, the price at which it is transferred varying according to the credit conditions prevailing at the time. Interest at an agreed rate is paid, usually half-yearly. The terms of issue state whether the stock shall be redeemed within a certain time or at the option of the government.

See also COMPANY.

Stock Car Racing, see MOTOR RACING.

Stock Exchange. The function of a stock exchange is to provide a market in which stocks and shares of all descriptions can be freely bought and sold, and in which the provision of new finance for governmental or industrial purposes can be facilitated through the flotation of new issues of capital.

Stockhausen, Karlheinz (1928–), German composer. Since 1953 he has worked at a studio for electronic music at Cologne, and in 1955 founded with Herbert Eimert the periodical *Die Reihe* for the propagation of serial and electronic music. His composition courses at Darmstadt, started in 1957, have become a regular forum for the avant-garde. His works include *Gesang der Jünglinge*, 1956, for treble and electronic tape, *Gruppen* for three orchestras, 1957, and *Für kommenden Zeiten*, '17 texts for intuitive music', 1970.

Stockholm, capital of Sweden, situated where Lake Mälaren joins Saltsjön, an inlet of the Baltic Sea thickly dotted with islands. The oldest part of the city is built on the island that separates the two stretches of water. Here it grew up in the middle of the 13th century round the fortress that had been erected to guard the vital entrance to the trading centres of Lake Mälaren. On the foundations of this old fortress there now stands the imposing royal palace, built to the design of Nicodemus Tessin the younger (1697–1754).

Stockholm extends north and south of the old town across the so-called 'malm' areas—Norrmalm, Östermalm, and Södermalm—which were first built on to any extent during the 17th century, and which are now completely covered by the many blocks of flats and offices that were built here as a result of the 19th-century industrialisation. The turn of the century saw the development of garden suburbs, e.g. Djursholm and Saltsjöbaden, and somewhat later the municipal garden suburbs of Bromma and Brännkyrka, west and south-west of Stockholm, were established. Stockholm's inner harbour, which gives the city much of its aesthetic appeal, is both large and deep, and is kept open all the year round, sometimes with the help of ice-breakers in the winter. In the northern part of Djurgården is Frihamnen, the 'Free Harbour'. There is passenger traffic from Stockholm not only to most of the Swedish coastal towns but also to the USSR and Finland. Commercial traffic is worldwide. The city has many big industries such as shipbuilding, engineering, ironfounding, sugar refining, brewing, tanning, and the manufacture of silk, cotton, soap, tobacco, cork, and leather. Population (1978) 653,929.

Stockings, see HOSE.

Stockport, industrial town on the River Mersey, 10 km from Manchester, and now part of Greater Manchester Metropolitan County, England. The Mersey is formed here by the confluence of the rivers Tame and Goyt, and their valleys were favourable sites for textile mills. Until recently, Stockport's river banks were lined with mills. The decline

Stockholm. *The historic centre of the city, with the three-storeyed Royal Palace to the left.*

of cotton has been offset by the growth of other industries, including chemicals and engineering. Population (1981) 136,496.

Stocks, device which was used for the punishment of certain criminal offenders. It consisted of two baulks of timber so padlocked together as to imprison the feet, sometimes also the hands and even the neck, in holes made for the purpose. They were last used in England in the middle of the 19th century. In the USA they survived until before the Civil War as a punishment for slaves.
See also PILLORY.

Stockton, Harold Maurice Macmillan, 1st Earl of see MACMILLAN, (MAURICE) HAROLD, 1ST EARL OF STOCKTON.

Stockton, county seat of San Joaquin county, California, USA, 115km south-east of San Francisco, on an arm of the San Joaquin river. Its chief industries are the manufacture of agricultural implements, lumber products, flour and food preparations, and there is a trade in the fruit, cattle, and grain of the rich San Joaquin valley. Population (1980) 149,779.

Stockton-on-Tees, town of Cleveland, England, 5km west of Middlesbrough. The chief buildings of interest are those connected with the first passenger railway from Stockton to Darlington. In addition to the old-established heavy industries of iron, steel, chemicals, and engineering, there is varied manufacturing. Population (1981) 154,585.

Stockwood, Arthur Mervyn (1913–), English churchman. He was vicar of the University Church, Cambridge, 1955–59, and bishop of Southwark, 1959–81. His books include *There is a Tide*, 1946, and *Cambridge Sermons*, 1959.

Stoics, sect of ancient philosophers and moralists opposed to the Epicureans in their views of human life. Its founder was Zeno (fl.3rd century BC) who opened his school in the Stoa Poikile (Painted Porch), at Athens, whence its name. The Stoic doctrine is a materialist theory, with matter, the one constituent of the world, considered as governed by reason. Stoics took a thoroughly tolerant

attitude towards religion, regarding the various practices as symbolic of the truth. Stoicism was thus eminently suitable as a general outlook for a world empire. It was introduced to the Romans between 200 and 50 BC and, under the Empire, the best known Stoic philosopher was the Emperor Marcus Aurelius Antoninus. Stoicism prevailed widely in the Roman world, although not to the exclusion of Epicurean views.

Stoke Mandeville Games, also known as the Paraplegic Olympics. The Games were first held at the Stoke Mandeville Hospital in England in 1948 to encourage physically disabled men and women to participate in sport. The Paraplegic Olympics, attended by disabled competitors from all over the world, are held annually at the Stoke Mandeville Hospital and also every fourth year in the country hosting the Olympic Games. Entry is open to those confined to wheelchairs. Events include track and field athletics, swimming, weight-lifting, fencing, archery, table tennis, basketball, bowls and snooker.

Stoke-on-Trent, city of Staffordshire, England, 23km north of Stafford on the Trent and Mersey Canal. It includes the six towns of Burslem, Hanley, Longton, Fenton, Tunstall, and Stoke-upon-Trent. Stoke-on-Trent is famous for the manufacture of pottery and porcelain, often being referred to as 'The Potteries'. Other major industries are coal-mining, iron and steel production, light engineering and rubber tyre manufacture. Population (1981) 252,351.

Stoke Poges, town and parish of Buckinghamshire, England, 3km north of Slough. The poet Gray is buried in the churchyard, which is identified with the scene of his *Elegy*. Population (1971) 4850.

Stoker, Bram (1847–1912), Irish novelist. An invalid in childhood, he developed into a fine athlete while at university, and also had a brilliant academic career. Afterwards he worked for ten years in the civil service, eventually becoming Inspector of Petty Sessions in Ireland. In 1878 he became Henry Irving's acting manager at the Lyceum theatre, London, and later wrote *Personal*

Reminiscences of Henry Irving, 1906. He published several novels, but is remembered above all for *Dracula*, 1897, one of the most spine-chilling horror stories in English literature.

Stokowski, Leopold (1882–1977), American conductor, born in London of Polish and Irish parents. From 1912 to 1936 he conducted the Philadelphia Orchestra, and later other American orchestras. One of the most gifted and colourful performers of the century, he appeared in films, made many orchestral arrangements (notably of Bach), and was an advocate of modern music. He still conducted and recorded at the age of 95.

Stole, ecclesiastical vestment consisting of a long band of silk or rich stuff, coloured according to the season, and often embroidered, usually with crosses at the centre and ends (which may be widened for decorative purposes).

Stolen Goods. Possession of stolen goods recently after their loss is *prima facie* evidence, in English law, that the person in possession stole the goods or received them knowing then to have been stolen; but if many months have elapsed between the loss and the discovery the possessor cannot, in the absence of any other circumstances implicating him in the theft, be called upon to account for the manner in which he came by the goods. This is the doctrine of 'recent possession'. Under the Theft Act 1968, a person convicted of an offence in relation to the theft of goods may be ordered e.g. to restore the goods, to pay the value of the stolen goods.
See also HANDLING STOLEN GOODS; THEFT.

Stolypin, Pëtr Arkadevich (1862–1911), Russian statesman. Stolypin's policy was, on the one hand, firm suppression of the revolution and, on the other, reforms designed to remove the causes of discontent. He did not shrink from unpopular measures (dissolution of two Dumas). Stolypin's agrarian reforms (1906–11) enabled the peasants to leave the village communities and set up separate farms. Stolypin also facilitated purchase of land by the peasants. A liberal conservative, Stolypin was opposed both by the radicals and the extreme Right. He was assassinated by a Socialist Revolutionary terrorist who was also a police agent.

Stoma (plural stomata), a pore in the epidermis of a leaf or a herbaceous stem which allows interchange of gases between the plant and the atmosphere during the processes of respiration and photosynthesis, and the escape of water vapour by transpiration. A stoma is bounded by two guard cells which, by the varying thickness of their walls, alter shape according to the amount of water they contain (depending e.g. on the sugar content of the guard cells), temperature, and light.

Stomach, in Man, the pear-shaped digestive sac situated in the upper part of the abdomen. It is entered by the oesophagus at the *cardiac orifice*, where the circular muscle is thickened to form a sphincter. Its opening into the intestine is called the *pylorus*. The innermost coat of the stomach consists of mucous membrane resting on connective tissue. Outside this are three coats of unstriped muscle. The whole of the organ is covered by peritoneum, the serous membrane which lines the interior

1513

of the abdominal cavity and covers the viscera.

The mucous coat contains gastric glands which secrete gastric juice and mucus. Entering the stomach by the cardiac orifice, the food is acted upon by the gastric juice, which contains hydrochloric acid and the enzyme pepsin. The juice is effectively mixed with the salivated food by the movements of the muscular walls of the stomach. When the food has been rendered acid by the action of the gastric juice and has been propelled by peristalsis to the pyloric canal, the pylorus opens to admit the food to the small intestine. The effect of digestion in the stomach is to convert proteins into polypeptides. The gastric juice has also some bactericidal influence.

Stone, see METROLOGY.

Stone Age. The earliest of the three technological stages in man's development, as defined by C. J. Thomsen, in which man used stone tools and weapons. The Stone Age has been divided into the Old Stone Age (Palaeolithic), when stone implements were merely chipped into shape, Middle Stone Age (Mesolithic) and the New Stone Age (Neolithic), when implements of stone were ground and polished.

Palaeolithic men were hunters, and their remains have been found in the caves in which they lived, and in the sedimentary deposits of river gravels. The *Early Palaeolithic* belongs to the Riss-Würm interglacial period, when the 'warm' fauna included *Elephas antiquus*, a rhinoceros, and *Hippopotamus major*, whereas in the *Middle Palaeolithic*, a period of glaciation, Neanderthal man lived with a 'cold' fauna which included the mammoth, horse, ox and reindeer. The *Upper Palaeolithic* occurred during the retreat of glaciation and a dry and cold subsequent period.

The walls of certain caves lived in by Palaeolithic man were decorated with sketches and paintings whose association with hunting is unmistakable. The best-known series of paintings are in a cave at Lascaux, France.

There are several distinct cultures in the Mesolithic period, all of them based on a food-gathering economy. The climate had much improved, and hunting and fishing are well represented by the presence of microliths (very small implements mounted to serve as arrow-heads or saws) and fish-spear barbs. The Neolithic, with its colonisation across the mainland of Europe and along the Atlantic coast route, saw a higher civilisation based upon agriculture and stock-raising; there was a wide trade in flint and stone axes, and the period was also marked by the spread of megalithic tombs and the construction of earthwork camps with causeways or interrupted ditches. There is one type of pottery, based in design on vessels made of leather. Plants, both cereal and textile, were cultivated. Sheep, oxen, goats and swine were domesticated.

See also BEAKER FOLK; BRONZE AGE; GREAT BRITAIN, ARCHAEOLOGY. IRON AGE; PREHISTORY.

Stone Carving. Sculpture in hard material, stone or wood, differs from sculpture in plastic material, clay. The former is a paring down of material, the latter is a building up. A clay model lends itself to reproduction by someone other than the artist (indirect method), whereas the essential point of carving is that it must be carried out by the sculptor's own hand (direct method). Stone carving has been associated with architecture in all the great periods of art—Egyptian, Mesopotamian, Greek, Maya, Aztec. In the cathedrals of the European Middle Ages ceilings were intricately carved, and the stone pillars were carved at base and capital. The tradition of architectural stone carving or monumental sculpture, a particular feature of Indian art, has been revived in modern times. A large number of modern sculptors, including Jacob Epstein and Henry Moore, have since devoted themselves to 'direct' stone carving.

See also CARVING; SCULPTURE.

Stone Circles, rings of standing (or now fallen) stones. They are found usually on level ground and are nearly all religious or astronomical monuments, most of them belonging to the Bronze Age. Some, such as Stonehenge, Avebury, Callanish in the island of Lewis, and Stenness in Orkney, are remarkable for their size and state of preservation. They are very rare in Europe outside Britain. See AVEBURY; CARNAC; MEGALITHIC MONUMENTS; STONEHENGE.

Stone Flies, see PLECOPTERA.

Stonechat, *Saxicola torquata,* a small bird related to the robin and nightingale, in family Muscicapidae, order Passeriformes. The male bird has a black head and throat, dark back and tawny breast, and the female differs from it in that its head is brown. It occurs in Europe, Asia and Africa.

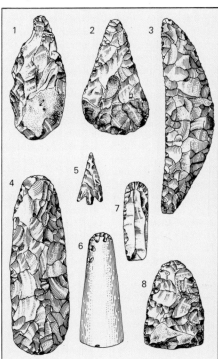

1. Hand-axe, Fordwich, Kent
2. Middle Acheulean hand-axe, Swanscombe, Kent
3. Sickle
4. Neolithic axe, Great Bealing, Suffolk
5. Tanged arrow-head
6. Neolithic polished axe, Teddington, Greater London
7. Upper Palaeolithic scraper
8. Late Acheulean hand-axe, Bournemouth, Hampshire

Stone Age. Implements of flint are the earliest man-made objects known.

Stonehenge, great circles of standing stones on Salisbury Plain, Wiltshire, England; a prehistoric site of various periods.

The first late Neolithic monument about 2800 BC was a low circular earth bank with a shallow outer ditch, inside and close to which was a circle of pits known as the Aubrey Holes. This is thought to have had a lunar alignment.

The first stones were erected in two concentric circles c.2150 BC. The stones were not as large as at the roughly contemporary Avebury but were brought from as far away as the Prescelly Mountains, Wales, indicating the importance of the site in contemporary culture. It seems that the entrance of this Blue Stone double circle was aligned on the present axis of the monument, that is the orientation on the mid-summer sunrise marked by the Avenue, suggesting a shift in the site's focus from lunar to solar.

The next building stage, c.2100 BC and associated with Beaker pottery created the spectacular monument of today. Larger blocks of local sarsen stone were erected to form a horseshoe of five capped pairs of sarsens, called trilithons, within a circle of sarsens, each linked to the next by a capstone. A final phase, c.1600 BC, saw the re-erection of the Bluestones into a horseshoe and circle within the sarsen monument.

The sarsen phase of Stonehenge is unique in that other great stone circles are of Neolithic date, while the many other Beaker circles in Britain tend to be smaller in scale and plan. It may represent Beaker adoption of the astronomical preoccupations of previous builders, although there has been much debate as to exactly what these were.

See also ARCHAEOLOGY; AVEBURY; MEGALITHIC MONUMENTS; STONE AGE.

'Stonewall' Jackson, see JACKSON, THOMAS JONATHAN.

Stoneware, name for all objects made of clay and baked in a high-temperature kiln at approximately 1200–1400°C, so that the body is vitrified and is therefore no longer porous. This term does not include objects made of porcelain.

Stonework, see MASONRY.

Stools, see FAECES.

Stopes, Marie Carmichael (1880–1958), British advocate of birth control. In 1904 she became instructor in palaeobotany at Manchester University, being the first woman to be appointed to its scientific staff. She was co-founder with her husband, H. V. Roe, of the mothers' clinic for constructive birth control, and became president of the Society for Constructive Birth Control and Racial Progress. She wrote many books on marriage and contraception.

Stoppard, Tom (1937–), English playwright. *Rosencrantz and Guildenstern are Dead,* 1967, was a great success on both sides of the Atlantic, and was followed by *The Real Inspector Hound,* 1968; *After Magritte,* 1970; *Jumpers,* 1972; *Travesties,* 1974; *Dirty Linen,* 1976; *Night and Day,* 1978; and *The Real Thing,* 1982.

Stoppard is a brilliant exponent of a form which is perhaps best described as 'philosophical farce'. He portrays man desperately seeking some ultimate sanction for his existence, but failing to find any rational system

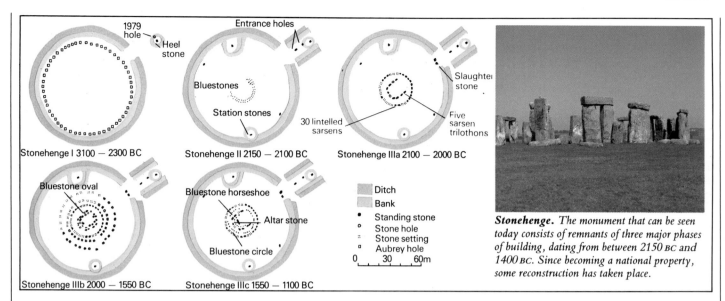

Stonehenge I 3100 — 2300 BC

Stonehenge II 2150 — 2100 BC

Stonehenge IIIa 2100 — 2000 BC

Stonehenge IIIb 2000 — 1550 BC

Stonehenge IIIc 1550 — 1100 BC

1979 hole
Heel stone
Entrance holes
Bluestones
Station stones
Slaughter stone
30 lintelled sarsens
Five sarsen trilothons
Bluestone oval
Bluestone horseshoe
Altar stone
Bluestone circle

Ditch
Bank
Standing stone
Stone hole
Stone setting
Aubrey hole
0   30   60m

Stonehenge. *The monument that can be seen today consists of remnants of three major phases of building, dating from between 2150 BC and 1400 BC. Since becoming a national property, some reconstruction has taken place.*

which can provide the key to an incomprehensible universe. He does not, however, like Beckett or Pinter, emphasise the bleakness of this failure, but rather the extraordinary ingenuity and energy with which we construct our logical systems, even though they are built on totally unverifiable, or absurd, premises.

Storey, David Malcolm (1933–), English novelist and playwright. He became known as a novelist with *This Sporting Life*, 1960, dealing with the life and emotional inadequacy of a professional rugby player. *Flight into Camden*, 1960; *Pasmore*, 1972; *A Temporary Life*, 1973; and *Saville*, 1976; followed. Storey wrote his first play, *The Restoration of Arnold Middleton* in 1959, though it was not performed until 1967. It was followed by *In Celebration*, 1969; *The Contractor*, 1969; *Home*, 1970; *The Changing Room*, 1971; *The Farm*, 1973; *Cromwell*, 1973; *Life Class*, 1974; and *Mother's Day*, 1976. His plays concentrate on the various aspects and implications of what Storey believes to be our acutely alienated society.

Stork, any birds of the Ciconiidae, a family of 17 species of wading birds with long conical bills, long three-toed legs and large wings in the order Ciconiiformes. The white or house stork, *Ciconia ciconia*, is widely distributed in Europe and central Asia, in many parts of which it is strictly protected for its service in destroying reptiles, small mammals and insects, and in devouring offal. Its great, clumsy nest is often to be seen on a house top or church spire. Its plumage is greyish white, its quills and longest feathers on the wing coverts black, and the beak and legs red. It migrates to Africa in winter. In the black stork, *C. nigra*, the upper surface is black and the lower parts are white. It is widely found in southern and central Europe, Asia and parts of Africa. The adjutant, ibis, heron and spoonbill are related birds. New World species include the jabiru of South America, *Jabiru mycteria*, and the wood ibis, *Mycteria americana*.

Storm, a wind force of 10 on the Beaufort scale, i.e. between 24·5 and 28·4 metres/second (m/s). The term is used to cover any strong wind, for example gales, which vary from 17 to 30m/s, but especially those accompanied by heavy rain, snow, hail, or dust. A tornado is caused by and moves with the Inter-tropical Front on its migration from West Africa northwards during late April and early May.

Storm Surge, a change in the sea-level caused by atmospheric phenomena. They are caused by severe storms and hurricanes. There is a gradual change in sea-level several hours before the storm approaches, a sharp rise or fall as the storm passes, followed by periodic oscillations, which last for between one and two tidal cycles, as the water level returns to normal. Surges are higher in an estuary which has a wide entrance, and so surges travelling down the east coast of Britain and entering the Thames estuary pose a considerable flood threat to London. A barrage has been built across the river below Tower Bridge.

Storm surges occur whenever there are hurricanes, mainly in the tropics, or severe storms in the mid-latitudes. They are frequent in the English Channel and North Sea where they are caused by severe atmospheric depressions. The maximum amplitude in the North Sea is 2–3m but can be larger, and in 1953 a large surge breached many of the dykes of the Netherlands, flooded 25,000km² of land, killed 2000 people, and forced 600,000 people from their homes.

Other severe surges have occurred in the Bay of Bengal due to the monsoon winds and in the Gulf of Mexico due to hurricanes.

Storm Troops (*Sturmabteilung*), see SA AND SS.

Stormont, castle in east Belfast which from 1921 to 1972 was the seat of government in Northern Ireland. Its legislative powers were limited to domestic affairs. Following the outbreak of sectarian violence in the province in 1969, Parliament was suspended and Britain resumed direct rule.

Stornoway (Stjarna's Vagr or Bay), seaport and most important town of Lewis Island (east coast), Outer Hebrides, Scotland. It is the centre of the Harris tweed industry, and a fishing centre. There is also some offshore oil-related industry. Population (1971) 5152.

Stoss, Veit (c.1440–1533), German sculptor. He worked in Cracow, 1477–96, carving a large wooden altarpiece with the *Death of the Virgin*, for St Mary's Church, and the stone tomb of the King Casimir IV Jagellio (in the Cathedral). He spent the remainder of his life in Nuremberg and Bamberg. His style, deriving to a great extent from that of the Netherlands and Upper Rhine, is a dramatic, realistic, and personal version of the late Gothic idiom.

Stoup, stone bowl near the door of a church, containing the holy water with which those who enter make the sign of the cross. The iconoclasts at the Reformation smashed most of the old stoups in England, but many have been restored and are in use.

Stour, English river which forms the boundary between Suffolk and Essex; it flows into the estuary of the Orwell at Harwich, and is navigable to Catawade. Length 76km.

Stour, a tributary of the Hampshire (England) Avon. The river is 88km long, rises in Wiltshire and, flowing through Dorset, joins the Avon at Christchurch.

Stour, river rising in the West Midlands county in the borough of Dudley, a tributary of the Severn, which it joins at Stourport. It was an important source of water power during the earlier part of the Industrial Revolution. Its length is 32km.

Stour, Great, rises near Lenham in Kent, and flows past Ashford, Canterbury, and Sandwich, before entering Pegwell Bay. Length 64km. It has two tributaries, East Stour and Little Stour.

Stourbridge, market town of West Midlands metropolitan county, England, 19km west of Birmingham, on the River Stour. The district has glass manufactures established by Hungarian immigrants c.1557, brickworks, manufactures of fire clay, leather, and galvanised and enamelled holloware. Population (1981) 54,661.

Stourhead, mansion at Stourton, Wiltshire, England. Henry Hoare, the banker, commissioned Colen Campbell to build the house in 1722, and the landscaped gardens were laid out c.1741–50. The house contains works of art and furniture by Thomas Chippendale the Younger.

Stout, one of the stronger beers, popular in Britain. It is brewed from highly kilned malt with a proportion of roasted malt of barley which gives it a characteristic flavour. It may be strongly or lightly hopped. There are varieties of stout, such as oatmeal and glucose.

See also BEER.

Stowe, Harriet Elizabeth Beecher (1811–1896), US novelist and philanthropist. Her first publication was *The Mayflower*, 1843. *Uncle Tom's Cabin* appeared in *The National Era*, in serial form, in 1850, and on its appearance in book form two years later attained an almost unequalled popularity. Half a million copies were sold in the United States, and it was translated into 22 foreign languages. It had a great influence in stirring up public opinion in the northern states against slavery.

Strabismus, see SQUINTING.

Strabo (c.63 BC–c. AD 22), Greek geographer and historian. He travelled extensively in Greece, Italy, Egypt, Sardinia, and Ethiopia. His historical memoirs remain only in fragments, but his *Geography*, one of the most important works of antiquity on that subject, is extant.

Strachey, (Giles) Lytton (1880–1932), English biographer and critic. Strachey became famous in 1918 with *Eminent Victorians* (lives of Cardinal Manning, Florence Nightingale, Arnold of Rugby, and General Gordon), which was followed in 1921 by his famous life of *Queen Victoria*. Strachey was a leading figure in the revolution in attitude towards the Victorians, mercilessly attacking their moral hypocrisy. His next major biography was *Elizabeth and Essex*, 1928. He also contributed some 90 full-length reviews to the *Spectator*, 1904–14.

Stradivari, Antonio (c.1644–1737), one of the greatest Italian violin-makers associated with Cremona. He was an apprentice under Nicolo Amati, and until 1684 devoted himself chiefly to models in the Amati style. In 1690 he began making 'long Strads'; after 1700 he discarded the Amati style and pursued original lines. He is famous also as a maker of violas and cellos.

Strafford, Thomas Wentworth, 1st Earl of (1593–1641), English statesman. He entered Parliament in 1614 but was not active there until the early 1620s when he soon became prominent as a critic of royal policy. Then, in 1628, he went over to the King's side, eagerly accepting the presidency of the Council of the North. There he ruled autocratically, and sometimes ruthlessly, for the next five years, firmly upholding the royal prerogative.

In 1633 Wentworth was appointed lord deputy of Ireland. For six years he dominated the country, reorganising the law courts, the financial system, the army and the navy. Charles I only gave Wentworth his full support when, in 1639, it was too late. Then, after the first Bishop's War, he created him earl of Strafford. Strafford urged the King to summon Parliament, apparently hoping that national hatred of the Scots would persuade the opposition to vote supplies. But Parliament refused to do so until its grievances had been dealt with. Meanwhile the Scots occupied Northumberland and Durham, Charles was forced to come to terms at Ripon and to summon another Parliament. The first act of this, the Long Parliament, was to move the impeachment of Strafford. Charles signed his death warrant in fear of the London mob attacking his wife and family if he failed to do so and Strafford was executed.

Strain and Stress. Strain is the change in size and/or shape of a body under the action of stress; stress is a set of forces in equilibrium maintaining a strain.

See also ELASTICITY; MATERIALS, STRENGTH OF; METALLURGY; MODULUS.

Straits Settlements, general name before 1946 for the British Crown Colony which comprised Singapore, Penang, and Malacca in Malaya; Labuan, off the northern coast of Borneo; and Christmas Island and the Cocos Islands to the south of Sumatra. It was dissolved by the Straits Settlements (Repeal) Act 1946, Singapore becoming a separate colony, Penang and Malacca part of the Federation of Malaysia, and Labuan part of North Borneo (now Sabah). Christmas Island and the Cocos Islands were administered with Singapore, but were transferred to Australian control in 1958 and 1955 respectively.

See also MALAYA, HISTORY OF.

Stralsund, port of the German Democratic Republic, 69km north-east of Rostock. It was an important member of the Hanseatic League. Its churches include the fine 14th-century Nikolaikirche; the old town still preserves its medieval appearance. There are boat-building, engineering, and chemical industries. Population (1971) 72,000.

Strangulation, a term used to describe constriction of the trachea (windpipe) often causing death from asphyxia; or the constriction of parts of organs resulting in restriction of their blood supply.

See also HERNIA.

Stranraer, seaport and royal burgh of Wigtown District, Dumfries and Galloway Region of Scotland, on Loch Ryan, 13km north-east of Port Patrick. Its large tidal harbour is used as the terminus of the shortest cross-channel service with Ireland. It trades in dairy produce, and has oatmeal mills and nurseries. Population (1981) 10,837.

Strapwork, in Flemish and Elizabethan architecture, a form of ornament in stone, stucco or wood carving, composed of interlacing bands, resembling straps, with 'rivets' at their intersections.

Strasbourg (German *Strassburg*), French city, capital of the *département* of Bas-Rhin. It lies 445km east of Paris, on the River Ill, 3km west of the Rhine, near its junction with the Rhine-Rhône and Rhine-Marne canals. In the 13th century Strasbourg became a free city, but was seized by Louis XIV, and formally ceded to France by the Treaty of Rijswijk in 1697. In 1870 the town surrendered to the Prussians after a seven-week siege, and was returned to France only in 1918.

Strasbourg has been important from early times as a centre of communications; it is now a railway junction for Paris, the Netherlands, West Germany, and Switzerland. Its river, harbours, and canals make it the chief inland port of France, trading in potash, iron ore, oil, and grain. Its industries include the manufacture of rolling-stock, electrical equipment, river boats, perfumes, soap, chemicals, oil-refining, and textiles, and breweries, flour mills, sugar, and tobacco processing. The long-established printing and publishing trades are still important. It was at Strasbourg in the 15th century that Gutenberg invented his printing press. The town was selected as the headquarters for the Council of Europe in 1949. Population (1975) 253,384.

Strategic Arms Limitation Talks (SALT), a series of negotiations between the USA and the USSR, begun in 1969 on the initiative of US President Johnson, and aimed at limiting and reducing strategic nuclear weapons. Limited agreements were reached in 1974 (SALT 1) and 1979 (SALT 2).

Stratford, town of Ontario, Canada, through which pass six lines of the Canadian National Railway, which has repair shops here. Furniture and agricultural implements are made; other industries include woollen goods and food processing. Population (1976) 25,657.

Stratford-upon-Avon, market town in Warwickshire, England, 35km south-south-east of Birmingham, in the valley of the Avon. The town is famous as the birthplace of Shakespeare, and is visited every year by travellers from all parts of the world. The original theatre built by public subscription as the Shakespeare Memorial Theatre, was destroyed by fire in 1926. The present building, which changed its name in 1961 to the Royal Shakespeare Theatre, opened in 1932. Population (1981) 20,858.

Strathclyde, early British kingdom, c.560, covering, at its zenith, the western part of the lowlands of Scotland, the greater part of Westmorland, and Cumberland. Its capital was Alclyde, the rock fortress at Dumbarton. It was finally absorbed into the Scottish kingdom in the middle of the 10th century.

Strathclyde Region is the largest and most populous of the new (1975) administrative units of Scotland. The total population is 2,397,827 (1981), i.e. about 50 per cent of Scotland. Its area is 14,000 km². The name is that of a British kingdom which flourished from the sixth century in the Clyde basin, with its capital at Dumbarton. The present region has the Clyde basin as its centre, extends south and west into hilly country, including the Lowther Hills, and north and west into the highlands; among the western islands included are Mull, Coll, Tiree, Colonsay, Jura, Islay and Arran. Tourism is very important in the highland and island areas and around the Firth of Clyde, and agriculture is important in the upper Clyde Valley, but the economic life of the region depends on the industrial Clydeside conurbation. Heavy industries such as steel, shipbuilding and heavy engineering are now being overtaken by electronics and diverse manufacturing, but the process has been slow and there has been much attendant unemployment. Coal is still important in Ayr, but mining has declined in Lanark. Barite is extracted at Muirshiels and Gass Water. The regional capital is Glasgow, an industrial, financial, service and educational centre.

Strathmore, wide valley of Scotland, bounded on the north by the Grampians, and on the south by the Lennox, Ochil, and Sidlaw Hills. It runs for some 160km north-east to south-west across Scotland from the North Sea through Grampian and Tayside Regions.

Stratification, geological term used to describe the layered or bedded character of a sequence of rocks.

Stratigraphy, see GEOLOGY.

Stratosphere, see ATMOSPHERE.

Strauss, Johann, the elder (1804–48),

Austrian composer. In 1825 he founded his own orchestra with which he became famous abroad. He composed waltzes, marches, quadrilles and polkas.

Strauss, Johann, the younger (1825–99), Austrian composer. From 1849 to 1863 he led his father's orchestra, then concentrated on composition. He achieved great popularity as the 'waltz king', by his expressive talent, gift for melody and rhythm and apt instrumental technique. *The Blue Danube* is perhaps the most famous of his waltzes. His operettas include *Die Fledermaus, A Night in Venice* and *The Gypsy Baron.* He composed over 500 dances, including waltzes, polkas and galops.

Strauss, Richard (1864–1949), German composer. He became chief conductor at Meiningen in 1885, and began to cultivate the symphonic poem; his best examples include *Don Juan,* 1888; *Till Eulenspiegel,* 1895; and *Don Quixote,* 1897. His operas *Feuersnot* and *Salome* scandalised Dresden. Hugo von Hofmannsthal was librettist for *Elektra,* 1909; *Der Rosenkavalier,* 1911; *Ariadne auf Naxos,* 1916; *Die Frau ohne Schatten,* 1919; and *Die Aegyptische Helena,* 1928; these, and *Arabella,* 1933, were soon accepted as among the greatest German operas. The autobiographical *Intermezzo* was produced in 1924. In *Die schweigsame Frau,* 1935, he collaborated with Stefan Zweig, and in *Friedenstag,* 1938, *Daphne,* 1938, and *Die Liebe der Danae,* 1942, with Josef Gregor. The last opera, *Capriccio,* 1942, had a libretto by himself and Clemens Krauss. Other works include two ballets, choral works, an oboe concerto, two horn concertos, and chamber music. Among the more than 120 songs are many classic examples of the *Lied.*

Stravinsky, Igor Fyodorovich (1882–1971), US composer of Russian birth. From 1939 Stravinsky settled in the USA. He was a pupil of Rimsky-Korsakov, after whose death a new stimulus came from Diaghilev, who produced *The Firebird,* 1910. His second ballet, *Petrushka,* 1911, revealed a new personality, while *The Rite of Spring,* 1913, proved of revolutionary significance, causing a riot in Paris at its first performance. *The Wedding* and *The Soldier's Tale* demonstrate Stravinsky's continued desire to vary his style, sometimes using older models as a basis—folksong, Bach, Tchaikovsky. After the First World War, Stravinsky's work showed a new austerity, as in the one-act opera buffa *Mavra,* 1921–22, or the piano concerto, 1924. He turned to the classical manner in the octet for wind instruments, 1923, the oratorio *Oedipus Rex,* 1927, and the ballet suite *Apollo Musagetes,* 1928. *The Fairy's Kiss,* 1928, *Capriccio* for piano and orchestra and the *Symphony of Psalms,* 1930, filled old forms with new ideas. A movement towards definite classicism was made in the symphony in C. In the opera *The Rake's Progress,* 1951, he reverted to *bel canto* and opera in set numbers, and showed a new interest in English words. Other works include a septet for strings, wind and piano; two cantatas; *Movements* for piano and orchestra, 1960; and *The Flood,* a musical play for television, 1962. Stravinsky's experiments influenced his contemporaries. In his last works he used an individual form of 12-note serialism.

Straw, the stalk or stem of various corn crops such as wheat, barley, oats, rye, maize, leguminous crops, and also flax and hemp. It is put to many uses for litter, thatching, plaiting, and also, when other feeding-stuffs are scarce, as a food for livestock.

Strawberry, various species of the genus *Fragaria* in the family Rosaceae. Botanically, the edible flesh is neither a berry nor even a true fruit; the true fruits or achenes are the so-called seeds on the outside of the fleshy receptacle. The fruit of the wood strawberry, *F. vesca,* is small and delicately flavoured. The cultivated varieties are mostly derived from the Chilean strawberry, *F. chiloensis,* and the scarlet strawberry, *F. virginiana.*

Strawberry Tree, see ARBUTUS.

Strawson, Peter Frederick (1919–), British philosopher, who in 1968 became Wayneflete professor of metaphysical philosophy at Oxford. In his *Introduction to Logical Theory,* 1952, he discusses the character of formal argument and shows how ordinary discourse differs from formal systems. In *Individuals,* 1959, he shows that the basic feature enabling us to recognise things as individual is location in space and time.

Stream, see HYDROLOGY; RIVER.

Streicher, Julius (1895–1946), German politician. Streicher founded a special weekly paper entitled *Der Stürmer,* which specialised in Jew-baiting. After Hitler's triumph in 1933 the views of *Der Stürmer* soon prevailed throughout Germany, and when Hitler decided on boycotting Jewish shops Streicher was made Aktionsführer (riot leader). Later he became governor of Franconia. Streicher was sentenced to death at the Nuremberg trial in 1946 and executed.

Streisand, Barbra (1942–), US singer and actress. She won an Oscar for her first film, *Funny Girl,* 1968, and also starred in *Hello Dolly,* 1969, and *A Star is Born,* 1976. In 1970 she broke away from musicals to establish herself as a talented comedy actress in *The Owl and the Pussycat,* 1970. Other films include *What's Up Doc,* 1972, and *The Way We Were,* 1973.

Strelitzia, a genus of Musaceae which occurs exclusively in Africa. *S. reginae* is known as the queen's flower, bird's-tongue flower, or bird-of-paradise flower, because of its showy and beautiful orange and blue flowers.

Streptocarpus, a genus of the Gesneriaceae, found in Africa, usually known as Cape primrose. It contains downy herbs, bearing beautiful flowers, generally of a purple or blue colour, which are much grown as house plants.

Streptococcus, a genus of bacteria responsible for many virulent forms of inflammation. See also BACTERIA.

Streptomycin, an aminoglycoside antibiotic which interferes with the synthesis of proteins. Its most important use is in the treatment of tuberculosis, when it is often combined with other drugs.

Stresa, Italian town in Piedmont, on the western shore of Lake Maggiore, a tourist and health resort. Population (1971) 4000.

Stresemann, Gustav (1878–1929), German statesman. In August 1923 he became, briefly, chancellor of the Republic, being later succeeded by Wilhelm Marx. He was foreign minister in various governments until his death, and it was largely through his efforts that Germany was admitted to the League of Nations. Stresemann shared the Nobel Peace Prize with Briand in 1926.

Stress, see STRAIN AND STRESS.

Stress, in psychology, condition causing anxiety, tension or depression. The condition may be due to physical stress, such as that produced by an emergency, or exposure to excessive noise, fumes, and so forth; or it may be caused by anticipating or imagining a stressful situation. Psychological stress, if prolonged, may lead to actual physical symptoms, such as peptic ulcers.

Stricture, or stenosis, narrowing of a tube in the body or of its opening, by inflammatory or other changes in its walls or from outside pressure. The term is most commonly used of urethral stenosis, caused by ulceration due to gonorrhoeal infection.

Stridor, a noise caused by obstruction to the passage of air, into or out of the lower respiratory tract. In adults it is often accompanied by other symptoms such as hoarseness or shortness of breath, but in young children and babies stridor may be the only symptom of a potentially serious obstruction. Inspiratory stridor in children is known colloquially as 'croup' and it is caused by inflammation in the larynx.

Strike, The General (1926), 'sympathetic' strike by the trade unions of Great Britain,

The General Strike. A mass meeting of strikers at St Pancras goods station.

undertaken in support of the Miners' Federation in their dispute with the coal-owners. The vast majority of the organised workers ceased work, though the essential services were partially carried on by volunteers acting upon plans outlined by the government in the light of the experience of the railway strike of 1919 and the miners' strike of 1920. In the absence of newspapers the government took control of the radio, and issued a journal of its own, the *British Gazette*, whilst the TUC published the *British Worker*. The TUC, feeling that the other unions had gone as far as they could in supporting the miners, advised the executives of its constituent bodies to call the strike off, and it ended inconclusively after 10 days on 13 May. The miners stayed out for another six months but were eventually driven back to work by starvation. They returned on the owners' terms, to longer hours, lower wages, and district agreements—and the owners did nothing to improve conditions.

The General Strike involved over 2 million employed persons, and caused the loss of about 162 million working days.

Strike and Lock-out. A strike is generally taken to be a cessation of work by employed persons acting together, or their refusal to continue work in order to compel their employer(s), or to aid other employed persons to compel their employer(s), to accept or not to accept conditions of employment. A lock-out is the refusal of an employer, by means of closing the place of employment, to continue to employ persons in order to compel them, or to aid other employers to compel persons employed by them, to accept conditions of employment.

See also INDUSTRIAL RELATIONS; TRADE UNION.

Strindberg, Johann August (1849–1912), Swedish novelist, dramatist, poet and essayist. Strindberg was an extremely prolific author. His novel *The Red Room*, 1879 (trans 1913), was acclaimed as Scandinavia's first realist-social novel. He adopted much of Nietzsche's doctrine, being one of the supreme examples of Idealism, distorted by extreme introspective pessimism. Strindberg was thrice married and divorced; his hatred of women and peculiar conception of paternity, seen in embryo in *The Red Room*, and becoming almost maniacal in the collections of short stories, *Marriages*, 1884, 1885, and the plays *The Father*, 1887 (trans 1907), and *Miss Julie*, 1888 (trans 1911), had their origin in his own abnormality and acute inferiority complex, and eventually became an obsession. He spent some time in a mental sanatorium. Strindberg never fully recovered from the breakdown he suffered when prosecuted for blasphemy on the publication of *Marriages*. In later years he turned from Nietzschean Idealism to evolve a religious mysticism, which found expression in the dramatic trilogy *To Damascus*, 1898–1904 (trans 1933–35).

Strindberg was Sweden's greatest dramatic artist, and possibly its greatest literary figure. There can be no doubt about the emotional power of his plays, or of their remarkable, if distorted, insight into sexual relations. Nor is their any doubt about the influence of his work on later dramatists, especially the Expressionists.

String, see ROPE AND ROPE-MAKING.

Strobilanthes, a large genus of Acanthaceae. *S. cusia*, growing in South-East Asia, yields a blue dye. *S. dyerianus*, is a dwarf evergreen shrub, with long iridescent leaves, purple beneath, and violet flowers in spikes.

Stroboscope, device for causing a moving object to appear stationary. It emits a series of light flashes exactly synchronised with the frequency of the object's motion. The stroboscope was developed and named by Simon R. von Stampfer in 1832.

Stroheim, Erich von (1885–1957), Austro-American film actor and director. Between 1918 and 1928 he directed eight films of great power; but thereafter his uncompromising methods prevented him from obtaining backing and so he concentrated on film acting, often appearing as Prussian villains. His films include, as director: *Blind Husbands*, 1918; *Foolish Wives*, 1921; *Greed*, 1923; *Merry Widow*, 1925; *Wedding March*, 1927; *Queen Kelly*, 1928 (unfinished); and as actor: *Blind Husbands*; *Foolish Wives*; *Wedding March*; *La Grande Illusion*, 1937; *Five Graves to Cairo*, 1943; *La Danse de Mort*, 1947; and *Sunset Boulevard*, 1950.

Stroke, see CEREBRAL HAEMORRHAGE.

Stromboli, see LIPARI ISLANDS.

Strontium, metallic chemical element, symbol Sr, atomic number 38, atomic weight 87·6; one of the alkaline earths. It occurs in nature as strontianite, $SrCO_3$, and celestine, $SrSO_4$. The metal is obtained by the electrolysis of the fused chloride. It is a white metal with a low relative density (2·6), chemically similar to, though more reactive than, calcium. It readily oxidises in air and decomposes in water at ordinary temperatures. Excepting the sulphate, carbonate, and phosphate, the salts of strontium are soluble in water. They impart a crimson colour to flame, and are therefore used in pyrotechny. The hydroxide is largely used in the manufacture of beet sugar. The isotope of atomic weight 90 has become of great general importance on account of its toxic effects associated with radioactive fall out. Because of its similarity to calcium, radioactive strontium replaces calcium in animal and human bones, and its radioactive decay causes leukaemia.

Strophanthus, a genus of the Apocynaceae, found from southern Africa to China. They consist of small trees or shrubs bearing flowers which have long thread-like lobes on their petals. *S. hispidus* yields the poison strophanthin and the seeds have been used to stimulate the action of the heart. *S. sarmentosus* yields an acid from which cortisone may be produced.

Structural Formula, in chemistry, a formula expanded in such a way as to represent the relative arrangements of the atoms in a molecule. Thus the structural formula of alcohol, C_2H_6O, is $CH_3 \cdot CH_2 \cdot OH$. Further expansion gives a graphic formula, e.g.

$$\begin{array}{ccc} H & H & \\ | & | & \\ H-C-C-O-H. \\ | & | & \\ H & H & \end{array}$$

See also FORMULA.

Structural Geology, the study of individual structures such as folds, faults, and lineations within rock units. The structures seen within a rock unit may be of primary or secondary origin; primary structures are those developed during the original formation of the rock, and include depositional textures such as graded bedding and depositional structures such as load casts and worm burrows. These features are classed as sedimentary structures; by far the greater part of structural geology is concerned with the secondary structures, which are those developed when the rock is deformed by forces acting in the Earth's crust. Rock structures include the effects of plastic yielding, as in the case of folding, and of fracturing, as in the formation of faults and joints.

Structural Steelwork, a form of construction in which the main strength lies in the steelwork. The advantages of this method include tensile strength and erection speed; the disadvantages include corrosion liability and low resistance to fire damage unless suitably encased.

Structuralism, a term used in several disciplines with differing shades of meaning. It is basically a system of analysis. In psychology, structuralists analyse conscious experience by breaking it down into its component sensations. Linguistic structuralists analyse language from the point of view of its structure rather than from an historical or comparative standpoint. In general, structuralists strive to erect models of the component parts of their discipline by logical deductions from first principles. In science, this allows of theorising from paradigms to attempt to explain natural phenomena. There is some doubt about the value of structuralism in dealing with social sciences. The leading figure in the structuralist movement is the social anthropologist Claude Lévi-Strauss.

Struve, family whose members were distinguished astronomers for four generations. Friedrich Georg Wilhelm von Struve (1793–1864), born at Altona, Germany, was director of the observatory at Dorpat in Russia (now Tartu, Estonia, USSR), 1820–39; in 1839 he supervised the construction of the new central observatory at Pulkovo, near St Petersburg, of which he was director until 1861. He is best known for his pioneer work in measuring and cataloguing double stars, and for the measurement of the parallax of Vega, in 1837. One of his 18 children, Otto Wilhelm von Struve (1819–1905), born at Dorpat, was his father's assistant at Pulkovo from 1839, and became director, 1862–90.

Two sons of Otto Wilhelm became astronomers: Karl Hermann von Struve (1854–1920), born at Pulkovo, founded the Berlin-Babelsberg observatory in 1913; Ludvig von Struve (1858–1920), born at Pulkovo, was professor of astronomy at Kharkov University.

A son of Ludvig, Otto Struve (1897–1963), born at Kharkov, fought with the White Russian army, escaped to the USA as a refugee in 1921, and obtained a post at Yerkes Observatory near Chicago. He founded the McDonald Observatory of the University of Texas and was first director of the National Radio Astronomy Observatory, 1959–62. He was most prolific and published over 500 papers on many aspects of stellar spectroscopy, stellar rotation, binary stars, and interstellar gas. Publications include *The Universe*, 1962.

Strychnine, an alkaloid occurring in *Strychnos nux-vomica* and other trees of the same genus. The alkaloid is contained with brucine in the bark, leaves, seeds and root. Strychnine, usually in the form of a more soluble salt, has long been used, with or without iron, as a bitter tonic or stimulant, but there is no evidence that it is particularly effective. It has been given as a respiratory stimulant especially in the treatment of poisoning by depressants of the central nervous system. It should not be used as a laxative due to its toxicity. Strychnine in larger doses acts as a powerful poison. A volatile anaesthetic should be rapidly administered until it is possible to give an intravenous dose of a barbiturate and a muscle relaxant such as curare. The patient should be kept in complete darkness. An emetic should not be given.
See also POISONS.

Strychnos, a genus of tropical plants of the family Strychnaceae. Most are poisonous. *S. nux-vomica* is an Indian tree containing several alkaloids, the chief of which are strychnine and brucine. *S. toxifera* of South America yields curare used as an arrow poison and for relaxing muscles in surgery.

Stuart, Charles Edward Louis Philip Casimir (1720–88), known as the 'Young Pretender' and 'Bonnie Prince Charlie', the elder son of the Chevalier de St George, the 'Old Pretender'. In 1743 he headed an unsuccessful French invasion of England, but in 1745 succeeded in landing at Eriskay in the Hebrides. Marching southwards, he entered Edinburgh and held his court at Holyrood. He defeated Cope at Prestonpans. With a troop of 6500 men he invaded England, and marched as far south as Derby. Retreating to Scotland he was again victorious at Falkirk (1746), but was overwhelmed by the Duke of Cumberland at Culloden, and for many months hid in the Highlands with a price of £30,000 on his head. Before the end of the year he escaped to France, from where he was expelled in 1748. He spent the remainder of his life wandering in Europe, living for some time in Rome, and became a drunkard. He married Louisa von Stolberg in 1772, but the marriage was extremely unhappy and childless.
See also MACDONALD, FLORA; STUART, JAMES FRANCIS EDWARD.

Stuart, Henry Benedict Maria Clement, Cardinal York (1725–1807), last of the Stuarts, the second son of James Stuart, the 'Old Pretender'. He went to France in 1745 to support his brother, Charles Edward, and after his return to Italy was created cardinal deacon with the title of York by Pope Benedict XIV. In the following year he was ordained priest and nominated arch-priest of St Peter's. In 1759 he was consecrated as titular Archbishop of Corinth, in 1761 appointed Archbishop of Frascati, and in 1763 vice-chancellor of St Peter's. On the death of his brother in 1788 the Cardinal styled himself 'Henry IX, not by the will of men, but by the Grace of God' but no other ruler, not even the Pope, acknowledged his title. In 1799 he accepted from George III an annual pension of £4000. He died in Rome and was buried in St Peter's, leaving to the Prince of Wales certain crown jewels.

Stuart, James Francis Edward (1688–1766), Prince of Wales, later known as the 'Old Pretender', the son of James II by his second wife, Mary of Modena. His birth precipitated the revolution of 1688. In 1701 James II died and his son was accepted by the Jacobites as king of England and Scotland under the style of James III. He served with distinction in the French army before the Peace of Utrecht, and in 1715 went to Scotland to take part in the unsuccessful Jacobite rising. He married Maria Clementina Sobieski in 1719 and was the father of Charles Edward Stuart, the 'Young Pretender'. The rising of 1745 was the last attempt to secure his restoration.

Stuart, House of, see STEWART.

Charles Stuart, the Young Pretender.

Stubbs, George (1724–1806), British painter. He served an artist's apprenticeship, but studied anatomy, and even lectured at York hospital. He is famous for sporting or animal pictures, and scenes of rural life, e.g. *Gimcrack*, c.1765 (Private Collection); *Mares and Foals*, c.1763 (Tate Gallery); *The Reapers*, 1784 (Private Collection). He was also in demand as a portrait painter, especially of family groups. Stubbs published *The Anatomy of the Horse*, 1766, illustrated by his own engravings, and experimented in working in enamel on copper, or china plaques provided by the Wedgwood potteries.

Stubbs, William (1825–1901), British historian and churchman. In 1866 he became regius professor of modern history at Oxford. In 1884 he was consecrated bishop of Chester, and three years later translated to the see of Oxford. His chief publication, *Constitutional History of England*, 1873–78, is a work of monumental scholarship. Stubbs's work gave a new direction to the study of medieval English history.

Stucco, Italian word applied in most languages to plaster of any kind used as a coating for walls to give them a finished appearance.

Stupa (Sanskrit, mound), Buddhist monument erected to commemorate, or enshrine relics of, the Buddha or his disciples. The stupa is usually in the form of a tumulus of masonry shaped like a dome or tower, and often surrounded by an elaborately carved stone railing with lofty gateways at the cardinal points. There are numerous examples in India and South-East Asia, which archaeologists date between 200 BC and modern times.
See also INDIA, *Architecture*.

Stupor, the state of partial unconsciousness in which the patient can be roused by pain or may respond vaguely to questions. The deeper state of unconsciousness, in which nothing rouses the patient, is coma.

Sturgeon, any fish in the family Acipenseridae of the infra-class Chondrostei. They are large and have elongated bodies, bearing five rows of large bony projections; the mouth is small, has no teeth, and in front of it are four barbels. Sturgeon are voracious feeders on small animals and plants. Caviare is sturgeon roe (eggs), and isinglass is made from the swimbladders of several Russian and American species.

Sturm und Drang, see GERMAN LITERATURE.

Sturt, Charles (1795–1869), Australian explorer. On his first expedition in 1828 he traced the course of the inland rivers of New South Wales. The next year he followed the River Murrumbidgee to its junction with the Murray and then the Murray to its mouth, solving the problem of where the inland rivers flowed. In 1844 he set out from Adelaide and penetrated to the centre of Australia. His contribution to the knowledge of the interior of Australia was of great importance, for it opened the way for rapid expansion of settlement inland.

Stuttering, see STAMMERING AND STUTTERING.

Stuttgart, city of south-west Federal Republic of Germany, capital of the *Land* of Baden-Württemberg. It is situated in a natural basin, open only towards the Neckar, which flows through the suburb of Bad Cannstatt. In 1482 it was made the provincial capital of the counts of Württemberg, but its fortunes declined after the Thirty Years' War. Its modern importance dates from the raising of Württemberg to the status of a kingdom in 1806. Stuttgart is one of the leading industrial cities of the country. Its manufactures include electrical goods (Bosch, Standard, AEG, IBM, Bauknecht), cars (Daimler-Benz, Porsche), metallurgical goods, optical instruments, clothing, and food industries. It is a publishing, banking and major exhibition centre. Population (1979) 581,989.

Stuyvesant, Peter (1592–1672), Dutch colonial governor who became director-general of the New Netherlands in 1646, until the surrender of New Amsterdam (New York) to the English in 1664. His farm (Bouwerij) gave its name to the Bowery.

Stye (also sty) or hordeolum, an inflammation of the modified sweat glands between the eyelashes, or of the hair follicles of the eyelashes themselves. Strictly speaking, a hordeolum is an inflammation of the gland and a stye is an inflammation of the hair follicle. It commences with a hardening of the skin about the part, followed by swelling and soreness. Suppuration of the lower layers of the skin follows and the central core subsequently sloughs off. Hot fomentations tend to ease inflammation.

Styrax, a genus of shrubs and trees, chiefly deciduous, in the family Styracaceae, *S. japonica*, of Japan, is cultivated for ornament; *S. benzoin*, of Sumatra, is the source of benzoin, a drug that forms part of 'Friar's Balsam'.

Styrene, $CH_2:CHC_6H_5$, vinyl benzene, or phenylethene, formed by the thermal desaturation of ethylbenzene. Styrene is the monomer for the plastic polystyrene. Styrene is a colourless liquid with boiling point 145°C.

Styria (German *Steiermark*), province of south-east Austria, bordered on the east by Hungary and on the south by Yugoslavia. It was part of the Roman province of Noricum. It became Austrian in 1192, ceded to the Hapsburgs in 1276. The province is mountainous, containing the outlying ranges of the eastern Alps (Dachstein, 2996m), and it is bisected west–east by the valleys of the Mur and Mürz. The other main river is the Enns. Forestry is a major industry although the economy of the province has always been dependent on its minerals, for example iron ore and brown coal. Agriculture employs more than 40 per cent of the working population. There are large iron and steel works at Donauwitz-Leoben. The capital is Graz. Area 16,385km². Population (1981) 1,184,175.

Styx (Greek, hateful), river of Peloponnesus which was supposed by the ancients to flow round the underworld. When the gods swore by Styx they dared not break the oath, under pain of a year's unconsciousness and nine years' exile. To mortal oathbreakers its waters were deadly poison. The tradition originated probably in some form of trial by ordeal.

Suarez, Francisco (1548–1617), Spanish philosopher and theologian, he entered the Society of Jesus in 1564. He wrote his first work, *De Verbo Incarnato*, in 1590, noted for its attempts to reconcile the Thomist view of the Redemption as the final cause of the Incarnation with that of Duns Scotus. Suarez was appointed professor of theology at Coimbra in 1597, where he lectured until 1616. He was an adherent of Thomas Aquinas but was opposed by strict Dominican Thomists for tending towards Molinism. His *Defensio fidei* attacked the doctrine of a divine right of kings and the English oath of allegiance in particular. Suarez is considered the greatest Jesuit theologian and his opinions continue to be important.

Subjectivism, in philosophy, is the opposite of objectivism. The latter holds that there is an objective order existing independently of the person who seeks to know it. By contrast, subjectivism denies that there is such an independent order. Moreover, the subjectivist would argue that even if there were such an order, we could never know that there was. The most extreme form of subjectivism is solipsism, the view that a person can assert the existence only of himself.

Sublimation. When a solid, on the application of heat, passes straight to the vapour state without first becoming liquid, it is said to sublime. On cooling, the vapour becomes solid without first becoming liquid. Sublimation depends on the fact that the boiling-point of the solid is lower than its melting-point at atmospheric pressure. Thus by increase of pressure a substance which sublimes can be made to pass through a liquid stage. By sublimation, non-volatile impurities are left behind, and thus a method of purifying those substances which sublime is established.
See also DISSOCIATION; TRIPLE POINT.

Submachine-gun. Its German name, *Maschinen-pistole*, shows at once its origin and function, i.e. a weapon intended to be to the pistol what the machine-gun is to the rifle. Developed probably from the Mauser Parabellum, an automatic pistol of heavy calibre with detachable stock and a magazine containing some two dozen rounds, the first submachine-gun to be extensively manufactured was the Thompson (whence 'Tommy gun') under US patent. A similar weapon, the 'Suomi pistol', was used by the Finns in the 'winter war' of 1940–41, and at the same period the German patrols on the western front were armed with Schmeisser submachine-guns. These were all-metal weapons with folding stock and straight vertical magazine. The Suomi pistol inspired the prototype of the Russian submachine-guns. Other makes used in the Second World War were the Steyr-Solothurn and the Beretta.

A simple type of submachine-gun, the Sten, was evolved in Great Britain. Its parts were mainly of stamped steel, and especially suited for mass production.

Submarine, a vessel designed to operate beneath the surface of the sea. Until nuclear power, submarines were in fact surface craft capable of limited operations submerged.

Submarines are submerged by flooding ballast tanks; to rise again the water is discharged by compressed air. These tanks are outside the pressure hull which is of circular section, strengthened by transverse frames to withstand the pressure of water at depths of up to 300 m. The conning tower above it houses the periscopes, snort or Snorkel tube, and radar and radio masts. The diving planes are fitted on each side of the conning tower. The first reliable attempt at building a submarine vessel appears to have been in the 17th century when a Dutchman, Cornelius Drebbell, navigated a boat manned by twelve rowers in the Thames. The first practical submarines were the *Holland* class ordered by the British Admiralty in 1899.

Nuclear-powered submarines are capable of higher speeds submerged than would be possible on the surface, and can maintain such speed indefinitely. The first built was the *Nautilus*, completed for the US navy in 1955. The introduction of nuclear power points to an expansion of this type of warship at the expense of surface vessels.

Subpoena, in English law, the name of the writ for calling a witness to give evidence.

Subsidies were taxes in aid formerly granted to the kings of England. They were imposed not immediately on property, but upon persons in respect of their reputed estates.

Modern subsidies take the form of government grants to industries and commercial undertakings, such as those made to shipping and air lines.

Subsoil, a term dating from the period when soil was conceived of as two parts, topsoil and subsoil. It refers to the B horizons, which are not penetrated in normal cultivation practices.
See also SOIL.

Subspecies represent distinct forms of a species, which can often be recognised by their morphology and distinct distribution, and which breed true.

Substance, in philosophy, that which exists in itself. A created substance is that which exists in itself and arrives as a subject in which attributes (accidents) inhere. Such is the teaching of Aristotle and the Scholastics, who classified substances according to their perfection as complete (e.g. God, angels) and incomplete (e.g. human and animal souls), and according to their degree of unity as single (God, angels, souls) and complex (man, animal, plant). This view was repudiated by Locke and others, who held that every object has some *fundamental* or *essential* quality, which, being present, preserves its identity, and which being removed, renders it no longer the same substance, but another. According to this system, therefore, substance is unknowable, or at least unknown. According to Descartes, there are two substances: matter, whose essence is extension, and minds, whose essence is thinking. Spinoza recognised only a single substance, namely the world as a whole, which he identifies with God. Matter and minds are then regarded as aspects of the one substance. Leibniz, on the other hand, held that there were infinitely many substances, which he called monads. The atoms of Democritus in Greek philosophy, as much as those of physical science till the late 19th century, were uncreated substances which, as unchanging elements, were used as principles for explaining change in complex things.

Substitution. In orthodox economics the assumption that substitution is possible between the factors of production.
See also ELASTICITY; MARGIN; SUPPLY AND DEMAND.

Substitution Reactions, in chemistry, occur when a compound of the type R-X undergoes reaction to become R-Y (i.e. one group has been substituted for another). The study of the various possible mechanisms of substitution, first classified by Ingold (1930s), is of great theoretical interest.

Succession. The law of succession is that according to which the succession to property is regulated. In English law, this may be: (1) where a deceased party has died intestate when the order of succession follows fixed rules, or (2) according to a settlement under which property stands in trust for any person by way of succession.
See also HEIR; PRIMOGENITURE; WILLS AND TESTAMENTS.

Succession, Royal. Inheritance by heirs male, when applied to the royal office, is the Salic Law, which prevailed in France and other countries. Down to 1688 the English succession was regulated by custom, Parliament claiming some right to intervene. In 1700, when it became evident that both William III and his sister-in-law, Anne, would probably die without issue, the Act of Settlement was passed to provide for the succession after their deaths. This is the act under which, as modified by the Act of Abdication of Edward VIII, the Crown is still held. The Act of Settlement: (1) declared that if a Roman Catholic obtains the Crown the subjects of the realm are thereby absolved of their allegiance; (2) settled the Crown on the Electress Sophia and the Protestant heirs of her body; and (3) expressly excludes any person holding communion with the Church of Rome, professing the popish religion, or marrying a Papist.

Succulent Plants, those which have developed very fleshy leaves or stems, or both, capable of retaining moisture in long spells of dry, hot weather. They are native to arid areas in tropical or subtropical regions and include cacti, *Agave, Aloe, Crassula,* and *Mesembryanthemum.* They are popular indoor plants in temperate countries. Plants growing in strongly saline conditions, e.g. *Salicornia* in salt marshes, are also typically succulent, again for water conservation.

Sucking-fish, any member of the family Echeneidae, the remoras, in the order Perciformes, so named on account of the suctorial oval disc they bear on the upper part of the head. This sucker is in fact a highly modified dorsal fin. By means of this disc they attach themselves to sharks, and they are to be found in all warm seas. They feed, at least in part, on the external parasites of oceanic sharks. Other sucking-fish are the suckers, which form the family Gobiesocidae, order Gobiesociformes, and the lump-suckers, which form the family Cyclopteridae, order Scorpaeniformes.

Suckling, Sir John (1609–42), English poet, playwright, and prose writer. Though he wrote in more than one genre, it is as a poet that he is best known. Some of his shorter pieces are incomparable for charm and delicacy, such as his 'Ballad upon a Wedding' and 'Why so pale and wan, fond lover?'

Sucre, capital town of the department of Chuquisaca, Bolivia, and legal capital of Bolivia itself (La Paz being the actual seat of government). Its altitude is 3390 m but it has a mild climate. Sucre is the seat of the judiciary and the archbishop. The best buildings, besides the cathedral, are the legislative palaces, from which Bolivia's independence was declared in 1825, and the palace of justice. Population (1974) 88,000.

Sudan
Area: 2,506,000 km²
Population: 18,400,000
Capital: Khartoum

Sudan, or Soudan, a republic of north east Africa, is bounded by Egypt on the north; Libya, Chad, and the Central African Empire lie to the west; Zaire, Uganda, and Kenya lie to the south; and Ethiopia and the Red Sea are to the east. The estimated area of Sudan is 2,506,000 km², making it the largest state in Africa.

The physiography of the Sudan is dominated by the drainage basin of the River Nile, most of which is below 750 m. There are highlands rising to 2200 m along the shore of the Red Sea in the east, and in the west of Darfur province the Marra Mountains rise to over 3000 m. The northern Sudan is desert, mostly sandy to the west of the Nile but stony to the

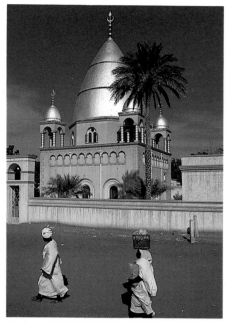

Sudan. The Mahdi's Tomb at Omdurman.

east. Southern Sudan has extensive areas of flat clay plains along the Blue Nile, where the river floods seasonally, and along the White Nile the clay plains are permanently flooded to form the Sudd, a vast area of marshland.

The total population of Sudan in 1980 was estimated at 18,400,000, partly Arab, partly Negroid, and partly Nubian. The main cities are Khartoum (the capital), Omdurman and Port Sudan. The most fertile regions lie east and south of Khartoum watered by the Atbara and the Blue and White Niles. Here there are large areas under dura (the staple native food), millet, sesame and pulse. The Gezira irrigation scheme enables an area of 370,000 ha to be cultivated between the Blue and White Niles. One-quarter is under cotton, Sudan's major export crop.

Most of Sudan's limited industrial capacity is centred on Khartoum. The textile industry is the largest single employer of labour. Sugar refining is increasing in importance. The cement industry is also expanding.

The Sudan is a democratic republic. A new constitution was proclaimed in 1973. Under this the executive authority lies with the President and his cabinet. The legislature is the National People's Assembly which sits for four-year terms. In the assembly, 274 of the seats are filled by elected representatives and 30 are appointed by the President.

The language of the Sudan is Arabic in the north and various African dialects in the south.

History. In the 6th century northern Sudan was converted to Christianity; a century later the Muslims arrived, and eventually Christianity was replaced by Islam. Southern Sudan cut off by the Sudd, remained untouched by foreign influences until the 19th century. Mehemet Ali, the Viceroy of Egypt, conquered the Sudan in 1820. Egypt nominally governed the Sudan for the next 65 years; it was in fact governed by nobody. Britain, through the control that it exerted on Egypt, appointed Gen. Charles Gordon as governor-general of the Sudan (1877–79) and attempted its reorganisation. Around 1880 Mohammed Ahmed, a Muslim agitator, proclaimed him-

self Mahdi and organised a revolt in Egyptian Sudan. He besieged Khartoum and Gen. Gordon was killed. In 1898, a joint British and Egyptian army marched against the Sudan, and shattered his power at the battles of Atbara and Omdurman. Under an Anglo-Egyptian agreement signed on 19 January 1899 the two countries governed the Sudan jointly on a condominium basis.

On 1 January 1956 the Sudan became a sovereign state, and joined the Arab League. During the period since independence Sudanese politics have been dogged by instability, which can be attributed to divisions between pro-Western and pro-Egyptian factions, splits within the parties, to the economic difficulties in administering Africa's largest country, and to the civil war, which lasted for 17 years (1955–72), between the north and the non-Muslim, non-Arab south.

In 1969 Col. Numeiry assumed control of the government by coup d'etat. Under Numeiry Sudan tightened links with the Eastern bloc, and firms, both local and foreign, were nationalised. Political parties were banned. In July 1971, Numeiry was ousted for three days by a Communist-led coup. Thereafter Numeiry set up the Sudan Socialist Union as the sole political organisation, and in October was elected president. The orientation of the regime was turned towards the West and the more conservative Arab governments. Numeiry managed to survive, in 1976, a serious attempted coup, which was probably mounted with Libyan assistance. In April 1977 Numeiry was re-elected president for a second six-year term.

Sudan, French, see MALI.

Sudbury, city of north-western Ontario, Canada, 482 km north-west of Toronto on the Canadian Pacific and Canadian National railways. In the district 90 per cent of the world's nickel supply is produced; also a large output of copper. The town is the chief commercial centre of northern Ontario. Population (1976) 97,604.

Sudetenland, land formerly occupied by the German minority in Bohemia, concentrated chiefly near the German frontier formed by the Sudetic Mountains. This German minority was a useful lever in Hitler's hands to force the gateway into Czechoslovakia. After the German annexation of Austria, their leader, Henlein, called on the Czech government to transfer the Sudetic region to the German Reich. This demand was, of course, rejected, but by the Munich Pact 'the orderly taking over of the Sudetenland by Germany' was provided for. On the basis of the Potsdam Conference some 3,300,000 Germans were evicted from Czechoslovakia after the end of the Second World War.

See also CZECHOSLOVAKIA, *History.*

Sue, Joseph Marie (1804–57). French novelist, known as Eugène Sue. His novels, realistic and ingeniously constructed, were very popular, perhaps the best-known being *Les Mystères de Paris,* 1842, describing the underworld of the capital. In 1848 Sue, a socialist, was elected a representative of the Assemblé Nationale, but on the election of Napoleon III was expelled from French territory, and he retired to Annecy.

Suede, any leather finished with a nap on the flesh side.

Suetonius, full name Gaius Suetonius Tranquillus (c.70–c.140), Roman historian. He became confidential secretary to the Emperor Hadrian. The most important of his surviving works is the *De Vita Caesarum*, a collection of 12 imperial biographies from Julius Caesar to Domitian. Though often scandalous in content, it is based on good sources.

Suez, seaport town and province of Egypt, situated at the head of the Gulf of Suez and west of the mouth of the Suez Canal, 120 km east of Cairo. Suez is a refuelling station for ships passing through the canal. The town was largely deserted after the Arab-Israeli War of 1967, and was rebuilt as a new town. Population (1976) 193,965.

Suez, Gulf of, western arm of the Red Sea after its bifurcation in latitude 28°N, whence it extends north-west for 300 km to latitude 30°N. It lies between Egypt and the Sinai Peninsula. Average breadth, 50 km.

Suez, Isthmus of, neck of land connecting Asia and Africa, having the Gulf of Suez to the south and the Mediterranean to the north, and through which is cut the Suez Canal. Minimum width, 116 km.

Suez Canal. A French businessman, Ferdinand de Lesseps, founded a company in 1856 to build a canal linking the Mediterranean Sea at Port Said on the northern coast of Egypt with Suez on the Red Sea. Work was started in 1859 and completed 10 years later. This canal provided a direct link between Europe and the Indian Ocean, as shipping no longer had to circumnavigate the Cape of Good Hope.

Britain bought shares worth £4 million in 1875, and acquired a controlling interest in the company after occupying Egypt in 1882. In 1956, the Egyptian government under Nasser nationalised the Suez Canal Company 12 years before the company's operating concession was due to expire.

The canal was closed for an eight-year period as a result of the June 1967 six-day war when Israel occupied the Sinai bank. Following the October 1973 war, the canal was reopened.

Suffocation, see ASPHYXIA.

Suffolk, most easterly, and one of the largest English counties (381,000 ha), bounded by Norfolk to the north, by Cambridgeshire to the west, by Essex to the south, and by the North Sea to the east. The coastline, which is generally low and singularly regular, has been locally encroached upon by the sea, as in the famous cliffs at Dunwich.

Interesting remains of monastic buildings may be seen (Bury St Edmunds), and there are castles (Framlingham). Many of the numerous churches are of great size and beauty. Lavenham is probably unrivalled in Britain in its wealth of medieval buildings. On the coast are the well-known seaside resorts of Lowestoft, Southwold, Aldeburgh, and Felixstowe. The surface of the county is flat on the east and undulating on the south and west. In the north-east are the Broads as in Norfolk, and around Brandon is the Breckland, originally heathland, but now largely afforested or reclaimed for agriculture. Nearly all the county is under cultivation, and farming is in a very flourishing condition. Cattle, sheep, and pigs are reared. The thriving fishing industry is concentrated at Lowestoft. Until 1974 the

Suez Canal. A vessel passes through the 103-mile-long canal linking the Mediterranean and Red Sea.

county was divided into two divisions of East and West Suffolk. Population (1981) 596,354.

Suffrage, Women's, see WOMEN'S SUFFRAGE.

Sufism (a European formation from the Arabic *suf*, wool), the name of the mystical movement in Islam. Mohammed preached the worthlessness of this world as compared with the world to come, and some took his words literally and led an ascetic life. They wore wool, probably in imitation of monks, and the individual was called a Sufi. Sufis used the images of wine and earthly love to describe their relation to God, and it is often impossible to tell whether a Persian poem is to be taken literally or in a religious sense.

Sugar, name of a class of sweet-tasting carbohydrates, which is subdivided into simple sugars or monosaccharides and the compound sugars, di- and trisaccharides, etc. The mono compounds are termed pentose, hexose, heptose, according to the number of carbon atoms in the molecule. They are polyhydroxy derivatives of paraffin hydrocarbons with an aldehyde or ketone group in the molecule (hence termed aldose or ketose sugars) from which their property of reducing Fehling's solution is due. Pentoses have the general formula $C_5H_{10}O_5$ and hexoses $C_6H_{12}O_6$. Examples of the former are arabinose and xylose and of the latter dextrose (glucose or grape-sugar) and laevulose (fructose or fruit-sugar). The disaccharides have the general formula $C_{12}H_{22}O_{11}$ and include sucrose (cane-sugar, the ordinary sugar of commerce, whether derived from cane or beet), maltose, and lactose (milk-sugar). Raffinose, $C_{18}H_{32}O_{16}$, is the best-known trisaccharide. Di- and trisaccharides can be split into constituent monosaccharides by heating with dilute acids or by action of enzymes. In this reaction one or two molecules of water are absorbed and the change is termed hydrolysis. Sucrose on hydrolysis yields glucose and fructose, the mixture being known as invert sugar because the optical rotation of the solution is changed from the positive to the negative. Invert sugar with a little sucrose constitutes the major part of honey and, with rather more sucrose, golden

syrup, the remainder being water and salts. In jam manufacture some inversion of sucrose is due to acidity of the fruit. Maltose on hydrolysis yields two molecules of glucose, and lactose one molecule each of glucose and galactose. Sucrose, the most important sugar, is very soluble in water; it is insoluble in absolute alcohol, but will dissolve in aqueous alcohol. It crystallises from water in monoclinic prisms and melts at 188°C, giving a glassy mass on cooling (barley-sugar). Prolonged heating causes gradual dehydration, darkening, and production of caramel.
See also NUTRITION.

Sugar Beet, see BEET; SUGAR.

Sugar Beet Yellows, a virus disease in which the middle and old leaves of an infected plant become yellow and die. The young leaves usually remain green. The disease is caused by at least two viruses, beet yellows virus and the commoner beet mild yellows virus. The viruses are spread by aphids, especially *Myzus persicae*, from overwintering members of the genus *Beta*; beet mild yellows virus also overwinters on some weeds.

Sugar Cane, *Saccharum officinarum*, a large tropical grass with shoots reaching 3–4 m in height and having thick solid stems (unlike the hollow ones of most grasses) which yield a sugary juice when crushed. Sugar cane is thought to be native in South-East Asia, but is now cultivated very widely in moist tropical and subtropical regions as an extremely productive crop, being one of the world's main sources of sugar. The cane is generally propagated vegetatively, by planting pieces of the stem.

Suger (c.1081–1151), French prelate, historian, and statesman. He was abbot of St-Denis. Minister and counsellor to Louis VI and Louis VII, he was regent of France during the Second Crusade. He wrote a life of Louis VI and a history of the reign of Louis VII.

Suharto (1921–), second president of Indonesia. As a result of his military training, he quickly attained high rank during the independence struggle and thereafter. He early befriended both Untung and Latief, who were later involved in the unsuccessful pro-

Sukarno coup of 1965. Having apparently encouraged them to stage the coup, which eliminated his six main army rivals, he turned on them, suppressed the coup, and presided over the slaughter of some million left-wing sympathisers. After the fall of Sukarno he was confirmed in power as president by the MPRS (Provisional People's Consultative Assembly) in 1968. Corruption has, however, continued to flourish under his rule; the bankruptcy of the state oil combine, Pertamina, indicates the trend.

Suicide. By the Suicide Act 1961, suicide ceased to be a criminal offence in English law. If, however, two persons agree to commit suicide together and one dies and the other survives, the survivor is criminally liable, but he cannot be prosecuted without the consent of the director of public prosecutions. If the survivor killed the deceased, he will be guilty of manslaughter; if the deceased killed himself, he will be guilty of aiding and abetting suicide. The former offence carries a maximum penalty of life imprisonment; the latter fourteen years' imprisonment.
See also HOMICIDE.

Suite, in music, a series of dances unified by key. The suite originated in the coupling of two contrasted dances in the 16th century. Then followed the grouping of several dances of different kinds, sometimes thematically related. The wealth of characteristic dances in the French ballet led to the composition of orchestral suites for concert performance: German composers were particularly influenced by Lully's dance style. The keyboard suite also developed in Germany, France and England. The binary form usual in suite movements became extended and more organised with regard to the repetition of material and the key-scheme so that it contributed to sonata form. Today the term is used for a collection of short pieces, for example, derived from a ballet or film score.

Sukarno, Achmed (1901–70), first president of Indonesia. By 1927 he was prominent enough to be one of the founders of the Indonesian Nationalist party (PNI). Arrested in 1929, he spent much of the following decade in captivity or exile.
The Japanese, however, gave him free rein, and on the declaration of independence in 1945 there was no challenge to his claim to be Indonesia's first president. For the next two decades, he epitomised in the minds of both Indonesians and others the dearly won independence. His progressively more nationalist and anti-imperialist policies, particularly during 1957–65, attracted to him the hostility of Western leaders, and he was eased from power in stages from 1965 to 1968.

Sukhumi, capital of the Abkhazian ASSR, Georgian SSR, USSR, on the Black Sea. The town, which is a popular resort, has fruit canning, tobacco, and leather industries, and a famous botanical garden. Originally it was an ancient Greek colony, then a Turkish fortress town, passing to Russia in 1810. Population (1981) 114,000.

Sukkur, town of Pakistan, on the Indus, opposite Rohri. Sukkur is principally known for the Sukkur or Lloyd Barrage, a great irrigation project on the Indus, built between 1923 and 1932. It irrigates an area of 2·4 million ha. Population (1972) 159,000.

Sulawesi, formerly known as Celebes, island of Indonesia, separated from Kalimantan to the west by the Makasar Strait, with an area of 188,784 km². Most of the island is rugged upland above 450 m, with numerous rift-like lowlands, and soil erosion and leaching are prevalent. However, despite difficult terrain, swamps are absent and the soil (though not rich) supports a relatively productive shifting agricultural system and lowland wet-rice farming. Good agricultural land is concentrated in the south-west peninsula and Minahasa, associated with volcanic soils. The island is rich in nickel, iron, gold, silver, and a variety of other minerals. Seventy per cent of the island is forested; most of the southern forests are tropical deciduous.
Total population in 1980 was 10,409,533. Major groups are the Makasarese, the Menadonese and the Bugis, all of Deutero-Malay stock. Major towns are Makasar (population 500,000) and Menado (185,000).
Sulawesi's main food crops are rice and maize. Coconuts are grown over much of lowland Sulawesi, especially in Minahasa. Sulawesi's main agricultural exports are copra, coconut oil, peanut oil, palm oil, castor oil, and kapok. The main port is Makasar in the south-west.
History. During the 17th century Makasar was a major port for Java-Moluccas trade. It remained strongly independent of European control until Dutch conquest in 1667. The subduing of Makasar was followed, during the 18th century, by a period of Bugis ascendancy. This threat to Dutch influence led, after 1755, to open war between the Dutch and Bugis, and the Dutch gradually contained Bugis influence. By 1880 Sulawesi was effectively under Dutch political control. After Indonesia achieved independence in 1949, regional separatist moements developed into a military revolt on the island. A state of emergency was declared in 1957, and the rebellion was broken by 1961.

Suleiman the Magnificent (c.1496–1566), Sultan of Turkey. He became sultan in 1520, seized Belgrade in 1522, captured Rhodes from the Knights of St John in 1523, defeated and killed King Louis of Hungary at Mohacs in 1526, took Armenia and the cities of Tabriz and Baghdad from the Persians in 1534, conquered Croatia in 1537, established a pasha in Buda in 1541, and, in 1560, gained a decisive naval victory over a Christian confederacy at Djerbeh. He was succeeded by Selim II, his son by a Russian slave; Suleiman murdered his legitimate offspring to further this end.

Sulla, Lucius Cornelius (138–78 BC), surnamed Felix, Roman general and statesman. He served under Marius until Marius's undisguised jealousy drove him to take a command under Q. Lutatius Catulus.
Sulla's ability and reputation had led the Optimates to look to him as their leader, and thus political animosity was added to professional jealousy and personal hatred on the part of Marius. At this stage, however, the outbreak of the Social War hushed all private quarrels. Both men took an active part in hostilities against the common foe; Sulla gained some brilliant victories, and ended the war by taking Nola. Meanwhile he had obtained command in the Mithridatic war, and set out to oppose Mithridates at the beginning of 87. During the next four years he

won a series of amazing victories, and collected a large amount of plunder. Having sacked Athens (86), and driven the enemy from Greece, he crossed the Hellespont in 84 and in the same year concluded peace with Mithridates.
In 82 the struggle in Italy was brought to a close by the great victory over the Samnites before the Colline Gate at Rome.
Sulla was now absolute master of Rome and Italy; he resolved to take revenge upon his enemies and to destroy all potential opposition to the Optimates. The steps he took are known as the 'Sullan proscription'. He was given the office of dictator and drew up a list (*proscriptio*) of men who were said to be outlaws and enemies of the state. The reign of terror spread to the whole peninsula. His constitutional and administrative reforms were in effect a restoration of the Senate to its old legislative and executive supremacy.
When he withdrew into private life (79), he died the following year of a long-standing disease.

Sullivan, Sir Arthur Seymour (1842–1900), British composer. With W. S. Gilbert as librettist he wrote the light operas *Thespis, Trial by Jury*, 1875; *The Sorcerer*, 1877; *H.M.S. Pinafore*, 1878; *The Pirates of Penzance*, 1879; *Patience*, 1881; *Iolanthe*, 1882; *Princess Ida*, 1884; *The Mikado*, 1885; *Ruddigore*, 1887; *The Yeomen of the Guard*, 1888; *The Gondoliers*, 1889; *Utopia Limited*, 1893; and *The Grand Duke*, 1896. Sullivan also composed choral works, the grand opera *Ivanhoe*, 1891, other operettas, incidental music, overtures, church music and songs.

Sullivan, John L(awrence) (1858–1918), US prizefighter, known as 'the Boston Strong Boy'. He won the bare-knuckle championship of America against Paddy Ryan, 1882, and was undefeated for ten years. A contest with the English champion, Charley Mitchell, at Chantilly, France, resulted in a draw after 39 rounds, preventing him from claiming the world championship. His greatest victory was over Jake Kilrain in 1889, when he knocked out the latter in the 75th round. At a further attempt at world status, he was beaten by James J. Corbett in a contest with gloves in 21 rounds. His autobiography, *Reminiscences of a 19th Century Gladiator*, was published in 1892.

Sullivan, Louis Henry (1856–1924), US architect. He designed many commercial and other buildings, generally favouring a variant of the Romanesque style; but in his Wainwright Building at St Louis (1890–91) he adopted a more functional style of design, expressing directly the metal-frame structure, and in his Transportation Building at the World's Fair, Chicago (1893), he made a remarkable attempt to evolve a definitely original and American design, not based on any traditional type. This idea has since been developed by his most distinguished disciple, Frank Lloyd Wright. Other widely admired works are the Guaranty Building, Buffalo (1894), and the Carson, Pirie, Scott Store, Chicago (1899–1904).

Sullom Voe, long, deep coastal inlet in the northern part of Mainland in the Shetland Isles, Scotland. It lies 35 km north of Lerwick. There is a huge complex for storing and transhipping oil from the North Sea.

Sully, Maximilien de Béthune, Duc de (1559–1641), French statesman. In 1572 he entered the service of Henry, the young King of Navarre, and after the assassination of the French king, Henry III, Sully did much to establish his master's diplomatic position as rightful king of France.

He was appointed a member of the great council of finance (1596). He was soon afterwards promoted superintendent of finance. Sully decreased taxation and reformed the corrupt system of collection, and greatly improved the finances of the country. His success led to his appointment as grand-master of the artillery, director of the marine, master of works, and director of bridges and highways. He became in fact sole minister of France. The murder of Henry IV in 1610 terminated the career of Sully as minister.

Sully-Prudhomme,   René-François-Armand (1839–1907), French poet, born in Paris. His works include *Stances et poèmes*, 1865; *Les Épreuves*, 1866; *Les Solitudes*, 1869; *Les Destins*, 1872; *Les Vaines tendresses*, 1875; *La Justice*, 1878; *L'Expression dans les beaux arts*, 1883; *Le Prisme*, 1886; *Le Bonheur*, 1888; *Réflexions sur l'art des vers*, 1892; a metrical translation of the *De rerum natura* of Lucretius, and a study of *Pascal*, 1905. His best work has severe beauty of form and a serene melancholy of thought, while often showing great intellectual power. He was awarded the Nobel Prize for literature in 1901.

Sulphonamides. These drugs were discovered in 1935 by Domagk, working for the German firm of Bayer; he showed that the aniline dye prontosil was effective in controlling infection of mice by the lethal bacteria known as haemolytic streptococci.

The sulphonamides inhibit the synthesis of folic acid (an essential growth factor for some bacteria, e.g. streptococci) from para-aminobenzoic acid. (Man uses preformed folic acid and thus his cells are not affected by sulphonamides.) Sulphonamides have a broad spectrum of antibacterial activity and individually vary in their efficiency of absorption and duration of action. They are used in patients who are sensitive to antibiotics and also for infections of the urinary tract and respiratory tract, trachoma, and meningococcal meningitis. Their use has declined due to the development of resistant bacteria which metabolise sulphonamides to an inactive form. However, they are still frequently administered with other drugs, e.g. with trimethoprim.

Sulphur, non-metallic chemical element, symbol S, atomic number 16, atomic weight 32·06. It occurs in the free state in two forms: a volcanic deposit, found in lava fissures and extinct volcanoes; and in combination with gypsum (from which the sulphur has been thermally reduced). In combination with other elements, sulphur is widely distributed, occurring as sulphides in many important ores, such as those of zinc (blende), lead (galena), mercury (cinnabar), antimony (stibnite), and iron and copper (pyrites). Sulphur is found in the sulphates gypsum ($CaSO_4$), heavy spar ($BaSO_4$), and Epsom salts ($MgSO_4$). Sulphur is present in trace quantities in organic products such as garlic, mustard, hair and eggs.

Native sulphur is a pale yellow solid, soluble in carbon disulphide and in benzene, turpentine, etc. It is an extremely bad conductor of electricity and heat. At 444°C it boils to a deep red vapour. Sulphur combines directly with many metals and non-metals, forming sulphides. It is used as an insulator, in pyrotechnics, in medicine as an aperient, and in vulcanising rubber.

The more important sulphur compounds include hydrogen sulphide (H_2S), a colourless, poisonous gas smelling like rotten eggs; sulphur dioxide (SO_2), formed whenever sulphur is burned in air; and sulphur trioxide (SO_3) which combines violently with water to form sulphuric acid.

Sulphuric Acid, hydrogen sulphate, or oil of vitriol, H_2SO_4, is a colourless, oily liquid (relative density 1·84) which has a great affinity for water and is used as a drying agent. The mixing of the acid with water is accompanied by a great evolution of heat, hence care must be taken when mixing. Sulphuric acid is used in the Leblanc process for carbonate of soda, in galvanising, tinplate, explosives, plastics and aerated water industries and many others, and in the production of dyes and many important organic 'intermediates'. The acid is dibasic, forming both normal and acid salts. Of the normal salts, several occur in nature, for example, barytes, $BaSO_4$, and Epsom salts, $MgSO_4$. The sulphates are mostly soluble in water; those of lead, calcium, and strontium are only sparingly soluble, while barium sulphate is insoluble in water and in acids. The precipitation of this last salt is, therefore, used as a test for the presence of the sulphate ion.

The acid is produced commercially by dissolving sulphur trioxide in sulphuric acid to produce fuming sulphuric acid which is diluted with water to reconvert it to sulphuric acid. Sulphur trioxide is obtained from sulphur dioxide and oxygen in the presence of a platinum or vanadium pentoxide catalyst.

Sulphurous Acid, a solution of sulphur dioxide in water. The solution smells strongly of sulphur dioxide and gradually oxidises in air to sulphuric acid. It is dibasic and forms two series of salts: normal sulphites, prepared by the action of excess of hydroxide or carbonate of the metal on the acid, e.g. sodium sulphite (Na_2SO_3); and acid sulphites, such as potassium hydrogen sulphite ($KHSO_3$), prepared by having excess of acid acting on the hydroxide. The metabisulphites (e.g. $K_2S_2O_5$) and the bisulphites are also derivatives of the acid and are used in photography. Chemically the sulphites, bisulphites, and the acid are mild reducing agents.

Sultana, see RAISIN.

Sulu Archipelago, archipelago of the southern Philippines, having the Sulu Sea on the north-west and the Celebes Sea on the south-east. There are about 400 islands, divided into six groups stretching some 270 km. Products include cassava, fruits, coconuts, rice, hemp, sesame, indigo, and cocoa. The sea provides the mainstay of the economy including pearl beds, coral, and turtle fisheries in addition to commercial fishing. The province is mainly populated by Muslims (Moros) who are fiercely independent; the archipelago has witnessed violent exchanges between Muslim separatists and government forces. The capital is Jolo on the island of Jolo. Area 2688 km². Population (1970) 427,386.

Sumatra (Indonesian *Sumatera*), the largest island of the Indonesian archipelago wholly under Indonesian control. Area 425,092 km². A mountain spine stretches down the west coast from the Aceh highlands, through the Batak plateau and Menangkabau highlands, to the Benkulu Mountains. Along the west coast are occasional coastal plains and a continuous belt of steep foothills, heavily forested and with major timber potential (especially teak and ebony); while the east coast is characterised by a wide belt of freshwater and tidal swamp (as wide as 250 km in east-central and south Sumatra) separating the foothill zone of the range's eastern flank from the coast.

Total population in 1980 was 28,016,160. There are four main ethnic groups each numbering three million or more: the Acehnese, Menangkabau, Sumatran coast Malays, and Bataks; they are all of Deutero-Malay stock except the Bataks, who derive from earlier Proto-Malay stock. Urban centres are nowhere as large as the largest Javanese cities: Medan, Palembang, and Padang are the biggest.

Sumatra has long been Indonesia's major source of cash crop exports (other than timber). Since 1870 the *Cultuurgebied* (Plantation District), a swamp-free, fertile lowland area along the north-east coast between the Asahan river and Aceh, has been a principal growing area for tobacco (grown around Medan), rubber, tea, coffee, palm oil, and sisal. As a whole, Sumatra is the main producer of Indonesian rubber; it is also the main producer of palm oil, coffee, tea, and pepper. Timber is an important export, mainly from South Sumatra, where half the forest area is under cutting licence. Of the major food crops, Sumatra is the main producer of rice outside Java. Other food crops include maize, cassava, sweet potatoes, peanuts, and soybeans.

Sumatra is the main oil producing region in Indonesia. Since 1967 important new oil and natural gas fields have been developed, mainly off the south-east and north-east coasts. Other minerals include gold and brown coal. There is a hydroelectric and aluminium smelting complex based on the Asahan river in north-east Sumatra.

Between the 7th and 12th centuries, the Indianised maritime power of Sri Vijaya, based in Palembang, controlled Sumatra's east coast as well as the west coasts of the Malay Peninsula and Kalimantan. While the Java-based Majapahit empire consolidated its hold over south and west Sumatra, before a brief period of ascendancy in the 14th century, the Hindu-Malay Menangkabau kingdom established itself firmly in the north, leaving, after its eclipse, one of the most advanced cultures in Indonesia. From the 15th century, the Muslim influence was dominant, and from 1496 onwards the sultanate of Aceh (or Achin) was dominant in the north. Aceh developed as one of the most distinctive Muslim territories in Indonesia, bringing a large body of Mogul culture into Sumatran social and political life. Its sultans resisted both Portuguese and Dutch attempts at domination, but after an expensive war was begun in

1873, the Dutch gained sovereignty over Aceh in 1908, making it the last part of Indonesia to come under formal Dutch control. After Indonesia gained independence in 1949, a separatist movement set up an autonomous military régime in central Sumatra in 1956. However, the rebellion, like the related rebellion in North Sulawesi, was broken by 1961.

Sumer, or Sumeria, term which the ancient Semites of Akkad, Mesopotamia, applied to the country of the lower valley of the Tigris and Euphrates rivers, namely south Babylonia.

Little is known of the early history of Sumer or of the origins of the Sumerians. The Sumerians represented the dominant cultural group of the Near East until c.2000 BC, strongly influencing such distant places as Mari on the Euphrates, and Ashur. They invented the earliest known system of writing, first attested about 3100 BC (gradually developed into the cuneiform writing), and produced a vast and highly developed literature. Even after the loss of political independence, the Sumerian cultural supremacy continued for many centuries. The Accadians adopted from them the script, the literary and liturgical language, and a large part of their literature.

See also BABYLONIA.

Sumerian Language (Accadian *lišan šuméri*, language of Sumer), spoken by the Sumerians, who, in the 4th, 3rd, and early 2nd millenniums BC, inhabited southern Mesopotamia.

Sumerian was an agglutinative speech, combining into single words various linguistic elements, each having a distinct, fixed connotation and a separate existence. The Sumerian language is preserved in about 250,000 clay tablets, of which more than 95 per cent are economic in character (contracts, wills, receipts, and letters). About 3000 tablets contain literary compositions, and about 600 are building and dedicatory inscriptions, some of them being very important historical sources.

Summary Jurisdiction. The summary jurisdiction of justices of the peace in England is a power to try certain minor offences without the aid of a jury and to make orders for payment of money on complaint.

See also CRIMINAL LAW.

Summer, the second of the four seasons, defined astronomically as the interval between the summer solstice and the autumnal equinox but in popular usage taken to mean the period from the beginning of May to the end of August in Great Britain and from the beginning of June to the end of August in North America. Midsummer Day is 24 June, i.e. two or three days after the actual solstice.

Summer Time, see DAYLIGHT SAVING.

Summerskill, Edith Summerskill, Baroness (1901–80), British politician, qualifying as a doctor in 1924. She entered Parliament as Labour MP for West Fulham in 1938 and represented Warrington, 1955–61. From 1945 to 1950 she was parliamentary secretary to the Ministry of Food; and minister of national insurance (1950–51). A prominent exponent of women's rights, she was made a life peer in 1961.

Summons, in English law, a citation to appear in court. It is a written notification, signed by the proper officer, to be served on a party to an action to warn him to appear on a specified day to answer the claim of the plaintiff.

See also POLICE.

Sun-birds, *the malachite sun-bird,* Nectarinia famosa, *of South and East Africa.*

Sun, the centre of our solar system, is a typical medium-sized star whose distance from the Earth averages 149,600,000 km. It is in a gaseous state and so has no definite boundary. It only appears to have a relatively sharp edge because of its 'photosphere', a layer only a few hundred kilometres thick, from which most light reaches us. With the exception of hydrogen and helium, the photosphere seems to have a relative abundance of elements similar to Earth. The 'chromosphere', a thin red transition layer, and the 'corona', a very high temperature $(1,000,000 \text{ K})$, low density layer, stretching far out into interplanetary space, form the solar atmosphere above the photosphere. The corona gives rise to 'solar wind' which blows continuously from the sun at about 450 km/s. Short-lived solar disturbances range from cold 'sunspots' and hot 'plages' to violent 'flares'. Sunspots appear to be shallow depressions in the photospheric level, many becoming larger than Earth. Their slow movement across the disc shows that the Sun rotates round an axis at $82°45'$ to the ecliptic and that most of the angular momentum of the solar system comes from the planets, and not from the Sun which contains 99.86% of the mass. Flares are explosive events in the chromosphere in which large amounts of energy are released in small volumes over a short period, their charged particles producing terrestrial magnetic storms. These disturbances seem to occur at random, but have a maximum activity at intervals of around 11 years. They appear to be connected with the solar magnetic field and may disturb the Earth's upper atmosphere. When solar activity is at a minimum, the Sun is said to be 'quiet'.

The most important property of the Sun is the vast energy it is pouring out into space by the conversion of hydrogen into helium deep in its interior, where the temperature is about 15,000,000 K. The age of the Sun is about 4.5×10^9 years; mass 1.99×10^{30} kg; diameter 1,384,000 km; mean density 1.409 g/cm^3. The estimated period for which it can maintain its present energy output is another 5×10^9 years, after which it is expected to evolve into a red giant, burning up the Earth and other inner planets.

'Sun, The', British newspaper which first appeared in 1964 as a successor to the *Daily Herald*, and the first new mass-sale paper in Britain for over 30 years. In 1969 the title was bought by the Australian publisher Rupert Murdoch, and the paper became a heavily illustrated sensational tabloid, growing rapidly in circulation and overtaking the *Daily Mirror* as Britain's largest selling daily newspaper.

See also NEWSPAPERS.

Sun-birds, various species of birds in the family Nectariniidae, order Passeriformes. They are inhabitants of tropical parts of the Old World, frequenting Africa, India, and northern Australia. In appearance they are extremely brilliant, shining with metallic colours, and very small.

Sun-bittern, *Eurypya helias,* heron-like bird, the only member of the family Eurypygidae order Gruiformes, which occurs in Central America. It is fairly large, about 42 cm, with a long neck and slender bill. Its plumage is mottled, but the chief shades are brown, black and white. It frequents the marshy banks of large rivers.

Sun Worship has been universally common at all times, the sun being naturally regarded as the source of life. The sun-god was worshipped in Egypt as Ra, in Greece as Apollo, and under other names in Peru, North America, and North Europe. In Egypt the reforming Pharaoh, Akhnaten, husband of Nefertiti, made the solar disc (the Aten) the object of a monotheistic religion.

Sun Yat-sen (Chinese *Sun Zhongshan*) (1866–1925), Chinese statesman and first president of republican China.

In 1894, following the outbreak of war between China and Japan, Sun Yat-sen went to Honolulu and founded the Society for the Restoring of China. He returned to China the next year and plotted an armed rising. But the plot failed and he fled to Europe. He returned to the East and lived in Japan from 1898 to 1900, where he met the leaders of the popular parties. During 1906–11 he took part in, or directed, numerous uprisings, most of them abortive, but that at Wuchang, on 10 October 1911, was successful, and some 13 of 18 provinces responded to the revolutionary call and declared their independence of the Manchu dynasty. Later in the year the newly formed Senate elected him provisional president of the republic and in 1912 the Nanjing Assembly inaugurated him president, but he resigned his office after 14 days in favour of Yuan Shikai.

But Yuan proved to be a reactionary and a traitor to the republic, and in the ensuing few years a bitter struggle went on between Sun Yat-sen's newly organised party, the Guomindang (the Nationalist party), and the reactionaries under Yuan, who died in 1916. In 1917 Sun had himself elected president of a Southern Chinese Republic, at Canton. In 1924 he undertook a radical reorganisation of his party on the model of the Communist party in Soviet Russia; later, however, differences arose between the Guomindang and the Communists.

See also CHINA, *History*.

Sunburn, see SUNSTROKE; SUNTAN.

Sunda Islands, islands of the Indonesian archipelago. The Greater Sunda (or Sunda Raya) group comprises the larger islands of

Sumatra, Java, Kalimantan, Sulawesi, and adjacent smaller islands, and, with the exception of Sulawesi, corresponds to the Indonesian extension of the Sunda continental shelf. The Lesser Sundas (or Nusa Tenggara) lie to the south-east and include the smaller islands of Bali, Lombok, Sumbawa, Timor, etc. Nusa Tenggara is an administrative province of Indonesia.

Sunday, first day of the week. The word is derived from the Old English *Sunnandæg* (day of the Sun).

See also SABBATH.

Sunday School, an organisation which gives religious instruction to children and young people on Sundays and is usually attached to a church or chapel.

The idea of Sunday Schools to rejuvenate religious life was suggested by St Charles Borromeo and by Luther. However, in England the Sunday School movement developed as an effort to combat illiteracy as well as to impart religious instruction. The founder of the movement was Robert Raikes, who, with his friend Stocks, rector of St John's, set up Sunday Schools in Gloucester in 1780.

Sunderland, port of Tyne and Wear, England. It developed as a port during the Middle Ages, with a coal trade which grew until 1914. The first shipyard was established in 1775 and the wet dock was built in 1840. Sunderland became one of the leading shipbuilding centres in Britain. Although the industry has declined, some yards remain. Sunderland also has marine and general engineering industries, and manufactures glassware, radio components, and furniture. Population (1981) 196,152.

Sundew, common name for *Drosera* a genus of insectivorous plants growing in boggy places throughout the world. The leaves form a rosette and are covered with sticky glandular hairs, whereby insects are trapped and held while they are digested by means of enzymes secreted from the hairs ('tentacles') onto the leaf surface. The flowers, usually white or pink, are borne on a leafless stalk. *D. rotundifolia*, the common or round-leaved sundew is an acrid and caustic plant used in Italy in making the liquor called Rossoli.

See also INSECTIVOROUS PLANTS.

Sundial, an instrument for measuring the time from the position of the shadow of a fixed object (the gnomon) cast by the Sun. Now chiefly decorative, sundials were of great importance before the days of cheap reliable mechanical clocks, and very many ingenious forms were developed. A properly constructed and orientated sundial may be expected to give the local apparent solar time to the nearest minute from which the standard time can be easily derived by applying the appropriate corrections for longitude and the equation of time.

Sundsvall, Swedish seaport in Västernorrland, on the east coast, on a wide bay of the Baltic Sea. Its harbour is sheltered by Alnö Island. Sundsvall is the regional centre for central Norrland. There is a large concentration of timber processing industries in the vicinity of the town. Population (1978) 94,375.

Sunfish, any fish of the family Centrarchidae, in order Perciformes. They inhabit fresh water in North America. The species, of which about 30 are known, are compressed and have a somewhat oval body and a spot on the operculum (gill cover). Most of them build nests, all are voracious, and many are valued as food. The genus *Micropterus*, the black bass, is found in Europe.

Sunflower. *Helianthus annuus* is the common sunflower, an annual, native to North and Central America, grown in gardens; *H. rigidus* is the perennial sunflower, of running habit; both are in family Compositae. Varieties are grown for their seeds, yielding oil for commerce, and cattle cake.

Sunflower Oil (iodine value 130 ± 5) comes from the seeds of the plant *Helianthus annuus* (common sunflower), indigenous to Mexico but extensively cultivated in the USSR and to a lesser extent in Yugoslavia, Turkey, and South Africa. The seed varies in colour from white to brown or black; it has a hard, fibrous husk constituting about 45 per cent of the whole seed, and contains 22–30 per cent of oil. It may be eaten directly, but by far the greater part of the world crop is crushed in hydraulic or continuous screw presses, or is solvent-extracted, for the production of edible oil. Sunflower oil is a clear pale yellow; it is liquid at low temperatures, and resembles olive oil in many respects. Component fatty acids are: saturated, total 5–15 per cent; unsaturated, oleic (25–42 per cent) and linoleic (52–66 per cent). It is also used for making compound cooking fats, soap, as a lubricant, and, due chiefly to the high linoleic content and absence of linoleic acid, in the production of non-yellowing alkyds and artists' colours.

Sung, see SONG.

Sungari, large river of Manchuria, rising near the North Korean frontier in the Ch'ang-pai Shan. Its upper reaches join the River Nen; it then flows north-east to join the River Amur south-west of its confluence with the Ussuri. Its total length is about 1850 km.

Sunni, or Sunnite, a member of the majority group of Muslims who accept the first three caliphs as the legitimate successors of Mohammed.

See also ISLAM.

Sunrise, see TWILIGHT.

Sunset, see TWILIGHT.

Sunspots, see SUN.

Sunstroke, or heatstroke, a condition of prostration or fever brought about by excessive exposure to the sun's rays, or to a high temperature. The primary cause is probably the disturbance of the temperature-regulating centre in the brain. The body temperature rises, and there are disturbances in the respiratory and circulatory processes akin to those seen in shock. Thus, fainting may be the predominant symptom; the patient is sick and giddy, and has a very weak pulse before he faints. He should be placed in a recumbent position. The form of sunstroke known as heat cramps, or miner's cramps, is caused by shortage of salt due to the loss of salt in sweating.

Suntan, and sunburn, are changes in the skin due to exposure to sunlight. The body gets most of its vitamin D from sunlight, hence moderate exposure is beneficial. Exposure causes production of melanin in the basal layers of the epidermis and this darkens the skin, forming the suntan. The tan protects the skin from harmful radiation emanating from the Sun. However, overexposure will damage the skin and burn it.

Suoche, see SHACHE.

Superconductivity. The electrical conductance of most metals increases as the temperature is lowered, i.e. their resistances are lower at lower temperatures. For certain metals and alloys the remarkable phenomenon of superconductivity begins abruptly at well-established temperatures a few degrees above absolute zero, i.e. some 270°C below the freezing-point of water. The resistance of the specimen below the transition temperature is zero, and currents less than a critical value can flow indefinitely without generating any heat. Application of a magnetic field can destroy superconductivity.

Superfluidity. The viscosity of liquid helium decreases by a very large factor and its thermal conductivity becomes extraordinarily large when its temperature is reduced below the so-called λ-point at $2 \cdot 186$ K (approximately -271°C). The phenomenon has some interesting parallels to superconductivity but has so far found no applications outside pure research. It occurs only for the ^{4}He isotope, indicating that it is quantum statistical in origin.

Superior, Lake, largest and most westerly of the five Great Lakes of North America, and the second largest freshwater body in the world. It is 616 km long (east–west), and 260 km at its widest; its maximum depth is 407 m. Area $82,100$ km^2—$29,000$ km^2 in Canada, the rest in the USA. The St Louis river, 260 km long, enters at Duluth, Minnesota. The lake discharges by way of St Mary's river (100 km long) into Lake Huron. The region has valuable iron-ore deposits. This results in an immensely important iron-ore traffic upon the lake, mainly from the ports of Duluth and Superior.

Supernovae, see NOVAE.

Supersonic Flight, flight faster than the local speed of sound. The most important difference between airflow at supersonic speed and subsonic speed is that at high speed irreversible phenomena, in the form of shock waves, are set up. These give rise to a very considerable increase in drag and thus power consumed, and fundamentally affect the airflow. For the transonic range considerable sweep-back on all surfaces, a low aspect ratio wing, or a combination of the two is desirable. For the supersonic range thin aerofoils and slender fuselages show performance gains although they introduce structural problems. Production SSTs (supersonic transports) have all been slender delta-wing aircraft. In plan form these look like an obtuse-angled isosceles triangle travelling apex first. Control is by combined aileron elevators, known as elevons, on the wing trailing edge when no tailplane is fitted.

See also SONIC BOOM.

Supersonics, see SOUND.

Superstition is a term often used to dismiss beliefs and practices one does not agree with. However, the term is usually employed when such beliefs and practices contradict the weight of evidence and conception of reasonableness present in a given society.

Suppé, Franz von (1819–95), Austrian composer of Belgian descent. His best-known works are the *Poet and Peasant* and *Light Cavalry* overtures. He wrote five operas, 25 operettas and other music for the theatre.

Supply, grant of money provided in order to meet the expenses of government by the representatives of the people. The power of voting supplies in Britain is vested in the Commons.

Supply and Demand. According to orthodox micro-economic theory, bargaining between individuals in the market for goods and services produces a pattern of supply and demand which determines which goods are produced and what their relative prices will be in the future.

Supremacy, Royal, exercise of supreme ecclesiastical authority by the Crown. In the medieval Church authority descended from pope to bishops, but in practice kings exercised a good deal of power and influence. Royal supremacy was first enforced in England by Henry VIII in 1534. Repealed by Mary, it was reimposed under Elizabeth in 1559, and acceptance was enforced by an oath of supremacy. In 1689 the Convention Parliament required all holders of office in Church and State to take 'the oath of supremacy', but in a form that merely denied the papal supremacy; it contained no positive statement of the royal supremacy. By an Act passed in 1791 it was provided that no person should be liable to be summoned to take the oath of supremacy, or prosecuted for not obeying such summons. Roman Catholics, upon taking an oath in which the civil and temporal authority of the pope is abjured, could hold office without taking the oath of supremacy.

Suprematism, Russian abstract art movement c.1914; related to Cubism and led by Kasimir Malevich.

Supreme Court of Judicature. The Supreme Court consists of the Court of Appeal and the present High Court of Justice, which consists of Chancery, Queen's Bench, and Family Divisions.

Sur, see TYRE.

Surabaya, second largest city in Indonesia, located in north-eastern Java at the mouth of the Kali Mas river, opposite Madura Island. It has Indonesia's second largest port (Tanjung Perak), and is now headquarters of the Indonesian Fleet Command. Surabaya is a manufacturing centre (second to Jakarta), with most activity concentrated on shipbuilding and repair, some motor assembly, and rubber processing.

During the 13th and 14th centuries, Surabaya was a powerful port-kingdom thriving on the Moluccan spice trade and its strategic role in the Majapahit empire's expansion from Java. The walled city resisted attack by the Mataram kingdom until it was subjugated in 1625. The Dutch conquered it in 1707. Estimated 1975 population 1·8 million.

Surakarta, formerly Solo, city in Central Java province, Indonesia, on the River Solo. Surakarta is a key railway centre and trade centre for the rich agricultural area of the Surakarta basin. It also manufactures leather, plastic, textile, and batik products. Historically, Surakarta is best known as the capital of one of the two residual *vorstenlanden* (or princely states) into which the Mataram empire was divided in 1755; the other was

Yogyakarta. Population (1975) 497,000.

Surat, city of Gujarat state, India, on the Tapti river 25 km from its mouth. It was the chief port of the Moghul empire in the 16th and 17th centuries. The town, once with 800,000 people, declined until the cotton boom of the 1860s and its railway junctions made it more important. Industrial suburbs based on textiles have grown up to the east. Population (1981) 776,004.

Surd. If *a* and *n* are integers then the radical $a^{1/n}$ is either an integer or an irrational number. A surd is an expression that contains one or more irrational radicals. A surd is said to be in simplified form when all the radicals in it are in simplified form, e.g.

$$\sqrt{8} = 2\sqrt{2}$$

Surf, see SEA WAVES AND SWELL.

Surf-bird, *Aphriza virgata,* a bird of family Charadriidae, order Charadriiformes, closely related to the turnstone. Its plumage is brown with white markings, and it occurs on the Pacific coast of America.

Surface Soil, the soil moved by ploughing or cultivation, i.e. the uppermost 10 to 20 cm. It can be used with reference to soil erosion and conservation to denote the amount of soil lost, e.g. 50 per cent of the original surface soil was lost by erosion.

Surface Tension. Many phenomena show that liquids behave as though they were enclosed in a stretched membrane. The shape assumed by a given volume of liquid, minimising its surface area, is a sphere. Small drops of mercury spilled on a table likewise assume the spherical form under the influence of surface tension, though large drops deviate from this shape because of the distorting effect of gravity. The spherical shape adopted by soap bubbles, where weight plays a negligible part, is due to surface tension. The effect of surface tension is due to the different conditions that obtain at the surface of a liquid as opposed to those within the main bulk. A molecule near the surface is subjected to downward attractions by the molecules below it, which are much greater than any attractions due to gaseous molecules above it. The capillarity of liquids (an essential for the life of plants and trees) is due to surface tension. Petrol spreads rapidly on the surface of water because its surface tension is less. Thus it can form a film covering a pool, a fact of significance in destroying mosquito larvae which hang from the surface in order to breathe but cannot do so from an oily surface.

Surfing, riding or planing, with or without a board, on the front part of a breaking wave as it moves towards the shore. Surfing originated in Polynesia and became popular in Australia in the early 20th century, and later in the USA. There are several forms: body surfing, accomplished by keeping one's body rigid in the water and using it as a board; belly-board surfing, by lying prone on a short board or surf mat; long-board surfing, the most popular form, performed by standing upright on a board of between 1·8 and 3 m in length.

Surgery, that branch of medicine which treats diseases and damage, wholly or in part, by manual and operative procedures. It has been practised since the early civilizations of Mesopotamia, Egypt, India and China. The science of surgery was transmitted to Europe

by Byzantine writers, and somewhat later by writers who followed the Arabian tradition. Because of pain, speed in surgery was essential before the development of anaesthetics in the 19th century. There was also a high mortality due to operative infection. The inauguration of antiseptic methods by Lord Lister is generally acknowledged to be the single most important advance in surgical history. It made possible safe operations on parts of the body that were previously particularly liable to infection, such as the abdomen, and overall greatly diminished the mortality rate. Following Lister's ideas came the modern practice of aseptic surgery, in which everything that might come into contact with the wound is sterilised. The development of antibiotic and sulphanomide drugs has diminished the danger from septic conditions already present in the body.

Recent advances include the replacement of damaged joints, such as hips and knees, and microsurgery, in which tiny vessels are joined under the microscope, enabling, on occasions, the replacement of severed limbs.

See also AMPUTATION; ORTHOPAEDIC SURGERY; TRANSPLANT.

Surinam
Area: 163,265 km²
Population: 375,000
Capital: Paramaribo

Surinam, formerly Netherlands Guiana, a republic on the north coast of South America between latitude 2° and 6°N and longitude 53° and 58°E, having an area of 163,265 km². It is bounded on the east by the River Maroni (or *Marowijne*) which separates it from French Guiana, on the west by the Courantyne (Dutch *Corantijn*), which divides it from Guyana, and on the south by dense forests bordering on Brazil. The general direction of the rivers in the interior is from south to north, but near the coast, most flow in a westerly direction. A few kilometres from the coast there is a narrow zone of savannas, and beyond a region of thick rain forest and jungle stretching to the frontier of Brazil. Its population was estimated to be 375,000 in 1979.

The country contains very large deposits of bauxite. Most is exported directly but the world's first mining, refining and smelting complex for aluminium was opened in 1966 in Paranam.

Rice is the principal agricultural export, the main food staple, and occupies three-quarters of the cultivated land. Sugar cane and citrus fruits are also important products. The country also contains large timber reserves and exports wood and wood products.

The currency in use is the *florin*.

A new constitution was drafted in 1981. The government consisted of the President and the Council of Ministers, responsible to an elected legislature. This was suspended in 1982 after the 1980 *coup d'etat*.

The official language is Dutch, although a wide range of other languages are also spoken and pidgin English is the native dialect.

The first attempt at the settlement of this area was made in 1630 by an Englishman, Capt. Marshall but it was not until 1650 that a permanent settlement was effected by Francis Lord Willoughby of Parham. In 1666 the colony capitulated to the Dutch, and was ceded to the Netherlands in exchange for New Amsterdam, now New York, which thus became a British possession. Surinam remained a poor colony with a population hardly exceeding 60,000 and an economy that depended on exports of sugar-cane and cacao until, after 1870, the Dutch government sponsored Asiatic immigration. Cacao production was hit by disease after 1900, and was gradually replaced by coffee. Sugar-cane was displaced by rice and tobacco. From 1945 bauxite was developed on such a scale as to make Surinam the world's third largest producer.

In 1954 Surinam became a self-governing part of the Netherlands until independence in 1975. A National Military Council, formed in 1980, achieved sole effective power by 1982.

Surplice (Latin *superpelliceum*, above the fur dress), loose white linen garment with wide sleeves, worn over the cassock by clergy and laity in choir or when serving in the sanctuary, etc. The surplice reaches to the knees, is pleated from the yoke, and made with simple sleeves. It was once worn over furs by priests when conducting service in cold churches. A shortened surplice with a square neck, sometimes edged with lace, is called a cotta.

Surrealism, art movement expressed largely in painting, though possessing much influence in sculpture and literature. Its main tendency consists in the relation of forms and symbols, seldom found together in everyday life, producing dreamlike sensations or an expression of the subconscious. Surrealism owed something to the iconoclastic outburst of Dadaism towards the end of the First World War, but is an essentially romantic movement, reaching full fruition c.1930–35, when it was a revolt against the purely aesthetic and abstract values that were then dominant in the advanced circles of art. There were two main trends, one towards pure fantasy using collage and frottage and juxtaposing unlikely objects to produce surprising relationships. The other consisted of elaborate, highly-detailed paintings of hallucinatory clarity expressing the complexity of the subconscious. Among the precursors of Surrealism in the present century was Giorgio di Chirico. Paul Klee and Marc Chagall are sometimes regarded as Surrealist, but more representative are Max Ernst, Joan Miro, Yves Tanguy, René Magritte, and Salvador Dali. For a time Picasso also worked along surrealistic lines.

Surrender, see CAPITULATION.

Surrey, Henry Howard, Earl of (1517–1547), English poet, the son of Lord Thomas Howard, afterwards Duke of Norfolk. He was earl marshal at Anne Boleyn's trial in 1536, and the same year accompanied his father against the Yorkshire rebels. Imprisoned on a charge of treasonably quartering royal arms (these were the mythical Arms

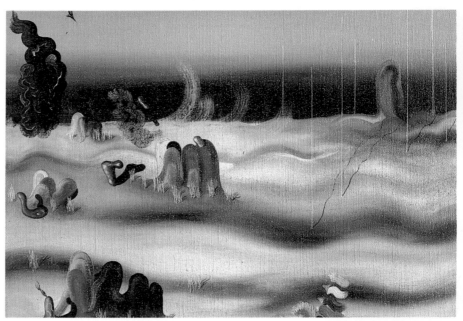

Surrealism. Shadow Country *by Yves Tanguy, 1927.*

of the Confessor), he was executed on Tower Hill. He introduced blank verse into English. For the sonnet on the Italian model cultivated by Wyatt, Surrey substituted the less elaborate and easier English form, which Shakespeare afterwards adopted, of three quatrains with different rhymes, ending with a couplet. He introduced blank verse, of five iambic feet, into English in his translation of the second and fourth books of the *Aeneid*.

Surrey, south-eastern county of England, bounded by Greater London, East and West Sussex, Hampshire, Kent, Berkshire, and a small area of Buckinghamshire. Boundary changes in 1974 meant the loss of Gatwick to West Sussex. The main rivers are the Mole, Thames, and Wey. There are large areas of heath and common land, especially in the west; market gardening is carried on extensively in the Thames Valley, elsewhere there is mixed agriculture.

One of the smaller counties, Surrey is now densely populated, particularly in the northeast and along the main commuter road and rail links to London. The rural areas are mainly south of the Downs and most of the county is now protected from further urban encroachment by designation as 'open space', green belt etc. In total about 14,500 ha is open to the public and includes the important North Downs long distance footpath from Farnham eastwards. Administratively, Surrey is still divided between Guildford, the county town, and Kingston-upon-Thames, which has county hall and many administrative departments, but the former has become increasingly the focus, with redevelopment in its old centre, and with the new cathedral and university on Stag Hill. Population (1981) 999,393.

Surrogate, in the Church of England, one appointed by the chancellor and the archdeacon in a diocese to act as their deputies in granting marriage licences. He is also empowered to take affidavits in matters within the jurisdiction of these principals, and to perform any other judicial business which may be specially deputed by them.

Surtees, John (1934–), British racing motorcyclist and racing driver; Surtees took up motorcycle racing in 1951, and won seven World Championships before transferring to cars in 1960. Riding for the Italian MV company, his last major victory came in the Isle of Man TT in 1960. Surtees became a member of the Ferrari team in 1963, and won the World Championship the following year. He is the only man ever to win World Championships on two and four wheels.

Surtees, Robert Smith (1803–64), English novelist. He founded the *New Sporting Magazine* in 1831, and in it he published the sporting career of Jorrocks, a character who achieved lasting fame. Episodes appeared in book form in 1838 as *Jorrocks's Jaunts and Jollities*, and Jorrocks figured also in *Handley Cross*, 1843. His other works include *Mr Sponge's Sporting Tour*, 1853, and *Mr Facey Romford's Hounds*, 1865.

Surtsey, island to the south of the Vestmannæyjar in Iceland, created by volcanic eruption in 1963. It has been the subject of intense scientific study. Landing is strictly controlled.

Surveying determines the relative positions of points on the Earth's surface and portrays this information in an ordered form, graphically as in a map, or numerically as in a list of co-ordinates. With most methods, the determination of horizontal position and of vertical height above a datum surface, normally taken as mean sea-level, are treated separately, the latter by the method of levelling. Relative position may be defined by measured angles and measured distances. A control framework may be obtained by triangulation (using angles), or by trilateration (using distances). An economical combination is to use successive angles and distances; this is termed traversing.

Geodetic surveys establish national and international control frameworks with triangulation points some 50 km apart, situated on prominent hill-tops. Precise intercontinental connections are made using an Earth satellite as an intermediate and commonly visible station. Topographical surveys, at map scales of 1/20,000 to 1/100,000 are normally produced by aerial surveying. Large-scale engineering surveys provide a basis for the planning of services or construction and may be at scales of 1/100 to 1/2500.

The basic instrument for measuring horizontal and vertical angles is the theodolite. It is used on a tripod or a pillar to enable it to be accurately levelled. For hydrographic work, where levelling and steadiness is impossible, the sextant is used.

Electronic distance measurement equipment falls into two groups: those employing microwave frequencies which have high resolution but a restricted range; and those using visible or near-visible frequencies, with a long range but low resolution. The use of small portable, battery-powered lasers has now largely overcome these problems.

Surveyors, skilled inspectors employed by governments, insurance companies, classification societies, and prospective home purchasers, whose duty it is to ensure that certain rigid standards of construction and maintenance required by the respective bodies and by careful home buyers are complied with. In maritime matters, the Department of the Environment and Lloyd's Register of Shipping are employers of surveyors.

Surya, in Hindu mythology, the Sun. He is represented as the son of Dyaus and the husband of Ushas the Dawn, and he moves in a car drawn by fiery horses. He is the preserver of all things stationary and moving, the source of life, and beholds the good and bad deeds of mortals.

Susa, ancient city of Persia, situated in southeast Dizfūl (Khuzistan). The site was settled from c.4000 BC on, and was one of the main centres of the various Elamite dynasties from about the middle of the third millennium BC; destroyed by Ashurbanipal, c.645–40 BC. It was incorporated into the old Persian Empire by Cyrus II the Great. After its capture by Alexander the Great, it was granted Greek city status by the Seleucidae, and continued a relatively prosperous existence under the Parthians and Sassanidae.

Susceptance, a measure of how easily a coil, capacitor, or other 'lossless' electrical component conducts alternating current. It is the reactive component of the admittance. See also ADMITTANCE; IMPEDANCE; REACTANCE.

Suspension Bridge, see BRIDGE.

Sussex, East, maritime south-east county of England, fronting the English Channel and bounded by West Sussex, Surrey, and Kent. Antiquities are numerous and there are castles, abbeys, prehistoric earthworks and Roman villas. Noted events include the Battle of Hastings (1066).

Sussex derives much of its character and charm from the combination of Weald, downland, marsh, and sea. In the east the coastline is generally unbroken, with the Beachy Head promontory providing the eastern terminus of the South Downs which lie generally within 15 km of the sea. The rivers Ouse and Cuckmere break through the Downs at Lewes and just east of Seaford, while the eastern Rother flows southeastwards to reach the sea near Rye on the borders of Romney Marsh. There is a thriving cross-channel ferry service from Newhaven. Noted seaside resorts include Brighton, Hastings, Bexhill-on-Sea, Eastbourne, and St Leonards. East Sussex is one of the most wooded counties in England. The Weald is now a dairy farming area with scenic but agriculturally difficult small fields. Population (1981) 652,568.

Sussex, West, a somewhat enlarged county due to 1974 reorganisation which took in parts of East Sussex and Surrey. Hampshire bounds it to the west. Landscapes of Weald, Downs, coast, and marsh are all present, together with the wide and fertile coastal plain stretching westwards from Worthing, and the intricate channels of the Chichester harbour area.

The county includes the castles at Arundel and Bramber, the city of Chichester and the large houses and grounds of Petworth, Uppark, and Goodwood. There are many flourishing coastal resorts, as well as the busy port of Shoreham. Agriculturally the county is very dependent upon cereals, especially wheat and barley, dairying, market gardens, and fruit. Population (1981) 658,562.

Sutcliffe, Herbert (1894–1978), English cricketer. He first played for Yorkshire in 1919, and quickly established himself as an opening batsman. With his great Yorkshire partner P. Holmes he established the world record opening stand of 555 v. Essex, 1932, which stood until 1977. Their partnerships exceeded 100 74 times; 23 times they exceeded 200. In 54 tests he made 4555 runs; his career aggregate was 50,135 (highest score 313).

Sutherland, Graham Vivian (1903–80), British painter. An etcher and engraver to begin with, he made a dramatic new start as a painter in 1935, and was official war artist in 1940. His semi-abstract landscapes, studies of inanimate objects, fine series of war paintings and heavy industry, and later imaginative works, brought him international prominence. His works include a Crucifixion, 1946, for the church of St Matthew, Northampton, portraits of Somerset Maugham and Lord Beaverbrook, and the design of the tapestry in Coventry Cathedral.

Sutherland, Dame Joan (1926–), Australian soprano. She made her Covent Garden début in 1952 as First Lady in *The Magic Flute*. She sang many roles with the company until 1959, when her performance in Donizetti's *Lucia di Lammermoor* turned her into a celebrity. She then appeared at every major opera house in the world, specialising in the coloratura roles of Handel, Rossini, Bellini, Donizetti and others. She married the conductor Richard Bonynge.

Sutlej, river of India and Pakistan, rising in Tibet, crossing the Himalayas to flow east to south-west across the Punjab plain, receiving the Beas, and ending, with the Chenab, in the Indus after almost 1500 km.

Suttee, or Sati, Sanskrit word meaning 'a virtuous wife', applies to a practice once prevalent among the Brahmins of India. On the death of her husband a Brahmin or high-caste widow would proclaim herself *sati*, and at the cremation throw herself over her husband's body on the funeral pyre, having first distributed her jewels among the assembled mourners. The custom, frowned upon by enlightened sections of Indian opinion, was prohibited in 1829 by Lord William Bentinck.

Sutton, a London borough created on 1 April 1965, comprising the former municipal boroughs of Beddington and Wallington, Sutton and Cheam, and the urban district of Carshalton. Population (1981) 168,407.

Sutton Coldfield, town of West Midlands county, England, 11 km north-east of Birmingham, and a residential town. Population (1981) 86,494.

Sutton Hoo, site of Saxon burial ship in Suffolk, England. It was excavated in 1939 and was found to consist of a 38-oared vessel containing a large quantity of finely worked metal artefacts: jewelled sword, bronze helmet, sceptre, drinking vessels and jewellery, as well as coins and precious stones.

Sutton-in-Ashfield, industrial town in Nottinghamshire, England, 22 km from Nottingham. Sutton-in-Ashfield has collieries, and manufactures cotton, hosiery, thread, light engineering products, plastics, tin, cardboard boxes, and precision tools. Population (1981) 41,270.

Suture, term in surgery and anatomy. In surgery: (1) a verb meaning to join tissue using stitches, as in closing a wound; (2) a noun meaning the material (catgut, silk, wire, nylon, etc.) used in stitching tissues together. In anatomy: a special kind of joint or articulation found only in the skull, by which the separate bones of the skull are joined together.

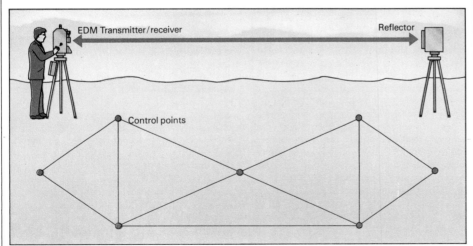

EDM Transmitter/receiver

Reflector

Control points

Surveying. Electronic distance-measuring equipment, which measures the lengths of the sides in a triangulation system, is now used to establish the accurate control points on which a survey is based.

Suva, capital of the Fiji Islands, on the south-east coast of the island of Viti Levu, chief port of Fiji and seat of government. It is a commercial and light industrial centre; industries include coconut-oil processing, soap manufacture, biscuit making, small boat building, and the manufacture of cigarettes. Population (1979) 66,018.

Suvorov, Aleksandr Vasilievich, Count (1730–1800), Russian soldier. He commanded the Russian forces in Poland in 1768 and 1794. When Emperor Paul I joined the anti-French coalition in 1798 Suvorov was given the task of halting the French advance in Italy; in a series of brilliant attacks he defeated the French and conquered northern Italy. Transferred to Switzerland, he was surrounded by the French, but avoided disaster by one of the most daring feats in military history—he marched through the St Gotthard pass.

Suwannee, river of the USA. It rises in Georgia, flows south, and enters the Gulf of Mexico. It is navigable as far as White Springs. Length 400 km.

Suzhou (Soochow), city in Jiangsu province of eastern China, built on a group of islands east of the lake, Taihu. There are silk and cotton mills. Suzhou, with its dozens of stone bridges, temples, and pagodas, has been regarded as the 'Venice of the East'. In recent years the city's old-established silk industry has been augmented by chemical production and paper making. Population (1970) 1,000,000.

Svalbard, see SPITSBERGEN.

Sverdlovsk (formerly *Ekaterinburg* or *Yekaterinburg*), capital city of Sverdlovsk *oblast* and one of the major economic and cultural centres of the USSR, situated in the central Urals. It has large heavy engineering industries (metallurgy, electrical equipment), also chemical and diverse food processing and light industries. It is the centre of Uralmash, the largest machine-building plant in the USSR, and is also an important transport centre. The city was founded in 1723 as a metal-works and fortress. Tsar Nicholas II and his family were shot by the Bolsheviks here in 1918. Population (1980) 1,225,000.

Svevo, Italo, pseudonym of Ettore Schmitz (1861–1928), Italian novelist. The subject-matter of his work is the inner reality of the human conscience. With *La coscienza di Zeno*, 1923 (*Confessions of Zeno*, 1962), he gave Italy its first psychoanalytical novel. It was acclaimed abroad and established Svevo as one of Europe's major writers. He also wrote several plays and short stories.

Swabia (German *Schwaben*). The name comes from the Suevi, the original inhabitants of the area. A medieval German duchy, whose territory is now largely included in the *Länder* of Baden-Württemberg, Hessen, and Bavaria, it occupied an important strategic position between the Rhine and the Danube. The name Swabia is still generally applied to the region of the former duchy. Its chief cities were Augsburg, Ulm, Freiburg, and Konstanz.

Swahili, farming people of the coastal region of East Africa, particularly Tanzania. Of Bantu origin, Arab cultural and linguistic influence is strong and most are Muslim. A form of their language, Kiswahili, is used as East Africa's *lingua franca*. They number about 1 million.

Swale, river of North Yorkshire, England, rising in the mountains on the border of Cumbria, and flowing east and south-east to the Ure, which it joins to form the Ouse. It is 97 km long and is noted for its fishing.

Swaledale, dale in North Yorkshire, England, is 32 km in length from Keld to Richmond. It is the narrowest and grandest of the north-west dales, and is a well-known beauty spot. Up to 1880 lead mining supported a larger population in the dale than today's agriculture. Swaledale gives its name to an important breed of horned sheep.

Swallow, *Hirundo rustica*, in North America known as the barn swallow, a well-known bird of family Hirundinidae, order Passeriformes, that is widely distributed throughout Europe, central Asia and North America during the summer, but winters in Africa, tropical Asia, and South America. Its two outside tail feathers are elongated into a graceful fork, which is more pronounced in the male. Its nest, somewhat like a flattened cup, is made of mud, straw, hair and feathers, and is usually attached to the rafters of barns. Other species include the red-rumped swallow, *Cecropsis daurica*, of the eastern Mediterranean, and the martins. *Delichon urbica*, the house martin, is smaller than the swallows and also differs in having feathered feet, a less sharply forked tail and shorter wings. *Riparia riparia* is the sand martin.

See also SWIFT.

Swallowing, a complex co-ordinated reflex that is initiated voluntarily, mainly by tongue movements, and completed by the involuntary contractions of the oesophageal musculature. The contraction of the tongue muscles pushes the food on the tongue backwards to the fauces. The soft palate is then raised by reflex action to prevent the food entering the nasal cavity, and the larynx is also protected by reflex closures. The constrictor muscles of the pharynx then urge the food into the gullet, where it is impelled towards the stomach by peristaltic action. Swallowing is assisted by the secretion of saliva.

Swammerdam, Jan (1637–80), Dutch naturalist. He used the microscope as an instrument of continuous biological research. He was the first to describe (in 1658) the red blood corpuscles, and in addition studied the movements of the heart, lungs, and muscles. He also studied the life histories and structure of insects and published observations on tadpoles, including their cells, in *Biblia Naturae*.

Swan, Sir Joseph Wilson (1824–1914), British inventor. The carbon process of printing in photography, the development of the 'rapid' photographic plate and many improvements in the processes of electro-reproduction are due to him. He is best known, however, for the incandescent-filament electric lamp, 1879, which was the first successful lamp of its kind.

Swan, *Cygnus*, a genus of birds in order Anseriformes, with an elongated body and neck and short feet. The base of the bill is fleshy and naked, and the sexes are similar in plumage. About six species are known. The mute swan, *C. olor*, native to Eurasia but introduced to North America and Australasia, is the semi-domesticated bird of rivers and ornamental waters. The front part of the bill is orange. Closely related to the mute swan are the Australian black swan, *C. atratus*, and the South American black-necked swan, *C. melanocorphyrus*.

The remaining species of swans are white and are all northern species breeding in or near the arctic regions of Eurasia and North America. In Europe there are the whooper swan, *C. cygnus cygnus*, and Bewick swan, *C. columbianus bewicki*, both with yellow in different proportions on their otherwise black bills. In North America their equivalent subspecies are the trumpeter swan, *C. cygnus buccinator*, and the whistling swan, *C. columbianus columbianus*. These two have all black bills.

Swan, The, constellation, see CYGNUS.

Swannee River, see SUWANNEE.

Swansea (Welsh *Abertawe*), seaport and city of West Glamorgan, South Wales, 70 km west of Cardiff, at the mouth of the River Tawe. Most of the Welsh steel sheet and tinplate works are situated within a radius of 15 km of the city. Swansea's metallurgical importance was founded on copper ore, and copper works multiplied from the early 18th century. Long recognised as the chief metal port of Great Britain, Swansea is now also a large oil port. The oil-refining industry yields a wide range of products. Other industries are paint, batteries, brewing, bricks, building and structural engineering, chemicals, concrete, electrical fittings, machinery, ship-repairing, zinc, and sulphuric acid manufacture. Population (1981) 167,796.

Swastika (from Sanskrit *svasti*, well-being) a very ancient decorative motif. In form the swastika is a Greek cross, the arms of which are like elbow-joints, all bent at right angles. If the arms go to the right it is the female form; if to the left, the male form. It is to be found on early Elamite ceramics of the 4th millennium BC, as well as on ceramics of the 2nd and 1st millennia BC from Troy, Greece, Cyprus, India, Tibet, China and Japan. It is also found in Christian inscriptions from the 2nd century onwards, as well as among the Amerindians. It was often used as a charm against 'the evil eye', and as a religious symbol by the Buddhists and Jains. Adopted in 1910 by some German groups as the symbol of the 'Aryan race', the female swastika later became the official symbol of the Nazis.

Swatow (Chinese *Shan-t'ou*), port in Guangdong province of south-east China, and one of the first treaty ports to be opened to trade with the West in the 1850s. As a port, it serves the Han river basin but is of little more than local and regional significance. Population (1970) 400,000.

Swazi, Bantu farming people numbering over 1 million. The Swazi live in Swaziland and adjacent parts of South Africa. Until the end of the 19th century, the Swazi, under their king, were organised into regiments which fought in the eastern part of South Africa. Today this structure remains but it has been neutralised by the South African government. Political and religious power is divided between the king and the queen mother, and the power of the ancestors is respected.

The Swazi 'homeland' in South Africa is situated in the eastern Transvaal, bordering Swaziland in the south.

Swaziland
Area: 17,185 km²
Population: 563,733
Capital: Mbabane

Swaziland, kingdom of southern Africa, bounded on the north, west and south by Transvaal, South Africa, and separated from Natal, South Africa and Mozambique by the Lubombo Mountains. Area 17,185 km².

The country can be divided into four topographical regions running north-south: the mountainous Highveld (1250 m) in the west; the Middleveld (600 m); the Lowveld or Bushveld (300 m); and the Lubombo Mountains in the east.

In 1979 the population of Swaziland was estimated at 563,733. The Swazi people are a branch of the Bantu-speaking group. The main towns are Mbabane (the capital) and Manzini.

About 40 per cent of the land is held on freehold terms, largely by whites. This area includes estates producing sugar, rice and citrus fruit under irrigation, commercial ranches, and large areas of commercial pine forest. The remainder is Swazi Nation land, on which plots are allocated by chiefs. Maize is the main subsistence crop, and there is some cotton, sorghum and tobacco.

Sugar and wood-pulp milling account for most manufacturing. Coal production in the Lowveld is growing.

The King of Swaziland is head of state (*Ngwenyama*). In 1973 he assumed supreme executive power; the constitution was abolished in 1976. An indirectly-elected Assembly was set up in 1978.

The official languages are English and Siswati.

The Swazi migrated southwards from central Africa in the 15th to 16th centuries and finally settled in Swaziland about the beginning of the 19th century. Often in conflict with the Zulus, they appealed in 1840 for British protection. In the 1860s the South African Republic tried to annex Swaziland so as to obtain an outlet to the sea, but was stopped by the British and Portuguese governments.

By the first Swaziland Convention (1890), the country was controlled dually by the South African Republic and the British government. It was not successful and, after the Anglo-Boer War, Swaziland came under British administration and in 1906–07 became a protectorate. Independence was granted in 1968.

In 1977 King Sobhuza II announced that he would resort to government based on traditional tribal communities, known as *Tikhundla*. After his death in 1982, this government continued under a regency.

Sweating, see DIAPHORETICS; SKIN.

Sweating Sickness, a curious malady first observed in England in 1485: subsequent epidemics occurred in 1508, 1517, 1528 and 1551. It also occurred in Germany in 1529; and in France (Picardy sweat) in 1718 and later. The onset was sudden, and was heralded by profuse, often foetid, sweating: malaise, fever, headache, abdominal pain, and cerebral symptoms were common. A rash appeared in a few days. The disease was often fatal. It may have been a form of relapsing fever.

Sweden (Swedish *Sverige*), country of northern Europe comprising the eastern portion of the Scandinavian peninsula; it is bounded on the north-west by Norway, on the east by Finland, the Gulf of Bothnia, and the Baltic Sea, on the south by the Baltic Sea, and on the west by the Kattegat. Its area (449,800 km²) includes the great lakes of Vanern, Vattern, Mälaren and Hjälmaren.

The north-west part of the country is mountainous, the highest peak, Kebnekaise, reaching about 2100 m; the remainder is flatter, sloping to the east and divided by many rivers, notably the Dal, Indal, Angerman and Skellefte. Physically, the country is traditionally divided into the three regions of Norrland, Svealand and Götaland.

Norrland is the most northerly, a region of high mountains and dramatic scenery. Svealand covers the lower slopes of the highlands and the central lowlands studded with lakes. South of Svealand lies Götaland, a region of hills and plains. The Skåne plains at the southern tip of the country are the most fertile and thus the most densely populated region. The Swedish coastline is typified by hundreds of small offshore islands.

In 1979 the population totalled 8,300,000. Nearly 90 per cent of Sweden's population live in the southern half of the country and about 80 per cent live in towns or urban areas, the most important being Stockholm (the capital), Göteborg, Malmö, Uppsala, Vasteras and Norrköping.

Sweden
Area: 449,800 km²
Population: 8,300,000
Capital: Stockholm

Swedish agriculture is concentrated in the fertile south of the country; most of the output consists of cereals, potatoes and dairy products. Sweden's forests provide the materials for paper, rayon and other industries. Half the country is covered with productive forests. Sweden has long been famous for her mineral resources, and especially iron ore. Other minerals include zinc, lead, tungsten, manganese and copper. There are important metalworking, engineering, electronic, textile and chemical industries.

In Swedish currency 100 *öre* = 1 *krona*. Sweden is a monarchy, but under the constitution that came into effect on 1 January 1975 the king has no political power. Parliament, the *Riksdag*, consists of one chamber of 349 members, elected every three years by a system of proportional representation. A peculiar feature of the Swedish constitution is that government and administration are two separate functions. For administrative purposes, the country is divided into 24 counties (*län*).

The official language of Sweden is Swedish; some Lappish and Finnish are spoken in the north.

History. The early history of Sweden is contained in legend and saga. The country appears to have been inhabited by two separate but closely related races, the Swedes and the Goths. These played some part in the great Viking expansion, although their penetration of the Baltic and Russia was more important. By about the end of the 13th century Finland had been incorporated in the Swedish kingdom. The Middle Ages in Sweden are marked by a centralisation of power in the country, but also by clashes between rival claimants to the throne and between the king and the nobility. By the Union of Kalmar in 1397, the kingdoms of Denmark, Norway, and Sweden came under the common regency of Margaret of Denmark. The union came to an end in the reign of Christian II, after his brutal treatment of the leaders of a rebellion (the Stockholm Bloodbath, 1520). Eric XIV (1560–68) embarked on a campaign of expansion in the southern Baltic and took

Sweden. Kalmar Castle was built in the 16th century for Eric XIV.

Estonia under Swedish protection in 1561. War with Russia in the early 17th century gave Sweden control of what is now the Baltic coast of Russia, whilst war with Poland confirmed Sweden in possession of Livonia and gave it a grip on the mainland of Germany. Under Gustavus Adolphus the army was reformed; and Sweden for the next century was one of the great powers in Europe. Gustavus Adolphus was succeeded by his daughter Christina, whose minority was made famous by the statecraft of the Chancellor, Axel Oxenstierna. The success of Sweden was seen in the Treaty of Westphalia, which marked the zenith of Swedish power. In 1654 Christina became a Catholic and abdicated in favour of her cousin Charles X. He continued the work of Gustavus Adolphus, attacking Denmark and establishing Sweden's natural frontiers along the western and southern coasts.

The Swedish empire was dismembered in a series of treaties, 1719–21. Most of the German provinces were ceded to Britain, Hanover, and Prussia, while Russia was confirmed in possession of Estonia, Livonia, and Ingermanland. On Charles XII's death the Swedish monarchy lost its absolute power, and under Frederick I (king 1720–51) and Adolphus Frederick (king 1751–71) a form of parliamentary government prevailed.

In alliance with France, Russia invaded and occupied Finland, and in 1809 this part of the Swedish kingdom had to be ceded to the tsar. Charles XIII was infirm, and to secure the goodwill of Napoleon the *Riksdag* accepted Napoleon's marshal, Bernadotte, as Crown Prince Charles John. He made war on Denmark to secure Norway as recompense for the loss of Finland, and later invaded Norway, whose union with Sweden was confirmed by the great powers in 1814.

His son Oscar I, who reigned from 1844 to 1859, introduced many democratic reforms. In the reign of Oscar II (1872–1907) Norway seceded from Sweden (1905). Oscar II was succeeded by his son Gustavus V (1907–50), during whose reign democracy was further extended, social services introduced or expanded, and a universal franchise introduced. Sweden has maintained its neutrality of the Second World War, refusing to follow Norway and Denmark in joining the North Atlantic Treaty Organisation. An important constitutional reform was the replacement of the bicameral parliament by a one-chamber assembly in 1971. The rights of the king were also curtailed after the death of Gustavus VI Adolphus, who was king from 1950 to 1973; the present king, Charles XVI Gustavus, has only a symbolic function.

Language. Swedish is an important member of the group of Scandinavian languages, which up until the medieval period could be described as Norse languages. With the exception of about 200,000 Finns, about 5000 Lapps (inhabiting the extreme north of the country), and some thousand speakers of other languages, the population of Sweden, numbering over 8,000,000, speaks Swedish. Moreover, this language is also spoken in western and southern Finland and the Åland islands (by about 375,000 people), by Swedish immigrants in Norway, Denmark, and other European countries, in the United States, in

Canada, and in some other countries.
See also DENMARK, *Language;* ICELAND, *Language;* NORWAY, *Language.*

Literature. There are four periods in the history of Swedish language and literature: archaic or common Scandinavian, 800–1225 (before Swedish emerged as a separate language), including mainly oral literature; classic, 1225–1375, which includes the earliest surviving document, a fragment of *Västgötalag,* a legal document, about 1250; middle Swedish, 1375–1525, producing mainly religious literature; and modern Swedish, which begins with the Lutheran translation of the New Testament in 1526, and other writings of Olaus Petri. The most important early work written in modern Swedish is the Bible of Gustavus I, 1541.

In the 17th century, Georg Stiernhielm, the most important writer of the time and a versatile, learned man, was the first Swedish author to use classical verse metres. A unique place in 18th-century literature is held by the great mystic Emanuel Swedenborg, while noted poets include Johan Henrik Kellgren and Carl Michael Bellman. About the beginning of the 19th century the Romantic movement was very strong and prominent among the Romantics was Per Daniel Amadeus Atterbom, with his long verse dramas. The novel developed towards the middle of the 19th century; Carl Jonas Love Almqvist was an early master. A central position in the cultural life of the time was held by Abraham Viktor Rydberg, novelist, poet, and an advocate of liberal idealism and modern Bible criticism. Naturalism was less pronounced in Sweden than in France, the most outstanding representative of the movement being August Strindberg, the greatest genius of Swedish literature, and one of the creators of the modern theatre.

During the first decade of the 20th century appeared many writers of the modern realistic novel. The foremost is Hjalmar Söderberg, ironical sceptic and a fine stylist. Of the succeeding generation, Pär Lagerkvist was a novelist, poet, and dramatist of great significance. Swedish literature of the post-war period has been preoccupied with horror at man's situation, both in historical terms and in a metaphysical, Existentialist (see Existentialism) sense. Apart from the poets Karl Vennberg (1910–) and Erik Lindegren (1910–68), the most important figure of the 1940s is Stig Dagerman (1923–54), while more recent novelists include Sara Lidman (1923–) and Per Olof Sundman (1922–).

Swedenborg, Emanuel (1688–1772), Swedish scientist, philosopher, and theologian. Swedenborg is so generally known as a theologian of heterodox views which have found acceptance by the New Church, sometimes called 'Swedenborgian', that it is seldom appreciated that he was one of the foremost scientific minds of his day and had gained a European reputation for science and philosophy before he ever turned to theology. The wide range of his mind over all the known branches of science is comparable only with that of Leonardo da Vinci.

His system of theology presents Christ not as the second person of the Trinity, but as the one God, the whole Trinity being in Him as soul, embodiment, and operation. Redemp-

tion consisted in the conquest, in the human, of temptations from all the hells and the subsequent control of the hells by the divine human. Swedenborg asserts that the word of God has an internal or spiritual meaning throughout, and the *Arcana Caelestia,* 1749 consists of a detailed exposition of the 'spiritual sense' of Genesis and Exodus, and incidentally of many other parts of Scripture. The *Apocalypse Revealed,* 1766, and the posthumously published *Apocalypse Explained* deal similarly with the Book of Revelation. In the former work he declares that the Holy City, New Jerusalem, signifies a new 'Church' or dispensation of truth then being effected through these revelations. One of his first critics was Kant who directed *Träume eines Geistersehers,* 1766, against him.

Sweelinck, Jan Pieterszoon (1562–1621), Dutch organist, harpsichordist and composer. His works include four books of psalms, *Cantiones Sacrae* for several voices, organ works and harpsichord pieces.

Sweet, Henry (1845–1912), British phonetician and philologist. Sweet devised two types of phonetic alphabet: an 'organic notation', a revised version of A. M. Bell's 'Visible Speech', which used completely new characters; and a 'Romic notation', using the Latin alphabet augmented by additional characters, which was based on A. J. Ellis and Isaac Pitman's 'Phonotypes' and which itself became the basis of the International Phonetic Alphabet (1888, with later revisions). He also produced a scheme for a limited reform of English orthography, and, like Passy, was interested in the teaching applications of phonetics (*The Practical Study of Languages,* 1899). Bernard Shaw partially based his character of Professor Higgins (*Pygmalion*) on Sweet.

Sweet Bay, see BAY; LAUREL.

Sweet Corn, see MAIZE.

Sweet Gale, see BOG MYRTLE.

Sweet Marjoram, see ORIGANUM.

Sweet Pea, *Lathyrus odoratus,* a popular annual garden plant. It is a typical member of the subfamily Papilionoideae of family Leguminosae. The large petal at the back is the standard, the two wings are laterals, and in front is the keel, formed from two petals which adhere along their lower edges. It originated in southern Europe but it is now widely cultivated for its fragrant flowers.

Sweet Potato, *Ipomoea batatas,* a species of the family Convolvulaceae, allied to the morning glory, that has tuberous, edible roots, and is grown in tropical and subtropical regions.

Sweet William, *Dianthus barbatus,* a perennial herb of the Caryophyllaceae. It is a native of eastern and southern Europe often grown in gardens as a biennial.

Sweetbread, name given to certain glands of animals used as food. The pancreas of the ox or calf is most generally used, as it is palatable and digestible, when gently cooked, with seasoning to enhance the subtle flavour. It is particularly nutritious, as the flesh is mainly protein and is a store of iron and vitamins A and D.
See also MEAT.

Sweyn I (d.1014), surnamed Forkbeard, King of Denmark, the father of Canute the Great, King of England. Sweyn himself led numerous invasions against England, but his wars were carried on more with a view to extort money from the English than with the idea of attempting any colonisation.

Swidden Agriculture, also called 'slash-and-burn' agriculture, is a method of land-use in which a portion of forest is cut down and burnt for growing crops (swiddens) fertilised by the wood ash. Dry rice, millet, taro, yams, and maize are frequently grown in this way in the tropics and sub-tropics. The only basic implements necessary are the axe or adze, and the hoe or digging stick. Generally, yields decline after the second or third year, and the clearing is abandoned to allow the forest to reconstitute itself, for some ten or twenty years, depending on the soil type, forest type, and other ecological factors. The cultivators meanwhile move to a new area, repeating the process.

Swift, members of the family Micropodidae in order Apodiformes, closely related to the humming-birds, but not to the swallow, which they resemble superficially. The main European species, *Apus apus*, arrives at its breeding grounds in May, leaving in August for its winter quarters in Africa. It feeds entirely on small winged insects and in its search for them exhibits remarkable powers of flight. The tail is long and forked. Common in the Mediterranean region and Asia Minor in summer is the white-bellied or Alpine swift, *A. melba*. Close relatives of these two species are the edible-nest swiftlet, *Callocalia* species, the nests of which are used to make soup in China and other far-eastern countries. North American species include the scissor-tailed swift, *Panjyptila hieronymi*, and the white-throated swift, *Aeronautes saxitalis*.

See also NESTS, EDIBLE.

Swift, Jonathan (1667–1745), the greatest English satirist. Born in Ireland, he attended Trinity College, Dublin, but after the Revolution of 1688 left Ireland to join his mother, then at Leicester. He joined the household of Sir William Temple at Moor Park as secretary, where he met Esther Johnson (Stella), who was afterwards to enter so largely into his life. During this time he wrote *A Tale of a Tub*, one of his best works, a satire on 'corruptions in religion and learning', and *The Battle of the Books*, describing in mock-heroic style a contest between Ancients and Moderns.

After Temple's death in 1699, Swift returned to Ireland as chaplain to the Lord Deputy, the Earl of Berkeley. In 1710 he attached himself to the Tories Robert Harley and Viscount Bolingbroke. The next few years were filled with political controversy, during which he published his celebrated pamphlets attacking the Whigs. Thereafter, when he received no further advancement, due to the hostility of Queen Anne, he again settled in Ireland and gained extraordinary popularity there with his *Drapier's Letters*, 1724, directed against English policy in Ireland. *Gulliver's Travels*, Swift's most widely and permanently popular work, was written during this period and published in 1726; a bitter satire, it has by a curious irony become, in expurgated form, a favourite children's book.

Swimbladder, or airbladder, a structure found in some fishes which is filled with gas and serves as an organ of flotation. It occurs in the position occupied in air-breathers by the lungs, and is now believed to have derived from primitive lungs during the course of evolution. It acts to keep the density of the fish the same as that of the water at the level where the fish wishes to swim.

In some cases the bladder has become modified for other purposes, such as sound production (e.g. catfish) or hearing (e.g. some herrings and catfish).

Jonathan Swift, a portrait by C. Jervas.

Swimming, the art of propulsion in water without artificial assistance. The first 'modern' competitive races were held in Australia in the 1840s. The world's oldest swimming organisation, the direct ancestor of the present English Amateur Swimming Association (ASA), was formed in 1869.

In the early days the first widespread technique was the *breaststroke*, in which the body and limbs remain submerged in a prone position, propulsion being obtained by simultaneous and virtually symmetrical movements of the limbs. From the breaststroke developed the *crawl* in which the arms recover alternately above the water and also pull backwards alternately, while the legs make a balancing flutter kick. The crawl (and its variations) has been the world's fastest stroke for over 70 years.

Swimming on the back was at first a trick, and the first *backstroke* races were swum using a sort of inverted breaststroke. Both backstroke and breaststroke had their débuts as separate ASA championships in 1903.

The *butterfly* developed from the breaststroke in the 1930s when ambitious breaststrokers exploited a loophole in the rules and began to recover their arms over the water. In 1952 the butterfly was recognised as a distinct stroke.

Freestyle swimming has never been defined: it has always been simply the fastest stroke, and for many years this has been the front crawl.

Medley races are made up of equal legs of backstroke, breaststroke, butterfly and free-style.

Swimming competitions can take two basic forms. There are simple head-to-head contests between teams scoring points in a number of events, and championship events, involving eliminating heats. These range from the Olympic Games and world championships down to local events. The fastest swimmers on a time basis go through to a final.

The international programme centres on the Olympic Games and the world championships (first held 1973 and biennially thereafter). Other important international occasions include the European championships (first held 1926), the British Commonwealth Games (first held 1930), and the Pan-American Games (first held 1951). The basic international list of events recognised for world records is as follows: *freestyle*: 100, 200, 400, 800, 1500 metres; 4 × 100, 4 × 200 m relay; *breaststroke, butterfly* and *backstroke*: 100 and 200 m; *medley*: 200 and 400 m; 4 × 100 m relay.

The world governing body for swimming (and diving, water polo and synchronised swimming) is the Fédération Internationale de Notation Amateur (FINA), founded in 1908.

Synchronised swimming, or 'synchro', is essentially a water ballet developed from individual displays of graceful or ornamental swimming. As a competitive event it almost always features only women and, like an ice-skating contest, is held in two parts—set stunts followed by a free-routine section. The event forms part of two world championship programmes.

See also CHANNEL SWIMMING; DIVING; WATER POLO.

Swinburne, Algernon Charles (1837–1909), English poet. At Oxford he met D. G. Rossetti, to whom he dedicated his first published poetical drama *The Queen-Mother*, 1860. This, with a similar work, *Rosamond*, was inspired by Shakespeare, and neither succeeded. In 1865 Swinburne published two much more successful poetic dramas, *Atalanta in Calydon* and *Chastelard*.

In 1866 his *Poems and Ballads* provoked scandal and a storm of abuse from the critics who were repelled by the sensuality which they declared characterised its pages. However, Swinburne had made his name as a writer, and from then on produced a great number of poems and poetic dramas, and also several critical essays.

He identified himself with the Pre-Raphaelite Brotherhood, and enthusiastically upheld the cause of Italian independence. His dissipated life caused a breakdown in health and in 1879 he moved to Putney, where he lived under the care of Theodore Watts-Dunton, until his death.

Swindon, town in Wiltshire, England, 123 km west of London, on the main railway line to Bristol and South Wales. An industrial town grew around the workshops of the former Great Western Railway, which was established in 1841. Swindon was approved as suitable for expansion under the Town Development Act 1952. Population (1981) 91,136.

Swine, see PIG.

Swiss Guards, regiment of Swiss mercenaries, forming the French royal bodyguard constituted in 1616. They were conspicuous for their bravery in the defence of the Tuileries (1792), which was commemorated in 1821 by the great lion outside one of the gates of Lucerne. Swiss Guards also form part of the Papal forces. They are recruited from every Swiss canton.

Switch, in electrical engineering, a mechanism for making or breaking a circuit, or for transferring a current from one conductor to another.

Switchgear, collective name for all the controlling and protective electrical apparatus in power stations, transmission networks, and large industrial premises connected with the operation and control of the network, machines, and buildings, and the safety of personnel.

Swithin, Saint, also Swithun (d.862). He was ordained and became chaplain to Egbert, King of the West Saxons, and tutor to his son Ethelwulf, who made him bishop of Winchester on his accession (852). The origin of the popular legend that if it rains on his day (15 July) it will do so for 40 succeeding days is uncertain.

Switzerland
Area: 41,290 km²
Population: 6,365,960
Capital: Bern

Switzerland (French *Suisse*; German *Schweiz*; Italian *Svizzera*; Latin *Helvetia*), republic of central Western Europe, consisting of a confederation of 23 self-governing cantons (three of them subdivided), bounded on the north by West Germany, on the west by France, on the east by Austria and Liechtenstein, and to the south by Italy. It is 355 km in length from east to west and about 220 km from north to south. Its area is 41,290 km² (half the size of Scotland).

The country is divided into three main regions: the Jura Mountains, extending along the north-western boundary, the Swiss Plateau (*Mittelland*), and the Alps. The chief physical feature is the vast Alpine system, known by various names in different localities, e.g. the Rhaetian Alps, Bernese Alps or Oberland, Valais Alps, Lepontine Alps, Rheinwald Alps, Glarner Alps and Urner Alps. The highest peak is Monte Rosa, on the Italian frontier, which is 4638 m.

The main rivers flowing through Switzerland are the Rhine, Rhône, Inn, Aar, Reuss, Limmat and Thur. Forests cover 24 per cent of the country. The largest cities are Zürich, Basel, Geneva, Bern (the capital), Lausanne, Winterthur, St Gallen and Lucerne. The population in 1980 was 6,365,960.

The productive land is owned mainly by farmers who grow wheat, barley, maize and potatoes, and also make cheese and milk products. Much stock is raised, mainly cattle, sheep, goats and horses (mainly in the Jura). Fruit is grown, and there are some 20,230 ha of vines.

Switzerland thrives by importing raw materials and exporting costly finished products. The lack of coal and oil has hampered industrial development, but this has been offset by the use of hydroelectric power, and now nuclear energy. The manufacture of machinery is very important. Other industries include dairy products, the manufacture of silk and cotton goods, clocks and watches, optical and scientific instruments, chemicals, aniline dyes, aluminium, chocolate, cheese, lace, embroidery and footwear. Tourism is important

The unit of currency is the Swiss franc of 100 rappen or centimes.

Switzerland is a federal republic with legislative and executive authority vested in the Federal Assembly, consisting of a National Council (directly elected members) and a Council of State (two members from each canton). Executive power is vested in a Federal Council of seven members, presided over by the president, which sits at Bern, members being elected for four years by the Federal Assembly.

The referendum and the initiative are essential features of Swiss democracy. Every constitutional amendment requires ratification by a popular and a cantonal majority. Each canton has its own written constitution, government and assembly.

The Swiss official languages are German, French, Italian and Romansch.

History. Between 700 and 1200 the country was under the influence successively of the descendants of Charlemagne, the German emperors, and the Zähringen dynasty.

In 1273 Rudolf of Hapsburg became emperor, with control of what is now German-speaking Switzerland. The extension of his power caused alarm and a few days after Rudolf's death, in 1291, the first Perpetual League of the three Forest States (Uri, Schwyz, Unterwalden) was formed, which, in 1315, defeated the Austrian forces at Morgarten. In 1481 Fribourg and Solothurn came into the confederation. The recognition of Switzerland's independence dates from the victory over the Empire at Dornach in 1499, by which the confederation was released from the Imperial tax.

Switzerland became a centre of the Reformation which led to internal dissension, as the north generally followed the reformist teachings of Zwingli, while the Forest States remained Roman Catholic. In the hostilities that resulted the Catholic troops were victorious, Zwingli was slain (1531), and a truce was arranged, whereby each canton was left free to determine its own religion.

In the peace treaty of Westphalia, 1648, the political separation of Switzerland from the German Empire was recognised by the powers. During the French Revolution Switzerland was seized by France, which made it the Helvetic Republic (1789). Only in 1815 was Switzerland's independence restored, and its permanent neutrality guaranteed by the powers at the Congress of Vienna.

In 1847 a savage war broke out between Protestants and the Seven Roman Catholic cantons, the latter having formed a separatist league or Sonderbund. After a short campaign, G. H. Dufour, at the head of the Federal army, defeated the Catholics. In 1848 a new federal constitution was adopted.

Switzerland's economic development has been peaceful and prosperous since the end of the Second World War, although not unaffected by the unsteadiness of the capitalist world market. Tourism has been a growth industry in Switzerland, bringing in large amounts of foreign currency.

The formation of a new canton (Jura) along the Franco–German linguistic frontier in 1979 caused some friction between the two communities.

Sword, a weapon with a long metal blade, either straight or curved, and usually

Switzerland. Alpine pasture near Tavetsch. In summer, cattle are brought up from the lowlands for grazing.

sharpened along the edge or edges. Varieties of swords are countless. The curved riding sword or hanger became the naval cutlass. In Asia one finds the curved scimitar, the progenitor of the sabre, which became the European cavalry sword, principally a cutting sword, but which could be used with the point also. In Japan the making of sword blades was carried out with great skill, and swords by famous makers were handed down in the aristocracy and were objects of veneration. Swords have been a symbol of justice and knighthood, and are still worn by officers of all services on ceremonial occasions. See also ARMOUR; FENCING.

Swordfish, *Xiphias gladius,* the single species of the mackerel-like family Xiphiidae in order Perciformes. Its distribution is practically universal. The average size of the fish is 2 m, but in some cases it attains a length of nearly 6 m. It is peculiar in possessing an elongated, sword-shaped snout formed from the upper jaw that is strong enough to pass through the planks of boats. It feeds on small fishes, sometimes slashing at them with the 'sword'.

Sybaris, ancient Greek town in Lucania, Italy, near the Gulf of Tarentum. Founded 720 by Achaeans and Troezenians it quickly rose to great prosperity, and the word 'sybarite' was used as synonymous with 'voluptuary'. In 510 BC Sybaris was attacked and destroyed by the Crotonians, who diverted the River Crathis over its ruins. The site was identified by means of electronic instruments in 1963.

Sycamore, name originally given to the European fig tree, now used in North America for *Platanus* species, and in England for the European *Acer pseudoplatanus,* a handsome spreading tree (family Aceraceae), introduced into Britain during medieval times and now thoroughly naturalised. The wood is white and fine-grained, and is much used by turners.

Sydney, chief port of Australia, and capital of New South Wales, situated on Port Jackson inlet. Sydney was founded by Captain Arthur Phillip, who had been sent to Australia to establish a penal colony. The harbour at Sydney has a safe entrance and is regarded as one of the most beautiful and perfect harbours in the world. Sydney carries practically all the overseas trade of New South Wales, and nearly half that of Australia. The harbour is crossed, in one span of 503 m, by a steel arch bridge, the Sydney Harbour Bridge, opened in 1932, carrying a roadway, two footways, and four railway lines. Sydney's impressive opera house was opened in 1973. Sydney is the manufacturing as well as the commercial centre of New South Wales, and most types of products, except basic iron and steel, are produced there. Population (1979) 3,193,300.

Sydney, seaport of Cape Breton Island, Nova Scotia, Canada. It is the centre of a coal-mining region. Metal fabricating plants have been attracted to the area by the availability of iron and steel. Population (1976) 30,645.

Syenite, a coarse-grained igneous rock composed of alkali feldspar and up to 20 per cent ferro-magnesian minerals (usually biotite).

Syktyvkar (formerly *Ust Sysolsk*), town in

Sydney, Australia, straddles the picturesque harbour. The Opera House is on the left.

the north-east European RSFSR, USSR, the capital and cultural centre of the Komi ASSR. It has a large timber industry, and has been known since the late 16th century. During the 17th and 18th centuries it had a flourishing grain and fur trade. Population (1980) 175,000.

Sylhet, town and district in north-eastern Bangladesh, the centre of the Surma Valley area where much tea is grown. Sylhet was formerly included in Assam, but the area became part of East Pakistan after a plebiscite. Population (1974) 45,000.

Syllogism (Greek *sun,* together, and *logos,* thought; i.e. the joining together in thought of two propositions), in logic 'the act of thought by which from two given propositions we proceed to a third proposition, the truth of which necessarily follows from the truth of these given propositions' (Jevons). The first two propositions in the syllogism are called the premisses and the last the conclusion.

Sylvester II, Gerbert d'Aurillac, Pope, 999–1003, Benedictine monk and scholar who succeeded Gregory V. He obtained letters from the emperor recognising the temporal authority of the Holy See.

Symbiosis (Latin, living together), a constant intimate relationship between separate and dissimilar organisms. Symbiosis includes many types of associations which are often further specified as: *Mutualism,* a bilaterally advantageous symbiotic association; *Commensalism,* a situation in which only one of the partners profits. It is also applied to situations characterised by no obvious advantages or disadvantages.

Symbolism, the representation, particularly in religion or art, of an idea or an emotion by a natural or material image. For example, the lion occurs frequently as a symbol of courage, while the lamb is one of meekness. Symbols include types, enigmas, parables, fables, allegories, emblems, and hieroglyphics. Some readily suggest what they represent; others often seem in no way related, the connection in some cases perhaps being due to a long-forgotten association of ideas.

Ancient and often universal symbols are frequently embodied in oral tradition, folk tales, and mythology, and the relationships between such symbols and religious belief were investigated by the psychologists Freud and Jung. While Freud concluded that religion derived from fundamental sexual and family images, Jung proposed that there are certain recurring images, or archetypes, common to all cultures and which exist in what he termed the 'collective unconscious'; symbols such as the underworld and the tree of life.

In 19th-century France there arose the Symbolist movement in poetry, a deliberate protest against naturalism and realism. In seeking more suggestive, allusive, and subtle images, the Symbolists took Romantic theory a step forward. They were inspired by music and particularly the *leitmotifs* of Wagner.

The French Symbolists introduced the concept of *modernismo* to Spanish and Portuguese literature, and influenced both T. S. Eliot and W. B. Yeats. Symbolism also influenced Russian literature, and the work and ideas of Ezra Pound and the Imagists, Rilke, and Paul Valéry, while painters attempted to emulate Symbolist poets by conveying emotion directly on to canvas.

Symbolist Movement, The, in painting, evolved from the literary movement in France c.1886 and likewise had its roots in 19th-century Romanticism. An idealistic reaction against the scientific objectivity of Impressionism and Realism, it rejected naturalistic representation in favour of painting from memory and exercising the imagination to distil the 'idea' of a subject and transcend physical appearance. Synthesism and Cloisonnisme are synonymous with Symbolism. In 1889 Gauguin and other Pont-Aven artists exhibited 'Synthesist' paintings which expressed subjective mood and emotion and were executed in bright areas of colour separated by black lines. The simplified, decorative features of Symbolism are found in Gauguin and Van Gogh and in Maurice Denis and the Nabis. The more literary side of the style is expressed by Gustave Moreau, Puvis de Chavannes, and Odilon Redon with whom the Symbolists claimed kinship.

Symboliste, L'École, French literary movement representing a reaction against the objective, impersonal poetry of the Parnassians. Their aim was to write poetry that was not 'plastic' and descriptive like that of the Parnassians, but 'fluid', suggestive and evocative, expressing the poet's innermost feelings and impressions and the depths of his soul by means of symbols.

They sought to go even further than the Romantics in breaking away from the rigid traditional French versification and so they introduced *vers libéré* (which employed new metres and made innovations in the use of the traditional 12-syllabled alexandrine, but still depended on syllabic patterns and rhyme) and the even more revolutionary *verse libre* (which dispensed both with metrical regularity and with rhyme). The ideals of the movement are expressed in Verlaine's poem 'L'art poétique', and its beginnings may be dated about 1884.

Symbols. A symbol is a conventional sign employed to convey a meaning, and is to be distinguished from impromptu, unintentional, or accidental signs. Objects and even gestures are sometimes employed as symbols, e.g. a bishop's crosier, a salute. Civilised man characteristically employs graphic or written symbols, of which an enormous number and variety are in common use. Examples are afforded by the letters of any alphabet, which are symbols standing for uttered sounds. Special subjects of study, such as the sciences and music, have their own codes of symbols, and these are usually internationally recognised.

A capital letter symbol in chemistry usually means one atom of an element. Thus, O means one atom of oxygen. O_2 means one molecule of oxygen, consisting of two atoms. O_3 means one molecule of triatomic oxygen or ozone. Some symbols are derived from the Latin or Greek names of the elements, such as Fe (*ferrum*), iron; Au (*aurum*), gold; Hg (*hydrargyrum*), mercury. Such symbols are used in constructing chemical formulae, such as H_2O, which means one molecule of water, consisting of two atoms of hydrogen and one of oxygen.

Symmetry. In geometry a figure is symmetric with respect to a point, a line, or a

Symbolist Movement. Sappho, *by Moreau.*

plane if it consists of pairs of points which are symmetric about the point, line, or plane. If a plane figure is symmetric about an axis, or a surface or solid is symmetric about a plane, then the axis or plane divides the figure into two parts each of which is the reflection of the other in the axis or plane.

A symmetric function is a function of two or more variables whose values are unchanged by the interchange of pairs of variables. For example, the function $f: \mathbf{R}^3 \to \mathbf{R}$, given by

$$f(x, y, z) = xyz + x^2 + y^2 + z^2,$$

is symmetric.

The term is used more loosely to describe crystalline repetitive similarity, for bilateral and radial symmetry in zoology, for botanic structures, and in art and material objects generally.

Symonds, John Addington (1840–93), English poet and critic. He wrote good critical lives of Shelley, 1878, Sir Philip Sidney, 1886, and Michelangelo, 1893, and his *Autobiography of Benvenuto Cellini*, 1888, and his versions of the sonnets of Michelangelo and Campanella, show his flair for translation. Other works are his *History of the Italian Renaissance*, 1875–86, *Studies of the Greek Poets*, 1873–76, and *Shakespeare's Predecessors in the English Drama*, 1884.

Symons, Arthur (1865–1945), Welsh poet and critic. Influenced by the French Symbolists, in 1889 he published a book of verses, *Days and Nights.* His next two volumes of poetry, *Silhouettes*, 1892, and *London Nights*, 1895, showed the influence of Verlaine, but the decisive influence upon his work was the aesthetic doctrine of Walter Pater. Symons deserves to be remembered as a critic for such works as *Introduction to the Study of Browning*, 1886; *Studies in Two Literatures*, 1897; *Aubrey Beardsley*, 1898; *The Symbolist Movement in Literature*, 1899, a work in which he introduced to England the French poets of the later 19th century; *Studies in Seven Arts*, 1906; and his *Confessions: a Study in Pathology*, 1930, in which he analysed his own mental collapses of 1908.

Among his later works were *The Romantic Movement in English Poetry*, 1909, and *Studies in the Elizabethan Drama*, 1919.

Symphonic Poem, or 'tone-poem', an orchestral form finding its inspiration in an extra-musical work. A distinction can be made between the narrative tone-poem, such as Strauss's *Till Eulenspiegel*, the character piece, such as Elgar's *Falstaff*, and the atmospheric tone-poem which does not attempt to portray characters or events.

Symphony, musical composition for orchestra, generally on a large scale. It evolved partly in Italy from the operatic overture and partly in the works of the Mannheim school of composers under the leadership of Johann Stamitz. It became one of the most important genres allied to sonata form and achieved its first definitive form in the hands of Haydn and Mozart: that of a generally four-movement work, the first movement (and sometimes others) in sonata form, the second being slow and the third dance-like. Beethoven substituted the more robust scherzo for the minuet-type of third movement. Berlioz and Liszt introduced programmatic elements and the principle of themes appearing in different movements. Nationalist elements made themselves felt in symphonies of Dvořák, Borodin and Tchaikovsky. Hyper-expressive, almost confessional, elements were represented in the work of Mahler, while Sibelius stood for the ideal of perfection of form and organic unity of material. In the 20th century the form has assumed many strange guises but it continues to represent the largest statement a composer can make in purely musical terms.

Symposium (Greek *sumposion*, a drinking party). The title was used by both Plato and Xenophon for books describing the conversations of Socrates and others, and the term has therefore come to mean a conference or general discussion. It is also used to signify a collection of opinions on a given subject by various contributors.

Symptom, any change that an individual notices himself when suffering from an illness. The term originally meant the disease itself, but with increasing knowledge about the unseen causes of disease (e.g. bacteria or biochemical changes) it has come to mean a way in which a disease shows itself to the patient, for example by pain, loss of appetite, weakness, loss of sensation, or a change in bowel habit.
See also CLINICAL SIGN; DIAGNOSIS.

Synagogue (Greek *sunagōgē*, an assembly), Jewish place of worship. The date of origin is uncertain. At Jerusalem, an inscription records the existence of a synagogue in the 1st century BC. The best preserved among a few ruined examples is at Capernaum, Galilee (late 2nd century AD), which is oriented southwards in the form of a basilica. Persecution during the Middle Ages accounts for the scarcity of European examples, but at Worms there is a Romanesque synagogue and at Prague a Gothic synagogue. In the West, a Moorish style was adopted. There are important Renaissance examples at Amsterdam (1675) and Bevis Marks, London (1710). The plan of a synagogue is normally rectangular, with seats downstairs for men and a gallery for women. There is a curtained niche for the Ark opposite the entrance, with a rostrum or pulpit (*bimah*) in front of it.

In Jewish traditions, the synagogue has functioned as the *bet ha-tefilah* (house of prayer), *bet ha-midrash* (house of study), and *bet ha-knesset* (house of assembly). Its importance from ancient times rests in its democratisation of worship, removing religion from the monopoly of priests and placing the authority on the community, thus creating patterns later adopted by the Christian church. The destruction of the temple in AD 70 marked the emergence of the synagogue as a preserving centre of Jewish life to modern times.

Synchrocyclotron, or frequency-modulated cyclotron, machine to accelerate atomic particles to energies greater than those obtainable with a conventional cyclotron. The construction is similar to that of the cyclotron, but instead of a fixed-frequency electric field between the 'dees' there is a changing frequency. As the particle attains higher energies it suffers a relativistic increase of mass and takes longer to traverse the half-circle within the dee. The frequency of the applied electric field is therefore reduced steadily to keep in step with the particle, and a synchronising action takes place which allows much higher energies to be attained. For yet higher energies the synchrotron is used.

See also CYCLOTRON; SYNCHROTRON.

Synchroniser, relay-operated automatic switch for connecting an alternator to the busbars when it has been run up to the speed, phase, and voltage of other alternators on the same busbars. It is used in tele-control of power stations. For manual operation a synchroscope is used.

Synchroscope, instrument indicating when two alternators are running at the same speed and phase. When an alternator is to be connected to busbars which are already connected to one or more other alternators it is necessary that the speed, phase, and voltage of the incoming machine should be the same as those of the busbars. The synchroscope is an instrument for indicating the speed and phase differences.

Synchrotron, or proton synchrotron, machine designed to accelerate protons to energies greater than those obtainable with the cyclotron and synchrocyclotron. The principle of action is an extension of those described for the lower-energy machines mentioned. By the simultaneous application of an increasing magnetic field and a high-frequency electric field of decreasing frequency it is possible to keep the proton in a stable orbit of fixed size whilst gradually increasing its energy. The size and cost of magnets is greatly reduced because of the fixed size orbit, so that above 1000 MeV (1 GeV) proton synchrotrons are more economic than synchrocyclotrons.

See also CYCLOTRON; SYNCHROCYCLOTRON.

Syncopation, displacement of the musical accent to the weak beats or off-beats in the bar, the effect being that of a syncope or missing heart-beat.

Syndicalism. In France, where syndicalism originated, a syndicate did not mean, as in English, a trading company, but an organisation of working men. The fundamental difference between syndicalism and socialism lies in their attitude to the state and in the purpose for which industry is to be organised. The syndicalist, like the anarchist is in active hostility towards the state which he repudiates. He sees social organisation as purely industrial and aims at organising all the workers in a trade into one union, and then to federate these unions into a national, and eventually into an international, organisation. Syndicalism organises industry in the interests of the workers in it. In theory, if not always in practice, socialism organises industry in the interests of the community as a whole.

Syndicate, The, see MAFIA.

Syndrome, a collection of features that taken together imply that a patient has a specific disease. Since the features may not obviously be related to each other, many syndromes are only recognised for the first time by perception or luck and are therefore named after the doctor who first described them. Many syndromes carry different eponyms in different countries which is confusing for doctors as well as patients.

Syngas, or SNG, synthetic gas to replace natural gas as the latter becomes less readily available. Processes based on coal, oil shale, and tar sands are under investigation. Some of the gases are similar to coal gas.

Synge, John Millington (1871–1909), Irish dramatist. His first play, *In the Shadow of the Glen*, 1903, was attacked by Irish critics for its portrayal of the peasantry, but that and *Riders to the Sea*, 1904, a one-act tragedy, were well-received when performed in London. When the Abbey Theatre became the home of the Irish dramatic revival Synge's plays entered its repertory, and he became its literary adviser and then a director. His masterpiece, *The Playboy of the Western World*, 1907, provoked riots when it was performed in Dublin, because patriotic audiences refused to believe that Irish peasants would protect a self-proclaimed murderer. It is now regarded as one of the classics of Irish theatre. The chief qualities of his work are his insight into the life of the Irish peasantry, and his lyrical feeling for their language, which he makes into a rich dramatic prose.

Other works are *The Aran Islands*, 1907; *In Wicklow, West Kerry and Connemara*, 1911; and *Poems and Translations*, 1909.

Synonym (Greek *sun*, together; *onoma*, word), in its narrowest sense a word which in all contexts has identical meaning to another word in the same language. Perfect synonyms barely exist, so in practice the term is used for words that are approximately equivalent. For example, *snuff* it and *decease* differ in formality, *house* and *home* in emotive associations, *rob* and *steal* in grammatical construction following them.

See also SEMANTICS.

Synovial Membrane, the membrane covering the articular extremities of bones and the inner surface of ligaments entering into the formation of a joint. It secretes a clear lubricating fluid with an alkaline reaction. Synovitis is the result of the inflammation of the synovial membrane.

See also JOINTS.

Synthesiser, electronic musical instrument capable of both imitating conventional musical instruments and of generating original sounds. The tones are derived from signals produced by a bank of oscillators, amplified and modified by filters. The Moog synthesiser, invented by Robert Moog in 1965, is played from a keyboard and is capable of only one note at a time. Polyphonic synthesisers, which can produce several tones at once, have been available since 1976.

Synthetic Materials are materials that have been built up from simple chemical substances, and which simulate a natural product. See also FIBRES AND FIBROUS SUBSTANCES; PLASTICS; RUBBER; SYNTHETIC RESINS.

Synthetic Resins, man-made polymers of many types used in a variety of ways: (1) as a film-forming emulsion, with water as the continuous phase—polyvinyl acetate, polyvinyl alcohol, and many synthetic rubbers, also polystyrene; (2) as a solution in a volatile solvent—all types of synthetic resins; (3) as a heat-sensitive or pressure-sensitive film—polyvinyl alcohol, urea formaldehyde, and phenol formaldehyde; and (4) as two separate components, a low polymer and a polymer catalyst, which when mixed shortly before use, react together in the joint to form a higher solid polymer—urea formaldehyde, phenol formaldehyde, and polyester resins.

Synthetic resin adhesives, developed by the modern plastics industry, set on being heated, cannot be resoftened by heat, and are water-resistant; they are being increasingly used in the manufacture of plywood and other composite timber products.

See also ADHESIVE; GLUE; PLASTICS.

Syphilis, a venereal disease due to infection by the bacterial organism *Treponema pallidum*. The disease occurs in three stages: primary, secondary and tertiary. The primary stage usually consists of a small nodule which breaks down to become an ulcerative sore (chancre), most often on the genitalia. This primary manifestation then recedes and gives way to the secondary during the next one or two months: the chancre heals, and a rash appears distributed over the trunk, palms, face and legs. A moderate constitutional upset occurs during this phase, consisting of a sore throat and raised temperature. This resolves also during the ensuing months, and often treatment is not sought owing to a mistaken belief that the disease has resolved spontaneously. The tertiary stage occurs with extreme variability, but usually appears some years after the secondary stage, presenting with destructive lesions of bone and soft tissues (gumma) and serious damage to the central nervous system and heart. Treatment is by antibiotics.

Congenital syphilis is syphilis caused by transmission of the organisms from the mother to infect the foetus during pregnancy, usually resulting in a stillborn infant or an abortion. A viable infant with congenital syphilis shows skin rashes, evidence of a generalised infection, and fails to thrive. The teeth are characteristically deformed, and central nervous system defects become apparent during puberty.

Non-venereal syphilis or bejel is an acute infectious disease also due to the *T. pallidum*, but not showing the presence of a primary chancre, and only rarely progressing to serious tertiary central nervous system and cardiac disorder. It is not fatal.

Syr Darya (ancient *Jaxartes*), river of Soviet Central Asia, rises in the Tien Shan range and flows north-west 2212 km through the Kirgiz, Uzbek, and Kazakh SSRs into the Aral Sea. The Amu and Syr Darya rivers supply water to over half of the cultivated land of the central Asiatic republics of the USSR.

Syracuse (Italian *Siracusa*), seaport in Sicily, capital of Syracuse province on the south-east coast, 200 km south-east of Palermo. In ancient times it was the richest and most populous city in Sicily. It was founded c.734 BC by settlers from Corinth led by Archias the Corinthian. Among the remarkable ancient remains are a fortress built by Dionysius, an immense Greek theatre, a Roman gymnasium, temples, aqueducts, and quarries now turned into gardens. There are 2nd–3rd century Christian catacombs, and the church of St Lucy has the saint's tomb. It is a centre in conjunction with Augusta of chemical and petrochemical industries. Population (1979) 116,755.

Syracuse, city in New York state, USA. Originally an Indian settlement, it owed its early growth to the coming of the Erie Canal, which passed through the site. Electrical machinery is the most important product, followed by non-electrical machines, food, and paper products. Population (1980) 170,292.

Syria
Area: 185,680 km²
Population: 8,330,000
Capital: Damascus

Syria, Republic of, an Arab state bounded to the west by the Mediterranean, the Lebanon, and by Israel, to the north by Turkey, to the east by Iraq, and to the south by Jordan. The total area is 185,680 km².

The physiography of Syria may be divided into four sections. The first is a narrow coastal zone backed by the Jebel Ansarieh, a range of mountains running from north to south at an average height of 1200 m. The range is bounded on the east side by the Ghab, a lowland rift valley 80 km by 150 km occupied by the Middle Orontes river; east of the Ghab is the open irregular plateau around Hama and Idlib. Further east is the mountain range of Ansarieh, and the Anti-Lebanon, which divides Syria from Lebanon. The west contains nearly all the cropped land and 95 per cent of the total population. A number of towns and villages however lie along the transitional zone of steppe between the western mountains and the inner deserts of Arabia. Chief of these is the capital Damascus. The total population was given in 1979 as 8,330,000.

Cotton is the main crop, and grain production is also important. Textiles are the longest established and most important industrial activity. The main extractive industries are oil and phosphates.

Syria. The ruins of the agora at Palmyra.

The 1973 constitution defines Syria as democratic, republican, popular and socialist. It provides for a seven-yearly elected President, a four-yearly elected People's Assembly, and a Council of Ministers. Supreme power resides with the President in conjunction with the Ba'ath party. The President of the Republic is required to be Muslim, and Islamic law is recognised as a principal source of legislation.

The controlling party in government is the Syrian Regional Command of the Arab Socialist Ba'ath party.

Arabic is the official language. The Kurdish, Turkish, Armenian, Assyrian, Circassian and Jewish minorities may speak their own languages as well.

History. Syria fell to the Muslims as they expanded out of Arabia in the 7th century and the Ummayad Caliphate ruled its vast empire between 661 and 750. In the 11th–13th centuries Syria was part of the Crusaders' battleground. With the fall of Acre in 1291 the last Crusader foothold was removed by the Turkish Mamelukes, who ruled until 1517. The period spent within the Ottoman Empire was one of slow decay. Egypt conquered Syria between 1831 and 1840.

Under the terms of the Sykes-Picot agreement of 1916, Syria (and Lebanon) were assigned to the French area of influence. The San Remo conference of April 1920 conferred the mandate of Greater Syria to France. Independence was granted in theory in September 1941, but did not become a reality until April 1946. Instability has since been the hallmark of Syrian politics.

Union with Egypt came into being, under the name of the United Arab Republic, in February 1958, but growing discontent at Egyptian domination led to a military coup in September 1961, and separation. The secessionists were in turn ousted by Ba'athist officers in March 1963, led by Gen. Amin Hafez, who became president. But the Ba'athists themselves were divided and the circle of coup and counter-coup was unbroken.

Involvement in the 1970 war in Jordan ex-

acerbated divisions in the Ba'ath party and resulted in Gen. Assad taking over in November, and being elected president. Syria became deeply involved in 1975–76 in Lebanon's civil war, at first as a mediating influence and then on the side of the rightwing Christians against the Muslims and Palestinians. Further involvement in Lebanon in 1982 brought Syria into fresh conflict with Israel and in 1983 with Lebanese and UN peace-keeping forces.

Syriac Language. Syria and Syrians were the Greek terms for biblical Aram and Aramaeans. Syriac is a late stage of Aramaic as spoken by the Christian population of Syria and has an extensive literature, dealing with Christian matter. Syriac script was an offshoot of a cursive Aramaic writing, perhaps of the Palmyrene cursive in its early stage.

In the second century, the Syriac spoken in Edessa (now Urfa) was adopted in the valley of the Euphrates as a *lingua franca*, was used far and wide, and became after Greek the most important language in the Eastern Roman Empire. From the 7th century onwards, however, Arabic everywhere put a speedy end to Syriac, which, however, has remained in use for liturgical purposes.

Syringa, the botanical name of lilac but sometimes used also as a common name for Philadelphus, the mock orange bush.

Syros (Greek *Síros*), island of Greece in the Aegean Sea, belonging to the Cyclades group. It is barren and has little natural vegetation, but olives, figs, cereals, and vines are cultivated. Its position and importance in coastal trade have made it the most prosperous and densely populated of the island group. Its capital is Hermoupolis. Area 85 km²; population (1971) 13,500.

Systole (Greek *systole*, contraction), the phase in the sequence of a heart beat, when the heart chambers contract and pump out the blood which collected in the previous diastole. First the atria contract, followed by the ventricles.

See also HEART.

Szczecin, province of North-West Poland, bordered on the north by the Baltic Sea, on the east by Koszalin, on the south by Zielona Góra, and on the west by East Germany. It is low-lying, mainly agricultural, and drained by the River Oder. Until 1945 it was part of Germany. Area 12,754 km²; population (1979) 887,000.

Szczecin (German *Stettin*), city of Poland, capital of the province of Szczecin and formerly the capital of Pomerania, 450 km west of Warsaw. It is on the River Oder, 25 km above the entrance of the river to the Baltic Sea by way of the Zalew Szczeciński. From 1278 a member of the Hanseatic League, Szczecin was held by Sweden from 1648 to 1720, when it became Prussian. In 1945 it passed to Poland. It is a very important port in Baltic trade, owing to its central position, and to its rich hinterland, served by rail and the navigable Oder. Its industries include shipbuilding, engineering, and the manufacture of chemicals, textiles, paper, soap, cement, and sugar. Population (1979) 388,000.

Szeged, town of Hungary, near the Yugoslav border, 24 km south-west of Hódmezővásárhely. It stands at the confluence of the rivers Tisza and Mureşul and has been a river port since the 9th century; its prosperity then depended on the salt trade from Transylvania. Szeged has a large trade in cereals, poultry, paprika, and fruit from the Alföld, and there are textile and river-fishing industries. Population (1980) 175,000.

Székesfehérvár (German *Stuhlweissenburg*), town of western Hungary, capital of the county of Fejér, 58 km south of Budapest. In the Middle Ages it was, with Esztergom, one of the two centres of government, and 36 Hungarian kings were crowned in its cathedral. There are aluminium, textile, and distilling industries and there is a trade in agricultural produce, tobacco, and wine. Population (1980) 102,000.

Szent-Györgyi, Albert (1893–), Hungarian biochemist. He discovered vitamin C in paprika and received the 1937 Nobel Prize for chemistry for his discoveries on the role of organic compounds, especially vitamin C, in cell oxidative processes. His work on the organic acids of living cells led directly to Krebs' elucidation of the tricarboxylic acid cycle. His next work was devoted to the biochemistry of muscle; he discovered actin and showed the need for adenosine triphosphate in muscle contraction.

Szymanowski, Karol (1882–1937), Polish composer. At first influenced by Debussy, he arrived at a mastery which showed itself in skill of form as well as in his love of folk-music. He wrote three symphonies, two violin concertos, the operas *Hagith* and *King Roger*, many songs and piano works.

T

T, twentieth letter of the English alphabet, derived through Latin and Greek from the North Semitic alphabet. English spelling uses the digraph *th* to represent the sound as in *this, thin*; it was originally a function of *t*.
See also ALPHABET.

Tabard, a loose surcoat, originally worn by peasants, adopted in the 15th century to be worn by knights over their armour and on which armorial bearings were displayed (whence the term 'coat of arms'). Today tabards are the ceremonial garb of heralds.

Tabari, (c.839–923), Persian writer. He travelled widely in search of learning before he settled in Baghdad. He composed the first history of the world in Arabic, which is most important for the early history of Islam, and compiled a vast commentary on the Koran.

Tabernacle (Latin *tabernaculum*, diminutive of *taberna*, hut, temporary dwelling), term generally applied in the scriptures to the portable sanctuary of the Jews, which was erected by Moses. It was a magnificently constructed tent containing the Holy Place and the Holy of Holies, which contained the Ark of the Covenant and the mercy seat. Similar portable shrines were used in Egypt before the time of Moses. In the New Testament the tabernacle is symbolic of heavenly things. Later in England 'tabernacle' was applied to places of worship not dignified by the name 'church', e.g. temporary churches in London after the Great Fire, 1666; certain Nonconformist chapels of the 18th–19th centuries, however substantial; temporary galvanised iron churches erected by all denominations in the 19th century.

Tabernacles, Feast of (Hebrew *Sukkoth*, huts, or *hag ha'asiph*, feast of Ingathering), Jewish festival, celebrated from 15 to 23 Tishri, commemorating the dwelling of the Israelites in the wilderness. All meals for eight days are eaten in an outdoor booth with a roof of branches.

Tabla, dissimilar pair of kettle-drums of north Indian classical music. Both drums are braced with leather thongs. The right-hand drum has a wooden body, and cylindrical wooden blocks under the thongs with which it can be tuned to the keynote of the music being played. The left-hand drum, usually made of metal, is not tuned; the player alters its pitch by pressure with the heel of the hand on the skin while playing. Both drums are played with the fingers. The tabla are the most important accompanying instruments in north Indian music, a performance by sitar and tabla being the equivalent of a violin and piano recital.

Tablature, various old systems of writing music, especially for organ and for lute, by means of letters, numbers or other signs. The ukelele and similar guitar types still use a tablature notation. Tonic sol-fa notation may be said to be a kind of tablature.

Table, see FURNITURE.

Table Bay, inlet of the Atlantic Ocean on the south-west coast of the Cape of Good Hope, on the south side of which Cape Town is situated.

Table Mountain, or Tafelberg, mountain of the Cape peninsula, South Africa, overlooking Cape Town and Table Bay. The level top gives it the appearance of a table; highest point, Maclear's Beacon (1113 m).

Table Tennis, a racket-and-ball game for two or four players. The standard table measures 274 cm by 152·5 cm, with a 15·25 cm-high net. The bats may be of any size, shape or weight. The balls weigh between 2·4 g and 2·53 g and are of celluloid or similar plastic. Each player serves five times successively, and no volleying is allowed. The game is played up to 21 points when a lead of at least two points must be obtained before the game is completed and won. The score is always called by stating the server's score first. The International Table Tennis Association was formed in 1926.

Tableland, see PLATEAU.

Taboo, from the Maori *tapu*, signifying the propensity of certain phenomena to influence other phenomena. Broadly speaking, it is associated in the Maori culture with male spiritual forces and raw food, and counteracted by female forces and cooked food. Similar concepts are found all over the world. Breach of taboo, i.e. contact of the phenomena to be separated, is often seen as spiritually polluting and as a cause of sickness. Birth, initiation and sexual practices are commonly brought under taboo to protect them from hostile influences. A widespread taboo is that enforced on pregnant or menstruating women who are seen as being dangerous to, and to be avoided by, males. A universal taboo is the incest taboo.

Tabor, drum used to accompany a pipe since the 13th century. The size has varied according to place and period, ranging from 7·5 cm to 40 cm diameter. It is slung from the player's wrist or shoulder and the pipe is played with the same hand; the other hand holds the beater.

Tabora, town and region in the centre of Tanzania, founded by Arabs about 1820 and formerly a great centre of trade in slaves and ivory; today it is important as a trade centre and regional headquarters. Population (1978) 67,392.

Tabriz, ancient city, capital of the Iranian province of East Azerbaijan, and a commercial and industrial centre of Iran. The carpets manufactured here are of fine designs and quality, and are well known all over the world. It was the capital of Iran in the time of Shah Ismail I and Ghazan Khan. Population (1976) 598,576.

Tachisme (French *tache*, stain), name given to the method used by some contemporary French artists of exploiting the quality of freely flowing oil-paint for its own sake, one aspect of a tendency to seek new effects in paint substance and colour without representation or formal design, pursued in Europe and America.
See also ABSTRACT EXPRESSIONISM.

Tachometer, instrument for measuring the speed of rotation of a shaft, such as an engine crankshaft. Mechanical tachometers are similar in principle to a governor; the centrifugal force produced by rotating weights moves a pointer against the action of a spring. Electrical tachometers use a small generator, either coupled to a voltmeter which is calibrated in revolutions per minute or driving a motor which in turn drives a magnetic drag cup indicator.

Tachycardia (Greek *tachys*, swift, *kardia*, heart), medical term denoting an excessively rapid heart beat, usually of more than 100 beats per minute. Tachycardia can be a normal, temporary response to exercise or emotional excitement. It can also be a sign of disease of the heart. It is classified as an arrhythmia. When the tachycardia is due to heart disease, treatment is usually directed towards the causative disease. Certain medications can help and the elimination of tea, coffee and other stimulants is desirable.

Tachygraphy, see SHORTHAND.

Tacitus, Publius Cornelius (c.AD 55–c.120), Roman historian. His extant works are: *Dialogus de Oratoribus*, a treatise on the decline of rhetoric; *Agricola* (98), a portrait of his father-in-law; *Germania*, a valuable ethnographical work; *Historiae*, a history of the empire from Galba to Domitian (69–

96) in 12 or 14 books of which only iv and part of v remain; and *Annales* (115–17), a history of the empire from the death of Augustus to that of Nero, of which books vii–x and parts of v, xi and xvi are lost. Though Tacitus did not, perhaps, quite attain his ideal of writing without prejudice, he remains the most reliable witness for the period covered by his works. His style is unique in ancient literature—rapid and condensed, combining great force with biting epigram. His power derives from his knowledge of the human mind and its motives.

Tack, in shipping, rope or wire used to secure the windward clews or corners of the courses to the ship's side, and the windward lower end of a fore-and-aft sail amidships. The term tack is also used for the lower forward corner of a fore-and-aft sail or the weather clew of a course. A ship sailing to windward is said to be on the port or starboard tack according to the side of the vessel towards which the wind is blowing. A ship is said to tack when she changes direction, passing head-to-wind, so as to bring the wind on the opposite side from which it was before she went about. See also STAYS.

Tacna, capital of Tacna department in Peru, it is linked with Arica in Chile, 60 km away, by a railway. Copper is mined in the department and there are plans to turn Tacna into an industrial centre. Altitude 558 m. Population (1972) 42,000.

Tacoma, city of the state of Washington, USA, situated near the head of Puget Sound. It is an excellent port although 250 km from the open sea. The first settlement consisted of a few sawmills but the city was selected as the Pacific coast terminus of the first transcontinental railway to the north-west (the Northern Pacific) in 1883. Tacoma has lumber and paper industries, and two smelters of national importance, one producing aluminium and the other mainly copper. Population (1980) 158,500.

Tacsonia, see PASSION FLOWER.

Tadpole, see FROGS.

Tadzhik Soviet Socialist Republic, or Tadzhikistan (also known as Tajik SSR or Tajikistan), constituent republic of the USSR bordering on Afghanistan in the south and on China in the east. It was formed as an autonomous republic in 1924 and acquired the status of a union republic in 1929. It is mainly mountainous and includes the whole of the Pamirs, and the Turkestan, Zeravshan and Gissar ranges. The main river is the Syr Darya. The economy is based on the growing (Vakhsh valley) and processing of cotton. Food grains (wheat, barley and millet) are grown in the south-east, and oil grains (flowering flax) in the south-west. There is a considerable cattle breeding industry. Lead and zinc are mined. Other industries include silk weaving (Leninabad), textile weaving (Dushanbe), and fruit canning. There is a large carpet factory at Kayrakkum. The capital is Dushanbe. Area 143,100 km². Population (1980) 3,900,000; mainly Tadzhiks (56 per cent), Uzbeks (23 per cent), and Russians (11 per cent).

Taegu (Japanese *Taikyu*), one of the main cities of South Korea, about 90 km north-west of Pusan; its textile industry contributes 30 per cent of the country's total output. Population (1980) 1,607,458.

Taff (Welsh *Tâf*), river of Wales rising in the Brecon Beacons. It flows through Mid and South Glamorgan and enters the Bristol Channel at Cardiff. Its main tributary is the Rhondda. Merthyr Tydfil stands where it enters Mid Glamorgan and Pontypridd at its confluence with the Rhondda. Length 64 km.

Taffeta, or taffety (Persian *tafta*), plain weave silk fabric introduced into England in the 14th century. It is woven so that warp and weft threads are evenly interlaced. Taffeta is either yarn-dyed, which gives a crisp taffeta, or dyed in the piece, which makes the fabric more pliable. 'Shot taffeta' has warp and weft of different colours making the fabric apparently change colour with the fall of light on its surface.

Tafilalt, or Tafilet, oasis on the south-east of the Atlas Mountains, Morocco, noted for dates and leather. It contains some 300 villages, is a caravan centre and the home of the reigning Moroccan dynasty.

Taft, William Howard (1857–1930), 27th President of the USA and chief justice. He was elected president by a large majority in 1908. Taft improved the financial position of the country, and sought peace agreements with several foreign powers. Though nominated by Theodore Roosevelt, Taft did not carry on his predecessor's policy to the satisfaction of its originator, the 1910 Tariff Acts being particularly unpopular. Roosevelt in 1912 stood once more as presidential candidate. Taft was chosen, but the resultant split in the Republican party permitted the return of the Democratic Woodrow Wilson. Taft then became a law professor at Yale. From 1921 to 1930 he was chief justice, his real ambition achieved.

Taganrog, seaport city in the RSFSR, USSR, on the Sea of Azov, 75 km west of Rostov-on-Don. It is an important industrial centre: iron and steel (since 1897), engineering (combine-harvesters, boilers, machine-tools, aircraft), leather, and food industries. It was founded by Peter the Great in 1698. Population (1980) 278,000.

Tagore, Rabindranath (1861–1941), Indian poet and author. Between 1900 and 1901 he established a self-governing experimental school at Śāntiniketan, which flourished and expanded in spite of financial difficulties, so that 20 years later he was able to found an international university, Viśvabhāratī, and realise his belief that men of different races and civilisations should study together in an atmosphere of peace, brotherhood and joy in life and work. He was the first Indian to be awarded the Nobel Prize for literature (1913). His poem *Conscience of the People* was chosen in 1950 (with music by Herbert Murrill) as the national anthem of India. Tagore brought new life to Indian literature by turning for inspiration to Bengali folklore and everyday life.

Tagua, a name of Araucan origin for a palm-tree (*Phytelephas macrocarpa*) also known as the corozo. The seed of the tree has a hard, white, opaque endosperm that can be polished and carved, and is known as 'vegetable ivory'. There are a great many groves of tagua palms in Colombia.

Tagus (Spanish *Tajo*; Portuguese *Tejo*), chief river of Spain and Portugal, which rises in the Sierra de Albarracín on the border between Cuenca and Teruel. It flows past Toledo, and after Alcántara forms the Spanish-Portuguese frontier for 50 km. It then crosses Portugal to its estuary on the Atlantic Ocean at Lisbon. It is navigable for 200 km from the sea. Length 1005 km.

Tahiti, main island of the Windward Islands of the Society group; it contains Papeete, the administrative centre of French Polynesia. It has a mountainous interior surrounded by a fertile alluvial belt; high rainfall and equable climate. The island exports copra, phosphates, pearl shell and vanilla. Discovered in 1606 by Quiros, Tahiti became a French Protectorate in 1847. Area 1040 km²; population (1977) 95,604.

Taiga, sub-Arctic coniferous forest zone, lying south of the tundra and north of the steppe. Spruce, firs, pine and larch are the chief trees. The taiga exists in North America, Europe and Asia, and forms about one-third of the area of the USSR. It contains many swampy low-lying areas, and during the spring thaw is often flooded.

Tailor-bird, *Orthotomus sutorius*, bird of family Muscicapidae, order Passeriformes, native to India and other parts of Asia, where it feeds on insects. It is about 15 cm long and olive-green, with markings of other tints. Its nest is a dainty structure of leaves stitched together with silk, wool, hair and vegetable fibre. Three or four varicoloured eggs are laid.

Tailoring (Old French *taillour*), cutting and making of clothes. Tailors originally made garments for both men and women, as well as the padding and lining of armour, for which reason the earliest charter of the Merchant Taylors Company was made out to the 'Taylors and Linen Armourers'. 'Bespoke' means simply that the garment is made to order for an individual customer. Social and economic changes are contributing to a decline in bespoke tailoring, with the consequent strengthening of the market in the lower and middle lower ranges.

Taimyr National Okrug, district in Krasnoyarsk *krai* of the RSFSR, USSR, comprising the Taimyr Peninsula with the adjacent mainland and islands. It includes Cape Chelyuskin, the northernmost point of Asia. Nickel, copper, uranium and coal are mined; other activities include fishing, reindeer breeding and fur trapping. The *okrug* was formed in 1930; capital, Dudinka. Area 862,100 km². Population (1975) 42,000 (62 per cent urban); mostly Nentsy people, a group of Samoyeds.

Tainan, city on the south-west coast of Taiwan, the old capital and oldest city on the island. It is the industrial centre of southern Taiwan, and the seat of Cheng-kung University (engineering). Population (1972 estimate) 490,000.

Taine, Hippolyte Adolphe (1828–93), French philosopher and critic, awarded his doctorate for an important thesis on La Fontaine (1853). In 1856 he began a series of articles on English literature, published in 1864. In 1858 appeared a first collection of *Essais de critique et d'histoire*. The originality of his critical theories lies in the application of the scientific and naturalistic method to literature. *L'Intelligence*, 1870, was a return to philosophy. His later years were mostly devoted to the series on *Les Origines de la France contemporaine*, 1875–94. Taine was a follower of Hegel and, more indirectly, of Spinoza. His determinist and materialist outlook had a great influence upon contemporaries, especially on Zola.

Taipei, principal city and capital of Taiwan in the China Sea. Since 1949 it has been the capital of the Nationalist government of China in exile. Taipei occupies a basin site surrounded by mountains in the north of the island. It is 36 km from the sea, its outport being Chilung. A centre for overseas trade, it also has industries, including textiles, electrical goods, canning of foodstuffs and plastics. Population (1979) 2·1 million.

Taipings, followers of Hung Hsiu-ch'üan, a Chinese peasant Christian leader, who rose against the Manchu emperor in 1851. By 1853 the rebels occupied all southern China, and their leader proclaimed himself emperor in Nanking. In 1860 France and Britain assisted in the suppression of the rebels, partly owing to the threat posed to their interests in Shanghai.

Taiwan
Area: 36,000 km²
Population: 17,480,000
Capital: Taipei

Taiwan (formerly *Formosa*) a large island and independent state off the south-eastern coast of China, separated from the mainland by the shallow Taiwan Strait about 150 km wide. Taiwan extends 320 km from its most northerly to its most southerly point and its total area is 36,000 km². Off the west coast are the P'enghu or Pescadores islands. In addition, the Chinese Nationalist government, which controls Taiwan, has possession of two small islands near the Chinese mainland coast, Matsu and Kinmen (or Quemoy).

In the central part of the east coast are the Taitung Mountains, which are so steep and rugged as to make communication along the coast virtually impossible. Immediately west of these is a deep rift valley. The flat valley floor is intensively cultivated in parts. West of the Taitung valley lies the rugged mountainous backbone of Taiwan, which is heavily forested and rather remote. Population is sparse, the most remote parts being inhabited only by scattered aboriginal tribes who pre-date the Chinese colonisation of the island. Nearer to the west coast, the mountains are succeeded by undulating and hilly land which is terraced for agriculture at the lower levels and interspersed with wide valleys where both agriculture and settlement are intensive. Along the coast itself lies an alluvial plain.

Population (1979) 17·48 million. Principal cities are Taipei (the capital), Kaohsiung and Tainan.

About one-quarter of the land can be used for agriculture, the main area being the western coastal plain. Rice is the principal farm crop, two crops a year being possible everywhere.

In those parts where it is not possible to grow rice, sweet potatoes are the staple item of the diet. Vegetables are grown around all the villages, while major non-subsistence crops are sugar cane, tea and pineapples. The forests contain important resources of camphor wood and Taiwan is the leading world producer of camphor. In recent years machinery and electrical industries have grown rapidly as has the manufacture of textiles. Taiwan now also produces a wide variety of manufactured consumer goods, such as rubber footwear, clothing and plastic toys, for export.

The structure of the central government is based on the constitution of December 1947. The president, who has supreme power, appoints the chairmen of the five *yuans* or councils (namely executive, legislative, judicial, control and examination). The councils form the executive government; legislative power lies with the National Assembly and Legislative Yuan, both elected bodies.

History. In 1684 the Manchu government established its administration on the island, which formed a prefecture of Fukien province. During the 18th and 19th centuries Chinese immigration increased significantly as population pressure in relation to available cultivated land mounted in the nearby mainland provinces. Taiwan was made a separate province in 1886. In the 1894–95 Sino-Japanese War Japan occupied the P'enghu archipelagoes, and by the Shimonoseki Treaty China ceded Taiwan to Japan. In the following ten years 13 major uprisings against the Japanese took place. After the Second World War Taiwan was returned to China in accordance with the Three-Power Cairo Declaration of December 1943. When, in 1949, Chiang Kai-shek was defeated in China he fled to Taiwan and set up a government there under the protection of the US 7th Fleet. In September 1954 the Kuomintang (KMT) government in Taiwan was forced to give up the Ta-ch'en islands after bombardment from the mainland. In December 1954 Taiwan and the USA signed a bilateral defence agreement. In 1958 bombardment of Quemoy resumed, and has continued at intervals ever since. In 1971 Taiwan's 'Republic of China' lost its place in the UNO to Peking. In 1975 Chiang Kai-shek died and was succeeded as party leader by his son, Chiang Ching-Kuo, who was also elected president in 1978.

Taiyuan, walled capital city of Shanxi province, northern China, on the Fenhe. It lies in a rich coal- and iron-mining district, and is at present the most important centre of heavy industry, especially heavy-machine factories, in northern China (excluding Manchuria). Population (1970) 1,250,000.

Taizé Community, interdenominational monastic order established at Taizé in southern France since 1944. The Rule of Taizé (1952) is similar to that of other orders, with much emphasis on co-operative work, but members wear ordinary lay clothing. The community has played a positive rôle in Franco-German reconciliation and in the ecumenical movement.

Taj Mahal, mausoleum at Agra, Uttar Pradesh State, India, in which lie the bodies of Shah Jahan, Moghul emperor (1627–58)

Taj Mahal, India, the 17th-century Moghul mausoleum, built by Shah Jahan in memory of his wife.

and his favourite wife, Mumtaz Mahal, who died in 1631. The Taj Mahal is one of the great sights of the world. Splendidly situated above the River Yamuna, it is built mainly of white marble, beautifully carved in open traceries and designs, and largely inlaid with semi-precious stones, many of which have been stolen. The proportions and balance of the main structure, together with the four supporting minarets, show Moghul architecture at its peak. It took 22 years to build.

Tajik, or Tadjik, or Tadzhik, term originally used to describe the Iranian peoples of central Asia. Today it is applied to Iranian-speaking peoples living in northern Afghanistan and Soviet central Asia, in Tadzhikistan and Uzbekistan. There are also some 15,000 in north-west China. Traditionally they are sedentary agriculturalists. From Persia their culture diffused to China. They are mainly Sunni Muslims, but there are some Shiites and some followers of the Aga Khan.
See also ISLAM.

Takahe, *Notornis mantelli,* flightless bird of New Zealand. It is a species of moorhen belonging to the Gruiformes, weighs just over 2 kg and is about 46 cm high. The tail and back are bronze-green, the head and breast bluish-black, and the bill red and short. Its fossil remains were found in the 1840s and it was thought to be extinct, but living specimens were later caught. It is now protected.

Takin, *Budorcas taxicolor,* a heavily built, goat-like mammal with the horns thickened at the base and growing outwards. It ranges from Bhutan in the Himalayas to Central China. Its only close relation is the musk ox.

Tal, Mikhail (1936–), Soviet world chess champion, 1960–61. He became a national master at 16 and in 1957 an international grandmaster. In 1960 he defeated Botvinnik and became world champion. In 1961 he lost the crown to his old rival and though he has played regularly for the USSR since then, ill health has affected his play.

Talbot, William Henry Fox (1800–77),

English pioneer photographer. He is best remembered for his invention in 1834 of the photogenic drawing process, an early form of photography, and for a subsequent improvement on it, the calotype, or Talbotype, process in 1840. The negative-positive principle which these methods incorporated is the basis of modern photography. His later inventions include the first successful method of photoengraving. His life and work are commemorated in a museum at his ancestral home in Lacock, Wiltshire.

Talc, $Mg_6Si_8O_{20}$ $(OH)_4$, hydrous bisilicate of magnesia, which crystallises in the rhombic system (hardness 1, relative density 2·8). Crystals are rare, and the massive form 'steatite' or 'soapstone' is more common. French chalk, potstone and figure-stone are all varieties of talc. It is used as a filter for paints and paper, a toilet powder, for insulation and acid resistance, in soap as a lubricant, and for making ornaments.

Talca, capital of Talca province in Chile, 240 km south of Santiago. It was founded in 1692 and completely rebuilt after the 1928 earthquake. At the centre of a rich agricultural area, it is also an important trading and manufacturing town and a railway junction. Its manufactures include matches (it has the largest match factory in Chile), shoes, paper, tobacco, flour and biscuits; there are also several distilleries and foundries. Population (1975) 115,130.

Talcahuano, city in Concepción province, Chile, lying to the north-east of the city of Concepción for which it serves as a port. It is the Chilean fleet's main port and a major commercial, fishing and industrial centre. Population (1975) 183,591.

Talent (Latin *talentum*, Greek *talanton* from verbal root *tla-*, to bear), unit of weight in use among the ancient Greeks. Its use to denote intellectual gift is derived from the Biblical parable of the talents.

Taliesin (fl.550), Welsh poet, possibly a mythical figure, famed as the leading bard of his day and said to have been a court poet in the kingdom of Rheged, in southern Scotland. His odes were written in praise of the victories of his patrons, Urien, King of Rheged, Cynan, King of Powis, and Gwallawg. Taliesin is first mentioned in the *Historia Brittonum* of Nennius.

Talisman, object allegedly having magical powers acquired from the influences of the planets and the celestial bodies operating at the time it is made. It is usually worn like an amulet.

Tallahassee, city of Florida, USA, founded in 1823 to serve as state capital. Its main business is government, but it also serves as a market centre for the surrounding agricultural areas. Population (1980) 81,548.

Tallensi, a people living in northern Ghana, with a strong and elaborate clan system. Government is in the hands of chiefs and earth priests, who are ritually independent, and who represent two diverse stocks, said to have been the ancestral stock of the people. They speak a Gur language.

Talleyrand-Périgord, Charles Maurice de (1754–1838), French statesman. In 1788 he was appointed Bishop of Autun, and having accepted the civil constitution of the clergy, was excommunicated in 1791. Talleyrand

was appointed foreign minister by the Directory in 1797. He supported the foreign and domestic policy of Napoleon until he grew convinced that this policy could only lead to disaster for France, and then he worked for the restoration of the Bourbons. He became foreign minister to Louis XVIII in 1814. At the Congress of Vienna Talleyrand played a leading part, obtaining favourable terms for France. He supported Louis Philippe in 1830, and until 1834 was envoy in London where he played an important part in the creation of a neutral Belgium, and concluded the Quadruple Alliance of 1830 with Britain, Spain and Portugal.

Tallien, Jean Lambert (1767–1820), French revolutionary. In 1791 he became famous as the author of the Jacobin sheet, *L'Ami des Citoyens, journal fraternel*. He proved himself a fanatical terrorist as commissioner of the Convention, but later led the Thermidorian attack on Robespierre. From 1795 to 1798 he was one of the Council of Five Hundred.

Tallinn (formerly *Revel*; German *Reval*), capital of the Estonian SSR, USSR, and a major port on the Gulf of Finland opposite Helsinki. The leading industries are engineering and machine building (electrical equipment, excavators, oil industry equipment), with paper, textile, food and furniture factories. Tallinn is known from the 12th century. Originally a Danish fortress town, it became Russian in 1710. Population (1980) 436,000.

Tallis, Thomas (c.1505–85), English composer. He was organist at Waltham Abbey, and from c.1542 a gentleman of the Chapel Royal and, with Byrd, joint organist there. In 1575 they were granted the monopoly of music publishing and produced the *Cantiones Sacrae*. The second Prayer Book of Edward VI (1552) created the demand for new church music, which Tallis was one of the chief to supply. Other works by him are the motet *Spem in alium* in 40 parts, about 50 motets, and 30 anthems.

Tallow, substance composed chiefly of the triglycerides of palmitic, stearic and oleic acids, derived mainly from beef and mutton suet. Best quality tallow is edible; other grades are used for soap manufacture, fatty acid manufacture and lubricants. Tallow is now little used for candles.

Tallow Tree, *Sapium sebiferum*, a Chinese tree of the Euphorbiaceae, which bears yellow flowers followed by small fruits; the seeds yield a wax used for making candles. An oil can be expressed from the seeds. The wood of the tree is very hard and is used in making blocks for printing. The African tree, *Pentadesma butyracea*, of the family Guttiferae, also called the tallow or butter tree, bears large red flowers followed by edible berries. The butter substitute is obtained from sap and seeds.

Tally (French *tailler*, to cut), stick or rod of well-seasoned hazel or other suitable wood, squared with a knife, and marked on one side with transverse notches of different size. The notched stick, a primitive memory aid for recording numbers, was employed by some early peoples of Australia, North America, West Africa and Asia and as an aid in conveying messages. It was used also in European countries to express numbers. In England

exchequer tallies for recording payment made by the Crown or government were introduced shortly after the Norman conquest; they provided a perfect check for both parties, and could be understood by illiterate people. The amount of the transaction was cut by the 'tallator', who also split the tally into two unequal parts: the chamberlain retained the smaller part (leaf, foil or tally), the larger part (stalk, counterfoil or countertally) being held by the other party. Tallies were used officially until 1826.

Talmud, The (Study), collection of Jewish books containing traditions, laws, rules and institutions, by which, in addition to the Hebrew Bible, the conduct of Jewry is regulated. The *Torah*, the 'Written Law', was augmented by the 'Oral Law', the rabbinic interpretations recorded in the academies which became the Talmud.

Hillel is considered to be the first author of the arrangement of the *Mishna*, although it was not yet reduced to writing. The compilation of the *Mishna* was accomplished by Jehuda ha-Nasi, 'the Prince' (died c.AD 219), the official leader of the Jewish community in Palestine. The *Mishna* (from the root *shanah*, 'to learn by repetition') contains nearly 4000 rules, divided into six *sedarim* (orders), of agricultural regulations, festivals, marital laws, injuries (civil and criminal law), sacred things (sacrificial laws), and laws of cleanliness. The language of the *Mishna* is Hebrew, known as *Mishnaic* Hebrew, a more recent and colloquial form than Biblical Hebrew. The *Mishna* became the standard text-book for the study of the *Torah*, and itself, in turn, the subject of study and explanation in the academies of Palestine and Babylonia. The main object of such study was to verify the *halachah* by establishing its connection with *Torah*, elucidating its meaning, and, in certain respects, bringing it up to date by showing how it was to be applied to the circumstances of the time. Thus, the *Gemara* (from the root *gamar*, 'to complete'), or 'completion' was formed. The *Mishna*, together with its *Gemara*, makes up the *Talmud*. There is one *Mishna*, but there are two *Talmuds* known as the Palestinian (or Jerusalem) and the Babylonian respectively, from the countries where the *Gemara* was completed.

The *Talmud* is the product of Rabbinic Judaism, by Jews, who have always valued it highly. Taken as a whole, it presents the appearance of a conglomerate of the most heterogeneous material, relating to religion, ethics, history, legend, folklore, astronomy, mathematics, law, physical life, botany, etc. It has moulded the Jews' spiritual and religious life, promoting their intellectual activity, and regulating their conduct: in short, it has helped to preserve the existence of Jewry.

Tamale, town of northern Ghana, 50 km from the northern tip of Lake Volta. It is the administrative, communications and service centre for much of the north of the country. Population (1970) 120,000.

Tamarind, *Tamarindus indica*, a leguminous evergreen tree cultivated in India and other tropical countries for its hard, close-grained, heavy wood. It bears pinnate leaves and racemes of yellow, red-streaked flowers followed by legumes. The pulp of the fruit can be used as a gentle laxative.

Tamarisk, *Tamarix,* a genus of shrubs in the Tamaricaceae, native to India, the Middle East and southern Europe. The common tamarisk, *T. anglica,* has been planted in some areas to bind and cover sand-dunes. It is evergreen, having bright green, minute, scale-like leaves and spikes of rose-pink flowers.

Tambourine, percussion instrument consisting of a vellum head over a circular wooden frame in which 'jingles' (small cymbals) are inserted. It is played by rapping, rubbing or shaking.

Tambov, capital city, economic and cultural centre of Tambov *oblast,* USSR, south-east of Moscow. There are engineering (chemical apparatus, spare parts for agricultural machinery), food and chemical industries, and it is an important railway junction. It was founded in 1636 as a fortress. Population (1980) 273,000.

Tamerlane, or Timur (1335–1405), Sultan of Samarkand, of Mongol origin, a direct descendant of Genghis Khan. He assisted and then attacked Husein, Khan of North Khorasan and Jagatai, finally supplanting him in 1369. He made Samarkand his capital and rapidly made himself master of the whole of Turkestan and part of Siberia. After a series of bloody and cruel conflicts, the whole of Persia, Georgia, Armenia and the neighbouring states accepted him as suzerain. In 1398 he defeated the Indian army near Delhi. He later came into conflict with Europeans, when he attacked and took Smyrna, the property of the Knights of St John. He died at Otra as he was marching to attack China. He figures as the hero of Christopher Marlowe's great drama, *Tamburlaine.*

Tamil, a Dravidian language, the official language and script of the state of Tamil Nadu (Madras), India. It is the mother tongue of over 30,000,000 people (1961) in India, 2,000,000 in Sri Lanka, and of many more in South-East Asia and Africa.
See also INDIA, *Language;* INDIA, *Literature.*

Tamil Nadu, state of southern India, containing most Tamil-speaking areas, bounded on the north by Karnataka and Andhra Pradesh, Kerala on the west, and facing the Bay of Bengal and Indian Ocean on the east and south. Tamil Nadu's 130,066 km² consists mainly of coastal plains, including the Cauvery delta and the hilly hinterland of the Nilgiri Hills and extensions of the Western Ghats. Rainfall is unreliable, and multiple cropping of land for several rice crops, or rice-millet-groundnuts combination, is frequently dependent on irrigation. Sugar-cane, cotton, coconuts and pepper are important cash crops, with tea and coffee plantations in the interior hills. Cars, motors, chemicals, oil refining, fertilisers, cement, sugar and cotton mills are in large-scale production, together with significant consumer industries including a big film industry and cycle works. Most industry is concentrated in and around Madras, the capital, with Coimbatore, Salem and Tiruchirappalli as lesser centres. Of the population (1980) of 48,297,456, 90 per cent are Hindu, mostly Tamil-speaking. The government is based at Madras. The legislature is of two houses.
The Vijayanagar empire included all of modern Tamil Nadu in the 14th–16th centuries, after which petty chiefs set up their own states, and later a Muslim overlord, the nawab of Carnatic, ruled. The British trading post at Madras (Fort St George), was their most important factory before the conquest of Bengal. The 18th-century wars between the British and the French and their respective Indian allies led to the British governing the Carnatic. The British presidency of Madras included much of what is now Kerala and Andhra Pradesh. Demands for linguistic divisions and more conveniently-sized administrative units led to the reduction of the state to its present extent to cover primarily Tamilnad (land of the Tamils). The state was renamed Tamil Nadu in 1968.

Tammany Hall and Society, New York party organisation established in 1789 for social and charitable purposes. In 1805 it adopted the title Tammany Society. Twenty-five years after its foundation it entered politics, and allied itself with the Democratic party of New York, and from 1834 established its nominees in the New York mayoral office in the majority of cases. Tammany Hall became an instrument of corruption in public life. Much purged, it continued to control New York politics until 1934, when La Guardia was elected mayor on an anti-Tammany Hall platform. It still retained great influence in Democratic quarters, however, but again suffered a blow in 1964 when John Lindsay was elected mayor.

Tammuz, or Thammuz, Babylonian and Assyrian god, possibly to be identified with the Greek Adonis and the Egyptian Osiris. He represents the decay and growth of natural life, descending part of the year into the nether world, and being rescued from there by his sister, the heaven goddess, Innini (Innana) or Ishtar, the Phoenician Astarte.

Tampa, city of Florida, USA, at the head of Tampa Bay, on Florida's west coast, 40 km from the open sea. It is a major port on the Gulf of Mexico; among its chief products are cigars, chemicals and fertilisers, food products and paints. The bay's shrimp fishing fleet is famous. The best-known feature of the metropolitan area is its attraction as a place of retirement for the elderly. Population (1980) 271,523.

Tampere (Swedish *Tammerfors*), town in Finland, 164 km north-west of Helsinki, on both sides of the Tammerkoski, whose rapids were originally utilised for the textile industry. It is the chief industrial town of Finland, and manufactures textiles, engineering products, timber, paper and footwear. Population (1979) 165,880.

Tampico, port in the state of Tamaulipas, Mexico, on the Gulf of Mexico. It is the largest city in the state; one of Mexico's chief ports, its main industries are oil shipping and refining. It is an important fishing port, and fish processing and preserving forms a leading industry. Population (1977) 240,540.

Tamworth, market town in Staffordshire, England, at the junction of the Tame and Anker rivers, 24 km north-east of Birmingham. Industries include engineering, paper-making, and the manufacture of asbestos goods, sanitary ware, clothing and small wares. In the vicinity are large market gardens and the North Warwickshire coalfield. Population (1981) 64,315.

Tamworth, town of New South Wales, Australia, on the River Peel, 454 km north of Sydney. It stands in an agricultural and sheep-rearing district and is a regional centre for New England. Population (1976) 30,700.

Tan Waste, see BARK BED.

Tana (Tsana), Lake, in northern Ethiopia, some 75 km long and 70 km wide. It is the source of the Blue Nile some 1800 m above sea-level. James Bruce reached its shores in 1770. The Blue Nile leaves the lake by way of the Tisisat Falls (40 m high), harnessed for hydroelectric power. Area 3673 km².

Tanacetum, see TANSY.

Tanager, name for about 200 species of the bird family Emberizidae in order Passeriformes, natives of the Americas, nearly all with very brilliant plumage. One of the finest is the superb *Tangara chilensis;* its plumage has a remarkable metallic lustre; the head is sea-green, the breast violet, and there is a flame-coloured patch on the lower part of the back. It feeds on fruit and insects. *Piranga olivacea,* the scarlet tanager or summer red bird, has brilliant scarlet plumage in the male with black wings and tail. In autumn its plumage changes to dull green, like that of the female.

Tanagra, ancient town of Boeotia. Situated near the Attic border, it was exposed to attack by the Athenians. Statuettes found on the site of Tanagra are characteristic of the best Greek work in terracotta; they date from c.350 to 200 BC.

Tananarive, see ANTANANARIVO.

Tancred (1076–1112), leader of the First Crusade. He played a prominent part in the sieges of Antioch and Jerusalem, and became Prince of Galilee in 1099. When Baldwin became King of Jerusalem, Tancred took over the regency of Antioch (1100–03), and later became Prince of Edessa and Antioch.

Tang, Chinese dynasty that ruled over a large part of central Asia (AD 618–906). During this period, literature and the arts and sciences flourished. Tang expansion was checked in the west by the Arabs at the Talas River in 751.

Tanga, bay and seaport of Tanzania, north-east of Zanzibar, 119 km north from Mombasa by sea. Tanga, with an excellent harbour but no deep-water quays, is the coastal terminus of the railway to Moshi and Arusha and has several large factories including a fertiliser plant. Population (1978) 103,409.

Tanganyika, Lake, lake of east-central Africa, situated in the Great Rift Valley. It forms the border between Tanzania and Zaire and is shared by Burundi in the north and Zambia in the south. It is about 725 km in length (the longest lake in the world), with an average breadth of from 50 to 70 km, and an area of 32,893 km². With the exception of Lake Baikal, it is the deepest freshwater lake in the world, soundings of 1436 m having been taken. It is 766 m above sea-level.

Tange, Kenzo (1913–), Japanese architect and town planner. Tange was deeply influenced by the International Style, but he sought to reinterpret it within the Japanese tradition. His important buildings include many in Tokyo, especially the gymnasia for the 1964 Olympic Games. He was also responsible for the Skopje Reconstruction Project (1965) and the master plan for Expo 70, Osaka.

Tangent. The tangent at a point on a circle is the straight line which goes through that point and has no other point in common with the circle; it is perpendicular to the radius at that point, (A) on illustration. The same definition can be applied to other simple curves such as ellipses, but in order to define a tangent at a point *P* of any curve *L*, a different viewpoint must be adopted. The tangent at *P* is defined as the straight line which most closely approximates the curve in the neighbourhood of *P*. This means that the tangent must go through *P* and must be as near as possible to the curve on both sides of *P*. The definition is only concerned with what happens in the immediate neighbourhood of *P*. A line may be a tangent at one point of a curve although it intersects the curve at other points, (B) on illustration. In analytical geometry the equation of a tangent may be determined by differentiation.
See also TRIGONOMETRY.

Tangerine, see CITRUS FRUITS.

Tangier, or Tangiers, seaport of Morocco, on a bay on the Strait of Gibraltar, 58 km south-west of Gibraltar. Lying on a picturesque bank overlooking the Atlantic, the city is surrounded by old walls and dominated by a *kasbah* (fort). The 'Great Souk' (market place) is the end of the Saharan and Sudan caravan routes. Cigarette manufacturing is the main industry, and there are fisheries, market gardens and preserving industries. Tangier is the northern terminus of the Tangier-Fez railway. Population (1971) 187,894. The Algeciras Act of 1906 recognised Tangier and the surrounding territory (583 km²) as an international zone. In 1957 Tangier became a part of Morocco.
See also MOROCCO, *History*.

Tango, Spanish solo and ballroom dance. The Spanish version, thought to have Arabic origins, was popularised and developed in Cadiz. The music is rhythmically quite unlike the ballroom dance, which is thought to have originated in South America and developed from rhythms brought there by African slaves, blended with those of the Spanish tango. The music and dance were adapted and returned to Europe in a very different form.

Tangshan, city in eastern Hubei province, China, 160 km south-east of Beijing. The site of China's first railway in 1882, it carried coal to Tianjin. Development and modernisation of the city's coal, steel, and cement industries began after 1949. In 1976 it was devastated by two violent earthquakes.

Tangus, a Mongolian people living in parts of Kansu, in China, and the Kuku-Nor and Khan districts in north-eastern Tibet. Their way of life was nomadic but, by controlling the trade routes between central Asia and the West, they established the Hsi Hsia empire from the 11th to the 13th centuries. They were overrun by Genghis Khan in 1227. Buddhism was the state religion.

Tanguy, Yves (1900–55), French painter. Self-taught, he was directed towards imaginative painting by the work of de Chirico and became a member of the Surrealist group in 1926.
See also SURREALISM.

Tank, a self powered vehicle moving on chain tracks, and protected by armour plate and its own weapons system, usually compris-

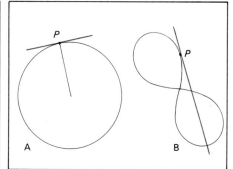

*A **Tangent** meets a circle only at the point of contact. With other curves, it may also intersect.*

ing machine guns or automatic cannon, missiles, or main armament artillery housed in a traversing turret. The first armoured vehicle was produced in 1902 by an Englishman, F. R. Simms; it failed commercially and it was not until the outbreak of the First World War that military commanders recognised the need for a vehicle invulnerable to machine-gun fire and able to cross no-man's land. In 1915 Lt Col. Ernest Swinton drew up specifications for an armoured vehicle; the name 'tank' was adopted to disguise the fact that a new weapon was being developed. Trials resulted in the production of the Mark I heavy tank which first saw action in 1916, during the Battle of the Somme. It was produced in two designs, had a crew of eight and a top speed of 4 km/h. Later developments included the traversing gun turret, first used in the French FT 17. In 1939 the Germans gave tank warfare its fullest expression in the *Blitzkrieg*, an attacking strategy employing an independent armoured force supported by infantry and aircraft. Design improvements followed quickly, sloped armour and low silhouettes adding new criteria to the classic factors of protection, fire-power and mobility. Today, tanks have become expensive pieces of high technology incorporating laser gun sights and laminated armours, such as the British Chobham armour, first seen in 1975.

Tanker, a cargo boat designed to carry liquids, especially oil or oil products. Most tankers are divided by two longitudinal bulkheads, giving an arrangement of three tanks across the ship and also a number of athwartship bulkheads. The total number of tanks depends on the trade of the ship. Oil tankers are loaded using shore pumps and discharged using the ship's pumps carried in a pumproom aft. Tankers are normally arranged in three main classes: crude oil tankers; product tankers, designed to carry refined petroleum; and parcel tankers, with double bottoms and sides, used to carry a range of chemicals, some of them dangerous.

Tannenberg, Battle of, fought in 1410, between the Teutonic Knights of Prussia on one side, and the Poles and Lithuanians on the other. It resulted in a great victory for the latter, marking the emergence of Poland as a great power.

Tannenberg, Battle of (1914), see WORLD WAR, FIRST.

Tannhäuser, legendary German knight who, wearying of the pleasures in the mountain of Lady Venus (Venusberg), travels to Rome to make his penance. Pope Urban IV, however, says that the staff in his hand could

no more blossom than Tannhäuser find forgiveness. Dejected, Tannhäuser leaves Rome and when, three days later, the pope's staff begins to sprout shoots, he can no longer be found. He has returned to the mountain of Venus, and the unforgiving pope must be eternally damned. Wagner's opera conflates this ballad with traditions deriving from the Singers' Contest in the Wartburg.

Tannin, or tannic acid, occurs in gall nuts and all kinds of bark. It is an almost colourless substance readily soluble in water, and difficult to purify and crystallise. Its solutions possess a very astringent taste, and with ferric chloride give a dark blue solution, and hence tannin is used in the manufacture of inks. Owing to its property of forming insoluble coloured compounds with many dyes, tannin is used largely as a mordant and is also extensively employed in 'tanning' leather. In medicine tannin is employed in cases of diarrhoea and haemorrhage. Tannin is actually the name of a large class of related substances, the chief being Turkish tannin, Chinese tannin and Hamameli tannin.

Tanning, treating animal skins with tannins to make them resistant to decomposition, and so to become leather. Tannins are substances related to the phenols and are found in many plants, especially in the bark of hemlock, oak, and the quebracho of South America.
Hides are steeped in solutions of tannins over a period of about three months. Mineral or chrome tanning, used for producing shoe uppers, is done with solutions containing bichromate of sulphur.
See also LEATHER.

Tansy, *Tanacetum* (now *Chrysanthemum*) a genus of perennial herbaceous plants of the Compositae, with much-divided leaves and yellow flowers usually in flat-topped clusters. The common tansy, *T. vulgare* of Europe and Western Asia, abounds in waste places and is often cultivated. Tansy is bitter and aromatic, and was employed as an anthelmintic and used in cooking and herb teas or tisanes.

Tanta, capital of Gharbiya province, Egypt, 80 km north of Cairo. It is a transport focus, is noted for its fairs and festivals, and has a branch of El-Azhar University. It is a market centre for cotton and sugar. Population (1976) 284,636.

Tantalum, metallic chemical element, symbol Ta, atomic number 73, atomic weight 180·9479. It occurs associated with niobium in the minerals tantalite and columbite. Both are the tantalates and niobates of iron, the former richer in tantalum, the latter richer in niobium. Tantalum is white in colour, has a relative density of 16·8, and can be drawn into wire of great tenacity and high melting point (2850°C). It was used in constructing the filaments of electric lamps, but has been replaced for this purpose by tungsten. It is used in the manufacture of acid-resisting chemical apparatus, and in electrical rectifiers.

Tantalus, a spirit case in which decanters are visible, but are held in position by a wooden collar, secured by a lock. They were current in the mid-19th century.

Tantric Buddhism, a complicated system of meditation and yoga, evolving within Mahāyāna Buddhism, based on the Tantras—Indian religious works of the 5th century. Two types of Tantricism developed: Buddhist and Hindu. The methods Tantricism employs in its teaching are unique in Buddhism. They involve a wide variety of esoteric practices, including ritual gestures (*mudras*), sounds having spiritual significance (*mantras*), and symbolical diagrams (*mandalas*). The cryptic nature of Tantricism makes it difficult to assess to what extent its rituals are to be interpreted symbolically, and to what extent literally. The body is emphasised as the means to Enlightenment, and yoga and ritual are aimed at transforming consciousness through the integration of energies within the body. The Tantric focus on sexual union as a method of gaining spirituality has led to much condemnation from outside observers, but scholars differ as to what extent it is to be taken literally, and to what extent metaphorically.

Tantric Yoga, in Hinduism, the path of transformation, worships the Divine as two principles, male and female, Being and Becoming. Śiva, the masculine, is eternal Being, pure perfection and timeless wisdom. Śakti, the supreme Mother, is the creative power of Becoming, the origin of created form, and the cause of time. It is to her that men turn when practising this yoga, for help and guidance towards perfection. She dwells in man as dynamic energy at the base of the spine (Kundalini). The aim of Tantric Yoga is to awaken Kundalini energy which will then travel up the spine to the brain to unite with Śiva, the Mind, in an embrace of love which is often portrayed sexually. It is represented as a supreme marriage between Being and Becoming, which is said to cause a flood of joy throughout body and mind.

Tanzania
Area: 937,000 km²
Population: 17,600,000
Capital: Dodoma

Tanzania, republic of East Africa, bounded on the north by Kenya, Lake Victoria and Uganda; on the west by Rwanda, Burundi, Lake Tanganyika, Zambia and Lake Malawi; on the south by Mozambique; and on the east by the Indian Ocean. Area 937,000 km².

Along the coast lies a plain, varying in width from 15 to 65 km, behind which the country rises gradually to a plateau constituting the greater part of the hinterland. This plateau falls sharply from a general level of 1225 m to the level of lakes Tanganyika (765 m) and Malawi (490 m), which mark the Great Rift Valley, and is also broken by the extensive basin of the Rufiji river. The highest points are in the north-east, where there are extinct volcanoes, Kilimanjaro (6010 m) and Mount Meru (4560 m). In the south-west are the Livingstone, or Kipengere, Mountains, where the highest peak is over 2743 m.

Tanzania contains many diverse ethnic groups, many from outside Africa. The total population (1979) is 17,600,000, and the main towns are Dar es Salaam, Tanga, Mwanza and Zanzibar. The capital is Dodoma.

The traditional economy is based on shifting

Tanzania. *Ruaha National Park, established in 1964, is a sanctuary for game animals.*

cultivation of millet and sorghum, increasingly supplemented by maize and cassava, bananas and sweet potatoes. Most farmers keep some cattle, and there is some animal husbandry in the north. Coffee, cotton and cashew nuts are grown for sale in specific regions. Plantation agriculture is also important, sisal, tea and sugar dominating. Cloves form the main cash crop of Zanzibar, and especially Pemba. Another important element in the rural economy is small-scale fishing along the sea and lake shores.

Mining is largely confined to the working of one diamond deposit, although other minerals exist, including both coal and iron ore.

The unit of currency is the shilling, of 100 cents.

On 5 February 1977 the two political parties were merged under the name of the Chama Cha Mapinduzi (CCM or Revolutionary Party), of which President Nyerere was unanimously elected chairman. Although the National Assembly is nominally the legislative body, the uncontested power and influence of the national executive of the CCM confirms it as the paramount policy-making body.

The official languages are Swahili and English, but the tribal languages retain their importance.

History. Arab traders visited the Tanganyika area in medieval times and later opened up the great slave route from Bangamoyo on the Indian Ocean to Ujiji on Lake Tanganyika. The British explorer, Richard Burton, first entered the territory in 1856, and was soon followed by Speke, Livingstone and Stanley. The territory was visited in 1884 by Karl Peters, who concluded several treaties with the local chiefs and so paved the way in 1885 for the establishment of a German protectorate. After the First World War virtually the whole of German Tanganyika was mandated to Britain.

Economic problems for the African peasant, and resentment of the privilege accorded to a minority of white settlers, encouraged, in 1954, the formation of the Tanganyikan African National Union (TANU) led by

Julius Nyerere. In December 1961 Tanganyika became an independent state within the Commonwealth, with Julius Nyerere as premier. It became a republic within the Commonwealth in December 1962 and Nyerere was the first president. In April 1964 Zanzibar united with Tanganyika and in October 1964 the composite state changed its name to Tanzania. Zanzibar won approval for a separate constitution in 1979.

Taoism (Chinese *tao*, way, path), a religious belief or approach practised in China up to 1949 and still having some scattered followers in China and other parts of the world. The Way is the way of life itself, to be discovered intuitively rather than intellectually and revealed in actual living. Thus Taoism has no dogma, for the ever-changing flow and growth of life itself cannot be bound by man-made categories but is free, unknowable and undifferentiated. It is One, the Tao, whole and unbound, to which each man must find his own relationship.

Taoism was first given form in the 6th century BC by Lao Tzu, who wrote the *Tao Te Ching*, the *Book of the Virtuous Way*, which is second only to the Bible in the numbers printed each year. It describes the Way as a perfect inner balance arising when man's heart responds to life with spontaneous harmony and virtue; conventional virtue as we understand it already belongs to a corrupt society. There is no doctrine of sin in Taoism (and indeed no word for it equivalent to the Western concept). Bad behaviour was regarded as stupidity and ignorance, for no one would knowingly violate the natural Way. Two major concepts of Taoism are stillness within movement and strength within gentleness. The penetrating profundity of Taoism always existed side by side with, and was eventually largely taken over by, more superficial beliefs in magical heavens where reigned the Immortals; in Blessed Isles of the West where the drug of immortality grew; in supernatural powers gained through yoga; and in magic of all kinds.

See also YIN AND YANG.

Tape Recorder, an instrument for recording and reproducing sound on magnetic tape. The transport system sends the tape at a constant speed, usually 3·75 or 7·5 in/s (9·525 or 19·05 mm/s), past three tape heads. The first two are used in the recording process, and are driven by the recording amplifier: one is known as the 'erase head', and wipes off any signal already on the tape, while the second, the 'record head', puts the new sound on. The third is the 'playback head', which reproduces the sound on the tape, passed through an amplifier to a loudspeaker.

Nowadays, all original recordings are made on magnetic tape. It is possible to mix a master tape, tailoring the original sound (by cutting or boosting certain frequencies, adding echo, phasing, etc.) to suit the desires of the producer. From the master it is possible to make copies and also disc matrices from which records can be pressed. The only real disadvantage of tape is 'hiss' (a random high-frequency sound) which can be reduced by filtering, usually by the Dolby system.

By making the contact between recording and reproducer electrical (tape-to-head), rather than mechanical (stylus-to-groove), the impossibility of making a point track with perfect accuracy in a modulated groove is obviated. There is no wear on tapes, and, unlike a worn stylus, a worn tape head does not damage the record material. In 1955 came the introduction of stereophonic tape records. The cartridge, using an endless loop and the cassette, enclosing two reels, has solved the handling problem.

See also STEREOPHONY; QUADRAPHONY.

Tapestry (French *tapis*, carpet), textile wall-hanging in which a design, often of a pictorial character, is woven on a loom by the use of different coloured threads in the woof. The weaver works from a full-scale cartoon. The word tapestry is used incorrectly to describe an embroidery such as the Bayeux Tapestry. The word is also used of coverings of furniture or carpets, and wool embroidery known generally as 'needlepoint'.

In antiquity textile wall-hangings were widely used in the East and by the Greeks and Romans. In the Middle Ages tapestries decorated domestic and ecclesiastical buildings, and their manufacture is particularly associated with France. The oldest surviving French tapestries are scenes from the Book of Revelation from Angers cathedral, woven in the late 14th century at Paris. Later the centre of manufacture moved to Arras, which became so famous as to give its name to the product. In the 16th century the main centre shifted to Flanders, and the famous Vatican tapestries of St Peter and St Paul were woven in Brussels between 1516 and 1519 after cartoons by Raphael. In the 17th century France

Tapir, the Malayan tapir, Tapirus indicus. *The colouration provides camouflage in forest.*

again became an important centre with the establishment of the state factory of the Hôtel Royal des Gobelins by Louis XIV in 1662. Another French tapestry manufactory was Aubusson, established in 1665. Aubusson tapestries are distinguished by subdued colouring and complex designs. Both Gobelins and Aubusson maintained their high standard of hand-woven manufacture until modern times. In 1954–57 the Aubusson factory executed the Coventry Cathedral hanging, *Christ in Glory*, designed by Graham Sutherland.

In England the Royal Manufactory of tapestries was established at Mortlake in 1619. It employed 50 Flemish weavers. Tapestries were woven from designs by van Dyck, Rubens and other artists. The factory closed in 1703. Foremost among 19th-century English tapestry designers were Sir Edward Burne-Jones and William Morris. Today tapestries are again recognised as works of art; one of the most famous modern designers is Victor Vasarely.

Tapeworm, see CESTODA.

Tapioca, see CASSAVA.

Tapir, any member of the family Tapiridae in suborder Ceratomorpha (tapirs and rhinoceroses) of the order Perissodactyla, which also includes the horse. They have a short, movable trunk, four front toes, and no horns, and form one of the oldest mammalian types. The skin is hairy and very thick, the tail is rudimentary. Tapirs frequent forests and are nocturnal, living chiefly on vegetable matter, though probably omnivorous. Of the four living species, *Tapirus indicus*, the largest, is Malayan. The rest occur in Central and South America. These are black when adult, the young being striped yellow and white. Tapirs are strong but shy and inoffensive.

Tapping, in surgery, an operation to draw off an accumulation of fluid in a body cavity. A puncture is made through the overlying tissues and a small tube inserted. The fluid then releases itself by its own pressure, or is withdrawn by suction.

Tar Sands, or bituminous sands, sandy or clayey material impregnated with petroleum-type materials, with similar origins to petroleum. The most outstanding example is the Athabasca deposits of North Alberta in Canada, which may have reserves equal to all known petroleum reserves in the world.

Tara, village of County Meath, Republic of Ireland, on the Boyne, 10 km south of Navan. The Hill of Tara (154 m) was in ancient times the religious, political and cultural capital of

Tapestry. The Lady with the Unicorn, *French c.1500.*

Ireland. It was a royal residence until 640.

Tarantella, lively courtship dance from southern Italy. It is danced by couples, the movement having a sharp and neat quality, and is performed at a quick tempo. One theory for the origin of its name is that a dance at this speed would allow a victim bitten by a tarantula spider to sweat the poison out of the body.

Taranto (ancient *Tarentum*), Italian seaport and capital of Taranto province in Apulia, on the Gulf of Taranto, 80 km south-east of Bari. It is a naval base. The large iron and steel works is one of the most ambitious projects of the government's regional policy. It also has chemical, oil refining, and oyster and mussel fishing industries. Population (1979) 247,680.

Taranto, Gulf of, inlet of the Ionian Sea, separating the 'toe' and 'heel' of Italy, bordered by Calabria, Basilicata and Apulia. The main town on the gulf is Taranto.

Tarantula, name originally applied to the wolf-spider *Lycosa tarentula* (family Lycosidae), of southern Europe, but now used for any member of the family Theraphosidae found in Europe and America. Theraphosids are large spiders, *Aphonopelma* reaching a body length of 5 cm and a leg span of 12·5 cm. They are no more poisonous than other spiders of similar size. They burrow in the ground and catch their prey by pouncing on it and not by means of a web.

Tarawa, see KIRIBATI AND TUVALU.

Taraxacum, a genus of herbaceous perennials, of the Compositae; there are many species, of which *T. officinale* is the dandelion, and *T. bicorne* is grown as a source of rubber in Russia. The dried roots, when roasted, make a coffee substitute.
See also CHICORY.

Tarbes, French town, capital of the *département* of Hautes-Pyrénées, on the River Adour. Tarbes has a 12th-century cathedral. It is noted for its horses and has a school of artillery, armament works and manufactures shoes, furniture, electrical apparatus, machinery and pottery. Population (1975) 57,765.

Tardigrada, or water bears, are microscopic animals up to 0·5 mm long with stumpy bodies carrying four pairs of claw-like legs. They feed on plant-cell contents. A few marine species are found among sand grains, but most live in the water films on terrestrial mosses and lichens.

Tare. The hairy tare is *Vicia hirsuta*, the slender tare, *Vicia tenuissima*; both are leguminous trailing annuals native to Britain. The tares of the Bible are probably darnel.
See also RYE GRASS.

Target, the object at which archers and riflemen aim. In archery a target is a circular frame of straw, painted with concentric rings of 122-millimetre width; there are five rings, counting respectively 1, 3, 5, 7 or 9 points. For some time 'match' targets of rectangular shape were solely used by soldiers; the 'bull' counted 4 points, the inner ring 3, a 'magpie' (a shot in the second of the target's rings) 2 points, and an 'outer' (outside any of the rings) 1 point. In most armies this type of target is used for elementary training. Advanced training is carried out with more realistic targets, for example, ones shaped like the head and shoulders of a man.

Tariffs, taxes paid on imports or exports for protection or revenue purposes. The General Agreement on Tariffs and Trade (GATT) is the international agency through which agreements on tariffs are made.

Tarkington, (Newton) Booth (1869–1946), US dramatist, novelist and essayist. He was successful with his first book, *The Gentleman from Indiana*, 1899, the model for further realistic novels of Middle West life. He twice won the Pulitzer Prize with *The Magnificent Ambersons*, 1918, and *Alice Adams*, 1921. He also wrote *The Conquest of Canaan*, 1905, and the *Plutocrat*, 1927.

Taro, or eddo, *Colocasia antiquorum* and its variety *esculenta*, tropical species of the Araceae, often used as a foliage plant. Its rhizomes are poisonous when raw, but once boiled form a nutritious starchy food.

Tarot. 18th-century Italian Tarot cards.

Tarot, a pack of cards of ancient origin, used as a method of divination. Its beginnings are uncertain although theories have linked it with Egypt and India. Its conception appears to be principally medieval and Western, but many Tarot scholars hold the view that at least the trump and pip cards date back to antiquity, and that the symbolism has evolved from an ancient occult tradition which contains a profound significance.

The pack consists of 78 cards divided into the Greater Arcana and the Lesser Arcana. The Greater Arcana comprise 22 trump cards (or tarots) considered the 'keys' of the pack, and named according to their picture symbols, e.g. the Juggler, the High Priestess and the Wheel of Fortune. They are said to correspond with the 22 letters of the Hebrew alphabet, each letter having an occult significance in the Kabbalah tradition. The remaining 56 cards (the Lesser Arcana) are similar to the ordinary playing cards pack except that they display pictures as well as numbers; the four suits are rods or wands, cups, swords, and shekels or pentacles, (corresponding to clubs, hearts, spades and diamonds), and as well as a king, queen and knave, each suit has a knight.

See also CARDS, PLAYING; DIVINATION; NUMEROLOGY.

Tarpaulin, coarse cloth, usually of jute, covered with tar to produce a waterproof material, used for roofing, etc.

Tarpeia, in Roman legend, daughter of Spurius Tarpeius, commander of the Capitol during the war that followed the rape of the Sabine women. Tarpeia offered to betray the Capitol to its besiegers if they would give her what they wore on their left arms, meaning their bracelets. The agreement was made, and Tarpeia opened one of the gates. But the Sabines obeyed the letter of their undertaking by crushing her to death with their shields.

Tarpon, *Megalops atlanticus*, in order Anguilliformes, a giant herring-like fish plentiful in warm American seas and off West African coasts. It grows to a length of 2 m or more, and to a weight of over 135 kg. Its scales are made into ornaments and are sometimes as much as 12 cm in diameter.

Tarquinius, name of an Etruscan family in early Roman history, to which the fifth and seventh legendary kings of Rome belonged. *Lucius Tarquinius Superbus*, the seventh and last king of Rome, 534–510 BC, though a tyrant at home, enhanced the power and prosperity of Rome, defeating the Volscians and taking Gabii. Following the rape of Lucretia in which his son was involved, Tarquinius Superbus and his family were exiled in 510 BC. He obtained the help of Lars Porsena, king of Clusium, who marched against Rome but then made peace with the Romans, and of his son-in-law, Octavius Mamilius, who induced the Latin states to declare war against Rome; but they were defeated at the battle of Lake Regillus. Tarquinius fled to Cumae, where he died.

Tarragon, *Artemisia dracunculus*, an aromatic perennial plant belonging to the Compositae, the green or dried leaves of which are used for flavouring vinegar, for cooking and salads.

Tarragona, city, capital of Tarragona province, Spain, on the Mediterranean coast at the mouth of the River Francolí. The older part of Tarragona stands on a high rock and has massive walls, portions of which date back to about the 6th century BC. The Romanesque and Gothic archiepiscopal cathedral stands on the site of a temple of Jupiter. The modernised port has a trade in the produce of the Ebro valley, including wine, and a petrochemicals industry. Population (1981) 111,689.

Tarrasa, town in Barcelona province, Spain, an important industrial centre, with cotton and woollen mills, and a trade in agricultural produce, oil and wine. Population (1981) 155,360.

Tarsier, *Tarsius spectrum*, small primate intermediate between lemurs and monkeys, a native of the East Indies. It is about the size of a small rat, has very large eyes, very long ankle bones, and sucker-like discs on the fingers and toes. The tarsier lives in trees, is nocturnal and feeds mainly on insects. Its skull closely resembles that of the ape.

Tarsus, city of Cilicia in Asia Minor, on the River Cydnus, about 32 km west south-west of Adana. It was the birthplace of St Paul and, from AD 72, capital of the Roman province of Cilicia.

Tartan (from French *tiretaine*, a linsey-woolsey cloth), has come to signify the distinctive woollen cloth in which coloured threads are woven into weft and warp to give a checkered or cross-striped effect, some patterns being regarded by certain highland Scottish families or clans as their exclusive property. In this modern sense tartans probably date from the upsurge of nationalism which led to the Scottish rebellion of 1745, after the failure of which they were proscribed for 35 years. The rescinding of the proscription led generally to new sets of designs being adopted by the qualifying families which did not correspond to those in earlier family portraits.

See also HIGHLAND DRESS.

Tartaric Acid, otherwise dihydroxysuccinic acid, or 2,3-dihydroxybutanedioic acid, $(CH(OH)\cdot COOH)_2$, commonly occurring vegetable acid, contained in grapes and other fruits. The acid forms large transparent crystals, is readily soluble in water and alcohol, but insoluble in ether (melting point $167°C$). Like other dicarboxylic acids, it forms both hydrogen and normal salts. The acid potassium salt is 'cream of tartar' and the potassium sodium salt is 'Rochelle salt'. Tartaric acid is used in the preparation of effervescing drinks and in baking powders. There are three optical isomers of the acid, viz. $(+)$-tartaric, $(-)$-tartaric and meso-tartaric (inactive). Racemic acid is a mixture of the $(+)$ and $(-)$ isomers in equal parts.

See also STEREOCHEMISTRY.

Tartars, see TATARS.

Tartarus, in Homer, a place of punishment reserved for the rebel Titans, as far below Hades as heaven is above the earth. Later poets use the name as synonymous with Hades.

Tartini, Giuseppe (1692–1770), Italian composer and violinist. In 1728 he started a violin school at Padua. His compositions for violin comprise about 150 sonatas (including the famous 'Devil's Trill'), 50 trios and about 140 concertos. He made improvements in the technique and construction of the bow.

Tartu (Russian *Yurev*; German *Dorpat*), city and cultural centre of the Estonian SSR, USSR, 160 km south-east of Tallinn. It has food, engineering and metal-working industries. Tartu was founded by the Russians in 1030 on the site of the Estonian village of Tarpatu, and belonged variously to the Livonian Order, Muscovy, Poland and Sweden. Population (1980) 106,000.

Tashkent, capital of Tashkent *oblast*, and of the Uzbek SSR. It is the largest city in Soviet Asia and the fourth largest in the Soviet Union. Situated in the valley of the River Chirchik, it is an important rail and air passenger transport centre. It has textile and mining machinery works, and a large number of light industries. Population (1980) 1,816,000.

Tasman, Abel Janszoon (1603–59), Dutch navigator and explorer. After journeys in China and India, he was sent by the Dutch East India Company to investigate the extent of Australia. On his second voyage, 1642–43, he discovered Tasmania (which he named Van Diemen's Land), New Zealand, Fiji and Tonga. In 1644, he explored the Gulf of Carpentaria.

Tasmania, state of Australia, an island once joined to the mainland but now separated by Bass Strait, which is c.225 km wide. It is the smallest of the six Australian states with an area of $67,800 km^2$. Over 50 islands are administered by Tasmania: the Furneaux group, at the eastern end of Bass Strait, and those off the north-east corner of Tasmania including Flinders islands, Cape Barren islands, and Clarke islands; besides these are Chapell islands and the Kent group.

Tasmania has two mountain chains which are continuations of the Dividing Range of the mainland. The eastern range has an average height of 1150 m and runs parallel with the east coast. The western chain is an elevated tableland in the centre of the island averaging 915 m in height; it contains large lakes. The main rivers are the Derwent, about 210 km long (on the estuary of which lies Hobart, the capital, with a deep and sheltered harbour), the Huon, about 160 km long, and the Arthur —these last two draining into the Southern Ocean. In the north, flowing into Bass Strait, are the Mersey and the Tamar, which is navigable up to Launceston 64 km from its mouth. The rivers Gordon and King on the west coast are of remarkable beauty.

The population in 1979 was 417,700.

The chief land-use is sown and natural pastures which are used for dairy cattle and sheep. The mild, moist climate is highly suitable for fruit and vegetable growing. Tasmania has a higher percentage of land under forest than any other Australian state. The forests have influenced the development of one of the most important industries— pulp, paper and newsprint. The state has important deposits of silver, lead and zinc at Rosebery; tin at Renison and Cleveland; copper and pyrites at Mount Lyell (near Queenstown); and iron ore in the Savage river area. There is tungsten and tin at Rossarden and mineral sands and tungsten on King Island. Mining has stimulated mineral refining and smelting. Of growing importance are industrial gases (liquid oxygen and nitrogen) which are manufactured at Hobart, Launceston and Burnie. At Devonport and Ulverstone vegetables are frozen and canned.

Tasmania has an upper house (Legislative Council) and a lower house (House of Assembly). Power of government is vested in the Governor, the Cabinet (10 members), and the two houses.

Tasmania was discovered by Tasman in 1642, and he called it Van Diemen's Land. It was proved an island by circumnavigation by Bass and Flinders in 1798. The earliest settlement, mostly of convicts, was established in 1803. In 1825 the island, previously part of New South Wales, was proclaimed a separate colony, and in 1856 the name was changed to Tasmania and responsible government granted. In 1901 Tasmania united with the states of the mainland in the Commonwealth of Australia.

Tasmanian Devil, *Sarcophilus*, a small mammal of the family Dasyuridae, order Marsupialia. It has a compact body with a large head, brownish-black fur with a white breastmark, and resembles a bear, although it is only about 65 cm long and has a bushy tail of about 25 cm. It has strong teeth and is irritable. It has recently become extinct in mainland Australia, but still occurs in remote parts of Tasmania.

Tass (Russian abbreviation for Telegraphic Agency of the Soviet Union), official Soviet Russian news agency attached to the USSR Council of Ministers. It was established in 1925, and is the only agency in the USSR for both internal and foreign news.

Tasso, Torquato (1544–95), Italian poet. In 1572 he entered the service of Duke Alfonso at Ferrara. In 1576 he showed signs of mental derangement, but escaped from his place of confinement, wandered through Italy, and, in 1579, returned to the court at Ferrara. The duke received him coldly and Tasso, wounded by some real or fancied insult, hurled denunciations at the whole household, and the duke confined him as insane. During his confinement he produced much admirable verse, a number of philosophical dialogues, and an *Apologia* for *La Gerusalemme Liberata*, which had been completed by 1575 and published without his consent, with many errors. The grotesque contrast between his fate and the rising fame of his masterpiece roused public interest and he was consequently released in 1586.

La Gerusalemme Liberata, an idealisation of the first crusade, had been submitted to several critics, and on his release Tasso rewrote his great epic in the light of his critics' suggestions. The result, *La Gerusalemme Conquistata*, 1592, was a pedantic effusion, in which he expurgated many of the passages that were to make the *Gerusalemme Liberata* for long the most popular work in Italian literature.

Taste, see TONGUE.

Tatar Autonomous Soviet Socialist Republic, formed in 1920, lies in East European RSFSR, USSR, occupying a lowland area crossed by the Middle Volga and Lower Kama. The northern part is in the mixed (mainly deciduous) forest belt, and the south is wooded steppe with black earth soils. There are extensive oil deposits and oil-extraction (largest in USSR), engineering, chemical, woodworking and fur industries. Grain, sunflowers and potatoes are grown, and horticulture and dairy-farming are widespread. The main urban centres are Kazan (the capital), Chistopol, Naberezhniye, Chelny, Almetyevsk and Bugulma. Area 68,000 km^2. Population (1980) 3,454,000; mostly Tatars and Russians.

Tatars (often, but wrongly, written 'Tartars'), peoples of mixed ethnic, linguistic and cultural origin, nowadays speaking Turkic languages. Originally they were dispersed over the steppes of eastern European Russia, central Asia and Siberia. In the 8th century the word 'Tatar' was used to denote the Mongolian-speaking peoples of the northern China frontier regions. It was later applied to Genghis Khan's Mongols, and particularly to Turkic peoples, such as the Bulgars, Qïpchägs, Turkomans and others, who preceded and followed the Mongolian invasion of Europe.

Today Tatars farm, fish and breed horses. They are Sunni Muslims, but retain shamanist practices. Traditionally many were teachers, traders, Islamic missionaries and craftsmen. They now number between five and six million and many are urbanised.

Tate, Sir Henry (1819–99), British merchant and art patron. He was a sugar merchant, and patented machinery for making sugar cubes. His firm of Henry Tate & Sons later became Tate & Lyle. He was instrumental in founding the Tate Gallery in 1897.

Tate, Nahum (1652–1715), English poet. He wrote some indifferent plays, including an adaptation of Shakespeare's *King Lear* which was defended by Dr Johnson and performed well into the 19th century. In 1682 he wrote, with Dryden's assistance, a second part to the poet's satire *Absalom and Achitophel*. In 1692 he was appointed poet laureate, as a result of which Pope pilloried him in the *Dunciad*; and in 1702 he was made Historiographer Royal. His chief original poem was *Panacea or a Poem on Tea*, 1700, but he is remembered mainly for the metrical version of the Psalms in which he collaborated with Nicholas Brady.

Tate Gallery, Millbank, London, contains the national collection of British painting from the 16th century to the present day, modern foreign painting from approximately 1880, and modern sculpture. The Tate Gallery has unique collections of the work of Turner and Blake, also one of the best collections of Pre-Raphaelite painting. More recently it has begun to form a major collection of modern British prints and an archive of modern British art.

Sir Henry Tate financed the building of the gallery, which was opened in 1897. This housed the Tate gift of 65 British paintings, the collection purchased under the Chantrey bequest the Vernon collection, bequeathed in 1847, and the Watts gift. Sir Henry Tate made possible the addition, in 1899, of eight further galleries, and in 1910, through the generosity of Sir Joseph Duveen senior, the wing to house the Turner bequest of 1856, was opened, while his son Lord Duveen, gave additional galleries in 1926 and an immense sculpture hall, opened in 1937. In 1977 a new extension made available 50 per cent more space for showing the permanent collections, and includes a large, well-equipped conservation department.

The nucleus of the collection of modern foreign art was established by the bequest of Sir Hugh Lane in 1915, and the endowment by Samuel Courtauld in 1923. An effort has been made since the war to clarify and extend its separate functions as the National Collection of Modern Art and National Collection of Historical British Painting.

Tati, Jacques (1908–82), French film actor and director; real name J. Tatischeff. He was a music-hall player before appearing in films. *Jour de fête, Monsieur Hulot's Holiday, Mon Oncle* and *Playtime* achieved great popularity and won awards; they depend on Tati's imagination as a director and exploitation of his long, thin figure and bird-like mannerisms. A later film was *Traffic*, 1971.

Tattersall's, name of the firm established in 1766 by Richard Tattersall to sell horses by public auction. Today it holds large bloodstock auctions at Park Paddocks, Newmarket, at fixed times annually.

Tattersall's Committee is in no way related to the above; it is an authority set up to settle questions relating to bets, wagers or gaming transactions on horse racing. It has the power to report defaulters to the Jockey Club. The defaulter is then warned off by the Jockey Club until the report is withdrawn.

Tatting, a lace worked with a small handheld shuttle and thread which is knotted at frequent intervals to produce the required formation. Tatting was known in England and Europe in the Middle Ages but its high point was in the 17th century. It is today enjoying a revival. Tatting is now generally worked with embroidery or crochet threads, stranded cotton or wool, and plastic shuttles. Old shuttles, now collectors' items, included ones of silver, mother-of-pearl and tortoiseshell. Tatting instructions are printed like knitting patterns. Technical terms include the basic ring (a loop of thread composed of tatted knots).

See also MACRAMÉ.

Tattoo (Dutch *tap toe*, literally 'tap shut', meaning the time of closing public-houses) is the signal, by drum-beat or bugle, for soldiers to return to their quarters at night, just before 'lights out'. The word is also applied to a military pageant consisting of spectacular evolutions with musical accompaniment, performed at night by artificial light. The Tattoo is a highlight of the Edinburgh Festival.

Tattooing. *The members of certain Japanese underworld sects are elaborately tattooed.*

Tattooing, custom of marking the skin with incisions which are filled with colouring matter to produce an indelible stain. Practised since Palaeolithic times, the Thracians used it as a sign of rank, and later it was used to identify convicts and slaves. In some societies tattooing is an indication of adult status and may be performed during initiation. In western societies it survives as decoration.

Tauber, Richard, real name Ernst Seiffert (1892–1948), Austrian-born tenor, conductor and composer. He made his operatic début in 1913 as Tamino in *The Magic Flute*, becoming an unrivalled interpreter of Mozart's tenor roles. Later he appeared in many operettas written for him by Lehár, including *The Land of Smiles*, in which he sang in London in 1931.

Taunton, the county town of Somerset, England, 50 km north-east of Exeter, 70 km south-west of Bristol, situated in the fertile valley of Taunton Deane. Taunton is an agricultural, educational and administrative centre, and an Army headquarters. It is the chief marketing centre for west Somerset and east Devon. Local industries include textile and leather goods; gloves; aeronautical instruments; agricultural, mining and other machinery, and cider-making. The Admiralty Hydrographic Establishment is here. Population (1981) 35,326.

Taupo, lake of North Island, New Zealand, situated in the centre of the island, 357 m above sea-level. Area 600 km², maximum depth 159 m, drained by the Waikato river.

Tauranga, town of North Island, New Zealand, on the Bay of Plenty. Its chief industries are tourism and farming. Population (1980) 49,300.

Taurus, 'the Bull', the second sign of the zodiac and a conspicuous northern constellation. In the conventional constellation figure Taurus represents only the forepart of a bull. The V-shaped Hyades cluster forms the head with the bright red Aldebaran (Alpha Tauri) as the fiery eye. The Pleiades, the best known of all star clusters, are in the shoulder. The tips of the horns are marked by Beta and Zeta Tauri. Close to Zeta Tauri are the remnants of the supernova of AD 1054 now known as the Crab Nebula. Visible as gaseous nebulosity, it is also a strong radio and X-ray source and the location of one of the first pulsars to be discovered. T Tauri is the prototype of a class of variable stars thought to represent an early stage of stellar formation.

Taurus Mountains (Turkish *Toros Dağlari*), range in the south of Asiatic Turkey, extending from the River Euphrates to the Aegean Sea. Portions of the range are known by different names as Ala Dağları, Bolkar Dağları and Bey Dağları. Heights exceed 3000 m in several places.

Tautology (Greek *tauto*, the same), figure of speech employing superfluous words that are in the same grammatical relation; in this way it differs from pleonasm. Needless repetition is seen in phrases such as 'free, gratis, and for nothing', 'the shortest and nearest way'.

See also FIGURE OF SPEECH.

Tautomerism, in chemistry, the phenomenon whereby some chemicals exist in more than one chemical form. Such substances are usually present as equilibrium mixtures of the interconvertible forms, and show the chemical properties of both forms, depending on the reaction conditions.

Tavener, John (1944–), British composer. His dramatic cantata *The Whale* delighted critics when it appeared in 1968; both it and *A Celtic Requiem* (1968–69) stamp Tavener as the most spirited English exponent of avant-garde collage. More recent works include the monodrama *The Immurement of Antigone* and *Akhmatova: Requiem*.

Tavern (Latin *taberna*, booth, hut), a house where wines and other alcoholic liquors are sold and where accommodation is given to travellers. Taverns existed in England as early as the 13th century. By an Act of 1284 they were ordered to be closed at curfew. In Edward III's reign only three were allowed in London. By Edward VI (1552–53) 40 were allowed in London, eight in York, six in Bristol, and three or four each in some 20 other towns.

Taverner, John (c.1495–1545), English composer. In 1526 he became choirmaster at Cardinal College, Oxford (later Christ

Church) and from 1530 lived in Boston, Lincolnshire. His works include eight masses, of which *The Westerne Wynde* is the best known. Especially important is his mass *Gloria tibi Trinitas*, from which was developed an instrumental piece known as an *In Nomine*. He also wrote motets, services, etc.

Tawney, Richard Henry (1880–1962), British historian. He was professor of economic history at London University, 1931–49. His *Religion and the Rise of Capitalism*, 1926, established him as the spokesman of a new school of thought on the growth of modern capitalist society. His other publications include: *The Agrarian Problem in the Sixteenth Century*, 1912; *Tudor Economic Documents* (with Eileen Power), 1951; and *Lionel Cranfield as Merchant and Minister*, 1958.

Tax Haven, a country or region that levies relatively low taxes and is therefore attractive to companies or individuals who pay high taxes in their country of origin. Companies can benefit by opening offices or subsidiary companies there and channelling part of their business through these.

Taxation, the method of raising the revenue required for public services through compulsory levies.

There are four canons set out by Adam Smith on the standards by which the quality of a tax should be judged. These are: (1) equality —the subjects of the state should contribute to the support of the state as nearly as possible according to their ability; (2) certainty, not arbitrariness; (3) convenience of payment; (4) economy of collection. Adam Smith recognised that a progressive tax system is more equitable than a proportional one.

Classification of Taxation. Taxes can be classified according to a number of different principles, e.g. the tax base (income tax, etc.), the regularity of levy (income tax to be paid annually), and taxes arising on specific events such as estate duty and capital gains tax. The distinction between direct and indirect taxes (e.g. between income tax and value-added tax) relates in practice rather to the method of collection than to incidence.

Taxicab, see CAB; HACKNEY CARRIAGE.

Taxidermy, the art of preparing the skins of vertebrate animals so as to give them the appearance of life and preserve their characteristics as nearly as possible. The art began to be practised in the 16th century. The body is removed and the skin is painted inside with a preservative soap. 'Setting up' may be done by wiring and filling in with fine wood wool. Another method is to retain the skeleton, wash it with carbolic acid, and work over it with tow or clay to produce a shape like that of the body. With larger birds and most mammals an alternative method is to prepare a mould of plaster by arranging the hardened carcase in a suitable attitude. Paper casts are made by pressing layers of paper into the dry mould, so that when the model is mounted and prepared the skin can be drawn over it. Today smaller animals and plants can be preserved by freeze-drying. The results are permanent and include the internal organs.

Taxing Master, in England and Wales, an official of the High Court who assesses the amount of costs payable by the loser to the winner of litigation in that court.

Taxodium, a small genus of deciduous coniferous trees in the family Taxodiaceae, native to North America. *T. distichum*, the swamp cypress, has a very thick trunk, the base often swollen, while knees or hollow protuberances rise from the roots when the tree grows in swampy soil. The timber is of considerable value. Other species include *T. heterophyllum*, the Chinese water pine, and *T. mucronatum*.

Taxonomy, the science of biological classification, involving the division of living organisms into taxa (biological categories, such as genera and species). Traditionally, taxonomy has been based on the morphological and anatomical similarities and differences between groups. An expert in a particular animal or plant group is usually able to classify an unknown species simply by looking at it and comparing it with known species. Sometimes this is insufficient, however, and techniques have been developed to provide a more objective basis for classification.

The new methods are known as 'experimental taxonomy' and the most important are chemotaxonomy, cytotaxonomy and numerical taxonomy. In chemotaxonomy, certain chemical constituents are extracted from organisms under investigation and the similarities and differences in molecular structure of these constituents are used as an aid in the classification of the organisms. Cytotaxonomy is the use of microscopic characters in classification, particularly the number and structure of the chromosomes. The electron microscope enables minute details of structure, such as surface sculpturing on pollen grains, to be used as taxonomic characters. Numerical taxonomy involves the use of computers to compare taxa in respect of large numbers of characters and produce a statistically based classification.

Besides its use in identifying individual species, taxonomic classification is used to arrange organisms into higher categories that define how closely they are related. The only natural category is the species; the classification groupings above this: genus, family, order, class, phylum or division, and kingdom, are theoretical.

See also CLASSIFICATION OF ANIMALS; CLASSIFICATION OF PLANTS; BINOMIAL SYSTEM OF NOMENCLATURE.

Taxus, see YEW.

Tay, river and firth of Scotland, rising in the Central Highlands, and flowing first northeast then, at the confluence with the Tummel, south-east. The Earn joins it at its estuary. The length of the river, including the firth, is 184 km. It is crossed at Dundee by the famous Tay Bridge. The chief port is Dundee, but the river is navigable as far as Perth. The total area of the Tay basin is nearly 6400 km².

Taylor, A(lan) J(ohn) P(ercivale) (1906–), British historian and journalist. As fellow and tutor of modern history at Magdalen College, Oxford, Taylor became known for his authoritative studies of German and Austrian 19th- and 20th-century constitutional history. He is also known from his broadcast and television appearances. His publications include: *The Course of German History*, 1945; *The Struggle for Mastery in Europe*, 1954; and *Essays in English History*, 1976.

Taylor, Brook (1685–1731), British mathematician. He became a Fellow of the Royal Society in 1712, and was its secretary from 1714–19. In 1716 he went to Paris and had an enthusiastic reception from the French savants. His *Methodus incrementorum* and a *Treatise on Linear Perspective* were published in 1715. The former contains the proof of Taylor's Theorem.

Taylor, Elizabeth (1932–), British-born film actress who became famous for her film appearances while still a child. These included parts in *Lassie Come Home*, *National Velvet* and *Little Women*. She later excelled in sultry rôles, and her films include: *Raintree County*, *Cat on a Hot Tin Roof*, *Cleopatra* and *Who's Afraid of Virginia Woolf?* Her only Oscar, however, was given for a most undistinguished film, *Butterfield 8*, made in 1960. She made her Broadway stage début as Regina in *The Little Foxes* in 1981.

Taylor, Jeremy (1613–67), English prelate. He took holy orders in 1634. His sermons attracted the attention of Laud, to whom he became chaplain, shortly afterwards becoming one of the king's chaplains. He later settled in Carmarthenshire, and wrote his well-known works, *The Liberty of Prophesying*, 1646 (a plea for toleration); *The Rule and Exercises of Holy Living*, 1650; and *The Rule and Exercises of Holy Dying*, 1651. His more formal treatises include *An Apology for Authorised and Set Forms of Liturgy*, 1646; *The Worthy Communicant*, 1660; and *Ductor Dubitantium, or the Rule of Conscience*, 1660, intended as a handbook of Christian casuistry.

Taylor, Zachary (1784–1850), 12th President of the USA. He entered the army in 1808. After the annexation of Texas he resisted the Mexican invasion, and gained the memorable victory over Santa Anna at Buena Vista in 1847. On his return he was elected president (1848) as a Whig, just at the time when the struggle over the extension of slavery had begun, but he died during the negotiations for the Compromise of 1850.

Tayside Region, in Scotland; an amalgamation of the former county of Angus and parts of the counties of Perthshire and Kinross-shire. It is subdivided into three districts— Angus, Perth and Kinross, and the City District of Dundee. Topography varies between that of the Grampians in the north and west, rising to 1214 m at Ben Lawers; the lower range of the Sidlaw Hills, parallel to the Firth of Tay, which forms the southern perimeter of the region; and several low-lying fertile areas such as the Vale of Strathmore, the Carse of Gowrie, and Strathearn. The area is drained by the River Tay which forms the central axis, and the rivers Earn, Isla, and North and South Esk. The city of Dundee is the largest urban centre, but there are several other large towns within the Tayside Region, notably Perth, Arbroath, Forfar, Montrose, Brechin, Carnoustie, Crieff, and Blairgowrie and Rattray. Area 750,305 ha. Population (1981) 391,529.

Tbilisi, or Tiflis, capital city of the Georgian SSR, USSR, and a major industrial and cultural centre situated on the River Kura. It has diverse engineering (machine-tools, equipment for food and textile industries, radio and telegraph equipment, etc.), food and light industries, and is an important transport centre. Known since the 4th century AD, it has been the capital of Georgia or

East Georgia since the 11th century. It became Russian in 1801 and was the capital of independent Georgia (1918–20), and of the Transcaucasian Federal Republic within the USSR (1922–36). Politically it was a stronghold of Social Democracy in Russia. It is a spa; its name derived from the presence of several hot sulphur springs nearby (Georgian *tbili*, warm). Population (1980) 1,080,000.

Tchad, see CHAD.

Tchaikovsky, Pëtr Ilich (1840–93), Russian composer. In 1862 he entered the St Petersburg Conservatoire, where he studied composition with Anton Rubinstein. In 1865 he became a professor at the Moscow Conservatoire. He met Balakirev, but did not join his circle: his music remained cosmopolitan, although it often has a Russian flavour. His early operas, the first two symphonies and the first piano concerto had won him recognition by 1875. Of his 11 operas *Eugene Onegin* and *The Queen of Spades*, both based on Pushkin, have remained in the repertory. The ballets *Swan Lake*, *The Sleeping Beauty* and *The Nutcracker*, three of the six symphonies and the first piano concerto are also favourites. Other characteristic works are the symphonic poems *Romeo and Juliet*, *Francesca da Rimini* and *Hamlet*, the *Capriccio Italien* and *1812 Overture*, the violin concerto and the piano trio. Tchaikovsky also composed church and secular choral works, and many songs and piano pieces.

Te Deum Laudamus ('We praise thee, O God'), non-metrical Latin hymn, found in the Roman breviary at the end of matins. Modern scholars have shown that it consists largely of borrowing from older sources. Its present form is probably due to Niceta, Bishop of Remesiana (d. c.414). It occurs, in English, in Anglican matins.

Te Kanawa, Dame Kiri (1944–), New Zealand soprano. In 1970 she joined the Royal Opera at Covent Garden, where her first major rôle was the Countess in Mozart's *Marriage of Figaro*. Her début with the Metropolitan Opera in New York was as Desdemona in Verdi's *Otello*. During the 1970s she also sang with Lyons Opera, at Glyndebourne, with the Paris Opéra, and in Australia, New Zealand and the USA. Her many other rôles include Fiordiligi, Pamina and Donna Elvira in Mozart operas, and Mimi in Puccini's *La Bohème*.

Tea, beverage used since a remote period in China, introduced into England in 1657. Though it attracted great interest, it was obtainable only by the wealthy until about 1750. At first it was infused and kept in barrels, being drawn like beer, and warmed for use. The first shipment of Indian tea was made from Assam in 1839. Tea is derived from *Camellia sinensis*. The young leaves and shoots (the 'flush') are picked from the bushes, taken to the factory, spread thinly over wire or bamboo trays, and placed on racks to wither. Withering takes, on average, 24 hours. The next process, that of rolling, is generally done by machine. It causes the juice to be exuded, and gives the leaf the twist characteristic of its manufactured state. The leaf is then spread out thinly in the fermenting room, where the air is kept moist, and there in a few hours it changes from green to copper colour. It is then 'fired' by being passed through a hot-air chamber, sorted or classified and packed.

More than one-third of the tea exported from tea-producing countries is consumed in the United Kingdom. In the past tea was always made by pouring water over loose tea-leaves, but nowadays tea-leaves are often contained in tea-bags in Western countries. In Japan traditional tea-drinking ceremonies are still held.

See also MATÉ.

Tchaikovsky. Portrait by N. Kuznetsov, 1893.

Tea Ceremony, Japanese custom, called *cha-no-yu*, which was first practised by Zen priests in the 14th century and spread throughout Japanese society. It is a ritualised performance aimed at achieving a contemplative calm, in which the ritual itself and its implements, chosen for their aesthetic appeal, are the sole focus of attention.

Teak, timber tree indigenous to India, Sri Lanka, Burma, Thailand and Indonesia, particularly Java. It is produced from *Tectona grandis* of the Verbenaceae family, and is a most useful timber, particularly because of its durability, good strength to moderate weight, and small movement when used in fluctuating atmospheres. The usual colour is golden brown, sometimes figured with dark markings. Teak has a variety of uses, especially in shipbuilding, furniture, veneer, and constructional work. Its resistance to a variety of chemical reagents makes it especially valuable in industrial chemical plants and laboratories.

Teal, *Anas crecca*, small freshwater duck, order Anseriformes. The male is dusky grey; the crown of its head deep cinnamon or chestnut; its eye is surrounded by a black band, glossed with green or purple, which unites on the nape; its wing markings are black and white; and its bill is black. The female is mottled brown. It is c.35 cm long.

Tear Gas, a lachrymatory irritant used as a riot control agent and as a harassing agent in warfare. The main tear gases are CA gas or Camite (brombenzylcyanide), CN gas or CAP (chloracetophenone), and CS gas (orthochlorbenzalmalononitrile). CA gas and CN gas were developed in the First World War and CS gas in 1928. They are used in the form of grenades that explode to give a spray or smoke containing the gas. The gases cause a burning sensation in the eyes and tears, difficulty in breathing, and sometimes nausea and vomiting. Although tear gases are often described as non-lethal, they are in fact lethal substances and casualties have been caused by their use. CS gas is widely used by police and armies for the dispersal of rioters. It was also used by the US army in Vietnam. The Geneva Protocol (1925), ratified by many nations, prohibits the use of asphyxiating and poisonous gases in warfare.

Tears, secretion of the lachrymal gland. See also EYE.

Teasel, *Dipsacus*, in the family Dipsacaceae, a genus of prickly biennial herbs, native to Europe, Asia and Northern Africa. *D. fullonum* has two subspecies, *sylvestris*, the wild teasel, and *fullonum*, Fuller's teasel, grown as a crop for its seed heads which are used for raising nap on certain cloths. *D. pilosus* is the small teasel. A rosette of basal leaves forms during the first year, then the plants throw up prickly, angled stems, with blunt, conical purplish flower-heads, held erect.

Tebaldi, Renata (1922–), Italian operatic soprano. She studied at Parma and made her début at Rovigo; by the 1950s she was recognised as one of the world's leading singers. Her powerful lyricism was particularly suited to Puccini and Verdi operas.

Tebbit, Norman (1931–), British Conservative politician. He was elected an MP in 1970 and from 1979 until 1981 he was under-secretary at the Department of Trade. From January 1981 he was a minister at the Department of Industry, a post held until September when he became secretary for Employment. In 1983 he was appointed secretary for Trade and Industry.

Technetium, originally masurium, chemical element, symbol Tc, atomic number 43. All the isotopes of this element are known to be radioactive and to exist in nature only as fission products of uranium.

Technical Education, term used to describe courses of instruction, in a variety of institutions, in subjects directly applicable to the purposes of agriculture, industry, trade or commercial life. A distinction is sometimes made between technical education and commercial education. In its limited sense technical education is provided for three categories of personnel: technologists, who make a scientific study of the practical or industrial arts, and are expected, in their careers, to initiate advances in their own field; technicians, who while specialists by virtue of their theoretical and practical training, usually require a good knowledge of the mathematics and science related to their speciality, and work under the general direction of technologists; and craftsmen, who represent the skilled labour of manufacturing industry. Each category has its appropriate qualifying examinations—degrees, technical diplomas and certificates.

Apart from the universities there are 522 (1981) technical or commercial training establishments in England and Wales. About one quarter of the students attend evening courses; many of the others are released by their employers to attend courses under the day-release scheme; around 17% are in full-time attendance. Industry co-operates in technical education through 'sandwich' courses: substantial periods of full-time study are alternated with periods of industrial training. The number of technically trained personnel in the UK compares unfavourably with other countries, particularly with the USA and USSR. See also EDUCATION; UNIVERSITIES.

Tecton, distinguished firm of British architects, established by Berthold Lubetkin (1901–80); Denys Lasdun was at one time a partner. They designed the Penguin Pool and Gorilla House at London Zoo, 1934–1938, in reinforced concrete; Highpoint and North Hill flats at Highgate, 1936–38; Finsbury Health Centre, 1938–39; and flats in Rosebery Avenue, 1946–49.

Tectonics, see GEOTECTONICS.

Tedder of Glenguin, Arthur William Tedder, 1st Baron (1890–1967), British airman, Marshal of the RAF. He went to France with the army in 1914 and was seconded to the Royal Flying Corps in 1916. He was given a permanent commission in the RAF in 1919. He became air officer, commander-in-chief Middle East, 1941–43, and air commander-in-chief, Mediterranean air command, in 1943. Tedder, appointed deputy supreme commander under Gen. Eisenhower for the Anglo-American expeditionary force, was the first British airman to assume so important a military post. He was a specialist in strategy, moulding to his own shape the current ideas on air cooperation with armies. Appointed chief of the air staff in 1945, he retired in 1950.

Tees, river of England, rising in Cross Fell, Cumbria, and flowing south-east and then north-east for 112 km, entering the estuary called Tees Mouth to join the North Sea. It is navigable to Middlesbrough, and has a port trade including oil and iron ore.

Teesside, industrial area in Cleveland, England, on either side of the Tees estuary including Stockton-on-Tees, Middlesbrough, Billingham and Redcar.

Teeth, calcareous structures occupying the upper and lower jaw, and serving to tear, cut or grind food.

In humans there are 32 permanent teeth, 16 in each jaw. They are divided as follows: two incisors, one canine, two premolars, or bicuspids, and three molars, in the lateral half of each jaw. The incisors have chisel-shaped crowns and are adapted for dividing food by cutting. The canine teeth are conical and are adapted for piercing. The premolars have a shearing action. The molars are at the back of the mouth and in humans are the largest teeth, being adapted to grinding and chewing. The last molar is known as the 'wisdom' tooth. Herbivorous animals have greatly enlarged molars with ridges across to provide a grinding surface, a special adaptation to the chewing of coarse plant food.

In humans the first permanent teeth erupt at about the age of six, and the last molar, the wisdom tooth, erupts at about 18–20 years. The permanent dentition is preceded by 20 'milk' teeth which erupt during the first 2½ years of life and are shed between the ages of six and 12 years. The structure of all the teeth is basically the same. The outer layer of the crown is enamel. This is the hardest biological tissue, consisting of a small amount of organic matrix and water and approximately 96 per cent mineral salts. The inner layer is dentine which consists of similar constituents but the organic matrix and water account for approximately 30 per cent of this tissue. See also DENTISTRY.

Tegea, town of Arcadia in ancient Greece, named after its reputed founder, Tegeates. It was long subject to the hegemony of Sparta, but became independent after the Theban victory at Leuctra (371 BC). Tegea was famous for its temple of Pallas Athene.

Tegucigalpa, capital of the Central American republic of Honduras, situated at an altitude of 975 m at the foot of the extinct volcano El Picacho. Silver and gold are mined nearby (as they have been since the 16th century). The main industries include cotton textile manufacture, clothing, construction materials, food processing, beverages and soap. Population (1980) 472,700.

Tehran, or Teheran, city and capital of Iran, built at an average altitude of 1220 m, on a gentle slope running south from the Elburz Mountains. Formerly a suburb of Rey, Tehran became the capital in 1785 under the Qajar dynasty and expanded steadily. Modern Tehran exhibits marked internal differences; the southernmost part, the poorest, is a reception area for migrants from all over Iran; further north, upslope, are the bazaar and many of the ministry buildings, while further north still the former 19th-century upper-class suburbs have most of the foreign embassies. The modern central business district is now centred on Takhte Jamshid and Firdausi avenues. Since the Second World War, however, there has been rapid residential expansion north from here towards Shemiran. The growth of modern Tehran has been at the expense of other Iranian cities. Population (1975) 3,400,000; Greater Tehran 4,171,000.

Tehuantepec, Isthmus of, situated in the south of Mexico with the Atlantic (Gulf of Mexico) to the north and Pacific to the south, the land at the narrowest point being about 208 km between the oceans.

Teilhard de Chardin, Pierre (1881–1955), French theologian, philosopher and scientist. He entered the Society of Jesus in 1899, and was ordained priest in 1911. He served throughout the First World War as a stretcher-bearer in the French army, earning the Legion of Honour. He then resumed the study of palaeontology and in 1919 became professor of geology at the Institut Catholique in Paris. In 1923 he went to China, where he studied its rich palaeontological remains. In 1951 he was attached to the Wenner-Gren Foundation for anthropological research, making trips to South Africa in 1951 and 1953. He published numerous papers and articles in learned journals from 1913. His major work *Le Phénomène Humain*, 1955, is a study of the process by which man has developed and which looks forward to man, controlling the evolutionary process, achieving his final fulfilment. Taken in conjunction with his theological study *Le Milieu Divin*, 1957, it has proved a source of inspiration to many Christians. Teilhard remains, however, a controversial figure, regarded by some as the major modern Christian thinker but dismissed by many scientists as lacking in rigour in his argument and evidence.

Tejo, see TAGUS.

Tel Aviv (Hebrew, Hill of Spring), largest city of Israel, situated on the coast of Sharon Plain, 77 km north-west of Jerusalem. Founded in 1909, on bare sand-dunes to the north of Jaffa, it was intended only as a suburb of the latter. It became a municipality in its own right in 1921, and absorbed its smaller neighbour in 1950. Tel Aviv was the capital of Israel from the state's declaration of independence until 1950. By 1930 it had become Israel's leading economic centre, its activities including chemicals, pharmaceuticals, confectionery, textiles, banking, and almost all of the country's publishing. Tel Aviv is also

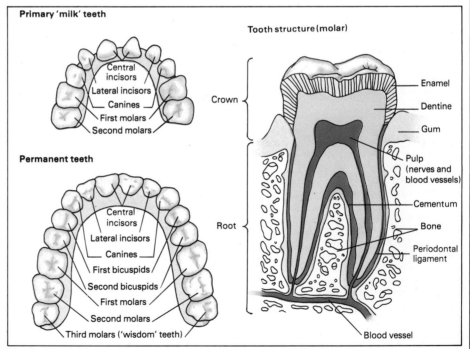

Teeth. *20 primary or 'milk' teeth give way to the permanent set of 32 from about six years.*

the seat of the national theatres (English and Hebrew), the state ballet and the Israel Philharmonic Orchestra. Population of Tel-Aviv –Jaffa (1976) 353,800.

Telecommunications, science of communication by electrical means.

See also TELEGRAPHY; TELEPHONY; TELEVISION.

Telegraphy, system for conveying information between two points. The first serviceable telegraphic device, invented by Chappe (France) in 1792, was a form of semaphore. In 1816 Ronald (Britain) produced his pith-ball telegraph, where an electric current caused two pith-balls to diverge, and their movement indicated a character. In 1819 Oersted discovered that an electric current deflected a neighbouring magnetic needle, the direction of movement depending on the direction of current flow. Cooke and Wheatstone, applying this principle, produced the first practical electric telegraph in 1837.

In the same year Morse produced his electromagnetic telegraph. The Morse code consists of two distinct signals in groups to define the various characters. One signal is a 'dot' and the other a 'dash', the dash being three times the duration of the dot. There are intervals between the letters and a longer interval between words. In the elementary Morse system the recorder at each end is replaced by a sounder; in later systems, dots and dashes were ink recorded on tape.

The Baudot system (1874) was a multiplex printing system which used a five-unit code in which each character was made up of a combination of five currents, each positive or negative. A multiplex system is a multiple-way arrangement of sending two or more messages over the same line by the allocation of the exclusive use of the line in rapid succession.

Stop-Start Teleprinter Working. Modern inland telegraphic communication is now carried out by teleprinters. The teleprinter consists of the transmitter and the receiver, which are mounted upon one base and are driven by a small electric motor. The transmitter consists of a keyboard, and a transmitting unit, controlled by the keyboard, which transmits electrical impulses. The receiver electromagnet causes the characters corresponding to the signals to be printed on paper tape.

Modern teleprinter working uses the Murray five-unit signal code. Here the signal time for each character is the same. Five electrical impulses of equal duration are transmitted for each character. Various formations of these impulses make up the different characters. The number of different characters that can be obtained is 32, and since it is necessary to transmit numerals as well as the alphabet, the machine is arranged to use the same combinations for figures as for letters. Start and stop pulses accompany every character combination. The motors run continuously, but when no signals are passing the transmitting and receiving mechanisms are at rest. When a key is depressed, both mechanisms make one revolution, during which time the start pulse, character combination and stop pulse are sent. The time for one revolution is approximately 150 ms and the system

Telegraphy. The Morse Code.

is capable of working at approximately 66 words per minute.

Where the traffic is too heavy for direct keyboard operation, automatic tape transmission may be used. The operator prepares the message, to the five-unit code, on perforated tape. This is fed through an automatic tape transmitter which transmits the signals to line at high speed.

Telegraph Signalling. DC signals are subject to distortion. On inland networks the modern method is to signal by alternating current (a.c.) in the voice-frequency range. Such signals can be passed over standard telephone trunk lines, and amplified by thermionic valve or transistor amplifiers. AC signals retain their shape in transmission with sufficient accuracy almost without distance limit.

Facsimile, or picture telegraphy, incorporates a sender, which is arranged to scan the picture by a light spot. The variations in tone are interpreted into variations in amplitude of a.c. passed to the telephone line to a receiver. Here a light from a constant source is arranged to fall on a piece of photographic material and scan this at the same rate as the sender. The variation of incoming current operates a light valve, which controls the intensity of the light falling on the photographic material to reproduce the original picture.

See also CABLES, ELECTRIC; SIGNALS AND SIGNALLING.

Telekinesis, the movement of objects by a person without that person having any physical contact with them. It is a common feature of physical phenomena in spiritualism.

See also PSYCHOKINESIS.

Telemachus, in Greek legend, son of Odysseus and Penelope, a child when his father set out for Troy. After about 20 years he set sail in search of news of him, returning to Ithaca in time to help his father in the famous fight with Penelope's suitors.

Telemann, Georg Philipp (1681–1767), German composer. He was mainly self taught in music, but in 1704 became organist at the New Church, Leipzig, and founded a students' music society, the Collegium Musicum. He was later music director of the Johanneum at Hamburg. Telemann was one of the most prolific and facile composers of the late Baroque period. His works are transitional in

style: Baroque procedures are mixed with the new, lighter 'rococo' manner. He wrote operas, oratorios, and chamber and church music.

Telenaipura, see JAMBI.

Teleology, in philosophy, is the theory that things are determined by the ends towards which they strive. This notion was central to Aristotle's metaphysics and his theory of causality. For example, on a teleological view of falling bodies one might say that bodies fall because they seek the centre. Vestiges of this way of talking survive in science. Aristotle developed this view from his interests in biology, where it has some semblance of plausibility. In natural science, the teleological notion of final cause has been totally superseded by what Aristotle called the efficient cause.

Teleostei, the largest group of fish, in class Osteichthyes, the bony fishes. This is the largest group of living vertebrate animals; more than 20,000 species are known. There are 30–40 orders of Teleostei. Some of the important ones are: Elopiformes, the tarpons and bonefish; Anguilliformes, the eels; Clupeiformes, which includes herring and anchovies; Salmoniformes, salmon, trout, whitefish, smelts and pikes; Cypriniformes, carp and some electric eels; Siluriformes, catfish; Gadiformes, cod, hakes; Lophiiformes, anglerfishes; Atheriniformes, flying fishes, swordtail; Perciformes, perch, swordfish, mackerel; Gasterosteiformes, sea horses; Pleuronectiformes, flat-fishes.

Telepathy, name given by F. W. H. Myers to the transference of knowledge from one mind to another without the use of any normal sensory channel of communication. The reality of this power was proved in the early days of the Society for Psychical Research, but it was generally supposed to be restricted to a few exceptional individuals. The more recent work of Dr J. B. Rhine has shown that it is much more widespread than was at first supposed, and that the paranormal acquisition of knowledge is not restricted to what is in another person's mind, since a fact not known to any other person may also be known without the use of any normal sense channel. Telepathy is thus only one example of a more general paranormal power of obtaining knowledge, often now referred to as extrasensory perception (or the *psi* capacity).

Telephony, system of reproducing sounds at a distance. The first practical telephone, which was based on electromagnets, was made by Alexander Graham Bell in 1876. In the modern transmitter, speech vibrates a diaphragm, varying the resistance of carbon granules between two electrodes, causing the current between them to fluctuate. In the rocking armature receiver, a current change causes an armature to rock slightly. This motion is conveyed to a conical diaphragm which reproduces the original speech vibrations.

Automatic Telephone Exchanges have a central battery which supplies current for both speech and signalling. When the receiver is lifted, a free selector switch is connected to the caller's line. Each digit dialled interrupts the current from the exchange a specific number of times. These impulses route the call on to contacts to which the called line is connected. When the call is answered, a speaking circuit is completed and the connection is held under the control of the caller, against whom it is automatically metered.

Exchange systems. The step-by-step system, introduced in Great Britain in 1912, is still widely used. It consists of line switches (uniselectors), and group and final selectors. These are of the electro-mechanical Strowger type which consist of stacks of horizontal contact layers. Operation is by vertical, then horizontal, selection. More compact is the Bell crossbar system, consisting of crossbar switches and multi-contact electronic reed relays. In both these systems, voice patterns are represented in analogue form by varying electric currents. New computer-controlled digital exchange systems have no moving parts but rely on micro-chips, giving much improved transmission quality and speedier connection. Voice patterns are represented by on-off digital pulses.

Call transmission. Between exchanges, many separate 'go' (caller) signals are usually carried over a single line, another line being used for 'return' signals.

'Frequency-division multiplex' allows many calls to be carried by a single coaxial cable, by superimposing the speech patterns on carrier waves of a range of high frequencies. These microwaves can be focused by parabolic reflectors and transmitted between high towers.

Time-division multiplex, now widely used, employs a rapid electronic switching system. Calls may be interleaved by sampling each modulated waveform at staggered time intervals. In pulse-code modulation the modulated-wave form samples are quantisised and transmitted in binary code. This device is used in conjunction with time-division multiplex.

The latest method of transmission uses glass fibres instead of metal cables, and lasers or light-emitting diodes to send light pulses. These 'lightlines' have the advantages of cheapness, greater capacity, less frequent amplification, and higher security and clarity.

Telephone messages over large distances may be relayed by communications satellites.

Teleprinters, see TELEGRAPHY.

Telescope, an optical instrument for examining distant objects. A Dutchman, Jan Lippershey, is usually given the credit for constructing the first telescope in 1608. Hearing of the invention in 1609, Galileo quickly constructed one for himself and went on to produce a succession of such instruments which he used from 1610 onwards for astronomical observations. His telescope consisted of a weak convex lens as objective and a stronger concave lens as eye-piece. Galileo's arrangement has the merits of simplicity and compactness but the disadvantage of a small field of view if large magnifications are used. It is an ideal arrangement for opera glasses for which the magnification is usually only 2 × or 3 ×.

Another simple telescopic system, sometimes attributed to Kepler, is that in which Galileo's concave eye-piece is replaced by a convex one. The magnification is the same, but the object appears upside-down. On the other hand the field of view is larger and a reticule or cross wires can be fitted at the common focus of the eye-piece and objective, making the telescope a very useful measuring or pointing device. This is the usual form of the astronomical refractor and of many of the reading telescopes used in laboratories.

However, nowadays astronomers rarely use telescopes for direct visual observations. For them a telescope is either a convenient method of collecting light from a celestial source to feed into some subsidiary apparatus such as a spectrograph, or it is a very large camera.

A mirror with a parabolic surface makes an ideal light collector since all rays parallel to its axis are reflected back through its focus where the light receiver can be mounted. If this is not convenient, or if a longer effective focal length is required, subsidiary mirrors can be introduced to deflect the light where it is wanted.

Unfortunately the field of good definition of a parabolic mirror is comparatively small, especially if its focal ratio, i.e. the ratio of its focal length to its diameter, is small. When it is desired to take photographs with an instrument having a small focal ratio it is better to use a Schmidt camera.

Basically what Schmidt pointed out was that a spherical mirror, unlike a paraboloid, has no particular axis and is thus automatically free from many of the aberrations that plague the conventional reflector. It does, however, suffer from spherical aberration, but he demonstrated that this could be corrected by a properly shaped correcting plate placed at the centre of curvature.

See also ASTRONOMY; HALE OBSERVATORIES; OBSERVATORY; RADIO ASTRONOMY.

Teletext, a system by which pages of information can be transmitted by television. Teletext uses four spare lines at the top and bottom of the TV screen which are not normally seen unless the set is maladjusted. The information carried by these lines is transformed into a picture by a decoder, built into or attached to the receiver. The decoder has a keyboard like a computer. By keying the appropriate number, the viewer can select any one of several thousands of pages of text and graphics being transmitted. In the UK two systems are available, *Ceefax*, transmitted by the BBC, and *Oracle*, operated by the IBA.

See also VIEWDATA.

Television is the transmission and visible reproduction of pictures or scenes by radio-communication, direct line or closed circuit. The earliest practical demonstration was given by J. L. Baird in 1926. In 1928 he transmitted a low-definition picture by radio to the USA. The first high-definition service began in November 1936 from Alexandra Palace. Radio Corporation of America produced an acceptable colour system in 1949.

Scanning. At the transmitter, the scene is focused on to the photoconductive target plate of the camera tube. The resistance of this is high, diminishing in illuminated areas. An electron beam, deflected by time bases, scans the plate and outputs an electrically varying current which represents, line by line and frame by frame, the light and shade of the picture. Cinematograph films are scanned with a high intensity cathode-ray tube; a photocell behind the film detects the changes in light intensity to produce the signal.

At the receiver, the picture is projected on to the screen of a cathode-ray tube by an electron beam which is deflected in step with that in the camera tube by synchronising signals transmitted with the picture. In British television, 625 lines are transmitted in 0.04 s (using two interlaced frames of $312\frac{1}{2}$ lines to reduce flicker).

Colour television. By splitting the light from the scene and filtering it to three camera tubes, chrominance (colour or hue) signals are obtained for the red, green and blue components. The luminance (brightness) signal is made from fixed proportions of the tube outputs, chosen to give an acceptable variation of grey tones when viewed in black and white.

A colour receiver has three electron guns and its screen is composed of over a million indiscernible dots, one-third of which emit red, one-third green and one-third blue light when struck by an electron beam. Between

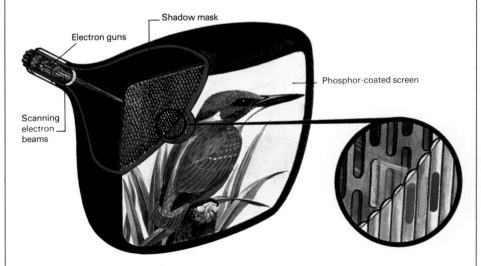

Television. *The cathode-ray tube of a colour television set has three separate electron guns, one for each colour. The shadow mask ensures that signals of a particular colour reach only the corresponding phosphor dots on the screen.*

the guns and the screen is a shadow mask containing very many tiny holes, precisely positioned so that the electron beam from a particular gun strikes the dots of one colour only. The simultaneous emission of electrons from the guns can therefore synthesize any colour, including white, by controlling the relative strengths of the beams.

Recent developments include the transmission of signals for cable television along glass fibres and the flat-screen television receiver.

See also BROADCASTING; SATELLITE COMMUNICATIONS.

Telford, Thomas (1757–1834), British civil engineer. He built the Severn bridges at Montford and Buildwas, 1793–96; the Ellesmere Canal, 1796–1801; the Caledonian Canal, 1801–23; and in the same period over 1600 km of road and 120 bridges throughout Scotland. His greatest achievement was the improvement of the London–Holyhead road (A5) with the building of the Menai suspension bridge. He also did much harbour work in Scotland; he built St Katherine Dock, London; the Gotha Canal, Sweden; and designed the Warsaw frontier road for Tsar Alexander. A man of talent, wholly self-educated, Telford often gave his services gratuitously.

Telford New Town, in Shropshire, England, 15 km west of the Wolverhampton–Birmingham urban complex, which the New Town is intended to relieve, drawing off population and industry. Telford was originally (1963) Dawley New Town, but was extended and renamed in 1968. Population (1981) 103,786.

Tell, William, romantic national hero of Switzerland. Although the form in which his story first appears, in a Swiss chronicle written between 1467 and 1476, is legendary, several Swiss authorities suggest that Tell really did live, and that his history has been obscured by folklore. His part in the uprising of the Forest Cantons against the oppression of the Austrian Hapsburgs seems to have been much exaggerated.

The story of William Tell and the apple has been popularised in the masterpiece by the German playwright, Friedrich Schiller, which was published in 1804. It is a patriotic play, reminding people of resistance to foreign oppressors in past times. The story centres on the struggle for independence of the cantons of Uri, Schwyz and Unterwalden, and is as follows: Tell, having refused to do homage to the ducal hat which Gessler, the Austrian governor, set up for the purpose, was taken prisoner, but was promised his liberty if he could shoot an apple in two, placed on his son's head, at the distance of 80 paces. He accomplished the task, but confessed on compulsion that his other arrow was meant for Gessler's heart had he killed his son, whereupon he was again seized and taken on the lake, bound for Küssnacht Castle. A storm arose, Tell was asked to steer the ship, and while doing so he escaped. He afterwards killed the landgrave, and his actions became symbolic of the courage of the Inner Cantons in their struggle against the Hapsburgs.

Tell el-Amarna, modern name of ancient site on the east bank of the Nile about 290 km south of Cairo. The ruins are those of Akhetaton, the capital of Akhnaton, who built it c.1375 BC. After his death the city was abandoned and has since been uninhabited. In 1887 peasants found there about 400 clay tablets, consisting of letters mostly in cuneiform from Asiatic potentates and Egyptian vassals in Palestine and Syria to Akhnaton and his father, which are of great historical importance. Later excavations uncovered palaces, villas and an Aton temple.

Teller, Edward (1908–), Hungarian-US physicist, researched at Leipzig and Göttingen but left Germany in 1933. In 1941 he became professor of physics at Columbia University, and in 1942 began his long association with nuclear weapons. He supported the development of the hydrogen bomb and was assistant director of Los Alamos Scientific Laboratory 1949–52. Since 1953 he has been a professor at the University of California and since 1954 director of the university's Lawrence Radiation Laboratory.

Tellurium, chemical element, symbol Te, atomic number 52, atomic weight 127·6; it occurs in the free state in nature, but is chiefly obtained in combination with other elements, as in tellurite (TeO_2) and tetradymite (Bi_2Te_3). With selenium, it is found in the 'anode mud' resulting from electrolytic copper refining, from which it is isolated by reduction with coke. It is a bluish-white solid with a metallic lustre (melting point 452°C; relative density 6·26), and burns in air to form a dioxide, TeO_2. It is oxidised by nitric and sulphuric acids and it forms tellurides with hydrogen and the metals, corresponding to the sulphides. Two oxides, the dioxide and trioxide, are known, which give rise respectively to the two acids, tellurous acid and telluric acid. The salts of tellurium are known as tellurates.

Telugu, a Dravidian language, the official language and script of the state of Andhra Pradesh, India. It is the mother tongue of nearly 38,000,000 people (1961).

See also INDIA, *Language.*

Tempe, valley of northern Thessaly, famous for its beautiful scenery. It was the traditional scene of Apollo's purification after the killing of Python, and of Daphne's metamorphosis.

Tempera, painting medium consisting of: (1) Pure *egg-tempera*, where well-ground inorganic pigments mixed on a white palette with egg-yolk and water are applied to a slightly absorbent gesso panel. (The yellow of egg-yolk bleaches out, whereas white of egg may turn brown.) In early Italian painting, the initial lay-in of a design was often done with *terra-verde*, hence the term *verdaccio*. Colours are first applied in a mixture with flake or zinc white, and then strengthened and modelled with glazes or hatches of pure transparent colour. (2) *Tempera-emulsion* uses for its medium a well-fused mixture of egg-yolk and stand-oil, which permits of dilution with water. It dries hard sooner and, being more flexible, can be used on canvas prepared with a waterground, i.e. with size and gesso. A variant of egg-tempera is *casein*, where the medium is fresh white curd and a little slaked lime, diluted with water.

Temperament, in music, is connected with the intonation of the notes in a scale, and with the tuning of instruments. In vocal, and in much instrumental, music the intervals of a scale are flexible. A string player with a keen ear will make a slight difference between A flat and G sharp, which on the piano or the organ are the same note. Before equal temperament, in which each octave is divided into 12 equal semitones, came into use for tuning keyboard instruments, some notes in certain keys were more noticeably out of tune than others. Bach's 48 preludes and fugues were composed in all the major and minor keys (*Well-tempered Clavier*) to demonstrate that, with equal-temperament tuning, keyboard instruments could deal with any key.

Temperance Movement, a series of campaigns that have tried to persuade people to reduce or to abstain from the intake of alcoholic beverages. Social, educational and legislative means have been employed, and women have been very active in the movement. It has also been closely connected with the Christian churches. The temperance movement started in the USA early in the 19th century. The Ulster Temperance Society was founded in 1829, the Church of England Temperance Society in 1862. Legislation has included prohibition of the buying or selling of intoxicating liquors for a time in the USA, Canada and a few other countries; state ownership of shops for the sale of alcoholic beverages; rationing; and various licensing laws that regulate who may sell alcoholic beverages and during what hours. Many countries now have laws making it illegal to drive a car after drinking. Alcoholics Anonymous has been among the active social and educational organisations in the campaign against alcoholism.

Temperature, the degree of hotness of a body. A body X is said to be at a higher temperature than Y if heat flows from X to Y when the two are placed in contact. Any property of a body which depends on temperature, e.g. its length or electrical resistance, can be used to define a scale of temperature. The property considered, e.g. the length of a column of mercury in a glass capillary, is measured at two fixed points and a relation is assumed to exist between the change in the property (length) and the change of temperature. The centigrade scale takes the ice point to be 0°C and the steam point to be 100°C. If L_0 is the length of the mercury column at 0°C and L_{100} that at 100°C, the temperature T°C corresponding to a length L_T is given by

$$T = (L_T - L_0)\,100/(L_{100} - L_0)\,°C.$$

Kelvin defined an absolute scale of temperature and showed that it was the same as the perfect gas scale.

Temperature in medicine. The temperature of the body varies with the different forms of life. In man it lies between 36·9° and 37·4°C in a state of health, varying slightly with the time of day, exercise, ingestion of food, and the temperature of the surrounding atmosphere. The temperatures of cold-blooded animals have a wider range and are much lower than in the warm-blooded ones. Thus the temperature of the frog may vary from 17·2° to 8·8°C, according to circumstances.

Temperature in meteorology. A fundamental

element in the study of weather and climate is the measurement and forecast of temperature at the ground surface and of the air at all levels of the atmosphere. The source of heat is the Sun, and temperature is modified by solar radiation (or insolation), of which about 45 per cent reaches the Earth's surface; this heat is released back into the atmosphere by terrestrial radiation, the most important aspect for meteorology.

Tempering, heat-treatment process for relieving certain stresses that may occur in hardened steels, and for recovering to specific limits the toughness and ductility essential to hardened steels. This process usually follows hardening of a steel by quenching from above its upper critical temperature into cold water or oil. Quench hardening produces martensite, which is commonly too hard and brittle for general engineering use and must be softened by tempering. The process consists of reheating the steel to a selected temperature in the range 200–650°C and then cooling in oil, water or air. This causes the martensite to decompose into a tough form of steel consisting of a fine dispersion of iron carbide particles in iron. The hardness of the tempered steel decreases with increase in the tempering temperature. This temperature is therefore chosen according to the purpose for which the steel will be used. The trend in modern methods of tempering is to use liquid baths for reheating, and pyrometer and thermo-electric control for accurate measuring of tempering temperatures.

Templars, or Knights Templars, military order founded in 1118 by nine French knights, led by Hugh de Payns. They received their rule in 1128 from Saint Bernard. Their original vow was simply to maintain free passage for the pilgrims who should visit the Holy Land. Pope Honorius II confirmed their rule and assigned a white mantle as their badge. Pope Eugenius III added a red cross on the left breast to the mantle. For more than 170 years the Templars formed the most renowned portion of the Christian troops. By 1300 the order had 15,000 members, and its property included 9000 castles and manors. It was suppressed at the Council of Vienne in 1312, many of its members executed, and its property confiscated. The name survives in the Temple, London, and the Temple, Paris.

Temple, Frederick (1821–1902), English prelate. He was ordained in 1847. In 1857 he became headmaster of Rugby, where he continued the work of Arnold, though Temple laid more stress on the place of orthodox religion in school life. His friendship with Gladstone, whose Liberal views he shared, led to his appointment in 1869 to the see of Exeter. He was appointed bishop of London in 1885, and in 1896 archbishop of Canterbury. He worked to prevent the influence of the Oxford Movement from resulting in a split within the fabric of Anglicanism.

Temple, Shirley Jane (1929–), US child actress. She made her screen début in 1932 in *Red Haired Alibi*. She was a leading figure in the *Baby Burlesque* series. Her appearance in *Stand Up and Cheer*, 1934, resulted in a highly successful career; she is probably

the best-known child star ever to appear in films. Her pictures include *Baby Takes a Bow, Bright Eyes, Our Little Girl, Curly Top, The Littlest Rebel, Poor Little Rich Girl, Heidi, Rebecca of Sunnybrook Farm, The Little Princess* and *The Blue Bird*. With the passing of childhood her popularity faded, although she made a number of later films and has appeared on television. As Shirley Temple-Black she has latterly played a part in Republican politics. She was appointed US ambassador to Ghana in 1974.

Temple, Sir William (1628–99), English statesman and man of letters. He was largely responsible for carrying through the triple alliance formed against Spain in 1668 between England, Holland and Sweden. He was later ambassador at The Hague, but was recalled in 1670, returning in 1674 to arrange the marriage between Princess Mary of England and William of Orange. When he moved to Moor Park he engaged Swift as his secretary, and was assisted by him in the composition of his *Memoirs*. His essay *Of Ancient and Modern Learning* provoked the Ancients and Moderns literary controversy, to which Swift contributed with *The Battle of the Books*.

Templars. The Chateau de Mer in Sidon is one of the best preserved Crusader castles.

Temple, William (1881–1944), English prelate, son of Frederick Temple. He was ordained in 1909, and was successively chaplain to the archbishop of Canterbury, headmaster of Repton School, rector of St James's, Piccadilly, canon of Westminster, bishop of Manchester, archbishop of York and archbishop of Canterbury. As a writer, his reputation rests chiefly on his essays in philosophy and on his application of that philosophy to social and economic problems. His Gifford Lectures, collected as *Nature, Man and God*, 1934, were an outstanding contribution to theology. Temple led the Life and Liberty Movement which resulted in the Enabling Act, 1919, and the setting up of the Church Assembly. The unity of the Church was an urgent and practical necessity to him. He made his greatest impact by pronouncements on Christian social theory.

Temple, structure designed for the worship of a deity or deities. The first *templum* of the Romans was simply the space of earth and sky marked off by an augur for divination. The ancient Egyptians built enormous temples by degrees over a long period; ancient India is noted for cave temples hewn out of the solid rock; Hindu temples always include the shrine in front of which it is customary to remove one's shoes. In the Far East and in South-East Asia the temple is known as *pagoda*, while the ancient Mexican temple was known as *teocalli*. In France Protestant churches are known as temples as also are some Jewish synagogues and Masonic halls. The most celebrated temples of antiquity were those of the Ancient Greeks.

The famous temples of the Jews are: *The First Temple,* the sacred edifice of the ancient Hebrews erected in Jerusalem on Mount Moriah, where Abraham is reputed to have attempted to sacrifice Isaac, the building of which was begun by Solomon; *The Second Temple,* built on the same site, by Zerubbabel, completed in 516 BC, 70 years after the first temple was destroyed; and *The Herodian Temple,* begun in 20–19 BC and finished in AD 64, six years before it was finally destroyed. The 'Western' or 'Wailing Wall' belongs to the remains of the enclosure walls of the Herodian temple.

Temple, Classical. The essential room in a Greek temple was the *cella* or *naos*, containing the cult statue. In small temples it might simply have a porch (*pronaos*) in front, the façade formed either by columns (usually two) between the extended side walls (*in antis*) or by columns standing in front of the extended walls (*prostyle*). In major temples there was a matching false porch (*opisthodomos*) at the rear of the cella and a colonnade round the whole building (*peripteral*), while colossal temples might have two surrounding colonnades (*dipteral*). Roman temples usually had a deep porch of free-standing columns in front of the cella, with half-columns attached to the side and rear walls (*pseudoperipteral*). The façades were always crowned by a low-pitched gable (*pediment*), which was often filled with sculpture, and a free-standing figure or other decoration (*akroterion*) might also be placed at its apex and lower angles. The roof was tiled, with decorative *antefixes* terminating the rows of cover tiles. The portico and pediment motif, derived from the temple, was a favourite one with Renaissance and later architects.

Temple Bar, formerly a gateway marking the boundary between the cities of London and Westminster. A barrier existed here from medieval times to 1669. In 1670–72 an archway was erected to Wren's designs. This was removed in 1878 and re-erected at Theobald's Park, in Hertfordshire, the site being marked by the Temple Bar Memorial, erected in 1880. In former times the sovereign sought permission of the lord mayor at Temple Bar before entering the City of London, an act still symbolically performed.

Tempo (Italian, time), musical pace. The speed of any musical composition is determined by the directions set above the stave at the opening of a piece or section (e.g. *allegro, andante, adagio*, etc.). The exact pace may be indicated by means of metronome marks.

Temporal Bone, part of the base and lateral walls of the skull. It has important nerves and vessels running through it and contains the middle and inner ear.

Temuco, city of southern Chile, capital of Cautín province, 688 km south of Santiago and the fourth largest city in Chile. Cereals, timber and apples are the main products. Population (1978) 156,900.

Ten Commandments (Decalogue). They were given to the Israelites on Mount Sinai and engraved on two tables of stone. These being broken, Moses was commanded to hew another two tables on which Yahweh again engraved the decalogue. Only four of the precepts are peculiar to the Hebrews, the 1st, 3rd, 9th and 10th—of the others, all six are found in some form in Babylonian, and four in Egyptian, texts. There is nothing in them inconsistent with Mosaic date.

Tenant, see LANDLORD AND TENANT.

Tench, *Tinca tinca,* order Cypriniformes, a European freshwater fish with exceedingly small scales, a slimy skin, and a short barbel at each angle of the mouth. It is olive green, shading into light grey on the belly. It spawns in early summer, the greenish ova numbering about 250,000. Like the carp, to whose family it belongs, it is omnivorous. It attains a length of c.45 cm and a weight of 2 kg.

Tender, in English law, offer of money in payment of a debt. To be valid it must be: (1) unconditional. (2) of the whole debt; though if the creditor's claim is made up of separate items the debtor may validly make a tender of payment of any one item provided he makes it clear in respect of which item it is made. (3) in legal tender.
A valid tender does not extinguish the debt, but a plea of tender, if sustained by the debtor, will result in the plaintiff having to pay costs.
A tender in commerce is a written offer of terms for executing a specific piece of work or for supplying a certain consignment of merchandise.

Tendon, immensely strong connective tissue composed of bundles of parallel collagen fibres. Tendons are attached at one end to the sarcolemma or connective tissue around muscle fibres, and at the other end to the periosteum, the connective tissue surrounding bone. Tendons have a relatively poor blood supply and if torn, healing is slow.

Tendon of Achilles, tendon attaching the muscles of the calf of the leg to the heelbone. It is capable of resisting a great tensional strain, and yet is sometimes ruptured by the contraction of the muscles in sudden extension of the foot.

Tendril, in botany, a thread-like growth by which some plants climb. Tendrils may be modified terminal shoots, as in vines, leaves as in peas, leaf-stalks as in clematis, or branch stems as in white bryony; they are sensitive to contact and react by twining around supports.

Tenerife, largest of the Canary Islands, in the province of Santa Cruz de Tenerife. It is divided in two by a mountain chain. The volcanic Pico de Teide rises to 3712 m. The island is known for early fruits and vegetables and is a tourist and health resort. The capital is Santa Cruz de Tenerife. Area 2020 km²; population (1981) 688,273.

Teng Hsiao Ping, see DENG XIAO PING.

Teniers, David, the Elder (1582–1649), Flemish painter. He studied painting under Rubens and Adam Elsheimer at Rome. His subjects were mainly religious; as a painter of Flemish life he was eclipsed by his son and pupil, Teniers the Younger.

Teniers, David, the Younger (1610–90), Flemish painter, son and pupil of David Teniers the Elder. He was a master in the Antwerp Guild (1632–33). He was appointed court painter to Archduke Leopold and keeper of his pictures. His work was a development of his father's style, influenced also by Brouwer, and was extremely popular. He was happiest in his portrayals of small figures in landscape or rustic interiors. His best picture, *Meeting of the Civic Guards,* 1642, is at Leningrad, while his *Village Fête,* 1643, and many other works are in the National Gallery, London. He continued the Flemish tradition of secular rustic scenes, epitomised in Brueghel.

Sir John Tenniel. *'The Trial of the Knave of Hearts' from* Alice in Wonderland, *1865.*

Tennessee (Volunteer State), central-southern state of the USA, having an area of 109,417 km². Its boundaries on the north are Kentucky and Virginia; on the east North Carolina; on the south Georgia, Alabama and Mississippi; and the Mississippi river on the west separates it from Arkansas and Missouri. Along the eastern boundaries rise the Unaka and Great Smoky Mountains, with peaks over 1830 m; between these highlands and the Cumberland Plateau, is the valley of east Tennessee.
There are 5·2 million ha of commercial forests, the greater part made up of valuable hardwoods, and industries like paper making, which are based on the forest products, are everywhere important. Agriculture is varied; crops include cotton in the west, and an important tobacco crop. The major sources of farm income, however, are livestock and dairy products. It was the poor condition of Tennessee's farms which lay behind the creation in 1933 of the Tennessee Valley

Authority (TVA), created to control floods on the Tennessee river and, to this end, to build dams and arrest erosion; as a by-product, electricity was generated at the dams. The availability of power attracted industry—so much industry that the Tennessee valley now relies far more heavily on thermal power stations than on the hydroelectricity which was the initial attraction. Mineral resources are varied; Tennessee is a leading US producer of zinc, pyrite and phosphates, and produces 8–9 million t of coal a year. Nevertheless, the average standard of living is low. The population of the state in 1980 was 4,590,750. The capital is Nashville. The state was first settled from North Carolina in the 1750s, and entered the Union in 1796.

Tennessee, river, tributary of the Ohio river, USA. The Holston and French Broad, which unite near Knoxville, Tennessee, are its headstreams. The river winds through eastern Tennessee, Alabama, western Tennessee and Kentucky, reaching the Ohio at Paducah. It is now navigable from its mouth 1005 km upstream. Length 1050 km.
See also TENNESSEE VALLEY AUTHORITY.

Tennessee Valley Authority, created by the Tennessee Valley Act in 1933, which was initiated by Franklin D. Roosevelt's administration as part of the New Deal. The authority initiated regional planning on an unprecedented scale. The reasons why the Tennessee Valley was selected for this great experiment included the existence of a large government-built nitrate plant, and the Muscle Shoals works at the Wilson Dam. Control of the Tennessee river was also crucial for the prevention of disastrous floods on the lower Mississippi river, while flood control could be readily related to improved navigation and the profitable generation of cheap electric power. The Tennessee valley was one of the most depressed areas of the USA, affecting parts of the states of Alabama, Kentucky, Tennessee, Virginia, Georgia and North Carolina. Its disastrous condition was due to exploitation by early settlers: the soils were eroded and the woods had been cut down, and the rivers frequently flooded. Under the Tennessee Valley Authority co-ordinated research was undertaken throughout the area, which is approximately 116,550 km². Soil regeneration, afforestation, water control, malaria control, and similar measures were scientifically applied. National parks were laid out, tourist facilities organised, and cultural and educational activities promoted. There was opposition, particularly to the idea that the federal government should sell electricity in competition with private companies, but these sales enabled the Tennessee Valley Authority to repay to the government the capital sums originally invested, and this source of income has been one of the key factors in the authority's success. The authority has created an optimistic atmosphere in the region and has provided power which, in turn, has attracted industry.

Tenniel, Sir John (1820–1914), British cartoonist and illustrator. In 1850 he succeeded Richard Doyle as joint cartoonist with John Leech in *Punch.* Some 2300 cartoons and many smaller drawings were executed by Tenniel before he severed his connection with *Punch* in January 1901. In them can be traced a political history of the period. His illustrations for Lewis Carroll's *Alice in Wonderland*, 1865, and *Through the Looking-Glass*, 1872, are his greatest claim to fame.

Tennis, Lawn, one of the most popular games and most lucrative sporting professions of the second half of the 20th century. The game that can be most directly linked with modern tennis developed in the 12th and 13th centuries in France. It was played in unenclosed spaces, initially, and was known as *jeu de paume*. It was also the forerunner of real tennis, which is played indoors.

Lawn (i.e. open-air) tennis was begun by Major Harold Gem and J. B. Perera in Warwickshire in 1858. Lawn tennis became associated with Wimbledon in 1875 when the All-England Croquet Club gave over one of their lawns for tennis, and the first championships were held there in 1877.

The first international tournament for lawn tennis was the Davis Cup (for men); other important competitions held annually are the Wightman Cup (competed for by British and US women's teams), the Federation Cup (also for women), and the Australian, US and French Championships.

The Game. Lawn tennis is played by two (singles) or four (doubles) players using rackets and a ball on a court 23·8 m (78 ft) long and 8·2 m (27 ft) (singles) or 11·0 m (36 ft) (doubles) wide, divided into two halves by a net 0·9 m (3 ft) high at its centre. There is nothing in the rules to state the size, shape or weight of the racket. The ball must be stitchless with a diameter maximum 6·668 cm (2⅝ in) and weighing around 57·5 g (2 oz).

The court can be grass, wood, carpet or any other suitable surface which must be approved by the relevant national association if used for sanctioned tournaments.

The court is divided into rectangles for service and the rally play which follows service. The object of the game is to win points by serving or hitting the ball either beyond the opponent's reach or so that he is unable to return it over the net.

In a singles game the server must stand behind the base-line and serve the ball diagonally across the court so that it falls within his opponent's service-court. If the server fails, the service is a 'fault'. Two faults count a point to the opponent. His opponent must hit back the ball after the first bounce. After this, the ball may be volleyed on either side, or it may be hit after the first bounce.

In a doubles game the service is received alternately by the opponents who keep to the same side of the court. The service is arranged so that each player serves one game out of four.

Scoring. A player on winning his first point counts 15; on his second, 30; on his third, 40; if he wins a fifth-stroke before his opponent has reached 40, the game is his. If, however, both players have won three strokes the score is 'deuce'. In this case the game is not complete until one player has won two points in succession. The player who first wins six games wins a set, but if the score is five all the set continues until either one player wins seven-five, or the score reaches six all. In this case a tie-breaking game is played in which one point is scored per winning stroke. Whoever wins seven points, with a margin of two

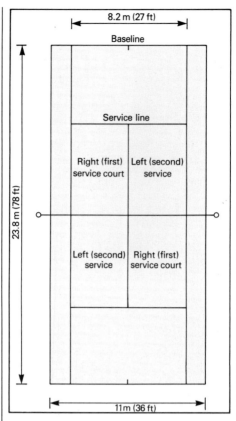

8.2 m (27 ft)

Baseline

Service line

Right (first) service court | Left (second) service

Left (second) service | Right (first) service court

23.8 m (78 ft)

11m (36 ft)

Lawn Tennis. Dimensions of the doubles court.

over his opponent, wins the set. In the event of six-six, the game continues until one player has a two-point lead.

Most matches are the best of three sets. At Wimbledon, and in the late stages of some other championships, men's matches are played to the best of five sets.

See also DAVIS CUP; FEDERATION CUP; KING'S CUP; REAL TENNIS; TABLE TENNIS; WIGHTMAN CUP; WIMBLEDON.

Tennyson, Alfred, 1st Baron (1809–92), English poet. An unhappy childhood may account for Tennyson's remarkable sensitivity and melancholia in later years. In 1830 he produced a volume of *Poems, Chiefly Lyrical*, containing some verse of great promise. In the same year he toured the Continent with Arthur Henry Hallam, and his impressions inspired many of his works. In 1833 he published *Poems*, including 'The Lady of Shalott' and 'The Lotus Eaters'; the volume was generally liked and acclaimed by Tennyson's friends, but was virulently attacked in the *Edinburgh Quarterly*. In the same year Arthur Hallam died suddenly and Tennyson began his brilliant elegy, *In Memoriam*, which grew over the years into a record of spiritual conflict and a confession of faith. In 1847 he published *The Princess*, a serio-comic epic. This was his first popular success. On Wordsworth's death in 1850, Tennyson accepted the poet laureateship.

'The Charge of the Light Brigade', showed the jingoistic aspect of Tennyson's work. It was published in the volume *Maud and other Poems*, 1855, which contained a number of fine pieces. 'Maud', an extraordinary study of murderous instincts and insanity, has passages of power and contains some beautiful lyrics. In 1859 *Idylls of the King*, variations in poetic form on the Arthurian romances, were pub-

lished. These contain some of Tennyson's most telling descriptive passages and have a musical quality. Few poets have excelled Tennyson in precision and delicacy of language. As a lyrist he ranks with the highest in English poetry.

Tenor, term in music denoting: (1) the highest natural adult male voice, the compass being from C on the bass stave to about B on the treble stave. It is so called because in polyphony it was the tenor part which 'held' the cantus firmus. (2) A musical instrument playing the part between bass and alto. (3) The largest bell of a set is known as the tenor. See also CAMPANOLOGY.

Tenor Drum, see DRUM.

Tenor Oboe, see COR ANGLAIS.

Tenpin Bowling, indoor game played on a bowling lane with balls made of hard rubber or plastic. Though played in Germany and the Low Countries from the 14th century, it attained its greatest popularity in the USA where it was introduced by Dutch immigrants. Up to 1840 the Dutch population of New York played the game on the green.

The indoor alley is 105 cm wide and 24·38 m long. On each side is a gutter of 23 cm to catch 'wides', and at the back a heavy curtain. The game is played with tenpins, or skittles, which are set up in front of a triangle with the apex to the front. The ball may not exceed 68·5 cm in circumference and 8·6 kg in weight; it has three holes for the thumb, middle and forefinger. The object of the game is to knock the pins down, each player rolling two balls (a frame), ten frames making a game. A mode of scoring by 'strikes' and 'spares' is used.

See also SKITTLES.

Tenrec (tenerec or tanrac), small mammals of order Insectivora. The 23 species are placed in the family Tenrecidae, confined to Madagascar and the Comoro Islands. The common tenrec is *Tenrec ecaudatus*, a tailless animal about 40 cm long, which is one of the largest insectivores. It has a brownish coat with spines along the top of the head and neck. Tenrecs usually have rounded bodies and large heads with a long snout. They eat insects, worms, other small animals and fruit, live in burrows and are nocturnal. The female gives birth to up to 21 young at a time, more than any other mammal.

Tense, in grammar, involves the expression of time; either the time sense expressed by the verb in a sentence, or the relation between time as expressed in the sentence and the time when the sentence was spoken or written. Three tenses, past, present and future, are common to many languages. Differences of tense are indicated mainly by the use of inflections and auxiliary verbs.

See also GRAMMAR; MOOD.

Tension, in physics, a force of stretching or pulling. Newton's third law states that action and reaction are always equal and opposite. Where the action and reaction tend to keep two bodies together they constitute a tension.

Tent, movable dwelling or shelter made of cloth, skins or tree bark supported by poles and secured by ropes and pegs. Tents have been used by nomadic peoples since the dawn of history. Those used by the Bedouin Arabs are made of strips of woven goat's hair. The *tepi* of the North American Indian is a conical-shaped tent made of skins or tree bark stretched over a tripod of poles. Probably the most luxurious tent used by nomadic peoples is the Mongol *yurt*, a felt-covered dwelling with walls of latticed hurdles; richly embroidered felt curtains line the interior and form partitions. Tents have long been used to house troops on active service. Modern tents vary in size from a one-man sleeping shelter to very large marquees.

Tenzing Norgay (1914–), Sherpa mountaineer who reached the summit of Everest (8850 m) with Edmund Hillary on 29 May 1953. Between 1935 and 1953 he took part in 19 expeditions to all parts of the Himalayas. He made several first attempts and became a distinguished sirdar ('Sherpa leader') and climber. He has for some time been a director of the Himalayan Institute of Mountaineering, centred at Darjeeling.

Teotihuacán (Abode of the Gods), remains of an ancient Toltec city, 39 km north-east of Mexico City. It is famous for its pyramids, which form the largest artificial tumuli on the American continent. The Pyramid of the Sun (709 m) has terraced sides and wide stairs leading to the top; the Pyramid of the Moon is 459 m high.

Teplice or Teplice-Šanov (German *Teplitz-Schönau*), town of Czechoslovakia, in northern Bohemia, in the Biela valley at the foot of the Erzgebirge. It is a popular spa. The district has coal-mines, and the town has several industries, including paper, glass and pottery. Population (1970) 51,000.

Terbium, metallic chemical element, symbol Tb, atomic number 65, atomic weight 158·9254. It is a member of the group of lanthanides.

Ter Borch, Gerard, also Terborch or Terburg (1617–81), Dutch painter. He was one of the most distinguished of Dutch genre painters, his small intimate works being characterised by a beautiful, cool tonality and an exquisite ability to render the texture of rich materials. His portraits, often painted on copper, are marked by a similar restraint and delicacy. Unlike most of his Dutch contemporaries, he travelled widely in Europe.

Terbrugghen, Hendrik (1588–1629), Dutch genre painter. He was one of the first northern followers of Caravaggio (with whom he may have been in direct contact in Rome), adopting the latter's chiaroscuro but developing a clearer, silvery light which anticipates the Delft School and Vermeer.

Teredo, the ship worm or woodworm, a genus of bivalve molluscs with a long worm-like body clothed in a thin shelly sheath. The shell is small and occurs at the thicker end where it protects the various organs. At the more slender end are two tubes, one of which conveys water to the gills and the other expels it with excavated matter. With its shell valves it bores into timber, and is very destructive to ships, piers and submarine cables.

Teresa of Avila, Saint, or Theresa (1515–1582), Spanish nun and monastic reformer, born Teresa Cepeda de Ahumada. She entered a Carmelite convent in Avila in 1533 but was not fully converted to her life of perfection till 1555. Soon afterwards she received her first ecstasy and an intellectual vision of Christ. Seeing the lax discipline within the religious orders, she set about founding a house in which all the original rules of the Carmelite order would be observed, and having obtained papal permission, she established (1562) the ancient Carmelite rule at a small house in Avila. Here Teresa herself, as she says, spent the five happiest years of her life. Between 1562 and her death she founded 15 new houses directly, and 17 through others, also establishing her reform among the Carmelite friars. Her work probably did much to prevent the spread of Protestantism to Spain, and it inspired the leaders of the Counter-Reformation all over Europe. Teresa combined common sense and industry with extraordinary mystical graces, which are described in her writings. These latter are classics of Spanish literature and masterpieces of mystical theology. She was canonised in 1622; her feast is 15 October. She was declared a doctor of the Church in 1970. Her works include *The Way of Perfection, The Castle of the Soul* and *The Book of the Foundations*.

Teresa, Mother (1910–), founder in Calcutta, in 1948, of the Order of the Missionaries of Charity, a Roman Catholic order of women dedicated to the relief of the poor, particularly in India. She was born in Macedonia, now in Yugoslavia, and went to India as a nun in 1928. In 1950 her order received papal sanction; in 1971 she was awarded the first Pope John XXIII Peace Prize; in 1979 she received the Nobel Peace Prize, and in 1983 was awarded the British Order of Merit.

Mother Teresa. Much of her work is concerned with the welfare of orphaned children.

Teresina, capital of the state of Piauí, Brazil, situated about 400 km inland on the Rio Paranaiba. It is the commercial centre of an agricultural and cattle-raising area. Population (1975) 290,000.

Term, or terminal figure, in classical architecture, representation of the upper half of a human figure, springing from a pedestal.

Terminal Velocity. If a body moves under the influence of a continuous force in a resisting medium, e.g. the atmosphere, there is a limit to the velocity it can attain. This terminal velocity is small for snowflakes, greater for drops of rain, and greater still for hailstones. It depends on the size, shape and density of the falling body, in addition to the humidity and density of the air.
See also VISCOSITY.

Terminator, the line which divides the dark from the illuminated portion of the disc of a moon or a planet.

Terminus, Roman god of boundaries and frontiers. His cult was supposed to have been introduced by Numa, who made everyone mark the boundaries of his land with stones consecrated to Jupiter, and offer yearly sacrifices at these stones. This festival was the Terminalia held on 23 February.

Termite, an insect in the order Isoptera. There are about 2000 species, mostly tropical, with a few in Europe. Termites are often misnamed 'white ants', but though they look something like ants and resemble them in being social insects, with caste systems, they are not related.

Generally speaking, a termite colony consists of a large queen, laying several thousand eggs a day; a king, who lives with the queen and fertilises her; workers; soldiers; and standby males and females, known as supplementary reproductives, which are available to replace the queen and king should they die.

Workers do all the chores of the colony, caring for and feeding the young, and also the queen and king, foraging for food, building, repairing and expanding the colony; and tending the fungus garden, where present. Soldiers defend the colony, and escort foraging workers. Some have large heads with powerful mandibles; others of the same species can discharge a repellent fluid from a gland on the head. Workers and soldiers are sterile, but may be male or female. Termite nests may be simple, but are often complex structures, full of corridors and chambers, and with an air-conditioning system. Some colonies survive for 100 years or more.

Terms, in English law, the portions of the year during which the High Court sits. There are four: Michaelmas (1 October to 21 December); Hilary (11 January to the Wednesday after Easter Sunday); Easter (Second Tuesday after Easter Sunday to the Friday before the Spring bank holiday); Trinity (Second Tuesday after the Spring bank holiday to 31 July).

Terms, in universities, colleges and schools, the time during which instruction is regularly given to students. In the UK there are usually three terms, the academic year starting in September/October, with breaks at Christmas, Easter and during the summer months. Many colleges and universities in the USA operate on a two-term (nine months) academic year and hold summer sessions during June, July and August.

Tern, or sea swallow, *Sterna*, a genus of birds in order Charadriiformes. They resemble the gulls, to which they are related, but are smaller and slender, with a forked tail. They are extensively distributed, especially in temperate climates. Though poor walkers and swimmers, they are very active on the wing, skimming the surface of the sea from sunrise to sunset in search of small fish and other marine animals. The Arctic tern, *S. paradisea*, is remarkable for the range of its migration, from Greenland, North America and northern Europe as far south as the Antarctic. The black tern and other similar species known as marsh terns are now placed in the genus *Chlidonias*. They are distinguished by their shorter bills, short and slightly forked tails, and less fully webbed feet.

Terni (ancient *Interamna Nahars* or *Interamna Umbrica*), Italian town, capital of Terni province, situated on the edge of a rich well-watered basin 80 km from Rome. Its site is believed to have been occupied since 1000 BC. It has steelworks (stainless steel is a major product), iron foundries, fertiliser, plastics, engineering and textile works. It is a centre of hydroelectric power production from the rivers Nera and Velino, particularly at the nearby Marmore waterfall. Population (1974) 111,043.

Terpenes, general name given to hydrocarbons which occur in essential oils and have a molecular formula $(C_5H_8)_n$. They can be classified as mono- ($n = 2$, e.g. *p*-cymene), sesqui- ($n = 3$), di- ($n = 4$) and tri-terpenes ($n = 6$). They are all volatile and unsaturated compounds, the most important being limonene, camphene and pinene, many of them being derivatives of *p*-cumene (*p*-methyl *iso* propyl benzene). There are also useful derivatives of terpenes such as alcohols (e.g. terpineol, menthol), terpene ketones (e.g. carvone, camphor, menthone), terpene ethers (e.g. cineole) and acyclic members (e.g. geraniol, citral and myrcene).

Terrace, bench in a river valley profile denoting a former level of the valley floor or floodplain. More or less constant in height, they are separated from each other and the present valley by low bluffs or scarps. Two types of terraces are generally recognised: erosional and depositional. The first are carved out of bedrock or an earlier accumulation of stream deposits, and the second results from the deposition of alluvium.
See also BEACH, RAISED.

Terracotta (Italian, baked earth), hard, unglazed pottery, used for bricks, tiles and architectural ornaments, as well as for tombs and coffins, vases and statues. It may be left with its natural brownish red surface, painted as was customary among the Greeks, or covered with enamel.

Terrapin, various tortoises of the families Testudinidae and Dermatemydidae of the order Chelonia. Some of them, especially the diamondback terrapin, *Malaclemys terrapin*, found in the salt marshes on the eastern shores of North America, are highly valued as food. Among the most important are the yellow-bellied, the red-bellied, the chicken and the salt-water terrapins. They are all active swimmers, their clawed digits being united by a web. They are almost omnivorous, but feed chiefly on aquatic animals. In North America and Australia they are fattened in captivity.

Terre Adélie, French sector of the continent of Antarctica, between longitudes 136° and 142°E. It was first visited by Dumont d'Urville in 1840 and named after his wife.

Terrier, term originally applied to dogs which pursue rabbits and other game into their burrows. The following are true terriers: Airedale, Australian, Bedlington, Border, Bull, Cairn, Dandie Dinmont, Fox, Irish, Kerry Blue, Lakeland, Manchester, Norfolk, Norwich, Scottish, Sealyham, Skye, Staffordshire Bull, Welsh and Welsh Highland White. The word is now also applied to a number of breeds of foreign origin, for example Boston and Tibetan terriers.

Territorial Army. The British Territorial Army has an establishment of about 73,000. Its rôle is to provide a national reserve for employment on specific tasks at home and overseas and to meet the unexpected when required; and, in particular, to complete the Army Order of Battle of NATO committed forces and to provide certain units for the support of NATO Headquarters, to assist in maintaining a secure United Kingdom base in support of forces deployed on the Continent of Europe. Men who have completed service in the Regular Army normally have some liability to serve in the Regular Reserve. All members of the TA and Regular Reserve may be called out by a Queen's Order in time of emergency or imminent national danger and most of the TA and a large proportion of the Regular Reserve may be called out by a Queen's Order when warlike operations are in preparation or in progress.

Territorial Waters. Most modern states recognise the sovereignty of every other state over its own territorial waters. The limit was generally fixed at one marine league (c.3 miles, 4·8 km) from the shore, measured from low-water mark. This distance is the subject of much criticism by writers on international law, because it was in its origin suggested by the supposed range of gun, and the tremendous range of modern artillery has therefore made it meaningless. Three miles (4·8 km) at low-water mark, however, remains the minimum claim by a coastal state to sovereign control of the seas. A more extensive jurisdiction to the waters surrounding their coasts is claimed by a great many states, though this extended claim may be restricted to certain specific purposes, i.e. fishing. UK courts have jurisdiction to try persons for crimes committed in territorial waters.
A conference on the law of the sea at Geneva in 1958 failed to agree that the limit of territorial waters should be extended to 12 miles (19·3 km). The general trend in thinking seems to be towards a 12-mile (19·3 km) territorial sea and a 200-mile (321·9 km) economic zone. In Europe, the situation came to a head in the 'Cod Wars' of 1972/3, and 1975/6 involving Iceland, the UK and West Germany. Although no international negotiations have been successful, bilateral agreements have been reached between interested parties over fishing rights.

Terrorism, Urban, the name given to the activities of the urban guerrilla, criminal acts undertaken by small groups of criminals or political dissidents as a means of securing funds, obtaining publicity, or seeking to blackmail governments into meeting their demands. The prefix 'urban' is used because the attackers employ the anonymity of the modern city and all the resources of modern society against its rulers, and to contrast them with the brigands and guerrillas of the past, essentially part of rural society.
See also GUERRILLAS.

Terry, family of illustrious English actors and actresses, of whom the parents, Benjamin (1818–96) and Sarah (Ballard) (1819–92) were well-known in the provinces, and later appeared in London with Macready and Charles Kean. Their eldest child Kate (1844–1924) was a successful actress. Her daughter, Mabel Gwynedd Terry-Lewis (1872–1957) was a well-known actress, while another daughter (also Kate) was the mother of Val and John Gielgud. Two other daughters of Benjamin and Sarah went on the stage: Marion (1852–1930), who was the first Mrs Erlynne in *Lady Windermere's Fan*; and Florence (1854–96). The youngest child, Fred (1863–1933), was a successful romantic lead, who often played opposite his wife, Julia Neilson. Their children, Phyllis (1892–) and Dennis (1895–1932) were both on the stage, and it was under Phyllis's management that John Gielgud made his first professional appearance. The most eminent member of the Terry family, however, was Benjamin and Sarah's second child, Dame Ellen Alicia Terry (1847–1928), who was leading-lady to Sir Henry Irving at the Lyceum between 1878 and 1902. Together, they played numerous Shakespearean and modern rôles. Dame Ellen later appeared under her own management at the Imperial Theatre, and in 1906 celebrated her stage jubilee at Drury Lane with a matinee in which 23 members of her family appeared with the leading theatrical figures of the day. As an actress, she is said to have had a fresh and lively technique, though without much talent for the weightier tragic rôles.

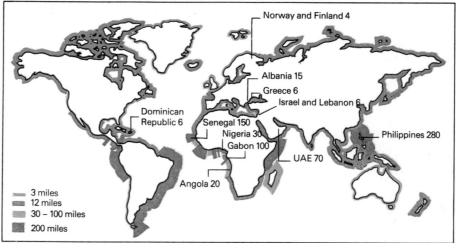

Territorial Waters fall largely into three width categories, 3, 12 and 200 miles. There are also seven or so countries with limits between 30 and 100 miles. Exceptions to the key are noted on the map.

Tertian Fever, see MALARIA.

Tertiaries, see FRANCISCANS.

Tertiary System, occurs above the Cretaceous and below the Quaternary Systems. It began about 64 million years ago and ended two million years ago. Tertiary rocks in Britain occur as two widely differing facies; shallow-water sediments in south-east England and volcanic rocks of lower Tertiary age in western Scotland, northern England and north-east Ireland. The Tertiary System is divided into a number of series, the lowest of which is the Palaeocene series; this is followed by the Eocene, Oligocene, Miocene and Pliocene series. Prior to the deposition of the Tertiary sediments, the Cretaceous strata of southern England were uplifted, tilted and eroded, and the succeeding Tertiary period saw a total change in the fauna from the dominant reptiles of the Jurassic and Cretaceous to the coming of the mammals. The flora also changed radically, with modern forms such as grasses appearing for the first time in the Tertiary.

Tertis, Lionel (1876–1975), British viola-player. He studied music at Leipzig and in London, and became a brilliant player and a great teacher. In 1938 he designed a deep-bodied viola which became widely used.

Tertullian, Quintus Septimius Florens (c.160–230), early Christian apologist. At Carthage, probably, he was converted to Christianity, around 190, and at once was ordained priest. About the end of the 2nd century he became a Montanist, probably because he was a rigorist, and violently opposed the restoration to communion of penitent adulterers and fornicators, a concession made by Agrippinus, Bishop of Carthage. Tertullian is one of the leading Latin fathers for learning and intellectual power. The *Apology*, written at Carthage, probably in the reign of Severus, contributed largely to the better understanding of Christianity and the mitigation of persecution.

Terza Rima, verse form consisting of three-line stanzas, the middle line of each stanza rhyming with the first and last lines of the succeeding stanza: *aba bcb cdc ded*. Terza rima originated in Italy in the 13th century and the most famous example of its use is Dante's *Divina Commedia*. At the time of the Renaissance it was introduced into English by Sir Thomas Wyatt, in his satires, and by Surrey, and also into French.

See also METRE.

Test Act. By the Test Act 1673 all office-holders of the English Crown, civil and military, were obliged within six months after appointment to take the sacrament in accordance with the ceremony of the Church of England, and take the oaths of allegiance and supremacy. This act was usually conjoined with the Corporation Act of 1661, which compelled all holders of municipal offices to take the sacrament. Lord John Russell in 1828 carried a motion for their repeal, but both by then were ineffective. The Test Act of 1678 excluded all Roman Catholics save the Duke of York from Parliament.

Test Match, although the term is now widely used in other sports to denote a major international fixture, is most usually associated with cricket. Test matches are generally held over five days, between the international sides of England, Australia, New Zealand, the West Indies, India, Pakistan and, since 1982, Sri Lanka. A former Test-playing nation, South Africa, is now excluded from international competition on political grounds. The first-ever Test match is generally held to be the game played between Australia and England in March 1877 in Melbourne.

Test-papers, paper slips impregnated with some chemical reagent. Litmus papers are used for testing for acids and alkalis, acids turning the blue variety to a red colour, and alkalis turning the red papers to blue. Paper containing lead acetate is used as a test for hydrogen sulphide, which turns it brown. Oxidising agents, such as chlorine, and ozone are tested for with papers containing potassium iodide and starch, which are turned blue by their presence. Turmeric paper, yellow in colour, is used as a test for alkalis and boric acid, which cause it to turn reddish-brown.

Test-tube Baby, a baby born in the normal way but conceived by fertilisation of ovum and sperm outside the woman's body 'in-vitro', literally 'in glass'. It is mainly used in cases where the woman is infertile due to a defect in her reproductive system, for example, blocked Fallopian tubes. Her ova can be removed from the ovary by a simple operation and put with the man's sperm in a culture medium where fertilisation occurs. The resulting embryo is then implanted in her womb at about the third day to develop as in a normal pregnancy. To date, only a few test-tube babies have been born. Some controversy has surrounded the status and future of spare embryos sometimes produced by this technique.

Testament, see BIBLE.

Testicle, see TESTIS.

Testis (testicle), the reproductive organ of the male animal, in which the reproductive cells (spermatozoa or sperm) that fertilise the egg (ovum) are produced. There is usually one pair of testes in each individual. In the human foetus the testes develop on the posterior abdominal wall, slowly descending as the foetus grows, until by the end of the eighth month of pregnancy they reach the scrotum. Occasionally for some reason a testis becomes halted in its descent and is not in the scrotum at birth, a condition known as 'undescended testis'. Unless it descends in the few months following birth, a simple operation is usually performed before the onset of puberty to bring the testis into the scrotum. The testes are the main source of the male sex-hormone testosterone.

Testosterone, the male hormone. It is secreted in the endocrine portion of the testes and controls the development of the adult male, including development of the genitalia and the growth of the beard. The hormone also controls the supply of seminal fluid. As a drug testosterone is given to correct hypogonadism (underdevelopment of the gonads).

Testudo, see TORTOISE.

Tetanus, a disease caused by *Clostridium tetani,* a bacterium capable of living and reproducing in the absence of oxygen and showing a predilection for wounds contaminated by debris and dirt. A toxin that is secreted by the multiplying bacteria causes the main symptom of the disease, painful muscular spasms (hence the old name lock-jaw), that may lead to respiratory failure and death. The microbe is widespread, being detectable in the faeces of most mammals, but no harm results from its presence in the gut. It is known to be associated with even very minor forms of injury, especially among gardeners. Burns also may be contaminated with *Clostridium* spores, as may the newborn's umbilicus.

Prevention is the aim, an effective vaccine being available in the form of the toxin (prepared from growing cultures in the laboratory), which is made harmless by treatment with chemicals. In this form, the immunisation is often given with diphtheria and whooping-cough vaccines (known as triple immunisation) during infancy, with booster doses every five to eight years.

Tethys Sea, the name given to an ancient ocean which covered much of southern Europe, the Mediterranean, North Africa, Iran, the Himalayas and South-East Asia in the Mesozoic era. Thick deposits of sedimentary rocks were laid down, and it later became the site of the Alpine orogenic belt in Tertiary times.

Tetracyclines, a group of antibiotic drugs with a wide spectrum of antimicrobial activity. They include tetracycline, chlortetracycline, oxytetracycline and dimethylchlortetracycline.

Tetraethyl Lead (TEL), $Pb(C_2H_5)_4$, first prepared in 1859, was found to be an extremely efficient anti-knock additive for petrol in 1921. Very small amounts (e.g. 0·06 per cent by volume) will increase the octane number of a fuel considerably (e.g. by 5 to 10 octane numbers). TEL is manufactured by heating an alloy of lead and sodium with ethyl chloride in a closed vessel at 60–80°C. It is a poisonous, colourless, stable liquid, immiscible with water. Recent concern over the effect of lead on the environment has led to legislation in many countries reducing the maximum permitted content of lead in petrol. See also KNOCKING.

Tetrafluoroethylene, $CF_2:CF_2$, prepared by the high-temperature condensation of difluorochloromethane, and used as the monomer in the manufacture of polytetrafluoroethylene.

See also PLASTICS.

Tetrazzini, Luisa (1871–1940), Italian soprano. She studied in Florence where she made her début in 1895. Later she toured Europe, Mexico and South America. With brilliant coloratura technique she achieved particular success in the title rôle of Donizetti's *Lucia di Lammermoor,* and as Amina in Bellini's *La Sonnambula.*

Tetzel, Johann (c.1465–1519), German Dominican friar. By the scandalous manner in which he carried on the traffic in indulgences, Tetzel roused Luther to precipitate the German Reformation in 1517 with the issue of his Ninety-Five Theses. Tetzel was later discredited.

Teutonic Knights, one of the great semi-religious orders of knights founded during the period of the crusades. It originated in a brotherhood formed by certain German merchants of Bremen and Lübeck to alleviate the sufferings of the attacking troops during the siege of Acre in 1190. A hospital was started, and as a result the Teutonic Knights of the

Hospital of St Mary of Jerusalem were founded. The new order, distinguished by a white mantle with a black cross, was formed on the model of the Knights Hospitallers and its members were also pledged to tend the sick, to protect the Church, and to wage war against the heathen. In 1198 the hospital was turned into an order of knighthood. The Teutonic Knights conquered Lithuania and the Baltic regions of Prussia during the 13th and 14th centuries. For a century their head-quarters were at Acre (1191–1291), but the seat of the order was transferred to Marien-burg in 1308. Their defeat at the hands of the Poles and Lithuanians at Tannenburg (1410) struck a great blow at their prestige and the order declined rapidly. In 1525 the 'high master', Albert of Brandenburg, secularised the order in Prussia, but it survived in Cath-olic Germany until suppressed by Napoleon in 1809. An Austrian branch survives in atten-uated form to this day as a purely religious community.

Teutons, or Teutones, a German people, first mentioned by the Greek navigator Pytheas as living on the coast of what was later called Holstein. They migrated and wandered with the Cimbri between 120 and 102 BC and, becoming a threat to northern Italy, were annihilated in battle by the consul Marius at Aix-en-Provence in 102 BC. The name 'Teu-tons' later became a synonym for Germans.

Tewkesbury, market town in Gloucester-shire, England, situated on the Avon, close to the point where that river joins the Severn, 16 km north-east of Gloucester. The Battle of Tewkesbury, 1471, was one of the most bitter battles of the Wars of the Roses, in which the Lancastrians were routed. The town's most magnificent building is its abbey church, all that is left of a great Benedictine abbey erected in the 12th century on a Saxon foundation. Population (1981) 9554.

Texas (Lone Star State), the southernmost of the central states of the USA and the largest (682,835 km²) in the Union before the ad-mission of Alaska, with a coastline along the Gulf of Mexico stretching for 595 km from Mexico north-east to Louisiana. It is separated from Mexico, on the south-west, by the Rio Grande; New Mexico and Oklahoma border it on the north, and Arkansas and Louisiana on the east. The general relief slopes from north-west to south-east. The Llano Estacado is a barren plateau in the west with a mean elevation of 915 to 1525 m. The descent to the coastal plain at a height of 300 m is swift, and then come fertile tracts of rolling prairie crossed by plentiful forests of yellow pine in the east, and with rich pastures alternating with corn lands—tracts which extend terrace-like to the fertile lowlands and barren swamps of the coastal belt. Behind Padre Island, which hugs the shore for over 160 km northward from the mouth of the Rio Grande to that of the Nueces, is a region of white sands, known as 'the desert'.

The largest share of the farm income is derived from livestock products. Cattle and sheep dominate western Texas, where some of the largest ranches in the USA are to be found. Among field crops, the largest areas are under cotton and grain sorghum. Fruit and vegetables are important. There are 5·2 million ha of commercial forests, and coastal fisheries are valuable to the ports of the Gulf coast. Petroleum is the most valuable mineral pro-duct, representing more than one-third of US total output. Texas also has natural gas, asphalts and pyrites; helium, clays, mag-nesium, sulphur and gypsum. The original agricultural processing industries have been augmented by petroleum-based industries and later by regional steel production, aircraft manufacture and vehicle assembly.

The Spanish explorers de Vaca and Coronado were the first to explore the region now known as Texas (the name was that of an Indian tribe), but the first permanent settle-ment was made by La Salle in 1685 at Fort St Louis. Texas was surrendered in 1713 by France to Spain. When Mexico became in-dependent of Spain in 1821, Coahuila and Texas formed one state. Texas was colonised to a large extent by Americans and British, and when trouble broke out with the Mexi-can government, Texas was constituted an independent republic in 1836. In 1845 it gained admission as a state of the USA.

In 1980 Texas had 14,228,383 people. The capital is Austin, but its three largest cities are Houston, Dallas and San Antonio.

Textiles, fabrics made from either natural or man-made fibres. They may consist of bonded or matted fibres, as in felt, or be made by weaving or knitting yarn spun from the fibres.

See also COTTON; FABRICS, TEXTILE; FIBRES AND FIBROUS SUBSTANCES; SILK AND SILK-WORMS; SPINNING; TEXTILE PRINTING; WEAV-ING; WOOL.

Textile Printing, the application of colour to specific areas of textile material. It can be performed by four main processes: block, roller, screen and transfer.

Block Printing. The block is covered with a liquid consisting of dyestuff, a thickener and a fixative. The block is placed on the cloth, hammered to ensure proper contact, and removed. Many colours can be applied by this method and the setting-up cost for preparing the blocks is relatively low, but the process is slow and is now only used on expensive cloths printed in short runs to 'exclusive' designs.

For *roller printing* the design is engraved and transferred to a copper roller. Each individual colour to be printed demands a separate roller, so that machines carrying as many as 20 copper cylinders may be employed.

In *screen printing* a very finely woven fabric or screen, formerly of silk but now nylon or metal, is processed so that in certain areas the holes between the weave are blocked. The screen is placed on the cloth and print paste pressed through the open parts of the screen by a flexible rubber blade. Many colours may be applied consecutively.

Transfer Printing has been developed since about 1965; paper is printed using textile dyes which are then transferred to fabric in dry heat by pressing the cloth on the paper at temperatures of 160–210°C.

Teyte, Dame Maggie (1888–1976), English soprano. She studied in London and Paris, and made her début at Monte Carlo in 1907. In 1908 Debussy chose her to sing the heroine in his *Pelléas et Mélisande*. She also sang at Covent Garden in Chicago, Boston and New York. She later excelled as an interpreter of songs, especially French.

Thackeray, William Makepeace (1811–1863), English novelist and essayist. In 1833 he became part owner of a weekly paper, the *National Standard*. When the paper came to an end in 1834, its losses were borne by Thackeray, and the remainder of his £20,000 inheritance from his father in 1815 dis-appeared with the failure of an Indian bank in 1833. At this time he was in Paris studying art as he now hoped to become an illustrator. In August he married Isabella Shawe, and became Paris correspondent of a daily newspaper, the *Constitutional*. This also failed, and in 1837 he returned to London. To this period belong his contributions to *Fraser's Magazine*. From this time Thackeray's life was clouded by his wife's insanity. The bril-liant *Barry Lyndon* appeared serially in *Fraser's* in 1844. Since 1842 he had contributed regularly to *Punch* and increased his reputa-tion with *The Book of Snobs*, which appeared there, 1846–47. He did not become really famous until the publication of *Vanity Fair*, which was brought out in monthly parts from January 1847 to July 1848. This is Thackeray's masterpiece; one of the greatest social satires in English. He at once began work on *Pendennis*, and the first of 24 monthly parts appeared in November 1848. These two satirical works placed him in the forefront of contemporary novelists. *The History of Henry Esmond* was published in 1852, and *The Rose and the Ring* was produced in 1854. In 1860 Thackeray became first editor of the highly successful *Cornhill Magazine*.

Thailand
Area: 514,000 km²
Population: 45,000,000
Capital: Bangkok

Thailand (formerly *Siam*), a country of mainland South-East Asia, bordered on the north by Burma and Laos, on the east by Laos and Kampuchea (Cambodia), and on the west by Burma. Thailand extends southward as a peninsula with the Gulf of Thailand to its east and the Indian Ocean to its west. In the south of the peninsula, it borders Malaysia.

The total area is 514,000 km² which can be divided broadly into four major natural regions: the northern valleys, the central plain, the north-east plateau, and the penin-sula. The central plain is drained by the Chao Phraya river. The valleys of the northern region are separated by high, forest-covered ridges and these extend southward as a line of mountains which form the eastern border of the country and constitute the backbone of the southern peninsula. A distinctly separate region is the low plateau of Khorat, the scarp of which overlooks the central plain in the east and which drains eastward and north-ward to the Mekong river which forms most of the boundary with Laos.

The population in 1979 was 45 million.

Most of the Thai population continue to live in the countryside, although the capital Bang-kok and its conurbation has grown to be one of the largest cities in the Orient.

Agriculture is dominated by rice production. Maize is grown chiefly in the north central

Thailand. *The Summer Palace is situated in Bangkok, which has been the capital since 1782.*

plain, cassava in the south-east, sugar cane in the west central plain, and kenaf in the north-east. In the southern peninsula, smallholder rubber cultivation remains an important enterprise.

Thai industry remains concentrated in the Bangkok metropolitan region. Manufacturing is mainly oriented towards import substitution of consumer goods, with food processing and textiles the most important sectors of employment. In the extractive sector, although limestone quarrying and lignite and fluorite mining are significant, the tin and tungsten mining industry of the peninsula is still most important. The vast salt and phosphate deposits underlying the north-east plateau have not yet been exploited; possible petroleum supplies have been explored in the Gulf of Thailand.

The Thai currency is the baht (100 satangs = 1 baht).

The constitution of 1978 was designed to restore democracy and provides for the continuation of the monarchy. There is an elected legislature.

Legislative power effectively lies with the prime minister, the cabinet and the Advisory Council.

The official language is Thai.

History. The Thais began to move into their present territory in the 8th and 9th centuries from the kingdom of Nan Chao in the Yunnan area of China. Small states were established in the 11th century and in 1238 the first major kingdom was founded at Sukhothai. By 1350 power had passed to the south where another prince, Ramatipadi, founded Ayuthya. From this capital, Thailand was involved in a protracted power struggle, first with Cambodia and then with Burma. The latter conflict led in 1767 to the obstruction of Ayutha. Order in Thailand was subsequently restored and in 1782 the present Chakri dynasty came to power in the new capital of Bangkok.

After 1851 King Mongkut (Rama IV) and his successor, King Chulalongkorn, employed Western advisers to assist in the modernisation of the country's administration and commerce. Siam remained a British sphere of influence in the early 20th century, but major financial difficulties hit the country in the 1930s and these precipitated a political coup in 1932. Throughout the 1930s politics were marked by increasing nationalism; exploited by the invading Japanese in 1940–41. By 1942 Thailand had declared war on the West. Military coups and periods of unstable government have marked the post-war years. A coup in 1977 led to a new constitution in 1978 and elections in 1979.

Thaler, the popular name of a German and Austrian silver coin which had a wide currency from the 16th to 19th century. The denomination was also popular outside Germany, hence the Italian *tallero* and English and American dollar.

Thales (c.636–c.546 BC), Greek philosopher, first of the Seven Sages. He taught that water or moisture was the one element from which all things evolved. He appears to have owed much to the astronomy of the Egyptians and the civilisation of Mesopotamia. He is regarded as the founder of abstract geometry, of the strict deductive form as shown in Euclid's collections.

Thalia, muse of comedy and idyllic poetry. See also MUSES.

Thalidomide is a hypnotic (sleep-inducing) and sedative drug synthesised in Germany in 1953. The harm caused to the foetus when it was administered to women during the early stages of pregnancy was realised in 1961 and the drug was withdrawn. Children born to women who took it had phocomelia (seal extremities), in which the long bones of the limbs were defective, but the hands and feet were normal.

Thallium, metallic chemical element, symbol Tl, atomic number 81, atomic weight 204·37. It was discovered in 1861 by Crookes in the seleniferous deposits from sulphuric acid manufacture. It occurs in small quantities in iron pyrites, and associated with copper, silver and selenium in the mineral 'crookesite'. Thallium compounds give a bright green line in the spectrum (Greek *thallos*, a green shoot); some of them are used in the manufacture of optical glass.

Thallus, term used of the plant body of an alga or fungus, where there is no differentiation into root, stem or leaf.

Thames, river of England, which rises near Cirencester in the Cotswold Hills and follows a course of 330 km through Oxford and Henley-on-Thames to the Nore, where it debouches into the North Sea. It is one of England's largest and most important rivers. At Gravesend, the head of the estuary, it has a width of a kilometre, gradually increasing thence to 16 km at the Nore. Tidal waters reach Teddington, 100 km from its mouth. Lying some 5 km south-west of the Nore is the mouth of the Medway estuary, at the head of which lie Chatham with naval dockyards, Gillingham and Rochester. Gravesend on the south bank of the river, some 40 km from the Nore, has developed at a point where vessels formerly awaited the turn of the tide. Tilbury Fort and Docks, important as the main London container terminal, lies opposite Gravesend on the northern bank. Between Tilbury and London Bridge (some 40 km upstream) stretches the old London dock system and many wharves. The Port of London Authority is responsible for the control and conservation of the river below Teddington; above Teddington the Thames Water Authority is responsible.

Thanet, Isle of, extreme eastern part of Kent, formerly separated from the mainland by the River Wantsum which remained in part navigable up to the end of the 15th century. Traditionally a cereal growing area, it has now become noted for green vegetables and potatoes. Margate, Broadstairs and Ramsgate are well-known resorts.

Thanjavur, town in Tamil Nadu state, India, 273 km south of Madras, standing at the head of the Cauvery delta which is heavily irrigated, densely populated, and very fertile. The town is a Brahmin centre and a noted political, literary and educational focus. Population (1981) 183,464.

Thanksgiving Day, annual festival of thanksgiving in the USA, celebrated as a national holiday on the fourth Thursday in November. It is in essence a national harvest celebration, and was first observed by the Pilgrim Fathers at Plymouth in 1621 after their first harvest.

Thant, U (1909–74), Burmese administrator and United Nations official. He was Burma's permanent representative at the UN, 1957–1961. After Dag Hammarskjöld's death, Thant, a compromise candidate, was acting secretary-general of the UN from November 1961 to November 1962, when he was confirmed as secretary-general, a post he held until 1971.

Thapsus, ancient city of north Africa, 48 km south-east of Susa. In 46 BC Julius Caesar here routed the Pompeians under Cato, Metellus Scipio and Juba II.

Thasos (Greek *Thásos*), island of Greece in the north of the Aegean Sea, off the coast of Macedonia. The Thasians once possessed territory on the coast of Thrace, and were one of the most powerful peoples in the northern Aegean. After subjugation by Persia, they regained their independence in 479 BC and joined the Delian League. The island was ruled by Romans, Byzantines and Turks before it was ceded to Greece in 1913. Area 378 km²; population (1971) 16,000.

Thatcher, Margaret Hilda (1925–), British politician. She began her career as a research chemist, but became a barrister before being elected Conservative MP for Finchley in 1959. From 1961 to 1964 she was parliamentary secretary, Ministry of Pensions and National Insurance. She was an Opposition spokesman from 1964–70 and entered the Cabinet as secretary of state for Education and Science in 1970, a post she held until the Conservative defeat of 1974. In 1975 Mrs Thatcher successfully challenged Edward Heath for the leadership of the Conservative party and thus became the first woman to lead a political party in Britain. In 1979 she became prime minister. Under her leadership, government policies have been characterised by the use of tight monetary controls as a method of checking inflation, and a desire to achieve cost effectiveness in government spending. Her awareness of the media and her strong personal leadership, particularly during the Falklands war, has given her a populist appeal, apparently unaffected by high unemployment, which has largely been attributed to her policies. She has a single-minded, authorative approach to government. She was returned to office after the general election of 1983 with a majority of 144 seats, the largest since 1945.

Thatching, art of roofing or protecting stacks of hay or grain with a covering of reeds, rushes, straw, etc. Thatch should be at least 30 cm thick and laid to a pitch of 45 degrees. Best or true Norfolk reed is used in thatching. Norfolk reed with an admixture of lesser reed mace lasts longer, besides being less expensive than best reed. Wheat or rye straw is considerably cheaper than reed, but may require renewal after 20 years, whereas reed thatch should last about 75 years. Thatching is now seldom used except for renovations.

Thaumaturgy, healing by means of some supernormal ability not yet usually verifiable by science. It includes faith healing (which is said to be effected by the patient's faith in divine power); spirit healing (which is claimed to be due to spirit doctors working through mediums); and contact healing (described as a transmission of healing energy from healer to patient through bodily contact of some sort).

Theatre, building or area specially designated for the presentation of a performance by an actor or actors in front of an audience; also, all the physical elements which make up the presentation. The first known Greek theatres were built on sacred sites in close proximity to temples. At first, plays were performed in theatres consisting of wooden stands or seats on a slope with an open playing area. Only later did a stage become the focus, and a scenic background added. The building was enclosed with high walls, also often architecturally elaborate. Playhouses of increasing splendour were built in many Roman towns and cities.
The staging of the liturgical plays of the medieval Church was governed by the physical conditions of the church or cathedral and by the devotional purposes of the music-drama. The vernacular religious plays—whether miracle play cycles, moralities or saints' plays—conformed in general to this convention of staging with two basic variations: the station-to-station form, in which moveable pageant wagons were used for performances at different locations in the town; and the stationary place-and-scaffold structures representing separate locations.
The Italian rediscovery of classical dramatists, especially Plautus and Terence, in the 15th century led to attempts in schools and academies to reconstruct the physical conditions of their original performance. The growing interest in the 16th century in perspective scenery, however, displaced to a large extent this original scholarly interest.
Regarding English playhouses of the Elizabethan period, a number of documentary sources, including the surviving contracts for the building of the Fortune Theatre (1600) and the Hope Theatre (1613), indicate that the acting platform was in general very large, and that the 'heavens' supported on pillars were apparently normal. Finally, playhouses of the Elizabethan or Jacobean periods could be circular, octagonal, or square in shape.

Theatre design through history has fallen roughly into two classes: the thrust style stage, whose origin lies in the Greek classical theatre, and the proscenium-arch style, which can be traced back to Roman times.

In the course of the 17th century, the conception of spectacle spread from Italy throughout Europe as a result of the efforts of such designers as Bernini, Torelli and Inigo Jones. In England, Inigo Jones developed, in his designs for masques and plays presented at Court, a system of flats which moved in grooves in and above the stage, the backcloth being formed of two shutters which could open to reveal another elaborate scene behind. Italianate stage practice spread from the court theatres of the 17th and 18th centuries to the public theatres. The tragedies of Corneille and Racine were played in a neutral palace setting derived from Italian precedent and the formal concern with the *Unity of Place*. The reopening of the English theatres, at the Restoration, signalled the triumph of the perspective and proscenium stage, though at first a traditional apron stage protruded in front of the proscenium arch.
The 18th and 19th centuries saw the elaboration of developments already apparent in the late 17th century. In Europe, generally, the 18th century was the age of the opera houses, with their sumptuously decorated horseshoe auditoria round the proscenium-arched stage. Towards the end of the century, especially in England, there developed a movement towards greater historical realism in costume, and later in scenery. This type of staging was associated especially with the Shakespearean productions of Charles Kean in the 1850s. Spectacle was also the keynote of the popular melodrama of the 19th century, and elaborate machinery was invented to reproduce, with maximum effect, such sensational events as train crashes, horse races and ships in storm-tossed seas. Most significant of all were the advances in stage lighting; the darkened auditorium; the illuminated and realistically decorated stage which had become entirely separated. The front curtain became increasingly vital, and behind the proscenium arch ever more naturalistic settings were sought. Stanislavsky is particularly associated with naturalist theatre in Moscow.
Early reaction against photographic naturalism in stage design is linked with two designers, Adolphe Appia and Edward Gordon Craig, who were part of a general movement called 'Theatricalism'. In France, the reaction against elaborate effects and naturalistic detail is evident in the work of Jacques Copeau during and after the First World War, and in the theories of Antonin Artaud, who was greatly influenced by Oriental conventions of performance, as well as in the work of such directors as Jean-Louis Barrault and Peter Brook. Experimental work was also done in the Russian theatre at the beginning of the century, especially in the period immediately following the Revolution. In Germany, the Expressionist movement developed a form of presentation in which stages of mind were evoked by stylisation of the décor and acting, and by the elaborate use of lighting effects. From this grew the Epic theatre of Bertolt Brecht and Erwin Piscator which set out to make the audience think critically.

Theatre of the Absurd, a term coined to describe those modern plays which dramatise some aspect of the philosophical belief that, since there is no God, there is therefore no essential meaning to human existence. Among the major recent dramatists whose work has been critically included within this category are Eugene Ionesco, Samuel Beckett, Jean Genet and Harold Pinter, though there is doubt as to what extent some of these playwrights would accept the ascription: Beckett, for example, has insisted that he is not an Absurdist. As a critical term, it has the merit of indicating the underlying common preoccupations and attitudes of much modern thought and drama.

Theban Legend, story of Oedipus, son of Laius, King of Thebes, in present-day Boeotia, Greece. The legend tells how Oedipus was cast out in infancy, returning on killing the Sphinx to marry his mother, Jocasta, and how the destruction of the city followed the disastrous rule of his sons, Eteocles and Polynices.

Thebes, name of ancient city of Upper Egypt, known latterly as Thebais. It survives today in the magnificent ruins of Karnak and Luxor, which mostly date from the New Kingdom, when it was the capital. It rose into prominence under the princes, who in the 11th Dynasty reunited Egypt. One of the princes, Mentuhotep II, enriched the whole area with monuments and began the long series of royal tombs in the Valley of the Kings. Thebes was the centre of worship of Amen-Ra, with his consort Mut, the vulture mother-goddess, and their son Khons. Each king added to the great temple of Amun at Karnak. Seti I and Rameses II built great additions to the temples of Karnak and funerary temples on the west bank. Rameses III built a temple and tower at Medinet Habu. The 25th Dynasty made Thebes their capital, but under them it was sacked by the Assyrians. Under the Ptolemies it ceased to be the capital of Upper Egypt, but as always it was liable to be the centre of nationalist movements. It was severely punished after a rising in 86 BC by Ptolemy IX and destroyed in the reign of Augustus for another rising.
See also EGYPT, ANCIENT.

Thebes, chief city of Boeotia in ancient Greece and the birthplace of Pindar. Situated in a plain surrounded by mountains, it was well defended. No place is more celebrated in Greek legend: here the alphabet was introduced from Phoenicia; here was the birthplace of Dionysus and Hercules, and here was the scene of the Theban Legend. The first historical trace of the city dates from Boeotian (Dorian) conquest, c.1100 BC. Thebes then became the chief city of a confederation. She became the closest ally of the Spartans, but in 394 BC she allied with Athens against Sparta. In 382 the citadel was occupied by Spartan troops, and its recovery by Theban exiles in 378 led to war with Sparta. After the battle of Leuctra (371 BC) for a short time she became, under Epaminondas, the most powerful state in Greece, but with his death at the battle of Mantinea, 362, Thebes lost her hegemony. In 335 BC she defied Alexander and was largely destroyed. The city was rebuilt by Cassander and the Athenians in 316 BC. In 290 it was taken by Demetrius Poliorcetes, and thereafter declined rapidly. The final blow was administered by Sulla, who gave half its territory to Delphi.

Theft is defined, in English law, by the Theft Act 1968 as the dishonest appropriation of property belonging to another with the intention of permanently depriving the other of it. The offence of theft replaces the old offences of larceny, embezzlement and fraudulent conversion.
See also BURGLARY.

Theme, in music, principal melodic feature in a composition, differing from a subject by greater length and more self-contained completeness. Sets of variations are usually based on a theme.
See also FUGUE; SONATA.

Themistocles (c.528–c.460 BC), Athenian soldier and statesman. He was appointed archon of Athens in 493 and instigated the construction of harbours in the bays of Piraeus. He persuaded the Athenians to employ the revenues from their silver mines in building 100 triremes, and to move the naval base from Phalerum to Piraeus. When Xerxes began his invasion (480), Themistocles commanded the Athenian fleet and was responsible for the victory of Salamis. However, his arrogance resulted in a decline of his popularity; he was accused of peculation and ostracised (which meant banished) in 471. He settled at Argos, but evidence was found apparently implicating him in the conspiracy of Pausanias, and envoys were sent from Athens to arrest him (468). Themistocles escaped to the coast of Asia Minor. Having spent a year learning the Persian language and customs, he was welcomed by Artaxerxes I, who provided him with a handsome maintenance, and he took up residence at Magnesia, where before long he died.

Theocritus (c.310–250 BC), Greek pastoral poet. Having studied under Philetas in Cos, he visited Alexandria and obtained the patronage of Ptolemy Philadelphus, in whose praise he wrote the 14th, 15th and 17th idylls. Theocritus was the creator of bucolic poetry; his idylls, of which 30 survive, are of a dramatic and mimetic character, and are pictures of the life of the ordinary people of Sicily.

Theodolite, an instrument used in surveying for measuring angles in horizontal and vertical planes. It consists essentially of a small sighting telescope mounted altazimuthly and fitted with graduated circles so that the amount of motion about both the horizontal and vertical axes can be recorded. Clamps and slow-motion screws allow the telescope to be quickly and accurately pointed. In a modern theodolite the graduated circles are etched on glass, are totally enclosed, and can be read from a position close to the telescope eye-piece. The optical train for doing this incorporates a micrometer device and views both ends of a diameter of the relevant circle. The base carrying the vertical axis is fitted with foot screws and an appropriate series of bubbles to allow the instrument to be accurately levelled when placed on a tripod. The vertical axis can be set immediately over a reference mark by the optical plummet which replaces the plumb-line formerly used. An automatic levelling arrangement is incorporated into the reading system of the vertical circle so that altitude readings are not critically dependent on the precise levelling of the instrument.
Many theodolites have horizontal 'stadia' lines ruled on the reticule in the telescope in addition to the usual cross. These allow the theodolite to be used as a tacheometer, i.e. in conjunction with a levelling staff to measure distances quickly.

Theodora (c.500–48), wife of the Byzantine Emperor Justinian I, notorious before her marriage as an actress, was proclaimed empress in 527. She showed great courage in the Nika insurrection (532), and was an able counsellor in all matters of state.

Theodorakis, Mikis (1925–), Greek composer, who studied with Messiaen and whose first work, the oratorio *Sinfonia*, was published in 1944. In the 1960s he led a revival of Greek folk music, including elements of it in his compositions, particularly his music for the film *Zorba the Greek*, 1964. He was elected to the Greek Parliament in 1964, but was imprisoned under the junta for his political activities (1967–70).

Theodore I Lascaris (c.1175–1222), Byzantine Emperor. After the Crusaders' conquest of Constantinople (1204), he created a Byzantine empire in exile in western Asia Minor, based at Nicea (1208), repelling attacks by the Latins and Seljuk Turks.
See also BYZANTINE EMPIRE.

Theodoric the Great (c.445–526), founder of the Ostrogothic monarchy in Italy. Theodoric, after some raids against the Emperor Zeno, set out to win Italy from Odoacer, whom he defeated at Verona and killed (493). Theodoric's 33-years reign was a period of peace and prosperity for Italy such as it had not known for centuries. He maintained his traditional Arian creed, but was tolerant in religious matters. His closing years were sullied with the judicial murders of Boethius and the latter's father-in-law, Symmachus.

Theodosius I, or Flavius Theodosius, known as the Great (347–395), Byzantine Emperor. He was proclaimed emperor of the East by Gratian in 379. He warred successfully against the Goths, and by skilful diplomacy enlisted them as his allies (382). He secured the Western throne for Valentinian II, and after Valentinian's death (392), defeated another usurper, Eugenius (394), and became sole emperor. A few months later, however, he died, and the empire was divided between his two sons. One of Theodosius's most important acts was the adoption of the Nicene definition of Christianity as the state religion.

Theodosius II (401–50), Byzantine Emperor, 408–50. He succeeded at the age of seven. His sister Pulcheria and the praetorian prefect, Anthemius, ruled during his minority. Wars with the Persians (421 and 441) and the Huns under Attila (441–448) occurred during his reign.

Theognis of Megara (late 6th century BC), Greek elegiac poet, and reputed author of a collection of political verses strongly aristocratic in temper.

Theology (Greek *theos*, god; *logos*, science), science of religion, dealing with God, and man in his relations to God. Systematic theology deals with the specific doctrines, principles and characteristics, for example of Christianity. Theology is treated under two main headings, Natural and Revealed Theology; but various causes, especially the application of the theory of evolution to religion and theology, gave rise to a Broad or Modernist school of thought, which sought to do away with hard-and-fast divisions.
Revealed theology may be analysed according either to its matter or to its method. The division according to its matter gives us the two branches of *Fundamental* and of *Dogmatic Theology*: the former is concerned with the grounds upon which Revealed theology and religion rest, the Fact of Revelation, the Founts of Revelation and the way in which it is received; the latter, dealing with the truths so revealed, falls into two branches, theoretical (or Dogmatic Theology) and practical (or Moral Theology). The division according to method gives us *Positive* and *Speculative Theology*. *Positive Theology*

seeks to establish, expound and prove the truths of theology; it is further divided into *Biblical Theology* (concerned with scriptual sources and proofs), *Patristic Theology* (drawing upon the Fathers), and *Symbolic Theology* (confined to the creeds and formularies of the Church). Akin to these (and to Fundamental Theology) are *Polemic* or *Apologetic Theology*, which seek to defend and to commend theological doctrine in a hostile, sceptical world. *Speculative Theology* makes use of philosophy and other rational inquiries to probe more fully into the nature and implications of the truths of religion.

The philosophy of religion, with which Natural Theology is now identified, concerns itself with the study of the idea of God, the freedom of God and the operation of Grace, and finally with the nature of immortality, which is also the subject of eschatology.

Theophrastus (c.370–c.286 BC), Greek philosopher. He became Aristotle's most able pupil and succeeded him as head of the Peripatetic school in 322 BC. From that time until his death he successfully consolidated and expanded the work of his master. A close follower of Aristotle's thought and method, he gave particular attention to natural science and botany. His surviving works include *The History of Plants* and *The Causes of Plants*, *From the Metaphysics*, and a very readable book called *Ethical Characters*, a collection of typical 'bad hats'.

Theorbo, bass lute with a long neck, bearing two pegboxes. The lower carries strings which run over the fingerboard; the higher carries bass strings which run beside the fingerboard and are retuned to vary their pitch. The theorbo was widely used for continuo parts into the 18th century.

Theory, the presentation of a set of facts as a connected account consisting of interdependent statements. The term literally means a sight-seeing, which is the source of the contrast made later between theory and practice, the latter indicating the doing of things. The function of theory is to account for the observed facts; it must 'save the appearances', to use Plato's phrase. The object of scientific research is to provide ever wider and more comprehensive as well as more accurate accounts of the world, i.e. to create increasingly satisfactory theories.

Theosophy (Greek *theos*, god; *sophia*, wisdom) is a term which in a general sense can be applied to those forms of religion which are pantheistic and which often claim esoteric knowledge. It is usually used in a more restricted sense to apply to the late-Victorian religious movement founded by Madame Blavatsky. As such, it may be defined as a syncretistic religion professing to afford a higher knowledge or more immediate approach to God than is offered by any single religion based on revelation or reason.

Therapsids, mammal-like reptiles of Permo-Triassic age from the Karroo beds of South Africa. They display radiation into several varied groups, and gave rise to the mammals.

Therapy or therapeutics, that branch of medicine that deals with the treatment of disease and the application of remedies. Some types of therapy used today include occupational therapy, physiotherapy, psychotherapy, radiotherapy and chemotherapy.

Theravāda (Teaching of the Elders), one of the two main forms of Buddhism, the other being Mahāyāna. The differences between the Theravāda and the Mahāyāna schools are mainly of emphasis; on the fundamental doctrines of Buddhism such as The Four Noble Truths and The Noble Eightfold Path, there is no disagreement. The two forms have on the whole co-existed peacefully.

See also BUDDHISM; MAHĀYĀNA.

Thérèse of Lisieux, Saint (1873–97), 'The Little Flower', French nun. At 15 she became Sister Teresa of the Child Jesus in the Carmelite convent at Lisieux, where she remained until she died of tuberculosis. Her autobiography, *Histoire d'une âme* was written at the command of her superiors, 1894–97, and was not seen outside the convent until after her death. Its publication evoked a world-wide wave of acclamation, and the shower of miracles immediately following her death led to her canonisation in 1925 (commemorated 3 October). Her 'little way' teaches the way of 'spiritual childhood'. She appealed especially to ordinary people by showing that a state of sanctity was possible by continual renunciation in small matters and not only through extreme mortification. She is the patroness of priests in their vocation of winning souls for Christ.

Therm, British statutory unit of heat. It is equal to 100,000 British Thermal Units (BThU).

Thermae, Roman public bath buildings comprising not only baths of various kinds but often also libraries, gymnasia, theatres, etc. The bathing suite consisted of a dressing-room (*apodyterium*), a cold room (*frigidarium*), a warm room (*tepidarium*), a hot room (*caldarium*), and often an open-air swimming pool (*natatio*). The procedure was similar to a Turkish bath, and the rooms were heated as required by hot air from a furnace passing under the floor and up flues within the walls.

Thermit, or thermite, a mixture of powdered aluminium and a metal oxide, most commonly iron oxide. When this mixture is ignited there is a strongly exothermic (heat-producing) reaction in which the aluminium combines with the oxygen from the metal oxide which is reduced to the metallic state. The heat evolved is sufficient to melt most metals. Red thermit contains the red oxide of iron (Fe_2O_3) and black thermit contains the black oxide of iron (Fe_3O_4). The thermite process, also known as the Goldschmidt process, is the use of the thermite reaction to reduce the oxides of metals which have high melting points and are difficult or impossible to reduce with carbon, e.g. chromium, manganese, molybdenum, vanadium and tungsten. In thermit welding, a mould is built around the parts to be joined. Thermit mixture is ignited in a crucible and the molten iron produced is poured into the mould. The superheat in the iron is sufficient to form a fusion weld.

Thermochemistry, science founded on the law of the conservation of energy and dealing with the thermal effects accompanying chemical reactions. Reactions in which heat is evolved are called 'exothermic', and where heat is absorbed 'endothermic'. Measurements are performed with a water calorimeter, where the reaction proceeds rapidly to the end and takes place at normal temperatures, or otherwise under pressure with oxygen in a container known as a steel bomb. In many cases, when it has not been possible to make direct determinations of the heat value of chemical changes, the thermal values can be calculated indirectly from Hess's law. This, the fundamental principle of thermochemistry, states that the heat change is dependent only on the initial and final stages of the reaction or system of reaction.

The unit of heat used in thermochemical measurements is the joule, J, or the kilojoule, kJ. The heat change, ΔH, is negative for an exothermic reaction and positive for an endothermic reaction, and measurements refers to 1 mole of the substances which react.

As well as being of theoretical importance, thermochemistry is invaluable in determining the heating power of fuels and energy values of foodstuffs.

Thermocouple, see THERMOMETERS AND THERMOMETRY.

Thermodynamics is the science of heat in relation to other forms of energy. It is based on two laws. It had its origin in an attempt by Carnot 'to determine mathematically how much work can be got out of a steam engine'. His work was based on consideration of an ideal heat engine, performing in a manner that enabled him to deduce the relation between the work done and the heat taken in from the furnace. His researches, published in 1824, were subsequently modified by Kelvin to accord with the First Law of Thermodynamics. In simple terms the First Law states that heat and work are equivalent energy forms. The Kinetic Theory of Matter regards heat as the kinetic and potential energy of the particles of a substance. This led to the recognition that heat, light, electricity and sound are all forms of energy.

Carnot's engine is an (impossible) ideal one, but it gives a start in the development of the subject of thermodynamics. From the fact that it is a reversible engine, and a study of its performance as such, comes the conclusion known as Carnot's Principle, viz: no heat engine working between two given temperatures (source and condenser) can be more efficient than a reversible one. The formal proof of this principle depends on the Second Law of Thermodynamics. Two equivalent statements of this law are: (1) 'It is impossible for a self-acting machine unaided by any external agency to convey heat from one body to another at a higher temperature.' (Clausius), i.e. heat cannot of itself pass from a colder body to a hotter body; (2) 'It is impossible by means of inanimate material agency to derive a mechanical effect by cooling a body below the temperature of the coldest of the surrounding bodies.' (Kelvin), i.e. work cannot be obtained by using up the heat of the coldest body of a system. As related to the entropy of the universe, which tends to a maximum at a point when all temperature differences have disappeared, the Second Law states that the Universe will ultimately suffer a 'heat-death'.

Based on the two laws, the science of thermodynamics developed along two main lines: (1) its applications to heat engines; (2) pure thermodynamics, a powerful method of analysis in deriving a variety of important physical and chemical results.

Thermoelectricity. Seebeck found in 1821 that if the junctions between two dissimilar metals in a circuit are kept at different temperatures, a steady current will flow. The two metals form a *thermocouple*, and this *Seebeck effect* is widely used for the measurement of temperature. In 1834, Peltier found that when a current was passed across a junction of two dissimilar metals reversible heating effects occur. Heat is evolved when the current passes one way across the junction and absorbed when it passes in the opposite way. This is called the *Peltier effect*. From thermodynamic reasoning, if a circuit were made of two dissimilar metals and one junction were kept at a constant temperature, the electromotive force in the circuit should increase as the temperature of the other junction is increased. It is found, however, that as the temperature of the second junction is gradually raised, the electromotive force increases to a certain limit, then decreases again and is finally reversed. Lord Kelvin predicted in 1851 and later observed that when a current flows along a wire the temperature of which varies from point to point, heat is liberated at a given point when the current is flowing in one direction, and absorbed when the current is flowing in the opposite direction. This reversible heating is known as the *Thomson effect* after William Thomson (Lord Kelvin).

Thermoluminescence, see DATING IN ARCHAEOLOGY.

Thermometers and Thermometry. A thermometer is an instrument that measures the variations of sensible temperature. The commonest form utilises the change with temperature of the volume of a liquid in a container, e.g. mercury in glass. Mercury as a thermometric liquid has many advantages such as its wide range (-40 to $356°C$, and up to $570°C$ under pressure) in the liquid state; its regular expansion; its utility in fine capillary tubes, which it does not 'wet'; and the expeditious way of obtaining it in a very pure form. On the other hand, alcohol has a lower range (to $-80°C$) while pentane can be used as low as $-200°C$.

Maximum and minimum thermometers for recording the highest and lowest temperatures vary in construction. Rutherford's maximum self-registering thermometer consists of an ordinary mercury thermometer placed in a horizontal position, with a small piece of steel inside the tube *beyond* the mercury. As the mercury expands it pushes the steel before it, and as it contracts it leaves the steel in the farthest position to which it has been driven. The instrument can be reset by means of a magnet. The minimum thermometer contains alcohol instead of mercury, and *inside* the alcohol contained in the tube there is a small index of glass, with the farthest end touching the surface of the alcohol. As the alcohol contracts it carries the glass index with it, but when it expands the index is left behind. The two are commonly combined in a single 'maximum-minimum' thermometer.

The metallic thermometer depends on the principle that if two strips of different metals with unequal coefficients of expansion be firmly fixed (e.g. riveted) together and wound into a spiral with the more expansible metal inside, a rise of temperature causes the spiral to unwind. A needle indicates temperature variation. In the platinum resistance thermometer use is made of the fact that the electrical resistance of most metals varies with temperature. The thermocouple thermometer is based on the thermoelectric effect—that electric currents can be produced by applying heat or cold to junctions in a circuit of two different metals. If a sensitive galvanometer is used to measure the current, temperatures up to $1500°C$ can be measured with great accuracy in this way. The colour and brightness of an electrically heated filament depend on its temperature, and by matching the filament to a furnace the temperature of the latter can be measured in terms of the current through the filament. This is the basis of the radiation pyrometer. A gas thermometer is more sensitive than ordinary thermometers, owing to the relatively large coefficient of expansion of gas, but it is cumbersome, and requires a large amount of the fluid whose temperature is to be found.

See also ABSOLUTE TEMPERATURE; CENTIGRADE; FAHRENHEIT; THERMODYNAMICS; THERMOSTAT.

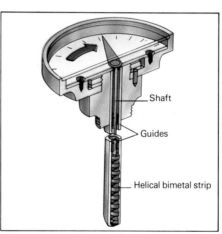

Thermometer. The metallic thermometer is operated by the differential expansion of a bimetallic strip.

Shaft

Guides

Helical bimetal strip

Thermonuclear Reaction, a reaction caused by an extremely high local temperature (e.g. 10 million degrees) which causes high velocity collisions between atomic nuclei. The reaction can lead to the fusion of two nuclei of low atomic weight to form a single nucleus, the mass of which is less than the sum of the masses of the two original nuclei. The excess mass appears as a relatively large amount of energy. This in turn can cause more light nuclei to react, and produce yet more energy, and a chain reaction can result. More complex nuclear reactions can also take place, but the ones of particular interest are those in which energy is produced by the transmutation of the mass of the original particles. A device designed on this principle can therefore explode, or may be controlled to act as a new source of nuclear power (fusion reactor). This has been realised in the hydrogen bomb or H-bomb,

which is many times more powerful than the conventional atomic bomb, which works by fission, i.e. the splitting, of heavy nuclei. The main difficulty is to produce a sufficiently high temperature for the thermonuclear reaction to be initiated.

See also MASS ENERGY.

Thermopylae, often called simply Pylae, pass from Thessaly to Locris. It is especially celebrated because of its heroic defence by Leonidas against the Persians in 480 BC.

Thermos Flask, see VACUUM FLASK.

Thermostat, device for maintaining an appliance at a preset temperature. The element sensitive to temperature can depend on the expansion of metals, the increase in volume of a liquid, or the increase in pressure of a fluid. Thermostats that depend upon the expansion of metals are known as the bimetallic type and consist of a composite strip of two metals with widely different coefficients of expansion. This strip may be used flat or formed into a coil, one end being free and the other fixed. When the temperature alters, the unequal expansion causes an appreciable movement at the free end, which moves a switch or lever. The second type consists of a cylindrical bulb, a capillary tube, and a metallic bellows. The system is filled with liquid and sealed; when the temperature rises the liquid exerts pressure on the bellows. It is used in most refrigerators and in some air-conditioning plants. In the vapour-pressure thermostat the system is only partially filled with a volatile fluid of a low boiling-point, leaving a vapour space. Movement is again produced by bellows.

Thesaurus, see DICTIONARY.

Theseus, legendary hero of Attica, son of Aegeus, King of Athens. Brought up at Troezen, when he reached maturity he went to Athens, where he killed the Cretan Bull and was acknowledged by Aegeus as his heir. Next he went voluntarily as one of the seven youths and seven girls the Athenians were obliged to send every year to Crete, to be devoured by the Minotaur. On his arrival, Ariadne, daughter of King Minos, fell in love with him and gave him a sword and a length of thread, with which he killed the Minotaur and found his way out of the labyrinth in which the monster was kept. On the way home Theseus abandoned Ariadne and, approaching Athens, forgot to hoist the white sail as the signal of his success; Aegeus, watching, thought his son had perished and threw himself into the sea. As king of Athens, Theseus fought the Amazons and carried off their queen, Hippolyte. He abducted Helen from Sparta but she was rescued by the Dioscuri, and he tried to abduct Persephone from Hades. Finally he was dethroned by the Athenians.

Thespiae, ancient Greek city near the foot of Mount Helicon in Boeotia. The neighbouring city of Thebes dismantled its walls in 423 BC, captured it in 372, and razed it to the ground. A famous statue of Eros by Praxiteles was preserved here.

Thespis (fl. 6th century BC), called the father of Greek tragedy, was the first to introduce an actor into what had been hitherto a merely choral performance. This individual took various parts in the same piece under the several disguises provided by linen masks.

Thessalonians, Epistles to the, written by St Paul probably from Corinth, between AD 51 and 53. They are among the earliest of St Paul's epistles, and their genuineness is universally acknowledged. The epistles were addressed to a Gentile audience. The immediate occasion of the first epistle is the good news brought by Timothy of the steadiness of the Thessalonians in the faith in spite of persecution by their countrymen. His letter, however, did not settle all difficulties: the expectation of the second coming of the Lord, which he had dealt with in the first epistle still caused great excitement and the neglect of the duties of daily life. The second epistle is intended to correct this.

Thessaloniki (Salonika) port of Macedonia, Greece, at the head of the Gulf of Salonika. The port was taken by the Turks in 1430. In 1908 the Young Turk revolution broke out there. In 1912 Thessaloniki was taken by a combined Greek and Bulgarian force, and it was annexed by Greece the next year. Thessaloniki is the second largest port in Greece, handling one-third of all exports. It has long traded in the products of the agricultural hinterland (tobacco, cereals, opium, cotton and vines) and local minerals (manganese, antimony and chrome), but its industrial development is recent. It is the second ranking textile-manufacturing centre in Greece, has food-processing factories, a 2·5 million-tonne capacity oil refinery, and a 1 million-tonne capacity steel mill. Population (1981) 402,443.

Thessaly, largest division of ancient Greece. Thessaly proper is a large plain, drained by the River Peneus and its affluents. About 113 km across, it is shut in by mountain barriers, broken only at the north-east corner by the valley and defile of Tempe, which separates Ossa from Olympus. There were two other districts included under the general name of Thessaly; one, called Magnesia, being a long narrow strip of country extending along the coast of the Aegean Sea from Tempe to the Pagasaean Gulf, and the other a long narrow vale at the extreme south of the country, lying between Mounts Othrys and Oeta. The Thessalians were a Thesprotian tribe, and invaded the western part of the country, afterwards called Thessaliotis, whence they subsequently spread. The area of modern Thessaly is 22,530 km² and its population (1971) is 659,243.

Thetford, market town in Norfolk, England, situated on the borders of the great state forest of Thetford Chase and the Breckland. Thetford was once the capital of the kingdom of East Anglia. Since 1960 the town has been greatly expanded to receive overspill from London. Population (1981) 19,591.

Thetis, Greek sea-goddess, daughter of Nereus and Doris, and mother of Achilles. Poseidon and Zeus sued for her hand; but when Themis declared that Thetis's son would outshine his father, both gods withdrew.

Thibaud, Jacques (1880–1953), French violinist. He studied under Marsick at the Paris Conservatoire, and his rise to fame as a virtuoso dates from 1898. He represented the technique of the great classical school passed down to him through Marsick and Ysaÿe. From 1905 he was especially associated in a trio with Cortot and Casals.

Thiers, Louis Adolphe (1797–1877), French statesman and historian. In 1821 he began writing for the *Constitutionnel*, and next collaborated with Félix Bodin in the production of *Histoire de la révolution française*, 1823–27. In 1830 with Carrel, he founded the *National*, which helped to provoke the revolution later that year. After Louis Philippe became king, Thiers became under-secretary of state to the Treasury (1831). He was minister of the interior in Soult's Cabinet of 1832 and in 1836 became head of the Cabinet, and adopted aggressive foreign policies. In 1840 he became president of the council and foreign secretary, but his policy did not have the support of Louis Philippe, and he was dismissed. He then wrote historical works, and published his huge *Histoire du Consulat et de l'Empire*, 1845–69. On the fall of the Second Empire he became president of the executive government, and supported the Paris Commune of 1871. In 1873 he was defeated and resigned.

Thigh, the part of the lower limb between the pelvis and the knee. The thighbone, or *femur*, is the longest bone in the human body, constituting about a quarter of the height from sole to crown. It articulates with the hipbone above, and with the *tibia* (shinbone) below.

Thimphu, see BHUTAN.

Thin-film Optics, the study of layers of transparent or absorbing materials, each of thickness of the order of magnitude of the wavelength of light. When light falls on a thin film, say the surface of a soap bubble, the light is reflected at both surfaces and the two reflected beams interfere; the interference effects depend on the thickness of the film, on its refractive index, on the angle of incidence of the light; and on its wavelength and state of polarisation, so that even with a single film complicated and beautiful effects are seen. When several films are used more complex effects occur. The properties of such a multilayer are calculated by a special calculus based on the electromagnetic wave theory of light. The most striking kinds of multilayer are those in which all are transparent. High-reflecting mirrors consist of alternate films of high and low refractive index, each a quarter of a wavelength thick; they reflect more than 99 per cent of the incident light over a wavelength range of about 100 nm and they show a brilliant metallic lustre, in spite of containing no metal layers. They are used as end mirrors in lasers, as reflecting coatings for Fabry-Perot etalons, and where a more highly reflecting surface than aluminium or silver is required.
See also BLOOMING OF LENSES.

Thíra, or Thera (formerly Santorini), island of Greece in the Aegean Sea, the most southerly of the Cyclades group, lying about 95 km north of Crete. Its steep cliffs vary in height from 150 to 350 m. The northern half of the island is composed of lava, and from earliest times the island has been a centre of volcanic activity. Thíra produces some cereals, figs and olives, but vines are the main crop. There is no fresh water on the island, except from rain collected in tanks. Area 75 km²; population (1971) 7750.
See also CYRENE.

Third Estate, that French social class which was represented in the states-general, as well as the clergy and nobility. If it was relatively easy to designate the clergy, of First Estate, or heterogeneous nobility of the Second Estate, the Third Estate contained everyone else and ranged from beggars to millionaires and those who were on the fringe of nobility.

Third Reich, term applied to the German National Socialist regime, formally begun 1 February 1934, which viewed itself as direct successor to the Holy Roman Empire and to the German Empire of 1871–1918.
See also GERMAN HISTORY.

Third Republic, in France, lasted from the fall of the Second Empire in 1870 to the surrender of the French government on 17 June 1940. The Third Republic survived the most terrible experience of the First World War, but after 1918 both the international and economic situations turned against France and the defeat of 1940 was complete.

Third World, The, a term used to refer to those countries which have neither fully developed capitalist nor planned socialist economies. Despite enormous differences in history, geography, social structure and culture, they have the following characteristics in common: their modern industrial sectors are relatively undeveloped; they are mainly producers of primary commodities for the capitalist countries; their populations are poor and chiefly engaged in agriculture.

Thirst, the desire for drink, made known by sensations projected to the pharynx. We become thirsty and take into our bodies water in varying quantities according to our needs. The sensation of thirst is due to several factors, the most important being the sense organs in a special centre of the hypothalamus of the brain, which are stimulated if the concentration of the blood rises. Drying of the mucous membranes of the mouth also helps to produce the sensation. Thirst is temporarily quenched partly by the subjective knowledge of having drunk, partly by the mouth being wetted and the stomach filled with liquid. However, unless the blood concentration is lowered, the sensation of thirst returns in a few minutes. Angiotensin also causes thirst via its action on the brain, both directly and indirectly.

Thirty-Nine Articles, articles of the Church of England described in their heading as 'agreed upon by the archbishops and bishops of both provinces and the whole clergy, in the Convocation holden at London in the year 1562, for the avoiding of diversities of opinions and for the establishing of consent touching true religion'.

On the death of Henry VIII in 1547, the government of the country was left in the hands of a group of nobles, of whom almost all were in favour of the reformed doctrines, and changes in the teaching and practice of the Church increased rapidly. In 1549 Parliament empowered Edward VI to appoint a commission for the drawing up of ecclesiastical laws. The commission, which included Cranmer, Ridley and Coverdale, was appointed in 1551, and drew up a code of 42 articles which were published in 1553. In the same year Edward VI died, and the Convocation of the first year of the Catholic

Queen Mary repudiated the articles. On the accession of Elizabeth, a Protestant, in 1558 a revised form of the 42 articles was submitted to Convocation. These were reduced in number to 39 and were finally promulgated in 1571. In 1604 they were settled in the form in which they are now used. The Thirty-Nine Articles were adopted by the Convocation of the Irish Church in 1635, and by the Scottish Episcopal Church in 1804.

Thirty Years' War, The. Practically it may be said that the Thirty Years' War was the result of the German Reformation and the Counter-Reformation. The war was begun in 1618 by the revolt of the Bohemians against their Hapsburg ruler, the Emperor Ferdinand II, and the acceptance of their crown by the Calvinist Elector Palatine, Frederick V. The emperor immediately drove Frederick out of Bohemia, depriving him also of the Lower Palatinate.

The Hapsburgs now developed their policy: Germany was to become an exclusive Hapsburg possession and the land lost to Catholicism by the Reformation was to be regained. The Imperial generals, Tilly and Wallenstein, swept all before them. Christian IV of Denmark came forward as the champion of German Protestantism, but was defeated and forced to make peace in 1629 at Lübeck. In 1630 Gustavus II (Adolphus) of Sweden, aided by French subsidies, took Christian's place as the champion of Protestantism, and began to turn the tide. Wallenstein had been dismissed at the Diet of Ratisbon because the German princes feared this 'mercenary upstart'. Gustavus Adolphus continued victorious. Tilly was defeated at Breitenfeld, and Gustavus marched to the south. In 1631 he again defeated, and killed, Tilly, and Wallenstein was recalled. Gustavus won the battle of Lützen (1632), but was killed, and much of his work was now undone.

From this point the religious motives of the war entirely disappear. France, anxious to break the power of the Hapsburgs, supported the Swedes and German Protestant princes. Richelieu played his hand well; enemies to the Hapsburgs were raised up in Germany, Italy and Spain; the Dutch were supported in their struggle against Spanish power; and Hapsburg power, both Austrian and Spanish, began to decline. After Richelieu's death Mazarin continued his policy, and the French generals Condé and Turenne won brilliant victories over the Imperialists. The end came in 1648, when the emperor agreed to terms of peace in the Treaty of Westphalia. The territorial gains of France and Sweden, and the independence of the German princes, were recognised. The attempted revival of the power of Catholicism by the sword had failed, and the imperial power became nominal except in Austria. The independence of Switzerland and the United Provinces (Holland) was also recognised by this treaty. The devastation which the war caused in Germany had political and social consequences of long duration.

See also GERMAN HISTORY.

Thisbe, see PYRAMUS AND THISBE.

Thistle, general name for a number of spiny plants, especially certain members of the Compositae, with characteristically-shaped flower-heads consisting of tubular florets. The most important species economically is the creeping thistle, *Cirsium arvense*, a persistent weed. Thistles of related genera include Scotch thistle, *Onopordum acanthium*, a tall plant with woolly white hairs among its spines; holy thistle, *Silybum marianum*, with edible roots and young leaves; scented musk-thistle, *Carduus nutans*; and carline thistle, *Carlina*. Globe thistle, *Echinops*, often grown in gardens, has spherical heads of complex compound structure. Sow-thistles (milk-thistles) belong to the genus *Sonchus*. Hedgehog thistle is a totally different plant, being a type of cactus, genus *Echinocactus*.

Thistle, Order of, see ORDERS OF KNIGHTHOOD.

Thirty Years' War. *The Defenestration of Prague, 1618, when Bohemian Protestants threw two imperial regents from a window, heralded the outbreak of war.*

Thistlewood, Arthur (1772–1820), British conspirator. He served in the army, and having absorbed revolutionary ideas in America and France, became a reformer and sought to achieve his ends by the use of violence. His project in 1820 to assassinate the entire Cabinet when gathered together at dinner in Grosvenor Square, failed owing to the presence of a spy among the conspirators. Thistlewood and his associates were caught in a loft in Cato Street, London, and the attempt became known as the Cato Street Conspiracy. Thistlewood was tried for high treason and hanged.

Tholos, in Greek architecture, either: (1) a prehistoric circular tomb with corbelled roof; or (2) a circular building surrounded by columns.

Thomas, Saint, one of the 12 apostles, called also Didymus, i.e. 'the twin'. All the information about him in scripture is given in the fourth gospel.

Thomas, Dylan Marlais (1914–53), Welsh poet. He was a reporter for a time on the *South Wales Evening Post*. His first book, *Eighteen Poems*, 1934, containing some surrealist verse, was praised by Dame Edith Sitwell. Rejected for service in the Second World War, Thomas worked for the BBC. In 1940 he published *Portrait of the Artist as a Young Dog*, a series of humorous autobiographical sketches. *Deaths and Entrances*, 1946, and *In Country Sleep*, 1951, are considered the finest volumes of his poetry, which has affinities with the works of Blake and Gerard Manley Hopkins. Regarded by some as the most outstanding poet of his generation, his heavy drinking contributed to his early death during a lecture tour of the USA. *Under Milk Wood*, 'a play for voices', was written for radio and first broadcast in 1954.

Thomas, (Philip) Edward (1878–1917), English poet and essayist. His first book, *The Woodland Life*, appeared in 1897. He lived in poverty while he tried to make a living by writing. On the outbreak of the First World War he enlisted and was killed at Arras. An intense love of the country is shown in his works, which include *Oxford*, 1903; *The Heart of England*, 1906; *The Country*, 1913; and *A Literary Pilgrim in England*, 1917. Thomas wrote no poetry until 1912, when he used the pseudonym Edward Eastaway; his *Collected Poems*, 1920, were praised by Walter de la Mare.

Thomas, R(onald) S(tuart) (1913–84), Welsh poet. Though he wrote in English, his verse is close to Welsh traditions in its concern for the threatened values and existence of the rural Welsh communities in which he lived. He was ordained a priest in 1937.

Thomas à Kempis (c.1380–1471), Augustinian canon and religious writer, called after his birthplace Kempen, near Düsseldorf. His real surname was Hammerken. He was educated at the school of the Brethren of the Common Life at Deventer. In 1399 he joined the Augustinians of Mount St Agnes at Zwolle. Here he remained almost continually for the rest of his life, copying manuscripts, writing, and directing novices. By far the most celebrated of his numerous treatises (though his authorship is sometimes denied) is the *Imitatio Christi*, which has been translated into more languages than any other book except the Bible.

Thomas Aquinas, see AQUINAS, THOMAS, SAINT.

Thomas Becket, see BECKET, THOMAS.

Thompson, Sir Benjamin, Count Rumford (1753–1814), Anglo-American scientist and administrator. Among the subjects he studied were ballistic experiments, a differential thermometer and lighthouse improvements; but he is chiefly noted for his researches in heat, the caloric notion of which was rejected when he noticed that the metal chips from the boring of a cannon were very hot. He entered the service of Bavaria as minister of war. In 1795 he visited England, devoting himself to the problems of smoke abatement. In 1799 he co-operated with Sir Joseph Banks in projecting the establishment of the Royal Institution, and selected Sir Humphry Davy as its first scientific lecturer.

Thompson, Flora (1877–1948), English novelist. She is best known for her autobiographical novels *Lark Rise*, 1939, *Over to Candleford*, 1941, and *Candleford Green*, 1943, forming a trilogy later published as *Lark Rise to Candleford*, 1945, which lovingly describe rural life at the turn of the 19th century.

Thompson, Francis (1859–1907), English poet. A Roman Catholic, he studied medicine but failed to take a degree. He worked in London in various occupations, until in 1888 he sent two poems to the magazine *Merry England*. These were recognised by Wilfrid Meynell as works of merit. Meynell rescued Thompson from poverty and opium addiction and helped him to publish his first volume of *Poems*, 1893. *Sister Songs*, 1895, and *New Poems*, 1897, both gained him recognition as a poet. His most famous poem is 'The Hound of Heaven'.

Thomsen, Christian Jürgensen (1788–1865), Danish archaeologist. As first curator of the National Museum of Denmark, his classification of the antiquities led him to devise the three-age system, whereby prehistory was divided into the three successive ages of Stone, Bronze and Iron.

Thomson, Sir George Paget (1892–1975), British physicist, son of Sir Joseph Thomson. He served in France 1914–1915, and worked on aerodynamic problems until 1919, when he returned to Cambridge. He was Master of Corpus Christi 1952–62. De Broglie's view that electrons possess both the properties of discrete particles and attributes of wave motion was strongly supported by experiments performed by Thomson, for which he shared the 1937 Nobel Prize for physics with C. J. Davisson. He was a member of the Aeronautical Research Committee 1937–41, and in 1946–47 was scientific adviser to the British delegation to the Atomic Energy Commission of the UN.

Thomson, James (1700–48), English poet. In 1725 he went to London to pursue a literary career. He published in 1726 *Winter*, which was highly praised, followed in 1727 with *Summer*. *Spring* appeared in 1728, and two years later he republished these, adding *Autumn*, under the title of *The Seasons*. It was the first lengthy nature poem in English and foreshadowed the work of the Romantics. In 1740, in collaboration with David Mallet, he wrote *The Masque of Alfred*, which is famous because in it first appeared the ode 'Rule Britannia'. *The Castle of Indolence*, 1748, an allegorical poem in the Spenserian stanza, is often reckoned his finest work.

Thomson, Sir Joseph John (1856–1940), British physicist. He was Master of Trinity College and professor of physics, his association with Cambridge lasting throughout his life. From 1884–1918 he was Cavendish professor of experimental physics. To Thomson belongs, by general consent, the credit for the discovery of the electron. His book, *Application of Dynamics to Physics and Chemistry*, 1888, was to a great extent the foundation stone on which the study of physical chemistry was built. This was followed by numerous papers on electrical theory and experiments on gases. After Röntgen had demonstrated the existence of X-rays produced by substances struck by cathode rays, Thomson (assisted by Rutherford) adapted the discovery and used the X-rays for producing more controllable ionised gas. He concluded that all matter is composed of electrically charged particles, and that electricity is atomic in nature. His subsequent researches into the nature of electricity resulted in the development of the study of

atomic physics. In 1906 he was awarded the Nobel Prize for physics, and was president of the Royal Society from 1916 to 1920.

Thomson, Virgil (1896–), US composer and music critic. Influenced by Satie and 'Les Six', he developed a deadpan style, often based on American folk material. His works include the operas *Four Saints in Three Acts*, *The Mother of Us All* and *Lord Byron*, the first two having texts by Gertrude Stein; and orchestral pieces, choral music, piano music and film scores.

Thomson of Fleet, Roy Herbert Thomson, 1st Baron (1894–1976), British newspaper proprietor. Born in Canada, he already owned a chain of provincial Canadian newspapers and three radio stations when in 1953 he acquired control of the *Scotsman* group of newspapers, and secured the independent television licence for Scottish television. In 1959 he took over Kemsley Newspapers Ltd, and in 1967 acquired *The Times* and its subsidiaries, which in 1980 were sold by his son to Rupert Murdoch. He became a British citizen in 1963 and was created a baron the following year.
See also NEWSPAPERS.

Thor. *The hammer of the god of thunder was a symbol of protection from the forces of evil.*

Thor, Teutonic god of thunder, identified by the Romans with Jupiter, or Jove, hence Thursday for *Jovis dies*, French *jeudi*.
See also MYTHOLOGY.

Thoracic Duct, the duct which conveys the greater part of the lymph and chyle into the blood. It does not, as its name would seem to imply, lie wholly within the thoracic cavity, but begins in the abdomen. It reaches the thorax by passing through the aortic openings in the diaphragm, passes upwards to the root of the neck, and then takes a curved course outwards and downwards, emptying into the left subclavian vein at its junction with the left internal jugular vein. The duct is, in the adult, between 37·5 and 50 cm long.

Thorax, the part of the body which is above, or in front of, the abdomen and below, or behind, the head. In insects, the thorax includes the three segments to which the legs and wings are attached. In crustaceans, such as lobsters, it is often fused with the

head, forming the cephalothorax. In vertebrate animals, it contains the heart and lungs, which are enclosed within the protective rib cage. In mammals, the division between the thorax and abdomen is the muscular diaphragm.

In humans, the thorax or chest is shaped like a truncated cone with the diaphragm as its base. The thoracic inlet is small, slopes downwards and forwards and contains the oesophagus (gullet) and trachea (windpipe), and those arteries and veins leading from and to the heart through the neck, together with certain nerves. The thoracic outlet is larger, slopes downwards and backwards and is filled by the diaphragm, which is convex above.

Thoreau, Henry David (1817–62), US writer. Through Emerson he came to know Hawthorne and Channing and was drawn to Transcendentalism. In 1845 he built a cabin on Emerson's land and lived there near Walden Pond for two years in an attempt to rediscover the essentials of life. *Walden, or Life in the Woods* was published in 1854. Thoreau's influential essay on civil disobedience appeared in 1849. This work was much admired by Gandhi and, through him, by Martin Luther King. He was also a poet, a collection of his nature poems appearing in 1895.

Thorium, metallic chemical element, symbol Th, atomic number 90, atomic weight 232·0381; one of the actinides. It was discovered by Berzelius in 1818, and its identity confirmed ten years later. It is present in several complex silicate ores (thorite, gadolinite and orangeite) found in Sweden and Norway, and also in the monazite sand of Brazil and the USA. Metallic thorium is difficult to isolate, owing to its chemical activity, but it has been prepared pure by reduction of the oxide and by electrolysis. It is a white metal, melting at 1842°C. When heated in air or oxygen it burns brilliantly. Thorium is radioactive and, under neutron bombardment in a nuclear reactor, the common isotope thorium-232 forms the fissile isotope uranium-233, which is a valuable nuclear fuel.

Thorndike, Dame Sybil (1882–1976), British actress. Her first professional appearance was in 1904 at Cambridge. After touring in America for four years, she was with Miss Horniman's Manchester Company, 1908–09. She married in 1908 the actor and producer Sir Lewis Thomas Casson (1875–1969), with whom she often appeared. From 1914 to 1918 she played leading rôles at the Old Vic, and at the Little Theatre from 1920 to 1922. Her creation of the title rôle in Shaw's *St Joan* in 1924 gained her wide recognition. Her range and quality were shown in the classical parts of Lady Macbeth, Medea and Lady Teazle, and in such modern plays as *The Corn is Green* and *The Linden Tree*. To celebrate her golden wedding she appeared with Sir Lewis in *Eighty in the Shade*, written for them by Clemence Dane, and they both appeared at the first Chichester Festival (1962) in *Uncle Vanya*.

Thornhill, Sir James (1676–1734), British painter. He was much employed by Queen Anne, who commissioned him to paint the interior of the dome of St Paul's, and the princesses' apartments at Hampton Court.

Thornhill's other decorative works include the great hall at Greenwich Hospital, the hall at Blenheim, and paintings in Kensington Palace. He also painted altarpieces for All Souls' and Queen's College chapels, Oxford, and portraits of Sir Isaac Newton and Steele. He founded a school of art in Covent Garden, attended by Hogarth, who became his son-in-law.

Thoroddsen, Jón (1818–68), Icelandic writer. He has rightly been called 'the father of the modern Icelandic novel'. His *Piltur og stúlka*, 1850, is a story of young love, while *Madur og kona*, 1876, also has a romantic plot but is more mature and humorous.

Thorough Bass, see CONTINUO.

Thorpe, (John) Jeremy (1929–), British politician. He was called to the Bar in 1954 and elected Liberal MP for North Devon in 1959. Thorpe succeeded Jo Grimond as leader of the Liberal party in January 1967. During his leadership the Liberal party won over six million votes, nearly one-fifth of those cast, in February 1974, securing the election of 14 MPs. The election of October 1974 was disappointing for the Liberals and Thorpe came under increasing criticism, eventually leading to his resignation in 1976.

Thorwaldsen, Bertel (1770–1844), Danish sculptor. He studied for a while in Copenhagen School of Art and later went to Italy, where he was influenced by Canova, and where he remained for 23 years. Soon after his death a permanent exhibition of his work was formed at Copenhagen, while his statue of Byron is now at Trinity College, Cambridge. The Lion of Luzern is also his work. Thorwaldsen established an international reputation during his lifetime, and examples of his monumental sculpture may be seen on buildings and in churches all over Europe.

Thoth, early Egyptian deity of wisdom and magic. He invented writing, and was the patron of scribes. Thoth was represented by a baboon or ibis, and associated with the moon, whose phases were used for reckoning.

Thousand and One Nights, see ARABIAN NIGHTS.

Thrace, or Thracia (Modern Greek *Thráki*; Turkish *Trakya*), was the name of the vast tract of country bounded on the north by the Danube, on the south by the Propontis and the Aegean, on the east by the Pontus Euxinus (Black Sea), and on the west by the River Strymon and the easternmost of the Illyrian peoples. It was divided into two parts by Mount Haemus (the Balkans) running from west to east and separating the plain of the lower Danube from the rivers which fall into the Aegean. Philip of Macedon, the father of Alexander the Great, reduced the greater part of Thrace; and after the death of Alexander the country fell to the share of Lysimachus. It subsequently formed a part of the Macedonian dominions.

Thrace was the centre of disturbances in more modern times. It was one of the theatres of war in the Balkan Wars of 1912 and 1913. Greece had obtained most of Thrace by 1920. In 1923 by the Treaty of Lausanne eastern Thrace as far as the Maritsa was given to Turkey, while western Thrace, except Karagach, was given to Greece.

Thrace in Greece has an area of 8586 km² and is divided into three *nomes*—Evros, Rhodope and Xanthi. Total population 356,000. Eastern Thrace, Trakya, or Turkey-in-Europe, has an area of 23,732 km² and includes the cities of Istanbul and Edirne (formerly Adrianople). Population, 3,210,792.

Thrale, Hester Lynch, see PIOZZI, HESTER LYNCH.

Thread, in textile terms, a continuous cord made by twisting fibres of such natural substances as cotton, wool and flax or those of man-made fibres such as nylon or polyester. The slightly twisted yarns used for weaving are strictly called threads, but the term is more commonly applied to the stronger and more highly finished cords used for hand or machine sewing. The cotton or other material is first twisted into yarn, which is doubled upon itself and twisted in the opposite direction to the original twist. The product is then two-ply thread. To make a stronger thread a number of two-ply yarns are twisted again in the opposite direction to the previous twist.

See also EMBROIDERY; FIBRES AND FIBROUS SUBSTANCES; SEWING-MACHINE.

Threadworm, see NEMATODA.

Threats are frequently crimes and so punishable by the English courts. A threat with a view to gaining property or money may be blackmail. A physical threat to injure someone may be an assault, and threats may open the way to a charge of rape. A threat to a witness or juror before or after a trial is contempt of court. Threats may also form the basis of the tort of intimidation or the tort of inducing a breach of contract.

Three Choirs Festival, British music festival established in 1724, held annually, alternately in the cathedrals of Hereford, Gloucester and Worcester. New works from eminent contemporary composers have always been a feature. Orchestral and chamber concerts are also included.

Three-day Eventing, an equestrian competition designed to test the skills of both rider and horse. It has its origins in competitions organised for the training of cavalry officers and is sometimes referred to as horse trials. The competition is in five distinct phases; dressage, speed, endurance, cross-country and show jumping, and is competed for over three days, hence the name. It is a part of the equestrian section of the Olympic Games.

Three Kings, Feast of, see EPIPHANY.

Three-Mile Limit, see TERRITORIAL WATERS.

Three-phase System, electric supply system to which are connected three alternating electromotive forces of equal peak values of the same frequency but displaced in time phase by one-third of a cycle (120 electrical degrees). In three-phase generators and transformers the ends of each of the three-phase windings may be so connected internally as to make necessary only three external conductors for carrying the current over transmission lines or distribution networks. A fourth conductor is usually added in distribution networks, connected to the 'star' point (neutral) and to earth. If the voltage between the lines of a distribution network is 415 V the voltage between any one of the lines and the fourth conductor (neutral) is $415/\sqrt{3} = 240$ V. In a three-phase system the power in watts is $V \times I \times \sqrt{3}$, where V and I are line values of voltage and current. Three-phase alternating current supply systems are standard over most of the world.

Thresher Shark, *Alopias vulpes*, a common species of shark of the family Alopiidae, suborder Galeoidei, found in the Mediterranean and the Atlantic and in most subtropical and temperate seas. Its chief characteristic is a very long tail which is nearly half the total length of about 6 m. The thresher shark follows the shoals of small fish, such as herrings, driving them together by lashing its tail.

Threshing, separation of the grain from the straw, or the seed from the haulm. Formerly the operation was performed by the flail, and this laborious but effective implement is still occasionally used by seed growers and on small holdings. The first workable threshing machine was invented by Andrew Meikel about 1786; the modern machine, besides effectively sorting out the products of the sheaf, delivers the straw unbroken and ready for trussing. The corn is passed by hand or self-feeder into the drum mouth and is threshed out by beaters. The straw is passed out after the grain has been shaken away by means of riddles, an air blast from a fan, and rotary screens which grade the corn. The combine harvester cuts and threshes in one operation and has a threshing mechanism similar to that of a stationary thresher. Since the grain is cut and threshed at the same time, and has no opportunity to dry naturally in the stook and stack, the moisture content may remain high, and unless it is then dried artificially it may heat or ferment when stored. The straw left by the combine tends to be much broken, but it can be collected.

Thrift, sea pink, *Armeria maritima*, a summer-flowering perennial plant of the family Plumbaginaceae. The globular heads of rosy flowers rise on slender stems from the tufts of leaves. Thrift grows wild by the sea, and also on mountains. *A. plantaginea* is the Jersey thrift.

Thrips, insect belonging to the order Thysanoptera. Thrips are minute, dark-coloured insects, measuring no more than 2–3 mm long. Because of their size they are seldom noticed, or they may be mistaken for a speck of soot or dust. They are abundant during the summer, when they are found on plants such as primroses and legumes. They are capable of inflicting irritating bites on the human skin. A number of species are pests of flowers, greenhouses and field crops such as onions, pears, cotton and citrus fruits.

Throat, the front of the neck; or the upper part of the respiratory passages in the neck. See LARYNX; PHARYNX; TONSILS.

Thrombosis, formation of a clot (thrombus) of blood, within a blood vessel or inside a heart chamber. The thrombus is usually attached to the inner lining (intima) of the vessel and obstructs the flow of blood through it. Among the various factors encouraging the process of thrombosis are: (1) damage to the intimal lining of the affected vessel; (2) an increase in the clotting properties of the blood; and (3) stagnation of blood in the vessel affected. If thrombosis takes place in one of the arteries, the tissues supplied by that artery may be deprived of oxygen and nutrition, causing damage or death of the tissue (gangrene). If the vessel to a vital organ is affected, e.g. the heart (coronary thrombosis) or the brain (cerebral haemorrhage), the person may be severely crippled or killed.

As the flow of blood is usually much slower in the veins than in the arteries, thrombosis occurs more often in veins. It usually occurs in the deeper veins of the legs, sometimes following surgery. Often this only produces an ache, swelling and slight congestion of the affected area, and may heal spontaneously. Sometimes a part of the clot breaks off and circulates in the blood. This is called an embolus. It will soon lodge in a vessel that is too small to allow it to pass, usually in the lungs, causing a pulmonary embolus. Various drugs are used in the treatment of thrombosis and drugs which break down the clots are currently being tested.

Throwing events in athletics generally consist of discus, hammer and javelin throwing, and putting the shot (or weight). A Scottish variation is 'tossing the caber'.

The discus is thrown from a circle 2·50 m in diameter. It must land within a 45° sector and, as in the shot and hammer, the thrower must not leave the circle before the implement has landed, and only then from the rear half. The men's modern discus weighs 2 kg, with an outer diameter of 219 mm. The women's discus weighs 1 kg, with a diameter of 180 mm to 182 mm.

The hammer, unlike the discus, javelin and the shot, is a men-only event. The modern hammer weighs 7·26 kg; the head, having a diameter of 10·2 cm to 12·0 cm, must be completely spherical in shape. The handle is made of spring steel wire which must not stretch appreciably when the hammer is being thrown. The length of the hammer measured from the inside of the grip must be between 117·5 cm and 121·5 cm. The rules are similar to the discus and shot.

The javelin weighs 800 g in the men's event and must be between 260 and 270 cm long. The women's weighs 600 g, length 220 to 230 cm. The throw is made from behind a scratch line at the end of a runway 36 m long and 4 m wide. The throw is not a good one unless the tip of the javelin strikes the ground first. The thrower must not cross the scratch line until the throw has been measured.

Putting the shot (or weight). This event, using large stones, is of great antiquity; the modern event uses a round implement weighing 7·26 kg (for women, 4 kg) which probably owes its size and weight to cannonballs. The shot is put from a circle 2·13 m in diameter, the rules being as for the discus.

Thrush, see CANDIDIASIS; MYCOSIS.

Thrush, about 300 species of the bird family Muscicapidae, order Passeriformes, with very extensive distribution and of omnivorous diet. The typical genus *Turdus* includes the blackbird, ring ouzel, redwing and fieldfare, to which the name thrush is not commonly applied. The song thrush, or mavis, is one of the best-known European song-birds. The mistle thrush or holm thrush, *T. viscivorus*, is a larger bird with a slightly forked tail.

Thucydides (c.455–c.401 BC), Greek historian. He possessed gold mines in Thrace, opposite the island of Thasos, where he was a person of great consequence. In the Peloponnesian War he commanded an Athenian squadron at Thasos (424). Failing to save Amphipolis, he was exiled, and retired to Thrace. He spent 20 years in exile, returning in 404 BC, under a general amnesty. Some accounts say he was later assassinated in Athens.

The Peloponnesian War forms the subject of the history of Thucydides. Though he was engaged in collecting material during the whole of the war, he continued re-writing his history throughout. He did not, however, live to complete it. His work is noted for its accuracy and impartiality.

Thugs, roving bands of fanatical murderers and robbers who used to infest parts of central and northern India. Devotees of the goddess Kali, the Thugs regarded those they murdered and a certain part of their belongings as sacrifices to her. The systematic suppression of the Thugs was begun about 1830 by Capt W. H. Sleeman, Bengal Army, and continued until this century.

Thuja, a genus of conifers in family Cupressaceae, native to western Asia and North America, pyramidal in habit, with scale-like leaves on flattened branchlets. *T. occidentalis* is the American arbor-vitae or white cedar; *T. orientalis*, Chinese arbor-vitae; and *T. plicata*, western arbor-vitae or western red cedar.

Thule, name given by the ancient Greeks to the most northerly part of Europe known to them. Pliny said it was an island in the northern ocean, six days' sail from the Orcades. Müllenhoff plausibly identifies it with the Shetlands. Procopius and others use the name for Scandinavia. It appears to be a Greek form of the Gothic *Tiel* or *Tiule*, meaning 'remotest land'.

Thulium, metallic chemical element, symbol Tm, atomic number 69, atomic weight 168·9342, belonging to the group of lanthanides. It was discovered in 1879 by Cleve, but was first prepared pure by James in 1911. Its salts are pale green in colour. Thulium is extracted from the minerals gadolinite, euxenite, etc.

Thumbscrew, iron instrument of torture for compressing or breaking the thumbs. It was used by the Spanish Inquisition and in the persecutions of the Covenanters in Scotland, where its last recorded use was in the late 17th century.

Thun, town in Bern canton, Switzerland, 23 km south-east of Bern, on the River Aar just below its exit from the Lake of Thun. It is a castle town and has a tourist industry (centre for the Bernese Oberland). The lake is 19 km long and has an area of some 48 km²; maximum depth 217 m. Population (1980) 36,900; mainly German-speaking Protestants.

Thunbergia, genus of tender climbing plants, also called clock vines, and named after the Swedish botanist Carl Peter Thunberg (1743–1828), pupil and successor of Linnaeus at Uppsala. *T. alata* (black-eyed Susan) has orange-yellow petalled flowers with dark brown centres. It is native to South Africa. *T. grandiflora*, from India, is a vigorous purple-flowered climber.

Thunder Bay, city of Ontario, Canada, created in 1970 by the amalgamation of Fort William and Port Arthur. It is situated on the north-west coast of Lake Superior and is the lakehead terminus of the Canadian National Railway. It is a major wheat exporting port with the biggest number of grain elevators in the world. Its other industries include shipbuilding, timber and woodworking plants, paper and pulp mills. The city's importance has been increased by the St Lawrence Seaway, of which it is virtually the terminus. Population (1976) (city) 111,476; (metropolitan area) 119,253.

Thunderbolt, or thunderstone, common name for objects once thought to have been formed by thunder and lightning, the belief being that thunder somehow sent out a destructive bolt or dart (such as Zeus's bolts in Greek mythology). The thunderbolt myth recurs in many lands.

A so-called thunderbolt is really a discharge of lightning from one part of the sky to another, and especially one which strikes the Earth, causing damage. Lightning in certain cases does leave behind it a vitrified tube, called a fulgurite, which is created by vitrification or fusing on the spot where it is found. The term thunderstone is used especially for objects having more or less a dart or arrow shape, for belemnites, meteorites, and the pyritous nodules to be found in Cretaceous rocks.

Thunderstorm, a rain, snow or hail storm with thunder and lightning. Lightning is an electrical discharge which causes rapid expansion and contraction of the air, producing the sound of thunder. The light from a stroke travels at 299,000 km/s, but thunder at only 335 m/s, so that, although both occur simultaneously, thunder is heard some time later, 3 seconds for every 1 km away. Since different parts of the lightning flash are at different distances and heights, and the speed of sound decreases with height, the thunder is not normally heard as a single crack but as a succession of rolling sounds. As a rule thunder can be heard only at distances up to 16 km, but this varies with the conditions, and thunder has on occasion been heard up to 300 seconds after the lightning flash—from 100 km away.

A thunderstorm consists of several convective cells, each up to 24 km in diameter, starting with an up-current extending up to more than 6000 m and often attaining more than 100 km/h. A thundercloud (cumulonimbus) is essentially a gigantic electricity generator which works, like all generators, by separating positive and negative charges. It is now generally agreed that almost all thunderclouds have a positive charge at the top and a negative charge at the base. The violent up-and-down air currents within the cloud supply the energy necessary to effect the separation of charge. According to recent research, the charge separation is a thermoelectric effect arising when super-cooled droplets of water freeze suddenly and disrupt. In a very short time the outer shell of a frozen droplet becomes colder than the inner liquid core and is positively charged owing to the greater mobility of the positive (hydrogen) ions.

See also ATMOSPHERE; ELECTRICITY, ATMOSPHERIC; LIGHTNING.

Thurber, James Grover (1894–1961), US humorist. He worked as a journalist and artist, and in 1926 became a leading member of the staff of the *New Yorker*. Perhaps his best known story is 'The Secret Life of Walter Mitty', the tale of an escaper into fantasy. His work has been described as a mixture of absurdity, inconsequence and irony.

Thurifer (Latin *thus*, incense; *fero*, I bear), the server who bears the incense in Catholic worship.

Thuringia (German *Thüringen*), name given to a region of central Germany. The chief states referred to as Thuringia were: Saxe-Weimar, Saxe-Coburg-Gotha, Saxe-Meiningen, Saxe-Altenburg, Schwarzburg-Rudolstadt, Schwarzburg-Sondershausen and the two Reuss principalities. In 1945 Thuringia became a *Land* of the German Democratic Republic, but in 1952 it was divided into the *Bezirke* of Erfurt, Gera and Suhl. The most important town in Thuringia was Weimar.

Thuringian Forest (German *Thüringer Wald*), range of wooded hills in the German Democratic Republic, extending for about 130 km south-east to north-west, from the River Werra near Eisenach to the Saale. The highest point is the Grosse Beerberg (980 m) in the north-west.

Thurloe, John (1616–68), English politician. He was appointed secretary of the Council of State in 1652, and, effectively, all the principal civil business of the Commonwealth, foreign and domestic, passed through his hands during the next eight years. His life was spared at the Restoration and he remained in England, although declining to serve Charles II. The *Thurloe Papers* are one of the major original sources for the history of the Protectorate.

Thursday, fifth day of the week, named after Thor, the Scandinavian god of thunder. In the Roman calendar the fifth day was Jupiter's Day.

Thursday Island, lies 40 km off the northern tip of Cape York Peninsula, Queensland, Australia; it is the centre of the Torres Straits pearling industry. Area 3·8 km². Population (1971) 2350, most of which is Aboriginal.

Thylacine, or Tasmanian wolf, *Thylacinus cynocephalus*, a carnivorous mammal of order Marsupialia, found in Tasmania. It somewhat resembles a wolf. The fur, however, is close and short, and the tail long and tapering; its fur is grey-brown and striped with black. The four young are carried in the pouch until they outgrow it. The species is probably now extinct.

Thyme, *Thymus*, a genus of small-leaved aromatic plants in family Labiatae. The commonest thyme of northern Europe is *T. arcticus*. The lemon-scented thyme of gardens is a variety of *T. serpyllum*. The thyme used for seasoning and flavouring is *T. vulgaris*, a native of southern Europe.

Thymus Gland, a roughly triangular lymphoid organ which lies in the chest immediately behind the upper part of the breastbone. It reaches its greatest size in relation to the rest of the body at two years of age and thereafter only grows slowly. After puberty the thymus ceases to grow and gradually becomes smaller. Its rôle is still not fully understood. The thymus is the first lymphoid tissue to develop, appearing in the human embryo during the eighth week of pregnancy. It has long been associated with the production of lymphocytes both pre- and post-natally, although there is some dispute as to whether the lymphocytes actually originate in the thymus. There is clear evidence that, in post-natal animals at least, there are primitive cells which develop in the bone marrow and then circulate to the thymus where they develop into 'T-lymphocytes'. Some of these T-lymphocytes then migrate to 'thymus-dependent' zones of lymph nodes and the spleen.

The explosion of research in this field resulted from the finding in 1961 that if the thymus is removed from a newborn animal, its blood and lymphoid tissue later contained fewer lymphocytes than normal. Furthermore, the thymectomised animals showed impaired immunological development, particularly in their ability to reject transplanted skin.

Children born without a thymus gland have Di George's syndrome and do not develop cell-mediated immunity; they are thus more susceptible to fungal and viral diseases.

Thyroid Gland. One of the endocrine glands, the thyroid is situated in the front of the neck; it consists of two lobes and is applied to the front of the larynx. It also (in the case of man) contains two to six para-thyroid glands whose rôle is quite separate. The most important activity of the gland is to manufacture the two thyroid hormones: tri-iodothyronine and tetra-iodothyronine (thyroxine). Since both of these hormones require iodine for their synthesis, the thyroid is very dependent on the availability of iodine in the diet.

Unlike most endocrine glands, the hormones are stored within the substance of the gland, contained in a storage colloid called thyro-globulin. T_3 and T_4 are released from thyro-globulin under the influence of a hormone produced by the anterior pituitary gland, thyroid stimulating hormone (TSH).

The effects of T_3 and T_4 on the body are very profound. The two hormones speed up almost every biochemical process, and are essential for normal growth. The two hormones seem to be universally distributed throughout the animal kingdom, and one of the first of their activities to be described was their rôle in the metamorphosis of tadpoles into frogs.

Tianjin, (Tientsin), municipality and port in China, at the junction of the Haihe with the Grand Canal, 120 km south-east of Peking. It is the main trading centre for north China and is located in Hebei Province. Its industrial development began after it was made a treaty port in 1860. Population (1980) 7.39 million.

Tian Shan (Tien Shan), mountain chain of Central Asia, forming part of the boundary between the USSR and China, and extending north-east from the Pamirs to the western fringe of the Gobi desert. The highest summit is Pobeda Peak (7439 m).

Tiara, jewelled head ornament, specifically the papal triple crown, which is a symbol of sovereign power (not sacred like the mitre), a high cap of gold cloth or metal, encircled by three coronets and surmounted by a gold cross. In a general sense a tiara is a jewelled head ornament, usually of precious metal or diamonds, worn on the forepart of the head. It often begins in a foliage or scroll design at the sides of the head, rising to a higher central group. The modern gem-set tiara dates from a Napoleonic court fashion.

Tiber (Italian *Tevere*; Latin *Tiberis*), third longest river of Italy, rising in the Apennines on the eastern borders of Tuscany and flowing generally south past Perugia and Rome to the Tyrrhenian Sea near Lido di Roma. It is joined near Narni by the Nera, its most important tributary; other tributaries are the Aniene, the Chiani and the Paglia. The Tiber empties into the sea via two channels: the southern one (*Fiumara*) is silted up; the other (*Fiumicino*) is canalised. Small ships can sail up river as far as Rome. Length 400 km.

Tiberias, capital of Galilee; town on the west shore of the Sea of Galilee, Israel, 207 km below sea-level, founded by Herod Antipas, AD 26, and named in honour of the Emperor Tiberius. After the destruction of Jerusalem in AD 70, many Jewish scholars and rabbis settled in the town and much of the Jerusalem Talmud was written there. The city fell to the Arabs in 687, and later to the crusaders who fortified it and built a church, but lost it in 1187. Most of the old city is built of black basalt. The modern residential quarter stands on the hills to the west of Tiberias. To the south are the renowned hot baths, famous from Roman times, which have curative properties for rheumatism and skin infections. In 1968 the population was 23,600. At the north end of the lake is the traditional site of the Sermon on the Mount.

Tiberias, Sea of, see GALILEE.

Tiberius, full name Tiberius Claudius Nero Caesar (42 BC–AD 37), Roman Emperor, son of Tiberius Claudius Nero and Livia, afterwards wife of Augustus. Tiberius was married to Vipsania Agrippina, but about 12 BC Augustus compelled him to divorce her and marry his daughter Julia. In AD 4 he was adopted by Augustus, now married to his mother, and given command of the armies in northern Germany. On the death of Augustus (AD 14) he returned home, and secured the throne without opposition. Tiberius made his rule absolute. He governed with justice and moderation from AD 14 to 23, then in 26 left Rome, never to return. He moved to Capri. Meanwhile his minister Sejanus was plotting to obtain for himself the imperial throne. Tiberius realised this in AD 31, and had him put to death. In the last six years of his life, his mind was almost certainly unbalanced, and in AD 37 he was found dead.

Tibesti Mountains, range of the central Sahara, on the borders of Libya, Niger and Chad. They are some 500 km long and 300 km wide and their highest peak (3415 m) is the highest point in the Sahara. The mountains are a block of volcanic rocks that have forced their way through the surrounding sandstone plateau.

Tibet Autonomous Region (Chinese *Xizang Zizhiqu*), formerly a dependency, now an integral part of China. It is bounded by the Kunlun Mountains on the north, separating it from the Sinkiang Uighur Autonomous Region, and by Qinghai and Sichuan provinces to the east, by the Himalayas to the south, and by Kashmir on the west. The boundaries are, in some cases, ill defined, e.g. with Bhutan where the bamboo forests are regarded as the frontier.

Tibet may be divided into three major physical regions: (*a*) the Northern Plains, Qing Zang, a region of plains and valleys, averaging over 4880 m and rising several hundred metres higher in its peaks and ridges. This region extends south to the valley of the upper Brahmaputra. (*b*) South Tibet, consisting of the valleys of the upper Indus and Sutlej in the west and the great valley of the Brahmaputra (or Zangbo) in the south and east. (*c*) East Tibet, comprising the mountains and valleys lying between the Qing Zang and the Chinese frontier. On the eastern slopes rise the great rivers of South-East Asia, the Salween, Mekong and Changjiang; somewhat to the north rises the Huanghe. The Northern Plains are treeless owing to the great elevation; vegetation is scanty grass, but sufficient to graze large numbers of yaks, asses, goats, sheep and other animals. Because of the rigours of the climate this region, almost two-thirds of Tibet, is very thinly populated. South Tibet is Tibet proper, and here are the chief towns, Lhasa (the capital), Shigaze and Gyangze. East Tibet is a land of considerable natural resources; grazing is abundant, agriculture is possible, and mineral wealth is known to be considerable. Gold is found in Tibet, but amounts extracted are now small. Iron pyrites is found and lapis-lazuli and mercury in small quantities, also salt and borax among the lakes of the north. Sheep and cattle are reared, also goats, pigs and poultry; horses, mules and donkeys are used. Area 1,221,700 km². Population (estimated 1980) 1,800,000. The population mainly lives in the districts between Lhasa and the Chinese border.

Tibet. *The valley of Drepang lies deep in the Himalayas in southern Tibet.*

Tibetan Book of the Dead, English rendering of the Tibetan *Bardo Thödol*, meaning 'Liberation by Hearing on the After-Death Plane'. The *Bardo Thödol* is a Tantric work of the Nyingmapa School of Buddhism and consists of advice on after-death experience.

Tibetan Mastiff, ancient breed of dog, used in Tibet as a watch-dog; it is a very powerful animal with a long coat. Mentioned in old Chinese literature and by Marco Polo, it is regarded as the ancestor of many present breeds. Its height is about 71 cm and its weight 60 kg; colour is black or black and tan.

Tibia, the larger of the two bones in the lower part of the leg, popularly called the shinbone. It articulates with the femur above to form the knee joint, the fibula externally at its upper and lower ends, and with the talus below, forming the ankle-joint.

Tibullus, Albius (c.54–19 BC), Roman elegiac poet. His poetry addressed to two mistresses, Delia and Nemesis, is notable for its quiet tenderness and spirit of self-denial. His bucolic elegies are among the most charming pieces in Latin poetry.

Tichborne Case, famous English criminal trial. The accused, Thomas Castro, otherwise 'Bullocky Orton', a butcher from Wapping, was tried and convicted of perjury in putting forward in the civil courts a bogus claim to the Tichborne title and estates in 1872. Not only did Orton, in posing as Sir Roger Tichborne, son of Sir J. F. Doughty Tichborne, who had died in 1862, answer with astonishing skill every question put to him in the civil actions, but even the real Tichborne's mother at first 'identified' him as her missing son. The whole proceedings cost the Tichborne family some £70,000 in legal expenses. In 1874 Castro was sentenced on two counts to two cumulative terms of seven years.

Ticino, river of Switzerland and northern Italy, which rises in the canton of Ticino on the St Gotthard Pass, flows through Lake Maggiore between Piedmont and Lombardy, and joins the Po 6 km south-east of Pavia. Length 246 km.

Ticks, animals of the families Argasidae (the soft ticks) and, more commonly, Ixodidae (the hard ticks) of the order Acarina (ticks and mites), in the class Arachnida of phylum Arthropoda. They have flat bodies protected by horny shields. During part of their existence they are blood-sucking parasites on animals and birds, for which they have developed a rostrum or beak composed of two barbed harpoons above and a dart below. Their eggs are laid on rough herbage and hatch into white six-legged larvae, which climb up the legs of passing animals and in some species complete their life history on the animal's skin, but in others return to the grass for a period. Ticks cause irritation and anaemia, but their chief dangers to their hosts are the numerous diseases of veterinary and medical importance they transmit, such as Rocky Mountain spotted fever.

Tiddley-winks, game of flicking counters into a receptacle. Each player has six discs and flicks one in turn. If he flicks it into the cup he has another go; if not, the next flick must be taken from the place where the disc lies. If one player's disc is covered by that of another, he cannot flick it until he has put all his free discs into the cup. If the covered disc is his only remaining one he must miss a turn before flicking it.

Tides, regular disturbances of the fluids on the Earth's surface produced by the action of gravitational forces of the Moon and Sun. The Moon's orbit around the Earth and the Earth's orbit around the Sun are ellipses not circles. Since the gravitational attraction

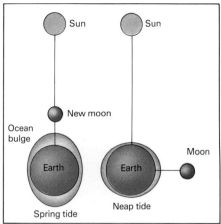

Tides. *Spring tides occur when the Sun and Moon pull together; neap tides when they pull against one another.*

depends upon the distance between two bodies, the Moon tides are larger when the Moon is closest to the Earth, called its perigee, and smaller when the Moon is farthest away from the Earth, called its apogee. Similarly the Sun's tide is larger and smaller when the Earth is closest and farthest away from the Sun, at the December and June solstices respectively. When the Sun and Moon are pulling together the tides are larger, spring tides. When they are pulling against each other they are smaller, neap tides.

There is very little tide in an enclosed sea such as the Caspian; only a small tide is generated in each basin of the Mediterranean because the Straits of Gibraltar are too narrow to allow the ingress and egress of the tidal wave from the Atlantic. Tides are generally uniform along the open coast bounding an ocean such as the Atlantic, but they are subject to great changes in bays and gulfs, e.g. the Bay of Fundy, where the tidal range is 18 m. High tides can also occur where the tidal waves from two different oceans meet.

Tides and Practical Navigation. The Admiralty Tide Tables contain astronomical data for the prediction of tidal information at ports throughout the world. At certain well-known ports called standard ports, tidal predictions are tabulated for every day in the year. These predictions can generally be relied upon to give the times of high and low water within a few minutes and the heights within a few centimetres; times and heights at secondary ports are considerably less exact than those predicted in the tables for standard ports; times and heights found from the tidal constants may be considerably in error.

Tieck, Johann Ludwig (1773–1853), German writer. Tieck was drawn to the Romantic school by the brothers Schlegel. He tried his hand in many fields of literature but he was especially successful as a writer of short stories. His *Phantasus*, 1812–17, is a collection of old tales and legends. In later years he freed himself from the Romantic, and wrote many *Novellen*, which rank amongst his best work. He made his own translations of Shakespeare and also helped in the great translation by August Schlegel.

Tien Shan, see TIAN SHAN.

Tientsin, see TIANJIN.

Tiepolo, Giovanni Battista (1696–1770), Italian painter. He trained under Lazzarini and, almost from his earliest works (painted in the style of Piazzetta), rose to a position of peerless eminence which he held for half a century. He was constantly sought after and his output was prodigious: he did a great deal of work on the huge ceilings and walls of the villas and palaces of Venice, and worked in other parts of Italy, in Germany and in Spain. He brought new freedom and lightness to the fresco medium in which he principally worked, but although his clear, bright colours and airy sense of space are Rococo in feeling, the monumental grandeur of his figures and his firmness of design are Baroque. He revived the glories of 16th-century Venetian painting and enriched his work with new perspective techniques. His son, Giandomenico (1727–1804), was a faithful follower and in 1757 worked with his father on the decoration of the Villa Valmarana near Vicenza, perhaps his greatest masterpiece.

Tierra del Fuego, group of islands separated from the southern extremity of Chile by the Strait of Magellan. The main islands are Tierra del Fuego or Isla Grande (area 48,100 km²), Navarin, Hoste, Clarence and Santa Inez. Tierra del Fuego was discovered by Magellan in 1520. Half of Tierra del Fuego Islands, and the islands west of it, belong to Chile; the rest forms an Argentinian territory (its capital is at Ushuaia), with an area of 20,900 km² and a population (1980) of 19,000. Punta Arenas is the major Chilean town.

Tiflis, see TBILISI.

Tiger, *Panthera tigris,* a large, powerful mammal of the cat family, Felidae, in order Carnivora. They live in Asia, from Siberia south to Sumatra. The Indian tiger rarely exceeds 3 m in length, the female averaging about 2·6 m. Fine males weigh 170–230 kg. Young animals, which are characterised by their canine teeth being hollow throughout, are handsomer than older ones, the tawny orange colour being richer and the stripes darker and closer together. Tigers are monogamous, though there is no reason to sup-

Giovanni Tiepolo. *A fresco in the Villa Valmarna Vicenza, on which he worked with his son.*

pose that they pair for life. The period of gestation is 14 or 15 weeks, and from one to six cubs are born, though no more than two are usually reared. They will eat carrion, but generally kill for themselves. Their food consists principally of deer, antelopes and smaller animals, but they sometimes kill wild boar. The tiger has been crossed experimentally with the lion; the resulting hybrid, the *tigon,* is faintly striped; it is sterile. Tigers are now in grave danger of extinction in the wild, due to over-hunting and the high prices paid for the pelt.

Tiger Beetle, any member of the family Cicindelidae in the order Coleoptera. Some 2000 species have been recorded, mostly in the tropics. They are typically found on sand or dry soils. Most adult tiger beetles are brightly coloured in shades of blue, bronze or green, with yellow or white markings. They generally have long legs and antennae. The most striking feature is the large eyes. The adults move rapidly and fly readily. The larvae live in burrows in the soil, where they lie in wait with their powerful mandibles ready to grab any insect that passes by.

Tiglath-pileser I, King of Assyria (c.1115–1060 BC). He restored his country's declining power by a series of campaigns which re-established control as far west as the Mediterranean.

Tiglath-pileser III, or Pul, Assyrian king, 745–727 BC. In a series of extensive wars, he initiated a system of provinces owing direct allegiance to his court and enforced by the deportation of recalcitrant populations.
See also ASSYRIA.

Tigridia, tiger flower, a genus of bulbous plants in the Iridaceae, natives of tropical America. *T. pavonia* and its varieties are particularly beautiful but the flowers only last a few hours.

Tigris, one of the two large rivers of Iraq, the other being the Euphrates. It rises in Turkey on the southern slopes of the Taurus range, and flows east across Turkey through Diyarbakir, entering Iraq east of Nusaybin. Then it flows south-east to Mosul and Samarra and then south through Baghdad. It is joined by the Euphrates 80 km north-west of Basra to form the Shatt-al-Arab, which flows into the Persian Gulf. Length 1850 km. It is navigable to within 50 km of Mosul.

Tijuana, city in Baja California (Norte) state, Mexico, on the US border near the Pacific coast. A popular tourist centre, it has developed as a border resort, particularly for Californians. Irrigation has opened up vast areas of surrounding farmland growing wheat, barley and grapes. Population (1978 est.) 534,993.

Tilak, Bal Gangadhar (1856–1920), a Brahmin from Maharashtra, the first Indian nationalist to unite religious and cultural sentiment with positive political action. He interpreted British government action as a threat to Hinduism. His militant action led to imprisonment. He called for *Swarej,* complete independence. Until Ghandi appeared, he was seen as the leader of Indian nationalism.

Tilburg, town in North Brabant province, Netherlands, 24 km south-west of 's Hertogenbosch. It is a great industrial centre, manufacturing cloth, woollens and soap. Population (1980) 151,800.

Tilbury Fort and Docks, fortification in Essex, England, on the Thames opposite Gravesend, enclosed by a moat. Originally built by Henry VIII, it was enlarged by Charles II. The docks were opened in 1886, and formerly belonged to the London and East India Dock Company. The great development of trade since 1886 has rendered frequent changes necessary. Tilbury is now the major dock complex of the Port of London Authority.

Tilden, Bill (1893–1953), US tennis player. Though he did not win a major title until he was 27, he was the first US citizen to win Wimbledon, which he won twice thereafter, and also won the US Championship seven times. He won 11 Davis Cup Challenge Round singles in succession.

Tile, thin plate of various materials, e.g. earthenware, porcelain, marble and glass, used for roofing, flooring, walls and fireplaces. Roofing tiles of marble-coloured clay were used in ancient Greece and Rome; coloured glazed roofing tiles were known in ancient China and Japan; and unglazed red earthenware roofing tiles were used in medieval Europe. During the 16th to 18th centuries glazed roofing tiles, especially those intended as finials, were often fashioned in fantastically elaborate, tall forms. Floor tiles of medieval Europe were made of red earthenware often with a lead-glaze and slip decoration. The use of earthenware tiles for wall decoration is of Near-Eastern origin, as early as 500 BC. The mosaic type of tile work, cutting to shape from slabs of tin-glazed earthenware, spread from North Africa to Spain under the Moors. Spanish tiles with coloured glazes, lustred, stamped in relief and painted, were imported by the Italians who imitated them and created Maiolica tiles for flooring. In the Netherlands the maiolica technique was extended to pictorial representations extending over many tiles for wall and fireplace decoration, the great Dutch tile manufacturers of the 17th century favouring blue-and-white designs. These were copied in northern France, Germany and Britain, where, in about 1756 at Liverpool, transfer-printed decoration was used. Painted porcelain tiles were made at Meissen and Fürstenberg. In the 19th century came the invention of the process by which ceramic tiles were pressed from clay dust, and many factories were established. Technical innovation over the last fifty years includes the automatic pressing of tiles, firing by tunnel kiln, automatic glazing, and decorating. Ceramic tiles are now manufactured in most countries.
See also MOSAIC; ROOF.

Tillage, see CULTIVATION.

Tillandsia, a genus of the Bromeliaceae, native of tropical and subtropical America and usually epiphytic. *T. usneoides* is Spanish moss or old man's beard, which hangs from trees in the tropics and resembles the lichen *Usnea.* Several species are cultivated as pot plants or epiphytes.

Tillett, Benjamin (1860–1943), British labour leader and politician. He organised the Dockers' Union of which he became general secretary. Tillett played the principal part in organising the dock strike of 1889. He was Labour MP for North Salford (1917–24 and 1929–31), and president of the TUC (1929).

Tilley, Vesta, real name Matilda Alice Powles (1864–1952), British music-hall performer, best remembered for her male impersonations: her father was a music-hall chairman under the name of Harry Ball, and she made her first appearance with him in Nottingham at the age of three. In 1873 she first appeared in London, playing three halls a night. Among the songs she made famous were 'The Piccadilly Johnny', 'The Girl who Loves a Soldier' and 'Six Days' Leave'. She retired at the height of her popularity in 1920.

Tillich, Paul (1886–1965), German theologian. He was ordained as a Lutheran minister. His sympathy with socialism led to his emigration to the USA after the Nazis took power. Tillich's insistence on a contemporary and relevant form of Christian belief appears in his writings, above all in his three-volume *Systematic Theology*, 1950–63.

Tilly, Johan Tserclaes, Count von (1559–1632), German soldier. In 1607 he became general of the Bavarian army and Catholic League, greatly distinguishing himself during the Thirty Years' War. He won the great battle of the White Mountain, near Prague, in 1620. In the same year he was appointed commander-in-chief of the Imperial forces, and took Magdeburg. Four months later, however, he was defeated by Gustavus Adolphus at Breitenfeld, and, shortly afterwards, on the banks of the Lech, where he was mortally wounded.

Tilsit, see SOVETSK.

Timaru, seaport of South Island, New Zealand, on the east coast between Christchurch and Dunedin, the chief town of the southern Canterbury district. Industries include the manufacture of woollen goods, flour and allied products. Population (1980) 30,100.

Timber, term for wood other than fuel-wood, that is either sawn or prepared in some way; it is also used to denote a group of trees from which timber may be obtained (hence, 'standing timber'), or for wood used in heavy construction, for example, shipbuilding.

Timber is described as either 'softwood' or 'hardwood', depending on whether it originates from coniferous or broadleaved trees, respectively. These terms are widely used, although many 'hardwoods' are soft, for instance the balsa (*Ochroma lagopus*), and some 'softwoods' are quite hard, the yew (*Taxus baccata*) for example, is almost as hard as oak. However, the terms are also used literally to denote the actual hardness of the timber.

Timber, in the English law of real property, means oak, ash and elm by general custom, and various other trees by local custom.
See also WASTE.

Timbrel (Old French *timbre*), 16th-century name for the tambourine, used in the authorised version of the Bible to translate the Hebrew *tof*.

Timbuktu, see TOMBOUCTOU.

Time. We are subjectively aware of the passage of time, which can be measured objectively by counting the cycles of a recurring phenomenon. Experience has gradually made us familiar with the concept of *uniform time* which is probably best defined as the independent variable in the accepted dynamical equations of motion. Its present practical expression is the system of *Co-ordinated Universal Time* (UTC), which is based on a series of extremely accurate electronic clocks maintained at various institutions round the world and regularly compared with each other. Its second is defined as the duration of 9,192,631,770 periods of the radiation corresponding to the transition between the two hyperfine levels of the ground state of the caesium-133 atom.

Standard Time. In the UK the passing of the Statutes (Definition of Time) Act in 1880 made *Greenwich Mean Time* the standard for the whole country. An international conference held at Washington in 1884 selected the meridian of Greenwich as longitude zero, and suggested that the meridians selected as standard for time-keeping should be those whose longitudes were a whole number of hours or half hours. The use of half hours has been gradually discontinued and the world is now divided into 24 time zones, each forming a belt of approximately $7\frac{1}{2}°$ on either side of its standard meridian, the exact boundaries being determined by political and geographical considerations.

'Time', US weekly news magazine founded in New York in 1923. It issues overseas as well as American and Canadian editions.
See also MAGAZINES.

Time of Troubles, period in Russian history (1598–1613) between the extinction of the house of Rurikidae and the establishment of the house of Romanov. During this time there were five tsars in Moscow whose claims were dubious, as well as Polish and Swedish invasions, and widespread popular and Cossack unrest.

Time Signature, see SIGNATURE NOTATION.

'Times, The', British daily newspaper, founded in 1785 as the *Daily Universal Register* and re-titled *The Times* in 1788. In 1817 Thomas Barnes was appointed editor. An outstanding journalist, as the champion of middle-class opinion, he won for *The Times* the nickname 'The Thunderer'. Family disputes ultimately made necessary the public sale of *The Times* in 1908. In 1966, in an attempt to increase circulation, *The Times* modernised its layout and news replaced classified advertisements on the front page. Financial difficulties remained, however. In

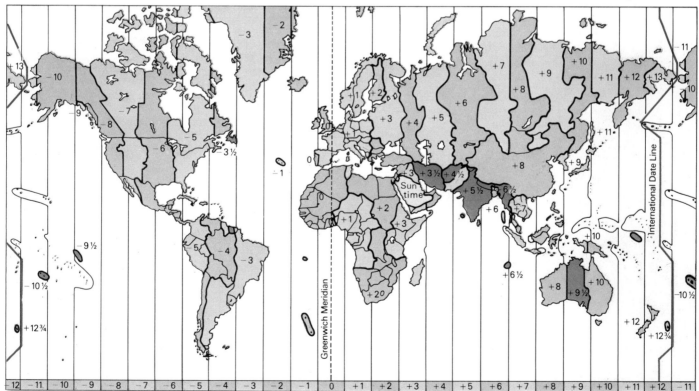

Time. *The internationally recognised time zones on land and at sea. Time in relation to GMT can be found by adding or subtracting the numbers indicated. The time shown on land relates to standard or 'legal time' and does not take into account daylight saving.*

1967 *The Times* was taken over by Lord Thomson of Fleet and in 1980, after a long industrial dispute, it was bought by Rupert Murdoch's News International. Closely connected with *The Times* are *The Times Educational Supplement*, founded in 1910, and the *Higher Education Supplement*, published separately in 1972. *The Times Literary Supplement*, founded in 1902, is one of the leading literary weeklies in Britain.

Timişoara (Hungarian *Temeşvár*), town of Romania, on the River Bega, capital of Timis province, near the Yugoslav border. In 1920, by the Treaty of Trianon, it passed from Hungary to Romania. Industries include brewing and distilling, chemicals, engineering and leather goods. Population (1979) 281,320.

Timor, largest and most easterly island of the Lesser Sunda Islands, partitioned until 1976 between Indonesian West Timor (14,931 km²) and (formerly Portuguese) East Timor (18,982 km² including the western Oé-Cusse enclave in Indonesian territory). The island is the driest in the Indonesian archipelago, being strongly affected by the south-east monsoon. Consequently, the soil is dry and relatively infertile, and vegetation is scrub-like with tropical deciduous forest stands. Timor has a dissected mountainous landscape, rising to over 3000 m. Out of a total population of 1·2 million (estimated 1975), 658,000 live in West Timor. The coastal peoples, of mainly Deutero-Malay stock, include the Belunese and Atonis groups, and are predominantly Muslim in the western half of the island and Christian in the east. The interior peoples, of Australoid and Melanesian stock, are animist-Christian in religion. The main towns of the two territories are Kupang (population 25,000) in West Timor and Dili (about 27,000) in East Timor. The local economy is based on shifting cultivation and both wet and dry settled rice farming, with cash crops of coffee, cocoa, coconut and sandalwood, and some cattle and specialised pony rearing. The staple food crop, in the predominant shifting cultivation system, is sago.

By virtue of a fortified post there, Timor was part of the Portuguese 'garrison empire' in Asia from the 15th century. The island was divided between Portugal and Holland by treaty in 1859, with boundaries settled by arbitration in 1914. After western Timor became part of independent Indonesia in 1949, the Portuguese sector remained a colony. The colony was scheduled to become independent in October 1978, but civil war broke out in 1975. Indonesian fears of a left-wing victory, and Indonesian intervention during 1975, led to annexation by Indonesia in 1976.

Timoshenko, Semën Konstantinovich (1895–1970), Soviet marshal. Called up for military service in 1915, he rose to the rank of general. In 1920 he was in the Russo-Polish campaign. It was Timoshenko who retrieved the Russian military position in the Russo-Finnish War of 1939–40. When the Germans invaded Russia, Timoshenko, who, as defence commissar, had reorganised the Red Army and introduced many reforms, was entrusted with the defence of Moscow. After he had repulsed the Germans, Stalin sent him to stem the enemy's advance in the Ukraine in

November 1941. From 1939 to 1952 he was a member of the Central Committee of the Communist Party.

Timothy, Saint (d.AD 97), young friend and fellow-labourer of St Paul. He accompanied St Paul on the second missionary journey, and the lives of the two are henceforward closely connected. Timothy was left as the apostle's representative at Ephesus. Eusebius says that he met his death there in a popular riot, after denouncing the worship of Artemis.

Timothy, Epistles to, form with the Epistle to Titus the group known since 1703 as the Pastoral Epistles, which give detailed instructions for the appointment of officers and the pastoral care of the Christian churches. The Pastorals are strongly doctrinal. The Christian life must show no incongruity between creed and practice. The Christian is to fight a good fight and expect suffering, and his swan song will be a song of victory. Other points are the unity of God; the inspiration of scripture; and the danger of riches.

Timothy, common name of *Phleum pratense*, a perennial grass native to Britain, and widely grown as fodder for livestock.

Timpani, the orchestral kettle-drums. Imported from the Turkish armies through Hungary at the end of the 15th century, they were adopted as royal instruments in the courts of Europe. They were introduced into the orchestra in the 17th century. They can be turned to precise pitches by varying the tension of the skin with tuning handles. Modern instruments can be tuned instantaneously by a pedal which acts on all the tuning handles simultaneously. A set from two to six, each of a different size and producing a different range of pitches, is used in the orchestra. Timpani are normally played with felt-headed sticks though other materials are used for special effects.

Tin, metallic chemical element, symbol Sn, atomic number 50, atomic weight 118·69; one of the seven metals of the ancients. It occurs free in nature in scattered deposits, but the oxide—tinstone or cassiterite—found in Cornwall, Australia, Malaysia, Nigeria and South America, is the only commercial source. Tin melts at 232°C. There are at least two allotropic forms: grey tin (relative density 5·8) exists below 13°C; above this temperature, white tin (relative density 7·3) is stable. White tin is crystalline in structure and when bent emits a curious crackling sound called the 'cry of tin'. Tin is not acted upon by the air, and is therefore used for tinning iron. Tin forms two series of salts, the stannous, in which it is bivalent, and the stannic, in which it is quadrivalent. The alloys of tin are of great value, and include gunmetal (copper 88, tin 10, zinc 2 per cent), bronze (copper and tin), phosphor bronze (0·5 per cent phosphorus), pewter (tin 80, lead 20 per cent), modern pewter (tin, antimony, copper, with a little bismuth), solder, bell metal, as well as a large number of alloys with other metals such as gold, iron and bismuth.

Tin-plate and Sheet, basis of low-carbon unalloyed mild steel coated by hot-dipping or electrodeposition with pure tin. It is used chiefly for the manufacture of cans and boxes. See IRON AND STEEL; METALLURGY.

Tinamou, any game bird of the family Tinamidae, inhabiting the forests of tropical and

South America and placed in a separate order, Tinamiformes. They resemble partridges in appearance, but have little or no tail: tinamous have a number of anatomical features in common with the flightless ratites. Despite their large flight muscles, they are slow, clumsy flyers. The coloration of their plumage provides good camouflage. They feed largely on vegetable matter supplemented by insects. Polygamy appears to predominate; often several females lay eggs in one nest; one hen may also lay eggs in nests guarded by different males. The males build the nests and incubate the eggs.

Tindemans, Leo (1922–), Belgian politician. He entered the Chamber of Deputies in 1961 as a member for the Christian Socialist party. In 1972 he was appointed deputy prime minister and was given responsibility for the budget in the Cabinet. He was prime minister from 1974 to 1978; a member of the European Parliament from 1979, and minister of Foreign Affairs from 1981.

Tinnitus, ringing in the ears. It is a frequent symptom of ear disease and may be described by the patient as a buzzing, humming, hissing, whistling, crackling, jangling or roaring sound. It may be due to trivial conditions in the external or middle ear such as a plug of wax or a blocked Eustachian tube. Disorders of the middle ear which give rise to tinnitus are otosclerosis and otitis media. The causes of tinnitus in the inner ear are not known. Diseases of the auditory nerve or the higher auditory centre in the temporal lobe of the brain also cause tinnitus. Unfortunately there is no medical or surgical treatment for tinnitus, although it may fade of its own accord or following treatment of the underlying condition.

Tintagel, coastal village on the north coast of Cornwall, England. The correct name of the village proper is Trevena, which merges with Bossiney. On Tintagel Head, a promontory 91 m high on the Atlantic coast, are the ruins of a castle, famous in the Arthurian romances. Population (1971) of parish, including Trevena and Bossiney, 1372.

Tintern Abbey, famous ruins at Tintern village, beautifully situated on the Wye river, north of Chepstow, Gwent, Wales. They date from 1131, when Walter de Clare founded a Cistercian house which became one of the wealthiest foundations in England. The building was mainly erected between 1269 and 1287 by Roger Bigod, Earl of Norfolk. The chief remains are the ruins of the magnificent cruciform church, the chapter-house and refectory. The great west window is one of the finest examples of curvilinear tracery.

Tintoretto, Jacopo Robusti (1518–94), He studied under Titian, and was considerably influenced by Michelangelo, writing on the wall of his studio the precept 'Michelangelo's drawing, Titian's colour'. His industrious life was spent almost entirely in Venice where he had a workshop which included his sons Domenico (c.1560–1635), Marco (d.1637) and daughter Marietta (c.1556–90?). There he painted his great *Miracle of St Mark*, 1548, his decorations for the Scuola di San Rocco (including the vast *Christ before Pilate* and *Last Supper*), and the *Paradise* for the Doge's Palace, 1588. The *St George and the Dragon* (National Gallery, London) shows his characteristic originality in depicting figures in rushing movement, and *The Origin of the Milky Way* (National Gallery) is one of the most beautiful allegories. He also painted a large number of portraits, e.g. *Vincenzo Morosini* (National Gallery).

Tipitaka (Sanskrit *Tripitaka*) or Triple Basket, the canonical writings in Pāli of Theravāda Buddhism. The name derives from the containers in which the scrolls were originally stored. These scriptures, otherwise known as the Pāli Canon, were first written down (on ola leaves) at a special council held in Sri Lanka in c.80 BC, and are among the earliest existing records of the *Buddha Dhamma* (Teaching of the Buddha).

Tipperary, inland county of the province of Munster, Republic of Ireland, bounded by Galway and Offaly in the north, Cork and Waterford to the south, Laois and Kilkenny to the east, and Clare and Limerick to the west. To the north and west lies a mountainous region with Keeper Hill (672 m), and in the south are the Galtee Mountains with Galtymore (920 m), the Knockmealdown Mountains and, farther east, the Slieveardagh Hills. The Bog of Allen adjoins Kilkenny, while in the south-west lies the Golden Vale, one of the most fertile regions in all Ireland. The principal river is the Shannon in the north-west. Agriculture is the chief industry, barley and oats being the main crops, but most of the area is under pasture. Dairy farming flourishes, and there are a number of butter factories. There are also flour and meal mills. Coal, copper, lead and zinc are mined, also slate and limestone, and peat production is being extended. The county town is Clonmel. Area 4296 km²; population (1979) 133,740.

Tippett, Sir Michael (1905–), British composer. He studied at the Royal College of Music. His humanitarian views first found significant expression in *A Child of Our Time*, 1941, a wartime oratorio. From 1940 to 1951 he was musical director of Morley College. Tippett's works show closely concentrated craftsmanship and great originality. He owes nothing to current systems or fashions, but his work is modern in a very personal way. It includes four symphonies; concertos; four string quartets; three piano sonatas, the cantata *Boyhood's End* (W. H. Hudson); the song-cycle *The Heart's Assurance*; the operas *The Midsummer Marriage*, 1955; *King Priam*, 1962; *The Knot Garden*, 1970; and *The Ice Break*, 1977; and also the oratorio *The Vision of Saint Augustine*, 1966.

Tipstaff, in England and Wales, an officer of the High Court whose function it is to arrest and take to prison any person committed by the court. The name is connected with the staff tipped with metal or a small crown which was formerly his badge of office.

Tipu Sahib (1749–99), Sultan of Mysore, succeeded his father Haider Ali in 1782. As sultan he concluded a treaty with the British in 1784, but in spite of this invaded the protected state of Travancore in 1789. War followed, and in 1792 he was obliged to resign half of his dominions. He continued his intrigues, urging the French to stir up war with Britain, the result of which was the storming of his capital, Seringapatam, by the British, during which action Tipu was killed.

Tiranë, capital of Albania and of Tiranë district, 27 km from the Adriatic Sea, on the River Ishm, situated in a fertile plain. The town was chosen as the capital in 1920 and in the 1930s King Zog commissioned Italian architects to replan it. Districts of the old town and several old mosques are preserved. Tiranë is the country's industrial and commercial, as well as administrative, centre and its industries include metallurgy, textiles, cigarettes, foodstuffs and timber. Population (1978) 198,000.

Tintoretto. A detail from The Origin of the Milky Way.

Tiresias, legendary blind soothsayer of Thebes. After the defeat of Thebes, he fled—or, according to another version, was carried off captive—but on the road he drank from the spring Tilphusa, and died. He was believed to retain his powers as a seer in the underworld.

Tirol, or Tyrol, former crown land of the Austro-Hungarian Empire, now part of a province of Austria (see below). In Roman times it was part of Rhaetia. It was later ruled by the bishops of Brixen and Trent, and came into the possession of the house of Hapsburg in 1363. By the Treaty of St Germain-en-Laye in 1919, it was divided, the part north of the Brenner Pass becoming a province of the new Austrian republic, and the part south of the pass being ceded to Italy.

Tirol, or Tyrol, Alpine province of western Austria and the northern half of the former crown land (see above). It is bounded on the north by Bavaria and on the south by Italy. East Tirol, the part south of the Hohe Tauern, is detached from the rest of the province. The main part contains the valleys of the Inn and the Lech—both trending south-west to north-east. The Alpine ranges separating these valleys are broken up by many small rivers flowing south-north. Grossglockner (3798 m), the highest peak in Austria, is at the

junction of the borders of East Tirol, Salzburg and Styria. The valley of the upper Drau crosses East Tirol. The province is heavily forested. The chief occupations are dairy-farming, stock-raising and forestry. Lignite, nickel, lead and other minerals are found; there are textile and chemical industries, and several hydroelectric installations. Tourism is a major source of revenue. The capital is Innsbruck. Area 12,650 km². Population (1981) 586,297.

Tirpitz, Alfred Peter Friedrich von (1849–1930), German grand-admiral. In the 1870s Tirpitz, a lieutenant-commander, prepared memoranda on torpedoes, which led to the creation of a torpedo-section in 1885. In 1897 he became secretary of state for the navy. In 1898 he presented to the Reichstag his first Navy Bill, the beginning of the serious growth of the German navy. His second bill, brought in in 1900, started the naval armament race. He was made grand-admiral in 1911. At the beginning of the First World War he was still secretary of state for the navy, but did not succeed in his purpose of making full use of the navy from the beginning. He resigned in 1916. He was a member of the Reichstag from 1924 to 1928.

Tiruchirappalli, or Trichinopoly, town of Tamil Nadu state, India. It is an important rail centre at the head of the Cauvery river delta with textile, cement and railway goods manufacturing at Golden Rock. Population (1981) 360,919.

Tiryns, ancient city of Argolis, traditionally founded by Proetus, who was said to have built the walls with the aid of the Cyclopes. Tiryns existed in the 3rd millennium BC. It was finally destroyed by the people of Argos in 468 BC.
See also AEGEAN CULTURE.

Tissot, James Joseph Jacques (1836–1902), French painter. Initially he was influenced by Degas and shared his interest in Japanese prints. He settled in England after 1870 where he did illustrations for London journals. He also illustrated the life of Christ, spending ten years in Palestine, but is better known for charming pictures of late-Victorian life.

Tissue, a collection of associated cells having in common form, function and/or other characteristics. The study of tissues is histology. Tissues may be named according to the types of cells composing them, e.g. muscular tissues of animals, and parenchymatous tissues of plants; or according to their function, e.g. connective tissues of animals, storage tissues of plants; or according to their position, e.g. epithelial tissue of animals and dermal tissues, such as bark, of plants. The discovery of nutritional media in which living tissues may be cultivated *in vitro* has added much to the knowledge of cell division and differentiation and of the behaviour of strains of cancer cells.
See also DEVELOPMENTAL BIOLOGY; EMBRYOLOGY.

Tissue Culture, a technique of cutting out small portions of living tissues and placing them in conditions where the cells can grow and develop autonomously. The conditions required are: nutritive elements suitable for cell growth and division, an oxygen supply, a suitable temperature near that of the organism from which the tissue was taken, removal of excretory products or the reculturing of the cells in fresh media, and aseptic conditions.

Tisza (German *Theiss*; Serbo-Croatian *Tisa*), river of the Ukraine, Hungary, and Yugoslavia. It rises in two headstreams in the Carpathians and flows across the Alföld, generally parallel with the Danube, which it joins at Novi Sad. The principal tributaries are the Körös and the Mureşul. Length 1350 km.

Tit, or titmouse, birds of the family Paridae in order Passeriformes. All are insect-eaters. The blue tit, or tomtit, *Parus caeruleus*, is blue with green above, yellowish underneath, and a black throat. The great tit, *P. major*, is about 15 cm long and is green on the back, with grey wings and tail, and black and white head and black throat. Both species are confined to the Old World. In North America tits are called chickadees; the best known is the black-capped chickadee, *P. atricapillus*.

Tit-lark, see PIPIT.

'Titanic' Disaster, caused when the White Star liner *Titanic*, then the largest vessel afloat, collided with an iceberg on the night of 14 April 1912, while on her maiden voyage to New York. She sank within three hours of impact and of her 2206 passengers, only 703 were saved.

Titanium, metallic chemical element, symbol Ti, atomic number 22, atomic weight 47·9. Titanium ranks ninth in abundance amongst the elements in the Earth's crust, but owing to its reactivity at high temperatures its extraction from its ores: anatase, ilmanite, rutile, brookite and aeschinite, is particularly difficult. The metal is prepared by the reduction of titanium tetrachloride with sodium or magnesium. Titanium is a white, lustrous metal of low density (relative density 4·5) and high strength, and is resistant to corrosion. It is used in aircraft manufacture, in the manufacture of propeller shafts and other marine parts, and in surgery, because it is resistant to corrosion and is physiologically inert. Titanium dioxide (TiO_2) is an important white pigment, particularly useful in that it is non-toxic and does not discolour with age.

Titanotheres, extinct mammals of order Perissodactyla (horses) that lived in Eocene and early Oligocene times. They were of considerable size, and had large horn-like processes on the front of the skull. The teeth were primitive and the animals probably lived on soft vegetation.

Titans, fabulous beings in Greek mythology. Uranus and Gē (Heaven and Earth) had, among other children, six sons and six daughters called Titans, the most important being Cronus and Rhea. The Titans deposed Uranus, and Cronus married Rhea and became their king. But he had been warned by his parents that one of his children would destroy him; so he swallowed them at birth: Hestia, Demeter, Hera, Pluto and Poseidon. Rhea, therefore, when carrying Zeus went to Crete, bore her child in the Dictaean cave and gave Cronus a stone wrapped in a cloth, which he swallowed believing it to be his son. When Zeus grew up he gave Cronus a potion which caused him to vomit up the children he had swallowed. Together with his brothers and sisters Zeus then began his

Titian. Sacred and Profane Love, *a study of the conflicting elements of human nature.*

struggle with the ruling Titans which lasted ten years and ended in victory for Zeus.

Tithe, a 'tenth part of annual agricultural or other produce, or personal profits, payable for the maintenance of the parish priest. Tithes were payable before the Christian era. In the Christian Church they were first given by the faithful as spontaneous offerings in kind, e.g. wool, corn, or other agricultural or farm produce. Canon law later enjoined payment as a legal obligation in accordance with the divine law of the Old Testament. The system was only finally abolished in Britain by the Tithe Act, 1936.

Titian, otherwise called Tiziano Vecelli (c.1487/90–1576), Italian painter. He was a pupil of Giovanni Bellini and worked with Giorgione. He emulated the latter's style so successfully that their contributions are inseparable in works which Titian completed after Giorgione's death in 1510. These include the Dresden *Venus* and the *Concert Champêtre* in Paris. His *Assumption of the Virgin* altarpiece in the Frari secured his reputation in Venice and was an important innovatory development in Venetian painting. His *Christ and the Tribute Money* (Dresden Gallery) was spoken of by Vasari as something stupendous and miraculous. In 1516 he was made official painter to the council in Venice. In 1522 he went to Ferrara, and executed amongst other works the glorious masterpiece *Bacchus and Ariadne* (National Gallery, London). In 1532 the Emperor Charles V commissioned a portrait of himself. Titian was now of European eminence. In 1545 he went to Rome where he painted portraits of Pope Paul III as well as *Danaë* (Naples Museum). In 1548 he joined Charles V at Augsburg, and painted the well-known portraits of Philip of Spain. From this time he was chiefly occupied in Venice where his large workshop included his son, Orazio. Titian's works are remarkable for their magnificent colouring and technical skill.

Titicaca, Lake, mountain lake in the Andes, half in Bolivia and half in Peru, between the main Andean range and the Cordillera Real. It is 3750 m above sea-level and is said to be the highest navigated lake in the world. Area about 9100 km² (including its 36 islands); maximum depth about 450 m. There is a steamer service between Guaqi in Bolivia and Puno in Peru.

Title Deeds, documents showing title to interests in land (for example, a conveyance, a lease and a mortgage).

Titles, additions to a person's name, indicative of some honour, office or dignity, e.g. emperor, prince, chancellor, primate, duke, mayor. Some titles are held by virtue of office; others are hereditary, while others still, like that of knight, are conferred for life. See also NAME; NOBILITY; ORDERS OF KNIGHTHOOD.

Titmouse, see TIT.

Tito, originally Josip Broz (1890–1980), Yugoslav soldier and statesman. After the First World War he became a Communist, and spent some time in Moscow. In 1937, he became general secretary of the Yugoslav Communist party, which he dissolved and ordered re-registered, thus ensuring that he was surrounded by loyal adherents. During the Second World War, Tito, unlike most European Communist leaders, was in his own country organising resistance to the Nazis. His other antagonists included the Mihajlović partisans, and the NKVD observers in his own Politburo. By welding peasants, factory workers and intellectuals into a victorious guerrilla partisan army he felt he had contributed a new Communist experience and something novel in Stalinist doctrine. His independent attitude and popular national following did not suit Moscow. In mid-1948 the Cominform expelled Tito and urged the Yugoslav people to turn him out of office if he did not change his policy. The quarrel with Soviet Russia made serious political and economic difficulties for Yugoslavia; but Tito was still genuinely popular with supporters from all classes in all parts of Yugoslavia. The idea of Moscow controlling Yugoslav internal affairs roused national pride and rallied Yugoslavs hitherto hostile to his government round Tito. The Cominform countries therefore imposed economic sanctions, hoping to bring about the collapse of the Yugoslav economy; but Tito, adhering to his five-year plan, made trade treaties with over twenty countries, many of them in Western Europe, and received economic aid from Britain, France and the USA. After Stalin's death he resumed relations with USSR, though maintaining his country's independence. When the Yugoslav constitution was revised in 1953 Tito became

Marshall Tito, the founder of modern Yugoslavia.

president and in 1974 he was made president for life.

See also YUGOSLAVIA, *History*.

Titograd (formerly *Podgorica* or *Podgoritza*), town in Yugoslavia, capital of the republic of Montenegro, at the confluence of the rivers Ribnica and Morača. It was renamed in 1946 in honour of the Yugoslav leader, Marshal Tito. Population (1971) 98,800.

Titration, method of quantitative chemical analysis. The weight of a substance in a definite volume of solution is determined by causing it to react with a solution of another reagent of known strength. This reagent is contained in a burette and run out into the other solution till reaction is complete, as shown by change of colour of an indicator such as litmus, or by cessation of effervescence, etc. The volume is noted, and the weight of reagent contained is thus known. From the chemical equation and the atomic weights, the weight of the other solute can then be calculated.

Titus, Saint, friend and companion of St Paul who consecrated him bishop of Crete. All that is known of him is learned from the canonical epistle addressed to him by St Paul. Eusebius says that Titus remained unmarried and died in old age.

Titus, full name Titus Flavius Sabinus Vespasianus (c.AD 40–81), Roman Emperor, son of Vespasian. He succeeded to the Empire in 79, and at once put away Berenice, sister of Agrippa, his attachment to whom had made him unpopular. The first year of Titus's reign was memorable for the eruption of Vesuvius and a great fire at Rome. He completed the Colosseum and built the baths named after him. His death was greatly mourned by the Romans, especially after the accession of his brother Domitian.

Tiv, a people living in the Benue province of Central Nigeria. Originally they were subsistence farmers growing yams and millet; today they produce cash crops of soya beans. In the traditional system there was no centralised political authority but their markets served as forums for debate on public issues. Their social organisation is based on a system of segmentary lineages and their religion, or a belief of the power of forces (*akombo*), is manifested in emblems and fetishes. The Tiv number about 1·5 million.

Tivoli (ancient *Tibur*), Italian town in Lazio, 25 km north-east of Rome. It stands on the Aniene, at the point where the river forms a series of falls down to the Campagna di Roma; these cascades have been celebrated for their beauty since classical times. Ruins still exist of fine Roman villas, in particular a magnificent villa built by Hadrian, and of mausolea, aqueducts, and a temple of Vesta. Vast quantities of travertine, used as a decorative building stone, are quarried in the vicinity. Population (1974) 28,400; municipality (1971) 41,000.

Tlaxcala, capital of Tlaxcala state in Mexico, its full name being Tlaxcala de Xicotencati. Situated at an altitude of 2240 m at the foot of La Malinche volcano, it is the commercial centre of an agricultural and cattle-raising district; its chief industries are cotton and woollen textile manufacturing. Population (1970) 13,000.

Tlemçen, capital of Tlemçen department in Algeria, 130 km south-west of Oran. It exports blankets, olive oil and alfalfa, and manufactures leather work and native carpets. Population (1974) 115,054.

TNT, see TRINITROTOLUENE.

Toad, common name for frog-like, tailless, rough-skinned, hopping members of order Anura, class Amphibia. The name is used loosely, but the true toads belong to the family Bufonidae, with about 300 species, and especially the genus *Bufo* with over 200 species. They differ from frogs chiefly by the absence of teeth, and in certain other anatomical features. In toads, a large gland, called the parotid, occurs, which is absent in frogs. The gland provides a noxious substance when its secretion is mixed with the toad's blood, through an abrasion or other means, and thus affords some protection to the animal when attacked. The skin of the toad is drier and more warty than that of the frog. The value of toads to the farmer and gardener cannot be exaggerated, as they feed entirely on insects, millipedes, woodlice, slugs and snails. They are harmless to man.

European toads such as the common toad, *B. vulgaris*, and North American species such as the spadefoots, *Scaphiopus*, range in size from 2 to 25 cm. They live mostly on land, are nocturnal and hibernate in burrows. Breeding takes place in winter and the eggs are laid in water in the spring. Toads migrate long distances (up to 1·5 km) from their land quarters to suitable breeding waters. The eggs are laid in two long strings, not in a mass as with frogs.

Toadflax, *Linaria*, a genus of the Scrophulariaceae; the flowers resemble small snapdragons (*Antirrhinum*) with a spur at the base of the petal tube. Bastard toadflax belongs to the family Santalaceae.

Toadstool, common name for the fruiting body of a fungus in subdivision Basidiomycotina that resembles a mushroom but is inedible.

See also FUNGI.

Tobacco, plant of the genus *Nicotiana* in family Solanaceae, from which are manufactured smoking and chewing tobacco, cigarettes, cigars and snuff. There are over 50 varieties of the plant, many of which are cultivated in gardens, but only a few varieties are used for smoking purposes. The varieties of most importance to smokers are *N. tabacum* and *N. rustica*. The former, a native of the West Indies, bears pink or rose-coloured flowers and grows from 1 to 3 m high. The bulk of tobacco used in the trade of most countries of the world is produced from this variety. The latter, a native of Mexico, bears greenish-yellow flowers, and is a much smaller plant than *N. tabacum*. *N. rustica* was cultivated by the ancient Mexicans and by the North American Indians, but early in the 17th century it was largely superseded by *N. tabacum*.

Tobago, island of the West Indies about 121 km south-east of Grenada and 34 km north-east of Trinidad. The island is 42 km long and 12 km wide and has an area of 301 km². Tobago is mountainous in the centre and at the north-east end, and undulating and flat in the south and west. The highest peak is 641 m. Deep fertile valleys run down from either side of the main ridge. The principal river is the Courland, named after the Viking duke who in the 17th century ruled the island. Scarborough on the south coast, formerly called Port Louis, is the capital. The only other major town is Roxborough. Population (1970) of Tobago 39,000. Cocoa, coconuts and limes have taken the place of sugar which was the staple industry before being ruined by foreign sugar bounties.

Sir Robert Dudley, natural son of the Earl of Leicester, is believed to have hoisted the English flag in Tobago in 1580. Nearly 36 years later British colonists from Barbados effected the first settlement. For 40 years the island's history was a struggle between Dutch colonists and some Baltic settlers from Courland, varied by French and British invasions. In 1814, it was finally ceded to Britain. It became part of the independent Commonwealth state of Trinidad and Tobago in August 1962.

See also TRINIDAD AND TOBAGO.

Tobey, Mark (1890–1976), US painter. Regarded as the leader of the 'West Coast' School in the USA, he was noted for his calligraphic use of the brush derived from the East, which he called 'white writing', and his elaborately patterned abstract paintings.

Tobogganing, descending an ice track on a vehicle comprising a platform resting on runners.

Luge tobogganing (or lugeing) originated in 1879 in Switzerland. World championships began in 1955. The luge is made of wood with twin metal runners and is steered by the feet, a handrope and weight transference, the rider adopting a backward-leaning sitting posture. The absence of any mechanical means of steering or braking is a clear distinction from bobsledding. The single-seater is limited to 1·5 m in length, 44 cm in width, 15 cm in height and 20 kg in weight. The double-seater, although longer, has the same weight restriction. Senior courses, banked and usually steeper than for bobsledding, are about 1000 m long with at least 12 bends. Speeds of 130 kmph are possible. Championships are determined, as in bobsledding, by the aggregate times of four descents.

Cresta Run skeleton tobogganing, uniquely characterised by riding prone and head first, takes place on only one course, the Cresta

Run at St Moritz, Switzerland, built in 1884. With steeply banked bends, including the notorious Stream Corner, the course from Top is 1213 m long, with an elevation of 156·7 m. The fastest descents have exceeded an average speed of 80 kmph.

The skeleton toboggan comprises a flat wooden platform on steel runners. There is no restriction as to weight, size or design. Events are normally decided by the aggregate times of three descents by each rider.

Tobolsk, city in Tyumen *oblast* of the RSFSR, USSR, in West Siberia, on the River Irtysh, the centre of a lumbering and dairy-farming area and supply point for the northern part of the *oblast*. The city was founded by Russian Cossacks in 1587. It was capital of Siberia, 1596–1824, and provincial capital until 1923. It was formerly a place of banishment, including that of Nicholas II (1917–18). Population (1970) 48,000.

Tobruk, seaport of Libya, North Africa. It has an excellent harbour, and was occupied by Italy in 1912. It was the scene of much fighting in the Libyan campaign of the Second World War. The town now has a modern oil refinery linked by a 560-kilometre pipeline to the Spirit oil-field. Population (1970) 28,000.

Toc H, a movement to bring together into interdenominational Christian fellowship men and women of every class and opinion for the purpose of social service of all kinds, with groups and branches throughout the world. The name Toc H comes from the army signallers' designation of the initials TH, which stood for Talbot House, opened in 1915 at Poperinghe in Flanders as a chapel and club for soldiers. It was a memorial to Gilbert Talbot, who was killed in 1915, founded by his brother, Neville Talbot, later Bishop of Pretoria, and the Rev P. B. ('Tubby') Clayton.

Toccata (from Italian *toccare*, to touch; figuratively, to play), in the 17th century, simply 'a thing to play' as distinct from *cantata*, 'a thing to sing'. It acquired a sense of touching a keyboard instrument, for the purpose of trying or testing it, which meant that it usually contained scales and brilliant figuration interspersed with slow chordal passages. Modern toccatas usually lay stress on brilliance and rapid execution.

Tocqueville, Alexis Charles Henri Maurice Clérel de (1805–59), French historian. He went to America to study prisons in 1831, and took the opportunity to collect materials for his *De la Démocratie en Amérique*, 1835–40, a work of peculiar interest as the first reasoned and more or less unbiased exposition of popular government in that country. A moderate Liberal in politics, he was elected vice-president of the Assembly in 1849, was dismissed when Louis Napoleon became emperor, and met with an enthusiastic reception from John Stuart Mill and other prominent Whigs when he visited England.

Todd, Reginald Stephen Garfield (1908–), New Zealand-born Zimbabwean politician. He became a missionary in Rhodesia, entering politics in 1946. He formed the United Rhodesia party and was returned to power as premier of Southern Rhodesia, 1953–58, but lost office when his progressive policies were rejected by the electorate. In 1965, after his outspoken criticism of the Smith government, he was placed under restriction until 1976.

Toddy, in cold and temperate countries, usually a drink of spirits, sugar and hot water with a slice of lemon; in tropical countries, beverages fermented from the sap of various palms.

Toga, the formal dress of a Roman citizen obligatory on public occasions. Made of white wool, it was semicircular in shape and elaborately folded and draped. Curule magistrates and boys wore a purple border; on attaining manhood the *toga virilis*, without the border, was assumed. After Augustus, the emperors commonly wore a purple toga.

Togliatti, Palmiro (1893–1964), Italian Communist politician. He lived in exile in the USSR during the Mussolini regime, and returned to Italy in 1944. In a speech made in Salerno in that year he announced that the Italian Communist party was prepared to collaborate with all democratic parties, so laying the basis for strategy in the post-war years. He was vice-premier 1944–45 and minister of justice 1945–46. With the onset of the cold war the PCI (the Italian Communist party) was excluded from the government, and Togliatti retained leadership in opposition. He died in the USSR.

Togo, Heihachiro (1847–1934), Japanese admiral. He was commander-in-chief of the Japanese navy on the outbreak of the Russo-Japanese War and succeeded in destroying the Russian fleet at Port Arthur and later in defeating that of Adm. Rozhdestvensky at the battle of Tsushima in 1905.

Togo
Area: 56,000 km²
Population: 2,470,000
Capital: Lomé

Togo, Republic of, small republic in West Africa, sandwiched between Ghana on the west and Benin on the east; the country is barely 100 km wide at any point but extends inland to a northern border with Upper Volta, a distance of 560 km (area 56,000 km²).

The sand-bar coast gives way to sheltered lagoons, backed by a coastal plain forming a productive farming area called the 'Terre-de-Barre', extending into neighbouring Benin. Inland a range of quartzitic hills traverses the country obliquely from the south-west (the Togo Mountains reach 850 m) towards the north-east where they pass into Benin as the Atacora Mountains (700 m).

Most of the country is covered by forms of savanna grassland or woodland, much modified by farming, especially in the south. The Togo–Atacora Mountains, however, are well wooded and carry good crops of coffee and cocoa.

The total population in 1979 was an estimated 2,470,000. The capital is Lomé.

Agriculture occupies 90 per cent of the working population. The chief crops are yams, millet, cassava and maize; the chief cash crops are coffee, cocoa, cotton, groundnuts and palm kernels. Livestock breeding and fishing also contribute to the internal economy.

Industry is small but growing, mainly processing agricultural products and producing consumer goods. There is a steel works, an oil refinery and two cement plants. Phosphates have long been the country's leading export. Limestone and marble are also quarried.

The constitution of 1979–80, establishing the third Togolese Republic, provides for an executive president, directly elected for 7 years. He appoints the Political Bureau of the sole legal party which, in turn, nominates the candidates for the National Assembly.

The official language is French.

History. The Ewe, who form the largest ethnic group in present-day Togo, migrated to that country from the area of the Niger from the 14th to the 16th centuries. The first Europeans to establish coastal trading stations were the Portuguese, who shipped slaves to work on Brazilian plantations.

The export trade in slaves gave way during the 19th century to legitimate commerce, mainly the export of palm oil. In 1884, the

Togo. Stilt dwellings on Lake Ganvié.

Germans made a number of treaties with local chiefs, and attempted to create a model colony in Togo; but there was popular resentment against German systems of forced labour and heavy taxation. In 1914 British and French troops forced a German surrender. German Togo was divided into British and French spheres.

After 1946 the movement for unification of the two Togos gained momentum. But there were separatist movements also, and plebiscites in British Togo showed a majority in favour of union with the Gold Coast. British Togo now forms part of Ghana.

In 1955 French Togo had been granted a considerable degree of autonomy, and in 1958 the elections for the legislative assembly saw the majority victory of the Committee of Togolese Unity (CUT) led by Sylvanus Olympio, who became prime minister in 1958 and president of the newly independent republic in 1960. In 1963 Olympio was killed in the course of the military coup which overthrew his government.

The leading opposition leader, Nicolas Grunitzky, formed a coalition government, and later assumed full powers. By November 1966 civil war was imminent, and it was to prevent this course of events that the army, led by Col. Etienne Eyadéma, seized power in the coup of 13 January 1967.

In 1968 he founded a new political party, the Movement of the Togolese National Rally, overtly a party of national unity. Ninety-nine per cent of the population approved of Eyadéma's position as president in the referendum of January 1972.

In 1980, under a new constitution, he was re-elected as president of the Third Togolese Republic.

Tojo, Hideki (1884–1948), Japanese politician and general. In 1940, when Prince Konoye founded his National party, Tojo, as war minister, was one of the two leading figures in the Cabinet formed by Konoye, whom he succeeded as prime minister. It was Tojo who ordered the attack on Pearl Harbor. He assured his position at home in 1941 by dissolving the Diet and appointing a National Service Political Council to control the Diet in the interests of the government. In 1944 Tojo reorganised the High Command, himself taking the posts of war minister and army chief of staff and combining the posts of navy minister and navy chief of staff. When Saipan fell, he resigned. After the Japanese collapse Tojo was tried in Tokyo (1947–48) and hanged.

Tokaj (English *Tokay*), town of Hungary, in Borsod-Abaúj-Zemplén county, near the junction of the rivers Tisza and Bodrog, 45 km east of Miskolc. The town is at the foot of Mount Tokaj (515 m), which gives its name to the celebrated wine produced on its slopes and in the surrounding hilly district of Hegyalja. Population (1970) 5000.

Tokay, see HUNGARIAN WINES.

Tokelau Islands, formerly Union Islands, group of islands, central Pacific ocean, about 434 km north of Apia, Western Samoa. They comprise three atolls, Atafu, Nukunono and Fakaofu. In 1948 they were included in the territorial boundaries of New Zealand. Total area of the islands, 1012 ha. The main export is copra. Population (1980) 1620.

Tokyo. *Crowds throng the Ginza, the city's most famous shopping street.*

Tokyo (formerly Edo or Yedo), capital of Japan, sited in south-east Honshū, on the north-west shore of Tokyo Bay, on the delta of the Sumida river, which separates the city proper on the west bank from the Kōto on the east. It was founded in 1457 by Ota Dokan, who built his castle here, and received its present name when the court moved from Kyōto in 1868; the following year, it was opened to foreigners. The magnificent palace, in a blend of Japanese and European styles, stands in the Fukiage park, not far from the ancient castle. To the east of the palace lies the commercial and industrial part of the city, while the northern part is mainly educational and contains many universities, colleges and beautiful temples. In the west and south-west are the foreign embassies and legations. Tokyo has its own seaport, Yokohama, 30 km away.

Although heavy industries are concentrated in neighbouring cities, Tokyo is important as a manufacturing centre in its own right. A high proportion of its factories are small-scale enterprises, many of them manufacturing components which are assembled in plants outside the city boundaries. Industries include food and beverages, printing and publishing, chemicals, textiles, electrical machinery, cameras, optical goods, precision instruments and rubber. Industrial development has brought about serious problems of atmospheric pollution and the city also suffers from traffic congestion and many other problems associated with acute shortage of land. The population of the city (as distinct from the wider area of Tokyo-to) amounts to 8,200,000 (1979).

Toledo, city of Spain, capital of Toledo province, built on a rock above the River Tagus. In 1085 it became a capital of Castile, and later, of Spain. Toledo has the great five-aisled Gothic cathedral (13th–17th centuries) of the primate of Spain. Several churches preserve paintings by El Greco. Toledo sword blades were long famous, and fine knives are still manufactured, as well as silks, ceramics and objects of church art. Population (1970) 44,434.

Toledo, city and county seat of Lucas county, Ohio, USA, on Maumee Bay of Lake Erie, 153 km west of Cleveland. It is a railway centre and oil pipeline terminus, and a principal Great Lakes port. Important for shipbuilding and oil refining, it also manufactures glass, automobiles, electrical equipment and steel. Population (1980) 354,265.

Tolkien, J(ohn) R(ouald) R(evel) (1892–1973), English writer, born in South Africa, but brought up in England. He was professor of Anglo-Saxon at Oxford, 1925–45, then Merton professor of English language and literature until 1959. He published studies and editions of Anglo-Saxon and Middle English works, but is best known for his unique and vastly popular imaginative writings, especially the *Lord of the Rings* trilogy, which was published between 1954–55. These books expand the adventures of dwarfs, hobbits, monsters and other creatures first created in *The Hobbit*, 1937, into a complete and self-contained world with its own history and geography, reminiscent of Norse myth.

Tolls, taxes imposed in consideration of some privilege. In the feudal system it meant the right to tollage villeins. Later it became the distinguishing mark of a turnpike road, i.e. a road with toll-gates or bars on it, called 'turns'. These 'turns' appear to have been first constructed about the middle of the 18th century, when interested persons subscribed among themselves for the repair of various roads, and exacted a toll for the privilege of using the roads so repaired. Popular resistance to these exactions led to the passing of acts to regulate tolls. Most road tunnels under rivers, ferries and some bridges impose a toll, as do motorways in Italy and the USA. A *port-toll* is a charge on goods carried into a port.

Tolpuddle Martyrs, six farm labourers of Tolpuddle, 11 km from Dorchester, Dorset, England, who in 1834 formed an association to resist wage reductions. They were sentenced to seven years' transportation on the charge of administering illegal oaths but after widespread protests were reprieved two years later. Theirs is perhaps the best known case in the early history of trade unionism.

Tolstoy, Count Lev Nikolaevich (1828–1910), Russian novelist and social reformer, born into an aristocratic family on their estate, where he spent most of his life. While with the Russian forces in the Caucasus he wrote the autobiographical works *Childhood*, 1852, and *Boyhood*, 1854, and a number of war stories which revealed what were to be the main features of his literary work; acute observation and perception, and moral sincerity. In 1857 and 1860 he travelled in western Europe, experiencing disgust at its materialism, and studying educational methods. In the 1860s and 1870s Tolstoy devoted much time to educational activities, including running a school on his estate, as a pioneer of 'free education'. This was also the period of his most intensive literary work. From 1863–69 he worked on *War and Peace*, a panorama of Russian society on the eve of, and during, the war of 1812 against Napoleon. In it Tolstoy expressed the view that history is made not by great men like Napoleon, but by the countless unconscious actions of individuals. His own search for a way to live is reflected in *War and Peace* and still more strongly in *Anna Karenina*, 1873–77, in which the ethics of marriage and broader questions of life and death are examined.

By 1877 Tolstoy had approached a spiritual crisis, which he resolved by working out a new religious and social teaching based on the conviction that the whole message of Christ was contained in the words 'that ye resist not evil'. Renunciation of violence, wealth and sex, a need for inner self-improvement and love for all living things are the main tenets of Tolstoyan Christianity. The imaginative works of his later years serve to illustrate and propagate his new philosophy. His rejection of Church and State brought him excommunication and government hostility.

Lev Tolstoy, pre-eminent Russian novelist.

His fame spread, and during the last 15 or 20 years of his life he was probably the most venerated man in the world. Tolstoy the artist has had much influence on subsequent literature. Tolstoy the thinker has proved much less influential, his only great disciple being Gandhi.

Toltecs, semi-legendary people of Mexico and Central America, to whom the Aztecs and Mayas ascribed many cities, monuments and arts. Though their certain origin is not known, they were the reputed conquerors of the Mayas. It is thought their main centre was at Tula (Tollán). They reached the zenith of their power between 700 and 1100, conquering many neighbouring peoples. Their name means 'builder', and they are famous for the great pyramids of Teotihuacán.

Toluca, town of Mexico, capital of the state of Mexico, 60 km south-west of Mexico City. It is the centre of an agricultural and stock-farming region. The chief industries comprise cotton and woollen textile manufacturing and the processing of agricultural products. Population (1975) 142,000.

Toluene, or methyl benzene, $C_6H_5CH_3$, mobile liquid (boiling point 110°C) which resembles benzene in most respects. It is prepared from the 90 per cent benzol obtained from coal-tar and from the cracking of petroleum, and is used in the preparation of aniline dyes, explosives and many aromatic compounds.

Tom Thumb (Charles Sherwood Stratton, 1838–83), US midget exhibited by Phineas Barnum. He grew to a height of 101·6 cm and married Lavinia Warren, herself a midget. He gave several command performances before Queen Victoria and amassed a fortune of around $750,000 before his death.

Tom-toms, see DRUM.

Tomato, *Lycopersicum esculentum*, an annual plant in the family Solanaceae, bearing globose or ovoid red or yellow fruit. Round fruits are generally grown in Britain; in Europe and America they are larger and irregular in shape. Its production is now an important world-wide industry.

Tomb, properly signifies a mass of masonry raised over a grave or vault used for interment; but it is applied, in a wider sense, to any sepulchral structure. Primitive sepulchres are of two classes: subterraneous, and raised mounds or tumuli. Monuments of the first kind are numerous in Egypt; the pyramids had no doubt a common origin with the tumulus. Tombs of the Middle Ages within buildings (churches, chantries, etc.) exhibit a variety of form and enrichment, from the primitive stone coffin to the lavishly decorated canopied monuments. Another class consists of altar or table tombs. The next in order is the effigy tomb, introduced in the 13th century, with a recumbent figure of the deceased upon it, extended, the hands slightly raised and joined in the attitude of prayer. See FUNERAL RITES AND BURIAL CUSTOMS; MAUSOLEUM; PYRAMID; SARCOPHAGUS.

Tombouctou, or Timbuktu, town of Mali, West Africa, situated near the most northerly point on the Niger river. Its position made it a focus of caravan routes between North and West Africa, and it flourished as a trade centre in the 12th century. European influence reoriented trade towards the coast

during the 20th century, and the town's population has fallen from a peak of 50,000 to about 9000 today.

Tommy Atkins, slang name for the British private soldier; more shortly 'Tommy' as in the opening poem of Kipling's *Barrack Room Ballads*, 1892. Originally the suppositious name used in a specimen form in an official handbook issued by the War Office after the Napoleonic wars, it was afterwards generally applied to describe the British regular soldier. The vogue of the name, which is used in a friendly rather than in any derogatory sense, was due largely to Kipling. The Scots equivalent is 'Jock'.

'Tommy Gun', see SUBMACHINE-GUN.

Tomsk, capital city and economic centre of Tomsk *oblast*, USSR; an important rail and river transhipment centre (sited on the River Tom, a tributary of the Ob), and a major cultural centre of Siberia. There are engineering, chemical and woodworking industries. It was founded in 1604 as a fortress town and played an important part in the Russian advance into Siberia, though it declined after it was bypassed by the Trans-Siberian Railway. Population (1980) 431,000.

Tomtit, see TIT.

Ton, see METROLOGY.

Tonality, in music, a synonym for key, but with the more specific implication of the feeling of a definite key suggested by a composition or passage. It might be viewed as the art of harmony projected onto the largest scale and affecting a composition as a whole. It is thus one of the most powerful determining factors in musical structure, operating through the establishment of, and rate of change in, dominating harmonies, by the agency of modulation and the sense of cadence.

Tone, (Theobald) Wolfe (1763–98), Irish rebel and patriot. With Thomas Russell and James Tandy he founded the Society of United Irishmen in 1791. In 1796 he was in Paris consolidating his plans for a French invasion of Ireland. In the resultant expedition the French failed to effect a landing. In 1798 there was a rebellion in Ireland; Tone was captured, tried by court-martial, and sentenced to be hanged for treason. He cut his own throat in prison.

Tone, in music: (1) The interval of a major second. In the scale of C the interval C–D is a major tone. (2) In American usage = note. (3) The quality of a musical sound, especially with reference to performance. (4) In plainsong the name of one of the eight melodic formulas used for chanting the psalms.

Tone, in painting. Just as colour is a quality of light, so tone is an amount of light. The range of tone becomes 'tonality' when it provides proportionable ratios just as form and colour do. Striking decorative effects can be obtained from well-planned areas of light, middle-tone and dark, which is the basis of chiaroscuro.

Another pictorial means of expression derives from what physicists call 'percentage reflectivity'. This means that if the illuminated side of a form reflects a certain percentage of the light falling upon it, and its shadow side the same percentage but only of scattered light, then any other forms, different in intrinsic tone but lit under the same conditions, will preserve the same percentage ratio between their lighted and shadowed sides. Thus the percentage will be constant but the amount of difference will be considerable, producing a 'variety in unity', the essence of art.

Tone Poem, see SYMPHONIC POEM.

Tonga
Area: 699 km²
Population: 90,128
Capital: Nuku'alofa

Tonga, or Friendly Islands, kingdom in the west Pacific, to the south-east of Fiji, between 15° and 23° latitude. Of about 170 small islands making up the group 36 are inhabited; estimated area, including inland water, 699 km². The population in 1976 was 90,128, nearly all Tongans. The islands on the east side are of coral formation, the chain on the west is volcanic. The Tongans are Polynesians, allied to the Maori and Samoans.

The economy is based on agriculture. The two chief crops are coconuts and bananas. Agriculture employs about three-quarters of the working population.

The government consists of the sovereign, a privy council, and cabinet, a legislative assembly and the judiciary.

History. Tonga was discovered by Tasman in 1643 and visited in 1773 by Cook, who called the islands the Friendly Islands. In the early 19th century Tonga was torn by civil wars between rival dynasties, from which it was rescued by a member of the 19th Tui Kanokubolu, or 3rd dynasty, Taufa'ahau Tupou, an able warrior and administrator who had been converted to Christianity in 1831. He gave the country stable government and his dynasty survives today. In 1900 Tonga became by treaty a British protected state; a revised treaty was signed in 1958 and another in 1967, giving Tonga increasing control over its affairs. On June 4, 1970 it became fully independent, joining the Commonwealth on the same date. The islands are ruled by King Tupou who succeeded his mother Queen Salote in 1965.

Tongue, the movable muscular organ attached to the floor of the mouth that is concerned in the operations of mastication, deglutition (swallowing), speaking and tasting. The base is attached to the hyoid bone; the upper surface, or dorsum, is free as are the edges and the anterior portion of the lower surface. The substance of the tongue is striped muscle, and is innervated by the hypoglossal nerve. The dorsum of the tongue is subdivided by a V-shaped groove, the sulcus terminalis. Immediately in front of the sulcus terminalis lie a row of vallate papillae which bear many taste buds. Small salivary glands are also scattered over the dorsum of the tongue. The tongue undergoes alterations during disease. The easily recognised phenomenon of furring may indicate a raised temperature (from any cause) but is generally of little medical significance. Deficiency of the B group of vitamins can produce a bald tongue as can iron deficiency anaemia. Ulcers of the tongue may be associated with infective

conditions of the mouth. Long lasting ulceration may be caused by cancer of the tongue. A cause of white patches on the tongue is the fungus *Candida albicans* or thrush.

Tonic, in music, the fundamental keynote of a scale.

See also OCTAVE.

Tonic, an old-fashioned medical concept; a tonic was considered to be an agent which re-established the proper performance of the body. Tonics differ from stimulants in that the latter produce a transient effect rapidly, while the former theoretically gradually build up a permanent effect. Tonics are used medically when the reasons for a patient's weakness and lack of enthusiasm for life cannot be attributed to any disease for which there is a remedy. Their value depends on suggestion and they are ineffective in children.

Tonic Sol-fa, see GUIDO D'AREZZO.

Tonic Water, see SOFT DRINKS.

Tonkin, or Tongking, the northern region of Vietnam and the part which has been longest under Vietnamese rule. It was governed as a separate protectorate by the French from 1883 till 1945, and since 1954 has been part of the Democratic Republic of Vietnam. Its capital is Hanoi.

Tonkin, Gulf of, an arm of the South China Sea, between Tonkin and the island of Hainan.

Tonle Sap, large tidal lake in north-west Cambodia, fed by the River Mekong. It is the centre of Cambodia's fishing industry and the source of irrigation.

Tonnage. A ship's capacity is measured in four different ways depending on what is required. The word 'ton' came from a tun of wine, which was a barrel holding 252 gallons (1145·6 l), and was the first measure of a ship's carrying capacity. The *gross tonnage* of a ship is the volume of all the enclosed spaces measured at 2·83 cubic metres to the ton less certain exemptions. *Register tonnage* (net tonnage) is the tonnage arrived at after certain spaces are deducted from the gross tonnage. Net tonnage is basically the space available in a ship for carrying cargo and it is on this that port and canal dues are levied. *Deadweight tonnage* is the maximum weight of cargo, fuel and stores that a ship can carry, and is a useful measurement for tankers and bulk carriers which are normally limited by the weight of cargo they can carry. *Displacement tonnage* is used for warships and is the weight of the ship which is equal to the amount of water displaced, 1 m³ of sea-water weighing 1·025 t.

Tonnage and Poundage. Tonnage, a tax levied on each tun of wine or liquor imported into or exported from the UK, seems first to have appeared in the 12th century; poundage, a similar tax on every pound of dry goods, was first levied in the 13th century. From 1415 they were allowed to sovereigns for life. The tax was abolished on the reorganisation of customs and excise in 1787.

Tonnage Dues, rates levied on the tonnage of ships entering ports or navigable public waters. The dues are devoted to the upkeep of harbours, wharves, the maintenance of buoys, moorings, river channels and docks. Light dues are generally paid separately for upkeep of lights. Pilotage dues are often paid

on tonnage, and all ships passing through the Suez, Panama and other such canals pay tonnage dues.

Tonsillitis, an acute inflammation of the tonsils causing difficulty in swallowing, usually associated with fever and painful enlargement of the regional lymph nodes. Commonly infection is viral, but in patients with severe symptoms, it may be due to haemolytic streptococci, glandular fever (infectious mononucleosis) or diphtheria. Only bacterial cases respond to treatment with antibiotics.

Tonsils, a pair of almond-shaped bodies situated in the pharyngeal cavity. Each consists of a mass of lymphoid tissue plentifully supplied with blood vessels. The tonsils form part of a ring of lymphoid tissue guarding the common entrance to the alimentary and respiratory tracts. Thus they function as a first line of immunological defence against infective agents. Because of their exposed position, they are a frequent site of inflammation from septic infection. When associated with ulcers the condition is known as quinsy.

See also TONSILLITIS.

Tonsure, the cutting of the hair in a certain form as a symbol of self-dedication to the monastic life. The custom first appears in the late 4th or early 5th century. In the ancient Celtic Church all the head was shaved in front of a line drawn from ear to ear. In the Roman Catholic Church the 'coronal of St Peter' has always been used, in which the crown of the head is shaved to leave a fringe of hair all round.

Tontine, form of mutual life insurance in which a number of people invest a sum of money in the purchase of a property. They share the income, and as each dies the shares become proportionately larger per survivor, until all the property eventually devolves to one. It owes its name to an Italian banker, Lorenzo Tonti, whose idea it was. In France and Great Britain in the 18th century, the state raised money by this means.

Tooke, John Horne (1736–1812), British politician and philologist. He was ordained in 1759, but resigned his living in 1773. His support for the American colonists and for the French Revolution brought him political notoriety. In 1801 he was elected to Parliament, but immediately after this an act excluding the Anglican clergy from membership was passed, which disqualified him. He wrote an important work on philology: *Epea Pteroenta, or the Diversions of Purley,* 1786–1805.

Tools, Machine. All machine tools must provide for relative motion between the cutting tool and the workpiece in two directions at right angles, to give a cutting movement and a feeding movement. Each may be obtained by moving either the tool or the workpiece. On the lathe the workpiece is rotated about a horizontal axis to give the cutting motion, its surface moving past the tool which is fed parallel to the axis. On the milling machine the cutter rotates and has teeth round its periphery; the workpiece is clamped to a horizontal table which is fed past the cutter. On the *drilling machine* the work is held stationary, both cutting and feeding motions being given to the tool. The work is also stationary on the *shaping machine*;

Machine Tools. *Computer-controlled tools in operation in the Mazda factory, Hiroshima, Japan.*

the tool is moved backwards and forwards across it and is given an intermittent feeding movement between cutting strokes. The *planing machine* is similar in principle except that the work moves to and fro past the tool. Nowadays each machine has its own motor with gearboxes providing a range of cutting and feeding speeds, and the frames are welded. The structure of the machine must be rigid to avoid distortion and vibration. The growing demand, especially in the motor industry, for the mass-production of large quantities of identical components has led to the development of machine tools which will automatically carry out a number of operations in sequence, so that the operator has only to load and unload the machine. A further development is the use of transfer machines: several machines carrying out successive operations on a component are linked together and the work is automatically transferred from one to the next by a conveyor, and correctly located. A system of automatic inspection stops the machine if errors occur in the components. Tape- or computer-controlled machine tools, in achieving greater utilisation of the tools with greater flexibility and accuracy, are becoming popular and economic for short production runs.

In *ultrasonic machining* the workpiece is subjected to repeated blows from a tool which is given a very small movement (about 0·025 mm) at a high frequency (approximately 10 kHz). The process is especially useful for piercing intricate shapes in hard, brittle materials such as tool steels, glass and ceramics.

Toothwort, *Lathraea,* a genus of plants of the Orobanchaceae, parasitic and lacking chlorophyll. *L. squamaria,* from Europe and Asia, has a fleshy branched rhizome clothed with tooth-like scales and dull, pink flowers, parasitic on hazel, beech and woody plants. *L. clandestina* is parasitic on willows and poplars. It has bright purple flowers rising from buds at ground level.

Toowoomba, second largest town in Queensland, Australia, in the centre of the rich Darling Downs, 162km west of Brisbane. It serves vast farming and dairying areas, where meat, wheat and wool are produced. Population (1980) 72,800.

Topaz, mineral crystallising in the orthorhombic system, with cleavage parallel to the basal face, a fluosilicate of aluminium, $Al_2[SiO_4](OH,F)_2$. The colour range includes colourless, yellow (pale to brown) and blue. Hardness 8; specific gravity 3·5. The pink topaz seen in jewellery is produced by heating brownish-yellow stones which change colour on cooling.

Topeka, capital of Kansas, USA, and county seat of Shawnee county, on the Kansas river, 85km west of Kansas City. It is a distribution and manufacturing centre, serving eastern Kansas, with processing industries for farm produce. Population (1980) 116,000.

Topiary, the training and clipping of trees and shrubs into ornamental shapes. The art was most greatly developed in Tudor times, and was a definite feature of old-world gardens: some of the more ambitious examples still exist at Elvaston Castle, Derby, and Leven's Hall, Westmorland. Evergreens are most popular for topiary work, though hawthorn stands up to clipping well and is often used. The two best species, being long-lived and able to withstand severe and constant clipping, are yew, *Taxus baccata,* and box, *Buxus sempervirens.* Holly, *Ilex aquifolium,* and evergreen oak, *Quercus ilex,* are also used.

Toplady, Augustus Montague (1740–78), English Anglican divine and hymn-writer. In 1775 he became minister at the French Calvinist Chapel in London. He is remembered for his hymn, 'Rock of Ages'.

Topography is the general form and configuration of the Earth's surface resulting from the geological agencies of erosion and deposition. Individual topographic features are known as landforms, and the science of landforms is termed geomorphology. The surface features of the Earth result from three main controlling factors, 'process, structure and stage'. Geology controls the initial large-scale landforms (structure), but the reworking and detailed sculpturing of these forms into their present configuration is achieved by different processes operating for varying periods of time (stage). The term process covers the different agencies of weathering and erosion, i.e. water (rivers, coasts), ice (glaciers), and gravity (mass movement). The stage at which a given landform evolves reflects its position within the 'geographical cycle' or 'cycle of erosion'.

According to this cyclic concept landforms evolve through a series of stages. Following uplift of the land-mass, the phase of youth, typified by rapid incision into the newly-emergent flat plain, gives way to maturity, characterised by further dissection and the establishment of a drainage system and maximum relief. Ultimately the whole land-mass is nearly reduced to sea-level at the old-age stage, marked by the emergence of a peneplain, a gently undulating, almost featureless plain. Interruption of the cycle caused by additional uplift results in a return to youth; such a phase is termed rejuvenation.

Recently the theory of the cycle of erosion has been seriously challenged on the ground that certain landforms achieve a state of dynamic equilibrium and undergo no further change of form through time. This occurs if the rate of weathering and erosion is sufficient to cause the height of the landform to be reduced commensurate with the amount of uplift.

Many different classifications of landforms have been attempted. One of the most widely adopted is based on a distinction between constructional and destructional landforms. The former are those landforms produced by accumulation of sediment or by diastrophism (uplift of the Earth's surface by tectonic forces). Included under the heading of constructional processes are volcanism, deposition, soil movement, and the various components of diatrophic activity. Destructional landforms are those which result from the removal of matter from the initial land surface. See also GLACIATION; LANDFORMS, STRUCTURAL.

Topology deals with the properties of continuous functions and is fundamental to large areas of mathematics, especially analysis. Certain characteristics of geometric figures are unaltered by changes in their shape, size and orientation. If a closed network is drawn on a surface then the number $V - E + F$, where V = number of vertices, E = number of edges, F = number of areas enclosed by the edges, is called the Euler characteristic of the network. If the network is one plane polygon then $V - E + F = 1$ because the polygon encloses 1 area ($F = 1$) and the numbers of vertices and edges are equal ($V = E$). $V - E + F = 1$ for any network which can be transformed into a *disc* (a circle and its interior) by bending and stretching without tearing (a circle is 1 edge which meets itself at 1 vertex enclosing 1 area).

A polyhedron can be transformed into a plane network only by making a hole in one enclosed area and flattening it out. Thus one enclosed area is lost, giving the 'circle' Euler characteristic of 1.

The Euler characteristic of 2 includes any network which can be transformed into a *sphere* by stretching and bending without cutting or puncturing.

All figures with the same Euler characteristic are in the same category and cannot be transformed without tearing or puncturing, into a figure in a different category. Topology describes 'allowable' transformations and the nature of the properties which they leave invariant.

Topsoil, a popular term used to describe variously (1) the surface layer which is ploughed (the Ap horizon); (2) the A1 horizon which varies in depth with different natural soils; (3) the total group of A horizons which, like (2) above, varies from soil to soil in the uncultivated state; and (4) soil material used for top dressing by gardeners. It is normally envisaged as the upper 20 cm which is dark in colour owing to the presence of organic matter and is characterised as the major zone of organic matter accumulation. Topsoil is the soil normally moved in tillage practices and is the major zone of root development carrying many of the nutrients and supplying much of the water available to plants. Ploughing, digging and cultivation modify its characteristics; thus it can be drained, and organic and chemical nutrients added to it and hence the productivity can be raised, lowered or stabilised. Topsoil contains approximately 45 per cent mineral matter, 5 per cent organic matter, 25 per cent air, and 25 per cent water, but air and water vary constantly.

Torah, the name given in the Jewish tradition to the five books of Moses. The term is also used in Judaism to denote all God's teachings, both written or orally recorded.
See also PENTATEUCH.

Tor Bay, on the south coast of Devon, England, the landing place of William of Orange (1688). On its shores are the towns of Torquay, Paignton and Brixham. Tor Bay provides one of the best yachting courses in Great Britain.

Torgau, town of the German Democratic Republic, on the River Elbe, 48 km north-east of Leipzig. In 1526 the Torgau League (of Protestant princes) was formed here. Chemicals and machinery are manufactured. Population (1981) 55,393.

Tormentil, *Potentilla erecta*, a perennial herb in the family Rosaceae, native to Europe and Asia. The leaves are divided into three, sometimes five, leaflets; the yellow flowers have four, rarely five, petals. The rootstock was used in tanning, having an astringent quality.

Tornado, see CYCLONE.

Toronto, capital of the province of Ontario, Canada, situated on a bay on the north shore of Lake Ontario, 535 km south-west of Montreal and 383 km east of Detroit. The site of the present city was chosen by Lord Dorchester, governor of Canada, as the seat of government for the newly created province of Upper Canada in 1793; it was incorporated as a city under the name Toronto in 1834. Its name, of Huron Indian origin, means 'a place of meeting'. The site is good for government, business and industry alike, being on a large low-lying plain opposite the great hooked spit which protects the harbour. The Humber and the Don valleys carry roads and railways inland. Toronto emerged at an early date as the major manufacturing, service and financial focus for southern Ontario. Its stock exchange accounts for about two-thirds of the value of Canadian

sales of stocks; insurance and banking are important. The chief industries are metal founding and machine shops, shipbuilding, and agricultural implements; together with meat packing, flour milling and canning; textiles, automobiles, furnishings and clothing; paper products, printing and publishing. Population (1976) (city) 633,318 (metropolitan area) 2,803,101.

Torpedo, or electric ray, a member of the elasmobranch family Torpedinidae in order Batoidei. Torpedos are characterised by the possession of electric organs which are present between the head and the pectoral fins. The shock which they are capable of producing is from 20 to 30 volts in *T. marmorata*. The largest species may be 180 cm long.

Torpedo, self-propelled submarine explosive device. In 1866 Robert Whitehead succeeded in producing a satisfactory torpedo by using a hydrostatic valve linked to the horizontal rudders and later to a pendulum, which overcame the depth-keeping problem. In 1876 the servo-motor was added and in 1895 a gyroscope, which solved the problem of straight running. These principles now form the basis of all torpedoes.
The shape of the modern torpedo resembles a blunt-nosed cigar. It is constructed of special steel, and divided into compartments: the explosive head, compressed-air chamber, balance chamber, engine room and buoyancy chamber. Torpedoes are normally housed in tubes, either above water or submerged, from which they are discharged by compressed air or by the ignition of a cartridge. Their use by aircraft has been superseded by rocket weapons for anti-ship work, but anti-submarine torpedoes have been designed for use by helicopters.

Torpedo-boat, warship which is now obsolete, having been replaced by the destroyer and motor torpedo-boat, now classified, together with motor gunboats, as fast patrol-boats. The first torpedo-boat was built by Thornycroft in 1873, for the 'towing' type of torpedo. In 1879 the same firm built the *Lightning*, 27 t, with a speed of 19 knots (25 km/h), fitted with a bow torpedo tube for launching a Whitehead torpedo. As these vessels grew in size and speed, it became necessary to evolve means of protecting battleships from their attack. Eventually the torpedo-boat gave way to the torpedo-boat destroyer, in which the functions of both torpedo-boat and anti-torpedo-boat were combined.
See also GUNBOAT.

Torpedo-boat Destroyer, see DESTROYER.

Torquay, administrative centre of Torbay, seaport and holiday resort in south Devon, England, on Tor Bay, 41 km south of Exeter. The development of Torquay as a resort dates back to the late 18th century when, with the threat of invasion by Napoleon, ships of the fleet constantly used Tor Bay as an anchorage, and houses were built on the shores for the families of the officers. Population of Torbay (1981) 115,582.

Torque, a dress ornament, usually of gold, worn around the neck like a collar; common from the Bronze and Iron Ages in Britain, Ireland and north-west Europe, especially among Celtic peoples.

Torquemada, Tomás de (1420–98),

Spanish Dominican friar and Grand Inquisitor, who in 1483 was entrusted by Queen Isabella with the establishment of the Spanish Inquisition. Ascetic in his private life, he was ruthless towards suspected or convicted heretics. Of 100,000 said to have been accused, about 2000 were put to death, others fined and penanced. He was one of the leading instigators of the conquest of Granada and of the expulsion of the Jews.

Torrens, Lake, large salt lake of South Australia, discovered in 1840 by Eyre, 56 km north of Port Augusta. Its average width is 32 km, length 209 km. It becomes a salt marsh in dry weather.

Torreón, town in the state of Coahuila, Mexico. An important railway junction, it lies at the centre of an oasis-like area called La Laguna which produces a substantial proportion of Mexico's cotton and wheat. The town has considerable industry including cotton gins, cotton-spinning and weaving mills, flour mills, smelting plants, oil-processing and meat-packing plants. Population (1975) 251,300.

Torres Strait, in the south Pacific Ocean, separating New Guinea and Australia by a channel 130 to 145 km wide.

Torres Vedras, town of Portugal, 43 km north of Lisbon. It was here that Wellington constructed the famous field-works called the 'Lines of Torres Vedras' during the Peninsular War, when he withdrew his forces, in face of Masséna's invasion of Portugal, for the winter of 1810. Torres Vedras is the centre of a wine-producing region. Population (1970) 13,100.

'Torrey Canyon', a Liberian tanker of 120,000 t deadweight which was bound from Mina al Ahmadi in Kuwait to Milford Haven in Wales on 18 March 1967, and became grounded on the Seven Stones reef north-east of the Scilly Isles. At that time she was the largest ship to be involved in a marine disaster, and the resulting oil pollution led to anti-pollution legislation in a number of countries.

Torricelli, Evangelista (1608–47), Italian physicist, succeeded Galileo as professor of mathematics at Florence and carried on Galileo's work in mechanics. In 1643 he up-ended a half-closed tube of mercury in a dish of mercury. Some of the mercury in the tube flowed out; the remaining column varied slightly in height from day to day; above the column was apparently a vacuum. Like Galileo, Torricelli believed that a vacuum could not exist. Torricelli believed his most important work was in mathematics where he succeeded in deriving a formula for the area bounded by an arc of a cycloid. He also deduced the first quantitative law of hydrodynamics: the flow of liquid through an orifice is proportional to the square root of the head of liquid.

Torrigiano, Pietro, or Torrigiani (1470–1522), Florentine sculptor. Torrigiano worked in Rome for Pope Alexander VI; he was also a hired soldier for a while in various states. He was invited to England to execute the tomb for Henry VII and his queen in Westminster Abbey, which he completed in 1519—a splendid work in the mature Renaissance style. A tomb for Henry VIII at Windsor was left unfinished.

Torsion, a strain produced by a twisting motion, by a couple acting in a plane at right angles to the axis of a body. The distortion produced is a type of shearing stress. The amount of 'torque' required to produce torsion in cylindrical bars of the same material varies as the fourth power of their diameters. In bars of section other than circular the rigidity is lessened, so cylindrical bars or tubes are best adapted to resist a twisting strain. See also ELASTICITY.

Tort, in English law, is the breach by act or omission of a duty imposed by law (as opposed to one assumed by the parties under a contract which gives the injured party a right to damages. The word is also used to mean the breach of a particular duty, such a breach being known as a tort: e.g. the tort of trespass, and the tort of nuisance, but is usually (though not invariably) a civil offence.

Tortelier, Paul (1914–), French cellist, composer and conductor. He won first prize at the Paris Conservatoire at the age of 16, and began his solo career in 1947. He composes mainly for the cello, although he has also written a piano concerto, a violin concerto and a symphony. He is also a noted teacher.

Tortoise, land animals of the order Chelonia. They are cold-blooded, four-footed reptiles, without teeth, and are protected by a large shell on top, called a carapace, with a thinner shell, the plastron, under the belly. All lay eggs, but otherwise there is wide diversity in their habits. The most familiar example of the land tortoises (Testudinidae) is the common tortoise (*Testudo graeca*), which occurs around the Mediterranean and is popular as a pet. It is entirely vegetarian in its diet, though frequently sold as an insect killer. Among the most interesting kind of tortoises are the giant tortoises formerly found in great numbers in the Galápagos and Mascarene islands. When discovered, these islands were uninhabited; the tortoises therefore enjoyed perfect security, and this, as well as their extraordinary longevity, accounts for their great size (as much as 1·5 m in length) and numbers.

Tortoise Beetle, any member of the subfamily Cassidinae of family Chrysomelidae in order Coleoptera. The outer margins of the wing covers and the prothorax (shield) are drawn out and form a convex shield reminiscent of the outline of a tortoise, hence their popular name. In general they are leaf-feeders in both adult and larval stages. They are often brilliantly coloured with a metallic sheen. The larvae generally have spiky outgrowths and cover themselves with excrement or cast skins as methods of camouflage. These beetles are usually found in the tropics.

Tortoiseshell, in commerce, is the horny plates of the hawksbill turtle (*Chelonia imbricata*). The largest of these plates are about 45 cm long by 15 cm broad, and rarely exceed 3 mm in thickness. Tortoiseshell is semi-transparent, and mottled with various shades of yellow and brownish-red. Its value depends on the brightness and form of the markings, and the finest tortoiseshell is derived from shells immersed in boiling water immediately after the death of the animal. Numerous imitations and substitutes are made. Tortoiseshell probably first began to be used to decorate furniture in northern Europe around 1640, and about 1680 it began to be employed in France by Boulle in conjunction with brass inlay. During the 18th century the fashion for tortoiseshell on furniture died out, but it continued to be used for small boxes, combs and other *objets de vertu*, often with a silver inlay: this is called *piqué* work.

Torture, the application of bodily pain as a prelude to, or an accompaniment of, capital punishment; as an act of vengeance upon defeated enemies; or as a means of extracting confessions or other evidence. It has taken a large variety of forms and has been employed by peoples and states of varying degrees of political and social sophistication. In England torture as punishment was virtually ended in 1640; in Scotland an act of 1709 was passed abolishing its use. Torture was used by both the Nazis and the Japanese during the Second World War. There have been many proven instances of torture, and many more allegations of its use, in the period since then, both in conflicts involving open warfare and in those where opponents of the regime in power have been active in lesser forms of rebellion. In 1975 the United Nations adopted a Declaration against the use of torture.

Totemism. *North American Indian totem poles consist of animals and mythological creatures associated with the ancestry of the tribe.*

Tory, synonym, though historically inappropriate, for a Conservative in British politics. The word 'tory' is Irish, meaning 'outlaw' and signified, particularly during the wars in Ireland in the reign of Elizabeth I, a bandit attached to neither army, who preyed generally upon the country. They were prominent during the Protestant massacres of 1641. The term then came to be applied to a body of men who, in 1680, appear to have ridiculed the Popish Plot and yet encouraged the Papists to revive it. Their political object was to banish the Duke of Monmouth and recall the Duke of York. They therefore opposed the Bill of Exclusion (from their abhorrence to which they were called 'abhorrers' and their opponents 'petitioners'). Ultimately the 'abhorrers' and 'petitioners' became identified with the Tories and Whigs respectively. See also WHIGS.

Toscanini, Arturo (1867–1957), Italian conductor. He studied cello and composition at the Parma Conservatory, and began his conducting career in 1886 at Rio de Janeiro. He was appointed to La Scala, Milan (1898) and in 1907 to the Metropolitan, New York. He was later conductor of the Philharmonic Symphony Society of New York and then of the NBC Orchestra. He was guest conductor at Bayreuth, Vienna, Salzburg, Paris, London and elsewhere. Many new Italian operas were presented by him.

Tostig (d.1066), Earl of Northumbria, brother of Harold II. In 1065 he was banished from his realm because of his cruel, repressive measures. The following year he returned with Harold Haardraade, King of Norway, and was killed at the battle of Stamford Bridge.

Totalisator, machine or apparatus, set up on racecourses for recording bets and payment of winnings on the principle that all money staked is pooled and shared (subject to a percentage deduction) by those who have backed winners.

Totalitarianism, social and political system involving the conscious political control of, and intervention in, all aspects of private and public life. Although many regimes have in the past attempted to exercise such control there is a distinction between such autocracies and totalitarianism. The latter is essentially a modern phenomenon made possible through the existence of sophisticated means of control and manipulation. The organisation of control is invariably through the monopolisation of the organs of the state by a centrally directed party, this party usually subscribing to an ideology involving fundamental social reorganisation. It should be noted, however, that single-party rule does not always involve totalitarianism.

Totemism (Algonquin Indian *totem*, guardian spirit), belief of descent from an original ancestor who is also the ancestor of certain plants or animals; the term is extended to any belief that one shares some common essence with a plant or animal. Totemism has been found among many peoples of the world, and certainly existed at one time among Europeans. The belief is frequently accompanied by a prohibition to harm the plant or animal with whom one shares a totemic ancestor, akin to a taboo; should this occur accidentally, elaborate rituals may be necessary to offset the believed damaging spiritual consequences.

Totila (d.552), King of the Ostrogoths in Italy, was proclaimed in 541. He at once began the restoration of the Ostrogoth kingdom of Italy and captured Rome. Owing to Totila's continued successes the Emperor Justinian sent a large army against him, led by the eunuch Narses, who killed him.

Toucan, any bird of the genus *Ramphastos*. The name is often applied to the whole family Ramphastidae of the order Piciformes. They are all natives of tropical America and are characterised by their enormous brightly-coloured bill. They live chiefly on fruit, seeds and insects. In the true toucans the ground colour of the plumage is generally black; the throat, breast and rump are adorned with yellow, red and white; the body is short and thick; the tail is rounded or even and can be turned up over the back when the bird goes to roost. The largest are about 60 cm long.

Touch, sensation due to the stimuli of pressure and contact acting on the body. The peripheral nerves supplying the skin terminate either on or between epithelial cells, or in special corpuscles. Certain of these act as transducers which change the mechanical energy of pressure into a nervous signal. Like all other sensations, that of touch is perceived by the brain, and is conveyed to it by afferent nerves or fibres which travel in special tracts of the spinal cord.

Toulon, French seaport in the *département* of Var, on the Mediterranean, 46 km south-east of Marseilles. Toulon has been an important naval station and is now one of the three naval headquarters in France. There are marine engineering, armament, chemical, oil and textile industries. Population (1975) town, 185,050; conurbation, 378,430.

Toulouse, French town, capital of the *département* of Haute-Garonne, 200 km south-east of Bordeaux, on the River Garonne. It was the old capital of Languedoc. Toulouse is a centre of communications and the seat of an archbishopric and of a university (founded 1229). It has aircraft, armament, chemical, footwear, metallurgical, textile and flour industries, and a large trade in agricultural produce. Population (1975) town, 383,176; conurbation, 509,939.

Toulouse-Lautrec-Monfa, Count Henri Marie Raymond de (1864–1901), French painter. He broke both legs in boyhood and this prevented their normal growth. He turned, in compensation, from aristocratic country life to painting and the contemplation of the amusements and vices of Paris. His prolific period was between 1885 and 1899. He visited England in 1895. Strongly influenced by Degas, he is more of a social commentator than that master. He excelled in graphic art, notably in the posters he himself lithographed in colour for various Parisian resorts, which show the influence of Japanese prints. His subject matter is intimately connected with the life he led; scenes in bars, dance-halls and brothels predominate.

Tour de France, the main professional event of the European cycling season. It is considered more prestigious than the World Championships. Originally it was a six-stage race of 2,410 kilometres, but has since varied in length. In 1971 the *Union Cycliste Internationale* decided that the race should be in 20 stages (one stage per day), and that the average length of the stages should be no more than 200 kilometres, with no one stage being longer than 260 kilometres. From the outset the event has been dominated by the trade teams and has been heavily commercially sponsored. In 1919 the 'yellow jersey' was introduced to mark the race leader. The race has been won a record number of five times by both Jacques Anquetil (France), 1957, 1961, 1962, 1963, 1964, and Eddie Merckx (Belgium), 1969, 1970, 1971, 1972, 1974.

Touraco, or turaco, a beautiful African bird of the family Musophagidae or plantain-eaters in the order Cuculiformes. The touraco has a small high bill, notched and serrated mandibles, short rounded wings and a long rounded tail. It has an erectile crest on the

Toulouse-Lautrec. A lithograph by Lender.

head. Many of them are brilliantly coloured with glossy blue, red, violet and green plumage. There are about 18 species.

Touraine, old province of France, now the *département* of Indre-et-Loire and a part of Vienne. Its capital was Tours and it was named from the local Gallic tribe of the Turones. With Anjou and Orléanais, it was a source of dispute between France and England. It came to England with Henry II in 1154, and was regained for France by Joan of Arc.

Tourcoing, French town in the *département* of Nord, 13 km north-east of Lille. It has an important textile industry, especially in woollens (dating from the 12th century), commercial activities, and forms part of the Tourcoing-Lille-Roubaix urban complex. Population (1975) 102,543.

Touré, Ahmed Sékou (1922–), Guinean politician. In 1946 he was a founder member of, later vice-president of, the African Democratic Rally (RDA). By 1948 he had widened the scope of his trade union activities to become secretary-general of the Territorial Union of the General Workers' Confederation (CGT—Confédération Générale du Travail) and in 1950 secretary-general of the Co-ordination Committee, for French West Africa and Togoland, of the CGT. In 1952, he became secretary-general of the Guinean Democratic party, and by 1956 was a deputy to the French National Assembly. He was co-founder, then president, of the General Union of Workers of Black Africa (UGTAN) formed in 1957. In May 1957 he became vice-president of the Government Council, and then president. After Guinea's declaration of independence he held the post of Head of State, becoming the first president of the Republic of Guinea in January 1961. He was re-elected in 1963, 1968, 1974 and 1980.

Tourischeva, Ludmila (1952–), Russian gymnast. She won the World Championship in 1970 and took the European title the following year in Minsk. She was overall champion at the 1972 Munich Olympics and in the 1973 European Championships she won every apparatus gold medal as well as finishing first overall. At Montreal in 1976 she shared the

team gold and won two silver medals for the floor and horse competitions, and a bronze in the individual title.

Tourmaline, a complex aluminium silicate mineral. It crystallises in the hexagonal system as prismatic crystals, often triangular in section. It also occurs massive and compact and in radiate fibrous masses. It is generally black, more rarely green, blue and red, and, still more rarely, colourless. The black variety is termed schorl. The mineral is pyro- and piezo-electric. On account of its hardness 7·5; (specific gravity 3), it is sometimes cut as a gem.

Tournai (Flemish *Doornik*), town in Hainaut province, Belgium, situated on the River Scheldt, 43 km north-east of Mons. It is an important railway junction. There are quarries of freestone and limestone, and the chief manufactures are Brussels carpets, pottery, and woollen and cotton goods. Population (1981) 69,718.

Tournament, also tourney or joust, a form of martial sport popular in the Middle Ages. Combats took place between men of noble rank, and a prize was given by the lady of the tournament to the knight who had displayed the greatest prowess. The custom was introduced into England from France during the 11th century. Tournaments were regulated by very strict etiquette and definite rules. The weapons used, spears, lances, swords or daggers, had to be blunted. Each jouster was attended by his squire, who acted as his second. In its earlier form the tournament often took the form of a private war; it was more than once banned (though ineffectively) by the Church. It was in the tournament that spectacular conventions of staging, including elaborate scenic emblems and rich symbolic costuming, were developed. In modern times the term is sometimes used for a military display, for example the Royal Tournament, which takes place annually at Earls Court, London, in which the three fighting services participate.

Tournefort, Joseph Pitton de (1656–1708), French botanist. His *Eléments de Botanique*, 1694, embodies a systematic arrangement of some 8000 species of plants, classified, mainly, according to the corolla (petals), a system long adopted on the Continent. His chief work was *Institutiones Rei Herbariae* (3 vols), 1700, which prepared the way for Linnaeus, whose system of classification eventually superseded that of Tournefort.

Tourneur, Cyril, also Tournour or Turner (c.1575–1626), English poet and dramatist. Very little is known of his life. He was a soldier much of the time, but in the six years which he devoted to literature Tourneur was a prolific writer. He wrote *The Atheist's Tragedy*, 1611; a poem, *The Transformed Metamorphosis*, which was discovered only in 1872; and a lost play, *The Nobleman*. Tourneur's masterpiece (although his authorship has been contested, some considering it the work of Thomas Middleton) is *The Revenger's Tragedy*, 1607. Having close affinities with the morality tradition, it is a revenge play which explores courtly corruption and evil. It combines sensation and horror with psychological intensity and, on occasion, poetry of lyrical beauty.

Tourniquet, a bandage or cuff which can

be tightened around the upper end of the thigh or arm to close the arteries to the limb and thus stop the flow of blood. Tourniquets should not be used in the First Aid treatment of bleeding, since direct pressure over a bleeding area is usually enough to stop the haemorrhage. The commonest use of tourniquets is in the operating theatre, to prevent bleeding during operations on the arm or leg.

Tours, French city, of the *département* of Indre-et-Loire, lying between the rivers Loire and Cher, south-west of Paris. It was formerly the capital of Touraine. It developed in importance after the time of St Martin, and it was here that St Gregory founded the abbey which became one of the great centres of learning in the Middle Ages. Machinery, textiles, electrical goods and chemicals are manufactured, there is a publishing industry, and a trade in agricultural produce, fruit, wines and spirits. Population (1975) town, 145,441; conurbation, 245,631.

Toussaint L'Ouverture, Pierre Dominique (1743–1803), Negro liberator of Haiti. Born a slave (although the grandson of an African chieftain), he taught himself to read, and this, together with his personal experience of the inhuman treatment of slaves, caused him to interest himself in the question of social justice. The French Revolution of 1789 had great repercussions in Haiti, one of France's most lucrative colonies. The outlawing of slavery by France caused considerable disturbances and conflicts here. By 1791 Toussaint found himself the leader of the Negro population and for ten years he and his Negro army successfully fought off French, British and Spanish efforts to suppress the freedom movement. In 1801 he appointed himself governor-general for life, an action which caused Napoleon Bonaparte to despatch a strong expeditionary force which finally forced Toussaint's surrender. He was sent to a French prison where he died. In 1804 Haiti achieved its independence.

Tovey, Sir Donald Francis (1875–1940), British composer, pianist and scholar. Tovey studied classics at Oxford. He gave concerts in London, Berlin and Vienna, and from 1914 was Reid Professor of Music at Edinburgh University. He conducted the Reid Orchestra, Edinburgh, and as a pianist was for some time in the front rank. He is remembered for his *Essays in Musical Analysis*, 1935–1938, which were intended as programme notes for performances by the Reid Orchestra.

Tower, lofty structure (other than a dome) rising above the general roof-level of a building.
See also CAMPANILE; MINARET; PHAROS; SPIRE; STEEPLE.

Tower Bridge, the easternmost bridge over the River Thames, built in 1886–94. It was designed by Sir Horace Jones and Sir John Wolfe Barry and it cost the city corporation £1·5 million. It has two high Gothic towers 60·9 m apart, and is connected with either bank by single-span suspension bridges. The span between the towers in the centre of the river consists of a pair of drawbridges, which can be raised in 1·5 minutes, and thus permit the passage of vessels.

Tower Hamlets, a London borough created on 1 April 1965, comprising the former metropolitan boroughs of Bethnal Green, Poplar and Stepney. The borough's population in 1981 was 142,975.

Tower of London, situated on the north bank of the Thames, the most historic building in London. It was first built by William the Conqueror to protect and control the City. His building, the Great Tower or Keep, generally called the White Tower, lay within the Roman walled city. Enlargement in the 12th century meant that part of the Tower lies outside the City, but it forms a Liberty in itself. Considerable additions and alterations have been made to the buildings, and they exhibit a variety of architectural styles from the 11th to the 20th centuries. The inner ward is defended by a wall flanked by 13 towers, the outer ward by another wall, flanked by six towers on the south, and by bastions on the north-west and north-east, the whole surrounded by a moat. At the south-west angle there were originally three drawbridges and three towers before entrance was gained to the outer ward. The Tower of London has been a fortress, a palace, a prison, has housed the public records, the Royal Mint, the royal menagerie, the Royal Observatory, and was for centuries the arsenal for small arms. It is now a museum of armour, in a limited sense a fortress (it has a military garrison), and the repository of the Crown Jewels. As a palace (the palace buildings have not survived), it was used by all sovereigns down to James I.

The White Tower contains the Armouries and the Chapel of St John, the earliest Norman building in London. In the inner ward is the Chapel of St Peter ad Vincula, rebuilt in 1512, where many famous people executed after incarceration in the Tower are buried. South of the chapel is Tower Green where executions took place within the Tower. The Bloody Tower, built by Henry III, is believed to be the scene of the murder of the 'Princes in the Tower'. Adjoining it is the Wakefield Tower, also built by Henry III, which houses the Crown Jewels. On its western side stood the Great Hall, demolished during the Commonwealth. The Beauchamp Tower, built probably in Henry III's reign, contains the inscriptions of many famous prisoners. Traitors' Gate, under St Thomas' Tower, became a convenient landing-place from the river for prisoners tried at Westminster. On Tower Hill, north-west of the Tower, a permanent scaffold was erected in 1465, the last execution there being in 1747.

Town and Country Planning. Many ancient and medieval towns, particularly colonial towns, were originally laid out on definite plans, often for military reasons, e.g. the Greek cities (Priene, Ephesus) and Roman towns (Chester). Most towns, however, grew organically. During the 18th and 19th centuries the industrial revolution led to a vastly increased concentration of production and wealth in cities. The resulting problems led first to public health legislation and then to the emergence of town and country planning as a new branch of government. Planning legislation in the modern sense came into vogue in the 1860s and 1870s, beginning in Italy, Sweden, Austria and Germany with laws to control the layout of suburban extensions, and gradually spreading to other countries. In Britain the Housing, Town Planning, etc., Act of 1909 was the first attempt to introduce an element of compulsion into the organisation of the city environment.

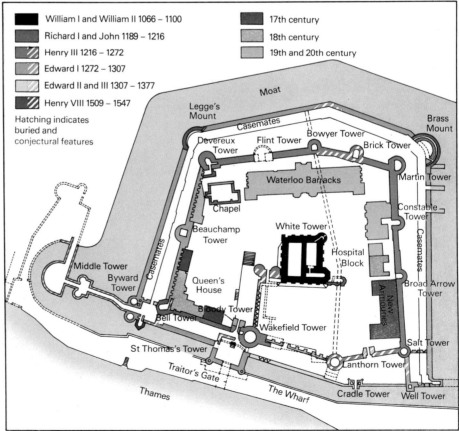

The Tower of London consists of many buildings, erected over ten centuries.

All previous Acts were replaced by the two Town and Country Planning Acts of 1947, for England and Wales and for Scotland, since consolidated by the Act of 1962. By these the town and country planning administration and procedure were revolutionised. Planning powers were transferred to county councils and county borough councils. All planning authorities made a full survey of physical and other resources and existing development, and devised a series of plans which were to be revised every five years.

In the USA the system of planning law and administration is very different and involves far less control of development. It relies principally on zoning laws rather than comprehensive plans and policies, and the administration has no permanent structure. In the USSR and other Communist countries of Europe a very elaborate system of planning exists. Town plans must conform to a hierarchy of other plans, e.g. at the regional, republic and national levels. All policies have to conform to the national economic plan. Other countries in Europe vary considerably in their town and country planning procedures. Some, such as Spain and Italy, have minimal sets of laws to control development, while others have systems that are similar in comprehensiveness to that of Britain, as in the case with the Netherlands and Denmark. In Germany and Sweden extensive ownership of land by cities has facilitated planned development.

Townes, Charles Hard (1915–), US physicist. He was at Bell Telephone Laboratories working on radar, 1939–47. In 1951 he conceived the idea of irradiating ammonia with low-intensity microwaves at the frequency at which the molecules naturally vibrated. Each molecule would then 'resonate' and emit its own microwave radiation which would affect other molecules in a chain reaction. This was the principle of the 'maser' (microwave amplification by stimulated emission of radiation). In 1953 Townes and his colleagues produced a working maser. In 1957 he proposed that the technique should be extended to visible light—the laser—and in 1960 T. H. Maiman succeeded in constructing such a device. Townes was awarded the Nobel Prize for physics in 1964 jointly with the Soviet physicists N. G. Basov and A. M. Prokhorov, who had independently worked out the theory of the maser.

Townshend, Charles Townshend, 2nd Viscount (1674–1738), English statesman. On George I's accession he was appointed secretary of state of the Northern Department. He lost favour in 1716, but in 1720 he was president of the council under Stanhope, and on Stanhope's death in 1721 became again secretary of state, a position he held until 1730, when he retired into private life. He took a considerable interest in agriculture, encouraged turnip growing, greatly improved the rotation of crops, and came to be known as 'Turnip Townshend'.

Townsville, port of Queensland, Australia, 1339 km north of Brisbane. It is the chief commercial and administrative centre for a large section of northern Queensland, contains a large bulk sugar refinery, and is the chief port through which are exported sugar, farm products and minerals. Population (1980) 84,300.

Toxaemia, the presence of toxins (poisons) in the blood. The term is generally used to mean the presence of toxins due to absorption from a local infection.
See also PREGNANCY.

Toxicology, the study of poisons. Its main branches deal with the chemical nature of poisons, their origin and preparation; their physiological action and tests to detect their presence; the pathological changes due to their presence and the recognition of them by post-mortem evidence; and their chemical reactions with a view to the determination of the antidote and its physiological action.

Toxin, any poisonous substance derived from a plant (particularly a fungus or bacterium), animal or virus.
See also PASSIVE IMMUNISATION; POISONS.

Toxophily, see ARCHERY.

Toy Theatre. A 19th-century example, set for a traditional pantomime.

Toy Theatre, as opposed to three-dimensional puppets, is a product of the 19th-century popular print trade in England and several European countries. Japan had its own version, dating from slightly earlier. Traditionally, European toy theatre consisted of printed paper scenery, characters and theatre proscenium to be pasted on card, cut out and mounted on a wooden structure with a stage, for model performances. Characters were moved by wires from above or the sides, with a slight agitation accompanying speech.

In England, prints were coloured by hand professionally or sold uncoloured for colouring at home, hence the phrase 'A Penny Plain and Twopence Coloured', made famous by Robert Louis Stevenson's essay of that title on English toy theatre. Called the 'Juvenile Drama', it originated in the theatrical souvenir portrait trade around 1811, developing by popular demand of children into complete plays with playbooks based on real London productions. The craze reached its peak in 1835, while generations of children revelled in cutting and colouring for family performances. A typical English toy theatre character stood 6 to 7 cm high and each was supplied in various costumes and poses. Favourite among hundreds published was Pocock's 'The Miller and His Men'. Diaghilev produced a ballet based on English toy theatre called 'The Triumph of Neptune'.

Toy theatre provides the collector with a unique record of 19th-century productions for which little other pictorial information survives.

Toynbee, Arnold (1889–1975), British historian. He became, in 1925, director of studies at the then newly founded Royal Institute of International Affairs (Chatham House) from which he retired in 1955. There he wrote contemporary history in the annual *Survey of International Affairs*. The 12 volumes which comprise *A Study of History*, published between 1934 and 1961, form a standard work on the evolution of civilisations. His other publications include: *Christianity and Civilisation*, 1940; *The Crucible of Christianity*, 1968.

Toynbee, (Theodore) Philip (1916–81), English novelist, son of Arnold Toynbee. He was the first Communist president of the Oxford Union. Later he resigned from the Communists and supported Labour, and in 1950 he joined the staff of the *Observer*. He wrote several experimental novels, *The Savage Days*, 1937; *The Barricades*, 1943; and *Tea With Mrs Goodman*, 1947; and several others in verse, including *The Fearful Choice*, 1958, and *Two Brothers*, 1964.

Toynbee Hall, Whitechapel, London, the first English university settlement, founded in 1885 by Canon Barnett, Rector of St Jude's, Whitechapel, and named after his friend, Arnold Toynbee.

Trabzon (ancient *Trapezus*, formerly *Trebizond*), seaport on the Black Sea coast of Asiatic Turkey, capital of Trabzon province. Trabzon was founded in 600 BC by Greek settlers from Sinope. In 1204 it became the capital of Trebizond, a kingdom which lasted until its capture by the Turks in 1462. In addition to its important transit trade it exports local agricultural products. Population (1980) 108,403.

Trace Element, a chemical element present in minute quantities. Trace elements are important in the nutrition of both plants and animals.
See also FERTILISERS; MINERALS IN FOOD.

Tracery, in architecture. At first it took the form of 'plate' tracery, in which a thin panel of stone or wood was inserted into the window frame, and this was pierced by circular and lancet-shaped openings. The next stage, first taken at Reims in the early 13th century was to reduce the masonry between the various openings to narrow vertical moulded bars of stone (mullion) and to continue these moulded bars around the tops of the lancets and around the circular window, thus forming 'geometrical tracery', so called because it consisted of regular geometrical shapes; it is characteristic of the period c.1250–1300 in England. In the third stage the masons introduced flowing curvilinear designs instead of regular geometric forms; these were introduced at the beginning of the 14th century in England and later became popular in France. Finally, the flowing designs gave way to nearly rectilinear 'lights' and, as the size of windows increased, both in width and height, horizontal transoms were introduced to strengthen the mullions. This 'rectilinear' or 'perpendicular' tracery, largely restricted to England, prevailed until the end of the true Gothic style in the middle of the 16th century.

Trachea, or windpipe, the air tube which leads from the larynx to the bronchi. It is about 11 cm long and is made up of fibro-elastic membrane which is kept open by C-shaped cartilaginous rings about 1·6 cm in diameter. The incomplete portion of the C is at the back where the trachea is in contact with the oesophagus. The interior is lined with submucous tissue and ciliated epithelium. The trachea begins at the larynx and proceeds downwards in front of the oesophagus until it bifurcates into the two bronchi.

Tracheid, a conducting cell in the wood, particularly of ferns and gymnosperms. It is a long, dead, narrow cell containing watery sap. Its walls are thickened with lignin, a complex carbohydrate, and it conducts water and solutes from the roots to other parts of the plant.

Tracheostomy, a surgical operation which consists of making an opening into the trachea (windpipe) below the larynx (voice-box). The opening may be held open by a curved trachaeostomy tube through which the patient breathes. A temporary trachaeostomy may be made (1) to allow a patient to breathe when the upper air passages are blocked; (2) to protect the lungs from blood or fluid falling through the larynx; (3) during respiratory failure to enable the lungs to be inflated by artificial respiration; or (4) in patients in whom the vocal cords are paralysed and not able to open widely enough to let air through the larynx into the lungs.

Trachoma, an eye disease of either rapid or insidious onset, caused by a small bacterium, *Chlamydia trachomatis*, regarded as being largely tropical or subtropical, and associated with poor hygienic conditions. Complications include blindness and severe scarring and deformity of the eyelids, as well as additional infection by other bacteria in later stages. No area of the world can be regarded as free of the disease; however, nutrition, prevalence of flies, dry conditions and overcrowding are factors influencing incidence. The disease is passed by contact, by fomites (materials soiled with discharges or other sources of infection), or possibly by flies. Vaccination has not been successful, so control measures are directed towards eradication of flies, improvement of the poor hygienic conditions and adequate treatment of cases. This last is of high importance, since the disease reservoir is man. The antibiotics used are tetracycline, oleandomycin, chloramphenicol, with sulphonamides as alternative chemotherapy.

Trachyte, an intermediate, fine-grained, igneous effusive rock composed essentially of alkali feldspar and ferromagnesian minerals. The coarse-grained intrusive rock of the same composition is syenite. Trachytes occur in several volcanic districts, notably southern Italy, the Auvergne, and East Africa. Trachytes containing the feldspathoid nepheline are termed phonolites, and those containing leucite, leucitophyres. The trachytes and syenites are the commonest alkaline igneous rocks.

Track and Field Sports, see ATHLETICS.

Trackways, term applied generally to prehistoric routes and particularly to pre-Roman ways in England. Their principal purpose was the conveyance of goods, and they ran roughly in a straight line, being sited by such natural objects as stones, stumps and ponds. It is probable that some of the Roman roads (e.g. Watling Street) followed at least in part these trackways. A different sort of trackway, of wood piles and hurdles, was used to cross bogland safely. Neolithic and Iron Age examples have been found in the Somerset Levels.

Tractor, a compact mobile power-unit, used primarily for agricultural purposes and generally deriving its energy from a petrol, fuel-oil or vaporising-oil engine. Steam-engined tractors were used extensively in the past, and are occasionally used today for heavier haulage and stationary belt-work. The food crisis of 1916 gave the real impetus to tractor design and production in Britain and the USA, and the utility tractor developed then is the forerunner of today's lightweight internal-engined tractor. Crawler types (track-layers) were developed to work under exceptionally heavy soil conditions and other types for requirements in row-crop work, for example. The tractor is now, in the main, a highly specialised item of modern farming machinery. Another major development is the mounting of an implement directly on the rear of the tractor and hydraulically controlling it by the tractor driver from his seat, giving better control and greater traction. The present trend is towards high-efficiency, light weight-to-power ratio engines of sturdy endurance. Engines fuelled by vaporising oil are popular throughout the world, while the fuel-oil compression-ignition and petrol engine are also used extensively.

See also PLOUGHS AND PLOUGHING.

Tracy, Spencer (1900–67), US actor. He made his New York stage début in 1922 in *RUR*; he later appeared in several other New York productions. He made his screen début in 1930 in *Up The River*, and his films include *Stanley and Livingstone, Edison the Man, Northwest Passage, Dr. Jekyll and Mr Hyde, A Guy Named Joe, Edward My Son, Father of the Bride, Bad Day at Black Rock, Inherit the Wind, Judgment at Nuremberg*. He won the Academy Award for the best actor in 1937 (*Captains Courageous*) and 1938 (*Boy's Town*).

Trade Cycle, term for the fluctuation of prices, profits and employment over a period of several years. Before the Keynesian revolution in economics it was generally held that it arose from faults in the monetary system. Keynes showed that these fluctuations were caused by uncertainty about the future and, more specifically, by the fact that expectations depend on current experience.

Trade-Mark. A trade-mark is a mark used to indicate a connection between goods and some person having the right as proprietor or as registered user to use the mark. No mark will be registered in the Register unless it contains certain essential particulars.

It is not lawful to register as a trade-mark, or part of a trade-mark, any matter the use of which would, by reason of its being likely to deceive or cause confusion or otherwise, be disentitled to protection in a court, or would be contrary to law or morality, or any scandalous design. No trade-mark should normally be registered in respect of any goods or description of goods that is identical with a trade-mark belonging to a different proprietor and is already on the Register in respect of the same goods or description of goods, or that so nearly resembles such a trade-mark as to be likely to deceive or cause confusion. There are various particulars that are not permitted, e.g. representations of any member of the royal family; words such as 'patent', 'registered' and 'copyright'.

In case of infringement, the injured party may choose between damages or having an account taken of the profits of the person infringing. Registration is a condition precedent to the right to sue. In regard to unregistered trade-marks, the common law recognises a person's right to prevent others from 'passing-off', i.e. trading in a manner as would lead customers to confuse his goods with those of a trade rival.

Special legislation exists for the protection of e.g. the Red Cross mark or the words 'Red Cross', and the words 'Port' and 'Madeira'. In certain cases goods have to bear a specified distinctive mark. In this regard, the 'Hall Mark' on gold and silver articles is the most familiar example.

See also COPYRIGHT; PATENTS.

Trade Union, organisation of workers formed primarily for the purpose of collective bargaining about wages and working conditions. Some trade unions are affiliated to political parties. Trade unions exist in agriculture and commerce as well as in industry.

Trade Unionism in Great Britain. Trade unionism originated and achieved its legal emancipation in Great Britain. Although unions existed before the Industrial Revolution, their growth as powerful national organisations was stimulated by the development of the factory system. From 1850 onwards powerful societies grew up, such as the Amalgamated Society of Engineers (1851). The Trades Union Congress was formed in 1868, and the trades unions secured more definite legal recognition under the Trade Union Act of 1871.

The trade unions emerged from the First World War with doubled membership and increased power resulting from the high wartime demand for labour, and the necessity for constant negotiations as prices rose and industrial methods had to be modified in war-time conditions. After a short-lived economic boom, post-war depression set in and unrest grew, reaching its climax in the General Strike of 1926. By the outbreak of the Second World War in 1939 membership was back to the six million mark of 1921, and the TUC and its unions were consulted by government on all matters affecting the interests of workers.

Craft unions, enrolling highly skilled workers of a particular trade, e.g. carpenters or compositors, were the earliest form of trade union organisation. Some, such as pattern-makers, still exist. Others became national multi-craft bodies, such as the Amalgamated Union of Engineers. Some industrial unions have sought to enrol all workers in a whole industry; examples are the National Union of Railwaymen and the National Union of Mineworkers. General unions began as organisations for groups of unskilled labourers but now negotiate for many grades of workers in a very wide range of industries. The Transport and General Workers' Union and the National Union of General and Municipal Workers are large unions of this type. Finally, there is a group of unions of non-manual employees or particular occupational categories, among them unions for teachers, post-office workers, civil servants, local government employees, journalists, musicians, airline pilots and professional footballers.

See also TRADES COUNCIL; TRADE UNIONISM, INTERNATIONAL.

Trade Unionism, International. There is international co-operation and fraternal association both between national centres of trade unions, and between unions representing specific trades in various countries, e.g. the International Transport Workers' Federation. The International Working Men's Association ('The First International') was formed in 1864 when it met in London. It was superseded by the International Federation of Trades Unions (IFTU), which existed for the formation of industrial policy applicable to its member countries. More prominent were the activities of the International Labour Organisation, set up under the League of Nations and now under the United Nations. The World Federation of Trade Unions (WFTU) first met in Paris in 1945. It superseded the IFTU, which was dissolved in 1945. The WFTU suffered a setback in 1948 as the result of a split between the representatives of the unions from Communist countries and those which were non-Communist, and the Trades Union Congress, the Congress of Industrial Organisation (USA), and the Dutch Federation of Trade Unions withdrew their membership in 1949. The Trades Union Congress then called a conference in London at the end of 1949, at which the International Confederation of Free Trade Unions (ICFTU) came into being, and within a year had the support of 50 million trade unionists from most of the democratic countries.

Trade Winds, winds which blow constantly, at a speed of approximately 5–6 metres per second, from latitudes 30°N and 30°S, converging towards the equator. The winds in the northern hemisphere blow from a north-easterly direction, while those in the southern hemisphere blow from a south-easterly direction. They are stronger and more consistent over oceans and were instrumental in the creation of sea routes.

Trades Council, local organisation in the British trade union movement, consisting of representatives from the branches of the various trade unions in a town or district. The trades councils emerged before 1850 and within the next 15 years became established in the larger industrial centres. They were active in consolidating the Labour movement and in 1868 some of them were instrumental in the formation of the Trades Union Congress. In 1895, however, they were excluded from the Congress to avoid dual representation of the members of the TUC's affiliated unions. In Scotland they helped to form the Scottish TUC, to which they remain affiliated. In England and Wales they concentrated increasingly on local trade union affairs, presenting a unified view on local issues, and gradually came to be recog-

Trade Union banners at a London May Day march, the labour movement's annual celebration.

nised as the local agents of the TUC by whom they are registered annually. They are now the channel for conveying information and ideas between the TUC and local trade union branches.

The TUC convenes an annual conference of the trades councils and has established a Joint Consultative Committee. The trades councils may not spend money on party political activities. They assist in improving trade union organisation; publicise TUC policy; and nominate representatives to serve on local committees dealing with such problems as national insurance, employment and hospital management.

See also TRADE UNION.

Trades Union Congress (TUC), a permanent association of British trade unions, which has had a continuous existence since 1868 and which each year turns itself into an annual assembly of delegates meeting together to discuss common problems. The executive body of Congress elected each year is a General Council of 37 members, first constituted in 1921 to replace the old Parliamentary Committee, which had been in existence since 1869. The principal officer of the TUC is the general secretary, who is elected by Congress.

Tradescant, John (c.1570–1638), English plant-hunter, gardener to Charles I. With his son John (1608–62) he introduced a number of plants now familiar in British gardens. He was the first botanist to visit Russia (1618). He and his son helped finance the colony of Virginia, the younger John returning with the Virginia creeper, phlox and michaelmas daisy. Curiosities collected on their travels became Britain's first public museum. By trickery Elias Ashmole secured it and gave it to Oxford as the Ashmolean Museum. The genus *Tradescantia* was named after him.

Tradescantia, a genus of plants of the family Commelinaceae, native to America. A number of species are cultivated in flower-gardens. *T. virginiana,* the common spiderwort, bears purple-blue flowers with three petals. Many other species are grown indoors.

Trading Stamps, gift vouchers in the form of stamps issued by retailers to their customers in accordance with the amount of their purchases. The introduction of trading stamps in Britain caused misgivings amongst

some retailers and sections of the public. This resulted in the passing of the Trading Stamps Act 1964, which provides that stamps should carry their cash value stamped upon them and that, where the customer had accumulated more than 25p worth, they should be redeemable in cash if so desired.

Trafalgar, cape on the southern coast of Spain, and the scene of the great naval victory of the British fleet under Lord Nelson over the combined French and Spanish fleets under Villeneuve on 21 October 1805. This battle shattered the sea power of France and Spain.

Tragedy, see DRAMA.

Traherne, Thomas (1637–74), English poet and mystical writer. His *Roman Forgeries,* 1673, and *Christian Ethics,* 1675, have only historical interest, but *Centuries of Meditation* consists of short reflections on religion in prose of measured cadence and occasional lyric flights, reflecting intense joy and mystical experience. His poems, discovered in manuscript in 1896, were at first thought to be the work of Henry Vaughan but Bertram Dobell identified them as Traherne's, and published them in 1903.

Trail, town of British Columbia, Canada, 77 km south-west of Nelson on the River Columbia. It is the centre of a rich mineral bearing district containing gold, silver, lead, zinc and copper. Lead and zinc are taken to Trail where they are smelted in a large metallurgical plant. Population (1971) 11,149.

Training, Industrial. The Industrial Training Act of 1964 empowers the Secretary of State for Employment in Britain to set up industrial training boards, and to give them certain responsibilities for the promotion of training. The principal duties of the boards, which consist of representatives of employers, employees and educational bodies, are to make recommendations about the nature of such training in different spheres of industry, to make grants to those firms whose training schemes are approved by the boards, and to make a periodic levy on employers. A Central Training Council advises the minister on the administration of the act and the running of the grant-aided Industrial Training Service. In some of the industries for which Industrial Training Boards have not been set up, apprenticeship training is provided in individual firms and by attendance at technical colleges in courses following national or regional schemes.

Trajan, full name Marcus Ulpius Trajanus (AD 53–117), Roman Emperor. In 97 he was adopted by Nerva, whom he succeeded as emperor in the following year. In 101 he set out for his first Dacian campaign and celebrated a triumph in 103, assuming the title Dacicus. The second campaign opened in 104 and was successful, Dacia being made a Roman province. Two campaigns (115–16) sufficed to overrun, though not defeat, the Parthians, and the province of Mesopotamia was formed. In 117 he fell ill and died at Selinus in Cilicia. Trajan had married Pompeia Plotina, who persuaded him to adopt Hadrian; he had no children of his own. Trajan is acknowledged as one of the truly great men of antiquity. His ability as a soldier and an administrator was outstanding; his purpose at all times was the welfare of his subjects. His public benefactions included a much improved water supply, several important roads, a number of libraries (notably the Bibliotheca Ulpia), baths on the Esquiline and the magnificent Forum Traianum, amid the ruins of which stands a column, once the repository of his ashes.

Trampolining, a gymnastic sport in which participants use a sprung 'bed' to be projected upward and perform routines consisting of somersaults and twists in flight. The trampoline is a nylon webbed bed 4·5 m by 2 m supported between a frame of 5·5 m by 3 m. The sport, which is also used as training for gymnastics and diving, was developed primarily in the USA in the late 1930s. It is now international, and is practised equally by men and women; World Championships, administered by the International Trampolining Association, were instituted in 1964.

Tramps, see VAGRANTS.

Tramways, a term used to denote two methods of railway transport—mineral lines and the street railway. It probably originated from the Scandinavian word, *tram*, meaning a beam. The early mineral tramway developed from wooden beams laid in the road to facilitate the smooth passage of cars, to a specialised way on which the vehicles were retained by flanged wheels. In the 18th century the plateway with angle-iron rails to take ordinary carts or wagons with flangeless wheels was evolved.

The street tramway, invented by John Stephenson, transferred the railway to public streets, and was introduced by the New York and Harlem undertaking in 1832. Two horses could haul, say, 46 passengers on a tram, compared with 26 on a bus. Horse tramways were introduced in Paris, 1853, and London, 1861; but the projecting rails overturned carriages and the lines were removed. Only after the grooved rail, flush with the road surface, had been introduced to take the flanged wheels did the street tram develop. In Britain, steam traction was introduced on some lines after authorisation of mechanical power by an act of 1879. From the mid-1880s cable systems

Trajan. The marble reliefs on Trajan's column, Rome, commemorate his Dacian campaigns.

were built and the trams on Blackpool front operated electrically from conductor rails in a conduit from 1884; in Lytham St Annes gas engines were employed. The Roundhay Park line, Leeds, inaugurated overhead electric traction in 1891. The London United Tramways began electric traction in London in 1901.

There were at the peak in Great Britain 171 local-authority tramways, and in 1918, 103 tramways companies. Since that time there has been a rapid decline in the use of trams and there is only one system, at Blackpool, left. The last London tram was withdrawn in 1952. Owing to increasing traffic congestion interest in tramways revived during the 1970s, often under other names such as light rapid transit, or pre-Metro, to avoid the Victorian implications of the word tram. European cities which had retained tramways, e.g. Zürich and Munich, are improving and extending their systems.

See also ELECTRIC TRACTION.

Trance, a state, either induced or spontaneous, which is similar in some aspects to the sleep state, but which also has distinct characteristics quite different from the latter, the subject remaining conscious and usually capable of communicating intelligibly. There is often an insensibility to pain or other sensory stimulation. Hypnosis, catalepsy, certain types of hysteria and ecstasy are all categorised under the heading of trance.

Tranquillisers, drugs used to calm an anxious patient, but not to cause sleep; they are similar in action to the sedatives, but should have even less effect on sleep. The minor tranquillisers include barbiturates and meprobamate, and are used to treat psychoneuroses and to reduce anxiety, tension and restlessness. Major tranquillisers include reserpine and are used for the treatment of psychoses, such as schizophrenia, senile dementia and behavioural disorders in children.

Trans-Canada Highway, a coast-to-coast highway, 7837 km long, linking Victoria, British Columbia with North Sydney on Cape Breton Island, from where a ferry across Cabot Strait carries traffic to an extension of the highway in Newfoundland from Port-aux-Basques to St John's. The highway is designed as a two-lane all-weather motor road with a series of 'overnight parks' for camping. The route was decided by the provinces, subject to the approval of the federal government. The main criterion was that it be the shortest practical east–west route through each province. Thus the road passes through Vancouver, Calgary, Regina, Winnipeg and Port Arthur, thence skirting the Great Lakes to Ottawa and Montreal, where it crosses the St Lawrence and continues south of the river, turning east at Rivière du Loup and into New Brunswick. Passing through Fredericton and Moncton it enters Nova Scotia, crosses into Cape Breton Island, and ends its mainland section at the ferry terminus of North Sydney. The project was inaugurated by an Act of Parliament in 1949. By 1952 all provinces had agreed to participate except Quebec, which remained outside the scheme until 1960. The highway was formally opened in 1962; the Newfoundland section being finished in 1965–66.

Transcaucasia, important economic region

of the USSR, bounded by the Caucasus Mountains in the north, the frontier with Turkey and Iran in the south, and the Black and Caspian Seas in the west and east respectively. It includes the Armenian, Azerbaijan and Georgian SSRs. Area 186,100 km².

Transcendentalism has both a philosophic and a theological meaning. Philosophic transcendentalism is associated chiefly with Kant (whose use of the term differs, however, from that of previous philosophers), and his successors who defended the idea of *a priori* (or intuitive) as opposed to *a posteriori* (or experiential) cognition. In a broader sense, transcendentalism signified the spiritual or intuitive attitude of mind. Theological transcendentalism is associated with this meaning, and expresses the idea of a supersensuous religious consciousness, and intuitive perception of divine truth, as opposed to dogmatic rationalism.

Transducer, a device used for converting a physical variable or property (e.g. temperature, pressure, displacement, torque, flow, velocity, acceleration or vibration) into an electrical signal which is then used for instrumentation or control purposes. The transducer makes use of some effect of the quantity to be measured or controlled having a consequential electrical effect. Strain gauges are commonly used to convert force and pressure effects into electrical signals by means of bridge circuits. Other devices use (1) displacement of iron in magnetic circuits; (2) variation of inductance or capacitance, (3) piezo-electric effects to obtain electric output signals.

Transept, in architecture, that part of a cruciform church which lies across, or in a direction at right angles to, the main axis.

Transfer of Shares. Shares in limited-liability companies are transferred by a deed called a transfer. In Britain, both parties no longer have to sign such a document when a share changes hands. The transfer and share certificate are lodged with a registration fee. When the transfer has been registered a new share certificate is issued to the transferee, evidencing his title to the shares.

Transfiguration, Feast of the (6 August), commemorates the vision of glory given by Christ to the apostles Peter, James and John after Peter's confession. The feast was instituted in 1457 for the Western Church, but is several centuries older in the East.

•**Transformer,** a device for stepping up or down the value of alternating current (a.c.) voltages. It consists of two windings usually wound on an iron core, though air-cored or ferrite-cored transformers are used on high frequency. The windings have at least some magnetic flux common to both windings. If one winding (the primary) is connected to an a.c. supply, the current produces an alternating magnetic flux in the core which induces an electromotive force (e.m.f.) in the other winding (the secondary). The ratio of primary to secondary voltage is equal to the ratio of the number of primary to secondary winding turns, assuming that the flux links equally with both windings. When the secondary is supplying current to a load, the ratio of secondary current to primary current is equal to the ratio of the number of primary turns to secondary turns. This is the

transformation ratio, assuming no losses. The actual losses are partly copper losses due to resistance of the windings, and partly core or iron losses due to eddy currents and hysteresis. Transformer cores are built up of thin steel plates insulated from one another by paper, varnish or glass. Large transformers are immersed in oil which is cooled by air or water circulating in pipes. Transformers are also used for instrumentation (current and potential transformers), control systems (pulse transformers), electronic circuits (impedance matching and power supplies) and for d.c. applications with saturated cores.
See also ALTERNATING CURRENT; ELECTRICITY, CURRENT.

Transfusion, passage of fluid from one vessel to another, especially the introduction of fluid into the blood-vessel, usually to make up for fluid and salt loss in such conditions as dehydration, severe vomiting or diarrhoea, or after burns or surgery. Simple solutions of salt and sugar are most frequently used in medical practice, but a wide variety of different solutions are available for different purposes. If there has been blood loss, either whole blood or plasma (blood without the cells) may be transfused.
See also BLOOD TRANSFUSION.

Transistor, an electronic semiconductor device with three electrodes. It has replaced the thermionic valve in almost all applications. In 1948, Bardeen and Brattain of the Bell Telephone Laboratories constructed a device with two cat's whiskers touching an impure crystal and found that a current flowing into one of these point contacts, called the emitter, could cause a greater current to flow in the circuit attached to the second point contact, the collector. This device was thus capable of giving amplification in the same way as a diode valve. In 1949, Shockley suggested that junctions between different types of semiconductor be used instead of point contacts, which were unreliable.

Junction transistors consist of a series of wafers in n-type (negative) germanium crystal, which in the early days were treated on each side with indium, a p-type (positive) impurity, to produce a p-n-p structure in which the n-type wafer was the base and the indium-impregnated areas the emitter and collector. In modern methods of manufacture p-type and n-type impurities diffuse as gases onto the crystal wafers.

Planar transistors are made on oxidised wafers of single-crystal silicon by photoetching a precise pattern of windows onto which are diffused gaseous impurities. Many hundreds can be made at the same time. They are separated and the connecting wires welded on before being hermetically sealed.

Field Effect Transistors (FET) consist of a narrow channel of n-type (p-type) material attached at either end to electrodes known as the source and drain. The centre of the channel is in contact with two small pieces of p-type (n-type) material, which are connected to electrodes known as gates. The current in the channel can be controlled by altering the voltage across the gate. The effect of the FET is similar to that of the triode valve.

Transit Instrument, an instrument for determining the exact moment a celestial object crosses the meridian.

Transjordan, see JORDAN.

Transkei, the first African territory in South Africa to be raised to the status of an autonomous 'homeland', in 1963. It lies between the Kei river and the Natal border, and one district is detached from the remainder, because of intervening 'white' areas including Griqualand East. Area 38,541 km².
The population (1977: about 3,500,000) originated from a number of tribes which have a common language, Xhosa; the principal tribes are the Xhosa, Tembu and Pondo. The agricultural economy, although still chiefly one of subsistence, is being diversified through such crops as tea, coffee and New Zealand flax. Large deposits of titanium have been discovered and there are small deposits of copper, nickel, coal and marble. The economic dependence of the Transkei is such that over 80 per cent of all adult males have to work in 'white areas'.

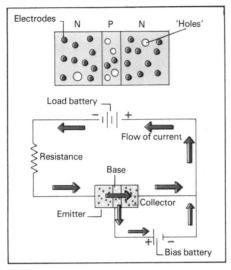

Transistor. An n-p-n junction transistor. Current flows when the base is positively biased.

Translation, in literature, the art of rendering the writings of one language into another language. The art of translation lies not only in conveying the literal sense but also in translating the feeling, thought and character of the work, so that the translation is equal in quality to the original. Translation allows the possibilities of creating a new work of art in the new language, and this has not infrequently happened; North's *Plutarch*, for example, and other major works of the late 16th and early 17th centuries (including the Geneva and Authorised versions of the Bible) fall into this category, as does Fitzgerald's translation of the *Quatrains* of Omar Khayyam. Translation has played a major part in alerting cultures to literary achievements and philosophic thought.

Transmigration of Soul, also called metempsychosis, the migration of the soul, as an immortal essence, into successive bodily forms, human or animal.
See also REINCARNATION.

Transmission of Electric Power, see ELECTRIC POWER: TRANSMISSION.

Transmitter, electronic device from which intelligence is sent out. A radio transmitter generates high frequency waves; it amplifies these, impresses upon them the intelligence to be conveyed and finally feeds them to an aerial which sends them into space, subsequently to be intercepted at the receiver.
A pure sine wave is generated by an oscillator, at a frequency kept constant by a quartz crystal maintained at a constant temperature. If the frequency to be transmitted is higher than can be generated by a crystal oscillator, a 'frequency multiplier' circuit is used. Subsequent stages of amplification generally use transistors, but in the final stages of high-power transmitters, valves are still used. When several kilowatts are to be generated, several pairs of valves are operated as push-pull amplifiers in parallel.
Most transmitters range from fractions of a watt to a few hundred watts. Army manpack radios comprise a complete transmitter-receiver ('transceiver') powered from batteries with a range of a few kilometres. Large units for vehicle use have correspondingly greater ranges, and are powered by batteries or generators. Special transmitters operating in the VHF (very high frequency) bands are used by police forces, fire services, etc. They are crystal controlled, and the portable versions operate at powers of about 10 W. Fixed VHF transmitters are of lower power than HF transmitters, since the aerial directivity can be made much greater.
Transmitters for radar and television have special features. The former are designed to be capable of producing pulses of 1 μs or less duration having very high peak power (exceeding 1 MW). As these pulses are of short duration and their repetition frequency is low, the average power is small. The valves have large cathodes capable of meeting the peak emission requirements, but the anodes are designed to deal with the average power dissipation. Television transmitters must possess wide-band characteristics if the full picture detail is to be radiated without distortion. The modern tendency is to design such transmitters to transmit the carrier and only one sideband, as this leads to maximum economy of frequencies and power rating of the final amplifier. The system is known as 'vestigial sideband' transmission.

Transmutation of the Elements, the conversion of one chemical element into another. The possibility of transmutation is a very old belief which formed one of the central ideas of the alchemists who were searching (among other things) for the philosopher's stone which would be the agent for the turning of base metals into gold. Early alchemist claims were based on a confusion between chemical replacement and transmutation. With the discovery of radium and radioactive substances in general a new era opened. Ramsay and Soddy found that radium bromide, by spontaneous change, gave rise to radon (a gas), and by spectroscopic examination helium gas was shown to be a product of the change. Now it is quite certain that radium itself is an element, so that here there appears to be a definite example of one element splitting up to give rise to two entirely different elements. Spontaneous changes of this nature do call to mind the ideal of the ancient alchemists. Natural radioactivity led to the discovery of many properties of the nucleus. Rutherford found that natural α-particles reacted with nitrogen nuclei to form oxygen and hydrogen—the

first example of artificial transmutation.
See also ACTINIDES.

Transom, in shipping, a board across the stern of a boat to which the after-ends of the side planking are fastened.

Transpiration, evaporation of water from the surfaces of green plants; in part directly from the cuticle or outer epidermal cells, but largely through the stomata. Factors affecting transpiration are: (1) relative humidity of the air; (2) temperature; (3) light; (4) wind; and (5) the nature of the leaf surface; the thickness of cuticle, hairiness, wax covering and texture. The functions of transpiration are chiefly to regulate temperature by the cooling effect of evaporation, and to initiate a flow of water transporting mineral salts from the soil through and up the plant, known as the transpiration stream. Excessive transpiration results in wilting. When water is forced up through the plant by root pressure more quickly than it can be transpired, drops are forced out through special glands around leaf margins, and this is called guttation.

Transplant, a section of tissue or an organ grafted in a new place on the same body or onto another individual's body. Grafting animal tissues is difficult because the transplant needs a good blood supply, nerve and other complex tissues may be involved, and the immunological defence system, which protects the body against foreign proteins that invade it, must be prevented from rejecting the graft. For a transplant to be accepted, it must resemble the recipient's tissues as nearly as possible. An *autograft* is one taken from another part of the same body, for example, a thin layer of skin from the thigh may be removed and grafted onto a burned arm. The next closest resemblance occurs in a transplant from an identical twin or, in animals, from another individual of a closely inbred strain. This is an *isograft*, and will be almost as acceptable to the immune defences. *Allografts*, transplants from other individuals of the same species, are rejected unless special measures are taken. In transplanting kidneys, for example, careful tissue typing is done to choose a donor with as similar tissue antigens and antibodies as possible to the recipient, and immunosuppressive drugs are given to inhibit the action of the recipient's immune defences. *Heterografts*, transplants from animals of different species, are always rejected.

Many kinds of tissue transplantation are now common, especially blood transfusion, in which matching the donor's and recipient's blood types is a routine task. The cornea of the eye is another common transplant, because it has no blood supply, so is inaccessible to most antibodies. Bone marrow, heart valves, pieces of bone, and sheets of connective tissue have been transplanted. Organs that have been transplanted include the kidney, heart, lungs and liver.

Transplant rejection is likely to occur in an individual (recipient) to whom tissues or organs are transplanted from another person (donor). The rejection is the result of an immune response of the cell-mediated type involving the activity of 'T-lymphocytes'. These T-lymphocytes respond to the presence of foreign antigens in the blood vessels of the graft tissue. Only when these antigens are identical in the recipient and donor are grafts accepted. This occurs only in identical twins who have the same genes, and in most cases elaborate tests have to be carried out to find a donor whose transplantation antigens will cause the mildest immune response in the recipient.

In order to minimise the chances of transplantation rejection the recipient can be treated with X-rays, immunosuppressant drugs such as azathioprine, or antilymphocytic serum (ALS).

Transplanting, moving of plants from one site to another. Newly germinated seedlings recover best when moved as young as practicable. Tap-rooted plants, e.g. brassicas, benefit from the breaking of the tap root, which induces a fibrous root system. Deciduous trees, shrubs and perennials transplant best in winter when the soil is workable; evergreens and conifers in early autumn or late spring. The roots must not be allowed to dry out, and firm planting in prepared soil is essential. With special preparation, mature plants are often moved when in full growth.

Transportation, the sending of convicts to penal settlements, probably first practised in England in the reign of Charles II, when pardons were granted to persons under sentence of death conditionally on their being transported for a number of years, usually seven. Transportation was unknown under the common law and was not legalised until 1719. During the 18th and the early 19th centuries numerous acts were passed by which various terms of transportation with alternative punishments were allotted to specific offences. Australia was the main destination of the transports (a term applied to the people as well as to the ships that carried them).

Transposing Instruments (music). Many wind instruments are built in fundamental tunings in which the major scale without key signature, written as C major, actually sounds higher or lower. A clarinet in B flat, for example, will automatically play the scale of that key when the music is written in C major; if it is to play a piece in F major, the music must be written in G major, and so on. Among the orchestral instruments, cor anglais, clarinet, horn and trumpet are transposing instruments.

Transposition (music). The process, either in composing or performing, of turning a piece from one key into another in such a way that the music remains exactly the same except for the change in pitch. All intervals remain of the same size, whatever the new key may be. Accompanists are often required to transpose at sight when a song is too high or low for a singer's voice.

Transsexuality, see SEXUALITY, HUMAN.

Trans-Siberian Railway, longest in the world, from Moscow to Nakhodka, near Vladivostok on the Soviet Pacific coast, a distance of 9334 km; it was built between 1891 and 1915. It greatly facilitated Russian colonisation of Siberia and the Far East, and large-scale geological prospecting, which laid the basis for the economic development of Siberia.

Transubstantiation (Latin *transubstantiatio*, change of substance), the change which is believed by Roman Catholics to take place in the Eucharistic elements of bread and wine, in virtue of the consecration, i.e. the whole substance of the bread and the whole substance of the wine is changed into the substance of the body and blood of Christ, the accidents of the original elements alone remaining. By 'accidents' is meant those qualities or conditions which produce upon the human senses the impression of the presence of bread and wine.

Transvaal, province of South Africa, bounded on the north by Zimbabwe, on the east by Mozambique and Swaziland, on the south by the provinces of Natal and Orange Free State, and on the west by Botswana. It was originally a Boer republic, conquered by the British in the Boer Wars. Area 286,065 km².

The Transvaal is part of the Southern African plateau. In the south the Highveld averages 1500 m above sea-level and the Waterberg plateau in the north-west is slightly higher. Between them lies the Bushveld basin, crossed by a series of ridges, of which the most important is the Witwatersrand (Rand). The Limpopo river forms the northern boundary with Zimbabwe, and other rivers include the Olifant, Letaba and Mogalakwena. The population in 1970 was 8,765,056, including 1,895,358 whites, 6,637,645 Africans (of whom 2,370,373 live in 'homelands'), 151,391 coloureds, and 80,662 Asians. The main towns are Johannesburg, Pretoria (the capital), Germiston and Krugersdorp.

The southern Transvaal is responsible for more than 40 per cent of the gross value of South Africa's industrial output and most of its gold-mines; more than half of its metal and engineering industries are located on the Witwatersrand. In the eastern Transvaal Lowveld area most of the country's citrus fruit is grown. Tobacco, groundnuts, castor-oil seed, grain and timber are the main agricultural products. Minerals mined are asbestos, iron ore, mica, platinum, manganese, granite, fire clay, phosphate, chrome ore, marble, corundum, copper, beryl, antimony and vermiculite. Large coal deposits exist to the west. In north-east Transvaal there are immense deposits of apatite at Phalaborwa and a plant has been built to produce phosphate concentrates in sufficient quantities to make the country self-sufficient in this fertiliser. The world's largest open-cast copper mine is at Phalaborwa. The Transvaal is a large producer of diamonds, mined and alluvial.

There is a Provincial Council elected on the same franchise as the House of Assembly.

Transvestism, see SEXUALITY, HUMAN.

Transylvania, historical province of eastern central Europe, since 1947 a district of Romania. It lies within the Carpathians, divided from the mountain mass by depressions, thus forming a self-contained tableland. It is drained by tributaries of the rivers Prut and Tisza. In the early 11th century the area was conquered by Stephen of Hungary, who settled a Magyar-speaking people, the Szeklers, as colonists; they enjoyed self-government under Hungarian and then (after 1526) Turkish suzerainty. From 1691 Transylvania came directly under Austrian domination. After the First World War it was granted to Romania by the Treaty of St-Germain-en-Laye. Transylvania is rich in minerals (copper, lead, salt, gold, silver and methane gas), and is a fertile agricultural region. The main towns are Cluj, Braşov, Sibiu and Tîrgu-Mureş. Area 57,000 km².

Trapdoor Spider, any member of the arachnid family Ctenizidae. They occur in tropical and subtropical regions of the world, are about 3 cm long, and have large jaws, each with a long fang, and horny teeth. They live in tunnels in the ground covered with a trapdoor that probably functions only to protect the spider from predators such as hunting wasps. Their diet includes insects, worms, millipedes and centipedes. Trapdoor spiders are related to the purse-web spiders of the New World.

Trapping and Trappers. Trapping is practised to some extent in many parts of the world where game animals form part of the food supply, but it is chiefly used as a means of capturing animals in order to secure their pelts or furs without damage. Since the fur-bearing animals live in the cold northern climates, northern Canada and the northern parts of the USSR are the main areas of the world where trapping is carried on on a large scale for commercial purposes. During the period of Canada's early history, furs were the main article of commerce and the basis of the country's economy, and they still contribute millions of dollars annually to the national income although fur-farming has developed rapidly. Muskrat and squirrel provide the greatest numbers of pelts taken annually; mink, beaver and muskrat lead in value. The conservation and management of fur-bearers is receiving increasing attention in Canada from the authorities. All Canadian provinces have trapping regulations, and trappers are licensed.

Trappists, a branch of the Cistercian order founded by Dominique Armand Jean le Bouthillier de Rancé (1626–1700); it is known officially as the Order of Reformed Cistercians, or Order of Cistercians of the Stricter Observance. Until the age of 34 de Rancé led the voluptuous life of a courtier-priest. Then in 1660 he retired to live a life of austerity and devotion in the Cistercian abbey of La Trappe, which had long formed part of his possessions. The abbey was lax in discipline, and it was with great difficulty that de Rancé introduced his strict observance. The new community devoted itself to the observance of strict silence and seclusion from the world, to hard labour, and to abstinence from wine and all seasoning of their simple diet of bread and vegetables. The reform of La Trappe spread to other houses, and is found today all over the world.

Trasimene, (Italian *Lago Trasimeno*), lake in Umbria, Italy. In 1898 it was partially drained into the Tiber, some 2225 ha of land being reclaimed. It is famous for Hannibal's great victory over the Romans under Flaminius, won on its shores in 217 BC. Depth 7 m. Area 128 km².

Travancore, former princely state of India, stretching along the Malabar coast from Cape Comorin to Cochin. In 1949 Travancore joined Cochin to form a state, which in turn was merged with Kerala state in 1958. The state capital was Trivandrum.

Traveller's Cheques, cheques issued by banks and certain travel agents for the benefit of persons travelling at home or abroad. They provide greater security than actual cash since they must be countersigned in the presence of the paying agent, who is able to identify the holder by comparing the signature with the one written on the cheque at the time of issue.

Traveller's Joy, see CLEMATIS.

Traveller's Tree, *Ravenala madagascariensis*, in the Musaceae, a tree with long, large fan-shaped leaves. At the base of the leaf stalks water collects, forming a useful store for travellers and animals.

Travelling Microscope, device for measuring short lengths. It consists of a microscope with cross-hairs in the image produced, mounted on an accurate carriage. The microscope is moved from one point to another and the distance read off a micrometer scale. See also MICROSCOPE AND MICROSCOPY, OPTICAL.

Travers, Ben (1886–1980), English novelist and dramatist. Influenced by A. W. Pinero, Travers wrote a series of classic farces which were first performed at the Aldwych Theatre in the 1920s. They included *A Cuckoo in the Nest*, 1925; *Rookery Nook*, 1926; *Thark*, 1927; and *A Night Like This*, 1930. He wrote many others, perhaps the most popular being *Banana Ridge*, 1938; *The Bed Before Yesterday*, his first play for 23 years, was produced in 1975. He also wrote novels and the screenplays of many of his farces, as well as an autobiography, *Vale of Laughter*, 1957, which has interesting comments on farce as an artform.

Trawler, see FISHING, COMMERCIAL.

Treacle, a by-product in the process of refining sugar. Treacle is removed at the second stage of refinement. After further refinement and bleaching, golden syrup is extracted, and after still further refinement, bleaching and evaporation, sugars are spun off. Treacle, which is extremely thick and sweet, is used in cake making.

Treadmill, known as 'the everlasting staircase', worked by persons treading on steps fixed on the periphery of a wheel. It was once used as a means of prison discipline, or to give useful employment in the shape of grinding corn or moving machinery to persons imprisoned for crime, and came under the category of 'hard labour'.

Treason, treachery against the sovereign. In England it is treason e.g. to compass the death of the king, queen or their eldest son; to levy war against the king; to adhere to the king's enemies in his realm, giving them aid and comfort; and to slay the chancellor, treasurer or king's justices. The punishment for treason is death.

In addition, the offence of treason felony, which is punishable by imprisonment for life, is committed when any person e.g. deposes the sovereign; or levies war against the Crown within the UK to influence the policies of government by force.

Misprision of treason is an offence committed by the failure to disclose information relating to a committed treason.

See also CRIMINAL LAW; POLITICAL OFFENCES; ROYAL FAMILY.

Treasure Trove, articles of gold or silver discovered hidden in the earth or some other secret place of which the owner is unknown. The established principle of English law is that the Crown is entitled to such treasure. Providing that the find is promptly and fully declared, the finder normally receives an *ex gratia* payment equal to the market value of his discovery. Whether the find is treasure trove or not is decided at a coroner's inquest. See also LOST PROPERTY.

Treasury, major department of State nowadays primarily responsible for the management of the financial resources of the UK and the development of Britain's overall economic strategy, the control of public spending, and international monetary relations. Its Public Services Sector is responsible for controlling aggregate public spending and most of the nation's public expenditure programmes; its Domestic Economic Sector is concerned with fiscal, monetary and counter-inflation programmes, and with the Department's contribution to industrial policies, including control of public expenditure on industry and agriculture; its Overseas Finance Sector is responsible for balance of payments policies, the management of Britain's foreign currency reserves, international monetary questions, financial relations with other countries, and the overseas aid programme; while the Treasury's Chief Economic Adviser's Sector is responsible for the preparation of short-term and medium-term economic forecasts and specialist advice on broad economic policies. The Treasury has general oversight of the Bank of England (effective instrument of much of its international and domestic monetary policy) and such 'sub-departments' as the Royal Mint, the Department for National Savings and the National Debt Office.

Constitutionally, the Treasury is governed by a board of seven Lords Commissioners: the First Lord of the Treasury (always the Prime Minister, who, however, takes no part in the control of day-to-day Treasury business), the Chancellor of the Exchequer and five junior Lords (who in practice are MPs acting as assistants to the Government Chief Whip).

Treasury Bill. Treasury bills originated in Britain in 1877 at the suggestion of Walter Bagehot. They are the means by which the British government borrows money for short periods. The bill itself is a promise to pay a stated sum within a period not exceeding one year, though normally the period is for three months. They form the largest part of the government's floating debt, and are offered for tender (sale) on Friday of each week. They are bought by the discount houses, overseas central banks, and sometimes by large corporations with cash in hand, for a short period on which they can earn some interest.

Treasury Solicitor, in England and Wales, legal adviser to the Treasury and government departments which do not have their own legal advisers.

Treaty, an agreement in writing between subjects of international law, usually states, which is intended to be governed by international law. The treaty-making power in the UK rests on the Crown.

Treaty Port, name given to certain seaports in China which were open to European trade by treaty. The earliest of these treaties was that of 1842. Between 1943 and 1947 the Treaty Powers relinquished the extraterritorial rights and privileges in China for which the various treaties made provision.

Trebizond, Empire of, founded in 1204 just before the sack of Constantinople, by Alexius and David Comnenus. It outlived its parent empire, the Byzantine, only falling to the Ottoman Mohammed II in 1461. At first it extended as far as Paphlagonia in the west and the Crimea in the north, but the Seljuk capture of Sinope in 1214 blocked any such expansion. From that time it was largely surrounded by the Turks, who encroached on its territory. Trebizond was, however, generally prosperous, profiting from the caravan route to the east.

See also TRABZON.

Treble, highest voice in a vocal composition in several parts, derived from the Latin *triplum,* which was the top part of the earliest three-part motets. The term treble is used for a boy's voice but not for the female soprano.

Tree, Sir Herbert Draper Beerbohm (1853–1917), British actor-manager. Educated in Germany, he took the name of Tree, and made his first appearance on the stage in 1878. His first success was in *The Private Secretary,* 1884. Manager of the Haymarket Theatre, 1887–96, he was thenceforth proprietor and manager of Her (His) Majesty's Theatre. Tree was especially famous for his production of Shakespeare's plays, in which he also acted, being particularly admired as Falstaff, Malvolio and Richard II. He also excelled in 'character' parts such as Fagin in *Oliver Twist,* and especially Svengali in *Trilby,* 1895, his greatest success. He founded at His Majesty's an academy for stage training which later became the Royal Academy of Dramatic Art.

Tree, a perennial plant with a woody stem and branches, differing from a shrub in its greater size and its possession of a main stem or trunk which is free of branches for some distance from the ground. Trees are divided into two groups, the Angiosperms and the Gymnosperms. The chief gymnospermous trees are the conifers; the majority of angiospermous trees are Dicotyledons, which yield the hardwoods, but one family of Monocotyledons, the palms, consists entirely of tree forms. Trees are either deciduous and lose their leaves in the winter, for instance, the birch and oak, or evergreen, for example, the pine and common holly.

Tree-creeper, small bird of the genus *Certhia,* order Passeriformes. Creepers inhabit woodlands in North America, Europe and southern Asia. They eat mainly insects and occasionally seeds.

Tree-fern, ferns with a trunk-like stem that somewhat resemble a tree in structure. Many belong to the family *Cyatheaceae.*

Tree-frog, about 600 species of the amphibian order Anura, family Hylidae. They are widely distributed, especially in America. The common tree-frog (*Hyla arborea*) is about 2·5 cm long, bright leaf-green above and white underneath, and possesses some powers of colour change. The male croaks loudly by means of a distensible throat sac. The digits bear adhesive discs, with which it readily climbs.

Tree of Heaven (*Ailanthus altissima*), a hardy tree native to China. It is fast growing and can reach a height of 25 m; because it withstands atmospheric pollution it is popular in cities in Europe and North America. It has a smooth, grey-brown bark, and produces greenish flowers which turn red-brown in autumn.

Tree Worship, in some form or other, is common world-wide. In Europe, the veneration of trees as sacred or the abode of deities survived late, and is found in many of the accounts of early Christian missions in the North. The sacred oak featured in the old Prussian religion, and the oak and its parasite the mistletoe were sacred to the ancient Britons. Tree-worship is of two types. In the more primitive the tree is itself regarded as an animate being. In the later and commoner form it is thought of as the residence of a separate being. There are legends about the tree from which the cross of Christ was made.

Trench Warfare. A French print of 1915 showing a star shell bursting over no man's land.

Treece, Henry (1912–66), Welsh poet, novelist and critic. As a poet he was a leader of the 'New Apocalypse' movement, which represented a reaction against the realistic and political poetry of the 1930s; he was joint editor of their anthologies *The White Horseman,* 1941, *The Crown and the Sickle,* 1945, and wrote *How I See Apocalypse,* 1946. Later volumes were *The Haunted Garden,* 1947, and *The Exiles,* 1952. His novels include *The Dark Island,* 1952; *The Golden Strangers,* 1956; and *Red Queen, White Queen,* 1958. In 1949 he published a study of Dylan Thomas.

Trees, Age of, see AGE OF TREES.

Trefoil, common name for species of *Trifolium* and related genera with 3-leaflet leaves. Bird's-foot trefoil is *Lotus corniculatus;* moon trefoil, *Medicago arborea;* scented trefoil, *Melilotus* species.

Trelleborg, on the island of Sjaelland, Denmark, is the site of a large Viking stronghold occupied between 950 and 1050, which was skilfully excavated in 1932–42. In this fortress 'aspiring youth was trained under discipline and fixed regulations for the craft of war and for the grim voyage over the sea'. The camp consists of a circular inner ward, with outer defences and other attributes, surrounded by a massive bank of earth strengthened with timber. Within is a regularly laid-out plan of streets and barracks.

Trematodes, a group of flatworms, with an oval non-segmented body, now divided into two separate classes, Monogenea and Digenea, both of which possess adhesive organs or suckers, often with hooks, to cling to their hosts. The former are mainly ectoparasites of aquatic vertebrates, e.g. *Polystoma* of frogs, and have a simple life-cycle, but Digenea include many important endoparasites, among them the liver fluke of sheep, *Fasciola hepatica,* and *Schistosoma mansoni* and *S. japonicum,* which are the cause of schistosomiasis. Digenea have complex life-cycles involving two or three intermediate hosts for the larval stages.

Trench Warfare. From the earliest times, particularly in siege operations, armies have made excavations in the earth to protect them from the enemy's fire. As small arms and artillery became more numerous and powerful, so the adoption of earthworks as protection increased. The climax was reached during the First World War on the Western Front when, between October 1914 and November 1918, both sides constructed elaborate trench systems extending from Switzerland to the English Channel. These trench systems included front line, support and reserve lines with communication trenches from rear to front for supply purposes. As the war progressed concrete machine-gun emplacements and shell-proof dug-outs were added. In some places the opposing front-line trenches were only a few yards apart, but the average was 275 or 365 metres. For additional security the fire-trenches were protected by extensive barbed-wire entanglements. The opposing sides mined under each other's trenches with a view to blowing them up. Operations were more fluid in the Second World War and trench warfare was not practised extensively.

Trenchard, Hugh Montague Trenchard, 1st Viscount (1873–1956), British soldier, airman and administrator. He entered the army in 1893. In 1912 he obtained his air pilot's certificate and in 1914, in the First World War, was commandant of the military wing of the Royal Flying Corps. He became chief of the air staff in 1915, and in 1918 was appointed to command the independent Air Force in France. In 1919 he was again chief of the air staff, which position he held until 1929 when he became air chief marshal. From 1931 until 1935 he was commissioner of the Metropolitan Police Force. Trenchard (nicknamed 'Boom') laid the foundations of the RAF and is popularly regarded as the 'Father of the Air Force'.

Trent, Jesse Boot, 1st Baron (1850–1931), British industrialist, founder of Boots Pure Drug Company. He opened his first chemist's shop in 1877 and in 1883 formed the company of J. Boot and Co. Ltd., which was among the first 'chain stores' in Britain. Boot was a munificent patron of education.

Trent, important English river, rising in Staffordshire and flowing through Derbyshire, along the county boundary of Leicestershire and through Nottinghamshire and Lincolnshire, eventually joining the Ouse to form the Humber. It is about 270 km long, and is connected with other rivers and with Birmingham and Merseyside by the Trent and Mersey and Grand Union canals.

Trent, Council of, the 19th ecumenical council of the Church, held mainly at Trento in Italy. It was convoked by Pope Paul III in 1545 to reinvigorate the Church, then on the defensive as a result of the attacks of Luther and other reformers. It sat till 1563 and passed a number of decrees defining doctrines questioned by the Protestants and reforming abuses. The Council was of considerable importance in initiating the Counter-Reformation. Its decrees were confirmed by Pope Pius IV in 1564.

Trentino-Alto Adige (formerly *Venezia Tridentina*), region of Northern Italy, comprising the provinces of Trento and Bolzano. Before 1919 the district belonged to the Austrian Tirol, thus leaving 400,000 Italians under Austrian rule. By the Treaty of St Germain-en-Laye it was ceded to Italy. After 1945 there was considerable agitation among the German inhabitants (most of Bolzano province is German-speaking) at their inclusion in Italy. This stopped after extensive local autonomy was granted. The region is entirely in the Alps and consists mostly of the Adige valley. Agriculture is efficient and limited to the valley floors; its chief products are wine, fruit and dairy products. Timber is an important industry. Using abundant hydroelectric power, successful industrial plants have been established at Bolzano and Merano (paper, chemicals, metals). The regional capital is Trento. Area 13,613 km². Population (1980) 878,296.

Trento (German *Trient*; ancient *Tridentum*), Italian city, capital of both Trento province and the region of Trentino-Alto Adige. It occupies a strategic position on the Brenner Pass route and the Adige, some 160 km northeast of Milan. It is of pre-Roman origin, and became part of the German Empire in the time of Otho I. It remained German, ruled by prince-bishops, until 1801. Most of the sessions of the Council of Trent (1543–63) took place in the Renaissance church of S. Maria Maggiore. The main industries are cement, agricultural machinery, and food and drink. Population (1974) 95,800.

Trenton, capital of the state of New Jersey, USA, situated on the Delaware river 50 km above Philadelphia. The Delaware is navigable up to the city, and Trenton is an old-established manufacturing centre; the first open-hearth steel furnace in the USA was opened here in 1868. Trenton became the state capital in 1790. Population (1980) 92,124.

Trepanning (Greek *trupanon*, bore), a surgical operation in which a circular hole is bored, usually in the cranium to permit access to the brain. The instrument used is a trepan (trephine), and resembles a carpenter's bit provided with a handle. The discovery of prehistoric skulls bearing circular scars with signs of healing shows that trepanning is an operation of great antiquity, being performed presumably for the purpose of releasing imaginary evil spirits and devils. Nowadays it is carried out in operations on the brain, and to relieve excessive intracranial pressure resulting, for instance, from a haematoma, or collection of blood, which may develop inside the skull following a fracture. Trepanning is also performed with miniature trephines on the eyeball.

See also GLAUCOMA.

Trevelyan, George Macaulay (1876–1962), British historian. He received the Order of Merit in 1930. He was regius professor of modern history at Cambridge University from 1927 until 1940 when he became master of Trinity College, retiring from this position in 1951. His publications include: *England in the Age of Wycliff*, 1899;

History of England, 1926; *English Social History*, 1944; and *A Shortened History of England*, 1959.

Trevelyan, Sir George Otto (1838–1928), British statesman and author, a nephew of Lord Macaulay. In 1865 he entered Parliament as Liberal for Tynemouth. Trevelyan was civil lord of the Admiralty, 1869–70; secretary of the Admiralty, 1880–82; chief secretary for Ireland, 1882–84; chancellor of the Duchy of Lancaster and member of the Cabinet, 1884–85; and secretary for Scotland, 1886 and 1892–95. He published a number of works including his famous *Life and Letters of Lord Macaulay*, 1876, and *Early History of Charles James Fox*, 1880.

Trèves, see TRIER.

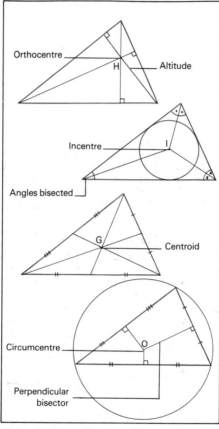

Triangle. *In a scalene triangle, the orthocentre, incentre, centroid and circumcentre all have different locations.*

Treviso (ancient *Tarvisium*), Italian town, capital of Treviso province, at the junction of the Sile and the Piavesella, some 26 km northwest of Venice. A prosperous medieval town, first as a free city and later under Venice from 1389, it is a picturesque walled town with canals, curious houses, winding alleys and arcades. Treviso has been a textile centre since 1900, but now has diverse small industries including ceramics and porcelain. It is a market town. Population (1974) 88,300.

Trevithick, Richard (1771–1833), British inventor of locomotives. About 1797 he made a steam engine for Herland mine, and in 1800 a double-acting high-pressure engine for Cook's Kitchen mine. In 1801 he completed the first steam carriage to draw passengers. In Wales, in 1804, he put the first practical rail locomotive into use; it had a flywheel and did not work long. Trevithick was the first to turn steam exhaust into the

chimney to increase the draught and to rely on friction of smooth rails and wheels. In 1809 he failed in an attempt to make a tunnel under the Thames. He made a steam threshing-machine in 1811. In 1816 Trevithick went to Peru, where his engines were being installed in the mines. He prospected for an inter-oceanic railroad in Costa Rica. He took out his last patent, 1832, for superheated steam; but he had numerous unpatented projects, including a stern driving propeller. He died penniless.

Trevor-Roper, Hugh Redwald, see DACRE OF GLANTON, HUGH REDWALD TREVOR-ROPER, BARON.

Triad. A Welsh form of literary composition depending on an arrangement of similar subjects, things or events in series of three under some general title suggesting that they were more or less connected. Among the best-known are the Triads of Horses, which are included in the 12th-century Black Book of Carmarthen; the Triads of Arthur and his warriors, believed to be 13th century; the Triads of the Island of Britain, in the Red Book of Hergest (a 14th-century manuscript in the possession of Jesus College, Cambridge); and the later Triads of Dyfnwal Moelmud, a legendary king of Britain. The Third Series of Triads in the *Myvyrian Archaiology of Wales* are 18th-century forgeries by Iolo Morganwg (Edward Williams).

Trial by Combat, or wager of battle, mode of trial introduced into England by William the Conqueror. In civil cases the duel was fought by hired champions, but in criminal cases the parties themselves fought until one was slain or gave in (when he was put to death unless the king intervened). Where the blood relations of a murdered person 'appealed' (meaning in this sense accused) the supposed murderer, the latter, where the accuser was not a woman, child, priest or infirm person, could claim trial by combat with his accuser.

Triangle, geometrical figure consisting of three distinct points joined by three distinct line segments. The points are called the vertices and the line segments the sides. In Euclidean geometry, the following types of triangle are distinguished: (1) equilateral, in which all sides are equal (and all internal angles are $\frac{1}{3}\pi$ rad or 60°); (2) isosceles, in which two sides are equal (and so are the two angles between the equal sides and the third side); (3) scalene, in which no two sides are equal (nor are any two angles); (4) right-angled, in which one angle is a right angle. The sum of the internal angles of a triangle is π rad (180°). An external angle is equal to the sum of the two opposite internal angles. If one side of a triangle is designated the base, then the perpendicular distance from the base to the opposite vertex is called the altitude. Also, a line drawn from a vertex that is perpendicular to the opposite side is called an altitude. The three altitudes meet at a common point called the orthocentre. The bisectors of the internal angles of a triangle meet at a common point, called the incentre, which is the centre of the incircle which just touches each side. The lines joining vertices and the mid-points of sides meet at a point which is the centroid of the triangle. The perpendicular bisectors of the sides meet at a point, called the circumcentre, which is the centre of the circle that goes through the vertices of the triangle.

The area of a triangle is half the product of a base and the corresponding altitude.

Spherical Triangles. A spherical triangle is one formed by three intersecting great circles of a sphere. The sum of the spherical angles is always greater than π rad (180°) and less than 3π rad (540°). The amount by which the sum exceeds π rad is called the 'spherical excess' of the triangle. The area of a spherical triangle is r^2E, where r is the radius of the sphere and E is the spherical excess (measured in radians).

See also TRIGONOMETRY.

Triangle, percussion instrument consisting of a steel bar bent into three-cornered form. It is struck with a short steel rod and produces a bright tinkling sound of indefinite pitch.

Triangulation. When a large area is to be mapped, one of the prerequisites is a system of points throughout the area, whose relative positions are known exactly. One method of coordinating such positions is to use triangulation, which involves covering the area with a network of triangles and measuring all, or most, of the angles in the system. If one of the sides has been measured and the position of one end of this side and its azimuth (normally measured using astronomical observations) is known, then the coordinate positions of all the other points can be calculated. If the network covers a very large area then a similar azimuth, position and length may be measured at the far end of the scheme as a check on the accumulation of error. The primary network of a country is subsequently densified by secondary, tertiary and lower order systems so that there is a close network of coordinated points throughout the area.

See also SURVEYING.

Triassic System, occurs above the Permian and below the Jurassic Systems. It began about 235 million years ago and ended about 210 million years ago. It is sometimes grouped with the Permian System as the New Red Sandstone. Triassic rocks in Britain cover a larger area than any other system; they are found in the Midland and Cheshire Plains, stretching north-east of the Pennines to the Durham coast and north-west of the Pennines to Cumbria. Triassic rocks also occur in Gloucestershire, South Wales, Somerset, Devon and parts of Scotland.

The Triassic period in Britain was a time of widespread continental conditions, but marine rocks occur on the continent. In Germany the Trias is divided into the Bunter at the base, followed by the Muschelkalk and the Keuper. The Muschelkalk represents a marine incursion from the Tethys Sea lying to the south.

Tribe, term commonly used to denote a group of clans under a recognised chief. Anthropologists use it in a technical sense to refer to a single, indigenous, territorially-defined political unit.

Tribune, name given to certain Roman magistrates and other officials, of whom the most important were the *tribuni plebis*, tribunes of the plebeians, whose office dated from 493 BC. At first their power was small and there were only two (increased to ten c.449), but soon they became formidable and

not only preserved the rights of the people, but could summon assemblies, propose laws, stop the deliberations of the Senate, and even veto its decrees and those of all other magistrates. Their authority was restricted by Sulla; but their privileges were restored by Pompey and Cotta. Augustus accepted the tribunician power for himself, and it was conferred upon all later emperors until Constantine, who abolished it. Other officials bearing the title were: (1) *tribuni militum*, officers in the Roman Army; (2) *tribuni cohortium praetoriarum*, officers of the Praetorian Guard; (3) *tribuni aerarii*, keepers of the military chest to defray the expenses of the army; (4) *tribuni voluptatum*, who had charge of popular entertainments.

Tribune, in architecture, either: (1) the apse of a basilican church; or (2) a rostrum; or (3) a gallery in a church.

Triceratops, a genus of Upper Cretaceous horned dinosaurs of the Ceratopsian group of the order Ornithischia. They were massive quadrupeds, up to 6 m long, with large heavy skulls extended into a neck frill at the rear, and with horns on the snout.

Trichinosis, or trichiniasis, a disease caused by the parasitic nematode *Trichinella spiralis*, which is found chiefly in man, the pig and the rat. The parasite finds its way into man from infected pork which has not been properly cooked. The young forms are encysted in the muscular fibres of the pig, and when the pork is eaten and the cysts reach the intestines, the calcified cyst capsule dissolves to set free the parasites, which grow rapidly and reproduce in enormous numbers. The young trichinae then develop and bore through the intestinal walls, ultimately reaching the muscles, where they become encysted by the secretion of lime salts. They are then quiescent, and can develop further only by reaching the intestines of another host if the present host is eaten. The acute symptoms of the disease are caused by the migration of the trichinae from the intestines. The early indications are nausea, fever and loss of appetite; later, exhausting diarrhoea may occur, together with delirium, swollen eyelids and tenderness and pain in the muscles. Preventive measures are important; meat should be regularly inspected and condemned if infected.

Trichomoniasis is an infection of the human genital tract with the parasitic protozoan, *Trichomonas vaginalis*. Infection is usually spread during sexual intercourse and produces a mild and chronic non-specific urethritis in the male, but an intensely irritating inflammation of the vagina and vulva in females, associated with a copious, white vaginal discharge. Treatment with metronidazole (Flagyl) by mouth is usually effective.

Trier (French *Trèves*), city in the Rhineland-Palatinate, Federal Republic of Germany, on the Moselle, near the Luxembourg border, 115 km west of Mainz. It was founded by the Emperor Augustus c.15 BC as *Augusta Treverorum*, and during the 3rd and 4th century was frequently an imperial residence. Trier has more important Roman remains than any other place in Northern Europe. The cathedral, rebuilt from a Roman basilica, was extended in the 12th and 13th centuries, and also has Baroque additions. Trier is an

important centre of the Moselle wine trade. Its main industries are tyres, machinery, artificial fibres, food, tobacco and beer. It is a river port (the Moselle was opened to navigation in 1964) and also a tourist centre. Population (1980) 95,736.

Trieste (Slovenian *Trst*; ancient *Tergeste*), seaport on the Gulf of Trieste at the head of the Adriatic Sea, 110 km north-east of Venice. It is the capital of the Italian region of Friuli-Venezia Giulia. It was settled by the Romans in 178 BC, and soon became a prosperous port. In the 13th and 14th centuries, it was controlled by Venice, and in 1382 it submitted to Austrian suzerainty. After 1719 it was a free port. During the 19th century it developed greatly, and was an important outlet for Austria. For long a centre of Italian irredentism, it was occupied by Italy in 1918, and formally ceded to Italy in 1920. There are shipyards, iron and steel works and oil refineries. Machinery, textiles, foodstuffs, spirits, paper and paints are manufactured. The city is a centre of shipping and marine insurance, and its port (with three basins) extends for 13 km along the Gulf of Trieste. It is the start of a major European oil pipeline to Ingolstadt in the Federal Republic of Germany. Population (1980) 257,697.

Territory of Trieste. At the end of the Second World War the city of Trieste and its environs were the subject of a dispute between Italy and Yugoslavia. As a compromise, under the terms of the Italian Peace Treaty of February 1947, the Free Territory of Trieste was formed, comprising the city and an Adriatic coastal strip. It was divided between Italy and Yugoslavia in 1954.

Trifolium, a genus of the Leguminosae (the pea family), including *T. pratense*, red clover; *T. arvense*, hare's-foot; *T. hybridum*, alsike; *T. repens*, white or Dutch clover; and *T. campestre*, hop trefoil, which are important fodder crops and often planted as ley pasture.

Triforium, or blind storey, in Romanesque and Gothic aisled churches, the stage of wall between the top of the nave arcade and the bottom of the clerestory, usually pierced with open arcading, with a wall passage behind; the term is often misapplied to a gallery or tribune.

Trigonometry, in its primary meaning, signifies the measurement of triangles; it has a much wider scope, however, embracing all types of geometric and algebraic investigations by means of trigonometric functions. The subject arose out of the study of astronomy, and was originated by the Greek astronomer Hipparchus (c.160 BC).

The trigonometric functions are defined by the following ratios of the lengths of the sides of a right-angled triangle with an acute angle.

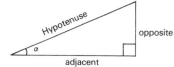

$\sin\alpha$ = opposite/hypotenuse
$\cos\alpha$ = adjacent/hypotenuse
$\tan\alpha$ = opposite/adjacent = $\sin\alpha/\cos\alpha$.

sin, cos and tan are abbreviations of sine, cosine and tangent, respectively. Sine and cosine are linked by Pythagoras' theorem

(hypotenuse)^2 = (adjacent)^2 + (opposite)^2
= {(cosα)^2 + (sin α)^2} (hypotenuse)^2
i.e. 1 = (cos α)^2 + (sin α)^2.

It is usual to write (cosα)^2 as cos$^2\alpha$ etc. Triangles that are not right-angled can be dealt with by using the following formulae.

$a^2 = b^2 + c^2 - 2bc$ cos$A$. (cosine rule)
$a/\sin A = b/\sin B = c/\sin C$. (sine rule)

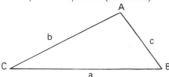

A, B and C are angles; a, b and c are the corresponding opposite sides.

The trigonometrical functions for an obtuse angle, β (between 90° and 180°) are defined as:

sinβ = sin($\pi - \alpha$) = sinα
cosβ = cos($\pi - \alpha$) = $-$cosα
tanβ = tan($\pi - \alpha$) = $-$tanα.

where π radians = 180°; this can be extended for reflex angles (between 180° and 360°). It is found that trigonometrical functions repeat themselves at periods of 2π(360°) for sines and cosines and π(180°) for tangents.
It is sometimes easier in calculations to use the following three reciprocal functions:

cosecα = 1/sinα
secα = 1/cosα
cotα = 1/tanα.

The abbreviations are for cosecant, secant and cotangent respectively.
Functions of Complementary Angles. In a right-angled triangle with an acute angle α, the other acute angle is equal to $\frac{1}{2}\pi - \alpha$. Applying the elementary definitions to that angle gives the following relations:

sin($\frac{1}{2}\pi - \alpha$) = cosα
cos($\frac{1}{2}\pi - \alpha$) = sinα
tan($\frac{1}{2}\pi - \alpha$) = 1/tanα = cotα.

Addition and Other Formulae. The following identities are true for all values of x and y.

sin ($x \pm y$) = sin$x$ cos y $\pm$ cos x sin y
cos ($x \pm y$) = cos x cos y $\mp$ sin x sin y
tan ($x \pm y$) = (tan x $\pm$ tan y)/(1 $\mp$ tan x tan y)
sin $2x$ = 2sin x cos x
cos $2x$ = cos$^2 x -$sin$^2 x$
tan $2x$ = 2 tan x/(1 $-$ tan$^2 x$)
sin $\frac{1}{2}x$ = $\pm\sqrt{\{\frac{1}{2}(1 - \cos x)\}}$
cos $\frac{1}{2}x$ = $\pm\sqrt{\{\frac{1}{2}(1 + \cos x)\}}$
tan $\frac{1}{2}x$ = sin x/(1 + cos x)
         = (1 $-$ cos x)/sin x
1 + tan$^2 x$ = sec$^2 x$
1 + cot$^2 x$ = cosec$^2 x$.

Where alternative signs are given, take either both upper signs or both lower signs.
Three-dimensional and Spherical Trigonometry. The methods of elementary trigonometry can be used to solve problems in three dimensions by considering triangles in different planes that have a side in common. Spherical triangles can be solved using the trigonometric functions, though the formulae are not the same as those employed for plane triangles.

Trilling, Lionel (1905–76), US critic. He held various teaching positions at Columbia University after 1931, becoming a professor in 1948. His best-known work is *The Liberal Imagination*, 1950.

Trillium, a genus of perennial plants in family Liliaceae from Asia and North America, with thick rhizomatous stems, and a solitary nodding white, pink or purple flower borne in the centre of a whorl of leaves. *T. grandiflorum*, the wake robin, is often grown in gardens.

Trilobites, an extinct group (Trilobito-morpha) of marine Palaeozoic arthropods in which the dorsal exoskeleton is divided into three lobes. Longitudinally, the dorsal shield is also divided into three distinct parts, the head or cephalon, the flexible thorax, and the tail or pygidium. The body was divided into segments, each bearing a pair of appendages, but these are only rarely preserved. Some trilobites were burrowing or bottom-dwelling forms, while others were planktonic (floating). Highly developed trilobites occur in the oldest Cambrian rocks; they reached their acme in Ordovician times, and died out in the Permian. They are valuable as index fossils.

Trimurti, in Indian religion, the later Hindu triad, Brahmā, Vishnu and Śiva, considered as an inseparable unity. Trimurti implies the unity of the three principles of creation, preservation and destruction, and is an expression of philosophical, rather than popular belief. Trimurti as the representation of the Hindu triad consists of a human body with three heads: Brahmā in the middle, Vishnu on the right and Śiva on the left.

Trincomalee, seaport on the north-east coast of Sri Lanka, with an excellent harbour. It is the site of the Temple of the Thousand Columns, a pilgrimage resort, reduced to ruins by the Portuguese during the 17th century. It was a British naval base in Ceylon during the Second World War, and was taken over by the government in 1957. Population (1981) 44,913.

Trinidad and Tobago
Area: 5129 km²
Population: 1,157,000
Capital: Port-of-Spain

Trinidad and Tobago, two islands forming the southernmost part of the West Indies, Trinidad lying within sight of Venezuela, its companion island of Tobago being 32 km to the north-east. Trinidad has an area of 4828 km² and is crossed by three mountain ranges, the highest point being El Cerro del Aripo at 940 m. Tobago has an area of 301 km², a range of conical hills and ridges running along its length giving rise to rugged country reaching a height of 576 m.
The combined population of the islands was estimated at 1,157,000 in 1979. In the 1970 census the population accounted for a great diversity of nationalities and races: Africans, 43 per cent; Indians, 40 per cent; Europeans, 1 per cent; Chinese, 1 per cent; others, 15 per cent.
Until the 20th century Trinidad's economy relied mainly on the cocoa and sugar crops; but in recent times oil and asphalt deposits have greatly increased her source of wealth. Trinidad is the leading Caribbean producer of oil. The government investments include an aluminium smelter, increased domestic food production, and the development of industries such as plastics, electronics, fertilisers, iron and steel and petrochemicals. Sugar, molasses, rum, fruit juices and textiles are also important.
Under the 1976 republican constitution, the head of state is a president elected in secret ballot by members of both houses of parliament. This body consists of a Senate and a House of Representatives.
History. For almost two centuries after its discovery by Columbus in 1498 the island remained undeveloped. Under Spain in 1783 a royal proclamation was issued by which extraordinary advantages were offered to foreigners of all nations to settle in Trinidad, on condition that they were Roman Catholics. The result was a large influx of population, which was soon augmented by many French families who were driven from St Domingo, Haiti, and elsewhere, in consequence of the French Revolution. On 18 February 1797 articles of capitulation were signed by the Spanish by which Britain's sovereignty over the island was recognised. The final cession of the colony took place in 1802 under the Treaty of Amiens.
In August 1962 Trinidad, with Tobago, became an independent state within the Commonwealth, Eric Williams being the first Prime Minister.
The country became a republic in 1976.

Trinitrotoluene (TNT), highly explosive chemical, $C_6H_2(NO_2)_3CH_3$, largely used in the two world wars. It is a pale yellow crystalline solid, melting-point 80·8°C, prepared by acting upon toluene with a mixture of concentrated sulphuric and nitric acids. It combines high explosive power with a good degree of safety in handling and ease of manufacture and utilisation. It is used mixed with ammonium nitrate and aluminium, or as a commercial blasting explosive.
See also EXPLOSIVES.

Trinity, the highest mystery of the Christian faith, the doctrine that God, while one in nature and being, is three distinct persons, the Father, the Son and the Holy Spirit. In the Old Testament this doctrine is absent, and in the New Testament the synoptic gospels contain only one convincing reference (Matt. xxviii. 19); but there are many examples in the Gospel according to St John and the Epistles. The development of this concept was the work of the early centuries, and the clear expression of the doctrine was the fruit of Greek thought. In the West the great exponent of Trinitarian doctrine is St Augustine of Hippo (*De Trinitate*). The fullest expression, however, is found in the *Quicunque Vult*, or Athanasian Creed.

Trinity House, see CORPORATION OF TRINITY HOUSE.

Trinity Sunday, the first Sunday after Pentecost, or Whitsunday, observed by the Roman Catholic and Anglican churches. Gervase of Canterbury says that St Thomas Becket instituted it in England soon after his consecration in 1162. It was made a universal observance by John XXII.

Trinidad and Tobago. *Port of Spain, on the site of an old Indian village, has been capital since 1783.*

Triple Jump, see JUMPING.

Triple Point, the point of temperature and pressure at which the liquid, solid and vapour phases of a substance can coexist in equilibrium.

Tripoli, seaport, capital and largest city of Libya in North Africa. It is also the capital of Tripolitania, a region of Libya. Situated on a promontory of the Mediterranean, 600 km west of Benghazi, old Tripoli is a typical Moorish city. It is at the junction of caravan routes to Tombouctu (Timbuktu), Lake Chad and Darfur, and three railway lines diverge from it to Zuara, Garian and Tagiura. The port exports fruit, olive oil, and is a fishing port. Population (1973) 735,000.

Tripoli (ancient *Tripolis*), town of the Lebanon, 65 km north-east of Beirut, its port being El Mina. It was founded about the 7th century BC and was the capital of Tripolis, a Phoenician federation of three cities (Sidon, Tyre, Aradus). A varied trade is carried on including oranges and cotton. The oil refinery is important as it is the terminus of the pipeline from Iraq. Population (1978) 175,000.

Tripolitania, region of Libya, stretching from the Mediterranean some 1300 km into the Sahara Desert. Total population (1970) 1,141,000. The greater part of the coastline is low and sandy, and unfit for harbourage. There are no rivers of importance. Along the coast all kinds of Mediterranean fruit, palms, olives, etc., are produced. The hinterland grows barley, wheat, olives, tobacco, mulberries, figs, almonds, dates and the vine. There is good pasture land for cattle and sheep. Farther inland are sand dunes, which during the Italian occupation were afforested with poplar, pine, acacia and robinia; next comes the mountain district, which produces vines, figs and olives. The sub-desert zone, still farther inland, produces only alfalfa, and farther south still is the desert itself, barren save for a few fertile oases. Libya's major oil-fields are in the Sirte Basin, not far inland from the Mediterranean coast. Other centres are Sirte, Aziez, Nofilia, Misurata, Homs and the oasis of Gadàmes.

Roman Tripolitania enjoyed a long period of prosperity. It was rich in grain and olive oil, and supplied one-third of the corn imported by Rome. In later centuries Arabs from the east conquered Tripolitania. During the 16th century it came under Turkish rule, and in 1835 was made into a vilayet of the Ottoman Empire. Tripolitania was annexed by Italy in 1911 and united to Cyrenaica in 1938 to form Italian Libya.

Tripos, final examination for the honours degree at Cambridge University. The name recalls the three-legged stool (Greek *tripous*) on which an 'ould bachelour' sat in front of the Proctors to argue with the candidate. The 'ould bachelour' was known as Mr Tripos and made a satirical speech in Latin on the subject of the examination, which in the early days was mathematics.

Triptych (Greek, threefold), a tablet, picture or altarpiece, made in three sections that fold together.
See also DIPTYCH.

Tripura, former Indian princely state and Union Territory of India from 1957, and since 1972 a state. It is located east of Bangladesh, area 10,477 km², and contained 2,060,190 people in 1981, mostly hill tribes who practise shifting cultivation of hill rice, millet, maize and fruits. Timber, jute and cotton are also produced. The capital is Agartala.

Trisagion (Greek *tris*, thrice; *hagios*, holy), short chant in the Eucharistic liturgies of the Eastern churches, so called from the threefold inclusion of the word *hagios*. In the Western churches it is found in the liturgy of Good Friday at the 'adoration of the cross'.

Tristan, or Tristram, hero of a tragic love story, later attached to Arthurian legend. Tristan wins Iseult (also Isolt, Isolde) of Ireland as a bride for his uncle Mark, King of Cornwall, but a magic potion, intended for the bridal pair, is mistakenly given to Tristan and Iseult, who are thereafter bound by love. After many adventures, Tristan leaves for Brittany and marries Iseult of the White Hands. Wounded by a poisoned weapon, he sends for his love, who alone can save him. If she comes, her ship is to show white sails; if not, black. She comes, but his jealous wife reports seeing black sails. Tristan dies of despair, and Iseult dies of grief at his side. From their graves two trees grow and intertwine.

Tristan da Cunha, best known island of a group discovered by the Portuguese navigator of that name, lying in latitude 37°6′S and longitude 12°2′W, some 3218 km west of the Cape of Good Hope. Area 98 km². The other islands, Inaccessible, Nightingale, and Gough Islands or Diego Alvarez, are uninhabited. They are British possessions which in 1938 were made dependencies of St Helena. Tristan da Cunha, a volcano (2060 m) with a crater lake near its summit, was annexed by a military force in 1816. When the garrison was withdrawn in 1817 William Glass, a corporal of artillery, and his wife elected to remain, and they were joined by two ex-naval men; these, with some later arrivals were the founders of the present settlement. Until 1880 the settlement thrived, being on a main sailing route, but with the replacement of sail by steam it became isolated. In 1961 the volcano, believed extinct, erupted and the islanders were evacuated to Britain. After two years, following a secret ballot, all but 14 returned to the island, but in 1966 some 40 returned to Britain, leaving a population of 294. They keep cattle, sheep and poultry, and grow potatoes, living in the settlement of Edinburgh at the north of the island.

Triton, legendary son of Poseidon and Amphitrite, represented as human above the waist and dolphin below, usually blowing a shell to raise or calm a storm.

Triumph, highest honour accorded to a victorious commander in republican Rome. Only a dictator, a consul, or a praetor holding imperium was entitled to the distinction, and then only after success in true warfare, not rebellion, civil strife, etc. The honour with necessary expenses was granted by the Senate, who received the victorious general outside the city. The celebration took the form of a procession, led by the Senate, to the Capitol through the city. Next came trumpeters, then the spoils and trophies, and the crowns presented to the general by provincial towns. Following these came the sacrificial bulls, captives in chains, lictors, musicians and priests. Then the triumphal car, gilded, garlanded, and drawn by white horses; in this stood the general wearing the garb of the Capitoline Jupiter, the purple *tunica palmata* and the *toga picta*, the former decorated with palm shoots, the latter with golden stars. An ivory sceptre surmounted by a golden eagle was carried in the left hand, a branch of bay in the right. Over the general's head a slave held the golden crown of Jupiter. Then followed the soldiers. At the Capitol, sacrifice was made, and general festivity followed in the city.

Triumviri, in the Roman republic, were boards of three magistrates. The most famous triumvirates were (1) that of Caesar, Pompey and Crassus in 60 BC (which was constitutionally not a triumvirate at all, merely a political alliance); and (2) that of Antony, Lepidus and Octavian (Augustus), which lasted from 43 BC to 33 BC (though Lepidus was deposed in 36 BC).

Trivandrum, capital of Kerala state, India. It has many palaces: there is a legend that each maharaja built a new one. Its industries include rubber products, chemicals and textiles, and there is an international airport. Population (1981) 499,168.

Trobriand Islands, a small cluster of islands in north-west Melanesia. The inhabitants are among the anthropologically best-known peoples in the world, due to the writings of Bronislaw Malinowski. The islands are administered by Papua New Guinea.

Troglodytes, general Greek name for un-civilised cave dwellers of the Caucasus, Ethiopia, and along the south Red Sea coast of Egypt.

Trogon (Greek *trōgein*, to gnaw), a genus of birds, family Trogonidae, order Trogoni-formes, widely distributed in tropical and subtropical regions, especially in America. They are about the size of a thrush, and have soft plumage of varied and generally brilliant colouring, particularly marked in the quetzal, and spasmodic flight. They are primarily birds of woodland, living in trees, and feeding mainly on insects, arthropods, and fruit.

Troilus, legendary son of Priam, King of Troy, who was killed in battle or taken captive by Achilles. The story of Troilus and Cressida is of medieval origin.
See also BRISEIS.

Trois-Rivières, town of Quebec, Canada, on the northern shore of the St Lawrence river, at the mouth of the St Maurice river. It is a natural ocean port. Trois-Rivières was founded in 1634, and the first Canadian manufacturing industry, 'The Old Forges', was established there in 1737. The city is now a large producer of newsprint, metals and textiles. Population (1980) 50,000.

Trojan Planets, a group of minor planets having the same orbital period as Jupiter. In 1772 Lagrange showed that a large body (the Sun), a small body (Jupiter), and a very small body of negligible mass (a minor planet) will, if situated at the vertices of an equilateral triangle, remain in that relative position while revolving about the centre of gravity of the system. There are two Lagrangian points, one east, the other west of Jupiter, and a number of minor planets have been found near each. They have been named after Homeric heroes, those to the west of Jupiter mainly after Trojans and those to the east after Greeks.

Trojan War, see ACHILLES; ATREIDS, LEGEND OF THE; MENELAUS.

Troll, or Trold (Old Norse, demon, giant), in Scandinavian folklore an ogre (sometimes a gnome) of either sex with evil powers which can only be exercised at night. In English stories many of the giants (as in Jack and the Beanstalk) and gnomes are descendants of trolls in Scandinavian folklore.

Trollope, Anthony (1815–82), English novelist and civil servant. He became a clerk in the Post Office in 1834 and in 1841 took a surveyorship in Ireland, where he acquired a taste for hunting, shown in his stories. He published his first novel, *The Macdermots of Ballycloran* in 1847. Appointed inspector of postal deliveries, Trollope toured England on horseback for two years. He instituted pillar-boxes in 1853, made official visits to Egypt and the West Indies, 1858, and on his return published *The West Indies and the Spanish*

Trompe l'oeil. A mural at Plas Newydd, Isle of Anglesey, painted by Rex Whistler, 1936.

Main, 1859, a book of shrewd comments on life there. He visited the United States in 1862 and published *North America*. He left the Post Office in 1867. He visited Australia, 1871–72, and South Africa, 1878, later writing books about those countries. Meanwhile, through serials published in the *Cornhill*, the *Fortnightly* and the *Pall Mall Gazette*, he had become a popular novelist. His greatest work is to be found in his two series: the 'Barchester' series, among which are *The Warden*, 1855; *Barchester Towers*, 1857; *Doctor Thorne*, 1858; and *The Small House at Allington*, 1862–64: and the 'Political' or 'Palliser' novels, including *Phineas Finn*, 1867–69; *The Eustace Diamonds*, 1871–73; *The Prime Minister*, 1875–76.

Trombone, brass wind instrument, developed from the medieval sackbut, made in five sizes from soprano to contrabass, of which only the tenor-bass is normally used today. The trombone's most characteristic feature is the slide, by means of which the tube can be adjusted to different lengths in seven positions, so that all the notes of the chromatic scale can be produced as natural harmonics. The intonation is not fixed, but depends on the player's ear and skill. The compass of the tenor-bass is from C below the bass stave to about C on the treble stave. In the 19th century valve trombones were invented and gained favour in military and brass bands as being easier to play, though inferior in tone. It never gained favour in Western Europe.

Tromp, Maarten Harpertszoon (1597–1653), Dutch admiral, associated with the 17th-century struggle for command of the seas between the Dutch and the British. In 1639 he destroyed a large Spanish squadron off Gravelines, and the same year defeated the combined fleets of Spain and Portugal off the English coast. When war broke out with Britain he was beaten by Blake in May 1652, but in November he encountered Blake off Dover and this time got the best of the fight. On 18 February 1653, while convoying mer-

chantmen, he kept up a running fight with the combined fleets of Blake, Monck and Deane, and had the worst of the encounter. He again appeared in the Channel in July 1653, and in a fierce battle with the British under Monck on 31 July, Tromp was shot through the heart.

Trompe l'oeil, a skilful painting technique, employed since classical times, where an artist aims to reproduce objects so that the spectator is deceived into believing that he is seeing the objects themselves.

Tromsø, capital of the county of Troms, in the north of Norway, on Tromsø island. It is the chief port for Spitsbergen, and does an important trade in fish and fish products. There are Lapp settlements in the area. Population (1981) 46,454.

Trondheim, also called Nidaros, city and seaport in Norway, and former capital; it lies at the mouth of the Nid, on Trondheim Fjord, 135 km north-east of Kristiansund. It is Norway's third biggest city. From early times the coronation of the kings of Norway took place in its celebrated cathedral, but the importance of the city began to wane after the Reformation. Population (1981) 134,976.

Troop, originally the unit of cavalry corresponding to the company in the infantry. It now corresponds to the infantry platoon, and is hence a subaltern's command in armoured regiments.

Trooping the Colour, a British military ceremony, held annually on Horse Guards Parade in London on the sovereign's official birthday. The colour or flag of a chosen regiment is carried in parade; this was originally done so that foreign mercenaries could learn to recognise it in battle.

Tropic, the latitude at which the Sun is overhead on the June solstice (Tropic of Cancer, 23 30′N) and the December solstice (Tropic of Capricorn, 23 30′S). 'The tropics' also describes the area lying between these latitudes.

Tropical Hygiene, see HYGIENE; TROPICAL MEDICINE.

Tropical Medicine. Owing chiefly to climatic conditions and poverty, many diseases rare or unknown in temperate and colder regions are common in the tropics. The tropical climate favours a great variety of parasites causing serious diseases in man. The parasites are transmitted directly from person to person by food and drinking water contaminated with faeces; by water harbouring parasites discharged from snails; by water containing crustacea infected with parasites; or by blood-sucking insect vectors which inoculate parasites when they bite. Other tropical diseases such as beri-beri and pellagra are due to deficiencies in diet.

The microscope made possible the identification and study of minute parasites. It led to the discovery of the causative organisms and transmission of such diseases as malaria, sleeping sickness (trypanosomiasis), leprosy and amoebic dysentery. The chief diseases due to protozoa are malaria, black-water fever, kala-azar (leishmaniasis), sleeping sickness and amoebic dysentery. Tsetse flies, carriers of the trypanosomes of sleeping sickness, are confined to Africa. Relapsing fever is caused by spirochaetes carried by ticks and lice. Typhus fevers are divided into three groups according to their transmission by lice, ticks and mites. Diseases due to viruses are yellow fever and dengue, transmitted by mosquitoes, and sandfly fever, carried by sandflies (*Phlebotomus*). Plague, a pandemic disease discovered by Kitasato and Yersin to be caused by the bacterium *Yersinia pestis*, is transmitted by rat fleas. Cholera, a waterborne disease, causes serious epidemics with a high mortality rate. Most of the above diseases are treated by drugs. Leprosy, an ancient disease long considered incurable, was discovered by Hansen (1874) to be due to *Mycobacterium leprae*. Brilliant research has been carried out in connection with the various parasitic worms causing ancylostomiasis, filariasis, guinea-worm, schistosomiasis and other diseases. The antibiotics, which have proved effective against many bacterial infections, and the powerful insecticides represent probably the most important of the recent advances in tropical medicine. Much is being done by the WHO to assist various tropical countries in introducing their own health measures.

Tropism, measurable movements made by various plant parts in response to certain environmental stimuli, the direction of the response being directly related to the direction of the stimulus. These stimuli are normally light (phototaxis) and gravity. When shoots and roots are displaced from their normal growing position differential growth occurs which causes the shoot tip to curve upward, the root tip downward, and the vertical positions are re-established. Many leaves behave similarly. This phenomenon is known as geotropism. In general, roots are positively geotropic, growing towards the gravitational pull, but many leaves and shoots are negatively geotropic.

Tropopause, see ATMOSPHERE.

Troposphere, see ATMOSPHERE.

Trossachs ('bristled terrain'), picturesque glen in Central Region of Scotland, between Lochs Katrine and Achray. This rugged and narrow defile is about 3 km in length, and overlooking it are Ben Venue, 729 m, and Ben A'an, 564 m.

Trotsky, Lev Davidovich, real surname Bronstein (1879–1940), Russian politician. He became prominent during the Revolution of 1905 as chairman of the St Petersburg Soviet, was arrested, but escaped abroad, where he tried to reunite all Russian Social Democratic factions, continuing the struggle against Lenin's dictatorial tactics. During the First World War Trotsky, with Martov, led the internationalist wing of the Mensheviks. After the February Revolution in 1917 he embarked for Russia, joined the Bolsheviks, and became Lenin's chief partner in organising the October Revolution. In 1917–18 he was commissar for foreign affairs. From 1918 to 1925 he was commissar for war, the chief organiser and leader of the Red Army in the Civil War. He was a Politburo member 1919–27, and repeatedly opposed Lenin. After Lenin's death Trotsky was ousted from power in Russia and in the world Communist movement by Stalin, Zinoviev and Kamenev, but continued to fight back, later joining forces with Zinoviev and Kamenev in the 'combined opposition' until he was expelled from the party in 1927, and from Russia in 1929. During the Great Purge he was accused of conducting espionage and subversive activities. He was murdered, probably by Stalin's agents, in Mexico City. His works include *The Revolution Betrayed*, 1937; and *Stalin*, 1946.

Troubadour, Provençal poet of the 12th and 13th centuries. Troubadours were required to *trobar*, that is, to compose songs, both words and music. Some of the troubadours were of high social standing; others were court poets, patronised and protected by the nobles of the Midi. Their main theme was that of *amour courtois*.

The maturity and technical perfection (complex stanza and rhyme patterns) of troubadour verse raise the question of its origins; folk-songs, late Latin verse, Arab literature and religious hymns may all have played a part, but none of these hypotheses has yet been substantiated and the question remains open. The influence of the troubadours was felt in Portugal, England and Germany (in the works of the Minnesingers). In northern France, their influence is seen in the works of the *trouvères*, lyric poets of the late 12th and 13th centuries.

See also PROVENÇAL LITERATURE.

Trout, several species of widely distributed freshwater fishes of the salmon family Salmonidae in order Salmoniformes. The colouring is variable, ranging from almost black to light olive, according to habitat, with the characteristic black or red spots. The eggs are laid in the gravel of streams, in winter, and hatch three to four months later, but the fish may move into lakes at other times. They feed chiefly on insects, their larvae, and small fish. Their size depends mainly on the abundance of the food supply; trout of over 9 kg have been caught, but the normal size is below half a kilogram.

The trout is prized for its culinary and sporting qualities, and is commercially bred and reared on fish farms to stock streams. The rainbow trout (*S. irideus*), an American species introduced to Europe, is more commonly reared for the table. The life history of salmon and trout can be determined by microscopic examination of their scales on which marks indicate age, growth rate and spawning history.

Trout Fishing, see ANGLING.

Trowbridge, market and manufacturing town in Wiltshire, England, famous for its West of England cloths. In addition to the traditional woollen industry, Trowbridge has bacon curing and meat processing, brewing, mattress and furniture making, printing, building engineering, glove making, agricultural seed processing, and the manufacture of heating and ventilating appliances and meat and cream products. Population (1981) 22,984.

Troy, or Ilium, ancient city of Asia Minor in the district of Troas, forming the north-west of Mysia. The district, usually known as 'the Troad', was bounded on the west and north-west by the Aegean and the Hellespont, east by a ridge of Mount Ida, and south by the Gulf of Adramyttium. Its greatest length is about 64 km, and its breadth about the same. The central part is drained by the Menderes (formerly Scamander), which rises in Ida and reaches the Hellespont east of Cape Sigeum.

In classical legend, the earliest king of the country was Teucer. His daughter married Dardanus, a neighbouring chieftain. The Trojans were probably a Pelasgian race, possibly descended from Thracian immigrants; Dardanus was grandfather of Tros, whose son Ilus founded Ilium, or Troy, the largest and strongest settlement in the Troad. The next king, Laomedon, was succeeded by his son Priam, in whose reign the famous siege of Troy by the Greeks took place. This was to avenge the rape of Helen, wife of Menelaus of Sparta, by Priam's son Paris. The siege lasted nearly ten years, and ended with the sack of Troy, probably about 1250 BC. The story forms the background of Homer's *Iliad*, and part of Virgil's *Aeneid*. Once considered purely legendary, the main outline is now regarded as factual, the rape of Helen, perhaps, representing some act of piracy. Among the Greek heroes of the siege were Achilles, Agamemnon, Ajax, Diomedes, Menelaus and Odysseus; and among the Trojans, Aeneas and Hector.

The Hissarlik mound is almost certainly the site of ancient Troy. Explorations here by Schliemann (1870–90) and Dörpfeld (1893–1894) brought to light much valuable information. Remains of some nine different cities were discovered, buried one beneath another, the earliest dating from c.3000–2560 BC. Probably the beginning of the seventh phase in the history of the city was the Homeric Troy. There are traces of two Greek settlements (1000 BC–1st century BC), and of a new Ilium (1st century BC–AD 500).

See also AEGEAN CULTURE.

Troy Weight, see METROLOGY.

Troyes, French town, capital of the *département* of Aube, 150 km south-east of Paris, on the River Seine. In the Middle Ages it was the capital of Champagne. It has a fine cathedral, an agricultural market, textile industries, and manufactures machinery and foodstuffs. Population (1975) town, 75,500; conurbation, 126,611.

Troyon, Constant (1810–65), French painter. He was an accomplished landscape painter of the Barbizon School and excelled as a painter of cattle.

Trucial States, see UNITED ARAB EMIRATES.

Truck Acts. 'Truck' means the payment of wages in kind. In the early stages of industrialisation there was much opposition to this practice since it restricted the freedom of workers to spend their wages on goods and services of their own choice. The Truck Acts of 1831 made it an offence to make payment by delivery of goods and thus eliminated the worst effects of the system. This and subsequent Truck Acts have now been repealed.

Truck Farming (French *troquer*, to barter), an American term for large-scale vegetable production in contrast to market gardening which is the intensive, small-scale production of a wide range of vegetables.

Trudeau, Pierre Elliot (1919–), Canadian politician. He was elected to the Canadian Parliament in 1965 as a representative of the Federal Liberal party. In 1966 he became parliamentary secretary to the prime minister, Lester Pearson, and in 1967 minister of justice and attorney-general. He became leader of the Liberal party and prime minister of Canada in April 1968. Trudeau generally fared well in dealing with the problem of Quebec separatism as his electoral successes there in 1968, 1972 and 1974 indicate. He made a solid appeal to the young and exploited his charismatic touch to the full. He has worked consistently to keep Confederation intact, mainly by insisting on official bilingualism, by wealth-sharing arrangements among the provinces, and by strong federal leadership. In 1974 he steered clear of committing his party to anti-inflationary pay and prices policy, but after re-election he instituted a policy remarkably similar to this. His party was defeated in 1979 but he returned as prime minister in 1980. He resigned the premiership in 1984 and was succeeded by John Turner.

Trueman, Fred (1931–), English cricketer. A right-arm fast bowler of great hostility, he played for Yorkshire, 1949–68, and in 67 Tests for England, 1952–65. Through much of his Test career he formed a fine opening bowling partnership with J. B. Statham. In 1964, at the Oval, he became the first bowler to take 300 wickets in Test cricket; his final total was 307. In 1972 he retired from competitive cricket. Altogether he took 2304 wickets in first-class matches. His autobiography is *Ball of Fire*, 1976.

Truffaut, François (1932–), French film director. He started his career as a journalist and film critic, publishing the influential magazine *Cahiers du cinéma*, which helped to launch the *nouvelle vague*. His own films include *Les Quatre Cent Coups, Tirez sur le pianiste, Jules et Jim, Farenheit 451, La Sirène du Mississippi, L'Enfant sauvage, La Nuite Americaine* (*Day for Night*) and *The Last Métro*.

Truffles, the fruiting-body, usually underground, of fungi of order Tuberales in subdivision Basidiomycotina. The British truffle (*Tuber aestivum*) is found just below the surface in beech and oak plantations in the autumn. When mature it is hard, black and warted externally. Inside it is mottled with white and yellowish brown. The truffle used in France is *T. melanosporum*, and the garlic-scented truffle of Italy is *T. marginatum*.

Trujillo, capital of the department of La Libertad, and one of Peru's largest cities. Founded in 1534 by Diego de Almagro, it is the centre of an important sugar-producing area. Trujillo is being developed as an important engineering city, with motorcycles and tractor assembly plants, amongst others. Population (1972) 241,880.

Truman, Harry S. (1884–1972), 33rd President of the USA. As Democratic vice-president he succeeded to the presidency on Roosevelt's sudden death in April 1945. One of his first major acts was to authorise the use of the atomic bomb against Japan in August 1945. In 1947 he initiated what became known as the 'Truman Doctrine': the policy of helping countries threatened by, and anxious to resist, communism. Later in 1947 he supported his secretary of state, Gen. Marshall, in the plan to aid Europe, and in 1948 launched the Economic Co-operation Administration. Truman's re-election as president in 1948 was a great and unexpected personal triumph. In June 1950, immediately following the invasion of the South Korean Republic, he announced the armed intervention of the USA. Truman's second term in office ended stormily. There was disillusion because the Korean peace-talks had been, so far, unproductive, and a vociferous wave of criticism was levelled at the Democratic administration's treatment of communists. Truman announced that he would not stand for the presidency again and retired to private life.

Trumpet, a brass wind instrument consisting of a long narrow tube, bent twice on itself. The mouthpiece is cup-shaped, and the other extremity broadens into a bell. Until the invention of the valves in the 19th century the trumpet was capable of producing only the natural harmonic notes: the valves made it a chromatic instrument. The trumpets in modern use are usually in B flat or C, transposing a whole tone down or sounding as written respectively, the written compass being from below middle C to C above the stave in the treble clef.

Trumpet Creeper, two species of the genus *Campsis*, of the family Bignoniaceae. They are vines with trumpet-shaped orange flowers.

Trumpeter, *Psophia*, genus of South American birds related to the crane in order Gruiformes. *P. crepitans* is a bird of lustrous and brilliantly-coloured plumage and is often domesticated. There are three species; very little is known about any of them in the wild.

Truro, cathedral city in Cornwall, England, on the River Truro, a branch of the Fal, 14 km north of Falmouth and 446 km from London. The ancient diocese was re-established in 1876, and the cathedral was the first erected in Britain after the rebuilding of St Paul's in the reign of Charles II. Population (1981) 16,277.

Trustee Investments, term used to describe investments authorised by statute for the investment of trust money. The law on this matter was radically altered, in Britain, by the Trustee Investment Act 1961, the general object of which was to permit trustees to invest up to half their trust funds in ordinary shares of established companies with a view to preventing the erosion of the real value of the trust property by inflation. The act also imposes on trustees a statutory duty to take advice before investing.

Trusts and Trustees. In English law a trust is an obligation binding a person (called a trustee) to deal with property over which he has control (called the trust property) for the benefit of persons (called the beneficiaries) of whom he may himself be one, and any one of whom may enforce the obligation. A trustee may be either an individual (of adult years) or a corporation. The Public Trustee is a statutory corporation, especially created to act as a trustee. A custodian trustee is a type of trustee who merely holds the trust property without otherwise acting in the administration of the trusts. The powers of trustees include powers of investment, of managing, maintaining and insuring the trust property, and of employing agents, and also discretionary powers for the maintenance of infant beneficiaries out of income and the advancement of beneficiaries who are interested in capital. Trustees have power to recover their actual out-of-pocket expenses from the trust property, but in general cannot charge for their services. Such charges may however be authorised, e.g. by an express provision in the trust instrument. The duties of trustees include duties to preserve and invest the trust property, to keep a fair balance as between beneficiaries interested in capital and income respectively, to keep accounts, not to obtain any unauthorised personal advantage from the trust, and generally to act in good faith and in the best interests of their beneficiaries. If all the beneficiaries are of full age, they can put an end to the trust. The court has wide power to vary or terminate trusts.

Truth is that which is true. The term true, with its opposite false, is defined by Plato as follows: an account is true if it states things as they are, and false if it states things as they are not. This accords well with the way we generally use these words. This view has been called the correspondence theory of truth, in that it seems to define a statement as true if it corresponds to the facts. However, this is not of much use, since we have no other way of formulating facts except stating them. There have been other theories of truth. The coherence theory, for example, sees truth as residing in a statement hanging together with or fitting into a system. Thus in mathematics a statement counts as true if it follows from the appropriate axioms or basic assumptions; however, this cannot show that the axioms are true. The pragmatic theory defines truth as that which has useful consequences. However, some truths may in fact have harmful effects. Indeed it is impossible to find a formal prescription which will always issue in true statements.

Trypanosomiasis, a parasitic disease of human beings, which has two very different forms: sleeping sickness in Africa south of the Sahara, and Chagas's disease in the American continent. *Sleeping sickness* is caused by protozoan parasites of the family Trypanosomatidae. The protozoan parasites multiply asexually in the blood and tissue fluids of the human subject, and are ingested by tsetse flies of the genus *Glossina* which constitute the intermediate hosts or vectors. In the human, the trypanosomes multiply, produce attacks of fever, and eventually invade the central nervous system and brain, leading to a comatose condition immediately preceding death, which has given rise to the name sleeping sickness. Infection in West Africa is maintained in humans, but in East Africa game animals and domestic cattle form the animal reservoir. Sleeping sickness can be treated with a variety of drugs.

Chagas's disease of the New World is caused by *Trypanosoma cruzi*. Its distribution extends from Argentina and Chile north to Texas. The life cycle is basically similar to that of the African trypanosomes, but the vectors are kissing-bugs or assassin bugs of the family Reduviidae of the order Hemiptera. At present there is no fully effective treatment.

Tsar (Latin *Caesar*), title of the emperors of Bulgaria, Serbia and Russia.

Tsaritsyn, see VOLGOGRAD.

Tsarskoye Selo, see PUSHKIN.

Tschudi, Aegidius, or Gilg von (1505–72), Swiss chronicler. His *Chronicon helveticum, 1000–1470,* contains one of the principal accounts of William Tell.

Tselinograd (formerly *Akmolinsk*), capital of Tselinograd *oblast*, USSR, on the Ishim river. It has agricultural machinery works and rolling-stock repair depots. Population (1980) 234,000.

Tsetse Flies, see GLOSSINIDAE.

Tshekedi Khama, see KHAMA, SIR SERETSE.

Tshombe, Moise (1918–69), Congolese politician. He became prominent in Katangese and Congolese politics from 1956, and from 1960 to 1962 was premier of the breakaway province of Katanga, which he declared independent. After his forces were defeated by UN troops in 1963 he fled to Spain. In 1964 he was appointed premier of the Congo republic. He was dismissed by the Congolese president in 1965. He returned to Spain but was kidnapped and taken to house arrest in Algiers in 1967, where he subsequently died.

Tsimshians, North American Indian people, who live along the shores of the Pacific, facing Queen Charlotte Island. They live mainly by hunting and fishing. They now number about 6500.

Tsinan, see JINAN.

Tsinghai, see QINGHAI.

Tsingtao, see QINGDAO.

Tsuga, hemlock or hemlock spruce, a genus of evergreen conifers in family Pinaceae, of which *T. heterophylla*, western hemlock, *T. canadensis*, eastern hemlock, and *T. mertensiana*, mountain hemlock, are North American forest trees, now widely grown. They are valuable plants because their bark is used in tanning, they yield pitch, and the timber is strong and useful.

Tsukahara, Mitsuo (1947–), Japanese gymnast. He won gold medals at the 1972 Munich and 1976 Montreal Olympics in the high-bar and team championship. He also won the bronze medal at Munich for the rings, and at Montreal gained a silver for the vault and bronze medals for the parallel bars and the individual overall title. He is especially remembered for the 'Tsukahara' vault, characterised by a twisting somersault.

Tsunami, a Japanese word meaning tidal wave which is now used for the wave system generated by a sudden, impulsive movement of the ocean. They occur mainly after earthquakes of magnitude greater than 6·5 on the Richter scale, landslides and volcanic eruptions. Therefore, they can be described as seismic sea waves. Tsunamis occur principally in the Pacific Ocean where seismic activity is high, but have also been recorded in the North Atlantic and North Indian Oceans.

Once formed in the deep ocean, a tsunami looks like the ripple pattern set up by throwing a stone into a shallow pond. The concentric rings of crests and troughs propagate outwards from the impulse at a speed proportional to the square root of the ocean depth. Thus in the Pacific they can travel at between 600 and 800 km per hour and the wavelength, or distance between successive wave crests, can be several hundred kilometres. In the deep ocean, the height of tsunami waves is only one or two metres, and so usually pass unnoticed. As the waves run into shallower water, however, the height increases dramatically. Where the coastal features are extensive flat shores or V-shaped inlets, the tsunami waves can become 10–20 m high and form a series of between four and eight waves which come ashore at intervals of between 15 minutes and an hour.

Tsushima, island of Nagasaki-ken, Japan, situated south of Korea. It is mountainous, and really consists of two islands, the uniting neck being dry only at low tide. Area 682 km²; population (1970) 58,000. Main town, Izuhara.

Tsvetaeva, Marina Ivanovna (1892–1941), Soviet poet. Strongly anti-Bolshevik, she was allowed to emigrate in 1922, and her best poetry was composed abroad. Quarrels with the emigré literary world and extreme poverty partly prompted her return to the USSR with her family in 1939. After the execution of her husband and the arrest of her daughter, she hanged herself in 1941.

Tswana, western group of the Sotho people of Botswana and South Africa, numbering almost 2 million. The basic units of organisation are wards comprising lineally related groups. The Tswana are divided into several tribes and the men of each tribe form age sets. They practise farming and animal husbandry, although nowadays many have to seek wage labour in the towns.

Tuamotu Archipelago (also called Paumotu, Low or Dangerous Archipelago), group of islands in French Polynesia consisting of a dozen fairly large atolls and countless small atolls and reefs, scattered over 15° of longitude and 10° of latitude, east of the Society Islands. Area 774 km²; population (1977) 8,537. It is noted for its pearling grounds. It was on Raroia, one of this group, that the famous raft Kon-Tiki ended its voyage from Peru in 1947.

Tuareg, a Berber-speaking nomadic pastoralist people living in the southern Sahara and numbering about 400,000, some of whom are formed into tribal confederations. Their society is hierarchical and is divided into noble, vassal and craft classes. In the 15th century they traded with Portuguese West Africa and controlled trade routes across the Sahara, which they continued to do until the 20th century. Their name derives from the Arabic *tawarek*, meaning 'God forsaken', and is attributable to their reputation as raiders and marauders. The adult men all wear veils. Today many are Muslims.

Tuatara (*Sphenodon punctatus*), New Zealand lizard, the only living member of the Rhynchocephalia. The body is covered on the upper part with small scales and tubercles, a crest of spines running the length of the back. It is amphibious in habit, and usually spends the day in a burrow of its own excavation, hunting for insects, crustaceans, worms, and even small fish by night. The eggs are deposited in sand and usually take more than a year to hatch. This reptile has traces of a median third eye, the pineal organ, on the roof of the brain.

Tuba, the bass instrument of the saxhorn family, used in the orchestra as the bass of brass instruments. It has four or five valves, and a chromatic compass of three octaves from F an octave below the bass clef. It is the main bass instrument in brass and military bands.

Tuber, a stem tuber is a swollen section of a rhizome which contains a food store, as in the potato; a root tuber is a swollen food-storing root, as in the dahlia.

See also VEGETATIVE REPRODUCTION.

Tuberculosis, chronic disease of humans and some animals, infectious by contact, ingestion or inhalation, and caused by the bacterial

Tuareg. A festival in Djanet, Algeria. The men wear the teguelmoust, *a combined veil and turban.*

pathogen *Mycobacterium tuberculosis*. World-wide, it kills between 1 and 2 million people annually. The disease (also called consumption or phthisis) most commonly begins with a lung focus known as the primary lesion. No disability appears to be conferred by the primary infection. As well as in the lung, a primary focus or complex may become established from ingestion of tuberculosis organisms, as when drinking unpasteurised milk containing the bacteria. Although the vast majority of initial exposures follow such a pattern, in some individuals the infection may progress to more overt disease forms: pulmonary tuberculosis of a more progressive type; miliary tuberculosis, in which small tubercles of infection are widely disseminated throughout the body; or tuberculous meningitis.

Preventive measures include large-scale examination to detect early cases by chest X-ray and skin-tests. Control is by restriction of contact with infected persons, education concerning the dangerous airborne (inhalation) mode of transmission, effective and early treatment of active cases, careful disinfection of tuberculous infected materials, and adequate tracing of contacts. Treatment is by general supportive measures, rest, good food, freedom from stress, and antibiotics.

Tübingen, city in Baden-Württemberg, Federal Republic of Germany, in the Neckar valley, 30 km south-west of Stuttgart. It was once a free city of the empire. There are many picturesque streets and fine old buildings. A publishing centre, it also manufactures surgical instruments, machinery and textiles. Population (1971) 67,800.

Tubman, William Vacanarat Shadrach (1895–1971), Liberian politician and 18th President of Liberia. He led the fight of the tribes people against the established and privileged position of the Americo-Liberians (those of American descent). He became leader of the True Whig party, and in May 1943 won the presidential election. He was president of Liberia until his death in 1971, and his presidency was notable for the 'open door' economic policy and the continual efforts made to achieve social and political unification.

Tubuai, see AUSTRIAL ISLANDS.

Tucana, 'the Toucan', a southern constellation containing the Small Magellanic Cloud.

Tucker, Sophie (1884–1966), US actress and entertainer. She first appeared as a singer in her father's café in Hartford in 1905, then went into cabaret and variety in New York. She visited England for the first time in 1922, as a cabaret singer and music-hall artiste, and soon became tremendously popular in London and New York as a 'Red Hot Momma'. She was equally at home in sentimental numbers like 'Yiddisher Momma' and in songs like 'The Lady is a Tramp'.

Tucson, city of Arizona, USA situated 105 km north of the Mexican border, at 700–750 m altitude. The winter sunshine record is far superior to that of the Florida resorts, which makes Tucson a favoured winter home for many Americans. With the coming of the railway in 1880 and the University of Arizona in 1891, the city developed service and manufacturing industries. Population (1980) 330,537.

Tucumán, capital of Tucumán province, Argentina, also known as San Miguel de Tucumán. The town is beautifully situated on the plain at the foot of the Sierra de Aconquija. It is the largest and most important town in the north-west of Argentina. Its industrial activity is based on sugar and its various by-products. It is also an important rail centre. Population (1980) 497,000.

Tudor, surname of an English dynasty, founded by a Welshman, Owen Tudor, who married Catherine, widow of Henry V. By her he was the father of Edmund, Earl of Richmond, who married Margaret Beaufort, great-granddaughter of John of Gaunt. Their son gained the crown after defeating Richard III at Bosworth, and as Henry VII reigned from 1485 to 1509. The other Tudor monarchs were: Henry VIII (1509–47), Edward VI (1547–53), Mary (1553–58), and Elizabeth I (1558–1603).

Tuesday, the third day of the week, from Old Norse *Tý* or *Týr*, Mars, because the first hour of Tuesday was supposed to be ruled by the planet Mars—hence the French *mardi* for Tuesday.

Tuff, see PYROCLASTIC ROCKS.

Tug, or tugboat, any small craft equipped to tow larger vessels or trains of barges. A tug must have good manoeuvrability, and tends therefore to be a shortish vessel, often with twin screws. She must have adequate power, and for propulsive efficiency usually has a comparatively large slow-turning propeller giving a good grip on the water. Nowadays geared diesel engines are common. The appearance of the Thames tug, 24–36 m long, is typical, but in other parts of the world local needs have given rise to vessels of very different appearance. Salvage tugs must be especially seaworthy and powerful; they are fitted with heavy towing gear, pumps and fire-fighting equipment.

Tug-of-war, one of the oldest of English sports in which two teams of equal numbers (usually eight) pull against one another by means of a rope. The event was included in the 1900 Olympic Games, but was discontinued after 1920.

The rope used for competition must be 10 to 12·5 cm in circumference and, for a team of eight, at least 32 m long. A coloured tape is fixed exactly in the middle of the rope and, at a distance of 2 m on either side, white tapes are fixed. There are similar ground markings. A pull is successfully completed when one team has pulled the other so far forward that the loser's white tape lies over the winner's ground line.

Tugela, river of Natal, South Africa, which has its source in the Drakensberg mountains, flowing in a south-easterly direction to the Indian Ocean north of Durban. At Isandhlwana and Rorke's Drift on the Tugela, actions were fought in the Zulu War (1879).

Tula, capital city, economic centre of Tula *oblast*, USSR, and main industrial centre of the Moscow Coal Basin, on the main Moscow–Simferopol road. There are large metallurgical and engineering works, and (since the 16th century) metal-working industries, among them the famous Tula samovars. It is a railway junction. Known since 1146, it was made the provincial capital in 1775. Population (1980) 518,000.

Tulip, *Tulipa*, a genus of bulbous plants in family Liliaceae, found in Europe, temperate Asia and North Africa. The range of garden tulips is held to stem from *T. gesneriana*, and includes a wide variety of forms. *T. clusiana*, lady tulip, and *T. greigii* and *T. kaufmanniana*, the water-lily tulip, are also widely grown.

Tulip Tree, *Liriodendron tulipifera*, a tall American tree of the Magnoliaceae, bearing unusual saddle-shaped leaves and large fragrant flowers which superficially resemble those of the tulip. It has several varieties, and is the source of the American whitewood.

Tull, Jethro (1674–1741), English agricultural writer. He tried out many ideas collected on his travels abroad and invented the first corn drill of note. In 1733 his major work, *Horse-Hoeing Husbandry*, was published in which he discussed the advantages of hoeing crops grown in rows.

Tulsa, city of Oklahoma, USA, second city of the state, situated on the Arkansas river just east of its confluence with the Cimarron. In 1901 prospectors from Pennsylvania struck oil nearby and the city experienced an oil boom. It became a manufacturing and service centre with a wide range of industries. Population (1980) 360,919.

Tulsī Dās (1532–1623), Brahmin Hindi poet and religious reformer. He is said to have been abandoned during infancy and found by a wandering sādhu from whom he learned the Sanskrit epic *Rāmāyana*, story of the divine hero Rāma. After his marriage he became an ascetic himself and lived at Ayodhyā, where legend has it that Rāma told him in a dream to write the story of the *Rāmāyana* in the language of the common people. His version, called *Rāmcaritmānas*, was his greatest work and remains the most popular religious and epic poem in Hindi literature.

Tumbrel, or tumbril, ducking-stool which was used to punish scolding women. It consisted of a stool or chair at the end of a long pole, which could be swung over a pond and lowered. It was also used to punish transgressing bakers and brewers. The same name was applied to carts constructed with a tipping body, especially dung-carts, to the covered carts for tools in a train of artillery, and also to the execution carts used in the French Revolution.

Tummel, river and loch in Tayside Region, Scotland. From the east end of Loch Rannoch, the River Tummel broadens into Loch Tummel, 1 km wide and 11 km long.

Tumour, a swelling; a mass of cells, resembling those normally present, but differently arranged, and proliferating at the expense of the organism without serving any useful purpose.

Tumours are classed, according to the tissues of which they are composed, into: simple tumours of normal tissue; hollow tumours or cysts; and malignant tumours or cancer. The essential characteristics of simple and hollow tumours are that they grow and divide without destroying or invading the surrounding cells, which are simply pushed aside as the mass of the tumour grows. Malignant tumours, on the other hand, tend to invade the surrounding tissues. Cancer cells may also be disseminated by the blood and lymph channels to other parts of the body, giving rise to secondary or metastatic tumours.

Tumulus (Latin *tumere*, to swell), an ancient grave-mound.

See also BARROW.

Tun (weight), see METROLOGY.

Tuna, see TUNNY.

Tunbridge Wells, town in Kent, England. There was an Iron Age hill-fort at High Rocks but the town came into being with the discovery of chalybeate springs in 1606. The town was also famed for its local industry of Tunbridge ware (wood-mosaic). Population (1981) 44,821.

Tundra, term applied to a geographical region in the USSR, but now generic for all such regions. Primarily, it is a region which by reason of high latitude, permanently frozen subsoil, and strong cold winds, is almost destitute of trees. The soil is completely frozen, except for a depth of up to a metre during summer, at which season the surface water forms pools, lakes and marshes. Tundra soils cover approximately 4 per cent of the Earth's land area. Soil processes are dominated by the presence of permafrost which prevents the movement of water down the profile to depth. Water moves laterally and may cause the soil to move under soli-fluction. As water is unavailable for plant growth for much of the year, plants are small and stunted, and organic matter production is low and decomposes slowly. The vegetation consists of mosses, lichens, dwarf birch and willow, and an Alpine flora. Except for the reindeer, caribou and musk-ox, the fauna consists of small fur animals, sought by hunters and trappers.

Tung Oil, or Chinese wood oil (iodine value 168 ± 8) is obtained from the nut kernel of two trees, *Aleurites fordii* and *A. montana*, of family Euphorbiaceae indigenous to southeast China, Indo-China and Burma, and now cultivated in many parts of the world. Tung oil is generally pale yellow, but also appears on the market in various grades ranging from clear or 'white' for best quality to yellow, red and black, etc., for the lower grades; it has a characteristic odour and is thick and viscous. On standing or heating it poly-merises, and is used in quick-drying paints and varnishes. The component fatty acids of the oil are—saturated: total 3–7 per cent; un-saturated: oleic, 1–16 per cent; elaeostearic, 78–85 per cent. The press cake is poisonous, and is used only as a manure.

Tungsten, metallic chemical element, symbol W, atomic number 74, atomic weight 183·85; it occurs in nature as wolframite (iron manganese tungstate), scheelite (calcium tungstate), and wolfram ochre (tungsten trioxide). The metal can be obtained by reducing the trioxide on charcoal with hydrogen. It is a hard grey metal (melting point 3380°C, relative density 19·3). It is a very magnetic material, a feature used in concentrating the crude ores by a magnetic separator. It forms three oxides: WO_2, basic and a reducing agent; W_2O_5, blue in colour; and yellow WO_3, which gives rise to the tungstates when treated with alkalis. Tungsten is used largely for electric-lamp and thermionic-valve filaments. It alloys well with aluminium and with chromium. Well-known steels containing tungsten are

Tundra. Autumn colours of Arctostaphylos *on the coast of Hudson's Bay, Manitoba, Canada.*

characterised by being very strong and hard, and not losing the 'temper' when heated. They are especially valuable for high-speed cutting tools.

Tunic (Latin *tunica*), originally a long, white shirt-like garment with short sleeves, worn by the ancient Romans; in female attire it reached to the ankles, but for men it was somewhat shorter and worn under the toga. The word tunic is now also applied to any tight-fitting jacket, particularly that of the military uniform.

Tunicata, invertebrate marine animals that form a subphylum of phylum Chordata. There are about 1600 species. The adults are either pelagic (drifting with the sea currents) or sessile, fixed to the sea bottom, rocks, sea-weed or the bottom of a ship. They are covered by a protective coat (tunic). The larvae, which resemble tadpoles, have a stiff internal supporting rod, the notochord, which is present in all chordates. They may be close to the ancestral chordate.

Males and females are usually separate and the eggs are discharged into the water where the male fertilises them. Other forms of reproduction occur, including budding, in which a part of the adult is pinched off and grows into a new animal. The digestive and nervous systems are well developed. The circulatory system is interesting because the heart pumps the blood in one direction for a while, then reverses and circulates it the other way.

There are three classes. Ascidiacea, the sea squirts, are sessile, ranging from a few mm to 30 cm long. They have two openings at the top end of the animal, a siphon to take in water in order to extract food and oxygen, and a siphon to excrete water containing wastes. Larvacea includes the smallest tuni-cates, a few mm or less long. They retain the larval tadpole shape and excrete a cellulose covering that is much larger than the animal. They are luminous by night and brightly coloured by day. Thaliacea are pelagic tuni-cates that form colonies up to 4 m long. Some swim by taking in water at one end and ejecting it forcefully behind them.

Tunicle (Latin *tunicella*), less ornate form of the dalmatic (*tunica dalmatica*), worn by sub-deacons as a liturgical vestment over the alb.

Tuning-fork, small instrument for establishing pitch, invented in 1711 by John Shore. It retains pitch very accurately and also gives out a very pure sound, free from harmonic upper partials. It is often tuned to A above middle C which is used by orchestras as their fundamental tuning-note.

Tunis, capital of Tunisia, which stands on a bay of the same name, surrounded by lakes and marshes, 15 km from the sea and 450 km north-west of Tripoli. Its port is Goletta, but a channel opened in 1893 has made Tunis directly accessible to ocean vessels. In the centre of the old town is the Medina, the focus of trade and industry, built mainly from the ruins of the towns of Thunes, Carthage and Utica. Tunis has chemical works, a lead smelter and distilleries. Velvets, silks, linen and fez caps are also manu-factured. Population (1975) 505,400.

See also CARTHAGE.

Tunisia
Area: 164,000 km²
Population: 6,030,000
Capital: Tunis

Tunisia, Republic of, in North Africa, lies on the Mediterranean Sea coast, bounded on the west by Algeria and on the south by Libya. The total area is 164,000 km².

There is a narrow discontinuous coastal zone stretching from Bizerte in the north to the island of Jerba in the south. Some 54 per cent of Tunisia's population live in this zone, which is only 16 per cent of the total area. Here too are most of the large urban centres. The second zone is the mountain area of northern Tunisia, called the Tell. The third zone, the steppe, lies south of the Tell. The most important centre of population here is

Tunisia. *The old town of Tamerza near the Algerian border was destroyed by floods.*

Kairouan. The fourth zone is an area of desert sand, salt lake and bare mountain.

The total population in 1978 was estimated at 6,030,000. The capital is Tunis. The four main towns after Tunis are Sfax, Sousse, Bizerte and Kairouan.

Half the population are engaged in agriculture. Citrus fruit is grown in the north-east, the northern valleys are cultivated for cereals (wheat, barley, maize, oats and sorghum), the Sahel produces olives, the desert oases dates, and the central plateaus provide pasture for sheep, cattle and goats.

Tunisia's major industrial products are minerals. It is one of the world's biggest producers of phosphates. There are several deposits of oil, rich iron ore and lead, and zinc is also mined. Crude oil is refined for domestic consumption at Bizerte, and there is processing of local raw materials: food, wool, leather and minerals. Of the first, vegetable oil and sugar refining, fish canning and creameries are the most important.

The unit of currency is the Tunisian *dinar* of 1000 millimes.

The constitution of independent Tunisia was proclaimed on 1 June 1959. It declares the president of the republic to be head of state, head of the executive, and commander-in-chief of the armed forces.

The national assembly is elected every five years by direct universal suffrage. All members belong to the only legal party, the Destour Socialist Party.

The official language is Arabic, but French is used everywhere.

History. Earliest records show that Phoenician colonies were founded on the coast during the 9th century BC, out of which the powerful empire of Carthage developed. It held naval and commercial supremacy in the Mediterranean, until in the 3rd century BC it was challenged by the Romans. The Punic Wars ended in the destruction of the Carthaginian culture, and the region was absorbed into the Roman Empire.

Arab incursions began soon after the conquest of Egypt was assured by the fall of Alexandria in 642. Tunisia was the focus of these lengthy campaigns, because of its fertile wheatlands. It was not until 705 that Carthage finally fell. At this time the town of Tunis was founded as the base for the Arab North African fleet.

Turkish corsairs and the Spanish tussled over Tunis during the 16th century: the Turks were the victors, and Tunisia nominally joined the Ottoman Empire for the next 250 years. In the wake of the Napoleonic Wars, Tunisia became a centre of European interests and rivalries. The country went bankrupt in 1869, and a triple control (by Italy, France and Britain) was established. The French forced the bey to recognise a French protectorate in 1883. After the First World War Tunisian nationalism grew apace with that of other Middle Eastern countries, and in 1920 the formative Destour (Constitution) party was founded. In 1934 its successor, the Néo-Destour, was formed by Habib Bourguiba. In March 1956 France recognised Tunisia's independence by protocol, and it became formally independent on 25 July 1957, with Bourguiba as president.

In 1964 the Néo-Destour changed its name to the *Parti Socialiste Destourien*. It set about promoting its 'Tunisian socialism' chiefly through the nationalisation of foreign-owned lands and agrarian reform. In 1974 Bourguiba was appointed president-for-life.

Tunnelling. With modern mechanical appliances, few technical limitations are imposed on tunnelling. Small-section tunnels are driven at their full dimensions; for larger sections, a pilot heading is often excavated and then enlarged. Modern CAP (Comprehensive All-Purpose) machines can bore through any kind of rock at the full tunnel section, automatically remove the rock cuttings, and position reinforced and pre-stressed-concrete lining sections. Where blasting is used, power drills on a platform, or jumbo, bore rounds of holes in the rock into which charges are placed. Liquid air or oxygen, when used as the explosive, have the advantage of leaving no blasting fumes. Wet boring and spraying the broken rock help in suppressing dust, and ventilation is provided by a forcing fan through air tubes. Cementation (injecting liquid cement at high pressure through advance boreholes) deals with water from rock fissures. In soft ground or under water, air pressure is used to keep out water. The laser-controlled tunnelling mole (essentially a sharp-edged cylindrical shield) is pushed forwards by hydraulic rams, and a supporting lining is inserted.

Another form of tunnelling is pipe jacking, in which steel and concrete pipes are forced through the ground by jacks. A recent invention employs compressed-air jacking, in which each pipe section is pushed forwards by the one behind it, thus considerably reducing the thrust required.

Tunny, *Thunnus thynnus,* a large teleost fish of the family Scombridae, in order Perciformes, allied to the mackerel. It is abundant in the Mediterranean, and is also found in the Indian, Pacific and Atlantic oceans. It attains a length of 3m and a weight of 670kg. Tunny-fishing is a popular sport, and tunny is an important commercial food-fish.
See also FISHING, COMMERCIAL.

Tupi-Guaraní, an important group of South American peoples, extending from the Amazon to the Lower Paraguay and the Peruvian Andes. A corruption of the Tupi language is spoken as the trade medium in the Amazon region. The Indians of Paraguay belong to the linguistic family of the Tupi-Guaraní, which is believed to have originated in the basin of the Paraguay and to have spread from the centre over much of South America east of the Andes. The Guaraní make up most of the coastal people of Brazil today, and even well in the interior of the Amazon country tribes speaking this same language are to be found. The Guaraní language is still the popular language of Paraguay.

Turban, headdress of Muslims in certain countries (especially India, Pakistan and Afghanistan), though no special religious significance attaches to it. It consists of linen, muslin, taffeta or silk strips wound round the head, sometimes over a fez or a tarbush. It may be white, coloured or striped (Pathans).

Turbidites, rock formations deposited by turbidity currents. They are characteristically coarse, poorly sorted sandstones interbedded with clay or shale.

Turbine, Hydraulic, machine for converting the potential energy of an elevated water supply into mechanical work. The potential energy is first converted wholly or partly into kinetic energy and the flowing water is then directed over curved blades attached to a rotor. The resultant change of momentum produces a torque on the rotor shaft. In impulse turbines, water jets hit the rotor blades radially and have only kinetic energy. Reaction turbines run full of water, which flows between vanes, providing both kinetic and pressure energy; flow may be radial or axial, the latter being preferred for low head of water.

Turbine, Steam, a device which receives steam at a high pressure and allows it to expand to a low pressure, so producing power at the expense of its internal energy. The steam expands in fixed blades or nozzles which it leaves with decreased internal energy and increased kinetic energy; it then passes over curved blades on the turbine rotor, the resultant change in momentum producing a torque on the rotor shaft. In the impulse turbine the whole pressure drop occurs in the fixed blades; in the reaction turbine part of the pressure drop occurs in the moving blades.

The turbine differs from the reciprocating engine in that the moving parts have a purely rotary motion and that the working forces are produced by changes in the momentum of a steady flow of steam rather than from the pressure of a fixed mass. The principal advantages over the reciprocating engine are that it is mechanically simpler, is much smaller for a given power output and has a higher efficiency. Moreover, the motion is barely perceptible and the turbine runs at constant speed for a constant load. It is therefore without rival as a prime mover for electric generators and for other similar applications. As only the shaft bearings need lubrication, the exhaust steam is uncontaminated by oil and is immediately available for heating and other processes.

Turbocharger, turbine form of supercharger, a device that compresses air fed into an internal combustion engine. Such a device aids combustion and increases engine efficiency. A turbocharger is driven by the exhaust gases of the engine, and is particularly useful in aeroplane engines because it tends to run faster at higher altitudes, when a greater degree of supercharging is needed.

Turbot, *Scophthalmus maximus,* a flat-fish found off European shores. It is a left-sided flat-fish, about 0·5 to 1 m long, with no scales, but covered with small bony knobs. It is carnivorous, and a highly valued food fish.

Turenne, Henri de la Tour D'Auvergne, Vicomte de (1611–75), French soldier, grandson of William the Silent. He was brought up as a Protestant. During the last eight years of the Thirty Years War he was the leading French commander, though superseded occasionally by his principal rival, Condé. During the Fronde revolt, Turenne eventually sided with the court, ensuring the victory of the monarchy over its internal and external enemies. He inflicted crushing defeats on Condé and the Spanish. In the war against the Dutch, 1672, he campaigned with his usual brilliance, though his devastation of the Palatinate (1674) is a blot on his character. He was killed at Sarsbach, fighting Montecuccoli. Turenne became a Catholic in 1668.

Turgenev, Ivan Sergeevich (1818–83), Russian novelist. His first work, *A Sportsman's Sketches,* 1847–52, is a series of understated stories about Russian peasants and landowners set against a poetic picture of the Russian countryside. The book made a deep impression on the educated classes of Russia by its picture of the harm and suffering caused by serfdom. In his novels he attempted to portray objectively successive stages in the development of the Russian intelligentsia. His efforts at objectivity were frequently misunderstood, and this in part prompted his decision to live abroad after 1855. Turgenev was the first Russian author to acquire an international reputation. His influence on the development of the novel in Europe generally was important. Among his most important works are *Rudin,* 1856; *A Nest of Gentlefolk,* 1859; *Fathers and Sons,* 1862; and the play *A Month in the Country,* 1850.

Turgot, Anne Robert Jacques, Baron de l'Aulne (1727–81), French minister of finance and political economist. On the death of Louis XV he was rapidly raised to the position of comptroller-general. By a series of enactments, some of which were repealed immediately after his removal from office, he aimed at making taxation more equitable, destroying the servitude of the peasant class, and removing the disabilities under which the urban dwellers suffered. But all the classes that had benefited by their previous exemption from taxation combined against him, and Louis XVI was too weak to resist. In 1776 Turgot was dismissed. He published several works on economics and literature.

Turin (Italian *Torino*; ancient *Augusta Taurinorum*), Italian city, capital of Turin province and the region of Piedmont. It stands at the foot of the Alps, at the junction of the Po and the Dora Riparia, in a position commanding road and rail routes between France and Italy. It was a duchy of the Longobards and eventually became an important possession of the House of Savoy. It was the capital of the kingdom of Sardinia from 1814 to 1860, and was the organising centre of the unification of Italy and the nation's first capital, 1861–65. During this century, especially since 1945, Turin has become a great industrial and commercial centre. Its economic fortunes are now inextricably linked with the motor car industry and with the largest corporation in Italy, Fiat, in particular. It also has textile, paper, chemical, foodstuff, wine (Vermouth) and publishing industries. Population (1979) 1,160,687.

Turin, Shroud of, see HOLY SHROUD OF TURIN.

Turkana, a Nilo-Hamitic people living in the near-desert conditions of northern Kenya. They are fierce and nomadic cattle-keepers. They have no centralised government and are organised through an age grade system. They are culturally close to the Jiye and Karamojong.

Turkana, Lake, (formerly Lake Rudolf) African lake partly in Ethiopia, but for most of its length in north-west Kenya. It is 298 km long, and 59 km wide at its widest point. Altitude 381 m; maximum depth 73 m. Lake Turkana is rapidly diminishing in area. It was discovered in 1881 by Teleki and von Höhnel, who originally named it after Crown Prince Rudolf of Austria-Hungary. The lake is famous for sporting fish including the Nile perch and tiger fish. It attracts great numbers of migratory birds, notably flamingos, pelicans and ducks. The scenery is remarkable for its beauty.

Turkey, the largest of the game birds, once believed to have come from Turkey but in fact native to North and Central America. *Meleagris gallopavo,* the origin of the domesticated varieties, formerly occurred throughout the North American continent. The wild birds are larger and more ornate than domesticated turkeys, which, however, have been improved by introductions of wild blood. The largest of the domesticated varieties is the 'American mammoth bronze'. *Agriocharis ocellata,* the other species, occurs in northern Belize and northern Guatemala and has plumage of great brilliancy with ocellated tail feathers.

See also POULTRY.

Turkey
Area: 779,452 km²
Population: 45,442,000
Capital: Ankara

Turkey, republic of Western Europe and Asia, at the eastern end of the Mediterranean, bordered on the east by the USSR and Iran, on the south-east by Iraq and Syria; East Thrace (Trakya), the south-eastern portion of the Balkan peninsula, is bounded by Greece and Bulgaria. Area, 779,452 km².

Interior Anatolia (Anadolu) comprises extensive plains in the west, of about 100 m above sea-level, with considerable semi-arid areas and a large salt lake (Tuz Gölü, 1642 km²), and in the east mainly mountainous terrain with numerous basins. The mountain systems of the Pontus in the north and the Taurus in the south, both with peaks over 2500 m, cut off the interior from the coasts. The highest peak, Mount Ararat (5165 m), is in the extreme east, close to the Soviet border. The Black Sea coastal plain is very narrow, but there are extensive plains in Trakya and around the Sea of Marmara, and broad valley lowlands in the Aegean coastal zone. On the Mediterranean coast there are lowlands around Adana and Antalya. The main rivers are the Firat (Euphrates), Dicle (Tigris) and Meric (Maritsa). There are numerous lakes, mainly in the western Taurus, but the biggest, Lake Van (3738 km²), is in eastern Anadolu. Vegetation in the coastal zones and on the mountains is mainly forest, usually of poor quality, but rich along the Black Sea. In the interior plains and basins there are large areas of steppe.

The estimated population in 1980 was 45,442,000.

The main cities are Istanbul, Ankara (the capital), Izmir, Adana, Bursa, Gaziantep, Eskisehir and Konya.

About 30 per cent of the land is arable. Except in coastal lowlands, soils are generally poor and productivity low. The interior is devoted mainly to cereals (especially wheat and barley) and livestock rearing with sugar beet, potatoes and vines. Cotton, tobacco and citrus fruits are also important.

Minerals inlude lignite, coal, iron ore, chrome ore, lead and zinc ores, copper (refined), and smaller quantities of mercury, sulphur, asbestos, barite, boron, sodium sulphate and emery. Turkey has one of the largest steel industries in the Middle East. The main manufacturing industry is cotton textiles, but there are engineering and chemical industries.

The unit of currency is the Turkish *lira* (TL), of 100 *kurus*.

The constitution and the elected Grand National Assembly were suspended in a military take-over in 1980; the National Security Council became the supreme legislative body, and its head, General Evren, head of state.

The main language is Turkish. Arabic and Kurdish are spoken near Syria and Iraq.

History. The Turks were converted to Islam in the 7th century and were subjugated by Tatar invaders, known as the Seljuk Turks, when Togul Beg captured Baghdad in 1058. The Turks were soon in possession of Asia Minor and the greater part of Syria. In the 14th century the Seljuks were ousted by the Ottomans who went on to subjugate Serbia (1389), Bulgaria (1396), Macedonia (1430), Greece (between 1456 and 1460), Syria (1515), and Egypt (1516). Under Suleiman the Magnificent (ruled 1520–66), the Turks captured Belgrade (1521), expelled the Knights of St John from Rhodes (1522), and defeated the Hungarians (1526). The Turks later acquired Cyprus (1571) and Crete (1669). The gradual but steady decline of Turkish supremacy dates from the end of the 16th century; the first serious disaster was the defeat of the Turkish fleet by Christian forces under John of Austria at Lepanto in 1571. A long series of Russo-Turkish wars began in 1730 and in 1774 Turkey relinquished its suzerainty over the Crimea, and Russia secured the approach to the Black Sea. In the Crimean War of 1853–56 Britain and France supported Turkey against the Russians. The whole of the 19th century was marked by a series of revolts; Turkish overlordship finally came to an end in Greece (1830) and Egypt (1879). By the Treaty of Berlin (1878), the independence of Bulgaria, Serbia, Romania and Montenegro was formally acknowledged. Bosnia and Herzegovina were occupied by Austria, and Cyprus was handed over to British control. By 1913 Turkey was left with only a small strip of territory in Europe. Despite attempts at domestic reform, the growing abuses of the government resulted in the formation, at the end of the 19th century, of the 'Young Turk' party. In 1909 the sultan was deposed and his brother came to the throne. In 1914 Enver Beg became minister of war. On 8 September, following Turkish naval attacks in the Black Sea, Russia and then Britain and France declared war. Turkey had no hope of victory and an armistice was signed with the Allies on 30 October 1918.

A movement towards the regeneration of Turkey began in 1919 in Anatolia, where Mustafa Kemal Atatürk convoked a Turkish nationalist Congress. At the 1919 election the Nationalist Party under Kemal was legitimised by its strong representation. It was further strengthened by Turkish protests against the Greek occupation of parts of Anatolia. A successful war against Greece followed and the treaty of peace was signed at Lausanne on 24 July 1923. In 1922 the sultanate was abolished and on 29 October 1923 Turkey was declared a republic with Kemal as president. After his death in 1938, the regime, under President Ismet Inonu, was sufficiently sturdy to survive. Turkey changed sides during the Second World War, being

Turkey. The travertine falls at Pamukkale are formed by mineral depositions from hot springs.

forced to ally with Germany in 1941 and then, in February 1945, declaring war on Germany and Japan.

In May 1960 the Menderes regime, which had been in power since 1950, was overthrown by an army coup. Parliamentary government was re-established during 1961. In 1971 the armed forces put pressure on the premier, Demirel, who resigned. After the lifting of martial law, elections were held in 1973 and the Republican People's Party under Bülent Ecevit won a slim majority. Ecevit's reputation was greatly enhanced as a result of the invasion and occupation of northern Cyprus in July 1974. After a period of political instability there was a further military take-over in 1980, and 1982 General Kenan Evren put a new constitution to referendum and was elected to a 7-year term as president.

Art and Architecture. From the 11th to the 17th century the Turks proved extremely susceptible to the artistic traditions of the countries they conquered. During the Seljuk era (11th–14th centuries) they employed Persian craftsmen at their capital, Konya, and important mosques were erected there. Geometrical decoration continued to be used freely, becoming more elaborate than ever. Though artistic development tended to be confined to mosques and other religious buildings up to modern times, domestic architecture of the 16th–18th centuries tended more and more to follow western European fashions.

Language. Modern Turkish is written in a modified Latin alphabet introduced in 1928. Turkish lacks grammatical gender, has a distinctive word order (qualifiers precede the words they qualify; verbs usually come last) and makes extensive use of suffixes, whose vowels normally harmonise with the preceding vowel. So, to *ev* (house) 'front vowelled' suffixes -*ler* (plural), -*iniz* (your), -*de* (in) are added to make *evlerinizde* (in your houses), but as *oda* (room) ends in a 'back vowel', 'in your rooms' is *odalarinizda*.

Turkey Oak, *Quercus cerris,* is common in southern Europe and south-west Asia. It has deciduous, short-stalked toothed leaves and bristly cups for the acorns.

Turkey Vulture, *Cathartes aura,* also mistakenly called turkey buzzard, a common bird of prey of North and South America, of the family Cathartidae in order Falconiformes. It is a large brown bird with a wingspan of about 2 m. It is said to use its sense of smell to detect its prey, which is any form of carrion; this is a very rare phenomenon in birds.

See also VULTURE.

Turkistan, or Turkestan, historic name of an extensive region in Central Asia now divided between China (the province of Sinkiang Uighur), the USSR (Kazakh, Kirgiz, Tadzhik, Turkmen and Uzbek SSRs), and Afghanistan (North-East Province). Its chief cities were Tashkent, Samarkand and Bukhara. Former area 2,600,000 km².

Turkmen Soviet Socialist Republic, or Turkmenistan, constituent republic of the USSR formed in 1924. It is bordered on the south by Iran and Afghanistan. The republic is mountainous in the south and west, with the extensive (about 80 per cent of the total area) Kara Kum desert in the centre and north. The main river is the Amu Darya. The economy is centred round agriculture, the main branches being cotton growing, sheep breeding and the production of raw silk. Industry includes oil from the important western oil-fields, chemical products, food processing and carpet making. The republic is crossed by the Krasnovodsk–Tashkent railway. Krasnovodsk is an important Caspian Sea port. There is navigation on the Amu Darya river and the Kara Kum canal. Capital, Ashkhabad. Area 488,100 km². Population (1980) 2,800,000; 65 per cent are Turkmen.

Turkmens (Turkomans), West-Turkic-speaking Sunni Muslims subdued by Russia between 1881–85. One million live in Turkmen SSR, USSR, and 500,000 in Iran, Afghanistan, Iraq, Syria and Turkey. Some are nomadic pastoralists, some settled agriculturalists and stock-breeders and some, Caspian Turkmens, are sailors and traders. Exceptionally among Asian Turks, Turkmens were stratified socially by occupation, not descent.

Turks, or Turkic peoples, are terms without any racial significance which can, however, be applied to the peoples linguistically and historically related to the 'Tu-Kiu', a nomad people, who stretched from northern China to the Black Sea. Apart from the Turks of the Turkish republic, the Turkic people have no common characteristic other than language, although most of them are Muslim. The Turkic languages, belonging to the Altaic family, closely resemble each other and have changed little since the 8th century.

The total number of the Turkic peoples is about 40 million, of whom about 18 million are in Turkey and 17 million in the USSR (in the Volga region, Caucasus and central Asia). Of the remainder about three million live in China and two million in Iran and Afghanistan. Linguistically the Turks may be divided into those of Europe and western Asia and those of central and eastern Asia.

Turks and Caicos Islands (or Cayos, or Keys Islands), group of islands lying to the south of the Bahamas. The group consists of six inhabited islands and several uninhabited rocks numbering about 30 in all. The total land area is 430 km². The largest island, Grand Caicos, is 40 km long by 19 km wide. The seat of government is on Grand Turk. Total population (1980) of the islands, 7436.

Products exported are mainly crayfish, salt, fish-meat and conch. The US government operates an important cable station on Grand Turk; also a weather bureau, a guided missile observer station, and an oceanographic measurement station.

The islands are a dependent territory within the Commonwealth. The governor is president of an Executive Council; there is also a Legislative Council of which the majority of members are elected.

History. The Turk Islands were discovered about 1512, but no attempt at occupation was made until 1678, when their value for the production of salt was recognised by the colonists of Bermuda. Towards the end of the 18th century the Bahamas government laid claim to the Turks and Caicos Islands, and despite the vigorous protests of the Bermuda salt-rakers it was determined by Order in Council in 1804 that the legislature of the Bahamas government should extend to them. At the end of a struggle lasting 50 years, a further Order in Council placed the Turks and Caicos Islands as an independent administration under the supervision of the governor of Jamaica. The Caicos Islands, which in 1848 were appended to the Turks Islands for governmental purposes, were formerly occupied by loyalist refugees from Georgia after the declaration of independence by the USA. The islands became a crown colony and a dependency of Jamaica until 1962 when, on Jamaica's independence, they became a separate colony. A new constitution was introduced in 1976.

Turku, or Åbo, important town in Finland, formerly the capital, situated on the Aurajoki river not far from its mouth. Turku has important shipbuilding, oil refining, cement, textile and machine industries, and a significant timber trade. Population (1975) 163,981.

Turner, Dame Eva (1892–1983), British dramatic soprano. She sang with the Carl Rosa Opera Company from 1916 to 1924. She then sang at La Scala, Milan, at Covent Garden and in North and South America. Her powerful, bright-toned voice made her an ideal exponent of Verdi's *Aida* and Puccini's *Turandot*, while she also sang Wagnerian rôles with great success. She was created DBE in 1962.

Turner, Joseph Mallord William (1775–1851), British landscape painter. In 1789 he entered the Royal Academy schools. He began as a topographical water-colourist, but first exhibited in oils in 1796 and was elected RA in 1802. He made extensive travels in Europe and in Britain in 1801–45, constantly recording the effects of sea, sky, mountain and plain in water-colour. He produced series of water-colour studies, which were issued to the public as engravings, throughout his life (e.g. *Rivers of France*, 1833–35, and *Rivers of England*, 1823–27), but his real aim was to make landscape paintings in oil as acceptable at the Royal Academy as figure compositions. His work was soundly based on the study of the European masters of landscape painting: van de Velde, Wilson, Claude and Poussin, and he produced works in their recognisably different styles, e.g. *Crossing the Brook*, 1815 (Tate Gallery, London), in the style of Claude; the *Destruction of Sodom*, 1805 (Tate Gallery), which has echoes of Poussin. But the great landscapes of this period, as indeed most of Turner's major works, were based on observed natural conditions and were also allegories of national power. Examples are *Hannibal Crossing the Alps*, 1812 (Tate Gallery), and *Ulysses Deriding Polyphemus*, 1829 (National Gallery).

Turner's later works show the original departures in the rendering of light and colour that are much admired today, such as *The Evening of the Deluge*, 1843 (Tate Gallery), and *Rain, Steam, and Speed—The Great Western Railway*, 1844 (National Gallery, London). He also produced the engraved plates of his *Liber Studiorum*, 1806–19, showing different styles of landscape composition. He intended his bequest of works to the nation to be exhibited together permanently, but at present they are mainly distributed between the Tate, the National Gallery, London, and the British Museum. Turner's work received much criticism during his lifetime. Ruskin defended his painting in *Modern Painters*, 1843.

Turnip, see BRASSICA.

Turnpike Roads, see TOLLS.

Turnstone, *Arenaria interpres*, shore bird related to the plovers, in order Charadriiformes. Its common name comes from its habit of turning over stones and shells on the seashore in search of marine insects and small crustaceans. It is widely distributed, but breeds chiefly on arctic coasts. It is about 23 cm long. The upper parts are chestnut with black spots, and the lower parts white, except on the breast.

Turpentine, a naturally occurring oil, obtained by distillation from the oleoresinous exudation of pine trees from America, France, India, Portugal and Spain. Chemically, oil of turpentine is a mixture of various terpenes in somewhat variable proportions and is a colourless liquid of relative density 0·86. It has a boiling range from 150 to 170°C. The oil is used in medicine externally as a counter-irritant. It is also a solvent for paints and varnishes; however, its place has steadily been usurped by white spirit, a petroleum fraction (often called turpentine substitute). Turpentine is also used in the preparation of polishes, leather dressings and synthetic camphor.

Turpin, Dick, properly Richard (c.1706–1739), English highway robber whose fictitious exploits on his mare 'Black Bess' have secured a legendary fame. Turpin was the son of an Essex inn-keeper, and began his career by cattle-stealing when apprenticed to a butcher. He was ultimately convicted at York of horse-stealing and hanged.

J. M. W. Turner, Rain, Steam, and Speed—The Great Western Railway, *1844.*

Turquoise, or callaite, $CuAl_6(PO_4)_4(OH)_8 \cdot 4H_2O$, a blue or bluish-green mineral, and a gem. It occurs only in massive cryptocrystalline form (hardness 6; specific gravity 2·7).

Turtle, aquatic reptile of the order Chelonia. Turtles differ from land tortoises in having the feet modified into paddles. Turtles resort to sandy shores to lay their eggs. The marine green turtle (*Chelonia mydas*) has long been valued for its meat and eggs, and is found world-wide in the warmer oceans. The hawksbill turtle (*Eretmochelys imbricata*) yields tortoiseshell.

Turtle Dove, *Streptopelia turtur*, a bird of the pigeon order Columbiformes. It is a summer visitor to Europe, wintering in Africa. It is about 30 cm long, with a long, rounded tail. The plumage is greyish brown, with yellow on the sides of the head and pink on the neck and breast. The back of the neck and crown are greyish blue, and the legs and toes are red. Two pure white eggs are laid in a rough structure of twigs placed in a tree near the ground. The male assists the female in incubation, and their devotion is proverbial. The collared turtle dove, *S. decaocto*, is often kept in captivity. This latter species is about 25 cm long with a short tail; the general colour is grey, tinged with red, and the upper parts are greenish-brown, with a black collar on the back of the neck.

Tuscany (Italian *Toscana*), region of central Italy, comprising the provinces of Massa e Carrara, Arezzo, Florence, Grosseto, Livorno, Lucca, Pisa, Pistoia and Siena. It lies mostly in the northern Apennines but also includes the plain of the lower Arno and the Maremma. The chief rivers are the Arno in the north and the Ombrone in the south. Tuscany is roughly co-extensive with the ancient Etruria. Since the rise of the Medici in Florence, the region has been dominated by that city. On the extinction of the Medici in 1737, Tuscany passed to the House of Hapsburg and later to Spain. In 1859 Tuscany voted for annexation to Sardinia, becoming part of united Italy in 1861. The Tuscan dialect has become Italy's literary language. Tuscany is the major mining region of Italy with lignite (Upper Arno), iron (Elba), mercury (Monte Amiata), and marble (Apuan Alps) being extracted. Agriculture is now prosperous, mainly producing cereals. The plain of the Arno supports market gardening and tobacco. Industry is concentrated along the coast of Piombino-Leghorn-Massa (Carrara) and on the Arno plain (Florence, Prato, Pistoia, Lucca and Pisa). Tuscany contains some of Italy's most important tourist centres, e.g. Florence, Pisa, Siena and Viareggio. The regional capital is Florence. Area 22,989 km². Population (1980) 3,600,000.

Tuscaroras, North American Indian people. Driven out of Carolina by the whites, they became one of the tribes of the Iroquois Confederacy. Today they number about 1000, mostly living in Canada and New York state.

Tusculum, ancient town of Latium, 24 km south-east of Rome. Its situation made it a favourite summer resort of the Roman aristocracy. Cicero had a villa at Tusculum, which he frequently mentions under the name of Tusculanum.

Tussaud's, Madame, waxworks established by Madame Marie Tussaud (1760–1850). She was drawing mistress to the children of Louis XVI of France and during the French Revolution was forced to make wax heads of many of those unfortunates who were guillotined. After arriving in England in 1802 she used her skill to set up an exhibition of waxworks at the Lyceum in the Strand. The present exhibition in Marylebone Road London, contains important international contemporary figures as well as historic personages and such set pieces as 'The Death of Nelson'. The 'Chamber of Horrors' contains effigies of notorious murderers and their victims, as well as instruments of torture and execution.

Tussock Moth, any member of family Lymantriidae of order Lepidoptera. The common name alludes to the tufts (tussocks) of long hairs on the caterpillars. Several species are major forest pests, in Europe and North America, e.g. the gypsy moth, *Lymantria dispar*; the nun moth, *L. monacha*; and the browntail moth, *Nygmia phaeorrhoea*. In some species, e.g. the white-marked tussock moth, *Hemerocampa leucostigma*, the females are wingless.

Tutankhamen. One of four small coffins found in the canopic urns.

Tutankhamen (fl. c. 1358 BC), Egyptian king of the 18th Dynasty, successor of Akhnaton. He came to the throne at the age of about ten as Tutankhaton, being married to Akhnaton's third daughter, Ankhesenpaaton, and died aged about 18. The religious reformation had left much dissatisfaction in the kingdom, and Tutankhamen had to re-adopt the worship of Amun and move the court from Akhetaton back to Thebes, changing his name to Tutankhamen. An unimportant king who died prematurely, he owes his fame to having been buried in a small tomb which was concealed by the soil from digging the larger tomb of Rameses VI nearby. Thus his came to be the only royal tomb of Egypt to survive almost intact until 1922, when it was discovered by Howard Carter. The sarcophagus, with the golden coffin, is still in the tomb, but the other contents fill most of the upper floor of the Cairo Museum, and are now one of the wonders of the world, although artistically verging on decadence and but a fraction of the magnificence with which the greater pharaohs must have been buried.
See also EGYPT, *Archaeology*.

Tutsi, politically dominant minority of Rwandi and Burundi since their arrival in the area in the 14th century. They herd cattle which are the symbol of power and wealth,

Tuscany. The mountain village of Sorano in the province of Grosseto.

and which enabled the Tutsi to dominate the agricultural Hutu. In the early 1970s the Tutsi massacred huge numbers of Hutu.

Tuva Autonomous Soviet Socialist Republic, in the RSFSR, USSR, situated in South Siberia, bordering on the Mongolian People's Republic. It consists of two mountain basins with mostly steppe vegetation, enclosed by the Western Sayan, Altai and other mountain ranges (maximum height over 3500 m), with forest and tundra vegetation. The region is crossed by the Upper Yenisei, and has gold, coal, asbestos, cobalt and salt deposits, Sheep, goats and cattle are raised, and there are mining and various other industries. The region was Chinese from 1757 to 1912, and became a Russian protectorate in 1914. The capital is Kyzyl. Area 170,500 km². Population (1980) 269,000.

Tuvalu
Area: 24 km²
Population: 7349
Capital: Funafuti

Tuvalu, formerly the Ellice Islands, an island group lying between latitude 5°30′ and 11°S, and longitude 176° and 180°E. There are nine main islands; the centre of administration is on Funafuti. Area, about 24 km². The population at the 1979 census was 7349, Polynesians. The main products are coconuts, fruit, vegetables and fish; many islanders are employed in the phosphate industry on nearby Nauru. Tuvalu has a governor-general, a prime minister and cabinet government.
History. The group separated from the Gilbert Islands, as the result of a referendum, in 1975. Having been a British protectorate since 1892, Tuvalu became an independent state within the Commonwealth in 1978.

Tver, see KALININ.

Twain, Mark, pseudonym of Samuel Langhorne Clemens (1835–1910), US novelist and humorist. He was apprenticed to a printer and wrote articles for the *Missouri Courier*. In 1857 he became an apprentice pilot on the Mississippi, where he remained until the outbreak of the Civil War. He then went back to journalism and as city editor of the Virginia City, Nevada, *Enterprise* he first used the pseudonym Mark Twain, the call of the pilots when taking soundings, meaning two fathoms. In 1865 his story *The Celebrated Jumping Frog of Calaveras County* was published, which made him famous as a humorist. He was then commissioned by the Sacramento Union to write travel articles, and ordered on a journey round the world. Instead, he joined a party going to the Mediterranean and wrote *The Innocents Abroad*, 1869, a debunking account of the trip, which established him as a writer of note. Returning to America, he now wrote his most famous books, including *The Adventures of Tom Sawyer*, 1876; *Life on the Mississippi*, 1883; and *The Adventures of Huckleberry Finn*, 1884, his classic novel, a vernacular, comic study of the problems of slavery, colour and innocent morality against social expectations.
In 1894 a bad investment left him penniless,

and he went on a world lecture tour, earning enough to pay his debts. During his later years he became a national legend. He was an artist in grotesque and somewhat obvious humour, but his achievement in establishing a vernacular tradition, and in analysing the contradictions of Gilded Age America was massive.

Tweed, river in the south of Scotland, draining most of the eastern portion of the Southern Uplands. It rises in the Tweedsmuir Hills and flows in a north-easterly direction, to form the boundary between Borders Region and Northumberland before entering the North Sea at Berwick-upon-Tweed. It drains an area of 4860 km², and is one of the best salmon rivers in Scotland. It is navigable only in its last 10 km. Length 155 km.

Tweed, a woollen woven fabric manufactured in Scotland, named because the word 'tweel' (twill) on an invoice in 1825 was misread. Tweed is today a general term dependent on place of origin. Harris tweed is a rough fabric; Donegal tweed is traditionally brown in colour. Tweeds are used for making clothing.

Tweedsmuir, Baron, see BUCHAN, JOHN, 1ST BARON TWEEDSMUIR.

Twelfth Night, see EPIPHANY.

Twelve-note Music, see SERIALISM.

Twelve Patriarchs, Testaments of the, a series of writings purporting to give the last speeches of the 12 sons of Jacob. Each speech is an exhortation to avoid some particular sin or practise some special virtue. It is a Jewish work of the 2nd century BC but early underwent Christian interpolation.

Twelve Tables, Law of the (*Lex duodecim tabularum,* begins the legal history of the Roman republic. Its importance lies in the fact that it substituted a public written body of laws, accessible to all citizens, for an unwritten code known only to a few. The law of the Twelve Tables, published 451–450 BC, was engraved on bronze tablets and fixed to the rostra. No part of the text survives in its original form.

Twickenham. Since its opening in 1908, this sports stadium in south-west London has become the home of the England rugby football team and the headquarters of the Rugby Football Union. It is also the home ground of the Harlequins Rugby Club, and is additionally the venue for most major events on the rugby football calendar played in England.

Twilight, the diffused light preceding sunrise (dawn) or following sunset (dusk) which is due to atmospheric scattering of sunlight. Since the atmosphere remains sufficiently dense to scatter light up to an altitude of 300 km, the last traces of daylight do not fade from the sky until the Sun is about 18° below the horizon.

Twill, woven fabric in which the warp is raised one thread and depressed two or more threads for the passage of the weft, with resultant diagonal surface ribs.

Twinkling, or scintillation, of stars is due to the refraction of their light rays in various directions by the Earth's atmosphere. The air near the Earth's surface is frequently in commotion owing to warm currents rising from the comparatively warm ground, cold currents descending, and horizontal movements of layers of different densities. There

are also pockets in the atmosphere which act as lenses—concave and convex—dispersing and collecting rays of light, and as these pockets are moved by the wind, stars seen through them are never steady. Twinkling is much more common with the stars and small planets, e.g. Mercury, because they do not present an appreciable disc to the eye, the light emanating from them like a ray, whereas the planets in general send bundles of light from the various portions of their discs.

Twins, generally denotes two individuals produced at one birth. In its strictest sense the word denotes the result of the division of an organism or of an organ into two equivalent organisms or organs. In consequence, although two animals may be developed and born at the same time, they are twins only if they are the products of the division of a single fertilised ovum. Human 'twins' resulting from the synchronous development of two fertilised eggs are not true twins. True or 'identical' twins are always of the same sex. Not infrequently one individual is larger than the other. Twins may be conjoined (Siamese Twins). There is some evidence to show that the tendency to beget twins is inherited by males.

Two Sicilies, Kingdom of the, see NAPLES, KINGDOM OF; SICILY.

Two-stroke Engine, see INTERNAL COMBUSTION ENGINE.

Tyburn, a tributary of the River Thames, England, now running through London completely underground, formed originally by the confluence of two streams from the Hampstead heights. It entered the flood plain of the Thames near the western end of St James's Park, then divided into three mouths, two of them forming the island of Thorney on which Westminster Abbey was built. The historic London gallows, known as Tyburn Tree, stood at the western end of Oxford Street. The first recorded execution took place in 1196, the last in 1783, when the place of execution was moved to Newgate Prison. A permanent gallows stood at the junction of Oxford Street and Edgware Road from 1571 to 1759.

Tyler, John (1790–1862), 10th President of the USA, 1841–45. In 1825–27 he was governor of Virginia, becoming a senator in 1827. In 1840 he was elected vice-president, succeeding on Harrison's death to the presidency. As president he stood midway between the two great parties, without the support of either. Besides the Ashburton Treaty, the most important act of his administration was the annexation of Texas in 1845.

Tyler, Wat, or Wat the Tiler (d.1381), leader of the Kentish men in the rebellion of 1381, the Peasants' Revolt, in the reign of Richard II. The rebels protesting against the Statute of Labourers and the imposition of a poll tax, marched on London. On 12 June they camped on Blackheath; London capitulated, and Tyler presented his demands, chief of which was the abolition of serfdom. On the 15 June took place the celebrated meeting between the rebels and the king at Smithfield when Richard is said to have offered himself as the rebels' leader after Tyler had been killed by the Lord Mayor of London, Sir William Walworth. In fact the rebels dispersed and their demands came to nothing.

Tympanum, in architecture, the triangular space enclosed by the horizontal and raking cornices of a pediment; or the semicircular space enclosed between the arch and the lintel of an arched doorway.

Tynan, Katharine (1861–1931), Irish poet and novelist. A well-known figure in the Celtic revival, her first book of poems, *Louise de la Vallière*, was published in 1885. Others are *Ballads and Lyrics*, 1891; *The Wind in the Trees*, 1898; *Innocencies*, 1905; *Experiences*, 1908; and *Irish Poems*, 1913; her *Collected Poems* appeared in 1930. The first of her pleasant, sentimental novels was *The Way of a Maid*, 1895, and she wrote over a hundred. She also published an autobiographical series, beginning with *Twenty-Five Years*, 1913, and ending with *Memories*, 1924.

Tynan, Kenneth Peacock (1927–1980), English writer. He was drama critic for the *Spectator*, 1951, and other periodicals, notably the *Observer*, 1954–63 (film critic, 1964–66). He was literary manager of the National Theatre, 1963–69, and literary consultant from 1969 to 1973. He devised and partly wrote the entertainment *Oh, Calcutta!*. His books include *A View of the English Stage*, 1975 and *The Sound of Two Hands Clapping*, 1975.

Tyndale, William (c.1494–1536), English translator of the Bible and reformer. He was chaplain in a household at Old Sodbury, but his sympathy with the new learning aroused suspicion and he moved to London. Finding it impossible to complete his translation of the New Testament there, he went to Hamburg and then to Cologne, where in 1525 he began printing the work. In 1528 he published *Parable of the Wicked Mammon* and the *Obedience of a Christian Man*, and was for a time in Henry VIII's favour, but having published *The Practice of Prelates* in 1530, he lost the king's goodwill. He was burnt as a heretic at Vilvorde, Netherlands. His fame rests on his translation of the Bible, consisting of New Testament, Pentateuch and Jonah.

Tyndall, John (1820–93), Irish physicist, professor of natural philosophy at the Royal Institution, 1854. He made important investigations in the Penrhyn slate quarries and in the Alps with T. H. Huxley. He investigated the scattering of light and explained why the sky is blue. He also showed that micro-organisms are normally present in the atmosphere.

Tyne, river of northern England, formed by the junction of the North and South Tyne near the town of Hexham, Northumberland, flowing east to the North Sea at Tynemouth. Its total length is 72km, and its principal tributary is the Derwent. Newcastle upon Tyne, Gateshead, Jarrow and South Shields are among the towns on its banks.

Tyne and Wear, county of England, formed in 1974 through the reorganisation of County Durham and Northumberland. It comprises the five districts of Newcastle upon Tyne, Sunderland, Gateshead, North Tyneside and South Tyneside, with an area of 534km², uniting the interests of the contiguous industrial towns along the estuaries of the rivers Tyne and Wear.

Several of the towns of Tyne and Wear originated as Anglo-Saxon settlements from the 7th century. These include the fortified monastery at Tynemouth, the monastery at Jarrow, Gateshead at the southern end of the Tyne crossing, North and South Shields by the sheltered waters upstream of the Tyne river mouth, and Monkwearmouth and Sunderland, respectively north and south of the Wear gorge.

Coal shipments began in the 13th century due to the coalfield's proximity with harbour facilities. The local invention of the iron-screw collier in 1852 reduced the cost of transport of coal to London and overseas but, on land, the development of the railway enabled other inland coalfields to compete in markets once monopolised by supplies from North-East England. Riverside sites were, however, attractive to 19th-century industry because of its dependence on large inputs of coal and bulky raw materials. The short constricted waterfront of the Wear was soon occupied by shipyards. On the Tyne, the narrowing and deepening of the channel allowed shipyards room to develop on either side of the estuary. Further upstream there was a large chemical industry, with heavy engineering and armaments above Newcastle. A local economy almost wholly based on coal and capital goods could not sustain growth in the 20th century. Government aid began in 1935 and has led to the establishment of new towns and industrial trading estates on the fringes of the older settlements. Newcastle has become the major office centre of the northern region of England and the chief shopping centre. A rapid transit system, the Tyneside Metro, extends and integrates the suburban rail network by underground lines beneath Newcastle city centre. Population (1981) 1,143,245.

Tynwald, Court of, legislative body of the Isle of Man, comprising the lieutenant-governor (representing the queen), the Council, and the House of Keys. The Legislative Council consists of the Bishop of Sodor and Man, the first deemster, the attorney-general (who may not vote), and seven members elected by the House of Keys. The House of Keys consists of 24 members elected for five years by adult suffrage.

Type and Typefounding. In the inception of typography the printer was his own type-founder; in fact, it was not until the 17th century that the arts of printing and letter-founding were separated. The process of typefounding remained much the same until the introduction of type-making machinery in the middle of the 19th century. With some modifications in the mould it is still to a minor extent in use for the casting of small quantities of seldom used sorts.

Point size refers to the depth of a type body measured column-wise. (One point is approximately 0·35 mm.) Set size, or thickness, is the width of a type body. The varying set of different letters is inherent in the alphabet we use; the letters *i* and *w* must be cast on different thicknesses of body. It is to be noted that in typefounders' parlance each portion of a single type has its own special name. There are now two standardised sizes of different types in use in the various countries of the world. One is the American 'point' system in use in the USA and the English-speaking countries; the other is the French 'Didot' system in general use on the European continent.
See also TYPOGRAPHY.

Typesetting, the process by which type is assembled ready for printing. Typesetting machines may be classified as: (1) those that set type that has been cast by some other machine; (2) those that cast their own type in the order in which it is required for printing and (3) those that assemble the matrices for a complete line and then cast that line as a single slug. Machines of class (1) have long been superseded by the other two classes. Of class (2) typesetting machines, Monotype machinery is an example. These machines consist of two separate parts, a keyboard, which perforates rolls of paper, and a caster, which these perforations guide in moulding the type. The 'Monotype' principle has been applied to Photosetting under the name 'Monophoto'.

The Linotype and Intertype machines are keyboard-operated linecasters of class (3). Their end-product is a single line or bar of metal type, in relief, known as. a slug. Each slug is the length and depth of a line of type, and has on its upper edge the type characters to print a complete line.
See also COMPUTER COMPOSITION; PHOTO-SETTING.

Typewriter, writing machine operated by means of a manual keyboard for producing characters similar to those of printing. In its modern commercial form it was invented by three Americans, Christopher Scholes, Carlos Glidden and Samuel Soulé, in 1868. Scholes also devised the standard keyboard layout still used.

In the conventional typewriter the platen or roller carrying the paper is mounted on a carriage which moves across as the keys are depressed. Many electric typewriters now have the type characters mounted on either a sphere or a wheel, which moves across, leaving the platen stationary. Electric typewriters are faster, easier to use, and produce a more even touch than conventional typewriters. In the 1970s electronic machines, with far fewer moving parts, were introduced.
See also WORD PROCESSOR.

Typha, a genus of aquatic plants in family Typhaceae, with sword-shaped leaves and long cylindrical brown spikes of female flowers, surmounted by a slender spike of male flowers. *T. latifolia*, great reed mace, cat-tail or bulrush, and *T. angustifolia*, lesser reed mace, are found throughout the world.
See also BULRUSH.

Typhoid Fever, or enteric fever, an acute infectious disease caused by *Salmonella typhi* and characterised by fever, headache, malaise and gastro-intestinal symptoms (first constipation and then diarrhoea). The onset is insidious and the symptoms become apparent only 10–14 days after ingestion of the organism in food or water. The temperature rises and remains elevated, a sparse rash may appear on the trunk, and the spleen is enlarged. Diagnosis is established by isolation of *S. typhi* from blood-cultures. The organism is regularly excreted in the faeces. Treatment with antibiotics cuts short the course of the disease, prevents many complications and reduces mortality, but despite treatment relapses are common. After clinical recovery

S. typhi may be isolated from the stools for a variable period, occasionally for life. Such carriers are the source of infection. Prevention is primarily based on hygiene; a vaccine is available and useful in special circumstances, such as travel to endemic areas.

Typhus Fever, an infectious disease of the rickettsiosis group, caused by microbes of the genus *Rickettsia*. The principal types of clinical typhus fever are scrub typhus, endemic typhus and epidemic typhus. The pathogenic microbe is transmitted mainly via an arthropod vector. The onset varies, but it is often sudden, with headache, fever, general malaise and muscle pains, development of a rash, sometimes a cough, and lymph node enlargement. Diagnosis is usually by means of serological blood tests, culture of the pathogens in fertile hen's eggs or in experimental animals.

Endemic typhus (also called murine typhus fever, flea-borne typhus) is an infectious disease caused by *Rickettsia typhi*, which lives intracellularly and multiplies in man and rats, and is transmitted by rat fleas (mostly *Xenopsylla cheopis*). The rat does not suffer serious debility from the infection; in man it is a severe illness. Transmission occurs when the infective flea sheds faeces onto the skin, and the *Rickettsia* organisms penetrate through the site of bite immediately or when it is scratched. Control is achieved by reduction of the rat population, the use of insecticides in rat-infested sites, and treatment of human cases by antibiotics.

Epidemic typhus (also called louse-borne typhus, classical typhus or jail fever) is a disease due to *R. prowazeki*, existing in man as the basic reservoir, but transmitted mainly by the body louse *Pediculus humanus corporis*. It is associated with squalor, poverty and malnutrition. One attack usually confers immunity. The fatality rate increases with age, being generally 100% over the age of 60. Man becomes infected by contamination of a cut or scratch with louse faeces or crushed louse debris, thus control is by cleanliness, application of insecticides, if necessary, to skin and clothes, and adequate housing and nutrition. A vaccine is available, usually reserved for people at special risk, especially health workers in poor communities. Antibiotics are usually effective, but the disease may recur.

Scrub typhus (also called Tsutsugamushi fever, mite-borne typhus, Japanese river fever) is a rickettsial disease caused by *R. tsutsugamushi*, a microbe capable of growing in the cells of the host. The disease is transmitted via the larvae of mites that live in human skin. There is some evidence that wild rodents harbour the mites and perpetuate the infection cycle. A skin sore (eschar) at the site of the larval bite often is an early sign. Treatment is by antibiotics, and is usually effective. A vaccine is available but is not of high specificity and so is not often used. Control of the disease is by chemicals aimed at mite destruction or repellents, rodent control, treatment of cases, and monitoring susceptible people in areas where the disease occurs.

Typography, a term which formerly embraced the whole craft of printing, but is today customarily used in the narrower sense to signify type designing.

The essence of typographic design is fitness to purpose, and typography which hinders the reader's understanding of the printed message is bad. Book typography should not obtrude itself on the reader. Its basic principles are strongly traditional and the policy of the manufacturers of modern typesetting equipment in reviving the best typefaces cut by printers of the past has been a major contribution to good typography today.
See also PRINTING.

Tyr (Old English *Tiw*), Teutonic god of war. His right hand was sacrificed as a pledge when the monster Fenriswolf, son of Loki, was to be fettered. At the Ragnarök he was to slay Garm, the hound of the cave leading to Hel, but was to be mortally wounded in the conflict. Perhaps originally the sky-god (his name is cognate with the Greek Zeus) he was, however, identified by the Romans with Mars (hence Tuesday corresponds with *Martis dies*, French *mardi*).

Tyrannosaurus, see DINOSAURS.

Cross ply tyre

Radial ply tyre

Modern safety tyre

Rubber Tyre. The structural differences between radial and cross-ply tyres. The safety tyre has a canister which, when there is a puncture, releases fluid that lubricates and partially reflates the tyre.

Tyrant (Greek *turannos*), name given by the ancient Greeks to a man who availed himself of popular discontent to overthrow the existing government and make himself supreme. Where a tyrant did not abuse his power, the people often fared better under a 'benevolent despot', and a tyranny often encouraged new developments in the state, gave impetus to trade and commerce, and encouraged the arts. Such tyrannies arose most often in the 7th and 6th centuries BC.
See also DION; POLYCRATES.

Tyre (modern Sur), ancient town of Syria, built partly on an island and partly on the mainland, said to have been founded in the 15th century BC. It was the main seaport of the Phoenicians, and as such known to the Greeks. As an island fortress Tyre withstood many sieges, but was sacked by Alexander in 332 BC and did not recover. It was Alexander who built a causeway linking the island to the mainland.

Tyre became a flourishing port under the early Roman emperors, and a place of considerable importance in medieval history, especially as the stronghold of the Crusaders (1124–1291). But after the fall of Acre the Christians deserted the city, which was then destroyed by the Muslims. In Roman and earlier times, it was famous for its silk and purple dye. The modern city of Sur is now a seaport in Lebanon.

Tyre, Rubber. Tyres are fitted to the wheels of road vehicles and aeroplanes to absorb shocks and to provide controlled steering behaviour. The pneumatic tyre was first invented by R. W. Thomson, a Briton, in 1845; his first tyre was fitted experimentally to horse-drawn carriages, but achieved little commercial success. In 1888 J. B. Dunlop, also a Briton, practising as a veterinary surgeon in Belfast, re-invented the pneumatic tyre. He used it to equip bicycles, where it was successful in reducing the effort needed to propel them.

Synthetic rubber is now often used for tyres. Other changes in tyre construction include the wide adoption of tubeless tyres, particularly for motor-cars; a prime advantage of the tubeless tyre lies in the ability to retain air pressure for long periods, even when punctured by a nail or similar object. Radial ply tyres have restraining layers of cord under the tread, to give extra stiffness and consequently better tread wear and road adhesion, though with some sacrifice in comfort at low speeds.

Tyrell, George William (1883–1961), British geologist. He specialized in the petrology of igneous rocks. His book *Principles of Petrology* was the standard text of its time.

Tyrol, see TIROL.

Tyrone, county of Northern Ireland, bounded on the west by Donegal, south by Monaghan and Fermanagh, east by Lough Neagh and Armagh, and north by Londonderry. It is hilly in the north and south, the main ridges being the Sperrin Mountains (812 m) in the north-east and the Slievebeagh (376 m) in the south. The main rivers are the Strule and its tributaries of which the chief is the Derg. The main area of lowland fronts onto Lough Neagh, from which narrow valleys lead inland to the bogs and moors of the Sperrins, which provide rough grazing for sheep. Elsewhere mixed farming predominates with the emphasis on cattle rearing. Agriculture provides the main source of employment and there are some small-scale manufacturing concerns in the larger towns. Omagh is the county town. Area 3328 km². Population (1971) 139,073.

Tyrrhenian Sea, is that part of the Mediterranean Sea which lies between the west coast of Italy and the islands of Corsica,

Sardinia and Sicily. It has a large central abyssal plain reaching a maximum depth of 3620 m, and is studded with many seamounts, one of which is some 2850 m high.

Tyumen, capital city, economic and cultural centre of Tyumen *oblast*, USSR, and the oldest city in Siberia. Its industries include shipbuilding, woodworking, tanneries and food industries. It is an important river and rail transhipment point. It was founded in 1586 on the ruins of a Tatar settlement, and was the 'Gate to Siberia' until the construction of the Trans-Siberian Railway. Population (1980) 369,000.

Tzara, Tristan (1896–1963), French poet. In Zürich in 1916 he founded, with Hans Arp and other refugee poets, the short-lived literary movement known as Dada, from which Surrealism developed. His works include *Sept manifestes dada*, 1924.

Tzu Hsi, see ZI XI.

U

U, twenty-first letter of the English alphabet, and the last of the five vowel sounds, closely connected with *v* and *w*. The purely consonantal North Semitic alphabet had a letter *w(aw)*, one form of which became the Greek *digamma*, while another form was used as the vowel *upsilon*. In the Etruscan and Latin alphabets the vowel *u* was written *v*. In the early Middle Ages *v* and *u* were used indifferently for both the consonantal and the vowel sound, and remained interchangeable until the end of the 17th century. The original sound of Middle English short *u* is preserved in such words as *put* and *pull*; the sound heard in *cut* and *mull* (away from the North of England) represents a recent development. The 'long' sound varies, as in *rude, music*.
See also ALPHABET.

Uccello, Paolo (1397–1475), name given to the Florentine painter, mosaicist and sculptor, Paolo di Dono. A pupil in Ghiberti's workshop, he developed a passionate interest in the study of perspective for which he is famous. His most famous works are the three battlepieces of *The Rout of San Romano*, c.1456 (one in the National Gallery, London), painted for Lorenzo de' Medici in his most decorative manner. A *St George and the Dragon*, c.1460, is also in the National Gallery, while *A Hunt in a Forest* is in the Ashmolean Museum, Oxford.

Udaipur, city and region of Rajasthan state, India. Situated by Lake Pichola, the walled city, founded in 1567, contains fine buildings, especially the imposing palace of the former princely state. A marble palace on an island in the lake now caters for Udaipur's increasing tourist trade. Handicrafts and modern chemical and asbestos manufacturing and zinc smelting employ increasing numbers. Population (1981) 229,762.

Udall, Nicholas (1505–56), English dramatist and scholar. From 1534 to 1541 he was headmaster of Eton, and in 1554 became headmaster of Westminster. He is best remembered for his *Ralph Roister Doister*, the first known English comedy to be modelled on those of Plautus and Terence.

Udine, Italian city, capital of Udine province, situated some 100 km north-east of Venice. It became the capital of Friuli in 1238. The 13th–18th century archiepiscopal cathedral has paintings by Tiepolo. The town is an administrative and market centre for the Friulian plain. In 1976 the surrounding area was devastated by an earthquake. Population (1979) 103,000.

Udmurt Autonomous Soviet Socialist Republic, lies in the east of European RSFSR, USSR, between the Kama and Vyatka rivers in an undulating well-forested plain that includes many swamps. There are engineering, iron and steel (since the 18th century), and timber industries. Coarse grain and flax are grown, and dairy-farming is widespread. The main towns are Izhevsk (the capital), Votkinsk and Sarapul. Votskaya Autonomous Oblast was formed in 1920, and renamed Udmurt in 1932. Area 42,100 km². Population (1980) 1,506,000, mostly Udmurts and Russians.

Ufa, capital city, economic and cultural centre of the Bashkir ASSR, USSR. It is one of the main industrial centres of the Urals, with engineering (aircraft engines, electrical and oil industry equipment), oil refining (pipelines from the Tuimazy and Ishimbay fields), chemicals (the largest petrochemical plant in the USSR), wood-processing, and diverse light and food industries, and is also an important transport centre. Ufa is the residence of the religious head of the Muslims of European Russia and Siberia (since 1788). It was founded in 1574 as a Russian fortress, has been a town since 1586, and a provincial capital since 1862. Population (1980) 986,000.

Ufa Directory, anti-Bolshevik government in Russia, set up in 1918 at the State Conference in Ufa which had been called by the Committee of Members of the Constituent Assembly. It was soon overthrown by Adm. Kolchak.
See also UNION OF SOVIET SOCIALIST REPUBLICS, *History*; CONSTITUENT ASSEMBLY, RUSSIAN; UFA.

UFO, common abbreviation of Unidentified Flying Object.

Uganda
Area: 236,860 km²
Population: 13,200,000
Capital: Kampala

Uganda, republic in East Africa, 800 km from the Indian Ocean, bounded on the west and north by Zaire and Sudan, on the east by Kenya, and on the south-west by Tanzania and Rwanda. Area 236,860 km².
Uganda has great mountains and vast forests and lakes. The Ruwenzori Mountains, the legendary 'Mountains of the Moon', are the main range and form the boundary between the Western Province and Zaire. The highest peaks are Margherita (5110 m) and Alexandra (5091 m). The White Nile river has several of its headwaters in these mountains. Below 4250 m the slopes consist of stretches of alpine

Uccello. St George and the Dragon, *painted around 1460.*

Uganda. The view south-east from the summit of Mount Elgon, towards the Rift Valley in Kenya.

meadow and bamboo forests, on the lower slopes equatorial forests, grading upwards to savanna.

The White Nile has its main source in Lake Victoria, flowing out at the Owen Falls near Jinja. From there the river flows through Lake Kyoga into Lake Mobutu; it is navigable between Namasagali and Atura.

The total population was estimated at 13·2 million in 1979 and the main towns are Kampala (the capital), Entebbe and Jinja.

Over 85 per cent of the population depend on the land for their livelihood, traditional farming systems ranging from shifting cultivation of millet and sorghum in the north to perennial cultivation in the south with the banana as the staple food. Maize, cassava, sweet potatoes and groundnuts are other important food crops, still grown largely for subsistence. Coffee and cotton are the main cash crops. Plantations are important only for sugar and tea.

Many mineral deposits are known but the only large mine is that producing copper at Kilembe. Manufacturing employs only a few thousand people, producing such goods as beer, cigarettes, textiles and cement.

The unit of currency is the shilling, of 100 cents.

Uganda has presidential government, with legislative power vested in an elected parliament.

English is the official language, with Luganda the most widespread of the local languages.

History. In 1862 Speke and Grant were the first Europeans to reach the capital of Mutesa, King of Buganda, near the present Kampala. In 1872 Sir Samuel Baker arrived at the headquarters of the young King of Bunyoro, Kabarega, and proclaimed the formal annexation of Bunyoro on 14 May 1872. In 1884 control of the British sphere in East Africa was assigned to the Imperial British East Africa Company, and in 1890 Lord Lugard was sent to establish the Company's influence in Uganda. On 1 April 1893 the British government assumed the responsibilities of the Company in Buganda. The formal establishment of a protectorate was postponed until 18 June 1894. In 1896 the protectorate was extended to most of the other regions which are now included within the present Uganda. There was increasing internal self-govern-

ment from 1920 onwards. In April 1962 elections were held and Milton Obote became prime minister. On 10 October 1962 Uganda became an independent state, a dominion with a federal structure, and remained within the Commonwealth. In 1963 Uganda became a republic.

Early in 1966 serious divisions became apparent in the government. In February Obote assumed absolute powers and dismissed the president, Mutes II, Kabaka of Buganda. On 24 May 1966 the Kabaka palace was stormed by Obote's troops. The Kabaka was arrested. In 1967 a second republican constitution was introduced.

Before Obote could implement new political and economic measures, the Chief of the Defence Staff, Maj.-Gen. Amin seized power in January 1971, while Obote was out of the country. Under Amin, people were subjected to a brutal oppression by the military. In 1972 Amin expelled the 40,000-strong Asian community from Uganda, and announced the repatriation of all African refugees living in Uganda.

Amin was overthrown in 1979 and a provisional government was set up which ultimately appointed the former Attorney-General, Dr. Binaisa, as President. He was put out of office by the army in 1980. Elections to a new parliament were held in December 1980 and Obote, returned from exile, claimed victory. The army is still powerful and there has been little progress in restoring social or economic stability.

Ugarit (modern Ras Shamra), seaport on Syrian coast, north of Latakiya, and capital of a small state which flourished in the 15th to 13th centuries BC. Excavations from 1929 produced ivories and thousands of inscribed clay tablets. The inscriptions were written in Akkadian, Hurrian and a special cuneiform alphabetic script, called Ugaritic.
See also CUNEIFORM WRITING.

Uhland, Johann Ludwig (1787–1862), German poet, literary historian and politician. With Justinius Kerner he was at the centre of the famous circle *Der Schwäbische Dichterkreis.* Three books, consisting mostly of national verses, published between 1815 and 1820, made him famous, and he rapidly became a political leader. The revolutionary year of 1848 saw him as a leading member of

the German National Assembly in Frankfurt-am-Main. Uhland's poems include mostly ballads, romances and folk songs.

Uhlans, Tatar name for a particular type of soldier, and adopted in Poland in the 18th century to denote light cavalrymen, who were armed with a lance and sabre, and later with a carbine. The name was later applied to Prussian cavalry regiments.

Uist, North, one of the larger islands of the Outer Hebrides, connected to Grimsay and Benbecula to the south by a stone causeway. Lochmaddy in the north-east is the main settlement. Elsewhere the crofting population is found on the north and west coasts. The interior consists of peat bogs and countless lochs. The population is 1726 and tourism, weaving, estate work and lobster fishing are of local importance.

Uist, South, one of the larger of the islands of the Outer Hebrides, connected to Benbecula by a road bridge. Lochboisedale in the south-east is the main town and port. Most of the population of 2281 (1971) live in crofting townships on the west coast. Weaving, tourism and salmon-rearing are locally important. There are hundreds of lochs in the central area but the east coast is mountainous and dissected by sea-lochs. In 1955 the north-west part of the island was leased for the army's guided-missile firing range.

Ujjain, town of Madhya Pradesh state, India. It is one of the seven sacred Hindu cities, and every 12th year is the scene of the great bathing festival, the Kumbh Mela. It was the capital of the ancient Avanti kingdom (6th–4th centuries BC) and in the 2nd–4th centuries AD was a centre of Sanskrit learning. It trades in grain. Population (1981) 281,878.

Ujungpadang, or Makasar, formerly Macassar, town on the south-west peninsula of Sulawesi, Indonesia. The town serves a rich volcanic hinterland, is the focus of the eastern archipelago's air links, and an important export port for timber, minerals, vegetable oils (including 'macassar' oil once used extensively in hair preparation) and leather. Population (1975) 521,000.

Ukelele, miniature guitar, introduced to Hawaii by the Portuguese in 1877 and thence back into Europe. It has four gut strings and is played from a tablature.

Ukraine, The, region in the south-west part of European USSR. The eastern Slav (Russian) people—Polyane, Severyane, Drevlyane, Volhynians, etc.—inhabited the forested and wooded steppe zones from the Early Middle Ages. After a short period of Khazar domination they were, in the 9th century, included in the Kievan state, whose capital and most other main centres were here. The steppe remained the home of the nomadic Pechenegs and Cumans. After the break-up of Kievan Russia, and particularly after the Tatar conquest in the 13th century, the centre of gravity shifted to the west. By the middle of the 15th century most of the Ukraine was under Lithuania, while in the south-east the Crimean Khanate was formed. The Lithuanian-held territory became Polish in 1569. The Cossacks, in the mid-17th century, rose and won independence from Poland for the central Ukraine, and brought about a union with Muscovy in 1653. The Ukraine to the west of the Dnieper remained Polish until the partitions of Poland in the 1790s. During the 14th–15th centuries the population of the Ukraine had developed a separate identity and a degree of national consciousness. A romantic literary Ukrainian movement began early in the 19th century. At the beginning of the 20th century a nationalised trend appeared which favoured autonomy for the Ukraine. This autonomy was granted, after the February Revolution in 1917, by the Provisional Government, which recognised the authority of the Ukrainian Central Rada (Council) over the central Ukraine. After the seizure of power by the Bolsheviks the Ukrainian Soviet Republic was proclaimed in December 1917. When the Union of Soviet Socialist Republics was formed in 1922 it became one of the four original constituent republics.

Ukrainian Directory, ephemeral nationalist government in the Ukraine 1918–19, headed first by the author V. Vynnychenko, then by S. Petlyura, commander of the Ukrainian nationalist troops. Composed of people of divergent political views, it soon disintegrated.

Ukrainian Hetman. From the late-16th century 'Hetman' was the title of the highest officer of the Zaporozh'e Cossacks; from 1648 to 1764 it was the title of the head of the Cossack state, with administrative authority. In 1918, under German occupation, the title was re-established and Gen. P. Skoropads'ki ruled the country as a hetman for seven months.

See also UKRAINE, THE.

Ukrainian Soviet Socialist Republic, or Ukraine (Russian *Ukraina*), lies in the south-west of European USSR, north of the Black Sea and the Sea of Azov, and bordered on the west by Romania, Hungary, Czechoslovakia and Poland. It takes second place in the USSR (after the Russian Soviet Federative Socialist Republic) in population (1980) 50,000,000, and third place (after the RSFSR and Kasakh SSR) in size, having an area of 603,700 km². It is divided into 25 *oblasti* (provinces). The capital is Kiev. The Ukraine lies largely in the Russian plain, which here forms the Polesye, Dnieper and Black Sea lowlands, and the Volhynia-Podolia, Dnieper and Donets uplands. In the west lie the Carpathians (maximum height 2061 m), and in the south the Crimean Mountains (maximum height 1545 m). The Ukraine has rich deposits of iron-ore (Kerch, Krivoi Rog), manganese (Nikopol), coal (Donets Basin), natural gas, oil, mercury, salts, etc. The main rivers are the Dnieper, Dniester, Southern Bug, and Severeski Donets, a tributary of the Don. There are mixed forests in the north, wooded steppe with beech and oak forests, and steppe in the south; the wooded steppe and steppe have fertile black earth soils.

The population density is higher than in the rest of the USSR (apart from the Moldavian SSR); it is highest in the industrial Donets Basin. Among the branches of industry, engineering occupies the first place, followed by metallurgy, chemicals, coal-mining and the sugar industry. Maize, wheat, barley, rye and oats are the main grain crops, and sugar-beet and sunflowers are also widely grown.

Ulan Bator (formerly *Urga*), capital city of the Mongolian People's Republic, on the River Tula north-west of Peking (China). Leather and woollen goods are manufactured. An important transport focus, it is in the process of being transformed into a modern industrial city. Population (1978) 400,000.

Ulanova, Galina (1910–), one of Russia's greatest ballerinas. Originally a member of the Leningrad Theatre of Opera and Ballet, where she created the rôles of Maria in the *Fountain of Bakhchisarai*, 1934, and Juliet in *Romeo and Juliet*, 1940, she joined the Bolshoi Theatre, Moscow, in 1944, where she created the title-role in *Cinderella*, 1945. She led this company on its visit to London in 1956, when she was acclaimed as the greatest present-day interpreter of Giselle. She retired from the stage in 1962 and now coaches younger dancers in her former rôles.

Ulan-Ude (formerly *Verkhneudinsk*), city in the RSFSR, USSR, in south-east Siberia, capital (since 1923), economic and cultural centre of Buryat ASSR. It is situated in West Transbaikalia on the Trans-Siberian Railway and is a major industrial centre (mainly since the 1930s—locomotives, ship repairing, glass, timber and food industries). It has been known since 1666 as a Russian fort, has been a town since 1775, and was made capital of the Far Eastern Republic in 1920. Population (1980) 305,000.

Ulbricht, Walther (1893–1973), German politician. He worked for the Communist party in Moscow, returning to Germany after the Second World War. As organiser of the Socialist Unity party (a fusion of Communists and Socialists), he quickly became the most powerful figure in East German politics. His authority rested on his position as first secretary of the Politburo (from 1950) in the German Democratic Republic. An unwavering supporter of Soviet policies, Ulbricht played the prime rôle in East Germany's development as a 'people's democracy'. In 1960 he succeeded Pieck as head of state.

Ulcer, a gradual destruction of tissue on the surface of the skin or mucous membrane due to any cause, but commonly the result of injury or infection. The most frequent sites are the skin and the lining of the alimentary tract. Ulcers of the skin are usually due either to simple infection, varicose veins and the consequent impairment of circulation, trauma or malignant disease.

See also PEPTIC ULCER; STOMACH; ULCERATIVE COLITIS.

Ulcerative Colitis, the condition characterised by the presence of inflammation and numerous ulcers in the bowel. Its symptoms consist of diarrhoea often accompanied by the passage of blood, slime and mucus in the faeces, abdominal pain, loss of weight and general weakness. It is more common in people of a nervous disposition and may be treated by drugs: severe cases may need surgical operation.

Uleåborg, see OULU.

Ulex, a genus of the Leguminosae, found in Europe and North Africa. The leaves are reduced to scales, their function being taken over by spiny green stems. *U. europaeus* has been introduced into many temperate areas and can be a serious weed.

Ullswater, the second largest lake in the Cumbrian Lake District, England, on the east side of Helvellyn ridge; it is 13 km long and 1 km wide.

Ulm, city in Baden-Württemberg, Federal Republic of Germany, on the Danube at its confluence with the Iller, 71 km south-east of Stuttgart. It is connected by bridges with Neu-Ulm on the right bank of the Danube in Bavaria. In the Middle Ages it was an important market on the trade route to Italy and the Orient. Ulm has a magnificent Gothic cathedral (begun in 1377). The city has machinery, electrical, textile and leather industries. Population 94,000.

Ulna, medial and larger of the two bones of the forearm, running from the wrist to the elbow. It articulates with the humerus and the head of the radius above and the radius and carpus below.

Ulster, ancient northern province of Ireland, the seat of the O'Neills, comprising the present counties of Cavan, Donegal and Monaghan (Republic of Ireland), and Antrim, Armagh, Londonderry, Down, Fermanagh and Tyrone (Northern Ireland).

Ulster King of Arms, see HERALD'S COLLEGE.

Ultra Vires (Latin, 'beyond one's strength or power'), legal phrase used particularly with regard to the limitation of the legal or constitutional powers of a person, court, company or corporation. In English law anything done by a company outside the powers given in the memorandum of association is *ultra vires* and void.

See also COMPANY.

Ultramarine, name given to a substance of a fine blue colour, originally obtained by grinding hydrated lapis-lazuli. It is now prepared artificially by heating sodium carbonate or sulphate with kaolin, charcoal and sulphur, at first with exclusion of air. The dull green product is converted into the blue compound by heating with sulphur with access to air. It is used as a pigment by artists, for colouring papers and in laundries.

Ultrasound, an instrument that transmits high frequency sound waves, too high to be heard by the human ear. Ultrasonic waves are reflected by soft tissue, so can be used in medicine to give a picture of parts of the body that would not show up in X-rays. The ultrasound is used commonly in obstetrics, as the reflected waves can give a picture of the state of the foetus and the uterus, and cause no known side-effects. The ultrasound can detect the presence of twins as early as seven weeks, can measure the rate of foetal growth, and detect gross abnormalities. It can also locate the site of the placenta. It detects growths in the uterus or on the ovaries, and also abnormalities of the brain, and of other soft tissues in the body.

Ultraviolet Radiation, electromagnetic radiation of shorter wavelengths than visible light, i.e. less than 400 nm (4×10^{-7} m). The lower limit can be anywhere between about 100 and 10 nm, depending on definitions; this is also the long end of the soft X-ray region. Ultraviolet radiation makes many materials fluoresce. Fluorescent light tubes are coated inside with materials which fluoresce under the ultraviolet radiation produced by the discharge. Most glasses are opaque to all but the longest wavelengths of the ultraviolet, but quartz and fused silica transmit well and these are used in 'sun-lamps'. Almost all detectors of radiation are very sensitive to ultraviolet. Air transmits down to a wavelength of approximately 200 nm but the upper atmosphere is opaque to radiation below 300 nm on account of the presence of ozone; life as we know it might not exist if it were not for this protective effect. The chemical, physical and biological effects of ultraviolet are broadly due to the fact that the energy in a quantum in the ultraviolet range is enough to shatter many chemical bonds; thus irreversible changes can be caused in protein and other living tissue.

Ultraviolet Spectroscopy, means of analysis which gives information on the characteristics of the groups within a molecule. The technique depends on the fact that energy of a suitable frequency and wavelength is able to be absorbed, producing highly energised or 'excited state' electrons. Electrons associated with different atoms and bonds require different energies to activate them, the energy being a characteristic of the group, or the chemical situation of the electron.

See also SPECTRUM AND SPECTROSCOPE.

Ultraviolet Spectrum, see SPECTRUM AND SPECTROSCOPE.

Ulyanov, see LENIN, VLADIMIR ILYICH.

Ulyanovsk (formerly *Simbirsk*), capital and economic centre of Ulyanovsk *oblast*, USSR; on the Volga, and a port on the Kuibyshev Reservoir. It has engineering (cars, machine-tools), food and light industries. It is an important transport centre (four railway lines), and a local cultural centre. It was founded in 1648 as a fortress town and starting-point of the Muscovite Simbirsk defence line. It has been a provincial capital since 1780, and is the birthplace of Lenin (Ulyanov). Population (1980) 473,000.

Ulysses, see ODYSSEUS.

Umbelliferae, a family of about 200 genera and about 2700 species, occurring mainly in north temperate regions. Typically they have a basal rosette of divided leaves and hollow upright stems, which bear the flower-clusters (umbels). The flowers usually have very small sepals, five white, pink or yellow petals, five stamens and an inferior ovary (formed below the attachment of the petals) of two fused carpels which separate as the fruit ripens. The Umbelliferae include many plants used as herbs and flavourings, also the carrot (*Daucus*) and parsnip (*Pastinaca*), but there are also a number of very poisonous species, notably hemlock, *Conium maculatum*.

Umber, natural pigment, containing hydrated oxides of iron and manganese. The earthy pigment is washed and dried at 100° C. It then constitutes 'raw umber', which, calcined, becomes a rich brown colour—'burnt umber'.

Umberto I, Ranieri Carlo Emanuele Giovanni Maria Ferdinando Eugenio (1844–1900), King of Italy (1878–1900), eldest son of Victor Emmanuel I. He won popularity by his generosity and by his interest in his people, who called him 'Umberto the Good'.

Umberto II (1904–83), King of Italy, son of Victor Emmanuel III. He was proclaimed king on the abdication of his father in May 1946, but a referendum in favour of a republic the following month led to his retirement to Portugal, where he then lived.

Umbilical Cord, see FOETUS.

Umbra, in astronomy, means either the darkest portion of the shadow cone cast by the Earth or Moon in an eclipse, or the dark central part of a sunspot.

See also ECLIPSES OF THE SUN AND MOON.

Umbrella (Latin *umbra*, shade), a portable protection from the sun or rain; it is of great antiquity. Its use was known in China as early as the 11th century BC, and ancient sculptures of it have been discovered in Nineveh, Persepolis and Thebes (Egypt). In the East the umbrella was an emblem of rank. In ancient Greece and Rome umbrellas were regarded as effeminate, but in the 12th century the Doge of Venice had an umbrella with the ceremonial significance of a canopy. The Spanish invaders of Mexico found the Aztec kings using umbrellas.

Umbrella Bird, three species of the genus *Cephalopterus*, in family Cotingidae, order Passeriformes. These birds have a large crest on the head, which they spread out like an umbrella when courting. They are black, 40 to 50 cm long, and are found in the tops of trees in northern South America and Central America. They have a wattle hanging from under the beak.

Umbrella Plant, alternative name for *Cyperus alternifolius*, also for *Peltiphyllum peltatum*, a perennial waterside plant of the family Saxifragaceae, having round leaves with the stalk attached at the centre.

Umbrella Tree, name given for reasons of shape to many plants, notably to *Schefflera* sp., *Brassaia actinophylla* and *Pariti guineense*.

Umbria, region of central Italy, comprising the provinces of Perugia and Terni. Umbria is essentially hilly Apennine country. The main rivers are the upper Tiber and the Nera. The region depends on low productivity agriculture. Cereals are the chief crop, grown in the rich valley of the Tiber and on the poor uplands. There is an important industrial area around Terni based on local hydro-electricity supplies and iron and steel. The regional capital is Perugia. Area 8456 km². Population (1980) 808,351.

Umiak, Eskimo boat, resembling the kayak but of greater size and capacity.

Umlaut (from German) has two meanings: (1) an internal vowel change (as in German *Hand* into *Hände*), usually caused by a vowel in the following syllable; it is common in Germanic languages, and traces of it remain in English, *man, men; mouse, mice*, and so on; (2) the diacritic mark placed over a vowel to indicate such change: *a-ä, u-ü, o-ö*.

Umm al-Quwain, see UNITED ARAB EMIRATES.

Umtali, see MUTARE.

Umtata, capital of the Transkei, South Africa, and terminus of the railway from East London. There is an Anglican cathedral. Umtata is an industrial growth point. Population (1971) 24,838.

Unalaska, see ALEUTIAN ISLANDS.

Unamuno, Miguel de (1864–1936), Spanish author. From a Catholic background, he lost his faith and until 1897 wrote in defence of agnostic Positivist, and then Marxist, ideas. As a result of a nervous breakdown he attempted to persuade himself of the truth of Catholic dogmas, but failed. He now began to write in defence of religious faith, arguing that without God existence is emotionally unbearable, while admitting that faith is offensive to reason. Unamuno became famous in his day, suffering exile twice, for progressive criticisms of Primo de Rivera in 1923, and for repudiating the second Spanish Republic of 1931. His works include the novels *Niebla*, 1914, and *Abel Sánchez*, 1917, both about the freedom of the will, and *Del sentimiento trágico de la vida*, 1913, his most famous book, an impassioned statement of his religious dilemma.

Unanimism, a minor movement in French literature which took place about the turn of the 19th and 20th centuries. Its beginnings were in the writings of *le groupe de l'Abbaye*, a number of young poets including Georges Duhamel, Chennevière and Vildrac. This group is described in Duhamel's *Pasquier* novels; another member, Jules Romains was the leader of the Unanimist movement.

Uncertainty Principle, or indeterminacy principle, a theory, enunciated by Heisenberg in 1927, which in simple terms states that it is impossible to measure or know exactly and simultaneously the position and momentum of a particle. If Δp is the uncertainty or range of possible values within which the momentum lies, and Δq is the uncertainty or range of possible values in the determination of the position of the particle, then the product $\Delta p \Delta q$ cannot be less than $h/(2\pi)$ where h is Planck's constant. Thus, if the momentum is determined with great precision so that Δp is very small, then Δq, the uncertainty in the position, is unavoidably large, and vice versa. This does not arise from experimental errors (which further increase the uncertainty in the results of measurement); it is a fundamental characteristic of the quantum nature of matter arising from its dualistic behaviour, and a consequence of our inability to describe it ultimately except in statistical terms.

See also ATOM; QUANTUM THEORY.

Uncle Sam, the USA, or rather the government of the United States, personified. It is said to be derived from the initials 'US' on government wagons during the War of 1812 and the nickname began to appear after 1813 in New York newspapers. Just before the Civil War it had found its way into dictionaries as the accepted sobriquet of the nation. The familiar costume of Uncle Sam was taken from that of 'Major Jack Downing', whom he superseded as the cartoonists' national symbol.

Unconformity, a surface separating older rocks below from younger rocks above. The plane of unconformity may be a surface which has been exposed to weathering, erosion and denudation before a new series of rocks are deposited on top of it; alternatively it may simply represent an interval of time during which no sediment was deposited, in which case it is termed a surface of non-deposition.

Unconsciousness, includes all types of impaired consciousness from drowsiness through stupor to coma. There are two main degrees of unconsciousness. Stupor is a state of extreme drowsiness, in which the person seems to be unconscious, but can be roused by pain, and may give vague responses to forceful questioning. The next state is coma. A person in coma does not feel any pain or respond to any stimulus. An anaesthetised patient is in coma. The cause of unconsciousness is a disturbance of the cerebral circulation, and this, in turn, may be traumatic, toxic or inflammatory in origin. Where the symptoms are unilateral and asymmetrical, the cause may be cerebral haemorrhage, embolism or thrombosis, cerebral tumour or abscess. Where they are bilateral and symmetrical, the causative condition may be concussion, post-epileptic coma, uraemia, diabetes mellitus, insulin hypoglycaemia, heatstroke, poisoning or infection.

Underdevelopment. An underdeveloped country is one which is below its potential economic level, where most of the population is engaged in food production, because industrialisation has not taken place. Until 200 years ago all countries were underdeveloped in this sense; the fact that industrialisation has since occurred in some but not in others has enabled the former to wield enormous economic and political power internationally.

See also THIRD WORLD, THE.

Underground Railroad, lines of communication formed in the Northern states of America before the Civil War in order to assist fugitive slaves to reach Canada, where they were safe from recapture. Guidance, shelter, food and clothing were provided by the sympathisers.

Underhill, Eveylyn (1875–1941), British mystic and writer. Her own religious experiences led her to a comprehensive study of the mystics, and her book *Mysticism*, 1911, remains a classic exposition. She also exercised wide personal influence as a spiritual director and a conductor of retreats. Her many other books include *The Path of Eternal Wisdom*, 1912; *The Life of the Spirit and the Life of To-day*, 1922; and *Worship*, 1936.

Underpinning, method of structural support to counter causes of foundation failure in which new foundations are built bit by bit below the existing ones.

Undset, Sigrid (1882–1949), Norwegian novelist. Her first successful novel was *Jenny*, 1911, the story of an idealistic young woman and her defeat in the face of harsh reality. After other works on a similar theme, she turned to the past, and in the trilogy *Kristin Lavransdatter*, 1920–22, created a dramatic story of passion which is perfectly blended with a meticulously observed 14th-century setting. This was followed by the two novels about *Olav Audunssøn*, 1925–27, in which the central character is a 13th-century chieftain torn between the pagan code of honour and the new Christian morality. Her conversion to Roman Catholicism in 1925 is reflected in novels such as *Gymnadenia*, 1929, and *Den trofaste hustru*, 1936.

Undue Influence. In English law a contract to which a party has been induced to give his consent by the exercise of undue influence on the part of another is voidable. So also a will can be attacked by interested parties on the

same ground. Presumptions of undue influence arise generally in connection with gifts. The relations of solicitor and client, parent and child, for example, are presumed to give the former in each case influence over the latter.

Undulant Fever, see BRUCELLOSIS.

Unemployment. During the period between the two World Wars, unemployment first became an acute world problem. The chief causes were: (1) disorganisation of the labour market; (2) a surplus of available labour, together with a surplus of manufactured goods; and (3) under-consumption. In the UK by 1932 unemployment had reached its highest total with 2,947,000 or 22 per cent of the insured working population.

In the USA during the years 1930–39, the average number of unemployed was 8·5 million out of a total working population of over 51 million. In the 1970s and 1980s unemployment, linked this time with inflation, again became a major problem, reaching 3,225,216 in the UK in January 1983.

See also SOCIAL SECURITY.

Ungaretti, Giuseppe (1888–1970), Italian poet. He was influenced by the work of the French poets Mallarmé and Valéry. Ungaretti became the chief exponent of the *poesia pura*; he believed that the poet's aim should be to convey an immediate impression by means of words and sounds. His theories had a great influence on younger poets, including those belonging to the Hermetic movement.

Ungava, former district of northern Labrador, Canada, occupying all the interior of the peninsula now known as the Territory of Ungava. The vast deposits of iron ore in the basin straddling the Quebec-Newfoundland boundary have been developed since the early 1950s.

Ungulates, terrestrial, mainly herbivorous mammals with the ends of the limbs generally bearing horny hooves. The former mammalian order of Ungulata is now split up into separate orders: Artiodactyla, eventoed hoofed mammals (pigs, peccaries, hippopotamuses, camels, deer, antelope, cattle, sheep and goats); Perissodactyla, odd-toed hoofed mammals (horses, tapirs, rhinoceroses); Proboscidea, elephants; and Hyracoidea, hyrax.

Uniats, Near-Eastern Christians in communion with Rome. Uniats keep their own liturgy and ancient rites, with married priests and communion in both kinds.

See also NESTORIUS.

Unicorn, fabulous Indian animal, referred to by Greek and Latin writers, resembling a horse and having one straight horn.

Unicorn, in Heraldry, see MONSTER.

Unidentified Flying Object (UFO) applies to objects seen in the air or on the ground and unidentifiable by the observer. Many people, either singly or in groups, attest to having sighted aerial objects unidentifiable with known atmospheric or astronomical phenomena, and in many cases photographs have been taken of the objects claimed to have been seen.

Unified Field Theory, a hypothetical theory to link electromagnetic, gravitational, strong nuclear and weak nuclear forces, describing their combined characteristics in one set of equations. Einstein spent his latter years

in attempts to link electromagneticism with gravitation.

Uniformitarianism, in geology, is the principle first formulated by the geologist James Hutton. It states that the structural and petrological evolution of the Earth's crust during the whole extent of geological time has been controlled by physical processes of types which are still in action today. The principle can be summed up in the phrase 'the present is the key to the past'. It contrasts with the old 'catastrophic' theory which postulated the occurrence, in the course of geological time, of events radically different from anything going on at the present day.

Uniformity, Acts of, series of Acts passed by Parliament for the regularising of public worship in England. The Act of 1549 directed the clergy to conform to the new prayer-book of that year. The new prayer-book of 1552 was accompanied by an Act which prescribed its use by laity and clergy. The Act of 1559 imposed the Elizabethan prayer-book on the whole kingdom and required all persons to attend their parish church. The best-known Act is that of 1662. This required the revised liturgy of that year to be used in all churches and places of worship. The Worship and Doctrine Measure of 1974 repealed the Act of Uniformity and transferred authority in matters of worship to the General Synod.

Union Group, see TOKELAU ISLANDS.

Union, Irish. The union of Great Britain and Ireland was effected on 1 January 1801. The Irish Parliament, whose members all belonged to the Church of Ireland, passed the bill after a liberal distribution of peerages and pensions had been made to its members. Moreover, Pitt had promised to link this measure with one of Catholic Emancipation. But George III refused to sanction Catholic Emancipation, and Irish Catholics therefore came to regard the Acts of Union as yet another example of English perfidy. The Act provided that 100 Irish members should become part of the House of Commons at Westminster, and 28 temporal with 4 spiritual peers, co-opted for each Parliament by their fellow peers, should represent Ireland in the House of Lords. Commerce was to be free from all restrictions. The union was dissolved in 1921, when the agreement setting up the Irish Free State was concluded.

See also IRELAND, *History*.

Union Jack, see FLAG.

Union of South Africa, see SOUTH AFRICA.

Union of Soviet Socialist Republics
Area: 22,402,200
Population: 264,500,000
Capital: Moscow

Union of Soviet Socialist Republics (abbreviations USSR, Soviet Union), quasi-federal state in Europe and Asia comprising 15 Soviet Socialist Republics. Area (1976) 22,402,200 km².

The official name 'Union of Soviet Socialist Republics' was adopted in 1922 at a congress of representatives of the four Soviet republics then in existence—the RSFSR, the Ukraine, Belorussia and Transcaucasia—when the USSR was officially founded as a federal state. Two more constituent republics were admitted in 1925, Turkmenia and Uzbekistan. Later several autonomous republics were raised to the status of constituent republics of the USSR (Tadzhik, 1929, Kazakh and Kirgiz, 1936, Karelian and Moldavian, 1940). The Baltic Republics of Estonia, Latvia and Lithuania, annexed in 1940, were also transformed into constituent republics. Real authority lies in the hands of the centralised Communist Party of the Soviet Union.

The USSR, with over 75 per cent of its territory in Asia and roughly 25 per cent in Europe, is bounded on the west by Norway, Finland, the Baltic, Poland, Czechoslovakia, Hungary and Romania; on the south by the Black Sea, Turkey, Iran, Afghanistan, China and Mongolia; on the east by the Pacific Ocean; and on the north by the Arctic Ocean; the Bering Strait, 35 km wide, separates the USSR from Alaska (USA) in the north-east. In the south the USSR reaches a latitude of 35°08′N, while its northernmost point is well within the Arctic Circle, reaching as far as 81°50′N. It extends from longitude 19°38′E to 169°02′W.

A broad division can be made into three lowland (the East European Plain and the West Siberian and Turanian lowlands), and two highland areas separating them (the Urals between the first two, the Kazakh Hills between the last two), a vast plateau (the Central Siberian plateau), and a mountainous rim on the southern and eastern borders.

The mountainous rim includes part of the Carpathians, the Crimean Mountains (highest point 1545 m), the Caucasus Mountains (5642 m), the Kopet-Dag, and the Pamirs-Alay (Communism Peak, formerly Stalin Peak, at 7495 m, the highest point in the USSR). Farther east are the Tien Shan (Victory Peak, 7439 m), the Dzungarian Ala Tau (4464 m), and Altai (4506 m), and the Sayan Mountains. East of Lake Baikal are complex mountain ranges, their maximum heights ranging from 1500 to 3650 m.

The chief rivers of European USSR have their sources in the central Russian upland. The Don and Dnieper flow south into the Sea of Azov and the Black Sea respectively; the Volga flowing east, is joined by the Kama from the Urals, and turns south to the Caspian; and the Western Dvina flows north-west to the Baltic. In addition the Neva in the north-west connects Lake Ladoga and the Gulf of Finland; the Dniester in the south flows into the Black Sea south-west of Odessa; the Kuban flows into the Sea of Azov; and the River Ural (traditionally considered the frontier between Europe and Asia) in the south-east, flows into the Caspian Sea. The chief rivers in Asiatic USSR have their sources in the mountains of the south, and flow north into the Arctic Ocean (the Ob, Yenisei and Lena), east into the Sea of Okhotsk (the Amur), or north-west into the inland Aral Sea (the Amu Darya and the Syr Darya). The total population of the USSR was estimated to be 264·5 million in January 1980. The average population density in the USSR is well below the world average and the distribution of the population is very uneven.

USSR. *Uplift of the valley floor has produced this spectacularly dissected topography in Armenia.*

Cities in the USSR with an estimated population in January 1980 of over one million were: Moscow (the capital); Leningrad; Kiev; Tashkent; Baku; Kharkov; Gorki; Novosibirsk; Minsk; Kuibyshev; Sverdlovsk; Tbilisi; Odessa; and Omsk.

Ethnically the population of the USSR is highly diverse and there are 100 separate peoples with more than 1000 persons in each, as well as many smaller groups. They all belong to two of the major racial groupings: the white, or European, and the yellow or Mongoloid. The most convenient classification is the one based on language.

After the Revolution, agriculture was reorganised on Communist principles with collective (*kolkhozy*) and state farms (*sovkhozy*) forming the basic farming units.

Grain crops are the most important (approximately 60 per cent of the total sown area) with wheat the major crop, others being rye, buckwheat and rice. The most favourable regions for grain production are the Ukraine, the North Caucasus, the Volga region, and the black earth belt to the south of the Ukraine. Industrial crops (for raw materials or foodstuffs) include cotton, flax, sugar beet, sunflower seed and tobacco. Potatoes and vegetables are grown chiefly near large industrial centres. Horticulture is also practised; and vineyards are found in the warmer south. Dairy-farming is carried on chiefly in the north of European USSR. Sheep-rearing is found both in rich grazing areas such as the lower Volga basin and in low-yield pastures, as in the Siberian steppes. Pigs are raised in the south of the European RSFSR and the

USSR. *A southern-Siberian village.*

Ukraine and also in the Baltic Republics and Belorussia. Poultry farming is carried on chiefly in the Ukraine.

Forests cover almost 40 per cent of the USSR, the largest area (515 million ha) being in the Soviet Far East.

The products of the fishing industry go largely to the home market. The main fishing grounds are in the North Atlantic and especially off the Baltic coast (cod, bass, eels, herrings, sprats), and in the Soviet Far East, where the most important catch is salmon. Seals, walrus and sea otters are caught for their furs in the Sea of Okhotsk and off the Komandorski Islands. Whaling is carried on in the North Pacific and the Antarctic.

The Soviet Union possesses the greatest fuel and mineral resources in the world. Much of the total mineral reserve is, as yet, untapped, lying beneath the inhospitable wastes and the permafrost of Siberia. The leading coalfields are those of the Donets, Kuznetsk, Karaganda and Pechora basins. The largest coal deposits lie, as yet untouched, in Asiatic USSR (the Central Siberian plateau and the Lena Valley). Lignite deposits occur to the south-west of Moscow. Coal has, however, been overshadowed since the discovery of oil and gas deposits in the Volga region and, more importantly, Central Asia and western Siberia.

Iron-ore deposits provide raw materials for the iron and steel industries. The traditional metallurgical industries of the Ukraine, the Urals, and central USSR have expanded, and new plants have arisen in Transcaucasia, Central Asia, Kazakhstan, the Soviet Far East, and the north-west. Non-ferrous metal ores include manganese ore, chromite, bauxite, aluminium, copper, lead, zinc and tin. Little is known about the uranium deposits, apart from the fact that uranium is extracted in important quantities in the Krivoi Rog district. Gold and diamonds are also mined.

After the fuel (coal, oil, gas) industries and the metallurgical industry, come the engineering and chemical industries. The textile industry too is fast growing. Light industries are developing in Siberia, producing such goods as man-made fabrics and footwear, but the centre for the majority of consumer goods is the European USSR.

Legislation is carried out formally by the

Supreme Soviet, a two-chamber arrangement of the Soviet of the Union and the Soviet of Nationalities; the volume of the laws and decrees and the large number of deputies concerned make the practice of parliamentary-type legislation unfeasible and it is, in any case, not wanted. The Supreme Soviet confirms the decrees of its Praesidium, which contains about 17 members, who are themselves leading members of party and state.

The official language is Russian, which is also the first language of over half the population. Languages of four big linguistic groups and some smaller ones are also spoken.

The USSR was formed as a non-federal union in 1922. A constitution worked out by Lenin and Stalin was enacted two years later; it phased out the old tsarist gubernates and introduced 'autonomous' republics, oblasts or krays, and smaller urban and country units; the basis of the new units of government was economic, in contrast to ethnic or political divisions only.

The constitution of 1936 ensured that the Communist Party, 'the leading core of all organisations, both public and state', remained motivator and activator of the life of the state. The 1936 constitution is still the basis of legality for state and civil law in the USSR and for the type of justice administered by Soviet courts.

History. (For pre-Revolution period, see Russian History.) The Bolsheviks originated as a radical wing of the Social Democratic party and remained so until after 1917. But the founder and leader of the Bolshevik party, Lenin, had early on concentrated on elaborating organisational and tactical principles of attaining and keeping power, and on training his followers in the implementation of these devices. After the February Revolution the Bolsheviks, led by Lenin and Trotsky, formed private armed detachments (Red Guards), gradually neutralised the armed forces and the majority of the population by propaganda, and in October seized power.

The Bolsheviks proclaimed a Dictatorship of the Proletariat, which was to be exercised by the Communist party through the Soviets and the Cheka, as well as directly. Armed resistance to the communist dictatorship developed into a civil war, which raged for three years (1918–21). With the country impoverished, industry and agriculture ruined, Lenin proclaimed the New Economic Policy (NEP) of concessions to peasants, private enterprise, and consumers. The period of the NEP (1921–27) was one of restoration of the economy, but also a period of consolidation of the political monopoly of the Communist Party. In the struggle for Lenin's succession Stalin was the dominant figure. Having ousted his opponents, Stalin launched his Five-Year Plans: policies of rapid expansion of heavy industry, forced Collectivisation of Agriculture, and the so-called cultural revolution, i.e. elimination of the old professional and technical intelligentsia and its replacement by a new one, indebted to the regime and indoctrinated. From 1934 Stalin ruled as unlimited dictator. Opposition among his own followers precipitated the universal terror of the Great Purge, 1937–38. In 1939 Stalin, who until then had let the

Soviet Union appear as champion of peace and anti-Fascism, suddenly concluded a pact of friendship with Hitler; this enabled the latter to attack Poland, which led to the outbreak of general hostilities between Germany and the western European countries. Despite the friendship pact, Hitler invaded the USSR in 1941. Britain and the USA immediately offered assistance, and the Soviet Union joined the anti-Hitler alliance.

As a result of the Allied victory in the Second World War the USSR retained all the territory annexed during the Stalin-Hitler friendship and also acquired new territories. The establishment of communist regimes in the countries of central and south-east Europe, Manchuria, and North Korea was a clear violation of the obligations undertaken by the Soviet government at the Yalta and Potsdam conferences, and under the United Nations Charter and the post-war peace treaties. It split the alliance and led to the formation of the two great ideological and power camps, the communist led by the USSR and the capitalist led by the USA.

Internally the post-war period under Stalin was characterised by the suppression of the comparative freedom of the war years and restoration of conformity, particularly in the cultural field, by mass deportations, xenophobia, obscurantism and anti-Semitism.

When Stalin died in 1953, a fierce struggle for power set in. Malenkov was ousted from the premiership in 1955, and in 1958 Khrushchev ousted Bulganin to add the premiership to his first secretaryship of the party's Central Committee. Having packed the latter's Praesidium, the Politburo, with his nominees he was now supreme.

The main policy issue between the warring cliques had been, and in fact continued to be, the scope and pace of de-Stalinisation. The great strikes and uprisings in the main corrective labour camp areas, 1953–55; the revolts in the satellite countries culminating in the Polish and Hungarian revolutions of October-November 1956; the appearance in the USSR itself of a radical reformist opposition among the intelligentsia (led by the Moscow writers) —all this frightened Stalin's successors. Many changes were made in economic matters, chiefly industrial administrative organisation and attempts to increase farm outputs.

Externally the tentative Soviet policy was to relax tension with the USA and the West. The detente policy, renewed after the reckless Soviet attempt in 1962 to install missiles in Cuba failed, exacerbated the Sino-Soviet dispute and led to a breach between the two great communist powers. Khrushchev's radical policy was one of the reasons for his colleagues' coup against him in October 1964, which made Leonid Brezhnev the first secretary of the party and A. N. Kosygin the premier. Criticism of all aspects of Khrushchev's policies gave rise to a firmer and more oppressive style of rule by his successors. This was shown in the policy of suppressing dissidence at home and sending military aid to communist governments, such as Czechoslovakia in 1968, to maintain the Soviet brand of Communism. The USSR's relations with the USA and Western Europe have in recent decades fluctuated between hostility and cautious approaches. The Soviet invasion of

Afghanistan in 1979 and the Solidarity protest in Poland have recently made East-West relations uneasy. In 1982 Brezhnev died and was succeeded as President by Yuri Andropov. Andropov remained in office for 16 months and on his death was succeeded by Konstantin Chernenko.

See also RUSSIAN ARCHITECTURE; RUSSIAN ART; RUSSIAN HISTORY; RUSSIAN LANGUAGE; RUSSIAN LITERATURE; RUSSIAN MUSIC.

Unionist, supporter of union between Ireland and Great Britain. Since the split in the Liberal party in 1886 between Home Rulers and Liberal Unionists, the Conservative party has been officially 'the Conservative and Unionist Party' and Conservatives have often stood for election under such labels as Unionist, and Conservative and Liberal Unionist. The Unionists were the ruling party in the Northern Ireland Parliament until direct rule in 1972.

Unit Trust, a method of investment through which small investors can gain two major advantages normally only available to those with large sums of money to invest: (1) a wide spread of risk and (2) the benefit of skilled management. They are proper legal trusts (hence unit-holders are not shareholders, as in investment trusts) with the funds provided by unit-holders invested in a variety of companies, usually from many industries, as decided by the managers in accordance with the Trust Deed, which must be approved by the Department of Trade before any units can be sold. The investor is further safeguarded since the investments are supervised by a Trustee, normally a bank or an insurance company, and by law not more than 5 per cent of the Trust Fund can be invested in any one company, nor can the Fund hold more than 10 per cent of the share capital of any one company.

Unitarianism, literally denotes simply belief in one God, and when thus understood is a generic term applicable not only to Christianity but to every form of monotheism. However, it is normally used to describe the belief held by certain Protestants who, while rejecting the scheme of orthodox theology as a whole, acknowledge the pre-eminent position of Jesus Christ in the world's history as a teacher of religion and a prophet of righteousness. A modern summary of the Unitarian faith enumerates the Fatherhood of God, the Brotherhood of Man, the Leadership of Jesus, the Victory of Good, the Kingdom of God, and the Life Eternal.

The English Unitarians trace their descent from those congregations, mainly Presbyterian, whose ministers were ejected in 1662, many of whose chapels are now in Unitarian hands. In 1928 the 'General Assembly of Unitarian and Free Christian Churches' was formed. The Assembly has about 200 ministers and 280 churches and other places of worship in Great Britain and Ireland. The American Unitarian Universalist Association, formed in 1961, has over a thousand churches and fellowships with 155,000 adult members.

United Arab Emirates, a group of seven independent federated sheikhdoms on the southern shore of the Persian Gulf, stretching about 525 km between Cape Masandam and the Qatar peninsula. They were formerly known as the Trucial States.

United Arab Emirates
Area: 92,100 km²
Population: 1,040,275

The physiography of the UAE is composed of a low desert plain, everywhere below 200 m except for the easternmost mountains on the Gulf of Oman.

The total population at the census of 1980 was 1,040,275. Dubai, Sharjah and Abu Dhabi are the principal towns and contain over half the total population.

Due to low, and unreliable, amounts of rainfall, there was virtually no agriculture until recently. Much effort has gone into agricultural research. Intensive irrigated and controlled cultivation produces alfalfa, cabbages, cauliflowers, tomatoes, turnips, cucumbers, onions, aubergines, radishes and strawberries. Abu Dhabi is the main oil producer in the emirates. Oil revenues have made it the richest state in the world in terms of per capita income, but the scope for industrial diversification is limited.

The Emirates are a federation headed by a President and a Supreme Council made up of the seven rulers. The Council appoints a Council of Ministers which drafts legislation. There is an elected National Council which may suggest amendments but has no legislative power.

Arabic is the official language, but English is also used for business purposes.

History. The federation of the United Arab Emirates (UAE) was proclaimed on 2 December 1971 by the sheikhdoms of Abu Dhabi, Dubai, Sharjah, Umm al-Quwain, Ajman and Fujairah. Ras al-Khaimah joined the UAE two months later.

The Portuguese, in the 16th century, were the first European power to take advantage of the Gulf's situation for trade with the East. By 1650 they had been replaced by the Dutch and British; the latter, through supremacy in India, won lasting control. When other powers showed interest in the Gulf towards the end of the 19th century, Britain entered into 'exclusive' treaties with the separate sheikhdoms, mortgaging them to British influence. After British withdrawal in 1971 from the base at Sharjah, which had succeeded Aden, attempts were made to form a union of Gulf states, but after Bahrain, Kuwait and Qatar opted for independence, the UAE was created. The oil-rich UAE maintains strong links with Britain and the West, and with the conservative element in Arab politics. The president is the Emir of Abu Dhabi, Shaik Zayed, and the Emir of Dubai is vice-president.

United Arab Republic (Al-Jumhūrīyah Al-'Arabīyah Al-Muttahīdah), name given to the political union of Egypt and Syria, effective 1958–61. Although the union was ended by Syria's secession in 1961 Egypt continued to use the name until 1971.

United Irishmen, society founded in Belfast in 1791 by Theobald Wolfe Tone. It was strongly influenced in its organisation and aims by the French Revolution. In 1795 it became a secret, oath-bound society, and it pursued revolutionary aims which culminated in the unsuccessful risings of 1798.
See also IRELAND, *History.*

United Kingdom, state of north western Europe properly called the United Kingdom of Great Britain and Northern Ireland. The United Kingdom includes England, Wales, Scotland and Northern Ireland; it does not include the Channel Islands or the Isle of Man which are direct dependencies of the Crown with their own legislative systems. Great Britain is a term denoting the main land mass in the British Isles which includes England Scotland and Wales.

For descriptions of landscape, population, agriculture and industry, see ENGLAND; IRELAND, NORTHERN; SCOTLAND; WALES.

The UK has no written constitution, although some parts are written down in the form of statute law and constitutional documents. In practice the constitution consists of statutes or acts of Parliament, various constitutional documents (e.g. Magna Carta, 1215, and the Bill of Rights, 1689), judicial rulings or precedents by the courts, customs and constitutional conventions (e.g. the Queen must act on the advice of the Cabinet and that advice must be unanimous).

The UK is a constitutional or limited monarchy, with a parliamentary system of government. Constitutionally Parliament consists of the Sovereign, Lords and Commons, and each must normally approve all bills before they become law. Political power lies in practice in the hands of the prime minister and Cabinet, who are normally drawn from the party or parties having a majority in the House of Commons. Ministers are constitutionally responsible to Parliament, both individually for their particular departments and collectively for the government's conduct of affairs. Between 1920 and 1972 Northern Ireland had its own parliament and government, with

United Kingdom
Area: 230,646 km²
Population: 54,321,000
Capital: London

power devolved from the UK parliament. The upper house at Westminster has a nominal membership of more than a thousand, but in practice its work is carried out by some two to three hundred regular attenders, whilst its judicial functions are carried out by specially-appointed law lords. The House of Commons consists of 650 members of Parliament, elected by universal adult suffrage for single-member constituencies, using the simple plurality or 'first-past-the-post' electoral system.

The official language is English.

History. England and Scotland came into being as a single political entity (Great Britain) with the Union of the Parliaments in 1707. The German-speaking Hanoverian kings who succeeded Queen Anne, the last of the Stuarts, in 1714, delegated attendance at ministerial councils to a 'first' or 'prime' minister among whom Walpole and the Pitts, father and son, were outstanding. Wealth came from new developments in manufacturing and from finance related to extensive overseas trade. Wars were fought mainly to protect profitable colonies and trading routes. The attempt to retain the American colonies (1775–83) brought conflict with America's allies (France, Spain and Holland). In 1793 war began once more against revolutionary France.

Great Britain became the United Kingdom in 1801 with its legislative union with Ireland. The country was then beginning to change from an agricultural to an industrial nation, and was still at war with France. After the war, demand for parliamentary reform was feared as the probable prelude to revolution. Catholic emancipation had been promised implicitly at the time of the Union with Ireland but George III had refused to countenance it and the Prime Minister, Pitt, had resigned. The king, who had been incapable of ruling since 1811, died in 1820 and his son, the Prince Regent, became king as George IV. In his reign religious toleration became a reality in spite of some violent opposition. In 1832, in the reign of William IV, agitation for a parliamentary Reform Bill at last resulted in the passing of the great Reform Act of 1832. Slavery was abolished, a Poor Law passed, and legislation for the protection of the worker was enacted.

In 1837 William IV died and was succeeded by his niece, Victoria, whose long reign witnessed much change and material progress.

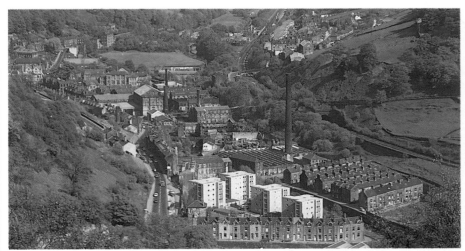

United Kingdom. *The traditional industrial landscape of the mill town of Hebden Bridge, W. Yorkshire.*

Commercially Britain was prospering and progressing and gradually the power and prestige of the of the House of Commons increased and its representative character was broadened. In the ministry of Robert Peel, the Corn Laws were repealed (1846) and free trade introduced. Peel was then defeated on the question of a Coercion Act for Ireland and resigned. The Tory Party was split and the Peelites, chief among whom were Gladstone and Lord Aberdeen, ultimately joined forces with the Whigs to form the Liberals, whilst the Protectionists, under Bentinck and Disraeli, eventually formed the modern Conservative party. From 1867 almost to the end of the 19th century politics were dominated by the duel between Gladstone and Disraeli. In 1868 Disraeli was succeeded as prime minister by Gladstone, who during the five years of his ministry passed more measures than almost any previous one. Education became compulsory, trade unions were legalised, and the Ballot Act was passed. The question of Irish Home Rule gradually forced itself to the fore. Disraeli, returned to power in 1874, put forward his imperial policy. In 1886 Gladstone formed his third ministry, with his majority dependent on the Irish. He determined, however, to introduce a Home Rule Bill, which was eventually defeated by a majority of 30. The measure seriously split the Liberal party, and from 1886 to 1906 the Conservatives were almost continuously in power. Queen Victoria died in 1901 and was succeeded by her son, Edward VII, who was, in his turn, succeeded in 1910 by his son, George V.

Britain's entry into the First World War on 4 August 1914 subdued domestic political difficulties until the end of the war in 1918, and in 1915 a coalition government was formed. In 1916 Irish volunteers seized the principal buildings in Dublin and civil war was proclaimed which was destined to end, eventually, in the formation of the Irish Free State and, subsequently, of the Republic of Ireland. In 1923 the Labour party assumed office for the first time, under the prime ministership of Ramsay MacDonald, although the Conservatives were returned to power by the 1924 election. In 1926 labour relations worsened and negotiations with the miners having failed, a general stoppage resulted, which led to the General Strike. By 1931 the financial and economic situation had deteriorated; unemployment figures exceeded 2.8 million, and a budget deficit of £40 million was shown to be imminent. Labour had again returned to power in 1929 but was succeeded in 1931 by a National Government of all parties under Ramsay MacDonald. The nation's financial outlook gradually improved, but soon domestic policy was overshadowed by considerations of foreign policy and the exigencies of national defence. In 1936 George V died and was succeeded by his son, Edward VIII. The new king reigned for less than a year, abdicating, uncrowned, in consequence of his proposed marriage to an American divorcée. His brother succeeded him as George VI.

During 1937 the international situation grew worse and German ambitions more dangerous. Chamberlain's policy of appeasement culminated in a humiliating meeting with Hitler and Mussolini in 1938 at Munich. In March 1939 Chamberlain announced that Britain would lend its support to Poland if that country was attacked. This pledge marked the end of the much-criticised appeasement policy. On the eve of the German invasion of Poland, Britain resolved to stand by its pledge – and went to war with Germany on 3 September. Winston Churchill took over from Chamberlain as prime minister in 1940, in which year the Battle of Britain, fought in the air, averted the danger of a German invasion. The war in Europe ended in May 1945 and was followed by a landslide victory for the Labour party at the General Election. The government, under Attlee, put forward an industrial programme for the nationalisation of the coal, gas and electricity industries. Among the outstanding social measures passed were the National Insurance Act and the National Health Service Act. Significant foreign policy decisions taken were the granting of dominion status to India, Pakistan, and Ceylon, and

United Kingdom. *Gilbert White's village of Selborne in Hampshire.*

independence to Burma. In 1948 Britain, France, 'Benelux', and the USA signed the North Atlantic Pact. The 1951 General Election resulted in a narrow Conservative victory, with Churchill as prime minister. In 1952 George VI died suddenly and was succeeded by his daughter, Elizabeth II. Britain's internal economic situation showed steady improvement. In 1955 Churchill resigned and was succeeded as prime minister by Eden, whose government was then returned with an increased majority. In 1956 Britain's ill-fated support, along with France, of Israel's invasion of Egypt after Nasser's nationalisation of the Suez Canal aroused bitter controversy. In 1957 Eden was succeeded as prime minister by Harold Macmillan, in whose term of office many former colonies gained independence. Thirteen years of Conservative government ended in 1964 with a narrow victory by the Labour party, under Harold Wilson. The basic British postwar problem of combining domestic expansion with international solvency, and of maintaining full employment without creating persistent inflation, remained. In 1970 a Conservative government was formed, led by Edward Heath, and British politics were dominated by serious inflation and rising unemployment. The situation in Ulster deteriorated steadily. In 1973 Britain joined the European Economic Community and the

economic situation began to look slightly brighter when the first of the North Sea oil came into production. Industrial unrest, however, remained acute, and there was concern at the levels of government borrowing and public spending. The Conservative party under Margaret Thatcher, won the election of 1979 with a policy of controlling the money supply and curbing union power. Her government was re-elected in 1983.

United Kingdom Atomic Energy Authority (UKAEA) was established in 1954 as a statutory corporation for research and development in atomic energy. It operates under the general supervision of the Secretary of State for Energy. Its main research centre is the Atomic Energy Research Establishment at Harwell, Berkshire.

United Methodist Church, see METHODISM.

United Nations (UN), an international organisation established in 1945 at the San Francisco Conference after considerable preparation by the victors in the Second World War. Its purposes are set out in Article 1 of its Charter. These are: (1) to maintain international peace and security; (2) to develop friendly relations among nations based on the principle of equal rights and self-determination of peoples; (3) to achieve international co-operation in solving international problems of an economic, social, cultural or humanitarian nature and in the promotion and encouragement of human rights and fundamental freedoms; (4) to be a centre for harmonising the actions of nations in the attainment of these common ends.

The principal organs of the UN are the Security Council, the General Assembly, the Economic and Social Council, the Trusteeship Council, the International Court of Justice and the Secretariat.

The Security Council has primary responsibility for the maintenance of international peace and security and acts on behalf of UN member states in carrying out its duties. The Council consists of five permanent members (Britain, France, USSR, USA and China) and ten non-permanent members elected for two-year terms. Decisions must have the affirmative vote of nine members including, except on procedural matters, that of the permanent members. Any permanent member can therefore veto a decision.

The General Assembly of the UN was originally intended to be merely a deliberative body. Pressures from the smaller states at the time of its establishment ensured it of a larger rôle. Although its decisions have no mandatory status and are only recommendations, it may discuss any subject and make recommendations on it to the Security Council or a member state.

The Economic and Social Council guides and co-ordinates the General Assembly's economic programme. It consists of 54 members elected for three years.

The Trusteeship Council supervises territories placed under the International Trusteeship System.

The International Court of Justice is the main judicial organ of the UN. Decisions of the Court are binding, but states are not obliged to submit cases to it. It consists of 15 independent judges of different nationalities elected by the General Assembly and the Security Council.

The Secretariat is headed by a Secretary-General appointed by the General Assembly on the recommendation of the Security Council. There have been five Secretaries-General: Trygve Lie (1946–53); Dag Hammarskjöld (1953–61); U Thant (1963–71); Kurt Waldheim (1972–81); Javier Pérez de Cuellar (1982–).

United Press International (UPI), the world's largest independent news-gathering organisation. Originally founded in 1907, today it combines the global facilities of United Press Associations and the International News Service, which were merged in 1958. It operates 240 bureaus throughout the world and employs more than 10,000 full and part-time reporters, photographers, editors, telegraphists and technicians. United Press International world headquarters are in New York. Newspapers and broadcasters in the United Kingdom are served by United Press International (UK) Ltd, in London.

United Provinces of Agra and Oudh, see UTTAR PRADESH.

United Reformed Church, formed in 1972 by the union of the Presbyterian and Congregationalist churches of England and Wales. Total membership in 1979 was 157,000.

United Society for the Propagation of the Gospel (USPG), formed in 1965 by the merger of the Society for the Propagation of the Gospel in Foreign Parts (founded in 1701) and the Universities' Mission to Central Africa (founded in 1857). Both societies were formed with the object of finding missionaries to work in parts of the church overseas. They continue to do so, and to supply grants to Anglican dioceses which will enable them to continue and extend their work. The society also supports a number of ecumenical activities among the newly united churches.

United States of America
Area: 9,363,122 km²
Population: 226,504,825
Capital: Washington D.C.

United States of America, a federal republic consisting of 50 states and a federal capital district. The United States lies roughly between 25° and 49°N latitude and between 69° and 125°W longitude, with Alaska reaching 71°N and the Aleutian Islands extending to 172°E longitude. It is bounded on the north by Canada, on the south by Mexico, on the east by the Atlantic Ocean, and on the west by the Pacific. Two of the states, Alaska and Hawaii, are detached sections of the national territory, but their political status is in every way identical with that of the other 48 states. The estimated area of the USA is 9,363,122 km², of which 202,710 km² are water area. Other territories of the USA include Puerto Rico (acquired 1899), Guam (1899), the

USA. Farmland in Pennsylvania. Around 30 per cent of the state is devoted to agriculture.

Virgin Islands (1917), and some lesser Pacific islands.

In its physical build, the USA consists of a system of five major units, some of which may be subdivided. They are:

(1) The coastal plain of the east. This is an east-dipping series of sedimentary rocks. Differential erosion has shaped a landscape of parallel ridges and vales from these rocks, and this extends down the entire Atlantic coast south of New York, and continues round the Gulf of Mexico coastlands.

(2) Inland from the coastal plain rises the Appalachian Mountains system. This is a four-fold feature. A rolling plateau (the Piedmont), a bold ridge (the Blue Ridge), a system of parallel ridges and valleys (the ridge-valley region), and a broad group of plateaus follow in succession from east to west.

(3) Beyond the Appalachian system opens the enormous and magnificently fertile interior basin, drained by the Mississippi and its major tributaries. To the west the surface rises gently to heights of 1525 m at the foot of the Rocky Mountains in a region of high plains to which the name Great Plains is given. In the south of the interior basin lies the compact but complex interior highland system, of which the dominant feature is the Ozark plateau.

(4) In the western third of the continent is a most complex mass of mountains and plateaus, sometimes erroneously given the general name of the Rocky Mountains, although these latter are merely the first mountain chain, extending from Canada to Colorado, in a system of north–south ridges, with high grassy valleys separating them in the south and great structural trenches in the north.

(5) The Pacific mountain system (sometimes improperly included in the Rocky Mountains) consists of two parallel north–south ranges separated by a deep discontinuous valley. The innermost range is the line of the Sierra Nevada–Cascades, while the Coast-Ranges extend in broken form along the

Pacific shore. Between the two is the rich Central Valley of California, continued north after a break in the region of the Klamath Mountains as the Willanette valley of Oregon and the Puget Sand lowland.

Numerous rivers drain from the Appalachians, across the 'grain' of the system, to the Atlantic. The Hudson, Delaware, Susequehanna, Potomac and James are the largest, but only the Hudson valley provides, via its tributary the Mohawk, an easy route through the mountains. The central lowlands are drained by the great Mississippi–Missouri system, and flood control is the major problem there.

West of the Mississippi, aridity and irregular flow in the rivers are general right across the south-west where, consequently, the major systems of the Rio Grande and the Colorado are quite inadequate for the demands placed upon them. Only in the north-west, in the Columbia-Snake basin, is there water and to spare. In Alaska, the Yukon system carries to the sea a huge volume of water at present largely unused.

At the 1980 census the population of the USA was 226,504,825.

The leading ethnic minorities were as follows: Blacks, 26,488,218; American Indians, 1,418,195; Asian and Pacific Islander, 3,500,636. The capital is Washington; the largest cities are New York, Chicago, Los Angeles, Philadelphia, Houston, Detroit.

Wheat, oats, barley and corn are the chief cereals grown. Wheat is grown chiefly in Washington, Minnesota, Indiana, North and South Dakota, Ohio, and Oregon. Corn is largely grown for fattening cattle, chiefly in Kansas, Nebraska, Iowa, Illinois, Missouri, Indiana and Texas. Tobacco is grown principally in Kentucky, South Carolina, North Carolina, Virginia, Georgia and Tennessee. Sugar is grown in Louisiana, but beet sugar is also manufactured from beets grown in Michigan, Nebraska, Colorado, Utah and California. Cotton is very largely grown in the south-east part of the country and under irrigation in the west.

Most of the dairy cows are in the north-east and north-central states; the sheep are almost wholly on the dry and mountain pastures of the west, where also a high proportion of lean store cattle is reared. But the corn belt of the Midwest is the great cattle fattening district, and here too is found the bulk of the pigs.

US forest lands (including Alaska and Hawaii) capable of producing commercial timber covered more than one-fifth of the total land area in 1980.

Manufacturing in the world's largest industrial power is still largely concentrated in a belt reaching from New England to the Midwest in Illinois and Indiana. In this great complex of industrial regions is located the bulk of the steel industry, the car industry, specialised and electrical engineering, and the textile and clothing trades. Almost 75 per cent of American industry is still located in this north-east and north-central belt, but parts of the south have gone through an industrial revolution in the last 30 years. The textile trades are now largely in the south-eastern states. The west coast dominates the American aircraft and aerospace industries and has other manufactures based on food processing, timber and oil refining.

The relative importance of the service trades as distinct from the manufacturing industries has increased.

There are seven main coalfields supplying bituminous coal, and there are immense lignite resources in the Great Plains and Gulf Coast areas. Much of the largest iron-ore resources is in a series of ranges near the western end of Lake Superior. Oil and natural gas comes from dwindling fields in the east, but chiefly from the very large fields in Texas, Oklahoma and California.

The United States Constitution dates from 17 September 1787. The constitution contains seven original articles and 26 amendments, and divides the national government into three branches—legislative, executive and judicial. Article I vests legislative powers in Congress, consisting of a Senate and a House of Representatives. Representatives are chosen every second year by the electors in the states, and the House of Representatives consists of 435 members. The Senate consists of 100 members, two from each state, serving a term of six years, one-third being elected every two years.

Executive power is vested by Article II in a president, who holds office for four years. He is elected by an electoral college and popular vote, each state having as many electors as it has representatives and senators.

The official language is English.

History. In the 16th century the great maritime nations (Spain, England, France and Portugal) led the exploration of the New World that had been discovered by Columbus. The Spaniards went to Florida, discovered the Mississippi and crossed into what is now Arkansas and Missouri. The French discovered the Gulf of St Lawrence and the English founded the first colony, in 1585, when Sir Walter Raleigh named the territory 'Virginia' after the 'Virgin Queen'. After the failure of this first colony, a second was established in 1607 at Jamestown.

Religious persecution in England led to the foundation of the New England colonies.

In the mid-18th century Britain and France were on opposite sides in wars in Europe, and the American colonies were soon involved. In 1754 the war started that was to decide the language and civilisation of North America, and in 1759 the British capture of Quebec brought to an end the sovereignty of France in North America. By the Peace of Paris (1763) Britain gave back Cuba and the Philippines to Spain and received Florida instead. France ceded to Spain New Orleans and Louisiana and to Britain everything except two islands in the Gulf of St Lawrence. The war helped to unite the colonists in the 13 settlements who began to reconsider their position with regard to Britain. The War of Independence started as the product of complex factors, but was basically due to Britain's refusal to recognise that the American colonies had attained a status which demanded an alteration in the theory and practice of their relations with Britain. On 4 July 1776 the American Continental Congress passed its Declaration of Independence. The peace treaty that brought war to an end in 1783 divided North America between Spain, the British Empire, and the USA. Spain received the land west of the Mississippi and south of a line which gave it Florida. Britain kept what is now Canada. France took a few West Indian colonies. In 1789 an entirely new government was instituted in the United States and George Washington and John Adams were chosen as the first president and vice-president respectively. Alexander Hamilton became the dominant figure in the Federalist party, with Thomas Jefferson and James Madison the architects of the Democratic Republican opposition.

In 1803 the purchase of Louisiana from the French was effected. At the beginning of the 19th century relations with Britain deteriorated, culminating in the outbreak of war in 1812. After a series of land and sea battles, with no decisive victory on either side, a treaty of peace was signed in 1814. In 1819 Spain ceded Florida to the USA. The

population of the United States was growing rapidly and the West was being settled. The question of admitting Missouri to the Union brought the slavery issue into prominence. The North wanted to prevent the admission of states in which slavery was allowed. Missouri was finally admitted in 1820 by the Missouri Compromise, which in addition decreed that slavery should be prohibited in all the remainder of Louisiana territory north of 36°30'N lat. The US annexed Texas from Mexico in 1845 and, after war with Mexico, annexed what are now the states of California, Nevada and Utah and parts of New Mexico, Arizona and Colorado. Only nine days before this treaty was signed, gold was discovered in California, and the famous gold rush began. After controversy over the issue of fugitive slaves, California was admitted to the Union. The slavery issue grew in importance until, in 1860, the South Carolinians held a convention at which they passed secessionist resolutions and proclaimed the union between South Carolina and the USA at an end. Mississippi, Florida, Alabama, Georgia, Louisiana and Texas soon followed their example. In 1861 Abraham Lincoln was inaugurated as president and in his speech asserted that no state could withdraw from the Union. The 11 Southern states were soon united in opposition to the North but, in the war that raged from 1861 to 1865, the fact that the North had greater wealth, was more advanced industrially, was self-sufficient, had better railways and a stronger navy, plus its greater manpower resources, proved decisive and by May 1865 the South had completely surrendered. Under President Andrew Johnson, Lincoln's successor, a pardon was given to the South and the 13th amendment, forbidding slavery in the USA, was passed.

The industrialisation of the country was made possible by the rapid building of railways after the Civil War had ended. The West was opened up, the Indians defeated, and the pioneers were followed by farmers. In the second half of the 19th century the cities grew rapidly. After preserving its neutrality for three years, the USA finally entered the First

USA. *The Rocky Mountains in Colorado. The entire state lies above 1000 m.*

World War in April 1917, and was responsible for hastening its conclusion. In the inter-war period the country consolidated its position as a leading world power while contending with the problems caused by the Depression at home. The 1932 presidential election saw a landslide victory for Franklin D. Roosevelt, the Democratic contender. He took measures to effect the 'New Deal' which he had promised the nation. The US attitude to the possibility of another war in Europe was shown by the passing of three Neutrality Acts in 1935, 1936, and 1937. The common ground for both isolationists and interventionists was the need to rearm the US and re-equip its forces. On 7 December 1941 Japan crippled the US fleet at Pearl Harbor, Hawaii, and on 11 December Germany and Italy also declared war on the USA. From 1942 onwards, US forces were engaged in North Africa, Europe and the Far East, playing a significant part in the Allied victory. After the war US aid was given to Europe to enable it to recover its normal economy, and to forestall intervention from the USSR. The communist invasion of South Korea in 1950 led to US military intervention and, at home, the period 1950–54 was marked by the campaign, conducted in particular by Senator McCarthy, against alleged communist infiltration into US public life.

At the 1960 presidential elections, popular reaction after eight years of Republican administration, swung the polls in the Democrats' favour and brought John F. Kennedy to the presidency. The end of recession and a new period of economic boom gave impetus to Kennedy's programme of social reform and to the acceleration of the US space programme. In 1963 Kennedy was assassinated and was succeeded by his vice-president, Lyndon Johnson, under whose presidency several of the liberalising measures instigated by Kennedy were passed. Increasing concern for the political status of blacks led to civil rights demonstrations in many US cities. Foreign affairs came to be dominated by the Vietnam War in which the US was militarily involved from 1965 until 1972. President Nixon, under whose presidency the war was ended, was forced to resign in 1974 after the Watergate scandal. After this crisis a period of relative calm followed in which inflation and economic depression emerged as dominant problems. In 1980 Ronald Reagan became president, promising economic reform and a 'Strong America' image overseas.

Architecture. Before the end of the 19th century American architecture consisted largely of revivals and adaptations of European styles. In the third quarter of the 19th century, the architect H. H. Richardson introduced a 'Romanesque Revival' which showed great originality; and on his early death his concepts were taken up by L. Sullivan, who developed a new American style, notably in the Wainwright Building, St Louis (1890), and the Guaranty Building, Buffalo (1893). His brilliant pupil Frank Lloyd Wright became, with his Prairie houses, Usonian houses, churches and factories, the leading architect of America well before the middle of the 20th century. Even so, from c.1900 to c.1940 most of the important buildings in the USA were designed by architects trained in the classical tradition at the École des Beaux Arts, Paris. The invention of the skyscraper in the latter part of the 19th century was due to the tremendously high cost of land in the centre of Chicago, New York, and other American cities.

Political and racial persecution in Germany and central Europe during the second quarter of the 20th century led to the immigration into America of many distinguished architects such as Gropius, Neutra, Saarinen and Van der Rohe.

In the varieties of post-international modern architectural styles, America is unsurpassed.

Art. During the colonial period art basically reflected European tastes, however, the founding of the Republic created some nationalist works such as those of John Trumbull. Later the Romanticism of the early 19th century re-established European influence in such works as those of Washington Allston; Primitive artists also came into their own in this period. Landscape, particularly that of the West, began to interest painters such as George Catlin, toward the middle of the century. Attempts to express American life in the later 19th century were accompanied by a desire to escape from earlier realism and can be seen in the symbolist work of Albert Pinkham. For many painters such as Whistler, this was a period of expatriation or else a return of European influences particularly in the form of French Impressionism. A return to American themes is noticeable during the early part of the 20th century particularly in the paintings of George Bellows, whilst Georgia O'Keefe was among the first to be influenced by advanced European painting. In the 1940s Abstract Expressionism led by Jackson Pollock gave American painting an international importance. In the early 1960s Pop Art, whose exponents included Andy Warhol, derived its influences from the mass-media. More recently a dichotomy has arisen between 'performance' artists such as Dennis Oppenheimer and the more traditional 'photorealists' such as the painter Richard Estes.

Literature. In the colonial period up to the Revolution, American literature was of necessity largely an offshoot of English, the earliest writers being immigrants who were born and educated in England. Early writers include the diarists William Byrd, Samuel Sewell (1652–1730) and Sarah Kemble Knight. Poetry had minor status, though some important figures exist. Anne Bradstreet is usually identified as the first significant poet. The writing of Benjamin Franklin demonstrates a developing national spirit. Political writing reaches its highest mark with Thomas Paine.

After the Revolution, American literature began gradually to develop on original lines. In prose the first really original figures were Washington Irving and James Fenimore Cooper. In poetry and prose, a key figure in American Romanticism is Edgar Allan Poe. Though New York and the South contributed, New England became the centre of American writing, evolving an established, 'genteel' tradition. A central figure was Henry Wadsworth Longfellow. The Transcendentalist movement of the 1830s to the 1850s was an important focus. Its central figure was Ralph Waldo Emerson, essayist, preacher, and poet. Emerson's most significant descendant was Walt Whitman, a genuinely revolutionary poet who did much to establish the distinctive 'Americanness' of subsequent writing in the United States. The other outstanding figure was the recessive Amherst spinster Emily Dickinson, whose very personal yet metaphysical poetry, about selfhood, nature, death and divinity led the way to 20th-century Imagism. The novel was also becoming a key American form; and in the pre-Civil War years it grew richly symbolist, gothic and metaphysical. Nathaniel Hawthorne and his friend Herman Melville created the American novel as a complex, ambiguous form—a vehicle for intense symbolism and speculation.

After the Civil War a vein of realism, and a wider subject-matter, entered American fiction; new writers from new cultural sources appeared including Mark Twain (Samuel Langhorne Clemens) and Henry James, the greatest American novelist of the later 19th century. With the turn of the century the naturalistic tradition was set deep in American prose. In Jack London it took the form of popular, socialistic, outdoor adventure tales; in Upton Sinclair it appeared in the horrifying exposé. The great figure was Theodore Dreiser, who probed the relationship between deterministic forces and the American dream of success. From 1912 onwards, a radical explosion affected American writing, bringing in new cultural and socially critical attitudes, and much influence from European modernist writers. The many new figures included poets Wallace Stevens, Ezra Pound, Conrad Aiken, T. S. Eliot, William Carlos Williams and Robert Frost. The 1920s saw a new and significant wave of American fiction, less dependent on English sources than ever before; a number of the novelists, like the poets, went as expatriates to Paris and were influenced by experimental sources, notably Gertrude Stein. They were also affected by the war itself; several had served in it as ambulance men. One was Ernest Hemingway, who wrote of war and its consequences. The disillusioned generational mood also expressed by Scott Fitzgerald. But a tighter experimentalism, also characteristic of the decade, is found in the middle work of William Faulkner, who explored his Mississippi in novels where modernist techniques express the dislocations of time and history. American theatre rose to high significance with the work of Eugene O'Neill.

With the 1940s, a new generation and mood appeared. In fiction, after a spate of war novels, a mood of some retrenchment, adapting experimental and realistic methods to the post-war existential climate, emerged. The morally-concerned Jewish-American novel became a central expression with the work of Bernard Malamud, Philip Roth, J. D. Salinger, author of the classic *Catcher in the Rye*, 1951, Saul Bellow and Norman Mailer. In theatre the outstanding figures were Tennessee Williams and Arthur Miller. By the later 1950s a new, more radical mood affected American writing, with the growth of the 'beat generation', represented in poetry by Allen Ginsberg and in fiction by Jack

Kerouac. In poetry, the confessional writing of Sylvia Plath, the new prosody of 'Black Mountain' poets like Charles Olson and the open field poetry of New York poets like Kenneth Koch marked a change away from the tighter, more academic poetry of the 1950s. In fiction, critics have discerned a 'post-modern' period of experimentalism and social withdrawal, dominated by the 'black humour' mood of novelists like Joseph Heller and Kurt Vonnegut; the self-conscious fictionality of Vladimir Nabokov and John Barth; and the documentary-fiction experiments of Mailer and Truman Capote. Among outstanding playwrights are Edward Albee, author of *Who's Afraid of Virginia Woolf?*, 1962, and in Black theatre Imamu Amiri Baraka (LeRoi Jones).

Music. The earliest composers of any importance emerged only at the time of independence. William Billings (1746–1800) wrote psalm settings with some stark effects and also patriotic songs for the revolution. Folk-music was used in the 19th century by William Henry Fry and by Louis Moreau Gottschalk. Later it became commonplace for composers to study in Germany and follow European models. Renewed interest in indigenous music came with the work of Henry F. B. Gilbert (1868–1928) and others. Gilbert was particularly eclectic, using American Indian, Negro and Latin American sources. Charles Ives largely abandoned European models and standards, exploring all manner of novel techniques.

Ives's music remained almost unknown until his last years and so had no immediate effect on composers born around 1900. Chief among these were Walter Piston, Aaron Copland and Elliott Carter. Other major composers of their generation include Roger Sessions and Samuel Barber.

The experimental direction was pursued by Henry Cowell, Harry Partch, and Edgar Varèse, who was among the first of many 20th-century immigrants to enrich American music. Milton Babbitt was a follower of serialist methods. John Cage has shown himself a more iconoclastic musician. Among those to follow Cage in the use of live electronics have been Robert Ashley, Gordon Mumma and La Monte Young.

Of popular composers, Stephen Foster had few successors until the great period of the American musical and popular song, dominated by George Gershwin and Cole Porter.

United States of Brazil, see BRAZIL, UNITED STATES OF.

Units, standards arbitrarily chosen, in terms of which quantities may be expressed. Scientifically, units are of two kinds, fundamental and derived, fundamental units being those in terms of which all others can be expressed.

See also METROLOGY; PHYSICAL UNITS.

Units, Electrical. The ampere (symbol A) is defined as the constant current which if maintained in two straight parallel conductors of infinite length and negligible circular section, placed one metre apart in vacuum, will produce a force between these conductors equal to 2×10^{-7} newton per metre length. The derived electrical units in the SI system include the coulomb, C (ampere-second); the volt, V (watt per ampere); the ohm, ω (volt per ampere); and the farad, F (ampere-second per volt).

See also METROLOGY.

Universal Language, see ESPERANTO; INTERNATIONAL LANGUAGE.

Universals, in philosophy, are abstract entities of a general kind, in terms of which ordinary concrete things are specified. For example, consider a red apple hanging on a tree. Its quality of being red ('redness') is a universal, as is its relation of height with regard to the ground ('higher than'). Likewise, the general entities of mathematics are universals. Since language is a system of symbols that can be applied repeatedly, all linguistic expression requires general features, and thus language involves universals. However, it does not follow that the universal is itself a symbol for an actual object. Those who maintain that there are such objects are called Realists, while those who argue that universals are only names are accordingly called Nominalists.

See also NOMINALISM; REALISM.

Universe, The, see COSMOGONY; COSMOLOGY.

Universities. At the end of the 14th century the word university began to be used with the exclusive meaning of a lawfully recognised community of teachers and scholars. The first university charters were granted by religious authorities. After the Reformation charters were increasingly granted by secular authorities, and today in the UK universities receive a royal charter. Originally the universities restricted themselves to the study of law, theology, and medicine.

Paris University, whose organisation influenced all the central European universities, including Oxford and Cambridge, grew out of the school opened by William of Champeaux during the first decade of the 12th century. Oxford and Cambridge Universities developed similarly in the course of the 12th century. In both a unique and permanent feature of English universities was established through the halls of residence, later known as colleges. The number of universities in Europe grew rapidly during the 14th century. Charters were granted to Prague, Kraków, Vienna, Heidelberg, and Cologne.

The secularisation of Paris University occurred as a consequence of the French Revolution and a new system of university organisation was promulgated by Napoleon in 1808. Development of universities in England only began in the mid 19th century, with the establishment of those at London, Manchester and Leeds, among others. The 20th century has seen a vast expansion in the size and number of UK universities, with eight new ones being founded between 1961 and 1965 alone. In addition the Open University in Britain has introduced a new concept in university education.

The inclusion of technological studies within the full university framework is, as far as Europe is concerned, peculiar to the UK. Elsewhere separate institutions providing courses at the highest level in technology have grown up.

In the USA the original settlers were quick to establish colleges for the preparation of the clergy. Harvard, Yale, William and Mary, Princeton, King's (later Columbia), Brown, Rutgers, and Dartmouth were all established before 1750. The older universities retain even today some of the conservatism of the European universities, but their curricular offerings have been modified by the pressure exerted by the large state universities. Today the state universities offer a wide range of professional courses at the highest level. This emphasis on professional, technical education is also apparent in the USSR. By contrast in Britain 44 per cent of university students continue to graduate in arts subjects.

Unknown Warrior, an unidentified soldier killed in the First World War, whose grave serves as a memorial to the dead of both World Wars. Several countries have such memorials; Britain's is in Westminster Abbey.

Unsaturated Compounds, in chemistry, are compounds that will form derivative substances by direct addition. Thus ethylene, C_2H_4, combines directly with chlorine to form ethylene dichloride: $C_2H_4 + Cl_2 = C_2H_4Cl_2$; and acetylene, C_2H_2, will combine directly with bromine to form acetylene tetrabromide: $C_2H_4 + 2Br_2 = C_2H_2Br_4$. Ethylene and acetylene are therefore said to be unsaturated, as contrasted, for instance, with methane, CH_4 which can form derivatives only by substitution. Thus, when methane reacts with chlorine, a hydrogen atom is removed for every chlorine atom that enters: $CH_4 + Cl_2 = CH_3Cl + HCl$; $CH_3Cl + Cl_2 = CH_2Cl_2 + HCl$; and so on.

Untouchables (Harijans), term formerly applied in India to Hindus of the lowest social status who do not belong to any caste. Caste Indians consider their touch polluting and must purify themselves if they come into contact with untouchables, who perform polluting activities such as leather working, sweeping, washing and fishing. In southern India they lived in separate villages and were barred from many areas of ritual and social life. Although the traditional divisions of pure and polluted caste groups persist, the use of the term and the disabilities of being an untouchable have been declared illegal in both India and Pakistan.

Unwin, Sir Raymond (1863–1940), British architect and town-planner. He began practice in 1896 with Barry Parker. In 1901–03 they planned the Rowntree Estate, near York, and in 1903 won the competition for planning the first Garden City at Letchworth, Hertfordshire. In 1906 Unwin planned the Hampstead Garden Suburb. From 1914 to 1928 he was employed as adviser on town planning by various government departments. In 1909 he published *Town Planning in Practice*.

Upanishads, the Hindu scriptures, the last-written section of the Vedas, probably composed between 800 and 400 BC. The name means literally 'to sit near' and comes from the sessions of secret teachings which were given to pupils by the forest-dwelling gurus —secret because much of the teaching was considered too profound for the common man, who would have misunderstood and misused it. The Upanishads are mainly about Vedanta, the end of the Vedas.

Upchurch Ware, a variety of Roman pottery, usually grey in colour and ornamented with burnishing and applied dots, which has been widely found at Upchurch on the

Medway in Kent and at places in Essex, England. There seems to be enough evidence that its manufacture formed a really important local industry.

Updike, John Hoyer (1932–), US writer. He worked for the *New Yorker* until, in 1959, he produced a collection of poems, a volume of stories, *The Same Door*, and a novel, *The Poorhouse Fair*. Subsequent novels, like *Rabbit, Run*, 1960, and *Couples*, 1968, show a morally anarchic world in which the characters search for secular deliverance through aesthetic or sexual sensation. Updike's own aesthetic fineness appears especially in stories like *Pigeon Feathers*, 1962. He frequently evokes the world of his Pennsylvania childhood. *Bech: A Book*, 1970, deals explicitly with problems of writing. He has also written poetry, plays and books for children. *The Coup*, a novel set in Africa, was published in 1979.

Upper Canada, see ONTARIO.

Upper Volta
Area: 274,200 km²
Population: 6,617,000
Capital: Ouagadougou

Upper Volta (French *Haute-Volta*), landlocked republic in West Africa, bordered to the north by Mali and Niger, and to the south by the Ivory Coast, Ghana, Togo and Benin (Dahomey). Area 274,200 km².

The land consists mainly of a low plateau at 250 to 300 m elevation, broken by steep-sided inselbergs where resistant rocks occur, and in which the various headwaters of the Volta river cut only slight depressions. The rivers are all marked by sharp seasonal variations of flow. The natural vegetation is savanna woodland everywhere, but the density of trees decreases northwards; agricultural productivity is restricted by soils of generally low fertility. The two main ethnic groups are the Mossi and the Mandingos, and in addition there are Hausa traders, Fulani herdsmen, and Tuareg. The population was estimated at 6,617,000 in 1979 and the main centres are Ouagadougou (the capital) and Bobo-Dioulasso.

Over 85 per cent of the population rely on settled agriculture or livestock raising for their livelihood. Settled agriculture is restricted to river valleys and oases and efforts are being made to increase the crop area. The drought of the early 1970s had an appalling effect on the country's livestock herds. Methods are still traditional and lack of water, disease and low soil fertility and erosion remain constant problems. The chief crops are sorghum, millet, yams, rice, groundnuts and maize. Tobacco and cotton are also grown.

A scheme exists for infrastructural, mining and industrial development on the borders with Mali and Niger to exploit minerals, including manganese at Tambao. Manufactures include textiles, foodstuffs and metal products.

A constitution was drawn up in 1977 and suspended following a military *coup* in 1980.

Executive power is held by an appointed council.

The official language is French, although there are three important native tongues, in turn giving rise to many dialects.

History. The area of present-day Upper Volta includes the former territory of three important Mossi states, Wagadugu, Yatenga and Gurma, which resisted the spread of Islam during both the medieval period and again during its resurgence in the 18th and 19th centuries.

These states, which were never populous, managed to preserve their autonomy, even after the French military conquest. In the area known as Mossi, the French forces were, in the end, sufficiently powerful to overthrow the Mogho Naba, the Emperor of the Mossi. It was during the colonial period that the region of the Upper Volta was established as a reservoir of labour for the Ivory Coast. The area now known as Upper Volta was 'constructed' in 1920 out of parts of the French colonies of Niger, Ivory Coast and Soudan.

In 1960 Upper Volta received its independence, and the Voltaic Democratic Union (UDV) formed the government, with Maurice Yameogo as president. The military intervened in 1966, as the nation was on the brink of a general strike, and deposed Yameogo. The new head of the government was Lieut.-Col. Sangoulé Lamizana.

In April 1970 the military government drew up a new constitution which would provide for a gradual return to a form of civilian government, in which Lamizana was to remain as president, and the military would act as a constitutional check on the civilian government.

Since then constitutional rule has been suspended twice: 1974–78 and again from 1980. Colonel Saye Zerbo, who seized power in 1980, was ousted by the army in 1982.

Uppsala, or Upsala, capital of Uppsala county in Sweden, situated on both sides of the River Fyris. The old town is on the west bank and the new town on the east, the two being joined by five bridges. The university, with which Linnaeus was connected, was founded in 1477. The cathedral is the greatest surviving achievement of Swedish Gothic architecture. Uppsala has a wide range of industries including food processing, ceramics, pharmaceuticals and engineering. Population (1978) 143,386.

Upwelling, the process in the ocean by which deep water is brought to the surface. Although slow vertical motions are a feature of oceanic circulation in general, upwelling is confined to ascending motions of restricted extent. The upwelled water is rarely from deeper than 200 m and is subsequently removed from the area by horizontal currents. Upwelling results in water rich in inorganic nutrients (phosphates and nitrates) being brought into the sunlight where they are converted to organic matter by plankton in the process of photosynthesis. Thus upwelling regions are associated with high organic productivity.

Ur, ancient city, possibly the biblical 'Ur of the Chaldees', modern Tell el-Mugayyar. The birthplace of Abraham, it was formerly on the Euphrates river near the Persian Gulf, 10 km west of Nasiriyah (Iraq). Ur was an influential Sumerian city-state. Remains of several prehistoric phases, named after Al-Ubayyid (6 km north), Uruk and Jemdet Nasr respectively, have been found in a number of pits dug down to virgin soil. Pottery and objects of the Ubayyid periods were found interrupted by a 2-metre deposit of clean water-laid clay which was interpreted as evidence of the Flood, recorded in Biblical and Babylonian texts. The date of this flood level is c.3500 BC, and is now considered to have been due to a local flood.

A series of 17 brick and stone tombs, dating to the Early Dynastic II Period (c.2700–2600 BC) were found. Some interpret these 'Royal Tombs' as part of ritual burials, connected with either the cult of Tammuz or the Sacred Marriage ritual. After a period under Sargon of Agade, and Naram Sin, Ur was most prosperous under its Sumerian 3rd Dynasty (2113–2006 BC), founded by Ur-Nammu, builder of the ziggurat and many temples and buildings dedicated principally to Nannar, the moon god and patron deity of Ur. Nebuchadnezzar II extensively rebuilt the temple area and the ziggurat, the lower two stages of which dominate the present ruins. A few Persian houses seem to have been occupied until as late as the 4th century BC, when the site was abandoned following a change of course by

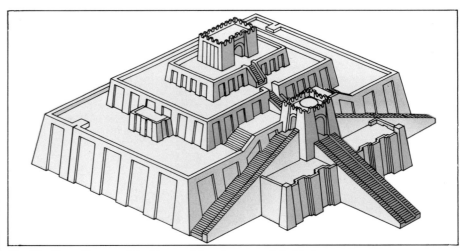

Ur. The Great Ziggurat of the Moon god dates from around the 22nd century BC.

the Euphrates river.

See also BABYLONIA; CHALDAEA.

Uraemia (Greek *ouron*, urine; *haima*, blood), toxic condition caused by renal failure, in which the waste products normally excreted by the kidneys into the urine are retained in the blood. Urea is one of these products, and a way of measuring the degree of uraemia is to estimate the urea in the blood. Normally the blood urea is about 20 mg of urea in every 100 ml of blood, but in severe uraemia it may rise to 200–300 mg. The blood 'electrolytes' (sodium and potassium ions) are also increased in uraemia. The most usual cause of uraemia is kidney failure due to kidney disease.

Ural, river in the Southern Urals, USSR, forming the boundary between Europe and Asia. It rises in the Urals and flows south into the Caspian Sea at Gurev. Length 2428 km. From the 17th century the banks of the river were colonised by Cossacks.

Ural-Altaic Languages, see ALTAIC LANGUAGES; FINNO-UGRIAN LANGUAGES.

Uralic Languages, see FINNO-UGRIAN LANGUAGES.

Urals, mountain system of the USSR on the boundary between Europe and Asia, extending north to south over 2000 km almost from the Kara Sea to the town of Orsk; breadth 60–150 km. The highest point is Mount Narodnaya (1874 m). The greater part of the mountains is covered with forest (to a height of 500 m in the north and 1000 m in the south); mainly conifers. The central section contains rich mineral deposits of iron, copper, chromium and nickel ores, precious stones, coal, oil and asbestos. The region (now comprising the Chelyabinsk, Orenburg, Perm and Sverdlovsk *oblasti* of the RSFSR, the Komi-Permiak National Okrug, and the Udmurt ASSR) is an important industrial centre, famous for its iron and steel works.

Uraninite, see PITCHBLENDE.

Uranium, metallic chemical element, symbol U, atomic number 92, atomic weight 238·029. It is used as a source of atomic energy. Uranium is radioactive, spontaneously disintegrating into radium, etc., and finally into lead, the complete disintegration taking an extremely long time. Its compounds are widely distributed in nature and are easily detected because of their radioactivity. In 1789 Klaproth concluded that the mineral pitchblende must contain a new element which he called uranium in honour of the newly discovered planet Uranus.

Two rich deposits of uranium in the ore pitchblende are those at Great Bear Lake, Canada and at Shaba in Zaire. Deposits of the ore carnotite are found in Czechoslovakia and in Colorado, Utah and Arizona in the USA. The goldfields of South Africa also produce uranium. Large deposits have recently been discovered in the Northern Territories and Western Australia. Generally, the ore is treated with a solvent, usually sulphuric acid, to dissolve the uranium compound in the ore. Uranium is then recovered from the solution by chemical precipitation or by ion-exchange or solvent-extraction methods. Usually uranium oxide is produced, and then reduced to the metal if necessary.

Uranium, a silvery-white metal (relative density 18·7, melting point 1132° C), is a reactive element, being readily oxidised and attacked by acids. Uranium trioxide and the sodium diuranate salt are used as dyes in glass and pottery. Its most important properties are those connected with its radioactivity. Nuclear fission is the name given to the reaction in which a free neutron, the uncharged constituent of the nucleus, strikes the nucleus of a fissile element and causes it to split into fragments of dissimilar mass with the release of nuclear energy. Natural uranium consists of a mixture of three isotopes in the following proportions: ^{238}U, 99·28 per cent; ^{235}U, 0·71 per cent; and ^{234}U, 0·005 per cent. Of these atoms only ^{235}U undergoes fission on the capture of a 'thermal' or slow neutron. Natural uranium is used in the 'thermal' type of nuclear reactor, where fission of the ^{235}U converts the non-fissile ^{238}U by the absorption of neutrons to ^{239}U, which rapidly decays to plutonium-239.

Uranus, in Greek mythology, Heaven, son and husband of Gē (Earth) and father of the Titans, Cyclopes and Hecatoncheires.

Uranus, in astronomy, the seventh planet in distance from the Sun, the first to be discovered with the telescope. It was found in 1781 by Sir William Herschel who named it 'Georgium Sidus' in honour of George III, but the name suggested by Bode ultimately prevailed. Its mean distance from the Sun is 2,862,000,000 km; orbital period 83·69 years; diameter 3·70 that of the Earth; mass 14·6 times the Earth's; mean density 1·71; surface temperature about 60 K (−213° C); rotation period 10 h 49 min.

Under very good conditions Uranus is just visible to the naked eye; in the telescope it appears as a small blue-green disc never more than four arc seconds in diameter. It has a very deep atmosphere in which hydrogen and methane are certainly present. So far five satellites (Miranda, Ariel, Umbriel, Titania and Oberon) have been discovered. These form a regular, compact system similar in size and arrangement to the inner satellites of Saturn. Their orbits lie in the equatorial plane of Uranus and are traversed in the same direction as the planet rotates. This plane is almost at right angles to the plane of the ecliptic. Consequently there are times during the orbital period, such as 1945 and 1967, when Uranus as seen from the Earth is 'pole-on' and the satellite orbits are seen 'in plan' as nearly perfect circles. At other times, such as 1966 and 2008, the satellite orbits are seen 'edge-on' so that the satellites appear to move backwards and forwards along straight lines. Uranus also has nine rings, which lie within the orbits of the satellites. The rings are best observed when they occult stars. The rings are generally only a few km wide, although one broad ring has a width of some 60 km.

See also PLANETS.

Urartu, ancient state in the Middle East, existing in the 9th–6th centuries BC on the Armenian plateau. Its capital was Tushpa near Lake Van. In the early 8th century Uratu achieved a dominant position among the states of the Middle East, but was finally destroyed by the Medes. Urartu culture, influenced by Assyrian, itself influenced Armenian and Georgian cultures.

Urban II, Blessed, Odo de Lagary, Pope, 1088–99; formerly Cardinal Bishop of Ostia. The major event of his pontificate was the Council of Clermont (1095), at which he initiated the first crusade.

Urban VI, Bartolommeo Prignano, Pope, 1378–89. It was his determination to reform the higher clergy that caused the election of the Antipope Clement VII at Avignon and precipitated the Great Schism of the West.

Urban VIII, Maffeo Barberini, Pope, 1623–44. Last of the popes to practise nepotism on a wide scale, he greatly increased the wealth of his family. In the political field Urban did much to strengthen Rome and the papal states. Regarding the Thirty Years' War as a mere secular conflict, he took the side of France. In 1633, because of a personal grudge, he allowed the condemnation of Galileo. To his credit, however, stand the revised Breviary (1631), the condemnation of Jansen (1644), and the erection of some noble structures in the Eternal City.

Urban and Rural District Councils, established by the Local Government Act 1894, they, together with non-county boroughs, consituted the second tier of local government in the administrative counties of England and Wales. Under the Local Government Act 1972, which came into operation in 1974, urban and rural districts were replaced by metropolitan and non-metropolitan districts.

See also LOCAL GOVERNMENT.

Urbanisation, the growth of towns and cities. The transition from agricultural to urban-based society began in the Middle East. Before 6000 BC techniques of arable and pastoral farming developed on the alluvial plains of Mesopotamia, an area where the availability of water (eventually used for irrigation) and technological advances encouraged the production of an agricultural surplus, leading to the trading of surplus goods and the development of specialist crafts. Towns, cities, and then states developed, and by 2500 BC Babylon, the major centre, had a population estimated at 80,000. From Mesopotamia urbanisation spread into the Indus and Nile river valleys and thence into south-east central Asia, China, and the eastern Mediterranean often as a by-product of the growth of large kingdoms and empires, which encouraged specialisation and trade. The most significant of these was the Roman Empire. By the middle of the 4th century AD there were 12 cities with populations over 100,000, of which five were in the Mediterranean area. When the Roman Empire collapsed, urban life in Europe waned, and throughout the 8th, 9th, and 10th centuries urban life flourished only in the Middle and Far East.

The urbanisation process began again in Europe with the political consolidation of the Holy Roman Empire. By 1200 Paris was among the world's 25 largest cities with a population of 110,000 and a century later it had been joined by Granada, Venice, Milan, and Genoa.

During the late 19th century the Industrial Revolution provided a great impetus to urban expansion in Europe and in North America. Of the processes important in the sudden growth of cities none was to be greater than the continual improvement in transport technology. The speed of movement on dense urban road and rail networks has meant that cities have been able to grow to great sizes.

The largest cities of China and India continued to exist and also grew but not at the same rate as those in the western world. Elsewhere in Asia and Africa urban growth was very restricted until after 1945, since when Japan in particular has undergone the most striking development.

Urbino (ancient *Urbinum Hortense*), Italian town in the Marches, built on a hill 30 km south-west of Pesaro. It has a fine 15th-century ducal palace of the Montefeltro family, once lords of Urbino, an archiepiscopal cathedral, and a university (non-state) founded in 1506. Population (1974) 7700.

Urdu, an Indo-Aryan language. Standard Urdu, written in a modified form of the Persian-Arabic script, is the official language of Pakistan and of the state of Jammu and Kashmir, India. Urdu is acknowledged as mother tongue by 23,000,000 Muslims in India, including some 10 per cent of the population of Uttar Pradesh, Bihar and Mysore, and by a further 3,000,000 (by immigration) in Pakistan (1961). Hindi and related dialects are acknowledged by some 150,000,000 persons, and the term Hindustani is now normally reserved for a more pidgin and Anglicised form of the vernacular used as a second language from Pakistan to Bangladesh and among expatriates throughout the world.

See also INDIA, *Language*; INDIA, *Literature*.

Urea, or carbamide, $CO(NH_2)_2$, compound which occurs in the urine of mammals and of carnivorous birds and reptiles. It forms about 3 per cent of human urine. It forms colourless crystals (melting point 132°C) soluble in water and alcohol, and combines with acids to form salts. It is decomposed on heating, and when heated with sodium hypobromite gives off nitrogen. This latter property is used as a method of estimation. Urea was discovered in urine in 1773, and was artificially produced by Wöhler in 1828, the discovery being of fundamental importance as the first indubitable example of isomerism. This production of urea (an organic compound) from ammonium cyanate (an inorganic compound) led to the abandonment of the 18th-century 'vital force' theory, which propounded the existence of a fundamental difference between inorganic and organic compounds. It is used in the manufacture of synthetic resin, fertilizer and in the preparation of various drugs.

See also ISOMERS; PLASTICS.

Urea Cycle, biochemical process first postulated by Krebs and Henseleit in 1932; the means by which nitrogenous waste is converted into urea, which is easily excreted. When proteins and amino-acids break down, ammonia, which is highly toxic, is formed. Most of the ammonia is converted into glutamate, and becomes usable for the synthesis of more amino-acids and proteins. Any excess is converted into the water-soluble compound, urea, which can be excreted as urine.

Urey, Harold Clayton (1893–), US

chemist. He was director of War Research Atomic Bomb Project (1940–45), professor of chemistry at the University of Chicago (1945–58), and professor of chemistry at the University of California from 1958. In 1934 he was awarded the Nobel Prize for chemistry for his discovery of deuterium; he is also known for his work on the separation of isotopes, the structure of atoms and molecules, the thermodynamic properties of gases, geochemistry and the origin of the planets.

Urfa, town of south-east Asiatic Turkey and capital of Urfa province. It was the ancient city of Edessa, the capital of an independent kingdom in 137 BC. The modern town is a centre of the wheat industry. Population (1980) 147,488

Urfé, Honoré d' (1567–1625), French writer. Besides various minor works he wrote a vast and influential pastoral romance, *L'Astrée*, the first part of which was published in 1607 and the fourth, posthumously, in 1627. The conclusion was written after Urfe's death by his secretary, Balthazar Baro, on the basis of Urfé's notes.

Urga, see ULAN BATOR.

Urial, *Ovis vignei*, known also as the Punjab wild sheep or shapu, ranges from sea level near the Caspian Sea to 4200 m in Tibet. The male has massive horns up to 1 m long. Some authorities suggest that the urial is no more than a race of the red sheep or Asiatic mouflon (*O. orientalis*).

Uric Acid, $C_5H_4N_4O_3$, product of the metabolism of the animal organism, which occurs in small quantities in human urine. It sometimes accumulates in the bladder, forming 'stones', or it is deposited in the tissues of the body, causing gout. The excrement of birds (guano) and of reptiles contains large quantities of the acid. Serpents' excrement consists chiefly of ammonium urate; the uric acid is prepared by boiling with caustic soda, and the clear alkaline solution precipitated with hydrochloric acid. The acid forms crystals which are insoluble in water. Evaporated with nitric acid, a yellow stain is left, which becomes intensely violet on addition of ammonia. Uric acid is a weak dibasic acid, and forms salts which are all sparingly soluble in water.

Urine, fluid excreted by the kidneys. It contains a large proportion of water as well as some of the waste products of metabolism. The kidneys extract these waste products from the blood and pour their secretions into the ureter, a muscular tube through which the fluid reaches the bladder, there to be retained for a while until it is discharged to the exterior through the urethra. Urine as excreted is normally clear and of straw colour, which may be pale or dark merely from variations in concentration. It is usually acid in reaction, but after a meal there may be an alkaline tide, and the urine after standing will deposit a cloud of phosphates. The most important of the nitrogenous products in the urine is urea which contains about 90 per cent of the total nitrogen excreted. Urea is formed from the amino-acids resulting from the digestion of proteins. The amount of urine discharged by an adult human is about 1·4 litres daily on average.

See also UROLOGY.

Urodela, or Caudata, an order of amphibia which has for its distinguishing characteristics a well developed tail which persists throughout life and usually two pairs of limbs. There are almost 300 species, and nearly all occur over the temperate northern hemisphere. Newts, salamanders and mud-eels are representative of the order.

Urology, the study of the urinary tract and its diseases. The chief parts of the urinary system are the kidneys, ureters, bladder and urethra. In addition to abnormalities, displacements and injuries, the kidneys may be affected by micro-organisms, as in tuberculosis and pyelonephritis, by tumours, stones (renal calculus) and other diseases. The chief abnormalities of the ureters, the ducts conveying the urine from the kidney to the bladder, are dilations and constrictions, abnormal bends and twists; the origin of the ureter from a position too high to drain the kidney; blind endings and the opening of the ureters into parts of the genito-urinary system other than the bladder. Inflammation of the ureter is frequently associated with infection of the kidney. Not infrequently the passage of the ureter is partially or completely blocked by stones. Diseases of the bladder are, mainly, cystitis, or inflammation of the bladder, stone in the bladder, and benign and malignant growths. Diseases of the prostate gland come into the field of urology, and the treatment of benign enlargement of the gland forms a large part of the work of the urologist. The urethra is subject to inflammation (urethritis), one of the commonest causes of which is gonorrhoea.

Ursa Major, 'the Great Bear', a large northern constellation seven of whose brighter stars form the most famous of all asterisms known variously as 'the Plough', 'the Big Dipper', 'Charles's Wain', 'the Seven Bright Shiners', etc. The first two stars of the Plough, Alpha and Beta Ursae Majoris, are called 'the Pointers' because the line joining them leads to Polaris, the Pole Star. The star in the middle of the handle of the Plough is Mizar (Zeta Ursae Majoris), which makes with the nearby fourth-magnitude Alcor a visual double star sometimes known as 'the Horse and Rider'. Many of the stars in this constellation are moving through space with the same speed and in the same direction. Sirius and several other stars in different parts of the sky share this common motion and so belong to the 'Ursa Major moving group'.

Ursa Minor, 'the Little Bear', a small constellation whose brighter stars form the asterism known in America as 'the Little Dipper'. The bright star at the end of the tail is Polaris (Alpha Ursae Minoris) which marks approximately the position of the north celestial pole.

Ursula of Cologne, Saint, legendary British princess said to have been put to death by the Huns at Cologne some time in the 4th century together with 11,000 other virgins.

Ursulines, an order of women in the Roman Catholic Church, founded under the patronage of St Ursula at Brescia, Italy, in 1535 by St Angela Merici for the education of girls. The members lived at first in their own homes, and later in communities approved as a religious order by Pope Paul V in 1612. This order was the first specifically teaching order of women. It spread rapidly throughout Europe and America, and later in the other continents.

Urticaceae, a plant family that includes about 40 genera and 500 species of herbs and shrubs, mainly tropical, often with stinging hairs on the leaves. The male and female flowers are generally separate but borne on the one plant. Male flowers have four or five sepals, and an equal number of stamens; in the female flowers the sepals surround a simple ovary. Pollination is by wind; the stamens are at first incurved and spring out sharply when ripe, scattering the pollen. *Urtica* (stinging nettle), *Parietaria* (pellitory of the wall), *Helxine* (mind-your-own-business) and *Pilea* belong to this genus.

Urticaria, or nettlerash, a skin reaction attributable to various causes. It is characterised by raised red and white weals similar to those produced by the sting of a nettle, and accompanied by a sensation of burning and irritation, the latter sometimes being intense. Urticaria is a symptom and not a disease. The most usual cause is allergic, but it may be toxic, psychological or endocrine, or arise from a combination of these factors.

Uruguay
Area: 186,926 km²
Population: 2,886,000
Capital: Montevideo

Uruguay, officially named República Oriental del Uruguay, the smallest of the South American countries, comprising an area of 186,926 km² and taking its name from the Uruguay river which forms its western frontier.

Uruguay lies on the south-east side of South America, forming a wedge or buffer between Brazil in the north and Argentina in the south and west. It has a coastline of about 200 km on the Atlantic Ocean and about 360 km on the Río del Plata; in the west it has a river boundary of about 432 km. The general character of the land is undulating grass-covered hills, lacking woods or forests except along the valleys of the numerous small rivers. The only major internal river is the Río Negro, rising in Brazil and flowing across the centre of Uruguay from north-west to south-west where it enters the Uruguay river.

In 1978 the total population was 2,886,000. Over 40 per cent of the total population lives in the capital city of Montevideo. About 90 per cent of the people are of European descent, mainly from early Spanish and Italian immigrants, though in more recent years there has been considerable immigration from other European countries as well. The remaining 10 per cent are mestizo, a mixture of European and Indian stock.

Uruguay is mainly a pastoral country dependent on livestock farming, especially cattle and sheep. Only some 10 per cent of farm land is cropped, the main crops being wheat, rice, maize, barley, oats and linseed. Sugar cane and beet are also important. Industry is confined to processing raw materials.

The unit of currency is the *nuevo peso*, introduced in July 1975 and equivalent to 1000 old *pesos*.

In November 1966 the country voted to return to presidential government after 15 years of being governed by a national council. Elections are supposed to take place every five years. Legislative power is vested in a general assembly made up of two houses. Executive power is exercised by the President and his council of ministers.

The official language is Spanish.

History. In the 16th and 17th centuries Uruguay was remote from the main Portuguese and Spanish settlements. In the late-18th century, small villages and towns were built, and Uruguay became a country of small scattered ranches. Montevideo was founded by the Spanish governor of Buenos Aires in 1726. When Brazil declared its independence in 1822 Uruguay was included as part of Brazilian national territory. In 1825 an Argentine army drove the Brazilians northward, and gained control of the whole of what is now Uruguay. In 1828 the British secured the agreement of both Argentina and Brazil to the establishment of an independent Uruguay as a buffer state.

Two political parties, the *blancos* (conservatives) and *colorados* (liberals), which still survive, emerged in the late 1830s. The Uruguayan economy continued to depend on meat exports. Since 1904 the *blancos* and *colorados* have co-existed peacefully. President José Batlle y Ordóñez (who was in office 1903–07 and 1911–15) sought to rebuild a vigorous, independent economy and was responsible for what some Europeans considered Latin America's first welfare state. This extensive welfare policy attracted European immigrants. The policy of state interventionism was not dramatically extended again until the 1950s, when rapid inflation followed from pressure for higher wages and heavy spending in the public sector. Economic stagnation was responsible for a series of ineffective governments—both civilian and military—and for frustration reflected in trade union agitation and guerrilla action by the Tupamaro group.

Juan Bordaberry Arocena became president after elections in 1971, and the following year declared a 'state of internal war' to suppress the Tupamaros. Congress was dissolved in June 1973.

A new constitution providing for a return to democratic government was prepared in 1980, and rejected by referendum. In 1981 Gregorio Alvarez was elected to the presidency and another constitution proposed.

Uruguay, river of South America, rising in southern Brazil and flowing westwards for 1600 km, first along the Brazil–Argentina border and then along the Uruguay–Argentina border. It then, with the River Parana, forms the Río de la Plata estuary. For much of its course it is navigable and is an important waterway.

Uruk (Biblical *Erech*, modern *Warka*), situated 56 km north-west of Ur. Prehistoric Uruk (c.3500–3100 BC) represents the succes-sor to the Ubaid phase in the cultural development of southern Mesopotamia. In the Early Dynastic period (c.2800–2400 BC), Uruk was one of the most important of the Sumerian city-states, and it is to this period that the reign of its famous king, the hero Gilgamesh, the fifth king of Uruk, must be dated. The political power of Uruk waned after this time, but it continued to play a very important part as a religious centre (seat of the sky god Anu).

Urumchi, or Tihwa, capital of Sinkiang Uighur Autonomous Region of China, on the east bank of the River Urumchi in the Dzungarian Basin at the northern foot of the Tien Shan. By the 1881 Sino-Russian treaty it was opened as a trading port. It is on the old Silk Route and has good communications with other cities in Sinkiang and Kansu. Its chief exports are wool, cotton, and fur. A small iron and steel plant was established in 1951, and the production of agricultural machinery and textiles has also developed. Population (1970) 450,000.

Ushant (French *Ouessant*), island in the *département* of Finistère, France, 43 km north-west of Brest. It has steep and rocky cliffs but inland the soil is fertile; fishing is the chief industry, and the small port of Ouessant is the only town. Population (1970) 1800.

Usk (Welsh *Wysg*), river of Wales, rising in the Black Mountains on the boundary between Powys and Dyfed. It flows through Powys and Gwent and enters the Bristol Channel at Newport. The Usk valley is famous for its scenery and fishing, and its upper half is in the Brecon Beacons National Park. Length 112 km.

Üsküb, see SKOPJE.

Üsküdar (formerly Scutari, ancient *Chrysopolis*), town on the east side of the Bosporus, Turkey, now a suburb of Istanbul. Behind the town is a large cemetery, the burial ground of British troops killed during the Crimean War. Üsküdar has textile and engineering industries. Population (1980) 255,899.

Ussuri, river of the Soviet Far East, joining the Amur at Khabarovsk. One of its tributaries forms the outlet of Lake Khanka, and for most of its 575 km it divides Manchuria from the USSR.

Ustinov, Peter Alexander (1921–), British actor, director, novelist and playwright. Trained by Michael Saint Denis, he first appeared in London in 1939 at the Players' Late Joys, where he gave a memorable sketch of the ageing opera-singer, Mme Liselotte Beethoven-Finck. After serving in the army during the Second World War he returned to the stage in *Crime and Punishment*, 1946, and has since appeared mainly in his own plays, which include *The Love of Four Colonels*, 1951; *Romanoff and Juliet*, 1956; *Photo-Finish*, 1962; *The Unknown Soldier and His Wife*, 1967; and *Beethoven's Tenth*, 1983. He has appeared in many films, among them *Topkapi* and *The Comedians*.

Ust-Kamenogorsk, town and capital of East Kazakhstan *oblast*, Kazakh SSR, USSR, on the Irtysh river east of Semipalatinsk. It has (non-ferrous) metallurgical and food industries, and a large hydroelectric power station near-by. Population (1980) 280,000.

Usury, formerly denoted any legal interest

for the use of money, but in present usage denotes only illegal or excessive interest. Many early ecclesiastical laws prohibited usury of any kind in Britain but these were all repealed in 1854.

See also INTEREST.

Utah (Beehive State), bordered by Nevada (west), Idaho and Wyoming (north), Colorado (east) and Arizona (south). The Wasatch Mountains (highest peak Timpanogos, 3660 m) shuts off the western section (which belongs to the Great Basin and consists of highland ranges running north to south separated by semi-desert valleys) from the east, which belongs to the Colorado basin and is remarkable for its elevated plateau, through which big canyons carve their passage. The Uinta Mountains, an off-shoot of the Wasatch system, contain the greatest elevations in the state (Kings Peak, 4114 m). A notable feature is the Great Salt Lake, 120 km long, 80 km wide, and with 20–27 per cent salinity.

The farm and ranch activity is basically three-tiered, as in most of the mountainous west; there are the natural range grasses, on which cattle and sheep graze, but whose carrying capacity is low; there are the dry-farmed wheatlands intermediate between the ranges and the oases; and there are the patches of irrigated farmland, on which fodder and fruit crops are grown. Utah is one of the few mountain states in which dairying is important; so too is the raising of turkeys. Utah produces salt from the desert, but the main output of the state is copper; the world's largest open-cast copper mine is at Bingham, south-west of Salt Lake City. There is a small production of petroleum and coal. The Salt Lake City-Ogden belt has developed a considerable amount of industry.

Utah was founded by the Mormon Church under Brigham Young in 1847. A year later the great California gold rush began, and the Mormons found themselves strategically placed on the main route to the west, and supplying the gold-seekers with food and necessities. Utah became a territory in 1850 and a state in 1896. The capital is Salt Lake City. In 1980 the population was 1,461,037. The total area is 219,931 km².

Utamaro (1754–1806), Japanese artist of the Ukiyo-e school, known chiefly by his colour woodcuts. Utamaro was the first Japanese artist to become well known in Europe, many of his prints being sent there during his lifetime by Dutch merchants resident at Nagasaki.

Ute, war-like North American Plateau Indians of Shoshonean stock, who used horses effectively for fighting. The 5000 survivors live in Colorado and Utah, which was named after them.

Uterus, or womb, the generative organ in which the development of the fertilised ovum takes place. It is a muscular pear-shaped organ flattened and about 7·5 cm long in the non-pregnant condition. Its position is between the bladder and the rectum, with the base directed forwards and upwards; the cylindrical neck or cervix is directed towards the vagina, with which it communicates. The wide portion, or *fundus*, of the uterus receives the Fallopian tubes at its two upper angles. The fundus is triangular in form, the apex being a constriction called the *os uteri internum* leading to the cervix. The walls of the uterus consist of mucous membrane, as its inner surface is continuous with that of the vagina, a thick layer of muscular tissue, and an outer surface of peritoneum. The chief function of the uterus is the development of the fertilised ovum. The ova are carried from the ovary to the uterus by way of the Fallopian tubes. After the ovum has been fertilised, it depends for nourishment and for carrying away its waste products on the placenta which forms on the uterine wall.

Inflammation of the mucous lining of the uterus is called endometritis. It is due to the extension of infective inflammation from other structures, or to sepsis following the expulsion of the foetus. The uterus is a very common seat of tumours, both benign and malignant. The commonest benign tumours are known as fibroids. Cancer of the uterus usually appears at a later age (55 to 65 years) and a common presenting sign is post-menopausal bleeding. Surgical treatment at an early period of the disease often cures it.

See also GYNAECOLOGY.

Utica, ancient city of North Africa, situated north-west of Carthage in the present district of Tunis. It was founded by the Phoenicians about 1100 BC and, after the destruction of Carthage (146 BC), rose to be the first city of Africa.

Utica, city in New York state, USA, one of the line of minor industrial and commercial centres which lie along the Mohawk river, the main rail, road and water route from New York to the American interior. Population 75,435.

Utilitarianism may be summarised by its own catch-phrase, 'the greatest happiness of the greatest number', such happiness being the criterion of ethical right and wrong, and pleasure and freedom from pain the desirable ends of life. The term originated with Jeremy Bentham as a purely philosophical and political expression. His *Principles of Morals and Legislation*, 1789, must be regarded as the origin of the movement, which culminated in John Stuart Mill. Mill defined Utilitarianism as 'the creed which accepts as the foundation of morals utility, or the greatest happiness principle, holds that actions are right in proportion as they tend to promote happiness, wrong as they tend to produce the reverse of happiness'.

See also ETHICS.

Utility, in economics, is a concept representing the satisfaction which an individual obtains from consuming a commodity. Originally basic to the classical theory of demand, it was introduced into economic theory by the neoclassical school of economists in order to provide an explanation of consumer behaviour. However, as it is a purely subjective notion, utility is, of course, unmeasurable, and the theory had eventually to be recast in terms of the consumers' revealed preferences, reflected in the purchases they make at various prices.

Utopia (nowhere; Greek *ou*, not; *topos*, place), name given by Sir Thomas More to the imaginary island of his *De Optimo Reipublicae Statu, deque Nova Insula Utopia*, 1516, where life is governed by reason. From it the adjective utopian has been formed to mean 'impracticable' or 'ideal'.

Utrecht, capital of Utrecht province, Netherlands, on the Oude Rijn (Rhine) river, 60 km east of The Hague. In the Middle Ages it developed into a powerful political, commercial and ecclesiastical centre under the church, but lost some of its status to Amsterdam in the 15th century. Utrecht is an important railway centre. Its industries include textiles, carpets, pottery, chemicals, engineering, musical organs and printing. Population (1980) 237,000.

Utrillo, Maurice (1883–1955), French painter. He was influenced at first by the Impressionists, but developed a personal style in painting the streets of Montmartre. His street scenes with their white walls and houses belong to what is known as the 'white period' from 1907 to 1910. The so-called 'white and blue period' followed, but from 1917 onwards the calm beauty of his early work was exchanged for strident colour and less careful drawing. His later work disclosed something of a return to the style for which he is most esteemed.

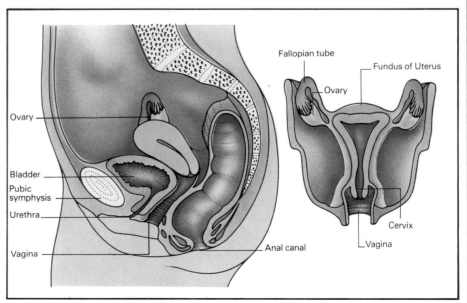

Uterus. *A cross-section of the trunk showing the female sex organs.*

Uttar Pradesh, state of India covering 294,366 km² in the central Gangetic Plain. Formerly the United Provinces, the state's boundaries have changed little since independence. It is bordered by Nepal and China to the north and north-east, and by Indian states to the west and south. The landscape is mostly the Ganges plain: generally arable, quite fertile, and better watered in the south-east than the north-west. Uttar Pradesh is the most populous state in India (110,858,019); 80 per cent is rural. Wheat and rice are the main crops with wheat and millet predominating in the drier north. New wheat varieties have increased food supplies markedly since the 1960s. Barley, sugar-cane, groundnuts, peas and cotton are also important. Some 30 per cent of the crop area is now irrigable. The state has enormous hydroelectric potential because of the Ganges, Yamuna and tributary rivers. Cement, aluminium and chemical industries have developed, Kanpur being the main centre. Handloom weaving and craft industries remain very important especially at Varanasi, Lucknow and Allahaba. State government operates through an elected assembly of 425 members and a nominated council of 108 based at Lucknow, the capital.

History. The region has been called the heart of India; it is the most heavily populated and longest-settled, and has formed part of every great empire of the Indo-Gangetic plain, experiencing invasions by Aryans, Turks, Mongolians, Persians and the British. The presidency of Agra came into being in 1833; it was joined to Oudh as the North-West Province in 1856, and the name was changed to United Provinces of Agra and Oudh in 1902. The name Uttar Pradesh has been used since 1950.

Uvula, the small cone-shaped process suspended from the middle of the border of the soft palate.

Uzbek Soviet Socialist Republic, or Uzbekistan, constituent republic of the USSR, formed in 1924, bordering on Afghanistan in the south; it includes the Karakalpak ASSR. Mountain ranges enter the republic in the east, but the greater part of it consists of a plain with large deserts interspersed with oases, the largest of which is the Fergana Valley. These oases are its economic centres. The east is drained by the Amu Darya, the Fergana Valley by the Syr Darya, the Tashkent oasis by the Chirchik and Angren rivers, and the Samarkand and Bukhara oases by the Zeravshan. The republic's most important product is cotton, of which it provides 65 per cent of the USSR's total requirements. It also produces half of the Union's output of silk cocoons. It is the largest producer of dried grapes and apricots. There are important mining, chemical and agricultural machinery industries. The republic is divided into 11 *oblasti.* Main cities are Tashkent, (the capital), Samarkand, Andizhan, Namangan and Kokand. Area 447,400 km². Population (1980) 15,800,000, mainly concentrated in the oases. 80 per cent of the population are Muslim.

Uzbeks, or Uzbegs, Turkic people named after Uzbek, a descendant of Genghis Khan. They appeared in Transoxania in the 15th century, and in the 16th century founded the kingdoms of Bukhara and Khiva. Six million Uzbeks now live in the Uzbek SSR, where they are dominated by the Tajik, and one million live in Afghanistan, where they are traders and craftsmen. A small group of Uzbeks live in north-west China. Once nomadic pastoralists, they are now sedentary agriculturalists; in the USSR they produce the majority of that country's cotton. They are Sunni Muslims, but retain shamanist practices. The Uzbeks speak Jagatai Turkish.

V

V, twenty-second letter of the English alphabet, interchangeable at various stages with *u, w, f, b* and *m.* The ancient Greeks had apparently no *v* sound, but the Romans used *v* to represent consonantal *v* or the vocalic *u.* Only from the later Middle Ages is the *v* constantly employed for the consonantal sound, and *u* for the vowel sound. The interchangeability of *v* with *f* and *w* appears not only in the Latin alphabet, where the letter *f* was an indirect descendant of the Greek *digamma,* but also in the modern German alphabet, where the letter *v* is pronounced *f,* and the English sound *v* generally expressed by the letter *w.*
See also ALPHABET.

V, roman numeral for 5.
See also NUMERALS.

V1 and V2 Weapons, see FLYING BOMB.

Vaal, river of South Africa, tributary of the Orange river, which rises in Mount Klipstapel, flows west and south-west separating the Orange Free State from the Transvaal, and crosses Griqualand West. The Vaal Barrage, 30 km downstream from Vereeniging, forms a reservoir for the Rand.

Vaasa, town of Finland on the coast of the Gulf of Bothnia, capital of Vaasa province which has rich agricultural coastlands and a productive forest interior. Industries include sawmilling and food-processing, ship-repairing, textiles and engineering. Population (1979) 53,720.

Vaccination (from Latin *vacca,* cow). The first vaccination was inoculation with cowpox in order to afford protection against smallpox. The idea of vaccination occurred to Edward Jenner in connection with observations of Benjamin Jesty, a Dorset farmer, that persons infected with cowpox were thereby rendered immune from smallpox. Vaccination against such diseases as measles, whooping cough and diphtheria has been made compulsory in a number of countries. However, many doctors oppose compulsory vaccination because, like any inoculation, it may cause infection and, rarely, it causes a severe allergic reaction.
See also ACTIVE IMMUNISATION; PASSIVE IMMUNISATION.

Vaccinium, a genus of deciduous and evergreen shrubs of the Ericaceae occurring in the northern hemisphere, chiefly North America and Asia. *V. angustifolium* is the blueberry; *V. myrtillus,* the bilberry or whortleberry; and others yield edible fruits of some importance. Many species are bog plants, and all prefer acid, lime-free soils. Cranberry (*Oxycoccus*) is sometimes placed in this genus.

Vacuole, a membrane-bound cavity within the cytoplasm of a cell. Vacuoles perform a variety of functions. They are not a common feature in prokaryotic cells such as bacteria, but occur occasionally in blue-green algae as flotation devices. In young plant cells, vacuoles may be extremely numerous, but at maturity usually a single vacuole occupies most of the cell volume, pressing the cytoplasm against the cell wall. This reduces the length of diffusion required to bring oxygen and nutrients from the environment to the cytoplasm, and to rid the cell of excretions. Plant vacuoles contain cell-sap comprising mainly water with various substances in solution, such as salts, sugars, organic acids, and frequently pigments and tannins. These may be by-products of metabolism or materials held in reserve for utilisation.

Many single-celled fresh water organisms such as *Amoeba, Euglena, Paramecium* and *Volvox* utilise vacuoles to expel the excess water which tends to enter their cytoplasm by osmosis or with food. These contractile vacuoles repeatedly fill with water and suddenly collapse, ejecting their contents to the exterior. They may also play a part in excretion. In phagocytic protozoans such as amoebae, and the phagocytes of more complex organisms, particles are taken into vacuoles where they are subsequently digested or sequestered.
See also CELL.

Vacuum, a space devoid of matter; but the term is extended to any enclosure in which gas pressure is considerably less than atmospheric. Hence one can have a low, high or ultra-high vacuum. It is impossible to obtain a perfect vacuum, present methods of exhaustion always leaving some residual gas —though the amount may be extremely minute. Modern diffusion pumps can reduce the pressure inside a vessel to approximately 10^{-4} Pa, a pressure of the order of 10^{-9} of atmospheric. By introducing substances which absorb gases, such as activated charcoal, vacua can reach approximately 10^{-5} Pa. Electromagnetic radiation will pass through a vacuum. Energy in the form of vibrating particles, heat and sound, is not transmitted. Interstellar space contains appreciable quantities of gas, albeit at extremely low pressure.
See also AIR-PUMP; BAROMETER.

Vacuum Cleaner, a type of air suction pump used for extracting dust from carpets and furnishings. The first vacuum cleaners, which were invented at the beginning of the present century, were operated by hand. The modern domestic suction cleaner is operated by a high-speed electric motor. The nozzle is connected to a dustbag that collects the dust and filters the dust-laden air before blowing it out. Domestic suction cleaners may operate at high suction or have less suction and utilise a revolving brush, which beats the surface of the carpet, loosening the dirt, which is picked up by the air stream and conveyed to the dustbag. Some high suction domestic cleaners now pick up liquids too, a metal container having replaced the dustbag for collection of wet and dry material.

Vacuum Flask, invented by Sir James Dewar to store liquid air. Very little heat enters by conduction because glass is a bad conductor, and the vacuum between the glass walls is an even worse one. This vacuum, if perfect, would entirely prevent convection. Since a vacuum allows the passage of radiation the walls are silvered inside the vacuum; any heat getting into the vacuum is reflected back. The idea has been exploited commercially under the trade-mark Thermos and other names. The vacuum flask keeps liquids hot for the same reasons that it keeps them cool.

Vacuum Pump, see AIR-PUMP; DIFFUSION PUMP.

Vadodara, see BARODA.

Vaduz, capital of Liechtenstein. Above the town stands the castle of the ruling prince. There is a textile industry, and the town trades in corn, wine, livestock and vegetables. It is a major tourist centre. Population (1979) 4892.

Vagina, in the human female, a hollow canal that lies behind the urethra and in front of the anus, and extends upwards and backwards from the vulva. The width and length of the vagina show considerable variation in normal women. Marriage and regular coitus result in some stretching of the vaginal walls, and this is also increased by childbearing, but the vagina can be narrowed voluntarily by regular exercising of the muscles in its walls.

The opening to the vagina lies between two 'lips', the *labia minora*, which in turn are protected by two larger pads of flesh, the *labia majora*. The labia and the general area from the pubic bone, surrounded by the pubic hair, are collectively called the vulva. Near the pubic bone, at the forward junction of the labia minora, lies the clitoris, which is the equivalent structure in the female to the male penis. It is a small, solid structure rich in nerves and blood vessels, and is the most erotically sensitive part of the vulva. Between the clitoris and the vaginal opening, the urethra (the tube from the bladder) opens to the outside.

See also UTERUS.

Vagrants. In English law the word 'vagrant' is applied to three categories of persons: (1) idle and disorderly persons; (2) rogues and vagabonds; (3) incorrigible rogues. The first category includes prostitutes behaving riotously or indecently in public places; pedlars trading without a licence; persons in any public place to beg alms. The second category includes persons wandering abroad (i.e. about the country) and lodging in barns, tents, etc. The third category includes those convicted a second time as rogues and vagabonds.

Vaishnavas, Hindu sect, especially prevalent in modern Hinduism, distinguished from others by the special worship of Vishnu and his incarnations, particularly as Rāma and Krishna, who they hold to be supreme in the Trimurti.

Valdivia, capital of Valdivia province of Chile, a commercial port 18 km up the River Valdivia, founded in 1552 by Pedro de Valdivar, the conqueror of Chile. Opposite the city is Teja Island, where are situated tanneries, shoe and furniture factories, shipyards, flour-mills, sugar refineries and breweries. Population (1978) 106,800.

Valence, French town, capital of the *département* of Drôme, built on an escarpment above the River Rhône 550 km south-east of Paris. It was once the capital of the Duchy of Valentinois. There is manufacture of foodstuffs, textiles, and leather goods, and a trade in agricultural produce. Population (1975) town, 70,307; conurbation, 104,330.

Valencia, region in Spain, on the Mediterranean, comprising the provinces of Alicante, Castellón de la Plana and Valencia. It was formerly a kingdom, was taken from the Moors by the Cid at the end of the 11th century, and was incorporated with Aragón in 1238. It remained a kingdom in name until the 18th century. Area 23,222 km²; population (1981) 3,646,765.

Valencia, capital of Valencia province, Spain (and, formerly, of the kingdom of Valencia), on the estuary of the Guadalaviar. It is the third city of Spain, and has a port, El Grao, on the nearby Mediterranean coast. The Gothic and Baroque cathedral was begun in 1262. There are textile, metallurgical, chemical, furniture, shoe and boatbuilding industries, and a large trade in oranges, rice and silk. Population (1981) 751,734.

Valencia, town of Venezuela, on the Cabriales river, 130 km west of Caracas. It is the capital of the state of Carabobo and the third largest city in Venezuela. It is highly industrialised and the centre of a highly developed agricultural region. Population (1971) 367,000.

Valenciennes, French town in the *département* of Nord. It has an important metallurgical industry, manufactures hosiery and glass, and has an oil refinery. The famous lace industry is being revived. Population (1975) 43,202.

Valency, or valence. Expressed in its simplest form, the valency of an element is the number of atoms of hydrogen, or of any other univalent element (or radical such as CH_3), capable of uniting with one atom of the element. The maximum known valency of an element is 8, shown by osmium and ruthenium. Elements are described as uni-, bi-, tri-, quadri-, penta-, hexa- and heptavalent when the valencies are 1 to 7 respectively. Measured by their combining capacity, elements do not always exhibit the same valency. Thus 1 atom of phosphorus unites with 3 atoms of hydrogen, but can combine with 5 atoms of chlorine; alternatively, 2 atoms of phosphorus (valency 3) can unite with 3 atoms of oxygen (valency 2), or 2 atoms of phosphorus (valency 5) can unite with 5 atoms of oxygen (valency 2). The valency of an element is therefore often a variable quantity and, in many cases, dependent upon temperature and pressure.

Valens (C.AD 328–78), Eastern Roman Emperor, 364–378, elevated by his brother, Valentinian I. During his reign, the Goths penetrated into the countries south of the Danube. In 378 Valens was defeated by them at Adrianople, and his body never found.

Valentine, Saint (fl. 3rd century), priest and physician of Rome who suffered martyrdom. The feast day on 14 February seems also to have commemorated Valentine, a bishop of Terni, who was martyred in Rome and whose remains were taken back to Terni. The custom of sending 'valentines' as a token of love may have had its origin in a heathen practice connected with the worship of Juno Februalis at the Lupercalia, or in the medieval belief that birds commenced to mate on 14 February; its association with the saint is wholly accidental.

Valentinian I (AD 321–75), Roman Emperor, 364–75. During his reign the frontiers of the empire were threatened by the Alemanni, who were twice repulsed (366 and 368). He was an able and wise administrator.

Valentino played the title rôle in the Son of the Sheik, *1926.*

Valentino, Rudolph (1895–1926), US film actor. He emigrated to the USA from Italy in 1914, became a dancer and appeared in his first film, *The Four Horsemen of the Apocalypse*, in 1921. He had a strong romantic charm which induced near-hysterical adulation in women filmgoers, ending in a climax of grief at his funeral. His major films were: *The Sheik*, 1922; *Blood and Sand*, 1922; *Monsieur Beaucaire*, 1924; *The Eagle*, 1925; and *The Son of the Sheik*, 1926.

Valera, Eamon de, see DE VALERA, EAMON.

Valeriana, valerian, a genus of perennial herbs and sub-shrubs in the family Valerianaceae, mostly of northern temperate regions, but a few tropical, with clusters of small white or pink flowers. Red valerian is *Centranthus ruber*.

Valéry, Paul (1871–1945), French poet. He

became a friend and pupil of Stéphane Mallarmé, the Symbolist poet. Some of his prose and verse appeared in magazines, and he worked out a scheme of what he called 'pure poetry'. *La Jeune Parque*, 1917, and another volume of poems, *Charmes*, 1922, 1926, were so irresistible in their mere incantation that they were soon known by heart.

Valetta, see VALLETTA.

Valhalla, in Norse mythology, the hall in Asgard of the slain (*valr*), where Odin receives the spirits of dead heroes. At Ragnarök they will fight with Odin against the giants.

Valium, see DIAZEPAM.

Valkyries (Old Norse *valr*, slain, *kjosa*, choose), in Norse mythology, maidens who play various rôles in the service of Odin, most notably that of guiding the course of a battle and choosing those warriors to be slain and taken to Valhalla.

Valla, Lorenzo (1405–57), Italian writer and humanist. His two major works are *Historiarum Ferdinandi regis libri tres* and *De elegantiis linguae latinae*. The latter established the standards of Renaissance Latin style. He was a great controversialist and in a famous pamphlet demonstrated that the so-called Donation of Constantine, on which the papal claims to temporal power were largely based, was a forgery.

Valladolid, capital of Valladolid province, Spain, on the River Pisuerga. It was the seat of the court at one time, and Philip II was born there. There are foodstuffs, textile, iron, paper and engineering industries. Population (1981) 330,242.

Valle d'Aosta, autonomous region of northwest Italy. It is a small bilingual (French and Italian) part of the Alps drained by the Dora Baltea. It includes many high peaks (Gran Paradiso, Mont Blanc, Matterhorn, and Monte Rosa). Two important routes across the Alps pass through it, the Mont Blanc Tunnel into France and the Great St Bernard Pass into Switzerland. Its chief activities today are industrial: the making of special steels, textiles, and the production of hydroelectricity. Tourism is also important; there are two big Alpine resorts, Courmayeur and Breuil-Cervinia. The capital of the region is Aosta. Area 3262 km². Population (1980) 114,600.

Valletta, Valetta, or La Valetta, capital of Malta, situated on the south-east coast of the island on a rocky peninsula, Mount Sceberras (2·5 km long, 1 km wide), which separates Marsamscetto Harbour (on the west) from the Grand Harbour (on the east). It is an important port of call and dockyard. It was founded by Jean Parisot de la Valette, Grand Master of the Knights of Malta, after the unsuccessful Turkish siege of 1565. Population (1981) 14,249.

Valois, Dame Ninette, de, see DE VALOIS, DAME NINETTE.

Valois, House of, French dynasty, ruling 1328–1589, and beginning with Philip VI (1328–50). On the death of Charles VIII without sons (1498) the crown passed to Louis of Orléans (XII), the first of the Valois-Orléans house. This was succeeded by the Valois-Angoulême branch in 1515, the Valois line finally dying out with Henry III, in 1589, when the Bourbons came to the French throne.

The first Bourbon king being Henry IV.

Valparaíso, capital of Valparaíso province in Chile and the main port and commercial centre on the west coast of South America, 186 km north-west of Santiago by rail. Copper, wheat, silver and nitrates are amongst the exports. Not many antiquities have survived the numerous earthquakes and other disasters (though a small part of the old colonial town exists in the hollow known as 'The Port'), and the palaces, churches, villas and fortifications are modern. Valparaíso has machine and railway workshops; the local products include textiles, sugar, petrol, paints, varnishes and enamels, shoes, chemicals, leather, pharmaceutical goods and cottonseed oil. Population (1975) 248,972.

Value, in economics, means value in exchange, which is the power a commodity or service possesses for obtaining other goods or services through the process of exchange. The value of an article may be expressed in terms of the article for which it exchanges, price being the value of an article in terms of money. According to the labour theory of value, first developed by Adam Smith but popularised by Karl Marx, all value is the creation of labour; but the cost of production theory widened the concept to include all the factors of production.

The so-called paradox of value arises from the observation that some apparently useless commodities (e.g. diamonds, old paintings) are precious, while essential goods, such as water, are cheap or even free. Value in use does not determine value in exchange.

Value Added Tax (VAT). From April 1973 purchase tax and selective employment tax were replaced in Britain by VAT, which is charged at every stage of the production process, unlike purchase tax, which was charged only at a single distribution stage. Each manufacturer, wholesaler or retailer accounts for tax on the full value of his taxable sales less any tax he has already paid on his purchases. Some goods are exempt or zero-rated, for example, food, children's clothing and exports.

Valve (US, vacuum tube). The first valve, invented (1904) by Fleming, consisted of a vacuum bulb with a heated filament (cathode) surrounded by a cylinder. Electrons were emitted from the filament to the cylinder when this was given a positive potential (anode)—in conventional terms, 'current' flowed from the anode to the filament. No current flowed if the cylinder was negatively charged. With alternating current this 'diode' acted as a half-wave rectifier, barring the negative part of the wave if applied to the anode. Using two diodes or a diode with two anodes full-wave rectification is obtained.

In modern diodes the filament is sometimes surrounded by a cathode consisting of a small metal tube coated with a substance that readily releases electrons; the tube is heated, and surrounding the whole is the anode. Lee de Forest (1907) added a third electrode, the 'grid', making the diode into a triode. Small variations in grid voltage produce large variations in anode current, which can be transformed into output voltage by a resistance in the output circuit. Thus a weak 'signal' fed to the grid is 'amplified'.

The efficiency of the triode as an amplifier is limited at high frequencies by the effect of stray capacitance between the electrodes. This led to the development of the tetrode, a valve having a screen grid between the anode and the first (or 'control') grid. The screen grid, at a potential lower than the anode, has the effect of reducing the capacitance between the anode and the control grid. The tetrode tends to suffer from 'secondary emission', a reverse flow of electrons from the anode to the screen grid. The pentode has a third (suppressor) grid at cathode potential between the anode and screen grid and is more generally satisfactory as an amplifier than the tetrode. The hexode and heptode, with six and seven electrodes, respectively, are used as frequency changers in superheterodyne radio receivers. Some multi-electrode valves constitute, in effect, two or more valves in one envelope, e.g. the diode-triode, double diode-triode and triode-hexode.

Conventional valves are unsuitable at frequencies above about 300 MHz, partly because of stray capacitance and partly because of the inductance of the internal leads between the electrodes and the valve pins. By using miniature valves or special valves with short connections the frequency limit may be raised to about 1000 MHz. At these higher frequencies, for example, in radar, devices such as the magnetron and klystron, employing cavity resonators, are used.

Gas-filled valves include the mercury arc rectifier and the thyratron. The thyratron is similar to a conventional triode but the envelope contains gas instead of being evacuated. It may be used as a rectifier and also as a form of switch or relay, requiring very little power to operate it.

Transistors have almost entirely replaced valves except in very high-power or high-voltage applications, for they are smaller, physically more robust, have a longer life, and since they have no heater they require no 'warm up' period.

See also COMPUTER; ELECTRONICS; OSCILLATORS; SEMICONDUCTORS; TELEVISION; TRANSISTOR.

Valves, Mechanical, devices to control the flow, or pressure, in a fluid system. They may be operated by the flow or pressure of the fluid itself; by the machine of which they form a part; independently by hand; or by a suitable signal, be it mechanical, hydraulic, vacuum, or electromagnetic.

The check valve is operated by the system fluid and may take the form of a hinged flap; a sphere in an enlarged section of pipe; or a disc. A variant is the shuttle valve, which is used in one branch of a T-shaped pipe. If the light return spring (or weight) of the check valve is replaced by one which requires the maximum permissible system pressure to lift it, we obtain a safety or relief valve.

Manually operated globe and gate valves, in which the valve disc is inserted to block the flow path, are widely used.

Mushroom-like poppet valves are common in internal combustion engines and multiported piston slide valves are widespread in hydraulic and pneumatic applications.

See also STEAM ENGINE.

Vampire, monster which figures largely in the folk traditions of Russia and Poland, and which, with modifications, pervades the folk-lore of many peoples. It is primarily the spirit of a dead person, which, leaving the grave by night, sucks the lifeblood of sleepers till they waste away and die, becoming vampires themselves.

Vampire Bat, common name for three species of blood-sucking bat (family Desmodontidae) occurring in the tropics of South America: *Desmodus rotundus*, the common vampire, *Diaemus youngi*, the white-winged vampire, and *Diphylla ecaudata*, the hairy-legged vampire. They are timid brown animals 6–9 cm long, which chiefly approach their prey by crawling and leaping. The incisors are used to make a small wound and the blood issuing from it is lapped up. They typically feed on large mammals, including occasionally man, and birds. Each individual requires about 1 cm³ of blood each night. Medically they are of importance as vectors of rabies.

Bats of genus *Vampyrus* are fruit- and insect-feeders. Several other genera of bats are carnivorous.

Van Allen Radiation Belts, two rings of high-energy charged particles in the Earth's magnetosphere which have been derived from some extra-terrestrial source, probably the Sun, and have become trapped by the Earth's own magnetic field. The inner, more energetic belt is about 3000 km above the Earth's surface, while the outer belt is about 16,000 km away. The belts were discovered in 1958 by the US physicist James Van Allen (1914–) on examining data collected by the US space satellite Explorer I.

Vanadium, metallic chemical element, symbol V, atomic number 23, atomic weight 50·941; widely distributed in the Earth's crust. It is a greyish metal with a high melting point (1730° C) and is used in making hard steels. Because vanadium tends to oxidise at the temperatures at which it is prepared, it is difficult to obtain pure. Many vanadium compounds find application in industry.

Vanbrugh, Dame Irene (1872–1949), British actress. Among her numerous parts were Rosalind in Barrie's play of that name, Agnes Ebbsmith in Pinero's *The Notorious Mrs Ebbsmith*, also Paula in the same dramatist's *The Second Mrs Tanqueray*, and Nina in *His House in Order*. Her autobiography, *To Tell My Story*, was published in 1948.

Vanbrugh, Sir John (1664–1726), English dramatist and architect. He was controller of the Board of Works, 1702–13. Although entirely untrained as an architect, he designed the huge mansions of Castle Howard (1699–1726), Blenheim (1705–20), Seaton Delaval (1720–29), and many others; also much of Greenwich Hospital. He was one of the few English architects to follow the Baroque style. His plays are distinguished by their wit and skill of situation, and he was a master of satire, which he used with great effect against the Puritans in *The Relapse*, produced in 1696. He was knighted in 1714.

Vanbrugh, Violet (1867–1942), British actress. She included among her many rôles Queen Katharine in *Henry VIII*, and Lady Carfax in *The Knave of Diamonds*. By the command of King Edward VII, she played

Sir John Vanbrugh. Castle Howard in North Yorkshire was his first architectural commission.

Portia in *The Merchant of Venice* at Windsor Castle, 1905. She also appeared in films, notably *Pygmalion*, 1938. The Vanbrugh Theatre at the Royal Academy of Dramatic Art, London, was named in honour of Dame Irene and Violet by their brother Sir Kenneth Barnes, principal from 1909 to 1955.

Van Buren, Martin (1782–1862), 8th President of the USA. He attached himself to the Democratic party, being elected to the US Senate in 1821. He became successively governor of New York state, secretary of state, vice-president of the Union, and president in 1837. The country was upset by financial panic and van Buren pressed his bill for an independent US Treasury, which was finally adopted in 1840.

Vancouver, third city of Canada, commercial metropolis of British Columbia and Canada's chief Pacific seaport; it lies on the southern shore of Burrard inlet. It has a fine ice-free harbour, and is the western terminus of the Canadian Pacific and Canadian National railways, and the northern terminus of the US Great Northern and North Pacific railways. It is also the western terminus of the mainland section of the Trans-Canada Highway, and of a 1144-km pipeline from the Alberta oil-fields. Chief industries are lumbering (of which it is the centre), canning, brewing, sugar and oil refining, saw and flour milling, and shipbuilding. Named after Captain George Vancouver, who surveyed the area in 1792, it was incorporated as a city in 1886. Population (1976) city, 410,888; Census Metropolitan Area, 1,166,348.

Vancouver Island, island off the coast of British Columbia, of which it forms part. It is separated from the mainland by the straits of Juan de Fuca, Haro, Georgia, Johnstone, and by Queen Charlotte Sound. It was first circumnavigated by Captain George Vancouver, a British navigator, in 1792. It was established as a crown colony in 1849 under the aegis of the Hudson's Bay Company. In 1866 it was united with the mainland colony of British Columbia. The island has an area of 32,136 km² with a deeply indented coastline containing many deep-water harbours. The land on the south and east coasts is comparatively level; the interior is mountainous and heavily timbered. Gold, copper, iron and coal are found, but the chief wealth is in its forests. Victoria, the capital, is on the southern tip of the island.

Vandals, The, a Teutonic people of east Germanic stock, who originally inhabited the area between the Vistula and the Oder. About 406 they began to swarm into Gaul, across the Pyrenees to Spain, where, after much bloodshed, they settled down with the Alans in Andalusia ('Vandalitia'). Genseric, the Vandal king, invaded Africa in 429. He captured Hippo (431) and Carthage (433) and was soon acknowledged master of the whole province. In 455 he sacked Rome; and his pirate bands terrorised the Mediterranean. The decline in the power of the Vandals began after Genseric's death in 477. In 534, Gelimer, having been defeated by Justinian's general, Belisarius, finally acknowledged the supremacy of Rome, and thus brought to an abrupt conclusion the independent history of his people.

Van de Graaff, Robert Jemison (1901–67), US physicist. He taught at Princeton, 1928–31, and at MIT, 1931–60. His name is remembered by the high-voltage electrostatic generator which he produced in 1931.

Van de Graaff Machine, an electrostatic machine for the production of high voltages. It consists of a moving belt of insulating material, one end of which is charged by passing near a point conductor attached to a high-tension supply at 5000–50,000 V. The other end of the belt enters an insulated hollow conducting sphere, and the charge of the belt is collected by a pointed conductor. The action of the point depends on induction which produces an opposite charge on the points, and in consequence there is locally a high electric field leading to a point discharge. The charge is transferred to the sphere irrespective of the voltage on the sphere; this is a result of the inverse square law of charges. The sphere can be charged to about 8,000,000 V, but the current obtained is small and the voltage stable, making the generator suitable for applications in atomic and nuclear research.

See also CYCLOTRON; ELECTROSTATIC MACHINES.

Vanderbilt, Cornelius (1794–1877), US financier. At the age of 16 he bought a boat and started a ferry, which he gradually developed into a large steamboat business round New York. In 1863 he started speculating in railways, acquiring enormous and commanding interests, and left a fortune of over $20 million. By his will the Vanderbilt University was founded. His eldest son, William Henry Vanderbilt (1821–85) joined him in business, acquiring further extensive railway control, and also left a vast fortune.

Van der Post, Sir Laurens Jan (1906–), South African author and explorer. After serving in the Second World War, he undertook several government missions in Africa. *Venture to the Interior*, 1952; *The Lost World of the Kalahari*, 1958; and *The Heart of the Hunter*, 1961, among other books, vividly and sensitively describe his exploration there. Later books include *Night of the New Moon*, 1970; and *A Far Off Place*, 1974.

Van der Rohe, Ludwig Mies, see MIES VAN DER ROHE, LUDWIG.

Van de Velde, see VELDE, ESAIAS VAN DE; VELDE, WILLEM VAN DE.

Van der Waals, Johannes Diederik, see WAALS, JOHANNES DIEDERIK VAN DER.

Van der Weyden, Rogier, see ROGIER VAN DER WEYDEN.

Van Diemen, Anthony (1593–1645), Dutch explorer and colonial governor. He went to India as a government accountant and in 1625 became a member of the supreme council. In 1631 he returned to Holland in command of the Dutch Indian fleet, and, the following year, was sent back as director-general. Later he became governor-general, in which capacity he greatly extended Dutch interests in the Far East. In 1642 he sent Abel Tasman on a voyage to the south, the result of which was the discovery of the island which was named after van Diemen but which was changed to Tasmania.

Van Diemen's Land, the original name for Tasmania, given in 1642 in honour of Anthony Van Diemen, governor-general of the Dutch East Indies, by Abel Tasman, one of his navigators, who discovered the island. It was renamed in 1856.

Van Dyck, Sir Anthony (1599–1641), Flemish painter. Early training was with van Balen. Some early religious paintings were noticed by Rubens, who made van Dyck an assistant. He visited England in 1620, where James I gave him a pension, and, soon after, leave to travel to Italy, where he studied Titian, Veronese and Tintoretto. Once more he visited England, 1632, where, knighted and made court painter, he received the patronage of Charles I. Fine portraits of the royal family came from this time. Van Dyck next embarked on his remarkable record of the English aristocracy. Some examples are not entirely by van Dyck, who tended to work on the painting in the final stage, studio assistants doing the laying-in from his careful drawing and studies. Van Dyck established a formula for the grand style in portraiture which was to be accepted for generations.

Vane, Sir Henry, the Elder (1589–1655), English statesman. From 1612 he held various posts in the royal household, becoming one of Charles I's leading advisers. He entered Parliament in 1614. In 1640 he was made a secretary of state, but after his part in the condemnation of Strafford he was dismissed from all his offices in 1641 and joined the Parliamentary party.

Vane, Sir Henry, the Younger (1613–62), English statesman, son of Sir Henry Vane, the Elder. He was governor of Massachusetts (1636–37). He returned to England, was appointed joint treasurer of the navy, and entered Parliament in 1640. In 1641 he was,

for his share in the impeachment of Strafford, dismissed from the treasureship of the navy. He then joined the Parliamentary party, and they appointed him to his old post, which he held until 1650. In the early years of the Commonwealth he was one of the leading spirits, but in 1653 he quarrelled on a political matter with Cromwell. After the Restoration, he was executed for high treason. Vane was not a regicide, and was a champion of religious toleration.

Van Eeden, Frederik Willem, see EEDEN, FREDERIK WILLEM VAN.

Vänern, largest lake of Sweden, 140 km long and 70 km broad. It is very indented, and receives several rivers. Its shores are high and rocky in the north, open and shallow in the south, and fringed by several islands.

Van Eyck, Jan, see EYCK, JAN VAN.

Van Gogh, Vincent, see GOGH, VINCENT VAN.

Vanilla, a genus of climbing orchids, in the family Orchidaceae, natives of tropical Asia and America, with fleshy leaves and large white and yellow flowers. The vanilla of commerce is derived from the long dried pods of *V. planifolia*, which is cultivated in tropical countries. The main component of the flavour is vanillin, which is now also produced synthetically.

Van Dyck. A portrait of William Fielding, c.1633.

Van Leeuwenhoek, Anthony, see LEEUWENHOEK, ANTHONY VAN.

Van Meegeren, Henricus Anthonius (Han) (1889–1947), Dutch painter and forger. He made eight fakes of 17th-century masters, including *Christ at Emmaus*, bought by the Beymons Museum, Rotterdam, as a supposed Vermeer, and which long deceived the world.

Vannes, French seaport and capital of the *département* of Morbihan. It is named after the Celtic Veneti tribe, whose capital was on the site. The town's industries include shipbuilding and tourism, and the manufacture of woollen fabrics, rope, tyres and agricultural machinery. Population (1975) 43,507.

Vansittart of Denham, Robert Gilbert Vansittart, 1st Baron (1881–1957), British diplomat and publicist. In 1930 he was made

permanent under-secretary in the Foreign Office. In 1938 he was moved to a specially created post of chief diplomatic adviser to the foreign secretary, which he held until his retirement in 1941. Vansittart constantly urged rearmament against the threat of German aggression and his views were held by the government to be a threat to any attempt to achieve conciliation with Hitler: hence his removal, in 1938, from the direction of foreign affairs to an office of little influence.

Van't Hoff, Jacobus Hendricus (1852–1911), Dutch chemist. His great work was in connection with stereochemistry. Taking up the discoveries of Wislicenus in connection with the lactic acids, he enunciated in 1874 his discovery that 'in carbon compounds which exhibit the property of rotating the polarised ray in either direction, the molecule in every case contains at least one atom of carbon combined in four different ways' (Tilden). Van't Hoff also developed Kekulé's ideas on the linking of atoms.

Vanuatu
Area: 14,762 km²
Population: 112,596
Capital: Vila

Vanuatu, formerly the New Hebrides, archipelago of Polynesia in the south-west Pacific Ocean, 1769 km east of Australia, lying between 13° and 20°S and 166° and 170°E, and extending over 804 km. Vanuatu (the total area of which is about 14,762 km²) includes the Banks and Torres groups. The largest islands of the group are Santo (120 km by 70 km) and Malekula (nearly as large). There are four good harbours, Vila and Havannah on Efate, and Ports Sandwich and Stanley on Malekula. The islands form an independent republic with headquarters at Vila, which is also the chief trade centre.

The islands are volcanic and free from coral reefs. The soil is rich and deep, densely wooded, and produces breadfruit, sago-palm, bananas, sugar-cane, yam, taro, arrowroot, oranges, pineapples and coffee, and particularly sandalwood. Manganese is mined at Forari in eastern Efate. The natives are Melanesians and Polynesians. Census population in 1979, 112,596. The main towns are Vila, the capital, (14,000), and Santo.

History. Vanuatu was discovered by the Portuguese navigator de Quieros (1606). Cook charted most of the archipelago in 1774.

By a convention of 16 November 1887 Britain and France set up a naval commission to protect the lives and property of the British and French subjects in the group, and the condominium government of the New Hebrides was established in 1906. Each power retained sovereignty over its nationals and business corporations. Independence was achieved under the name of Vanuatu in 1980.

Van Veen, Maerten, see HEEMSKERK, MAERTEN JACOBSZ.

Van Wyk Louw, Nicholaas Petrus, see LOUW, NICHOLAAS PETRUS VAN WYK.

Vaporisation, see EVAPORATION.

Vaporising Oil, see KEROSINE.

Vapour, see GAS.

Var, river of France, which rises in the Alpes Maritimes and flows across the *département* of Alpes-Maritimes to the Mediterranean 6 km south-west of Nice. Length 120 km.

Varanasi, or Benares, city of Uttar Pradesh state, India. It is one of the most ancient cities in the world and the most sacred of the seven holy cities of Hinduism. Varanasi is also sacred to Jains, Sikhs and Buddhists: Buddha came to Varanasi from Gaya and is believed to have preached in the Deer Park. Within the circle of the Panch Kosi road there are narrow twisting alleyways leading to the riverside temples and *ghats* (steps). Each year over a million pilgrims bathe here to wash away their sins. Riverside cremation continues and, according to Hindu belief, ensures a direct path to heaven. Despite extensive commercial exploitation of the religious situation, arts and crafts are still very fine, especially of silks, brocades and embroidery. Population (1981) 716,779.

Varèse, Edgard (1883–1965), French composer. He was one of the avant-garde composers of his day, anticipating some of the concepts of electronic music in his substitution of sound complexes for traditional harmony and counterpoint and in his exploitation of the spatial aspects of sound. His earliest compositions frequently employed many percussion instruments on an equal basis with pitched instruments: *Hyperprism*, 1922–23; *Octandre*, 1923; *Intégrales*, 1923–25; *Arcana*, 1926–27; and *Ionisation*, 1931. His interest in electronically synthesised sound was first exploited in *Ecuatorial*, 1934; in his use of two ondes musicales, and later in his use of musique concrète in *Déserts*, and in the *Poème électronique*, 1958.
See also ELECTRONIC MUSIC.

Vargas, Getulio Dornellas (1883–1954), Brazilian statesman. He was the focus of the revolution of 1930, and was president of the Republic (though not constitutionally elected) from 1930 to 1945 when he was forced to resign. Dictatorial and forceful, he crushed Brazilian constitutionalism, and by his efficiency won support from classes which had formerly sided with the constitutionalists. He was elected president in 1950 and held the office until, because of mounting economic and political problems, he committed suicide in 1954.

Variable Star, a star that varies periodically or irregularly in brightness. Of some 19,000 variable stars listed in modern catalogues, about four-fifths are 'intrinsic' variables, while one-fifth are eclipsing variables, or *eclipsing binaries*, pairs of stars in orbit around one another, whose combined light drops when one star eclipses the other. Eclipsing binaries yield much information about star structure.

'Intrinsic' variable stars fall into many classes, named after typical members. Cepheid, W Virginis and RR Lyrae variables pulse at regular intervals related to their distance from us and have become important landmarks in mapping galaxies lying at distances too great to be measured by paralax.

Variations, musical form, the principle of which is the statement of a theme followed by varied treatments of it. Sets of variations

first emerged during the 16th century, especially in England and Spain. The English virginal masters wrote sets on popular tunes; another favoured medium was the lute. In 17th-century England, variations were called divisions because they split up the theme into smaller rhythmic patterns over a ground bass. The later history continues to show the different tendencies of (1) varying the tune, and (2) maintaining the same bass, with greater or less incidental changes, while the superstructure can be handled very freely and need not keep to the melodic tune of the theme. Mozart's variations are predominantly melodic; and so are Beethoven's earlier sets, but he reverted to the 'ground' type in the Diabelli Variations, and in the 32 Variations for piano. In Elgar's 'Enigma' Variations and in R. Strauss's *Don Quixote*, the form is complicated by an element of programme music. In Schoenberg's Variations for Orchestra, Op. 31 his 12-note method enshrines the principle of developing variation, by which the variation process is continuous and extends to the whole fabric of the music.

Varicella, see CHICKEN-POX.

Varicose Veins, blood vessels enlarged, made tortuous, and elongated apparently by increased stagnation of blood in them. The valves of the veins, which normally allow the blood to flow only one way towards the heart, become leaky. This prevents the veins from emptying, and encourages the blood to pool in them, and to stretch their walls. The condition occurs in the veins that lie below the level of the heart, especially those of the calves and thighs or in the rectum, where they cause piles, or haemorrhoids. In most cases, there is an inherited deformity or weakness of the valves in the veins.

Variety, in botany, a morphologically unique plant or group of plants, distinct from the typical forms of a particular species. See CLASSIFICATION OF PLANTS.

Variola, see SMALLPOX.

Variscan Orogeny, period of mountain building that culminated in the Upper Carboniferous era, some 270–290 million years ago. The Variscan orogeny is also known as the Hercynean or Armorican orogeny, named after localities in Europe. The Variscan mobile belt runs east-south-east to west-north-west across south-west Ireland, south-west England, northern France and northern Germany, and can be traced in the Appalachian Mountains of the eastern USA. The Variscan orogeny predates the opening of the Atlantic Ocean, and during this period North America and Europe were still joined as part of the ancient continent of Pangea, and were separated by an ocean from the African continent lying to the south. Movements between the European/American plate to the north and the African plate to the south resulted in the gradual narrowing of this ocean and led eventually to uplift and orogeny as the two continental areas collided.

Varna (formerly *Stalin*, 1949–57), city of eastern Bulgaria, capital of Varna province, built on a sandy isthmus on the Black Sea, 370 km north-east of Sofia. It was founded by the Greeks in the 6th century BC, and was subsequently ruled by the Romans and

the Byzantines. The port is busy; it is a holiday resort and spa, and there are engineering (including shipbuilding), textile, leather, foodstuff and other industries. Population (1978) 278,827.

Varnish Tree, name given to several species of trees producing resin, or with sap, used in the preparation of varnish or in lacquer work. Several species of *Aleurites*, of the Euphorbiaceae, are of importance here: *A. fordii* and *A. montana*, the Chinese wood oil trees, produce tung oil or China wood oil. In addition, *A. moluccana* is the candleberry tree. The lacquer used in Japanese lacquer work is the sap of *Rhus verniciflua* (or *vernicifera*), of the Anacardiaceae, while black lacquer is due to *Melanorrhoea usitata*, also of the Anacardiaceae.

Varnishes, solutions of resins in solvent blends. The resins can be natural products, purely synthetic, or blends depending on the end use. Varnishes can be used as protective finishes for ink for the packaging industry or they can be applied direct to a substrate such as wood or metal. Resins containing no unsaturation are preferred where non-yellowing properties are required.

Where exterior durability is required siliconised resins are preferable. These can be polyesters, alkyds or polyurethanes. Polyurethanes, particularly the two-pack type based on a hydroxyl-containing component and an aliphatic diisocyanate, are used for wood finishing and for some metal structures such as coaches, containers and chemical works. Finishing varnishes for tinplate and aluminium capsule work can be based on terephthalate resins where a high deformation is required. Normal varnishes for this type of work are based on thermosetting acrylics containing acrylamide or carboxyl modified acrylics where the carboxyl group is reactive with epoxy resin. Alkyds blended with amine resins are also used. Paper and board varnishes are based on alkyd/amino-resin systems, nitrocellulose, acrylics, vinyls, polyamides, cellulose acetate butyrate and polyurethanes. For some purposes epoxy resins, i.e. condensation products of diphenylol propane and epichlorhydrin, are used as varnishes. These can be esterified but epoxy resins have a tendency to chalk on exterior exposure. Natural resins which can be used in varnishes are shellac, copal, dammar and congo resins. Clear varnishes drying by oxidation, either oleoresinous or alkyds, usually contain driers. The driers normally used are soaps of cobalt, manganese, calcium and zinc. Originally these were based on naphthenates but are now generally based on octoates or other short-chain synthetic fatty acids which can be branched, such as 'versatic acid'. Linseed oil alkyds have been replaced by alkyds containing safflower or soya oil fatty acids which have a high linoleic and low linolenic acid content. Linolenic acid containing alkyds give rise to yellowing on ageing.

Varve, the finest outwash material from a glacier deposited in proglacial lakes. The alternation of very fine and coarse sediment represents a seasonal oscillation in deposition. The coarser sediment constitutes deposition in the warmer season when silt and clay are brought into the lake, because stream erosion is at its maximum. The silts settle fairly quickly, but the clays stay in suspension for a considerable length of time and finally settle in the winter when no new material is being deposited in the lake. This cycle of a coarse–fine layer thus represents one year's sedimentation and has been used in Sweden as a dating mechanism.

Vas Deferens, a muscular tube that forms part of the male sexual apparatus. It leads from the epididymis of each testis to a point just above the prostate, where it is joined on each side by the duct of the seminal vesicle to become the ejaculatory duct.

Vasa, Gustavus, see GUSTAVUS I.

Vasarely, Victor de (1908–), Hungarian-born artist; he went to Paris (1930) and has lived in France ever since. He is regarded as having initiated Op Art with his dazzling compositions in colour and black and white.

Vasari, Giorgio (1511–74), Italian historian of art. He studied under Michelangelo, and during his lifetime was famous as a painter and architect. He made designs for the interior of the Palazzo Vecchio, Florence, and its frescoes (1555), and his painting can be studied in his house at Arezzo, now a museum. He is chiefly remembered as an art historian with wide interests and knowledge. An indispensable source book is his *Lives of the most eminent Painters, Sculptors and Architects*, 1550, which was enlarged in 1568, and contains his autobiography.

Vascular Bundle, or vein, in botany, the conducting strands in a stem, leaf or other plant organ, that include the xylem and phloem vessels and the surrounding cambium cells.

Vascular System (Latin *vasculum*, little vessel), the system of tubes or vessels present in most animals, which conveys the blood to and from different parts of the body. In the higher plants it comprises the wood or xylem which carries water and nutrients from the roots to the leaves, and the bast or phloem which distributes the products of photosynthesis from the leaves to various parts of the plant.

Vasectomy, see STERILISATION.

Vaseline, term coined by Robert A. Chesebrough about 1870 and used as the trade mark for several of the Chesebrough Manufacturing Company's products, the chief of which is petroleum jelly, a semi-solid mixture of hydrocarbons, distilled from petroleum and purified, and used largely as an unguent and lubricant.

Vasiliev, Vladimir (1940–), Russian dancer, trained in the Bolshoy School and now one of its greatest dancers. To a fabulous technique, Vasiliev adds strong dramatic conviction. His playing and dancing of the title role in *Spartacus* is unsurpassed; he gives heroic stature to the doomed leader of the slaves' revolt.

Vasodilators (Latin *vaso*, vessel, *dilatare*, to widen), drugs that widen the bore of blood vessels. They are normally used to improve the blood supply to parts of the body where the bore of the blood vessels is reduced, e.g. owing to thrombosis or atherosclerosis of the arteries.

See also ARTERIES, DISEASES OF.

Västerås, or Vesteras, capital of Västmanland county, Sweden. It is an old town with a cathedral and an episcopal library. It has major engineering factories, chiefly electrical, and is Sweden's largest island port. Population (1978) 117,600.

Vatican, residence of the popes since their return from Avignon in 1377. Previously their home had been the Lateran, but they had long possessed a palace on the Vatican hill next to St Peter's, Rome. In 1377 the Lateran palace was in ruins, and Pope Gregory XII decided to make the Vatican his permanent residence. Subsequent building has made it a vast collection of edifices, containing over 4000 rooms, used mainly for museums or administrative purposes, the residential part being relatively small.

Among its artistically famous units are the chapel of San Lorenzo, the Apartamento Borgia, the Sistine Chapel, containing the masterpieces of Michelangelo (*The Last Judgment* and the ceiling frescoes), Botticelli and Ghirlandajo, and the Loggie of Julius II.

Adjoining the palace are five museums containing the world's finest collection of Graeco-Roman sculpture, and including Egyptian and Etruscan departments. In the Pinacotheca and elsewhere are paintings by Raphael, Perugino, Domenichino and Titian. The grand corridor of the Vatican library is the longest room in the world, being $\frac{1}{3}$ km in length.

The Vatican is an institute of scientific research, for which its archives and its library make it the most important centre for historical research in the world. There is a Vatican observatory, the Polyglot Press, and the Galleria Lapidaria, containing 6000 stone inscriptions.

The Vatican is the administrative centre of the Roman Catholic Church. In particular, the cardinal secretary of state, who is in charge of foreign policy, has his offices here. The Vatican buildings cover an area of 351 m by 234 m. The policing of the Vatican is mainly in the hands of the famous Swiss Guards, formed in 1505.

Vatican City
Area: 43 ha
Population: 600

Vatican City, area adjacent to St Peter's, Rome, being the independent state governed by the pope, and the smallest state in the world (43 ha). It lies almost entirely north and west of the basilica of St Peter and is bounded by the Piazza di San Pietro, the Via di Porta Angelica, and the Via de Leone IV on the east; the Viale Vaticano with very high walls completes the enclosure on the other sides. The Vatican City came into being in 1929, when the papal states were renounced by Pope Pius XI at the signing of the Lateran treaty between Cardinal Gasparri and Mussolini.

The population, i.e. those having permanent residence in the Vatican, is about 600. The Vatican City has its own governor, post office, coinage and law courts.

See also VATICAN.

Vatican Council, First, ecumenical council of the Roman Catholic Church, 1869–70. It is principally famous for the promulgation of the doctrine of papal infallibility. The Council also promulgated an important constitution on the relationship between faith and reason.

Vatican Council, Second (1962–65), by Roman Catholic reckoning the 21st ecumenical council. It was summoned by Pope John XXIII, upon whose death it was reconvoked by his successor Paul VI. Its main purpose was to adapt the methods of the Roman Catholic Church to modern requirements. Among its most notable achievements were extensive liturgical reforms and a declaration of the episcopate's collegiality with

Vatican. A view of St Peter's Piazza from the Basilica. The walled Vatican City is on the left.

the pope in governing the Church. Above all, it brought the Roman Catholic Church into the mainstream of ecumenism, from which it had always remained aloof; and it provided a forum for the airing of discontent among 'progressives' with regard to ecclesiastical discipline, the consequences of which are likely to be far-reaching.

Vatnajökull, an icefield of south-eastern Iceland, extending across 8,400 km² with an average thickness of over 900 m. There are numerous active volcanoes. The icefield rises to 2119 m at Oraefajokull, the highest point in Iceland. Its meltwater feeds some of Iceland's largest rivers, incuding the Thjórsá, Skjalfandafljót, Fjöllum and Lagarfljót.

Vauban, Sébastien le Prestre de (1633–1707), Marshal of France, and military engineer. He served under Condé in Spain, and in 1658 he was France's chief engineer under Turenne. In 1678 he became *commissaire-général des fortifications* and proceeded to strengthen the frontier defences. Besides constructing or improving over 150 strongholds, he conducted 40 sieges.

Vaudeville, play or theatrical presentation in which dialogue is interspersed with songs. In the 15th century one Oliver Basselin, of Vire, composed a number of satiric songs, which spread over France, bearing the name of their native place, whence vaudeville (after *ville*, town) developed. Boileau in 1674 describes them as 'political ballads'. The tunes were used for the productions at the Paris fairs known as *pièces en vaudeville*, roughly corresponding to the English ballad-opera, and the name passed to light comedies and sketches, and so to the music-hall. In the USA the term means much the same as 'variety' in Britain.

Vaughan, Henry (1622–95), English poet, born at Llansantffraed, Breconshire, Wales. Coming from the land of the ancient Silures, he called himself 'Silurist'. His first book, *Poems, with the Tenth Satire of Juvenal Englished*, appeared in 1646. *Olor Iscanus* (The Swan of Usk), a collection of poems and translations, was surreptitiously published in 1651. About this time he had a serious illness which led to deep spiritual impressions, and thereafter his writings were almost entirely religious. *Silex Scintillans: Sacred Poems and Private Ejaculations*, 1650, his best-known work, consists of short poems in the 'metaphysical' manner, full of deep religious feeling; it contains 'The Retreat', a short, exquisite poem which suggested to Wordsworth his 'Ode on the Intimations of Immortality'.

Vaughan Williams, Ralph (1872–1958), British composer. He studied at Trinity College, Cambridge, at the Royal College of Music, and later with Ravel. His first major success was *Toward the Unknown Region*, 1907. It was followed by *On Wenlock Edge*, 1909, and the Tallis Fantasia, 1910. After the First World War he was professor of composition at the Royal College, for some 30 years.

An upholder of the finest English traditions and an enthusiast for English folk-song, he was also progressive. In works written when he was nearly 80, such as the sixth symphony and *Sinfonia Antartica*, he introduced new ideas or devices. His large output includes five operas; *Job*, 1930, a masque for dancing; incidental music; church and film music; *A Sea Symphony, Flos Campi, Five Tudor Portraits* and other choral works; *Serenade to Music*; symphonies, including *A London Symphony* and *Pastoral Symphony*; *The Lark Ascending* for violin and orchestra; concertos; two string quartets; and many songs.

Vault, in architecture, an arch forming a self-supporting roof over a building. The principle of vaulting was known in Babylonia and Egypt 6000 years ago. It was developed by the Romans, who made great strides in their skilful use of concrete; by the Sassanid rulers of Persia in the 6th–7th centuries AD using brickwork on the grand scale; and by medieval builders throughout Europe. The Romans used barrel or tunnel vaults; Roman barrel vaults were made of concrete and were massively thick.

During the Romanesque period vaults were built of masonry and were less massive; they were further lightened by the introduction of stone ribs, carrying a thin stone 'web', just as the steel ribs of an umbrella support the thin cover. This led to difficulties, especially where the nave of a church was twice the width of each aisle, because the wide round arch of the nave was far taller than the narrow arches over the aisles. In the early Gothic period the introduction of pointed arches solved this problem, for they could be made more or less pointed to suit the varying widths of nave and aisles. Vaulting became more complicated during the later Gothic period as intermediate ('lierne') ribs were added, and the thickness of the stone 'web' was reduced.

Fan vaulting was peculiar to England and introduced during the last phase of Gothic. The underside of the vault was carved into tracery, thus producing the effect of a fan as seen from below.

Vazov, Ivan Minchev (1850–1921), Bulgarian 'national' author. He was the first Bulgarian to adopt literature as a profession. From 1877 he lived in Bulgaria and Eastern Rumelia, except for a period of exile (1886–1889) in Odessa, where he wrote *Under the Yoke*, the Bulgarian national novel *par excellence*. Prolific in many genres, he excels as a poet, short-story and travelogue writer. He was inspired by a passionate but clear-sighted love of his country. He immensely improved the flexibility and expressiveness of Bulgarian as a literary instrument.

Vector, a single symbol used to represent the combination of an unlimited number of characteristics of a physical quantity; for example, the three co-ordinates of a point in space, or a velocity (speed and direction). The term was first used by Sir William Rowan Hamilton. It can be treated as an element of a mathematical structure called a vector space, in which a vector can be added to another or multiplied by any number and the result will be a vector.

See also ANALYTICAL GEOMETRY.

Vector, in biology, an animal carrier of disease organisms, e.g. the tsetse fly which carries the organism responsible for sleeping sickness and for various diseases in cattle. In strict usage, the term is restricted to carriers in which development of the disease organism takes place, such development being a condition for transmission by the vector.

Veda, general term for the ancient sacred literature of India, written in archaic Sanskrit, dating from c.1500–1200 BC. The Vedas proper are four collections of hymns meant to be used at sacrifices. The oldest of these is the *Rigveda*, which contains the poems from which the earliest information about the Aryans in India is derived.

Veddahs, aboriginal hunting and gathering people living in Sri Lanka. Their economy, material culture and social organisation were very simple. Today few are left in their indigenous state, having been merged into the Sinhalese and Tamil populations.

Vedism, the Aryan religion of ancient India, taking its name from the sacred Vedas. Great importance was attached to ritual, especially sacrifice, which became increasingly complex. Vedic gods, not easily distinguishable one from another, tended to be connected with cosmic and natural phenomena, such as fire, rain, storms, and were for the most part male. Vedism began to decline in the 5th century BC, giving way to classical Hinduism.

Vega, Alpha Lyrae, a first magnitude star in Lyra. It was the first star to be photographed and to have its spectrum recorded photographically. As a consequence of precession it will become the north polar star about AD 14,000.

Vega Carpio, Lope Félix de, or Lope de Vega (1562–1635), Spanish poet and dramatist. He served in the Armada in 1588, and was secretary to the Duke of Alva. In 1613 he took holy orders. He was a voluminous writer, producing epics, pastorals, odes, sonnets and novels; but it is to his dramatic works, of which he wrote over 700, that he owes his eminence. He worked out the formula for the regular *comedia*, which was to last into the 18th century. Essentially, this involved a mixture of entertainment based on fast-moving action, often centring on the honour theme, and edifying moral instruction, which was not usually allowed to be obtrusive. Vega produced a remarkable variety of plays: religious works, including autos; dramas on pastoral and mythological subjects like *La selva sin amor*; historical plays like *Peribáñez*; and 'cloak and dagger' and romantic pieces like *El Castigo sin Venganza*. The basis of his enduring fame is thus not only his individual qualities as a dramatist, such as his lyricism and technical skill, but his development of a form which was both commercially and artistically triumphant.

Vegetable Ivory, the seed of *Phytelephas macrocarpa*, the ivory nut palm, native to Colombia. When dried, the seeds can be carved and polished to simulate ivory.

Vegetarianism, the practice of eating a meatless diet. It is estimated that as much as half of the world's population is vegetarian, but for most this is from necessity rather than from choice. There are several types of vegetarians. *Lactoovovegetarians* eat vegetables supplemented with milk, cheese and eggs. *Lactovegetarians* eat vegetables supplemented only with milk and cheese. *Pure vegetarians* or *vegans* eat an all-vegetable diet and will not eat *any* foods of animal origin, including milk, butter and eggs.

See also NUTRITION.

Vegetative Propagation, the controlled

reproduction of plants by asexual means, where a single piece of one plant may be used to produce another complete plant with identical characteristics. This single piece of plant may form part of the particular plant's natural tendency to reproduce vegetatively by such specialised organs as bulbs, runners or suckers. Other plants are not so well adapted and horticulturists have developed techniques to facilitate vegatative propagation, such as layering. Other plants have the capacity to produce roots or shoots on detached portions of plants, which may be as small as tips of growing stems or as large as 30-cm pieces of dormant stem. These pieces of dormant stem, often called hardwood, are known as cuttings, of which there are several other kinds, including leafy shoots, leaf-buds, leaves and roots. The roots must produce vegetative buds, while the others must produce roots for survival.

A modern aid to the rooting of all cuttings is a rooting hormone, of which there are several proprietary powders, containing naphthalene acetic acid or indole butyric acid.

See also BUDDING; GRAFTING; MERISTEM CULTURE; VEGETATIVE REPRODUCTION.

Vegetative Reproduction, propagation of plants by organs other than seeds. Frequently the shoot is modified to store food and produce new plants. Since all types of vegetative reproduction are asexual, the offspring are exactly like the parent plant.

The *bulb* is a modified underground shoot consisting of a short, thickened, disc-like stem, or plate, surrounded by a number of overlapping leaves which contain reserve material for the next season's plant. The bulbs of the onion and hyacinth are said to be *tunicated*, i.e. the leaves completely enwrap the modified shoot like a tunic; the bulb of the lily is *scaly*, or *imbricated*, i.e. the leaves merely overlap one another. The *corm* is a short, swollen, underground stem, forming an organ of hibernation; the reserve food is used early in the year, in rapid growth, to give a flowering shoot or shoots. All roots grow from the stem. Some plants, e.g. the potato, may be propagated from the *eyes* which are dormant buds on the swollen underground stem or *tuber*. The *rhizome* is an underground stem growing more or less horizontally. Plants with rhizomes often spread very rapidly since any bud on a rhizome can produce a new plant. Some rhizomes, e.g. those of the iris, are swollen with stored food. The *bulbil* is an axillary bud which drops to the ground and becomes a new plant, as in some lilies. The *runner* is a prostrate shoot from the axil of a radical leaf that roots at the nodes or at the end to form a new plant, e.g. strawberry. A *sucker* is a shoot growing from the underground stem or stock of a plant. *Stolons* are stems that bend over to the ground, take root and produce independent plants when the parent stem dies or is cut, e.g. raspberry.

Vein, in anatomy, any of the blood-vessels that carry the blood from the tissues to the heart. Veins are composed of three coats, *tunica adventitia, tunica media* and *tunica intima*, and there is less muscular and elastic tissue than in the arteries. The veins are generally divided into three systems: the general venous system, the pulmonary system and the hepatic portal system. The general venous system

Velázquez, The Water-seller of Seville, *1618.*

returns the blood from the greater part of the organism to the heart. The pulmonary system brings back the oxygenated blood from the lungs to the left atrium of the heart. The hepatic portal system carries the blood from the stomach, intestines, spleen and pancreas to the liver by the hepatic portal vein, ramifying into numerous capillary vessels. The pulmonary and hepatic veins have no valves, but the general venous system has. The valves are so constructed as to prevent a reverse flow of blood. When these valves become incompetent varicose veins result. As a rule the course of the deeper veins is parallel to that of the arteries.

See also CIRCULATION OF THE BLOOD.

Vein, in plants, see VASCULAR BUNDLE.

Velázquez, Diego Rodriguez de Silva y, also Velasquez (1599–1660). From 1610 to 1616 he was apprenticed to Francisco Pacheco, becoming an independent master in 1617. His earliest works display a powerful ability to suggest weight and volume through strong lighting and show the influence of Caravaggio. He became court painter in Madrid in 1623; before this he had painted mainly religious works and *bodegones* (interior scenes with a strong still-life element), but he now concentrated on portraits, mainly of the royal family and courtiers. He remained at the court for the rest of his life apart from two visits to Italy.

Throughout his career naturalism was the basis of Velázquez's art but his means of expression continually grew in subtlety, his colour becoming cooler and his brushwork freer. With his technical development went an increasing psychological penetration, and whether he was painting the king of Spain or the court dwarfs, Velázquez approached his work with the same honesty, conviction and respect for his sitter's humanity. His portrait of *Pope Innocent X* (Doria Pamphili Gallery, Rome) is perhaps his greatest achievement in portraiture. He also painted some noble religious and mythological works, two exquisite landscapes of the Medici Gardens in Rome (Prado), one of the most celebrated of nudes, *The Rokeby Venus* (National Gallery, London), and a great con-

temporary history painting, the *Surrender of Breda*, (Prado). Velázquez's career was one of uninterrupted success, and he never adopted easy formulae or mannerisms. His greatest paintings unite virtuosity of technique and depth of feeling, and constantly reveal new subtleties.

Velde, Esaias van de (c.1591–1630), Dutch landscape painter. He was a pupil of Gillis van Coninxloo, but he broke away from the Mannerist style and became one of the leading pioneers of the realistic tradition in Dutch landscape painting. His fresh and direct vision was very influential, notably on his great pupil Jan van Goyen.

Velde, Willem van de, the Elder (1611–93) and the Younger (1633–1707), Dutch marine painters, father and son. They specialised in accurate portrayals of ships, and it is often difficult to separate the works of the two; indeed they probably collaborated on occasions. They frequently painted sea-fights, and their desire for accuracy led them to make drawings from a small boat in the heat of action. They went to England in 1672 where they were patronised by the crown and remained for the rest of their lives. Willem the Younger, with his great sensitivity to light and atmosphere, is generally regarded as the greatest Dutch marine painter, his work proving an inspiration to most English artists who worked in that genre, up to and including Turner. Adriaen van de Velde (1636–72), also the son of Willem the Elder, was less talented but more versatile than his relatives. He painted landscapes as well as seascapes, and a few religious works, and he often painted the figures in the landscapes of other artists, notably his master Wynants.

Vellum, the prepared skin of calves, lambs and other animals, finer in quality than parchment.

Velocity, rate of displacement of a moving point. It is sometimes applied to the rate at which a change of state or configuration may take place. To specify velocity, the direction in which the body is moving must be given, and hence it is a vector quantity. See also DIFFERENTIATION; MECHANICS; METROLOGY; VECTOR.

Velocity of Circulation, an economic concept which expresses the average number of times that a unit of money enters into transactions during a given period. The value of money can be influenced by the velocity of circulation, which depends on the quantity of money in circulation relative to the number of transactions performed, the structure of interest rates, the frequency with which workers are paid, and other factors. It tends to rise in periods of inflation.

Velour, or velure (French *velours*, velvet), imitation velvet, a woven fabric with thick short pile, traditionally used for headwear and upholstery.

Velvet (Latin *villosa*; French *velours*), fabric believed to have originated in the East, possibly in China, but known at least as early as the 13th century. Velvet is made of pure silk, its surface being a short, thick pile, produced by weaving a second set of warp thread over the already woven cloth, these threads being passed over wires and cut before the wires are removed. A similar material with a cotton back and silken face is termed velveteen. With the development of synthetic materials the term velvet is indiscriminately used in conjunction with the basic fabric from which it is made, such as rayon velvet, cotton velvet, etc. Velvet was produced in England from 1685 (Spitalfields). It is used for clothing, upholstery and interior decoration.

Venation, botanical term for the arrangement of veins in a plant organ such as leaves. In zoology the term is used by analogy for the arrangement of veins in the wings of insects.

Venda, homeland of the Vhavenda people, granted independence by the Republic of South Africa in 1979. Area, 6500 km²; population (1980 estimate) 343,480. The country is arid. Livestock-farming predominates; some crops, mainly maize and tea, are grown under irrigation. Minerals include coal, stone, graphite and magnesite. Venda is a republic with presidential government and a partly-elected National Assembly; tribal authorities also survive. The origin of the Vhavenda is unknown. They were formerly ruled by a king regarded as semi-divine. Their territory became a self-governing homeland in 1973.

Vendetta, a custom, similar to that of the blood feud, by which fellow kinsmen were bound to avenge any personal injury done to a member of their clan or family. The vendetta only occurs, however, when the relative has actually been murdered. The vendetta still exists in Corsica, and in parts of Sardinia and Sicily.

Vendôme, Louis Joseph, Duc de (1654–1712), Marshal of France, great-grandson of Henry V. In 1702 he was placed in command of the Franco-Spanish army in Italy, overthrowing the Austrians at Calcinato (1706). Defeated by Marlborough at Oudenarde in 1708, he was relieved of his command, but won further victories in Spain in 1710. Vendôme was one of the greatest of French generals.

Veneering, a highly skilled craft, consisting of glueing a thin sheet or sheets of fine quality wood over a foundation of woods or a coarser calibre. The craft originates from classical Greece and Rome and was rediscovered in the early 17th century following the introduction of ebony to France. Veneering is much practised in furniture making, and is the most popular and least expensive means of forming a decorative surface on plywood boarding.

Venereal Disease, any infection transmitted by means of sexual contact. The special study of venereal disease is known as venereology. Diseases regarded as venereal are: gonorrhoea, granuloma inguinale, lymphogranuloma venereum, syphilis, chancroid (an ulcer caused by the bacterium *Haemophilus duereyi*), and virus infections such as those of hepatitis and herpes. Many organisms, including non-pathogens as well as pathogens, may be transmitted between partners during sexual intercourse, without the term venereal being customarily applied to them, as for example streptococci, *Listeria*, and staphylococci. *Trichomonas* is one example of a sexually transmitted parasite, and *Candida* (a yeast-like organism) of a sexually transmitted fungus.

Venesection, or phlebotomy, cutting of a vein in order to let blood. In modern practice it is sometimes employed in conditions where the blood pressure needs to be reduced or in congestive heart failure, where the circulating volume of blood in the vessels is much increased. So-called physiological venesection involves putting tight bands around the arms and thighs, thus cutting off return of blood in the veins to the heart. The effect on the circulation is similar to that of actually bleeding the vessels, but is of course bloodless and temporary.

Venezia, or **Venetia,** see VENICE.

Venezuela
Area: 912,050 km²
Population: 14,540,000
Capital: Caracas

Venezuela, republic of South America. It lies on the northern coast of the continent and has a coastline of 3200 km on the Caribbean Sea. Colombia borders it in the west, Brazil in the south, and Guyana in the east. It has an area of 912,050 km².

The coastal lowlands comprise the Maracaibo lowlands, surrounding the Gulf of Venezuela and Lake Maracaibo to the south of the gulf, and the narrow coastal strip running between the Caribbean Sea and the Andes. The eastern end of the coastal strip joins the delta of the River Orinoco. Lake Maracaibo is 13,000 km² and its surrounding land is swampy and mosquito-infested.

The Andes mountains cut across the north-western corner of Venezuela running from the Colombian border nearly to the sea. Although comprising only 12 per cent of the area of Venezuela, about 70 per cent of the population lives here and it is in fact the economic and social heart of the country, apart from the oil-fields located round Lake Maracaibo and in the Ilaños.

The Orinoco lowlands or Ilaños (plains) stretch between the Andes and the River Orinoco and extend the breadth of the country. They are vast treeless grasslands intersected with small rivers and streams. The Guiana highlands cover the south-eastern half of Venezuela but have only 2 per cent of its population, the only significant economic activity being iron-ore mining.

In 1979 the total population was 14,540,000. The population is predominantly mestizo (mixture of Spanish and Indian). The largest city is the capital, Caracas, followed by Maracaibo, Valencia, Barquisimeto, Maracay and San Cristobal.

The most valuable products are milk, beef and eggs; arable production is less important, and the most valuable crops are sugar cane, coffee and bananas.

The largest manufacturing sectors are still in more traditional lines such as textiles, clothing and foodstuffs but the steel, aluminium and petrochemical sectors are growing.

Petroleum is very important and Venezuela is today the world's fifth largest producer.

The country also contains large iron-ore deposits which were nationalised in 1974, and abundant supplies of bauxite and some copper, coal, nickel and zinc.

The unit of currency is the *bolívar*.

Venezuela is one of the few genuine social democracies in the Third World with an open plural society, a free press, and an effective opposition. Executive power is vested in the President and his ministers. Congress consists of a senate and a Chamber of Deputies.

The official language is Spanish.

History. Venezuela was first sighted by Columbus in 1498. The country remained under Spanish rule until the revolution under Simón Bolívar, when its independence was won at the battle of Lastoguanes (1813) and Carabobo (1821). Venezuela was part of the Federal Republic of Colombia until 1830, but thereafter became absolutely independent. Between 1830 and 1935 Venezuela had more than a dozen rulers, but three were pre-eminent: Páez, the half-Indian peon, who declared the independence of Venezuela in 1830; Guzmán Blanco, who assumed office in 1870; and Juan Vicente Gómez (1909–35).

In October 1945 a revolt broke out against the

Venezuela, the skyline of Caracas. The city lies in a high mountain valley, near the coast.

reactionary government of Gen. Medina. The progressive leader of the revolt, Romulo Betancourt, assumed the presidency and instituted constitutional and economic reforms. He was succeeded by a military junta in November 1948 and Pérez Jiménez was elected president. His government was dictatorial and corrupt. After a revolution in 1958, and a new and democratic constitution was established, Betancourt was again president, 1959–64, and his progressive policies were continued by his successor, Raúl Leoni (1964–69). The Social Democrats under Carlos Andres Pérez came to power in 1974. Luis Herrara Campins (Acción Democrática) succeeded in 1979.

Venice (Italian *Venezia*; Latin, *Venetia*), Italian city and seaport, capital of Venezia province and the region of Veneto, situated on the lagoon of Venice some 250 km east of Milan. The city is built on numerous small islands divided into two groups by the Grand Canal which runs north-west to south-east and forms the main thoroughfare. The canal (a reversed 'S' shape) is lined with palaces and crossed by three bridges (from north to south: Scalzi, Rialto, Accademia), and from it branch about 150 smaller canals. There is no wheeled traffic in the city, and transport is traditionally by means of the boat known as the gondola.

The centre of Venice is the square of St Mark, which is surrounded by many of the main buildings of the city. The five-domed cathedral of St Mark (1063–94), with its marbles and mosaics is one of the most splendid Byzantine buildings in the world. The palace of the Doge is a Gothic structure of the 14th–15th centuries and is connected to the state prison by the covered Bridge of Sighs. In addition to its great schools of painters, the contribution of Venice to the arts has been very considerable. Its masons, mosaicists and glass-workers have been famous since early times, and in the 15th century the printing presses of Venice produced more books than those of Rome, Milan, Florence and Naples combined. The blown-glass industry still flourishes on Murano, and there are textile, jewellery, lace and publishing industries. Population (1979) of Greater Venice, 355,865. From its origin as a temporary refuge in the lagoons from the incursions of the barbarians, Venice grew into the most powerful of the Italian states. From the beginning of the 14th century its government was an oligarchy headed by the Doge, and it had to maintain its supremacy in the Adriatic against its rival Genoa, and against the Holy Roman Empire, the Turks and the Dalmatian pirates. The end finally came with the destruction of the republic by Napoleon I and the handing over of the city to Austria by the Treaty of Campo Formio in 1797. In 1866, after the war between Prussia and Austria, Venice passed to Italy.

Venice today is faced by two problems. Firstly, the physical decay of the city, pollution, the erosion of the islands on which it stands, and subsidence. Secondly, the economic decay of the old city due to the dominance of the industrial suburbs of Mestre and Marghera on the mainland.

Venizelos, Eleutherios (1864–1936), Greek statesman. He became Greek premier in 1910.

Venice. *The Grand Canal, looking towards the baroque church of St Maria della Salute.*

At the outset of the First World War he advocated Greek intervention on the side of the Entente, but received no support from King Constantine and resigned in 1915. In 1916 Venizelos set up a provisional revolutionary government at Salonika. Late in 1917 he returned to Athens, being recalled to office, after the abdication of Constantine, by King Alexander. He contributed to the success of the Allied army at Salonika, reorganising the Hellenic forces. After the revolution in Greece in 1922 he represented his country at the Lausanne Conference and in 1924 again became prime minister, the country having meanwhile become a republic. From 1928 to 1932, following a dictatorship, he was again in power; in Crete he inspired an anti-government revolt in 1935, but this was quelled and he was forced into exile in France.

Venn Diagram, diagram used in set theory to show the relationship between sets. They were invented by the British logician John Venn (1834–1923).

See also SET THEORY.

Ventilation, the replacement of stale air by fresh. Ventilation should be designed to remove smell, smoke, noxious gases or dusts before they cause discomfort or injury to health. In hot weather it may need also to supply a current of fresh air to promote evaporation of perspiration, whereby the human body keeps cool. Some air movement is always necessary for comfort, at rates of about 6–12 m per minute. The ventilation of a room is usually measured by the number of air changes per hour: thus a room 30 m³ in volume needs 60 m³ of air to enter to give two air changes. Domestic bathrooms and water-closets require 8–10 air changes per hour, larders 2, living-rooms rather less. Higher rates are generally required for public buildings and offices. In factories and mines ventilation demands special standards and standards are laid down in the Factories and Mines and Quarries acts.

In houses and other small buildings natural ventilation is usually adequate; indeed, it is often desirable to fit draught-excluding strips in the winter. On no account, however, should the ventilation below timber floors be interfered with, or decay such as dry rot may result; care should also be taken not to reduce ventilation below that necessary for coal or gas fires to draw properly.

See also AIR CONDITIONING.

Ventricle (Latin *ventriculus*, small belly), any small cavity but particularly the two lower chambers of the heart. The cardiac ventricle is one of the two lower chambers, muscular structures receiving blood from the atria and pumping it out into the pulmonary artery from the right ventricle and the aorta from the left ventricle.

See also BRAIN.

Ventriloquism, art of speaking in such a manner that the sound appears to be produced at a distance from the speaker. The origin of the word, from *venter*, belly, suggests that the voice was supposed to proceed from the speaker's stomach. The words are, however, produced in the usual manner, though some consonants may be masked by the immobility of the lips and teeth and the restricted use of the tongue. Since the 19th century ventriloquists have used a dummy with a moving mouth with which they carry on a conversation.

Ventris, Michael George Francis (1922–1956), British scholar He was an architect and helped design schools for the Ministry of Education. He is famous for his decipherment of the so-called 'Minoan Linear B script'. His book, *Documents in Mycenaean Greek*, written in collaboration with John Chadwick, was published within a few days of his death in a road accident.

Venturi, Adolfo (1856–1941), Italian art historian. He is largely remembered for his monumental survey of Italian art, *Storia Dell'-Arte Italiana*, published in 25 volumes between the years 1901 and 1939.

Venturi, Lionello (1885–1961), Italian art historian. He had a wide range of interests, and was the author of numerous surveys of art, including *History of Art Criticism*, 1936; *Italian Painting: The Creators of the Renaissance*, 1950; *The 16th Century from Leonardo to El Greco*, 1956.

Venus, in astronomy, the brightest of the planets, popularly known as the 'evening star'. The details of its orbit are: mean distance from the Sun, 0·723 astronomical units or 108,210,000 km; eccentricity, 0·0068; inclination to the ecliptic, 3°24′; sidereal period, 224·701 days; mean synodic period, 583·92 days. Its vital statistics are: equatorial diameter, 12,100 km; period of axial rotation, 243·0 days, the rotation being retrograde; mean density, 5·25 g/cm³. Seen from the Earth, the apparent diameter of Venus varies from 64 to 10 arc seconds as its distance varies. At its brightest Venus is visible to the naked eye during daytime. Venus is very disappointing telescopically. All that can be seen is sunlight reflected from the top of a dense layer of yellow clouds.

The little knowledge we have of the physical constitution of Venus is mainly derived from recent observations, particularly from the Soviet and US space probes that have either passed closely by or landed. Even the slow retrograde rotation was not discovered till the early 1960s when the results of the special radar observations came as a complete surprise to most astronomers. Even more surprising has been the extent and constitution of the atmosphere, which proved unexpectedly to be very many times more extensive than that of the Earth; 97 per cent of it is carbon dioxide, and the pressure that it exerts at ground level is 90 times greater than that produced by the terrestrial atmosphere. Moreover, the temperature at ground level is about 750 K (477°C), presumably because of a 'greenhouse effect' produced by the extensive atmosphere. The clouds lie in three distinct layers and are composed of droplets of sulphuric acid and particles of solid and maybe liquid sulphur. Radar studies of Venus have revealed two continent-like structures on the surface, one with mountains higher than Everest, and a rift-valley larger than Earth's Grand Canyon. There are also craters typical of those caused by the impact of meteorites as well as areas that appear to have a volcanic nature. No magnetic field has been detected.

Venus, Roman goddess, perhaps originally of garden fertility. Later identified with the Greek Aphrodite, she became above all the goddess of sensual love and physical beauty.

Venus's Fly-trap, *Dionaea,* a genus of Droseraceae. The leaves have a lower winged part and an upper expanded part fringed with teeth. Inside the upper part are numerous tiny digestive glands and hairs. If one of these is touched by an insect the sides of the leaf fold up, and as the captive decomposes, its products are absorbed by the plant.

Veracruz, one of Mexico's leading ports on the Gulf of Mexico (probably the chief as regards imports). The port, an artificial one whose channels have to be continually dredged, is used by coastal and international shipping. The town has a well-developed industrial complex in which oil plays a leading rôle backed by iron and steel plants, an aluminium plant, shipbuilding yards, in addition to cotton textiles, sugar refining, sisal manufacturing and foodstuff processing. Population (1975) 266,400.

Veratrum, false hellebore, a genus of perennial plants in the family Liliaceae, with decorative leaves and panicles of white, green or purple flowers. *V. album* yields the poisonous powder known as hellebore powder, which is mixed with water and used as an insecticide.

Verb, part of speech which indicates action or existence, a class of words distinguished by all languages.
See also PARTS OF SPEECH.

Verbano, Lago, see MAGGIORE, LAKE.

Verbena, vervain, a genus of herbaceous plants and shrubs in the family Verbenaceae, mainly indigenous to America. *V. × hybrida* is the verbena of gardens.

Verbenaceae, a family of dicotyledons, including mainly tropical trees, shrubs and woody climbers, with about 80 genera and 800 species. The most important species of the family is teak (*Tectona grandis*). Species of *Clerodendron* and *Callicarpa* are grown for their decorative flowers and coloured fleshy fruits. Verbena species are also grown in gardens.

Vercelli (ancient *Vercellae*), Italian town and capital of Vercelli province, situated 65 km north-east of Turin. There is a Baroque archiepiscopal cathedral and a 13th-century basilica. The town is the centre of Europe's main rice-producing area, and has chemical and man-made fibre industries. Population (1974) 58,000.

Vercingetorix (d.46 BC), chieftain of the Arverni, a Gallic tribe. He led a revolt against the Romans with great ability, but was delivered to Caesar on the surrender of Alesia (52 BC). After adorning Caesar's triumph in 46 BC he was put to death.

Verde, Cape, see CAPE VERDE.

Verde, Cesário (1885–86), Portuguese poet. One of the most original and best of Portugal's poets, Verde's descriptions of Lisbon, seen through the eyes of a countryman, retain their charm. For his profound insights into modern urban life he has been compared with the French poet Baudelaire.

Verdelho Wine, see MADEIRA WINE.

Verdi, Giuseppe (1813–1901), Italian composer. In 1831 he was sent to Milan with a scholarship but was over the entrance age for the Conservatoire. He studied, however, with the conductor at the Scala Theatre. Verdi's first opera, *Oberto,* was produced at La Scala in 1839. *Un giorno di regno* was a failure, but *Nabucco,* 1842, was a great success. *Ernani,* 1844; *Rigoletto,* 1851; *Il Trovatore,* 1853; and *La Traviata,* 1853, followed, and in 1871 Verdi excelled his previous efforts with *Aida.* After a long interval, he produced his two great Shakespearean masterpieces, *Otello,* 1887, and *Falstaff,* 1893. His other important operas are *Macbeth,* 1847; *Simon Boccanegra,* 1857; *Un ballo in maschera,* 1859; *La forza del destino,* 1862; and *Don Carlos,* 1867. Outstanding non-operatic works are the *Requiem,* 1874, the *Four Sacred Songs,* and the string quartet. Verdi was the artistic successor of Donizetti and Bellini, but showed a greater wealth of passionate feeling and craftsmanship. He enlightened pathos or tragedy by a simple and suggestive spirituality.

Verdict. In English civil trials the jury determine by their verdict all issues of fact and if they find for the plaintiff assess the damages. Juries are now rare in civil actions and there is a right for either party to demand a jury only in actions for defamation, false imprisonment, malicious prosecution or where fraud is alleged. Thus the functions of the jury in civil cases are now usually discharged by a judge sitting alone.
In criminal law, verdicts are said to be: (1) general, i.e. guilty or not guilty; (2) partial, i.e. guilty on one count and not guilty on the rest; (3) special, i.e. where the jury find a certain state of facts and leave it to the judge to decide upon those facts whether the offence charged has been committed.
In Scots law there is a middle verdict of not-proven, but English jurisprudence has never favoured any rule that militates against finality one way or the other in criminal trials. Where the jury cannot agree they must be discharged, and the accused is then tried before a new jury, except that a jury which has been out for at least two hours may return a majority verdict. At least ten jurors must agree where the total number is eleven or twelve; where the number has been reduced to ten a majority of nine will suffice.

Verdigris, see ACETIC ACID.

Verdun, French town in the *département* of Meuse, on the River Meuse. It has long been a fortress, commanding an approach to the Paris basin. There are brewing and textile and metallurgical manufactures. Population (1975) 26,927.
See also WESTPHALIA, TREATY OF.

Verdun, Battle of (1916), see WORLD WAR, FIRST.

Vereeniging, town of the Transvaal, South Africa, a manufacturing centre 56 km from Johannesburg, on the River Vaal. It is one of the most important coal-mining areas in South Africa. Iron and steel works, large electric power stations and other industries are situated there. Population (1980) 149,410, including 65,500 whites.

Vergilus Maro, see VIRGIL.

Verhaeren, Émile (1855–1916), Belgian poet. The influence of the French Symbolists on his work was profound, yet his poetry is often distinctly Flemish in inspiration, for example, *Les Flamandes,* 1883. His compassionate response to contemporary problems is reflected in such works as *Les Villes tentaculaires,* 1895. In the essays *Les Ailes rouges,* 1916, he reflects on Belgium's plight in the First World War.

Verlaine, Paul (1844–96), French poet. His early paganism, responsible for such Baudelairean works as the *Fêtes galantes,* 1869, inspired by the paintings of Watteau, was superseded (after 12 years of dissipation broken by illness) by devout Catholicism. *Sagesse,* 1881, is equal to the finest religious poems ever written. Verlaine gave to French poetry a new and original music; his poetry's music, the harmony of mood and sound, has found few rivals. He combined this power of sound with deep emotionalism, and the combination produced a poignant and extremely beautiful sense of poetry.

Vermeer, Jan (1632–75), the greatest of Dutch genre painters. He was admitted to the Guild of Painters of Delft in 1653 and was later Dean of the Guild. He probably studied under Carel Fabritius, a pupil of Rembrandt. After his death he was forgotten, his work being assigned to Pieter de Hooch and others. He was 'discovered' in 1866 by the French critic Théophile Thoré. Vermeer worked very slowly and only about forty paintings by him are known, but he is now acknowledged as one of the most important 17th-century painters. He stands apart from his contemporary genre painters through his superb draughtsmanship and skill in perspective, his compositions of almost abstract simplicity, subtle characterisation, fresh colour harmonies and an incomparable ability to suggest the fall of light on objects. Examples of his domestic genre scenes are *The Kitchenmaid,* c.1658 (Rijksmuseum, Amsterdam); *The Lacemaker,* c.1664–65 (Louvre); and *Young Woman Standing at a Virginal,* c.1670 (National Gallery, London). Two exterior scenes are known, *The Little Street,* c.1658 (Rijksmuseum), and *View of Delft,* c.1660 (Mauritshuis, The Hague). Several paintings

Vermeer, The Guitar Player, *painted in the 1670s, is a fine example of Vermeer's use of light.*

attributed to Vermeer, notably *Christ at Emmaus*, were proved in 1945 to be forgeries. See also VAN MEEGEREN, HENRICUS ANTHONIUS.

Vermicelli, see PASTA.

Vermiculite was originally thought to be mica which had undergone metamorphosis and was considered of no commercial importance until 1936. Today the USA and the Transvaal are the largest producers of vermiculite. It is formed from a micaceous ore, by heating to about 1100°C, and consists of a porous, flaky medium of small particles, sterile, highly absorbent, retentive of air and water, and light in weight. Its colour varies from white to yellow, brown and green, and it expands to about twenty times its original volume on heating. The heated product has a very low density, high refractoriness at low temperatures, low thermal conductivity, chemical inertness, and is a non-conductor of electricity. It is thus used extensively in the building trade, giving nearly ten times as much thermal insulation as does the same quantity of sand, gravel or concrete. Vermiculite plasters have excellent acoustic properties and are moisture-resistant and crack-proof. A specially prepared form, neutral in reaction, is used in horticulture as a medium for raising plants from seeds and cuttings, for which it is admirably suited. It is also employed in oil refining, and is one of the few materials whose supply is almost unlimited.

Vermilion, red variety of mercuric sulphide, HgS. It may be obtained by subliming the black sulphide formed by grinding mercury and sulphur together in a mortar. It is also prepared by heating the black amorphous sulphide for some hours in alkaline sulphides. Vermilion is used as a pigment, but is commonly adulterated with ferric oxide and red lead. It occurs naturally as cinnabar.

Vermin, general term for animals destructive of crops and game. Rats, mice, moles, weasels and foxes are vermin. The word is also used of the insect parasites of man, such as lice and fleas.

Vermont (Green Mountain State), a New England state of the USA, bounded on the north by Canada, on the east by New Hampshire, on the south by Massachusetts, and on the west by New York. Lake Champlain, 172 km long, forms part of the western boundary. The name has reference to the Green Mountains (highest peak Mount Mansfield, 1339 m), which cross it from north to south. Vermont is primarily an agricultural state. Eighty per cent of the value of all farm produce sold is derived from dairying. Eggs, apples and maple syrup supplement the income from dairying. There are few towns. Commercial forests cover some 1·8 million ha, and the state's other main natural resources are stone, asbestos and talc. Manufacturing is mainly in food processing and the production of paper and textiles. Vermont was the first state to be admitted to the Union formed by the original states, in 1791. Its total area is 24,887 km². The 1980 population was 511,456. The capital is Montpelier.

Vermouth (from German *Wermut*, wormwood), an aperitif made from white wine compounded with herbs and usually fortified. Noilly Prat is probably the best known of the French vermouths, which are mostly drier than the Italian vermouths, represented by Martini and Cinzano.

Vernadski, Vladimir Ivanovich (1863–1945), Russian scientist and thinker, one of the founders of geochemistry and the founder of bio-geochemistry; also the founder of many academic bodies (for example, the Institute of Radiology, 1922). As a public figure Vernadski was active in the Zemstvo movement. He opposed the Bolsheviks and rejected Marxist philosophy, building his own natural philosophy.

Vernalisation, a low-temperature treatment used to promote flowering in many plants. Many biennials and perennials must experience some exposure to a low temperature in order to induce flowering later at normal temperatures. Hence, some plants are restricted to climates in which the winters are fairly cold. In many plants, chilling is effective in the seed stage.

Verne, Jules (1828–1905), French novelist. He first popularised the type of romance in which all kinds of more or less plausible scientific discoveries provide the basis of the most extravagant and thrilling adventures. His stories remain very popular; among the best are *A Journey to the Centre of the Earth*, *Twenty Thousand Leagues under the Sea*, and *Around the World in Eighty Days*. Many of the books have been filmed successfully, and the stories influenced the development of science fiction.

Vernet, French family of painters: Claude Joseph (1714–89), marine painter, noted for his views of French seaports, and for dramatic shipwreck scenes; Antoine Charles Horace (1758–1836), son of the above, painter of horses and battle scenes; and Carle Vernet's son Emile Jean Horace (1789–1863), military and sporting painter.

Vernon, Edward (1684–1757), English admiral. He served at the siege of Gibraltar under Sir George Rooke (1704), and in 1739 captured Porto Bello with only six ships.

Verona, Italian city, capital of Verona province, situated on the Adige, 100 km west of Venice, at the point where the road from the Brenner Pass joins the Venice–Milan road. The city is of Roman origin, and has many Roman remains, including a magnificent amphitheatre, arches and a theatre. There is a Romanesque-Gothic cathedral, and among its churches is that of San Zeno (12th–13th centuries), one of the finest Romanesque churches in Italy. Verona is one of Italy's main marketing centres for fruit and vegetables and has large freezing and cold-store plants. It also has engineering, paper and printing industries. Population (1979) 269,763.

Veronese, Paul, real name Paolo Caliari or Cagliari (1528–88), Italian painter, born in Verona. He studied under Antonio Badile, and from 1555 lived in Venice. His gigantic paintings, including his religious works, exhibit rich colouring, broad composition and that love of pomp and wordly splendour which led to charges of irreligion against him by the Inquisition in 1573. The huge *Marriage at Cana*, now in the Louvre, with its 130 figures (many are portraits of famous people of the time), is typical of the exuberance of his art. The *Vision of St Helena* and the *Family of Darius* are in the National Gallery, London. His best paintings are in Venice, the illusionistic ceilings of the Doge's Palace, the church of San Sebastiano, the Accademia and the Villa Maser, near Treviso.

Veronica, speedwell, a genus of the Scrophulariaceae, herbs and shrubs with leaves in opposite pairs and blue, mauve or white flowers, borne in spikes or singly in leaf-axils. The flowers have four petals and two stamens. Many species are weeds in temperate areas. *V. spicata* and related species with long spikes of bright blue flowers are grown in gardens. The shrubby *Veronica* species belong to the genus *Hebe*.

Verrocchio, Andrea del, real name Cione (1435–88), Italian artist, was 'goldsmith, master of perspective, sculptor, carver, painter and musician', according to Vasari. He worked under Donatello, and Leonardo da Vinci was a pupil in his large workshop. The only authentic painting of his is the *Baptism of Christ* (Uffizi Gallery), though the *Virgin and Child* in the National Gallery, London, is ascribed to him. His renown has a sure foundation in the magnificent equestrian statue in bronze of Bartolommeo Colleoni, which adorns the piazza of SS. Giovanni e Paolo in Venice.

Verruca, see WART.

Versailles, French town, capital of the *département* of Yvelines, 18 km south-west of Paris. From 1678 to 1769, Versailles was the principal residence of the kings of France. On the site of a hunting-lodge of Louis XIII, Louis XIV built the magnificent palace of Versailles, the work of Le Vau and J. H. Mansard. The gardens were designed by Le Notre, and much of the interior decorations are the work of Le Brun. In addition to the great châteaux, there are two smaller châteaux: the Grand Trianon, and the exquisite Petit Trianon. Population (1975) 97,133.

Versailles, Treaty of (1919), signed on 28 June 1919 and ratified on 10 January 1920. Articles of the Treaty:

The League of Nations. In the forefront of the treaty were the clauses to establish the League of Nations and to provide for international action to preserve peace in the future.

Surrendered Territories. (1) Alsace-Lorraine was to go to France; (2) the great part of the provinces of West Prussia and Posen to Poland; (3) the greater part of East Silesia and of East Prussia to Poland; (4) a portion of Upper Silesia to Czechoslovakia; (5) Memel to Lithuania; (6) Danzig to be a Free State under the protection of the League of Nations; (7) part of Schleswig to Denmark.

War-guilt. Under the treaty, the Allies publicly arraigned the ex-Emperor William II (who had fled to Holland). In fact, the Dutch government could not and were not even expected to surrender their refugee.

Reparations. Provision was made for assessing the amount of compensation to be paid by Germany in kind or money.

See also EUROPEAN HISTORY; PEACE CONFERENCE (1919); REPARATIONS.

Verse (Latin *vertere*, to turn), a word used in three distinct senses in English. It can mean: poetical writing in general as opposed to prose; a single line of poetry; a set of lines, or stanza.

See also METRE; POETRY.

Vertebral Column or backbone, composed of a number of small bones called vertebrae; 33 in the human infant, but only 26 in the adult where the lower vertebrae become fused together, or ankylosed, to form the sacrum and the coccyx. The whole column forms the axial support of the body. It supports the skull at its summit; the ribs articulate with the thoracic vertebrae to support the upper limbs, while the pelvis forms a girdle with the sacrum, and serves as a support for the lower limbs. The vertebrae vary considerably in shape, but each possesses a body and an arch. The body is a cylinder that is connected above and below with the adjacent vertebrae by a disc of fibro-cartilage, which acts as a buffer in absorbing shock. The arch consists of two halves which spring out to unite medially behind, thus forming a ring. The whole succession of these rings forms the vertebral canal, or channel, containing the main nerve trunk known as the spinal cord. Viewed from the side, the vertebral column presents a series of curves. This curvature serves to maintain the strength of the structure and adapts itself to the movements of the body. The spinal cord occupies the upper two-thirds of the vertebral canal, and 31 pairs of spinal nerves arising from the spinal cord leave the vertebral canal through spaces at the sides between successive vertebrae.

Vertebrate Palaeontology. The study of the fossils of vertebrates. This science covers all aspects of vertebrate evolution from the dinosaurs to fossil man.

See also PALAEONTOLOGY.

Vertebrates, animals with backbones. They form the subphylum Vertebrata in the phylum Chordata. Vertebrates have a distinct head, with the skull enclosing the brain, and most sense organs are grouped on the head. Their skeleton is mostly bony, with some cartilage, and includes two pairs of limbs or fins and the segmented backbone made up of vertebrae. A notochord is present only in the embryo.

There are six classes of vertebrate: Agnatha, the hag-fishes and lampreys; Chondrichthyes, the cartilaginous fishes, such as rays and sharks; Osteichthyes, the bony fishes, such as trout and sole; Amphibia, which includes frogs and salamanders; Reptilia, which includes turtles, snakes and lizards; Aves, the birds; and Mammalia, the mammals, for example kangaroos, anteaters, bats, whales, deer and man.

The internal, jointed skeleton has enabled vertebrates to become the largest animals, by weight and bulk, though not by length, on land and in water. The limbs have adapted into forms as varied as fins, flippers, wings, and hoofed and toed feet. The body covering includes scales, feathers, fur and hair. Vertebrates live on land, and in salt and fresh water, and breathe through lungs or gills.

Vertical Take-off and Landing (VTOL), term used of aircraft which can leave the ground and land directly, without having to use a runway. The term normally excludes helicopters. The world's first operational jet fighter with a vertical take-off and landing capability, the Hawker Siddeley Harrier, uses jet thrust for its vertical or short take-offs and landings. The Harrier is powered by a Rolls-Royce Bristol Pegasus turbo-fan which has four jet nozzles, two discharging cool air from the front of the engine and two at the rear for the turbine efflux. The direction of the rotating nozzles is controlled by a single lever in the cockpit. For taxiing, conventional take-off and flight, the nozzles are pointed towards the rear. The nozzles are rotated downwards through 90° for a vertical take-off or landing, during which the whole weight of the aircraft is supported by the direct jet thrust.

See also AEROPLANE.

Vertigo, literally a sense of turning, but Gowers (1893) gave a more precise definition of the term as 'any movement or sense of movement, either in the individual himself or in external objects, that involves a defect, real or seeming, in the equilibrium of the body'. Disorders of the ear which may give rise to vertigo are: Menière's disease; labyrinthitis (inflammation of the inner ear), either as an epidemic or secondary to chronic otitis media (infection of the middle ear); and injury to the ear. Other causes of vertigo are epilepsy, migraine, decrease in cerebral blood flow as in fainting, and decrease in the blood flow to the brainstem, often due to interruption of the vertebral artery supply.

Verulam, Lord, see BACON, FRANCIS, BARON VERULAM, VISCOUNT ST ALBANS.

Verulamium, ancient Roman town near St Albans, Hertfordshire, England. It superseded the nearby Belgic city. The town was sacked by the Iceni under Boudicca (Boadicea) in AD 61, but afterwards the timber shops were rebuilt and a basilica was erected in 79. The town plan of the late first century was almost rectangular. In the early 2nd century there appears to have been a new plan, but the masonry wall with solid projecting bastions and elaborate gateways was not erected until the third century. Occupation in the centre of the town continued until c.450. Only the south-eastern gate foundations and adjoining wall, one mosaic pavement and its hypocaust or heating system, the theatre with its adjoining shops, and one large house, are visible today.

Verus, Lucius Aurelius, joint Roman Emperor, AD 161–69, with Marcus Aurelius, his brother by adoption.

Verwoerd, Hendrik Frensch (1901–66), South African politician. He became minister of Bantu affairs in 1950, and in this post implemented the apartheid policy. In 1958, when Strijdom died, Verwoerd succeeded him as premier of South Africa. Under his premiership, South Africa left the Commonwealth and became an independent republic. His domestic policies, while causing strong criticism abroad, broadened the Nationalist appeal to South African voters, and in the general election in March 1966 his party was returned with an increased majority. Verwoerd was assassinated in the Parliament buildings in September 1966.

Vesalius, Andreas (1514–64), Flemish anatomist, the founder of modern anatomy. In 1543 he published *De Humani Corporis Fabrica,* one of the greatest of all medical

Versailles, seen from the Place d'Armes. It was built between 1661 and 1756.

works. With this book and in his own teaching Vesalius replaced tradition in anatomy with observation and experiment, and did away with the reverence for authority in science, paving the way for the experimental era in medicine instituted by William Harvey. The *Fabrica* contains some magnificent plates, particularly of the muscles, and excellent descriptions of the bones and nervous system. It had a hostile reception from the Galenists, and Vesalius gave up his teaching to become physician to Charles V.

Vesicants, agents that cause blistering. A vesicant may be a substance applied to the skin, such as cantharides and mustard, or a physical agent in the form of heat or ultra-violet light rays.

Vesicle, a small sac containing liquid. It is the medical term for a blister or elevation of the epidermis containing serous fluid.
See also SKIN.

Vespasian, full name Titus Flavius Sabinus Vespasianus (AD 9–79), Roman Emperor, AD 69–79. In 43, as *legatus legionis* in Britain, he reduced the Isle of Wight. Vespasian was in Judaea, where he had been sent in 66 to conquer the Jews, when news reached him of his proclamation as emperor (69). Vitellius, his rival for imperial honours, was defeated by Antonius Primus. By his wife Flavia Domitilla, Vespasian had two sons, Titus and Domitian.

Vespucci, Amerigo (1451–1512), Italian navigator. He began his career at Seville, Spain, as a merchant, but his interest in the trade then beginning with the New World led him to undertake four voyages there between 1497 and 1504. The first discovery of the mainland of America was made by Columbus in 1498. In 1499 Vespucci reached a point farther south and thence went northwards to the Gulf of Paria, and after that to Venezuela, which he so named. Vespucci's account of the inhabitants of Venezuela was the cause of his name being given to the major continent of the western hemisphere.

Vessel, in botany, long cells fitted end to end in a tubular structure with thick pitted walls, reinforced with lignin. Xylem and phloem vessels are characteristic of the wood of angiosperms, and allow rapid movement of the sap.

Vesta, Roman goddess of the hearth, closely associated with the Penates and identified with the Greek Hestia. From Lavinium her worship was traditionally introduced to Rome by Numa, who was believed to have built her central shrine in the Forum between the Palatine and Capitoline hills. Here her fires were kept burning by the Vestal Virgins.

Vestals, six priestesses of Vesta, in her temple at Rome. They were chosen by lot from 20 maidens of free and worthy parentage. The violation of the vow of chastity was punishable by death, and retribution followed if they allowed the sacred fires to go out.

Vestdijk, Simon (1898–1971), Dutch author and critic. A prolific writer, his 38 novels, 10 collections of short stories, 28 books of essays, and 22 volumes of poetry exhibit technical brilliance and the penetrating intellect of a mind trained in medicine, philosophy, psychology and music.

Vestmannæyjar, or Westman Islands, some rocky islands on the south coast of Iceland, surrounded by excellent fishing-grounds. Harbour facilities are good, but communication with Reykjavík is now principally by air. Population (1975) 4396.

Vestments, Sacred, special garments worn at religious rites and festivals from time immemorial. Religious dress as part of a ceremonial rite and to convey rank is common to all countries and religions, ranging from the elaborate robes of Eastern Orthodox Christianity to the markings and tattoos of primitive societies.

As regards Christianity, mention of a special vestment is first made at Jerusalem in the 4th century. In the first centuries ordinary dress was used in sacerdotal functions, and this remained the Roman usage until the 6th and 7th centuries, when barbarian fashions conflicted with religious conservatism concerning dress, and turned the old everyday garments into ceremonial vestments. Those for a priest in the Western Church are amice, alb, girdle, stole, maniple and chasuble. At certain solemn services and in processions a cope is used. At choir offices and on other occasions the clergy wear a surplice. A stole is worn in the administration of the sacraments.

Vestry, room in a church where the vestments and other movable ornaments are kept.

Vesuvius (Italian *Vesuvio*), volcano in Campania, Italy, 15 km south-east of Naples. Its height varies by about a hundred metres, but averages 1220 m. Monte Somma, the Mons Summanus of the ancients, is a great semicircular girdle of cliff to the north and east, parted from the eruptive cone by the valley known as Atrio di Cavallo. The amazing fertility of its slopes, especially for grapes from which the wine '*Lacrimae Christi*' is made, explains why Vesuvius, in spite of its constant menace, has been the heart of a densely populated region. The destruction on 24 August AD 79 of the cities of Pompeii, Herculaneum and Stabiae ended a dormant period so long that the volcano had been presumed extinct. There has been no eruption since 1944.

Vetch, name applied mainly to tendril-climbers of the genus *Vicia*, belonging to the Leguminosae, but also to some species of *Lathyrus*. Vetches have pinnate leaves, with the terminal leaflets modified to tendrils.

Veterinary Science is the study of the care of animals in health and disease. It may be said to have begun in ancient Egypt. The Egyptians' knowledge of the horse and its diseases was passed on to the Greeks and Romans. The Roman Vegetius (c.AD 450–500) left writings on the subject, which in the 16th century were much studied, and stimulated interest in the science, especially in France, where the first veterinary college was established at Lyons in 1762. A Frenchman, St Bel, founded the Royal Veterinary College in London in 1791.

In modern times the most important function of the veterinary profession is the improvement of animal husbandry. This involves a knowledge of the proper selection of breeding farm animals, the management and feeding of herds and flocks, and the prevention of diseases. By far the largest employer of veterinarians in Britain is the Ministry of Agriculture, Fisheries and Food. Recognition and prevention of animal disease, particularly in the interest of public health, is of primary importance. There is an increasing demand for veterinary scientists to combat infectious diseases, especially cattle plague (rinderpest), which, in Africa, have devastated herds and caused large tracts of country to be uninhabitable. The veterinary surgeon, particularly in private practice, attends to cases of animal suffering of all kinds. Small animal practice has assumed an increasing importance, and great strides have been made in this area, particularly in anaesthesia, operative technique, X-ray diagnosis, preventive medicine and euthanasia.

Veto, term applied to the right of a king or other chief magistrate or officer to withhold his assent to the enactment of a law, or, generally, of one branch of the executive or legislature of a state to reject the bills, resolutions or measures of other branches. The term originates in the power of the tribunes of the plebs of ancient Rome to declare their protest against any unlawful measure, which they did by pronouncing the word 'veto' (I forbid). In Britain the power theoretically belongs to the Crown. The power of veto enjoyed by the House of Lords was reduced by an Act of Parliament of 1949 to one year. In the USA the president can veto a measure of Congress, but, notwithstanding his veto, the measure becomes law if subsequently carried by a majority of two-thirds from each house.

The exercise of the veto has been of great importance in the operations of the Security Council of the United Nations. Each of the five permanent members of the Council, the USA, the USSR, the UK, France and China, has the right to veto any resolution. The USSR originally proposed that unanimity among the five was necessary, but eventually agreed to the veto. Apart from China each of the powers has made use of the veto occasionally, the USSR most frequently.

Vevey, tourist resort in the canton of Vaud, Switzerland, situated on Lake Geneva, 18 km south-east of Lausanne. The chief manufactures are chocolate, machinery, watches and woodworking. Population (1974) 17,500, mainly French-speaking.

Via Aemilia, famous highway of ancient Italy which continued the Via Flaminia from Ariminum (Rimini) through Bononia (Bologna) to Mutina, Placentia, and Mediolanum (Milan). It was constructed by M. Aemilius Lepidus, consul in 187 BC.

Via Appia, ancient Roman road, begun in 312 BC by the censor Appius Claudius Caecus to consolidate the conquest of Samnite territory. It ran from the Porta Capena at Rome to Capua (210 km). By 244 BC it had been extended to Brundisium via Beneventum (375 km). Much of the old work remains, and the first few kilometres are lined with pagan and early Christian tombs. The 30 km from Forum Appii across the Pontine marshes was improved by Nerva, Trajan and Theodoric, as also by Pope Pius VI who built a new Via Appia from Rome to Albano.

Via Aurelia, ancient Roman road of uncertain date. It ran from the Janiculan gate at Rome northwards to Cosa, but was later extended to Vada Volaterrana. By the construction of the Via Aemilia in 109 BC it was carried to Gensa, Dortona and later still to Arelate (Arles).

Viability, in botany, the ability to germinate. In all plants there is a period of dormancy when growth is suspended and the metabolism is at a very low ebb. One form in which plants pass through this phase is as seeds. In seeds life can be maintained in cells which are relatively very dry and in which metabolic activity is barely measurable. Some of the oldest surviving seeds are those of *Nelumbo nucifera* (Indian lotus) which are 1200 years old. The viability of a package of seeds to be sown in the garden is the percentage that will grow; it is influenced by heredity and the care with which they were grown, harvested, packaged and stored.

Viaduct, see BRIDGE.

Via Flaminia, the chief northward highway from ancient Rome, named after the censor C. Flaminius, who in 220 BC continued an earlier road, from Spoletium to Ariminum. Leaving Rome by the Pons Mulvius, it ran to Forum Flaminii, thence to Nuceria and over the main ridge of the Apennines to Cales and Ariminum. The total distance was 334 km.

Viareggio, Italian seaside resort in Tuscany, on the Tyrrhenian Sea, 20 km west of Lucca. It is the oldest seaside resort in Italy and started when Giuseppe Barellai founded a health establishment for children here in 1861. Population (1974) 50,000.

Viaticum (Latin, provision for a journey), Holy Communion when given to a person in danger of death.

Viborg, capital of Viborg county, 60 km north-west of Århus. It is one of the oldest towns in Denmark, and has the largest granite church in Europe, founded in 1130. Viborg has textile mills and food-processing plants. Population (1974) 37,645.

Viborg, see VYBORG.

Vibraphone, see XYLOPHONE.

Vibrio, see CHOLERA.

Viburnum, a genus of deciduous and evergreen shrubs and trees in the family Caprifoliaceae. *V. opulus,* the guelder rose of Europe and Asia, is grown as an ornamental shrub. Many fragrant-flowered species, such as *V. farreri* (*V. fragrans*), called wintersweet, are grown in gardens for their early winter and spring flowers. *V. tinus* is the evergreen, winter-flowering laurustinus.

Vicar, strictly one who holds a benefice as deputy of the rector, who may be a layman and receives a share of the emoluments of the incumbency. Commonly a vicar is any incumbent who is not entitled to tithes. In France an assistant priest is called a *vicaire*.

Vicente, Gil, or Vincente (c.1465–1536?), Portuguese dramatist. Over 40 of his works survive, including moralities, farces, romantic comedies and allegorical spectacles devised for the lavish Portuguese court. Vicente had a gift for creating credible and sympathetic characters, and for structuring complex plots with skill. There is also a strong element of social criticism in his work.

Vicenza (ancient *Vicentia*), Italian city, capital of Vicenza province, situated on the Bacchiglione, 65 km west of Venice. It was the birthplace of Palladio, and the city contains many splendid buildings by him.

Vicenza manufactures textiles, glass and machinery. Population (1979) 117,570.

Viceroy, one who rules over a kingdom or country in the name of the sovereign with regal authority. Historical examples of recent times were the British viceroys in India and Ireland.

Vichy (-les-Bains), French spa in the *département* of Allier, 320 km south-east of Paris, on the River Allier. During the Second World War it became the seat of the government headed by Marshal Pétain and Pierre Laval. The waters of Vichy were known to the Romans; they are exported in large quantities. Population (1975) 32,250.

Vicksburg, town of Mississippi, USA. Although today only a small town, Vicksburg played a significant part in the Civil War. The siege and capture of the stronghold, between December 1862 and July 1863, may be said to have brought General Grant to prominence and led to his eventual appointment to supreme command. Population (1980) 25,434.

Victoria. A portrait by Winterhalter.

Vicky, pen name of Victor Weisz (1913–1966), cartoonist, born in Berlin of Hungarian parents. He first worked for the Berlin *12 Uhr Blatt* and published an anti-Hitler cartoon in 1928. When the Nazis came into power he went to England (1935), and drew for a number of papers, in particular the *New Statesman* and *Evening Standard*. A lifelong socialist, he was noted for the satirical wit with which he opposed power politics, and for his humorous assaults, alternating with serious drawings, exposing the plight of the poor, hungry and oppressed.

Vico, Giambattista (1668–1744), Italian philosopher, historian and jurist. In 1735 he was appointed historiographer to Charles III, king of Naples. His most important work is the *Scienza nuova* (revised edition 1744), in which he studies and defines the imaginative faculty, and propounds theories on the nature of poetry, the origin of speech, etc., and revives the ancient theory of recurring cycles in history. Vico's theories have greatly influenced modern thinking about history and literature, and play a considerable part in the philosophy of Croce.

Victor Emmanuel II (1820–78), King of Sardinia (1849–61) and of Italy (1861–78). He ascended the Sardinian throne on his father's abdication after the defeat of Novara. A new Italian kingdom had been created by the end of 1860, and Victor Emmanuel was proclaimed king of Italy in 1861. He showed considerable political skill in the handling of the crises with the papacy and those resultant on the conduct of Garibaldi. He became extremely popular, and proved a unifying influence in the new state.

See also ITALY, *History*.

Victor Emmanuel III (1869–1947), King of Italy. In the crisis which brought Mussolini to power, he ignored the advice of his ministers to disperse the Fascisti by force. After the March on Rome he offered Mussolini the premiership, and thereafter allowed himself to become the figurehead and spokesman of the Fascist regime, though he unsuccessfully opposed Italy's entry into the Second World War on Germany's side. He escaped from Rome in September 1943. He supported Badoglio, his new premier, and promised support to the Allies after Italy's surrender in September 1943. Reluctantly he ceded his royal powers to his son, Crown Prince Umberto, and abdicated in May 1946. See also ITALY, *History*.

Victoria, in full Alexandrina Victoria (1819–1901), Queen of Great Britain and Ireland and, from 1876, Empress of India; daughter of Edward, Duke of Kent, fourth son of George III, by Victoria, daughter of the Duke of Saxe-Coburg. She became queen in 1837. At her accession the ties between Britain and Hanover were broken as the crown of Hanover could not pass to a woman. Victoria reigned longer than any previous British monarch, proved herself a model for constitutional monarchy for the age in which she lived, and gave her name to a great period of British history and social life.

Princess Victoria was strictly brought up by her mother, and on her accession, her closest friend and adviser was Lord Melbourne, the Whig prime minister, who gained considerable influence over her. However, it soon became clear that the new queen had a mind of her own. In 1840 Victoria married her cousin, Prince Albert of Saxe-Coburg-Gotha. The queen was devoted to her husband and, after an initial reluctance to allow him to take part in state affairs, she came to rely almost wholly on his judgment. There were nine children; the second child and eldest son subsequently succeeded his mother as Edward VII. The marriages of Victoria's children, and their immediate descendants, linked the British royal family to practically every royal house in Europe. They also transmitted the disease of haemophilia (from which Victoria's son, Leopold, died) to the royal houses of Russia and Spain.

In 1861 Prince Albert died of typhoid. For the rest of her life, that is, for more than half her reign, Victoria mourned him, and although she worked laboriously at affairs of state, refusing to let the Prince of Wales relieve her of anything, for a long time she never appeared in public if she could avoid it. Her three great ministers of this long period were William Ewart Gladstone, whom she detested; Benjamin Disraeli, who was the perfect courtier, flattering his royal mistress and making difficult affairs of state appear simple and interesting; and Lord Salisbury, the great Conservative leader. In 1887 she held her first Jubilee, to be followed ten years later by the Diamond Jubilee. This last period of her life was a sort of apotheosis, in which she was accepted as the living and apparently immortal symbol of British greatness and Empire.

Victoria's influence on British history was considerable. She had immense character and will-power, and a lively intelligence, but no great intellect. As a girl she had received the crown when it was in disrepute. She reigned for 63 years, and she left it as a symbol of public honour and the highest private virtue. Victoria had little understanding of party politics, which evolved in their modern form during her reign. But she demonstrated by example the place which the Crown could fill in British political life and as a link between the peoples of the Empire, and established a tradition of work and service to the nation.

Victoria, Tomás Luis de (c.1548–1611), Spanish composer. He received a grant from Philip II to go to Rome, where he took holy orders and became a singer in the German College, and later choirmaster. In 1578 he became chaplain to the dowager empress Maria, and in about 1583 became choirmaster in the Madrid convent in which she lived. Victoria was the leading representative of the Spanish polyphonic school. He wrote 19 masses, 2 requiems, 45 motets and much other church music.

Victoria, state of the Commonwealth of Australia, in the south of the continent. It is bounded on the north and north-east by New South Wales, from which it is separated by the Murray river; on the west by South Australia; and on the south and south-east by the Southern Ocean, Bass Strait and the Pacific Ocean. The area is 227,600 km². The state is crossed from east to west by the Great Dividing Range, maximum height 1986 m. The rivers to the north of this watershed flow to the Murray basin, and those to the south into the sea. The rest of the state is undulating, interrupted only by outlying spurs of the main chain.

The chief products are wheat, hay, oats and barley. Vineyards produce wine, raisins and currants. A large area is under orchards, and tobacco and hops are also grown. The dairying industry has become very important, as has wool-production. There are extensive deposits of brown coal in the Latrobe Valley and major offshore oil and natural gas deposits in Bass Strait. Manufactured products include refined oil, alumina, machinery, cars, paper and pulp, electronics, textiles, processed food, chemicals and pharmaceuticals. More than 90 per cent of the state's overseas trade passes through Melbourne, but the ports at Geelong and Portland are also significant.

The government of Victoria consists of a governor appointed by the Crown, a Legislative Council (upper house), and an Assembly (lower house). The constitution was established in 1854. The state capital is Melbourne; other major towns are Geelong, Ballarat and Bendigo. Population (1979) 3,853,500.

History. The first permanent settlement in Victoria was formed at Portland Bay by Edward Henty, from Tasmania, in 1834. Other settlers followed, but no marked development ensued owing to the lack of good land and of safe harbourage. The capital was founded by two Tasmanian parties, one led by John Batman in May 1835, the other by John Pascoe Fawkner, who reached the site of Melbourne in August 1835. Others followed, bringing stock with them, and penetrated farther into the interior. Regular government was first established under Captain Lonsdale, who was sent from Sydney to take control, in 1839. In 1851 the colony was separated from New South Wales and named Victoria. Gold was discovered soon afterwards which led to a further influx of population. A new constitution giving responsible government to the colony was proclaimed in 1855.

Victoria Falls, on the Zambia-Zimbabwe border.

Victoria, capital of British Columbia, Canada, on the southern end of Vancouver Island, overlooking the Strait of Juan de Fuca, separated by 132 km of sea from the city of Vancouver on the mainland. Founded by the Hudson's Bay Company, in 1843, it was named in honour of the young Queen Victoria. It is a residential and tourist centre, but there are some industries, including shipbuilding, lumbering, saw-milling, flour-milling and canning. Victoria is the western terminus of the Trans-Canada Highway. Population (Greater Victoria, 1976) 218,250.

Victoria, capital of the Republic of Seychelles. It lies on the north-east coast of Mahé Island, and is the only large town in the group. It has a deep-water harbour, being the sole port of the archipelago, and an international airport nearby. Population (1975) 15,000.

Victoria, Lake, largest lake of Africa. The northern part is bounded on the west and north by Uganda and on the east by Kenya. The whole of the southern shore is in Tanzania. It is 410 km long and 250 km wide; altitude 1136 m. As a freshwater lake it is second only in size to Lake Superior. Lake Victoria is situated on the equator and forms the chief reservoir of the Nile, which leaves the lake at Jinja. There is an important fishing industry. Lakeside ports include Kisumu, Musoma, Mwanza and Jinja. Area 69,484 km².

Victoria and Albert Museum, South Kensington, London, one of the greatest museums of fine and applied art in the world. The collections are mainly of post-classical periods. The Museum originated in the Museum of Ornamental Art at Marlborough House in 1852, and became in 1857 the South Kensington Museum, combining collections of science and art. The original aims of the art sections of the Museum were both educational and academic.

Victoria Cross, highest British decoration for 'conspicuous bravery or devotion to the country in the presence of the enemy'. It was founded by Queen Victoria towards the conclusion of the Crimean War (1856) and has been cast from the metal of Russian guns taken at Sevastopol, save for brief periods during the two World Wars. It consists of a Maltese cross made of bronze, bearing in the centre the royal crown surmounted by a lion, and with the scroll superscribed 'For Valour'. In 1920 the blue ribbon of Royal Naval VC awards was changed to crimson to conform with the other Services. The winning of the VC carries with it a tax-free annuity of £100.

Victoria Falls (African name *Mosi-oa-tunya,* smoke that thunders), great waterfalls upon the Zambezi river, Central Africa, 1450 km from the sea. Their existence was first made known to the outside world by David Livingstone in 1855. Above the falls the river is some 1·5 km wide, and then plunges into a series of zigzagging gorges, the first of which extends the whole breadth. Its course is impeded by an opposite wall, nearly as high, the water escaping through a channel of 30 m width through the 'Boiling Pot', into the Grand Canyon.
See also KARIBA.

Victoria Falls, town and tourist centre near the Victoria Falls, Zimbabwe. It is the administrative and commercial centre for north-west Zimbabwe, has an international airport and tourist facilities, and is surrounded by the Victoria Falls National Park. Population 3454.

Victoria Land, region of Antarctica fronting on the west side of the Ross Sea, extending north from about 78°S to 70°30′S in 164°E. It was discovered in 1841 by Capt James Clark Ross and named by him for Queen Victoria. It lies within the Ross Dependency (New Zealand) and the Australian Antarctic Territory.

'Victory', British battleship of 2164 t, launched at Chatham on 7 May 1765, which flies the flag of the commander-in-chief at Portsmouth. She was the flagship of Howe at the relief of Gibraltar (1782), of Hood at Toulon (1793), of Jervis at St Vincent (1797), and of Nelson at Trafalgar (1805). The *Victory* is now at Portsmouth, maintained in a state of preservation.

Vicuña, *Vicugna vicugna,* a member of the camel family, Camelidae, of order Artiodactyla, related to the other South American camelids; llama, alpaca and guanaco. The grown animal stands about 30 cm at the shoulder. *V. vicugna* inhabits semi-arid grassland at 3600–4800 m in the central Andes. The soft silky fur or wool is brown, and much valued for the manufacture of choice fabrics. Vicuña are noted for their timidity and are in considerable danger of extinction due to the large number killed for their fur.

Vidal, Gore (1925–), US novelist and essayist. His novels include studies of contemporary morality and society, such as the satire *Myra Breckinridge*, 1968, and its sequel *Myron*, 1974; invocations of the ancient world, such as *Julian*, 1964, and *Creation*, 1981; and a powerful historical trilogy about American politics, *Washington DC*, 1967, *Burr*, 1973, and *1876*, 1976.

Video Games, games in which the players, instead of moving pieces or cards on a board, move images on a television screen. The images are produced electronically, the player giving his instructions on a computer keyboard and the computer's signals being decoded into pictures or other visible shapes.

Video Recording. The information content of pictures is greater than that of sound, and early attempts to record vision electrically foundered because of the very high 'bit rate' of many millions of items of information per second that is necessary to achieve record vision successfully. Gradually the technology improved until recorded video tape was indistinguishable, when broadcast, from live TV transmission, and could even accept the higher 'bit rate' needed by colour video.

Today there are two chief methods, VHS and Betacord, which though similar in capability and picture definition, are incompatible. Video tape was first used in industry and education in the USA and Japan, and by the early 1960s was becoming a mass consumer item, packaged in standard cassettes (hence the term video-cassette recording, or VCR). By 1965 VCR was common in the American home, and 15 years later reached Europe and most other countries. As the same recording system is compatible with a video (TV) camera, it is likely eventually to replace traditional cinematography. Mass-produced systems are available both to record television programmes and live events, in sound and colour vision. The tapes can be erased and reused in the same way as their audio counterparts.

Vielé-Griffin, Francis (1864–1937), French poet. He was one of the Symbolist poets and in some of his works used *vers libre* with great effect. He was founder and editor of the journal *Les Entretiens politiques et littéraires*, 1890–92.

Vienna (German *Wien*), capital city of the Republic of Austria, and until 1916 the capital of the Austro-Hungarian Empire. With the exception of the district of Floridsdorf it lies on the right bank of the Danube, a canalised arm of which also intersects the city. To the west and south-west are the beautiful wooded hills known as the Wienerwald. Vienna consists of a medieval inner city (*Altstadt*) and 23 outer districts. The skyline is dominated by the famous St Stephen's Cathedral (12th–16th centuries). Other notable buildings include the Hofburg, the Hapsburgs' imperial

palace, begun in the 13th century, the last addition being completed in 1913. Vienna has long been regarded as a musical centre, and has connections with many great composers. In 1137, Henry Jasomirgott made 'Wienn' his capital. Under the Babenbergs Vienna became a commercial centre, and the Babenbergs kept a brilliant court and encouraged the arts. In 1278 it became the capital of the Hapsburgs, and thus, in time, the seat of the German emperors. Under Maria Theresa it was the centre of a great empire, and continued into the 19th century as the 'Alt-Wien' of tradition. In the second half of the 19th century the population increased rapidly, particularly in industrial suburbs such as Floridsdorf. The walls were destroyed and replaced by the *Ringstrasse* in 1860, a broad boulevard which encircles the *Altstadt*. Since the Second World War Vienna's commercial importance has declined because of the restrictions on traffic between East and West Europe. Among the main manufactures are silk, velvet, clothing, porcelain, carpets, jewellery, mathematical, scientific and musical instruments, watches, fine cutlery, chemicals, leather goods, furniture and paper. Population (1981) 1,517,154.

Vienna, Congress of, a congress of European statesmen held in 1814 after Napoleon's exile to Elba, to settle the peace of Europe. There were four principal delegates to the Congress: Castlereagh for Britain, Talleyrand for France, Metternich representing the Hapsburgs, and Alexander I for Russia.
See also EUROPEAN HISTORY.

Vienne, river of France, which rises in northern Corrèze, and flows north past Châtellerault, Limoges and Chinon, to join the Loire 13 km south-east of Saumur. Length 350 km.

Vientiane, capital of Laos, situated on the left bank of the River Mekong. Once the capital of an independent Lao kingdom, it was sacked by Siamese invaders in 1827 and its people dispersed. Chosen as the seat of the French commissioner of Laos in 1899, the city began to grow again with the building of European-style villas and streets. Today the administrative capital, it houses foreign embassies and has an airport. Population (1979 est.) 90,000.

Viet Cong, name used by the US and South Vietnamese governments to refer to the forces of the National Front for the Liberation of South Vietnam, founded in 1960. It means literally 'Vietnamese Communists', and was used as a means of insisting on the Communist nature of the front. The leaders of the front rejected the appellation.
See also VIETNAM WAR.

Vietminh, abbreviated name of the *Vietnam Doc-Lap Dong-Minh*, or 'Vietnamese Independence League', founded in 1941 under the leadership of the Indochinese Communist Party. It was able to seize power in Hanoi in 1945 and create a provisional government. It was renamed the Lien-Viet front in 1951.
See also VIETNAM.

Vietnam, independent republic in South-East Asia, divided into two zones from 1954 until 1975, but reunified in 1976 following the Communist victory in the Vietnam War.
Covering an area of 329,500 km², the country is divided into lowland and highland regions.

Vietnam
Area: 329,500 km²
Population: 54,000,000
Capital: Hanoi

The lowlands, with the major part of the population, include the deltas of the Song Huong (Red River) in the north and the Mekong in the south, as well as a series of smaller lowland areas along the coast of the central region. The Song Huong rises in Yunnan province (China) and flows south-eastwards to reach the sea in the Gulf of Tonkin. The Mekong, also with its source in China, flows through Laos (for part of its length forming the boundary with Thailand) and then Cambodia, before dividing into two above the point where it enters southern Vietnam; its right branch is known as the Bassac. The highlands include the massif of the Annamite Chain, which is heavily forested over part of its area.

Total population was estimated at 54,000,000 in 1981. In 1974, Hanoi, the capital city, had a population of 736,000. Only two other urban centres in Vietnam, apart from Ho Chi Minh City, have more than 250,000 people: Da Nang and Haiphong.

The majority of the people are Vietnamese, living mainly in the lowland zones; there are also important Chinese and Indian communities, mainly in the south, and a Cambodian minority in the western part of the Mekong delta.

The most important sector of the economy is still agriculture, with the principal emphasis on irrigated rice production. Farming has been reorganised by Communist principles and there has been extensive and compulsory rural resettlement in the south.

Other important crops include sugar, coconuts, tea, maize, tobacco, coffee, oil palms, and various kinds of fruit. Another significant element in the economy is fishing.

French colonial policy was unsympathetic to any major development of industry in Indochina, apart from the exploitation of minerals, mainly in the north: notably coal, tin, zinc and other metals. Phosphates were also found and developed. The only significant manufacturing industries were cement and textiles. The main impulse towards industrial development came after the Communist take-over of north Vietnam in 1954, when coal and iron output were increased, and new industrial complexes were created.

The monetary unit is the *dong*.

The constitution of 1980 proclaims that Vietnam is a proletarian dictatorship committed to Marxism–Leninism. There is an elected National Assembly. All executive power is vested in the Communist Party.

History. Between 111 BC and AD 42, northern Vietnam came gradually under the political and cultural control of Han China, and remained a Chinese province until AD 900. Becoming independent in the 10th century, as the kingdom of Dai-Viet, it resisted Chinese attempts at reconquest in 982, 1075–77, and 1283–88, but was briefly subjected to Ming Chinese rule in the early 15th century.

Central Vietnam was ruled by a long series of Cham kings, at different capitals, from before AD 200 to 1471. Expansion into the southern region (including the Mekong delta) came during the period 1690–1790 and led to the annexation of territory formerly belonging to Cambodia. In 1802 the whole of present-day Vietnam was unified under one king or emperor for the first time. The French conquered the Mekong delta and Saigon in the period 1860–67, and made it the colony of Cochin China. In 1884 they established the protectorates of Tonkin and Annam. The Union Indochinoise (also including Laos and Cambodia) lasted from 1887 to 1945, when it was overthrown by the Japanese army. This opened the way for a Communist-led revolution, and the Vietminh (led by Ho Chi Minh) declared independence. There followed the Indochina War (1946–54) and then the Vietnam War (1960–75) before the revolution finally triumphed. In 1976 a National Assembly proclaimed the country's reunification under the name of the Socialist Republic of Vietnam. In 1978 Vietnam signed a treaty of friendship with the USSR, and relations with China deteriorated. After 1975 more than 750,000 refugees, many of Chinese origin, left Vietnam.

Vietnam War. Beginning gradually during the years 1959–60, and lasting till 1975, this was in some respects a continuation of the Indochina War, with the United States taking the place of France as the principal Western power involved. It was a war between the northern and southern zones of Vietnam as they emerged from the Geneva Agreements of 1954, and also a 'Cold War' struggle between the United States and the Soviet Union. At the height of the conflict, in 1967–68, there were over 500,000 American troops in Vietnam.

Relations between North and South Vietnam became critical during 1959, when the Ngo Dinh Diem regime in Saigon tried to eliminate the remaining Communists in the south, and the Communist government of Ho Chi Minh in Hanoi decided to assist a new rebellion south of the 17th parallel. By the end of 1960, the anti-Diem forces in the south had formed a national liberation front under the leadership of southern Communists. During 1961, Ngo Dinh Diem, who had depended on American aid since 1954, sought additional American protection. President Kennedy decided against sending regular combat units to Vietnam but agreed to send 'advisers', many of whom were units of special forces expert in covert warfare.

After Kennedy's death in 1963, President Johnson adopted a less cautious approach and during 1964 allowed the preparation of plans for both covert operations and open air-warfare against North Vietnam. Air attacks on the north, which became a daily feature of the war until 1968, began in February 1965 and in April the Americans also began to send in combat troops. The war situation became even more serious during 1966–67 as the Americans failed either to suppress the national liberation front in the south, or to destroy the determination of the leaders in Hanoi to drive the Americans out. In 1968 the Tet offensive seriously weakened American willpower to carry on the war and

President Johnson decided against sending any more men to Vietnam, and announced a limitation of bombing raids on the north. Before the end of 1968 the bombing had been halted completely and peace talks had opened. But the war dragged on throughout 1969–71, as the policy of 'Vietnamisation' replaced that of 'escalation'. President Nixon carried the war into Cambodia in 1970, and with heavy fighting now in Laos, the war again engulfed the whole of Indochina.

To break the stalemate, North Vietnam in spring 1972 launched a new and much heavier offensive. The Americans responded with intense bombing of the north. They held the situation, but it became clear that in the end they must take the risk of withdrawing completely before South Vietnam was secure against Communist pressure. American forces finally left South Vietnam (March 1973). The final North Vietnamese offensive came in late 1974. By March 1975 South Vietnamese morale had collapsed, and in April the Communist forces took Saigon. The war was over and the way opened for the reunification of Vietnam during 1976.

See also INDOCHINA WAR.

Viewdata, an electronic system of information storage and retrieval using a telephone linked to a domestic television screen. Text is transmitted along the telephone lines in coded signals and displayed on the screen. The user selects information from a central computer store by keyboard; he has direct access to all information in the store and may take it in any order. *Prestel* is the name given to the system operated by British Telecommunications.

Vigil, in Christian terms, a day of preparation before a great festival. In the early Church the vigil was spent in watching and prayer. Most were abolished in the Roman Catholic Church in 1956.

Vignola, Giacomo Barozzi da (1507–73), Italian mannerist architect. He designed the Villa Papa Giulio (1551–55), the church of Il Gesù (begun 1568), and other churches in Rome; also the palace or castle of Caprarola (1559). He compiled two important books on architecture and perspective.

Vigny, Alfred Victor, Comte de (1797–1863), French poet. He served in the army for 12 years. He published his first volume of poems in 1822, followed in 1826 by his famous prose romance *Cinq-Mars*, and by *Poèmes antiques et modernes*, including 'Moïse' and 'Le Cor'. In 1835 appeared his drama *Chatterton*. Vigny's poetry is notable for its grandeur, starkness, and constant theme of suffering. He saw man as a pygmy, with a God entirely uninterested in his suffering, and evolved a stoic philosophy as humanity's only solace and solution.

Vigo, Jean (1905–34), French film director. He shot his first film with the help of Boris Kaufman (brother of Dziga Vertov) and the Soviet example is clear in the very precise editing of his social documentary, *A Propos de Nice* (1929). A short study of a swimmer, *Jean Taris, champion de natation,* followed in 1931. He made his famous *Zéro de Conduite* in 1933, a film whose poetic grace and anarchist fervour were achieved despite Vigo's ill-health, a largely non-professional cast, and only eight days in the studio. Vigo's

last film, *L'Atalante* (1934) transformed a commercial assignment about a barge sailor into another lyrical masterpiece, but he died without seeing it completed.

Vigo, seaport in Pontevedra province, Spain, standing on an inlet on the Atlantic coast. In 1702 a British and Dutch fleet under Rooke sank Spanish and French ships in the inlet and took £1 million of treasure. Vigo is the principal port in Spain for trans-atlantic traffic. There are important fisheries, and shipbuilding and metallurgical industries. Paper, sugar, leather, soap, brandy and flour are manufactured. Population (1981) 258,724.

Vijayanagar, ruined city in Karnataka state, India. Founded in 1336, it was the seat of the Hindu Vijayanagar kings, who ruled much of southern India before 1565, when at the Battle of Talikota the Muslims of the Deccan inflicted a shattering defeat. The ruins, which lie on the south bank of the Tungabhadra river, cover 23 km². Although the city was thoroughly looted, many splendid buildings still exist, notably the King's, or Ladies', Bath, the Elephant Stables, the huge image of Narsingh Avatar, and the Śiva temple.

Vijayawada, city in Andhra Pradesh state, India, situated on the left bank of the Krishna river. It has long been a centre of communications by land and canal, and was once an important Buddhist religious centre. Population (1981) 460,598.

Viking Art. Fine wood-carving, tools beautifully engraved with interlaced linear design, and finely wrought personal ornaments in gold and silver are typical of the art of the Vikings. In England it did not in any sense replace that of the Celts and Saxons, and not until the latter part of the 10th century did its influence become at all marked.

It is usual to recognise three styles in Viking Art. The *Jellinge* style, named from a Danish royal grave in Jutland, is based on heavy animal designs, of which the Great Beast, to be seen on the famous Jellinge rune-stone itself, is one variety. The style also has affinities with the patterns of Irish manuscript illumination. In Britain it is well represented on the 2 m-high standing-cross in Gosforth, Cumberland, churchyard.

An elaborate foliage ornament and interlacing are to be noticed in the *Ringerike* style, named after the district in Norway where it is represented in local sandstone. One origin of the style can be found in the Winchester school of illuminated manuscripts. A particularly interesting example of it is an early 11th-century sculpture of a 'Great Beast' and serpent, originally coloured and rune-inscribed, which is part of a tomb found in St Paul's churchyard in 1852 and now in the Museum of London. Influence of the Ringerike style is well represented in English manuscripts, and there are also a few exceedingly competent carvings in ivory.

The carving on the wooden doors of *Urnes* church on the Sognefjord, Norway, gives its name to the third style. It found brilliant exposition in Irish metalwork, e.g. the 12th-century Cross of Cong, and it had an equally important place in English Christian art.

Vikings, Norsemen, or Northmen, common names for the inhabitants of Scandinavia in the period 800–1050. Although the

Viking Art. *Left, a silver-hilted sword, worked in the south English style. Right, a cast of a Viking tombstone found in St Paul's, London.*

Vikings are best known as pirates, some of their raids were political in nature, and they were equally energetic as colonists—with colonies stretching from North America to central Russia—and as traders, with main trading posts at Birka (near Stockholm) and Hedeby (near Schleswig). A signal for the start of Viking raids on the British Isles was the sacking of the monastery of Lindisfarne in 793. Soon Viking rule was established in the Orkneys, Shetlands, Hebrides and parts of north and western Scotland, in parts of Ireland, and increasingly in England. The kingdom of Wessex under Alfred the Great resisted strongly, however, and was victorious in 899. In the 10th century the Scandinavian settlers in England lost their power, but towards the end of the century raids from Denmark increased, culminating in the invasion and conquest of England under Sweyn I and Canute the Great.

Under Charlemagne and his successor, Louis the Pious, the Carolingian empire proved too strong for the Vikings, but after the latter's death in 840 they raided the areas round the Seine and the Loire frequently, sacking Paris in 845. As in England, they were prepared to be bought off by 'Danegeld'. In 912 the Viking Rollo was granted lands in France which were to form the nucleus of the duchy of Normandy. In Spain and the Mediterranean the Vikings met determined opposition from the Arabs and made only infrequent raids. In the Atlantic, they had colonised the Faeroes and Iceland by the end of the 9th century. Eric the Red began the settlement of Greenland in about 986, and his son Leif Ericsson discovered 'Vinland' in North America (possibly Newfoundland) in 1000, though the Viking colonies that were established there do not seem to have survived long. In the East, the Vikings (known as Rus) traded down the Dnieper and Volga rivers, establishing trading posts at Novgorod and Kiev, where they founded a dynasty. Vikings also served in the imperial guard in Byzantium, where they were known as Varangians.

Viking success was based very much on their superior ships and seamanship, whether in the military longship or in the colonists' broad *knarr*. The Vikings were not disorganised pirates, but had an established system of law and social organisation and a rich poetic culture.

Vikramaditya, legendary king of Ujjain (Malwa) in India who is associated with the Vikram Samvat, the Hindu era which commenced in the spring of 57 BC. No ruler of that date is historically traceable, the era having been for long called the Malava era (from Malwa).

Villa, Latin name for a country house with farm attached. In the Roman Empire, villas were the characteristic economic and social unit of the countryside. In exceptional cases they could be very grand. The most important of this type of rural palace is Hadrian's villa at Tivoli (built AD 125–134), whose temples, baths, pools, courtyards and theatre extend over a kilometre. A more normal scale was to be found in England, where villas were common in the south and midlands. Most had hypocaust heating and tessellated flooring.

In Italy the villa survived into medieval times, but frequently lost the occupation of its owner to a tenant farmer. Its conscious revival came with the Renaissance, when the owners of estates, stimulated by the reading of Roman authors, sought retreat from the increasing noise and pestilence of the towns. The splendid successor to Hadrian's villa was the Villa Madama in the papal vineyards near Rome, designed for Cardinal Giuliano de' Medici by Raphael, c.1516–17, though its enormous plan was never completed.

Andrea Palladio has always been considered the architect of the villa *par excellence*. His villas were villas in the true sense, not palaces, but noble dwellings with farm buildings attached. But he adopted the planning and decorative features of Roman public buildings to dignify them. His favourite motif was the façade adorned by a temple portico. However, Palladio's use of classical features was usually practical as well as ornamental: his pediments covered haylofts, and his colonnades sheltered farmcarts. His absorption of Roman logic and experience is shown in his ground plans, which were symmetrical,

well proportioned and convenient.

However, his most influential villa, the Villa Rotonda (c.1568) was a suburban retreat with no farm. Close English derivations from it are Colen Campbell's Mereworth Castle (1723) and Lord Burlington's Chiswick Villa (1725).

See also GREAT BRITAIN, ARCHAEOLOGY; HOUSE; RENAISSANCE ARCHITECTURE.

Villa–Lobos, Heitor (1887–1959), Brazilian composer. He toured as a pianist and collected Brazilian folk-music, took to composition, and in 1915 gave his first concert of his own works at Rio de Janeiro. From 1922 he studied in Paris, and in 1931 became director of musical education in the schools of Rio. His works include 5 operas, 12 symphonies, 18 ballets, 9 instrumental works entitled *Bachianas Brasileiras* and 16 called *Chóros*, church and choral music, orchestral works, chamber music, piano works and songs.

Villars, Claude Louis Hector, Duc de (1653–1734), Marshal of France. In 1702 he defeated the Margrave of Baden at Friedlingen. In 1709 he was sent to command the main army opposing Eugène and Marlborough on the northern frontier, but was wounded at Malplaquet. He saved his country by his victory at Denain in 1712.

Villehardouin, Geoffroi de (c.1160– c.1213), French historian. He took part in the Fourth Crusade, and was present at the capture of Constantinople in 1204. His chronicle of the crusades, *La Conquète de Constantinople*, is the first major prose work in French.

Villein. In feudal law, villeins were those who held land by base or servile tenure; villeinage existed in England from about the 11th to the 14th century. Legally a villein was bound to his native manor and all his earnings were his lord's. He held no property of his own. His corn had to be ground at his lord's mill, his loaves baked in his lord's oven. A payment (merchet) had to be made to the lord when he married off his daughter, and a fine paid to the lord when he sold an animal. His lord could claim a villein's best animal as heriot at his death. A villein and all his family could be sold to another owner, though it is unlikely that a villein would in practice be removed to another part of the country; generally such transfers meant only a change of lordship. However, a lord might voluntarily enfranchise a villein; in theory a villein could not buy his freedom, but in practice this did occasionally happen. If a villein lived for a year and a day in a chartered borough he could claim his freedom.

Villeneuve, Pierre Charles Jean-Baptiste Silvestre (1763–1806), French admiral. In the battle of the Nile he commanded the rear of the fleet. In 1804 he was in command of the Toulon squadron, and in 1805 was defeated and taken prisoner off Cape Trafalgar. In 1806 Villeneuve was freed and returned to France, where he committed suicide.

Villeroi, François de Neuville, Duc de (1644–1730), French soldier. He was brought up with Louis XIV, with whom he was a favourite, and in 1693 rose to be Marshal of France. But he showed great incapacity in the Netherlands, 1695–96, and in 1701 was defeated and taken prisoner by Prince Eugène in Italy. He was defeated by Marlborough at Ramillies, 1706, after which he was made governor of Lyons.

Villiers, Alan John (1903–), Australian sailor and travel writer. At the age of 15 he went to sea, and thereafter spent much of his life in sailing-ships. With the four-master *Pamir* he twice won the grain race from South Australia to England. During the Second World War he was a lieutenant-commander RNVR, and was awarded the DSC. In 1957 he captained the *Mayflower II*, a replica of the original ship of the Pilgrim Fathers, on a commemorative voyage across the Atlantic.

Villiers, Barbara, see CLEVELAND, BARBARA VILLIERS, DUCHESS OF.

Villiers, George, see BUCKINGHAM, GEORGE VILLIERS, 1ST DUKE OF.

Villiers de l'Isle-Adam, Philippe August Mathias, Comte de (1840–89), French writer. He was a Roman Catholic, a visionary, and an anti-materialist, and there is a strong element of fantasy (sometimes macabre and horrific) in many of his works. He is perhaps best known for his short stories.

Villon, François, or François de Montcorbier (1431–after 1463), French poet; he called himself Villon after a priest who became his guardian and benefactor. By 1452 he had taken his MA degree. Little is then known of him until 1455, when he fled from Paris after killing a priest in a street brawl. In 1456 he was involved in a robbery at the Collège de Navarre. He then wandered about the provinces; his association with thieves continued and he was imprisoned. Returning to Paris after his release, he had another street brawl, and was condemned to be hanged in 1463; the sentence was commuted to ten years' exile, and no more is heard of him. Villon wrote the *Lais* (*Petit Testament*), 1456, the *Testament* (*Grand Testament*), 1461 or 1462, and a number of short poems, mainly ballades—including some in thieves' jargon. His main works are in the form of mock bequests, gay, malicious and pathetic by turn, and full of sometimes obscure references to his acquaintances, benefactors or enemies.

Vilnius (formerly *Vilna*; German *Wilna*; Polish *Wilno*), capital and economic and cultural centre of the Lithuanian SSR, USSR. It has engineering, woodworking, food and light industries, and many old crafts are practised. It is also an important railway junction. Known since the 12th century, it became capital of Lithuania in 1323. At first it was predominantly Orthodox, and Russian (Belorussian), but from the 17th century it became Catholic, and Polish. It was the main seat of Jewish culture in Europe in the 17th–19th centuries. It was the constitutional capital of independent Lithuania from 1918, was Polish from 1920 to 1939 and occupied by the Soviet Army in 1939. Population (1980) 492,000.

Viña del Mar, residential suburb of Valparaiso, Chile, 8km from the port, with which it is connected by rail along the shore. Population (1970) 250,670.

Vincent de Paul, Saint (1576–1660), French priest and philanthropist. He became curé of Clichy, and then tutor to the children of the Gondi family. He soon devoted himself, under the guidance of Bérulle, to the relief of the poor, establishing what he called 'confréries de charité' in various towns in France. In 1625 he founded the Congregation of Mission Priests to train preachers who were to act as assistants to the regular clergy; and in 1633 the Daughters of Charity, who are devoted to the care of the sick. He was canonised in 1737.

Vincent of Beauvais (c.1190–c.1264), French Dominican friar, who compiled the *Speculum Majus*, a summary of knowledge which remained unsurpassed until the encyclopaedias of the 18th century.

Vine, name generally given to the climbing shrub bearing the grape, but sometimes applied to a variety of other climbing plants, especially in American usage.

Vinegar, a weak solution of acetic acid containing colouring matter, obtained by the acetic fermentation of wine, beer or other dilute alcoholic liquids.

Vingt-et-Un (French, twenty-one), or pontoon, old card game, the object of which is to make out of the cards one holds 'twenty-one'. One card is dealt, face downwards, to each player, including the dealer or banker. The players look at their cards and stake accordingly. The game proceeds thereafter by a second deal and by the exercise of the option to draw further cards so as by a certain combination to make the desired total. An ace counts as eleven or one, court cards ten. A player may either buy cards, and have them dealt face downwards or have them 'twisted', dealt face upwards. If he draws a card which brings his total over 21, he is said to have gone 'bust', and hands his stake to the dealer. If the dealer overdraws, he has to pay all round, except to those who have already handed in their stakes.

See also BLACKJACK.

Vinland, country of uncertain identity discovered by Leif Ericsson, probably somewhere on the east coast of North America, ranging from New England to northern Newfoundland. In 1965 an apparently early 15th-century map depicting a Vinland (whose eastern coastline related closely to that of Greenland) came into the possession of Yale University, but the map's authenticity was disproved by scientific dating tests in 1975, which showed that it could not have been drawn before 1920.

Vinnitsa, capital city, economic and cultural centre of Vinnitsa *oblast*, USSR, on the southern Bug south-west of Kiev. It has food (butter, fruit canning, meat), light (footwear, knitwear), chemical, engineering and metalworking industries. It has been known since 1363 when it was a Lithuanian fortress. From 1569 it was under Polish rule and in 1793 it became Russian. Population (1980) 323,000.

Vinyl Acetate, or ethenyl ethanoate, $CH_2:CHOCOCH_3$, prepared by the acetylation of acetylene in the presence of phosphoric acid. Vinyl acetate is used as the monomer in the manufacture of polyvinylacetate.

See also PLASTICS.

Vinyl Chloride, or chloroethene, $CH_2:CHCl$, prepared by the high-temperature chlorination of ethylene, and used as the monomer in the manufacture of polyvinyl-chloride.

See also PLASTICS.

Viol. A family of bowed string instruments with a flat back and sloping shoulders, gut frets on the fingerboard, and six strings. There are three normal sizes for chamber music: treble, tenor and bass, all of which are played resting on, or held between, the knees. A smaller bass, the division viol, was widely used as a solo instrument in the late 16th and early 17th centuries. The bass viol (viola da gamba) was the most important member of the family. The great bass (violone) was used interchangeably with the double bass of the violin family in orchestral music of the 17th and 18th centuries.

Viola, a genus of herbs in the Violaceae, found in temperate regions. The genus is botanically divided into sections, the more important being (1) the true violets, typified by *V. odorata* or sweet violet; and (2) the true pansies, such as *V. cornuta*, a parent of tufted pansies, and *V. tricolor*, wild pansy and parent of garden pansies (*V.* × *wittrockiana*).
See also PANSY.

Viola, see VIOLIN FAMILY.

Viola da gamba, see VIOL.

Viola d'amore, bowed string instrument larger than the viola of the violin family, with up to seven playing strings plus seven strings which are not touched by the bow or fingers but which add a silvery shimmer to the sound by sympathetic resonance. Possibly invented in England in the early 17th century, it was extensively used in Europe until the end of the 18th.

Violet, see VIOLA.

Violin Family, stringed musical instruments played with the bow. The *violin*, which was developed in Italy at the beginning of the 16th century, consists of: a resonant wooden box (the body) of which the top surface is called the belly and the under surface the back; the neck, a solid piece of wood to which is attached the fingerboard; and four strings, fastened at one end to the body by a projecting tailpiece, and at the other to pegs in the scroll-like termination of the neck. The body has two deep inward curves in its sides; *f*-shaped sound-holes are cut in the belly on either side of the bridge over which the strings pass. The strings are of steel wire or of silver wire covering gut or nylon; they are tuned in fifths, the highest to E on the fourth space of the treble stave, the others to the A, D and G below. Since the time of the early Italian masters there has been little alteration in the shape of the violin and modern makers still follow the model of Stradivari.

The *tenor violin*, tuned an octave below the violin, was little used and became extinct in the 18th century. The *viola* is larger than the violin and its tone is somewhat grave and melancholy. It is pitched a fifth below the violin. Viola music is generally written in the alto clef. The *violoncello*, or *cello*, is much larger than the violin and viola, and is held between the player's knees. It is tuned an octave below the viola. Cello music is written in the bass, tenor and treble clefs. The *violoncello piccolo* was a small cello with a fifth string in the treble. Bach and other composers wrote important solos for it. The *double bass* is the largest of the violin family, having a deep, rougher tone. It differs from the other instruments, chiefly in having sloping shoulders and in being differently tuned. Formerly double basses had three strings; a fourth string was added, sounding the E

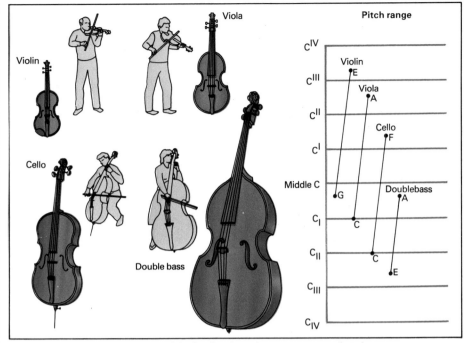

Violin Family. *The instruments of the family, their playing positions and pitch ranges.*

below the stave, and the strings are tuned in fourths (E, A, D, G). A fifth string tuned to low C is also sometimes added. The sound is an octave below the notes in the bass clef. See also AMATI; GUARNERI.

Viollet-le-Duc, Eugène-Emmanuel (1814–79), French architect and writer. After training in France and studying abroad, he began the restorations which made him famous. In 1840 he restored the church at Vézelay, and then worked on the Sainte Chapelle in Paris and Notre-Dame, 1845. Most of his later restorations have been criticised as being too drastic. They include the city of Carcassonne; the châteaux of Pierrefonds and Coucy; the abbey of St Denis; S. Ouen at Rouen and S. Sernin at Toulouse. His prodigious output of books included dictionaries of architecture and furniture.

Violoncello, or cello, see VIOLIN FAMILY.

Vionnet, Madeleine (1877–1975), French *haute couture* dress designer famous for bias-cut clothes which typified the best of the 1930s fashions.

Viper, common name for poisonous snakes of the family Viperidae, that are most abundant in Africa and south-west Asia. True vipers (*Vipera*) have a characteristic flattened triangular head and relatively short, thick body. The common viper or adder (*V. berus*) is the only poisonous British snake. Others of the genus are the horned viper (*V. cornutus*) and Russell's viper (*V. russellii*) of India, which causes many deaths. The rattlesnakes are related to this family.

Viper's Bugloss, *Echium vulgare*, a plant of the Boraginaceae from Europe and Asia, naturalised elsewhere. It has bristly stems and leaves, and spikes of blue flowers.

Vipers, Pit, see RATTLESNAKES.

Virchow, Rudolf Ludwig Karl (1821–1902), German founder of 'cellular pathology', a distinguished pathologist, physical anthropologist and statesman. In 1847 he founded the *Archiv für pathologische Anatomie* (Virchow's Archiv), one of the most im-

portant journals in medicine and still being published. The year 1858 saw the publication of his *Cellularpathologie*, one of the great books in medicine and one which caused a revolution in medical thinking (English edition: *Cellular Pathology*, 1972). He also made useful contributions to anthropology and archaeology.

Viren, Lasse (1949–), Finnish distance runner. One of the most outstanding 5000 and 10,000 m runners of modern times. In the 1972 Olympic Games he won Gold Medals for both the 5000 and 10,000 m races, the latter being completed in a world record time of 27 minutes 38·4 seconds. He repeated this triumph by winning the Gold medals for the same two events in the 1976 Olympic Games.

Virgil, Publius Vergilius Maro (70–19 BC), Latin poet. After completing his education, Virgil appears to have retired to his paternal farm. He probably became acquainted with Maecenas soon after finishing his *Eclogues* in about 37 BC. These are pastorals, following Theocritus; the landscapes are idealised, but some poems are touched with realism and contain veiled references to contemporary figures and events. His most polished work, the *Georgics*, was published in 30 BC. The four books deal with husbandry, the growing of crops, fruit and vines, the rearing of animals and beekeeping.

Virgil probably began the *Aeneid* about 26 BC. In 19 BC he caught a fever and died. The *Aeneid*, which he had wanted destroyed, was published by his executors on the order of the Emperor Augustus. Almost complete in 12 books, it tells the story of Aeneas's arrival in Italy after the fall of Troy and tries to claim the descent in direct line from Iulius, Aeneas's son, to Julius Caesar, whose heir Augustus was. It is the foremost poem of Latin literature, a national epic revealing, through the story of Aeneas, the greatness of Rome. Virgil was the greatest Latin poet to his countrymen and his influence on European literature has been immense.

See also EPIC; HOMER; LATIN LITERATURE.

Virgin Islands, consist of 100 small islands and cays 113 km east of Puerto Rico, between the Atlantic Ocean and the Caribbean Sea. Total land area is about 497 km² with an overall population of approximately 107,600 (1980). The islands form two distinct political units: the British Virgin Islands and the United States Virgin Islands. Tourism is the main industry in all the Virgin Islands.

Virgin Islands (British), comprises 36 islands, 16 of which are inhabited, 97 km east of Puerto Rico, adjoining the United States Virgin Islands (see below), and west and north of the Anegada Passage, an important channel connecting the Caribbean Sea and the Atlantic Ocean. Their area totals 130 km².

Tortola is the largest (54 km²) in the group, and is the site of Road Town, the capital and largest town. The population of the British Virgin Islands was estimated in 1980 to be 11,500; and that of Road Town, 3500.

Tourism is fast becoming the islands' chief source of income. Despite the highly inadequate water supply, agriculture and stock raising remain, however, the most important economic sectors, followed by fresh fish, gravel and sand. US currency is in use.

The British Virgin Islands are administered by a governor who, with added responsibilities as part of a new constitution introduced in 1967, presides over an executive council; there is a mainly-elected Legislative Council.

History. During his second voyage in 1493, Columbus discovered and named the island group Santa Ursula y las Once Mil Virgenes (St Ursula and the Eleven Thousand Virgins). Dutch buccaneers held Tortola from 1648 to 1666 when it was taken over and occupied by British planters. Annexed to the Leeward Islands in 1672, Tortola was granted a civil government 100 years later. Following the de-federation of the Leeward Islands in 1956, the islands became a crown colony; in 1967 they were given a ministerial form of government.

Virgin Islands (United States), three main and 50 smaller islands of 344 km² in area, towards the eastern end of the Greater Antilles, 64 km east of Puerto Rico in the Caribbean, and adjoining the British Virgin Islands (see above).

St Thomas, with an area of 83 km², has a good fertile soil. Throughout most of the island is an east-west ridge, the highest peak, Crown Mountain (472 m) rising north-west of the capital, Charlotte Amalie. St Croix, with an area of 216 km², presents a range of topography from 355 m in the north (Mount Eagle), to a flat southern coastline comprised mainly of lagoons. Total population of the islands in 1980 was 95,590.

The land is generally unsuitable for agricultural purposes, although cattle are raised on St Croix. The principal industries are tourism, jewellery, watches, rum, textiles and petroleum products. Sugar is produced on St Croix and exported to the USA, along with rum and gin, jewellery and perfume.

The governor and lieutenant-governor of the US Virgin Islands are elected, while the heads of the executive departments are appointed by the governor. There is a 15-member Senate.

History. Columbus discovered the Virgin Islands in 1493, landing at what is now St Croix. Emperor Charles V sent Spanish forces in 1555 annihilating the Carib inhabitants by 1596. Denmark occupied St Thomas island in 1666, and began exporting sugar, indigo, and cotton by 1671 (the date of colonisation). Apart from two brief periods of British occupation, Denmark held the islands until 1917, when they were sold to the USA for $25 million, becoming an unincorporated territory of the USA.

Virgin Land Campaign, measures for the cultivation of virgin lands and reclamation of waste land in the USSR, initiated by Khrushchev in 1953, and aimed at ensuring an adequate supply of grain. Between 1953 and 1961 nearly 35·6 million ha were brought under cultivation.

Virgin Mary, see MARY, VIRGIN.

Virginals, or virginal, small member of the harpsichord family, oblong in shape and especially popular in England c.1550–1620, when composers such as Byrd, Bull, Farnaby and Gibbons contributed excellent pieces to its repertoire.

Virginia (Old Dominion State), one of the 13 original states of the American Union, bounded on the north by West Virginia and Maryland, on the east by the Atlantic Ocean and Maryland, on the south by North Carolina and Tennessee, and on the west by Kentucky and West Virginia. It has an area of 105,703 km², and is divided into: tidewater Virginia, the low-lying coastal region consisting of four peninsulas; the Piedmont, the central part rising to the Blue Ridge Mountains; the Shenandoah valley between those mountains and the Alleghenies, a rich farming district; and south-west Virginia, extending to the west and including mountains and fertile valleys, and the highest point in the state (1746 m).

There are some 6·5 million ha of commercial forest land in Virginia, and about 4·3 million ha of farmland. There are many small hill-farms. The largest crop area is under maize, but the leading crop by value, as in the earliest days of Virginia, is tobacco. Apples and peanuts are other farm specialities. Important industries include lumber and timber products and tobacco manufactures. (Richmond is the world's largest cigarette-manufacturing centre.) Virginia also produces cotton and synthetic textiles, especially rayon and nylon. The chief minerals are coal, stone, gravel, sand and zinc; others include titanium, cement, feldspar, clay, lead-gypsum, manganese, mica, pyrites and salt. The 2415 km of tidal shore on the Atlantic, Chesapeake Bay and the river estuaries have important fisheries, especially of oysters and crabs. The chief ports are Norfolk and Newport News, on Hampton Roads, formed by the estuary of the James, on which stands Richmond, the capital, and other important cities.

The first permanent English settlement was made at Jamestown in 1607 under the leadership of John Smith. Virginia seceded with the Southern States in 1861. The western part of the state, which was against secession, broke away during the civil war and became the state of West Virginia. In 1980 the state had a population of 5,346,279.

Luchino Visconti directs Helmut Berger in The Damned, *1970.*

Virginia, West, see WEST VIRGINIA.

Virginia Creeper, see PARTHENOCISSUS.

Virgo, 'the Virgin', an extensive northern constellation and sixth sign of the zodiac. Its brightest star, the first magnitude Spica (Alpha Virginis), marked 'the Ear of Wheat' held by Virgo when it was regarded as representing Ceres, the goddess of tillage and corn. There are many relatively bright galaxies in this constellation.

Virus, submicroscopic particles which are the causative agents of many diseases in Man (e.g. influenza, measles, poliomyelitis, yellow fever), animals (e.g. foot-and-mouth disease, distemper, rabies), birds (e.g. fowl pest), fish (e.g. haemorrhagic septicaemia of salmonids), plants (e.g. potato leaf-roll, rice dwarf diseases, tobacco mosaic) and insects (e.g. polyhedroses). Unlike bacteria, viruses cannot grow on non-living media and require living cells to survive and replicate. They rely entirely on their cellular hosts for the machinery of protein synthesis and energy. On entering the host cell a virus is capable of 'dictating' to the cell, directing it to produce new virus.

Several viruses are known to multiply in, or are associated with, more than one type of host. Many viruses infecting plants or animals also multiply in their arthropod vectors, for example, potato leaf-roll virus in aphids and yellow fever in mosquitoes. Most infections produce no visible signs of illness in the host. Viruses enter the body via the skin, the respiratory tract or the alimentary canal. The virus may multiply at the site of entry with or without causing an obvious lesion. Signs and symptoms in generalised infections are usually associated with virus multiplication in various 'target' organs such as skin (e.g. measles and chicken-pox), glands (e.g. mumps) and the central nervous system (e.g. rabies, encephalitic viruses).

In vertebrate species, infection with a virus produces an immune response with the production of specific antibodies. This generally produces lifelong immunity to further infection with this virus (e.g. mumps, measles, rubella). Specific antibodies can be transferred during pregnancy from mother to foetus, and these antibodies persist in newborn babies for several weeks after birth. Recurrent attacks of the same disease are usually due to antigenically different strains of virus. In addition to acute infections, viruses can sometimes cause 'latent' infections over very long periods.

Vaccines are available for many common viral diseases, but antibiotics have no effect.

Visby, seaport of Sweden, capital of Gotland island in the Baltic, on its west coast. St Mary's cathedral was founded c.1200. Visby was an important member of the Hanseatic League, and gave its name to a maritime legal code of the 13th century. It is a popular holiday resort. It became Swedish in 1648. Population (1970) 19,000.

Viscacha, *Lagostomus maximus*, a large, heavily built rodent related to the chinchillas in the family Chinchillidae. It inhabits the pampas of Argentina. The head and body are about 60 cm long. The viscacha is nocturnal and lives in warrens. It is mottled grey and black. A stiff brush of bristles on the third digit of the hind foot is used as a fur-groomer.

Visconti, name of a noble Lombard family which ruled Milan for nearly two centuries. Their lordship was established by Ottone, who was appointed to the archbishopric of that town in 1262. In the 14th century the Visconti were in constant conflict with the papacy. During this century they were supreme in Milan, and Galeazzo II refounded a university at Pavia, and was a patron of Petrarch. He was succeeded by the joint sovereigns, Barnabo and Gian Galeazzo (died 1402), the latter of whom was the most powerful of all the Visconti.

Visconti, Luchino (1906–76), Italian film director; also well known as a director of drama and opera. His films include *La Terra Trema*, 1948; *Senso*, 1955; *Rocco and his Brothers*, 1960; *The Leopard*, 1962; *The Damned*, 1970; *Death in Venice*, 1971; and *Conversation Piece*, 1975.

Viscose, a synthetic fibre prepared by treating cellulose with caustic soda and then with carbon disulphide. The product is then filtered and spun to form filaments which coagulate in an acid bath. The fibre is one of the cheapest of all fibres and is quite strong when dry. Modification to the production process leads to the stronger high-tenacity fibres used in tyres and conveyor belts, and to the modal fibres which have superior wet strength. The fibres are used for linings, in continuous filament form, or blended with other fibres in carpets, blankets, etc. The fibres are marketed under many names such as Evlan, Sarille, Fibro or, for modals, as Vincel, etc.

Viscosity, property of a fluid whereby it resists the relative motion of its parts—a sort of internal friction. Thus, when tea is stirred, it is the viscosity that brings it to rest again under the action of friction between the layers of tea, and between the cup and the layer of tea next to it. All fluids, even gases, are viscous; the only exception known is liquid helium below 2·186 K.

Suppose a stream of liquid is moving over a horizontal bed. The velocity of any layer parallel to the bed depends on its distance above the bed; the layer next to the bed is at rest, while the surface layer is moving fastest. If we consider an intermediate layer we realise that the surface of the liquid immediately below it experiences a viscous force tending to bring it up to the speed of the faster-moving layer above it. The latter simultaneously experiences an equal and opposite viscous force, that acts as a drag, tending to reduce its speed to that of the slower-moving layer below it. As a result of these viscous forces the relative motion of the various layers will vanish unless there is some external force. Suppose the surface layer is moving with velocity v parallel to the bed. There is therefore a velocity gradient v/d, where d is the depth of liquid. The viscous force F per unit area of any layer parallel to the bed is given by $F = \eta v/d$, where η is constant for a given fluid at a given temperature, known as the coefficient of viscosity. The direction of this force is parallel to the bed.

See also LUBRICATION; SUPERFLUIDITY; TERMINAL VELOCITY.

Viscount (from Low Latin *vicecomes*, 'in place of a count/earl'), in the UK the title of the fourth degree of nobility, between earl and baron. Similar titles exist in other European countries.

Vishakhapatnam, port of Andhra Pradesh state, India. It is the sixth largest by tonnage handled and the major shipbuilding port in India, with an oil refinery and deep-water facilities. It exports iron ore from Mount Bailadila, manganese ore, sugar, and peanuts. Population (1981) 575,163.

Vishnu (the Pervader), one of the Hindu triad of creator deities, Brahma and Śiva being the other two. Vishnu represents the opposite tendency from Śiva, the disintegrator, for Vishnu is the power of cohesion and concentration. He holds the material of the universe together and is connected with light and life. Vishnu and Śiva are interdependent, life and death. Vishnu is the inner cause of life and whereas Brahmā gives it form, Vishnu is the 'idea' around which the form develops. He has four arms which represent the idea of personhood and the three qualities (Gunas) from which all existence takes its nature. Vishnu has had ten incarnations as Avatars, the most famous as Rama and Krishna.

Visibility, term used in meteorology and aviation to describe the transparency of the atmosphere. It is defined in terms of the horizontal distance to the farthest object that can be distinguished from the background.

Visigoths, see GOTHS.

Vision. The transference of part of the electromagnetic spectrum (light), impinging constantly upon our eyes, into a picture consistent with our experience of the real world is our vision or visual perception. Vision is a complicated optical, physiological, and psychological process and can be better understood if three interdependent aspects are considered. First, we are dependent on light —the visible spectrum—and the focusing of this light into images on the sensitive retina. It is light, being refracted into images, that constitutes a physical stimulus for vision. The optical system of the eye consists of the cornea and crystalline lens. These together form a powerful converging system. Objects at all distances cannot be in focus at the same time, and by the mechanism of accommodation the curvature of the crystalline lens can be changed to allow us to focus objects which are at different distances.

Secondly we know that vision involves an intricate sequence of events that is started when the image falls on the light-sensitive receptors, the rods and cones, of the retina. The light is absorbed by pigments contained in the receptors, subsequent physico-chemical reactions lead to the stimulation of the nervous parts of these receptors, then to stimulation of the fibres of the optic nerve and thence to the brain.

The third point is that vision is more than a bombardment of neural information set up by light. It consists, also, of a learning process started at birth and continued by our external environment for the first few years of life. People who have had their vision restored by operation after many years of blindness are often unable to recognise their surroundings, or even the simplest of objects. They have to pass through a long period of associating vision with touch, taste, hearing and smell before they can interpret their new world.

Colour vision is the sense by which the eye distinguishes and recognises colours. According to the Young-Helmholtz trichromatic theory of colour vision there are three kinds of sensory cones in the retina. A sensation of white is produced when the three types of cones are excited to the same extent, while other colour sensations are produced by the excitation of the three kinds of cones to different extents.

Vision and Colour Sense in Animals. The structure and functioning of the eye in other mammals, and indeed in all vertebrates, resembles in general that of man, though reptiles, amphibians and fishes accommodate for objects at varying distances by a backward and forward movement of the lens rather than a change in its shape, and some birds mould the cornea to different shapes. Amongst invertebrates a true eye capable of forming images is confined to some molluscs, such as the cuttlefish (which has eyes similar to those of mammals), and the arthropods, such as insects and crustaceans, in which the eyes are usually compound, with many facets, each of which forms a separate image. The compound eye is especially good at noticing movement. Most other invertebrates, as for instance the common earthworm and even some unicellular organisms, have at least one organ that is sensitive to the difference between light and darkness, but does not form an image.

The extent to which animals, apart from man, are able to distinguish various colours is still under investigation. An animal may be sensitive to a certain colour simply because that colour is brighter than the surroundings. Colour vision certainly occurs in birds, bony fish, some reptiles, and in primates. The majority of mammals (including, for example, dogs, but excluding primates) are probably colour-blind, despite the popular belief that red is a distinctive colour to bulls. The work of von Frisch has shown that the honey bee can distinguish blue and yellow, but not green or red; however, its vision extends into the ultraviolet. Colour vision is also present in other insects, e.g. the bluebottle *Calliphora*.

Binocular Vision. The preceding paragraphs have not taken into account the fact that most animals have two eyes. The use of two eyes has several advantages: there is a spare eye in case of damage to one; two eyes give a far wider field of vision than that given by one eye; and animals, such as the carnivores and primates, including man, that have the eyes placed together on the front of the face, have three-dimensional, or stereoscopic, vision that allows them to see in perspective and to judge distances.

Vision, Defects of. These may be due to affections of the nervous mechanism of the eye, to inflammatory and other changes in the transparent media through which light passes, or to errors of accommodation or co-ordination. The optical mechanism of the eye and the defects of vision arising from defective refraction are discussed in the articles on EYE and REFRACTION, ERRORS OF. Tumours in the brain may cause impairment of function of part or all of the visual centre. Toxic influences are usually responsible for amblyopia, in which the visual impressions are reduced. Paralysis or inflammation of the optic nerve may cause total or partial blindness. Glaucoma is a condition caused by a rise of pressure inside the eyeball; various visual defects are experienced. Keratitis, or inflammation of the cornea, is the result of injury or is secondary to conjunctivitis. Opacity of the lens is known as cataract; it may be due to injury, to degeneration of the tissues in old age, or to malnutrition. Iritis is a painful and dangerous condition dependent on a variety of causes, such as injury, constitutional disturbances of various kinds or extension of inflammation from other structures. Conjunctivitis may be catarrhal or purulent; most varieties are contagious, hence the necessity for care in dealing with discharges from a diseased eye. When the two eyes are not co-ordinated, double-vision exists; this is due to an affection of the oculomotor nerves.

See also BLINDNESS; COLOUR-BLINDNESS; SHORT-SIGHTEDNESS; SQUINTING; TRACHOMA; VISION.

Visitation of the Blessed Virgin Mary, Feast of the, Christian festival on 2 July commemorating the visit of the Virgin Mary to Elizabeth, John the Baptist's mother.

Visitations, periodic tours of the English counties, made by the kings of arms or other heralds between 1530 and 1686, in order to record arms and pedigrees of the gentry.

Vistula (German *Weichsel*; Polish *Wisła*), chief river of Poland, which rises in the Beskid Mountains, south of Cieszyn, and flows past Crakow, Warsaw, Plock and Toruń, to the Baltic Sea at the Gulf of Danzig. It enters the sea by several arms, of which the main arm, the Dead Vistula (Polish *Martwa Wisła*), passes Gdańsk. It is connected by canal with the rivers Oder, Neman and Bug. Its main tributaries are: on the right, the Skawa, Dunajec, Wisłoka, San, Wieprz, Narew and Drweca rivers; and on the left, the Nida, Pilica and Bzura rivers. Length 1078 km.

Vitalism, once popular belief that phenomena exhibited by living organisms are due to a special force and could not be explained by chemical and physical facts.

Vitamins. The vitamins are a group of unrelated organic compounds essential for growth and the maintenance of life. Vitamins generally function by acting as catalysts (substances that speed up the rate of chemical reactions) for specific reactions required by the body. Vitamins must be supplied by the diet because the body cannot make them. Several of the vitamins are referred to as a single substance for convenience, but are actually a group of compounds which are structurally related. Vitamins are classified as water-soluble or fat-soluble, as this property determines which foods supply them and how they are handled by the body. Most fat-soluble vitamins, since they can be stored in the body, are toxic if taken in excess.

Of the fat-soluble vitamins, Vitamin A affects skeleton growth and colour-vision; Vitamin D, the 'sunshine vitamin', enables the body to absorb and use calcium and phosphorus; Vitamin E interacts with other dietary requirements, though its function is not clearly understood; Vitamin K performs an essential rôle in blood coagulation.

Of the water-soluble vitamins, Vitamin C (ascorbic acid) plays a vital rôle in wound healing, and prevents scurvy; biotin is involved in reactions which release energy from carbohydrates; B_2 and B_{12} appear to be essential for the metabolism of protein, carbohydrate, and fat; B_9/B_{10} helps to make many compounds in the body; niacin helps in the breakdown of carbohydrates, fats, and proteins; B_6 is involved in the synthesis of regulatory compounds in the brain; B_1 functions in carbohydrate metabolism; B_3 is involved in overall body metabolism.

A (Retinol)	Liver, yellow vegetables, cod liver oil.
B1 (Thiamine)	Lean meat, whole wheat, yeast
B2 (Riboflavin)	Liver, cheese, milk, yeast
B3 (Pantothenic Acid)	Liver, cereals, beans
B6 (Pyridoxine)	Liver, yeast, potatoes.
B9/B10 (Folic Acid)	Liver, kidney, fresh vegetables
B12 (Cyanocobalamin)	Liver, milk, fish, eggs
Biotin	Yeast, peanuts
Niacin	Fish, meat, potatoes
C (Ascorbic Acid)	Fruit, fresh vegetables, nuts
D (Calciferol)	Sunshine, milk, fish, margarine
F	Vegetable oils, whole grains
K	Liver, green vegetables

Vitamins. Important dietary sources.

See also NUTRITION; NUTRITIONAL DEFICIENCY DISEASES.

Vitebsk, capital and economic and cultural centre of Vitebsk *oblast*, Belorussian SSR, USSR, on the Western Dvina, 220 km north-east of Minsk. There are textile, engineering (machine tools) and woodworking industries, and it is also an important railway junction. The city has been known since 1021; it became the capital of the independent Vitebsk principality in 1101 until it came under Lithuania in 1320, Poland in 1569, and Russia in 1772. Population (1980) 303,000.

Vitellius, Aulus (AD15–69), Roman Emperor, 2 January–22 December 69. He was proclaimed emperor by the troops at Cologne; his generals, Valens and Caecina, secured the throne for their master. In July Vespasian was proclaimed at Alexandria; his general, Antonius Primus, marched on Rome and put Vitellius to death.

Viterbo, Italian town, capital of the Viterbo province, 65 km north-west of Rome. It became the residence of the popes in 1257. There is a 12-century cathedral and a papal palace (1266–67). Engineering, construction and foodstuffs (sausages and cheese) are the main industries. Population (1974) 39,300.

Vitis, a genus of deciduous and evergreen climbing shrubs with tendrils in the family Vitidaceae. *V. vinifera* is the common grape vine in Europe and *V. coignetiae*, from Japan, is grown for its ornamental colourful leaves.

Vitoria, capital of Álava province, Spain. During the Peninsular War the French were decisively beaten here by Wellington in 1813. Agricultural machinery, vehicles, furniture, paper and leather goods are manufactured, and there is a trade in agricultural produce and wine. Population (1981) 192,773.

Vitória, capital of Espírito Santo state, Brazil. As a port its importance has been due to its railway connection with the mining and coffee-growing areas of the state of Minas Gerais. This is now being enhanced by the further development of iron-ore and manganese mining in Minas Gerais. Population (1975) 163,877.

Vitriol, Oil of, see SULPHURIC ACID.

Vitriols (Latin *vitrum*, glass), obsolete name for metallic sulphates that form glassy crystals. Blue vitriol is copper sulphate, white vitriol is zinc sulphate, green vitriol (copperas) is ferrous sulphate. Oil of vitriol is sulphuric acid.

See also SULPHURIC ACID; ZINC.

Vitruvius Pollio (active 1st century BC), Roman architect and writer. He appears to have served as a military engineer under Julius Caesar in Africa (46), and later dedicated to Augustus his celebrated work *De Architectura*, a treatise on architecture, construction, mechanics, etc. To it we owe much of our knowledge of Roman building methods and of Greek buildings which have perished since his day.

Vittorini, Elio (1908–66), Italian novelist and critic. He joined an underground communist group in Milan, became the director of *L'Unitá* and started the review *Il Politecnico*, 1945. He translated into Italian works by Faulkner, Steinbeck and D. H. Lawrence, finding his own early works blocked by the Fascist authorities. His novels include *Il Garofano Rosso*, 1933, 1948, and *Diario in pub-*

blico, 1957. Vittorini was one of the most persuasive influences on the post-war Italian literary scene.

Vittorio Veneto, Italian town in Veneto, 35 km north of Treviso. It manufactures motorcycles, textiles and cement. It was the scene of a great battle during the First World War. Population (1974) 25,500.

Vitus, Saint (3rd century), Italian martyr thought to have perished in the reign of Diocletian. His aid is invoked against St Vitus's dance (*Chorea*), hydrophobia and other complaints, and he is patron saint of dancers. His feast is on 15 June.

Vivaldi, Antonio (c.1675–1741), Italian violinist and composer. He was ordained priest in 1703, and taught music at the Ospedale della Pietà. Vivaldi is among the most individual of the Italian violinist composers of his time. He wrote over 40 operas, 2 oratorios, church music, secular cantatas, 23 symphonies, 46 *concerti grossi* and 73 sonatas for one and two violins and for cello, but his real importance lies in some 450 concertos for solo instruments and combinations of instruments.

Vivarium, a receptacle in which reptiles and amphibians can be kept. For lizards and snakes the major portion should be dry with a small pool of water. If frogs, toads, newts and terrapins are kept, there should be more water than land.

Vivekananda (1862–1902), Hindu sage famous for his exposition of modern Vedanta, and a disciple of Ramakrishna. Born in Calcutta as Narendranath Dutt, he studied at a Christian missionary college and became interested in western philosophy. In 1882 he met Ramakrishna and was later given the name Vivekananda and the title of Swami. He then spent six years as a recluse in the Himalayas. In 1893 he was appointed to represent Hinduism at the Parliament of Religions in Chicago where he spoke eloquently of Hindu teachings and achieved great success with western audiences.

Vives, Juan Luis (1492–1540), Spanish scholar and humanist. He was a friend of Erasmus and More and became tutor to Princess Mary of England in 1523, for whom he wrote *De Ratione Studii Puerilis Epistolae Duae*, 1523. He opposed Henry VIII's divorce, and from 1528 lived in Bruges. His works include a famous commentary on St Augustine's *City of God*, 1522.

Viviparous, describes animals such as mammals that give birth to young that have been nourished directly in the womb and have not developed within an egg.

Vivisection, dissection of, and experiment upon, living animals. In its present legal sense the term is limited to vertebrates. It is an ancient practice, Galen being one of its exponents. Under the Cruelty to Animals Act 1876, experiments on animals in the UK are controlled by the Home Office, which appoints inspectors to visit laboratories. Experimenters and their laboratories are required to hold a Home Office licence.

Vix, rich Iron Age burial site, 5 km northwest of Chatillon-sur-Seine, France. Most notable of the finds there was a large wine-container of bronze from Greece and several other Greek and Etruscan imported pieces dating to the end of the 6th century BC. Thus the burial, because of its Mediterranean connections, provides a key date for the Iron Age in France.

Vizcaya, Golfo de, see BISCAY, BAY OF.

Vizier (Arabic *wazir*), title first given to the chief minister of the Abbasside caliphs, subsequently applied to the chief minister of the Turkish sultan, and to the chief minister of other Muslim states.

Vladimir, Saint, also Vladimir I, Grand Duke of Kiev (956–1015), patron saint of Russian Christians. Before his marriage to the sister of the Byzantine emperor, Vladimir was baptised, and he called in the Greek clergy to evangelise his country. His feast is on 15 July.

Vladimir, capital city, economic and cultural centre of Vladimir *oblast*, USSR, on the Klyazma river 190 km east of Moscow. It has large engineering (tractors, automobile parts) and chemical industries, and is a treasury of Russian 12th- to early 19th-century art. It was founded by Vladimir Monomakh as a fortress in 1108, was the capital of central Russia 1157–1238, became Muscovite in 1364, and a provincial capital in 1778. Population (1980) 301,000.

Vladivostok, city on the western shore of the Sea of Japan, on a peninsula extending into Peter the Great Bay. It is the capital of the Primorski (Maritime) Krai of the RSFSR, USSR, and one of the most important economic and cultural centres of the Soviet Far East, where it is the largest city. It is a terminus of the Trans-Siberian Railway (9224 km from Moscow) and the Northern Sea Route, centre of communications for the Pacific territories, the largest Soviet port on the Pacific, and the chief base of the Pacific Fleet. There are engineering (shipbuilding, mining equipment), fishing and whaling industries. It was founded as a Russian port in 1860; it rapidly developed as a free port (handling supplies for the Soviet Far East and in transit from Manchuria), naval base and fortress, and had an international character until the 1930s. During 1918–22 it saw Allied occupation under Japanese leadership. Population (1980) 558,000.

Vlaminck, Maurice de (1876–1958), French painter. He worked with André Derain in early life and with him was one of the group associated with Matisse in the Fauvist Salon of 1905. He was much influenced at this period by the intense colour of Van Gogh but developed a darker mode of painting.

Vlissingen, see FLUSHING.

Vlorë (formerly *Avlona*), seaport of Albania on the Bay of Vlorë, 93 km south of Durrës. It was under the government of Venice until 1691. There is fishing and fish canning, and olive-oil refining. Its port is linked by pipeline with inland oil-fields. Population (1978) 58,400.

Vltava (German *Moldau*), river of Czechoslovakia, which rises in the Forest of Bohemia and flows north to join the Labe (Elbe) at Mělník. It passes through České Budějovice and Prague. Length 435 km.

Vocal Cords, see LARYNX.

Vocational Training, a term often contrasted with academic or liberal education, to describe training in skills and techniques of commerce or industry for the purpose of making competent practitioners. In Europe technical, commercial and professional courses at all levels are offered in special institutions, e.g. in technical universities or technical schools. This pattern has, to a greater or lesser extent, been copied in many areas of the world where European education has been influential. In contrast, the movement towards vocational and professional training at the highest level has been rapid in the USA.

Vodka, Russian national spirit, originally distilled from the cheapest grain available, needing neither nose nor palate for its appreciation, though for the *élite* there was a finer spirit with a more subtle flavour. Confined to the USSR and Poland until after the Second World War, vodka is now a popular drink in Western Europe. It is distilled with such a high degree of alcohol that it is practically tasteless and forms a neutral basis for mixed drinks. In the USSR and Poland the preferred form of vodka is distilled from potatoes.

Voice and Speech. Voice occurs when the vocal cords vibrate in such a way that sound waves are produced. This air stream passes from the glottis up through the throat (pharynx), mouth (oral cavity), and nasal cavities, which together constitute the supraglottic resonators. It is these resonators which modify the basic laryngeal note giving to each voice its individual tone or quality. The laryngeal vibration determines the pitch (frequency) and loudness (intensity). The term 'voice' generally encompasses both laryngeal phonation and resonance, though in a more restricted phonetic usage it may imply only the former.

Speech involves further highly detailed modification of the air stream by the organs of articulation, thus imparting to the sound the recognisable characteristics of vowels and consonants. The organs of articulation, principally the tongue, palate, lips and teeth, are used in such a way that the air stream is partially or completely obstructed in the case of consonant articulation, but remains unobstructed for the production of vowels. The latter are essentially voiced sounds, whereas consonants may or may not involve the vibration of the vocal cords.

The usual categories of the singing voice are, from high to low, soprano, mezzo-soprano, and contralto for women and tenor, baritone and bass for men. Boys have a soprano voice, and many men have a counter-tenor or alto range (falsetto) in addition to the normal range. The general quality of tone and the pitch range indicate the category to which a voice may belong. A female voice is approximately one octave higher than its male counterpart. Sensitivity of ear is of utmost importance to a singer, since an ability to produce the desired note depends upon mental perception of the sound rather than a direct control over the frequency at which the vocal cords vibrate.

Voile, a light-weight woven fabric of cotton, wool or silk, with a fine, open mesh.

Vojvodina, autonomous province of Serbia, Yugoslavia, lying north of the rivers Danube and Drava. Prior to the First World War it formed part of a Hungarian district established in 1849 as a concession to Serbian nationalism. The province is one of the chief agricultural regions of the country. The principal towns are Novi Sad (the capital), Subotica and Zrenjanin. Area 21,506 km²; population (1971) 1,950,000.

Volapük, see INTERNATIONAL LANGUAGE.

Volaterrae, called by the Etruscans Velathri, one of the 12 cities of the Etruscan Confederation. Its dominions extended eastwards to Arretium, westward to the Mediterranean, and southward to its colony Populonia. The modern town, Volterra, contains interesting Etruscan remains.

Volcano, a vent in the Earth's crust through which the various products of magma reach the atmosphere. The type of volcanic activity, and therefore the form of the volcano, depends upon the composition of the magma and the stage which the eruption has reached. Acid magma and lava is very viscous and results in explosive activity, such as that of the volcano Stromboli. Such activity produces large quantities of broken rock, both solidified lava and country rock, brought up from depth as the magma travels upwards to the surface. The broken material (pyroclastic rocks) forms a steep-sided cone surrounding the vent. During periods of relative calm lava may flow from the vent, breaching the crater wall and flowing down the sides of the volcano.

Basic (basaltic) magma and lava is relatively fluid and degasses freely as it ascends to the surface, causing little explosive activity—for

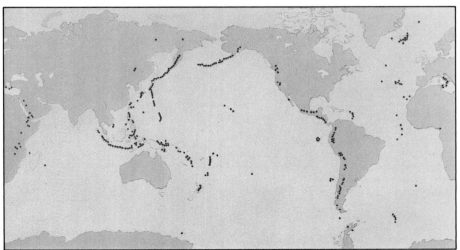

Volcano. *The incidence of volcanic activity is related to regions of geotectonic movement.*

example, the Hawaiian volcanoes. Basic volcanoes are predominantly lava producers with little pyroclastic material developed; consequently, the volcanoes tend to be dome shaped rather than conical. Lava is produced in great quantity, and basic volcanoes may be of enormous size.

The activity of a volcano or a volcanic area is usually periodic, with eruptions and periods of quiescence alternating over perhaps a million years. Most of the world's volcanic activity takes place deep under the oceans along the lines of the mid-ocean ridges, and along crustal plate margins as in the Circum-Pacific Belt, the so-called 'Ring of Fire.'

Vole, various species of rodents in the family Cricetidae which also includes hamsters and lemmings. The water vole (*Arvicola amphibius*) is about 30 cm long including the tail. Its fur is thick and shining, reddish-brown above and yellowish-grey beneath. Its feet are not webbed, although it takes readily to water. It feeds chiefly on the stalks of aquatic plants, and helps to keep watercourses clear. It is often incorrectly called a water rat. The field vole (*Microtus agrestis*) occasionally occurs in swarms, heavily damaging crops.

Volga (ancient *Rha*), longest river (3530 km) and one of the chief waterways of Europe. It lies entirely in the RSFSR, USSR, rising in the Valdai Hills, north-west of Moscow, and flowing roughly east to Kazan, and then south in a big curve near Kuibyshev and into the Caspian Sea, where it forms a large delta (120 km wide). Typical of the Volga is a low left bank and high right bank, especially between Gorki and Volgograd. It is free from ice for 200 days a year (near Astrakhan 260 days), and is largely fed by water from melting snow, therefore having high and long spring floods. Its chief tributaries are the Kama on the left and the Oka on the right, both longer than the Rhine. Total drainage area 1,360,000 km². The river is navigable almost throughout its course, except for the largest vessels, and has about 200 tributaries; the total length of the waterways is some 574,000 km (including temporary watercourses). The Volga and its tributaries carry two-thirds of the goods and over half of the passengers transported on internal waterways of the USSR. The main goods transported are timber, oil, mineral building materials, grain and salt. The chief ports on the river are Gorki, Kazan, Kuibyshev, Volgograd, Astrakhan, Saratov, Yaroslavl and Rybinsk. Artificial waterways connect the Volga with the Baltic Sea (Volga-Baltic Waterway) and the White Sea, (White Sea–Baltic Canal), the Don (Volga–Don Canal), and Moscow (Moscow Canal). The Kuibyshev, Volgograd, Saratov, Gorki and other large hydroelectric stations on the river make it one of the main sources of the country's power supply.

Volga–Baltic Waterway, artificial waterway connecting the River Volga with the Baltic via the Rybinsk Reservoir, lakes Onega and Ladoga, a number of small rivers, and connecting canals. It was built in 1810 as the Mariinskiy Waterway; after a reconstruction completed in 1964 it received its present title. It can take vessels of up to 5000 t capacity and is 368 km long.

Volga–Don Canal, artificial waterway connecting the Volga near Volgograd with the Don. It was built, 1948–52, largely by forced labour. Length 101 km; there are 13 locks, the first nine of which raise ships 88 m.

Volgograd (until 1925, *Tsaritsyn*; 1925–61, *Stalingrad*), capital city, economic and cultural centre of Volgograd *oblast*, USSR, extending for over 70 km along the right bank of the Volga. It is one of the main industrial and transport centres of the Volga region with large engineering (tractors, river vessels), iron and steel, timber, chemical, food and light industries; it is a major river port at one end of the Volga–Don Canal, and has five railway lines. It has been a major centre of timber trading and for the transhipment of Baku oil since 1862; its industrial development dates from 1875. Population (1980) 939,000.

See also SECOND WORLD WAR.

Volleyball, a six-a-side court game having affinities with badminton and lawn tennis, invented in the USA in 1895. The game consists in banging the ball over a net (height 2·43 m for men; 2·24 m for women) with the hands, the aim being to force the ball on to the ground in the opponents' court or to induce them to hit into the net or out of play. Only the serving side scores, service changing as soon as the serving side makes an error or commits a fault. The first team to reach 15 points wins. The six players of each team are ranged three at the net, three at the rear of their court, the right back serving. Each team is allowed three successive hits, but no player may hit twice consecutively, hold on to or throw the ball, touch the net, reach into his opponents' court, or strike the ball from below knee level. The court is 18 m by 9 m, and the ball about the size of a football.

World championships were instituted in 1949. The sport was introduced to the Olympic Games in 1964.

Volsci, an Italian people from east Latium, akin to the Oscans and Umbrians, living on both sides of the Liris down to the Tyrrhenian Sea. They were at war with Rome in the 5th and 4th centuries BC, but were subdued in 338 and enjoyed Roman citizenship by 304.

Volt, practical and SI unit of electromotive force (e.m.f.) or potential difference, so called after Alessandro Volta. Voltage is unity when a current of 1 ampere dissipates a power of 1 watt.

See also UNITS, ELECTRICAL; METROLOGY.

Volta, Alessandro Giuseppe Antonio Anastasio, Count (1745–1827), Italian physicist. He invented the electrophorus, the electrical condenser (1782), and the hydrogen lamp (1777). He studied Galvani's work on muscular movements induced in frogs and concluded in 1793 that they were caused by electricity generated by the contact of dissimilar metals. This interpretation was disputed until Volta built his first 'pile'—a battery made from layers of metal plates—in 1799. The SI unit of electric potential difference $(1 \, J \, A^{-1} \, s^{-1})$ is named the volt in his honour.

Volta, major river basin in Ghana, West Africa. The headwaters (White Volta, Red Volta and Black Volta) rise in the interior uplands of the Republic of Upper Volta, uniting to flow the length of the Republic of Ghana to reach the Gulf of Guinea 75 km east of Accra. The Volta Dam at Akasombo, 60 m high, impounds a vast lake more than 400 km in length and covering 8000 km² of land, thus changing fundamentally the internal geography of Ghana. Length 1600 km (including Volta Lake).

Volta Redonda, town in the state of Rio de Janeiro, Brazil. This new steel city stands on a broad bend (hence its name) of the Rio Paraiba, an an altitude of 554 m, 112 km along the railway from Rio to São Paulo. Population 155,000.

Voltaire, pseudonym of Jean François Marie Arouet (1694–1778), French sceptic, dramatist and historian. Voltaire, as writer, philosopher, scientist, moralist and historian personified in many ways the Age of Enlightenment. By the age of 18 his literary abilities had gained him entrance into the most brilliant intellectual circles. In 1715 he was banished and, on his return in 1717, imprisoned for writing a scurrilous lampoon on the regent. He had already written the tragedy Œdipe, and on his release in 1718 it was performed with brilliant success. In 1725, he was exiled to England, where he became versed in English politics, literature and philosophy. He returned to Paris in 1729, but in 1734, threatened with arrest for his *Lettres philosophiques*, retired to Cirey, where his writings included the *Traité de metaphysique* and part of *Le Siècle de Louis XIV*. Meanwhile, he had become the intimate correspondent of Frederick the Great (Voltaire was a voluminous letter-writer) and visited Frederick at Berlin, 1750–53. Later he settled at Geneva and then at nearby Ferney where he dominated the 'philosophic' movement. Works of this period include *Candide*, 1759, a novel; the *Dictionnaire Philosophique*, 1764; and the *Traité de la tolérance*, 1763.

Voltaire's contemporary fame rested chiefly on his verse tragedies; later the stories and histories were given more consideration. He sought to treat history scientifically as the story of the human mind and the advance of civilisation. He was an enemy of theocracy and the coercive power of the Church. He was a deist, and believed in a social morality common to all men in all ages. He developed a theory of a conscience implanted by God, and came to a belief in a God who is goodness itself, standing in some direct relationship to man. To the gift of a unique artistry in words Voltaire added industry and daring, and a life of service to mankind in the ideals of tolerance, justice and freedom.

Voltmeter, instrument for measuring voltage.

See also ELECTRIC METERS.

Volturno, river of Italy, rising in the central Apennines and flowing past Capua into the Tyrrhenian Sea 35 km north-west of Naples. Its main tributary is the Calore.

Völuspá (The Sybil's Prophecy), a cosmological poem preserved in the Edda, and believed to have been composed shortly before 1000, most probably in Iceland. It covers the whole history of the pagan Norse cosmos from its creation to the *Ragnarök* (Doom of the Gods) and beyond.

Volvox, a genus of small, colonial, chlorophyll-containing, flagellate Protozoa, common in ponds, and resembling green algae.

VORTIGERN

Botanists place the genus in Chlorophyta.

Vomiting, the reflex act by which the contents of the stomach are violently ejected up through the oesophagus and out of the mouth. It is usually caused by the presence of irritating substances in the stomach, and under such circumstances is a protective effort of the organism. It may, however, be produced by a variety of different causes: by certain drugs; by diseases such as peritonitis, gastric ulcer, kidney disease, liver disease or intestinal obstruction; by certain visual, olfactory or other sensations; by reflex nervous stimuli; or by hormonal changes as in the 'morning sickness' of pregnancy. The treatment of vomiting consists of removing the cause, if possible, and administration of drugs which exert a sedative action on the stomach and reduce the irritability of the 'vomiting centre' in the brain.

Vondel, Joost van den (1587–1679), Dutch poet and dramatist. He was deeply religious and became a Roman Catholic in 1641. He expressed his convictions with fearless integrity in polemical verse on religious and political matters, and selected the themes of his tragedies because of their moral relevance. The finest of these, *Joseph in Dothan*, 1640; *Lucifer*, 1654; *Jeptha*, 1659; and *Adam in Ballingschap*, 1664, are, like most of his drama, biblical. He also translated a number of classical tragedies.

Vonnegut, Kurt (1922–), US novelist, noted for the black humour with which he views contemporary society, and for his science fiction techniques. His best-known work, *Slaughterhouse Five*, 1969, is based on his own experience as a prisoner-of-war during the fire bombing of Dresden in 1945. Other books include *Breakfast of Champions*, 1973, and *Slapstick*, 1976.

Von Neumann, John (1903–57), US mathematician. He contributed to many areas of both pure and applied mathematics including mathematical logic, quantum theory, partial differential equations and hydrodynamics. In 1928 he proved the 'minimax theorem' in the theory of games and, in collaboration with Oskar Morgenstern, developed the theory of games and its applications to economics. In hydrodynamics he was an expert on shock and detonation waves and joined the Manhattan Project building the atomic bomb in 1943. The work on hydrodynamics also gave him an interest in improving methods of computation (he had a remarkable ability to perform complex calculations mentally at lightning speed) and from 1945 directed the electronic computer project at the Institute for Advanced Study, Princeton. Von Neumann made a crucial contribution to computer design by analysing a computer's functions in terms of logical instead of arithmetical operations. At the time of his death he was working on the structure of human thought processes. His publications include *Theory of Games and Economic Behaviour*; *Mathematical Foundations of Quantum Mechanics*; and *The Computer and the Brain*.
See also GAMES, THEORY OF.

Von Sternberg, Joseph (1894–1969), Austrian film director, lived mainly in the USA from 1901. One of the cinema's most elegant pictorial stylists between 1925 and 1935, his experimental *The Salvation Hunters*, 1925, gained him notice, while *Underworld*, 1927, which inaugurated the gangster genre, and *The Docks of New York*, 1928, proved his mastery of atmospheric low-life milieux. In 1930 he made *The Blue Angel* in Germany, discovering Marlene Dietrich, whom he proceeded to transform into one of the screen's great temptresses in *Morocco*, 1930; *Dishonoured*, 1931; *Shanghai Express*, 1932; *The Blonde Venus*, 1932; *The Scarlet Empress*, 1934; and *The Devil is a Woman*, 1935. His later career was beset by clashes with producers, but he published a notable autobiography, *Fun in a Chinese Laundry*, 1965.

Voodoo, from Vodun, the name of a spirit in Dahomey Fon folk belief; religion practised by the Negro population of some West Indian islands, especially Haiti. It is a mixture of African and Roman Catholic belief and practice, the most important element being belief in *loa*, spirits or lesser gods, who possess the worshippers. The popular reputation of voodoo for 'black magic' is unjustified, though animal sacrifice and other features equated with black magic do occur.

Voortrekkers, name given to the groups comprising the Great Trek or Boer migration from Cape Colony and Natal between 1834 and 1838, during which time one in ten of the colony's population took part in an exodus by way of an organised attempt to seek a country away from the British in which they might develop along their own lines.
The Great Trek was in fact a piecemeal longdrawn-out movement. The trekkers moved across the drifts of the middle Orange River, and over the open country on each side of the Vaal. By the close of 1837, after the defeat of the Matabele, the high veld had fallen to the Voortrekkers by right of conquest. Subsequently Andries Pretorius, greatest of the Boer leaders, in December 1838 gained a decisive victory against the Zulu army at Blood River. In 1836 the only European settlement south of the Orange River had been Cape Colony; by 1848 Natal, the Orange Free State and the Transvaal were established as under European control.

Voronezh, capital city, economic and cultural centre of the central black earth region including Voronezh *oblast*, USSR, situated north-east of Kharkov. It has important engineering (agricultural and food industry equipment, excavators, diesel motors, etc), chemical (synthetic rubber, pharmaceuticals), building and food industries, and is an important railway junction. Known from 1177, the fortress of Voronezh was founded in 1586 as a Muscovite frontier post against the Tatars. It has been an important commercial and cultural centre since the 1830s. Population (1980) 796,000.

Voroshilov, Kliment Efremovich (1881–1969), Soviet Communist. After the seizure of power by the Bolsheviks in October 1917 he helped to set up the *cheka*. During the Civil War he distinguished himself both as a military and a political leader, and in 1921 became a member of the Communist Party's Central Committee. In the inner-party struggle after Lenin's death he took Stalin's side and became commissar for war and the navy in 1925 and member of the Party's Politburo in 1926; marshal of the Soviet Union in 1935. In 1940 he was appointed deputy prime minister. During the Second World War he was a member of the State defence committee. After Stalin's death he became titular head of the Soviet state until he retired in 1960. Linked by Krushchev with the 'Anti-Party Group' of Malenkov, Molotov and Kaganovich, he lost his membership of the Central Committee between 1961 and 1966.

Vorster, Balthazar Johannes (1916–), South African politician. He was a member of the Ossewabrandwag during the Second World War and was subsequently elected to the Nationalist party in 1953. He was deputy minister of education, 1958, and minister of justice, 1961. During his term as minister of justice Vorster instituted the law by which the South African police were empowered to arrest persons suspected of subversion for successive periods of 90 days without trial. On Verwoerd's assassination Vorster was elected prime minister, September 1966, promising to adhere even more strictly to the South African apartheid policy. He became president of South Africa in 1978 but was forced to resign in 1979.

Vortex, motion in a fluid in which the individual particles have a circular or rotatory motion. Vertex motion is represented by a straight-line vector perpendicular to the plane of rotation, and of length proportional to the vorticity. It can be shown that such a line or filament cannot start or end in the interior of the fluid, and that a vortex always consists of the same elements of liquid.
See also HYDRODYNAMICS.

Vorticism. At the Hippodrome, *1923, by William Roberts.*

Vorticism, exclusively English art and literary movement (and the only one to have its own manifesto) initiated c.1912 by Wyndham Lewis, who combined elements from Cubism and Futurism and sought a new relationship between art and industrial methods. Lewis and the poet Ezra Pound founded *Blast*, the magazine of the movement. Other artists connected with the movement were William Roberts, David Bomberg, C. R. W. Nevinson, Edward Wadsworth, and the sculptors Jacob Epstein and Henri Gaudier-Brzeska.
See also LONDON GROUP, THE.

Vortigern, or Wyrtgeorn (fl. 450), British king who, according to Gildas, invited Hengist and Horsa to come to England to help him against the Picts and Scots. They quarrelled with Vortigern and overran Kent.

Vosges, frontier *département* in eastern France, shut in to the east by the Vosges mountains. The rivers Moselle and Meuse have the largest drainage areas of any rivers in the region. Oats, wheat and the vine are cultivated, and cheese-making and cattle-grazing are important. Textile goods are the chief manufactures. The principal towns are Epinal (the capital), St-Dié and Neufchâteau. Area 7424 km²; population (1975) 397,300.

Voussoir, one of the stones (usually wedge-shaped) of an arch.

Voysey, Charles Francis Annesley (1857–1941), British architect and decorative designer. He set up practice in 1882 and was soon successful as a designer of wallpaper and textiles, his work showing the influence of Morris and Mackmurdo. From 1888 to c.1914 he had an international reputation as a designer of houses of extreme simplicity, in contrast to mid-Victorian pretentiousness. These included several near Windermere, and his own charming home, 'The Orchard', in Hertfordshire. He designed his houses in minute detail, including the furniture, fireplaces, door handles, etc.

Vuillard, Edouard (1868–1940), French painter, a life-long friend of Bonnard, with whom his work offers a parallel. Noted for his intimate paintings of domestic interiors with figures, he also produced brilliant colour lithographs. A number of decorative works included those for the Palais des Nations, Geneva, 1938.

Vulcan (Latin *Vulcanus*), Roman god of fire, called also Mulciber (averter of fire). An area with altar (called Vulcanale) was dedicated to him on the north side of the Forum.

Vulcanisation, see RUBBER.

Vulgate (Latin *Vulgata,* in common use), name sometimes given to the Septuagint, but principally to the Latin version of the Bible prepared by St Jerome in the latter part of the 4th century. He revised the New Testament at the invitation of Pope Damascus, and this part of the Vulgate was little more than a revision of the existing text; the Old Testament version was an independent translation from the Hebrew into Latin. It was declared authentic by the Council of Trent for use in the Roman Church. The decision of Trent did not concern critical but doctrinal accuracy, guaranteeing the conformity of the Vulgate with the original texts as well as its authority in matters of faith and morals.

Vulture. *The Griffon vulture,* Gyps fulvus.

Vulture, a bird of prey in order Falconiformes, with a strong, hooked beak. It eats carrion, which it discovers by its abnormally keen sense of sight and smell. The name is applied to two separate groups, the Old World vultures in the family Accipitridae and the New World vultures in the family Cathartidae. The former are large birds with a wingspan of 1·5 to almost 3·7 m, mostly with black or brown plumage. Most of them are devoid of feathers on their heads and necks. All but one feed on carrion, the exception being the palm-nut vulture, *Gypohierax angolensis,* which feeds mainly on the fruit of the oil palm, as well as fish and offal on the shore. Other examples include the Egyptian vulture, *Neophron percnopterus,* found throughout Europe, Asia and Africa and the griffon vulture, *Gyps fulvus.* The New World vultures include the king vulture, *Sarcoramphus papa,* the turkey vulture, *Cathartes aura,* and the condors.

Vyborg (Finnish *Viipuri*; Swedish *Viborg*), city in the Leningrad *oblast* of the northwest RSFSR, USSR, on the Gulf of Finland, 129 km north-west of Leningrad. It is an important industrial (electrical instruments, fishing equipment) and transport centre (seaport, five railway lines). It became Russian in 1710 (provincial capital), but was included in Finland in 1811. It was ceded to the USSR in 1940 (included in the Karelo-Finnish Republic), but came under Finnish occupation from 1941 to 1944. Population (1970) 65,000.

Vyshinski, Andrei Yanuar'yevich (1883–1954), Soviet lawyer and politician of Polish descent. From 1928 to 1931 he was head of the department of higher education at the commissariat of education. In 1931 he became procurator of the Russian Federal Republic, in 1935 of the USSR, and in 1939 deputy chairman of the council of people's commissars. Vyshinski was the most prominent exponent of Stalinism in legal theory and practice. He played a leading rôle in the Moscow show trials of 1928–38. From 1940 to 1949 and again 1953–55 he was deputy minister of foreign affairs under Molotov, and from 1949 to 1953 minister.

W

W, twenty-third letter of the English alphabet. As a letter it appeared only in the 11th century. Its phonetic value in English is that of a 'consonantal *u*'. The North Semitic *waw*, and its descendant the Greek *digamma* (ƒ), probably had a similar phonetic value to that of the English *w*, as possibly did the Latin *v*. The Germans have no sound like English *w* and employ the letter *w* for the sound written in English as *v*. In English, the letter *w* is either a semi-vowel (as in *war*, *wine*), or part of a vowel digraph (as in *law*, *few*). In Welsh names it is generally a vowel (*Betws-y-Coed* or *Braich-y-pwll*).

See also ALPHABET.

Waals, Johannes Diederik van der (1837–1923), Dutch physicist. He was the first person to try to modify the 'ideal-gas' equation, $pV = RT$, so that it would account for the behaviour of real gases. In 1881 he deduced the van der Waals equation:

$$(p + a/V^2)(V - b) = RT,$$

where p is pressure, T thermodynamic temperature, V molar volume, R the gas constant ($\simeq 8·31434\,\mathrm{J\,K^{-1}\,mol^{-1}}$) and a and b are constants. He was awarded the Nobel Prize for physics in 1910.

Wace, Robert (c.1100–c.1174), Anglo-Norman poet. His two most important works are his historical poems, written mostly in octosyllabic verse. The first is the *Roman de Brut*, a history of the Britons, based on Geoffrey of Monmouth's *Historia Regum Britanniae*; the second is the *Roman de Rou*, based on Dudo of St Quentin and William of Jumièges. Wace's influence on medieval Arthurian romance was immense.

Wade, Virginia (1945–), English tennis player. She was ranked in the world top-ten women players continuously from 1967 until 1979. In 1977, she set a firm seal on a brilliant career by winning the Wimbledon title in the year of the Wimbledon Centenary and Queen Elizabeth II's silver jubilee. She had previously held the US title in 1968 and the Australian title in 1972. She also holds the record for the most appearances in both the Wightman Cup and Federation Cup competitions. In 1982 she became the first woman to be elected to the All-England Committee.

Wad Medani, town of Blue Nile province, Sudan, which owes its growth to the Geizira irrigation scheme; it is the scheme's research headquarters some 160km south-east of Khartoum. Population (1973) 106,776.

Wadi (Arabic) or arroyo (Spanish), a desert ravine or valley through which water flows only after rare floods. They do not always reflect the current climatic regime; thus the wadi drainage in the Ahaggar massif in the Sahara is too complex to be a response to present runoff. It is therefore assumed to have been created during a much wetter climate in the past.

Wadi Halfa, town in Northern Province, Sudan. It is the frontier town and lies on the shore of a southern extension of Lake Nasser. The Sudan railway across the Nubian Desert from Wadi Halfa to Abu Hamad was begun in 1897; it now extends, via Atbara, to El Obeid. Population (1965) 11,000.

Wading-bird, name given to any long-legged bird, such as the heron and curlew, that obtains its food by wading in water.

Wadsworth, Edward Alexander (1889–1949), British artist. In 1913–14 he made a remarkable series of semi-abstract woodcuts. He became ARA in 1943. He was primarily a painter of inanimate objects; his paintings of nautical subjects are outstanding.

Wages, price of labour, or that part of wealth which is given in exchange for labour. The ultimate source of wages, as of profits, is the value of that which capital and labour jointly produce, but in practice wages are paid in the first instance out of capital. Competition between employers tends to raise wages, between workers, to lower them. The results of competition are checked by: (1) agreements between employers and trade unions, and (2) minimum wage legislation.

Wagga Wagga, town of New South Wales, Australia, on the Murrumbidgee river, midway between Sydney and Melbourne. It is the centre of a rich agricultural and pastoral region. Population (1976) 35,600.

Wagner, Richard (1813–83), German composer, dramatist and essayist. He studied music at the Thomasschule in Leipzig. In 1834 he became conductor of the opera at Magdeburg. By then he had composed the opera *Die Feen*; *Das Liebesverbot* followed in 1836. He lived in Paris in poverty from 1839 until 1842, when *Rienzi* was produced at Dresden, and he was appointed second conductor at the court opera there. *Der fliegende Holländer* (1843) met with less approval. Its concentration on the central couple, its theme of the redemption of man by woman, and its musical economy, reappear in *Tannhäuser* and *Tristan und Isolde*.
The period from 1848 to 1874 saw the gestation of *Der Ring des Nibelungen*, *Tristan und Isolde* and *Die Meistersinger*. *Der Ring* crystallised Wagner's ideals as expounded in his writings (e.g. *Opera and Drama*, 1850–51). As always, he wrote his own text, adapting the kind of ancient saga which he believed was ideal material, with its possibilities of

Wagner with his second wife Cosima, the daughter of Liszt, photographed in 1872.

timeless and universal symbolism. The four parts of *The Ring—Rheingold*, *Die Walküre*, *Siegfried* and *Götterdämmerung*—are unified by *leitmotifs*. In this cycle Wagner replaces the 'number opera' by a continuous symphonic fabric in which a fragmentary vocal line often seems to be fitted into the orchestral texture, and in which no recitative, aria or conventional orchestral accompaniment are discernible. *Der Ring* and his last opera, *Parsifal*, were produced at Bayreuth in 1876 and 1882 respectively, in the theatre Wagner designed for his own works.
Wagner was one of the first to use his works as an expression of himself, for example in Walther (*Die Meistersinger*), the artist with new ideas struggling against the reactionary establishment, or in Tristan, the great lover. He realised Weber's dream of a German national opera, and his music profoundly influenced subsequent western music.

Wagram, village 16 km north-east of Vienna, Austria. Here was fought the battle of Wagram (July 1809), in which Napoleon defeated the Austrians under the Archduke Charles.

Wagtail, *Motacilla*, genus of insectivorous birds in the family Motacillidae, order Passeriformes, related to the pipit.

Wahlenbergia, a genus of annual and perennial herbs in family Campanulaceae, mostly of southern temperate countries. *W. hederacea*, ivy campanula, is a creeping perennial found in wet places in southern and western Europe. *Wahlenbergia* species in New Zealand are known as bluebells.

Wailing Wall, or Western Wall, a portion of the wall which used to surround the Temple in Jerusalem. The Wailing Wall reaches the height of 18 m. The Jews call it the *Kotel Ma'arabi* or "Western Wall', and only by Gentile onlookers has it been associated with 'wailing', because the Jews foregathered here to mourn the destruction of Jerusalem and the Temple. Today, it is used as a sacred site for services by all Jews who visit Israel. Traditional Jews still place slips of paper with petitional prayers between the stones of the Wailing Wall and 13-year-old boys celebrate their *bar mitzvah* (religious coming of age) there.

Wain, John Barrington (1925–), English writer. Wain achieved fame with his first novel, *Hurry on Down*, 1953, which made him a reputation as one of the 'angry young men'. His verse is extremely witty and drily ironic; it includes *A Word Carved on a Sill*, 1956, and *Feng*, 1975. He has also written several critical studies, including *Preliminary Essays*, 1957, and *Samuel Johnson*, 1975. He was Professor of Poetry at Oxford from 1973 until 1978.

Wajda, Andrzej (1926–), Polish film director, best known for his trilogy *A Generation* (1954), *Kanal* (1956) and *Ashes and Diamonds* (1958). Among his many other films are *The Birch Wood* (1971), *Man of Marble* (1976), *Man of Iron* (1981), and *Danton* (1983).

Wake (Old English *wacu*, a watch); or lyke-wake, or lych-wake (Old English *lyc*, a body), ancient observance by which the body of a dead person was watched all night by friends and relatives. Wakes were also observed on the eves of saints' days, and became fairs, as in Lancashire, and at Bradford (where they

were known as tides). Annual holidays are still called 'wakes' in Lancashire. The corpse wake survives in Ireland.

Wakefield, Edward Gibbon (1796–1862), British colonial statesman. He wrote *The Letter from Sydney*, 1829, exposing the evil effects of 'transportation' and roughly sketched a system of colonisation. He formed a colonisation society in 1830, and the bill to make South Australia a British province followed as a result. The scheme failed, but in 1837 he turned his attention to the acquisition of New Zealand as a British colony. Fundamentally his ideas were sound, and the New Zealand settlements achieved prosperity more rapidly than any of their predecessors elsewhere.

Wakefield, city in West Yorkshire, England, on the River Calder. A medieval town of some importance, Wakefield became a prominent centre for the cloth trade in the 16th century. Today the industries of Wakefield include worsted spinning, woollen manufacture, shirt and blouse-making, wire-drawing, coal-mining, and the manufacture of engineering and machine-tool products, chemicals, glass and sheet metal. The offices of the West Yorkshire Metropolitan County Council are here. Population (1981) 60,540.

Wailing Wall. The faithful at prayer.

Walafriedus Strabo, that is, 'squinting Wilfred' (c.808–49), German monk and scholar. He entered the Benedictine order at 15. His best-known works are *De Exordiis et Incrementis quarundam in Observationibus Ecclesiasticus Rerum*, a handbook on matters of archaeological and liturgical interest; *Visio Wettini*, c.830, a poem that foreshadowed Dante's work; *Glossa Ordinaria*, for centuries the most widely-used commentary on the Bible, attributed to him; and *Hortulus*, describing his herb garden.

Walbrzych (German *Waldenburg*), town of Poland, in Wroclaw province, in the foothills of the Sudeten Mountains, 69 km southwest of Wroclaw. It was formerly in Lower Silesia, and is a coal-mining centre. Chemicals, glass and pottery are manufactured and engineering is an important industry. Population (1974) 127,701.

Walburga, Saint, also Walpurgis or Walpurga (c.710–779), sister of Sts Willibald and Winebald. She became a nun at Wimborne, Dorset, England, and followed St Lioba to Germany, becoming abbess of Heidenheim until her death. Her relics were transferred to Eichstädt, where a convent was erected in her honour. Throughout Germany, and in

France, the Netherlands and England, churches were dedicated to her. The feast of Walpurga falls in some German calendars on 1 May.

Walcheren, island in Zeeland province, Netherlands, lying between the east and west Scheldt rivers. The fertile land is protected from the sea by dykes. The chief towns are Middelburg and Flushing.

Waldheim, Kurt (1918–), Austrian statesman. He held office as the fourth secretary-general of the United Nations (1972–81) succeeding U Thant of Burma. After a period as director-general for political affairs in the Austrian Foreign Ministry, Waldheim acted as the permanent representative of Austria to the UN (1964–68). From 1968 to 1970, prior to his second term of office as ambassador and his appointment as secretary-general, he was the Austrian federal minister for foreign affairs.

Wales (Welsh *Cymru*), one of the constituent countries of the United Kingdom forming a great westerly promontory (area 20,766 km²) of Britain, jutting out into the Irish Sea. Wales is bounded on the east by (north to south) the English counties of Cheshire, Shropshire, Hereford and Worcester, and Gloucester. To the north and west lies the Irish Sea, and to the south the Bristol Channel and the Severn estuary. The island of Anglesey is divided from the north-west coast by the Menai Strait. Cardiff is the capital city.

Since April 1974 Wales has been divided into eight geographical counties: Clwyd, Dyfed, Gwent, Gwynedd, Mid Glamorgan, Powys, South Glamorgan and West Glamorgan.

Practically the whole of Wales lies within the Highland zone of Britain; the Cambrian Mountains, lying north-east to south-west, occupy most of the country. The highest mountains are those of the Snowdonia range in the north-west, and Snowdon (1085 m) is the highest mountain in England and Wales. The main rivers are the Wye, Usk, Taff, Neath and Tawe; Vyrnwy and Bala are the two largest lakes.

The total population of Wales at the 1981 census was 2,790,000. They are also predominantly English-speaking. The Welsh language is spoken in central Wales, the north and west. Welsh agriculture employs only 2·6 per cent of the population and is dominantly pastoral in character. Sheep rearing is dominant in the upland core of the country but is combined with, and eventually gives way to, dairying and beef rearing along the larger valleys and in the coastal and border fringes.

The industry of Wales developed on the two coalfields, the larger in the south and the smaller in the north-east. In the south an early metallurgical tradition gave rise to the modern steel industry. There are two major centres: Margam near Port Talbot (where there are bulk ore importing facilities), and Llanwern near Newport. Virtually all the UK tin plate is produced in South Wales. The import of oil has produced associated refineries and petro-chemical industries at Milford Haven and Llandarcy (near Swansea). Owing to the rationalisation of heavy industry and the consequent loss of jobs, a wide range of light industries has been developed.

History. On the conquest of Britain by the Saxons (c.450–600) the Celts were driven back into Cumberland, Wales and Cornwall. Henceforth Wales became the main stronghold of the Celts or Britons. Powerful native princes arose in Wales, and extended and consolidated their dominions. The Welsh people were for a time united under Cadwallon. They made repeated attempts to recover the northern parts of England from the Saxons, but their defeat by Ethelfrith of Northumbria, the Angle king, at the battle of Chester (c.613), severed Strathclyde and all north Britain from Wales. For the next 600 years the struggle was between a king who regarded himself as the champion of the Britons, wearing 'the crown of Arthur', and the princes who were descended from the tribal princes. The country was again united under Rhodri the Great (844–78), who resisted the onslaughts of the Danes, but was defeated and slain by the Mercians. Howel the Good (c.909–49), made himself master of most of Wales, but did homage to King Athelstan of England. He collected and codified an elaborate system of laws. A period of anarchy was followed by the rule of two strong princes, Llewelyn ap Seisillt and his son Griffith (Gruffydd). Llewelyn freed his country from Danish raids. Griffith (1039–63) expelled the Saxons from Gwynedd, conquered south Wales, consolidated his dominions, and made war against England. Eventually the English subdued south Wales and defeated Griffith (1063).

The Norman kings of England made encroachments, in particular placing on the Welsh borders a number of powerful barons who took advantage of the disorganised state of Wales to expand their territories. The next two centuries (roughly, 1066–1282) form an epoch of continual struggle.

The most significant figure in medieval Welsh history is Llewelyn ap Iorwerth (Llewelyn the Great), who reigned from c.1196 to 1240. Married to the daughter of King John, Llewelyn tried to secure for Wales continuing peace by placing it in feudal dependence on the king of England through a treaty which gave away the semblance of Welsh independence while retaining its reality. But Edward I twice invaded Wales, and in 1282 the Welsh king Llewelyn, grandson of Llewelyn the Great, was killed. From this date Wales ceased to have any separate political existence.

The period from 1350 to 1400 was one of disintegration, due mainly to the tyrannies of the great marcher barons. The most formidable rising in Wales against the new order and the barons' tyranny was the national movement associated with the name of Owen Glendower (c.1359–1415). In 1404 Glendower was supreme in Wales, holding his own parliament; but his political ideals vanished with his death, leaving only a vague sense of nationality. The principal results of these risings were the appropriation by Englishmen of all positions of trust, the enactment of severe and unjust laws against the Welsh, and the consequent growth of bitter racial feeling. The Act of Union of 1535 united Wales to England, and by its operation the former was politically assimilated in all respects to the latter. See further under ENGLISH HISTORY; UNITED KINGDOM, *History*.

Language. Welsh (known to its speakers as *Cymraeg*) belongs, together with Breton and the now extinct Cornish, to the Brittonic branch of the Celtic languages.

It is likely that the Welsh language emerged as distinct from the other members of the Brittonic group by the 6th century. The history of the language is divided into the following periods: Early Welsh (pre-8th century); Old Welsh (9th–11th centuries); Middle Welsh (12th–14th centuries); Modern Welsh (15th century onwards).

In Wales, the language has been waning in the face of English for several centuries and in spite of the fact that Welsh is now widely taught in schools, that it is widely used on radio and television, and that the government accepted in 1965 a recommendation that Welsh should have equal validity with English in Wales, the language is still losing ground and there can be little reason for optimism regarding its future. The proportion of the Welsh population recorded as speaking Welsh dropped from 50 per cent in 1901 to 19 per cent in 1981.

Literature. The earliest period of Welsh literature is that of the *Cynfeirdd* or early poets. Much of their work is anonymous, but the major part is associated with the names of Aneirin and Taliesin, poets of the late 6th century, and Llywarch Hen, a dramatic figure in a 9th-century saga.

The next period is that of the *Gogynfeirdd* or the medieval poets, the court poets of the Norman period, chief among whom were

Wales. *Slate quarries in the Snowdonia region of North Wales.*

Gwalchmai, Cynddelw Brydydd Mawr and Prince Hywel ab Owain. This was the period of the bardic schools which elaborated the rules of versification that have now become traditional in Welsh poetry.

The next, or third, period is dominated in the 14th century by the genius of Dafydd ap Gwilym, who wrote in a simpler style than the court poets and developed a new form of metre in his *cywyddau* or lyrical odes. The first eisteddfod was held in the 15th century.

The religious movement was a major influence in the revival of Welsh literature in the 18th century. It had its finest expression in the flashing lyricism of William Williams, known as Williams Pantycelyn (1717–91), although many more fine hymns were written during the Methodist Revival. The rich variety of Welsh poetry in recent years is illustrated by the work of Waldo Williams (1904–71), Alun Llywelyn-Williams, Euros Bowen, Bobi Jones, and Gwyn Thomas.

Wales, Church in, disestablished 31 March 1920, comprises six dioceses: St David's, Llandaff, Bangor, St Asaph, Monmouth, and Swansea and Brecon (a diocese which, with Monmouth, was formed after 1920). The office of Archbishop of Wales is filled by the election of one of the bishops to it. Until the Welsh Church Acts of 1914 and 1919, Wales was included in the province of Canterbury; a Welsh archbishopric was formed on disestablishment. The languages used in services are Welsh and English.

Wales, Prince of, title conferred at discretion by the British sovereign upon his or her eldest son, the conferment sometimes being accompanied or followed by a ceremony of investiture at Caernarvon Castle. Edward (afterwards King Edward II), son and heir apparent of Edward I, was summoned to and sat in Parliament as Prince of Wales; his presentation at Caernarvon is legendary. The earliest documented grantee was Edward II's grandson, Edward the Black Prince, with limitation 'to him and his heirs the kings of England'. Consequently when a Prince of Wales succeeds to the throne his title merges in the Crown and requires a new creation for its separate existence.

Walesa, Lech (1943–), Polish trade union leader. In July 1980 he headed a strike of shipyard workers at Gdansk in Poland. It gained for Poland the right to free strikes and trade unions and the union Solidarity was formed, with Walesa as chairman. With a membership of 10,000,000 out of a workforce of 17,000,000 its powers were immense, and Walesa became a world figure. In 1981 Solidarity was outlawed and Walesa, with 5000 others, imprisoned. He was released nearly a year later and continued his trade union activities but has curtailed them in response to government pressure. In October 1983 he was awarded the Nobel Peace Prize.

Waley, Arthur David, originally Schloss (1889–1966), English poet and translator. He became one of the greatest authorities on Chinese literature, but is chiefly known for his renderings of Chinese lyrics, which are so effective that they deserve to be regarded as poems in their own right. He also translated Japanese classics, including *Tale of Genji*, 1925, and wrote philosophical studies.

Walker, John (1952–), New Zealand middle-distance runner who came to notice in the Commonwealth Games of 1974, when he won the Silver Medal. In 1975 he was the first to break 3 minutes 50 seconds for the mile, with a time of 3 minutes 49·4 seconds. He won the Gold Medal for the 1500 metres in the 1976 Montreal Olympics.

Walker, Peter Edward (1932–), British politician. He was elected Conservative MP in 1961 and entered the Cabinet as secretary of state for the Environment in 1970, a post he held until 1972 when he was appointed secretary of state for Trade and Industry. In 1979 he became minister of Agriculture, Fisheries and Food and in 1983 was made secretary of state for Energy.

Walker Cup, a golf tournament similar in concept to the Ryder Cup, save that it is open only to amateurs and that the traditional teaming of the United States versus Great Britain and Ireland still applies. The trophy was first competed for in 1922, since when the American amateurs have proved just as overwhelmingly superior as their professional Ryder Cup counterparts. A trophy for women amateurs, known as the Curtis Cup (after former US Amateur Champion Margaret Curtis), is also played bi-annually along Walker and Ryder Cup lines and again the Americans are dominant.

See also, RYDER CUP.

Walking (sport) is defined as 'progression by steps so taken that unbroken contact with the ground is maintained'. In recent years, track walking has largely given way to road walking mainly over distances of 20 and 50km. The sport is included in the Olympic Games.

Wall, vertical structure forming the perimeter of a building, normally expected to prevent passage of water, be windproof, offer resistance to fire, transmission of sound, and provide thermal insulation. In traditional construction, walls are used to carry roof and floor loads; in frame construction they do not have this function.

Wall Pennywort, see PENNYWORT.

Wall Street, street of New York City, and its financial centre. It is a narrow thoroughfare seven blocks long which runs along the site of the town wall of the Dutch New Amsterdam. In Wall Street and the skyscraper office blocks in the immediate proximity are located most of the great banks, trust companies, insurance corporations and other financial institutions of New York.

Wallaby, medium-sized members of the kangaroo family, Macropodidae, order Marsupialia, native to Australia. There are 11 species of the genus *Wallabia*, which resemble the kangaroo, but are smaller. There are about 13 other wallaby species, some of which live in Tasmania, New Guinea and a few other islands near Australia.

Wallace, Alfred Russel (1823–1913), British naturalist. In 1848 Wallace and H. W. Bates set out for the Amazon, but separated later. From 1854 to 1862 Wallace was in the Malay Archipelago; here he established the Wallace Line, zoologically separating Lombok and Celebes from Bali and Borneo. His own work and the reading of Malthus's *Essay on Population* led him to the idea of the 'survival of the fittest', as a correlation of natural selection, and his own formulation of the law that every species originates in the same locality as a pre-existing closely allied species. He wrote immediately to Darwin, who, noting the coincidence of views, communicated with Sir C. Lyell and Sir Joseph Hooker. As a result a joint paper was read, containing Darwin's views, to the Linnaean Society in 1858. Wallace's *Contributions to the Theory of Natural Selection* appeared in 1870, and contained his views on evolution, differing in certain aspects from Darwin.

Wallace, Edgar (1875–1932), English novelist and playwright. He was in the army in South Africa during the war of 1899 to 1902. On leaving the army he decided to become a journalist and returned to South Africa as war correspondent for Reuter's agency. His first story was *The Four Just Men*, 1905. After this Wallace wrote over 175 novels in 20 years. He found his true medium in 'thrillers'. Other titles are *Sanders of the River*, 1911; and *The Crimson Circle*, 1922.

Wallace, George Corley (1919–). US politician. He was elected Democratic governor of Alabama in 1962 and served until 1966, being re-elected in 1970 and again in 1975. He was the victim of an assassination attempt as he campaigned for the Democratic presidential nomination in 1972, which left him paralysed from the waist down. He was returned as governor of Alabama in 1982 for an unprecedented fourth time.

Wallace, Lewis (1827–1905), US diplomat and novelist. From 1881 to 1885 he was US minister to Turkey. His greatest success as a writer was with *Ben Hur*, 1880, a novel about the early days of Christianity.

Wallace, Sir William (c.1272–1305), Scottish patriot. He first took up arms against the English in 1297 after Edward I had taken possession of Scotland. The English barons and clergy were in revolt against Edward I, and Wallace seized his opportunity, organised the Scottish insurgents in the name of King John de Baliol, and became guardian of Scotland. He drove the English out of Perth, Stirling and Lanark shires, and went on to ravage Northumberland, Westmorland and Cumberland. He was defeated by Edward I at Falkirk in 1298 and resigned the guardianship of Scotland, but continued waging guerrilla war. He was declared an outlaw by Edward I in 1304, and was captured by treachery at Glasgow and brought to London, tried, and executed in 1305.

Wallachia, former province of Romania, lying between the Carpathians and the River Danube, the Black Sea and Yugoslavia. Wallachia was one of the two Danubian principalities (the other being Moldavia), on which the kingdom of Romania was instituted under the Treaty of Paris, 1856. Wallachia is the principal agricultural area of the country. Area 77,700 km².

Wallasey, town in Merseyside Metropolitan County, England, on the south-west bank of the Mersey estuary, opposite Liverpool. Wallasey serves as a suburb for Liverpool and Birkenhead. Population (1981) 90,057.

Wallenstein, Albrecht Eusebius Wenzel von (1583–1634), Duke of Friedland, German soldier. On the outbreak of the Bohemian revolt he obtained the command of an army, defeated Count Mansfeld, and conquered a great stretch of country. He was created duke of Mecklenburg by the Emperor Ferdinand II. Dismissed in 1630 on the insistence of the German princes, he was recalled to combat Gustavus Adolphus and succeeded in curbing the Swedes, though he was defeated at Lützen. The emperor had decided that Wallenstein had become too powerful for Hapsburg safety. He was charged with treachery, and murdered.

Waller, Edmund (1606–87), English poet and politician. He was MP successively for Ilchester, Chipping Wycombe and Amersham, and in 1640 sat in the Long Parliament. Waller was at heart a Royalist, and having been caught plotting to seize London for Charles I, was arrested and expelled from the House in 1643. He was a prisoner in the Tower (1643–44), but his sentence of death was commuted to a heavy fine and banishment. He was, however, pardoned in 1651 by Cromwell's influence, and published laudatory verses upon him in 1655. But he also wrote poems of rejoicing on Cromwell's death (1658), and in 1660 published *To the King, upon his Majesty's Happy Return*. He is now chiefly known for the lyrics to 'Sacharissa', identified with Lady Dorothy Sidney.

Waller, Thomas ('Fats') (1904–43), American jazz composer, pianist and organist. He played the organ at church when he was ten, and three years later he played a theatre organ in Harlem. Waller, with others in the Harlem 'school', developed from ragtime a freer style known as 'stride' piano playing. This demanded extensive use of the left hand. He recorded prolifically as accompanist, as soloist on piano and organ, and with his own group. He appeared in films, combining his talents as jazzman and comedian to great effect. Best known compositions include *Ain't Misbehavin'* and *Honeysuckle Rose*.

Wallflower, *Cheiranthus cheiri*, a fragrant cruciferous perennial plant, often grown in gardens. The orange or yellow Siberian wallflower is *Cheiranthus × allionii*.

Walling, Curtain, a system of external walling for framed buildings, in the form of a lightweight skin attached outside the frame so that it is uninterrupted by columns, beams or floor slabs.

Wallis and Futuna, an Overseas Territory of France comprising two groups of islands in the central Pacific, north-east of Fiji and west of Samoa. The Wallis archipelago (area 96 km²) was named after the English navigator Samuel Wallis who visited it in 1767; the Îles de Horn (area 159 km²) were named by their discoverer, Jakob Le Maire of Holland, after the Dutch city of Hoorn. The Îles de Horn have two main islands, Futuna and the uninhabited Alofi. The main island of the Wallis archipelago is Uvea; the capital of the Territory is Mata-Utu on Uvea. The islands have been French since 1842, and gained the status of a Territory in 1961. They are hot and humid, and crops include yams, taro, some copra and timber. The inhabitants are Polynesian. Population (1976) 9192.

Wallis, Sir Barnes Neville (1887–1979), British aeronautical engineer and inventor. In the 1920s and 1930s he worked for Rolls Royce, and designed the airship R100. During the Second World War he invented the bouncing bomb, which was used to destroy the Ruhr dams in 1943, and designed the Wellington bomber. He later invented the swing-wing aircraft, and also worked on Concorde.

Walloon, Romance dialect spoken in eastern Belgium, in the provinces of Liège, Luxembourg, Namur, Hainaut and part of Brabant. The dialect differs markedly from standard French and, in the view of some philologists, should be considered as a distinct language.

Walnut, *Juglans*, a genus of deciduous trees belonging to the family Juglandaceae, growing mainly in northern temperate regions. *J. regia*, the common walnut of eastern Europe, provides fine timber for cabinet-making, and edible nuts yielding oil. *J. nigra*, the black walnut of eastern America, is a valuable timber species; *J. cathayensis* is the Chinese walnut; and *J. cinerea* is the butternut of North America. The walnut fruit has crisp flesh, surrounded by a hard shell enclosed in a green husk.

Walpole, Horace, 4th Earl of Orford (1717–97), English author and letter-writer, son of Robert Walpole. He visited France and Italy with the poet Thomas Gray. He entered Parliament in 1741, holding a seat continuously up to 1768. Walpole lived at Strawberry Hill, Twickenham, from 1747. This he converted into 'a little Gothic castle' and his house became the centre of fashionable learning in England. He set up a printing press there and published much of his own, and his friends', work, including his *Castle of Otranto*, 1765, (published under a pseudonym), which established the vogue of the 'terror novel'. His memoirs include: *Reminiscences*, 1805, and *Journal of 1771–83*, 1859, but his greatest work was his *Letters*, which show something of the polish and refinement of Madame de Sévigné and the epigrammatic skill of Voltaire.

Walpole, Sir Hugh Seymour (1884–1941), English novelist. His first novel, *The Wooden Horse*, appeared in 1909, and he established himself in Chelsea as a writer. His first major success was *Fortitude*, 1913. Walpole's later writing is dominated by the massive and gorgeously tapestried historical work, the tetralogy of *Rogue Herries*, 1930; *Judith Paris*, 1931; *The Fortress*, 1932; and *Vanessa*, 1933, which form his 'Lakeland saga', a product of the modern romantic revival and one which endowed historical fiction with a new life. An

Robert Walpole. A portrait by Kneller, 1710–15.

able critic, he wrote studies of Conrad, 1916, and Trollope, 1928.

Walpole, Robert, 1st Earl of Orford (1676–1745), English statesman. A Whig by persuasion and upbringing, he entered Parliament in 1701 as MP for Castle Rising, and in the next Parliament, the first of the reign of Queen Anne, for Lynn. He quickly distinguished himself but when the Tories came to power in 1710 he was accused of peculation, and was dismissed from his office and sent to the Tower. The Protestant succession, however, restored him to favour, and in 1715 he became chancellor of the Exchequer. He succeeded Sunderland at the Treasury (1721–40) but his position was not undisputed until Sunderland's sudden death (1722). Walpole's handling of the South Sea crisis showed to the full his common sense, tenacity, and skilful, unprincipled manipulation of people and events. In 1739 the war of 'Jenkins's Ear' was declared, and Walpole ought to have resigned, since he had declared war much against his will, but he clung to office and only resigned when his majority had dwindled to two. He was raised to the peerage as Earl of Orford. The position which he occupied and the doctrine of ministerial cohesion which he applied are generally considered to justify his being regarded as the first effective British prime minister.

Walrus, or sea cow, *Odobenus rosmarus*, a large marine mammal of the family Odobenidae in order Carnivora (Pinnipedia). The Pacific walrus occurs around Alaska and the Siberian coasts. The Atlantic walrus is found in Spitsbergen and other European islands of the far north. The walrus has been ruthlessly hunted for its immense tusk-like upper canines, its hide and its oil. It is a gregarious animal, and quiet and inoffensive in disposition except during the breeding season, or if attacked, when it is capable of fighting fiercely. It averages 3–3·6 m in length, though specimens nearly twice as long are recorded. The muzzle is divided between the nostrils and bears bristly moustaches. The eyes are small, and there is no external ear. The adult animal has only one incisor and three premolar teeth at each side of the upper jaw besides the tusks; in the lower jaw only three premolars and one small canine occur on each side. Bivalve molluscs are its main diet. The tusks are used to dredge up the walrus's prey or as ice picks to enable the creature to lever itself onto icy surfaces.

Walsall, market town of West Midlands Metropolitan county, England, 12 km northwest of Birmingham. The town has a trade in harness, saddlery and leather goods as well as in engineering. Population (1981) 178,909.

Walsingham, Sir Francis (c.1532–90), English statesman. He travelled in Europe during the reign of Mary Tudor, but on the accession of Elizabeth I returned to England, and in 1569 acted as chief of the secret service in London. He was ambassador to France 1570–73, and secretary of state 1573–1590. His administration of foreign affairs was supported by a very efficient and widespread system of espionage, largely paid for out of his private fortune, but his diplomatic methods were balanced by personal integrity and disinterested patriotism. His ardent Protestantism led him into frequent disagreements with the queen and Burghley over their temporising policies. He unravelled numerous plots against the queen, including the Babington Conspiracy in 1586.

Walsingham, village in Norfolk, England, famous for its Chapel of Our Lady, with which miracles have been associated since before the Norman Conquest. From then until the Reformation Walsingham was un-rivalled in England as a centre of pilgrimage, being visited by every king and queen of England. Population (1971: Little Walsingham and Great Walsingham) 970.

Walter, Bruno (1876–1962), US conductor. He conducted in German opera houses and was influenced by Mahler, whom he accompanied to Vienna, (1901) where he became assistant conductor at the Court Opera. He became director of Munich Opera and from 1922 was associated with the Salzburg Festival. He conducted in Berlin and Leipzig and at the State Opera in Vienna. In 1939 he settled in the USA and conducted major orchestras and at the Metropolitan Opera in New York.

Waltham Forest, borough of Greater London created on 1 April 1965. It comprises the former boroughs of Chingford, Leyton and Walthamstow. Population (1981) 215,092.

Walther von der Vogelweide (c.1170–c.1230), German minnesinger. He served many masters, including Emperor Frederick II, and wandered all over Europe. The greatest of German medieval poets, his mastery lay in his wealth of tone and feeling.

Walton, Izaak (1593–1683), English author. Before 1619 he had begun to write verses, and in 1640 he prefixed a life of the author to the first folio edition of Donne's *Sermons*. In 1651 he published *Reliquiae Wottonianae* with his *Life of Sir Henry Wotton*, and two years later produced his famous treatise *The Compleat Angler, or the Contemplative Man's Recreation*, one of the most delightful books in the English language. In 1665 he published his *Life of Richard Hooker*, and in 1670 appeared the *Life of George Herbert*, followed in 1678 by that of Bishop Sanderson.

Walton, Sir William (1902–83), British composer. He studied at Oxford, but was mainly self-taught. In 1923 *Façade*, an entertainment to poems by Edith Sitwell, caused a furore at its first performance. Soon, however, his works began to inspire respect. *Belshazzar's Feast* put new and vivid life into the oratorio tradition and in 1934 his First Symphony was performed to great acclaim. Walton did not espouse post-war developments, though there are traces of 12-note influence (serialism) in the Second Symphony. His works include an opera, *Troilus and Cressida*; a ballet; incidental music for *Macbeth*; film and radio music; *Te Deum* for the coronation of Elizabeth II; *In Honour of the City of London* and other choral works; overtures *Portsmouth Point, Scapino* and others; *Sinfonia concertante* for piano and orchestra; concertos; chamber music; church music; and songs.

Waltz. This rhythm in 3-4 time was derived from the popular folk-dance landler found in Austria and Bavaria. The dance was adapted and taken to the courts in the late 18th century, becoming a favourite in Germany and France. In England, although waltz melodies were appreciated, the position taken by the dancing couples so shocked the public sense of decorum that the dance itself was not accepted in the ballroom until 1812. Even then it was performed at half the tempo. The waltz changed in form and tempo, and its variations included the French waltz, the sauteuse in a 6-8, the German or Viennese waltz, and the jete or quick sauteuse waltz, also in a 6-8 and often referred to as *valse à deux temps*. This dance became very popular in the early 19th century in Vienna; it was called *langaus* and was a type of frenzied gallop. The present modern waltz is smooth and flowing; much slower in tempo and technically very different from the original dance.

Walvis Bay, bay on the coast of South West Africa (Namibia); an enclave of South Africa. Most of the imports of South-West Africa are landed at Walvis Bay, the only good harbour on that coast. Important fishing and canning factories have been established. Population (1971) 21,725, of whom 7353 are whites.

Wampum, North American Indian perforated shell beads worn as adornment and used as currency, for sealing treaties, and as a means of recording events. Broad belts or collars were formed of strings of wampum arranged in patterns, sometimes representing pictographs depicting a story.

Wandsworth, a London borough created on 1 April 1965, comprising the former borough of Wandsworth (except for its eastern part, which is now incorporated into Lambeth) and the old villages of Roehampton and Clapham. Wandsworth's population in 1981 was 255,723.

Wanganui, port on the west coast of North Island, New Zealand, on the Wanganui river, 215 km north of Wellington by rail. It is the regional centre for a large area of pastoral and agricultural country. The chief industries are flour mills, freezing works, dairy factories, engineering works, woollen mills, steel-pipe works and chemical works. Population (1980) 40,000.

Wankel Engine, form of four-stroke internal combustion engine in which a rotor replaces the pistons. It was invented in the 1950s by Felix Wankel, a German engineer. A triangular rotor is mounted to revolve eccentrically inside the engine's combustion chamber in such a way that three gas-tight chambers are formed in which the fuel is drawn in, compressed and ignited in turn. It has the advantage of being able to drive directly without a crankshaft, but is less fuel-efficient than a conventional petrol engine.

Wankie, see HWANGE.

Wapentake (Old Norse *vápnatak*, brandishing of weapons), subdivision of those English counties which were settled by the Danes, corresponding to the hundred elsewhere.

Wapiti, *Cervus canadensis*, a large and magnificent deer once widely distributed throughout North America, now limited to the Rockies and the Cascades. It is also found in northeast and central Asia. In North America it is known as the elk.

War, Civil, see CIVIL WAR.

War, First World, see WORLD WAR, FIRST.

War, Great, see WORLD WAR, FIRST.

War, Second World, see WORLD WAR, SECOND.

War Crimes, see CRIMES, WAR; NUREMBERG TRIAL.

War Office, the name by which the headquarters of the British army was known until 1 April 1964, when the integrated Ministry of Defence was formed.

Warbeck, Perkin (c.1474–99), pretender to the English throne in the reign of Henry VII. He was a native of Tournai, and appeared in 1490 at the Burgundian court as the younger of the two princes whom Richard was said to have murdered in the Tower of London. He was acknowledged as her nephew by Margaret Duchess of Burgundy. Warbeck went to Scotland, where he was received by James IV. In 1498 he invaded the south-west of England, but was captured and taken to the Tower. The following year he escaped, but was recaptured and hanged at Tyburn.

Warble Fly, see DIPTERA; OESTRIDAE.

Warblers, birds of order Passeriformes, placed in two families. The Old World warblers are in the family Muscicapidae, while the New World warblers are members of the Parulidae. They are distinguished from the thrushes by their more delicate structure. They include some of the choicest songsters: the chiffchaff, *Phylloscopus collybita*; the garden warbler, *Sylvia borin*; the lesser whitethroat, *S. curruca*; the reed warbler, *Acrocephalus scirpaceus*; and the sedge warbler, *A. schoenobaenus*.

Warburton, William (1698–1779), English prelate and editor. He was dean of Bristol in 1757 and bishop of Gloucester in 1759. He was a friend of Pope, who made Warburton his literary executor, and he brought out an edition of Pope's works in 1751. He also published an edition of Shakespeare which was severely criticised.

Ward, James (1769–1859), British painter and engraver. In 1794 he was appointed painter and mezzotint engraver to the Prince of Wales, in 1807 became an ARA, and in 1811 an RA. In his animal studies he was influenced by his brother-in-law, George Morland, but his large landscape *Gordale Scar*, 1815 (Tate Gallery), reflects his ambition to paint dramatic history subjects.

Ward, Sir Leslie, known by his pseudonym 'Spy' (1851–1922), British artist, born in London. He became famous as a caricaturist for *Vanity Fair* (1873–1909).

Ward, Mary Augusta (1851–1920), English novelist, better known as Mrs Humphry Ward. She is best known for her novel *Robert Elsmere*, 1888. Mary Ward was an indefatigable social worker, establishing a settlement in Bloomsbury, and a member of the highest literary circles of her day.

Ward, in English law, a minor who has been legally placed under the care of a guardian.

Ward, electoral division of a parliamentary seat or of a district council in an urban area.

Warden, in England, officer appointed for the naval or military protection of some particular district. The position of Warden of the Cinque Ports was created by King John in 1214 with extensive jurisdiction over the adjacent coast land. The wardens of the marches were appointed to protect the boundaries between England and Scotland or Wales.

Wardmote, in the City of London, an annual court or meeting held in each ward of the city under the presidency of the alderman, at which the common councillors are elected. Its powers, which formerly extended to matters concerning the watch, the police, etc., are now merely nominal.

Wardroom, in the days of wooden warships, a large cabin in the after part underneath the captain's apartments. The term, of uncertain origin, dates from about 1750, the wardroom being used as a lieutenants' mess and sleeping-quarters. In modern times the wardroom is the mess for commissioned officers in a warship.

Wardship and Marriage, incidents of English feudal tenure found at all tenurial levels from tenants-in-chief downwards. The lands of a minor heir remained in the hands of the lord, who used them as he wished, until the heir came of age (males at 21 and females at 14). Marriage generally went with the wardship, while marriages of all widows of tenants-in-chief were in the king's gift. They were abolished under the Commonwealth.

Warfarin, an anticoagulant related in structure to coumarin. It is also used as a rat poison.

Warhol, Andy (1931–), US artist and filmmaker. Warhol was one of the originators of Pop Art with items such as his silkscreen prints of Marilyn Monroe. His 'underground' films: *Sleep* (1963); *Blow Job* (1964); *Chelsea Girls* (1966); etc., have acquired some reputation. One of his characteristics is the use of household objects in deliberate contradiction of traditional concepts of beauty.

Andy Warhol. Liz, *1965, a silkscreen Pop-Art representation of Elizabeth Taylor.*

Warlock, Peter, real name Philip Heseltine (1894–1950), British composer. The two great influences on his life and music were Elizabethan lute songs, which he edited, and Delius, a friend and mentor. His songs, numbering about 120, are among the best produced in England, and alternate between high spirits and melancholy, the latter at its most impressive in his Yeats cycle, *The Curlew*. Other works include the *Serenade* and *Capriol Suite* for strings.

Warm-bloodedness, see HOMOIOTHERMY.

Warp, see WEAVING.

Warrant, instrument authorising a person to do something which otherwise he has no right to do. In England a police warrant is issued by a justice of the peace on a written and sworn information of an offence; it is addressed to the constables of his district, specifies the offence, describes the person accused, and commands the police to arrest him and bring him before the justices to answer the charge. A 'general warrant' (i.e. one which purports to authorise the arrest of unnamed persons without previous evidence of their guilt or knowledge of their persons) and a general 'search warrant' are now both illegal. The term 'warrant' is also used for documents authorising the payment of dividends or the delivery of goods out of bond. A 'distress warrant' authorises the seizure of goods for arrears of rent.

Warranty. In English law a warranty is a term in an agreement, the breach of which gives a right to sue for damages, but not to treat the contract as at an end.

Warren, Robert Penn (1905–), US poet, novelist and critic. Warren was one of the leaders of the Southern agrarian movement and a proponent of the New Criticism, a critical method based on close reading of the text. He contributed to *I'll Take My Stand*, 1930, and was a founder and editor of *The Southern Review*. Though his reputation rests primarily on his poetry, his best-known book is probably *All the King's Men*, 1946. In 1938 he edited the influential *Understanding Poetry*, 1938, with Cleanth Brooks.

Warren, enclosure made for the breeding of rabbits, or any area where there are numerous colonies of wild rabbits. The term also denotes a fish or game preserve.

Warrington, town of Cheshire, England, 25 km from both Liverpool and Manchester. From Roman times it was of significance as a crossing-place of the Mersey. The industrial tradition of Warrington goes back to the medieval period, both in textiles and tools, this being stimulated when the Mersey was made navigable in the 18th century and the Manchester Ship Canal opened in 1894. Warrington has retained its industrial variety with metal trades, leather, brewing, sawmilling, printing and clothing. The chemical industry exists here also, but less prominently than at Runcorn and Widnes. Population (1981) 135,568.

Warsaw. The Market Square, part of the old town reconstructed after the destruction of 1939–45.

Wars of the Cross, see CRUSADES.

Wars of the Roses, see ROSES, WARS OF THE.

Warsaw (Polish *Warszawa*), capital of Poland in the eastern central part of the country, on the River Vistula. Warsaw developed around the castle of the Dukes of Mazowsze and in the 15th century became the capital of the duchy. In 1596 it succeeded Cracow as capital of Poland. In the Second World War it fell to the Germans in September 1939. In 1944 the Polish resistance movement rose against the occupying Germans and was subdued only after a battle lasting 63 days in which 160,000 Poles were killed. When the Red Army entered the city in January 1945, 90 per cent of its buildings were in ruins.

Reconstruction began immediately after the war. The new city was developed on the axis of an east-west main thoroughfare, which passes under the faithfully rebuilt 'old' town (Stare Miasto) through a tunnel. In layout the city consists of a series of north-south belts, with government offices along the riverside escarpment, the shopping, entertainment and commercial districts to the west, and industrial estates in the suburbs. The industries include metallurgy, textiles, chemicals, engineering (electrical goods, precision instruments and motor vehicles), food processing, and printing and publishing. Population (1979) 1,572,000.

Warsaw Pact, a treaty signed in 1955 between the USSR, Albania, Bulgaria, Czechoslovakia, the German Democratic Republic, Hungary, Poland and Romania, pledging mutual military support. Albania has not taken an active part since 1962.

Wart, in botany, a disease of potatoes, due to a fungus, *Synchytrium endobioticum*. It causes nobbly excrescences which become black and render the tubers inedible. Immune varieties of potato must be grown. An outbreak must be notified to the Ministry of Agriculture, Fisheries and Food.

Wart, or verruca, an excrescence caused by excessive growth of the tissues of the papillae of the skin. Little is known of the manner in which warts are formed, and they usually appear and disappear without any apparent cause, especially in the young. In some cases the cause seems to be infection by a virus. They are very vascular, and are covered with fairly thick, scaly epidermis, which easily becomes rubbed off. In children, plantar warts (i.e. verrucas on the soles of the feet) may be painful on walking, and, since they are very infectious, should always be treated at once.

Wart Hog, *Phacochoerus aethiopicus*, a species of African pig. Resembling the wild boar, it is distinguished by the large head, two large tusks, and at each side of the face large, wart-like pads. It has a mane of bristly hair on its neck and back. Like the pig, it belongs to family Suidae, suborder Suiformes, of order Artiodactyla.

Wartburg, Walther von (1888–1971), Swiss Romance philologist. His major work is *Französisches etymologisches Wörterbuch*, begun in 1922 and nearly complete at his death.

Warwick, Richard Neville, Earl of (1428–1471), 'the king-maker'. He was the most active and influential of all the supporters of the Yorkist house. For the first three years of Edward IV's reign Warwick was the real ruler of England, but he and Edward quarrelled, and Warwick went over to the Lancastrians. He was killed at the battle of Barnet in 1471. Warwick's title of 'king maker' does not seem to have been used until half a century after his death. Throughout his life, Warwick's actions were dictated solely by personal ambition.

See also ROSES, WARS OF THE.

Warwick, market town and county town of Warwickshire, England, on the River Avon, 33 km south-east of Birmingham. Its history is closely linked with that of its castle, which stands on a site fortified since Saxon times. The Hospital of Lord Leycester was founded by Robert Dudley, Earl of Leicester, in 1571. Manufactures include agricultural implements, edible gelatines, lozenges and other sweetmeats, mechanical and motor-engineering products, carpets and pistons. Population (1981) 21,936.

Warwickshire, midland county of England, bounded on the north by Staffordshire, on the south by Gloucestershire and Oxfordshire, on the east by Leicestershire and Northamptonshire, and on the west by Worcestershire and the West Midlands county. The surface is very variable, though there are no great elevations. The principal rivers are the Avon, with its numerous tributaries, which runs right across the county, the Stour and the Tame. Since the county reorganisation of 1974, which deprived Warwickshire of Birmingham, Coventry and the coalfields (all of which became part of the West Midlands Metropolitan county), agriculture has been the most important industry, although there is scattered light industry. Almost the whole county is under cultivation. The most important towns are the boroughs of Leamington, famous for its spa, Nuneaton, Rugby, Stratford-upon-Avon, the birthplace of Shakespeare, and Warwick, the county town, famous for its antiquities. The area of the county is 198,052 ha; population (1981) 473,620.

Wash, The, inlet (35 by 24 km) of the North Sea, on the east coast of England, between Norfolk and Lincolnshire, receiving the Welland, Ouse, Nene and other rivers. Its shores are low and marshy. Over the years the stretches bordering on salt-marsh have been reclaimed for agriculture.

Washington, Booker T(aliaferro) (1856–1915), US educator and reformer, born a slave. He became an educator, founding the Tuskegee Institute, Alabama (1881). The Institute grew and by his death had become the major educational institution for blacks. Washington was skilful in obtaining funds for the school, and in so doing became a prominent black leader. His personal philosophy and public policy is made clear in *Up from Slavery*, 1901. Shunned by many black intellectuals, Washington also set up the National Negro Business League.

George Washington, after a portrait by Peale.

Washington, George (1732–99), 1st President of the USA. He was of British descent, his great-grandfather having migrated from Northamptonshire in 1657. He inherited the Mount Vernon estate from his brother and settled down as a country gentleman, becoming lieutenant-colonel of the Virginia military. In 1758 he resigned command of the Virginia troops and married a rich widow, Martha Custis. The union of their plantations made Washington one of the wealthiest men in his state. He was elected in 1759 to the Virginia House of Burgesses. He displayed interest in the disputes between the colonies and the British Crown, and Virginia elected him a delegate to the first Continental Congress. He bought arms and ammunition, and when the congress adjourned, returned to Virginia to train the raw soldiers. When the second Continental Congress met, John Adams proposed Washington as commander-in-chief of the colonial armies, which were already at war with Britain, and in June 1775 Washington took command.

The American troops were often ill-equipped and Washington had to combat faction and treachery among his generals. His occupation of Dorchester Heights compelled Howe to evacuate Boston in March 1776. He then had a succession of reverses, notably at Brooklyn Heights, but in New Jersey he beat his enemy at Trenton and Princeton. Following his defeats at Brandywine and Germantown in autumn 1777, Washington led his 11,000 men into winter camp at Valley Forge, near Philadelphia. The spring brought better news for the Americans: the French were coming into the war. Clinton, who succeeded Howe, had been ordered to give up Philadelphia and return to New York. Washington harassed his troops, notably at the battle of Monmouth. When Clinton reached New York, Washington took up a position at White Plains and for three years, while fighting was going on elsewhere, the two armies watched each other. At last, Washington's chance came when Cornwallis met with difficulties in North Carolina and finally shut himself up in Yorktown. Here Washington, who had hurried south, forced him to surrender (1781). When the British moved out of New York for home, the American army under Washington entered the town. A few days afterwards Washington went to Maryland, where Congress was sitting, and on 23 December he resigned as commander of the armies.

For four years he strove to recoup his shattered fortunes. It was then decided to call a convention to frame a constitution, and Washington was chosen as one of the Virginia delegation. The convention opened in May 1787 in Philadelphia, and Washington was unanimously chosen to preside. Others wrote the constitution, but it was Washington who did much to remove difficulties. He was unanimously chosen first president of the republic. He was inaugurated on 30 April 1789. He wished to retire at the end of his first term, but at the instance of the rival leaders, Thomas Jefferson and Alexander Hamilton, he was elected to a second term by a unanimous vote. He declined a third term.

See also UNITED STATES OF AMERICA, *History*.

Washington, capital city of the United States of America. It is usually referred to as Washington DC (to distinguish it from the state of the same name) because it is situated in, and co-terminous with, the District of Columbia. The distinctive feature of Washington as a city is that it was planned from the first as a capital. The most prominent feature of the plan was the setting of the Congress building, known as the Capitol, (the present structure was begun in 1818, but not completed until the 1860s) on an eminence overlooking the 3·5-kilometre Mall, a grass-covered vista stretching west to the Potomac River, with government buildings flanking it. Washington became a beautiful and impressive city of wide avenues, white stone and marble, and over 300 statues or memorials. But the tendency of the federal government to think of the city as simply a setting for the national government has led to the neglect of Washington as a community of 637,650 people (1980) and one moreover where 71 per cent of the people are black, where 91 per cent of the primary school enrolment consists of black or Puerto Rican children, and where the birth rate is almost double the national average.

The city's economy has two main bases: government and tourism. Apart from local supply industries, the major industrial activity is printing and publishing.

See also WHITE HOUSE.

Washington (Evergreen State), Pacific state of the USA, formerly part of Oregon. It is situated in the extreme north-west, bounded on the north by Canada, east by Idaho, south by Oregon, and west by the Pacific Ocean. It was created a territory in 1853, and in 1889 was admitted to statehood. The state is divided from north to south by the Cascade range, whose general altitude is between 1800 and 2100 m, but there are several volcanic peaks rising above 3000 m. Mount Rainier reaches 4392 m and is surrounded by a national park. There is also a lower, coastal range in the west, the Olympic Mountains (Mount Olympus 2428 m). In the north-west, between the two ranges, lies Puget Sound, an inlet with many harbours, and the site of Seattle, Tacoma and Olympia; it forms the commercial nucleus of the state. The Columbia river enters the state from British Columbia on the north and flows along 480 km of its southern boundary. Its chief affluent is the Snake river, which joins it near Pasco.

East of the Cascades are stretches of arid or semi-arid land, where irrigation is necessary. Here are great cattle and sheep ranges, with apple-growing valleys, the Columbia Basin Project lands, and the wheat district of the Palouse. Wheat is also grown in the west, which receives heavy rainfall and has a profuse vegetation. Larger than the farmland area is that under forest; it covers 7·5 million ha, of which national forests account for nearly a quarter. Washington and Oregon are the US's great suppliers of softwoods, particularly Douglas fir. The Columbia river is a prime source of hydroelectricity. Industries include lumber and planing mills, aluminium refining and flour mills; meat-packing and the manufacture of dairy products are important, while shipbuilding and aircraft manufacture expanded greatly during the Second World War. Seattle is the landing place of the North Pacific fisheries.

There are 18 Indian reservations in the state, the largest being that of Coleville, and three national parks. The capital is Olympia. The population in 1980 was 4,130,163.

Washington, Mount, culminating peak of the White Mountains, in the Presidential range, Coos county, New Hampshire, USA. It is 1916 m high and ascended by a rack-railway (1869) and a road (1861). It is the highest peak in New Hampshire and in north-eastern USA.

Washington New Town is situated in Tyne and Wear, England, 8 km south-east of Newcastle upon Tyne. Washington was designated as a new town in 1963 in an area of dense industrial and mining settlement between the River Wear and the Durham motorway. Washington Old Hall, a largely 17th-century house near the centre of the new town, was, in its original form, the home of George Washington's ancestors in the 14th century. Population (1971) 38,000.

'Washington Post', US newspaper, founded in 1877. It is generally acknowledged as the most influential of the United States liberal-intellectual newspapers, and achieved wide fame through the investigations of its reporters Bob Woodward and Carl Bernstein into President Nixon's involvement in the 'Watergate' affair, 1973–74.

Wasp, any insect in several families of the suborder Apocrita in the order Hymenoptera.

In the female true wasp the ovipositor is modified into a stinging organ, but the male wasps do not have a sting. There are also parasitic wasps, in which the ovipositor is adapted for piercing and drilling. True wasps include both solitary and social species. The adult wasps of both types feed on fruit juices and nectar. There are various forms of nesting behaviour; some make their own from vegetable material or dig nests in the ground, some take over nests made by others.

Solitary wasps include digger wasps, *Sphex* and *Bembix*, and sand wasps. In the temperate zone, the social wasps include members of the genera *Vespula* (hornets), *Vespa* (wasps) and *Polistes* (paper wasps), which have similar life histories. All belong to the family Vespidae. See also GALL-WASP; WOOD-WASP.

Wassail (Old English *wæs hal*, be whole, of good health), originally an expression of good wishes at festivities, especially a 'toasting' or salutation in drinking. Later it was used for a drinking-bout or carouse, and then for the beverage used, especially at Christmas and on Twelfth Night.

Wassermann, August von (1866–1925), German bacteriologist and immunologist who invented the test for syphilis which bears his name. He carried out important investigations on toxins and anti-toxins, diphtheria antitoxin, cholera immunisation, cancer, diagnosis of tuberculosis, and blood grouping. By modifying the complement-fixation reaction of Bordet and Gengou he devised and perfected the Wassermann reaction, a specific blood test for the diagnosis of syphilis (1906).

Waste, in English law a term denoting any act of alteration done or permitted by the tenant to houses, woods, lands, or other corporeal property during the continuance of his particular property. Waste is said to be: (1) *ameliorating*, i.e. acts of improvement; or (2) *voluntary*, i.e. acts of commission, such as pulling down buildings, felling timber or opening mines; (3) *permissive*, i.e. acts of omission, such as non-repair of buildings; or (4) *equitable*, i.e. wanton destruction. A tenant for life, even though expressly declared by the settlement to be 'not impeachable' for waste, is nevertheless liable for equitable waste.

Watch, time-measuring instrument similar to a clock, but smaller and generally carried on the person. The watch became a practical possibility in about 1510 with the invention of the mainspring, which is generally attributed to Peter Hele, or Henlein, a Nürnberg locksmith. Most spring-driven watches are made with jewelled bearings for better wear. Early watches were made to carry in the pocket. The wrist watch made its appearance soon after 1900, and is now the usual type. The first self-winding watch, in which a pivoted weight acts on the mainspring, was invented in 1924.

The first electric watches appeared in 1952, as soon as suitable miniature batteries were available. The first electronic watch was devised in 1960, in which time-keeping was obtained through a small tuning-fork. The quartz-crystal electronic watches in general production today were introduced in 1967, followed by solid-state watches in which digital displays eliminate the conventional

hands and dial. Developments in the 1980s include watches combined with alarms and calculators, and, of particular interest to the blind, watches that speak the time when a button is pressed.

Watch, the seven periods of time into which the day is divided on board ship: midnight to 4 a.m., middle watch; 4 a.m. to 8 a.m., morning watch; 8 a.m. to noon, forenoon watch; noon to 4 p.m., afternoon watch; 4 p.m. to 6 p.m., first dog-watch; 6 p.m. to 8 p.m., last dog-watch; 8 p.m. to midnight, first watch. The purpose of the dog-watch is to produce an odd number of watches in each 24 hours so that regular watch-keepers do not keep the same watches each day. Time is denoted on board ship by striking a bell. The crew are generally divided into port and starboard watches.

Water covers 72 per cent of the surface of the globe and occupies depressions greater than the land above sea-level could fill. It solidifies and evaporates at normal Earth temperatures, and in the state of vapour forms a minute but extremely important constituent of the atmosphere. It freezes at 0°C and boils at 100°C. On freezing it expands by one-twelfth its bulk; 1 m³ weighs 1000 kg at 4°C. This is its greatest density, and it forms the unit of relative density. Plants and animals contain a large proportion of water combined in the tissues. Land plants contain about 60 per cent water; aquatic plants, 95 per cent; fish, 80 per cent; land animals (including humans), 70 per cent.

Chemically it is composed of 2 atoms of hydrogen combined with 1 of oxygen. It may be prepared by exploding a mixture of these gases or by burning one in the other. Water is, when pure, a faint greenish-blue and odourless; it is very slightly compressible and a bad conductor of heat and electricity. It has one of the highest specific heats known, and is thus an excellent coolant.

Water-boatman, also known as a 'back-swimmer', insects belonging to the family Notonectidae in order Hemiptera (suborder Heteroptera). They are aquatic bugs mostly living in fresh water. The adults are about 15 mm long. They rest upside down at the water surface to breathe. When disturbed they dive, carrying with them a supply of air trapped under the wings. They also swim upside down (hence 'backswimmers') with their long oar-like hind legs outstretched and rowing (hence 'boatmen').

Water Buffalo (Indian Buffalo), see BUFFALO.

Water Bugs belong to the order Hemiptera (suborder Heteroptera), and the majority of them, with the exception of the pond-skaters, belong to the Hydrocorisae (=Cryptocerata), a subdivision of Heteroptera. The antennae of water bugs are hidden, in contrast to the land bugs which have noticeable antennae. In general, water bugs are less brightly coloured than land bugs; they are usually varying shades of black or brown. They tend to inhabit the bottom strata of ponds, lakes and streams. They may or may not have wings. All stages of the life-cycle (adult, larva and egg) occur in the water; the eggs are usually attached to water plants.

In China giant water bugs (family Belostomatidae), over 100 mm long, are a much sought-after delicacy for the table.

See also POND-SKATERS; WATER-BOATMAN; WATER-SCORPION.

Water Chestnut, *Trapa,* in the Onagraceae. *T. natans* occurs in Europe, Asia and Africa. The fruit is an edible nut of peculiar four-pointed shape. The water chestnut of Chinese meals is the tuber of *Eleocharis tuberosa* (*E. dulcis*), a plant related to the sedges.

Water-colour, painting medium where the pigments are prepared with gum-arabic and glycerine by a fairly complex process. The pigments are diluted with water and applied with soft brushes (often sable or 'camel' hair) to fine-quality linen paper.

Water-colour first established itself as a specialist art-form in England in the later 18th century, thanks to three social factors: the 'Grand Tour' led to albums of water-colours recording sites visited; the Romantic Movement popularised mountains and atmospheric effects; the gentry found a social accomplishment in an unexacting medium. Great water-colourists included Gainsborough, Sandby, Cozens (father and son), Cotman, Girtin, de Wint, Turner, Cox, Towne, the Varleys, Bonington and Rowlandson. Exquisite work in an imaginative rather than landscape vein was done by Blake, Palmer, Calvert, Rossetti and Burne-Jones. *Gouache* is a form of water-colour using paints rendered opaque by the admixture of white fillers. A notable exponent was Paul Sandby.

See also PAINTING; PAINTING TECHNIQUES.

Water-cress, see CRESS.

Water Culture, see HYDROPONICS.

Water Cure, see HYDROPATHY; HYDROTHERAPY.

Water Divining, see DIVINING ROD.

Water Dropwort, marsh plants of the genus *Oenanthe,* of the Umbelliferae, having much-divided pinnate leaves and compound umbels of white flowers. *O. crocata,* the hemlock water dropwort, of Europe and North Africa, is a poisonous plant, as are, probably, the other species.

Water-flea, see CLADOCERA.

Water Gas is a gas formed by the action of steam on coke at 1200–1400°C. The process produces a gas with a calorific value of about one-third that of natural gas containing hydrogen (50 per cent), carbon monoxide (40 per cent), methane (0·5 per cent), and carbon dioxide and nitrogen. The process is often combined with the manufacture of producer gas. Water gas has been used in the past in the manufacture of hydrogen and synthetic ammonia. Carburetted water gas is water gas enriched with gases from cracked oils, and was used to supplement coal gas supplies.

Water Hemlock, *Cicuta virosa,* a large waterside plant, belonging to the Umbelliferae, which is highly poisonous. The name is also applied to some forms of water dropwort.

Water Hyacinth, see NYMPHAEA.

Water-lily, the various species of *Nymphaea, Nuphar* and also of *Nelumbium,* all belonging to the family Nymphaeaceae.

See also LOTUS.

Water Melon, see CUCURBITACEAE.

Water Plants, see AQUATIC PLANTS.

Water Polo a team ball game played in water with the object of scoring goals. It originated in England in about 1880. Teams are made up of 11 players, four of whom may be in the water at any one time. Except for the goalkeepers, players are not allowed to walk, jump, punch the ball, or handle it with two hands.

International matches are played in deep water in an area of 30 × 20 m with goals 2·5 m wide and 0·9 m high. The game is made up of four 5-minute periods (actual play), with a 2-minute break between.

Water Rat, see VOLE.

Water-scorpion, insects belonging to the family Nepidae in order Hemiptera (sub-order Heteroptera). These water bugs are strikingly dissimilar from other water bugs, in that their first pair of legs is modified into prehensile organs for grasping prey. They are carnivorous, feeding on smaller insects. The prey is held between their first pair of legs while they suck up its body fluids. Another characteristic feature of these bugs is their apical respiratory tube. While the bug remains at the bottom of the water, the respiratory tube reaches up to the surface, thus renewing its supply of air. This apical respiratory tube is often wrongly believed to be a stinging organ; it is in fact by means of their first pair of legs that they inflict painful wounds.

Water Skiing, sport which consists of towing a skier across water, holding the handle of a rope limited in length to 23 m, and attached to a motor boat. Modern conventional skis measure about 16·5 cm wide by 1·75 m long and have a short rubber keel at the back to act as a stabiliser and adjustable rubber footholds.

For competition the sport is divided into three categories: trick skiing, slalom and ski jumping. The trick skier has to perform gymnastic feats while being towed; the more difficult the manoeuvre, the more points are awarded. Trick skiing is performed at low speeds of about 30 kmph and short thick skis are used (23 cm wide by 1·2 m long). A slalom event is similar to the snow sport of the same name. The skier has to weave in and out between a course of marker buoys without actually touching them. This is usually done on one ski at speeds of up to 65 kmph. The slalom race is judged by speed. In ski jumping the skier is towed up to a wooden ramp with a greased surface, 3·5 m in length and 1·75 m high at the top. He approaches it at about 55–65 kmph. The longest recorded jumps have exceeded 50 m. Competitions are also held for straight speed and records have exceeded 190 kmph. A barefoot version of the sport also exists. World championships began in 1949.

Water Softening. Hardness of water is due to the salts of calcium and magnesium which occur commonly in natural waters. Hardness causes wastage of soap and scaling of kettles. Hardness due to calcium bicarbonate can be removed by boiling; hardness due mainly to calcium sulphate cannot be so removed.

There are two main methods of water softening:

Lime is added as a cream, a precipitate of calcium carbonate forms and settles out, leaving partially softened water.

Base Exchange makes use of zeolites. When hard water is passed through a bed of zeolite, the calcium and magnesium ions are removed from the water and replaced by sodium ions.

Water-spout, see CYCLONE.

Water Stoma, a pore derived from stoma, for active excretion of water (guttation). Hydathodes occur at the tips and in the serrations of leaves, or singly at the ends of main veins.

Water Supply. An adequate supply of wholesome water is the foundation of the health of any community. In providing a water supply consideration must be given to its quantity and quality. Diseases such as cholera, typhoid and dysentery can be transmitted by water. Contamination with sewage is the main cause of pollution, and strict control is essential to ensure purity and safety of water supplies.

Rain is the prime source of all water which runs off into lakes and rivers, or percolates down through the soil into the permeable strata to build up underground sources of supply.

Rain is collected directly for public water supplies in some parts of the world and is usually free from dangerous pollution; the main hazard comes from bird-droppings on the surfaces from which water is collected.

Streams and lakes of mountains and high moors generally provide soft water of good quality, but most large rivers of the industrialised countries are greatly contaminated with sewage, effluents from factories, and trade wastes.

Underground sources of water consist of springs and wells. Springs are flows of natural water which occur where the water table reaches ground level at the junction of pervious and impervious geological layers. As their quantity and quality vary seasonally, they are only useful for small communities.

Sea-water is distilled to provide drinking water to land-based populations which have an inadequate catchment area. Distillation can make use of waste heat, as from a power station; or desalination can be carried out by electro-dialysis, reverse osmosis, successive freezing and thawing, or demineralisation with synthetic resins.

Water for large public supplies needs storage, filtration and disinfection. Water is stored in a reservoir where a certain amount of natural purification takes place. Suspended solid matter settles, and organic pollutants are broken down and oxidised. Filtration through large open sand filters, or under pressure using aluminium sulphate as a coagulant, removes fine particles. A chemical agent, such as chlorine or ozone, is used to destroy any contaminating bacteria. Fluoride is sometimes added, where it does not occur naturally, to provide protection for children's growing teeth. The water is then distributed through the mains to the consumers. Adequate pressure and a reserve for fire-fighting are maintained by service reservoirs and water-towers sited at suitably elevated places in the area.

Public water supplies need regular bacteriological testing and chemical analysis for safety.

See also ARTESIAN WELL; IRRIGATION; PUBLIC HEALTH; RESERVOIR; RIVER; SEWAGE; WATER SOFTENING.

Water Table, see HYDROLOGY.

Water Wheel, a simple type of prime mover utilising the energy of falling water and the oldest form of inanimate power. Water wheels are of two basic types: horizontal wheels driving a vertical axle, and vertical wheels driving a horizontal axle which in turn transmits its power through gears. Vertical wheels are of three sorts: undershot, which simply dip into a stream and are driven by the flow of water; overshot, which are supplied with water at the top and are turned because the buckets on one side of the wheel are full of water, and therefore heavier than the empty buckets; and breast wheels, which take in water at about the level of the axle and are turned partly by the water's weight and partly by its velocity.

Waterbuck, see ANTELOPE.

Waterbury, city in Connecticut, USA, situated on the Naugatuck river, 30 km north of New Haven and the shore of Long Island Sound. Its most wide-reaching product is the Waterbury watch, made by the Ingersoll company, but there is also an important brass industry. Population (1980) 103,266.

Waterfall, abrupt torrent of water in a river course caused by a stratum of relatively hard rock resisting erosion while the softer rock beneath it (horizontally or dipping upstream) has worn away. The feature is typical of rivers that are young and have not graded their courses. Falls are numerous where coastal plains of younger and poorly resistant strata abut an older land-mass; a fall-line will then develop along the inner margin of the plain, as on the eastern coast of North America.

Waterford, city and capital of County Waterford, Republic of Ireland, on the River Suir. Fragments of the old city walls remain, notably Reginald's Tower, dating from the 11th century, and a number of well-preserved Norman towers. Waterford is now a distribution centre. Industries include bacon-curing, flour-milling, brewing, paper and board, and electrical equipment. Glass-making, for which Waterford was once famous, has been revived. The harbour is formed by the estuary of the Suir and Barrow. There is steamer traffic, largely freight and livestock, with Fishguard and other Welsh ports. Container traffic is especially important. Population (1979) 32,617.

Waterhouse, Alfred (1830–1905), British architect. He began practice as an architect in Manchester in 1853 where he won competitions for the Assize Courts, 1859, and for the Town Hall, 1868, both designed in the Gothic style. He moved to London in 1865. Among the chief buildings in his enormous subsequent practice were the Natural History Museum, 1873–81, the Prudential Assurance Company's head offices (1879 and 1899–1906), University College Hospital—all in London; the Metropole Hotel, Brighton; the universities of Manchester, Leeds and Liverpool; and Caius College, Cambridge. He favoured the Romanesque style, and used terracotta freely.

Waterloo, village situated 23 km south of Brussels, Belgium, chosen by the Duke of Wellington as the most advantageous place to resist the advance of Napoleon on the Belgian capital in 1815. Napoleon crossed the Belgian frontier and fighting began on

Waterloo. A 19th-century aquatint of the battle. Nine hours of fighting left over 60,000 casualties.

16 June, as the Prussians contested his advance to gain time for the concentration of the main Allied forces. The Prussians then retreated, but to the north, and not to the east. Detaching Grouchy to follow the Prussians, Napoleon advanced with his main body on Wellington's defensive position at Waterloo. The duke learned during the night of 18–19 June that Blücher could support him, and determined to stand and fight. He had 49,608 infantry, 12,402 cavalry, 5645 artillery with 156 guns (of which total scarcely 24,000 men were British). Napoleon had 48,950 infantry, 15,765 cavalry, 7232 artillery, with 246 guns.

The battle opened at 11.30 a.m. with a French attack. As Napoleon's Guard fell back at 8 p.m. Wellington set his whole force moving and the French Army disintegrated, the Prussians taking up the pursuit. The casualties were heavy; the French lost over 40,000, the Prussians 7000, and Wellington over 15,000.

Waterloo Bridge. The original nine-arched bridge, crossing the Thames in London between Blackfriars Bridge and Charing Cross, was built by Sir John Rennie between 1811 and 1817. It was demolished and replaced by a bridge designed by Sir Giles Gilbert Scott, which was opened in 1945.

Waterloo Cup, major event in the sport of coursing. The competition takes place during the second week in February on the Sefton estate at Altcar in Lancashire. Over the years the original eight-dog stake has expanded to a 64-dog stake. The event is so named because at the first meeting the entrants dined at the Waterloo Hotel.

Watermark, design impressed into paper, first invented at Fabriano in Italy.

Waterproofing and Water Repellency. For textiles, water repellency implies that a globule of water will not spread on and into the fabric; waterproof implies that the cloth is impervious to air as well as water. If the garment is to be comfortable, water vapour must pass from the body to the outside air; a water-repellent fabric is therefore more comfortable in wear than a waterproof one.

Waterproof fabrics were first produced by Macintosh in 1819, who supported a thin layer of rubber with a cotton fabric; rubbers, linseed oil and waxes are still used to produce proofed fabrics. Polyvinyl chloride sheet, which needs no support fabric, is used for the 'plastic mac', the seams being heat welded. Modern repellency treatments are often based on silicones and the finishes have excellent resistance to washing and dry-cleaning. The ability of cotton to swell as it absorbs water is made use of in the 'Ventile' fabric. The fibres in a very tightly woven cloth swell sufficiently to close up the fabric structure and so achieve water repellency whilst still allowing water vapour to be absorbed by the inside surface of the fibre. These cloths are used in mountaineering anoraks.

Watershed, geographical term used by European authors to denote the boundary line between one drainage area and another. See also RIVER.

Watford, town of Hertfordshire, England, on the Colne, 24 km north-west of London. Its wide variety of light industries includes printing, paper-making, engineering, brewing and electronics. It is also a London dormitory town. Population (1981) 74,356.

Watling Island, Bahamas, see SAN SALVADOR ISLAND.

Watling Street (*Waeclinga Straet*), early Roman highway in Britain, running from Dover, through Canterbury to London, and then through St Albans (*Verulamium*) on the same general line as the A5 to Wroxeter and perhaps to Chester. Branch-roads were added later, and branches from the Kentish ports, focused on Canterbury, became the highway from the Channel ports to London. The road in London still bears this name. The name is also used in modern times for some other stretches of road of Roman origin.

Watson, James Dewey (1928–), US biochemist. For his part in the determination of the three-dimensional structure of DNA, the molecular carrier of heredity, Watson shared the 1962 Nobel Prize for physiology and medicine with F. H. C. Crick and M. H. F. Wilkins. His major interest is the role of RNA in protein synthesis.

Watson, Tom (1949–), American golfer. The heir-apparent to Jack Nicklaus as the world's greatest player. Since his first professional season in 1972, Watson has won golf's three major prizes—the Open, the American Open and the US Masters—at least once, and has amassed earnings well in excess of one million dollars. In 1982, he won both the Open Championship and the American Open within the space of a few months to cement his title as the world's best player.

Watson-Watt, Sir Robert Alexander (1892–1973), British scientist and inventor. After working in the Meteorological Office and the Department of Scientific and Industrial Research, he was from 1933 to 1936 superintendent of the radio department of the National Physical Laboratory. Here, following the investigations of the Americans Breit and Ture, he established the science of radar as a military weapon. From 1938 to 1940 he was director of communications development at the Air Ministry. In 1940 he became scientific adviser on telecommunications at the Air Ministry and in 1942 vice-controller of communications at the Ministry of Aircraft Production.

Watt, George Fiddes (1873–1960), Scottish portrait painter. He studied at the Royal Scottish Academy School and became noted mainly for portraits of celebrated men of his time, following Raeburn in style.

Watt, James (1736–1819), British engineer. He was employed on surveys for the Forth and Clyde Canal (1767), as well as for the Caledonian and other canals, and he was also concerned with the deepening of rivers, including the Forth and Clyde, and with the improvement of the harbours of Ayr, Port Glasgow and Greenock. In 1764, while repairing a model of John Newcomen's pumping engine, he realised that its efficiency, which was extremely low, could be considerably improved by condensing the steam in a separate vessel instead of in the cylinder itself. In making his calculations he was handicapped by a lack of information about specific heats and about the properties of steam, so he determined the values he needed experimentally. In 1765 he constructed the first steam engine to have a separate condenser. Later he entered into partnership with Matthew Boulton of Birmingham. The firm started by making engines which were purely reciprocating but soon realised the advantages of delivering power by a rotating shaft and Watt decided to make use of a crank mechanism. Before he could patent the device he was forestalled by one of his own workmen, Pickard, so he determined to evolve an alternative method and designed a sun-and-planet wheel mechanism which he used instead. Among his other inventions are the 'straightline' mechanism which bears his name, the engine indicator, the double-acting engine, and copying ink. He was the first man to apply the centrifugal governor to the control of engine speed.

Watt, SI unit of power, defined as a rate of work of 1 joule per second. In electric direct current, watts = volts × amperes. In alternating current circuits watts = volts × amperes × power factor.
See also METROLOGY.

Watteau, Jean Antoine (1684–1721), French painter. He went to Paris in 1702, and after enduring much privation he was eventually recognised, being made a member of the French Academy in 1717, and painter to the king in 1718. His great *Embarkation for Cythera* (Louvre) was his 'diploma piece'. Despite his premature death, Watteau exercised a profound and lasting influence on French art, and left a great number of pictures behind him. He excelled in his imaginative portrayal of scenes from Italian comedy, and elegant party groups, *fêtes champêtres*, such as were given by his patron, Crozat.

Watthourmeter, meter installed in consumers' circuits for recording energy consumed.
See also ELECTRIC METERS.

Wattle, see ACACIA.

Wattmeter, instrument for measuring electrical power.
See also ELECTRIC METERS.

James Watt, from a painting by Sir W. Beechey.

Watts, George Frederic (1817–1904), British painter and sculptor. He studied art in the studio of William Behnes, the sculptor, and also at the Royal Academy schools. In 1843, when several prizes were offered for cartoons to decorate the Houses of Parliament, Watts competed with his *Caractacus*, and won £300. In 1864 he married Ellen Terry. Among his best-known paintings are *Hope* and *Love and Death* (Tate Gallery), represented by large symbolical figures. His sculpture *Physical Energy* and his portraits of eminent Victorians represent him at his best.

Watts, Isaac (1674–1748), English minister and hymn-writer. In 1702 he took the Independent pastorate at Mark Lane Chapel in London. Owing to ill health he retired in 1712 and spent the rest of his life in the homes of his friend Sir Thomas Abney, where he compiled educational manuals and published theological works. He wrote between five and six hundred hymns, including 'O God, our help in ages past', and 'When I survey the wondrous Cross'.

Watts, William Whitehead (1860–1947),

British geologist, who worked on the geology of south Shropshire and Charnwood Forest.

Waugh, Alexander Raban, or Alec (1898–1981), English novelist, brother of Evelyn Waugh. He held commissions in the Dorsets in both World Wars. His first novel, *The Loom of Youth*, 1917, written when he was 17, was a realistic story of school life which provoked considerable controversy. Waugh went to Tahiti in 1926, and afterwards wrote much about the South Seas, including *Island in the Sun*, 1956. *My Brother Evelyn and Other Profiles*, 1967, is mainly autobiographical.

Waugh, Evelyn Arthur St John (1903–1966), English novelist. He was a schoolmaster for a time, but soon began to travel and devote himself to writing. In 1928 he published the first of his brilliant satirical novels, *Decline and Fall*; others are *Vile Bodies*, 1930; *Black Mischief*, 1932; *A Handful of Dust*, 1934; *Scoop*, 1938; *Put Out More Flags*, 1942; and *The Loved One*, 1948. These novels are riotously funny, but are nevertheless bitingly satirical attacks on contemporary society. In 1930 Waugh joined the Roman Catholic Church, and after the Second World War, in which he served as an officer in the Commandos, his writing took a more intentionally serious turn. His war trilogy, *Men at Arms*, 1952; *Officers and Gentlemen*, 1955; and *Unconditional Surrender*, 1961, attempted to analyse the war as a struggle between good and evil. The earlier novel, *Brideshead Revisited*, 1945, is openly religious. *The Ordeal of Gilbert Pinfold*, 1957, an account of a middle-aged writer's nervous breakdown, is considered by some his best novel. His son Auberon Waugh (1939–) is a journalist and novelist.

Wave, in physics a periodic disturbance travelling in space. All material substances have some degree of elasticity, and any molecular disturbance will be propagated through a body by virtue of this elasticity. Elasticity may appear as the resistance offered to change of shape. The former is bulk elasticity or degree of incompressibility, and the latter rigidity. In gases and most liquids, such as water, bulk elasticity is the only one which exists, and any propagation through these fluids is due to this type of elasticity. Such waves are termed longitudinal, and consist of periodic variations of density.
See also ELECTROMAGNETIC WAVES; HEAT; LIGHT; QUANTUM THEORY; SEA WAVES AND SWELL; SIMPLE HARMONIC MOTION; SOUND.

Waveguide, a system of conductors for electromagnetic waves at or near microwave frequencies, e.g. from transmitter to aerial in a radar or UHF television. Although a coaxial transmission line, consisting of an inner conductor surrounded by a cylindrical conducting sheath, may be regarded as a waveguide, the word usually means a hollow conducting tube with no inner conductor, transmission being effected by an electromagnetic wave travelling in the space within the tube. Waveguides are usually made of copper or brass, and are often rectangular in cross-section. To avoid excessive power loss they must be manufactured with great precision, their dimensions being critical and related to the wavelength.

Wave Mechanics, see QUANTUM THEORY.

Wavell of Cyrenaica, Archibald Percival Wavell, 1st Earl (1883–1950), British soldier and administrator. In the First World War he was sent in 1916 to Russia as military attaché to the army of the Caucasus. When Russian resistance collapsed he was transferred to Allenby's staff in the Middle East. In 1937 he was appointed commander of the British troops in Palestine. After the Munich pact he was given the Southern command in Britain, and in June 1939 was sent to Cairo as commander-in-chief of the British forces in the Middle East. After the collapse of France in 1940 he was called on to defend the entire Middle East with a few divisions of British troops and a handful of planes. During the three years of Britain's delaying fight Wavell sustained defeat after defeat, but the net gain of his battles, which disrupted the whole German time-table, was incalculable. After the Greek débâcle and the loss of Cyrenaica, Wavell was sent to India, but soon after he was promoted to supreme command in the Far East against Japan, and after the fall of all the British and Dutch colonial possessions in the South Pacific he returned to India to organise the stand against the Japanese there and in Burma. He became field marshal on 1 January 1943. He was viceroy of India, 1943–48.

Waveney, river of England, rising near the Little Ouse and forming part of the boundary between Norfolk and Suffolk. It flows past Diss, Bungay and Beccles, and has a course of nearly 80 km, being navigable as far as Geldeston. The Waveney joins the Yare 6 km south-west of Great Yarmouth.

Wax. The various kinds of wax are usually mixtures of esters of the higher monobasic carboxylic acids with the higher mono- or occasionally di-hydric alcohols, with free acid and alcohol and often hydrocarbons. Waxes are of considerable commercial value and at various times have been used in making wax figures, candles, polishes, gramophone records, soaps, etc. Mineral waxes are also known, e.g. ozokerite and paraffin wax. The latter is a by-product from the petroleum distillation industry.

Wax Flower, or honey plant, *Hoya carnosa,* an evergreen climbing plant of the Asclepiadaceae, with thick leaves and white, starshaped waxy-looking flowers.

Wax Myrtle, see BAYBERRY.

Waxwing, a bird of the family Bombycillidae, order Passeriformes, of which there are three species. The Bohemian waxwing, *Bombycilla garrulus,* has a cinnamon-brown plumage changing in parts to grey or chestnut, relieved by black, white and a yellow band to the tail. It is easily distinguished from all other birds by the curious expanded shaft at the tip of some of its wing feathers which gives the appearance of scarlet sealing-wax droplets. *B. garrulus* is found in northern parts of Scandinavia, Asia and western Canada, feeding on insects and berries.

Wayfaring Tree, see VIBURNUM.

Wayland the Smith (Norse *Völand,* German *Wieland*), in Norse mythology, an elfish metalworker, enslaved and hamstrung by King Nidud. Wayland kills the king's sons and ravishes his daughter, then escapes on wings made from birds' feathers.

'Wayland's Smithy' is a chambered long barrow between White Horse Hill and Ashbury in Oxfordshire. According to folklore, a wayfarer might leave a groat at this 'smithy' and on his return find his horse shod by the unseen smith.

Way of the Cross, see STATIONS OF THE CROSS.

Wayne, John, real name Marion Michael Morrison (1907–79), US film actor. Wayne first starred in John Ford's *Stagecoach* (1939), creating an image of easy-going toughness sustained over thirty years in Westerns and war films. *True Grit,* 1969, won him an Academy Award.

Waziristan, tract of land, now forming part of Pakistan, lying on the border between Afghanistan on the north-west, Baluchistan on the south, and the North-West frontier province on the east. It is about 250 km from north to south and 100 km from east to west. The western half is mountainous. The land slopes towards the east and is, when irrigated, fertile in the north round Bannu.

Weald, region in England, specifically the area between the North and South Downs and Butser Hill, Hampshire. Much of Kent, Sussex, the southern part of Surrey, and eastern Hampshire are included in this 190 km-long and 48 km-wide anticlinorium with its ESE–WNW axis. The oldest rocks have been exposed by denudation at the centre and are surrounded by horseshoe-shaped outcrops of progressively younger rocks giving the Wealden Series, Weald Clay, and the complex Hastings Beds formation. By the time of the Saxon kingdom of *Andredesweald*, iron-ore had been mined here for many centuries with wood providing charcoal and oak for shipbuilding. In medieval England the Weald was a major provider of armaments.

See also CRETACEOUS SYSTEM.

Wealth. The mercantilists regarded wealth as money or 'treasure', measuring the profit of international trade by the amount of treasure, of gold and silver, they could thereby amass. The physiocrats brought the idea down to earth, teaching that increase in wealth is to be measured by *produit net*, the surplus of agricultural and mineral products over cost of production. For Adam Smith, *An Inquiry into the Nature and Causes of the Wealth of Nations* meant a study of exchange values of every kind. While air and sunlight had enormous value in use, only things with value in exchange were measurable wealth and the subject-matter of economics. Jean-Baptiste Say insisted that services are wealth equally with material things. It may seem fanciful to reckon a song as wealth: but the modern statistician cannot reconcile his national wealth figures if he ignores the fee of the singer. National wealth statistics have made great strides in recent years. Since 1941 a series of British government White Papers and Blue Books has given official estimates of the annual production of national wealth (goods and services).

The term 'national income and expenditure' denotes two aspects of one thing. The essential quality of the national income (everybody's income) and the national expenditure (everybody's spending) is a particularly modern conception which is bound up with the economic notion that to achieve full business activity it is essential to see that spending is adequate. Since spending is the mainspring of trade and production, the dynamic approach to national income is via national expenditure.

See also PERSONAL PROPERTY; PHYSIOCRATIC SCHOOL.

Wear, river of England, rising in the west Durham Pennines near Wearhead close to the border with Cumbria, from where it flows eastwards for nearly half its total length of 104 km along a narrow valley, Weardale, to Bishop Auckland, and then north-eastwards past Durham and Chester-le-Street to the North Sea at Sunderland (Wearmouth).

Weasel, *Mustela nivalis,* a widely distributed mammal of family Mustelidae in order Carnivora, native to Europe. Its body is about 20 cm long, and its tail about 6 cm. Its head is small and flattened, with lively black eyes and short, rounded ears. The fur is reddish-brown above and white below. It feeds principally on rodents and small birds.

Weather, see METEOROLOGY.

Weathering, a series of processes induced by physical, chemical and biological agents which lead to the breakdown and alteration of the materials of the Earth's surface. Physical weathering is the breakdown of materials by physical means, the forces originating within the rock or externally leading to stresses and eventual disintegration. Chemical weathering is normally aided by the presence of water giving rise to alteration products, whilst biological weathering can be physically induced, e.g. the breakdown in rocks by root action or by bacteria and organic acids which lead to complex biochemical reactions.

Weaver Birds. *The black-headed weaver* Ploceus cucullatus.

Weaver Birds, birds of the order Passeriformes in two families: true weavers belong to the family Ploceidae, weaver finches to the Estrildidae. They make remarkable nests, which in some cases are immense structures occupied by a colony of birds. They are most numerous in Africa, but extend to Asia and Australia. Most of them are brightly coloured, particularly in the breeding season. Their bodies are somewhat elongated and the tails long, and the prominent conical bill is very powerful. They eat insects and may eat cultivated grain. The male makes a typical enclosed nest on a branch, entered from beneath, then hangs from it calling and flapping its wings to attract a female.

Weaving, the formation of cloth by inter-lacing two sets of threads at right angles to each other; the *warp* running lengthwise down the cloth and the *weft* running across the width of the cloth. The warp beam, measuring just over the required width of the cloth, may weigh many tonnes and contain many thousands of yarns or ends, each end being up to several thousand metres in length. On a power-loom, shafts are lifted or lowered to form a shed or separation of the warp ends, and the shuttle which contains a bobbin of weft yarn is fired at speeds of up to 130 km/h through the shed, across the width of the warp, trailing behind it a length of weft. The reed presses the length of a weft or pick into the fell, creating a small length of woven cloth. Weaves such as plain weave, the twills, bara-thea and honeycomb, are achieved by a fixed arrangement of interlacings, which is brought about by programming which shafts will be up, which down, and the way the ends are threaded into the shafts. Many fabric names are derived from the weave; these names became associated with certain types of cloth, yarns, tightness of weave, etc. In weaving patterns and checks more than one colour is put into the warp, and more than one shuttle is used. A power-loom can be programmed to weave the required numbers of each weft colour to produce the required pattern.

Recent developments include means of inserting weft which do not involve pro-pelling a shuttle weighing several kilograms to introduce a pick weighing a fraction of a gram. The rapier, carrier, shuttle and jet methods of weft insertion have allowed speeds of weft insertion to rise from 500 m per minute for some shuttle looms to 1300 m per minute for jet.

The mechanism invented by Jacquard about 1800 is for weaving cloth where the com-plexity of the weave design demands more versatility than could be obtained with a shaft method of warp control.

See also COTTON; FABRICS, TEXTILE; WOOL.

Webb, Beatrice (Lady Passfield) (1858–1943), British social reformer. In 1891 she published *The Co-operative Movement in Great Britain*. Soon after this she met Sidney Webb, whom she subsequently married (1891). The first joint publication of the Webbs was their well-known book *The History of Trade Unionism*. A firm believer in the efficacy of royal commission, she herself served on many. She joined the Fabian Society and later became its president. She and her husband carried out researches in the history of trade unionism, the Poor Law and Russia, and their publications on these subjects are recognised as standard works.

See also PASSFIELD, SIDNEY JAMES WEBB, BARON.

Webb, Mary Gladys (1881–1927), English novelist. She wrote a book of essays and four novels before *Precious Bane* was published in 1924. This book was awarded the Femina Vie Heureuse Prize and became suddenly and immensely popular. Shropshire is the scene of all her novels, which depict a curiously primitive rural life, with unusual imaginative power and pathos.

Webb, Matthew (1848–83), British swimmer. He was the first man to swim the English Channel without artificial aids. On 25 August 1875 he swam from Dover, England, to Calais, France, in 21 hours 45 minutes, and not until 1923 was his feat emulated. After his Channel crossing he hoped to establish himself as an entertainer, but in an attempt to boost falling attendances at his vaudeville show he was drowned trying to swim across the rapids at Niagara.

See also CHANNEL SWIMMING.

Josiah Wedgwood. Jasper-ware medallions were imitations of the cameos of antiquity.

Weber, Carl Maria von (1786–1826), German composer. His first opera, *Peter Schmoll*, was produced in 1803. Weber became opera director of the German theatre in Prague, and later took up a similar post at Dresden. Here he became involved in the opposition of German opera against Italian. He consolidated the success of the former with *Der Freischütz*, which is based on a German legend and exploits the supernatural element which was to be popular in German Romantic opera. Italian coloratura was re-placed by a simplified vocal style, and by the use of arias in the manner of folksongs and dances. The chorus is integrated musically and dramatically into the structure and Weber employs his orchestra more subtly than Italian opera of the period. The more ambitious opera *Euryanthe* was less successful, but Weber's fame led to the commission of *Oberon* by the Covent Garden Theatre in London. Apart from numerous operas, Weber wrote chamber music and concertos, especi-ally featuring the clarinet as soloist, piano music, and songs.

Weber, Max (1864–1920), German soci-ologist, regarded as one of the founding fathers of sociology, even though some of his work remained unfinished. He held the chair of economics at Heidelberg. He made sub-stantial contributions to the idea of social action, to the theory of ideal types, to the study of the relationship between economic behaviour and religion, and of bureaucracy.

Webern, Anton (1883–1945), Austrian composer. He studied musicology at Vienna University, but turned to composition and came under the influence of Schoenberg, whose 12-note system he adopted. He wrote little and was able to perform his works only against great opposition (they were banned during the Nazi domination of Austria). Compositions include five choral works, six for orchestra, instrumental and vocal chamber music, variations for piano and 20 songs.

See also SERIALISM.

Webster, John (c.1580–c.1625), English dramatist. He wrote a number of plays in collaboration with Heywood, Dekker, Middleton and Chettle, as well as poetry and pageants. His reputation is based on two tragedies in the revenge tradition, *The White Devil*, 1612, and *The Duchess of Malfi*, c.1614. Both plays investigate the decadence and evil which centred on the Renaissance courts, and they do so with a vision which is dark, obsessive in its concern with death and decay, and yet constantly producing poetry of extra-ordinary power. They have been much revived in recent years, always with success. Webster also wrote *The Devil's Law Case*, c.1610, a tragi-comedy.

Webster, Noah (1758–1843), US lexi-cographer. His patriotic *American Spelling Book*, 1783, was tremendously popular and later editions (influenced by the more extreme proposals of Benjamin Franklin, about 1786), introduced the now standard American spellings such as 'center' and 'honor'. In 1828 he published his monumental two volume *American Dictionary of the English Language*, which owes much to Samuel Johnson, but established a distinct standard American English.

Weddell Sea, ice-filled sea which indents Antarctica between the Antarctic Peninsula and Coats Land (British Antarctic Territory), centring in about 73°S and 45°W. It was dis-covered in 1823 by the Scottish sealer, James Weddell.

Wedekind, Frank (1864–1918), German playwright. He was a founder and editor of *Simplicissimus*, and for a time an actor and producer. He ridiculed bourgeois morality, pointing out its hypocrisies, and insisted on the need for social acceptance of sexuality, as in *Spring Awakening*, 1891, and the 'Lulu' plays *Erdgeist*, 1895, and *Die Büchse der Pandora*, 1904. Wedekind has affinities with German Expressionism and Brecht.

Wedgwood, Dame Cicely Veronica (1910–), British historical writer. She has written extensively and sympathetically on a wide range of historical subjects, in particular on 17th-century England. Her publications include: *The Thirty Years War*, 1938; *Oliver Cromwell*, 1939, revised ed., 1973; *The King's Peace*, 1955; *The King's War*, 1958, and *The Trial of Charles I*, 1964.

Wedgwood, Josiah (1730–95), English potter. He was apprenticed in his brother's pottery, 1744–49, and worked with Thomas Whieldon, 1754–59. In 1759 he established a factory, Ivy House, Burslem, Staffordshire, where he soon made cream-coloured earthenware. In 1769 his new factory, Etruria, began producing Greek-style vases, black 'basalte' and other stonewares, especially the fine jasper (first produced 1774) stoneware for reliefs, either on vases or cameos. His published pamphlets and catalogues were translated into many European languages. In the 19th and 20th centuries his factories produced fine chinaware.

See also EARTHENWARE; PORTLAND VASE; STONEWARE.

Wedmore, village in Somerset, England, on a slight rise above the Somerset Levels, noted for the treaty (sometimes called the Treaty of Chippenham) concluded here (878) between Alfred and Guthrum. By this treaty the country north of Watling Street was ceded to the Danes. Population (1971) 2400.

Wednesday (Anglo-Saxon *Wodnesdaeg*, Woden's Day), fourth day of the week. It was the *dies Mercurii* (Mercury's Day) of the Romans, from which came French *mercredi*.

Week (Old English *wice*), period of seven successive days, as in Jewish and Christian calendars, especially such a period beginning with Sunday and including in addition to that day Monday, Tuesday, Wednesday, Thursday, Friday and Saturday. The names of the days of the week are derived from the planets, the hours being allotted to the seven planets in the order of their supposed distances from the Earth, and each planet being regarded as presiding over the day whose first hour belonged to it. Thus the days of the Roman week were assigned in order to the Sun, the Moon, Mars, Mercury, Jupiter, Venus and Saturn. The Latin nations have retained the names derived from these deities, but in the Germanic languages they are replaced by names derived from those of the corresponding Germanic deities, Tyr being regarded as the equivalent of Mars, Woden of Mercury, Thor of Jupiter, and Freyja of Venus.

Weelkes, Thomas (c.1575–1623), English organist and composer. He was organist at Winchester, then took the B Mus at Oxford and became organist at Chichester Cathedral. His madrigals and similar works show him as one of the greatest masters of the serious madrigal, often on deeply melancholy texts. He also wrote numerous services and anthems.

Weevil, any member of the insect family Curculionidae in order Coleoptera. In general they are less than 5 mm long and are readily distinguished from other beetles by their pronounced snout-like rostrum, which sometimes exceeds the entire length of the rest of the body. The rostrum (a prolongation of the head, bearing the mouthparts) is usually convex and curved, and is used for boring into plant stems and trees, both for feeding and, in the female, for depositing eggs. Weevils are generally plant feeders in both adult and larval stages. The larvae usually feed on their plant hosts internally or at root level. Weevils exhibit great specificity with regard to the plant host. There are also a number of weevils that feed on grains and stored products, e.g. species of the genus *Calandra*. The larvae of weevils are usually legless, pale, fleshy grubs. Adult weevils are mostly dark coloured, although some, e.g. *Phyllobius*

species, are bright green. Over 40,000 species of weevils have been identified, of which the most notorious is the cotton boll weevil, *Anthonomus grandis*, which is a serious pest of cotton crops in the USA. The genus *Rhynchophorus* includes the palm weevils of the tropics.

Weft, see WEAVING.

Wegener, Alfred Lothar (1880–1980), German geophysicist who pioneered the theory of continental drift. His ideas were not widely accepted until the discovery of seafloor spreading in the 1960s, and the development of plate tectonics theory.

See also GEOTECTONICS.

Weigel, Helene (1900–), German actress, who was married to Bertolt Brecht and who created the leading female rôles in—among others of his plays—*The Mother; Mother Courage and her Children;* and *The Caucasian Chalk Circle.* From Brecht's death in 1956 she directed the Berliner Ensemble.

Weigelia, see DIERVILLA.

Weight. The force acting upon a body due to gravity. If m is its mass and g the acceleration due to gravity, the weight w is given by $w = mg$, and is expressed in newtons or kilograms weight (1 kilogram weight = g newtons). Since g is not a universal constant, the weight will be different in space or on the Moon, for example, and will vary slightly at different locations on the Earth. Mass will always be constant.

Weight-lifting, competitive sport for men consisting of raising barbells (iron bars), evenly loaded with metal discs. The sport of weight-lifting as it is now practised originated in the late 18th and 19th centuries.

Although strength is the prime requisite, correct technique and speed both assist in the lifting of heavy weights. There are two methods permitted at international and Olympic level: the snatch and the clean and jerk. In the snatch, the bar is pulled evenly from the ground in one movement and is then affixed overhead while the competitor squats or splits (i.e. one leg forward and one leg back) beneath it. In the clean and jerk the competitor is able to raise even larger weights by first pulling the bar up to shoulder height and into his neck and then, using the initial impetus of his legs, pushes it overhead. Both moves must end with the feet in line and the body erect.

In Olympic weight-lifting there are nine bodyweight classes ranging from flyweight (under 52 kg) to super-heavyweight (over 110 kg). Lifters have three attempts in each of the two permitted styles. The highest efforts on the two techniques are aggregated and the person with the greatest total wins.

A variation of weight-lifting is powerlifting in which competitors participate on the squat (or deep knees bend), the bench press and the dead lift. Powerlifting has its own annual world championships, but its techniques are less popular than those of the Olympic events.

See also ATHLETICS; CLASSICAL GAMES; GYMNASTICS.

Weights and Measures, see METROLOGY.

Weil, Simone (1909–43), French writer. She had a varied life, which included studying and teaching philosophy, serving in the International Brigade in the Spanish Civil War, and working at the London headquarters of

the French provisional government during the Second World War. Her profound interest in philosophical and spiritual problems led her to write a number of works which were published posthumously. These include *La Pesanteur et la grâce*, 1948; *Enracinement*, 1950; *Attente de Dieu*, 1950; *La Source grecque* (on Greek philosophy, translations and studies), 1953; *Oppression et liberté*, 1955; and volumes of *Cahiers*.

Weill, Kurt (1900–50), German composer. He studied with Humperdinck and Busoni in Berlin. His *Dreigroschenoper*, a version of *The Beggar's Opera* incorporating jazz elements, inaugurated a period of collaboration with the dramatist Bertolt Brecht (*Happy End, Mahagonny*). Denounced by the Nazi regime, in 1933 he settled in America, where he wrote several musicals. His output includes two symphonies, a violin concerto, cantatas and songs.

Weimar, town of the German Democratic Republic on the river Ilm, 21 km east of Erfurt. In 1547 it became the capital of Saxe-Weimar, and in 1815 of the Grand Duchy of Saxe-Weimar-Eisenach. Later it was the capital of Thuringia. After the First World War it became the seat of the new German Republic. Weimar's cultural past is paid tribute in the Goethe National Museum, the German National Theatre, the Franz Liszt College of Music, and the archives of the philosopher Nietzsche. Its industries include chemicals, railway stock, furniture and building materials. Population (1981) 63,700.

Weinberger, Jaromír (1896–1967), Czech composer. The success of his opera *Švanda the Bagpiper* was not repeated by his four later operas, but the orchestral variations on *Under the Spreading Chestnut Tree* were briefly popular.

Weismann, August (1834–1914), German biologist. In 1860 he was appointed physician to Archduke Stephen of Austria, and in 1866 became professor of zoology at Freiburg im Breisgau, remaining there for the rest of his life. He began important microscopical studies, but abandoned them owing to deteriorating eyesight, turning instead to the study of evolution. His theory of the unbroken continuity of the germ plasm and his evidence that acquired characteristics are not directly transmitted were at first opposed but subsequently accepted. The second, which overthrew the Lamarckian theory of acquired characteristics, is of far-reaching social significance, showing that moral qualities are not transmitted to children but have to be acquired by intensive early training.

Weiss, Peter (1916–), German-born dramatist, now a naturalised Swede. He achieved international success with *Marat/Sade*, 1964. This was followed by *The Investigation*, 1965, and *Song of the Lusitanian Bogey*, 1967, which portrays with music and dance the Portuguese exploitation of Angola and Mozambique. *Vietnam Discourse*, 1968, traces the political history of Vietnam, and satirically portrays such figures as Winston Churchill and US presidents Kennedy and Johnson. More recent work includes *Trotsky in Exile*, 1970, and *Hölderlin*, 1971. His work has affinities with the plays of Georg Büchner and Brecht. He has also written novels and made some experimental films.

Weissmuller, Johnny (1904–84), US swimmer. He was the world's finest swimmer in the 1920s, winning five gold medals in two Olympic Games (100, 400 and 4 × 200 m freestyle in 1924, and 100 and 4 × 200 m in 1928). He set 24 world records, some of which stood for over 10 years. He also won an Olympic bronze medal for water-polo. He later turned professional and was a natural for the cinema rôle of Tarzan, through which he became still more widely known.

Weizmann, Chaim (1874–1952), Zionist leader and chemist, born in one of the Jewish 'pales' in Grodno, Russia. He became lecturer in chemistry at Geneva and reader in biochemistry at Manchester University in 1904. During the First World War, when he was director of the Admiralty laboratories, he made the brilliant discovery of a process for the manufacture of acetone, the basis for high explosives. Between 1917 and 1930 Weizmann, as president of the World Zionist Organisation, was mainly responsible for the political relationship between the British Colonial Office and the Jewish Agency in Palestine. Weizmann always stood for co-operation between the Jewish people and Britain in the development of Palestine, with the ultimate ideal of a Jewish Commonwealth in Palestine. He became president of the Provisional Council of Israel in 1948, and was sworn in as first president of Israel on 17 February 1949.

Weld, or dyer's rocket, *Reseda luteola*, a tall plant in the family Resedaceae, with long spikes of yellow flowers. It was formerly grown to furnish a yellow dye similar to that obtained from dyer's greenweed, *Genista tinctoria*.

Welding, the process of joining metals together without the use of dissimilar bonding materials. Energy in some form, usually heat, is supplied to the joint so that the parts can be united. Contaminating surface films must be prevented from forming during the welding process. The atmosphere, therefore, must usually be excluded by using a flux, or by welding in an inert gas or a vacuum. There are two main classes of process, pressure welding in which the parts to be joined are heated

and pressure is applied, and fusion welding where a filler of a similar metal is melted into the joint. Oxy-acetylene flames and a variety of forms of electric arc are the principal sources of heat. Electron beams and lasers are used for specialised applications. In spot welding the metal is melted between the opposite point of a pair of electrodes.

Welensky, Sir Roy (1907–84), Rhodesian politician. He was an engine driver, then took up professional boxing, becoming heavyweight champion of the Rhodesias, 1926–28. He formed the Northern Rhodesia Labour party in 1941. He took an active part in the formation of the Federation of Rhodesia and Nyasaland. He became deputy prime minister on federation and was prime minister, 1956–63, fighting hard to prevent the dissolution of the federation. After the federation was dissolved he attempted to make a political comeback in Southern Rhodesia (Zimbabwe), but failed and retired from politics.

Welfare State, name applied to a social system under which the state not only sets standards of, for example, health, education, housing and pensions, but provides the finance necessary and in most cases also supplies the services themselves.

Welkom, town of Orange Free State, South Africa, founded in 1947 following gold discoveries and now the second largest town in the province. Population (1980) 176,608, including 38,027 whites.

Well, see ARTESIAN WELL; WATER SUPPLY.

Welland Ship Canal, originally built 1824–1829, between Lake Ontario (Port Weller) and Lake Erie (Port Colbourne), parallel with the Niagara river. By the enlarged route (completed 1888) it was 44 km long.

The present Welland Canal was begun in 1913, and opened to ships in 1931. With the opening of the St Lawrence Seaway in 1959 the canal became part of the system and now has eight new locks, each 262 m long, 24 m wide, and 24 m deep, allowing ships of 220 m length and 23 m beam to pass through the canal.

Welles, Orson (1915–), US actor, film and theatre director. He made his first appearance on the stage in Dublin, and then returned to the USA to tour with Katharine Cornell. His most spectacular exploits in the theatre were his modern-dress *Julius Caesar* in 1937, and his broadcast, *War of the Worlds*, in 1938, which caused panic throughout America. A film director of genius, his first film, *Citizen Kane*, 1940, is one of the classics of the cinema; others include *The Magnificent Ambersons*, 1942; *The Lady from Shanghai*, 1947; *Macbeth*, 1948; *Othello*, 1951; *Chimes at Midnight*, 1966; and *The Immortal Story* 1968. He acted in most of these, and his suave, weighty presence lent distinction to *The Third Man*, 1949, and many lesser films.

Wellesley, Arthur, see WELLINGTON, ARTHUR WELLESLEY, 1ST DUKE OF.

Wellesley, Richard Colley Wellesley, 1st Marquess (1760–1842), British statesman, brother of the 1st Duke of Wellington. He went to India in 1797 as governor-general, a position he held for eight years, during which time he proved an enlightened and efficient administrator. In 1809 he became foreign secretary in Perceval's ministry. He

was lord-lieutenant of Ireland from 1821 to 1828, and again in 1833–34.

Wellesz, Egon (1885–1974), Austrian musicologist and composer. He studied musical science at Vienna university and composition under Schoenberg, whose influence showed in his work for a time, together with that of Mahler and Debussy. He settled at Oxford in 1939. As a scholar he particularly distinguished himself as an expert in Byzantine music. His compositions include six operas; four ballets: choral and orchestral works (nine symphonies); piano and violin concertos; chamber music; and piano pieces and songs.

Wellington. *A portrait by Lawrence, 1814.*

Wellington, Arthur Wellesley, 1st Duke of (1769–1852), British soldier and statesman. He began his military command at the head of a brigade in Holland in 1794. He then went to India where, as a colonel in the war against Tipu Sahib, Wellington first gave signs of military genius. Left in command of the troops at Mysore, he baffled Napoleon's plan of a descent on southern India from Egypt, by invading Mysore and destroying or scattering the 40,000 followers of Dhoondyah Waugh before French forces could be sent there. In 1803 he was appointed chief political and military agent in the Deccan and the southern Maratha states, and on the fresh outbreak of trouble with the native chiefs he added to his reputation by the signal defeat of an overwhelming force at Assaye. He received the thanks of Parliament and was knighted, but he resigned in 1805 and returned to England.

In 1806 he became MP for Rye, and in 1807 chief secretary for Ireland and a privy councillor, but with the threat of a French invasion he was soon in active service again. After a short campaign in Denmark, which ended in the humiliation of the Danes, he was sent to Spain in 1808, and was soon involved in difficulties with incompetent rivals. In 1809 he returned to England and resigned, but was afterwards sent out in sole command, and began a series of victories which resulted in the evacuation of Portugal and Spain by the French. Ill-supplied with men and materials, Wellington defeated a succession of French

Orson Welles *in* Citizen Kane, *1940.*

marshals and proved that Napoleon's military system was not invincible. Though not of a character to win deep affection, he gained the profound respect of his troops, displaying the highest strategical and tactical qualities and a fine control of supply and organisation.

In 1815, loaded with honours, Wellington was ambassador to the restored Bourbon court, and British representative at the Congress of Vienna, when news came of Napoleon's escape from Elba. There followed his best-known campaign, that of Waterloo. In 1818 he recommenced his political career, a staunch Tory, becoming prime minister in 1828. He carried through Roman Catholic emancipation, but resigned in 1830, refusing to agree to electoral reform. He was foreign secretary under Peel (1834–35) and minister without portfolio (1841–46), supporting Peel's repeal of the corn laws. He is buried in St Paul's Cathedral by the side of Nelson. See also PENINSULAR WAR; WATERLOO.

Wellington, port and capital city of New Zealand, in the North Island, bounded by Cook Strait to the south. The city was founded in 1840, as Britannia, by the New Zealand company. As a result of its situation and being the seat of government, Wellington has become the headquarters of the chief commercial institutions of the country. The harbour is one of New Zealand's principal ports. After Auckland it is the second largest manufacturing centre of New Zealand, with engineering, electrical appliances, textiles, food and footwear industries. Population (1979) 350,100.

Wellingtonia, see SEQUOIA.

Wells, H(erbert) G(eorge) (1866–1946), English novelist and sociologist. He was a draper's assistant, an apprentice chemist, a schoolmaster and took a first class degree in science, before he broke a blood vessel in his lungs, in 1893 and was forced, probably willingly, into a career of authorship.

His first real literary success was in 1891 when Frank Harris accepted his *The Rediscovery of the Unique* for the *Fortnightly Review*. He first won nationwide recognition with his *War of the Worlds*, 1898. His earlier novels, which include *The Time Machine*, 1895 and *The Invisible Man*, 1897, are scientific romances. These were highly imaginative stories which were among the first science fiction novels. His social novels explored with sympathy the condition of ordinary lower middle- and working-class people. They include *Love and Mr Lewisham*, 1900; *Kipps*, 1905; and *The History of Mr Polly*, 1910. Wells was a Fabian, and a prophet of world organisation. His ruling theme was the need for man to impose his mastery upon his own creations; and, in pursuance of this concept, he became a leading advocate of social planning. *The Outline of History*, 1920, was an ambitious attempt to illustrate the continuity of history from the beginnings of life to the treaty of Versailles, and was the first volume of a trilogy planned to popularise the historical, scientific and sociological ideology appropriate to the task of creating a world state.

Wells, city and bishop's see in Somerset, England. The cathedral, of the diocese of Bath and Wells, was begun in the late 12th century. Among Wells's industries are the manufacture of paper, brushes, cheese, electronic equipment and textiles. Population (1981) 8374.

Wells Cathedral, Somerset, England was begun in the late 12th century, and the transepts, east bays of nave and west bays of choirs are in the transitional style of that period. The rest of the nave, the west front and the north porch are all superb examples of Early English architecture. The other main features of Wells are in the Decorated style, the retrochoir and Lady Chapel being completed c.1325, the chapter-house by 1319, the crossing tower, 1315–22 (but the exterior altered c.1440), the strainer arches beneath the tower, c.1338–40, and the new east end, 1345. The most famous feature of the cathedral is the west front, once painted, which is a gallery of medieval statuary unrivalled in England. The cathedral also contains excellent 14th-century stained glass.

Welsh Corgi, small Welsh cattle-dog; the advantage of its small size is that cattle are unable to get their horns low enough to harm it. There are two distinct varieties, the Pembroke and the Cardigan. The former weighs from 8 to 11 kg and has a maximum height of 30 cm at the shoulder. The head is foxy in outline, the chest broad and deep, the body of medium length and the legs short and straight. The tail is short. The favourite colour is red, or red and white. The Cardigan variety is somewhat larger and heavier. The Welsh corgi makes a reliable guard dog and is a popular pet.

'Welt, Die', Federal German newspaper, published in Hamburg, with subsidiary presses in Essen and Berlin. Founded in 1946 and independent in outlook, it has a wide circulation in Germany and is sold in numerous foreign countries. *Die Welt* is one of the many Federal German newspapers and periodicals owned by Axel Springer.

Welwitschia, a unique gymnosperm with one species, *W. bainesii*, in its own family the Welwitschiaceae. Native to almost rainless parts of south-west Africa, the trunk is conical, up to 1 m in diameter, and 7–30 cm high, with two, ribbon-like, leathery leaves. They grow continuously from the base, the ends splitting into thongs and wearing away.

Welwyn Garden City, town of Hertfordshire, England, situated 34 km north-west of London. It was the second of Ebenezer Howard's garden cities, established in 1920. It has about one hundred industries of a wide variety including light engineering, radio and electronics, pharmaceuticals, chemicals, printing, plastics, fashion goods and food products. Population (1981) 40,496.

Wembley Stadium. Opened in 1923 to coincide with the British Empire Exhibition, this north London stadium is England's international football ground. The first event held at Wembley, the 1923 FA Cup Final between Bolton and West Ham, attracted an estimated 250,000 people to a stadium designed to hold only 127,000; the capacity is now limited to 97,500 for safety reasons. Since then, Wembley has become the home ground of the England international soccer team and is also used to stage the annual FA Cup and Football League Finals and the FA Charity Shield. The Rugby League Cup Final is also held at Wembley and the stadium has also staged a wide variety of other sports and also non-sporting events. Wembley was also used during the 1948 Olympic Games and was the venue of England's World Cup victory in 1966.

Wenceslaus, Saint, also Wenzel (c.907–929), Duke of Bohemia. He received a Christian education from his grandmother, St Ludmilla, and as ruler tried to bring Bohemia into closer contact with the Western world. In consequence of this and of his efforts to stem the tide of pagan reaction he was assassinated by his brother Boleslav. St Wenceslaus is the patron of Bohemia and 'Good King Wenceslas' of the carol.

Wenceslaus IV (1361–1419), King of Bohemia and Holy Roman Emperor, son of the Emperor Charles IV, whom he succeeded in 1378. Wenceslaus was an incompetent ruler, and in 1394 the Bohemian nobles rebelled and made him a prisoner. In 1400 four German electors pronounced him deposed from the Imperial throne, but he recovered Bohemia in 1404 and retained it until his death.

Wensleydale, dale in North Yorkshire, England, usually described as that part of the valley of the Ure beginning near Jervaulx Abbey and continuing until near the source of the river in Lunds. Wensleydale gives its name to a breed of long-woolled sheep and a type of cheese.

Wentworth, Thomas, see STRAFFORD, THOMAS WENTWORTH, 1ST EARL OF.

Werewolf (Old English *wer*, man), a man-wolf. Folklores throughout the world contain traditions of men turning into wolves (and other wild animals) at certain times, frequently at the new moon. The term *lycanthropy* (Greek *lukos*, wolf; *anthropos*, man) is used in medicine to denote a mental state in which the patient believes he is an animal.

Werfel, Franz (1890–1945), Austrian Jewish author. He settled in Vienna in 1918 but went to France at the time of the *Anschluss* in 1938 and to the USA in 1940. His early poems are Expressionistic, condemning wars and the politics which leads to them. His first play was a modern adaptation of Euripides's *Trojan Women*, published in 1915. It is perhaps in his novels that his best work is found, the most famous being *Verdi*, 1924, and *Das Lied von Bernadette*, 1941, the story of the miracle of Lourdes.

Wergeland, Henrik Arnold (1808–45), Norwegian poet. He was a polemicist of tireless energy and a patriot who embodied the new national spirit of 1814. He was given a 'literary pension' in 1839, and in 1840 became keeper of the state archives. His popular influence has continued to this day. Wergeland is best known for his extraordinarily beautiful lyrics, which reveal a deep love of nature, and a rich imagination, as in *Digte—Første Ring*, 1829. His most ambitiously conceived work was the epic poem *Skabelsen, Mennesket og Messias*, 1830, a legend of the Creation. The latter part of his life was embittered by the many feuds rising from his outspokenness, but his early death was the cause of national mourning.

Wergild, or wer-geld, in Anglo-Saxon England, a money compensation for murder or manslaughter. Every man's life had a fixed pecuniary value called the wergild; the amount was graduated according to the rank of the person. The wergild of a murdered freeman was payable as compensation to his kin; that of a serf was paid to his master.

Werner, Abraham Gottlob (1750–1817), German geologist, who taught that all rocks were marine and championed the 'Neptunists' against the 'Plutonists' led by Hutton, who maintained that igneous rocks had solidified from molten material. Werner is regarded as a founder of mineralogy and petrology.

Weser, one of the largest rivers in the Federal Republic of Germany, formed by the junction of the Werra and Fulda rivers, the latter rising in Bavaria. From the junction at Münden, the river flows towards the North Sea. The lower reaches are canalised, and the river is navigable by large vessels to Bremerhaven, and by smaller vessels to Bremen. Length 440 km.

Wesker, Arnold (1932–), English playwright. His East End background, RAF experience and work as a pastry cook are all utilised in his plays. A trilogy about an East End Jewish Communist family and their disillusions—*Chicken Soup with Barley*; *Roots*; *I'm Talking about Jerusalem* (1959–60)—made his reputation; other plays are *The Kitchen*, 1959; *Chips with Everything*, 1962; *The Four Seasons*, 1965; and *The Friends*, 1970. He has also written for television, and founded Centre 42 (1961–70), an organisation devoted to bringing the theatre and similar arts to the working class.

Wesley, Charles (1707–88), English hymnwriter, brother of John Wesley, whom he helped in furthering the cause of Methodism. His greatest contributions were the hymns he wrote, numbering over 6000, and including such well-known examples as 'Jesu, Lover of My Soul' and 'Love Divine, All Loves Excelling'.

Wesley, John (1703–91), English founder of Methodism. He was a scholar at Christ Church, Oxford, and took holy orders in 1725. He was his father's curate at Wroot, (1727–29), then returned to Oxford as tutor and fellow in Lincoln College until 1735. At Oxford his younger brother, Charles, had formed a small group of undergraduates who followed very strictly the ordinances of the Church and were dubbed 'Methodists'. John joined the party and became its leader. From 1735–36 he was in America in charge of the Georgian mission. On his return he was influenced by Peter Böhler, a Moravian, and became a member of that society's chapel at Fetter Lane, London. About this time he experienced a personal conviction of salvation, and his new movement now developed. In 1739 he began open-air preaching at Bristol. In 1742 he went to Yorkshire and Newcastle-upon-Tyne, and his teaching took root everywhere. He is said to have delivered over 40,000 sermons. He and his brother Charles, Whitefield and others set up an independent society which met at the Foundery near Moorfields, London. Wesley made Bristol his headquarters, and he divided his followers into classes, with rules for their conduct and each with its own leader. He was especially successful with the poorer classes. It was not until 1784 that Wesley executed the 'deed of declaration', from which dates the beginning of modern Methodism. At his death his followers numbered 100,000. Wesley wrote many books and pamphlets, and edited the first popular series—*The Christian Library*.

Wesley, Samuel (1766–1837), British musician, son of Charles Wesley. He was a celebrated musical prodigy, writing an oratorio, *Ruth*, when he was eight. He became one of England's finest organists, and devoted considerable energy to popularising J. S. Bach.

Wesleyan Methodist Churches, see METHODISM.

Wessex, kingdom of Anglo-Saxon England. The chalk uplands of Wessex form an archaeological province, the distinctive cultures of which can be demonstrated from the time of the Bronze Age. The heart of Wessex, and the key to its archaeology, is Salisbury Plain. The historical kingdom of Wessex is said to have been founded by West Saxons under Cerdic and his son, Cynric, in 519. The invaders were defeated at Mons Badonicus (520), but won a great victory at Cerdicolea (527). Cerdic died in 534, and Cynric extended his kingdom beyond what is now Hampshire. His son, Ceawlin (560–592), was a warlike king and made repeated inroads on his British neighbours. But in 592 his own subjects rebelled against him at Woddesbeorg, and Ceawlin died in exile. The territory he had conquered beyond the Thames was seized by the Mercians, and Wessex ceased to be a powerful state. Egbert (802–839), who had spent his youth in exile at the court of Charlemagne, restored Wessex to its former power. He ultimately brought the whole of England into submission and before 828 was acknowledged overlord by all the peoples south of the Tweed. Wessex's territory was further increased and its power strengthened under Alfred; he and his son, Edward the Elder, transformed the kingship of Wessex into that of England.

See also ENGLISH HISTORY; HARDY, THOMAS.

West, Benjamin (1738–1820), American historical painter. Initially a sign and portrait painter in Philadelphia, in 1759 he went to Italy and in 1763 to London where he was a founder-member of the Royal Academy, being made president in 1792. West's importance is due to his establishing a new approach to history painting, as for example in his famous *Death of Wolfe*, 1770, where the hero and his companions appear in contemporary dress instead of that of classical antiquity. West was a respected teacher, especially of fellow American artists in London, e.g. J. S. Copley, and through them exercised a strong influence on American painting.

West, Nathanael, pseudonym of Nathan Wallenstein Weinstein (1904–40), US novelist. A remarkable surrealistic novelist who leads the way to modern black-humour writing, West produced only four novels before he was killed in a motor accident. They are *The Dream Life of Balso Snell*, 1931, an elaborate psychic comedy; *Miss Lonelyhearts*, 1933, the story of a gossip columnist who takes on responsibility for the destructive tensions of his correspondents; *A Cool Million*, 1934, an ironic romp at the expense of the American dream of success; and *The Day of the Locust*, 1939, his best, an apocalyptic work about Hollywood and the grotesques who are lured there, finally producing the riotous destruction of the city.

West, Rebecca, pseudonym of Dame Cicily Isabel Fairfield (1892–1983), English novelist and critic. She was an actress for a short time, and took the name Rebecca West from the heroine of Ibsen's *Rosmersholm*, one of the parts she played. After writing as a journalist, her first book was a study of the novelist Henry James, 1916. Her novels include *The Return of the Soldier*, 1918; *The Judge*, 1922; *Harriet Hume*, 1929; *The Harsh Voice*, 1936; *The Thinking Reed*, 1936; *The Fountain Overflows*, 1957; and *The Birds Fall Down*, 1966. She also wrote two books about the Nuremberg war trials.

West Africa, geographical term covering the region south of the Sahara, north of the Gulf of Guinea, and west of the Cameroon and Bamenda Highlands. The total area of West Africa is 6·3 million km², in which

John Wesley preaching at Oxford. Methodism's success was due to his energy and popular appeal.

reside over 100 million people. The political divisions of West Africa are, north to south along the coast, Mauritania, Senegal, Gambia, Guinea-Bissau, Guinea, Sierra Leone, Liberia, Ivory Coast, Ghana, Togo, Benin, Nigeria, Cameroon and Equatorial Guinea; inland are Mali and Upper Volta. For the geography, economy, government and history of each country, see under their respective entries.

West Africa, British, see GAMBIA, THE; GHANA; NIGERIA; SIERRA LEONE, REPUBLIC OF.

West Africa, French, see BENIN, PEOPLE'S REPUBLIC OF; FRENCH EQUATORIAL AFRICA; GUINEA; IVORY COAST; MALI; MAURITANIA; NIGER; SENEGAL.

West Africa, German, see SOUTH-WEST AFRICA; CAMEROON, UNITED REPUBLIC OF; TOGO, REPUBLIC OF.

West Bank, land on the western bank of the Jordan River which was taken from Jordan by Israel after the Arab-Israeli war of 1967, and has since been disputed territory. It is the historic homeland of the Palestinians, who still claim it.

West Bengal, state of India covering 87,853km² comprising the part of Bengal allocated to India after the end of the British Indian Empire in 1947, and part of Bihar added in 1956. Most of the country is deltaic, alluvial land along the lower Ganges and its mouths, with a fringe of Himalayan mountain country to the north. The long settled, densely populated delta is cultivated wherever crops can be grown. Rice takes up 85 per cent of the crop area and jute occupies 10 per cent. Tea is the major crop of the hill-country based on Darjeeling and Jalpaiguri. Oilseeds, sugar, pulses and tobacco are also grown. Fisheries are significant food suppliers. The Raniganj coalfield is the basis of an important industrial complex for several iron and steel works (e.g. Durgapur), metal and engineering, aluminium refining, glass, chemicals and locomotive works. The major complex is along the Hooghly river where most of India's jute is processed. Cotton, printing and consumer goods production are very important, together with ship repairs and engineering. The state is increasingly urban: Calcutta is dominant with 9·1 million people. State incomes are below the national level and there is serious social instability. Bengali is the principal language. Bengal was the first area in India to come under British rule and Western education. The capital is Calcutta and state government operates through a single chamber. Population (1981) 54,485,560.

West Berlin, see BERLIN.

West Bromwich, town in West Midlands Metropolitan County, England, 9km northwest of Birmingham. The primary cause of the town's rapid development was the discovery of coal and iron ore nearby. Brindley's canal, completed in 1769, passed through West Bromwich. Heavy engineering and metal-working industries are still important. Population (1971) 166,000.

West Germany, see GERMAN FEDERAL REPUBLIC.

West Glamorgan, see GLAMORGAN, WEST.

West Highland White Terrier, breed of dog probably descended from the cairn terrier, and known as the Poltalloch terrier when first exhibited. The ears are small, triangular and erect, the body compact and firm, the chest deep, and the back level. The coat is white, about 5cm long, harsh and free from curl. The tail is fairly thick and carried erect. The dog's height is about 28cm and the weight 7kg.

West Indies, archipelago extending in a curved chain from the Florida Channel (North America) to within 11km of the coast of Venezuela (South America), i.e. between latitude 27° and 10°N, the islands varying in size from 114,524km², the area of Cuba, to several hectares. They and their waters represent the Spanish Main of history and romance and, with the northern coasts of Central and South America, enclose the Caribbean Sea, lying across the trade routes to the Panama Canal. The islands were called the West Indies because Christopher Columbus, who discovered them, believed when he cruised round Hispaniola (Santo Domingo) that he had reached India by a westerly route. The alternative name is the Antilles. The total land area is nearly 260,000km² (this area includes the Bahamas, which lie outside the West Indies proper).

The archipelago may be divided into three groups: (1) the Greater Antilles, consisting of Cuba, Haiti, the Dominican Republic and Jamaica, all independent; the Turks and Caicos Islands and the Caymans (British); and Puerto Rico (American); (2) the Bahamas; and (3) the Lesser Antilles, the semicircle of smaller islands to the east of the Greater Antilles.

West Indian Federation. A series of conferences beginning at Montego Bay, Jamaica, in 1947 led to the signing in 1956 of an agreement to set up a Federation of the West Indies comprising Barbados, Jamaica, the Leeward Islands excluding the British Virgin Islands, Trinidad and Tobago, and the Windward Islands. But on the eve of the Federation's independence in 1962, first Jamaica and then Trinidad voted to secede, and the Federation was dissolved.

West Irian (Indonesian *Irian Jaya*), easternmost province of Indonesia and western portion of the island of New Guinea. Until 1963 it was Dutch New Guinea. Area 411,808km². West Irian is marked by extensive swamps along the south-west coast and a broad high belt of mountains extending east-west in the centre. Since the 1960s, intensified prospecting has revealed extensive deposits of oil, copper, nickel and other minerals. Eighty per cent is forested.

Total population in 1980 was 1,173,875. The main town is Jayapura (formerly Hollandia), population (1975) 56,000.

West Kennet, site of what is probably the best known neolithic long barrow in Britain. It lies near Avebury, Wiltshire, 1km south of Silbury Hill. There is a main entrance at the east end leading into a chamber about 11m deep with two chambers on each side. These were all constructed of large stone slabs and then covered with an earth mound 100m by 20m. The chambers contained many cremated and inhumed bones and the barrow seems to have been a collective burial place or a chieftain's family vault.

West Midlands Metropolitan County, midland English county created under the local government reorganisation of 1974 from parts of Staffordshire, Warwickshire and Worcestershire. It comprises Birmingham, Coventry, Dudley, Sandwell, Solihull, Walsall, West Bromwich, Wolverhampton and other urban centres, forming in effect a single conurbation. The county was sparsely inhabited for centuries, though towards the end of the Middle Ages Coventry became an important centre of the cloth trade. Metalworking began at Birmingham in the 16th century, but the town remained very small until the Industrial Revolution, when the presence of coal and ironstone transformed it into an industrial boom town. The Birmingham area and the nearby Black Country (now the north-west part of the West Midlands county) became a highly industrialised, notoriously grimy, and densely populated area, manufacturing an enormous range of metal goods. Recent redevelopment schemes include a massive programme of high-rise building and new shopping centres. Population pressure has been relieved by the designation of new towns, such as Telford New Town in Salop. Engineering and the manufacture of motor cars and aircraft remain major West Midlands industries. Area 775 km². Population (1981) 2,644,634.

West Point Military Academy. The US Military Academy is situated at West Point, on the right bank of the Hudson River, about 80km north of New York City.

West Prussia, see POLISH CORRIDOR.

West Sussex, see SUSSEX, WEST.

West Virginia ('Mountain State'), state of the USA. It has an area of 62,628km², and a curious configuration. Its north-eastern borders with Pennsylvania were determined by surveyors' lines, including the Mason-Dixon Line, and these left the state with a narrow strip of territory between Pennsylvania and the Ohio river. The southern and south-eastern boundaries result from the events of 1861–63, when the state of Virginia, the original claimant to this whole area, decided to secede from the Union and join the southern Confederacy in the Civil War. The mountainmen in western Virginia, having little in common with the planter-aristocracy of the Atlantic coast and owning few slaves, decided to remain loyal to the Union and so seceded from their native state. West Virginia is a mountainous state, composed entirely of the Appalachian Mountains and the Allegheny plateau; the average elevation is almost 500m although the highest point is below 1500m. The plateau section is forested, deeply dissected, and difficult to penetrate; its population has traditionally been one of independent but backward smallholders ('hillbillies'), cultivating small patches of clearing in the valley bottoms. Livestock is the state's principal farm product and hay the chief field crop; apples, tobacco and eggs represent the cash-crop production. As the area in farms has declined, so that under forest has increased; it is now 5 million ha, and much of this area consists of valuable hardwoods. The great Appalachian coalfield underlies the Allegheny plateau, and the state is the leading US coal producer. There is also production of natural gas. The 1980 population was 1,949,644. Charleston is the capital.

West Wall ('Siegfried Line'), German line of fortifications constructed opposite the

French Maginot line before the Second World War. The view taken by the German general staff was that this huge fortified girdle could be held by very small forces against the entire French and Belgian armies, so that Germany's main offensives could be conducted freely elsewhere. The West Wall proved a formidable obstacle to the advance of the Anglo-American armies in 1944–45.

West Yorkshire, see YORKSHIRE, WEST.

Western Australia, state of the Commonwealth of Australia, amounting to nearly one-third of the Australian continent; total area 2,525,500 km².

The southern and western coasts are more or less flat and sandy, with comparatively few natural harbours until the Kimberley division is reached, where the character of the coast becomes broken, and fringed with numerous islands. The greater portion of the interior is as an immense arid tableland, with an altitude of from 300 to 600 m above sea-level. Mount Bruce (1226 m) in the Hamersley range is the highest summit in the state.

The population is concentrated in the south-west of the state. Perth, the capital, is the largest city. Other large regional centres are Bunbury, Albany, Geraldton, Kalgoorlie-Boulder and Kwinana. The state population in 1976 was 1,114,300.

The aridity limits agriculture in Western Australia; the south-west has the most favourable climate for farming and it is here that most development has taken place. The main products are wheat, barley, oats, wool and fruit. In the north the Ord river scheme will eventually irrigate 72,000 ha, mainly for cotton growing. Other crops include grain sorghums, linseed, rice, peanuts and pasture crops. Forestry covers only a small area of the state, most of it in the south-west. Reserves of high grade iron ore in the Pilbara region are estimated at about 20,000 million t. Annual production is now about 80 million t. The Kambalda area has major nickel resources. A nickel smelter has been constructed at Kalgoorlie, and from there the concentrate is sent to Kwinana for refining. The bauxite deposits of the Darling Range (and in future years the Mitchell Plateau) provide the raw material for the alumina refineries at Kwinana, Pinjarra and Muchea. The state also contains oil and natural gas, uranium and mineral sands and coal. Gold was discovered at Coolgardie in 1892 and is still important. Perth is the main manufacturing centre, with a wide range of industries including metal-working, foodstuffs, electronics and household equipment. Most industry is based on the vast mineral resources of the region and offshore oil and natural gas. Responsible government was granted to Western Australia in 1890. The legislature consists of two houses, both elected. Enrolment is compulsory for all but Aborigines, and voting is compulsory.

In 1791 George Vancouver took formal possession of the country above King George Sound for Great Britain; in 1801 Matthew Flinders explored the south coast, which, at his suggestion, subsequently received the name Australia; between 1818 and 1822 Philip Parker King charted the north coast. In 1827 James Stirling surveyed the coast from the Sound to Swan river and in 1829 Charles Fremantle in HMS *Challenge* took possession of the territory, and founded the Swan River Settlement, which is now the state of Western Australia, and the towns of Perth and Fremantle. In 1901 Western Australia became one of the federated states of the Commonwealth of Australia.

Western Bug, see BUG, WESTERN.

Western Dvina, see DVINA, WESTERN.

Western European Union was formed originally as the Western Union to implement the Brussels Treaty, 1948, 'for collaboration in economic, social and cultural matters and for collective self-defence'. In 1950 its defence functions were transferred to the newly-created North Atlantic Treaty Organisation. Following the failure to establish the European Defence Community in 1954, Federal Germany and Italy were invited to sign the Brussels Treaty and to join NATO, and the seven signatories of the former treaty constituted the Western European Union, i.e. the five original members, the UK, France, Belgium, the Netherlands and Luxembourg, together with Federal Germany and Italy. In its present form the WEU therefore dates from 1955 and consists of a Council, comprising the foreign ministers of the member-states, and an Assembly, comprising the member-states' representatives to the Consultative Assembly of the Council of Europe.

Western Front, see WORLD WAR, FIRST.

Western Isles Islands Area, Scottish regional administrative unit which is equivalent to the Outer Hebrides group of islands. These islands include Lewis, Harris, North and South Uist, Benbecula and Barra, as well as numerous smaller inhabited and un-inhabited islands such as St Kilda, Rockall, Pabbay and Mingulay with a total land area of 2900 km² and a population (1981) of 31,766 which is mainly Gaelic-speaking. Open to the Atlantic Ocean on the west and the stormy Minch to the east, the islands are now almost treeless and mainly covered by extensive peat bogs. Areas of hills and mountains are found on all the islands. The only fertile land is the sandy machair of the west coast. A long history of settlement has left Stone, Bronze and Iron Age remains, including those of Callanish.

From the 8th to the 13th centuries the area remained subject to the Scandinavians. Language, customs and place names are strongly related to this period. Today the main occupations of farming, weaving and fishing are related to the crofting form of land holding and settlement. The larger settlements are all ports on the indented east side of all the main islands. Apart from the Harris tweed mills there is little industry. Tourism is increasingly important. There are good air and sea connections from the larger islands. Stornoway is the administrative centre.

Western Sahara, Moroccan-occupied area of West Africa, formerly a Spanish province (Spanish Sahara), where sovereignty is claimed both by Morocco and by the native *Frente Polisario* who hold much of it and have named it the Democratic Saharan Arab Republic. Western Sahara has an area of 266,769 km²; it is bounded on the west by the Atlantic, north by Morocco, north-east by Algeria, east and south by Mauritania. The principal town is El Aaiún. There is livestock farming, production of dried fish, potash and iron ore, but the main source of revenue lies in the huge phosphate deposits found at Bu Craa in 1963.

Spain agreed to transfer the province to Morocco and Mauritania in 1976. The country was duly partitioned, but in 1979 Mauritania withdrew and its portion was taken over by Morocco. Algeria, which had objected to the partition, objected again and supported native claims to independence; anti-Moroccan guerillas have since been operating with Algerian backing. Population (1979) 165,000.

Western Samoa
Area: 1820 km²
Population: 157,000
Capital: Apia

Western Samoa includes the islands of Upolu, Savai'i, Apolima, and Manono, together with several small islets. Savai'i is 77 km long and 40 km wide, with an area of 1820 km². It is mountainous, rising to 1857 m.

Western Samoa. *The coastal village of Papa on the island of Savai'i, the largest in the group.*

The extinct crater of Mua on Savai'i rises to over 1219 m. Upolu, 72 km long and 21 km wide, with an area of 692 km², rises to over 1097 m. Upolu is the more fertile of these two islands, and contains the port and capital, Apia. The constitution which came into force after the granting of independence in 1962 provides for a head of state to be elected for five-year terms, though the present ruler, Maleiota Tanumafili II, holds the office for life. The head of state has executive control and appoints the Prime Minister and the eight-member cabinet (the latter on the premier's advice). There is an elected legislative assembly of 47 members.

The chief export is copra, the only other significant crops being bananas and cocoa.

The estimated population in 1978 was 157,000, of whom approximately 75 per cent were in Upolu (including Apolima and Manono) and the rest in Savai'i. For history, see SAMOA, *history*.

Westmacott, Sir Richard (1775–1856), British sculptor, son of a sculptor of the same name. He studied in Italy from 1793 to 1797, working under Antonio Canova. After his return, he was commissioned to execute a number of monuments to politicians and heroes of the Napoleonic Wars. The most successful of these are the monuments to Fox in Westminster Abbey, to Gen. Abercrombie in St Paul's Cathedral, and the statue of Fox in Bloomsbury Square. Westmacott's heroic classicism is displayed in the bronze *Warrior*, raised in honour of the Duke of Wellington (in Hyde Park), but he was also capable of sentiment, as in the monument to Mrs Warren in Westminster Abbey.

Westmeath, inland county of Leinster province, Republic of Ireland, bounded on the north by Cavan, south by Offaly, east by Meath, and west by Roscommon. The surface is varied and is some 76 m above sea-level. It contains some very fine scenery and is a county of loughs. The principal rivers are the Shannon, the Inny and the Boyne. Cattle rearing for the Dublin and British markets is the main type of farming. The chief towns are Athlone and Mullingar, the county town. Area 1094 km²; population (1979) 59,885.

Westminster, City of, pre-eminent among the London boroughs because in it are situated the Houses of Parliament, Westminster Abbey, Buckingham Palace, and the chief government offices. By the London Government Act of 1963 Westminster became a London borough enlarged by the addition of the former metropolitan boroughs of St Marylebone and Paddington. The fact that it was a royal residence from Edward the Confessor's time, if not earlier, close to the City of London, led to its supplanting Winchester as the legislative capital of the country. Some courts of law and of finance were set up by Norman and Angevin kings in their palace here. The setting up of the Wool Staple in the 14th century accelerated the development of Westminster in the Middle Ages. After a fire in 1512 Westminster Palace ceased to be a royal residence. The city's development was considerable in subsequent centuries. It was created a metropolitan borough in 1899, and in 1900 a city by royal charter. The City of Westminster's estimated population in 1974 was 218,500.

Westminster Abbey. *The choir, looking west. The abbey is perhaps Britain's finest medieval building and contains the country's finest sepulchral art.*

Westminster, Palace of, see PARLIAMENT, HOUSES OF; WESTMINSTER HALL.

Westminster, Statute of (1931), British act of Parliament which established the relation of Britain and the Dominions as defined at the Imperial conference in 1926. It abolished the power of Parliament to legislate for the Dominions and to veto Dominion acts; and it acknowledged the right of the Dominion parliaments to amend or repeal any act of the British Parliament applying to them.

Westminster Abbey. About 1050 Edward the Confessor began building an immense church on this site, the island of Thorney. Fragments of this church, which was consecrated in 1065, are embodied in the present structure. The style was that of the advanced schools of Romanesque architecture. In the early 13th century Henry III decided on a new building and a fitting shrine for the canonised Confessor. Demolition began in 1245, and by 1258 the new east sanctuary was completed. In 1258 the demolition of the Norman nave was begun, and in 1269 the body of St Edward was placed in a splendid gold shrine which stood on the present marble mosaic base. The original design of the east part was by Master Henry de Reyns. In 1275 the remainder of the Norman nave was demolished, and it was completed in a style similar to that of the 13th-century work, by Henry Yevele (d.1400), designer of the Perpendicular nave of Canterbury. The west towers are the work of Wren and Hawksmoor, c.1722–40.

Henry VIII's Chapel, which replaced the Lady Chapel of 1220, was begun in 1503. This was the work of the brothers Robert and William Vertue. The vault is technically remarkable from the fact that the architects discarded the use of ribs.

Design, Architecture, Ornaments. Structurally, Henry III's is a French church, but much of the detail is English. The royal chapels at the east end contain several monumental tombs of the highest medieval craftsmanship, especially those of William de Valence, Edward III, Eleanor of Castile, Edmund Crouchback and Henry VII. On the back of the tomb of

Philippa of Hainault is the Westminster Retable, a 13th-century oak altarpiece with what is considered to be probably the finest early medieval painting in Europe.

Westminster Abbey is not only the scene of the crowning of British sovereigns (the Coronation Chair of 1300–01 and the Stone of Scone are in the Confessor's Chapel), but the great national mausoleum, and many kings, statesmen, soldiers, writers and others are buried or commemorated there.

The chapter-house was built in 1245–50 and is one of the largest in England. From the reign of Edward I until 1547 Parliament generally met here. It was completely restored by Sir Gilbert Scott in 1865. The tile pavement dates back to c.1250.

Westminster Bridge, crossing the Thames in London, was originally built between 1739 and 1750 by the Swiss architect, Charles Labelye. Until this time London Bridge had been the only bridge to cross the Thames. A new, steel Westminster Bridge, replacing the old, was erected between 1854 and 1862. It is 246·8 m long and was designed by Thomas Page. At the western end of the bridge is a large statue of Boudicca, the work of Thomas Thorneycroft, placed there in 1902.

Westminster Cathedral, English Roman Catholic Metropolitan church, London. The architect, J. F. Bentley, designed a remarkable building in Early Byzantine style. The Stations of the Cross on the piers were carved by Eric Gill. The interior is intended to be covered with mosaic; work was resumed in 1955 but is not yet complete.

Westminster Hall, London, was built by William II in 1097–99 as the banqueting hall for his Palace of Westminster. Under Richard II the hall was rebuilt, and a wonderful hammerbeam roof constructed by Hugh Herland, the earliest dateable example (c.1395) of its kind. Except for modern steel erections, it is probably the largest roof unsupported by pillars. Westminster Hall has been the meeting-place of the chief law courts and some early parliaments, the scene of coronations and other festivals, but is most famous for the great state trials held there, including those of Thomas More, Guy Fawkes and Charles I. It is now used mainly for royal receptions and lyings-in-state.

Weston-super-Mare, seaside resort in Avon, England, 32 km from Bristol, on the Bristol Channel. Population (1981) 57,980.

Westphalia (German *Westfalen*), name given to that part of the North German Plain which is bounded by the Netherlands, Hanover, Hessen and the Rhine. The name was given to the Duchy of Westphalia, which was part of the old Saxon Duchy and which belonged to the Elector-archbishop of Cologne. After the sequestration of the Church lands, Westphalia went to Prussia and Hesse-Darmstadt. Westphalia is now part of the *Land* of North Rhine Westphalia.

Westphalia, Treaty of, peace treaty signed at Münster and Osnabrück on 21 October 1648, ending the Thirty Years' War. By its articles France was confirmed in its possession of Metz, Toul and Verdun, and also obtained the sovereignty of Alsace; Sweden, Bavaria, Brandenburg and Saxony also received accessions of territory. The structure of the Holy Roman Empire was weakened, and the larger among its constituent territories gained almost complete independence. The independence of Switzerland and the United Provinces of Dutch Netherlands was recognised. The treaty marks both the failure of the Austro-Spanish attempt to restore Roman Catholicism in central Europe and the beginning of French hegemony in Europe.

Westward Ho!, seaside resort in north Devon, England, incorporated in Northam. Westward Ho! takes its name from Charles Kingsley's novel. A remarkable pebble ridge juts out into the Taw-Torridge estuary. Population with Northam (1981) 8715.

Wetterhorn, mountain in the Bernese Oberland, Switzerland, east of Grindelwald. It has three peaks, of which the middle, or Mittelhorn, is the highest (3710 m). It was first climbed in 1844.

Wexford, maritime county in the province of Leinster, in the south-east corner of the Republic of Ireland. The surface is hilly in the north and west, the greatest heights being Mount Leinster (796 m), and Blackstairs (753 m). Owing to sandbanks, the coast is dangerous, and the only opening of importance is Wexford Harbour and Bay, while Waterford Harbour divides it from the county of that name in the south. The principal rivers are the Barrow and the Slaney, both navigable for a long distance. Agriculture is successfully carried on, the county being one of the most intensive arable areas in Ireland. The main crops are wheat, barley and beet. Sheep rearing on the hill-slopes, and dairying are also of significance. The main fishing port is in the south at Kilmore Quay. The principal towns are Wexford (the county town), New Ross, Enniscorthy and Gorey. Area 2352 km²; population (1979) 96,421.

Wexford, municipal borough and seaport, capital of County Wexford, Republic of Ireland, on the River Slaney. Its initial importance was mainly due to the harbour, which is formed by the estuary of the river, but owing to a bar across the mouth big vessels are unable to enter at ebb tide, and in consequence the harbour of Rosslare was built and connected by rail with Wexford (some 13 km). The town is of ancient foundation. The chief industries are the manufacture of agricultural machinery and farm implements, food processing, textiles, laminated springs and furniture. Population (1971) 13,293.

Weygand, Maxime (1867–1965), French soldier. He served in the colonial army until 1914, when he became chief-of-staff to Foch. In 1930 he became chief of the general staff, and in 1931 vice-president of the supreme war council. On 19 May 1940 he was appointed chief of the French general staff and commander-in-chief in all war theatres, but after the German breakthrough it was he who advised Pétain to seek an armistice. Thereafter it was never clear on which side he was really acting. In 1940 he was appointed high commissioner for French Africa, and in 1941 governor-general of Algeria. However, later in 1941 he was dismissed, at Hitler's express command, and in 1942 was arrested by the Germans and interned until 1945. In 1948 the sentence of infamy, passed upon him as a member of the Vichy government, was quashed.

Weymouth, and Melcombe Regis, a seaport and holiday resort in Dorset, England, at the mouth of the Wey. Its popularity as a seaside resort dates from the time of George III. Weymouth is the port for the Channel Islands. Population (1981) 46,260.

Whale, name for most of the members of the order Cetacea, in the class Mammalia. The Cetacea are divided into two suborders, the toothed whales (Odontoceti) and the whalebone whales (Mysticeti), the former including the sperm whale, or cachalot, the largest toothed-whale, the dolphins, porpoises and narwhal; the latter the right whales and the rorquals, from which are derived oil and whalebone. Whales are the most thoroughly aquatic of all mammals, the forelimbs being reduced to fin-like paddles and all external traces of the hind limbs having virtually disappeared. They occur in all seas. Most whales are inoffensive creatures and swim in herds. When they rise to the surface the heated air expelled condenses and forms a spray, the 'spout'. The whalebone whales still develop rudimentary teeth before birth, but these are displaced by a large number of flattened plates of bone or baleen fringed at the edges, which strain the food from the water. Whalebone is strong, light and flexible. Whales stranded on shore die by suffocation, their own weight crushing the lungs.

Whale Fisheries are of ancient origin, the Norwegians and the Basques having hunted whales as early as the 9th century; the Russians and Japanese are foremost in this industry. In modern times whale fishing, chiefly of rorquals, has become so profitable commercially that the whale, a slow-breeding animal, is in danger of extinction. Practically the whole of the animal is utilised in one form or another: the oil as a lubricant, or for making soap, candles and margarine; the whalebone is employed by corset manufacturers and in the brush trade; the prepared flesh is used as cattle-food; the flesh and ground bones as soil fertilisers; ambergris, found in the intestines of sperm whales, is used in the manufacture of perfumes. Some parts of the flesh are edible, and are used chiefly in petfood manufacture.

See also BELUGA; SPERM WHALE.

Whangarei, port of North Island, New Zealand, 210 km north of Auckland by rail. It is the chief town and seaport for an extensive dairying and fat lamb area. It is the site of New Zealand's only oil refinery (opened 1964) and has cement and ceramic industries. Population (1980) 39,700.

Wharfedale, in West and North Yorkshire, England, strictly speaking that part of the valley of the Wharfe beginning at Wetherby, and continuing until the source of the river on Cam Fell. Ilkley, the largest town, was the Roman settlement of *Olicana*.

Wharton, Edith Newbold (1862–1937), US novelist. She excelled in her short stories, collections of which include *The Greater Inclination*, 1899; *Tales of Men and Ghosts*, 1910; and *Here and Beyond*, 1926. During the First World War she organised a French ambulance unit, and in 1924 was made an officer of the Legion of Honour. Of her novels, *Ethan Frome*, 1911, is sometimes thought the greatest. *The Age of Innocence*, 1920, a satire on society, was awarded the Pulitzer Prize, as was *Old New York*, 1924, in its dramatic form with the title *Old Maid*.

Wheat, grass belonging to the genus *Triticum*, in the family Gramineae. Its geographical centre of origin is probably the Caucasian region. There are several species and many hundreds of varieties in cultivation. Wheat is, with rice, one of the principal food crops of the world. Einkorn, or one-grained wheat (*T. monococcum*), possesses a short flattened ear, each spikelet producing only a single ripe grain. It is sometimes cultivated on poor soils in southern Europe and Asia Minor. Hard or macaroni wheat (*T. durum*), is grown around the Mediterranean. Common wheat (*T. aestivum*) includes all the most important varieties for bread or biscuit making grown in the great wheat areas. Perhaps the most important diseases of wheat are the fungal diseases, rust and smut.

Wheatear, *Oenanthe oenanthe*, of family Muscicapidae, order Passeriformes, is a summer migrant to Europe, central and northern Asia and Alaska, often arriving in February. It winters in tropical Africa and India. It is about 15 cm long, grey on the upper parts with a black streak from beak to ear and with black quill feathers, wing coverts and tail feathers. In flight a white patch on the lower back and tail is conspicuous. The underparts are white with a buff tinge on the breast. Its food consists chiefly of insects.

Wheatley, Phyllis (c.1753–84), American poet, born in Africa. Sold as a slave to the Wheatley family, she became the first Negro poet to establish any reputation in a Western sense. Her first published poem, 'An Elegiac Poem on the Death of John Whitefield', was published in 1769. *Poems on Various Subjects, Religious and Moral*, 1773, was published while she was in England. Given her freedom, she married disastrously and died in poverty.

Wheatstone, Sir Charles (1802–75), British physicist, with an early interest in acoustics. He became professor of experimental philosophy at King's College, London, in 1834. He invented many intriguing instruments (including the English concertina). In 1837, with Sir W. F. Cooke, he took out the first patent for the electric telegraph. He invented the rotating-mirror method for examining vibrating bodies, and used a similar apparatus to measure the velocity of an electric discharge in conductors, obtaining a value close to that of light. He was a gifted cryptographer, invented the stereoscope, and did work on colours and spectra. His polar clock measured the position of the Sun, and therefore the time, by means of the plane of polarisation of scattered light. Wheatstone recognised the value of a measuring device first described by Samuel Hunter Christie and now known as the Wheatstone bridge.

Wheel, Breaking on the, a form of capital punishment once common in France and Germany, and employed on a few occasions in Scotland. The victim was stretched on a cart-wheel, which then revolved slowly while his limbs were broken with an iron bar. It was abolished in France at the Revolution, but used in Germany until 1827.

Wheeler, Sir (Robert Eric) Mortimer (1890–1976), British archaeologist. He directed excavations at Segontium (Caernarvon), Brecon, Caerleon, Lydney, Verulamium (St Albans), at the Iron Age fort of Maiden Castle in Dorset, and in northern France. As director-general of archaeology in India, 1944–48, and later as adviser to the government of Pakistan, he revitalised Indian archaeology and his excavations at Harappa and other sites revealed the extent of the Indus valley civilisation and its trading links with the west. His many publications included exemplary excavation reports as well as more popular works.

Wheels are most generally first found during the Bronze Age in all areas, but are also known to have existed during the Neolithic period, showing that metal tools were not required for their construction. The wheeled cart was known in Mesopotamia about 3000 BC, in Egypt not before 1600 BC, in Britain during the Late Bronze Age, while in America and other places it was not known until it was brought by modern European trade and settlement. The earliest wheel was a slice from a log attached solidly to an axle; later it revolved upon a fixed axle. Spokes were introduced about 2000 BC in the Near East, thus lightening the structure and providing levers to propel the vehicle if the need arose. The invention of the potter's wheel before 3000 BC is likely and wheel-thrown pots are known from Mesopotamia.

Whelk, any member of family Buccinidae of class Gastropoda of phylum Mollusca. Whelks mostly feed on other molluscs. The family is marine and occurs world-wide, mostly in colder waters. The name is commonly applied to *Buccinum undatum*, a carnivorous mollusc which is often eaten. The shell is grey or brownish white, spirally grooved, and with numerous raised ridges. Offshore individuals may attain 15 cm in length but littoral forms are smaller. The egg capsules form large spongelike capsules. There are other species to which the name is also applied, especially the dog whelk, *Thais lapillus*, and the netted dog whelk, *Nassarius reticulata*.

Whewell, William (1794–1866), British philosopher. He was professor of mineralogy (1828–32) and of moral philosophy (1838–1855), and is important in the development of scientific method. It was Whewell who coined the term 'scientist', in his *Philosophy of the Inductive Sciences*, 1840. While insisting on the importance of induction, he took a somewhat Kantian line. Accumulating observations is one thing, but making a theory out of them is quite another; that requires the formulation of a suitable hypothesis, which binds the observations together. Whewell also wrote a *History of the Inductive Sciences*, 1837.

Whieldon Ware, a type of earthenware made originally by Thomas Whieldon of Fenton (1719–95), the most prominent potter of his time in Staffordshire. It is characterised by decorative multi-coloured lead-glazes to produce marbling, clouding and 'tortoiseshell' effects.

Whig, name of the political party opposed to the Tory party in the late-17th, 18th and early-19th centuries in England. The word is probably a shortening of the Scots *whiggamore* (horse-drover), this having been applied to West Scottish insurgents of 1648; Whig was thus originally a term of contempt, like Tory. The name was first used in its established sense during the 1679 struggle to exclude the Roman Catholic James from succession to the throne, then denoting Nonconformity and rebellion. During the 18th century the Whigs stood for limited constitutional monarchy, religious toleration and expansive foreign policy, representing above all the interests of the aristocratic landowning families and the wealthy middle classes. A Whig party as such came into being only after 1784 and, led by Charles James Fox, stood for religious dissenters, industrialists and others seeking electoral, parliamentary and social reforms. After 1815 the Whig party gradually became the Liberal party of Russell and Gladstone.

Whig Party, in the USA, formed in opposition to Andrew Jackson and the new Democratic party. Its members took the name of Whigs about 1834. The party was in power from 1841 to 1845, and 1849 to 1853; its presidents were Harrison, Tyler, Taylor and Fillmore. It ceased to exist in the early 1850s when sectional divisions caused a general upheaval in the party system. The party's leading statesmen were Henry Clay and Daniel Webster.

Whimbrel, *Numenius phaeops*, a wading bird of the order Charadriiformes, related to the curlew.

Whinchat, *Saxicola rubetra*, bird of family Muscicapidae, order Passeriformes, that favours heaths and open places where it feeds principally on insects. The centre of the throat and breast are a light cinnamon-red, as also are the sides of the body, and the abdomen; the general colour above is brown; the head-feathers are edged with sandy-buff. It is a summer visitor to most parts of Europe, and breeds as far north as the Arctic Circle.

Whip-poor-will, *Caprimulgus vociferus*, a bird of the order Caprimulgiformes, commonly known as the North American goatsucker, or nightjar, so called from its cry during the nights of its breeding season. It is about 25 cm long, mottled tawny brown in colour, with a white collar on the throat, and long, stiff bristles at the base of the bill.

Whippet, dog originating in the north of England, where it was much used for races, being capable of tremendous speeds. The whippet was probably produced by crossing a terrier with the Italian greyhound, and then breeding back to the English greyhound. It is bred in various colours, including black, red, white, fawn and brindle, and its appearance is that of a greyhound in miniature. The height is about 47 cm for dogs, 44 cm for bitches, and the weight 9 to 10 kg.

Whips, officials of British parliamentary parties through whom party discipline in matters of attendance and voting is exercised. They are also channels of information between leaders and party members, and through them 'pairing' arrangements to assist MPs unable to attend any particular sitting are made. Both the Conservative and the Labour parties have a chief whip and a number of assistant whips. A 'whip' may also mean the note requesting a member's attendance at a particular sitting when a division is anticipated, the most urgent being a three-line 'whip', which takes its name from the triple underlining of the text.

Whirligig Beetle, insect in the family Gyrinidae of order Coleoptera. Both adults and larvae are aquatic. The adults are steel-black, oval, with flattened bodies. Their second and third pairs of legs are exceptionally short and broad, and are used for paddling in the water. About 400 species have been recorded. They are usually found in groups whirling around on the water surface. When disturbed they dart into the water. Both adults and larvae are carnivorous, feeding on small insects that fall onto the water. The adults have well developed wings and are capable of flying from one pond to the next.

Whirlpool, a circular eddy in a river or the sea. It may be caused by the meeting of two currents, or, especially in rivers, by the conformation of the water-channel. One of the most famous whirlpools is the Maelstrom, between two of Norway's Lofoten Islands. Another is the Garofalo, in the Strait of Messina, between Sicily and mainland Italy, the Charybdis of classical legend.

Whirlwind, see CYCLONE.

Whisky (Scotch and Canadian), or whiskey (Irish and American), derived from the Gaelic *uisge beatha*, the 'water of life'. Scotch whisky is of two different types: Scotch malt whisky which is made from malted barley only, and is distilled twice, and Scotch grain whisky, which is made by continuous distillation from malted and unmalted barley mashed with maize. Scotch whisky leaves the still colourless, with a rough aroma and flavour. The final smooth, mellow flavour is supplied by years of maturation in wooden casks. In the 1860s the practice began of blending whiskies from malt and grain groups to obtain a product of consistent flavour and character. Such blended whiskies proved acceptable to a far wider public, and were responsible for the growth of a market for Scotch whisky in England, and later throughout the world. Irish whiskey is either a pot-still product, triple-distilled from a fermented mash of barley malt and other cereals or a blend of pot-still and grain whisky. Bourbon whiskey, first distilled in Bourbon County, Kentucky, is the product of a fermented mash in which at least 51 per cent of the grain must be maize, with a balance of barley malt and rye, and which must be matured in new charred-oak casks for at least two years. Rye whiskey is distilled from a grain mash containing a minimum of 51 per cent rye.

Whispering Gallery, a circular construction in which whispered speech produced near any part of the wall is echoed and clearly audible at any other part of the gallery.

Whist, card game for four players in which a full pack of 52 cards is used. It is one of the oldest card games in existence and was first referred to in 1529. It derived its name, apparently, from the Cornish *huist* (silence), owing to the concentration it demanded.
The four players cut for partners, and the cards are dealt face downwards to each of them in turn by the player who draws the lowest card. The dealer exposes his last card, which determines the trump suit. The object of each deal is to take as many tricks as possible. The player to the dealer's left leads to the first trick. The remaining players must follow suit if they can; those who cannot may either trump or discard. The winner of a trick leads to the next one until the 13 have been played. Every trick made in excess of six scores one point. In *short* whist five points makes a game, and a score of two games out of three wins the 'rubber'; in *long* whist ten points makes a game.
See also BRIDGE.

Whistler, James Abbott McNeill (1834–1903), US painter, lithographer and etcher. In 1856 he went to Paris, entering the studio of Gleyre. He was greatly influenced by the newly discovered Japanese colour print, by the work of Courbet, and the Impressionists' techniques. In 1859 he settled in London, there producing his exquisite series of Thames etchings. In portraiture and landscape he evolved his own style, his so-called 'nocturnes', showing the Japanese influence. In 1877, when some were shown at the Grosvenor Gallery, they were so fiercely assailed by Ruskin in *Fors Clavigera* that Whistler sued him for libel, claiming £1000. The case resulted in Whistler being granted one farthing damages. His most famous works include *Thomas Carlyle* (Glasgow), the *Portrait of the Painter's Mother* (Louvre), and the *Old Battersea Bridge* (Tate Gallery). He aimed at balance and harmony in his works. The delicacy of his art is seen to advantage in his etchings, lithographs, pastels and watercolours. His 'Peacock Room' (now at Washington) was an original departure in interior decoration. The Ruskin trial is documented in Whistler's book, *The Gentle Art of Making Enemies*, 1890, which embodies also stimulating critical comment on art.

Whistler, Rex (1905–44), British painter, illustrator and stage designer. He excelled in a romantic style of illustration, exquisite examples being for *Gulliver's Travels* and *Hans Andersen's Fairy Tales*. He painted many murals with a 'period' flavour, mainly for private patrons. His mural for the Tate Gallery restaurant is widely known. His brother, Laurence, is well-known as a glass engraver.

Whit Sunday, or Pentecost (Greek, fiftieth), festival of the Christian Church celebrated on the seventh Sunday and the fiftieth day after Easter, to commemorate the descent of the Holy Ghost on the Apostles. Its name is probably an abbreviation of White Sunday, from the white robes then worn by the newly baptised. Whitsuntide corresponds with the Jewish Feast of Pentecost, which commemorates the delivery of the Law on Mount Sinai, 50 days after the Passover.

Whitaker, Joseph (1820–95), British publisher. He began business in 1855 as a publisher of theological and fine-art works, and in 1858 founded the *Bookseller*, which is today the major journal of the British book trade. In 1869 he brought out the first issue of *Whitaker's Almanack*, a comprehensive one-volume reference book which is still published annually.

Whitby, seaport and health resort in North Yorkshire, England, at the mouth of the River Esk 32 km north-west of Scarborough. The Abbess Hilda built a monastery at Streoneshalh, near Whitby, in AD 656, and here too lived the poet Caedmon. Whitby has associations with Captain James Cook. The manufacture of jet ornaments is still important on a small scale. The fisheries are also important. Population (1981) 13,763.

Whitby, Synod of, or Council of Whitby, held in 663, convened by Oswy, King of Northumbria, to decide whether to follow Celtic or Roman Church practices. The Roman party was represented by St Wilfrid and the Celtic by Bishop Colman. Oswy's decision for Rome was quickly followed by the other English kingdoms.

White Dwarf, see STAR.

White, Gilbert (1720–93), British naturalist. He took holy orders and held curacies at Selborne and elsewhere. He devoted himself to the study of natural history around Selborne, which is in Hampshire and is where he was born and spent most of his life. In 1788 he published his famous work *The Natural History and Antiquities of Selborne*, which had been in preparation since 1771. It is founded on letters and retains the epistolary style throughout; it reflects White's unrivalled powers of observation, and is simple and informal in manner.

White, Patrick Victor Martindale (1912–), Australian author. He travelled widely in Europe and the Near East and was there in Intelligence in the Second World War. He then settled in Sydney where he wrote his first major novel, *The Aunt's Story*, 1948. *The Tree of Man*, 1954, strengthened his reputation and *Voss*, 1957, winning critical acclaim and the W. H. Smith award, made it international. In a complex style, sometimes involuted and 'poetical', White mingles acerbic social comedy (also evident in his short stories and his drama) with celebration of the isolated artistic or religious sensibility in a savage and inimical world. The Nobel Prize for literature, awarded him in 1973, was the first to any Australian.

White Ant, see TERMITE.

White Army, general name for the anti-Bolshevik forces in the Russian Civil War, 1918–20.
See also USSR, *History*.

White Bryony, see BRYONY.

White Fly, insect in family Aleyrodidae in order Hemiptera (suborder Homoptera).

James McNeill Whistler, Thomas Carlyle*, painted 1872–3.*

They are related to plant lice (aphids) and scale insects. The adults are tiny four-winged insects which barely exceed a length of 3 mm; their wings are dusted with a powdery white wax which they secrete. In temperate countries they may be found in glasshouses, where they are pests of plants, such as cucumber and tomato. They are widely distributed in the tropics, where they attack citrus trees. They injure the plant by feeding on the sap and excreting honeydew, which encourages sooty black mould to grow. In general the eggs are laid on the undersurface of leaves in a characteristic circular or arch-shape, and are attached to the leaves by means of a stalk.

White Horses and Hill-figures are among the most interesting and popular features of the chalk downlands of south England. Nearly 50 hill-figures are known in Britain, of which all but four are in the chalk country.

The most widely known are the Uffington White Horse, below Uffington Castle, a hill-fort on the Berkshire Downs; the Cerne Giant, on the hillside above Cerne Abbas village, near Dorchester, Dorset; the Long Man of Wilmington on Windover Hill on the escarpment of the South Downs; and the Bledlow and Whiteleaf Crosses, close together on the Chiltern Hills. These figures are in all probability of ancient construction. With a very few possible exceptions, all the others are modern and the purpose of each hill-figure must be considered on its own merits. Some are landmarks, others have a religious purpose or are memorials, while one at least, the Cerne Giant, is associated with a pagan fertility cult.

Hill-figures. The Cerne Giant in Dorset, 55 m long, is thought to be a fertility symbol.

The Uffington White Horse is now thought to have been made by the Belgic tribes occupying south-east England between 50 BC and AD 50; its attenuated form is similar to designs on contemporary Celtic coins and metalwork. The Cerne Giant has been convincingly identified with Hercules and associated with a fertility cult or Priapus worship revived by the Emperor Commodus in the later 2nd century AD. The origin of the Long Man of Wilmington is much more debatable, and may be associated with the nearby priory of Wilmington, which was dissolved in 1414.

White House, official residence of the President of the USA, in Washington, DC. The building was designed in neo-classical style by

White House. The semi-circular south portico was built in the 1820s.

Philadelphia architect James Hoban and constructed between 1792 and 1800 of greyish limestone, later painted white; it has three storeys and over 100 rooms, of which the best-known is the Oval Office of the President. The original interior and part of the walls were burned by British troops in 1814, but it was reconstructed and extended under Hoban's direction. In 1949 the interior structure was found to be unsound, and extensive repairs were made.

White Lead, basic carbonate of lead, $2PbCO_3 \cdot Pb(OH)_2$. The compound is manufactured by several processes, the simplest of which consists of grinding litharge with water and sodium bicarbonate. White lead is a poisonous heavy powder, which is used as a pigment.

White Metal, metallurgical term applied either to the copper sulphide produced in the primary stages of obtaining blister copper from copper matte or to a range of low-melting, anti-friction and bearing alloys. These alloys consist of various proportions of lead, tin and antimony and include solder type metal and Babbit metal.

White Nile, see NILE, WHITE.

White Paper, proposes policy to be undertaken by the British government on a particular area, e.g. defence or trade union reform. It does not incorporate final Cabinet decisions and comes to the House of Commons as a basis for discussion. It is known as a White Paper simply because it is bound in the same (white) paper as the text.

White Russia, see BELORUSSIAN SOVIET SOCIALIST REPUBLIC.

White Sea, gulf of the Barents Sea in North European USSR. The main rivers flowing into it are the Northern Dvina, the Mezen and the Onega. The chief port is Archangel. From November to May there is drifting ice over much of the area, and solid ice forms in the bays. It is linked by the White Sea–Baltic Canal to the Baltic, and by the Volga–Baltic Waterway with the Black Sea and the Caspian. Area 90,000 km²; average depth 60 m, maximum depth 330 m (the eastern half is much shallower).

White Sea–Baltic Canal, waterway in the USSR, connecting the White Sea with Lake Onega, and through it with the Baltic Sea and the Volga. Length 227 km, of which 37 km are artificial; there are 19 locks. The idea was first mooted at the time of Peter the Great. Surveying was carried out in 1915–1916, and it was built in 1930–33 by forced labour.

White Shark, the genus *Carcharodon* in family Isuridae, suborder Galeoidei of order Selachii. *C. rondeletii* is the great white shark or man eater which is the most dangerous shark known to man. Its teeth may be up to 5 cm long and the shark itself up to 13 m long. The white shark is viviparous (the young are hatched within the parent) and is found in all the warm seas of the world.

White Vitriol, see ZINC.

Whitebait, the fry of herrings and sprats. In the winter and spring young sprats form the great proportion of what is sold under this name, but in the summer whitebait consists chiefly of young herrings.

Whitefield, George (1714–70), English founder of the Calvinistic Methodists in England, and one of their leaders in Wales. He was ordained deacon in 1736 and joined the Wesleys in America the following year. He returned in 1738 and began that course of preaching in association with Wesley which established Methodism as a popular faith. Whitefield set the example of open-air preaching (1739) near Bristol, and made a great impression as an orator. His stern Calvinism led to a breach with the Wesleys, but he received great support from others, who in 1741 built a tabernacle for him in Moorfields, London. He now spent most of his life on evangelising tours in Britain and America. He was provided with a centre in Tottenham Court Road, London, where the Whitefield Tabernacle was built. His type of Methodism developed in the Calvinistic Methodist Church.

Whitehaven, seaport, coal-mining town (some workings extend out under the sea), and manufacturing centre in Cumbria, England, south-west of Carlisle. Population (1981) 26,714.

Whitehead, Alfred North (1861–1947), British mathematician and philosopher. He was a Fellow of the Royal Society and of the British Academy, and gained the OM. He collaborated with Bertrand Russell in *Principia mathematica* in three volumes, 1910–1913. His first work in the field of logic and mathematics was *A Treatise of Universal Algebra*, 1898. His *Principle of Relativity*, 1922, supplies an alternative rendering to that of Einstein. Whitehead's *Process and Reality*, an essay in cosmology, 1929, along with his Lowell Lectures *Science and the Modern World*, 1926, and *Adventures of Ideas*, 1933, form a trilogy.

In Whitehead's Tarner Lectures (1919) he propounded the view that events constitute the ultimate components of reality. *Process and Reality* shows the close correspondence between his philosophy and that set forth in Plato's *Timaeus*. The fundamental idea is a process of divine development through which order is gradually evolved out of primeval chaos.

Whitehorse, capital of Yukon Territory, Canada, situated on the Yukon river. It was founded at the time of the Klondike gold rush when its situation at the head of navigation and the northern terminus of the White Pass railway route was of prime importance. The Yukon government sits at Whitehorse, and it is also the regional headquarters of the Royal Canadian Mounted Police. Population (1981) 14,814.

Whitelaw of Penrith, William Stephen Ian, Viscount (1918–), British politician. He is a farmer and landowner and was elected Conservative MP for Penrith and Border in 1955. From 1964 to 1970 he was Opposition chief whip, becoming lord president of the Council and leader of the House of Commons in 1970. In 1972 he became secretary of state for Northern Ireland, following the imposition of direct rule. Prior to the miners' strike of 1974 he was appointed secretary of state for Employment, but was unable to avert the strike. In 1975 he unsuccessfully contested the Conservative leadership. In 1979 he became secretary of state at the Home Office and in 1983 was created a viscount and became leader of the House of Lords.

Whiteman, Paul (1890–1967), US bandleader. He started his own band in 1919. The band's subsequent fame was due to the experimental orchestrations of Ferdé Grofe and such works as Gershwin's *Rhapsody in Blue*, which it premièred in 1924. Whiteman played a large part in commercialising jazz and dance music.

Whitethroat, a migratory bird of the genus *Sylvia*, classified among the warblers in the family Muscicapidae, order Passeriformes. Two species occur in western Europe, *S. communis* and *S. curruca*. *S. communis*, the common whitethroat, is greyish-brown, with an ashy-grey head, the tail feathers dark greyish brown, the under-surface of the body white, and the breast pinkish. It is a summer visitor, overwintering in Africa. The general colour of *S. curruca*, the lesser whitethroat, is rather greyer.

Whitgift, John (c.1530–1604), English prelate (1583–1604). Doctrinally he was a Calvinist, but he strongly defended the liturgy and discipline of the Church of England against the Puritans, notably in a long-drawnout controversy with Thomas Cartwright and in his administrative capacity as archbishop. He founded an almshouse and Whitgift School at Croydon (1595).

Whiting, *Merlangius merlangus*, one of the important European members of the cod family in order Gadiformes. It is abundant in shallow water round the coasts of western Europe, and extends into the Mediterranean. It is slender in form and differs from most of the other species of the genus in the absence of a barbel. It grows rapidly, but rarely exceeds 50 cm in length or 1 kg in weight. It is an important food fish.

Whitlam, Edward Gough (1916–), Australian politician. He joined the Australian Labor party in 1945 and has represented Werriwa, New South Wales, since 1952. He succeeded Calwell as leader of the party and of the federal Opposition in 1966. In 1972 Whitlam became prime minister of the first Labor government since 1949, and was elected again in 1973 for a further term. He brought about far-reaching changes, particularly in social welfare, trade practices and foreign policy, steering Australia away from support for the United States. Labor won the forced 1974 election but began to lose support with a series of personal scandals. Matters came to a head in 1975 when Malcolm Fraser, with a majority in the Senate, refused passage to budget bills concerning money supply. After a deadlock of some weeks, Sir John Kerr, the governor-general, dismissed Whitlam and appointed Fraser caretaker prime minister. A month later Fraser won a clear majority in the polls. Following his defeat in the 1977 elections, Whitlam resigned from the party leadership.

Whitley Councils, or Whitleyism, device for securing improved relations between employers and employed. In 1916 the government set up the Committee on Relations between Employers and Employed, known, from its chairman, J. H. Whitley, as the 'Whitley Committee'. Its recommendations regarding conciliation and arbitration were embodied in the Industrial Courts Act 1919. Later the Committee recommended the formation of joint industrial councils of employers and employees for consideration of a variety of questions. Some of the most important Whitley Councils are found in central and local government.

Whitlow, an infection of the pulp of the fingers. It usually occurs when the bacteria responsible (*Staphylococcus*) enter the tissues through a small, often unnoticed, puncture wound. The symptoms are pain, throbbing and tenderness. Antibiotics may help to resolve the condition, but sometimes it is necessary to drain the pus through an incision in the skin.

Whitman, Walt, originally Walter (1818–1892), US poet. He worked as printer, teacher and journalist. He found an outlet for expressing his democratic sentiments in writing verse, which he published in 1855 under the title *Leaves of Grass*. The metre he employed was entirely original. He discarded the conventional laws of feet and rhyme, and wrote in musical, rhythmic sentences of varied length, modelled on the rhymes of the Old Testament. He was accused of indecency and immorality for his frankness in speaking of subjects usually tabooed, but the book was given high praise by Emerson and Thoreau. The worth of *Leaves of Grass*, Whitman's masterpiece, was not fully acknowledged until after his death. The controversies aroused during his lifetime were largely due to his frank enjoyment of physical beauty and physical love. His poems on death have few equals in any language especially his poem on Lincoln, 'When Lilacs Last in the Dooryard Bloomed'. His triumphant 'Pioneers, O Pioneers' has become almost a national hymn.

Whittier, John Greenleaf (1807–92), US poet. He became a journalist, and in 1833 published an anti-slavery work, *Justice and Expediency*. For 30 years he devoted himself to the cause of abolishing slavery, and was venerated as the apostle of human freedom. His volumes of verse include *The Panorama*, 1856, containing the well-known 'Maud Muller' and 'Barefoot Boy'; *In War Time*, 1864, containing the famous 'Barbara Frietchie'; and *Snow Bound*, 1866, named from a poem that is sometimes accounted his best. At his best in nature pieces, he was in his day the most popular American poet after Longfellow.

Whittington, Richard (d.1423), Lord Mayor of London. He was a London mercer, who held several municipal offices, and was thrice lord mayor of London (1397, 1406 and 1419). He became extremely rich, was a liberal benefactor of the City, and lent money successively to Richard II, Henry IV and Henry V. Around him has grown a legend, the original basis of which is lost.

Whittle, Sir Frank (1907–), British inventor. He entered the RAF as a boy apprentice and gained a cadetship to Cranwell College. While still a cadet he became interested in jet-propulsion, but received little encouragement until 1936, when he was placed on the special duties list. His first engine ran in the following year, and in 1941 it powered the Gloster E 28/39. He was made a Fellow of the Royal Society in 1947. He published an autobiography, *Jet*, 1953.

Whitworth, Sir Joseph (1803–87), British engineer. After serving his apprenticeship as a mechanic, he set up in 1833 as a toolmaker in Manchester, and made experiments in rifles, cannons, etc. The Whitworth rifle was invented in 1857, and was adopted by the National Rifle Association in 1860 and by the War Office in 1869. His development of standards for screw-thread and gauge measurements was of great importance. See also ARMSTRONG, WILLIAM GEORGE ARMSTRONG, 1ST BARON.

WHO, see WORLD HEALTH ORGANISATION.

Whooping Cough (pertussis), an acute infectious disease of children causing paroxysmal cough, the episodes of coughing ending with vomiting and often a whoop (sharp indrawing of breath). The causative organism is the bacterium *Bordetella pertussis*, but a similar pattern of symptoms may occasionally be due to other causes, such as virus respiratory tract infections, measles or pressure on the windpipe by external structures. The cough tends to last for one to two months, and minor complications are common, the most serious being bronchopneumonia and convulsions.

Immunising vaccine, included in the routine DTP (diphtheria tetanus pertussis triple vaccine) given in clinics has recently been a cause of controversy, as there are very occasionally adverse reactions. However, the risks from the disease are much higher than those from the vaccine and decline in vaccination rapidly results in whooping cough reaching epidemic proportions.

Whorf, Benjamin Lee (1897–1941), US linguist. He was for most of his life a chemical plant fire insurance inspector. From 1924 he pursued linguistics as a hobby, studying the languages of the Mayas and Aztecs, and particularly the Hopi Indians of Arizona. The striking nature of the Hopi Indian language, compared to familiar European ones, prompted his famous 'new principle of relativity' often referred to as the '(Sapir-) Whorf hypothesis'. It holds that speakers' thinking is influenced by the way their language categorises reality, a proposal like that of Wilhelm von Humboldt (hence also called 'neo-Humboldtianism') and one which psychologists have since attempted to verify
See also LINGUISTICS.

Whorl, in botany, a ring of leaves or other plant organs arising in one plane from the axis of a stem. It is also used in zoology to denote a set of parts arranged in a similar fashion.
See also INFLORESCENCE.

'Who's Who', British biographical reference work founded in 1848, initially as a list of names of titled and official figures, with no biographical details beyond dates of birth and appointment. Bought for £30 by the publishers Adam and Charles Black in 1896, it was extended to include all the most prominent people in Britain and now includes other nationalities besides British. Since 1897 the entries removed from *Who's Who* on the subject's death have been collected in a series called *Who Was Who*. *International Who's Who*, first published in 1937, is produced by Europa Publications Ltd.

Whyalla, town of South Australia, on the western side of Spencer Gulf, 402 km from Adelaide by road. It is the shipping outlet for iron ore mined at Iron Knob, 56 km inland, and has steel works and shipyards. Population (1976) 33,426.

Whymper, Edward (1840–1911), British artist, author and mountaineer. He travelled among the Alps (1860) to sketch Alpine scenery, and ascended Mont Pelvoux (1861). His ascent of the Pointe des Écrins with a party (1864) was a remarkable mountaineering feat. Whymper made the first ascent of the Aiguille Verte and in 1865 the famous first ascent of the Matterhorn north-east ridge at his seventh attempt; in the descent four of the party of seven were killed. He next visited Greenland (1867, 1872), Ecuador and the Andes (1879–80), and Canada (1901–5). His works include *Ascent of the Matterhorn* and *Scrambles Among the Alps in the Years 1860 to 1869*, 1871; *Chamonix and Mont Blanc* and *The Valley of Zermatt and the Matterhorn*, 1897–1901.

Wichita, county seat of Sedgwick county, Kansas, USA, the largest city in the state, 338 km south-west of Kansas City on the Arkansas river. It stands in the centre of a farming, agricultural and oil district, the chief product being wheat, for which the city is a milling centre. There are also oil refineries, packing plants, motor-vehicle works, foundries and machine shops. Population (1980) 279,352.

Wick, small town of Caithness District, Highland Region, in the extreme north of Scotland, situated at the mouth of the River Wick. It has a good harbour, a white fish industry and a cattle market. It is a local administrative and shopping centre. Population (1981) 7933.

Wick and Lamp Time Measurers. Among primitive time-measuring devices adopted by the ancient Chinese was a flax or hempen wick, so treated that when ignited it smouldered slowly without breaking into flame. Knots were tied at definite intervals in the wick and intervals of time were represented by the distance between the knots. Of more recent date are lamp-clocks, which measured time by the amount of oil they consumed. The construction embodied a glass reservoir fixed on a stand, with a graduated scale to indicate the hours. The wick was led from the reservoir through an upturned projecting arm, where it was lit, and time was told by the amount of oil left. According to the historian Asser, Alfred the Great used candles 12 in (30 cm) long which burnt away completely in four hours. They were protected by a wooden lantern.

Wicklow, maritime county of Leinster, Republic of Ireland, bounded on the north by Dublin, south by Wexford, east by St George's Channel, and west by Carlow and Kildare. The county is famous for its beautiful scenery. Running through the centre from north to south are the Wicklow Mountains with the heights of Lugnaquilla (926 m), Kippure (754 m), and Duff Hill (723 m), between which lie many fine gorges and valleys. Wicklow and Arklow are the two main harbours. The rivers Slaney and Liffey rise in the Wicklow Mountains. Glendalough is the site of a monastery city (7th century). Granite is mined at Aughrim and Ballyknockan. Industries include stock-raising (a special breed of Wicklow mountain sheep), dairy products, wheat, oats, seed potatoes and bulbs. The chief towns are Wicklow (the county town), Bray, Arklow and Baltinglass. Area 2025 km²; population (1979) 83,950.

Widgeon, *Anas penelope*, a duck of order Anseriformes that visits temperate parts of Europe in winter, usually breeding farther north. It is about 46 cm long. The plumage is grey and brown pencilled with black, the head and neck reddish-chestnut, the underparts white. The American widgeon, *A. americana*, is a larger bird.

Widgery of South Molton, John Passmore Widgery, Baron (1911–81), English judge. He became lord chief justice of England, 1971. He conducted the inquiry into the deaths during disturbances in Londonderry on Sunday, 30 January 1972.

Widnes, town in Cheshire, England, linked with Runcorn on the other side of the Mersey by road and rail bridges. It is an industrial town, especially for chemicals and metallurgy, and some expansion is occurring due to industry and housing moving out from Merseyside. Population (1981) 54,411.

Widor, Charles Marie (1844–1937), French organist and composer. He succeeded Franck as organ professor at the Paris Conservatoire and later became professor of composition. He is principally remembered for his ten organ symphonies. He also wrote songs, concertos, ballets and operas.

Widow, woman whose husband is deceased and who has not remarried. For her legal rights, see also SUTTEE; WILLS AND TESTAMENTS.

Wieck, Clara, see SCHUMANN, CLARA.

Wieland, Christopher Martin (1733–1813), German poet and novelist. His religious, optimistic outlook, as seen in *Moralische Briefe in Versen*, and *Anti-Ovid*, was influenced by Klopstock. In 1760 at Warthausen Castle he came into contact with English and French rococo; his novel, *Der Sieg der Natur über die Schwärmerei*, 1764, ridiculed the romantic novels of his time. Then followed several important works: the educational novel *Agathon*, 1766; the educational poem *Musarion, oder die Philosophie der Grazien*, 1768; and prose translations of 22 of Shakespeare's plays, 1762–66. Wieland greatly influenced Goethe and Schiller, and the school of the later German Romantics. His work was the peak of German rococo poetry.

Wien, see VIENNA.

Wiener, Norbert (1894–1964), US mathematician, founder of cybernetics. He gained his PhD from Harvard when he was 18 and studied under Bertrand Russell, David Hilbert, G. H. Hardy and George Santayana. Wiener's work arose from an interest in randomness, irregularity and non-linearity. He advocated collaboration between research workers in different fields to prevent duplication and to achieve greater progress in problems of mutual interest, and was interested in the social impact of science. He invented the term 'cybernetics' to describe the mathematical theory of feedback and control systems and produced the theoretical framework which enabled technologists to realise the science-fiction dreams of automatic factories and computer-controlled manufacturing. His publications include *The Human Use of Human Beings*, 1950; *Exprodigy*, 1953; *Nonlinear Problems in Random Theory*, 1958; *The Tempter*, 1959; and *Cybernetics*, 1961.

Wiesbaden, city of the Federal Republic of Germany, capital of the *Land* of Hessen, situated on the Rhine, 30 km west of Frankfurt. It has been known as a spa since Roman times; its springs are the *Aquae Mattiacorum* mentioned by Pliny. The city is a cosmopolitan resort. It produces a sparkling wine (*Sekt*), and has textile, pharmaceutical and electrical industries. Population (1979) 273,267.

Wig, an artificial head of hair. The name is a shortened form of 'periwig', from the French *perruque*, which became 'wig' by 1675. Wigs were worn by the ancient Egyptians, who shaved their heads, and have been sporadically fashionable since the 18th century, for example, women wore elaborately dressed separate wigs, powdered white, and with a multitude of trimmings. Since the 1960s the wearing of wigs and 'false pieces' has again become fashionable.
See also DRESS; HAIRDRESSING.

Wigan, an old market town equidistant from Liverpool and Manchester, on the River Douglas, in Greater Manchester Metropolitan County, England. Well established, long before the Industrial Revolution, it profited from the abundant coal locally available and welcomed the cotton industry as well as engineering. Despite the heavy decline in the cotton trade, and the end of mining locally, the food, paper and engineering industries have expanded. The population in 1981 was 79,535.

Wight, Isle of, island off the coast of Hampshire, England, separated from the mainland by the Solent and Spithead, now forming a complete county. The island covers an area of 38 km²; its greatest length is 38 km and its greatest breadth 20 km. It has chalk cliffs and downs, the highest elevation being St Boniface Down (240 m). Off the west coast are the rocks known as the 'Needles'. The scenery of the island is picturesque, with its ravines or 'chines'. Yachting is a favourite sport in the island, and Regatta Week at Cowes is an outstanding annual event. The Isle of Wight was the Roman *Vectis*, and there are Roman remains. There is a castle at Carisbrooke, and Osborne House was a favourite residence of Queen Victoria. Agriculture and tourism are the chief industries; there are also boat and shipbuilding yards and sawmills. The most important towns are Newport (the capital), Ryde, Shanklin, Ventnor, Cowes, Sandown and Freshwater. Parkhurst Prison is just outside Newport. Population (1981) 118,192.

Wightman Cup, is a Lawn Tennis contest played annually between women players from Britain and the USA. It was founded in 1923 and the trophy was the gift of Mrs George Wightman, one of the outstanding US players. The competition is made up of five singles and two doubles rubbers.

Wigtown, royal burgh (since 1457) and former county town of Wigtownshire, now in Wigtown District, Dumfries and Galloway Region of Scotland. Population (1981) 1015.

Wigwam, hut or cabin made by North American Indians, which consists of a rough conical framework of poles stuck into the ground below and converging above, covered with bark, matting or tanned hides.

Wilberforce, Samuel (1805–73), English churchman, son of William Wilberforce. He upheld the traditions of Anglican orthodoxy during the days of the Tractarian movement and the submission to Rome of Newman, Manning and others. He became bishop of Oxford, 1845, and Winchester in 1869. See also OXFORD MOVEMENT.

Wilberforce, William (1759–1833), British reformer and philanthropist. The acknowledged leader of the Clapham Sect, and prominent in many philanthropic movements, the great work of his life was the abolition of slavery. The committee for the abolition of the slave trade was formed in 1787 with Wilberforce at its head. It worked steadily for its cause until 1807 when a bill banning trade in slaves was finally passed. Wilberforce continued to work for the abolition of slavery itself and died in 1833, a few months before the bill effecting this was passed. See also ANTI-SLAVERY.

Wilbye, John (1574–1638), English composer. He went into the service of Sir Thomas Kytson near Bury St Edmunds about 1595 and remained with the family all his life. He produced two volumes of madrigals which show him to have been one of the finest exponents of that form.

Wilcox, Ella Wheeler (1850–1919), US poet. Educated at the University of Wisconsin, she first became famous with her *Poems of Passion*, 1883, which were criticised as immoral, though they seem quite innocuous to modern readers. In 1884 she married Robert M. Wilcox, a silversmith. She published nearly 40 volumes of verse, which were widely popular.

Wild Boar, see BOAR, WILD.

Wilde, Oscar Fingall O'Flahertie Wills (1854–1900), English writer, born in Dublin. While a student at Oxford he was a disciple of Pater, and founded an aesthetic cult. In 1882 he went to America and lectured on aesthetic philosophy. In 1881 he had published a volume of poems, which, in spite of affectations, attracted attention. Seven years later he issued *The Happy Prince and Other Tales*, *Lord Arthur Savile's Crime and Other Stories*, and his only novel, *The Picture of Dorian Gray*, both appeared in 1891. *Dorian Gray* shows Wilde's aestheticism in all its aspects: the search for intense or rare sensations, the ban on every feeling which sets a limit to the faculty of enjoyment, the superiority of the true artist over the rules of society or morality.

Oscar Wilde at the Royal Academy; from a painting by W. P. Frith, 1881.

Wilde is remembered chiefly as a dramatist. With the exception of *Salome*, 1893, his successes were in the realm of light comedy, where he could give full play to his wit. *Lady Windermere's Fan*, 1892; *A Woman of No Importance*, 1893; and *The Ideal Husband*, 1895, were all successful, but his masterpiece was *The Importance of Being Earnest*, 1895. Here, Wilde finally rejected the melodramatic elements present in his previous efforts (though largely undercut by his satirical wit at the expense of established values), and produced a finely controlled 'society' farce, with brilliant dialogue and richly comic characterisations, which he called 'a trivial comedy for serious people'. In 1895, following Wilde's libel action against the Marquess of Queensberry, who had accused him of perversion, he was convicted of homosexual conduct and sentenced to two years' imprisonment. From 1897 until his death in obscurity and poverty, Wilde lived mainly in Paris. In his humilia-

tion he found the inspiration of the most powerful lines he ever wrote in *The Ballad of Reading Gaol*, 1898.

Wildebeest, see GNU.

Wilder, (Samuel) Billy (1906–83), US film director, initially a scriptwriter, born in Austria. He emigrated to Hollywood in the 1930s, where he worked on the script of *Ninotchka*, 1939. He had major successes with *Double Indemnity*, 1943, and *The Lost Weekend*, 1945, both unsparingly realistic in their treatment of greed and alcoholism, respectively. Other noted films include *Sunset Boulevard*, 1950, and *Some Like It Hot*, 1959.

Wilder, Thornton Niven (1897–1975), US novelist and playwright. His first novel, *The Cabala*, was published in 1925. In 1927 appeared *The Bridge of San Luis Rey*, which brought him international fame and the Pulitzer Prize. His play, *Our Town*, won the Pulitzer Prize in 1938, and he won this prize for the third time in 1942, with another play, *The Skin of Our Teeth*. *The Ides of March*, a study of Caesar's downfall in letter form, was published in 1948. His novel, *The Eighth Day*, appeared in 1967.

Wilfrid, Saint (634–709), English ecclesiastic. He was a Northumbrian, educated at Lindisfarne. He travelled in France and Italy, and returned to Ripon to found an abbey where he introduced the Benedictine rule. He was consecrated bishop of York at Compiègne in 664, and in the same year was the leading advocate of the Roman view at the Synod of Whitby. Wilfrid did much missionary work among the Frisians and South Saxons. His lengthy absences from his see led to efforts to supplant him, against which he appealed successfully to Rome. However, he agreed on his return to resign in favour of St John of Beverley.

Wilhelmina, in full Wilhelmina Helena Paulina Maria (1880–1962), Queen of the Netherlands. In 1890, after the death of her father William II, Wilhelmina succeeded him on the throne, but until her majority was under the regency of her mother. She was enthroned at Amsterdam in 1898. Her only child Juliana was born in 1909. After the German invasion in 1940, Queen Wilhelmina and her government went to London. After the liberation of her country she returned to the Netherlands. In 1948 she abdicated in favour of her daughter, who succeeded her as Queen Juliana, Wilhelmina taking the title of Princess of the Netherlands.

Wilhelmshaven, seaport city in Lower Saxony, Federal Republic of Germany, 165 km north-west of Hanover. It is on the western arm of Jade Bay, at the end of the Jade-Ems canal. It was founded in 1853 and after the opening of the harbour in 1869 became the headquarters of the Prussian North Sea fleet. The city is now the third largest German port, catering for supertankers which unload into the 390-km pipeline to the Rhine–Ruhr region. It is still a major naval base but also has an oil refinery, machinery (typewriters), textile, and furniture industries. Population (1976) 102,540.

Wilkes, John (1727–97), British politician. He entered Parliament in 1757 and became active in opposition to George III's Scottish first minister, Bute. In 1762 he founded the *North Briton*, a newspaper whose title indicates its anti-Scottish standpoint. The paper campaigned virulently against the ministry of Lord Bute. In 1763 Wilkes was arrested on a general warrant (i.e. one not naming the persons to be arrested) for a libel uttered in the famous number 45, in which he described the king's speech as false. He was found guilty but pleaded privilege as a Member of Parliament. He was unseated, however, and went abroad for four years to avoid arrest. After his return he was elected member for Middlesex by a large majority, but was expelled in 1769 for another libel. He was thrice returned for Middlesex on the strength of his enormous popularity, but was not allowed to sit until 1790. In 1774 he was elected Lord Mayor of London. Wilkes was a debauchee and a political adventurer, but his career was of constitutional importance in hastening the end of the much-abused general warrants system, giving the Press recognised entry to parliamentary debates, and establishing the right of an elected member to take his seat.

Wilkie, Sir David (1785–1841), British painter. He is famous for such pictures of popular life as *The Blind Fiddler*, 1806, and *The Village Festival*, 1811 (both in the Tate Gallery). He became an RA in 1811. He died at sea during his return from travels in Turkey and Palestine, and his death was commemorated by Turner in *Peace-Burial at Sea*, 1842 (Tate Gallery).

Wilkins, Sir George Hubert (1888–1958), Australian pioneer in polar aerial exploration. He joined Stefansson's Canadian Arctic Expedition, 1913–17, as a photographer. He was knighted in 1928 for a flight of 3380 km across the Arctic Ocean from Point Barrow (Alaska) to Spitsbergen. He led an expedition in 1928–1929 which made the first Antarctic flight, was commander of the *Nautilus* submarine expedition to the Arctic in 1931, and was manager of the Ellsworth trans-Antarctic expeditions of 1933–39.

Wilkinson, Ellen Cicely (1891–1947), British politician. She was Labour MP for Middlesborough East from 1924 to 1931, and for Jarrow from 1935 until her death. She was minister of education, with a seat in the Cabinet, 1945–47.

Will, a term used in a variety of senses in psychology and philosophy to cover the decisions, commitments and practices of the individual, and to refer to the mind's control of its impulses. A person acting under an impulse to take what he wants is acting under a conative drive. His will comes into play when he himself decides to check the impulse, or equally when he himself decides to implement it. Many psychologists and philosophers believe that will in this sense is illusory; that in all cases the strongest impulse wins, i.e. that will itself is determined by forces outside it. There seems sufficient reason to believe that both our decisions and our feelings affect our conduct and that although impulses and desires push us in certain directions, we also have a capacity to consciously choose our actions, according to the extent to which we are conscious of our feelings and impulses. Freud's work, which is consistently deterministic, represents will by other concepts.

Willemstad, city, port and capital of the Netherlands Antilles on the island of Curaçao, noted for its 17th-century Dutch-style gabled houses. It has one of the finest harbours in the Caribbean, and a large oil refinery. Population (1970) 50,000.

William I (1027–87), surnamed 'The Conqueror', King of England, bastard son of Robert I, Duke of Normandy. He succeeded at the age of seven to the duchy of Normandy and the suzerainty of the French Vexin, and had a bitter struggle to keep his inheritance. In 1053 he strengthened his position by marrying Matilda, daughter of Baldwin IV, Count of Flanders. In 1064 he conquered Brittany. William visited Edward the Confessor in 1051, when it seems that he was recognised by Edward as his heir. It is traditionally said that in 1064 Harold (later Harold II) promised to support William's claim to the English throne on Edward's death. But in 1066 Harold ascended the throne himself. William then invaded England, landing at Pevensey near Hastings, with about 10,000 men, and on 14 October defeated Harold's army at a place since called Battle; Harold was killed.

William I, portrayed in the 15th-century Great West Window of Canterbury Cathedral.

By an economic blockade William secured London, and was crowned by Aldred in Westminster Abbey on 25 December. In 1067 he returned to Normandy, leaving his half-brother, Odo of Bayeux, and William Fitz-Osbern as regents. The result was a series of rebellions by the barons lasting from autumn 1067 until 1072, when the last of them was ruthlessly quelled. All English and foreign resistance to William had now been crushed. Some historians have represented the Conquest as an almost entirely destructive *coup de main*, organised by a tyrannous governing clique imbued with alien traditions and intent on the extirpation of Anglo-Saxon culture and institutions. This is an oversimplification. While modern historians no longer underestimate the great achievements of Anglo-Saxon England, nor the suffering caused by the Conquest, William's invasion was ultimately to confer many benefits. He brought England within the western European system, gave it a government, an administrative system, an army, and a reformed Church subject to the common law. A system of dependent military tenure became the normal form of land tenure. Though the process by which William granted land is not known, its outcome is given in detail in the survey known as Domesday Book. In the grant of fiefs to his supporters William kept about one-fourth of the land of England for himself, and the immediate effect of his feudal settlement was greatly to enhance the power of the Crown.

See also HASTINGS, BATTLE OF; NORMAN CONQUEST.

William II (c.1056–1100), known as William Rufus, King of England, third and favourite son of William I, whom he succeeded to the English throne on his death in 1087, his elder brother, Robert, becoming duke of Normandy. In 1090 William acquired French Normandy and Fécamp from Robert; his intervention in Scottish affairs met with mixed success, but in 1092 he annexed Cumberland and Westmorland to the English crown. Much of William's reign was occupied in disputes with the Church, which became intense after Anselm's appointment to Canterbury. William's policy has received much criticism from monastic chroniclers; he was grasping, tyrannical, homosexual, and apparently irreligious, but in fact he was following, though with much less finesse and fewer scruples, the policy of his father. He was killed, probably murdered, while hunting in the New Forest.

William III (1650–1702), King of England, Scotland and Ireland, and Stadtholder of Holland, posthumous son of William II, Prince of Orange, and Mary, daughter of Charles I. The most far-reaching event of his life was his marriage, in 1677, to Mary, daughter of James, Duke of York, afterwards James II of England. This was the triumph of the Earl of Danby and William over Louis XIV of France. William cultivated the growing opposition to James II, and when eventually overtures were made to him to invade England he accepted them, and landed with a small force at Torbay, on 5 November 1688. He was crowned joint sovereign with Mary in 1689. In 1690 he defeated James II at the battle of the Boyne, and, having conquered Ireland, proceeded to subdue Scotland. He went to Holland in 1693 and commanded the Dutch army. The Peace of Ryswick (1697) was his greatest diplomatic achievement. William was a generally unpopular, though respected, king. His reserve, his apparent neglect of his wife, his Dutch favourites, and his obvious use of England primarily as an instrument for saving Holland from France alienated English affection. His treatment of the Whig party was skilful; though he in fact owed his throne to them, he established himself sufficiently to rule independently, and often in opposition to their views.

William IV (1765–1837), King of Great Britain and Ireland, third son of George III. He served in the navy from 1779 to 1790, reaching the rank of rear-admiral, and was created duke of Clarence in 1789. Shortly after this he became the lover of the actress, Dorothea Jordan. In the interests of the royal succession he married in 1818 Adelaide, daughter of George, Duke of Saxe-Coburg-Meiningen, but none of their children survived infancy. In 1830, on the death of

George IV, he succeeded to the throne. He was boisterous, tactless, but good-hearted, and occasionally as king showed unexpectedly sound common sense, as in his handling of the constitutional crisis of 1830–32.

William I (1797–1888), King of Prussia (from 1861) and Emperor of Germany. He found in Bismarck a minister anxious to govern according to his own view, and it may be said that between them they had a large part in the making of Germany as it was before 1914, though William was always prepared to make some compromise with progressive forces, and proved a popular monarch. During the Franco-Prussian War, he commanded the Prussian army and led his soldiers to the victories of Gravelotte and Sedan. He was proclaimed emperor of Germany in 1871.

William II (Friedrich Wilhelm Victor Albrecht) (1859–1941), German Emperor and King of Prussia, son of Frederick III, whom he succeeded in 1888. His obvious intention of reducing Bismarck, the Chancellor, to a mere instrument of his own will led to Bismarck's resignation in 1890. He attempted, however, to pursue the main lines of Bismarck's policy. William's chief ambition was to strengthen Germany's power in Europe by colonial expansion. In his strenuous endeavours to this end, he visited Abdul-Hamid at Constantinople in 1889 and 1898; and, while maintaining the Triple Alliance between Germany, Austria and Italy, he tried also to cement a friendship with Russia. He was a frequent and welcome visitor to Britain until 1895, but the British resented his congratulatory telegram to Kruger after the Jameson Raid in 1896.

When news of the Sarajevo assassination reached him on 28 June 1914, he pushed on with war preparations so openly that Russia, France and Great Britain were soon irrevocably committed, and a world conflict was inevitable. On 3 October 1918, when defeat of the German forces was imminent, he appointed Prince Max of Baden to the chancellorship. In November Prince Max demanded his abdication, and William thenceforth resided in Holland.

William of Malmesbury (c.1059–c.1143), English chronicler, a Benedictine monk at Malmesbury and inter-librarian and precentor. His *De Gestis Regum Anglorum* gives the history of kings of England from the Saxon invasion to 1127. He also wrote *De Gestis Pontificum Anglorum*, 1125 (revised 1135–40); *De Antiquitate Glastoniensis Ecclesiae*, an account of the church of Glastonbury; *Historiae Novellae* (a sequel to the *De Gestis Regum*); and a *Life of St Dunstan*. William gives a careful record of contemporary events at the Council of Winchester against Stephen in 1141. Master of a vivid and elegant style, he enhanced the interest of his narrative by introducing lively anecdote and pictorial description.

William of Ockham, see OCKHAM, WILLIAM OF.

William of Orange, see WILLIAM THE SILENT, PRINCE OF ORANGE; WILLIAM III.

William of Tyre (c.1130–c.1186), French prelate and chronicler. He was appointed Archdeacon of Tyre at the request of Amalric, King of Jerusalem, in 1167, and was consecrated Archbishop of Tyre in 1175. William was among the foremost of medieval historians, his chief work, *Historia Rerum in Partibus Transmarinis Gestarum*, being one of the main authorities for events in the Latin kingdom of the East in the 12th century.

William of Wales, Prince (William Arthur Philip Louis), born 21 June 1982, the son of Prince Charles and Princess Diana. He is second in line, after his father, to the throne of the United Kingdom.

William of Wykeham, see WYKEHAM, WILLIAM OF.

William the Lion (1143–1214), King of Scotland. He succeeded in 1165. In 1174 he invaded England in alliance with Henry II's own sons, was defeated at Alnwick, and agreed to do homage to Henry for Scotland and all his other territories. By the Treaty of Canterbury (1189) between him and Richard I the independence of Scotland was recognised on payment of 10,000 marks.

William II. *The Kaiser with his staff in 1916, during the First World War.*

William the Silent, Prince of Orange (1533–84), soldier, statesman and founder of the Dutch Republic. In 1555 Philip II appointed him Stadtholder of Holland, Zeeland and Utrecht. William led the movement against Spanish rule and the persecution of Protestants that culminated in the unsuccessful 1566 rebellion. In 1567 he went into self-imposed exile and became a Protestant. Following the capture of Den Brielle in 1572, he joined the Sea-Beggars (Les Gueux). A grim and bloody struggle ensued, but, eventually, Holland and Zeeland threw off Spanish rule. In 1576, when the Netherlands revolted, William became the national leader, reconciling Protestants and Catholics in the Pacification of Ghent. But this did not last: Protestants formed the Union of Utrecht, which became the constitutional basis for the Dutch Republic, and Catholics formed the Union of Arras. William continued his fight against Spain, despite this setback, to his main objective of a free, united Netherlands. He was assassinated by a Spanish agent.

See also NETHERLANDS, *History*.

Williams, Emlyn (1905–), British actor, dramatist and producer. He made his first appearance at the Savoy Theatre, 1927, in *And So to Bed*. His first big success as actor-dramatist was in 1935 with his play *Night Must Fall* at the Duchess Theatre, which ran for over a year. Among the subsequent successes in his own plays were *The Corn is Green*, 1938; *The Light of Heart*, 1940; *The Wind of Heaven*, 1945; *Trespass*, 1947; *Accolade*, 1950; and *Someone Waiting*, 1953. He made a great success in dramatic readings from the works of Dickens and Dylan Thomas. He produced his own play *Beth* in 1958. In 1961 he published his autobiography, *George*, and in 1966, *Beyond Belief: A Chronicle of Murder and its Detection*.

Williams, Eric (1911–), West Indian politician. He was a professor in the USA for several years. Williams founded the People's National Movement in 1956. He was Trinidad's first chief minister later that year, and its first premier in 1959. He led the independence talks in 1961, becoming premier of Trinidad and Tobago in the same year. One of the most forceful leaders in the Caribbean, he is also a prominent author and spokesman for anti-racialism.

Williams, John (1941–), Australian lutenist and guitarist, now settled in the UK. He studied with Andreas Segovia and at the Royal College of Music. He also performs and composes rock and jazz.

Williams, J(ohn) P(eter) R(hys) (1949–), Wales' most capped rugby union player with 55 test appearances (54 as full back and one as flanker) between 1969–81. He also holds the record as the world's most-capped full back with 62 appearances (including eight for the British Lions). He retired in 1979, but was recalled in October 1980 to play against the All Blacks. He finally retired in 1981.

Williams, Ralph Vaughan, see VAUGHAN WILLIAMS, RALPH.

Williams, Roger (c.1603–83), founder of Rhode Island, USA. Born in England, he took orders, but became a Puritan, and in 1630 sailed for the New World in search of religious freedom. He founded in 1636 the city of Providence, where all believing in religious freedom might live. He was president of Rhode Island, 1654–57.

Williams, Shirley Vivien Teresa Brittain (1930–), British politician, daughter of Professor Sir George Catlin and the novelist Vera Brittain. She was general secretary of the Fabian Society, 1960–64, was elected Labour MP for Hitchin in 1964, and was MP for Hertford and Stevenage from 1974 to 1979. Between 1966 and 1970 she was successively parliamentary secretary, Ministry of Labour, minister of state, Department of Education and Science, and minister of state at the Home Office. In 1974 she entered the Cabinet as secretary of state for Prices and Consumer

Protection. In addition to this post she was appointed paymaster-general and chairman of several important Cabinet committees by James Callaghan, following his appointment as prime minister in 1976. Later in 1976 Mrs Williams became secretary of state for Education and Science, still retaining the office of paymaster-general. She lost her seat at the general election in 1979. In 1981 she was a co-founder of the Social Democratic Party and re-entered Parliament as member for Crosby. She lost her seat in the 1983 general election.

Williams, Tennessee, originally Thomas Lanier Williams (1911–83), US playwright. His first real success was *The Glass Menagerie*, 1945. *A Streetcar Named Desire*, 1947, cemented his reputation on Broadway, and a succession of plays followed: *Summer and Smoke*, 1948; *The Rose Tattoo*, 1951, a comedy about sex; *Camino Real*, 1953, a symbolic drama based on Don Quixote; and *Cat on a Hot Tin Roof*, 1955, about family tensions. Many of his earlier plays feature a gothic Southern background and an obsession with violence and evil, elements which recur in his later work, including *Suddenly Last Summer*, 1958, and *Sweet Bird of Youth*, 1959. *The Night of the Iguana*, 1961, was a success both as a stage-play and a film, though *The Milk Train Doesn't Stop Here Any More*, 1962, was a notable Broadway failure. *Period of Adjustment*, 1960, was a successful 'serious' comedy. More recently, *The Two Character Play*, 1967; *The Seven Descents of Myrtle*, 1968; and *In the Bar of a Tokyo Hotel*, 1969, had a mixed critical reception, though *Small Craft Warnings*, 1972, was warmly received in London in 1974. Williams published a collection of one-act plays, volumes of short stories, and a novelette, *The Roman Spring of Mrs Stone*, 1950.

Williams, William Carlos (1883–1963), US poet and novelist. He studied medicine. As a poet Williams set himself to develop a distinct American technique which would be non-derivative. His volumes of verse include his 'personal epic', *Paterson*, 1946–51, which received the National Book Award. He also wrote novels which form a trilogy, *White Mule*, 1937; *In the Money*, 1940; and *The Build-Up*, 1952. He published two books of critical essays, *The Great American Novel*, 1923, and *In the American Grain*, 1925; and an *Autobiography*, 1951.

Williamsburg, city in Virginia, USA. It grew after the first English settlement in Virginia, Jamestown, had proved unhealthy and badly sited; it is located some 10 km inland from the James river and became the first capital of Virginia. The College of William and Mary, one of the oldest institutions in the USA, was founded here in 1693. By the early 20th century, the town had greatly declined and John D. Rockefeller, Jnr, now provided the capital to restore the old government buildings and much of the original aspect of the town. As a result, it has become one of the major tourist attractions on the east coast of America. The Williamsburg-Jamestown area now comprises the Colonial National Historical Park. Population (1980) 9870.

Williamson, Henry (1897–1977), English novelist and nature writer. He first came into prominence through his tetralogy, *The Flax of Dreams*. He is best known for his animal stories such as *Tarka the Otter*, 1927, which was awarded the Hawthornden prize; *The Old Stag*, 1926; *Salar the Salmon*, 1935; and *Tales of Moorland and Estuary*, 1953.

Williamson, Malcolm Benjamin Graham Christopher (1931–), British composer. He studied at the Sydney Conservatoire under Eugene Goossens and Erwin Stein. Resident in England from 1953, he was made Master of the Queen's Music in 1975. He is a versatile and active composer who aims at a wide public. His operas include *Our Man in Havana*, *Julius Caesar Jones* (for children), *Dunstan and the Devil* (for church performance), *Lucky-Peter's Journey*, and the *Red Sea*. Other works include the ballets *The Display* and *Perisynthyon*, five symphonies, concertos, church music, chamber music, keyboard works and songs.

Willibald, Saint, also Willebald (c.700–86), English missionary, a cousin of St Boniface. He was sent to Germany by the pope to help St Boniface, and by the latter was consecrated bishop of Eichstädt (742). He founded a double monastery at Heidenheim of which his sister, St Walburga, became abbess after his death. Willibald was canonised in 938.

Willibrord, Saint, also Willebrod (c.658–739), English Benedictine monk of Ripon. Trained in Ireland for the missionary life, he sailed with 11 companions to Friesland (c.690). He was consecrated archbishop of the Frisians six years later and established his see at Utrecht. In 698 he founded the monastery of Echternach, in Luxembourg, where he died. He is regarded as the apostle of the Netherlands.

Willis, Ted (Edward Henry, Baron Willis of Chislehurst) (1918–) British writer of plays and novels. His plays, which usually have a working class background, include *Hot Summer Night*, 1959; *Woman in a Dressing Gown*, 1962; and *Queenie*, 1967. Novels include *The Churchill Commando*, 1977, and *The Naked Sun*, 1980. He has also written for television, notably for the series *Dixon of Dock Green*.

Willis, Thomas (1621–75), British physician who is famous for his description of the anatomy of the brain. His *Cerebri Anatome*, 1664, was the most complete and accurate account of the nervous system which had hitherto appeared. Willis was a remarkably observant clinician; he was the first to note the characteristic sweet taste of diabetic urine, described whooping cough, myasthenia gravis and hysteria, gave the first account of epidemic typhoid and epidemic cerebro-spinal fever, and was the first to describe and name puerperal fever. He described the anatomical relations of the main cerebral arteries, discovering the Circle of Willis, the circle of arteries supplying the base of the brain.

Will o'the Wisp, also called Jack o' Lantern, an eerie, moving light seen hovering over marshy ground. In legend it has been represented as a lost soul, or as a diabolical attempt to lead astray benighted travellers. The light is the flame of methane or marsh gas, released by the decomposition of vegetation under water, and ignited by the spontaneous combustion of decaying matter.

Willow, see SALIX.

Willow Pattern, a generic term for a kind of design in the pseudo-Chinese style for underglaze blue transfer-printing on English pottery and porcelain. A popular form of this decoration was introduced by Thomas Turner (1749–1809), the proprietor of the Caughley porcelain works near Broseley, Shropshire (1772–99), though it was widely copied at many other English factories. The legend attached to the scene, of lovers transformed into swallows, is of English and not of Chinese origin. Chinese porcelain examples are later than the English, from which they are copied.

Willow Warbler, *Phylloscopus trochilus*, bird of family Muscicapidae, order Passeriformes. It breeds in open woodland. It is very similar to the chiffchaff, *P. collybita*, from which it is most easily distinguished by its song.

Willowherb, herbaceous plants of the genus *Epilobium* (family Onagraceae). The species generally have narrowly oval leaves and flowers with four pink petals. The fruit is a long pod-like capsule containing numerous very small seeds which are wind-dispersed by means of long hairs attached to one end. Rosebay willowherb or fireweed, *E. angustifolium*, was formerly placed in a separate genus *Chamaenerion*.

Wills and Testaments. In legal usage a will is a form of declaration, generally in writing, of a person's wishes as to the disposal of his property after death. Domicile is the place which a person regards as his permanent home, and every will of a person domiciled in England or Wales and appointing an executor is entitled to a probate if executed in accordance with the Wills Act 1837. Section 9 of the Wills Act requires that a will shall be in writing, which has been interpreted to include printing, lithography, photography and typewriting. At least two witnesses must subscribe the will in the presence of the testator after he has signed when all of them are present. Alterations and additions can be made by codicil.

It was formerly held that the power of a testator to dispose of his estate was unfettered, but the Inheritance (Family Provision) Act 1938, as amended by the Intestates' Estate Act 1952, enacted that a court may make an order for reasonable provision to be made for any of the testator's family if it is of the opinion that the will does not do so.

Willy-willy, see CYCLONE.

Wilmington, city in North Carolina, USA, the principal seaport of that state. It is situated on the Cape Fear river, 50 km up-channel, and access has been provided by dredging to the depth of 10 m. The port handles some 4 million t of freight annually, mainly agricultural produce and petroleum. Population (1980) 44,000

Wilson, Sir Angus (1913–), English novelist. He was deputy to the superintendent of the British Museum Reading Room, resigning in 1955 to become a full-time writer. In 1966, he was appointed professor of English literature at the University of East Anglia. His novels include *Hemlock and After*, 1952; *Anglo-Saxon Attitudes*, 1956; *No Laughing Matter*, 1967 and *As If By Magic*, 1973. Wilson's fiction is traditional in its concern for plot and character and in its serious analysis of modern society. He has written numerous short stories and several plays and television scripts.

Wilson, Edmund (1895–1972), US critic and novelist. He became a reporter, in 1920 was appointed editor of *Vanity Fair*, and from 1944 to 1948 was book reviewer for the *New Yorker*. One of the leading critics and cultural reporters of his time, he published *Axel's Castle*, 1931, a study of the Symbolist movement, and *To the Finland Station*, 1940, a history of revolutionary traditions. Wilson also wrote several plays including *This Room and This Gin and These Sandwiches*, 1937, and *Little Blue Light*, 1951. *I Thought of Daisy*, 1929, is a pleasing novel, and *Memoirs of Hecate County*, 1946, collects powerful stories. Wilson was the great modern example of the American all-round man of letters.

Wilson of Rievaulx, (James) Harold Wilson, Baron (1916–), British politician. He had a brilliant academic career, becoming lecturer in economics and fellow, at New College, Oxford. During the Second World War he was seconded to the ministry of Fuel and Power. He became Labour MP for Ormskirk in 1945 and represented Huyton from 1950 to 1976. In 1952 he was elected to the National Executive Committee of the Labour party and became leader of the group opposing German rearmament. Subsequently he took a more conformist line, supporting Hugh Gaitskell's candidature for the party leadership in 1955. On Gaitskell's sudden death in 1963, Wilson was elected leader of the Labour party. Though formerly criticised by many of his party for divisiveness, his authority and vigour now did much to revitalise and unify his party, and in October 1964 Labour won the general election after 13 years in Opposition, and Wilson became prime minister. He skilfully maintained stable and positive government for 18 months with a tiny majority, and the return of the Labour party in 1966 with a greatly increased majority was a personal triumph for Wilson. Economic difficulties now led to harsh economic policies, including a statutory incomes policy, which alienated many Labour supporters, as did proposals for the reform of industrial relations.

During the Conservative government of 1970–74 Wilson, who had, as prime minister, initiated further negotiations for British entry to the European Economic Community, shifted his ground and the Labour party became committed first to renegotiation of the terms of entry and then to a referendum on British membership. In February 1974 Wilson formed a minority Labour government and in October 1974 he won a small majority and consolidated Labour's hold on power. His tactics on receiving a large vote in favour of continued membership of the EEC in 1975 again illustrated Wilson's political skill in handling opponents in his own party. In March 1976 he announced his retirement as prime minister and leader of the Labour party. He was knighted in 1976 and received a life peerage in 1983.

Wilson, Henry Maitland Wilson, 1st Baron (1881–1964), British soldier. At the outbreak of the Second World War he was appointed commander-in-chief of British troops in Egypt. From 1942 to 1943 he was commander-in-chief in Syria, Iran and Iraq and in 1943 became commander-in-chief, Middle East. In 1944 he became supreme commander, Mediterranean.

Wilson, John (1785–1854), Scottish poet and essayist, his pseudonym was Christopher North. From 1820 he was professor of moral philosophy at Edinburgh University. He published two poems, *The Isle of Palms*, 1812, and *The City of the Plague*, 1816, but is best known for his *Noctes Ambrosianae*, 1822–35, a series of dramatic dialogues on multifarious topics.

Wilson, John Dover (1881–1969), British scholar. One of the greatest modern authorities on Shakespeare, he was joint editor of the New Cambridge edition. His works include *Life in Shakespeare's England*, 1911, and *The Essential Shakespeare*, 1932.

Wilson, Richard (1714–82), British painter. His pictures were little in demand during his lifetime but he was later recognised as the first great British master of landscape painting. When he went to Italy (1750) Wilson's intention was to improve his portrait painting, but on the advice of Claude Vernet he abandoned it for landscape. The principal sources of his inspiration while in Italy were the 17th-century French masters Claude Lorraine and Gaspard Poussin. He returned to England in 1756 and for the rest of his life painted landscapes in the classical style. Nonetheless he found inspiration in the Welsh mountains and his *Cader Idris* (Tate Gallery) and *Mount Snowdon*, 1760 (several versions, including Walker Art Gallery, Liverpool), are among his best known works.

Wilson, (Thomas) Woodrow (1856–1924), 28th President of the USA. In 1910 he was elected Democratic governor of New Jersey, and his reforms made him a prominent public figure. In 1912 he was nominated Democratic candidate for the presidency, and was overwhelmingly elected. His domestic policies were very successful, the principal Acts being the Underwood Tariff Bill, the Federal Reserve Act, the Clayton Anti-Trust Act, which gave organised labour its charter of freedom, and the repeal of the Panama Canal Tolls Act. His foreign policies were less fortunate, and for a time war in Mexico seemed imminent. When the First World War broke out, in accordance with the fixed policy of America to remain free from alliances and European wars, Wilson issued the usual neutrality proclamation.

At the election of 1916 Wilson was narrowly re-elected. His 'peace without victory' address in January 1917 was his last effort to end the war by peaceful methods. On 2 April 1917 he asked Congress to declare war on Germany and its allies. When the war ended and the peace conference met at Versailles, Wilson led the American delegation, and helped draw up the Covenant of the League of Nations. Returning to America in 1919 with the draft of the Covenant, he found a hostile Senate controlled by the Republicans. In July 1919 he declared that the peace treaty and the Covenant were interdependent and that one could not be adopted without the other. He appealed to the people over the heads of the Senate, and undertook a national speech-making tour. He had a mainly cool reception, and in September he had a stroke, from which he never fully recovered. As the controversy continued, the majority of the people veered into opposition, because of traditional feeling that the USA should not be entangled in foreign undertakings. The election of 1920 was an overwhelming win for Harding, the Republican.

Wilson never achieved great popularity, but he was keenly aware of the suffering and fears of ordinary people. He saw beyond national boundaries and gave inspiration to the ideal of international government. He failed because most of the world, including the USA, was not ready for his solution. He received the Nobel Peace Prize for 1919. See also UNITED STATES OF AMERICA, *History*; WORLD WAR, FIRST.

Wilton, market town in Wiltshire, England, celebrated for its carpets since the time of Elizabeth I. Wilton House is the seat of the Earls of Pembroke. Wilton gave its name to the county and is a military headquarters. Population (1981) 4005.

Wiltshire, south-western county of England, bounded on the north by Gloucestershire, on the south by Dorset and Hampshire, on the east by Hampshire and Berkshire, and on the west by Gloucestershire, Avon and Somerset. The surface is for the most part hilly, and includes Salisbury Plain (32 km by 25 km), which lies at about 120 m above sea-level, and to the north-east the Marlborough Downs and the Savernake Forest. The principal rivers are the Kennet, the Lower or Bristol Avon, the Salisbury Avon and the Nadder. Wiltshire is famous for its prehistoric monuments, of which Stonehenge and Avebury are the best known. There are numerous ecclesiastical ruins of later periods, including the abbeys of Malmesbury and Lacock. Salisbury Cathedral is a fine example of the Early English style. There are castle ruins at Old Sarum. Longleat House and Wilton House are two of the great historic houses of England; at Stourhead the gardens are a fine example of 18th-century design.

Mixed farming is carried on, and a considerable area of the county is under permanent pasture. Dairy-farming flourishes, cloth and carpets are manufactured, and Portland stone is quarried. There are important engineering works at Chippenham. The chief town is Salisbury, but Trowbridge is the centre for county administration. Area 388,104 ha; population (1981) 518,167.

Wimbledon, the site of the most famous tennis courts in the world and the venue of the Wimbledon All-England Lawn Tennis Championships. The first championships were held in 1877 at Worple Road, Wimbledon by the then All-England Croquet and Lawn Tennis Club. In 1882 the Club changed its name to the 'All-England Lawn Tennis and Croquet Club'.

The club acquired the present site in Church Road, Wimbledon, which holds over 30,000 spectators, in 1922. The centre and no. 1 courts hold approximately 14,000 and 7,500 spectators respectively.

Winchester, a cathedral city and the county town of Hampshire, England, on the River Itchen, 19 km north-east of Southampton. During the Roman occupation of Britain,

Winchester Cathedral was built in the 11th century on the foundations of an earlier Saxon building.

Winchester, called *Venta Belgarum*, was a route-centre and a commercial and administrative capital. The Saxon kings of Wessex, who made Winchester capital of Saxon England, are said to have been crowned in the old cathedral. During the Saxon period the Winchester illuminators became famous. Winchester College was founded by William of Wykeham in 1382. Winchester is a market for agricultural produce from the surrounding district. Population (1981) 30,642.

Winchester Cathedral. The present cathedral was begun in 1079 by Bishop Walkelin. Of his Norman building, only the crypt, transepts, crossing tower and some of the hidden structure of the nave remain. He gave the building its present exterior length of 170 m, making it then as now the longest cathedral in northern Europe. The retrochoir and Lady Chapel were rebuilt in 1189–1204, and the nave was remodelled in the Perpendicular style by William of Wykeham, from c.1394. Wykeham's master mason was William de Wynford. He recut the sturdy Norman piers and gave them refined vertical mouldings, rising to a lierne vault. The Early English Lady Chapel was remodelled in 1486–92, and the choir in 1500–1528, with a wooden vault and fine carved bosses. Noteworthy features of the choir are the altar screen, the carved stalls, and chests containing the bones of Saxon kings. There are several fine chantry chapels. Some kings of England were crowned here.

Winchester College, a school for boys founded by William of Wykeham in 1382. A substantial number of the original buildings, including the chapel, the central quadrangle known as Chamber Court, and the cloisters, are still in use; notable additions include School Hall (1687), possibly by Wren.

Winckelmann, Johann Joachim (1717–1768), German archaeologist and art critic. He became librarian to the cardinal-secretary of state in Rome, and in 1736 president of the Collection of Antiquities in the Vatican and Vatican Librarian. His main work was a comprehensive study of ancient art in two parts. The first part was *Gedanken über die Nachahmung der griechischen Werke*, 1755. The second part, *Geschichte der Kunst des Altertums*, 1764, became world-famous. This comprised a general theory of art and a history of art from the so-called Daedalos Period. His influence has been mainly in painting.

Wind, a movement of air over the Earth's surface. It is caused by uneven heating of the Earth by the Sun; hot air rises, producing low pressure, and is replaced by cooler air moving in from an area of high pressure. Surface irregularities cause turbulence, but this is not felt above 450 m. Changes in wind direction are termed *veering* if clockwise, and *backing* if anticlockwise. Speeds have been assessed since 1805 on the Beaufort scale, which ranges from 0 (calm) to 10 (hurricane). They are measured accurately at a standard height of 10 m by anemometers, while upper winds are measured by tracing the ascent of hydrogen-filled balloons or by radio-sonde.

Northern and southern hemispheres each have three pressure belts: polar high, sub-polar low, and sub-tropical low, divided by the equatorial low. From the polar highs, prevailing easterlies blow into the sub-polar lows, which also receive westerlies from the sub-tropical highs. *Trade Winds* flow easterly into the equatorial low. The sub-tropical highs are a source of wind outflow and therefore are a region of calms. They are known as the *Horse Latitudes*. The equatorial belt is an area of light winds, the *Doldrums*. Westerlies are stronger on the southern hemisphere, in the *Roaring Forties*, because of lack of land masses to slow them down by friction.

Many parts of the world have their own peculiar winds caused by local conditions. In coastal areas, the different rates at which the land and sea heat and cool cause sea breezes by day, and offshore winds at night. Such breezes can make otherwise enervating tropical coasts more pleasant for human occupation; hence the name, the *Freemantle Doctor*, for a wind such as this in North Australia. In other areas winds occur which are warmer than the prevailing conditions. These, for example the *Chinook* of North America, the *Föhn* of the Alps, the *Zonda* of Argentina, and the *Nor' wester* of South Island, New Zealand, are produced by air passing over high mountain areas, where it releases its moisture content through precipitation, and warming as it descends the leeward slope. In still other cases, locally recurrent pressure differences produce specific winds, at certain times of the year, that are colder than their surroundings. These include the *Bora* of south-eastern Europe; the *Mistral* of the Mediterranean coasts, between Perpignon and Genoa; the *Gregale* of Malta; the *Tehuantepec* or *Papagayos* of the west coast of Mexico, Nicaragua and Guatemala; the *Pampero* of Argentina; and the *Berg winds* of South Africa. Warm winter winds which bring storms and fog include the *Khamsin* of North Africa, the *Sirocco* of southern Italy, and the *Levanter* or *Solano* of southern Spain.

Wind Instruments are of three classes: (1) keyboard, e.g. organ, concertina, played by bellows; (2) woodwind, e.g. flute and the reed instruments, oboe, clarinet, bassoon, saxophone, bagpipes; (3) brass, e.g. bugle, cornet, horn, trumpet, trombone and other instruments with cup-shaped mouthpieces.

Wind-tunnel, a tubular structure in which models and full-sized objects are subjected to artificial winds in order to test their aerodynamic properties. The first wind-tunnel was made by the British aeronautical pioneers Wenham and Browning in 1871. Wind-tunnels are used chiefly by designers of aircraft, rockets, ships, bridges and automobiles.

Windermere, the largest lake in England. It lies in Cumbria, and is 18 km long and in places over 2 km wide. The lake drains southwards into Morecambe Bay via the River Leven. The small town of Windermere is a

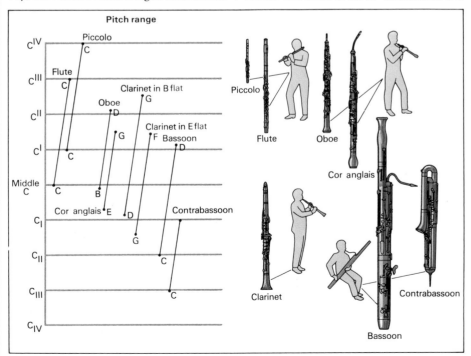

Wind Instruments. The orchestral woodwind instruments; their playing positions and pitch ranges.

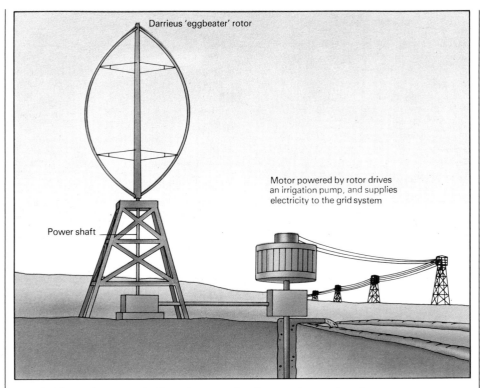

Darrieus 'eggbeater' rotor

Power shaft

Motor powered by rotor drives an irrigation pump, and supplies electricity to the grid system

Windmill. *'Eggbeater' windmills are being tested in the USA for providing electric power.*

favourite Lake District holiday and residential centre. It merges into Bowness further along the lake shore.

Windflower, see ANEMONE.

Windhoek, capital of South-West Africa (Namibia), 405 km from Walvis Bay. It has an international airport and is the world centre of the karakul industry. Other industries are being developed. Population (1970) 61,260.

Windlass, a machine used for lifting weights through a considerable distance, as in raising water from a well. It consists of a cylindrical roller made to rotate upon its axis by a crank and a handle. The weight is attached to a long rope which is coiled round the roller as the handle is turned.

Windmill, a machine driven by adjustable sails set to catch the wind. Windmills have been used in Britain to grind corn since the 12th century. A series of wheels and gears transmits the power from the revolving sails to the upper of two heavy circular millstones, which turns up to 150 times per minute.

There are three types of windmill. The post mill is the oldest; the body is supported by a massive wooden post, and the whole structure can rotate to face the wind. In the later tower mill, the machinery is contained in a round or octagonal body, and only the cap at the top which carries the sails is turned to face the wind. The smock mill, whose appearance resembles a countryman's smock, is a clapboard-covered wooden frame on a brick base. Only the cap turns.

Marsh mills, once used to pump water from the fenland, and so-called windmills which generate electricity by wind power, bear little resemblance to the traditional corn mill.

Windmill Hill, hill 2·5 km north-west of Avebury, England, is the site of a causewayed camp, an earthwork with interrupted ditches, which has given its name to the earliest culture of the English Neolithic. These

farmers bred cattle, cultivated wheat in small plots, dug out flint for tools and weapons, and traded in these products. They introduced, particularly from Switzerland and France, a distinctive type of pottery which in the first instance was derived from leather prototypes.

Window, an opening, usually glazed, in a wall or roof of a building to admit light and air and allow occupants to look out or objects inside to be seen. The Greeks and Romans used windows, occasionally glazed in Roman times, but during the Middle Ages they were seldom provided except in churches and important buildings. Glazing became common in dwelling-houses in the Tudor period. The top of a window opening is the head, the bottom is the sill, the sides are the jambs. Each light may be divided into panes. Before the invention of sash-windows (properly 'double-hung sashes') in the late 17th century, windows were wooden or occasionally iron casements, generally side-hung to open inwards or outwards.

In Britain between 1697 and 1851 a tax was imposed on houses with more than six windows. This decreased their use in small buildings but also led to the use of larger glazed areas since the tax was based on numbers, not on size. Modern structures present new problems with windows. Where buildings are air-conditioned the windows often have no opening sash. Where insulation against heat loss or noise transmission is required the windows may have to be double-glazed.

See also CASEMENT; JOINERY.

Windscale, see SELLAFIELD.

Windsor, Duke of, see EDWARD VIII.

Windsor, (Bessie) Wallis Warfield, Duchess of (1896–), widow of the Duke of Windsor, formerly King Edward VIII. She was born at Baltimore, Maryland, USA, and married E. W. Spencer, a US naval officer, in 1916, divorcing him nine years later. She

married Ernest Simpson in 1928. The Simpsons became close friends of the then Prince of Wales. They were divorced in 1936, and in June 1937 Mrs Simpson (who had reverted to her maiden name of Warfield) married the ex-king in France. Her memoirs were published as *The Heart Has its Reasons* in 1956.

Windsor, House of. Family name of the present royal house of Great Britain. In 1917 King George V gave up for himself and his family all German titles, together with the dynastic names of Saxe-Coburg-Gotha acquired through the marriage of Queen Victoria with Prince Albert. On 17 July 1917 King George V declared by proclamation that thenceforth his family should be known as 'The House and Family of Windsor'. In 1960 the queen declared that all her descendants (other than those titled Royal Highness and Prince or Princess) would be surnamed Mountbatten-Windsor.

Windsor, borough (since 1277), in full the Royal Borough of New Windsor, in Berkshire, England, on the Thames, 35 km from London. The town owes its importance to the castle, which is one of the royal residences, and the Great Park. Eton College lies just outside Windsor. Population (1981) 28,330.

Windsor, city and lake port of Ontario, Canada, 1 km east of Detroit, USA, with which it is connected by the Ambassador Bridge and Detroit-Canada Tunnel. It is the centre of Canada's motor-car industry, and also produces two-thirds of the country's pharmaceutical output. Its other industries include machine tools, adding machines, clothing, paint, forgings and stampings. The city is the market and service centre for the surrounding mixed farming region. Population (1976, city) 196,526.

Windsor Castle, England, a royal palace. Constructed by William the Conqueror as an earthwork surmounted by wooden palisades, it has been in continuous royal possession ever since. The work of replacing the palisades with stone walls and towers was started by Henry II (1165–79), and finished in the following century. Stone walls were followed by stone buildings, to which succeeding centuries have made many alterations and additions. The most notable are: those made in the 14th century by Edward III; in the 17th century by Charles II, whose architect was Hugh May; and in the 19th century by George IV, with Sir Jeffry Wyatville as architect.

Architecturally, the main feature of the castle is St George's Chapel, a masterpiece of Perpendicular architecture, where many English sovereigns are buried. It was built from 1475 to 1511. Opposite the chapel are the lodgings of the Military Knights of Windsor, dating from the 14th and 16th centuries. To the south of the castle is Windsor Great Park, comprising 1940 ha, connected with the castle by an avenue, known as the Long Walk.

Windsurfing, the sport of sailing on a long board, resembling a surfboard, to which is fitted a mast and sail (also known as board-sailing and sail-boarding). The sailboard was first devised in the USA c.1966–67. Several nations have established associations and competitive events, and there is now a windsurfer world championship.

Windward Islands, group in the West Indies, lying north-east of Venezuela, comprising Martinique, St Lucia, St Vincent, the Grenadines and Grenada.

Wine is the fermented juice of freshly gathered ripe grapes. The term is also applied to alcoholic beverages made from other fruit, and from vegetables. The juice pressed from the grapes is set fermenting by yeasts of genus *Saccharomyces* in the bloom of the berry. When the grapes, black or white, have been pressed for white wine, the juice is run off into vats, where it ferments apart from the stalks, skins and pips. For red wines, the juice ferments in contact with the skins, which contain the colouring matter, soluble as soon as alcohol has been formed, the pips, and a proportion of the stalks. The time required for the first fermentation varies; it ceases when it has transformed almost all the sugar into alcohol. Probably the highest alcoholic degree of naturally fermented wine is 17 per cent, occasionally reached by Châteauneuf-du-Pape. Wine, after it has ceased to be must (new, unfermented wine), goes on living with what is left of the fermenting yeasts, which need oxygen to exist. In the cask wine receives through the wood enough air to keep it developing, and wines which cannot be long-lived are drunk from the wood. Certain wines go on improving when they are more completely cut off from the outer air in the sealed bottle in which the air bubble is very sparingly reinforced with oxygen from outside. A special filter has been invented to remove from young wine every living organism, so that it can be sold younger without any danger of secondary fermentation in the bottle; but such wines only deteriorate with time. In bad years sugar is added to the must in northern vineyards to increase the alcoholic degree, but this dulls the flavour. See FERMENTATION; FRENCH WINES; GERMAN WINES.

Wingate, Orde Charles (1903–44), British soldier. In Palestine he organised and led a force for night operations during the Arab revolt (1936–38), and was head of the Jewish counter-guerrillas. In the Second World War he was selected for special service under Wavell, as leader of the Abyssinian partisans. Later he organised guerrilla war in Burma. His famous brigade of 'Chindits', consisting of British and Gurkha columns with intelligence detachments from the Burma Rifles, penetrated great distances across jungle ranges and valleys, skilfully infiltrating through the Japanese outposts and garrisons. He was killed in a plane accident in Burma, during an operational flight. Yemin Orde, a 'children's village' for orphans, was set up in Israel, as a memorial to Wingate.

Wings, see BIRD.

Winifred, Saint (Welsh Gwenfrewi) (d. c.650), patron saint of North Wales. She was beheaded (or wounded) by Caradoc of Hawarden for refusing to submit to his attempted seduction but was miraculously restored by her uncle, St Beuno. Miraculous cures at Holywell in Clwyd are attributed to her intercession. Her feast is on 3 November.

Winkelried, Arnold von (d.1386), Swiss knight, hero of Unterwalden. During the struggle for independence from the Austrians by the Swiss, a battle was fought at Sempach, a small village near Lucerne, in 1386. The Austrians, numbering about 4000, were opposed by 1500 Swiss, who could make no impression upon the phalanx of heavily armoured pike-bearing soldiers. Winkelried therefore rushed upon the spears, and embracing a number of the long spikes cleared a road for his companions in arms over his pierced body. At close quarters the Austrians, hampered by their armour, were annihilated, and the independence of Switzerland was won.

Winkle, see PERIWINKLE.

Winnipeg, capital of Manitoba and fourth largest city in Canada. It is situated at the confluence of the Red and Assiniboine rivers, in the south-east of the province, 65 km south of Lake Winnipeg and 30 km north of the US border. The Northwestern Company established the fur-trading post of Fort Gibraltar about 1810, and this was re-established by the Hudson's Bay Company as Fort Garry in 1882. Winnipeg was later the centre of the Red River Settlement. In 1870 the province of Manitoba was created, and Winnipeg declared its capital. Winnipeg is an administrative and service centre; it has a thriving agricultural engineering industry, flour mill, slaughterhouses, and food processing plants. It is also a major market and shipment centre for the produce, mainly wheat, of the three prairie provinces. Population (1976) 560,874.

Winnipeg, Lake, lake in the province of Manitoba, Canada. It is 400 km long, and from 8 to 11 km wide. The Winnipeg river, which enters at the south-east corner, drains from the Lake of the Woods and has a number of hydroelectric plants on its lower reaches, which have many falls and rapids. Area 23,553 km².

Winston-Salem, city and county seat of Forsyth county, North Carolina, USA. It is the commercial centre of a fertile agricultural region, especially noted for its tobacco, and the manufacture of cigarettes and flat plug tobacco here is most important. Textiles and furniture are also manufactured. Population (1980) 131,211.

Wint, Peter de, see DE WINT, PETER.

Winter, the fourth of the four seasons, defined astronomically as the interval between the winter solstice and the vernal equinox. Biologically, it is the annual period of suspended animation for many forms of life.

Winter Aconite, see ACONITE, WINTER.

Winter Berry, or black alder, a shrub, *Ilex verticillata*, of the Aquifoliaceae, indigenous to eastern North America. The bark has medicinal properties.

Winter Bud, a special type of bud surrounded by tightly packed bud-scales which protect the delicate embryonic tissues within from damage by freezing or desiccation during the dormant winter period.

Winter Olympics, a quadrennial series of sports competitions on snow and ice, held over a period of two weeks during February. Ice figure skating became an Olympic sport in 1908 and ice hockey was added in 1920. The first separate Winter Olympics, at Chamonix, France, in 1924, comprised nordic ski racing, ski jumping, ice hockey, four-man bobsledding, and figure and speed skating. Subsequent additions have been Cresta-Run tobogganing, two-man bobsledding, alpine ski racing, biathlon, luge tobogganing and ice dancing.

Winter Sports, physical recreations and organised competitions on snow or ice, largely developed from primitive forms of hunting and winter transportation. Leading winter sports are skiing (alpine and nordic), ice skating (figure, dance and speed), ice hockey, bobsledding, tobogganing and curling. Others include bandy, biathlon, broomball, ski-bobbing, dog-sledding, ski-jöring, snow-mobiling and ice yachting.

Wintergreen. In Britain, herbaceous plants of genus *Pyrola* in the family Pyrolaceae. In America, evergreen shrubs in the genus *Gaultheria* of the Ericaceae. It is from these that the oil of wintergreen is extracted, although it has now been largely replaced by synthetic esters of salicylic acid.

Winterhalter, Franz Xavier (1806–73), German portrait painter. He studied painting in Munich and is best known as an international court painter; he painted portraits of the Empress Eugenie and Queen Victoria.

Winter's Bark, the bark of *Drimys winteri*, an evergreen tree in the family Winteraceae of South America. It resembles cinnamon, and is used as a tonic and as a spice.

Wintersweet, see CHIMONANTHUS; VIBURNUM.

Winterthur, industrial commune of Switzerland in the canton of Zürich, manufacturing textiles, locomotives, machinery and cotton. A good wine is produced in the neighbourhood. There is some fine medieval architecture. Population (1980) 107,752; mainly German-speaking.

Winthrop, John (1588–1649), English colonist, governor of the colony of Massachusetts. He sailed in the *Arabella* from Yarmouth to America with several hundred persons in 1630, and helped to found Boston.

Wireless, see RADIO.

Wireless Telegraphy, system of radio-communication other than telephony. Intelligence is conveyed either by turning the transmitter carrier wave on and off in accordance with code symbols, by keying modulation on and off to a continuous carrier, or keying both carrier and modulation, or by carrier shift, i.e. moving the frequency of the carrier a few cycles for the positive code symbols. The codes used may be the International Morse Code or five-unit teleprinter code for direct operation of teleprinter machines.

Wireworm, see CLICK-BEETLE.

Wirral, a peninsula between the Dee and the Mersey estuaries, England, mainly a residential area but with some industrial development, notably at Birkenhead, Port Sunlight and Ellesmere Port.

Wisbech, town in Cambridgeshire, England, on the River Nene, in the centre of an agricultural and fruit-growing district. Agricultural implements, beer and baskets are manufactured. There are engineering works, and canning, preserving, timber, can-making, shipbuilding and printing industries. Wisbech is a small port, being used by vessels up to 2000 t. Population (1981) 17,332.

Wisconsin (Badger State), north-central state in the USA, bounded in the north by

Michigan and Lake Superior, east by Lake Michigan, south by Illinois, south-west by Iowa and Minnesota, and west and north-west by Minnesota. Its length north to south is 485 km and its greatest width 450 km; total area 145,438 km². The St Croix and Mississippi rivers separate it from Minnesota and Iowa. Other rivers are the Menominee (part of the Michigan state line), the Wisconsin and the Chippewa (tributaries of the Mississippi), the Fox and the Rock. The biggest lake is Lake Winnebago (557 km²). Wisconsin has nearly 6 million ha of commercial forests, but suffered greatly from a lumber boom in the late 19th century which destroyed much of the best timberland. It is the leading dairy state of the USA. The cattle are fed on corn (maize, usually cut green), hay and oats. Other crops are beetroots, sweet corn and green peas. Industries are mainly concentrated in the Milwaukee-Racine-Kenosha area in the extreme south-east. The pulp and paper industry, which is strongly developed in Wisconsin, is distributed throughout the central areas of the state, according to the availability of raw materials and water, and is especially concentrated in the Wisconsin and Fox river valleys.

The first permanent settlement was at Green Bay in 1701. Britain took Wisconsin in 1763, and ceded it to the USA in 1783. It became a state in 1848. The 1980 population was 4,705,335. The state capital is Madison.

Wisden Cricketers' Almanack, annual handbook dealing with cricket and cricketers. It was first issued in 1864 by John Wisden (1826–84), a cricketer and sports outfitter. It records all scores, averages and descriptions of first-class matches played in the preceding year.

Wise, Thomas James (1859–1937), British book collector, bibliographer and forger. His extensive forgeries of 'rare originals', made over a period of 20 years, were exposed in 1934 by John Carter and Graham Pollard in their *Enquiry into the Nature of Certain Nineteenth Century Pamphlets*, 1934. Wise became very famous as a book-collector, and his Ashley Library, catalogued in 11 volumes, is in the British Museum. This collection of the works of the English poets formed the basis for his numerous bibliographies ranging from Wordsworth to Conrad, still valued as works of reference.

See also LITERARY FORGERY.

Wiseman, Nicholas Patrick Stephen (1802–65), British Roman Catholic prelate, born at Seville. He became rector of the English college at Rome. He was nominated first archbishop of Westminster and cardinal in 1850 on the re-establishment of the Roman Catholic hierarchy in England. He was a distinguished scholar, and as such had a special sympathy with the writers who inaugurated the Oxford Movement. It was his essay on the Donatists in the *Dublin Review*, of which he was one of the founders, which first shook Newman's belief in the soundness of his Anglican position.

Wisent, see BISON.

Wismar, port of the German Democratic Republic, on the Baltic Sea. It became a member of the Hanseatic League in 1266, and was later ruled by Sweden, Denmark and then Mecklenburg-Schwerin. It has a big engineering works. Population (1971) 56,000.

Wisteria, a genus of leguminous climbing plants with twining woody stems. *W. sinensis, W. floribunda* and *W. venusta* are grown for ornament.

Wit (Old English *witan*, to know) originally meant simply intelligence and the power to know. This meaning has remained (cf. the plural 'wits'), but the singular form has in addition changed its sense to quickness of mind, then to the power of joining ideas in an unusual and humorous way, until wit is now almost synonymous with humour and satire. Strictly speaking, it is not essentially humorous; Hazlitt remarked that lying was a species of wit. It is the power to make an intelligent remark arising out of the situation or circumstances; the fact that such apt remarks are usually humorous has led to the narrower meaning of humorous repartee.

Witangemot (from Anglo-Saxon *wita*, wise man; *gemot*, assembly), in Anglo-Saxon England the national Council, consisting of members of the royal family, the archbishops, bishops, abbots, ealdormen and king's thanes. The *de jure* powers of the witangemot were very great, but were practically limited by a strong king or ruling clique.

Witch-Doctor, or medicine man, a practitioner devoted to combating evil, witchcraft and sickness, found in many pre-industrial societies throughout the world.

Witch-hazel, *Hamamelis* in the family Hamamelidaceae, more specifically *H. virginica*, a North American shrub resembling the hazel. The bark and leaves have an astringent property useful in medicinal preparations. Chinese witch-hazel is *H. mollis*.

Witchcraft. *The finger of accusation points at George Jacobs at the trial of the Salem witches.*

Witchcraft includes, broadly, any claim of possessing the ability to produce effects by compact with a supernatural power. In Europe, witchcraft cults may go back to fertility cults indigenous since palaeolithic times, the chief festivals being Candlemas, May Eve, Lammas and November Eve. The few surviving direct accounts of rituals show that a horned god symbolising the fertility of cattle, sheep, goats or occasionally deer was venerated, and that the local leader of the cult impersonated (and was regarded as the in-carnation of) this god. This explains Christian traditions of a 'devil' with horns and tail. Such ceremonies are depicted in the palaeolithic cave murals of Altamira, Ariège, etc. The object of the seasonal rites was probably to promote fertility by sympathetic magic. In time the original cult received discarded beliefs from other cults which tended to obscure its origins. At times it appears to have coalesced with Christian heresies.

It is commonplace to seek reasons for misfortunes, but what distinguishes witchcraft accusations from deductive reasoning is the basic assumption that certain people may be responsible for such events through some supernatural action, whether consciously and intentionally or not. Sorcerers are distinguished from witches in that they use mechanical means to achieve their aims (fetishes, potions or charms), whereas witches are thought to cause misfortune by the mere fact of their existence.

By the time of the Reformation, witchcraft had assumed the form of a secret society organised in 'covens' or groups of 13 members of both sexes, of which the leader was always a man. By this time it is unlikely that there were many people who believed in the cult and what had once been a serious enemy of the Church remained only as a convenient scapegoat, both religious and political. As members of a secret society, 'witches' could equally easily be denounced on charges of treason, heresy or demonolatry. English laws against witches are known from the time of Canute, and ecclesiastical and secular courts had concurrent jurisdiction in cases of witchcraft. In the case of the former, offences were punished by penance and fine up to 1542, when witchcraft was made a common felony (it was already indictable at common law). Apart from the statutes of 1542 and 1562, the Act of 1601, defining and prescribing the punishment for witchcraft, remained the principal Act up to the Act of 1736. Under all these Acts the prosecution had to prove that injury to person or property had been done or attempted (but not in the case of love philtres), or that gain had been made. Trials for witchcraft were most numerous in the 17th century.

In the hundred years following the accession of James I (himself a devout believer in 'Demonologie'), a profound change in the attitude of the educated classes towards 'witches' occurred, which can best be indicated by the fact that whereas justice under Queen Elizabeth I could condemn a proven 'witch' to the stake or the pillory for a crime against God and man, justice under Queen Anne would on the same evidence either dismiss the case or sentence her to a prison for a special type of fraud.

Witte, Count Sergei Yulievich (1849–1915), Russian statesman of German origin. He was minister of finance from 1892 to 1903, greatly stimulating the industrial development of Russia. From 1903 to 1906 he was prime minister. He negotiated the Treaty of Portsmouth, which ended the Russo-Japanese War, and suggested to Nicholas II the granting of a constitution providing for a legislative Duma. Witte incurred the suspicion of the emperor, who suddenly dismissed him.

Wittenberg, town of the German Democratic Republic, on the River Elbe, 64 km north-east of Halle. It was the capital (1273–1422) of the Duchy of Saxe-Wittenberg. It was one of the strongholds of the Reformation and it was on the door of its 15th-century *Schlosskirche* that Luther nailed his 95 Theses in 1517. Paper, machinery, chemicals and foodstuffs are produced. Population (1981) 53,870.

Wittgenstein, Ludwig (1889–1951), Austrian philosopher. *Tractatus logico-philosophicus*, 1921, was a revolutionary study of the function of language that greatly influenced the later schools of Logical Positivism and linguistic philosophy. Among Wittgenstein's posthumous works, which show how much he later changed his ideas, are *Philosophische Untersuchungen* (Philosophical Investigations) and *Bemerkungen über die Grundlagen der Mathematik* (Remarks on the Foundations of Mathematik). In the *Tractatus*, Wittgenstein expounded a logical atomist view: the basic elements are atomic propositions which picture the real world. Out of these are constructed complex propositions which depend only on the truth or falsehood of their atomic constituents. The later Wittgenstein of the *Investigations*, while retaining the aim of determining what can be said, departs radically from his earlier position: he now considers that we must ask not for the meaning but for the use of words. It is by examining the various ways in which language is used ('language games') that we grasp its scope.

Witwatersrand (Afrikaans, ridge of white waters), full name of the district in the Transvaal, South Africa, famous for its goldfields and more usually known as the Rand.

Woad, *Isatis tinctoria*, a herb in the family Cruciferae, with yellow flowers and pendulous pods. It was formerly cultivated extensively for blue dye.

Woburn Abbey, Bedfordshire, England, seat of the earls and dukes of Bedford since 1547. The present building contains an altered 17th-century wing but is otherwise of the 18th century, its main west range by Henry Flitcroft (1747–61), who also built the stables, and its south range (1787–90) built by Sir William Chambers or Henry Holland. Holland also enclosed the court with an east range (demolished 1950), and designed some of the major rooms.

Wodehouse, Sir P(elham) G(renville) (1881–1975), English author. His first novel was *Love Among the Chickens*, 1906, which introduced one of his immortal characters, Ukridge. In *The Lost Lamb*, 1909, he introduced Psmith, and then Bertie Wooster and the incomparable 'gentleman's gentleman', Jeeves, in 1919. Wodehouse used these characters repeatedly in entertaining novels set in a mythical upper-class world that for devotees became an institution of English social life. His career was marred when he was tricked by the Germans into making a propaganda broadcast after he had been interned in France in 1940, but by the 1960s his popularity in England had regained a high level. He became an American citizen in 1955. His *Selected Stories* appeared in 1958, and he also wrote many plays and was co-author of 18 musical comedies.

Woden, see ODIN.

Woffington, Peg, properly Margaret (c. 1714–60), British actress, born in Dublin, where she appeared as a child, and again in 1732. In 1740 she was engaged by Rich for Covent Garden, making her début in a 'breeches' part—Sir Harry Wildair in *The Constant Couple*. She was an immediate success, particularly as highborn ladies and elegant women. She was not very good in tragedy, and seldom attempted it. She was for a time the mistress of Garrick. She made her last appearance in 1757 as Rosalind. She is the subject of Charles Reade's play *Masks and Faces*, 1852, on which he based his novel, *Peg Woffington*, 1853.

Wolcot, John (1738–1819), English satirist. He wrote satires and lampoons on politics, society, and their prominent figures, under the pseudonym of Peter Pindar, which were popular in their day.

Wold (Old English *wold*, forest), term applied to open, hilly country. It is used specifically of certain areas in England to which this description applies, e.g. Yorkshire Wolds and Cotswolds.

Wolf, a name properly given to two species of the genus *Canis* (family Canidae, order Carnivora) which includes also dogs and jackals. The coyote is sometimes called the prairie wolf. The common wolf (*C. lupus*) is a species occuring in the more remote areas of North America, Europe and Asia. Wolves vary in size but are up to 1·4 m in length and usually grey. They may live alone or in packs, particularly in winter, and feed on large mammals such as deer, which they hunt as an organised team. Their eerie howl is heard more often than the animals are seen, for hunting pressure has driven them into the thicker forests. The maned wolf (*Chrysocyon brachyurus*) from Brazil and Paraguay is related. In general, foxes differ from wolves in having a more slender head with longer, tapering jaws.

Wolf-Ferrari, Ermanno (1876–1948), German-Italian composer. He settled in Munich in 1909 after seven years as director of the Liceo Benedetto Marcello in Venice. He composed several successful operas, including the realistic *I gioielli della Madonna*, the light and graceful *Il segreto di Susanna*, and the comic opera *I quattro rusteghi*.

Wolf, Hugo (1860–1903), Austrian composer. He studied music with his father and later at the Vienna conservatory. The 242 songs for voice and piano published in his lifetime are chiefly contained in the *Mörike-Lieder*, the *Eichendorff-Lieder*, the *Goethe-Lieder*, the *Spanisches Liederbuch*, the *Italienisches Liederbuch* and the *Michelangelo-Lieder*. Wolf's revolutionary effect on the German *Lied* has been likened to Wagner's on German opera. There is in his songs something of the continuous symphonic texture, the fragmentary vocal line and the chromaticism characteristic of Wagner. Some songs are almost atonal; Wolf also breaks up the rhythm and structure, so that there are no longer fully shaped 'tunes'. He also wrote an opera, *Der Corregidor*, and choral and instrumental pieces, including the *Italian Serenade* for string quartet.

Wolfe, James (1727–59), British general. He joined the army in 1741 and during the Seven Years' War had charge of Britain's operations in America under Amherst. In 1758 the task of taking Louisbourg was assigned to him, which he accomplished successfully. In 1759 he was given command of the expedition against Quebec, and on 26 June began the 12 weeks' siege. The first attempt at assault on 31 July failed. Later, Wolfe, in a night assault, succeeded in placing an army on the heights called the Plains of Abraham. The Marquis de Montcalm, the French commander, at once gave battle. The British were victorious, and Wolfe, three times wounded, died in the hour of victory. The capture of Quebec, which followed, marked the beginning of the end of French rule in Canada.

See also CANADA, *History*.

Wolfenden of Westcott, John Frederick
Wolfenden, Baron (1906–), British educationalist. In 1934 he became headmaster of Uppingham School, and in 1944 headmaster to Shrewsbury School. He was vice-chancellor of Reading University from 1950 to 1963. In the same year he was appointed chairman of the Departmental Committee on Homosexual Offences and Prostitution: the Wolfenden Report was published in 1957.

Wölfflin, Heinrich (1864–1947), German historian of Renaissance art and its interpretation. He believed 'composition' to be the basis of aesthetics, and the human figure the basic subject of all great art. He used the terms 'linear' and 'painterly' to describe the techniques whereby the art of different periods might be contrasted and evaluated, as in his *Renaissance and Baroque*, 1888, and *Classic Art*. He also wrote *The Art of Albrecht Dürer*, 1905, and the major work, *Principles of Art History*, 1932.

Wolfit, Sir Donald, real name Woolfitt (1902–68), British actor-manager. He specialised in Shakespeare, whose plays he toured for many years with his own company, founded in 1937. He made his first appearance in York in 1920, toured with Fred Terry and Matheson Lang, and was with the Old Vic and Stratford-upon-Avon companies between 1929 and 1936. During the Battle of Britain he gave over 100 lunch-time performances of Shakespeare in London at the Kingsway, the theatre on one occasion being slightly damaged by enemy action. A powerful actor, and perhaps the last in the 'grand manner', he was at his best in such parts as Sir Giles Overreach, Lord Ogleby and Tamburlaine. His autobiography is *First Interval*, 1955.

Wolfram, German name for tungsten.

Thomas Wolsey, Lord Chancellor of England, *1515–29.*

Wolfram von Eschenbach (c.1170–c.1220), German poet. He belonged to a noble Bavarian family and spent some time at the court of Hermann of Thuringia. One of the greatest medieval German poets, he possessed a great sense of humour, and great learning, although he professed to be a knight and not a scholar. His most famous work is the courtly romance *Parzival*, dated about 1200–10, a deep, philosophical interpretation of the Holy Grail legend.

Wolframite, name given to a group of minerals from which the metal tungsten is extracted. The wolframite minerals form a complete series between an iron-rich and a manganese-rich tungstate. Its general formula is $Fe,Mn\ WO_4$.

Wolf's Bane, see ACONITUM.

Wolfsburg, city in Lower Saxony, Federal Republic of Germany, on the Mittelland Canal, 20 km east of Brunswick. It was founded in 1938 as 'Stadt des KdF-Wagens', and later renamed. The town has grown around the main factory of Volkswagenwerke AG. Population (1980) 126,800.

Wolfson, Sir Isaac (1897–), British businessman and financier. He joined Great Universal Stores as a junior employee in 1932 and became its chairman in 1946. Wolfson acquired many companies and made a large fortune. He has given generously to charity in both Britain and Israel. In 1955 he founded the Wolfson Foundation, whose funds are used principally for the advancement of education, health and youth work in Britain and the Commonwealth. He endowed colleges named after him at both Oxford and Cambridge.

Wollongong, town of New South Wales, Australia, situated on the coast about 82 km south of Sydney. It is the main residential area and business centre of the Illawarra district and is situated on the southern coalfield. There are industries here including iron and steel, copper, fertilisers, oxygen and acetylene. Greater Wollongong, which includes Port Kembla, has a total population (1979) of 224,000.

Wolseley, Garnet Joseph Wolseley, Viscount (1833–1913), British soldier. He served in the Crimea, was at the relief of Lucknow during the Indian Mutiny, commanded the Canadian Red River expedition of 1870, and took part in the Ashanti War of 1873. In Egypt he won the battle of Al-Tall al-Kabir in 1882. He was made adjutant-general in 1885. (He was the prototype of Gilbert's 'Modern Major General' in the *Pirates of Penzance*.) From 1895 until 1900 he was commander-in-chief of the forces.

Wolsey, Thomas (c.1473–1530), English cleric and statesman. He took holy orders and in 1501 was appointed domestic chaplain to Henry Deane, Archbishop of Canterbury. Henry VII made him one of his chaplains in 1507, and preferments followed rapidly. By 1514 he was archbishop of York and in 1515 Leo X created him a cardinal. It was said that his magnificence outshone the king's, and that, as lord chancellor, which he also became in 1515, he made the Star Chamber more important than the king's court. He directed the plan of campaign against France in 1512, arranged the treaty of 1512 with that country, and accompanied Henry VIII to the Field of

Wolverine, or glutton, Gulo gulo.

the Cloth of Gold. In 1520, when Charles V became Holy Roman Emperor, Wolsey reversed his policy of alliance with France, and in 1521 allied with Charles against Francis, who was defeated at Pavia. Wolsey's policy was purely opportunist, the constant factor being his wishes to make English influence felt abroad and to satisfy his own ambitions.

Though opposed to Anne Boleyn, Wolsey conducted negotiations with Clement VII for the annulment of Henry's marriage with Catherine of Aragon (1527) and sat as a judge at the hearing with Campeggio. His failure to solve this question satisfactorily led to his fall from favour. He was indicted in 1529, but pardoned and allowed to keep and administer his diocese of York, which he did well. But he involved himself in plots in 1530, was arrested for treason and died on his way to London.

Wolverhampton, town in West Midlands metropolitan county, England, 21 km northwest of Birmingham. Industry is diversified (including tyres, rayon, heavy and light engineering of all kinds, aircraft and components, engines, buses and commercial vehicles, and locks, keys, safes and strong rooms). There has been much redevelopment. Population (1981) 252,447.

Wolverine, or glutton, *Gulo gulo*, the largest member of the weasel family, Mustelidae, in order Carnivora, measuring up to 1 m. Its underside and back are dark brown, its sides somewhat lighter. The coat is long and thick, and is prized as a trimming for garments. The wolverine hunts by lying in ambush and feeds mainly on small mammals, although large deer may occasionally be taken. It is sometimes called the glutton as it may break open and eat stores of food left by humans, and food it is unable to eat is coated with a repulsive secretion, rendering it inedible to other creatures.

Womb, see UTERUS.

Wombat, *Vombatus,* two species of burrowing mammals in family Vombatidae of order Marsupialia, found in southern Australia and Tasmania. *V. ursinus*, the ursine wombat, is about 1 m long, with a short tail, stout limbs, a blunt muzzle, and thick coat with long and coarse brownish-grey woolly hair. The head is large, flat and broad with small eyes and ears. The forefeet have five and the hindfeet four digits, and the soles are broad and naked. The pouch is more towards the rear of the body than is usual in marsupials, the young hanging between the hind legs of the mother. The dentition resembles that of the Rodentia. The wombat lives nocturnally and feeds exclusively on vegetables, digging up roots with its claws.

Women's Institute, see NATIONAL FEDERATION OF WOMEN'S INSTITUTES.

Women's Royal Air Force (formerly Women's Auxiliary Air Force) existed in the First World War as the WRAF and was reformed as the Women's Auxiliary Air Force (WAAF) in June 1939. The WAAF became the WRAF in February 1949 and has continued on a voluntary basis as a permanent feature of the armed forces.

Women's Royal Army Corps, title since February 1949 of the British Women's Army Corps, which came into being as the Auxiliary Territorial Service in 1938. Of the women's corps in the Second World War they were the most numerous body. Many units served abroad.

Women's Royal Naval Service. The WRNS was formed in 1917 but disbanded in 1919. It was re-formed in 1939 and throughout the Second World War performed duties ashore, releasing men for service afloat. 'Wrens' were employed on administrative, domestic, secretarial and communications work, plotting, meteorology, air radio, and many other duties. On 1 February 1949 the WRNS became established as a permanent, integral part of the Royal Navy.

Women's Royal Voluntary Service, formed in Britain in June 1938 to stimulate the enrolment of women in Air Raid Precaution services. Its work was later extended to welfare for the Services, schemes for old people ('Meals on Wheels' delivers around 11 million meals annually), children (Holiday Schemes and Play Centres), and the disabled. Clothing and furniture are collected and distributed, and non-medical work in hospital is carried out. Other WRVS activities include prison welfare and after-care, and schemes to provide homes for people with small fixed incomes. As a national service it has centres in every local authority area in England, Scotland and Wales, and gives help in any emergency.

Women's Suffrage. Bills on women's suffrage in Britain passed second readings in

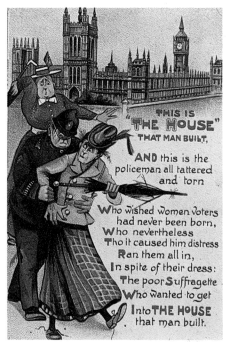

Women's Suffrage. A contemporary postcard.

the Commons six times between 1886 and 1911, but never proceeded beyond that stage. The organised violence of women in the 'suffragette' movement was abruptly terminated by the war in 1914. Owing to the work of women during the war, opinion turned in their favour. Early in 1918 a bill granting limited franchise to women was passed and ten years later, in 1928, the bill which equalised the franchise passed the House of Lords.

In the USA the struggle for women's suffrage was prolonged, but finally women over 21 were given the vote on the same terms with men. This became law in 1920.

Wonders of the World, Seven, see SEVEN WONDERS OF THE WORLD.

Wood, Ellen (1814–87), English novelist; she was better known as Mrs Henry Wood. She married her banker husband in 1836. Her great success was *East Lynne*, 1861, a novel of middle-class life which sold over half a million copies and was dramatised repeatedly. Other highly popular books were *Mrs Halliburton's Troubles* and *The Channings*, both published in 1862. The *Johnny Ludlow Papers*, 1874–87, were contributed to the *Argosy*, a magazine she owned and edited.

Wood, Sir Henry (1869–1944), British conductor. He was an assistant church organist in 1879. He later studied at the Royal Academy of Music. He gave organ recitals and conducted the Carl Rosa Opera Company and other organisations. From 1895 he conducted the Queen's Hall promenade concerts. He visited America in 1904, 1925 and 1926. Between 1895 and 1919 he presented over 200 English works, many for the first time, and introduced modern Russian, German and French works. He did much to foster an appreciation of orchestral music and leading musicians.

Wood, John, the Elder, commonly called 'Wood of Bath' (1704–54), English architect. He rebuilt and developed much of Bath, with the intention of restoring its Roman character. At Liverpool he designed the Exchange or Town Hall, 1749–54. After his death, his son John Wood the Younger (1728–81) completed some of his buildings in Bath and also designed the Royal Crescent, 1767–75, the New Assembly Rooms, 1769–1771, and the Hot Baths (1776–78).

Wood, the part of the stem of a tree or shrub between the pith and the bark. It consists of the xylem towards the centre and the phloem outside. These are conducting tubes that have walls made of two substances, cellulose and lignin. The function of these cells is to lend strength to the stem, to conduct water and minerals from the roots to the leaves, and nutrients formed by photosynthesis from the leaves throughout the plant. Wood also contains various quantities of substances such as gums, resins, oils and other materials which affect its durability, colour, taste, smell or working properties.

Wood-carving, see CARVING.

Wood-engraving. Though closely allied to woodcuts, wood-engravings differ from them in two essential ways: gravers are used to make the incisions which are made on the end grain of the wood rather than along the plank; and boxwood is the timber most in favour, having a close, hard grain. The small,

wedge-shaped gravers vary in section, to plough out different thicknesses of line. The chief advantage of engraving over cutting is that it offers infinitely greater possibilities for fine lines and details.

Although Thomas Bewick of Newcastle-upon-Tyne did not invent the process of end-grain engravings (as is sometimes thought), he was the first to see its possibilities. Instead of imitating the black lines of copper engravings, he used the white line which is the natural result of the process. During the 19th century wood-engraving sank to the level of a reproductive craft, although used with consummate skill by such men as the Dalziel brothers to facsimile the works of Leighton, Millais, Keene, Tenniel and other contemporary artists. Eventually photography and the introduction of process-engraving brought about its decline.

Early in the present century a number of artists saw in wood-engraving a medium of direct expression. Until recently the medium flourished as an art, and was considered by many to be *par excellence* the best for book illustration. The works of Eric Gill, Joan Hassall, Gwen Raverat, Robert Gibbings and many others have been so used. Wood-blocks are prepared 'type-high' so that when engraved they can be locked in a printing forme and printed at the same time as the type, thus producing a decorated book and not a book with plates.

Wood-ibis, name usually applied to *Mycteria americana* of family Ciconiidae, in the order Ciconiiformes, but also to ibises in general. It breeds in the southern United States and in South America.

Wood-lice, terrestrial arthropods in order Isopoda of class Crustacea. Wood-lice are the most completely terrestrial Crustacea. However, they are restricted to damp situations where they feed on decaying vegetable matter, although they will also eat any of their own relatives that have just sloughed their 'skins' and are unprotected.

Wood-pigeon, ring-dove or cushat,

Woodcut, Madame Lepere, The Convalescent*, by Auguste Lepere.*

Columba palumbus, a member of the family Columbidae, order Columbiformes. It receives one of its names from the white patches which ring its neck. It is distributed throughout the Palaearctic region. Besides the white neck patches, it also has a white wing-bar. The eggs are white, usually numbering two.

Wood Spirit, a mixture of methanol and acetone obtained by the distillation of pyroligneous acid (produced by the distillation of wood in iron vessels) after neutralisation with lime. Pure methanol can be obtained from wood spirit by combining it with anhydrous calcium chloride and distilling the resulting alcoholate. Crude methanol and naphtha are added to ethanol to render it unfit to drink. See also ALCOHOLS.

Wood-wasp, or horntail, insect in the family Siricidae, order Hymenoptera (suborder Symphyta). In general they are fairly large and black or metallic blue, often with yellow bandings. Morphologically, the adult females differ from the wasps or social wasps in that their ovipositor still retains its egg-laying function. The long lance-like ovipositor of the female wood-wasp is used for drilling holes into wood. Usually a single egg is deposited into each hole, and the larva on hatching bores through the heartwood, causing much damage.

The common wood-wasp, *Sirex juvencus*, is about 30 mm long and blue-black with a metallic sheen. The male may be distinguished from the female by its short triangular spine or horn at the tip of its abdomen and also by a brown-red stripe on its back. The female has a syringe-like ovipositor which she uses to bore holes into the wood of conifers.

Woodchuck, *Marmota monax*, popular name of a species of American marmot. It is a burrowing rodent, 60 to 70 cm long; grizzled above and reddish below. It has a stout body, broad, flat head and short, thick legs and is easily tamed.

Woodcock, George (1904–79), British trade union leader. Woodcock was secretary to the TUC research and economic department, 1936–47; assistant general secretary of the TUC, 1947–60, and TUC general secretary, 1960–69. Woodcock had considerable influence on trade unionism in Britain.

Woodcock, *Scolopax rusticola*, a game bird found throughout temperate parts of Eurasia. It belongs to the long-billed section of the snipes, in order Charadriiformes. It has large eyes, placed well back in the head, so that the hinder margin is just above the orifice of the ear. The wing is more rounded than in the snipes. It has 12 tail-feathers, and the upper leg is feathered. The adult male is about 40 cm long, and its general colour above is reddish, black and grey, the whole aspect of the upper surface being mottled; the breast and sides of body are buff, the latter having light brown bars, edged with blackish lines. The American woodcock is *Philomela minor*; it is found only in Eastern USA.

Woodcreepers, or woodhewers, family (Dendrocolaptidae) of small tropical and subtropical American birds, found from northern Argentina to Mexico. They have long bills and curved claws, which enable them to cling to the bark of trees. They are coloured in a range of dull browns and vary in size from 140 mm to 360 mm. They nest in natural hollows or old woodpecker holes and feed on small insects and spiders.

Woodcut. The art of the woodcut consists of cutting from the surface of a plank of wood, with a short-bladed knife and gouges, the white portions of a design, leaving untouched those parts which are to print black. Proofs are taken by coating the untouched surface of the block with printer's ink and then, either in a printing-press or with a burnisher, pressing a sheet of paper against the inked surface. Unlike engraving or etching on copper, in which the ink is pressed into the lines, in woodcutting it is the surface from which prints are taken, the lines showing white. Chestnut, pear and other even-grained woods are most suitable.

Blocks of wood cut in this way were first used for printing on fabrics. The earliest extant examples on paper are believed to date from the 9th century in China and from 1418 in Europe. The earliest European examples are playing-cards and religious prints. The 16th-century woodcuts of Dürer and Holbein (the latter's designs cut by Hans Lützelburger) make masterly use of simple and broad contrasts of strong blacks and white. But by the 17th century the development of more sophisticated techniques meant that woodcutting was used only for popular printing. It was revived as a medium for original expression at the end of the 19th century by artists like Gauguin and Munch and found particular favour with the German Expressionists.

See also BLOCK-BOOK; WOOD-ENGRAVING.

Woodhenge, a probable predecessor, of Neolithic date, to Stonehenge, situated 4 km north-east of the latter, and consisting of six concentric circles of wooden posts laid out very exactly, perhaps to a standard measurement. Nearby Durrington Walls, a large bank and ditch about 450 m in diameter probably contained several structures similar to Woodhenge.

Woodpeckers, Picidae, family of birds in the order Piciformes. The Picidae are adapted for climbing up the bark of trees, and picking out insects to eat from the crevices. The feet, though very short, are usually strong; the nails are broad and crooked and the toes placed in pairs, two forward and two backward. Woodpeckers have a long extensile tongue which is furnished with muscles enabling the bird to dart it forth and to retract it again quickly. They are found in all continents except Australasia and include the greater spotted, *Dendrocopus major*, the lesser spotted, *D. minor*, the green, *Picus viridis*, and the wryneck, *Jynx torquilla*, an aberrant form.

Woodrush, common name for the cosmopolitan genus *Luzula* of the family Juncaceae.

Woodstock, market town of Oxfordshire, England, on the Glyme. After the battle of Blenheim (1704), land was granted to the Duke of Marlborough, and Blenheim Palace was built near Woodstock. Gloves are manufactured. Population (1981) 2036.

Woodville, Elizabeth, see ELIZABETH (wife of Edward IV).

Woodwind Instruments, a group of musical instruments, traditionally made of wood though sometimes now of metal, which are blown to produce a sound. The flute and piccolo are played by blowing across a mouth hole, the remainder by blowing into a mouthpiece containing either one or two reeds. The saxophone (always made of metal but classified as woodwind) and the clarinet are single reed instruments, the oboe, bassoon and cor anglais are double reed.

Woodwork, see CARPENTRY; CARVING; FRETWORK; FURNITURE; INLAYING; JOINERY; MARQUETRY.

Woodworm, see TEREDO.

Wookey Hole, village in Somerset, England, 3 km from Wells. It is noted for its caves, also called Wookey Hole, the source of the River Axe. Objects dating from the palaeolithic to the Romano-British period have been found here. The papermill in the village is one of the oldest in Britain (1610). Population (1971) 1000.

Wool is the hair of certain animals, used to make knitted or woven fabrics. Sheep's wool (fleece) is the most important. There are four main types: the merino, the British, the cross-bred, and the Asian. The growth between annual shearings is between 5 and 10 cm.

The surface of wool is covered with scales overlapping from tip to root. These scales are responsible for the lustre of the fibre and are an essential part of the milling or felting process. Felting is a disadvantage in knitted garments, and wool is often treated to prevent felting when the material is machine-washed. Wool fibres have a natural crimp or wavy nature. This waviness is important in imparting bulk and therefore warmth; the closer the crimps the warmer the fabric. Man-made fibres are treated or bulked to make them take up a crimpy nature. Wool is highly elastic; it absorbs water from the atmosphere and, in normal conditions of use, will absorb moisture from the skin.

Other animal fibres which have properties similar to sheep's wool are:

1. Mohair, from the angora goat. It is a long, lustrous fibre, much coarser than wool and very durable. It originally came from Turkey.

2. Camel hair, from the Bactrian camel of China and Mongolia. The short, fine fibre is naturally a pale reddish-brown colour.

3. Cashmere, from the cashmere goat of Tibet and China. It is much finer than the best wool, and very soft.

4. Vicuña, from the wild vicuña (a species of llama) of Peru. It has the softest feel and the best drape of all the animal fibres.

Mildews, fungi and the larvae of certain insects such as the clothes moth attack wool and hairs.

See also MOTH RESISTANCE.

Woolf, (Adeline) Virginia (1882—1941), English writer. In 1912 she married Leonard Woolf. At their home in Gordon Square they became the centre of a literary group which championed the cause of modernism in English writing and became known as the 'Bloomsbury group'. At Hogarth House she and her husband set up the Hogarth Press. She did not achieve a really characteristic work until *Jacob's Room*, 1922. Her early works had been realistic studies but in this she followed James Joyce in adopting the 'stream of consciousness' method, hoping to mirror in prose the subjective inner experience of life as it was

Virginia Woolf, photographed in 1902.

lived. Later novels which won an international reputation include *To the Lighthouse*, 1927, and *The Waves*, 1931. She was also a skilled critic. *A Room of One's Own*, 1929, is a lucid essay about the special problems of a woman writer, and *A Writer's Diary*, 1953, reveals a great deal about her working methods. She drowned herself, leaving her last novel, *Between the Acts*, 1941, unfinished.

Woolley, Sir (Charles) Leonard (1880–1960), British archaeologist. While assistant keeper in the Ashmolean Museum, Oxford, he excavated at Corbridge in Northumberland. He went with the Eckley B. Coxe expedition to Nubia, 1907–11, and was in charge of the British Museum excavations at the Hittite city of Carchemish until 1914. From 1922–34 he conducted excavations at Ur. The spectacular results of this expedition made known to the public the ancient Sumerian civilisation. In 1935–39 and 1946–1949 he excavated in the Hatay near Antioch. From 1943 he was archaeological adviser to the War Office, responsible for the protection of monuments in the war areas. In addition to many detailed archaeological writings, he wrote books for the general reader, including *Digging up the Past*, 1950; *Ur of the Chaldees*, 1950; *A Forgotten Kingdom*, 1953; and *Spadework* (autobiographical), 1953.

Woolsack, seat of the lord high chancellor in the House of Lords. It is a large square bag of wool, with a backrest but no arms, covered with red cloth. It is traditionally held to have been placed in the House during the reign of Edward III as a mark of the importance of the wool trade to English prosperity.

Woolworth Family, US merchants and businessmen. Frank Winfield Woolworth (1852–1919) in 1879 opened a '5-cent' store in Lancaster, Pennsylvania, later adding 10-cent goods and including among his partners his brother Charles Sumner Woolworth (1857–1947). The partnership opened 5- and 10-cent stores in other cities, and was incorporated in 1911 as the F. W. Woolworth Company. Frank left a fortune estimated at $65 million. Britain copied the system of having only two, attractively low, prices and for 30 years the Woolworth stores sold goods at 3d and 6d only (1p or 2½p). The limitation of store prices to 5 and 10 cents was abandoned during the Second World War. Following years of poor trading results, in 1982 the UK part of the organisation, comprising some 1100 stores, was sold to a British consortium of companies for £310 million.

Woomera, space research centre and rocket launching station in South Australia, 440 km north of Adelaide. It is operated jointly by Australia and the UK, and was also an important testing ground for the projects of the European Launcher Development Organisation (ELDO). Activities there were curtailed after 1976.

Wootton of Abinger, Barbara Frances Wootton, Baroness (1897–), British economist and sociologist. She did research for the TUC and Labour party, 1922–26, and was professor of social studies, London University, 1948–52. From 1950 to 1956 Lady Wootton was a governor of the BBC. She was made a life peeress in 1965. Amongst her publications are *Freedom Under Planning*, 1945; *Crime and the Criminal Law*, 1964; and *Contemporary Britain*, 1971.

Worcester, a make of porcelain from the factory established by Benjamin Lund and William Miller in 1751, originally at Bristol. The factory became the most productive in England, especially for tableware. The best period, 1752–83, is known as the 'Dr Wall Period', from the name of one of the founders.

See also PORCELAIN, *Soft-paste*; CHINAWARE.

Worcester, cathedral city, market town, and county town of Hereford and Worcester, England, 35 km south-west of Birmingham. It is situated upon both banks of the Severn, though principally on the left bank. Worcester has been an episcopal see since 680, but its early history is obscure. In 964 St Oswald founded a new church there for Benedictine monks, and Bishop Wulfstan began rebuilding on a large scale in 1084. From medieval times Worcester was the centre of a prosperous glove trade. The firms of Dent's and Fownes', founded in the 18th century, carry on this tradition. The Royal Worcester Porcelain Works was founded in 1751. Engineering is the leading modern industry in Worcester, and includes mining and electrical engineering. There are also iron and brass foundries, pattern shops, and machine and fitting shops. Other industries include the manufacture of Worcester sauce, printing, footwear, furniture and agricultural machinery. Population (1981) 74,247.

Worcester, city in Massachusetts, USA, situated on the Blackstone river, 70 km west of Boston. It became a permanent settlement in 1713. Like other New England towns, it grew with industrialisation. Population (1980) 161,799.

Worcestershire, see HEREFORD AND WORCESTER.

Word Processor. A word processor generally comprises a keyboard, very similar in design to that of an ordinary typewriter, an electronics unit, a display screen, a diskette unit and a printer. Information is stored on diskettes. Programme diskettes enable the operator to type material, store it, and, if

necessary, revise it before printing; some word processors have built-in electronic dictionaries, others have accounting facilities. The concept of word processing was invented by IBM in the 1960s. Since then the idea has been developed, and the word processor has evolved into a highly technical electronic machine.

Worde, Wynkyn de, (d.c.1535), English printer, assistant to Caxton from 1476, succeeding him at his printing office in 1491. He made improvements in the art of printing, especially in type-cutting.

See also PRINTING.

Wordie, Sir James Mann (1889–1962), British scientist and explorer. He was geologist and chief of scientific staff to Shackleton's Antarctic expedition of 1914–16, and led expeditions to Spitsbergen, Greenland, Jan Mayen Island and Baffin Island.

Wordsworth, Dorothy (1771–1855), English diarist, sister of the poet William Wordsworth. From 1795 she kept house for her brother, accompanying him, with Coleridge, to Germany (1798–99). She later settled with Wordsworth and his wife at Grasmere, moving to Rydal Mount in 1813. The poet acknowledged how much he owed to her inspiring companionship, and dedicated to her the *Evening Walk*, 1793. Her own *Journals* display great powers of description and a keen appreciation of natural beauty.

Wordsworth, a portrait by Haydon, 1818.

Wordsworth, William (1770–1850), English poet. In 1791 he travelled in France and was converted to republicanism. He also fell in love with Annette Vallon and they had a daughter, but various obstacles prevented their marriage and he returned home alone. Meanwhile the excesses of the French republicans turned his admiration to horror, and he now embraced the rationalist philosophy of William Godwin. In 1793 his first published work appeared, *The Evening Walk* and *Descriptive Sketches of a Pedestrian Tour in the Alps*. With his sister Dorothy he settled in Somerset near where Coleridge was living. His fine poem 'The Ruined Cottage' seemed too good for separate publication; instead he made it part of his projected philosophical poem *The Recluse*. Wordsworth and Coleridge collaborated in the *Lyrical Ballads*, 1798, to which Wordsworth contributed 'Tintern Abbey', a meditation on his response to nature, and other

pieces. They then went to Germany where Wordsworth wrote some of his best short poems including 'Strange fits ...' and 'A slumber did my spirit seal'. In 1799 he and Dorothy moved to Dove Cottage at Grasmere. In 1802 he married his cousin Mary Hutchinson. In 1805 he completed *The Prelude*, a long autobiographical poem on the development of his mind. The early part, describing his childhood, contains some of Wordsworth's best poetry. The *Poems* of 1807 include the famous 'Intimations of Immortality from Recollections of Early Childhood' which develops the themes of 'Tintern Abbey'. In 1814 *The Excursion* (the middle part of *The Recluse*) appeared. Encouraged by a growing reputation, Wordsworth published some early work, and visited London literary circles, where his egotistical behaviour displeased some admirers. In 1843 he succeeded Southey as poet laureate.

Wordsworth is best known as the poet who, as a leader of the Romantic Movement, re-awakened his readers to the beauty of nature, describing the emotional fervour and perceptive insights which natural beauty aroused, recollected in tranquillity. In advocating a poetry of simple feeling and a use of the language of ordinary speech, he probably influenced his contemporaries most, but his nature-mysticism had a no less strong, though diffuse, effect on his successors.

Work, in mechanics and engineering, the effect produced in any mass by a force acting against inertia or in overcoming resistance. Work is measured as the product of the force and the distance over which it is overcome. This is so whether the motion is direct, inclined or curved. In the case of a force inclined at an angle θ to the resultant motion, the effective force is $f \cos\theta$. *Power* takes account of time; it is the rate of doing work. The SI unit of work is the joule, or newton-metre. *Energy* is the capability of doing work. See also METROLOGY.

Work Study, the activity of systematically examining, analysing and measuring the methods by which humans perform work. It is also known as time and motion study or methods engineering. There are two main components; method study and work measurement. Method study is concerned with making a job easier to perform so that a worker can be more productive and less fatigued. Work measurement aims at establishing how long a qualified worker should take to perform a job when he is working without over-exertion.

Workhouse, see POOR LAW, HISTORY OF.

World, see EARTH.

World Bank, popular name for the International Bank for Reconstruction and Development.

World Council of Churches, formed in Amsterdam in 1948, one of the chief products of the movement for Christian unity. Its headquarters are in Geneva. The Council has over two hundred member churches including all the main branches of Protestantism and most of the Orthodox churches. The Roman Catholic Church sends observers, and has increasingly undertaken joint activities with the World Council. Its three major divisions are Faith and Witness, Justice and Service, and Education and Communication.

World Cup, world's premier international soccer tournament. Initially known as the Jules Rimet Trophy, after the then President of FIFA whose idea the tournament was, the competition was first held in 1930 in Uruguay. The host nation won, beating Argentina 4–2 in the final.

The cup has been won by Italy, three times; Uruguay, twice; West Germany, twice; Brazil, three times; England, once; and Argentina, once.

On their victory in 1970, Brazil became the first club to win the cup three times and gained outright possession of it. The cup was then replaced by another trophy known as the FIFA World Cup. For the 1982 tournament in Spain, 24 countries (as opposed to 16 in previous tournaments) reached the final stages. They comprised the host nation and defending champions, both of whom are granted automatic entry, together with 22 qualifiers. Italy beat West Germany 3–1.

World Health Organisation (WHO), international body charged with the responsibility of protecting and promoting the health of all peoples. It is a specialised agency in relationship with the United Nations. The work of WHO is carried out at the request of governments and mostly takes the form of projects designed to improve health services and to stimulate national initiative. In addition to the prevention and control of specific diseases its basic activities are concerned with: strengthening of health services; family health; environmental health; development of manpower; and information and literature services. The headquarters are in Geneva, Switzerland.

World Scale, in shipping, a method used for calculating tanker freights. The World Scale Committee use a notional tanker of 19,500 t deadweight. They calculate the cost of a voyage using this ship and this becomes 'world scale flat' or 'world scale 100' for that voyage. Owners and charterers then negotiate a freight rate around this figure. World scale 70 is 70 per cent of the world scale flat. The world scale freight rates are published in *World-wide Tanker Nominal Freight Scale.*

World War, First (1914–1918). Intense nationalism, economic, military and naval rivalry were some of the causes of the First World War. At the beginning of the 20th century the balance of power in Europe was no longer stable. German military and industrial expansion since the defeat of France in 1870 alarmed her neighbours: colonial expansion and the need for a larger German navy to protect the colonies led Britain to regard the growth of German naval power as a threat to its own superiority at sea. Europe became divided into two camps: the Triple Alliance (1879–82) of Germany, Austria–Hungary and Italy, and the Triple Entente (1893–1904) of France, Russia and Britain. From 1906 onwards, crises regularly occurred every two or three years, e.g. Algeciras, Bosnia, Agadir—and in each crisis the Triple Entente faced the Triple Alliance.

The actual occasion for war arose out of conflict between Austria–Hungary and Russia in the Balkans. The Archduke Francis Ferdinand of Austria, heir to the Austro–Hungarian throne, was assassinated by a Serb at Sarajevo, in Bosnia, on 28 June, 1914. Austria–

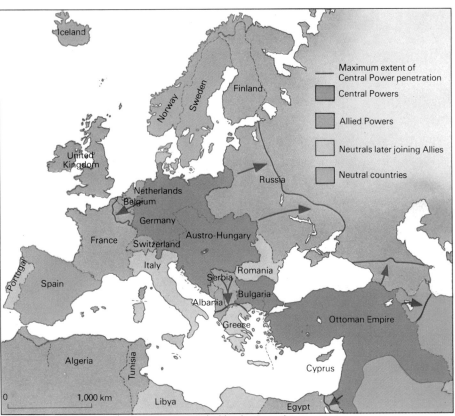

First World War. The furthest positions reached by the Central Powers.

Hungary, supported by Germany, declared war on Serbia. Russia mobilised in support of Serbia and Germany declared war on Russia (1 August) and on France (3 August). On 4 August, Germany invaded Belgium in order to strike at France. This brought Britain into the war on the same day. Britain, France, Russia and Belgium were later joined by Japan, Serbia, Italy (1915), Portugal (1916), Romania (1916), USA (1917) and Greece (1917). Germany and Austria–Hungary were joined by Turkey (1914) and Bulgaria (1915).

On the Western Front the German offensive was based on the Schlieffen Plan, a flanking movement through Belgium which was to approach and take Paris from the south. At the first battle of the Marne, the German advance was checked by the British Expeditionary Force (BEF) and the French under Joffre. Between 5 and 13 September, the Germans were forced to retreat across the River Aisne. The German attempt to reach the Channel was similarly thwarted at the first battle of Ypres. The final attack on Ypres began on 20 October and with the arrival of reinforcements on 17 November, the Germans ceased their attempt to break the line and the period of trench warfare began.

The year 1915 saw three major battles and great loss of life: at Neuve-Chapelle the attack began on 10 March but Allied gains were small; at the second battle of Ypres, the Germans used chlorine gas for the first time (22 April); the battle of Loos in September was bloody and inconclusive. In December 1915, Sir Douglas Haig replaced Sir John French as commander of the BEF.

In February 1916, the Germans launched an all out attack on the French fortress of Verdun. At first the French fell back and later began to retreat to prepared positions. At this point Pétain took over the defence and drove

back the enemy. On 24 October, the French attacked and some positions which the Germans had won at great cost were retaken within a few hours. The battle of the Somme, which had the object of driving the Germans north towards the coast, began on 1 July, 1916. Although the Allies made some advance, it was at the cost of the loss of some 600,000 men. German losses were about 650,000. During the first quarter of 1917, Allied pressure compelled the Germans under Ludendorff to withdraw to the prepared defensive positions of the Hindenburg line. By 11 April, Haig had taken Vimy Ridge at a cost of 132,000 men. The French attack on the southern part of the Hindenburg line failed and the commander-in-chief, Nivelle, was replaced by Pétain. By now, the USA had joined the Allies and in the third battle of Ypres (the Battle of Flanders), Passchendaele was taken at the cost of 245,000 British losses. The German offensive in the spring of 1918 failed to break the Allied line and German advances were neutralised by Foch's counter-offensive in the second battle of the Marne. The German forces retreated to the Hindenburg line which was broken in September by Haig. By October 1918, Germany was making overtures for peace. On 11 November, fighting ceased on the Western Front.

On the Eastern Front in 1914 the Russian armies advanced rapidly into East Prussia and by 25 August there was intense alarm in Berlin. Hindenburg was appointed to stop the Russian advance and at the battle of Tannenburg the Russians were defeated and 92,000 prisoners taken.

When Turkey entered the war in November 1914 and attacked Russia, the Allies mounted first a naval operation in the straits of the Dardanelles, March 1915, and then a military landing at Gallipoli where Australian and New Zealand troops (ANZAC) played an important part. Both operations were costly in ships and men and by January 1916 the Allies had been forced to withdraw.

By 1915, it was plain to Germany that Russia would be more easily defeated than France; Mackensen's drive into Galicia resulted in the expulsion of the Russians from Poland and most of the Baltic States (Lithuania, Latvia). The German armies were also victorious in Serbia and the Russians were pushed back well beyond the 1914 frontier. In an attempt to help the Serbs, the Allies landed at Salonika but the small Allied force could do little more than harass the flanks of the Bulgarian advance into Serbia. Defeats by the superior German army and the failure of its allies to aid Russia led to that country's collapse and the Russian Revolution of 1917. Hostilities on the Eastern Front ceased on 2 December, 1917.

The Middle East. Shortly after the outbreak of war in 1914, the Mesopotamian campaign began with the Allies landing Indian troops at Abadan. They took Basra at the junction of the Tigris and Euphrates and in this way controlled the delta and safeguarded the oil installations. The Turks made little progress against these British operations in the Persian Gulf. However, farther north the Allies failed to take Baghdad in November 1915 and the evacuation of Gallipoli left the Turks free to attend to Mesopotamia. Kut al Amara was captured by the Turkish forces in April 1916 but was retaken in February 1917. Finally, Baghdad fell to the British in March and, aided by the Arab revolt, the Allies invaded Palestine: Allenby took Jerusalem in December. The capture of Damascus and Aleppo (1918) completed the defeat of the Turks.

Italy entered the war in 1915 and maintained her front with Austria–Hungary through a succession of battles until 1917. In that year a combined German and Austro–Hungarian force inflicted a crushing defeat at Caporetto. Later, Italy was assisted by French and British units and the Austrians were heavily defeated at Vittorio-Veneto in October–November, 1918.

Naval Warfare. Throughout the war, Britain enjoyed naval supremacy in surface ships over Germany and demonstrated this effectively in 1914. Defeated at Coronel, in November 1914, when older British ships encountered two armoured German cruisers, *Scharnhorst* and *Gneisenau*, the Royal Navy's response was swift and effective. At the Battle of the Falklands in December, a squadron under Admiral Sturdee confronted *Scharnhorst* and *Gneisenau* and three German light cruisers. All the German ships except the light cruiser *Dresden* were sunk. British sea-power had thus safeguarded British sea-routes and also enabled the German colonies to be seized during the next two years. German naval raids in 1914 on Great Yarmouth, Scarborough, Whitby and the Hartlepools ceased after Beatty's victory at Dogger Bank when the heavy cruiser *Blücher* was sunk. The Battle of Jutland (May 1916), however, cast doubts on the superiority of the British navy. No less than fourteen ships of the Royal Navy, with a total tonnage of 115,000, were lost. The German losses were eleven ships with a total

tonnage of 61,000. Germany's most effective naval weapon was the submarine. U-boats effectively preyed on British shipping-lanes and sank some 6000 ships during the war. In 1917 they were made less effective by the adoption of the convoy system. UK's shipping losses during the First World War were 7,925,000 tonnes, about half its mercantile marine.

The War in the Air. Flying was in its infancy when the war started and, although aircraft developed rapidly, their rôle was mainly in support of the other services. Towards the end of the conflict, British and French aircraft bombed Germany and German aircraft bombed France and UK. Early in the war German Zeppelins raided UK cities, notably London. By modern standards these raids were ineffective and had little influence on the course of the war. The principal air forces involved were British, French and German; most air battles took place between fighter aircraft over the Western Front. In 1918, the Royal Air Force was formed from the Royal Flying Corps and the Royal Naval Air Service.

With the end of the war, after the defeat of Turkey and Bulgaria (September 1918) and Austria–Hungary and Germany (October 1918), revolution broke out in Germany and Kaiser Wilhelm II fled to the Netherlands. The Armistice was signed on 11 November 1918 and a peace treaty, the Treaty of Versailles, on 28 June 1919. The four years of war cost the Allies approximately 5 million lives and the Central Powers some 3·5 million.

World War, Second (1939–45). The Second World War began on 1 September 1939 with Germany's invasion of Poland. In 1938 Germany had annexed Austria and, following the Munich Agreement, occupied the Sudeten districts of Czechoslovakia. The rest of Czechoslovakia was seized in March 1939. This aggressive policy of the German National Socialist government headed by Adolf Hitler, led to Britain, France and Poland making an agreement of mutual assistance in August 1939. The Russo-German Non-Aggression Pact of August 1939 freed Hitler to make war on the West. In June 1940, Germany was joined by Italy and in December 1941 by Japan. These Axis Powers were opposed by the Allied Powers, consisting of Great Britain and the Commonwealth, France (the Free French after June 1940), the Soviet Union (from June 1941 when Germany attacked that country), and the USA and China from December 1941, when the Japanese attacked Pearl Harbor.

The War in the West. The Blitzkrieg technique with its large-scale use of tanks and aircraft enabled Germany to overrun Poland by 27 September. Soviet forces occupied eastern Poland and the Baltic States. A British Expeditionary Force under Gort was sent to France but for the next six months the only serious fighting occurred at sea as the Allies attempted to blockade Germany and the enemy retaliated with mines and submarine warfare. The German battleship *Admiral Graf Spee* was scuttled at the battle of the River Plate in December 1939.

In April 1940, Germany invaded Denmark and Norway. The failure of the brief but gallant Allied campaign in Norway led to Chamberlain being replaced by Churchill as British prime minister. The German invasion of Belgium and the Netherlands, which began on 10 May, soon crushed those countries and led to the Battle of France. On 14 May, von Rundstedt's armour crossed the Meuse between Sedan and Namur and thrust towards the Channel, reaching Amiens

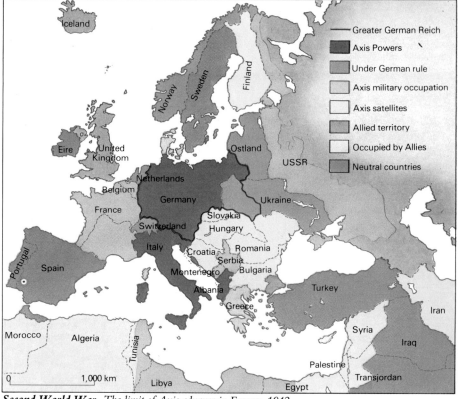

Second World War. The limit of Axis advance in Europe, 1942.

on 21 May. On 26 May the Allies gave the order to evacuate and some 338,000 Allied troops were rescued from Dunkirk by the Royal Navy and small civilian craft while the Royal Air Force gave air cover. On 14 June the Germans entered Paris and by 22 June the French government under Marshal Pétain accepted the German terms for an armistice. Fighting ceased on 25 June. In London, de Gaulle organised the Free French to continue resistance.

Britain now stood alone and in imminent danger of invasion. Between July and September 1940, the Battle of Britain was fought between the Royal Air Force and the Luftwaffe: the daylight air raids, the recognised preliminary to the Blitzkrieg, resulted in the loss of 915 aircraft by the RAF and some 1700 by the Luftwaffe. Fighter Command under Dowding won the day and by October the Luftwaffe had switched to night bombing. The failure to break British air power caused Operation Sealion, the German plan for the invasion of Britain, to be postponed and then abandoned. With the major ports of Western Europe under Axis control, sea warfare was intensified and Allied shipping was subjected to attacks by German submarines, aircraft and surface ships. The Battle of the Atlantic reached its peak in 1943, after which the Allied navies regained control through the use of escort carriers and radar-equipped warships and aircraft. Nevertheless, Allied and neutral shipping losses totalled some 21,900,000 tonnes from 1939 to 1945.

Italy and North Africa. In June 1940, Italy declared war on the Allies; in September, Italian troops led by Graziani advanced from Libya into Egypt. They were defeated by an Allied force led by Wavell which drove them out of Egypt and back into western Libya. Later, however, Wavell's force was weakened by the transfer of troops to Greece in the face of an Axis invasion. Both Jugoslavia and Greece fell to the Germans in April 1941. Meanwhile German troops under Rommel had reinforced the Italians in North Africa. Auchinleck, Wavell's successor, launched an attack against Rommel's forces, but by early 1942 the Allied forces in the Western Desert had been driven back to El Alamein, inside the Egyptian frontier. In August 1942, Montgomery was appointed commander of the Eighth Army and in October 1942 the Axis forces were defeated in the decisive battle of El Alamein. Rommel's forces were pushed back to the Tunis-Tripoli frontier. Throughout the campaign the RAF was the spearhead of the Eighth Army. On 8 November 1942 an Allied force under Eisenhower landed at Casablanca, Oran and Algiers and advanced through Tunisia to link up with the Eighth Army in April 1943. On 13 May 1943 the Axis forces surrendered. El Alamein was a decisive battle for it freed the Mediterranean sea routes and excluded the Axis powers from Africa, the Italians having been defeated by Wavell in Ethiopia and the British Somaliland in 1941.

The sequel to the Allied victories in North Africa was the landings in Sicily (July 1943) by the Eighth Army under Montgomery and the US Fifth Army. On 3 September the Italian armistice was signed. The Germans evacuated their troops to the mainland of Italy where they put up stiff resistance to the Allied advance northwards along the Italian peninsula. Rome fell on 4 June 1944, Bologna and Milan in April 1945 and the unconditional surrender of the German and Fascist forces on the Italian front became effective on 2 May 1945.

Eastern Europe and the USSR. The German drive into the Balkans (Yugoslavia and Greece) in the spring of 1941 was the prelude to the opening of the Eastern Front. On 22 June, Germany, supported by Finland, Hungary and Romania, invaded the Soviet Union. At first the campaign went well for the invaders and by November the German forces had cut off Leningrad, occupied the Crimea and the Ukraine and were within reach of Moscow itself. The winter of 1941/2 showed, however, that the Germans were no match for the Russians in winter-campaigning. Zhukov raised the siege of Moscow and the German troops were forced back. With the thaw, the Germans advanced again, approaching the Maikop oil fields and besieging Stalingrad. But by November 1942, von Manstein had been forced to withdraw from the Caucasus and the German Sixth Army besieging Stalingrad was destroyed and its commander, von Paulus, captured. In spite of temporary losses of territory after the early spring thaw of 1943, the Russians had by September defeated a further German offensive and regained Kharkov and Smolensk. The German armies were finally expelled from Soviet soil in August 1944. Romania signed an armistice with USSR and Finland followed suit in September. A final offensive took Soviet troops into Germany, Poland, Austria, Hungary and Czechoslovakia. On 2 May 1945 Berlin surrendered to the Russians.

Japan. With the entry of Japan in 1941, the war became a world conflagration. On 7 December, Japanese carrier-borne aircraft bombed the US naval base of Pearl Harbor and other US and British bases. Japan and Germany then declared war on the USA. In the next six months, Japanese forces occupied Hong Kong, Manila, Rabaul, the Solomon Islands, Singapore, the Dutch East Indies (Indonesia), part of New Guinea and Malaya, and thrust into Burma. India and Australia were greatly endangered until the Japanese expansion was stopped by the US air and naval victories of the Coral Sea (May 1942), Midway Island (June 1942) and Guadalcanal (August 1942). Finally, the Japanese fleet was crushingly defeated in the naval battle of Leyte Gulf in October 1944. Allied reconquest of Manila, the Philippines and Borneo followed in 1945. Meanwhile Burma was re-conquered by the Fourteenth Army— the 'forgotten' army, under Slim, between January and May 1945. RAF Transport Command played a vital role in ferrying supplies to the US army. Japan finally surrendered on 14 August 1945 after the Allies had dropped atomic bombs on Hiroshima and Nagasaki. The Allied victory was celebrated on VJ Day, 15 August 1945.

Allied Victory in the West. On the Western Front the final assault on land did not begin until June 1944. From 1940 to 1944 the Royal Air Force was the sole immediate weapon for use against Germany and the occupied countries. Fighter Command carried out offensive sweeps over Western Europe; Coastal Command and naval forces waged war against German submarines and shipping lanes as well as attacking submarine pens and installations from Norway to France. However, the primary role of the RAF was the strategic bombing of Germany and the occupied countries. In 1940–42, 90,000 tons of bombs were dropped. By 1944 this had risen to 525,000 tons. When the time came to invade France and finally defeat Germany, the RAF had a vital part to play. The invasion of mainland Europe, under the supreme command of Eisenhower, began at 2.00 am on 6 June 1944, 'D-Day', with mass paratroop landings behind the German lines; two US divisions, two British and one Canadian division were landed. By 11 June a beachhead had been established and further troops and equipment landed. By 2 July a million troops had disembarked. On 26 June Cherbourg surrendered. On 8 July the British under Montgomery launched a successful attack on Caen and on 18 July the Americans took St-Lô and later swept into Brittany against negligible opposition. On 15 August US and French troops landed on the Mediterranean coast of France and moved north up the Rhône valley and its environs. By 17 August the Canadians had taken Falaise and on 25 August Paris fell to the Allied armies. The Allies now pursued Montgomery's plan for a drive into the Ruhr from Belgium and Holland. In support of this plan, airborne troops were landed in the Rhine Delta in Holland and armoured units of the British Second Army established contact with all the airborne forces except those in the Arnhem area who suffered heavy casualties in the face of strong German counter-attacks. In December the Germans launched a strong offensive in the Ardennes region. This was initially successful but by the end of January 1945 the Allied armies had re-established their previous line. German resistance stiffened as the Allies reached the Reich frontier but the Rhine was crossed in March and shortly afterwards the Ruhr was encircled. On 4 May German forces in north-west Germany, Holland and Denmark surrendered to Montgomery and three days later a general surrender was signed. 8 May 1945 was celebrated as VE Day.

Worms, city in the Rhineland Palatinate, Federal Republic of Germany, on the Rhine, 25 km north of Ludwigshafen. It is one of the oldest cities of Germany; its Roman name was *Borbetomagus.* It was made a free city of the empire in the 11th century. More than a hundred Imperial Diets met in the city: at the Diet of 1122 the investiture question was settled by Emperor Henry V and Pope Calixtus II; at the Diet of 1521 Luther appeared before Emperor Charles V. The impressive Romanesque cathedral dates from the 11th century.

The city's industries include lorries, chemicals and an oil refinery, and it has a new Rhine harbour handling 1·2 million t annually. The well-known *Liebfraumilch* wine takes its name from a 14th- to 15th-century church in the city. Population (1970) 78,000.

Worms, see ANNELIDS; NEMATODA; PARASITES; PLATYHELMINTHES.

Wormwood, *Artemisia absinthium,* a tall perennial plant in the family Compositae, now a cosmopolitan weed, with silky leaves of feathery form and numerous small yellow flower heads. It is one of the chief ingredients from which absinthe is derived, and was formerly used as a tonic.

Worrell, Sir Frank (1924–67), West Indian cricketer. A right-handed batsman of especial grace, he played for Barbados and Jamaica, and in his 51 tests for West Indies scored 3860 runs. Highly acclaimed as a captain in the early 1960s, he moulded West Indian cricket into a world force. His 15,025 runs in first-class cricket was a record for a West Indian when he retired from first-class cricket in 1964.

Worsted, see SPINNING; WOOL.

Worth, Charles Frederick (1825–95), British dress designer. He went to Paris in 1841 where he made his name, first making 'ready-to-wear' clothing for the Maison Gagelin and, later, starting his own fashion house.

Worthing, town and seaside resort in West Sussex, England. Popularity came in the late 18th century and now the town includes other villages such as Broadwater (with a late Norman church), Durrington and West Tarring. Population (1981) 91,668.

Wotan, see ODIN.

Wotton, Sir Henry (1568–1639), English diplomat and poet. Under James I he was for 20 years in the diplomatic service. He was a lifelong friend of Donne, and wrote the lines addressed to Elizabeth of Bohemia, 'You meaner beauties of the night'. His years of service in Venice encouraged tastes in art and architecture in advance of his English contemporaries and these are set forth in his letters and *The Elements of Architecture*, 1624. Wotton's life, by Izaak Walton, was prefixed to the *Reliquiae Wottonianae*, 1651.

Wound, a rupture of the soft structures of the body. Wounds are usually classified as incised, punctured, contused and lacerated.

An incised wound is a clean cut, such as is made by a knife. The blood-vessels being cut clean, they bleed more freely than other kinds. The opening tends to gape on account of the retraction of the superficial structures. Punctured wounds are those produced by the thrust of a pointed instrument. They are dangerous according to their depth; a deep-seated organ may be injured or the instrument may have carried in septic germs. There is frequently little bleeding apparent, though there may be internal haemorrhage.

Contused wounds are caused by blunt instruments, or by falls. There is usually very little bleeding, though the parts may be extensively bruised. Owing to the injury to the small blood vessels, healing may be protracted. Lacerated wounds are produced by injuries from machinery, the teeth and claws of animals, etc. They are dangerous when extensive, as there is considerable danger of infection. A scar ultimately takes the place of the destroyed skin.

In treating wounds it is necessary first to arrest the bleeding and then close the wound. Where there is danger of septic infection, however, the wound should be cleaned and dressed with antiseptics. Antibiotics, both local and systemic, are now much used in the treatment of infected wounds. Skin grafts are employed for closure. Prophylaxis against tetanus is also important; tetanus antitoxin is also available.

Wren. St Lawrence Jewry, London, built between 1671 and 1677, is one of his 52 City churches.

Wouwerman, Philips (1619–68), Dutch painter. He studied under Hals, and was influenced by the Italian scenes of Bamboccio. He painted mainly Italianate landscapes and cavalry skirmishes in a bright, elegant style with a light touch. He was immensely prolific and highly prized in the 18th century.

Wrangel, Karl Gustav (1613–76), Swedish soldier. He distinguished himself at the battles of Wolfenbüttel (1641) and Leipzig (1642). He commanded the Swedish fleet against the Danes in 1644–45, and in 1646 succeeded Torstensson as commander-in-chief of the Swedish army in Germany, playing a prominent part in the later stages of the Thirty Years' War.

Wrangel, Pëtr Nikolaevich (1878–1928), Russian soldier. He served through the Russo-Japanese War and the First World War, after which he joined Kaledin. Kaledin committed suicide in 1918, and Wrangel joined Denikin's army. Denikin was defeated by the Bolsheviks in 1920 and resigned, leaving Wrangel in sole command of his disorganised army. Supported by the French, Wrangel continued successfully to withstand the Bolsheviks until after they ended the war with Poland. He was then compelled to evacuate his forces from the Crimea. He went to Belgium where he lived in exile.

See also UNION OF SOVIET SOCIALIST REPUBLICS, *History*.

Wrangel Island (Russian *Ostrov Vrangelya*), island in the Arctic Ocean belonging to the USSR; it lies between the East Siberian and Chukotsk Seas. The land is rugged with mountains rising to 1096 m. The Russian naval officer, Baron Wrangel, first postulated its existence in 1824; it was first explored in 1867 by the American, De Long, who named it after Wrangel. The Russians claimed the island in 1924. Area 7300 km².

Wrangler, term applied in the University of Cambridge, to those who have obtained first-class honours in the final examination for honours in pure and applied mathematics.

Wrasse, common name for a spiny-finned fish of the family Labridae in order Perciformes. The general shape is like that of the perch, but the back is straighter. There is a long dorsal fin, and the ventral fins are under the pectorals. Their coloration is generally brilliant and they often show elaborate courtship and nesting behaviour. Wrasse frequent rocky shores and coral reefs, usually in small shoals. They are also called rock fish. Wrasse are known to change their sex but it is unlikely that they can function as both sexes at the same time.

Wrath, Cape, most westerly point on the north coast of Scotland. It is one of a series of wild and rugged cliffs formed of gneiss, and is 90 m high.

Wreath, or torse, in heraldry a circlet formed from twisted skeins of silk of alternating tinctures, resting on top of the helmet and concealing the joint between helmet and crest.

Wrecks. The law on wrecks is contained in the Merchant Shipping Acts so far as British territorial waters are concerned. 'Wreck' means property cast ashore within the ebb and flow of the tide after shipwreck. It must be a ship or its cargo and includes all flotsam, jetsam and ligan, and derelicts, as well as wreckage cast ashore. The minister of Transport appoints local receivers to take charge of wreckage found or brought in (except that brought from extra-territorial waters by a foreign ship). It is the duty of all persons finding wreckage to notify the receiver. When wrecks occur in navigable waterways or harbours, the authorities responsible for the safety of such places have power to remove them, and claim expenses from the owners or underwriters. The term 'wreck', in Britain, applies only to tidal waters and to vessels and their contents; in the USA it applies also to inland lakes and large rivers.

The law relating to wrecks and salvage and to the duty of rendering assistance to vessels applies to aircraft on or over the sea or tidal waters in the same way as it applies to vessels.

Wrekin, The, isolated volcanic hill (407 m) rising from the north Shropshire plain, England, 4 km south-west of Wellington.

Wren, Sir Christopher (1632–1723), English architect and scientist. He had a brilliant career at Oxford as a scientist and mathematician and became a professor of astronomy in 1657; he did not turn to architecture until c.1662, when he designed the chapel of Pembroke College, Cambridge, followed by the Sheldonian Theatre, Oxford, 1662–69. His rebuilding of St Paul's Cathedral lasted from 1675 to 1710. He also rebuilt 52 of the City churches destroyed in the fire of London in 1666.

In 1669 Wren became surveyor-general of the King's Works, and in that capacity built, or altered, several royal palaces, including Hampton Court, Kensington, St James's, Westminster, Whitehall and Winchester; and also Windsor Castle, Chelsea Hospital (1682–85) and part of Greenwich Hospital. Among his numerous other buildings may be mentioned Emmanuel College Chapel (1665–76) and Trinity College Library (1676–84) at Cambridge; 'Tom Tower' at Oxford; the Royal Observatory, Greenwich; and the churches of St Clement Danes and St James, Piccadilly. His biography was written by his son under the title *Parentalia,* 1750.

Wren, a small bird of the family Troglodytidae, order Passeriformes. *Troglodytes troglodytes* is the common bird ranging throughout Europe, North Africa and Asia. It is about 10 cm long, has short, rounded wings, and usually carries its tail over the back. Its plumage is rich reddish brown; it builds a large domed nest, and additional nests are often built close at hand. Its song is remarkably loud. It feeds on insects.

Wrestling, one of the most basic sports, belonging to an ancient tradition, evidence of which dates back to the Sumerian civilisation, c.3000 BC. The sport was also practised in China and Babylon, but it was the ancient Greeks who did most to develop it. They founded wrestling schools called *palaestra,* where boys learned the theory and practice of the sport. Wrestling first appeared in the Olympic Games in 704 BC.

In modern times, the development of wrestling as an international sport did not begin until the 19th century. Two distinctive styles became prominent: Graeco-Roman and freestyle (formerly called 'catch-as-catch-can'). The latter form is the more spectacular, in which legal holds to all parts of the body are permitted. Graeco-Roman is a less open form of wrestling, and a much modified version of the style known to the Greeks as *triagmos.* Today, no holds below the waist are permitted. Graeco-Roman style wrestling featured in the first revived Olympic Games in 1896 in Athens and has been part of most Games since.

After the Second World War, wrestling began to expand greatly. On the professional side, the medium of television was largely responsible for 'all-in' wrestling, regarded more as entertainment than sport.

In both Graeco-Roman and free styles the object is to pin the opponent by the shoulders to the mat for one second. However, this aim is seldom achieved in world class wrestling where the most skill is exercised: the judges must assess which wrestler established the more control, awarding points for offensive moves. The international regulatory body is the Fédération Internationale des Luttes Amateurs (FILA).

A third wrestling style was recognised by the FILA in 1964, that of sambo, which originated from a combination of USSR wrestling styles. Regional variations of wrestling still exist in the UK, such as those of Cornwall, Lancashire or Cumberland. Sumo is the Japanese sport, attracting thousands of spectators to the championship events which are held six times a year. The competitors, who seldom weigh much under 130 kg, aim to force one another out of the ring, employing a good deal of aggressive ceremony.

Wrexham, market town in Clwyd, it is the largest centre in north-east Wales. Its industries include coal-mining, brewing, tanning and textiles, and it has a large industrial estate, but is also the centre of an agricultural district. Population (1981) 40,272.

Wright, name of two US brothers, inventors of the powered aeroplane. Wilbur (1867–1912) and Orville (1871–1948), were influenced by the work and death of Lilienthal. They made an exhaustive study of previous work in aviation, and in 1900 made the first of their three gliders. After perfecting their patented means of control (which consisted of warping the wing-tips in conjuction with a rear rudder, as well as using a front elevator for climb and dive) they designed and built their first powered aeroplane, including the engine, in 1903, and on 17 December, near Kitty Hawk, North Carolina, made the world's first powered, sustained and controlled flights, Orville making the first and third flights of four, Wilbur the others. Through a series of almost unbelievable circumstances their work for long remained unknown, despite flights of over 30 min in their *Flyer No. 3* in 1905. They did not fly

again until 1908, when Wilbur flew in public for the first time in Europe and Orville in the USA. Their known work on gliders had already been the largest factor in developing European aeroplanes, and when they emerged in 1908 they further revolutionised aviation. They thereafter constructed many excellent aircraft. Their first *Flyer* (now called the *Kitty Hawk*) is in the National Air Museum, Washington DC.

Wright, Frank Lloyd (1869–1959), US architect. He worked in various offices, including that of Louis Sullivan, and began practice in Chicago, 1893. His early fame rested on his so-called Prairie houses, notably the Willitts house, 1900, and the Robie house, 1909, Chicago. But his genius was revealed in many later works including Fallingwater, Mill Run, 1936, and his winter residence at Taliesen West, Arizona, 1938. He also designed the Unity Temple, Oak Park, 1906; the Imperial Hotel in Tokyo, 1915–22 (demolished); the Johnson Wax factory, 1936; the Usonian houses, 1939; and the Guggenheim Museum in New York, 1943–59. It was partly the originality of his work that made him the leader among American architects by the middle of the 20th century; but much of his wide influence internationally was due to his numerous books in which his ideas on architecture were expounded.

Wright, Judith (1915–), Australian poet. The poetry that first gained respect, responsive description of the past and present of the New England plateau in *The Moving Image,* 1946, remains among her best. Equally successful and even more influential are the lyrics of married love in *Woman to Man,* 1950. In *The Gateway,* 1953, and *The Two Fires,* 1955, poems of imaginative defeat, natural description and general meditation become conspicuous, and natural phenomena are the focus in *Birds,* 1960.

Wright, Richard (1908–60), US novelist. His grandparents had been Negro slaves. In 1938 he won a prize of $500 with his novelette *Uncle Tom's Children.* Later he was awarded a Guggenheim Fellowship. In 1940 his story

Frank Lloyd Wright. *Fallingwater, Pennsylvania, was built in 1936.*

Native Son received the Spingarn Medal, the highest award for work done in the Negro interest. *Twelve Million Black Voices*, 1941, is a history of the persecution of the American Negro, and *Black Boy*, 1945, tells of his own youthful hardships.

Wrist, or carpus, that portion of the arm between the hand and the lower arm. The joint is made by the articulation of the ulna and radius with the eight carpal bones. The mobility of the joint is combined with a great degree of strength, so that dislocations and sprains are not common. Fracture of the lower end of the radius is known as Colles's fracture.

Writ. In the literal sense of that which is written, writ is particularly applied to the Scriptures, or books of the Old Testament and New Testament, and in Scots law is sometimes used to denote a writing, deed or any legal instrument.

Writ, in English law, a writ is a precept under seal in the name of an executive officer, such as the lord chancellor or a judge, who has jurisdiction or authority in the particular matter, directed to a public officer such as a county sheriff or to a private person, commanding him to do something in relation to a suit or action. A writ of summons is the usual method of originating a civil action.

Writers to the Signet, see SIGNET.

Writing, is the most important method of recording and communicating ideas, by significant and convenient symbols, painted or drawn, traced or incised, on paper, stone, metal, or any other material.

Pictography, or picture-writing, is the first stage of true writing. In this, the painted or drawn or traced pictures, known as pictograms, speak for themselves. There are two forms:

(1) *Iconography*, which gives a static impression; the pictures are motionless, and they represent the things shown (the sketch of an animal would represent that animal, a circle might represent the sun, etc.).

(2) *Ideography*, synthetic or ideographic writing in which the pictures represent not only the things shown, but also the ideas associated with those things.

Analytic Writing. In this definite pictures, conventional and simplified, selected by agreement or custom from many experimental pictures, became fixed pictorial symbols, constantly used. Some eight or nine systems of writing belong to this category.

Phonetic Writing, in which each element corresponds to a specific sound in the language to be represented. Pure phonetic writing falls into two classes:

(1) *Syllabary or Syllabic Writing*, the less advanced stage of pure phonetic writing in which the single symbols represent syllables.

(2) *Alphabetic Writing* is the last, most highly developed, and at the same time simplest, system of writing; its development constitutes a story in itself.

See also ALPHABET; NUMERALS; PALAEOGRAPHY; SHORTHAND.

Wroclaw (German *Breslau*), city of Poland, on the River Oder, 306 km west of Warsaw. Its development dates from the 10th century, when it prospered from trade between the Baltic Sea and the Roman Empire, and between the Black Sea area and Western Europe. In 1138 it became the capital of Silesia. It was razed by the Mongols in the 13th century, but was rebuilt by German settlers. It became part of Bohemia in 1335 and joined the Hanseatic League. In 1526 it came under the domination of the Hapsburg family, until ceded to Prussia in 1741, when its name was changed to Breslau. The Polish community struggled to retain its national character, but its population was swelled by German colonists until, in 1910, it was an almost wholly German city of 500,000. Until 1945 it was capital of German Lower Silesia. Its industries are engineering and clothing, chemicals, foodstuffs and pottery manufacture. Population (1979) 608,000.

Wryneck, genus *Jynx* of small birds of the Picidae or woodpecker family, of which only two species are known. *J. torquilla* is the common wryneck of Europe. Its general colour is brown and grey with black markings; its length about 15 cm. It very rarely behaves like a true woodpecker, but usually stays in thick cover feeding on insects which it picks up from leaves or twigs. Its name is derived from its habit of twisting its neck as it picks insects. The other species is *J. ruficollis* of Africa.

Wryneck, in medicine, contracture of the sternomastoid muscle in the neck, usually on one side, causing an abnormal posture of the head. It may be present in infants from birth injury, and in longstanding cases the face and skull develop asymmetrically. Gentle manual stretching may be effective in straightening the neck, but in established cases division of the sternomastoid muscle is necessary. Wryneck of acute onset occurs in childhood as a result of trauma to the neck or local inflammation, such as tonsillitis, producing muscle spasm. In adults the muscle spasm is usually due to irritation of nerves by an abnormal cervical disc. Treatment consists of appropriate treatment of any underlying pathology and the wearing of a cervical collar.

Wuhan, a triple city on the Changjiang, the largest city of central China, and capital of Hubei province. It comprises the cities of Wuchang, Hankou and Hanyang. The triple city is an important centre of communications, since here the east-west river system of the Changjiang crosses the most important railway in China, the north-south line between Peking and Canton. Wuchang is the administrative and cultural centre of the municipality. The Hubei provincial government is located in this part of the city. It is the oldest of the three cities, and the most traditional part of the conurbation. Its industries include iron and steel, textile and paper mills and railway-repair yards. Wuchang was the starting-point of the revolution of October 1911, which eventually resulted in the overthrow of the Manchu dynasty and the establishment of the Republic of China. Hankou is the largest of the three cities; about two-thirds of the total population live there. It is a commercial and manufacturing centre, having been one of the first of China's inland cities to be opened to foreign trade in 1858. Hanyang is the major centre for heavy industry. Population (1977) 3,500,000.

Wulfstan (d.1023), English writer who was bishop of London, 996–1002, of Worcester, 1002–16, and archbishop of York, 1002–23.

His literary reputation rests upon a series of homilies, the best known of which is his *Sermo Lupi ad Anglos*. Wulfstan's intention was to castigate and move to repentance. He confronts his audience with all the vehemence of an Old Testament prophet, representing the depredations of the Danes as just retribution for the sins of the English.

Wuppertal, city in North Rhine-Westphalia, Federal Republic of Germany, in the valley of the Wupper, 27 km east of Düsseldorf. The textile industry, which dates from the Middle Ages, now includes the processing of artificial fibres. The city is famous for its monorail (*Schwebebahn*) built in 1902, suspended above the river, and still in operation. Population (1979) 394,600.

Württemberg, former republic (until 1918 a kingdom) in south-west Germany, bounded on the east by Bavaria and on the west by Baden. Hohenzollern formed an enclave in the south-west of its territory. The Counts of Württemberg obtained possessions in Swabia on the death of Conradin. These possessions were gradually increased, and in 1495 Württemberg became a duchy. In 1806 Napoleon created a kingdom of Württemberg, which lasted until 1918 when William II of Württemberg abdicated and a republic was proclaimed. After the Second World War, part of it was combined with Baden to form the *Land* of Württemberg-Baden in the American zone of occupation; the remainder was combined with Hohenzollern to form the *Land* of Württemberg-Hohenzollern in the French zone. In 1952 these two *Länder* became part of the new *Land* of Baden-Württemberg.

Würzburg, city in Bavaria, Federal Republic of Germany, on the Main, 219 km north-west of Munich. The *Marienberg* fortress, built on the left bank of the river, was formerly the castle of the prince-bishops; it has an 8th-century chapel. Of the city's many fine churches, the most notable is the Romanesque cathedral (1034). Würzburg is the centre of a wine-producing district. It also has machinery, chemical, metal and food manufacturing industries. Its harbour on the Main has traffic amounting to over 1 million t annually. Population (1979) 127,370.

Wyatt, James (1746–1813), British architect. He studied in Italy c.1762–68. His first known building was the Pantheon in Oxford Street, London (demolished in 1937). He designed many other important buildings in the classical style, including Heaton Hall, Lancashire (1772); Heveningham Hall, Suffolk (1788–1799); Castle Coole, Ireland; and two colossal Gothic mansions—Ashridge Park, Hertfordshire, and Fonthill Abbey, Wiltshire (1796–1807; demolished). He acquired the nickname of 'The Destroyer' for his drastic cathedral restorations. His son Benjamin Wyatt (1775–1850) was also a leading architect.

Wyatt, Sir Thomas (1503–42), English courtier and poet. He was one of the most accomplished men of his day and was held in high favour at court. For a time he appears to have shared the disgrace of Anne Boleyn, being imprisoned in the Tower, then banished to Allington Castle. Later, however, he was frequently employed by the king in positions of trust. He sat in Parliament as knight of the shire for Kent, and was named high steward of the king's manor at Maidstone in 1542. Wyatt's poems were published in 1557, and some are remarkable for their elegance and grace. He is chiefly remembered as the pioneer of the English sonnet, and historically is important for the introduction of Petrarchan forms and the concerns of the love sonnet, into English.

Wyatt, Sir Thomas (d.1554), English soldier and rebel, son of Sir Thomas Wyatt the poet. In 1554 he was involved in a conspiracy against the marriage of Queen Mary to Philip of Spain. He raised the Kentish men and marched on London, but was captured and beheaded.

Wycherley, William (c.1640–1716), English dramatist. His first play, *Love in a Wood*, produced in 1681, was followed by *The Gentleman Dancing-Master*, 1673; *The Country Wife*, 1675; and *The Plain Dealer*, 1677, which was inspired by Molière's *Misanthrope*. Wycherley's *Miscellaneous Poems* are forgotten, but his plays show remarkable skill in construction, and a vigorous mastery of characterisation and language. His social criticism was more perceptive than that of his colleagues, and his view of human nature more profound and pessimistic.

Wycliffe, John, (c.1329–84), English scholar and reformer. In 1374 he became rector of Lutterworth, and soon retired from Oxford, where he was Master of Balliol, living in Lutterworth until his death.

In 1374 he was sent to Bruges in the delegation which discussed the question of papal provisions with papal representatives. After his return he wrote his treatise *De Dominio*. Wycliffe's Realist speculations led him to a belief in predestination, and he went on to define lordship. He decided that the Church had no right to interfere in temporal affairs nor to temporal possessions. Though he never suggested a spoliation of the Church, such a move was the logical conclusion of his theory, and aroused clerical hostility. The general theory may have had a quite unintended influence in the Peasants' Revolt (1381), since the landless would see no reason to distinguish finely between ecclesiastical and civil lordship.

In 1377 Wycliffe was summoned to answer charges of heresy before the bishop of London, but his Lancastrian patrons ensured that the meeting ended inconclusively. With the papal schism of 1378, he took a more revolutionary attitude, asserting that papal decrees were binding only when in conformity with the word of God. He attacked the abuse of sanctuary and pardons and began to turn to the Scriptures as the criterion of Christian doctrine, a practice followed by later reformers. He questioned the sacerdotal system, and, by 1380, set aside the doctrine of transubstantiation in the Mass in favour of something approximating to the later

Lutheran doctrine of consubstantiation. This last conclusion branded Wycliffe as a heretic. It sprang directly from his scholastic Realism. His heretical views lost him the active support of the Lancastrians, whose prestige, however, was sufficient to enable him to end his days in peace. These views were officially condemned at Oxford, and never seem to have had any considerable following in England. Their violence secured the failure of the more orthodox aspects of his teaching. After his death Lollardry was eradicated from Oxford by Arundel and Courtenay, and with it the last brilliance of the medieval university.

In England his movement died soon after his death, despite the vernacular translation of the Bible, apparently made by his followers (known as Lollards) rather than Wycliffe himself. Lollardry survived longest among the poor in the Midlands. The fall of Oldcastle and a series of burnings under the statute of 1410 apparently suppressed the remnants. In Europe, Wycliffe influenced Huss, and through him probably Luther.

See also LOLLARDS, THE.

Wycombe, High, market town in Buckinghamshire, England, at the foot of the Chiltern Hills. Furniture making is a major industry; recent developments have brought in light engineering industries; postage stamps are printed and paper is manufactured. Population (1981) 60,516.

Wye, river of Welsh border country, which rises on Plynlimmon and after a course of 200 km enters the Severn 4 km from Chepstow. It has valuable salmon fisheries, and is noted for its scenery.

Wykeham, William of (1324–1404), English bishop, born at Wickham, Hants. He took deacon's orders at an early age, but was not ordained until 1362. In 1364 he became keeper of the privy seal; in 1366 he was appointed bishop of Winchester, and in 1367 he became lord high chancellor of England, holding office till 1371. Winchester College and New College, Oxford, were founded by him. He also rebuilt part of Winchester Cathedral. Wykeham was a sound administrator and a keen builder. He was one of the *episcopi curiales* and was not distinguished as a spiritual leader.

Wynants, Jan (c.1630–84), Dutch painter. He worked exclusively on landscape subjects, the figures and animals in his pictures often being painted by other artists, notably Lingelbach and Wouwerman.

Wyndham, Sir Charles (1837–1919), British actor. He made his stage début in 1862 but left for the USA, where he enlisted in the Federal Army, also making appearances on the stage. In 1865 he returned to England and after some varied experience took a company across America. In 1884 he took over the Criterion Theatre in London, and also built and ran Wyndham's Theatre. He was said

to have acted best in such plays as *Garrick, Rosemary* and *Mrs Dane's Defence*.

See also MOORE, MARY.

Wyndham, John, pseudonym of John Benyon Harris (1903–69), English writer. From 1930 he supported himself by his writing, publishing mainly in American magazines. After serving in the civil service and army during the Second World War, he wrote the first of the science fiction novels for which he became famous. His novels typically explore the reactions of ordinary people to extreme but apparently possible situations, as in *The Day of the Triffids*, 1951, when a strange plant mutation invades the Earth. His other novels include *The Kraken Wakes*, 1953; *The Midwich Cuckoos*, 1957; and *Trouble With Lichen*, 1960.

Wyoming (Equality State), mountain state of the USA, bounded on the north by Montana, east by South Dakota and Nebraska, south by Colorado, south-west by Utah, and west by Idaho. Wyoming is part of a plateau at about 1850 m above sea-level traversed by mountain ranges, including the whole breadth of the Rocky Mountain system. Gannett Peak, highest point of Wind River range, is 4202 m. Yellowstone National Park is situated in this state, and is noted for its scenery and geysers. Yellowstone, Bighorn and Powder rivers flow eastwards; the Snake river rises in the north. Almost one half of the state is owned by the federal government; its holdings include grazing districts which cover almost the whole of the south-west, and national forests which occupy much of the north-west, besides Yellowstone National Park and the Wind River Indian Reservation. Agriculture is largely confined to irrigated lands along the rivers. The state has only 700,000 ha in crops, mainly in animal feeds and sugar beet. Most land is in ranches. The carrying capacity of the natural livestock range is low, and there is a constant danger of overgrazing, which leads to the spread of sagebrush and other inedible plants. Mining is important; petroleum and coal are mined. Population (1980) 468,909. Wyoming has scattered small communities between which communication is costly and often difficult. Cheyenne is the capital. Total area 253,596 km².

Wyszyński, Stefan (1901–81), Polish cardinal. He was ordained in 1924, consecrated bishop of Lublin in 1946, and in 1948 appointed archbishop of Gniezno and Warsaw and Primate of Poland. On the eve of his elevation to the Sacred College in 1953, he was imprisoned by the Communist government of Poland, and was not released until 1956. In 1957 he visited Rome, where the pope conferred upon him the Red Hat. His championship of Church interests, and latterly the rise of free trade unions, several times brought him into conflict with the Polish government.

X

X, twenty-fourth letter of the English alphabet; it may be considered redundant as it can well be denoted by the consonants *ks* or *cs*.

The letter did not exist in the North Semitic alphabet, but was adapted in the classical Greek alphabet from a Semitic sibilant letter

to represent the sound *ks*, and given the name *xei*. After the Romans adopted the Etruscan alphabet (which had no *x*) they added X to

represent the sound *ks*, and it passed with the other Latin letters into the English alphabet, where it retains the same sound.
See also ALPHABET.

X, roman numeral for 10.
See also NUMERALS.

Xanthus, ancient city of Lycia, which stood on the west bank of the river Xanthus. It twice sustained sieges which terminated in the self-destruction of the inhabitants with their property, first against the Persians under Harpagus (c.546 BC), and later against the Romans under Brutus (43 BC). After the latter it was never restored.

Xavier, Francis, Saint (1506–52), Spanish Jesuit missionary, patron of the foreign missions and the Apostle of the Indies'. At the University of Paris he met Ignatius of Loyola with whom he was associated in the formation of the Society of Jesus (1534). He was ordained in 1537, and in 1540 he sailed for the East Indies as a missionary. Having made converts in Goa, Malacca, Travancore, the Banda Islands, the Moluccas and Ceylon, he founded a mission in Japan (1549–51) where, 40 years after his death, it has been estimated that there were 300,000 Christians. He was forbidden to enter China, and he died at Sanchian, a small island near Canton, where he was awaiting permission to preach. Xavier was one of the greatest of all missionaries. He was canonised in 1622.

Xenakis, Iannis (1922–), Greek composer and architect. He went to Paris in 1947 to study with Messiaen and collaborate with Le Corbusier. Recognised as a leading avant-garde figure in the 1950s, Xenakis has striven to explore the affinities between music and mathematics and he is the originator of so-called 'stochastic' music, based on Probability Theory; he has utilised computers and electronic tape in his compositions.

Xenon (Greek, a stranger), chemical element, symbol Xe, atomic number 54, atomic weight 131·3, heaviest of the group of inert gases, obtained by the fractional distillation of liquid air. It is present in the atmosphere to the extent of 1 part in 20,000,000. The spectrum of xenon shows prominent red and blue lines in the intermittent discharge. Xenon is not completely inert, but forms several fluorides and an oxide, in addition to being involved in several clathrate compounds. It is used in flash-lamps and lasers.

Xenophanes (fl.540–500 BC), Greek philosopher and poet. He settled at Elea in southern Italy, where he wrote several elegiac poems and one poem in hexameters, *On Nature*, of which fragments remain. Xenophanes condemned the anthropomorphism and polytheism of Homer and Hesiod. He taught that God is the One; that His existence is characterised by unity and immutability; and that the universe is permeated by this divine unity.

Xenophon (c.430–c.356 BC), Greek historian and Athenian general. He was a friend and disciple of Socrates. In 401 he entered the service of the Persian prince Cyrus the Younger, who was preparing to dispute the throne with Artaxerxes Mnemon. The Greek officers were treacherously killed after the battle of Cunaxa, and Xenophon, with great courage and skill, led the retreat from the Tigris to Trapezus. A history of the expe-dition is given in his *Anabasis*. He enlisted his soldiers in the service of Lacedaemon in 399, and soon afterwards was banished from Athens. In 396 he joined the Spartan army, fought under King Agesilaus at Coroneia (394) and was rewarded with an estate at Scillus. The decree of banishment against him was repealed (369), and he probably returned to Athens about 366 BC.
His other works include *Hellenica*, a history of Greece from 411 to 362 BC; *Memorabilia*, *Oeconomicus* and *Symposium*, which are ex-positions of the teachings of Socrates and attempts to vindicate him.

Xerophyte, a plant which is adapted to living where there is little water, or where, because of wind or high temperatures, water loss could be rapid. Succulents including cacti are typical examples. They have become adapted by increasing the water-storage area and reducing the surface area. Other adap-tations include reduction of size; reduction of the leaf-surface; a thick cuticle; or sunken stomata (pores). The cell walls may also be strengthened to prevent cell collapse under severe drought.

Xerxes (c.519–465 BC), King of Persia from 486 BC. After ascending the throne he sup-pressed revolts in Egypt and Babylon. He then set out against Greece at the head of a vast army. He first met resistance at Ther-mopylae, where he defeated Leonidas. He then marched through Phocis and Boeotia to Athens. He destroyed Athens and decided to engage the Greeks in a naval battle but was defeated at Salamis (480). He left Mardonius with a large army to complete the sub-jugation of Greece and, with the rest of his force, returned home. In 497 Mardonius was defeated at Plataea and the Persian navy at Mycale in Ionia. After this the Greeks success-fully 'liberated' the Greek city-states of the Asia Minor coast, and by 466 Xerxes had lost control of this area; he was assassinated.
See also PERSIAN WARS.

Xhosa, Nguni people living in the Transkei and Ciskei in South Africa. The Xhosa are farmers and cattle-herders; cattle have great social and religious importance to them.

Xiamen (Amoy), seaport on the island of the same name in Fujian province, south-east China, situated to the west of Taiwan. Xiamen exports porcelain and paper, and imports raw cotton and cotton manufactured goods. Communications inland were poor until the Yingtan (in Jiangxi) to Xiamen rail-way was built in 1956. Immediately offshore is the island of Quemoy which continues to be occupied by the Chinese Nationalists. Population (1970) 400,000.

Xi'an (Sian), capital of Shaanxi province on the Longhai railway in northern China, on the right bank of the Weihe, 125 km above its confluence with the Huanghe. It was the imperial capital during the Zhou, Qin, Han and Tang dynasties, and is considered to be the cradle of Chinese civilisation. Under the Tang dynasty it was known as Chang'an. Today industries include textile mills, a sewing-machine factory and a watch factory. Over 300,000 people have been transferred from Shanghai to Xi'an. Population (1970) 1,900,000.

Xining (Hsining), capital of Qinghai province in western China. An important communications centre established in the 16th century, it has experienced some growth through the development of the nearby Datong coal-field. There is a small iron and steel plant and some engineering and chemical industries. Population (1972) 300,000.

Xinjiang Uygur Zizhigu, see SINKIANG UIGHUR AUTONOMOUS REGION.

Ximénes de Cisneros, Francisco, also Jiménez (1436–1517), Spanish cardinal and statesman. He was ordained and led a life of extreme austerity, living for some time in a remote monastery until he became confessor to Queen Isabella in 1492. The queen ap-pointed him archbishop of Toledo in 1495, and sometime after her death in 1504 he was appointed regent (1506) until the return of Ferdinand from Naples in 1507. He founded the University of Alcalá de Henares, organ-ised the preparation of a new Polyglot Bible, and did his utmost to reform monastic life. In 1507 he became a cardinal, and in 1509 led in person an expedition against Oran in Africa. On the death of Ferdinand he again acted as regent (1516–17).

Xizang Zizhiqu, see TIBET AUTONOMOUS REGION.

X-rays were discovered by Röntgen in 1895 during experiments on electric discharges through highly evacuated tubes. He em-ployed a fluorescent screen to detect ultra-violet light and discovered that his screen continued to fluoresce even when the dis-charge tube was covered with opaque paper; he found that heavy objects interposed be-tween the tube and the screen stopped the fluorescence. It was clear that the radiation could penetrate opaque paper but was ab-sorbed by heavy objects. X-rays were identified as being electromagnetic waves by their insensitivity to deflection by electric or magnetic fields, and by von Laue's and W. L. Bragg's demonstration that they can be diffracted by the regular arrangement of atoms in a crystal. This showed X-rays to have wavelengths of 10^{-8}–10^{-11} m, com-parable with atomic sizes (10^{-10} m) and much shorter than the wavelength of light, 10^{-7} m.

Xuan Tong (Hsüan T'ung or Pu Yi) (1905–1967), last Emperor of China. The revolution that began in October 1911 ended in February 1912 with the establishment of a republic. Xuan Tong retained his title, received a hand-some allowance, and was allowed to remain in the Summer Palace of Peking. He was restored to the throne for a week in July 1917. In 1924, Xuan Tong's title and remaining privileges were abolished and he went to re-side under Japanese protection at Tianjin. He had cut off his queue, and called himself Henry Pu Yi. In 1934 he was proclaimed emperor of Manchukuo (Japanese-occupied Manchuria) by the Japanese. At the end of the Second World War he was captured by Russian troops and and sent to the USSR. After the establishment of the Chinese People's Re-public he returned to China to live in Shen-yang as a private citizen.
See also CHINA, *History*.

Xylem, or wood, the part of a perennial stem that includes the vessels that convey water through the plant. In the main stem of a tree or shrub, the xylem forms part of the cylinder of conducting tissues; in other organs it forms part of each vein. In leaves and herbaceous stems, it consists of tracheids and ground parenchyma cells with cellulose walls.

Xylol, commercial name given to the mixture of xylenes obtained traditionally from coal tar. There are three isomeric xylenes, *ortho-*, *meta-*, and *para-* dimethyl-benzene; they have similar physical properties but differ in chemical properties. Nowadays the xylenes are obtained with other aromatic compounds such as benzene and toluene by the catalytic reforming of petroleum fractions. They are used extensively as solvents and in the manufacture of other chemicals.

Xylophone, percussion instrument with a series of wooden bars tuned in a chromatic scale over 3½ or 4 octaves. It is played with hammers. Instruments of similar shape with metal bars include the glockenspiel and the vibraphone. An instrument with larger wooden bars is the marimba.

X Y Z Correspondence. President Adams of the USA used this term in the Congress reports on the letters of Marshall, Pinckney and Gerry, who were ambassadors to Talleyrand in France during a period of strained relations between the USA and France, 1797–98, and who reported that three French agents, to whom they referred as X, Y and Z, had offered them bribes.

Y

Y, twenty-fifth letter of the English alphabet, with the phonetic value of a consonantal *i*, as in *yes, young, yoke*; also used to denote any of several vowel sounds, e.g. *try, myth, martyr*. There was no *Y* in the North Semitic alphabet. The nearest letter in classical Greek was *upsilon*, which was pronounced like the French *u* or the German *ü*. After the Roman conquest of Greece (2nd century BC), the symbol *Y* was adopted in Latin for the Greek sound *u-y* in order to transliterate Greek words; Latin used a consonantal *i*, e.g. *iugum*, and the words in which the *y* occurs are not really part of the Latin language but are borrowed from the Greek, for example, *zephyrus*.

See also ALPHABET.

Yacht, generally a vessel used for pleasure-cruising or racing. The first British yachts were presented to Charles II by the Dutch at his Restoration. In 1661 Charles raced with the Duke of York from Greenwich to Gravesend and back, the first recorded yacht race in English waters. In 1720 the first yacht club was founded in Cork. Gradually there have evolved types of craft, moderate in size and capable of travelling all over the world. Yachts fall into two classes, sailing yachts and power-driven yachts. Sailing vessels are described by their rigging. Today almost all sailing yachts have tall masts and tall, narrow, triangular (Bermudian) mainsails.

Yachting, see SAILING.

Yak, *Bos grunniens*, a large Tibetan ox that exists both in the wild and the domesticated state, and can live at very high altitudes. Two of its chief characteristics are the fringe of long, pendulous hair along each flank and the huge whisk of hair at the end of the tail. In summer the coat is deep brown; the horns are black, large and strong. Domesticated varieties may be almost pure white as well as brown or black, and are used as beasts of burden, and for milk and meat.

Yakuts (Sakha), about 295,000 Turkic-speaking people of the Lena basin and eastern Siberia. They are sedentary stock-breeders, hunters and fishermen, subject to Russia since the 17th century.

Yakutsk, capital, economic and cultural centre of the Yakutsk ASSR, situated on the left bank of the middle Lena in East Siberia. Founded in 1632 by Russians, it became a centre for the conquest of much of north-east Asia and, in the 19th century, a supply centre for the gold-mining industry. It has saw-milling, leather and shoe, and food industries. Population (1980) 140,000.

Yakutsk Autonomous Soviet Socialist Republic, or Yakutia, lies in the RSFSR, USSR, in East Siberia; mainly mountainous with lowland in the north and centre, crossed by the Lena, Yana, Indigirka and Kolyma rivers, and largely covered by coniferous forests. The region has an extremely cold climate. There are gold-, coal- and diamond-mining industries, and livestock breeding, grain growing and fur trapping. The main towns are Yakutsk and Aldan. It became an area of banishment in the 19th century and of labour camps in the 1930s to mid-1950s. Area 3,103,200 km². Population (1980) 859,000.

Yale, Elihu (1648–1721), American patron of Yale University. He gave £800 and books to the collegiate school at New Haven, and the whole university was called after him.

Yalta, town on the Black Sea coast of the Crimea (part of the Ukrainian SSR), USSR, 50 km east of Sevastopol. Since the 1880s it has been the main centre of the Crimean health resorts. There are also tobacco and wine industries. Population (1970) 62,000.

Yalta Conference, held in February 1945 between Churchill, Roosevelt and Stalin to make plans for the final defeat and occupation of Germany. The Western Allies secured Stalin's promise to enter the war against Japan, but the USSR did not declare war until 8 August, six days before Japan's surrender.

Yam, *Dioscorea*, a genus of herbaceous plants in family Dioscoreaceae, which has edible tuberous roots. It grows in tropical countries where it takes the dietary place of the potato. Some species produce large single tubers up to 50 kg in weight, while others have many smaller tubers.

Yamagata, Aritomo (1838–1922), Japanese soldier and statesman. He played a significant military rôle in the Meiji Restoration and in the 1870s did more than anyone to shape the new conscript army. In later years he served as home minister and prime minister. After the death of Ito Hirobumi (1909) Yamagata became the most important *genro* (elder statesman) and was consulted by the emperor on all major issues.

Yangtse Kiang, see CHANGJIANG.

Yaoundé, town and capital of the United Republic of Cameroon. It is linked by rail with Douala, the main port in the south, and Ngaoundère in the north. Population (1976) 313,700.

Yap, see CAROLINE ISLANDS.

Yard (length), see METROLOGY.

Yarmouth, or Great Yarmouth, large sea-side resort, and port of Norfolk, England, 32 km east of Norwich. Yarmouth has a good harbour at the mouth of the Yare, with shipbuilding yards. In the past, the fisheries were prominent, but today the port serves as a base for North Sea gas platform-supply vessels and as a terminal for a roll-on/roll-off ferry to the Netherlands. Population (1981) 48,273.

Yarn, an assembly of textile fibres in a form suitable for the production of a fabric, or for other uses such as embroidery and sewing threads. Yarns may be classified as either staple or continuous filament. Staple yarns are produced from short lengths of fibres by twisting the fibres so that they adhere to each other usually by friction. Yarns may be produced as virtually continuous filament, either the natural fibres such as silk, spider's web fibre, or the synthetic or man-made fibres. The linear density or thickness of a yarn is now expressed in terms of tex, the weight in grams of 1 kilometre of yarn. The traditional methods of expressing linear density in terms of denier or hanks per pound, etc., are rapidly disappearing from the textile trade.

See also SPINNING.

Yaroslavl, capital city, economic and cultural centre of Yaroslavl *oblast*, USSR; the oldest town on the Volga, situated north-east of Moscow. It is an important industrial and transport centre with large engineering (automobiles), chemical (synthetic rubber and a nearby oil refinery), textiles (since 1722), and flour milling industries. It is also a river port. Known since 1071, Yaroslavl became the capital of its principality in 1216, Muscovite in 1463, and a provincial capital in 1777. The city was Moscow's Volga port until the construction of the Moscow Canal (1937). Population (1980) 590,000.

Yarrow, see MILFOIL.

Yawata, see KITAKYŪSHŪ.

Yawning, like sighing, is a deep inspiration, but yawning is accompanied by a stretching movement of the jaws and sometimes also of the limbs. It is not invariably a sign of tiredness or boredom; sometimes it is merely the physiological reaction to high carbon dioxide content of the blood following a long period with the body immobilised or from being in a vitiated atmosphere for some time. It may also be induced by the sight of another person in the act of yawning or by continually watching a slow, rhythmical movement. Yawning is commonly observed in other mammals, e.g. dogs and cats.

Yaws, or framboesia, an infectious disease due to the spirochaete *Treponema pertenue,* an organism morphologically indistinguishable from the causative organism of syphilis *T. pallidum.* In yaws destruction of skin and cartilage occurs, followed by bone changes. It is a chronic disease starting with a tumour-like skin lesion at the site of the microbe's inoculation into the skin. This yaw may regress, but secondary manifestations appear, including rashes and malaise, with more tumour-like lesions on the hands and feet. Often years later, destructive lesions occur. All phases of the disease are treatable by penicillin and occasionally other antibiotics. The occurrence is mainly tropical and subtropical, particularly among the poor. Transmission of yaws is by direct contact from disease lesions to healthy abraded skin, by contaminated clothing, and by flies feeding on the sores. The disease is non-venereal. It is generally contracted in early childhood, with development of considerable immunity to subsequent infection; there is also some cross-immunity to syphilis.

Yazd, or Yezd, town in Isfahan province, Iran. It produces silk and carpets, and functions as a route focus in the deserts of central Iran. There are several modern factories here. Population (1974) 118,000.

Year, basically the period in which the Earth goes round the Sun; more precisely the interval between successive passages of the Earth as seen from the Sun past certain chosen directions which are not necessarily fixed in space.

Yeast, a soft, light-brown, cheese-like material that consists of a mass of minute single-celled organisms belonging to the sub-division Ascomycotina of the Fungi. The usual species used in industry is *Saccharomyces cerevisiae.* Different strains of this are used in distilling and in baking. Yeasts are sometimes used medicinally and in the preparation of food extracts. Commercial yeast is prepared from molasses, to which are added yeast cultures, inorganic salts and sterile air. When given the correct conditions for multiplication—sugar, warmth and moisture—growth proceeds and a process of fermentation takes place. When yeast is added to a dough, aeration takes place owing to evolution of carbon dioxide. In warm conditions the carbon dioxide expands, increases the volume of the dough, and gives it lightness and porosity.

Yeats, Jack Butler (1871–1957), Irish painter, son of John Butler Yeats, a painter, and brother of W. B. Yeats (see below). His vigorous portrayals of Irish life and landscape make considerable use of the palette knife.

Yeats, William Butler (1865–1939), Irish poet and critic. He was inspired by the literary and mystic-religious heritage of his country, and later also influenced by European and Eastern thought. Yeats decided that he should be an Irish poet, not in the narrow nationalist sense, but by finding a 'unity of being' in himself, he felt he could create a kind of cultural and intellectual national unity. Such a vision lay behind the founding of the Irish Literary Theatre, later the Abbey Theatre, in 1899.

Yeats's early verse, *The Wanderings of Oisin,* 1889, for example, showed a mixture of

W. B. Yeats, a portrait by Augustus John.

Pre-Raphaelite romanticism, nationalist idealism, Irish mythology and mysticism. In 1889 he met Maud Gonne, an ardent supporter of Irish nationalism, and his love for her led him to join the cause, but although he was prominent in the Celtic revival, he was not an active nationalist. With the help of Lady Gregory, Yeats took on the management of the Abbey Theatre. His involvement with the theatre caused his poetry to become tighter and firmer, until, in the poetry of his middle and old age, his style combined rich and eloquent complexity with a firm sense of structure. Among the collections of Yeats's mature years are *The Wild Swans at Coole,* 1919; *The Tower,* 1928; and *The Winding Stair and Other Poems,* 1933. His plays were later influenced by the Japanese Noh play and, like his poetry, became more spare and resonant.

While his lyrics place him among the greatest of Ireland's poets, critics agree that in splendour of diction and imagery, and clarity of vision, Yeats was one of the outstanding literary figures of his age, and, of those writing in English, probably its greatest poet. Yeats won the Nobel Peace Prize for Literature in 1923.

Yellow, regarded, with red and blue, as a 'primary' colour. Artists use yellow ochre, cadmium and chrome yellow, lemon yellow (chrome, aureolin), and Naples yellow as yellow pigments.

'Yellow Book', British periodical, an illustrated quarterly magazine published by Matthews and Lane in London from 1894 until 1897. It was distinguished for its literary and artistic contributions by Aubrey Beardsley (who was for a time its art editor) and Max Beerbohm. Another leading contributor was Henry James.

Yellow Fever, yellow jack or amaryl, an acute infectious virus disease occurring in tropical and subtropical regions. The symptoms are fever, vomiting and rigor occurring after an incubation period usually of from one to four days. In severe cases, jaundice and haemorrhage are prominent symptoms. Blood appears in the faeces, the urine and in the vomitus, as well as from the gums. The urine also contains excessive albumen. The usual treatment for fevers is employed. An effective prophylactic vaccine is now in general use. A single dose produces lasting immunity. The American Commission of 1900 traced the disease to a virus conveyed by the mosquito *Aedes aegypti.* Other species of mosquito also transmit yellow fever.

Another type of yellow fever has been found to be enzootic in certain species of monkeys in Africa and South America. The disease is maintained in equatorial forests by monkeys and forest-dwelling mosquitoes. This monkey virus is transmitted to human beings living in or near forests, and there is little doubt that it is the reservoir of infection and is capable of causing epidemics when introduced by some traveller into a community where *A. aegypti* is prevalent. Air transport has increased the risk of spread of yellow fever to countries in which it has not previously occurred.

See also EPIDEMIOLOGY; TROPICAL MEDICINE.

Yellow-green Algae, see ALGAE.

Yellow Hammer, or yellow bunting, *Emberiza citrinella,* of the family Emberizidae, order Passeriformes. It is a common breeding bird of Eurasia. The males are distinguished by their bright yellow and chestnut plumage. The female has less yellow and is more of an olive brown. It is well known for its song. It occurs on farmlands, commons, heaths and roadsides.

See also BUNTING.

Yellow River, see HUANGHE.

Yellow Sea (Chinese *Huang Hai*), large gulf of the Pacific Ocean to the north of the East China Sea with China on the west and north and the Korean Peninsula to the east. Its length is about 1000 km, its greatest width 700 km, and its area 404,000 km². It is divided into three gulfs: Korea Bay, Liaodongwah and Bohai, and to the east is studded with islands. Its waters are shallow, average depth only 44 m, and are discoloured by the yellow mud carried down by the Huanghe and Changjiang rivers.

Yellow-tail, see AMBER-FISH.

Yellow-wort, see BLACKSTONIA.

Yellowknife, town and administrative capital of the North-West Territories, Canada, situated in Yellowknife Bay on the north shore of Great Slave Lake. It is the centre of a gold-mining region. The town was founded in 1935 after gold discoveries were made in the vicinity. Population (1979) 9918.

Yellowstone, river of the USA, tributary of the Missouri. Its source is in the Rocky Mountains of Wyoming. It flows north through Yellowstone National Park and a deep canyon, then east through Montana and North Dakota to join the Missouri. Length 1080 km; it drains 182,335 km².

Yellowstone National Park, US government reservation in the north-west of Wyoming, projecting about 3 km into Montana and Idaho. It is less a park than a series of parks formed by different valleys on the two sides of the Rocky Mountains. The scenery is famous for its brilliant colouring, and for natural phenomena, which include boiling springs and petrified forests. Yellowstone became a national park in 1872. Area 8956 km².

Yemen Arab Republic
Area: 190,000 km²
Population: 6,500,000
Capital: San'a

Yemen Arab Republic, (Arabic *ymn*, prosperity (in the Middle Ages and today) or right hand (i.e. of Mecca), state in the south-west corner of the Arabian peninsula, bounded north and east by Saudi Arabia, south and east by the People's Democratic Republic of Yemen, and west by the Red Sea. Total area c.190,000 km².

Fronting the Red Sea is a narrow coastal plain, the Tihama, 25–40 km wide. The population of this zone, including the coastal towns of Hodeida (50,000) and Mocha, is about one million. A further 200,000 people inhabit the second zone, a belt of foothills below 700 m, which receive negligible rainfall. The middle slopes of the Yemen plateau comprise a third region, above 750 m, where there is a more regular seasonal flow of water from streams originating in the high plateau. Here irrigated agriculture is possible and here live about 35 per cent of the population of 6·5 million people. The highest mountains rise to over 3700 m. Some 30 per cent of the total population live on the plateau highland and it contains most of the major urban settlements, including San'a, the capital, at 2500 m, with a population of 447,900. Eastward from the highlands is a descent to part of the Mesheq, the inner plateau of Arabia; there is greater aridity with a decrease in altitude.

The main cash crops are cotton, *qat* and coffee. Most of the cropped area is devoted to cereals for domestic consumption, however, and these include millet, sorghum, barley, wheat and maize. Vegetables and fruit are also significant.

The largest industrial enterprise is the San'a textile factory. Traditional handicraft activities include furniture manufacture. Salt extraction has long been of importance.

A provisional constitution was published in June 1974, replacing that of 1970. The chairman of the military Command Council has the powers of head of state. There are three other members of the council, which is the legislative and executive authority of the state. A People's Constituent Assembly was set up in 1978.

The official language is Arabic.

History. In ancient times the Yemen was the centre of several states which controlled one of the routes to the East and also the incense route. The opening up of the Persian Gulf-Palmyra route and of the direct sea route to and from India ruined their trade. In the Christian era the Abyssinians held the Yemen for a time, as did the Persians, but the Muslims soon conquered it. In 897 Zeidi sectaries (a branch of the Shi'a) under an imam founded a state there which lasted with vicissitudes till modern times.

In 1918 the Seidi Imam Yahya ibn Mohammad made himself master of the whole country. The Imam and two of his sons were murdered in February 1948; the rebel leader Sayid Abdullah Ibn Al Wazir declared himself king, but the Imam's eldest son, Ahmad,

defeated and killed the usurper in March and ruled until his death in 1962.

The Yemen joined the Arab League in 1945. In 1958 the Yemen was linked to the United Arab Republic in a federal union. This union lasted until 1961, when it lapsed after the defection of Syria.

In 1962 there was a republican revolt led by Sallal, an army officer, and civil war ensued. By 1966 the Yemen had become the principal area of conflict for the personal struggle for Arab leadership between Nasser and King Faisal. Sallal was deposed in November 1968 in favour of Qadi Iryani, a moderate, and by 1970 it had been agreed to include a number of royalists in the government. Tensions with southern Yemen were marked by border incidents. Nevertheless, efforts to unite the two countries continue. An agreement was signed in 1979.

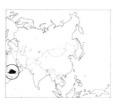

People's Democratic Republic of Yemen
Area: 287,682 km²
Population: 2,000,000
Capital: Aden

Yemen, People's Democratic Republic of, or South Yemen, a state in southern Arabia formed from the federation of South Arabia together with the territory of Aden, a former British crown colony. The state is bounded in the north by the Yemen Arab Republic and by the sandy desert of Rub 'al Khali in Saudi Arabia, in the east by the sultanate of Oman, and in the south by the Arabian Sea.

The physical geography consists of a narrow coastal plain rising rapidly inland to a series of plateaus and ranges, highest in the west and dropping to a low plain at the frontier with Oman. An important feature is the Wadi Hadhramaut, a deep valley running approximately east to west in the interior mountains of the eastern part of the country.

The total population of South Yemen was estimated at 2 million in 1980, with about 260,000 of these living in Aden.

Only one-fifth of the potential agricultural land is cultivated. Cotton is the main crop but cereals are also grown for local consumption. Fish production is important. There is some light industry. Aden is the capital.

The People's Democratic Republic is a one-party state, and the National Liberation Front is the only legal party. The Supreme People's Council exercises legislative power.

Arabic is the official language though many educated Yemenis also speak English.

History. From the earliest times Aden has been a key port in East-West trade. The Ottomans held tenuous control over it from the 16th century but it became increasingly of importance to Britain's imperial strategy, and was captured in 1839. Relations with Yemen in the north were persistently delicate and marked by border incidents and raids, as the north continued to press its territorial claims in the south. A treaty of friendship was signed with north Yemen in 1934.

During the 1950s Britain attempted to set up democratic institutions, of which the trade unions were most active. The presence of

Egyptian troops in north Yemen was an encouragement to the brutal competition between the rival nationalist groups NLF (National Liberation Front) and FLOSY (Front for the Liberation of Occupied South Yemen) to force independence from Britain. Violence increased, and the NLF overran the country in 1967. British forces withdrew. Qahtan al-Shaabi (the leader of the NLF) announced on 30 November 1967 the birth of the People's Republic of Southern Yemen (the country's present name was adopted in 1970).

In 1969 dissent within the NLF ranks led to Shaabi's replacement by Salim Rubai Ali. The new regime followed the Marxist line more strictly. Friction between the new state and the Yemen Arab Republic developed into war by 1979; hostilities ended with an agreement on eventual unity.

Yen (Japanese dollar), standard monetary unit of Japan since 1870. Originally the yen was a silver dollar-sized coin, but continued devaluation had, by 1955, reduced it to an aluminium coin, the size of a new penny.

Yenisei, or Yenisey, one of the largest rivers in the USSR, in Central Siberia. The river rises in two headstreams (the Great Yenisei, rising in the Sayan Mountains, and the Little Yenisei, rising in Mongolia), and flows north into the Kara Sea (an inlet of the Arctic Ocean). Length from the confluence of head-streams, 3487 km; if the River Selenga is accepted as the Yenisei's ultimate source, then its total length is nearer 5540 km; drainage basin 2,580,000 km². From below Krasnoyarsk to Dudinka it divides the West Siberian lowland from the Central Siberian plateau, forming a wide valley. The main tributaries are the Angara, Podkamennaya Tunguska and Nizhnyana Tunguska. The river freezes over between late October and early June. It is navigable almost throughout its course and is chiefly used for the transport of timber, grain and coal; it is accessible to sea-going vessels as far as Igarka. The chief ports are Dudinka, Igarka and Krasnoyarsk.

Yeoman, a term which has had varying meanings in English history but in the 15th century came to be wholly identical with the 40-shilling freeholder who exercised the franchise. More generally it has described a person of the middle class engaged in farming.

Yeomanry, name applied in Britain to mounted volunteer corps, not generally so called until 1794. Bodies of volunteer horse were raised before this during the reign of William III and at the time of the 1745 rising. The first unit of any permanence was the London and Westminster Light Horse Volunteers (1779). The yeomanry corps, which came into being in 1794, were not this time intended to fulfil a guerrilla role but to replace cavalry regiments of the line drafted overseas, in this instance, to the French Revolutionary Wars. By 1798 every country and several large towns had raised yeomanry. The yeomanry were bound to act as mounted police in case of riot. After 1816 their number was reduced but for many years, until the creation of county police forces, they played an important part in the maintenance of public order, being frequently called out to suppress riots and other disorders. When the

Territorial Force was constituted in 1908 the yeomanry was merged with it, and when the force was revived in 1921 as the Territorial Army it included 55 yeomanry regiments. They served in the Second World War, and still retain their individuality.

Yeomen of the Guard, a British royal bodyguard, employed on state occasions as part of the sovereign's retinue, founded by Henry VII in 1485. The term 'Beefeaters', given to both the Yeomen Warders of the Tower of London and the Yeomen of the Guard, is of uncertain derivation.

Yeomen Warders, guardians of the Tower of London, presumably in existence as a body since 1078, when William the Conqueror began the building of the White Tower.

Yerevan, or Erivan, capital city, economic and cultural centre of the Armenian SSR, USSR, situated on the River Razdan at an altitude of 850–1300 m. It has large aluminium, engineering, food and light industries, and manufactures synthetic rubber, tyres, chemicals and electrical equipment; its brandy is famous. It is first mentioned in Armenian history in the 6th century BC, but recorded in cuneiform as a fortress (Erebuni) in 782 BC. From 1440 it belonged variously to Persia and Turkey; it became Russian in 1827 and was the capital of independent Armenia from 1918 to 1920. Population (1980) 1,036,000.

Yesenin, Sergei Aleksandrovich (1895–1925), Soviet poet. His initial enthusiasm for the Revolution was dampened by his dislike of forced change in his beloved Russian countryside. He took refuge in debauchery and travel, in 1922 marrying the dancer Isadora Duncan. Disillusioned, and an alcoholic, he hanged himself in 1925. Yesenin's simple, mellifluous verse treats of peasants and the countryside, though in later life his tone became harsher.

Yeti (*yeh*, rocky place, *teh*, animal), name given by the Sherpas of east Nepal to an animal of the Himalayas, not yet identified by zoologists, reputedly inhabiting the deserts of scree at about 4000 to 5000 m. The first report was made in 1889, and the name 'abominable snowman' was a translation made by Henry Newman of a word used by porters on the 1921 Everest expedition. Footprints, up to 15 and 30 cm with a broad heel and separated toe, have been photographed and much discussed.

Yevtushenko, Yevgeny (1933–), Soviet poet, who achieved prominence with the poem *Zima Junction*, written shortly after Stalin's death in 1953. He became extremely popular with young people for his discussion of long-forbidden subjects (notably his attack on anti-Semitism in the poem *Babyi Yar*, 1961), and travelled widely in the West giving poetry readings. Though occasionally attacked for outspokenness, generally his communist ideals led to him being tolerated.

Yew, *Taxus baccata*, a European evergreen tree with linear leathery leaves and dioecious flowers, followed by seeds surrounded by bright red, waxy, cup-shaped arils (fleshy seed-covering). The tree attains a very great age; its wood is hard and close grained, but splits readily. It was formerly used for making long-bows. Its leaves and seeds are poisonous.

Yezd, see YAZD.

Yggdrasill, in Norse mythology, the vast ash tree which was the entire universe.
See also MYTHOLOGY.

Yi, Tibeto-Burman-speaking aboriginal people of south-west China, Vietnam, Thailand, Burma and Laos, numbering about 3·25 million. They were stratified into princes, aristocrats, commoners and debt-slaves. They are swidden agriculturalists growing rice and opium as a cash crop.

Yiddish (German *Jüdisch*, Jewish), the language of East European Jewry and of its many emigrants in other parts of Europe and overseas, originated in the Rhineland in the 14th century. Yiddish is based on Middle High German as it was spoken by Jews, who added to it several Romance words (Old Italian and Old French) and, particularly, many Hebrew words and phrases peculiar to Jewish life and observance. Yiddish employs the modern Hebrew alphabet (with slight modifications), and is written from right to left; it has a rich literature: the best-known modern Yiddish writers have been Sholom Aleichem and Sholem Asch.
See also HEBREW LANGUAGE.

Yin and Yang, Chinese symbols of complementary duality. Emerging from such a distant past in China that their history is unrecorded, the symbols of Yang and Yin were used extensively by both Taoism and Confucianism. It was thought that from the Tao—the undifferentiated One—arose all the dualities of nature, such as male and female, north and south, white and black, long and short. Yang and Yin are the principles inherent in all substance which eternally act and react upon each other.

The quality of Yin is dark, negative and feminine. Yin is the primordial chaos which gives rise to creativity and birth, and is thus a state of potentiality or of repose and rest, whereas Yang is motion, the principle of light, the sun, the male, the spirit. The diagram of Yang-Yin is a circle in which two shapes (somewhat like commas) appear to hold each other. Yang is white, and Yin is black; and because they are always interacting, the seed of one is shown as being contained in its opposite, a black point in the white and a white in the black. Although they are called opposites they are not to be confused with the western idea of the opposition of light to darkness, life to death, and good to evil, where one is to be cultivated and the other shunned. Yang and Yin are different aspects of the one system and the disappearance of either pole would be the disappearance of the system.

YMCA, see YOUNG MEN'S CHRISTIAN ASSOCIATION.

Ynys Môn, see ANGLESEY.

Yodel, primitive wordless song, or warble, practised by mountain dwellers in Switzerland, Tirol and Styria, characterised by rapid modulations from chest notes to falsetto. The yodel is first mentioned in Acts of Martyrs, AD 397, but is doubtless prehistoric.

Yoga, fourth of the six systems of Hindu philosophy, meaning literally 'to yoke', or to harness one's powers of mind and body towards spiritual union. Today the term Yoga has come to mean almost exclusively Hatha Yoga, but its wider sense is that of a training to experience realisation of the Self through the control of mind and body.

Rāja Yoga, 'King of yogas', is a harder and more specific path than other Yogas. It is also called the yoga of meditation, for it teaches the techniques of formal meditation, which include the bodily postures of Hatha Yoga. The method for following the Rāja path consists of eight steps. The first is *Yama*, the five restraints: non-injury, truthfulness, non-theft, spiritual conduct, non-greed. The second is *Nyama*, the five observances: purity, serenity, austerity, study, attentiveness to God. The third is *Hatha Yoga*, a Yoga for the body. The *asanas*, or postures, of this yoga are primarily intended for health. A healthy body creates its own harmonious energy and leaves the mind free from its demands. To keep the mind clear and tranquil is the real aim of this Yoga. The fourth step is the control of breathing, as uncontrolled breathing can destroy settled calm of mind. The fifth is control of the mind by withdrawing it from all distractions. The sixth is concentration. If the mind can flow towards the same thing for 12 seconds, this is concentration. Meditation is the seventh step. It is the flow of the mind towards an object of concentration *without interruption*. As the yogi meditates, he loses the feeling of himself as separate from the object of his concentration. The eighth is Samadhi, 'together with the Lord'; the integration of man's time-place-bound mind with the timeless and limitless Ground of existence.

Yoghurt, milk curdled with bacteria. Yoghurt is said to have been discovered accidentally by Asian nomads who carried their milk in bags made from the stomachs of sheep, which contained the bacteria that fermented the milk, warmed by the sun. Yoghurt today is made by boiling milk, cooling it to blood temperature, and then adding a small quantity of yoghurt to it. The milk curdles to produce a new batch in a few hours. The two basic bacteria involved are *Streptococcus thermophilus* and *Lactobacillus bulgaricus*.

Yogyakarta or Jogjakarta, town and principality in South Java province, Indonesia. The town is about 32 km from the active volcano, Mount Merapi, and 56 km south of Surakarta on the Jakarta-Surabaya railway. It is the cultural, political and trade centre for an extremely fertile agricultural area, an area of young volcanic soils, with population densities exceeding 1875 per km² in places. The agricultural basis is wet-rice cultivation, supplemented by cash cropping of sugar, rubber and copra.

Apart from being the cultural centre of the Sailendras, Yogyakarta was also the capital of the first Indonesian Republic (1945), when Sukarno withdrew here with the return of the Dutch. Yogyakarta is the only remaining principality in Indonesia. Population (town) 342,267; (principality) 2,750,813.

Yokohama, city of Kanagawa-ken, Japan, and seat of the prefectural government. Situated on the western shore of Tokyo Bay, 30 km to the south of Tokyo, Yokohama has developed since 1859 as a major seaport, and in terms of volume of trade ranks as the leading port of Japan. Industries include shipbuilding, oil refining, petro-chemicals, motor vehicles, flour milling and brewing. Improvement of communications with Tokyo has led to an increase in commuter

York. *The Minster seen from the 13th-century city walls. Large portions of the walls still exist.*

traffic between the two cities, and has helped to accelerate the growth of Yokohama's population. The city is now the second largest in Japan, next to Tokyo. Population (1979) 2,724,000.

Yokosuka, seaport and naval station of Kanagawa-ken, Japan, on Tokyo Bay, 20 km south of Yokohama. Population (1979) 414,000.

Yôm Kippur, see DAY OF ATONEMENT.

Yonge, Charlotte Mary (1823–1901), English novelist. She published various historical works, a *History of Christian Names*, 1863, and a monograph on Hannah More, 1888, but is remembered as the author of the novel *The Heir of Redclyffe*, which she published in 1853, and *The Daisy Chain*, 1856, both of which were popular with young and old alike. She wrote over 150 books.

Yonkers, city of New York, USA, on the Hudson river, north of and adjoining New York City, of which it is a residential suburb. Population (1980) 195,351.

York Cycle, see MIRACLE PLAY.

York, House of, branch of the English royal dynasty of Plantagenet, descended from Lionel, Duke of Clarence, third son of Edward III, and Edmund, Duke of York, fifth son of Edward III. The head of the house was Richard, Duke of York, who was killed at the battle of Wakefield in 1460. His sons, Edward IV and Richard III, and grandson, Edward V, were kings of England, 1461–85. Henry VII united the houses of York and Lancaster by marrying the daughter of Edward IV, Elizabeth. The title Duke of York has in recent times been borne by the second son of the reigning monarch.

York, Frederick Augustus, Duke of (1763–1827), British prince and soldier, second son of George III. In 1784 he was created Duke of York and Albany. He commanded the British forces in Flanders in 1793–95 and again on the occasion of the Helder expedition in 1799, both being campaigns in which British arms met with little success. He was made a field-marshal in 1795 and commander-in-chief in 1798. He was responsible for a number of army reforms and founded the Duke of York's Royal Military School, later Sandhurst.

York, Richard Plantagenet, 3rd Duke of, see YORK, HOUSE OF.

York, city in North Yorkshire, England, seat of an archbishopric, on the River Ouse, 319 km north-west of London. The Roman fortress of *Eboracum* was established at the junction of the rivers Ouse and Foss in AD 71. During the 300 years of the Roman occupation three emperors stayed here—Hadrian, Severus, and Constantius Chlorus. The latter two died in York. The son of Constantius, Constantine the Great, was proclaimed heir here on the death of his father. York was successively a Saxon and a Danish royal city, and was the capital of the kingdom of Northumbria. In the 8th century it was renowned as a seat of learning; Alcuin, the headmaster of its school of St Peter, was called by Charlemagne to found a school at Aachen, and a system of education for the Holy Roman Empire. Later York developed into an important commercial city, a centre of the wool trade, the small ships of its merchant adventurers sailing from the wharves of York to those of the Hanseatic towns. As the tonnage of ships increased the city's European trade declined. The 18th century saw a revival of its fortunes, when it became the fashionable resort for gentry, and in the 19th century its prosperity was again established by the railway. The chief glory of the city is York Minster. There are 16 other medieval churches in York, but some of these have been put to secular use. York is a great railway centre; its industries include carriage and wagon building, and the manufacture of chocolate and confectionery, beet sugar, scientific instruments, and glass and plastic ware. Population (1981) 99,787. See also YORK MINSTER.

York, town and county seat of York county, Pennsylvania, USA, on the Codorus Creek, 34 km from Harrisburg. It originated as a Quaker settlement. It has numerous manufactures and is the trade centre for a rich agricultural region. Population (1980) 44,619.

York Minster. Two churches were built on the site in the 7th century and are mentioned by Bede. In 1070 the first Norman Archbishop of York, Thomas of Bayeux, began to rebuild the Minster; the foundations of his choir remain under the present crypt. The choir and crypt were rebuilt in the 12th century by Archbishop Roger, and his crypt still exists. The present transepts were erected between 1220 and 1260 by Archbishop de Gray. The Norman nave was taken down and a new one built in the first half of the 14th century, shortly after the chapter-house was built. The fine west window was glazed in 1338. In 1354 a wooden vault was built, but this was replaced, after a fire, in 1840. The flying buttresses outside were added in 1905–07, but may have been planned originally. John Thoresby undertook the building of a new choir c.1380. In 1400–23 de Gray's Early English central tower, now unsuitable, was rebuilt. The north-west and south-west towers were added between c.1430 and 1471. This completed the Minster, and in 1472 its appearance was almost the same as at the present day, although fires in the 19th century necessitated considerable repairs.

Outstanding features of York Minster include its west front, its nave, its crypt, its chapter-house, its medieval stained-glass and a number of individual monuments. The chapter-house (c.1280–1310) is remarkable both for its large windows and for its wooden Gothic vault. The foundations of the Minster were strengthened in 1966–72. While engineers built a substructure of concrete, extensive and valuable excavations were carried out under the floor of the interior, revealing remains of a Roman basilica, Saxon tombs and parts of the Norman church. In 1984 the south transept was seriously damaged by fire.

Yorkshire, North, county of northern England created in 1974, out of the former North Riding of Yorkshire. The central administrative offices of the North Yorkshire County Council are in Northallerton. The west part of the county is crossed by the Pennine Range, cut by beautiful dales (Yorkshire Dales National Park), the principal ones being Swaledale, Wensleydale and Nidderdale. The middle part is a vast plain, the Vale of York. The east part has a variety of relief; to the north-east are the Cleveland Hills and the valley of the Esk. South of Eskdale lies Fylingdales Moor, North York Moors (and National Park), and Hambleton Hills. From these moors, several valleys run down to the Vale of Pickering drained by the Derwent which flows south-west from near the coast to join the Ouse between Selby and Goole. The county extends south of the Vale of Pickering to the Yorkshire Wolds. The coast from Runswick Bay in the north to Filey Bay in the south presents a variety of scenery, that between Whitby and Scarborough, with its high cliffs, being especially attractive.

With its pleasant coastline, two National Parks, and rural landscapes, North Yorkshire is important for tourism. Scarborough and Whitby are the largest coastal holiday resorts; their harbours are crowded with fishing and pleasure craft. Filey and many smaller places attract tourists, especially sea anglers. Numerous small market towns and villages within the two National Parks meet the needs of large numbers of visitors from the surrounding industrial regions. Nearby towns, e.g. Richmond, Ripon, Harrogate and Pickering, also serve the tourist, but in this respect they are overshadowed by York with its Minster, castle, medieval walls and streets, and museums. The most important economic activity in North Yorkshire is agriculture; dairying and mixed farming being widespread throughout the lowland plains of the Vales of York and Pickering, and sheep farming in the uplands of the Pennines and North York Moors. In the Selby District, rich coal seams have recently been discovered: their exploitation may initiate drastic changes in the area's economy. A large power station at Drax, on the Ouse, is already supplied by coal from the modern colliery at Kellingley. Population (1981) 666,610.

Yorkshire, South. This new metropolitan county came into being in 1974, and comprises the former county boroughs of Sheffield, Rotherham, Doncaster and Barnsley together with the southernmost urban and rural districts of the former West Riding of Yorkshire. Over 90 per cent of the population live in the urban areas. These are concentrated along the south-west to north-east axis of the Don valley, and along its main tributaries, the Dearne and the Rother. A high proportion of employed persons are engaged in coal-mining, steel manufacturing and processing, and in the glass, brass, wire and very varied engineering industries. Sheffield, the sixth largest city in Britain, is especially noted for its high-quality alloy steels, machine tools, heavy engineering and cutlery. The county contains a part of the Peak District National Park, and a rich diversity of rural landscapes formed between the barren Pennine moors in the south-west and the very low, flat carr-lands in the east. In contrast, the areas affected by coal-mining and manufacturing industry face problems associated with derelict and de-spoiled land, and the mushroom growth of settlement between 1830 and 1914. Population (1981) 1,301,813.

Yorkshire, West, a metropolitan county created in 1974 out of the former West Riding of Yorkshire. It is divided into five districts: Leeds, Bradford, Calderdale, Kirklees and Wakefield. The administrative offices are in Wakefield. The county stretches from the high Pennine moorlands in the west to the low-lying plain of the Vale of York to the east; the greater part lies within the valleys of the rivers Calder, Colne and Aire, but it extends northwards into the valley of the middle Wharfe and southwards into that of a tributary of the Don. Though the landscape is mainly industrial, more than half the total area (203,914 ha) remains semi-rural in character. In the west, there are unspoilt heather-clad gritstone moorlands, e.g. Rombalds (Ilkley) Moor and Haworth Moor (the Brontë country), intertwined with valleys along which sprawl textile villages. In the east, rich arable and pastoral land is interspersed with coal-mining villages. Centrally located are the larger manufacturing built-up centres of Leeds, Bradford, Halifax, Huddersfield, Dewsbury and Wakefield. The area already had a long-established woollen industry, when the application of steam power led to a rapid transformation. Inevitably, the coal seams were exhausted, and mining is now important only in the eastern parts of Wakefield and Leeds districts. Iron smelting, which reached its zenith about 1875, had disappeared by 1930. The engineering trades, mechanical and electrical, continued to expand and are found in all the major centres. The wool textile industry has transformed itself into a multi-fibre textile and clothing industry. Population (1981) 2,037,510.

Yorkshire Terrier, small, long-coated dog with straight, silky hair reaching to the ground from the back of the head to the tail and parted in the middle of the back. It is blue-grey, with tan on the head, ears and legs. The ears are small, V-shaped, and carried erect or semi-erect; the body is compact and level on top of the back. It weighs up to 3·2 kg; height 20 cm.

Yorktown, village and county seat of York county, Virginia, USA, on the York river. Here the last important battle of the American War of Independence was fought in 1781, when Lord Cornwallis surrendered to George Washington.

See also UNITED STATES OF AMERICA, *History*.

Yoruba, area, language and people in what is now south-western Nigeria and south-eastern Benin, West Africa. The spiritual, and at one time political, capital of the Yorubas lies in Ife. The Yorubas are divided into several groups such as the Egba, Ekiti, Ijebu and Oyo. In the past these groups formed their own city states although their kings, *Oba*, all owed allegiance to the ruler, Oni, of Ife town. Most Yoruba are farmers; cocoa is their major cash crop. Trade continues to be important and the markets are controlled by the women. Craft work is traditional and craftsmen are members of guilds. The bronze sculpture of Ife is well known. The Yoruba religion involved belief in an elaborate hierarchy of deities, at the head of whom were Ifa and Esu. Many Yoruba are today Christian or Muslim.

Yosemite Park, east-central California, USA, national park embracing the Yosemite Valley, and covering an area of 3060 km². The region is composed of granite, and the river valley is extremely beautiful. Discovered in 1851 by Bolling and his soldiers, it was made a national park in 1866 and is now one of the foremost tourist attractions in North America. The Yosemite Falls have a total descent of 739 m.

Yoshida, Shigeru (1878–1967), Japanese diplomat and politician. Because of his pro-Western and anti-militarist reputation, Yoshida became prime minister in 1946 when most politicians were removed by the Occupation purge. A forceful character who gained the soubriquet 'One-Man Yoshida', he was prime minister five times between 1946 and 1954.

Yoshkar-Ola (formerly *Tsarevokokshaysk*; 1919–27, *Krasnokokshaysk*), town in the RSFSR, USSR, 50 km to the north of the Volga, and capital and cultural centre of the Mari ASSR. It has engineering and food industries, and was founded in 1584 by the Russians as a fortress town and administrative centre in the territory of the Mari. Population (1980) 201,000.

Young, Arthur (1741–1820), British agriculturist. He was a practical farmer and wrote many books on agriculture and political subjects. His works include: *The Farmer's Letters to the People of England*, 1768; *Observations on the Present State of the Waste Lands of Great Britain*, 1773; *A Tour in Ireland*, 1780; and *Travels in France*, 1792. He was appointed secretary to the Board of Agriculture in 1793. Young was a pioneer in his promotion of modern agricultural methods, and his ideas were of European influence.

Young, Brigham (1801–77), US Mormon leader. He joined the sect in 1832, soon became important, and succeeded J. Smith as prophet and first president (1847). Under his leadership the Mormons when driven from Nauvoo finally settled in Utah, founding Salt Lake City (1847). Young proclaimed the doctrine of polygamy (1852). His capability as an organiser and administrator enabled the Mormon state to survive its early difficulties and become a flourishing area.

Young, Thomas (1773–1829), British physician, physicist and Egyptologist. He was elected Fellow of the Royal Society at the age of 21 for his discovery of the action of the ciliary muscles in the accommodation of the eye, and was its foreign secretary from 1802 until his death. Young gave the first description of astigmatism, 1801, and was the author of the theory that colour vision is due to retinal structures corresponding to red, green and violet, a theory later modified by Helmholtz. His famous experiments on interference, 1801–03, later developed by Fresnel, led to the eventual acceptance of the wave theory of light. In 1804 he stated the theory of capillary attraction, and in 1808 the laws governing the flow of blood in the heart and arteries. An accomplished Egyptologist, and the earliest decipherer of hieroglyphics, he was the first to decipher part of the Rosetta Stone.

Young England, section of the English Conservative party which about 1842 began a movement whose spirit and aim are well shown in Disraeli's *Coningsby*. Disraeli and Lord John Manners, later Duke of Rutland, led the movement, which aimed at better relations between different social classes.

Young Ireland, Irish political party formed in 1846 by seceders from the Repeal Association of Daniel O'Connell. Its aim was to unite the Catholics and Protestants of Ireland in an attempt to sever the union with England.

Young Men's Christian Association (YMCA), seeks to help young people to accept the Christian faith and live the Christian life, and to transcend the barriers of class, politics, race and creed by a variety of religious, educational, physical and social activities, designed to develop Christian character. The YMCA was founded in England in 1844 by Sir George Williams, then a clerk in a London drapery. The Association spread rapidly, especially after the Great Exhibition of 1851 and the establishment of the World's Alliance of YMCAs in 1855. The movement in the 1970s had a world membership of over 6 million in 80 countries.

'Young Pretender', see STUART, CHARLES EDWARD LOUIS PHILIP CASIMIR.

Young Women's Christian Association (YWCA), voluntary association founded in 1855 to promote the social, physical, intellectual and spiritual welfare of women and girls. Today the World YWCA, instituted in 1894, which has consultative status on the United Nations Economic and Social Council, has over 1·5 million members, as well as five million more who share in their activities in over 80 countries. Membership is open to women, girls, men and boys over 11 years, without distinction of race, nationality, politics or religion. The YWCA offers accommodation to single young people living away from home, friendship to visitors from overseas, and supports, with personnel and finance, associations overseas. Among expanding services are further education courses for girls in their first years at work, and courses for young unemployed people.

Younghusband, Sir Francis Edward (1863–1942), British explorer, administrator and mystic. Younghusband won early fame as an explorer and traveller, and was later known as a writer on India and for his work in connection with the organisation of conferences on world religions. He and Bell were the first Englishmen to reach India from China overland. He was *The Times* correspondent in South Africa (1895–97) and was in Johannesburg at the time of the Jameson Raid. Younghusband was British commissioner to Tibet (1903–04) and resident in Kashmir (1906–09). He was president of the Royal Geographical Society in 1919. He was devoted to the project of conquering Everest and was chairman of the Mount Everest Committee.

Youngstown, city in Ohio, USA, on the Mahoning river, 88 km from Pittsburgh. It is a major steel centre, and manufactures metal products and rubber tyres. Population (1980) 115,436.

Youth Hostels. The youth hostels organisations seek to satisfy the need for good overnight accommodation for the traveller of limited means. The International Youth Hostels Federation comprises over 40 associations, and encourages members to use hostels in any country within the Federation. The movement first assumed an organised form in Germany, where the first hostel was opened in 1910. In the 1920s the idea spread to other Continental countries, and since 1945 youth hostels have also been established in Eastern countries such as Israel, India and Japan. By 1974 there were 4340 youth hostels in 48 countries. Youth hostels are designed primarily for the use of young people, but in most countries there is no upper age limit. The buildings used vary from mansions to mountain huts, but all provide simple accommodation, separate dormitories for men and women, cooking and washing facilities.

Ypres, 1st Earl of, see FRENCH, JOHN DENTON PINKSTONE.

Ypres (Flemish *Ieper*), town in the province of West Flanders, Belgium, on the River Yperlée. It was famous in the Middle Ages as a centre of the Flanders cloth trade. The Menin Gate (1927) is a memorial to the British troops missing in the fighting around Ypres in the First World War. The chief manufactures are now linen and biscuits. Population (1970) 20,900.

Ypres, Battles of, see WORLD WAR, FIRST.

Ypsilantis, or Hypsilanti, noble Greek Phanariot family of the 18th and 19th centuries, who claimed descent from the Comneni, rising to great power in Constantinople. They fought for Greek independence.

Ysaÿe, Eugène (1858–1931), Belgian violinist and composer. He was known for his interpretations of Bach, César Franck and the Italian violinist-composers.

Ytterbium, metallic chemical element, symbol Yb, atomic number 70, atomic weight 173·04, a member of the group of lanthanides. It is obtained along with lutetium from gadolinite. Ytterbium forms an oxide, Yb_2O_3.

Yttrium, metallic chemical element, symbol Y, atomic number 39, atomic weight 88·9059, allied to aluminium; a member of the group of lanthanides. It yields colourless salts, and forms an oxide, Yt_2O_3.

Yuan, Mongol dynasty which ruled China from 1279 to 1368. It was founded by Kublai Khan.

Yuan Shikai (Yüan Shih-k'ai) (1859–1916), Chinese politician. When the revolution broke out in 1911 he became president of the council of ministers, and was premier for a short time. In 1912 he accepted the presidency of the Republic, but he had no sympathy with the revolution and in 1916 declared his intention of ascending the imperial throne. Discontent began, the south revolted, and Yuan had to abdicate.

Yucatán, peninsula of south-east Mexico, geographically including the Mexican states of Yucatán and Campeche and Quintana Roo together with parts of Belize and Guatemala; length 640 km; mean breadth 320 km; coastline 1120 km; area 144,040 km². It separates the Gulf of Mexico from the Caribbean Sea. The coast on the north and west is low and sandy, but higher and more indented on the east. The district contains many relics of the Maya civilisation, notably at Chichén Itzá and Uxmal.

Yucca, Adam's needle, a genus of slow-growing evergreen shrubs in the Agavaceae, bearing, when fully-grown, a huge erect panicle of pendulous flowers from the centre of a circle of thick linear leaves. The genus occurs in southern USA, Mexico and the West Indies. *Yucca* species are pollinated exclusively by a small moth, *Pronuba*. The female moth removes pollen from the stamens of one flower, rolls it into a ball and flies to another *Yucca* plant, inside the ovary of which she lays a few eggs, then places the pollen-ball on the stigma above the ovary. The larvae emerge from the eggs, and feed on the developing seeds, consuming about half, but allowing sufficient to remain for the perpetuation of the species.

Yugoslav Wines. The Riesling, Sylvaner and Traminer wines from Lutomer are established table wines, and the wines from Kapela, particularly the Kapela Rhine Riesling, grown from a noble variety of that vine, are wines of an equally high quality. Žilavka from Macedonia is an excellent dry white wine, and Tigermilk, pressed from the Ranina grape, mellowed like Sauternes by the *pourriture noble*, is velvety sweet. The red wines from Macedonia, Kavadarka and Prokupac are also of good quality.

See also WINE.

Yugoslavia, federal republic of South-East Europe (Socialist Federal Republic of Yugoslavia), the largest country of the Balkan peninsula, bounded on the north by Austria and Hungary, on the east by Romania and Bulgaria, on the south by Greece, on the south-west by Albania, on the west by the Adriatic Sea, and on the north-west by Italy. Area 256,177 km².

Yugoslavia has a long coastline (725 km) on the Adriatic Sea running parallel to the east coast of the Italian peninsula. In the north-east (the only low-lying part of the country) there

Yugoslavia, the town of Korcula on Korcula island, part of the Dalmatian archipelago.

Yugoslavia
Area: 256,177 km²
Population: 22,300,000
Capital: Belgrade

are extensive plains, very fertile and watered by the rivers Danube, Sava, Tisza and Drava. In the north there are spurs of the Alps, including the Julian and Karawanken Alps; in the north-west there is the karst; and running north-west to south-east above the littoral of Dalmatia are the Dinaric Alps. The south is a mass of mountain ranges (including, in the south-east, offshoots of the Balkan Mountains), with peaks of over 2440 m, cut by deep river valleys, notably those of the Morava and Vardar. The mountains are heavily forested. On the southern frontiers there are several large lakes (Scutari and Ohrid). Lying off the Adriatic coast are many small islands.

Population in 1980 was estimated at 22,300,000. Serbians form the largest group. About three-fifths of Yugoslavia is farmed and about one-third is forested. Collectivisation was abandoned in 1953 and most agriculture is in the hands of private landowners. The most favoured area is the Vojvodina plains in the north-east, where wheat, maize, sugarbeet, sunflowers and pigs are the chief products. Much land is forested, upland areas are used for pasture and mixed grains and potatoes are the chief crops.

The country is rich in mineral resources, including bauxite, lead, antimony, copper, mercury, chrome, gold, silver, salt and magnesite. The most important iron-ore mines are in Bosnia. The iron and steel industry uses imported coking coal and is still based in the north-west. Non-ferrous metallurgy is more widely dispersed and reflects the wide distribution of ores, but manufacturing is largely in the major towns and the north-west of the country. Food-processing industries are to be found in the rich agricultural areas of the north-east, but the manufacture of textiles and clothing is widespread. Tourism is important. Belgrade is the capital.

The unit of currency is the *dinar*, divided into 100 *paras*.

The constitution of 1963 (amended 1974) states that the Federal Socialist Republic of Yugoslavia consists of the socialist republics of Bosnia-Hercegovina, Montenegro, Croatia, Macedonia, Serbia (including the autonomous province of Vojvodina and the autonomous region of Kosovo-Metohija), and Slovenia. A collective Presidency, consisting of one representative of each republic and autonomous province and the President of the League of Communists, exercises the rights and duties of head of state. The Presidency, which is elected by the Federal Assembly, is assisted by a Federal Executive Council, the administrative branch of the government.

The supreme legislative body is the Federal Assembly, which has two chambers: the Federal Chamber and the Chamber of Republics and Provinces.

Serbo-Croat is the language of administra-

tion, but the state also recognises Macedonian and Slovene.

History. Yugoslavia, until 1929 known as the Kingdom of the Serbs, Croats and Slovenes, was created after the First World War from the former kingdoms of Serbia and Montenegro; Bosnia, Hercegovina, Dalmatia (except for a small part which went to Italy), and parts of Styria, Carniola and Carinthia from Austria; and Croatia, Slovenia and Vojvodina (parts of Baranja, Bačka and Banat) from Hungary. It was declared a constitutional parliamentary monarchy under the hereditary king of Serbia, but dissension between Serbs and Croats broke out, and in 1929 King Alexander I dissolved Parliament. At the same time the country was renamed Yugoslavia. The dictated constitution of 1931 vested the legislative powers in the king, the senate and the chamber of deputies. In 1934 Alexander was assassinated. During his son Peter's minority, Alexander's brother Prince Paul was regent. In April 1941, Germany invaded, penetrating the Monastir gap and eventually occupying Belgrade. The government of Peter II in exile had appointed a Serb, Gen. Mihajlović, commander-in-chief of what remained of the Yugoslav army in the fatherland. A rival force to Mihajlović's Cetnicks (Chetniks) arose under the leadership of Tito, a Croatian Communist. During the war, Tito became more powerful and in 1945 he was acclaimed at the general election. In 1946 the first constitution of the Federal People's Republic of Yugoslavia was adopted, and action taken to make Yugoslavia a fully Communist state.

Political and economic life in Yugoslavia from 1948 to 1953 was completely dominated by Tito's quarrel with the Cominform. Yugoslavia was able successfully to assert its independent status against Soviet claims, but while economic necessity forced it to trade with the West, its domestic policy continued to be conducted on generally Marxist lines, though with the emphasis on the 'peasant proletariat' rather than on the urban workers, and with rather less repression than was usual in a Communist state.

After the death of Stalin (in 1953) relations between Yugoslavia and the USSR gradually improved, though Tito continued to insist on Yugoslavia's independence of both the Eastern and the Western blocs.

The unique position of Yugoslavia in world politics since 1948 was very largely the personal achievement of Tito, whose influence over his country's affairs remained paramount until his death in 1980.

Language. The linguistic pattern of Yugoslavia is exceedingly complex. The great majority of the population speaks one or other of the South Slavonic languages, Slovene in the north, Macedonian, a dialect closely related to Bulgarian, in the south (each with about 1,500,000 speakers), or Serbo-Croatian (with about 14,000,000 speakers) over the greater part of the country. Macedonian exclusively and Serbian generally use the Cyrillic alphabet, while Slovene and Croatian use the Latin script with diacritic marks.

There are also numerous minority languages, the most important numerically being Albanian (with about 900,000 speakers), Hungarian (about 500,000 speakers); and Turkish

(about 200,000 speakers); others include Czech, Slovak, Romany, German, Romanian, Bulgarian and Italian. The minority languages are taught in schools and various periodicals and books are published in them.

Yukawa, Hideki, Japanese physicist. He became professor at the university of Kyoto in 1939 and was Director of the Research Institute for Fundamental Physics, 1953–70. He was later visiting professor at Columbia University. Yukawa is best remembered for his work on the meson. In 1935 he published work which showed that the existence of this particle would account for certain unexplained properties of the atomic nucleus.

Yukon, territory of north-west Canada, with an area of 531,845 km² (land) and 4480 km² (water). Almost the entire territory lies within the Cordilleran mountain system. The soils are highly acidic and of only marginal use for agriculture. Farming does take place around the mining communities and on the floors of the river valleys where alluvium has been deposited. The crops grown are limited to the hardy cereals, oats and rye, and to root crops and hay. Most farms have a few head of beef cattle and a milch-cow and close to the settlements market gardening is quite important. The territory owes its fame to the discovery of gold in the Klondike at the end of the 19th century and minerals continue to provide its main source of income. Gold, silver, lead and, more recently, zinc are mined in the vicinity of Dawson. The other major industries are lumbering, fur trapping and fishing.

The Yukon Territory was constituted a separate political region in 1898. It is governed by a resident commissioner appointed by the federal authorities and an elected legislative council. The seat of government is at Whitehorse. Population (1980) 24,138.

Yunnan, a province in southern China, bounded on the north and east by Sichuan, Guizhou and Guangxi Zhuang provinces, and on the south and west by Vietnam, Burma and Tibet. The province consists mainly of an elevated plateau broken by mountain ranges and river gorges. The mountains are highest in the north where they reach heights exceeding 5000 m; in the south heights of only 2–3000 m are reached. The headwaters of some of Asia's most important rivers lie in the province, including those of the Changjiang, the Mekong and the Salween (Nujiang). Level land for agriculture is exceedingly scarce and only about 5 per cent of the province is under cultivation. The timber of the mountains is a valuable resource. The principal crops are wheat, barley and maize; some sugar cane is grown in the valleys of the south-east. Yunnan has considerable mineral wealth, including tin, copper, gold, lead and jade. Gejiu is the most important tin-mining centre in China. Industrial development is continuing, particularly at Kunming, the province's capital. Yunnan has a varied population. About one-third of the people are not Han Chinese and some 28 different minorities are represented in the province including the Ya, Pai, Hani and Lisu peoples. Area 380,000 km². Population (1972) 24,000,000.

YWCA, see YOUNG WOMEN'S CHRISTIAN ASSOCIATION.

Z

Z, twenty-sixth and last letter of the English alphabet. In the North Semitic alphabet it occupied the seventh place; in the Greek and Etruscan the sixth. It was not required in Latin and was therefore dropped, and the letter G, created out of the letter C, was placed in its position. It was reintroduced after the conquest of Greece (2nd century BC), though only to transliterate Greek words, and was placed at the end of the Latin alphabet, from which it has been transferred to most European languages, though pronunciation varies. The name of the letter is *zed* in Britain, but *zee* in the United States.
See also ALPHABET.

Zaandam, port in the province of North Holland, Netherlands, on the River Zaan, 8 km north-west of Amsterdam. It has saw-mills and manufactures paper, metals, glue and dyes. Zaandam is the chief town of the municipality called Zaanstad created in a re-organisation of boundaries effective on 1 January 1974. Population of Zaanstad (1980) 128,809.

Zabrze (German *Hindenburg*), town of Poland, in Katowice province, 18 km north-west of Katowice. Until 1945 it was in Upper Silesia. It has coal-mines, and steel, engineer-ing, glass and chemical industries. The large mining town of Ruda Śląska lies to the east of the town. Population (1979) 196,000.

Zacharias, father of John the Baptist. All that is known of him is contained in Luke i. He was a priest in the Temple, and the angel Gabriel foretold to him that his ageing wife, Elisabeth, would bear a son. Zacharias was struck dumb for doubting. After the birth of the child, he named it John as the angel had commanded, and recovering his speech, uttered the Canticle, *Benedictus*.

Zadar, port in Croatia, Yugoslavia, on a peninsula of the Dalmatian coast. It was con-quered by Venice in the 15th century, became Austrian in 1797, and was ceded to Italy by the Treaty of Rapallo in 1920. Under the Italian peace treaty of 1947 it became part of Yugoslavia. Maraschino liqueur, glass and wax are manufactured. Population (1971) 43,000.

Zagorsk (formerly *Sergiev*), town in the Moscow *oblast* of the RSFSR, USSR, 70 km north-east of Moscow. It has been a centre of a wood-carving and toy-making craft since the 15th century, when a settlement had al-ready grown around its focal point, the famous Trinity Monastery of St Sergius (Troitse-Sergiyeva Lavra), founded in 1337. This is now a museum and residence of the Patriarch of Moscow. Population (1971) 94,000.

Zagreb (German *Agram*), capital of the republic of Croatia, Yugoslavia, on the River Sava. It has been the cultural centre of the Croats since 1557, and is the second city of Yugoslavia. It is divided into three parts. It manufactures textiles, machinery, paper, carpets, asbestos and electrical equipment, and it is an important centre of communi-cations. Population (1971) 602,200.

Zaire
Area: 2,344,886 km²
Population: 29,270,000
Capital: Kinshasa

Zaire, republic in Central Africa, bounded on the north by the Congo People's Republic, Central African Republic and Sudan, on the east by Uganda, Rwanda, Burundi and Tan-zania, on the south-east by Zambia, on the south-west by Angola, and on the west it has a short coastline on the Atlantic. Area 2,344,886 km².

The central zone of the country is a massive plateau with an average altitude of 900 m. This is well-drained land covered with wooded savanna. There are forests in the river valleys and in a region in the east and north which covers an area of 64,750 km². The long chain of the Mitumba Mountains runs from the south-east border north-eastwards to Lake Tanganyika, and then northward past Lake Kivu to Lake Mobutu. The western slopes descend gently to the basin of the Zaire River, but the east face is very abrupt in places, overlooking the Great Rift Valley. The river and its major tributaries provide a network of navigable waterways for 13,000 km.

***Zaire.** A village on the banks of the Zaire River.*

The earliest inhabitants of the Zaire river basin are believed to have been the pygmy people, of whom some 100,000 survive around lakes Tanganyika and Kivu and in the north-eastern river valleys. The majority of the population today are Bantu speakers who came to the region between the 10th and 14th centuries. There are also minorities of Sudanic peoples in the north, Nilotics in the north-east, and Tutsi around Kivu. The present population (1979) is 29,270,000. The main towns are Kin-shasa (the capital), Lubumbashi, Mbuji-Mayi, Kisangani, Kananga and Matadi.

Agriculture is helped by the rich soil which supports a wide variety of crops including cash crops of coffee, palm oil, cotton and rubber. Other important crops are cassava and bananas. Forest reserves cover 55 per cent of the country.

The country's chief riches lie in the Shaba copper mines. Manganese, zinc, uranium and other minerals are also mined and there are rich diamond deposits in Kasai provinces. Off-shore oil deposits have been exploited since the early 1970s. Zaire is the foremost producer in the world of industrial diamonds and pro-duces 60 per cent of the world's cobalt.

The country's sole political party is the Popu-lar Movement of the Revolution (MPR). The people elect, by universal suffrage, the chairman of the MPR, who is also the Presi-dent of the republic, for a seven-year term, renewable once only.

Executive power is shared with the National Executive Council acting as a form of Cabinet, although the President controls its pro-gramme and decisions, as well as appointing its personnel. Superficially, the legislative function is performed by a unicameral body of 268 members, the National Legislative Council.

The official language is French, but there is a widespread use of four national languages: Surahili, Tshiluba, Lingala and Kikongo.

History. In 1885 the Congo Free State was given international status by the Treaty of Berlin. Leopold II of Belgium was recognised as its sovereign. The Congo became a formal Belgian colony in 1908.

Belgium made enormous capital investments in the country, and its mineral wealth, notably in the province of Katanga (now Shaba) became considerable. The principal towns grew to thriving modern centres. But Africans were given few opportunities to take part in the administration of their country, and, when anti-colonial feeling became widespread, after the Second World War, it was extremist in character. Only in Katanga was there a poli-tician (Moise Tshombe) whose authority had reliable military backing. When the Belgians hastily granted Congo independence on 30 June 1960, chaos followed.

Neither Kasavubu, elected head of State in June, nor Patrice Lumumba, the leftist premier of an unwieldy coalition govern-ment, could maintain order. Katanga, under Tshombe, seceded from the republic. UN troops were sent to the Congo, but their effec-tiveness was limited. After an army coup in September Lumumba was arrested. In Febru-ary 1961 he was kidnapped and murdered by Katangese tribesmen.

Finally, in December 1961 the UN launched a determined military attack against Katanga, and in January 1962 Tshombe formally agreed to its reintegration in the Congo. In July 1964 Kasavubu appointed Tshombe as the new premier, as the only Congolese leader likely to be able to re-establish law and order. Tshombe used white 'mercenaries' to fight the rebellion, which was receiving material aid from various Communist countries and from the United Arab Republic. In the fighting which took place atrocities on a large scale were committed by both sides.

Tshombe's tactics and allies earned him the hatred of the Communist and Afro-Asian blocs. He was dismissed from the premiership in October 1965. In November 1965 Lieut.-Col. Mobutu overthrew Kasavubu and assumed supreme power, ruling by decree.

Mobutu's rule has been authoritarian, but has meant that the elements of peace and stability could enter into the Congolese political arena for the first time since independence. In May 1967 Mobutu founded the Popular Movement of the Revolution (MPR) as the sole political party; constitutional changes, and the new Constitution of 1978, have confirmed the power of the party's Political Bureau.

Zaire, formerly Congo, second river of the continent of Africa in terms of drainage area (3,690,733 km²) and also in terms of length (about 4828 km); in volume of water it is surpassed only by the Amazon and the Mekong. It drains the whole of Zaire. The actual source of the river is still disputed. Geographically the Lubudi, which flows into the Lualaba above Bukama, is the headstream of the Zaire, as from there to the mouth the river valley shows normal development. Up to the Stanley Falls, two rapids—those at Nyangwe and Ukassa—make the Zaire unnavigable. The middle Zaire which enters the alluvial plain of western equatorial Africa at an elevation of 396 m runs mainly in a westerly direction till it turns sharply southward near Bangala. There are many lacustrine expansions along the middle Zaire, the last being that of Malebo Pool, which is 305 m above sea-level, and beside which stand the cities of Kinshasa and Brazzaville. This is the end of the main navigable section of the river which then drops 259 m in 235 km. From Matadi to the Atlantic, the distance is about 145 km, and may be navigated by ocean-going vessels.

Zambezi, or Zambesi, river of Africa extending mainly through Zambia and Zimbabwe (the territorial boundary between the two countries from near Shesheke to Feira) and Mozambique. It has a length of about 2575 km, but its navigation is poor in proportion to its size. It has three navigable sections but they are divided by impassable barriers. Its drainage area is about 1,347,000 km². It rises in several streams in north-west Zambia, Angola and Zaire. Its general course is south-east through the Baroki Valley to the Victoria Falls; from here the river bends north-east and east nearly to Tete, Mozambique, when it resumes a south-easterly course to the delta, situated some 320 km north-east of Sofala in the Mozambique Channel. Its volume is largely increased by the Shire bringing the waters of Lake Malawi. For about 193 km towards its mouth, the Zambezi is navigable for shallow-draught steamers.

Zambia, independent republic of southern Africa, separated from Zimbabwe in the south-east by the Zambezi river, bounded on the south by Botswana, on the west by Angola, on the north by Zaire, and on the east by Tanzania, Malawi and Mozambique. Area 752,620 km².

The country is formed of thinly forested

Zambia
Area: 752,620 km²
Population: 5,600,000
Capital: Lusaka

plateau. Only the valleys of the Kafue, Luangwa and lower Zambezi rivers are below 1250 m, and the Tanzania plateau in the north-east averages 1550; the highest point is 1850 m. The swampy Lake Bangweulu is in north-western Zambia, and lakes Mweru and Tanganyika are on its northern borders.

Most of the indigenous peoples of Zambia belong to the group of Bantu speakers; the major tribes are the Bemba, the Nyanja and the Tonga. The main towns are Lusaka (the capital), Ndola, Kitwe and Kabwe. The total population in 1979 was estimated at 5,600,000. Commercial herds of beef and dairy cattle have declined with the departure of white farmers, but the state has invested in ranching. Crops include maize, groundnuts, sorghum, millet and beans.

The Copperbelt, an area 110 km by 50 km, flanks the Zaire border. Copper accounts for 96 per cent of Zambian mineral production and is almost all exported as unwrought metal. Zinc, cobalt and lead are mined and more recently low-grade coal in the Zambezi valley has been exploited.

The currency unit is the Kwacha.

The constitution formulated at the time of independence in January 1964 was amended in 1968 and again in December 1972, when Zambia officially became a one-party state, ruled by the United National Independence Party (UNIP). A new constitution was written, and received the approval of President Kenneth Kaunda in August 1973. This provided for a President who was elected by universal suffrage (over 18s) and was also the head of the United National Independence Party. Although the President is assisted in his executive function by the cabinet, the decisions of the cabinet are to be subordinate to that of the UNIP central committee. Legislative power is vested in the National Assembly, with the House of Chiefs operating in an advisory capacity.

The official language is English, although there are a number of important African languages including Nyanja, Bemba, Tonga, Lozi, Lunda and Luvale.

History. The early history of what is now Zambia is obscure. The first expedition of real geographical value was Livingstone's famous missionary journey of 1851 during which he discovered the Victoria Falls.

The great majority of the present African population of the area is of Bantu origin, descended from invaders who swept over the country about or a little after 1700.

Before 1899–1900 the whole territory had been vaguely included in the charter granted to the British South Africa Company, but thereafter the company's administration of the western and north-eastern portions of the country were put on a firm basis. These two territories were amalgamated in 1911 under the name of Northern Rhodesia. In 1924 the

Crown took over the administration of Northern Rhodesia from the British South Africa Company.

In 1953, the Federation of Rhodesia and Nyasaland, of which Northern Rhodesia was a component part, was created. Federation brought great economic benefits to Northern Rhodesia, but was bitterly opposed by African leaders. Kenneth Kaunda led a sustained campaign against Federation, and after elections held under a new constitution, 1962, his United National Independence party gained wide success. In March 1963 Britain agreed in principle to Northern Rhodesia's right to secede from the Federation, which was dissolved at the end of the year. In 1964 Northern Rhodesia became an independent republic within the Commonwealth, changing its name to Zambia. Kaunda became its first president.

Zambia's economy continued to be closely linked with that of Rhodesia, until the latter's unilateral declaration of independence in November 1965. In December 1965, when Britain imposed an oil embargo on Rhodesia, it arranged an air lift of oil into Zambia. Aided by Britain, Zambia pressed ahead to achieve its economic independence.

Zambia attempted to solve its problems by the construction of an oil pipeline from Dar es Salaam to the Copperbelt, and by the building of a railroad (with Tanzania and the People's Republic of China) from the Copperbelt to the coast in 1975.

During the Zimbabwe war of independence Zambia provided bases for the forces of the Patriotic Front, led by Joshua Nkomo.

Zamboanga City, in Zamboanga del Sur province on Mindanao in the Philippines. It is a busy and sheltered port with a large export trade. Its name is derived from the tropical flowers which grow everywhere, and its site and equable climate have made it a tourist resort; it is also a centre for brass and bronzeware. Population (1975) 261,978.

Zamenhof, Lazarus Ludwig (1859–1917), Polish-Jewish oculist and philologist, who invented the artificial language Esperanto.

Zamyatin, Evgeni Ivanovich (1884–1937), Soviet writer and critic. Though a Bolshevik in his youth, his attitude to the post-revolutionary regime was critical. In 1921 he formed an important group of writers, the Serapion Brothers. The 1920s produced his finest stories and plays, including the fantastic novel *We*, a critique of totalitarianism that influenced Huxley and Orwell. He emigrated to Paris in 1931.

Zanzibar, island situated 36 km off the East African coast. With Pemba island, 40 km to the north, it formed the independent state of Zanzibar in 1963–64 before becoming part of the United Republic of Tanzania. Zanzibar is a low platform of coral limestone, occupying 1660 km². The majority of the people are farmers, and cloves provide the chief export, although coconuts are also important. There is a large Arab element in the population, but its influence was sharply reduced by the 1963 revolution which overthrew the sultan. Despite its incorporation in Tanzania, Zanzibar retains autonomy in external and internal affairs. Area (Zanzibar and Pemba) 2640 km²; population (1978 census) 475,655.

History. At the end of the 15th century

Zanzibar was ruled by a 'king' of 'Moorish' descent. In the early 16th century the Portuguese made Zanzibar and Pemba tributary to the Portuguese Crown. After 1698 Zanzibar and Pemba under the nominal supremacy of Oman.

In 1888 the then Sultan Khalifa granted to a German East African company a lease of the whole coastline (including Mafia) of what was later Tanganyika. In the same year a similar lease was granted to the Imperial British East Africa Company of the Sultan's dominions to the north of the German concession. In 1890 Khalifa placed his dominions under British protection and abolished all traffic in slaves within those dominions. In 1906 the British government assumed more direct control over the Protectorate and re-organised the government. Increasing self-government began from 1920 onwards. In September 1963 Zanzibar became entirely self-governing internally, and in December 1963 became an independent state within the Commonwealth. In April 1964 Zanzibar united with Tanganyika, and in October 1964 the new state was renamed Tanzania.

Zanzibar, town on the west side of Zanzibar island, formerly capital of the state of Zanzibar, and now the second town of Tanzania. It is older than most East African towns, its period of greatest prosperity beginning when the ruler of Oman moved his court there in 1840, and has many fine Arab buildings. It has lost its entrepôt functions but it remains the chief commercial centre for both Zanzibar and Pemba islands. Population (1978) 110,669.

Zaporozhye (formerly *Aleksandrovsk*), capital city, economic and cultural centre of Zaporozhye *oblast*, USSR, on the Dnieper 70 km south of Dnepropetrovsk. It is a major industrial centre (metallurgical, electro-technical, engineering and chemical industries). It is also a transport centre (river port, airport and four railway lines). Zaporozhye was founded in 1770 as a fortress in the defence line against the Crimean Tatars. Population (1980) 799,000.

Zapotec, American Indian people who exercised control in the southern Mexican area of Oaxaca before the 16th century. There are now between 200,000 and 300,000 Zapotecs, who are mostly farmers.

Zaragoza (English *Saragossa*), capital of Zaragoza province, Spain, on the River Ebro. It was a capital of Aragón, but it declined in importance after the union of that kingdom with Castile. Zaragoza is a commercial and railway centre; its industries include foodstuffs, chemicals, machinery, glass and porcelain. Population (1981) 590,750.

Zarathustra, see ZOROASTRIANISM.

Zaria, town of North-Central State, Nigeria, 140 km south-west of Kano. The town was founded in the early 16th century and later the same century became the capital of the Hausa emirate of Zaria (or Zazzau). After the railway came into operation in 1910, cotton ginning became the most important economic activity, but now it is a collection point for tobacco, peanuts and hides as well, and there are textile, cigarette, cosmetics and publishing industries. Population (1975) 224,000.

Zátopek, Emil (1912–), Czechoslovak athlete, holder of 18 world records from the 5000 to the 30,000 m. Despite his unattractive, painful style, he electrified enthusiasts from 1948, when he won the 10,000-m Olympic gold medal and came a close second in the 5000 m, until 1956 when he came sixth in the marathon. He ran 10 miles in 48 minutes 12 seconds, running on to make a new one hour world record of 20,052 m (1952); he was the first man to run six miles inside 28 minutes and 10,000 m inside 29 minutes (1954).

Zealand (Denmark), see SJAELLAND.

Zealots, or Cananaeans, Jewish party implicated in two revolts against Rome. They were in full accord with the Pharisees in their devotion to the Law, but in politics much more intransigent and violent. From this party may have come Simon, one of the 12 apostles.

Zebra. *The extinct species,* Equus quagga.

Zebra, the fully striped species of the horse genus, *Equus*, in order Perissodactyla. There are three species, the largest being Grévy's zebra (*E. grevyi*), which stands some 1·3 m at the withers and lives in open, scrub-covered plains of the East African highlands. The mountain zebra (*E. zebra*) lives in southwestern Africa. The common zebra (*E. burchelli*) is widespread through Africa south of the Sahara, and several races are recognised. They have the boldest markings with the widest stripes and most races have faint 'shadow' stripes of black in the centre of each white one. The quagga (*E. quagga*), which became extinct in 1883, had a striped head and neck with a brown body and white tail and legs.

Zebrina, a genus of branching herbs in the family Commelinaceae, of Mexico and South America, akin to *Tradescantia*, and often known as Wandering Jew. *Z. pendula* is commonly grown as a house plant.

Zebu, see CATTLE.

Zechariah, minor prophet, a contemporary of Haggai, c.520 BC. His book is generally divided into two parts. The first part (chapters i–xiii) is universally regarded as the original work of Zechariah. The second part (chapters ix–xiv), called sometimes Deutero-Zechariah, is placed by some in Hellenistic times, while others claim that some pre-exilic material was used.

Zeebrugge, seaport in the province of West Flanders, on the North Sea, Belgium, 11 km north of Bruges, whose port it is. It has a fine breakwater, and a ship canal connecting it with Bruges which was opened in 1907. Port expansion here in recent years has led to the development of ferry services with England and also container handling facilities.

Zeeland, south-western province of the Netherlands. It consists of five islands lying in the River Scheldt estuary, and the region north of the Belgian province of East Flanders. The surface is very flat and much of it is below sea-level protected by dykes. The soil is fertile. Corn, butter and cheese are produced, and cattle reared. Chief towns are Middelburg (capital) and Flushing. A series of barrages are being built between the Zeeland islands. Area 2745 km²; population (1981) 351,662.

Zeeman Effect, the splitting of spectra by magnetic fields. In 1896 the Dutch physicist and Nobel prize winner (1902) P. Zeeman (1865–1943) discovered that the wavelengths of the lines of the spectra of atoms are changed when the atoms are in an intense magnetic field. In the simplest case each line appears split into two or three components, according as the observations are made on light emitted parallel to, or at right angles to, the field; the light is also found to be polarised. The explanation given by Lorentz, later shown to be over-simplified, was the first clear indication that the emission of light was to be attributed to atomic electrons. The phenomenon showed that magnetic fields exist in the Sun and stars, and allows the strength of these fields to be measured.

See also SPECTRUM AND SPECTROSCOPE.

Zeffirelli, G. Franco (1923–), Italian stage and film director and designer. Stage productions include *Othello* (Stratford-upon-Avon), 1961, and *Hamlet* (Old Vic), 1964, as well as numerous operas. Films include *The Taming of the Shrew*, 1966, and *Romeo and Juliet*, 1968, both noted for their visual richness and their cavalier treatment of the text. *Brother Sun Sister Moon*, 1973, is about St Francis of Assisi.

Zeiss, Carl (1816–88), German optician. He was apprenticed to various instrument makers at Weimar, Stuttgart and Vienna. In 1886, with Ernst Abbe and Otto Schott, he worked upon the microscope, perfecting the homogeneous immersion lens in 1878. In 1889 the firm was incorporated as the Carl-Zeiss-Stiftung, and gained a world-wide reputation, embracing every kind of optical instrument.

Zela, city of Pontus, near which Julius Caesar defeated Pharnaces in 47 BC. The words *Veni, vidi, vici,* so famous in connection with this battle, were not, as is commonly supposed, a laconic despatch to the senate. They were displayed on a decorated wagon at Caesar's Pontic triumph in 46 BC.

Zemlya Frantsa Iosifa (Franz Josef Land), Arctic archipelago of 187 islands in the north of the Barents Sea, belonging to the USSR (Arkhangelsk *oblast*), who annexed them in 1926. Area 16,090 km². Its population consists of temporary residents only, mainly meteorological observers and fur trappers. Divided into three parts: eastern, with the large islands of Wilczek Land and Graham Bell, separated from the others by the Austrian Straits; central, containing a large number of small islands, between the Austrian and British channels; western, west of the British Channel, with the largest island of all, George Land. Over 85 per cent of the archipelago is covered with glaciers, the highest of which, on Wiener-Neustadt island, rises to 620 m. The islands were discovered in 1873 by the Austro-Hungarian expedition of von Payer and Weyprecht.

Zen, one of the two major schools of Buddhism in Japan, the other being Shin. Zen teaching can be summed up in the four truths attributed to its founder, Bodhidharma: a special transmission (of Enlightenment) outside the scriptures; no dependence on words; direct pointing to the soul of man; seeing into one's own nature. Thus, to follow Zen is to embark on a practical path of self-reliance; without dependency on spiritual authorities; without trusting in the 'ping-pong' game of words; desiring only to 'see' clearly and 'know' directly and thereby attain *Satori* (the Zen term for Enlightenment). Broadly speaking, Zen is the result of a blending of Mahāyanā Buddhism with Taoist paradoxical quietism and Confucian pragmatism—and the later addition of Japanese characteristics. As a school it flourished in China for five centuries, having a tremendous and lasting impact on Chinese culture. The traditional Zen style was continued by Japanese artists when the power of Zen was transferred to Japan in the 13th century. More than any other religious teaching, Zen is renowned for its sense of humour. Zen principles have affected Japanese culture in general, sharing responsibility with Shinto for the simplicity, spaciousness and tranquillity that has for centuries characterised Japanese architecture, interior design, drama, music, flower arrangements and pottery. Peculiar to Zen is the famous Tea Ceremony and also the skills inherent in Japanese martial arts. Zen is becoming increasingly popular in the West.
See also BUDDHISM.

Zenith, the point on the celestial sphere immediately over the observer's head.

Zeno of Citium (335–263 BC), Greek philosopher, probably half Semitic, founder of the Stoic school, born at Citium in Cyprus. He opened a school in the 'Painted Porch', *Stoa Poikile*. Hence his disciples were called Stoics.

Zeno of Elea (fl. early 5th century BC), Greek philosopher, born at Elea in southern Italy. He was the favourite disciple of Parmenides, whom he accompanied to Athens c.448, and whose doctrine of the One he upheld in a series of famous paradoxes, e.g. Achilles and the Tortoise.

Zeolites are hydrous alumino-silicates of calcium, sodium and potassium. When heated they give off water, and the name zeolite is derived from the Greek word meaning 'to boil'. They are formed chiefly from the alteration of feldspars and feldspathoids and are therefore secondary minerals, occurring in cavities and veins. Basalts in which zeolites have formed in the gas cavities or vesicles are called amygdaloidal basalts. Heulandite, stilbite, laumontite and chabazite are hydrous calcium alumino-silicates.

Zephaniah, minor prophet, preached during the reign of Josiah. The two chief features of his prophecy are his vivid portrayal of the Lord's Day as a day of disaster, and his doctrine that a righteous remnant will survive it.

Zeppelin, Ferdinand, Count von (1838–1917), German inventor and designer. From 1897 he was occupied in the construction of his first airship, which first ascended in 1900.

Zermatt, village, spa and winter sports resort in the canton of Valais, Switzerland, at the head of the Visp valley and at the foot of the Matterhorn, 35 km by rail from Visp in the Rhône valley. It is one of the chief summer and winter resorts in the Swiss Alps. Altitude 1620 m. Population (1974) 3150.

Zero, a symbol used with two meanings: (1) the number 0 which has the property that $a + 0 = a$ for every number a; (2) a numeral used to denote an empty place in a place-value notation for numbers. Place-value systems with zero were first used in India (earliest dated inscription AD 595). Zero was undoubtedly used many centuries before the dates of the earliest inscriptions. The earliest Indian symbol was a dot and this was the symbol adopted by Arab mathematicians who introduced the Indian numerals to the rest of the world (so that they are now known as 'arabic' numerals). The circle symbol appears on an Indian inscription dated AD 870 and it also appears in 9th-century Chinese texts; it has been used in Western Europe since the 12th century.

The Indian (Sanskrit) word for zero was *sūnya*, 'empty place'. The Arabs translated this into the Arabic *as-sifr*, 'the empty'. This was latinised as *cifra* (from which 'cipher' derives) or as *zefirium* from which 'zero' derives.
See also NUMERALS.

Zetland, see SHETLAND.

Zeus, in Greek myth, the chief of the Olympian gods. He was originally the principal deity of the Hellenic invaders of Greece, the personification of the bright sky, and perhaps also of the sky as sender of fertilising rain. In Homer Zeus is called father of gods and men, the most powerful of the immortals. He is the supreme ruler who manages everything; author of kingly power and of law and order. He was identified by the Romans with Jupiter. For the legend of his birth, see TITANS.

Zhangjiakou (Kalgan), city in Hebei province of northern China. It is situated near the Great Wall, and lies about 185 km northwest of Peking. It occupies an important position commercially, being the southern gateway to Mongolia. Once a station for caravan routes, it has cotton and woollen mills, and also manufactures drilling equipment. There is iron ore mining and smelting in the vicinity. Population (1972) 1 million.

Zhdanov (until 1948, *Mariupol*), city in the Donetsk *oblast* of the Ukrainian SSR, USSR, on the northern coast of the Sea of Azov. It is a major industrial centre with large iron and steel plants using ore from Kerch, plus engineering and other industries. It is the seaport of the Donets Basin. It was founded in 1775 by Greek colonists and has been a seaport since 1780. Population (1980) 507,000.

Zhejiang (Chekiang), a coastal province of south-east China. It consists mainly of southeast trending uplands which continue into the neighbouring province of Fujian. The hills reach the sea, and the coastline is rugged with the exception of a few small delta areas. It is the smallest of the Chinese provinces, but wherever cultivation is possible population is dense. There is a network of waterways and irrigation ditches in the Changjiang delta area and the chief crops are rice, wheat, jute and cotton. The capital of the province is Hangzhou. Area 101,800 km², population (1968) 31 million.

Zhengzhou (Cheng Chow), capital (since 1954) of Henan province in eastern China. An ancient capital of China, it stands at the junction of two major railway lines. Industry includes textile manufacture, and food processing is also important. Population (1970) 2,000,000.

Zhenjiang (Chen-chiang), city and port in Jiangsu province, eastern China, on the south bank of the Changjiang, 70 km below Nanjing. It is situated at the junction of the Changjiang and the Grand Canal and may have been the head of the Changjiang delta at one time. It became a treaty port in 1861. Population (1970) 250,000.

Zhitomir, or Jitomir, capital city, economic and cultural centre of Zhitomir *oblast*, USSR, 165 km west of Kiev. It has engineering, light, wood-processing and food industries, and it is a railway junction. Founded in the second half of the 9th century, it became Lithuanian in 1320, Polish in 1569, and Russian in 1793; it became a provincial capital in 1804. Population (1980) 250,000.

Zhu De (Chu Teh) (1886–1976), Chinese military leader and chairman of the Standing Committee of the 2nd, 3rd and 4th National People's Congresses. Zhu De was in command of a brigade in 1919. He went to Germany in 1922 for further studies in military science, and joined a branch of the Chinese Communist party there. He returned to China in 1925. When the Nanchang uprising broke out in 1927 he joined the mutiny forces and organised the first Chinese Red Army. In 1928 he joined forces with Mao Tse-tung. From 1930 to 1934 Chiang Kai-shek assembled forces several times greater than those of the Red Army. As Communist commander-in-chief Zhu De showed considerable military genius in repeatedly beating off and outmanoeuvring Chiang's forces. He was vice-chairman of the Republic, 1954–59. In 1955 he was honoured as the first marshal of the Republic. In January 1975 he was re-elected chairman of the standing committee of the National People's Congress.

Zhukov, Georgi Konstantinovich (1896–1972), Soviet soldier, the most outstanding Russian military leader of the Second World War. He took a leading part in planning the operations of Soviet forces in the battles for Moscow (1941), Stalingrad (1942), in the relief of Leningrad (1943), and the advance on Berlin. He received the surrender of the German High Command in Berlin on 8 May 1945 and became head of the Soviet Central Control Committee in Germany, 1945–46. He became minister of defence in 1955, and was promoted later to full member of the Praesidium.

Zi Xi (Tzu Hsi) (1835–1908), Chinese regent, known in the West as the Empress Dowager. She became co-regent in 1862, and in 1881 sole regent. She allied with the conservative court establishment, and blocked reform. When the Emperor Guang Xu agreed to more radical reform in 1898 she sided with the reactionaries in a coup. In 1900 she at first gave some backing to the anti-imperialist Boxer rebellion, presumably to divert popular anger from the court. She fled Peking when imperialist troops seized it. She was forced to agree to humiliating peace conditions. She and her coterie then themselves began to look to reform for salvation. She died in 1908, and the puppet emperor, Guang Xu, died, probably poisoned on her orders, hours later.

Ziegfeld, Florenz (1867–1932), US producer and showman. In 1893 he was a showman at the Chicago World Fair. Two years later he arrived penniless in London, but succeeded in assembling another show and engaging Anna Held, the most popular showgirl of the day. Ziegfeld was noted for his lavish musical productions, including *Showboat*, 1927, but more especially for his spectacular and exotic revues, the Ziegfeld Follies, which he staged for 24 years.

Ziggurat, Babylonian word for the temple tower which was a characteristic architectural feature of Sumerian, Babylonian and Assyrian cities. Ziggurats were constructed of baked clay bricks and bitumen mortar with three to seven terraces, each of diminishing size and surmounted by a small temple which was used only on special occasions. Access to the various levels was by ramps and stairways, and some ruins show that trees and other plants were grown on the upper terraces, for example, the Hanging Gardens of Babylon. The best-preserved ziggurat is at Ur; the remains of the lower two stages measure 60 m by 45 m by 20 m (height). The best-known is the Tower of Babel.

Zimbabwe, site of massive ruins in the modern state of Zimbabwe, 27 km south-east of Fort Victoria, 193 km east of Sofala. They present the general appearance of a fortress. In the ruins porcelain of the Ming period has been found and also a large quantity of golden ornaments. The site is now known to have been occupied since the 3rd century AD but the ruins date from c.1500, and are almost certainly the work of African peoples.

Zimbabwe
Area: 390,308 km²
Population: 7,360,000
Capital: Harare

Zimbabwe, formerly Rhodesia, African republic bounded on the north by the Zambezi river (separating it from Zambia), on the east by Mozambique, on the south by the Limpopo river (separating it from South Africa), and on the west by Botswana. Area 390,308 km².

Zimbabwe lies on the huge plateau of central Southern Africa and is almost everywhere over 1000 m above sea-level. The Highveld, an 80-km wide ridge which rises to 1200–1675 m, crosses the plateau from north-east to south-west. On either side the Middle Veld, 1000–1200 m, forms a lower plateau, and then the land slopes northwards to the Zambezi river basin and Lake Kariba, and southwards to the Limpopo and Sabi rivers; these bottom lands are known as the Lowveld

Most of the people belong to the Bantu-speaking Shona and Ndebele peoples. There are also some whites, Asians and people of mixed race (coloured). The total population was estimated at 7,360,000 in 1978, and the main towns are Harare (the capital), Bulawayo, Que Que, Gwelo and Umtali.

Millet and groundnuts are grown as well as the staple crop, maize. Tobacco is the leading crop, and livestock is important, especially cattle. Other products include cotton, coffee, tea and citrus fruit.

Zimbabwe's extensive mineral resources satisfy most domestic needs of basic raw materials except oil. Asbestos is important, followed by chrome, coal and coke, pig-iron, ferro-chrome, nickel, silver, copper and gold. Foodstuffs, textiles and clothing, paper and printing, wood and furniture industries all expanded rapidly in the late 1960s.

The unit of currency is the Zimbabwean dollar of 100 cents.

A constitution was agreed in 1979 and came into force in 1980. Zimbabwe has parliamentary government, with a cabinet of ministers responsible to parliament, and a president as head of state.

The official language is English. The main African languages are Sindebele and Chishona.

History. The main indigenous peoples living in the area are the Ndebele (or Matabele) and Shona (or Mashona), the descendants of the builders of the great medieval ruins of Zimbabwe. In 1889 the British South African Company obtained a charter and, largely owing to the efforts of Cecil Rhodes, annexed Mashonaland. The Matabele were conquered in 1893, and in 1896 the country was formally given the name 'Rhodesia'. In 1911 the territory was divided into Northern and Southern Rhodesia. In 1922 Southern Rhodesia voted for responsible government and rejected a proposal for a merger with South Africa. A government was established under a governor in 1923. The country's prosperity, founded on the tobacco crop, grew rapidly and there was steady immigration to Southern Rhodesia from both South Africa and Britain, particularly after the Second World War.

Pressures for full dominion status increased from 1945, the situation being complicated by the rise of an African nationalist movement in Southern Rhodesia. The Federation of Rhodesia and Nyasaland was established in 1953 but from the outset African leaders in all three territories opposed it, believing it implied perpetual domination by the white minority. In 1963 the Federation was dissolved. Nyasaland and Northern Rhodesia became independent African states, as Malawi and Zambia. Southern Rhodesia remained theoretically a British colony. Demand by the white Rhodesians for immediate dominion status had become vociferous. A new constitution for Southern Rhodesia had been promulgated in 1961 and was violently opposed by the African political leaders of the country. In 1962 the principal African opposition party, the Zimbabwe African People's Union (ZAPU) was banned. It had been assumed by both Britain and Rhodesia that the 1961 constitution was the prelude to Rhodesian independence, but whereas Britain wished to ensure ultimate majority (i.e. African) rule within a specified period, the Rhodesian government was not prepared to do this. On 11 November 1965 the Rhodesian prime minister, Ian Smith, issued a Unilateral Declaration of Independence (UDI), announcing that Rhodesia was now an independent dominion within the Commonwealth. Britain at once declared UDI and the Smith regime illegal and imposed a total embargo on trade to Rhodesia. Neither sanctions nor numerous protracted negotiations brought the desired results and it was not until the mid 1970s that, following the withdrawal of Portugal from its African territories in 1974 and the growing success of guerrilla raids on Rhodesia's northern borders, the Rhodesian government released Joshua Nkomo, leader of ZAPU, and the Rev. Ndabaningi Sithole, leader of ZANU, from detention as a preliminary, with Bishop Abel Muzorewa, to discussions for a national conference to work out a new constitution. After a conference in 1975, in which Smith made it clear that he had no intention of handing over Rhodesia to black majority rule, the rift between ZANU and ZAPU supporters intensified. The former, under Sithole, insisted that military struggle was the only solution and ZAPU, under Nkomo, urged a continuation of constitutional talks. The pressures for Smith to reach an accommodation with the moderate Nkomo wing increased. But all attempted settlements failed and the guerrilla war

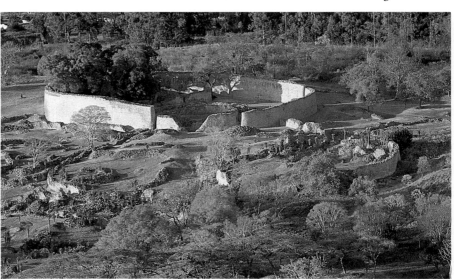

Zimbabwe. *The 500-year-old ruins of Great Zimbabwe are the vestiges of an ancient civilization.*

intensified until, by 1978, over 6000 had been killed. In March 1978 the Smith government and some Nationalist leaders agreed to form an interim government, including black members, while working towards majority rule. Elections were duly held in April 1979, and Bishop Muzorewa's party was returned to power; but the guerrilla leaders and their supporters boycotted the election and continued the war. A cease-fire was finally achieved by British intervention in December 1979 which led to talks in London to formulate a new constitution. Fresh elections, in which the whole electorate took part, returned ZANU, led by Robert Mugabe, with a large majority. Independence came in April 1980, although differences between ZANU and ZAPU continue to cause problems.

Zinc, metallic chemical element, symbol Zn, atomic number 30, atomic weight 65·37, generally met with in combinations as the carbonate (calamine), $ZnCO_3$, and the sulphide (zinc blende), ZnS. It also occurs as silicate (hemimorphite), $ZnSiO_3H_2O$, and as red zinc ore, ZnO. Silver, lead and zinc are often found together, notable instances being Broken Hill in New South Wales and Mount Isa in Queensland, both rich zinc areas. Mexico and the USA are large zinc producers. Blende is the ore generally employed, and this is converted to oxide by roasting in air. The crude oxide is mixed with coal or coke and strongly heated by gas-fired furnaces, in clay retorts or muffles, and the zinc vapour condensed in an iron box (Silesian process). In the Belgian process the mixture is heated in a horizontal fireclay tube connected by a conical clay tube to a sheet-iron condenser. The crude zinc is melted in a reverberatory furnace and further purified by distillation. Wet methods of extraction are by electrolytic processes, and by electric reduction furnaces.

Zinc is a bluish-white brittle metal (relative density 7, melting point 420°C, boiling point 907°C) which is malleable between 100 and 150°C. It is permanent in dry air at ordinary temperatures, and is used for galvanising iron for roofing purposes, etc. A number of alloys are formed by zinc with other metals, e.g. brass (copper and zinc) and bronze (copper, tin and zinc). Zinc burns in air, forming the oxide, ZnO (zinc white). The oxide is white at ordinary temperatures, but becomes yellow on heating. It is a basic oxide, and the salts of the metal can be prepared from its solution in acids. Zinc sulphate (white vitriol) is obtained by dissolving the metal, its oxide or carbonate in sulphuric acid, or is made on a large scale by roasting zinc blende in air. The sulphate crystallises from water, forming colourless rhombic prisms of the formula $ZnSO_47H_2O$, isomorphous with magnesium sulphate (Epsom salts). It has a metallic astringent taste, is poisonous, and is used as an emetic, in the dye industry as a mordant, and in the manufacture of varnishes. Zinc chloride is formed by dissolving the metal or oxide in hydrochloric acid, and boiling the solution down until it solidifies on cooling. It is a white, deliquescent substance, and made into a paste with zinc oxide rapidly sets to a hard mass. This mixture has been used in dentistry as a filling. A solution of the chloride is used as a flux in soldering.

Zinder, second town of Niger, West Africa. It is an ancient walled town, and was a centre for trade across the Sahara in salt and spices. It is now the terminus of a trans-Saharan motor route, but is chiefly a marketing centre for groundnuts and cattle. Population (1977) 58,436.

Zingiberaceae, the ginger family, a tropical monocotyledonous family including about 45 genera and 700 species of herbaceous plants, usually having spear-shaped or oval leaves with sheathing bases and thick underground stems (rhizomes). Many species contain aromatic substances much used as spices and flavourings, for example, cardamoms, ginger and turmeric. Species of *Hedychium*, *Alpinia* and *Kaempferia* are cultivated for ornament.

Zinnia, a genus of the Compositae from America. *Z. elegans* is an annual often grown in gardens.

Zinoviev, Grigori Evseevich, real surname Radomysl'sky (1883–1936), Russian politician. He emigrated after the Revolution of 1905, and from 1909 to 1917 was Lenin's closest collaborator in running the Bolshevik organisation. After the February Revolution in 1917 he returned with Lenin to Russia. He joined with Kamenev in opposing Lenin's policy of seizure of power by the Bolsheviks. After the October Revolution he was chairman of the Leningrad Soviet, and in 1926 became a full member of the Politburo. From 1919 to 1926 he was chairman of the executive committee of the Communist International (Comintern).

In 1924 a letter purporting to come from Zinoviev inciting rebellion was published in the London press and possibly helped in the defeat of the Labour government. Under Stalin he lost all his high offices and in 1935 was imprisoned for 'moral complicity' in the murder of Kirov. He was retried in 1936 at the first of the big show trials of the Great Purge, and executed.

Zionism, or Zionist Movement for the re-establishment of Jewish life in Palestine, is the modern expression in organised form of the traditional Jewish love for Zion, and of the hope of the ultimate ingathering of Israel from the Diaspora. Various proposals for the re-settlement of the Jews in their ancestral home were made from the end of the 17th century. Theodor Herzl published a pamphlet, *The Jewish State*, 1896, in which he advocated the creation of an autonomous Jewish state as the solution of the Jewish question, and in 1897 convened a congress in Basel to consider his project. This congress, attended by 200 delegates from all over the world, resolved that 'the aim of Zionism is to create for the Jewish people a home in Palestine secured by public law'. The congress founded a worldwide organisation which in 1908 began practical work in Palestine, establishing an office in Jaffa and engaging in urban and agricultural colonisation, and in education. Progress was slow owing to lack of funds, but the congress, the supreme organ of the movement, was held biennially from 1909. The Jewish National Fund was established in 1901 for the purchase of land in Palestine as the inalienable possession of World Jewry, and its resources were raised, and still are, by contributions from Jews the world over. In the First World War the movement finally followed the lead of Chaim Weizmann, who pinned his hopes to the Allied cause and set up Zionist headquarters in London. In November 1917 the British Government declared its sympathy in a letter from its Foreign Secretary to Lord Rothschild, which became known as the Balfour Declaration, and was incorporated in the preamble to the Palestine Mandate committed to Britain by the League of Nations in 1922. Zionism now entered a troubled, if constructive, phase down to the creation of the State of Israel in 1948. It is doubtful if it commanded the allegiance of the majority of Jews until the beginning of Jewish persecution under Hitler in 1933. The movement itself was split into factions, political and religious, and in 1946 Weizmann was forced to make way for the more activist policy of David Ben-Gurion, the future prime minister of Israel. Relations with the British government became progressively worse, the latter having somehow to reconcile the Balfour Declaration with its own promises to safeguard Arab nationalism. The local administration, in its endeavours to protect Arab interests, was regarded with suspicion by the Zionists. Zionism, however, grew in strength. Its financial organisation, the *Keren Hayesod*, settled Jewish immigrants and in building villages and towns. Until 1929, the Zionist Organisation was the Jewish Agency for Palestine, recognised by the Mandate, but in that year non-Zionist elements were added to the Agency. After the establishment of the State, the Organisation abandoned political activity, although the old parties have retained their independence. Its main work now is raising funds for settling immigrants.

Zircon, mineral, $ZrSiO_4$, found in Sri Lanka, the Urals and Canada. It forms tetragonal crystals, colourless to yellow, also green and red (hardness 7·5; specific gravity 4·7). Common zircon is colourless. If natural zircon is heated, it becomes a transparent blue crystal and is called 'starlite'. Zircon occurs as a common accessory mineral in igneous rocks and also as detrital grains in river and beach sands. It is the principal source of zirconium.

Zirconium, metallic chemical element, symbol Zr, atomic number 41, atomic weight 91·22. It occurs in nature as the silicate (zircon) and as the oxide (baddeleyite). It has been obtained in two forms, crystalline and amorphous. The metal is obtained by heating the tetrachloride with magnesium by vapour-phase decomposition of the tetra-iodide, or by electrolysis of its double potassium fluoride. The metal melts at about 1715°C. It resembles silicon chemically. The normal salts are prepared from the feebly basic tetravalent hydroxide $Zr(OH)_4$.

Zither, stringed instrument deriving from the psaltery, often with some strings which may be stopped and on which the melody is played, and a number of unstopped strings which are used for chordal accompaniment. The unstopped strings are sometimes grouped in chords to simplify the technique. On the auto-harp, these strings are provided with damper bars so that when one bar is pressed down and the strings plucked, only the desired chord is sounded. The zither is widely used in Europe and elsewhere.

Zizania, a genus of water-grasses, in the Gramineae, of which *Z. aquatica,* Canada rice or wild rice, an annual of North America, yields edible grain used as food by the Indians and considered a delicacy today. It is sometimes sown in ponds and lakes elsewhere for ornamental purposes and to provide food for waterfowl.

Zlatoust, city in the Chelyabinsk *oblast* of the RSFSR, USSR, in the southern Urals. It is an important industrial centre (machine-tools, precision instruments, agricultural machinery). There has been a metal-engraving craft here since the early 19th century. It was founded in 1754 as an ironworks, and was a centre of sword production by 1811. Population (1980) 199,000.

Zodiac, the zone of the sky in which the Sun, Moon and brighter planets appear to move. It is centred on the ecliptic and is usually considered to be 16° wide. The idea of such a zone is of great antiquity but the present name is of Greek origin and reflects the fact that the constellations through which it passes were named for living creatures, except Libra, which is almost certainly a later interpolation. At first various asterisms were chosen along the zodiac to serve as calendar reference points but as these were unequally spaced the zone was eventually divided into 12 equal 'signs', each stretching 30° along the ecliptic. The division into 12 was a natural consequence of 12 full moons per year.

The equinoxes occur as the Sun enters the signs of Aries and Libra, at which times the Sun passes directly above places on the equator. The solstices occur as the Sun enters the signs of Cancer and Capricorn and is passing directly over places on the 'Tropic of Cancer' and 'Tropic of Capricorn' which are circles of latitude 23°27' north and south of the equator.

Zodiacal Light, faint haze of light extending from the Sun along the ecliptic, visible just after sunset or before sunrise as a cone extending above the Sun. It is caused by light being scattered by a belt of interplanetary dust particles revolving around the Sun near the plane of the ecliptic.

Zoffany, Johann, also Zoffani (1733–1810), portrait painter, born at Frankfurt of a Czech family. He studied in Rome and went to England c.1758. He was a founder member of the Royal Academy (1768) and was patronised by the royal family, of whom he painted portrait groups e.g. *Queen Charlotte with her Two Eldest Sons,* c.1794 (Windsor Castle). Larger, crowded 'conversation pieces' include *The Academicians of the Royal Academy,* 1772 (Windsor Castle), which shows portraits of himself, Reynolds and Hayman, and *The Tribuna of the Uffizi,* 1780 (Windsor Castle), showing the old master paintings and antiques which were used for study at the Royal Academy, and groups of connoisseurs and students. Zoffany worked in India during 1783–89.

Zog, see ALBANIA.

Zohar (Book of Splendour), a central work of Jewish mysticism. A homily to the Pentateuch, it has been ascribed to R. Simeon ben Yochai (2nd century AD), but was written by the Spaniard, Moses de Leon (c.1270–1300), in Aramaic. It contains mystical speculations on the creation of primordial man, the nature of the soul and prayer. The Zohar is the most important text of the Kabbalah.

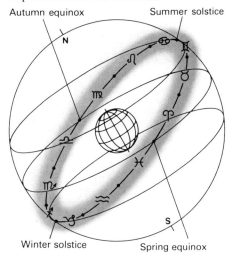

	CAPRICORN	22nd Dec – 19th Jan
♒	AQUARIUS	20th Jan – 18th Feb
♓	PISCES	19th Feb – 20th March
♈	ARIES	21st March – 19th April
♉	TAURUS	20th April – 20th May
♊	GEMINI	21st May – 20th June
♋	CANCER	21st June – 22nd July
♌	LEO	23rd July – 22nd Aug
♍	VIRGO	23rd Aug – 22nd Sept
♎	LIBRA	23rd Sept – 22nd Oct
♏	SCORPIO	23rd Oct – 21st Nov
♐	SAGITTARIUS	22nd Nov – 21st Dec

Zodiac. The signs of the zodiac derive from the constellations through which the Sun appears to pass on its annual journey along the ecliptic.

Zola, Émile Édouard Charles Antoine (1840–1902), French novelist and journalist. He made his name with *Thérèse Raquin,* 1867, a grim, powerful story of remorse. Having thus discovered his real talent, he planned the *Rougon-Macquart,* the story of a family during the decadence of the Second Empire, the 20 volumes appearing steadily over a quarter of a century. In the novels of the Rougon-Macquart series Zola proved himself, as an exponent of realism, the master of his age. In many of his novels the sense of impending doom is all-pervasive; a notable example is *La Débâcle,* 1892. Other important novels in the Rougon-Macquart series are *Germinal,* 1885; *La Terre,* 1887; and *La Bête humaine* 1890. Another series of novels was *Les Trois villes.* Some of his works subordinate characterisation, and even the story, to the inculation of socialist philosophy, which was Zola's solution to the material, and, to some degree, the spiritual problems of his age. His *Les Quartres Évangiles,* 1899–1903, exemplify this aspect of his work.

Zola earned the gratitude of opponents of anti-Semitism by his challenge to the French government to give Dreyfus a hearing. This appeared in the celebrated manifesto *J'accuse.* It resulted in Zola fleeing to England, but after Dreyfus's vindication he returned to France, a popular hero.

See also NOVEL.

Zollverein, literally customs union (German *Zoll,* customs; *Verein,* union). The word is especially applied to the Prussian or German customs union, founded through the efforts of the government of Prussia in 1833 from an amalgamation of smaller Zollvereins, and resulting in a considerable increase in Prussian influence in Germany.

Zomba, former capital of Malawi, situated on the lower slopes of Zomba Mountain, 67 km from Blantyre by road. There are many tobacco estates in the vicinity. Population (1977) 24,234.

Zonda, see WIND.

Zooantharia, see CORAL.

Zoological Garden, a park in which wild animals are kept in captivity. The earliest recorded zoological garden was in Egypt during the 4th century BC. Historically, zoological gardens were royal menageries and their rôle was to entertain. The first zoological garden intended for scientific study was opened in Regent's Park in 1828 by the Zoological Society of London. Thanks to Darwin and the continuous discovery of species hitherto unknown to science, zoos for a long time saw themselves as living museums of animal types. Today the emphasis is on ecology: breeding rare species for survival; keeping animals under the most natural conditions possible, and studying them in relation to their environment.

Zoological Society of London, founded in 1826 by Sir Stamford Raffles, Sir Humphry Davy and others. The Society opened the zoo in Regent's Park in 1828. It also owns Whipsnade Park, and has one of the largest collections of animals in the world.

Zoology, the branch of biology concerned with animals. It includes any aspect of the study of animal form and function. Anatomy is a major part of zoology. Histology is the microscopic study of the animals' cells and the different tissues made up of these cells. Cytology studies the interior of the cells and how their organelles function. Comparative anatomy compares the structure of various groups of animals to see how they are related to each other, and contributes to the study of evolution.

Studies of reproduction, growth and development include embryology and genetics. How animals function is studied through biochemistry, cytology and physiology, all of which help zoologists to understand the workings of the animal's body. The relation of the animal to its surroundings is studied in ecology and animal behaviour or ethology. The classification of animals, how each group is related to the others, is studied in taxonomy. Since many processes of life are common to plants and animals, the fields of zoology, botany and biology cannot clearly be separated.

Zorilla, *Ictonyx striatus,* the African equivalent of the skunk, to which it is very similar in shape and colouring. It belongs to the weasel family, Mustelidae, of order Carnivora. It has glands that secrete a foul fluid when the animal is alarmed.

Zoroastrianism, ancient Iranian religion as reformed by Zoroaster (Zarathushtra) probably c.800 BC. Probably a Magian, Zoroaster tried to purge the old Aryan religion of its polytheism. He preached an intensely ethical Dualism that was virtually monotheistic, since the victory of the Good Spirit, Ahura Mazda, over his rival, Ahriman, the spirit of Evil, was assured. He reduced the nature gods of the old pantheon, the *Daevas*, to servants of Ahriman. He taught a lofty morality, inculcating active charity, kindness to animals, truthfulness and purity, and the need for man to join with Mazda in his battle against the lying spirit of evil and all his manifestations, if man was to attain immortality and eternal happiness. He was killed by hostile Magi, but Zoroastrianism became the national religion of Persia, and remained so until it was driven out (to India, where it survives in Bombay as the religion of the Parsees) by Muslim invaders in the 7th century. Many of the old beliefs then returned and were amalgamated with his teaching. The central feature of Zoroastrian ritual was fire-worship, fire representing the divine essence and the source of life. Lesser deities were worshipped with Mazda, including *Mithras*, the 'eye of Mazda' associated with the Sun, as the god of light, to whom the finest hymn in the Avesta, the sacred writings of Zoroastrianism, is addressed.

Zorrilla y Moral, José (1817–93), Spanish playright and poet. One of the chief exponents of Spanish Romanticism, he is now almost exclusively remembered for his swashbuckling and colourful version of the Don Juan legend, *Don Juan Tenorio*, 1844, a play written in hours but performed every Easter throughout Spain. In marked distinction to Tirso de Molina's Catholic version, Zorrilla's Don Juan is saved by the power of love and ascends to Heaven.

Zuccarelli, Francesco (1702–88) Italian painter. His style was formed in Venice mainly on the model of Marco Ricci and he became noted for pastoral and decorative landscapes. He spent periods in England (1751–62 and 1768–72), having been employed in Venice by Joseph Smith (cf. Canaletto), and was a founder member of the Royal Academy in 1768. On his return to Venice he became president of the Venetian Academy.

Zuccaro, Federigo, also Zucchero (1542–1609), Italian painter, brother and pupil of the artist Taddeo Zuccaro (1529–66). He completed works including the frescoes at Caprarola and in the Vatican, left unfinished at his brother's death, and also completed Vasari's frescoes in the cathedral at Florence, and worked in Rome for Gregory XIII. In 1574 he travelled in Europe, drawing Elizabeth I's portrait in England (two drawings are in the British Museum). He also worked in Spain for Philip II. Later he helped to organise the Accademia di San Luca.

Zuckerman of Burnham Thorpe, Solly Zuckerman, Baron (1904–), British scientist, born in Cape Town. He was chief scientific advisor to the government, 1964–1971. He has been a member of numerous governmental, international and scientific committees. His many publications include *A New System of Anatomy*, 1961; *Beyond the Ivory Tower*, 1970; and an autobiography, *From Apes to Warlords*, 1978.

Zug, capital of Zug canton, Switzerland, situated on Lake Zug 24 km south of Zürich, at the foot of the Zugerberg (991 m). There are fine examples of 16th-century Baroque architecture. It has factories making electrical equipment, metal goods and textiles. Population (1976) 22,200.

Zugspitze, highest mountain in the Federal Republic of Germany, in the Bavarian Alps near the Austrian border, 85 km south-west of Munich. Height 2963 m.

Zuider Zee, formerly an arm of the North Sea penetrating into the north-west Netherlands, but now almost wholly reclaimed. Its area up to 1923 was 5250 km². A chain of islands (Texel, Vlieland, Terschelling, Ameland and Schiermonikoog) which separated it from the open sea were the remnants of the original coastline, breached in the 13th century. In 1918 the Dutch parliament decided to reclaim the Zuider Zee to provide a new province for the country, and work began in 1923.

See also POLDER; IJSSELMEER.

Zulu, Nguni people living in Natal Province in South Africa. In the 1820s they were formed into a nation by Shaka, who formed them into fighting regiments. They conquered many other Nguni tribes. Shaka was assassinated by his brother, Dingaan, who was himself defeated by the Boers in 1838. In 1879 the Zulus under Cetewayo were defeated by the British, and in 1887 Zululand was annexed by Britain; but it was not until 1907 that peace was finally established. Today the 3 million Zulus live in a Bantu 'homeland'. Many still live traditionally as agriculturalists. They form clans whose chiefs are the genealogically senior members, and divide into age sets which form sections of the army. Land erosion and lack of sufficient remaining land to support the population has meant that many Zulus have had to seek wage labour in the towns.

Zulu War (1879) arose out of Zulu-Boer disputes over the possession of lands on the Transvaal border. When the Transvaal was annexed by Britain in 1879, Cetewayo, the Zulu leader, was called upon by the British to disband his army, on the ground of the oppressive rule of the Zulus. Cetewayo refused and the British crossed into Zululand in five columns under Lord Chelmsford. One of these was promptly annihilated at Isandhlwana by 20,000 Zulus. This defeat was followed by the epic siege of Rorke's Drift. The Zulus were finally crushed at Ulundi in 1879.

Zululand, region of Natal, South Africa, proclaimed British territory in 1887 and incorporated in Natal in 1897. Under the South African government policy of separate development, or apartheid, its boundaries have been changed several times, but the territory, which remains fragmented, is now known as the 'homeland' of Kwa Zulu.

Zuñi, Pueblo people of New Mexico. Their 'Kingdom of Cibola' was first encountered by the Spaniards in 1539. Later they were subjugated by the Spanish. They now number about 4500.

Zürich, capital of the canton of Zürich, Switzerland, situated at the exit of the Limmat from Lake Zürich. It is the largest and most important city in Switzerland, and the centre of Swiss commercial life. Industries include textiles, machinery, paper and printing. Tourism is also important, and Zürich is one of the world's leading international banking and insurance centres (the 'Gnomes of Zürich'). The banking sector only employs some 6 per cent of the population, most people being engaged in retailing, admin-

istration and public services. The city joined the Swiss confederation in 1351. Formerly almost wholly Protestant, its population is now about one quarter Roman Catholic. Population (1980) 369,522.

Zweig, Arnold (1887–1968), German novelist. He served in the German Labour Corps during the First World War. Later he practised law, but subsequently devoted himself to writing novels and plays. In 1923 he settled in Berlin and became known as an enthusiastic socialist and Zionist and achieved world-wide fame with his novel of the First World War, *Der Streit um den Sergeanten Grischa*, 1927. In 1933 he was exiled from Germany, and lived in Palestine from 1934 until 1948 when he returned to Germany.

Zweig, Stefan (1881–1942), Austrian Jewish novelist and biographer. In 1920 he published *Drei Meister*, essays on Balzac, Dostoevski and Dickens, which were psychological in treatment. His later works in this genre dwelt more on the pathological side of genius, as in his studies of Tolstoi, Nietzsche, Hölderlin and Kleist. He wrote a number of short stories, technically brilliant but morbid in subject, often dealing with mental derangement and sexual abnormalities, the best, perhaps, being *Amok*, 1922. Forced out of Salzburg by the Nazis, he settled in Britain. His later work included *Ungeduld des Herzens*, a striking novel of woman's psychology set in imperial Austria, which ranks among his finest. Zweig later committed suicide in Petropolis, Brazil.

Zwickau, city of the German Democratic Republic, on the Zwickauer Mulde river, 32 km south-west of Karl-Marx-Stadt. It was a free city of the Holy Roman Empire, 1290–1323. During the Reformation the Anabaptist movement spread from here. The district has vehicle manufacture, coal-mining, chemicals and steel industries. Population (1979) 123,475.

Zwingli, Huldreich, or Ulrich (1484–1521), Swiss religious reformer. In 1519 he became preacher at the *Grossmünster*, Zürich. He now began to attack Catholic ceremony and doctrine and declared the Scriptures the sole rule of faith, denying papal authority. Under his influence, shrines were desecrated, sacred images destroyed, and pictures removed from the churches. Zwingli won over Zürich council in 1523, and in 1525 the Mass was abolished there. He declared that the Eucharist was merely symbolic, and on this point he quarrelled with Luther. Zwingli and Luther met at Marburg, only to part as bitter enemies. Zwingli took an active part in the war between Zürich and the Catholic Forest Cantons and was killed at Cappel, where his party met with a disastrous defeat. His break with traditional beliefs and practices was more extreme than that of Luther and in many ways he anticipated Calvin as in his views on predestination.

Zwolle, capital of Overijssel province, Netherlands, 64 km north-east of Arnhem. The town is an important centre of transit trade, manufactures iron and cotton, and has shipyards. Population (1981) 83,711.

Zygote, the fertilised egg cell formed by the fusion of a male gamete (spermatozoon or male sexual cell) with a female gamete (ovum or female sexual cell).